CHUMASH
INTERLINEAR

THE SCHOTTENSTEIN EDITION

חמשה חומשי תורה

INTERLINEAR CHUMASH

The ArtScroll Series®

Rabbi Nosson Scherman / Rabbi Meir Zlotowitz
General Editors

A PROJECT OF THE

Mesorah Heritage Foundation

ספר בראשית
BEREISHIS/GENESIS

Published by
Mesorah Publications, ltd

THE SCHOTTENSTEIN EDITION

INTERLINEAR CHUMASH

THE TORAH, HAFTAROS AND FIVE MEGILLOS
WITH AN INTERLINEAR TRANSLATION
AND AN ANTHOLOGIZED COMMENTARY

Edited by
Rabbi Menachem Davis

Contributing Editors:
Rabbi Nosson Scherman
Rabbi Meir Zlotowitz
Rabbi Avie Gold

Designed by
Rabbi Sheah Brander

FIRST EDITION
First Impression . . . October 2006

Published and Distributed by
MESORAH PUBLICATIONS, Ltd.
4401 Second Avenue / Brooklyn, New York 11232

Distributed in Europe by
LEHMANNS
Unit E, Viking Business Park
Rolling Mill Road
Jarrow, Tyne & Wear NE32 3DP
England

Distributed in Israel by
SIFRIATI / A. GITLER — BOOKS
6 Hayarkon Street
Bnei Brak 51127

Distributed in Australia & New Zealand by
GOLDS WORLD OF JUDAICA
3-13 William Street
Balaclava, Melbourne 3183
Victoria Australia

Distributed in South Africa by
KOLLEL BOOKSHOP
Shop 8A Norwood Hypermarket
Norwood 2196, Johannesburg, South Africa

THE ARTSCROLL SERIES® / SCHOTTENSTEIN EDITION
INTERLINEAR CHUMASH — Vol. 1: BEREISHIS

4401 Second Avenue / Brooklyn, N.Y. 11232 / (718) 921-9000 / www.artscroll.com

---

THE ANTHOLOGIZED COMMENTARY IS ADAPTED FROM
THE ARTSCROLL STONE EDITION OF THE CHUMASH
© MESORAH PUBLICATIONS, LTD.

Hard cover — ISBN-10: 1-4226-0202-8 / ISBN-13: 978-1-4226-0202-7
Deluxe Leather (Maroon) — ISBN-10: 1-4226-0203-6 / ISBN-13: 978-1-4226-0203-4

Typography by CompuScribe at ArtScroll Studios, Ltd., Brooklyn, NY
Bound by **Sefercraft, Inc.,** Brooklyn, NY

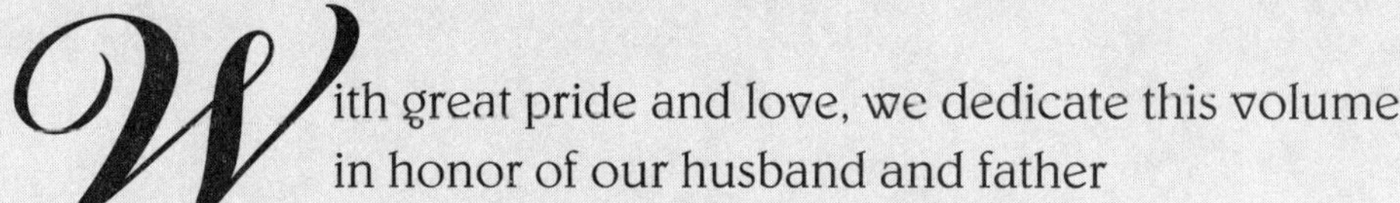

With great pride and love, we dedicate this volume
in honor of our husband and father

Jay Schottenstein

To some he may be a leader or a benefactor.
To others he may be business associate or advisor.
To many he is a friend. To us he is our hero.
His strength is what keeps us grounded.
We are constantly surrounded by his love for us.

His dedication to principle, integrity, humility
and his zeal to spread Torah learning and observance are public knowledge.
But we know better than anyone how much he is devoted to his family
and to maintaining the legacy of his forebears.

This Interlinear Chumash is one of many examples
of his imaginative, innovative, incredibly generous devotion
to the enrichment of Torah life.
It is fitting that this inaugural volume be dedicated to him.

He takes great pride in being a Kohen
and giving the Priestly Blessings to the congregation.
It is only right that he who blesses should be blessed.
So we pray that Hashem should shower those Priestly Blessings upon him:
to bless him and safeguard him;
to shine the Divine countenance upon him and be gracious to him;
to be generous to him and grant him peace.

Jeanie Schottenstein

Joseph and Lindsay

Jonathan Jeffrey

☙ Table of Contents

Publisher's Preface	*ix*
Editor's Preface	*xii*
An Overview: The Torah	*xv*
Blessings of the Torah	*xxii*
Pronouncing the Names of God	*xxii*
Cantillation Marks	*xxiii*
Blessings of the Haftarah	320

☙ ספר בראשית – Bereishis/Genesis

	TORAH	HAFTARAH
Bereishis / בראשית	2	322
Noach / נח	32	324
Lech Lecha / לך לך	60	326
Vayeira / וירא	86	328
Chayei Sarah / חיי שרה	116	332
Toldos / תולדות	135	335
Vayeitzei / ויצא	157	337
Vayishlach / וישלח	186	341
Vayeishev/ וישב	217	343
Mikeitz / מקץ	243	344
Vayigash / ויגש	274	346
Vayechi / ויחי	295	348
Shabbas Erev Rosh Chodesh / שבת ערב ראש חודש		349
Shabbas Rosh Chodesh / שבת ראש חודש	352	352
Shabbas Chanukah I / שבת חנוכה א	355	362
Shabbas Chanukah II / שבת חנוכה ב	359	364
Bibliography of Sources Cited in the Commentary		367
Scriptural Index for the Book of Bereishis/Genesis		374

◆§ Publisher's Preface

In 1993, the publication of ArtScroll's Stone Edition of the Chumash was a landmark event. It quickly became the standard Chumash in the English-speaking world, with hundreds of thousands of copies in print. Countless people have told us that their discovery of the Chumash marked a turning point in their lives. Its new translation and inspirational commentary gave them a new appreciation and understanding of the depth and beauty of the Torah.

In recent years, the publication of the SCHOTTENSTEIN EDITION INTERLINEAR SIDDURIM, MACHZORIM, and TEHILLIM, in a new, patented format, inaugurated a revolution in the comprehensive quality of prayer. The response to these works has been so positive that it was virtually a mandate to publish the Chumash in a similar format.

This new volume merges two classics: the Schottenstein Interlinear format and the Stone Edition of the Chumash. We hope that additional multitudes will study the Chumash with a comprehension they have never had before, and that אי״ה the publication of this "interlinear" Chumash will initiate the same sort of awakening in the lives of many people as the Stone Edition has achieved for many years.

The Torah is the eternal, living monument of God's rendezvous with Israel, the nation's *raison d'etre,* the soul that enables the nation to survive every trial, to rise to undreamed of spiritual heights, and to realize the goal and hope of its Creator.

Whenever the Torah is read, Jews relive the Revelation at Sinai, when our ancestors gathered around a lowly mountain and heard God speak to them. As they did then, we seek now to come closer to our Maker by hearing His teachings and rededicating ourselves to their fulfillment.

With this Chumash, our goal is to present the ancient wine of Sinai in the vessel of today's vernacular. The history of the various ArtScroll Series — on Tanach, Mishnah, Talmud, liturgy, and so on — has proven that English-speaking Jews are as eager as their ancestors were to hear and read the word of God. Let the barrier of language be removed and they will say to Him in the words of the bride in Song of Songs (1:4), "*Draw me, and we will run after You.*"

A look at a typical page of this work demonstrates why it is so unique. Even someone fluent in Hebrew will often come across an unfamiliar word or phrase. To look at an adjoining column or facing page for the translation will solve the problem, but often at the price of a loss of concentration. Next time, the reader may well decide to forgo the translation, especially during the synagogue Torah reading, in favor of continuing to listen to the Torah reading without a lapse. The result is a frequent tug of war between the desire for understanding and the need not to interrupt the reading, especially if one is praying with the congregation.

This new format provides the best solution yet to this problem. It is called "interlinear," a word that may sound cryptic, but whose meaning is immediately obvious when one looks at the page. The translation is directly beneath each word or phrase — not opposite the line, but intermingled with it. Instantly, the reader sees the meaning without interruption.

This approach had not been a common feature of Judaica, because the sentence structure of Hebrew is very different from that of English, and this complicates the task of translation. For example, take the very familiar phrase תְּהִלַּת ה׳ יְדַבֶּר פִּי, which the ArtScroll *Tehillim* and *Siddur* translate quite accurately and understandably as *May my mouth declare the praise of HASHEM.* But a literal, word-by-word translation

is *The praise of HASHEM will declare my mouth* — literally accurate, perhaps, but hardly comprehensible. Undoubtedly, the difficulty of making an interlinear translation both accurate and readable led to its disuse. Thus, the editors of this interlinear translation had to be masters of both syntax and meaning, often adding a word here and there in order to do justice to both translation and comprehensibility.

But there is another, more basic, problem — the discrepancy between the Hebrew that reads right to left, and the English that reads left to right. The eye is confused, as it were, like an American stepping off a curb in England, and instinctively looking to his left, while traffic speeds toward him from the right. Consequently, in order to make this interlinear treatment convenient and practical, a way had to be found to solve the right-left problem. Another glance at a page in this edition will show the solution. After each English word or phrase, there is a barely obtrusive arrow, which directs the eye in the direction of the Hebrew. We have tested this device, and found that it solves the problem to an amazing degree. These arrows keep the reader's eye moving in the direction of the Hebrew without interfering with his reading of the English. To indicate a comma or pause, there is a double arrow, and to indicate a period at the end of a verse, the double arrow is bold. This system, developed in conjunction with RABBI BENYAMIN GOHARI, whose efforts we gratefully acknowledge, is so innovative and user-friendly that it has been granted an international patent.

This new Interlinear Series is dedicated by JAY AND JEANIE SCHOTTENSTEIN. We are deeply gratified that, with their typical vision, Mr. and Mrs. Schottenstein have enlisted their children, JOSEPH and LINDSAY, JONATHAN, and JEFFREY as partners in this and their other charitable endeavors. The Jewish world should be proud that the next generation of this distinguished family is being added to the honor roll of guarantors of Torah's growth. The Schottensteins are familiar to Jews worldwide as the Patrons of Hebrew and English editions of ArtScroll's Schottenstein Edition of the Babylonian Talmud, and the new and monumental Hebrew and English Editions of the Jerusalem Talmud. With this Chumash they extend their vision to a new dimension of Torah study. The three pillars of the universe are Torah, service, and kind deeds (*Avos* 1:2). Jay and Jeanie and their children strengthen all three pillars: The Schottenstein Talmud, and now the Chumash, are raising Torah study to a new plateau; the generosity of the extended Schottenstein family has been legendary for generations; and the Interlinear Series of prayer books elevate the service of God for countless thousands of people.

This work is adapted from the now-classic Stone Edition, which was dedicated by the late IRVING STONE ז״ל, of Cleveland, Ohio, who was one of the outstanding pioneers in fostering the growth of yeshivos and day schools, not only in his hometown, but in many other cities. He was confident that the Stone Edition of the Torah would be a great contribution to English-speaking Jewry, and history has borne out his vision.

We are grateful to his son-in-law and successor MORRY WEISS, who gave warm encouragement to this interlinear project and is very pleased that the Stone Edition has been adapted for inclusion in this new work.

TRANSLATION AND COMMENTARY

THE TRANSLATION IN THIS VOLUME ATTEMPTS TO RENDER THE TEXT AS OUR SAGES understood it. Where there are differing interpretations, we follow *Rashi,* the "Father of Commentators," because the study of Chumash has been synonymous with *Chumash-Rashi* for nine centuries. As *Ramban* says in his introduction to the Torah, לוֹ מִשְׁפַּט הַבְּכֹרָה, *to him [Rashi] belongs the right of the firstborn.*

Drawn from Talmudic literature and the classic Rabbinic commentators from ancient times to our day, the commentary is an anthology in the sense that it draws from many sources, but it is original in its choice and blend of material. Given the need for brevity, it should be understood that many attributed comments are shortened or given only in part. Also, unattributed comments often contain strands from several sources that the author has woven into an idea that is an amalgam of many.

Major events, narratives, or conceptual themes are generally prefaced by introductory material, and

sometimes passages are summarized in a manner that blends the narrative with commentary. The commentary also includes insights of Torah leaders of the last generation.

We use "HASHEM," or "the Name," as the translation of the Tetragrammaton, the sacred Hebrew Four-letter Name of God. In the commentary we frequently refer to it as "the Four-letter Name." For the Hebrew *Elohim,* which is the more general and less "personal" Name of the Deity, we use the translation "God."

TRANSLITERATION

TRANSLITERATION PRESENTS A PROBLEM IN ALL WORKS OF THIS SORT. ASHKENAZI, PURE Sephardi, current Israeli, and generally accepted scholarly usages frequently diverge, and such familiar names as Isaac, Jacob, and Moses differ from them all. We have adopted a cross between the Sephardi and Ashkenazi transliterations, using Sephardi vowel and Ashkenazi pronunciations. Thus: *Akeidas Yitzchak,* rather than *Akeidat Izhak* or *Akeidas Yitzchok.* True, this blend may require some adjustment on the part of many readers, but it has proven successful. In the translation of the Text, however, we have generally followed the commonly accepted English usage, such as Abraham, Moses, Methuselah, and so on.

ACKNOWLEDGMENTS

HEARTY PRAISES ARE DUE TO THE SCHOLARS AND EDITORS WHO RESEARCHED, translated, and commented. Writing, editing, and supervising the project was RABBI MENACHEM DAVIS, who brought uncommon literary and scholarly skills to this very difficult task, and accomplished it brilliantly. He is a distinguished scholar who exhibits a rare combination of sensitivity to the subtleties and nuances of both the Hebrew and English languages, and the ability to discover ways of converting even the most complex syntactical constructions into the interlinear word-by-word format. With exemplary dedication he has produced an edifying work that will enhance the ability of our people to understand the Word of the One Above.

The design of the page was a challenge even for our cherished friend and colleague REB SHEAH BRANDER, the acknowledged genius in this demanding field. His achievement in the entire Interlinear Series is truly extraordinary.

REB ELI KROEN designed the cover with good taste and imagination.

RABBI AVIE GOLD, whose name is familiar to ArtScroll readers, provided the translation of the *Haftaros* and made many suggestions in the course of his meticulous reading of much of the text. AVROHOM YITZCHOK DEUTSCH proofread the Hebrew text to assure the greatest degree of accuracy. MENDY HERZBERG managed the flow of the production, unobtrusively and efficiently.

MRS. EDNA DAVIS made valuable comments and suggestions, in addition to proofreading. MRS. MINDY STERN, MRS. FAYGIE WEINBAUM, and MRS. TOBY GOLDZWEIG proofread diligently and efficiently. MRS. CHUMIE LIPSCHITZ did the beautiful and eye-pleasing pagination. SURY REINHOLD typeset and prepared the manuscript for pagination.

We are grateful to them all. They can have no greater reward for their work than the knowledge that they are bringing more and more Torah to our people.

We are confident that the new interlinear format will be a great boon for countless people and we look forward to the publication of forthcoming works in this new series, so that more and more people can learn and pray with increased feeling and comprehension. This volume will help sincere people achieve that goal, and for being able to help accomplish that, we are grateful to the One Who listens to the prayers of His people.

Rabbi Meir Zlotowitz / Rabbi Nosson Scherman

Tishrei 5767 / September 2006
Brooklyn, N.Y.

Editor's Preface

This year has seen the Interlinear Project expand in a new direction. The previous volumes in the series focused on the texts of prayer — *Tehillim, Siddurim* for Shabbos and for Weekdays, and *Machzorim* for the *Yamim Noraim,* the Days of Awe. The goal of those works was to enable us to understand the eloquent words of our standard prayers and eliminate a potential impediment to our connecting with our Creator, שׁוֹמֵעַ כָּל תְּפִלּוֹת, *Who hears all prayers.*

However, with the *Schottenstein Interlinear Edition of Megillas Esther,* published in Adar / March of this year, and now with this premier volume of the *Schottenstein Interlinear Edition of the Chumash,* the direction is reversed. It is not our words to the Creator that we are clarifying, but His words to us that we seek to understand. It is the words of the eternal Torah, God's gift to Israel, that we are separating into one-word bites and translating into a language that didn't even exist until thousands of years after Sinai. Any translation is considered as an act of betrayal of the original text, since its myriad nuances of meaning are reduced to one often inadequate interpretation. To maintain the syntax of the original in a foreign garb as well, is a twofold betrayal. And yet we undertook the task and completed it with a degree of סַיַּיעְתָּא דִשְׁמַיָּא, *assistance from Heaven,* that can be attributed only to the combined merit of those who will study this volume and of the Schottenstein family, who are acknowledged as Torah benefactors to the entire Jewish world.

Words are vehicles to probe the depths of ourselves — in prayer, and the majestic heights of the eternal — in the Torah. But there is a practical difference between the interlinear translation of the Torah to be *studied* and the translation of prayers to be *recited.* In this work it was deemed appropriate to forego, somewhat, the eloquence of the text, and to present a more literal rendering, in order to improve the accuracy of the translation. As a result there may be passages that read with less fluidity, but we hope we have provided greater precision.

Especially when we listen to the reading of the Torah, it often seems that words stream past, begging to be understood and explained. Now, hopefully, we will be able to fulfill that call without interrupting our attention to the Torah reading. One of my teachers taught me over forty years ago: When studying a text, if you can't find a purpose for a word, it is a sign that you have not understood the text. An interlinear translation compellingly demonstrates that every word counts.

The Interlinear Project, since its inception almost six years ago, could only have been produced inside the ArtScroll intellectual milieu.

The vision and energy behind the unique ArtScroll dynamic is RABBI MEIR ZLOTOWITZ. Reb Meir has been involved not only in the broad outlines of the interlinear project, but also in the intricate details. However, in this *Chumash Bereishis,* Reb Meir's portion is amplified. His anthologized commentary in the ArtScroll *Tanach* series proved invaluable. May he succeed in envisioning and incubating many more projects — to enlighten and inspire.

RABBI SHEAH BRANDER is one of the wonders of the publishing world. Although the earlier interlinear projects were daunting tasks that he met with alacrity, the juggling of at least five graphic elements on each page of this project, including the incredibly difficult interlinear translation, brought the challenge to unbelievable heights — heights that Reb Sheah magically scaled. Someone once defined the hallmark of a work of genius as being obvious in retrospect but seemingly impossible in prospect. Reb Sheah's work is that of genius.

Many scholars contributed to the interlinear project in those subtle ways that inspire and spur one's efforts to unexpected heights: RABBI NOSSON SCHERMAN, who is renowned for his eloquence and depth in expressing so many of the ideas of the ArtScroll oeuvre, and who was always available for consultation; RABBI MENACHEM SILBER, whose encyclopedic knowledge was readily proffered, and who provided access to critical volumes from his personal library; RABBI AVIE GOLD, whose knowledge and sage advice were vital to this volume, for he translated the *Haftaros,* reviewed the translation of all of the text, and provided many valuable suggestions; RABBI MOSHE ROSENBLUM, a consummate scholar of Hebrew, *Mikra,* and *Parshanus;* and RABBI AVROHOM SHERESHEVSKY, an expert in Hebrew grammar and *Mikra.*

In this volume my wife Edna served as an editor par excellence. She guided me over many hurdles with difficult translations and proofread much of the text. This is in addition to her inspiration and enthusiasm that is ever encouraging me to greater achievement. May Hashem grant that we be *zocheh* together to enjoy the further growth in Torah and *yiras Shamayim* of our children and grandchildren.

Menachem Davis

Tishrei 5767 / October 2006

An Overview — The Torah

I. Creation and Redemption

There was another creation, a creation that was much more meaningful than that of all the solar systems.

God created the world so that there would be a nation that would accept the Torah.

Ramban, in explaining the relationship between the themes of the Books of Genesis and Exodus, sheds light on the underlying message of the Chumash — and, indeed, on Creation itself. He describes the Book of Genesis as סֵפֶר הַיְצִירָה, *the Book of Creation,* but he makes clear that he is referring not merely to the physical creation of the universe and all its hosts. There was another creation, a creation that was much more meaningful than that of all the solar systems, stars, and the infinity of the cosmos. That greater creation was the story of the Patriarchs and Matriarchs, the progenitors of the Jewish people, because God created the world so that there would be a nation that would accept the Torah and remain loyal to it. As *Ramban* and other classic commentators set forth, and as will be discussed in the course of this commentary to the Chumash, מַעֲשֵׂה אָבוֹת סִימָן לַבָּנִים, *the events of the Patriarchs are portents for their descendants.* Thus the events of Genesis have a significance that far transcends its 2255-year narrative.

All the miracles of the Exodus, the Revelation at Sinai, and the building of the Tabernacle were to bring the nation back to the exalted level of the Patriarchs and Matriarchs.

Ramban goes on to describe the Book of Exodus as the story of the first Divinely ordained, national exile and redemption. His definition of redemption is basic and enlightening. Superficially, it would seem that the exile ended with Israel's triumphant march out of Egypt after the Ten Plagues and the Splitting of the Sea. But *Ramban* does not stop there, because the newly freed nation was still "exiled" in a Wilderness that was not theirs. They could not be called truly free until after they had accepted the Torah at Mount Sinai and built the Tabernacle. Only then, when God rested His Presence upon them, could they finally be called free. And the importance of that event, *Ramban* says, was that שָׁבוּ אֶל מַעֲלַת אֲבוֹתָם, *they returned to the eminence of their forefathers.* In other words, all the miracles of the Exodus, the Revelation at Sinai, and the building of the Tabernacle were to bring the nation back to the exalted level of the Patriarchs and Matriarchs (see *Ramban*'s introduction to Exodus).

Mission of Return

With the above comment, *Ramban* provides an insight into not only the first two Books of the Torah, but into the mission of Israel and mankind throughout history. It is not politics, economics, or military might that define freedom and redemption. Israel can be called free and redeemed only with the Torah, the Tabernacle — and

later the *Beis HaMikdash,* the Holy Temple in Jerusalem — and God's Presence. This was the goal of Israel in its national infancy in the Wilderness, and it remains the goal throughout our history. And just as the Book of Redemption ended only when Israel *returned to the eminence of their forefathers,* so must we still strive to return to that spiritual summit, and aspire to the coming of Messiah when the long climb will be successfully completed.

The Torah was the blueprint of the universe.

The formula for achieving that goal is contained in the Torah, for the Torah was the blueprint of the universe. As the Midrash relates, God looked into the Torah and created the world, meaning that He created it only as a medium for the performance of the Torah's commandments.

The universe without the Torah would be like a body without a soul.

The Sages (*Shabbos* 33a) interpret God's word to Jeremiah (33:25), אִם לֹא בְרִיתִי יוֹמָם וָלָיְלָה חֻקּוֹת שָׁמַיִם וָאָרֶץ לֹא־שָׂמְתִּי, *If not for My covenant* [i.e., the Torah] *day and night, I would not have established the laws of heaven and earth:* Were it not for the Torah, its study and observance, there would have been no Creation. God states that the universe without the Torah would be like a body without a soul. If the planet is the body, the Torah is its soul.

Free Will — Indispensable

The purpose of Creation was that there would be a species that was capable of making a free-willed choice to recognize and obey God — or ח״ו to refuse to do so. That creature would be man. If he made the right choice, he would be worthy of God's reward and bring Creation to its pre-ordained fruition. If not, the final redemption would be delayed, the world would suffer privation and strife, and the violators would be punished.

An exquisite balance: His Presence is not so obvious that it cannot be ignored, but if someone seeks it sincerely, he will perceive it.

God could just as easily have created man without free choice, so that he would automatically follow the commandments of the Torah — but robots are not rewarded for acting as they are programmed; they could not have acted differently. In order to provide the conditions for such a choice, God created the world with an exquisite balance: His Presence is not so obvious that it cannot be ignored, but if someone seeks it sincerely, he will perceive it. That is why life is such a challenge and why man must struggle to find the truth, refine his desires, and subdue the animal elements of his nature. It *can* be done, as shown by the spiritual attainments of both great and simple people throughout the ages, but it demands introspection and effort.

God wanted a species that would serve Him *voluntarily.* That species is man. Angels are spiritually beyond our comprehension, but they have no evil inclination. They *must* serve God. Animals are creatures of instinct. As illustrated in the imagery of *Perek Shirah* (see ArtScroll's *Song of the Universe*), every creature, whether living or inanimate, "serves" God by carrying out its function in Creation. For example, the Psalmist says, הַשָּׁמַיִם מְסַפְּרִים כְּבוֹד־אֵל, *The heavens declare the glory of God* (*Psalms* 19:2). Has anyone ever heard the heavens speak? How do they declare God's glory? Not audibly. Simply by carrying out their mission with uncanny accuracy and without deviation. If an astronomer can predict the flash of Halley's comet a hundred years into the future with split-second accuracy, is that not testimony to the glory of its Creator?

From Black Hole to Chariot

But the first eleven chapters of Genesis are a litany of failure. As recounted in *Pirkei Avos* 5:2-3, there were ten generations from Adam to Noah and ten generations from Noah to Abraham. Until the advent of Abraham, God's will was frustrated, as it were. In the words of *Avos,* the generations from Adam to Abraham were not merely lacking, "all those generations angered [God] increasingly."

Then came Abraham. He succeeded where his predecessors had failed, and, as a result, "he received the reward of them all." Abraham was a turning point in history. It was not only that he was so righteous. The key to his greatness is that He proved that a person *can* recognize God, *can* overcome the influence of his environment, *can* become so worthy that he and his offspring can justify the existence of the universe.

Abraham proved that a person can recognize God, can overcome the influence of his environment, can become so worthy that he and his offspring can justify the existence of the universe.

The Sages describe the Patriarchs — Abraham, Isaac, and Jacob — as God's "chariot" (*Bereishis Rabbah* 47). A royal chariot is dedicated totally to the king. The Patriarchs were His chariot because it was through them that His Presence found a place on earth. Their very existence — every moment of it — was an exercise in perfect, selfless service, and that is why they could unreservedly become the bearers of His *Shechinah,* or Presence. The Patriarchs were God's chariot because they were the realization of His original plan, and that is why He sealed an irrevocable covenant with them and their offspring.

To best appreciate the revolution sparked by Abraham and Sarah, we should note the dictum of the Sages that from the time of Creation, there were שְׁנֵי אֲלָפִים תֹּהוּ, *two thousand years of desolation* (*Avodah Zarah* 9a). It was as if all of history until then was a black hole, so to speak. Those 2,000 years included the fall of Adam, the murder of Abel, the introduction of idolatry, the Flood, the Tower of Babel and the resultant Dispersion. In the year 2,000 from Creation, at the age of 52, Abraham began gathering people in his homeland of Haran and teaching them to serve God. With that, a new era began, the era of Torah. The millennia of desolation were over and the light of Torah, embodied by Abraham and his descendants, began to glow. That glow became a blinding light when God appeared at Mount Sinai and proclaimed to the Children of Israel, "*I am* HASHEM*, your God, Who has taken you out of the land of Egypt.*"

At the age of 52, Abraham began gathering people in his homeland and teaching them to serve God. With that, a new era began, the era of Torah.

From that moment on, Israel became the nation of Torah, the national chariot that accepted the privilege of embodying God's message to the world.

The Book of Genesis tells how two great individuals, Abraham and Sarah, became the forerunners of a family that became God's nation. That nation emerged from the slavery of Egypt to proclaim: כֹּל אֲשֶׁר־דִּבֶּר ה׳ נַעֲשֶׂה וְנִשְׁמָע, *Everything that* HASHEM *has spoken, we will do and we will obey* (*Exodus* 24:7).

Portentous Events

The Oral Torah and the commentaries are replete with exegeses on the portentous deeds of the Patriarchs and Matriarchs. Every event in their lives, every utterance of their lips enwrapped the destiny of their posterity; for Jewish history, no less than Jewish offspring, is a product of their fatherhood and motherhood. Just as commentators throughout the ages have found the nation's history foreshadowed in the narrative of the Patriarchs, there is no doubt that the tale is not yet complete.

Events yet to unfold will surely cast new light on the pregnant words of Genesis, as more of the future comes to be recognized in the allusions of the past. A recitation and elucidation of the classic writings on this subject would fill tomes; let us illustrate its broad sweep, however, with *Maharal*'s commentary to *Avos* (*Derech HaChaim* 5:4):

Events yet to unfold will surely cast new light on the pregnant words of Genesis, as more of the future comes to be recognized in the allusions of the past.

Abraham's life began in suffering and flight as King Nimrod sought to execute him and silence his teaching, but from the time God plucked him from Ur Kasdim, his life was secure, serene, and productive, with few exceptions. Israel, too, lived in distress during the early years of its national history. It was exiled to Egypt and enslaved by rulers who wanted to destroy it. But from the time God pronounced Israel as His *firstborn son* and redeemed it from Egypt, the nation prospered and, despite periodic setbacks, advanced to the zenith of David's and Solomon's reigns, the construction of the Temple, and the universal acclaim that marked the golden years of the First Commonwealth.

Maharal goes on to say that Isaac began his life basking in the glow of Abraham's eminence. But Isaac became ill and blind in his later years, and his Canaanite and Philistine neighbors did not show him the same reverence they had displayed to Abraham. The middle period of Israel's Biblical history paralleled Isaac's life. Though it began in glory that reached its zenith in Solomon's time, its fortunes then began to decline as it split into two kingdoms, and foreign nations conquered Eretz Yisrael and extinguished the nation's light — the Holy Temple (see *Bava Basra* 4a) — and exiled the people.

The middle period of Israel's Biblical history paralleled Isaac's life. Though it began in glory that reached its zenith in Solomon's time, its fortunes then began to decline.

Jacob, the last Patriarch, embodied the final chapters of Israel's history. Nearly all of his life was a succession of tribulation and anguish, until the last seventeen years, when he enjoyed peace and serenity in Egypt, with his family reunited and flourishing. As the Talmud (*Taanis* 5a) expounds, "Jacob did not die." True, his physical shell left the world and was interred, but the *essential* Jacob, his exalted spiritual life, remains embodied in his children. So, too, Israel. It is beset by exile and pogrom, driven from country to country and continent to continent, reviled by foe and pseudo-friend. But the End of Days — like Jacob's final years — will bring fulfillment and vindication. The Temple — the *eternal* Temple — will be built and Israel will be reunited in a spiritual summit that will be a vindication of all that has gone before. Then the truth and holiness of the Torah will illuminate the world, and all of mankind will stream to do His will with a complete and sincere heart.

II. Two Kinds of Sun, Two Kinds of Darkness

Even familiar phenomena exist on levels beyond our physical abilities of perception. The Sages sometimes say that "the sun should have set in the middle of the sky" (*Sanhedrin* 91b). The Sabbath liturgy says that God "splits the windows of the firmament and removes the sun from its place." How can the sun drop

from the sky in midday? Is this possible in the literal sense? From what "place" does God "remove" the sun?

Although the heavenly bodies are physical entities, they also symbolize metaphysical concepts, and God uses them to infuse spiritual life into Creation, the Sages are referring to a higher world, the spiritual world.

The truth is that although the heavenly bodies are physical entities, they also symbolize metaphysical concepts, and God uses them to infuse spiritual life into Creation. When the Sages refer to astronomical phenomena that contradict observable facts, they are referring to a *higher world,* the spiritual world. There are holy places on earth, such as study halls, synagogues, Eretz Yisrael, homes that are founded on the dictates of the Torah, and people who live that way. When the sun passes over such people and places, God permits it to radiate spiritual blessing upon them. He "opens the windows of His higher realm" and lets the sun shine upon His blessed ones. When it passes over people who are undeserving of blessing, it "sets in the midst of the sky," in the sense that its spiritual nature is blocked and it becomes merely a gaseous mass that provides planets with light, heat, and energy, rotating endlessly as it carries its solar system through the cosmos.

Astronomers have recorded reams of information about the sun, but they cannot see its spiritual nature. One of the pioneers of pathology once said that he had performed thousands of autopsies and never found a soul. True. He hadn't, because he did not have the eyes that could see it.

Darkness by Day

The Psalmist writes: תָּשֶׁת חֹשֶׁךְ וִיהִי לָיְלָה, *You make darkness and it is night* (*Psalms* 104:20). The plain meaning of the verse seems obvious: God lowers the sun behind the horizon and night falls, shrouding the world in darkness. But the Sages see a deeper meaning. "The Psalmist refers to This World, which is likened to the night" (*Bava Metzia* 83b). There are two kinds of darkness. The first affects the eyes. The second affects the mind and heart.

There are two kinds of darkness. The first affects the eyes. The second affects the mind and heart.

Blindness of the mind and heart is worse, because it can cause man to stumble and suffer injuries far more serious than skinned knees. Blindness of judgment has caused all sorts of disasters throughout history. It has made people worship real and figurative idols. It has killed millions in needless wars. It has led people away from God and convinced them that power and wisdom are theirs. It lets people rationalize and justify heinous wrongs. It caused Israel to lose two Temples, be forced into crushing exiles, and deluded multitudes of its children into thinking that the Torah is open to change or even ח״ו abrogation.

In the same sense, *Rashi* cites a puzzling statement of the Sages. On the first day of Creation, God brought light into existence, but the heavenly bodies had not yet been created. At that time, *Rashi* writes: *Light and darkness were intermixed* (*Genesis* 1:4). Surely, if there was light there could not have been darkness. At best, the light and darkness would have blended into twilight, not have existed as separate, identifiable entities. Clearly, the Sages are speaking about the higher, spiritual forms of light and darkness. They are the "light" that enables man to see the truth of God's will and his own role in carrying it out, and the "darkness" that convinces man that the truth lies elsewhere. These two entities cannot blend; they are in continuous conflict with one another. It is for us to identify them and choose between them.

The Sages are speaking about the higher, spiritual forms of light and darkness. They are the "light" that enables man to see the truth of God's will and his own role in carrying it out.

How can one avoid the darkness that deadens the mind and the heart? How can one see the inner glory of the sun?

The Light Is Here

Rashi (ibid.) also cites another teaching of the Sages:

רָאָהוּ שֶׁאֵינוֹ כְּדַאי לְהִשְׁתַּמֵּשׁ בּוֹ רְשָׁעִים וְהִבְדִּילוֹ לַצַּדִּיקִים לֶעָתִיד לָבֹא

[God] perceived that it was improper for [the wicked] to make use of the [primeval light], so He set it aside for the benefit of the righteous in time to come.

Where did He hide that intense spiritual light? asked Rabbi Dov Ber of Mezritch, successor of the Baal Shem Tov, and seminal figure in the growth and spread of the Chassidic movement. He answered: The great light that God created at the beginning of Creation was the light of the Torah. At first, that light was meant to be available to everyone, but God saw that few people were worthy of enjoying it, so He clothed it in the Torah, and there it still remains.

The great light that God created at the beginning of Creation was the light of the Torah.

We bemoan the lack of that primeval light whose spiritual brilliance made the sun pale by comparison. We long for the day when we will see it again. But it is not gone. It is here. It is available. It awaits the diligent, indefatigable efforts of the righteous to discern it from between the lines and letters and wisdom of the Torah.

We long for the day when we will see it again. But it is not gone. It is here. It is available.

Can we accomplish this? The Torah itself assures us that we can.

For this commandment that I command you today — it is not hidden from you and it is not distant. It is not in heaven, [for you] to say, "Who can ascend to the heaven for us and take it for us, so that we can listen to it and perform it?" Nor is it across the sea, [for you] to say, "Who can cross to the other side of the sea for us and take it for us, so that we can listen to it and perform it?" Rather the matter is very near to you — in your mouth and in your heart — to perform it (*Deuteronomy* 30:11-14, see commentary).

Let us begin the search by studying the Torah, with dedication, curiosity, and faith.

Rabbi Nosson Scherman

Elul 5766/September 2006

§ The Interlinear Translation — How to Read it

There is a difficulty inherent in any interlinear translation of Hebrew to English: the fact that English and Hebrew are read in opposite directions. ArtScroll has developed a system of patented notations that helps the reader navigate the two languages simultaneously, without confusion.

These notations consist of the following:

1) single arrow notations ‹ between English phrases direct the reader's eye toward the next English phrase, reading right to left, for example:

וַיְהִי־אוֹר		אוֹר		יְהִי
« light. ‹ and there was,	‹‹	light,	‹	Let there be

2) Double arrow notations ‹‹ indicate a logical break between phrases, equivalent to a period, semicolon, dash, and many commas.

3) Bold double arrow notations **«** indicate the completion of a sentence at the end of a verse.

With these double arrows, the reader need not search for commas, semicolons, and periods. This was done to make the translation as user-friendly as possible; it allows the reader to continue following the Hebrew moving to the left, without the distraction of looking for English punctuation marks on the *right* side of the English words.

The arrows also identify the specific Hebrew word or words that are translated by the English phrase. This is especially useful where two or more Hebrew words are translated as a unit.

For quotations, one further convention was used: Wherever text would normally be set off by quotation marks, the quotation has been set in italics.

BLESSINGS OF THE TORAH / ברכות התורה

THE READER SHOWS THE *OLEH* (PERSON CALLED TO THE TORAH) THE PLACE IN THE TORAH. THE *OLEH* TOUCHES THE TORAH WITH A CORNER OF HIS *TALLIS*, OR THE BELT OR MANTLE OF THE TORAH, AND KISSES IT. HE THEN BEGINS THE BLESSING, BOWING AT בָּרְכוּ, AND STRAIGHTENING UP AT 'ה.

בָּרְכוּ אֶת יהוה הַמְּבֹרָךְ.

« the blessed One. ‹ HASHEM, ‹ Bless

CONGREGATION, FOLLOWED BY *OLEH*, RESPONDS, BOWING AT בָּרוּךְ, AND STRAIGHTENING UP AT 'ה.

בָּרוּךְ יהוה הַמְּבֹרָךְ לְעוֹלָם וָעֶד.

« and ever. ‹ for ever ‹ the blessed One, ‹ is HASHEM, ‹ Blessed

OLEH CONTINUES:

בָּרוּךְ אַתָּה יהוה אֱלֹהֵינוּ מֶלֶךְ הָעוֹלָם, אֲשֶׁר בָּחַר בָּנוּ

‹ us ‹ selected ‹ Who « of the universe, ‹ King ‹ our God, ‹ HASHEM, ‹ are You, ‹ Blessed

מִכָּל הָעַמִּים, וְנָתַן לָנוּ אֶת תּוֹרָתוֹ. בָּרוּךְ אַתָּה יהוה,

« HASHEM, ‹ are You, ‹ Blessed « His Torah. ‹ us ‹ and gave ‹ the peoples ‹ from all

נוֹתֵן הַתּוֹרָה. (אָמֵן. –CONG.)

« of the Torah. ‹ Giver « (Amen.)

AFTER HIS TORAH PORTION HAS BEEN READ, THE *OLEH* RECITES:

בָּרוּךְ אַתָּה יהוה אֱלֹהֵינוּ מֶלֶךְ הָעוֹלָם, אֲשֶׁר נָתַן לָנוּ

‹ us ‹ gave ‹ Who « of the universe, ‹ King ‹ our God, ‹ HASHEM, ‹ are You, ‹ Blessed

תּוֹרַת אֱמֶת, וְחַיֵּי עוֹלָם נָטַע בְּתוֹכֵנוּ. בָּרוּךְ אַתָּה יהוה,

« HASHEM, ‹ are You, ‹ Blessed « within us. ‹ He implanted ‹ of eternity ‹ and the life « of truth, ‹ the Torah

נוֹתֵן הַתּוֹרָה. (אָמֵן. –CONG.)

« of the Torah. ‹ Giver « (Amen.)

PRONOUNCING THE NAMES OF GOD

The Four-Letter Name of HASHEM [י־ה־ו־ה] indicates that God is timeless and infinite, since the letters of this Name are those of the words הָיָה הֹוֶה וְיִהְיֶה, *He was, He is, and He will be.* This Name appears in some editions with vowel points [יְ־הֹ־וָ־ה] and in others, such as the present edition, without vowels. In either case, this Name is *never* pronounced as it is spelled.

During prayer, or when a blessing is recited, or when Torah verses are read, the Four-Letter Name should be pronounced as if it were spelled אֲדֹנָי, *Adōnoy,* the Name that identifies God as the Master of All. At other times, it should be pronounced הַשֵּׁם, *Hashem,* literally, "the Name."

In this work, the Four-Letter Name of God is translated "HASHEM," the pronunciation traditionally used for the Name to avoid pronouncing it unnecessarily.

The following table gives the pronunciations of the Name when it appears with a prefix. In all these cases, the accent is on the last syllable (*noy*). The phrase "מֹשֶׁה" מוֹצִיא "וְכָלֵב" מַכְנִיס is used as a mnemonic. The prefixes מ, ש, and ה do not absorb or assimilate the vowel from the first letter of God's name, while the prefixes ו, כ, ל, and ב do absorb the vowel that follows.

בַּי־ה־ו־ה — *Ba-dōnoy*
הַי־ה־ו־ה — *Ha-adōnoy*
וַי־ה־ו־ה — *Va-dōnoy*
כַּי־ה־ו־ה — *Ka-dōnoy*
לַי־ה־ו־ה — *La-dōnoy*
מֵי־ה־ו־ה — *May-adōnoy*
שֶׁי־ה־ו־ה — *She-adōnoy*

Sometimes the Name appears with the vowelization יֱ־הֹ־וִ־ה. This version of the Name is pronounced as if it were spelled אֱלֹהִים, *Elōhim,* the Name that refers to God as the One Who is all-powerful. When it appears with a prefix לֵי־הֹ־וִ־ה, it is pronounced *Lay-lōhim.* We have translated this Name as HASHEM/ELOHIM to indicate that it refers to the aspects inherent in each of those Names.

ספר בראשית
Bereishis/Genesis

Cantillation Marks / טעמי המקרא

קַדְמָ֨א מְּ֣נַח זַרְקָא֮ מְּ֣נַח סֶגּוֹל֒ מֻּ֣נַּח ׀ מֻּ֣נַּח רְבִ֗יעִ֗י מַהְפַּ֤ךְ
פַּשְׁטָא֙ זָקֵף־קָטָ֔ן זָקֵף־גָּד֕וֹל מֵרְכָ֥א טִפְּחָ֖א מֻנַּ֣ח אֶתְנַחְתָּ֑א
פָּזֵ֡ר תְּ֠לִישָא־קְטַנָּה֩ תְּ֨לִישָא־גְדוֹלָה קַדְמָ֨א וְאַזְלָ֜א
אַזְלָא־גֵּ֜רֵשׁ גֵּרְשַׁ֞יִם דַּרְגָּ֧א תְּבִ֛יר יְ֚תִיב פְּסִ֣יק ׀ סוֹף־פָּסֽוּק׃
שַׁלְשֶׁ֓לֶת קַרְנֵי־פָרָ֟ה מֵרְכָא־כְפוּלָ֦ה יֵרֶח־בֶּן־יוֹמ֪וֹ׃

PARASHAS BEREISHIS / פרשת בראשית

[א] א בְּ*רֵאשִׁית בָּרָא אֱלֹהִים אֵת הַשָּׁמַיִם
[1] 1 ‹ In the beginning ‹ of God's creating ‹ the heavens
וְאֵת הָאָרֶץ׃ ב וְהָאָרֶץ הָיְתָה תֹהוּ וָבֹהוּ וְחֹשֶׁךְ עַל־פְּנֵי תְהוֹם וְרוּחַ
and the earth, ‹‹ 2 when the earth ‹ was ‹ astonishingly ‹ empty, ‹‹ with darkness ‹ upon ‹ the surface ‹ of the deep, ‹‹ and the Presence ‹

* ב' רבתי

אונקלוס

א בְּקַדְמִין בְּרָא יְיָ יָת שְׁמַיָּא וְיָת
אַרְעָא׃ ב וְאַרְעָא הֲוָת צָדְיָא וְרֵיקַנְיָא
וַחֲשׁוֹכָא עַל אַפֵּי תְהוֹמָא וְרוּחָא

רש"י

(א) **בראשית.** אמר רבי יצחק, לא היה צריך להתחיל את התורה אלא מהחדש הזה לכם שהיא מצוה ראשונה שנצטוו בה ישראל, ומה טעם פתח בבראשית, משום כח מעשיו הגיד לעמו לתת להם נחלת גוים (תהלים קיא:ו; תנחומא ישן יא) שאם יאמרו אומות העולם לישראל ליסטים אתם שכבשתם ארצות שבעה גוים, הם אומרים להם כל הארץ של הקב"ה היא, הוא בראה ונתנה לאשר ישר בעיניו, ברצונו נתנה להם, וברצונו נטלה מהם ונתנה לנו (ב"ר א:ב): **בראשית ברא.** אין המקרא הזה אומר אלא דורשני, כמ"ש רז"ל בשביל התורה שנקראת ראשית דרכו (משלי ח:כב; תנחומא ישן ה) ובשביל ישראל שנקראו ראשית תבואתה (ירמיה ב:ג; תנחומא ישן ג; ויק"ר לו:ד). ואם באת לפרשו כפשוטו כך פרשהו, בראשית בריאת שמים וארץ והארץ היתה תהו ובהו וחשך ויאמר אלהים יהי אור. ולא בא המקרא להורות סדר הבריאה לומר שאלו קדמו, שאם בא להורות כך, היה לו לכתוב בראשונה ברא את השמים וגו', שאין לך ראשית במקרא שאינו דבוק לתיבה שלאחריו, כמו בראשית ממלכת יהויקים (ירמיה כז:א) ראשית ממלכתו (להלן י:י) ראשית דגנך (דברים יח:ד). אף כאן אתה אומר בראשית ברא אלהים וגו' כמו בראשית ברוא, ודומה לו תחלת דבר ה' בהושע (הושע א:ב) כלומר תחלת דבורו של הקב"ה בהושע ויאמר ה' אל הושע וגו'. וא"ת להורות בא שאלו תחלה נבראו, ופירושו בראשית הכל ברא אלו, ויש לך מקראות שמקצרים לשונם וממעטים תיבה אחת, כמו כי לא סגר דלתי בטני (איוב ג:י) ולא פירש מי הסוגר, וכמו ישא את חיל דמשק (ישעיה ח:ד) ולא פירש מי ישאנו, וכמו אם יחרוש בבקרים (עמוס ו:יב) ולא פירש אם יחרוש אדם בבקרים, וכמו מגיד מראשית אחרית (ישעיה מו:י) ולא פירש מגיד מראשית דבר אחרית דבר, אם כן תמה על עצמך, שהרי המים קדמו, שהרי כתיב ורוח אלהים מרחפת על פני המים, ועדיין לא גילה המקרא בריאת המים מתי היתה, הא למדת שקדמו המים לארץ, ועוד, שהשמים מאש ומים נבראו (חגיגה יב.), על כרחך לא לימד המקרא בסדר המוקדמים והמאוחרים כלום: **ברא אלהים.** ולא נאמר ברא ה', שבתחלה עלה במחשבה לבראתו במדת הדין וראה שאין העולם מתקיים, הקדים מדת רחמים ושתפה למדת הדין. והיינו דכתיב ביום עשות ה' אלהים ארץ ושמים (להלן ב:ד; ב"ר יב:טו, יד:א; ש"ר ל:יג; פס"ר מ (קסו:)): (ב) **תהו ובהו.** תהו לשון תמה ושממון, שאדם תוהה ומשתומם על בהו שבה: **תהו.** אשטורדישו"ן בלע"ז: **בהו.** לשון ריקות וצדו (אונקלוס): **על פני תהום.** על פני המים שעל הארץ:

PARASHAS BEREISHIS

1.

We begin the study of the Torah with the realization that the Torah is not a history book, but the charter of Man's mission in the universe. Thus, in his very first comment, *Rashi* cites Rav Yitzchak who says that since the Torah is primarily a book of laws, it should have begun with the commandment of the new moon (*Exodus* 12:2), the first law that was addressed to all of Jewry as a nation. He explains that the reason for the Torah's narrative of Creation is to establish that God is the Sovereign of the universe: *He declared to His people the power of His works in order to give them the heritage of the nations (Psalms* 111:6). If the nations accuse Israel of banditry for seizing the lands of the seven nations of Canaan, Israel can respond, "The entire universe belongs to God. He created it and He granted it to whomever He deemed fit. It was His desire to give it to them and then it was His desire to take it from them and give it to us."

As *Ramban* notes, even after reading how the world and its central character, Man, came into being, we still do not understand the secret or even the process of Creation. What we *do* know is that Adam and Eve, the forerunners of humanity, had the mission of bringing about the fulfillment of Creation by carrying out God's commandment. They failed, and were driven into exile.

Man's mission did not change, however, only the conditions in which it would be carried out changed. God punished the transgressors, but did not discard them. They could repent; indeed, the concept of repentance was a prerequisite to Man's existence, because he could not have survived without it. Adam and Eve repented. So did the subsequent sinners Cain and Lamech. This, too, is one of the major lessons of the narrative of Genesis: Man may sin, but he can come back, and God allows him the opportunity to do so.

All this is a prelude to the story of Israel. God was patient for ten generations between Noah and Abraham, but each of these generations failed to carry out the mission for which it had been created. After that failure, God chose Abraham and his offspring to be the bearers of the mission that had originally been universal (see *Avos* 5:2). *Ramban* maintains that this is why Genesis is called the Book of Creation: The essence of Creation is not primarily the story of mountains and valleys, of oceans and deserts, or even of human and animal life. Creation is the story of the birth of Israel, the nation that inherited the task of Adam and Eve. In this first Book of the Torah we trace Israel's story from the life of Abraham and Sarah until their offspring develop into a family and then a nation.

Ramban comments that the Torah relates the story of the six days of Creation *ex nihilo* to establish that God is the sole Creator and to refute the theories of those who claim that the universe is timeless or that it came into being through some massive coincidence or accident.

1. בְּרֵאשִׁית בָּרָא אֱלֹהִים — *In the beginning of God's creating.* This phrase is commonly rendered *In the beginning God created,* which would indicate that the Torah is giving the sequence of Creation — that God created the heaven, then the earth, darkness, water, light, and so on. *Rashi* and *Ibn Ezra* disagree, however, and our translation follows their view.

According to *Ramban* and most other commentators, however, the verse is indeed chronological. It begins with a gen-

אֱלֹהִים מְרַחֶפֶת עַל־פְּנֵי הַמָּיִם: ג וַיֹּאמֶר אֱלֹהִים

« — God said, 3 « of the waters ‹ the surface ‹ upon ‹ hovered ‹ of the Divine

יְהִי אוֹר וַיְהִי־אוֹר: ד וַיַּרְא אֱלֹהִים אֶת־הָאוֹר

‹ the light ‹ God saw 4 « light. ‹ and there was « *light,* ‹ *Let there be*

כִּי־טוֹב וַיַּבְדֵּל אֱלֹהִים בֵּין הָאוֹר וּבֵין הַחֹשֶׁךְ: ה וַיִּקְרָא אֱלֹהִים ׀

‹ God called 5 « the darkness. ‹ and between ‹ the light ‹ between ‹ and God separated « it was good, ‹ that

לָאוֹר יוֹם וְלַחֹשֶׁךְ קָרָא לָיְלָה וַיְהִי־עֶרֶב וַיְהִי־בֹקֶר יוֹם אֶחָד: פ

« one day. ‹ morning, ‹ and there was ‹ evening ‹ And there was « *Night.* « He called: ‹ and the darkness « *Day,* « the light:

מִן קֳדָם יְיָ מְנַשְּׁבָא עַל אַפֵּי מַיָּא: ג וַאֲמַר יְיָ יְהֵי נְהוֹרָא וַהֲוָה נְהוֹרָא: ד וַחֲזָא יְיָ יָת נְהוֹרָא אֲרֵי טָב וְאַפְרֵשׁ יְיָ בֵּין נְהוֹרָא וּבֵין חֲשׁוֹכָא: ה וּקְרָא יְיָ לִנְהוֹרָא יְמָמָא וְלַחֲשׁוֹכָא קְרָא לֵילְיָא וַהֲוָה רְמַשׁ וַהֲוָה צְפַר יוֹמָא חָד:

רש"י

ורוח אלהים מרחפת. כסא הכבוד עומד באויר ומרחף על פני המים ברוח פיו של הקב"ה ובמאמרו כיונה המרחפת על הקן (חגיגה טו.; מדרש תהלים צג:ה) אקוצטי"ר בלע"ז: (ד) **וירא אלהים את האור כי טוב ויבדל.** אף בזה אנו צריכין לדברי אגדה, ראהו שאינו כדאי להשתמש בו רשעים והבדילו לצדיקים לעתיד לבא (חגיגה יב.; ב"ר ג:ו). ולפי פשוטו כך פרשהו, ראהו כי טוב ואין נאה לו ולחשך שיהיו משתמשין בערבוביא, וקבע לזה תחומו ביום ולזה תחומו בלילה (ב"ר שם; פסחים ב.): (ה) **יום אחד.** לפי סדר לשון הפרשה היה לו לכתוב יום ראשון כמו שכתוב בשאר הימים, שני, שלישי, רביעי, למה כתב אחד, לפי שהיה הקב"ה יחיד בעולמו, שלא נבראו המלאכים עד יום שני. כך מפורש בב"ר (ג:ח): (ו) **יהי רקיע.** יחזק הרקיע, שאע"פ שנבראו שמים ביום הראשון עדיין לחים היו וקרשו בשני מגערת הקב"ה באמרו יהי רקיע, וז"ש עמודי שמים ירופפו (איוב כו:יא) כל יום ראשון, ובשני יתמהו מגערתו (שם) כאדם שמשתומם ועומד מגערת המאיים עליו (ב"ר ד:ב, ז, יב:י; חגיגה יב.): **בתוך המים.** באמצע המים, שיש הפרש בין מים העליונים לרקיע כמו בין הרקיע למים שעל הארץ. הא למדת שהם תלוים במאמרו של מלך (ב"ר ד:ג):

eral statement: *At the very first moment* — from absolute nothingness — *God created the heaven and the earth,* i.e., the basic substance from which He then fashioned the universe as we know it, as expounded in the following verses. The chapter continues the day-to-day process until it reaches its climax in the Creation of Man — the prime goal of Creation.

Homiletically, the word בְּרֵאשִׁית can be rendered בִּשְׁבִיל רֵאשִׁית, [*the world was created*] *for the sake of* [*the things that are called*] *"beginning,"* meaning that God brought the world into being for the sake of things that are of such basic importance that the Torah calls them רֵאשִׁית, *first* or *beginning.* These things are the Torah and Israel; thus the reason for Creation is that Israel would accept and fulfill the Torah (*Rashi*). The Midrash adds other things called רֵאשִׁית, such as the commandments regarding the firstborn, first fruits, and gifts to the Kohanim, which must be taken from crops and dough before they may be consumed. The implication is that the purpose of Creation is to enable Jews to dedicate their first efforts and successes to the service of God.

אֱלֹהִים — *God.* This Name denotes God in His Attribute of Justice [מִדַּת הַדִּין], as Ruler, Lawgiver, and Judge of the world. By using this Name exclusively in the narrative of Creation, the Torah indicates that Justice is the ideal state of the world, meaning that Man should be treated exactly as he deserves, according to his deeds. However, because Man is not virtuous enough to survive such harsh scrutiny, God added His Attribute of Mercy to the story of Creation, so that judgment would be tempered with mercy (see 2:4).

2. חֹשֶׁךְ — *Darkness*. This is not merely the absence of light, but a specific creation, as is clearly stated in *Isaiah* 45:7: יוֹצֵר אוֹר וּבוֹרֵא חֹשֶׁךְ, *He Who forms the light and creates darkness.* This is also indicated by the Sages' characterization that until light and darkness were separated from each other, they functioned "in a mixture," implying that patches of light and darkness were intermixed with each other.

4-5. וַיַּרְא אֱלֹהִים . . . כִּי־טוֹב — *God saw . . . that it was good*. In the plain sense, God saw that the light was good, so He decreed that it should not be mingled with the darkness, but should function independently during the day (*Rashi*). *Ramban* maintains that the term *saw that it was good* means that God expressed His approval and decreed permanence to the phenomenon under discussion, in this case it means that the light required no further perfection. Then (v. 5), "God summoned the light and appointed it for duty by day, and He summoned the darkness and appointed it for duty by night" (*Pesachim* 2a).

Throughout the narrative, the term *that it was good* means that the creation of the item under discussion was completed. Thus, for example, the light is described as good, because its existence and function were now final. The waters, however, did not receive their final form until the third day, when they were gathered into seas and oceans. Consequently, they were not called *good* until the third day (*Rashi* to v. 7).

5. וַיְהִי־עֶרֶב וַיְהִי־בֹקֶר — *And there was evening and there was morning.* The first day is now complete. Scripture uses the cardinal number אֶחָד, *one* day, instead of the ordinal number רִאשׁוֹן, *first* day, to indicate that on this day God was One [because this phrase can be rendered *the day of the One and Only*]. On this day, God was still the only spiritual being in existence, for the angels were not created until the second day (*Rashi*).

6 וַיֹּאמֶר אֱלֹהִים יְהִי רָקִיעַ בְּתוֹךְ הַמָּיִם וִיהִי
God said, « Let there be < a firmament < in the midst < of the waters, « and let it
מַבְדִּיל בֵּין מַיִם לָמָיִם: 7 וַיַּעַשׂ אֱלֹהִים
separate < between < water < and water. « 7 So God made «
אֶת־הָרָקִיעַ וַיַּבְדֵּל בֵּין הַמַּיִם אֲשֶׁר מִתַּחַת
the firmament, « and He separated < between < the waters < which were < beneath <
לָרָקִיעַ וּבֵין הַמַּיִם אֲשֶׁר מֵעַל לָרָקִיעַ וַיְהִי־כֵן: 8 וַיִּקְרָא אֱלֹהִים
the firmament < and between < the waters < which were < above < the firmament. « And it was < so. « 8 God called «
לָרָקִיעַ שָׁמָיִם וַיְהִי־עֶרֶב וַיְהִי־בֹקֶר יוֹם שֵׁנִי: פ 9 וַיֹּאמֶר אֱלֹהִים
the firmament: « *Heaven.* « And there was < evening < and there was < morning, « a second day. « 9 God said, «
יִקָּווּ הַמַּיִם מִתַּחַת הַשָּׁמַיִם אֶל־מָקוֹם אֶחָד וְתֵרָאֶה הַיַּבָּשָׁה וַיְהִי־כֵן:
Let the waters be gathered < beneath < the heaven < into < one area, « and let appear < *the dry land.* « And it was < so. «

ו וַאֲמַר יְיָ יְהֵי רְקִיעָא בִּמְצִיעוּת מַיָּא וִיהֵי מַפְרִישׁ בֵּין מַיָּא לְמַיָּא: ז וַעֲבַד יְיָ יָת רְקִיעָא וְאַפְרֵישׁ בֵּין מַיָּא דִּי מִלְּרַע לִרְקִיעָא וּבֵין מַיָּא דִּי מֵעַל לִרְקִיעָא וַהֲוָה כֵן: ח וּקְרָא יְיָ לִרְקִיעָא שְׁמַיָּא וַהֲוָה רְמַשׁ וַהֲוָה צְפַר יוֹם תִּנְיָן: ט וַאֲמַר יְיָ יִתְכַּנְשׁוּן מַיָּא מִתְּחוֹת שְׁמַיָּא לַאֲתַר חָד וְתִתְחֲזֵי יַבֶּשְׁתָּא וַהֲוָה כֵן:

רש"י

(ז) **ויעש אלהים את הרקיע.** תקנו על עמדו והיא עשייתו, כמו ועשתה את צפרניה (דברים כא:יב): **מעל לרקיע.** על הרקיע לא נאמר אלא מעל לרקיע, לפי שהן תלוין באויר (ב"ר שם). ומפני מה לא נאמר כי טוב ביום שני, לפי שלא היה נגמר מלאכת המים עד יום שלישי והרי התחיל בה בשני, ודבר שלא נגמר אינו במלואו וטובו. ובשלישי שנגמר מלאכת המים והתחיל וגמר מלאכה אחרת כפל בו כי טוב שני פעמים, אחד לגמר מלאכת השני ואחד לגמר מלאכת היום (שם ו): (ח) **ויקרא אלהים לרקיע שמים.** שא מים, שם מים, אש ומים, שערבן זה בזה ועשה מהם שמים (שם ז; חגיגה יב.): (ט) **יקוו המים.** שטוחין היו על פני כל הארץ והקווס באוקינוס הוא הים הגדול שבכל

6-8. Second day. The heavens had been created on the first day, but they were still in a state of flux. On the second day, at God's command, *"Let there be a firmament,"* they solidified, creating a division between the waters above and the waters below (*Rashi*). According to *Ramban*, however, the separation mentioned in this verse is between the wholly spiritual aspects of Creation and the tangible world that is within the province of Man [which would include even the furthest reaches of the solar system]. He states, "Do not expect me to write anything about [the creation of the second day] since Scripture itself did not elaborate upon it . . . The verses in their literal sense do not require such an explanation. Those who understand the explanation are forbidden to reveal it. For those of us who do not understand, [it is forbidden to speculate about the unknown]." *Ramban's* implication is clear: The "firmament" and the "upper and lower waters" are among the mysteries of Creation that are either unknowable to Man or must be limited to those qualified to know them.

Since there is no solid dome encircling the earth, the commentators, including *Ibn Ezra, Malbim,* and *R' Hirsch,* discuss the meaning of the word "firmament." Generally, they comment that the term refers to the atmosphere that encircles the world.

This is the only day regarding which the Torah does not say כִּי טוֹב, *it was good. Rashi* explains that this term is used only for a finished creation, but the waters, which were begun on the second day, were not completed until the third day. The Midrash gives a different reason. The waters were divided on this day, symbolizing strife, which occurs when the bonds that unite people are broken. Schism and dispute cannot be called good.

9-13. Third day. Up to now, the entire earth was submerged under water. On the third day, God decreed boundaries for the water, making way for the development of land, vegetation, animal life, and, ultimately, Man.

Scarcely had God uttered the words, *"Let the waters be gathered,"* when mountains and hills appeared, and the waters collected in the deep-lying valleys. But the water threatened to flood the earth until God forced it back into the seabed, walling in the sea with sand (*Pirkei d'Rabbi Eliezer; Zohar*). This aspect of God's activity means that He determines the proper limits — to Creation itself and to an individual human being's resources and sufferings. The concept of God as determining what is sufficient and setting limits is alluded to in His Name *Shaddai,* from the word דַּי, *enough*, or *sufficient.* As Talmudic literature puts it: מִי שֶׁאָמַר לְעוֹלָמוֹ דַּי, *He Who said to His world, "It is enough!"* [See 17:1.]

9. וְתֵרָאֶה הַיַּבָּשָׁה — *And let appear the dry land.* The earth had been created on the first day, but it was neither visible nor dry until the waters were commanded to assemble in their designated areas (*Rashbam*).

י וַיִּקְרָא אֱלֹהִים ׀ לַיַּבָּשָׁה אֶרֶץ וּלְמִקְוֵה הַמַּיִם

< of waters < and the gathering << *Earth,* << the dry land: < God called 10

קָרָא יַמִּים וַיַּרְא אֱלֹהִים כִּי־טוֹב: יא וַיֹּאמֶר אֱלֹהִים

<< God said, 11 << it was good. < that < And God saw << *Seas.* << He called:

תַּדְשֵׁא הָאָרֶץ דֶּשֶׁא עֵשֶׂב מַזְרִיעַ זֶרַע עֵץ פְּרִי

< of fruit < trees << seed, < yielding < herbage << vegetation: < Let the earth sprout

עֹשֶׂה פְּרִי לְמִינוֹ אֲשֶׁר זַרְעוֹ־בוֹ עַל־הָאָרֶץ וַיְהִי־

< And it was << the earth. < on < is within it, < its seed < that << [each] after its kind, < fruit < yielding

כֵן: יב וַתּוֹצֵא הָאָרֶץ דֶּשֶׁא עֵשֶׂב מַזְרִיעַ זֶרַע לְמִינֵהוּ וְעֵץ עֹשֶׂה־פְּרִי

< fruit, < yielding < and trees << after its kind, << seed < yielding < herbage << vegetation: < And the earth brought forth 12 << so.

אֲשֶׁר זַרְעוֹ־בוֹ לְמִינֵהוּ וַיַּרְא אֱלֹהִים כִּי־טוֹב: יג וַיְהִי־עֶרֶב וַיְהִי־בֹקֶר

< morning, < and there was < evening < And there was 13 << it was good. < that < And God saw << [each] after its kind. < was within it, < its seed < that

יוֹם שְׁלִישִׁי: פ יד וַיֹּאמֶר אֱלֹהִים יְהִי מְאֹרֹת בִּרְקִיעַ הַשָּׁמַיִם לְהַבְדִּיל

< to separate < of the heaven < in the firmament < luminaries < Let there be << God said, 14 << a third day.

בֵּין הַיּוֹם וּבֵין הַלָּיְלָה וְהָיוּ לְאֹתֹת וּלְמוֹעֲדִים וּלְיָמִים וְשָׁנִים: טו וְהָיוּ

< and they shall serve 15 << *and years;* < *and for days* < *and for festivals,* < *as signs,* < *and they shall serve* << *the night;* < *and between* < *the day* < *between*

י וּקְרָא יְיָ לְיַבֶּשְׁתָּא אַרְעָא וּלְבֵית
כְּנִישׁוּת מַיָּא קְרָא יַמְמֵי וַחֲזָא יְיָ
אֲרֵי טָב: יא וַאֲמַר יְיָ תַּדְאֵית אַרְעָא
דִּיתְאָה עִסְבָּא דְּבַר זַרְעֵהּ מִזְדְּרַע
אִילַן פֵּירִין עָבֵד פֵּירִין לִזְנֵהּ דִּי בַר
זַרְעֵהּ בֵּהּ עַל אַרְעָא וַהֲוָה כֵן:
יב וְאַפֵּקַת אַרְעָא דִּיתְאָה עִסְבָּא דְּבַר
זַרְעֵהּ מִזְדְּרַע לִזְנוֹהִי וְאִילַן עָבֵד
פֵּירִין דְּבַר זַרְעֵהּ בֵּהּ לִזְנוֹהִי וַחֲזָא יְיָ
אֲרֵי טָב: יג וַהֲוָה רְמַשׁ וַהֲוָה צְפַר יוֹם
תְּלִיתָאי: יד וַאֲמַר יְיָ יְהוֹן נְהוֹרִין
בִּרְקִיעָא דִּשְׁמַיָּא לְאַפְרָשָׁא בֵּין יְמָמָא
וּבֵין לֵילְיָא וִיהוֹן לְאָתִין וּלְזִמְנִין
וּלְמִימְנֵי בְהוֹן יוֹמִין וּשְׁנִין: טו וִיהוֹן

רש"י

הימים (פדר"א פ"ה; ב"ר ה:ב; ת"כ שמיני פרשתא ג): (י) **קרא ימים.** והלא ים אחד הוא, אלא אינו דומה טעם דג העולה מן הים בעכו לדג העולה מן הים באספמיא (ב"ר שם ח): (יא) **תדשא הארץ דשא עשב.** לא דשא לשון עשב ולא עשב לשון דשא, ולא היה לשון המקרא לומר תעשיב הארץ, שמיני דשאין מחולקין כל אחד לעצמו נקרא עשב פלוני, ואין לשון למדבר לומר דשא פלוני, שלשון דשא היא לבישת הארץ בעשבים כשהיא מתמלאת בדשאים: **תדשא הארץ.** תתמלא ותתכסה לבוש עשבים (ר"ה יא.). בלשון לע"ז נקרא דשא ארבדי"ץ כולן בערבוביא, וכל שרש לעצמו נקרא עשב: **מזריע זרע.** שיגדל בו זרעו לזרוע ממנו במקום אחר: **עץ פרי.** שיהא טעם העץ כטעם הפרי, והיא לא עשתה כן אלא ותוצא הארץ וגו' ועץ עושה פרי, ולא העץ פרי, לפיכך כשנתקלל אדם על עונו נפקדה גם היא על עונה ונתקללה (ב"ר ה:ט): **אשר זרעו בו.** הן גרעיני כל פרי שמהן האילן צומח כשנוטעים אותו: (יב) **ותוצא הארץ וגו'.** אע"פ שלא נאמר למינהו בדשאים בצוויהן, שמעו שנצטוו האילנות על כך ונשאו ק"ו בעצמן, כמפורש באגדה בשחיטת חולין (ס.): (יד) **יהי מארת וגו'.** מיום ראשון נבראו וברביעי צוה עליהם להתלות ברקיע (חגיגה יב.) וכן כל תולדות שמים וארץ נבראו ביום ראשון וכל אחד ואחד נקבע ביום שנגזר עליו (תנחומא ישן א־ב; ב"ר יב:ד). הוא שכתוב את השמים לרבות תולדותיהם ואת הארץ לרבות תולדותיה (ב"ר א:יד): **יהי מארת.** חסר וי"ו כתיב, על שהוא יום מארה ליפול אסכרה בתינוקות. הוא ששנינו ברביעי היו מתענים על אסכרה שלא תפול בתינוקות (תענית כז:; מס' סופרים פי"ז): **להבדיל בין היום ובין הלילה.** משנגנז האור הראשון, אבל בשבעת (ילק"ש מז; ב"ר יא:ב, יב:ו) [ס"א בששת] [ס"א בשלשת (ב"ר ג:ו; סדר א"ז כא)] ימי בראשית שמשו האור והחשך הראשונים זה ביום וזה בלילה (ב"ר ג:ו; פסחים ב.; חגיגה יב.) [ס"א [שניהם] יחד בין ביום ובין בלילה]: **והיו לאתת.** כשהמאורות לוקין סימן רע הוא לעולם, שנאמר מאותות השמים אל תחתו וגו' (ירמיה י:ב) בעשותכם רצון הקב"ה אין אתם צריכין לדאוג מן הפורענות (סוכה כט.): **ולמועדים.** ע"ש העתיד, שעתידים ישראל להצטוות על המועדות והם נמנים למולד הלבנה (ב"ר ו:א, ש"ר טו:ל): **ולימים.** שמוש החמה חצי יום ושמוש הלבנה חציו, הרי יום שלם: **ושנים.** לסוף שס"ה ימים [ורביע יום] יגמרו מהלכן בי"ב מזלות המשרתים אותם, והיא שנה (ברכות לב:) [וחוזרים ומתחילים פעם שניה לסבב בגלגל כמהלכן הראשון]:

12. וַתּוֹצֵא הָאָרֶץ — *And the earth brought forth.* Rav Assi noted the apparent contradiction with the Torah's statement that nothing had grown prior to the creation of Adam (2:5). He explains that the herbs began to grow on the third day, as they had been commanded, but stopped before they broke through the soil. It remained for Adam to pray for them, whereupon rain fell and the growth was completed — God longs for the prayers of the righteous (*Chullin* 60b).

14-19. Fourth day. The luminaries, which had been created on the first day, were set in place on the fourth (*Chagigah* 12a). Indeed, all the potentials of heaven and earth were created on the first day but each was set in place on the day when it was so commanded (*Rashi*).

The *Vilna Gaon* notes that the creations of the first three

לִמְאוֹרֹת בִּרְקִיעַ הַשָּׁמַיִם לְהָאִיר עַל־הָאָרֶץ וַיְהִי־

‹ And it was ‹‹ the earth. ‹ upon ‹ to shine ‹ of the heaven ‹ in the firmament ‹ as luminaries

כֵן: טז וַיַּעַשׂ אֱלֹהִים אֶת־שְׁנֵי הַמְּאֹרֹת הַגְּדֹלִים

‹‹ the large ones, ‹ luminaries, ‹ the two ‹ And God made 16 ‹‹ so.

אֶת־הַמָּאוֹר הַגָּדֹל לְמֶמְשֶׁלֶת הַיּוֹם וְאֶת־הַמָּאוֹר

‹ and the luminary, ‹‹ of the day; ‹ for the dominion ‹ the greater one ‹ the luminary,

הַקָּטֹן לְמֶמְשֶׁלֶת הַלַּיְלָה וְאֵת הַכּוֹכָבִים: יז וַיִּתֵּן

‹ And set 17 ‹‹ and the stars. ‹‹ of the night; ‹ for the dominion ‹ the lesser one,

אֹתָם אֱלֹהִים בִּרְקִיעַ הַשָּׁמָיִם לְהָאִיר עַל־הָאָרֶץ: יח וְלִמְשֹׁל בַּיּוֹם

‹ by day ‹ to have dominion 18 ‹‹ the earth, ‹ upon ‹ to give light ‹ of the heaven ‹ in the firmament ‹ [did] God ‹ them

וּבַלַּיְלָה וּלֲהַבְדִּיל בֵּין הָאוֹר וּבֵין הַחֹשֶׁךְ וַיַּרְא אֱלֹהִים כִּי־טוֹב:

‹‹ it was good. ‹ that ‹ And God saw ‹‹ the darkness. ‹ and between ‹ the light ‹ between ‹ and to separate ‹‹ and by night,

יט וַיְהִי־עֶרֶב וַיְהִי־בֹקֶר יוֹם רְבִיעִי: פ כ וַיֹּאמֶר אֱלֹהִים יִשְׁרְצוּ הַמַּיִם

‹ *Let the waters swarm* ‹‹ God said, 20 ‹‹ a fourth day. ‹ morning, ‹ and there was ‹ evening ‹ And there was 19

שֶׁרֶץ נֶפֶשׁ חַיָּה וְעוֹף יְעוֹפֵף עַל־הָאָרֶץ עַל־פְּנֵי רְקִיעַ הַשָּׁמָיִם:

‹‹ *of the heavens.* ‹ *of the expanse* ‹ *across the face* ‹ *the earth* ‹ *over* ‹ *that shall fly about* ‹ *and fowl* ‹‹ *that are alive,* ‹ *beings* ‹ *with crawling creatures,*

לִנְהוֹרִין בִּרְקִיעָא דִשְׁמַיָּא לְאַנְהָרָא עַל אַרְעָא וַהֲוָה כֵן: טז וַעֲבַד יְיָ יָת תְּרֵין נְהוֹרַיָּא רַבְרְבַיָּא יָת נְהוֹרָא רַבָּא לְמִשְׁלַט בִּימָמָא וְיָת נְהוֹרָא זְעֵרָא לְמִשְׁלַט בְּלֵילְיָא וְיָת כּוֹכְבַיָּא: יז וִיהַב יָתְהוֹן יְיָ בִּרְקִיעָא דִשְׁמַיָּא לְאַנְהָרָא עַל אַרְעָא: יח וּלְמִשְׁלַט בִּימָמָא וּבְלֵילְיָא וּלְאַפְרָשָׁא בֵּין נְהוֹרָא וּבֵין חֲשׁוֹכָא וַחֲזָא יְיָ אֲרֵי טָב: יט וַהֲוָה רְמַשׁ וַהֲוָה צְפַר יוֹם רְבִיעָאי: כ וַאֲמַר יְיָ יִרְחֲשׁוּן מַיָּא רְחֵשׁ נַפְשָׁא חַיְתָא וְעוֹפָא יְפָרַח עַל אַרְעָא עַל אַפֵּי רְקִיעָא דִשְׁמַיָּא:

רש"י

(טו) והיו למאורת. עוד זאת ישמשו שיאירו לעולם: **(טז) המארת הגדולים.** שוים נבראו ונתמעטה הלבנה על שקטרגה ואמרה אי אפשר לשני מלכים שישתמשו בכתר אחד (חולין ס:): **ואת הכוכבים.** ע"י שמיעט את הלבנה הרבה צבאיה להפיס דעתה (ב"ר ו:ד): **(כ) נפש חיה.** שיהא בה חיות: **שרץ.** כל דבר חי שאינו גבוה מן הארץ קרוי שרץ. בעוף כגון זבובים (תרגום יונתן ויקרא יא:כ). בשקצים כגון נמלים (מכות טז:) וחיפושים ותולעים (ת"כ שמיני פרק יב). ובבריות כגון חולד ועכבר וחומט

days and those of the next three days paralleled and complemented one another. Light was created on the first day, and the luminaries were set in place on the fourth. The seas and atmosphere were created on the second day, and aquatic and bird life were created on the fifth. The dry land and vegetation were created on the third, and populated on the sixth.

The Midrash notes this phenomenon and comments that the Sabbath came and protested to God, as it were, saying, "You have given a 'mate' to each of the days, but You have not given me a mate." God responded that the Jewish people would be its mate, because Israel would accept the commandment to observe the Sabbath.

16. **שְׁנֵי הַמְּאֹרֹת הַגְּדֹלִים** — *The two luminaries, the large ones. "Large"* cannot refer literally to size, for the stars are larger than the moon. Rather, the luminaries are described as large because of the *visible* intensity of their illumination. Since the moon is closer to the earth than the stars, its light is perceived as stronger than theirs (*Radak; Malbim*).

R' Yosef Dov Soloveitchik offers a homiletical insight into the concept of great and small. The greatness of the sun is that it is a *source* of light, while the moon is small because it can only reflect what it receives from the sun. In this sense, we pray at a *bris milah,* "May this small one become great" — for a growing child is the recipient of wisdom and training from parents and teachers. We pray that the infant will grow up to become an independent source of greatness, who will enlighten others.

20-23. Fifth day. Marine and bird life.

שֶׁרֶץ נֶפֶשׁ חַיָּה — *Crawling creatures, beings that are alive.* This term refers to any living creature that does not rise much above the ground (*Rashi*).

כא וַיִּבְרָא אֱלֹהִים אֶת־הַתַּנִּינִם הַגְּדֹלִים וְאֵת כָּל־

< and every < the great ones, < the sea-giants, < And God created 21

נֶפֶשׁ הַחַיָּה | הָרֹמֶשֶׂת אֲשֶׁר שָׁרְצוּ הַמַּיִם לְמִינֵהֶם

<< according to their kinds; < the waters swarmed < with which << that moves about, < that is alive < being

וְאֵת כָּל־עוֹף כָּנָף לְמִינֵהוּ וַיַּרְא אֱלֹהִים כִּי־טוֹב׃

<< it was good. < that < And God saw << according to its kind. < with wings < fowl < and all

כב וַיְבָרֶךְ אֹתָם אֱלֹהִים לֵאמֹר פְּרוּ וּרְבוּ וּמִלְאוּ

< and fill < and multiply, < Be fruitful << saying, < God blessed them, 22

אֶת־הַמַּיִם בַּיַּמִּים וְהָעוֹף יִרֶב בָּאָרֶץ׃ כג וַיְהִי־עֶרֶב וַיְהִי־בֹקֶר יוֹם חֲמִישִׁי׃

<< a fifth day. << morning, < and there was < evening < And there was 23 << *on the earth.* < *shall increase* < *[however,] the fowl* << *in the seas;* < *the waters*

פ כד וַיֹּאמֶר אֱלֹהִים תּוֹצֵא הָאָרֶץ נֶפֶשׁ חַיָּה לְמִינָהּ בְּהֵמָה וָרֶמֶשׂ

< and creeping thing, < animal, << [each] according to its kind: << that are alive, < beings < Let the earth bring forth << God said, 24

וְחַיְתוֹ־אֶרֶץ לְמִינָהּ וַיְהִי־כֵן׃ כה וַיַּעַשׂ אֱלֹהִים אֶת־חַיַּת הָאָרֶץ לְמִינָהּ

<< according to its kind, < of the earth < the beast < God made 25 << so. < And it was << *[each] according to its kind.* < *of the land* < *and beast*

וְאֶת־הַבְּהֵמָה לְמִינָהּ וְאֵת כָּל־רֶמֶשׂ הָאֲדָמָה לְמִינֵהוּ וַיַּרְא אֱלֹהִים

< And God saw << according to its kind. < of the ground < creeping thing < and every << according to its kind, < and the animal

כא וּבְרָא יְיָ יָת תַּנִּינַיָּא רַבְרְבַיָּא וְיָת כָּל נַפְשָׁא חַיְתָא דְּרָחֲשָׁא דִּי אַרְחִישׁוּ מַיָּא לִזְנֵיהוֹן וְיָת כָּל עוֹפָא דְּפָרַח לִזְנוֹהִי וַחֲזָא יְיָ אֲרֵי טָב׃ כב וּבָרִיךְ יָתְהוֹן יְיָ לְמֵימַר פּוּשׁוּ וּסְגוּ וּמְלוּ יָת מַיָּא בְּיַמְמַיָּא וְעוֹפָא יִסְגֵּי בְּאַרְעָא׃ כג וַהֲוָה רְמַשׁ וַהֲוָה צְפַר יוֹם חֲמִישָׁאי׃ כד וַאֲמַר יְיָ תַּפֵּק אַרְעָא נַפְשָׁא חַיְתָא לִזְנַהּ בְּעִיר וּרְחֵשׁ וְחֵיוַת אַרְעָא לִזְנַהּ וַהֲוָה כֵן׃ כה וַעֲבַד יְיָ יָת חֵיוַת אַרְעָא לִזְנַהּ וְיָת בְּעִירָא לִזְנַהּ וְיָת כָּל רִחֲשָׁא דְּאַרְעָא לִזְנוֹהִי וַחֲזָא יְיָ

רש"י

וכיולא בהם (ויקרא יא:כט-ל) וכל [ס"א וכן] הדגים: **(כא) התנינם.** דגים גדולים שבים. ובדברי אגדה, הוא לויתן ובן זוגו, שבראם זכר ונקבה והרג את הנקבה ומלחה לצדיקים לעתיד לבא, שאם יפרו וירבו לא יתקיים העולם בפניהם [התנינם כתיב (ב"ר ז:ד)] (בבא בתרא עד:): **נפש החיה.** נפש שיש בה חיות: **(כב) ויברך אותם.** לפי שמחסרים אותם וצדין מהם ואוכלין אותם הוצרכו לברכה, ואף החיות הוצרכו לברכה, אלא מפני הנחש שעתיד לקללה לכך לא ברכן שלא יהא הוא בכלל (מדרש תדשא א; מדרש אגדה): **פרו.** לשון פרי, כלומר עשו פירות: **[ורבו.** אם לא אמר אלא פרו היה אחד מוליד א' ולא יותר, ובא ורבו שאחד מוליד הרבה:] **(כד) תוצא הארץ.** הוא שפירשתי שהכל נברא מיום ראשון ולא הוצרכו אלא להוציאם (תנחומא ישן א-ב; ב"ר יב:ד): **נפש חיה.** שיש בה חיות: **ורמש.** הם שרצים שהם נמוכים ורומשים על הארץ ונראים כאילו נגררים שאין הלוכן ניכר. כל לשון רמש ושרץ בלשוננו קונמוברי"ש: **(כה) ויעש.** תקנם בצביונם [בתקונן] ובקומתן (חולין ס.):

21. וַיִּבְרָא אֱלֹהִים — *And God created.* This term refers to something unprecedented. On the first day, it referred to Creation from a total vacuum; here, it refers to the huge size of some of the fish; in verse 27 it refers to the Creation of Man, intelligent life in the image of God (*Abarbanel*).

22. פְּרוּ וּרְבוּ — *Be fruitful and multiply*. Had the verse not added וּרְבוּ, *and multiply,* each creature would produce only one offspring — *multiply* adds multiple births to the blessing, so each would bring forth many (*Rashi*). In this context, the phrase is a blessing that the creatures would have the capacity to populate the earth. Later (v. 28), with relation to Man, it was also a commandment that he engage in procreation.

24-31. Sixth day. The climax of the physical creation is at hand. Animal life was created first, and then Man, the being whose performance for good or ill would determine the destiny of the universe. This sequence implies that God was telling Adam, in effect, the complete world is now placed in your hands. Your task is to make it function properly.

24. תּוֹצֵא — *Bring forth*. This term implies that a concealed, dormant presence was being brought into existence (*Ahavas Yonasan*). For, as explained earlier, the potential for everything was created on the first day; it was necessary only to *bring them forth (Rashi)*.

נֶפֶשׁ חַיָּה — *Beings that are alive.* These were independently living, breathing beings, capable of reproducing their own species . . . The term could also include any living thing not specifically mentioned, as, for example, germs (*R' Munk*).

לְמִינָהּ — *According to its kind.* The singular form implies that

כִּי־טוֹב: כו וַיֹּאמֶר אֱלֹהִים נַעֲשֶׂה אָדָם בְּצַלְמֵנוּ

‹ in Our image, ‹ Man ‹ Let us make « And God said, 26 « it was good. ‹ that

כִּדְמוּתֵנוּ וְיִרְדּוּ בִדְגַת הַיָּם וּבְעוֹף הַשָּׁמַיִם

« of the sky, ‹ over the birds « of the sea, ‹ over the fish ‹ that they shall rule « after Our likeness,

וּבַבְּהֵמָה וּבְכָל־הָאָרֶץ וּבְכָל־הָרֶמֶשׂ הָרֹמֵשׂ עַל־

‹ upon ‹ that creeps ‹ creeping thing ‹ and over every « earth, ‹ over the whole « and over the animal,

הָאָרֶץ: כז וַיִּבְרָא אֱלֹהִים ׀ אֶת־הָאָדָם בְּצַלְמוֹ בְּצֶלֶם אֱלֹהִים בָּרָא

‹ He created ‹ of God ‹ in the image « in His image, ‹ Man ‹ So God created 27 « the earth.

אֹתוֹ זָכָר וּנְקֵבָה בָּרָא אֹתָם: כח וַיְבָרֶךְ אֹתָם אֱלֹהִים וַיֹּאמֶר לָהֶם אֱלֹהִים

« and God said to them, « God blessed them, 28 « them. ‹ He created ‹ and female ‹ male « him;

אֲרֵי טָב: כו וַאֲמַר יְיָ נַעֲבֵיד אֱנָשָׁא בְּצַלְמָנָא כִּדְמוּתָנָא וְיִשְׁלְטוּן בְּנוּנֵי יַמָּא וּבְעוֹפָא דִשְׁמַיָּא וּבִבְעִירָא וּבְכָל אַרְעָא וּבְכָל רִחְשָׁא דְּרָחֵשׁ עַל אַרְעָא: כז וּבְרָא יְיָ יָת אָדָם בְּצַלְמֵהּ בִּצְלֵם אֱלָהִין בְּרָא יָתֵהּ דְּכַר וְנוּקְבָא בְּרָא יָתְהוֹן: כח וּבָרִיךְ יָתְהוֹן יְיָ וַאֲמַר לְהוֹן יְיָ

רש"י

(כו) נעשה אדם. ענותנותו של הקב"ה למדנו מכאן, לפי שהאדם בדמות המלאכים ויתקנאו בו (פדר"א יג) לפיכך נמלך בהן, וכשהוא דן את המלכים הוא נמלך בפמליא שלו, שכן מצינו באחאב שאמר לו מיכה ראיתי את ה' יושב על כסאו וכל צבא השמים עומד עליו מימינו ומשמאלו (מלכים א כב:יט) וכי יש ימין ושמאל לפניו, אלא אלו מימינים לזכות ואלו משמאילים לחובה. וכן בגזירת עירין פתגמא ומאמר קדישין שאלתא (דניאל ד:יד). אף כאן בפמליא שלו נמלך ונטל רשות (תנחומא שמות יח; סנהדרין לח:) א"ל יש בעליונים כדמותי אם אין כדמותי בתחתונים הרי יש קנאה במעשה בראשית (ב"ר ח:יא; ברכות לג:): **נעשה אדם.** אע"פ שלא סייעוהו ביצירתו ויש מקום למינים לרדות, לא נמנע הכתוב מללמד דרך ארץ ומדת ענוה שיהא הגדול נמלך ונוטל רשות מן הקטן, ואם כתב אעשה אדם לא למדנו שהיה מדבר עם בית דינו אלא עם עצמו. ותשובת המינים כתובה בצדו ויברא את האדם ולא כתב ויבראו (סנהדרין לח; ב"ר שם ח־ט): **בצלמנו.** בדפוס שלנו: **בדמותנו.** להבין ולהשכיל (ב"ר שם יא; חגיגה טז.): **וירדו בדגת הים.** יש בלשון הזה לשון רידוי ולשון ירידה. זכה, רודה בחיות ובבהמות. לא זכה, נעשה ירוד לפניהם והחיה מושלת בו (ב"ר שם יב): **(כז) ויברא אלהים את האדם בצלמו.** בדפוס העשוי לו (כתובות ח.) שהכל נברא במאמר והוא נברא בידים, שנאמר ותשת עלי כפכה (תהלים קלט:ה; אדר"נ סוף פ"א). נעשה בחותם כמטבע העשויה ע"י רושם שקורין קוי"ן בלע"ז וכן הוא אומר תתהפך כחומר חותם (איוב לח:יד; סנהדרין לח.): **בצלם אלהים ברא אותו.** פירש לך שאותו צלם המתוקן לו צלם דיוקן יוצרו הוא (ב"ב נח.): **זכר ונקבה ברא אותם.** ולהלן הוא אומר ויקח אחת מצלעותיו וגו' (להלן ב:כא). מדרש אגדה, שבראו שני פרצופים בבריאה ראשונה ואח"כ חלקו (ב"ר ח:א). ופשוטו של מקרא, כאן הודיעך שנבראו שניהם בששי, ולא פירש לך כיצד בריאתן ופירש לך במקום אחר (ברייתא דל"ב מדות יג):

God endowed each of the species with whatever senses and faculties it required to thrive (*Sforno*), and endowed each with its own peculiar nature and instincts (*Minchah Belulah*).

25. **כִּי־טוֹב** — *That it was good.* As noted above, this expression of approval always applies to a completed facet of Creation. Animal, vegetable, and mineral existence were complete and good as soon as they were created, because they had neither the ability nor the requirement to develop themselves further. Man, however, is in a different category. His creation, which is about to be recounted, is not followed by a similar declaration of approval, because Man's creation is never complete; he must always strive to better himself and his world.

26. **נַעֲשֶׂה אָדָם** — *Let us make Man.* This preamble indicates that Man was created with great deliberation and wisdom. God did not say, *"Let the earth bring forth,"* as He did with other creatures; instead, Man was brought into being with the deepest involvement of Divine Providence and wisdom (*Abarbanel*).

Targum Yonasan paraphrases: "And God said to the ministering angels who had been created on the second day of Creation of the world, 'Let us make Man.' "

When Moses wrote the Torah and came to this verse (*let* **us** *make*), which is in the plural and implies ח״ו that there is more than one Creator, he said: "Sovereign of the Universe! Why do You thus furnish a pretext for heretics to maintain that there is a plurality of divinities?" "Write!" God replied. "Whoever wishes to err will err . . . Instead, let them learn from their Creator Who created all, yet when He came to create Man He took counsel with the ministering angels" (*Midrash*). Thus God taught that one should always consult others before embarking upon major new initiatives, and He was not deterred by the possibility that some might choose to find a sacrilegious implication in the verse. God's response, "Whoever **wishes** to err," implies that one who sincerely seeks the truth will see it; one who looks for an excuse to blaspheme will find it.

כִּדְמוּתֵנוּ — *After Our likeness.* With the power of understanding and intellect (*Rashi*).

27. **בְּצַלְמוֹ בְּצֶלֶם אֱלֹהִים** — *In His image, in the image of God.* Among all living creatures, Man alone is endowed — like his Creator — with morality, reason, and free will. He can know and love God and can hold spiritual communion with Him; and Man alone can guide his actions through reason. It is in this sense that the Torah describes Man as having been created in God's image and likeness (*Rambam*).

זָכָר וּנְקֵבָה — *Male and female.* Although Eve was created later (2:21), she and Adam were created on the same day (*Rashi*). Although all living creatures were created male and female, this fact is specified only in the case of human beings, to stress that both sexes were created by God in His likeness (*R' Hirsch*).

פְּרוּ וּרְבוּ וּמִלְאוּ אֶת־הָאָרֶץ וְכִבְשֻׁהָ וּרְדוּ בִּדְגַת

‹ over the fish ‹ and rule ‹‹ and subdue it; ‹ the earth ‹ fill ‹ and multiply, ‹ Be fruitful

הַיָּם וּבְעוֹף הַשָּׁמַיִם וּבְכָל־חַיָּה הָרֹמֶשֶׂת עַל־

‹ on ‹ that moves ‹ living thing ‹ and over every ‹‹ of the sky, ‹ over the bird ‹‹ of the sea,

הָאָרֶץ: כט וַיֹּאמֶר אֱלֹהִים הִנֵּה נָתַתִּי לָכֶם אֶת־כָּל־

‹ all ‹ to you ‹ I have given ‹ Indeed, ‹‹ God said, **29** *‹‹ the earth.*

עֵשֶׂב ׀ זֹרֵעַ זֶרַע אֲשֶׁר עַל־פְּנֵי כָל־הָאָרֶץ

‹‹ earth, ‹ of the entire ‹ the surface ‹ on ‹ that is ‹ seed ‹ yielding ‹ herbage

פּוּשׁוּ וּסְגוּ וּמְלוּ יָת אַרְעָא וּתְקוּפוּ עֲלַהּ וּשְׁלוּטוּ בְּנוּנֵי יַמָּא וּבְעוֹפָא דִשְׁמַיָּא וּבְכָל חַיְתָא דְּרָחֲשָׁא עַל אַרְעָא: כט וַאֲמַר יְיָ הָא יְהָבִית לְכוֹן יָת כָּל עִסְבָּא דְּבַר זַרְעֵהּ מִזְדְּרַע דִּי עַל אַפֵּי כָל אַרְעָא וְיָת כָּל אִילָנָא דִּי בֵהּ פֵּירֵי אִילָנָא דְּבַר זַרְעֵהּ מִזְדְּרַע לְכוֹן יְהֵא לְמֵיכָל: ל וּלְכָל חֵיוַת אַרְעָא וּלְכָל עוֹפָא דִשְׁמַיָּא וּלְכֹל דְּרָחֵשׁ עַל אַרְעָא דִּי בֵהּ נַפְשָׁא חַיְתָא יָת כָּל יְרוֹק עִסְבָּא לְמֵיכָל וַהֲוָה כֵן: לא וַחֲזָא יְיָ יָת כָּל דִּי עֲבַד וְהָא תַקִּין לַחֲדָא וַהֲוָה רְמַשׁ וַהֲוָה צְפַר יוֹם שְׁתִיתָאי:

וְאֶת־כָּל־הָעֵץ אֲשֶׁר־בּוֹ פְרִי־עֵץ זֹרֵעַ זָרַע לָכֶם יִהְיֶה לְאָכְלָה: ל וּלְכָל־

‹ And to every **30** *‹‹ for food. ‹ it shall be ‹ for you ‹‹ seed; ‹ yielding ‹ of a tree ‹ the fruit ‹ on it ‹ that has ‹ tree ‹ and every*

חַיַּת הָאָרֶץ וּלְכָל־עוֹף הַשָּׁמַיִם וּלְכֹל ׀ רוֹמֵשׂ עַל־הָאָרֶץ אֲשֶׁר־בּוֹ

‹ within it ‹ which has ‹‹ the earth, ‹ on ‹ that moves ‹ and to everything ‹‹ of the sky, ‹ bird ‹ to every ‹‹ of the earth, ‹ beast

נֶפֶשׁ חַיָּה אֶת־כָּל־יֶרֶק עֵשֶׂב לְאָכְלָה וַיְהִי־כֵן: לא וַיַּרְא אֱלֹהִים אֶת־כָּל־

‹ all ‹ And God saw **31** *‹‹ so. ‹ And it was ‹‹ is for food. ‹ herb ‹ green ‹ every ‹‹ that is alive, ‹ a soul*

אֲשֶׁר עָשָׂה וְהִנֵּה־טוֹב מְאֹד וַיְהִי־עֶרֶב וַיְהִי־בֹקֶר יוֹם הַשִּׁשִּׁי: פ

‹‹ the sixth day. ‹‹ morning, ‹ and there was ‹ evening ‹ And there was ‹‹ it was very good. ‹ and indeed ‹ He had made, ‹ that

רש"י

(כח) וכבשה. חסר וי"ו, ללמדך שהזכר כובש את הנקבה שלא תהא יצאנית (ב"ר שם). ועוד ללמדך שהאיש שדרכו לכבוש מצווה על פריה ורביה ולא האשה (יבמות סה:): **(כט-ל) לכם יהיה לאכלה. ולכל חית הארץ.** השוה להם בהמות וחיות למאכל, ולא הרשה לאדם ולאשתו להמית בריה ולאכול בשר, אך **כל ירק עשב** יאכלו יחד כלם (בראשית רבתי להלן ט:ג; מדרש אגדה). וכשבאו בני נח התיר להם בשר, שנאמר כל רמש אשר הוא חי וגו' כירק עשב, שהתרתי לאדם הראשון, נתתי לכם את כל (להלן ט:ג; סנהדרין נט:): **(לא) יום הששי.** הוסיף ה"א בששי בגמר מעשה בראשית לומר שהתנה עמהם ע"מ שיקבלו עליהם ישראל חמשה חומשי תורה (תנחומא א). ד"א, יום הששי, כלם תלויים ועומדים עד יום הששי הוא ששי בסיון [ס"א שביום ו' בסיון] שקבלו ישראל התורה נתחזקו כל יצירות בראשית ונחשב כאילו נברא

28. **פְּרוּ וּרְבוּ** — *Be fruitful and multiply.* In accordance with the Divine wish, the world is to be inhabited . . . One who neglects this has abrogated a positive commandment, incurring great punishment, because he thereby demonstrates that he does not wish to comply with the Divine will (*Sefer HaChinuch*).

29-30. Most commentators group these verses together, *for you it shall be for food and to every beast of the earth . . .*, indicating that Man and beast shared the same herbal diet. At this time, Man was forbidden to kill animals for food; such permission was granted to Noah, only after the Flood [cf. 9:3 and *Sanhedrin* 59b].

31. **וְהִנֵּה־טוֹב מְאֹד** — *And indeed it was very good.* Everything was fit for its purpose and able to act accordingly (*Rambam*).

The Torah declares that Creation in its entirety was not only *good*, as the individual components were described above, but it was *very* good. As the *Vilna Gaon* explains, something may be good in isolation, but not when it is combined with other things. God's works, however, are good in themselves and also with others.

Even things that seem to be evil — such as suffering, death, and temptation — appear to be so only when viewed in isolation, but in the total context of existence they can be seen as good, even *very good*. If we could but perceive at one glance the entire picture of God's management of intertwining events, we would agree with this verdict (*R' Hirsch*).

יוֹם הַשִּׁשִּׁי — *The sixth day.* The definite article ה, *the,* before the word שִׁשִּׁי, *sixth,* indicates that this day is distinguished from the other days of Creation, because this is the one in which all His productive work was completed (*Chizkuni*). *Rashi* cites the Midrash that the appellation of distinction — **the** *sixth day* — alludes to the sixth of Sivan, when the Torah would be given. It was because of that auspicious day that the world was created.

[ב] א וַיְכֻלּוּ הַשָּׁמַיִם וְהָאָרֶץ וְכָל־צְבָאָם׃
[2] 1 And [thus,] finished were < the heaven < and the earth, < and all < their hosts. «

ב וַיְכַל אֱלֹהִים בַּיּוֹם הַשְּׁבִיעִי מְלַאכְתּוֹ אֲשֶׁר
2 God completed < on the seventh day < His work < which <

עָשָׂה וַיִּשְׁבֹּת בַּיּוֹם הַשְּׁבִיעִי מִכָּל־מְלַאכְתּוֹ אֲשֶׁר עָשָׂה׃ ג וַיְבָרֶךְ אֱלֹהִים
He had done, « and He abstained < on the seventh day < from all < His work < which < He had done. « 3 God blessed <

אֶת־יוֹם הַשְּׁבִיעִי וַיְקַדֵּשׁ אֹתוֹ כִּי בוֹ שָׁבַת מִכָּל־מְלַאכְתּוֹ אֲשֶׁר־
the seventh day < and He sanctified < it, « because < on it < He abstained < from all < His work < which <

בָּרָא אֱלֹהִים לַעֲשׂוֹת׃ פ שני ד אֵלֶּה תוֹלְדוֹת הַשָּׁמַיִם וְהָאָרֶץ בְּהִבָּרְאָם*
God created < to make. « 4 These are < the developments < of the heaven < and the earth < when they were created, «

א וְאִשְׁתַּכְלָלוּ שְׁמַיָּא וְאַרְעָא וְכָל חֵילֵיהוֹן: ב וְשֵׁיצִי יְיָ בְּיוֹמָא שְׁבִיעָאָה עֲבִדְתֵּהּ דִּי עֲבַד וְנַח בְּיוֹמָא שְׁבִיעָאָה מִכָּל עֲבִדְתֵּהּ דִּי עֲבָד: ג וּבָרִיךְ יְיָ יָת יוֹמָא שְׁבִיעָאָה וְקַדִּישׁ יָתֵהּ אֲרֵי בֵהּ נַח מִכָּל עֲבִדְתֵּהּ דִּי בְרָא יְיָ לְמֶעְבַּד: ד אִלֵּין תּוּלְדַת שְׁמַיָּא וְאַרְעָא כַּד אִתְבְּרִיאוּ

* ה' זעירא

רש"י

העולם עתה, וזהו יום הששי בה"א, שאותו יום ו' בסיון (פס"ר כא (ק.); שהש"ר א:ט)] המוכן למתן תורה (שבת פח.): (ב) ויכל אלהים ביום השביעי. ר' שמעון אומר, בשר ודם שאינו יודע עתיו ורגעיו צריך להוסיף מחול על הקודש, אבל הקב"ה שיודע עתיו ורגעיו נכנס בו כחוט השערה ונראה כאלו כלה בו ביום. ד"א, מה היה העולם חסר, מנוחה, באת שבת באת מנוחה, כלתה ונגמרה המלאכה (ב"ר י:ט; ור' פירש"י מגילה ט. ד"ה ויכל): (ג) ויברך ויקדש. ברכו במן, שכל ימות השבת ירד להם עומר לגלגולת ובששי לחם משנה, וקדשו במן, שלא ירד בו מן כלל (ב"ר יא:ב). והמקרא כתב ע"ש העתיד: אשר ברא אלהים לעשות. המלאכה שהיתה ראויה

2.

1-3. The seventh day / the Sabbath. The Sabbath is introduced with the declaration that the work of heaven and earth were complete, and that they stand before us in their final intended state of harmonious perfection. Then, God proclaimed His Sabbath. This passage, the first paragraph of the Sabbath *Kiddush,* proclaims that God is the Creator Who brought the universe into being in six days and rested on the seventh. Israel's observance of the Sabbath laws constitutes devoted testimony to this.

The Sabbath is a day saturated with purpose. The Torah states that God sanctified it *because on it He abstained from all His work* (v. 3), implying that the essence of the day is to commemorate cessation from work, but in the very next phrase, the Torah says *to make,* implying that accomplishment was simultaneous with rest. There is no contradiction. God rested from *physical* creation, but He created the *spiritual* universe that comes into being every Sabbath. The world of the Sabbath is far above that of the six days it succeeds, but they are not separate from each other. The bridge between the mundane and the sacred, between the weekdays and the Sabbath, is Man. Adam and Eve were created last, just before the Sabbath, because only Man has the intelligence and wisdom to bring the holiness of the Sabbath into the activities of the workweek. Of all the creatures in the universe, only he can *create* holiness. Angels *are* holy, but they are static. They cannot improve themselves or the world. Only Man can do both. The Sabbath is God's seal, and Man is the one who must impress it upon God's universe; indeed, Man's activities transform the universe from an apparently aimless amalgamation of matter into the mirror of God's will.

2. וַיְכַל . . . וַיִּשְׁבֹּת — *Completed . . . abstained.* The word *completed* indicates that God's work of Creation was finished; nothing new was created after the first six days. The word *abstain*, however, suggests that the work was interrupted — adjourned — but not ended. It tells human beings that there is always more to do, but that Man must abstain from his creative work when the Sabbath arrives (*Vilna Gaon*).

3. וַיְבָרֶךְ . . . וַיְקַדֵּשׁ — *Blessed . . . and sanctified.* God *blessed* the Sabbath with abundant goodness, for on it there is a renewal of physical procreative strength, and a greater capacity to reason and exercise the intellect. He *sanctified* it that no work was done on it (*Ibn Ezra*).

לַעֲשׂוֹת — *To make.* This word implies that there was an ongoing process of creation. The living creatures of the universe were given the ability *to make,* i.e., *to reproduce* themselves, each according to its species (*Radak*).

4-14. Man and Creation take shape. Chapter 1 described Creation only in outline because, as noted above, the Torah did not mean for Man to understand that entire process — that is beyond human capacity — but to know that God is the Creator. Now, the Torah reverts to elaborating on the narrative by focusing on the events that led to the emergence of Man (*B'chor Shor, Akeidas Yitzchak*). Since this narrative leads to the incident of the Tree of Life and Tree of Knowledge, it begins by describing how plant life came about (*Radak*).

4. בְּהִבָּרְאָם — *When they were created.* The letters of this word

בְּיוֹם עֲשׂוֹת יְהֹוָה אֱלֹהִים אֶרֶץ וְשָׁמָיִם: ה וְכֹל ׀
< And [now] all 5 << and heaven. < earth < God < [by] HASHEM < of the making < on the day

שִׂיחַ הַשָּׂדֶה טֶרֶם יִהְיֶה בָאָרֶץ וְכָל־עֵשֶׂב
< the herbs < and all << on the earth, < to be < were yet < of the field < the trees

הַשָּׂדֶה טֶרֶם יִצְמָח כִּי לֹא הִמְטִיר יְהֹוָה אֱלֹהִים
< —[He,] HASHEM God, < He had not sent rain < for << to sprout, < were yet < of the field

עַל־הָאָרֶץ וְאָדָם אַיִן לַעֲבֹד אֶת־הָאֲדָמָה: ו וְאֵד יַעֲלֶה מִן־הָאָרֶץ
< the earth, < from < would ascend < A mist 6 << the ground. < to work < was not there < and man < the earth < upon

וְהִשְׁקָה אֶת־כָּל־פְּנֵי־הָאֲדָמָה: ז וַיִּיצֶר יְהֹוָה אֱלֹהִים אֶת־הָאָדָם עָפָר
< of dust < the man < And HASHEM God formed 7 << of the ground. < surface < the whole < and it watered

בְּיוֹמָא דִּי עֲבַד יְיָ אֱלֹהִים אַרְעָא
וּשְׁמַיָּא: ה וְכֹל אִילָנֵי חַקְלָא עַד
לָא הֲווֹ בְאַרְעָא וְכָל עִסְבָּא דְחַקְלָא
עַד לָא צְמַח אֲרֵי לָא אַחִית
מִטְרָא יְיָ אֱלֹהִים עַל אַרְעָא
וֶאֱנַשׁ לַיִת לְמִפְלַח יָת אַדְמְתָא:
ו וַעֲנָנָא הֲוָה סָלִיק מִן אַרְעָא
וְאַשְׁקֵי יָת כָּל אַפֵּי אַדְמְתָא:
ז וּבְרָא יְיָ אֱלֹהִים יָת אָדָם עַפְרָא

רש"י

לעשות בשבת כפל ועשאה בששי, כמו שמפורש בב"ר (שם ט): (ד) **אלה.** האמורים למעלה: **תולדות השמים והארץ בהבראם ביום עשות ה'.** למדך שכלם נבראו בראשון (תנחומא ישן א־ב; ב"ר יב: ד). ד"א, בהבראם, בה' בראם, שנאמר ביה ה' צור עולמים (ישעיה כו:ד) בב' אותיות הללו של השם יצר שני עולמים. ולמדך כאן שהעולם הזה נברא בה"א [ס"א רמז כמו שהה"א פתוחה למטה כך העולם פתוח לשבים בתשובה (פס"ר כא (קט:)) ועוה"ב נברא ביו"ד לומר שצדיקים שבאותו זמן מועטים כמו י' שהיא קטנה באותיות (מנחות כט:).] רמז שירדו [הרשעים] למטה לראות שחת כה"א זאת שסתומה מכל צדדיה ופתוחה למטה לרדת דרך שם (ב"ר יב:י; מנחות שם): (ה) **טרם יהיה בארץ.** כל טרם שבמקרא לשון עד לא הוא (אונקלוס) ואינו לשון קודם, ואינו נפעל לומר הטרים כאשר יאמר הקדים, וזה מוכיח, ועוד אחר, כי טרם תיראון (שמות ט:ל) עדיין לא תיראון. ואף זה תפרש, עדיין לא היה בארץ כשנגמרה בריאת העולם בששי קודם שנברא אדם, **וכל עשב השדה** עדיין לא צמח. ובשלישי שכתוב ותוצא הארץ לא יצאו אלא על פתח קרקע עמדו עד יום ששי, **כי לא המטיר.** ומה טעם לא המטיר, לפי שא**דם אין לעבוד את האדמה** ואין מכיר בטובתן של גשמים. וכשבא אדם וידע שהם צורך לעולם התפלל עליהם וירדו, וצמחו האילנות והדשאים (חולין ס:): **ה' אלהים.** [ה'] הוא שמו, אלהים שהוא שליט ושופט על כל [העולם]. וכן פירוש זה בכ"מ לפי פשוטו ה' שהוא אלהים: (ו) **ואד יעלה.** לענין בריאתו של אדם, העלה התהום והשקה עננים לשרות העפר ונברא אדם, כגבל זה שנותן מים ואח"כ לש את העיסה, אף כאן והשקה ואח"כ וייצר (ב"ר יד:א; ש"ר ל:יג): (ז) **וייצר.** שתי יצירות, יצירה לעולם הזה ויצירה לתחיית המתים (ב"ר יד:ה) אבל בבהמה שאינה עומדת לדין לא נכתב ביצירתה שני יודי"ן (תנחומא תזריע א):

can be rearranged to spell בְּאַבְרָהָם, meaning that God created the world *for the sake of Abraham (Midrash)*, because he was the epitome of kindness, one of the pillars of the world *(Zohar)*. This suggests further that Abraham was the one who achieved God's purpose for the universe, because until he came on the scene, humanity consistently failed to live up to its mission. That is why Abraham earned the right to be the progenitor of Israel, the nation that was chosen by God to receive the Torah (*Zohar*).

In the above context, it may be that the letter ה of this word is small to symbolize that Abraham's name Abram had a ה added to it (*R' Avie Gold*).

ה' אֱלֹהִים — *HASHEM God.* This is the first mention in the Torah of the Hebrew Four-letter Name י־ה־ו־ה, which denotes God in His Attribute of Mercy. At first, God created the world exclusively with the Attribute of Justice [*Elohim*], because the ideal state is for Man to be judged according to his deeds, without a need for special mercy, but God knew that Man cannot survive without mercy and forbearance. Therefore He added the Name signifying mercy, to teach that He would temper justice with compassion (*Rashi* to 1:1). The Name י־ה־ו־ה also signifies the eternity of God, because its letters are also those of the words הָיָה הֹוֶה וְיִהְיֶה, *He was, is, and will be.* In the words of *Rambam's* fourth principle of faith, God "is the very first and the very last." Everything in the created universe must have a moment when it came into existence, but God is infinite; He transcends time. In recognition of this concept, the Four-letter Name is often translated the Eternal One. This is also the proper Name of God. In respect for its intense holiness, it is not pronounced as it is spelled. In prayer or when reciting a complete Scriptural verse, it is pronounced *Adonoy.* Otherwise, it is referred to as HASHEM, or the Name.

5. כִּי לֹא הִמְטִיר — *For He had not sent rain.* He had not sent rain because *man was not there to work the soil,* and there was no one to recognize the utility of rain. But when Adam was created, he recognized its importance for the world. He prayed, and rain fell, causing the trees and vegetation to spring forth (*Rashi*). As noted above, plant life had already been created and was waiting just below the surface for Adam to pray (see 1:12). This demonstrates a basic article of faith: God provides what Man needs, but it is up to Man to pray and otherwise carry out his spiritual responsibilities. As the Sages say regarding the Matriarchs: Sarah, Rebecca, Rachel, and Leah were each, by nature, incapable of bearing children. God created them that way because He knew that they and their husbands would pray for children, and God desires the prayers of the righteous.

מִן־הָאֲדָמָה וַיִּפַּח בְּאַפָּיו נִשְׁמַת חַיִּים וַיְהִי הָאָדָם

‹ and man became ‹‹ of life; ‹ the soul ‹ into his nostrils ‹ and He blew ‹‹ the ground, ‹ from

לְנֶפֶשׁ חַיָּה: ח וַיִּטַּע יהוה אֱלֹהִים גַּן בְּעֵדֶן

‹ in Eden, ‹ a garden ‹ HASHEM God planted 8 ‹‹ that is alive. ‹ a being

מִקֶּדֶם וַיָּשֶׂם שָׁם אֶת־הָאָדָם אֲשֶׁר יָצָר:

‹‹ He had formed. ‹ whom ‹ the man ‹ there ‹ and He placed ‹‹ to the east,

ט וַיַּצְמַח יהוה אֱלֹהִים מִן־הָאֲדָמָה כָּל־עֵץ נֶחְמָד

‹ desirable ‹ tree ‹ every ‹ the ground ‹ from ‹ And HASHEM God caused to sprout 9

לְמַרְאֶה וְטוֹב לְמַאֲכָל וְעֵץ הַחַיִּים בְּתוֹךְ הַגָּן וְעֵץ הַדַּעַת טוֹב וָרָע:

‹‹ and Bad. ‹ of Good ‹ of Knowledge ‹ and the Tree ‹‹ of the garden, ‹ in the midst ‹ of Life ‹ and [also] the Tree ‹‹ for food; ‹ and good ‹ to the sight

י וְנָהָר יֹצֵא מֵעֵדֶן לְהַשְׁקוֹת אֶת־הַגָּן וּמִשָּׁם יִפָּרֵד וְהָיָה לְאַרְבָּעָה

‹ four ‹ and becomes ‹ it is divided ‹ and from there ‹ the garden, ‹ to water ‹ from Eden ‹ issues forth ‹ A river 10

רָאשִׁים: יא שֵׁם הָאֶחָד פִּישׁוֹן הוּא הַסֹּבֵב אֵת כָּל־אֶרֶץ הַחֲוִילָה אֲשֶׁר־

‹ which is ‹‹ of Havilah, ‹ land ‹ the whole ‹ the one that encircles ‹ it is ‹‹ is Pishon, ‹ of the one ‹ The name 11 ‹‹ headwaters.

מִן אַדְמְתָא וּנְפַח בְּאַנְפּוֹהִי נִשְׁמְתָא דְחַיֵּי וַהֲוַת בְּאָדָם לְרוּחַ מְמַלְלָא: ח וּנְצִיב יְיָ אֱלֹהִים גִּינְתָא בְעֵדֶן מִלְּקַדְמִין וְאַשְׁרֵי תַמָּן יָת אָדָם דִּי בְרָא: ט וְאַצְמַח יְיָ אֱלֹהִים מִן אַרְעָא כָּל אִילָן דִּמְרַגַּג לְמֶחֱזֵי וְטַב לְמֵיכַל וְאִילַן חַיַּיָּא בִּמְצִיעוּת גִּינְתָא וְאִילָן דְּאָכְלִין פֵּירוֹהִי חַכִּימִין בֵּין טַב לְבִישׁ: י וְנַהֲרָא הֲוָה נָפִיק מֵעֵדֶן לְאַשְׁקָאָה יָת גִּינְתָא וּמִתַּמָּן יִתְפָּרֵשׁ וַהֲוָא לְאַרְבְּעָה רֵישֵׁי נַהֲרִין: יא שׁוּם חַד פִּישׁוֹן הוּא מַקִּיף יָת כָּל אֲרַע דַּחֲוִילָה דִּי

רש"י

עפר מן האדמה. צבר עפרו מכל האדמה מארבע רוחות, שכל מקום שימות שם תהא קולטתו לקבורה (תנחומא פקודי ג). ד"א, נטל עפרו ממקום שנאמר בו מזבח אדמה תעשה לי (שמות כ:כא) הלואי תהא לו כפרה ויוכל לעמוד (ב"ר יד:ח): **ויפח באפיו.** עשאו מן התחתונים ומן העליונים, גוף מן התחתונים ונשמה מן העליונים. לפי שביום ראשון נבראו שמים וארץ, בשני ברא רקיע לעליונים, בשלישי תראה היבשה לתחתונים, ברביעי ברא מאורות לעליונים, בחמישי ישרצו המים לתחתונים, הוזקק הששי לבראות בו בעליונים ובתחתונים ואם לאו יש קנאה במעשה בראשית, שיהיו אלו רבים על אלו בבריאת יום אחד (שם יב:ח): **לנפש חיה.** אף בהמה וחיה נקראו נפש חיה אך זו של אדם חיה שבכולן, שנתוסף בו דעה ודבור (אונקלוס): **(ח) מקדם.** במזרחו של עדן נטע את הגן. ואם תאמר, הרי כבר נאמר ויברא וגו' את האדם וגו'. ראיתי בברייתא של ר' אליעזר בנו של ר' יוסי הגלילי מל"ב מדות שהתורה נדרשת (מדה יג) וזו אחת מהן, כלל שלאחריו מעשה הוא פרטו של ראשון. ויברא את האדם וגו' זהו כלל, סתם בריאתו מהיכן וסתם מעשיו, חזר ופירש וייצר ה' אלהים וגו' ויצמח לו גן עדן ויניחהו בגן עדן ויפל עליו תרדמה, השומע סבור שהוא מעשה אחר, ואינו אלא פרטו של ראשון. וכן אצל הבהמה חזר וכתב ויצר ה' וגו' מן האדמה כל חית השדה (להלן פסוק יט) כדי לפרש ויבא אל האדם לקרות שם, וללמד על העופות שנבראו מן הרקק (חולין כז:): **(ט) ויצמח.** לענין הגן הכתוב מדבר (ב"ר יג:א): **בתוך הגן.** באמצע הגן (אונקלוס): **(יא) פישון.** הוא נילוס נהר מצרים, וע"ש שמימיו מתברכין ועולין ומשקין את הארץ נקרא פישון כמו ופשו פרשיו (חבקוק א:ח). ד"א פישון שהוא מגדל פשתן שנאמר אצל מצרים ובשו עובדי פשתים (ישעיה יט:ט; ב"ר טז:ב):

7. וַיִּפַּח בְּאַפָּיו נִשְׁמַת חַיִּים — *And He blew into his nostrils the soul of life.* God thus made Man out of both lower [earthly] and upper [heavenly] matter: his body from the dust and his soul from the spirit (*Rashi*). In the words of the *Zohar*, "one who blows, blows from within himself," indicating that Man's soul is part of God's essence, as it were. This soul made Man *a being that is alive,* which *Onkelos* defines as *a spirit that speaks.* Accordingly, the life that is unique to Man and which only God could "blow" into him is the rational soul that includes the power of intelligent speech. This is what elevates a human above animal life: the ability, and therefore the responsibility, to use his intelligence in God's service.

9. וְעֵץ הַדַּעַת טוֹב וָרָע — *And the Tree of Knowledge of Good and Bad. Nefesh HaChaim* explains the effect of eating the fruit of the tree, which God would forbid (v. 17). As Adam and Eve were originally created, their natural impulse was to do good. Although they knew in the abstract that there was such a thing as sin, it was not something that they craved. By eating of the tree, which embodied a *mixture* of good and evil — hence its name, the Tree of Knowledge of Good and Evil — they brought evil into themselves and made it part of their nature. Once they ate from the tree, they changed the nature of Man. From then on, Man was born with evil impulses, such as greed, selfishness, and lust for whatever suits his developing appetite. Through study, thought, and self-discipline, he must curb his base nature and desires, and inculcate into himself a desire for good and a revulsion for evil.

Sforno explains the name of the tree differently. It refers to

שם הזהב: יב וזהב הארץ ההוא טוב שם הבדלח

« the bedolach, ‹ there is [found] « is good; ‹ of that land ‹ The gold 12 « the gold. ‹ where there is

ואבן השהם: יג ושם־הנהר השני גיחון הוא

‹ it is « is Gihon, ‹ of the second river ‹ The name 13 « of shoham. ‹ and the stone

הסובב את כל־ארץ כוש: יד ושם־הנהר השלישי

‹ of the third river ‹ The name 14 « of Cush. ‹ land ‹ the whole ‹ the one that encircles

חדקל הוא ההלך קדמת אשור והנהר הרביעי

‹ and the fourth river « of Assyria; ‹ toward the east ‹ the one that flows ‹ it is « is Hiddekel,

תמן דהבא: יב ודהבא דארעא ההיא טב תמן בדלחא ואבני בורלא: יג ושום נהרא תנינא גיחון הוא מקיף ית כל ארעא דכוש: יד ושום נהרא תליתאה דיגלת הוא מהלך למדנחא דאתור ונהרא רביעאה הוא פרת: טו ודבר יי אלהים ית אדם ואשרה בגינתא דעדן למפלחה ולמטרה: טז ופקיד יי אלהים על אדם למימר מכל אילן גינתא מיכל תיכול: יז ומאילן דאכלין פירוהי חכימין בין טב לביש לא תיכול מנה ארי ביומא דתיכול מנה מימת תמות: יח ואמר יי אלהים לא תקין למהוי אדם בלחודוהי

הוא פרת: טו ויקח יהוה אלהים את־האדם וינחהו בגן־עדן לעבדה

‹ to work it ‹ of Eden, ‹ in the Garden ‹ and He placed him ‹ the man ‹ HASHEM God took 15 « the Euphrates. ‹ is

ולשמרה: טז ויצו יהוה אלהים על־האדם לאמר מכל עץ־הגן

‹ *of the garden* ‹ *tree* ‹ *Of every* « saying, ‹ the man, ‹ upon ‹ And HASHEM God commanded 16 « and to guard it.

אכל תאכל: יז ומעץ הדעת טוב ורע לא תאכל ממנו כי ביום אכלך

‹ *you eat* ‹ *on the day* ‹ *for* « *of it;* ‹ *you shall not eat* ‹ *and Bad,* ‹ *Good* ‹ *of Knowledge* ‹ *but of the Tree* 17 « *you may surely eat;*

ממנו מות תמות: יח ויאמר יהוה אלהים לא־טוב היות האדם לבדו

« alone; ‹ that the man should be ‹ good ‹ It is not « HASHEM God said, 18 « *you shall surely die.* ‹ *of it,*

רש"י

[(יג) **גיחון.** שהיה הולך והומה והמייתו גדולה מאד, כמו וכי יגח (שמות כא:כח) שמנגח והולך והומה:] **(יד) [חדקל.** שמימיו חדין וקלין (ברכות נט:): **פרת.** שמימיו פרין ורבין (שם; ב"ר שם ג,ז) ומברין את האדם (כתובות עז:):] **כוש ואשור.** עדיין לא היו וכתב המקרא ע"ש העתיד (ב"ר שם ג; כתובות י:): **קדמת אשור.** למזרחה של אשור (אונקלוס): **הוא פרת.** החשוב על כולם הנזכר על שם א"י (ספרי דברים ו; ב"ר שם): **(טו) ויקח.** לקחו בדברים נאים ופתהו ליכנס (ב"ר שם ה): **(יח) לא טוב היות וגו'.** שלא יאמרו שתי רשויות הן, הקב"ה יחיד בעליונים ואין לו זוג וזה יחיד בתחתונים ואין לו זוג (פדר"א יב):

Man's unwholesome capacity to choose what is superficially sweet [*good*] even though it is harmful to him, and to reject what is superficially bitter [*bad*] even when it is truly beneficial.

15-18. Man in the Garden. Adam was placed in the Garden of Eden *to work it and to guard it* (v. 15). The Midrash interprets this allegorically, since the Torah mentioned above that the trees of the garden grew of their own accord and the river provided the necessary irrigation. Rather, Adam was to work the garden through the study of Torah and the performance of positive commandments, and to guard it by refraining from forbidden activities (*Pirkei d'Rabbi Eliezer*). This means that Man's task in this world is to serve God. If he does that, then his material needs will be satisfied, as Adam's were in Eden, for to think that only physical exertion can bring success is to believe in an illusion.

17. מות תמות — *You shall surely die.* Since Adam lived to the age of 930, it is clear that he was not to die as soon as he ate the fruit. Rather, he would become *subject* to death, whereas if he had never sinned, his holiness would have kept him alive forever.

18-25. A companion for Adam. This passage does not describe a new creation; it merely elaborates upon the making of the creatures mentioned in 1:25. God knew that Adam needed a companion. God wanted Adam to have the companionship, support, and challenge that is present in good marriages, and He wanted the children who would be born to Adam and his future mate to be reared by both a father and a mother. The needs for such assets in human life are too obvious to require elaboration. But before creating Adam's helpmate, God brought all the creatures to him so that he could see for himself that none was suited to his needs, and *he* would ask for a companion. Then he would appreciate his newly fashioned

אֶֽעֱשֶׂה־לּוֹ עֵזֶר כְּנֶגְדּוֹ: יט וַיִּצֶר יהוה אֱלֹהִים מִן־
< from out < [Now], HASHEM God had formed 19 « corresponding to him. < a helper < for him < I will make

הָאֲדָמָה כָּל־חַיַּת הַשָּׂדֶה וְאֵת כָּל־עוֹף הַשָּׁמַיִם
< of the sky, < bird < and every < of the field < beast < every < of the ground

וַיָּבֵא אֶל־הָאָדָם לִרְאוֹת מַה־יִּקְרָא־לוֹ וְכֹל
< and every [name] « each one [of them]; < he would call < what < to see < the man < to < and brought [them]

אֲשֶׁר יִקְרָא־לוֹ הָאָדָם נֶפֶשׁ חַיָּה הוּא שְׁמוֹ: שלישי כ וַיִּקְרָא הָאָדָם שֵׁמוֹת
< names < And the man called 20 « its name. < that [remained] « that is alive, < each being < the man would call it < that

לְכָל־הַבְּהֵמָה וּלְעוֹף הַשָּׁמַיִם וּלְכֹל חַיַּת הַשָּׂדֶה וּלְאָדָם לֹא־מָצָא
< he did not find < but for man, « of the field; < beast < and to every < of the sky < and to the birds < the animals < to all

עֵזֶר כְּנֶגְדּוֹ: כא וַיַּפֵּל יהוה אֱלֹהִים | תַּרְדֵּמָה עַל־הָאָדָם וַיִּישָׁן וַיִּקַּח
< and He took « and he slept; < the man < upon < a deep sleep < So HASHEM God cast 21 « corresponding to him. < a helper

אַחַת מִצַּלְעֹתָיו וַיִּסְגֹּר בָּשָׂר תַּחְתֶּנָּה: כב וַיִּבֶן יהוה אֱלֹהִים | אֶת־הַצֵּלָע
< the side < Then HASHEM God built up 22 « in its place. < with flesh < and He closed over < of his sides < one

אֶעְבֵּד לֵהּ סָמֵךְ לְקִבְלֵהּ: יט וּבְרָא יְיָ אֱלֹהִים מִן אַרְעָא כָּל חֵיוַת בָּרָא וְיָת כָּל עוֹפָא דִשְׁמַיָּא וְאַיְתֵי לְוָת אָדָם לְמֶחֱזֵי מַה יִקְרֵי לֵהּ וְכֹל דִּי הֲוָה קָרֵי לֵהּ אָדָם נַפְשָׁא חַיְתָא הוּא שְׁמֵהּ: כ וּקְרָא אָדָם שְׁמָהָן לְכָל בְּעִירָא וּלְעוֹפָא דִשְׁמַיָּא וּלְכֹל חֵיוַת בָּרָא וּלְאָדָם לָא אַשְׁכַּח סָמֵךְ לְקִבְלֵהּ: כא וּרְמָא יְיָ אֱלֹהִים שִׁינְתָא עַל אָדָם וּדְמֵךְ וּנְסִיב חֲדָא מֵעִלְעוֹהִי וּמְלֵי בִשְׂרָא תְּחוֹתַהּ: כב וּבְנָא יְיָ אֱלֹהִים יָת עִלְעָא דִּנְסִיב מִן

רש"י

עזר כנגדו. זכה, עזר. לא זכה, כנגדו להלחם (יבמות סג.; פדר"א שם): **(יט) ויצר וגו' מן האדמה.** היא יצירה היא עשייה האמורה למעלה, ויעש אלהים את חית הארץ וגו' (לעיל א:כה) אלא בא ופי' שהעופות נבראו מן הרקק, לפי שאמר למעלה מן המים נבראו וכאן אמר מן האדמה נבראו (חולין כז:). ועוד למדך כאן שבשעת יצירתן מיד [בו ביום] הביאם אל האדם לקרות להם שם (אדר"נ פ"א). ובדברי אגדה, יצירה זו לשון רידוי וכבוש, כמו כי תצור אל עיר (דברים כ:יט), שכבשן תחת ידו של אדם (ב"ר יז:ד): **וכל אשר יקרא לו האדם נפש חיה וגו'.** סרסהו ופרשהו, כל נפש חיה אשר יקרא לו האדם שם הוא שמו לעולם: **(כ-כא) ולאדם לא מצא עזר: ויפל ה' אלהים תרדמה.** כשהביאן הביאן לפניו כל מין ומין זכר ונקבה. אמר, לכלם יש בן זוג ולי אין בן זוג, מיד ויפל (ב"ר יז:ד). **מצלעותיו.** מסטריו כמו ולצלע המשכן (שמות כו:כ) זהו שאמרו שני פרצופים נבראו (ב"ר ח:א): **ויסגור.** מקום החתך (ברכות סא.): **ויישן ויקח.** שלא יראה חתיכת הבשר שממנו נבראת ותתבזה עליו (סנהדרין לט.): **(כב) ויבן.** כבנין, רחבה מלמטה וקצרה מלמעלה לקבל הולד, כאוצר של חטים שהוא רחב מלמטה וקצר מלמעלה שלא יכבד משאו על קירותיו (ברכות שם): **ויבן**

mate and not take her for granted.

Adam named her gender *Ishah* [Woman], because she was taken from *Ish* [Man] (v. 23); but why is Man called *Ish*? That name is related to fire, *eish* [אִישׁ = אֵשׁ], because Man is unique in the characteristics symbolized by fire: verve and enthusiasm, lust and initiative. These characteristics enable Man to achieve dominance, attain wisdom, and develop culture. But the same fire can cause the mass destruction that has marred humanity almost since the beginning of time. Controlled and directed, that fire can create spiritual kingdoms that surpass the angels.

The presence of Godliness in human beings is expressed by the letters that are added to their names: י in the name אִישׁ and ה in אִשָּׁה. These letters spell the Divine Name יָהּ — because God must be present in the union of a man and wife. If they allow Him in, their union is Godly; if not, they are left with אֵשׁ, a destructive *fire*, that will harm not only their own relationship, but may unleash a conflagration that will harm all around them.

18. עֵזֶר כְּנֶגְדּוֹ — *A helper corresponding to him* [lit., *a helper against him*]. If the man is worthy, the woman will be *a helper;* if he is unworthy, she will be *against him (Yevamos* 63a; *Rashi)*. Many have noted that the ideal marriage is not necessarily one of total agreement in all matters. Often it is the wife's responsibility to oppose her husband and prevent him from acting rashly, or to help him achieve a common course by questioning, criticizing, and discussing. Thus, the verse means literally that there are times a wife can best be a helper by being against him (see 21:10-12).

20. שֵׁמוֹת — *Names.* In the Torah's concept, a name is not simply a convenient convention, but it reflects the nature of each creature and its role in the total scheme of the universe. Thus, as we find over and over in the Torah, the names of people had a profound significance that expressed their mission. Adam had the power to recognize the essence of every animal and name it accordingly (*Radak*). Having this insight into every creature, he realized that none of them corresponded to his essence, socially and intellectually.

אֲשֶׁר־לָקַח מִן־הָאָדָם לְאִשָּׁה וַיְבִאֶהָ אֶל־הָאָדָם׃
that He had taken from the man into a woman, and He brought her to the man.

כג וַיֹּאמֶר הָאָדָם זֹאת הַפַּעַם עֶצֶם מֵעֲצָמַי וּבָשָׂר
23 And the man said, *This time [it is] bone of my bones and flesh*

מִבְּשָׂרִי לְזֹאת יִקָּרֵא אִשָּׁה כִּי מֵאִישׁ לֻקְחָה־
of my flesh. This shall be called Woman, for from man was taken

זֹּאת׃ כד עַל־כֵּן יַעֲזָב־אִישׁ אֶת־אָבִיו וְאֶת־אִמּוֹ
this [woman]. **24** For this reason, a man shall leave his father and his mother

וְדָבַק בְּאִשְׁתּוֹ וְהָיוּ לְבָשָׂר אֶחָד׃ כה וַיִּהְיוּ שְׁנֵיהֶם עֲרוּמִּים הָאָדָם
and cling to his wife and they shall become one flesh. **25** They were — both of them — naked, the man

וְאִשְׁתּוֹ וְלֹא יִתְבֹּשָׁשׁוּ׃ [ג] א וְהַנָּחָשׁ הָיָה עָרוּם מִכֹּל חַיַּת הַשָּׂדֶה אֲשֶׁר
and his wife, but they were not ashamed. **[3] 1** Now the serpent was cunning beyond any beast of the field that

עָשָׂה יהוה אֱלֹהִים וַיֹּאמֶר אֶל־הָאִשָּׁה אַף כִּי־אָמַר אֱלֹהִים לֹא תֹאכְלוּ
HASHEM God had made; he said to the woman, *Is it so that God said: 'You shall not eat*

מִכֹּל עֵץ הַגָּן׃ ב וַתֹּאמֶר הָאִשָּׁה אֶל־הַנָּחָשׁ מִפְּרִי עֵץ־הַגָּן נֹאכֵל׃
of any tree of the garden'? **2** The woman said to the serpent, *Of the fruit of [any] tree of the garden we may eat.*

אָדָם לְאִתְּתָא וְאַיְתַהּ לְוַת אָדָם׃
כג וַאֲמַר אָדָם הָדָא זִמְנָא גַּרְמָא
מִגַּרְמַי וּבִסְרָא מִבִּסְרִי לְדָא יִתְקְרֵי
אִתְּתָא אֲרֵי מִבַּעְלָא נְסִיבָא דָא׃
כד עַל כֵּן יִשְׁבּוֹק גְּבַר בֵּית מִשְׁכְּבֵי
אֲבוּהִי וְאִמֵּהּ וְיִדְבַּק בְּאִתְּתֵהּ וִיהוֹן
לְבִסְרָא חָד׃ כה וַהֲווֹ תַרְוֵיהוֹן
עַרְטִילָאִין אָדָם וְאִתְּתֵהּ וְלָא
מִתְכַּלְמִין׃ א וְחִוְיָא הֲוָה חַכִּים
מִכֹּל חֵוַת בָּרָא דִּי עֲבַד יְיָ אֱלֹהִים
וַאֲמַר לְאִתְּתָא בְּקוּשְׁטָא אֲרֵי
אֲמַר יְיָ לָא תֵיכְלוּן מִכֹּל אִילַן
גִּינְתָא׃ ב וַאֲמֶרֶת אִתְּתָא לְחִוְיָא
מִפֵּירֵי אִילַן גִּינְתָא נֵיכוּל׃

רש"י

וגו' את הצלע וגו' לאשה. להיות אשה כמו ויעש אותו גדעון לאפוד (שופטים ח:כז) להיות אפוד: **(כג) זאת הפעם.** מלמד שבא אדם על כל בהמה וחיה ולא נתקררה דעתו בהם (יבמות סג.): **לזאת יקרא אשה כי מאיש וגו'.** לשון נופל על לשון מכאן שנברא העולם בלשון הקדש (ב"ר יח:ד): **(כד) על כן יעזב איש.** רוה"ק אומרת כן, לאסור על בני נח את העריות (שם ה; סנהדרין נח.): **לבשר אחד.** הולד נוצר ע"י שניהם ושם נעשה בשרם אחד (שם ושם): **(כה) ולא יתבששו.** שלא היו יודעים דרך צניעות להבחין בין טוב לרע (תרגום ירושלמי) ואע"פ שנתנה בו דעה לקרות שמות (ב"ר יז:ד) לא נתן בו יצר הרע עד אכלו מן העץ ונכנס בו יצר הרע וידע מה בין טוב לרע (עי' שם יט:ט): **(א) והנחש היה ערום.** מה ענין זה לכאן, היה לו לסמוך ויעש לאדם ולאשתו כתנות עור וילבישם. אלא ללמדך מאיזו עצה קפץ הנחש עליהם, ראה אותם ערומים ועסוקים בתשמיש לעין כל ונתאוה להם (שם יח:ו): **ערום מכל.** לפי ערמתו וגדולתו היתה מפלתו, ערום מכל ארור מכל (שם יט:א): **אף כי אמר וגו'.** שמא אמר לכם לא תאכלו מכל וגו', ואע"פ שראה אותם אוכלים משאר פירות, הרבה עליה דברים כדי שתשיבנו ויבא לדבר באותו העץ:

22. אֶת־הַצֵּלָע . . . לְאִשָּׁה — *The side . . . into a woman.* Unlike man's, the woman's body was not taken from the earth. God built one side of man into woman — so that the single human being became two, thereby demonstrating irrefutably the equality of man and woman (*R' Hirsch*).

24. יַעֲזָב־אִישׁ — *A man shall leave.* The Torah does not mean that a man should not continue to serve or honor his parents. It implies only a *physical* separation; his attachment to his wife should be so strong that he will move out of his parents' house and establish a new home with her (*Radak; R' Meyuchas*).

לְבָשָׂר אֶחָד — *One flesh.* Let him cling to his wife and to none other, because man and wife are in reality one flesh, as they were at the beginning of Creation (*Tur*). But that can happen only if they also become one mind, one heart, one soul . . . and if they subordinate all their strength and effort to the service of God (*R' Hirsch*).

25. וְלֹא יִתְבֹּשָׁשׁוּ — *But they were not ashamed.* People are ashamed of their nakedness because they associate vileness and lust with their private parts. But not Adam and Eve. As *Sforno* explains, they used all their organs exclusively to do God's will, not to satisfy their personal desires. To them, even cohabitation was as innocent as eating and drinking, so they had no reason to cover their bodies.

3.

1-14. The serpent's enticement. The Torah does not say how much time elapsed between the creation of Adam and Eve and their expulsion from the Garden of Eden. The Sages, however, tell us explicitly that *all the events related here* — including

ג וּמִפְּרִי הָעֵץ אֲשֶׁר בְּתוֹךְ־הַגָּן אָמַר אֱלֹהִים

« has God said: ‹ of the garden ‹ in the center ‹ that is ‹ of the tree ‹ But of the fruit 3

לֹא תֹאכְלוּ מִמֶּנּוּ וְלֹא תִגְּעוּ בּוֹ פֶּן־תְּמֻתוּן׃

« you die.' ‹ lest ‹ it, ‹ and you shall not touch ‹ of it ‹ 'You shall not eat

ד וַיֹּאמֶר הַנָּחָשׁ אֶל־הָאִשָּׁה לֹא־מוֹת תְּמֻתוּן׃

« [that] you will surely die; ‹ It is not so « the woman, ‹ to ‹ The serpent said 4

ה כִּי יֹדֵעַ אֱלֹהִים כִּי בְּיוֹם אֲכָלְכֶם מִמֶּנּוּ וְנִפְקְחוּ עֵינֵיכֶם וִהְיִיתֶם

‹ and you will be ‹ your eyes will be opened ‹ of it ‹ you eat ‹ on the day ‹ that ‹ God knows ‹ for 5

כֵּאלֹהִים יֹדְעֵי טוֹב וָרָע׃ ו וַתֵּרֶא הָאִשָּׁה כִּי טוֹב הָעֵץ לְמַאֲכָל וְכִי

‹ and that « for food, ‹ the tree was good ‹ that ‹ And the woman saw 6 « and bad. ‹ good ‹ who know « like the godly [ones],

תַאֲוָה־הוּא לָעֵינַיִם וְנֶחְמָד הָעֵץ לְהַשְׂכִּיל וַתִּקַּח מִפִּרְיוֹ וַתֹּאכַל וַתִּתֵּן

‹ and she gave « and she ate; ‹ of its fruit ‹ and she took « for awareness, ‹ was the tree ‹ and that desirable « to the eyes, ‹ it was ‹ enticing

גַּם־לְאִישָׁהּ עִמָּהּ וַיֹּאכַל׃ ז וַתִּפָּקַחְנָה עֵינֵי שְׁנֵיהֶם וַיֵּדְעוּ כִּי עֵירֻמִּם הֵם

« were they; ‹ naked ‹ that ‹ and they realized ‹ of both of them ‹ the eyes ‹ And then [were] opened 7 « and he ate. ‹ with her ‹ to her husband ‹ also

ג וּמִפֵּירֵי אִילָנָא דִּי בִמְצִיעוּת גִּינְתָא אֲמַר יְיָ לָא תֵיכְלוּן מִנֵּהּ וְלָא תִקְרְבוּן בֵּהּ דִּילְמָא תְמוּתוּן: ד וַאֲמַר חִוְיָא לְאִתְּתָא לָא מוֹת תְּמוּתוּן: ה אֲרֵי גְּלֵי קֳדָם יְיָ אֲרֵי בְּיוֹמָא דְתֵיכְלוּן מִנֵּהּ וְיִתְפַּתְּחָן עֵינֵיכוֹן וּתְהוֹן כְּרַבְרְבִין חַכִּימִין בֵּין טַב לְבִישׁ: ו וַחֲזַת אִתְּתָא אֲרֵי טַב אִילָן לְמֵיכָל וַאֲרֵי אַסֵּי הוּא לְעֵינִין וּמְרַגַּג אִילָנָא לְאִסְתַּכָּלָא בֵהּ וּנְסִיבַת מֵאִבֵּהּ וַאֲכָלַת וִיהָבַת אַף לְבַעְלַהּ עִמַּהּ וַאֲכָל: ז וְאִתְפַּתַּחָא עֵינֵי תַרְוֵיהוֹן וִידָעוּ אֲרֵי עַרְטִילָאִין אִנּוּן

רש"י

(ג) **ולא תגעו בו.** הוסיפה על הצווי לפיכך באה לידי גרעון (סנהדרין כט.), הוא שנאמר אל תוסף על דבריו (משלי ל:ו; ב"ר שם ג): (ד) **לא מות תמתון.** דחפה עד שנגעה בו אמר לה כשם שאין מיתה בנגיעה כך אין מיתה באכילה (ב"ר שם): (ה) **כי יודע.** כל אומן שונא את בני אומנותו, מן העץ אכל וברא את העולם (שם ד): **והייתם באלהים.** יוצרי עולמות (שם): (ו) **ותרא האשה.** ראתה דבריו של נחש והנאו לה והאמינתו (שם): **כי טוב העץ.** להיות כאלהים: **וכי תאוה הוא לעינים.** [כמו שאמר לה] ונפקחו עיניכם: **ונחמד העץ להשכיל.** [כמו שאמר לה] יודעי טוב ורע: **ותתן גם לאישה [עמה].** שלא תמות היא ויחיה הוא וישא אחרת (פדר"א יג; ב"ר יט:ה): **גם.** לרבות [כל] בהמה וחיה (ב"ר שם ו): (ז) **ותפקחנה וגו'.** לענין החכמה דבר הכתוב ולא לענין ראיה ממש, וסוף המקרא מוכיח:] **וידעו כי עירמים הם.** אף הסומא יודע

the birth of Cain and Abel — occurred on the day Adam was created. He had been given only one commandment: not to eat from the tree, and now his resolve would be tested to see if he could withstand temptation.

The consensus of the commentators is that the *serpent* was literally a serpent. They differ regarding what it represented: the Evil Inclination, Satan, or the Angel of Death. According to the Midrash, before this cunning beast was cursed, it stood erect and was endowed with some faculty of communication.

3. פֶּן תְּמֻתוּן — *Lest you die.* According to *Avos d'R' Noson* (1:5) Adam transformed the nature of the prohibition when he transmitted it to Eve. The command to Adam was: *You shall not eat ... for ... you shall surely die* (2:17) — an absolute prohibition based only on God's command and with an unequivocal outcome. The version Eve states here sounds like a health advisory: *Beware of the fruit because it is dangerous to health.* In Eve's version, the addition not to touch the "dangerous" fruit is quite understandable, but the addition of touch has no relationship to the original absolute prohibition, which is not dependent on the nature of the fruit. *Bereishis Rabbah* (15:7) suggests that it was Adam's haughtiness that led him to the sin. [Perhaps Adam did not wish to admit to Eve that God's word must be obeyed without questioning.]

5-6. כִּי יֹדֵעַ אֱלֹהִים — *For God knows.* The serpent used a ploy familiar to those who try to rationalize away the Torah. They contend that those who convey and interpret the Law of God are motivated by a selfish desire to consolidate power in themselves. "God did not prohibit this tree out of any concern for your lives, but because He is aware that by eating from it you will attain extra wisdom, and become omniscient like Him. Then you will be independent of Him" (*R' Hirsch*). The tempter did not explicitly tell the woman to eat the fruit, but he had enveloped her in his spell. She looked on the tree with a new longing — its fruit was good to eat, a delight to the eyes, and it would give her wisdom. Then she brought it to Adam and repeated everything the serpent had told her. He was עִמָּהּ, *at one with her,* and not blameless, and therefore liable to punishment (*Radak; Ibn Ezra*).

7. וַיֵּדְעוּ . . . — *And they realized . . .* The serpent was right: They had become enlightened people. But their first realiza-

וַיִּתְפְּרוּ עֲלֵה תְאֵנָה וַיַּעֲשׂוּ לָהֶם חֲגֹרֹת׃

« waistcloths. ‹ themselves ‹ and they made ‹ of a fig [tree] ‹ a leaf ‹ and they sewed

ח וַיִּשְׁמְעוּ אֶת־קוֹל יְהוָה אֱלֹהִים מִתְהַלֵּךְ בַּגָּן

‹ in the garden ‹ moving about ‹ God ‹ of HASHEM ‹ the sound ‹ They heard **8**

לְרוּחַ הַיּוֹם וַיִּתְחַבֵּא הָאָדָם וְאִשְׁתּוֹ מִפְּנֵי יְהוָה

‹ HASHEM ‹ from before « with his wife ‹ and the man hid « of the evening [sun]; ‹ in the direction

אֱלֹהִים בְּתוֹךְ עֵץ הַגָּן׃ ט וַיִּקְרָא יְהוָה אֱלֹהִים אֶל־

‹ to ‹ HASHEM God called out **9** « of the garden. ‹ of the tree ‹ in the midst « God,

הָאָדָם וַיֹּאמֶר לוֹ אַיֶּכָּה׃ י וַיֹּאמֶר אֶת־קֹלְךָ שָׁמַעְתִּי בַּגָּן וָאִירָא כִּי־

‹ *because* ‹ *and I was afraid* « *in the garden,* ‹ *I did hear* ‹ *The sound of You* « He said, **10** « *Where are you?* « to him, ‹ and said ‹ the man

עֵירֹם אָנֹכִי וָאֵחָבֵא׃ יא וַיֹּאמֶר מִי הִגִּיד לְךָ כִּי עֵירֹם אָתָּה הֲמִן־הָעֵץ

‹ *the tree* ‹ *Could it be that from* « *you are naked?* ‹ *that* ‹ *you* ‹ *told* ‹ *Who* « And He said, **11** « *and [so] I hid.* « *am I,* ‹ *naked*

אֲשֶׁר צִוִּיתִיךָ לְבִלְתִּי אֲכָל־מִמֶּנּוּ אָכָלְתָּ׃ יב וַיֹּאמֶר הָאָדָם הָאִשָּׁה אֲשֶׁר

‹ *whom* ‹ *The woman* « The man said, **12** « *you have eaten?* ‹ *of it* ‹ *to eat* ‹ *not* ‹ *I commanded you* ‹ *that*

נָתַתָּה עִמָּדִי הִוא נָתְנָה־לִּי מִן־הָעֵץ וָאֹכֵל׃ יג וַיֹּאמֶר יְהוָה אֱלֹהִים

‹ And HASHEM God said **13** « *and I ate.* « *the tree,* ‹ *of* ‹ *me* ‹ *gave* ‹ *— she* « *to be with me* ‹ *You gave*

וְחַטִּיטוּ לְהוֹן טַרְפֵּי תְאֵנִין וַעֲבַדוּ לְהוֹן זְרָזִין׃ ח וּשְׁמָעוּ יָת קַל מֵימְרָא דַייָ אֱלֹהִים מְהַלֵּךְ בְּגִינְתָא לִמְנַח יוֹמָא וְאִיטַּמַּר אָדָם וְאִתְּתֵהּ מִן קֳדָם יְיָ אֱלֹהִים בְּגוֹ אִילַן גִּינְתָא׃ ט וּקְרָא יְיָ אֱלֹהִים לְאָדָם וַאֲמַר לֵהּ אָן אָתְּ׃ י וַאֲמַר יָת קַל מֵימְרָךְ שַׁמְעִית בְּגִינְתָא וּדְחֵילִית אֲרֵי עַרְטִילַאי אֲנָא וְאִיטַּמָּרִית׃ יא וַאֲמַר מָן חַוִּי לָךְ אֲרֵי עַרְטִילַאי אָתְּ הֲמִן אִילָנָא דִּי פַקֶּדְתָּךְ בְּדִיל דְּלָא לְמֵיכַל מִנֵּהּ אֲכַלְתְּ׃ יב וַאֲמַר הָאָדָם אִתְּתָא דִּי יְהַבְתָּ עִמִּי הִיא יְהָבַת לִי מִן אִילָנָא וַאֲכָלִית׃ יג וַאֲמַר יְיָ אֱלֹהִים

רש"י

כשהוא ערום:] [אלא מהו] וידעו כי עירמים הם. מלוה אחת היתה בידם ונתערטלו הימנה (ב"ר שם): **עלה תאנה.** הוא העץ שאכלו ממנו, בדבר שנתקלקלו בו נתקנו (ברכות מ.) אבל שאר העצים מנעום מליטול עליהם. ומפני מה לא נתפרסם העץ, שאין הקב"ה חפץ להונות בריה, שלא יכלימוהו ויאמרו זהו שלקה העולם על ידו. מדרש רבי תנחומא (וירא יד): **(ח) וישמעו.** יש מדרשי אגדה רבים, וכבר סדרום רבותינו על מכונם בב"ר ובשאר מדרשות, ואני לא באתי אלא לפשוטו של מקרא ולאגדה המישבת דברי המקרא דבר דבור על אפניו, ובמשמעו. שמעו את קול הקב"ה שהיה מתהלך בגן (ב"ר שם ז): **לרוח היום.** לאותו רוח שהשמש באה משם [ס"א לשם] וזו היא מערבית, שלפנות ערב חמה במערב (שם ח) והמה סרחו בעשירית (סנהדרין לח:): **(ט) איכה.** יודע היה היכן הוא, אלא ליכנס עמו בדברים (תנחומא תזריע ט) שלא יהא נבהל להשיב אם יעניישהו פתאום (עי' דרך ארץ רבה ה). וכן בקין אמר לו אי הבל אחיך (להלן ד:ט), וכן בבלעם מי האנשים האלה עמך (במדבר כב:ט) ליכנס עמהם בדברים, וכן בחזקיהו בשלוחי מרודך בלאדן (ב"ר שם יא): **(יא) מי הגיד לך.** מאין לך לדעת מה בשת יש בעומד ערום: **המן העץ.** בתמיה: **(יב) אשר נתתה עמדי.** כאן כפר בטובה

tion was — that they were naked! . . . Man need not be ashamed of his body as long as it stands in the service of God . . . Otherwise he feels shame in his nakedness. This shame awakens the voice of conscience that reminds us we are not meant to be animals (*R' Hirsch*).

8. וַיִּשְׁמְעוּ — *They heard.* God caused His sound to be heard to afford them the opportunity of hiding (*Radak*), and also to teach etiquette: Do not look upon a man in his disgrace. God did not appear to them immediately after they sinned and felt ashamed; He waited until they had sewn fig leaves together and only then did they hear *the sound of HASHEM God.* The verse also teaches that one should never enter another's home suddenly and unannounced (*Derech Eretz Rabbah* 5).

9-12. אַיֶּכָּה — *Where are you?* God knew where Adam was, of course. The question was merely a means of initiating a calm dialogue with him so he would not be too terrified to repent [or: to reply], as he would be if God were to punish him suddenly. But Adam did not confess. Instead, as v. 12 shows, he hurled against God the very kindness of the gift of Eve, by implying that God was at fault for giving him his wife (*Midrash Aggadah*).

A further meaning of God's question is not that He inquired after Adam's *physical* whereabouts; rather, the significance of the question was, "Consider well how you have fallen from the heights; where is your exalted status?" (*Aderes Eliyahu*).

12. וָאֹכֵל — *And I ate.* In an astounding interpretation, the Sages note that the verb is in the future tense, as if Adam were

לָאִשָּׁה מַה־זֹּאת עָשִׂית וַתֹּאמֶר הָאִשָּׁה הַנָּחָשׁ
< The serpent << The woman said, << that you have done! < is this < What << to the woman,
הִשִּׁיאַנִי וָאֹכֵל: יד וַיֹּאמֶר יהוה אֱלֹהִים | אֶל־הַנָּחָשׁ
<< the serpent, < to < And HASHEM God said 14 << and I ate. << deceived me,
כִּי עָשִׂיתָ זֹּאת אָרוּר אַתָּה מִכָּל־הַבְּהֵמָה
< cattle < than any < are you < more accursed << this, < you have done < Because
וּמִכֹּל חַיַּת הַשָּׂדֶה עַל־גְּחֹנְךָ תֵלֵךְ וְעָפָר תֹּאכַל
< shall you eat < and dust << shall you go, < your belly < upon << of the field; < beasts < and than any
כָּל־יְמֵי חַיֶּיךָ: טו וְאֵיבָה | אָשִׁית בֵּינְךָ וּבֵין הָאִשָּׁה וּבֵין זַרְעֲךָ וּבֵין זַרְעָהּ
<< her offspring. < and between < your offspring < and between < the woman, < and between < between you < shall I put < Enmity 15 << of your life. < the days < all
הוּא יְשׁוּפְךָ רֹאשׁ וְאַתָּה תְּשׁוּפֶנּוּ עָקֵב: ס טז אֶל־הָאִשָּׁה אָמַר
<< He said, < the woman < To 16 << [his] heel. < will hiss at him [and bite] < and you << [on your] head, < will crush you < He
הַרְבָּה אַרְבֶּה עִצְּבוֹנֵךְ וְהֵרֹנֵךְ בְּעֶצֶב תֵּלְדִי בָנִים וְאֶל־אִישֵׁךְ תְּשׁוּקָתֵךְ
<< shall your craving be, < your husband < And [yet] for << children. < shall you bear < in pain << and your childbearing; < your suffering < I will greatly increase

לְאִתְּתָא מַה דָא עֲבַדְתְּ וַאֲמֶרֶת
אִתְּתָא חִוְיָא אַטְעֲיָנִי וַאֲכָלִית:
יד וַאֲמַר יְיָ אֱלֹהִים לְחִוְיָא אֲרֵי עֲבַדְתָּ
דָא לִיט אַתְּ מִכָּל בְּעִירָא וּמִכֹּל חֵיוַת
בָּרָא עַל מְעָךְ תֵּיזִיל וְעַפְרָא תֵיכוּל
כָּל יוֹמֵי חַיָּיךְ: טו וּדְבָבוּ אֲשַׁוִי בֵּינָךְ
וּבֵין אִתְּתָא וּבֵין בְּנָךְ וּבֵין בְּנָהָא הוּא
יְהֵי דְכִיר לָךְ מַה דַעֲבַדְתָּ לֵהּ
מִלְּקַדְמִין וְאַתְּ תְּהֵא נָטִיר לֵהּ
לְסוֹפָא: טז לְאִתְּתָא אֲמַר אַסְגָאָה
אַסְגֵי צַעֲרִיכִי וְעִדּוּיַיכִי בְּצַעַר תְּלִידִי
בְּנִין וּלְוַת בַּעְלֵיךְ תְּהֵא תְּאוּבְתִּיךְ

רש"י

(ע"ז ה:): (יג) **השיאני.** הטעני (אונקלוס) כמו אל ישיא לכם חזקיהו (דברי הימים ב לב:טו; ב"ר שם יב): (יד) **כי עשית זאת.** מכאן שאין מהפכים בזכותו של מסית, שאילו שאלו למה עשית זאת היה לו להשיב דברי הרב ודברי התלמיד דברי מי שומעין (שם כ:ב; סנהדרין כט.): **מכל הבהמה ומכל חית השדה.** אם מבהמה נתקלל מחיה לא כל שכן, העמידו רבותינו מדרש זה במסכת בכורות (ח.) ללמד שימי עיבורו של נחש שבע שנים: **על גחנך תלך.** רגלים היו לו ונקצצו (ב"ר כ:ה): (טו) **ואיבה אשית.** אתה לא נתכוונת אלא שימות אדם כשיאכל הוא תחלה ותשא את חוה (שם; אדר"נ א) ולא באת לדבר אל חוה תחלה אלא לפי שהנשים קלות להתפתות ויודעות לפתות את בעליהן (פדר"א שם) לפיכך ואיבה אשית: **ישופך.** יכתתך, כמו (דברים ט:כא) ואכות אותו ותרגומו ושפית יתיה: **ואתה תשופנו עקב.** לא יהא לך קומה ותשכנו בעקבו ואף משם תמיתנו, ולשון תשופנו כמו נשף בהם (ישעיה מ:כד) כשהנחש בא לנשוך הוא נושף כמין שריקה, ולפי שהלשון נופל על הלשון כתב לשון נשיפה בשניהם: (טז) **עצבונך.** זה צער גידול בנים (עירובין ק:): **והרנך.** זה צער העבור (שם): **בעצב תלדי בנים.** זה צער הלידה (שם): **ואל אישך תשוקתך.** [תאוותך] לתשמיש, ואעפ"כ אין לך מצח לתובעו בפה (שם) אלא **הוא ימשל בך,** הכל ממנו ולא ממך: **תשוקתך.** תאוותך, כמו ונפשו שוקקה (ישעיה כט:ח):

saying, "I ate and I will eat again!" *Michtav MeEliyahu* explains that Adam assessed himself objectively and said that if he were to be faced with a similar temptation, he would probably succumb again. A sinner cannot hope to escape from his spiritual squalor unless he is honest with himself.

13. מַה־זֹּאת עָשִׂית — *What is this that you* [i.e., Eve] *have done.* This rhetorical question was not to elicit information, but to give Eve an opening to express remorse and to repent (*Sforno*).

Since only Adam had been commanded, why was Eve punished? *Ramban* explains that Eve had been included in the prohibition since she was part of him — *bone of his bones.* Additionally, she was punished for misleading Adam and causing him to sin; that was a greater sin than her own eating.

14-21. The sinners are punished. By assimilating into their nature an awareness of and a temptation to sin, Adam and Eve became unworthy to remain in the spiritual paradise of Eden; consequently they were expelled. As a result, life changed in virtually every conceivable way. Death, the need to work hard physically as well as spiritually, the pain of giving birth, and the millennia-long struggle to regain that lost spiritual plateau are all part of the decree God was about to pronounce.

16. Before the sin, Adam and Eve lived together and she conceived and gave birth immediately and painlessly. From now on, conception would not be automatic, and there would be an extended period of pregnancy and labor pains (*Sforno*).

וְהוּא יִמְשָׁל־בָּךְ — *And he shall rule over you.* Her punishment was measure for measure. She induced her husband to eat at her command; now she must follow his commands (*Ramban*). The new conditions of life that made sustenance the product of hard labor would naturally make women dependent on the physically stronger men. Obedience to the Torah, however, restores her to her former and proper status as the *crown of her husband* and *pearl of his life* [*Proverbs* 12:4, 31:10] (*R' Hirsch*).

The Sages ordained that a man should honor his wife more than himself, and love her as himself. If he has money, he should increase his generosity to her according to his means.

וְהוּא יִמְשָׁל־בָּךְ: ס יז וּלְאָדָם אָמַר כִּי שָׁמַעְתָּ
‹ you listened ‹ Because ‹ He said, ‹ To Adam 17 ‹‹ over you. ‹ shall rule ‹ and he

לְקוֹל אִשְׁתֶּךָ וַתֹּאכַל מִן־הָעֵץ אֲשֶׁר צִוִּיתִיךָ
‹ I commanded you ‹ about which ‹ the tree ‹ of ‹ and you ate ‹ of your wife ‹ to the voice

לֵאמֹר לֹא תֹאכַל מִמֶּנּוּ אֲרוּרָה הָאֲדָמָה בַּעֲבוּרֶךָ
‹‹ because of you; ‹ is the ground ‹ accursed ‹‹ of it,' ‹ 'You shall not eat ‹‹ saying,

בְּעִצָּבוֹן תֹּאכְלֶנָּה כֹּל יְמֵי חַיֶּיךָ: יח וְקוֹץ וְדַרְדַּר
‹ and thistles ‹ Thorns 18 ‹‹ of your life. ‹ the days ‹ all ‹ shall you eat [of] it ‹ through suffering

וְהוּא יִשְׁלַט בִּיךְ: יז וּלְאָדָם אֲמַר אֲרֵי קַבֵּילְתָּ לְמֵימַר אִתְּתָךְ וַאֲכַלְתָּ מִן אִילָנָא דִּי פַקֵּידְתָּךְ לְמֵימַר לָא תֵיכוּל מִנֵּהּ לִיטָא אַרְעָא בְּדִילָךְ בַּעֲמַל תֵּיכְלִינַהּ כָּל יוֹמֵי חַיָּיךְ: יח וְכוּבִין וְאַטְדִּין תַּצְמַח לָךְ וְתֵיכוּל יָת עִסְבָּא דְחַקְלָא: יט בְּזֵעֲתָא דְאַפָּךְ תֵּיכוּל לַחְמָא עַד דְּתֵיתוּב לְאַרְעָא דְּמִנַּהּ אִתְבְּרֵיתָא אֲרֵי עַפְרָא אַתְּ וּלְעַפְרָא תְּתוּב: כ וּקְרָא אָדָם שׁוּם אִתְּתֵהּ חַוָּה אֲרֵי הִיא הֲוַת אִמָּא דְּכָל בְּנֵי אֱנָשָׁא: כא וַעֲבַד יְיָ אֱלֹהִים לְאָדָם וּלְאִתְּתֵהּ לְבוּשִׁין דִּיקַר עַל מְשַׁךְ בִּשְׂרֵיהוֹן וְאַלְבִּישִׁנּוּן:

תַּצְמִיחַ לָךְ וְאָכַלְתָּ אֶת־עֵשֶׂב הַשָּׂדֶה: יט בְּזֵעַת אַפֶּיךָ תֹּאכַל לֶחֶם עַד
‹ until ‹ bread ‹ shall you eat ‹ of your brow ‹ By the sweat 19 ‹‹ of the field. ‹ the herb ‹ and you shall eat ‹‹ for you, ‹ shall it sprout

שׁוּבְךָ אֶל־הָאֲדָמָה כִּי מִמֶּנָּה לֻקָּחְתָּ כִּי־עָפָר אַתָּה וְאֶל־עָפָר תָּשׁוּב:
‹‹ shall you return. ‹ dust ‹ and to ‹ you are, ‹ dust ‹ For ‹‹ were you taken: ‹ from it ‹ that ‹‹ the ground, ‹ to ‹ you return

כ וַיִּקְרָא הָאָדָם שֵׁם אִשְׁתּוֹ חַוָּה כִּי הִוא הָיְתָה אֵם כָּל־חָי:
‹‹ the living. ‹ of all ‹ the mother ‹ was ‹ she ‹ because ‹‹ Eve, ‹ of his wife ‹ the name ‹ The man called 20

כא וַיַּעַשׂ יהוה אֱלֹהִים לְאָדָם וּלְאִשְׁתּוֹ כָּתְנוֹת עוֹר וַיַּלְבִּשֵׁם: פ
‹‹ and He clothed them. ‹‹ of skin, ‹ garments ‹ and for his wife ‹ for Adam ‹ And HASHEM God made 21

רש"י

(יז) **ארורה האדמה בעבורך.** מעלה לך דברים ארורים כגון זבובים ופרעושים ונמלים. משל ליוצא לתרבות רעה והבריות מקללות שדים שינק מהם (ב"ר ה:ט): (יח) **וקוץ ודרדר תצמיח לך.** הארץ, כשתזרענה מיני זרעים תצמיח קוץ ודרדר קונדס ועכביות (שם כ:י) והן נאכלין ע"י תקון (ביצה לד.): **ואכלת את עשב השדה.** ומה קללה היא זו, והלא בברכה נאמר לו הנה נתתי לכם את כל עשב זורע זרע וגו'. אלא מה אמור כאן בראש הענין, ארורה האדמה בעבורך בעצבון תאכלנה, ואחר העצבון וקוץ ודרדר תצמיח לך, כשתזרענה קטניות או ירקות גנה היא תצמיח לך קוצים ודרדרים ושאר עשבי שדה, ועל כרחך תאכלם: (יט) **בזעת אפיך.** לאחר שתטרח בו הרבה: (כ) **ויקרא האדם.** חזר הכתוב לעניינו הראשון ויקרא האדם שמות (לעיל ב:כ) ולא הפסיק אלא ללמדך שעל ידי קריאת שמות נזדווגה לו חוה, כמו שכתוב ולאדם לא מצא עזר כנגדו (שם) לפיכך ויפל תרדמה. וע"י שכתב ויהיו שניהם ערומים (שם כה) סמך לו פרשת הנחש, להודיעך שמתוך שראה אותם ערומים וראה אותם עסוקים בתשמיש נתאוה לה (ב"ר יח:ו) ובא עליהם במחשבה ובמרמה [ס"א זו] (אדר"נ א): **חוה.** נופל על לשון חיה (ב"ר כ:יא) שמחיה את ולדותיה, כאשר תאמר מה הוה לאדם (קהלת ב:כב) בל' היה: (כא) **כתנות עור.** יש דברי אגדה אומרים חלקים כצפורן היו, מדובקים על עורן. וי"א דבר הבא מן העור כגון צמר הארנבים שהוא רך וחם,

He should not cast fear upon her unduly and his conversation with her should be gentle — he should be prone neither to melancholy nor anger. They have similarly ordained that a wife should honor her husband exceedingly and revere him . . . and refrain from anything that is repugnant to him. This is the way of the daughters of Israel who are holy and pure in their union, and in these ways will their life together be pleasant and praiseworthy (*Rambam, Hil. Ishus* 15:19-20).

19. כִּי־עָפָר אַתָּה — *For dust you are.* The implication is that death was not a curse but a natural consequence of Man's nature. Since he originated from the earth it is only natural that age and deterioration would return him to his origin. Had he not sinned, however, he would have purified his physical nature and risen above his origin (*Radak, Aderes Eliyahu*). In this regard, it is noteworthy that the bodies of outstandingly righteous people that have been exhumed were found not to have decomposed. They had so exalted their behavior that their bodies had become holy and no longer subject to the ravages of the earth. This is why Elijah and Enoch were able to ascend to heaven at the end of their lives without dying, and why Moses could live among the angels for forty days without eating or drinking.

20. חַוָּה — *Eve.* The Hebrew word חַוָּה means the same as חַיָּה, *living.* Thus her name alludes to her status as *the mother of all the living.*

21. וַיַּלְבִּשֵׁם — *And He clothed them.* Not only did God Himself make them comfortable garments, He Himself clothed them to show that He still loved them, despite their sin (*R' Bachya*).

רביעי כב וַיֹּ֣אמֶר ׀ יְהוָ֣ה אֱלֹהִ֗ים הֵ֤ן הָֽאָדָם֙ הָיָה֙ כְּאַחַ֣ד

22 And HASHEM God said, Indeed Man has become like the Unique One

מִמֶּ֔נּוּ לָדַ֖עַת ט֣וֹב וָרָ֑ע וְעַתָּ֣ה ׀ פֶּן־יִשְׁלַ֣ח יָד֗וֹ

among us, to know good and bad; and now, lest he put forth his hand

וְלָקַח֙ גַּ֚ם מֵעֵ֣ץ הַֽחַיִּ֔ים וְאָכַ֖ל וָחַ֥י לְעֹלָֽם׃

and take also of the Tree of Life, and he will eat and live forever!

כג וַֽיְשַׁלְּחֵ֛הוּ יְהוָ֥ה אֱלֹהִ֖ים מִגַּן־עֵ֑דֶן לַֽעֲבֹד֙

23 [So] HASHEM God expelled him from the Garden of Eden, to work

אֶת־הָ֣אֲדָמָ֔ה אֲשֶׁ֥ר לֻקַּ֖ח מִשָּֽׁם׃ כד וַיְגָ֖רֶשׁ אֶת־הָֽאָדָ֑ם וַיַּשְׁכֵּן֩ מִקֶּ֨דֶם

the ground which he was taken from. 24 [And having] driven out the man, He stationed to the east

לְגַן־עֵ֜דֶן אֶת־הַכְּרֻבִ֗ים וְאֵ֨ת לַ֤הַט הַחֶ֙רֶב֙ הַמִּתְהַפֶּ֔כֶת לִשְׁמֹ֕ר אֶת־דֶּ֖רֶךְ

of the Garden of Eden the Cherubim and the blade of the sword that was ever turning, to guard the way

עֵ֥ץ הַֽחַיִּֽים׃ ס [ד] א וְהָ֣אָדָ֔ם יָדַ֖ע אֶת־חַוָּ֣ה אִשְׁתּ֑וֹ וַתַּ֙הַר֙ וַתֵּ֣לֶד אֶת־קַ֔יִן

[to] the Tree of Life. [4] 1 [Now] the man had known Eve his wife, and she conceived and she bore Cain,

וַתֹּ֕אמֶר קָנִ֥יתִי אִ֖ישׁ אֶת־יְהוָֽה׃ ב וַתֹּ֣סֶף לָלֶ֔דֶת אֶת־אָחִ֖יו אֶת־הָ֑בֶל

and she said, I have acquired a man with HASHEM. 2 And she continued giving birth to his brother to Abel.

כב וַאֲמַר יְיָ אֱלֹהִים הָא אָדָם הֲוָה יְחִידִי בְּעַלְמָא מִנֵּהּ לְמִידַע טַב וּבִישׁ וּכְעַן דִּילְמָא יוֹשִׁיט יְדֵהּ וְיִסַּב אַף מֵאִילַן חַיַּיָּא וְיֵיכוּל וְיֵחֵי לְעָלַם: כג וְשַׁלְּחֵהּ יְיָ אֱלֹהִים מִגִּנְּתָא דְעֵדֶן לְמִפְלַח בְּאַרְעָא דְּאִתְבְּרִי מִתַּמָּן: כד וְתָרֵיךְ יָת אָדָם וְאַשְׁרֵי מִלְּקַדְמִין לְגִנְּתָא דְעֵדֶן יָת כְּרוּבַיָּא וְיָת שְׁנַן חַרְבָּא דְּמִתְהַפְּכָא לְמִטַּר יָת אוֹרַח אִילַן חַיַּיָּא: א וְאָדָם יְדַע יָת חַוָּה אִתְּתֵהּ וְעַדִּיאַת וִילִידַת יָת קַיִן וַאֲמֶרֶת קָנִיתִי גַבְרָא (מִן) קֳדָם יְיָ: ב וְאוֹסִיפַת לְמֵילַד יָת אֲחוּהִי יָת הָבֶל

רש"י

ועשה להם כתנות ממנו (ב"ר שם יב): (כב) היה כאחד ממנו. הרי הוא יחיד בתחתונים כמו שאני יחיד בעליונים, ומה היא יחידתו, לדעת טוב ורע, מה שאין כן בבהמה וחיה (אונקלוס; ב"ר כא:ה): ועתה פן ישלח ידו וגו'. ומשיחיה לעולם הרי הוא קרוב להטעות הבריות אחריו ולומר אף הוא אלוה (ב"ר ט:ה). ויש מדרשי אגדה אבל אין מיושבין על פשוטו: (כד) מקדם לגן עדן. במזרחו של גן עדן חוץ לגן: את הכרובים. מלאכי חבלה (ב"ר כא:ט): החרב המתהפכת. ולה להט, לאיים עליו מליכנס עוד לגן. תרגום של להט שנן, והוא כמו שלף שננא (סנהדרין פב.) ובלשון לע"ז למ"ה. ומדרשי אגדה יש, ואני איני בא אלא לפשוטו: (א) והאדם ידע. כבר קודם הענין של מעלה, קודם שחטא ונטרד מגן עדן, וכן ההריון והלידה (סנהדרין לח:) שאם כתב וידע אדם נשמע שלאחר שנטרד היו לו בנים: קין. על שם קניתי [איש]: את ה'. כמו עם ה'. כשברא אותי ואת אישי לבדו בראנו, אבל בזה שותפים אנו עמו (ב"ר כב:ב): את קין את אחיו את הבל. ג' אתים ריבויים הם, מלמד שתאומה נולדה עם קין

22-24. Man's expulsion from Eden. God grieved at the sin and its results, for Adam had now made it impossible for God to let him stay in the garden. By eating from the Tree of Knowledge, Man had become כְּאַחַד מִמֶּנּוּ, *like the Unique One among us,* meaning that he had become unique among the terrestrial ones, just as God is unique among the celestial ones, for now Man can discriminate between good and bad, a quality not possessed by cattle and beasts (*Rashi,* following *Targum*). Because Man has this unique ability to know good and evil, and his desire for sensual gratification had become enhanced, there was a new danger. If Man kept the capacity to live forever, he might well spend all his days pursuing gratification and cast away intellectual growth and good deeds. He would fail to attain the spiritual bliss that God intended for him. If so, Man had to be banished from Eden so that he would not be able to eat from the Tree of Life and live forever (*Rambam; Sforno*).

24. הַכְּרֻבִים — *The Cherubim.* These were destructive angels, who have the responsibility of preventing man from discovering and re-entering the garden.

4.

1-16. Cain and Abel. In accordance with the decree that Man must earn his sustenance through labor, Cain and Abel, the sons of Adam and Eve, engaged in different forms of work. They diverged also on their concept of how to serve God, and this led to jealousy and the first murder in history.

1. וְהָאָדָם יָדַע אֶת־חַוָּה אִשְׁתּוֹ — *[Now] the man had known Eve his wife.* The translation in the past-perfect follows *Rashi*, that the conception and birth of Cain had occurred *before* the sin and expulsion of Adam and Eve from Eden.

קָנִיתִי אִישׁ אֶת־ה׳ — *I have acquired a man with HASHEM*, as partners with Hashem. "My husband and I were created by God

וַיְהִי־הֶ֙בֶל֙ רֹ֣עֵה צֹ֔אן וְקַ֕יִן הָיָ֖ה עֹבֵ֥ד אֲדָמָֽה׃

« of the ground. ‹ a worker ‹ became ‹ and Cain «of sheep, ‹ a herder ‹ And Abel became

ג וַֽיְהִ֖י מִקֵּ֣ץ יָמִ֑ים וַיָּבֵ֨א קַ֜יִן מִפְּרִ֧י הָֽאֲדָמָ֛ה מִנְחָ֖ה

‹ an offering ‹ of the ground ‹ from the fruit ‹ [that] Cain brought «of a period of time, ‹ at the end ‹ And it was 3

לַֽיהוָֽה׃ ד וְהֶ֨בֶל הֵבִ֥יא גַם־ה֛וּא מִבְּכֹר֥וֹת צֹאנ֖וֹ

‹ of his flock ‹ of the firstborn « —himself as well — « brought ‹ And Abel 4 « to HASHEM.

וּמֵֽחֶלְבֵהֶ֑ן וַיִּ֣שַׁע יְהוָ֔ה אֶל־הֶ֖בֶל וְאֶל־מִנְחָתֽוֹ׃

« his offering, ‹ and to ‹ Abel ‹ to ‹ HASHEM turned « and from their choicest.

ה וְאֶל־קַ֥יִן וְאֶל־מִנְחָת֖וֹ לֹ֣א שָׁעָ֑ה וַיִּ֤חַר לְקַ֙יִן֙ מְאֹ֔ד וַֽיִּפְּל֖וּ פָּנָֽיו׃

« and his countenance fell. « exceedingly, ‹ Cain ‹ This angered « He did not turn. ‹ his offering ‹ and to ‹ Cain ‹ but to 5

ו וַיֹּ֥אמֶר יְהוָ֖ה אֶל־קָ֑יִן לָ֚מָּה חָ֣רָה לָ֔ךְ וְלָ֖מָּה נָפְל֥וּ פָנֶֽיךָ׃ ז הֲל֤וֹא אִם־

‹ *if* ‹ *Surely,* 7 « *has your countenance fallen?* ‹ *and why* ‹ *are you angry,* ‹ *Why* « Cain, ‹ to ‹ And HASHEM said 6

תֵּיטִיב֙ שְׂאֵ֔ת וְאִם֙ לֹ֣א תֵיטִ֔יב לַפֶּ֖תַח חַטָּ֣את רֹבֵ֑ץ וְאֵלֶ֙יךָ֙ תְּשׁ֣וּקָת֔וֹ

« *is its desire,* ‹ *And toward you* « *rests.* ‹ *sin* ‹ *at the door* « *you do not improve [yourself],* ‹ *But if* « *you will be forgiven.* ‹ *you improve [yourself],*

וְאַתָּ֖ה תִּמְשָׁל־בּֽוֹ׃ ח וַיֹּ֥אמֶר קַ֖יִן אֶל־הֶ֣בֶל אָחִ֑יו וַֽיְהִי֙ בִּהְיוֹתָ֣ם בַּשָּׂדֶ֔ה

‹ in the field, ‹ when they were ‹ And it happened « his brother. ‹ Abel ‹ to ‹ Cain said 8 « *it.* ‹ *can conquer* ‹ *yet you*

וַהֲוָה הֶבֶל רָעֵי עָנָא וְקַיִן הֲוָה פָּלַח בְּאַרְעָא: ג וַהֲוָה מִסּוֹף יוֹמִין וְאַיְתִי קַיִן מֵאִבָּא דְאַרְעָא תַּקְרֻבְתָּא קֳדָם יְיָ: ד וְהֶבֶל אַיְתִי אַף הוּא מִבַּכִּירֵי עָנֵהּ וּמִשַּׁמִּנְהוֹן וַהֲוַת רַעֲוָא מִן קֳדָם יְיָ לְהֶבֶל וּלְקוּרְבָּנֵהּ: ה וּלְקַיִן וּלְקוּרְבָּנֵהּ לָא הֲוַת רַעֲוָא וּתְקֵף לְקַיִן לַחֲדָא וְאִתְכְּבִישׁוּ אַפּוֹהִי: ו וַאֲמַר יְיָ לְקַיִן לְמָא תְּקִיף לָךְ וּלְמָא אִתְכְּבִישׁוּ אַפָּיךְ: ז הֲלָא אִם תֵּיטִיב עוֹבָדָךְ יִשְׁתְּבֵק לָךְ וְאִם לָא תֵיטִיב עוֹבָדָךְ לְיוֹם דִּינָא חֲטָאת נְטִיר וְדַעֲתִיד לְאִתְפְּרָעָא מִנָּךְ אִם לָא תְתוּב וְאִם תְּתוּב יִשְׁתְּבֵק לָךְ: ח וַאֲמַר קַיִן לְהֶבֶל אֲחוּהִי וַהֲוָה בְּמֶהֱוֵיהוֹן בְּחַקְלָא

רש"י

ועם הבל נולדו שתים, לכך נאמר ותוסף (שם ג): (ב) **רעה צאן.** לפי שנתקללה האדמה פירש לו מעבודתה (מדרש אגדה): (ג) **מפרי האדמה.** מן הגרוע (ב"ר כב:ה) ויש אגדה שאומרת זרע פשתן היה (תנחומא ט): (ד) **וישע.** ויפן. וכן ואל מנחתו לא שעה, לא פנה. וכן ואל ישעו (שמות ה:ט) אל יפנו. וכן שעה מעליו (איוב יד:ו) פנה מעליו: **וישע.** ירדה אש ולחכה מנחתו (מדרש אגדה): (ז) **הלא אם תיטיב.** כתרגומו פירושו: **לפתח חטאת רובץ.** לפתח קברך חטאך שמור (אונקלוס): **ואליך תשוקתו.** של חטאת הוא יצר הרע, תמיד שוקק ומתאוה להכשילך (ספרי עקב מה; קדושין ל:): **ואתה תמשל בו.** אם תרצה תתגבר עליו (שם ושם): (ח) **ויאמר קין.** נכנס עמו בדברי ריב

alone, but through the birth of Cain we are partners with Him" (*Rashi*). *Ramban* renders: "This [newborn] man shall be my acquisition for the sake of God" — she dedicated her son to become the servant of God after she and Adam would die.

2. **רֹעֵה צֹאן** — *A herder of sheep.* Because Abel feared God's curse against the ground, he turned to caring for sheep and herds (*Rashi*). Although Man was still forbidden to eat meat [see 9:3], he was allowed to use milk, butter, wool, and the skins of dead animals. Abel's work consisted of shearing the sheep and milking the cows (*Mizrachi*).

Like the Patriarchs, Moses, and David, Abel chose a profession that permitted him to spend his time in solitude and contemplation of spiritual matters (*HaK'sav V'HaKabbalah*). Cain, however, chose an occupation that, though essential, can lead its practitioners to worship nature and enslave others to do the hard work of the fields (*R' Hirsch*).

3-5. From the subtle contrast between the simple description of Cain's offering and the more specific description of Abel's offering — *of the firstborn of his flock and from their choicest* — the Sages derive that Cain's offering was from the inferior portions of the crop, while Abel chose only the finest of his flock. Therefore, Abel's sacrifice was accepted, but not Cain's (*Ibn Ezra; Radak*).

6-7. God wished to teach Cain how to repent: A sinner can atone for his sins if he will but repent sincerely (*Radak*).

7. **לַפֶּתַח חַטָּאת רֹבֵץ** — *At the door sin rests.* At the entrance to your grave, your sin will be kept (*Rashi*), i.e., punishment will await you in the future world unless you repent. If you succumb to your Evil Inclination, punishment and evil will be as ever-present as if they lived in the doorway of your house (*Sforno*).

וְאֵלֶיךָ תְּשׁוּקָתוֹ וְאַתָּה תִּמְשָׁל־בּוֹ — *And toward you is its desire, yet you can conquer it.* This phrase is almost identical to the phrase

וַיָּקָם קַיִן אֶל־הֶבֶל אָחִיו וַיַּהַרְגֵהוּ: ט וַיֹּאמֶר יהוה
[that] Cain rose up < against < Abel < his brother < and killed him. « 9 HASHEM said <

אֶל־קַיִן אֵי הֶבֶל אָחִיךָ וַיֹּאמֶר לֹא יָדַעְתִּי הֲשֹׁמֵר
to < Cain, « Where is < Abel < your brother? « And he said, < I do not know. « Is it the guardian <

אָחִי אָנֹכִי: י וַיֹּאמֶר מֶה עָשִׂיתָ קוֹל דְּמֵי אָחִיךָ
of my brother < that I am? « 10 [Then] He said, « What < have you done? « The voice < of the bloods < of your brother <

צֹעֲקִים אֵלַי מִן־הָאֲדָמָה: יא וְעַתָּה אָרוּר אָתָּה מִן־הָאֲדָמָה אֲשֶׁר
are crying out < to Me < from < the ground! « 11 And now, « cursed < are you < from < the ground < which <

פָּצְתָה אֶת־פִּיהָ לָקַחַת אֶת־דְּמֵי אָחִיךָ מִיָּדֶךָ: יב כִּי תַעֲבֹד אֶת־הָאֲדָמָה
opened wide < its mouth < to receive < the bloods < of your brother < from your hand. « 12 When < you work < the ground, «

לֹא־תֹסֵף תֵּת־כֹּחָהּ לָךְ נָע וָנָד תִּהְיֶה בָאָרֶץ: יג וַיֹּאמֶר קַיִן אֶל־יהוה
it shall not continue < to yield < its strength < to you. « A wanderer < and an exile < shall you be < on earth. « 13 Cain said < to < HASHEM, «

וְקָם קַיִן בְּהֶבֶל אֲחוּהִי וְקַטְלֵהּ: ט וַאֲמַר
יְיָ לְקַיִן אָן הֶבֶל אָחוּךְ וַאֲמַר לָא
יָדַעְנָא הֲנָטֵר אָחִי אֲנָא: י וַאֲמַר מֶה
עֲבַדְתָּא קַל דַּם זַרְעִין דַּעֲתִידִין לְמִפַּק
מִן אָחוּךְ קַבִילִין קֳדָמַי מִן אַרְעָא:
יא וּכְעַן לִיט אַתְּ מִן אַרְעָא דִּי פְתַחַת
יָת פּוּמַהּ וְקַבִילַת יָת דְּמֵהּ דְּאָחוּךְ
מִן יְדָךְ: יב אֲרֵי תִפְלַח בְּאַרְעָא לָא
תוֹסִיף לְמִתַּן חֵילַהּ לָךְ מְטַלְטַל וְגָלֵי
תְּהֵא בְּאַרְעָא: יג וַאֲמַר קַיִן קֳדָם יְיָ

רש״י

ומלה להתגולל עליו להרגו. ויש בזה מדרשי אגדה אך זה ישובו של מקרא: (ט) **אי הבל אחיך.** להכנס עמו בדברי נחת, אולי ישיב ויאמר אני הרגתיו וחטאתי לך (ב״ר יט:יא; במ״ר כ:ו): **לא ידעתי.** נעשה כגונב דעת העליונה (במ״ר שם; תנחומא ישן כה): **השומר אחי.** לשון תימה הוא, וכן כל ה״א הנקודה בחטף פתח: (י) **דמי אחיך.** דמו ודם זרעיותיו (סנהדרין לז.). ד״א שעשה בו פצעים הרבה שלא היה יודע מהיכן נפשו יוצאה (שם לז:): (יא) **מן האדמה.** יותר ממה שנתקללה היא כבר בעוונה (ב״ר ה:ט), וגם בזו הוסיפה לחטוא, **אשר פצתה את פיה לקחת את דמי אחיך וגו׳,** והנני מוסיף לה קללה [אלך], לא תוסף תת כחה (מכילתא בשלח שירה פ״ט): (יב) **נע ונד.** אין

said to Eve: וְאֶל אִישֵׁךְ תְּשׁוּקָתֵךְ וְהוּא יִמְשָׁל בָּךְ, *And [yet] for your husband shall your craving be, and he shall rule over you* (3:16). *Bereishis Rabbah* (20:7) identifies four desires: *the desire of a woman for her husband, the desire of the Evil Inclination for Cain and those like him, the desire of the rain for the land, and the desire of God for Israel.* Now the desire of the rain for the land is not an expression of a need or a lack, and the desire of God for Israel cannot be to supply something missing from God! Rather, both are indications of a desire to give to the other. It is the desire of one who, out of fullness, wants to give to one who is needy. As the Talmud states (*Pesachim* 112a), *More than the calf wants to suck, the cow wants to suckle.* Although the calf has a hunger that must be satisfied, the desire of the cow to satisfy that hunger is even greater. Similarly, the desire of a woman for a man is the desire to give, and, paradoxically, the Evil Inclination has something powerful to give as well. The Midrash (*Bereishis Rabbah* 9:7) makes the astonishing statement, *and indeed it was very good* (*Genesis* 1:31) *— this is the Evil Inclination. Could it be? Rather, if not for the Evil Inclination a person would not build a house, marry a woman, have children, or engage in business.* A person's passion and drive are not inherently evil, as long as they are controlled. This is God's admonition to Cain: *Yet you can conquer it* (*R' David Fohrman*).

8. וַיָּקָם קַיִן — *Cain rose up.* Abel was the stronger of the two, and the expression *rose up* implies that Cain had been thrown down and lay beneath Abel. But Cain begged for mercy saying: "We are the only sons in the world. What will you tell Father if you kill me?" Abel was filled with compassion, and released his hold, whereupon Cain *rose up and killed him* (*Midrash*).

9. אֵי הֶבֶל אָחִיךָ — *Where is Abel your brother?* The question was rhetorical, for God knew full well where he was. He engaged Cain in a gentle conversation to give him the opportunity to confess and repent (*Rashi; Radak; Sforno*), but Cain misunderstood. He took God's question to indicate ignorance about Abel's whereabouts, so he denied knowledge. The reference to Abel as his *brother* was to allude to Cain that he had a responsibility for Abel's welfare, but he denied that brotherhood imposed responsibility upon him.

10. דְּמֵי — *The bloods.* The word is in the plural, implying that Cain's crime was not limited to one person; he had shed Abel's blood and the blood of his potential descendants. Alternatively, this teaches that Abel bled from many wounds. Not knowing which organs were vital to life, Cain stabbed him all over (*Rashi; Sanhedrin* 37a).

12. לֹא־תֹסֵף תֵּת־כֹּחָהּ — *It shall not continue to yield its strength.* Cain would always strive to find new areas to cultivate, for, never finding blessing, he would wander aimlessly in search of more fertile land (*B'chor Shor; Ralbag*). He would know no more peace than his brother's blood (*Tzror HaMor*).

13-14. Cain pleaded for mercy, finally acknowledging the

גָּדוֹל עֲוֺנִי מִנְּשֹׂא: יד הֵן גֵּרַשְׁתָּ אֹתִי הַיּוֹם מֵעַל

[Is it too] great — my iniquity — to be borne? **14** Indeed You have banished me this day from upon

פְּנֵי הָאֲדָמָה וּמִפָּנֶיךָ אֶסָּתֵר וְהָיִיתִי נָע וָנָד בָּאָרֶץ

the face of the earth — from Your Face can I be hidden? if I become a wanderer and an exile on earth,

וְהָיָה כָל־מֹצְאִי יַהַרְגֵנִי: טו וַיֹּאמֶר לוֹ יהוה לָכֵן

it will be that whoever meets me will kill me! **15** HASHEM said to him, Therefore,

כָּל־הֹרֵג קַיִן שִׁבְעָתַיִם יֻקָּם וַיָּשֶׂם יהוה לְקַיִן אוֹת

whoever slays Cain! — [who after] seven generations will be punished. And HASHEM placed upon Cain a mark,

לְבִלְתִּי הַכּוֹת־אֹתוֹ כָּל־מֹצְאוֹ: טז וַיֵּצֵא קַיִן מִלִּפְנֵי יהוה וַיֵּשֶׁב בְּאֶרֶץ־

to preclude him being killed by anyone who would meet him. **16** Cain went forth from the presence of HASHEM and settled in the land

נוֹד קִדְמַת־עֵדֶן: יז וַיֵּדַע קַיִן אֶת־אִשְׁתּוֹ וַתַּהַר וַתֵּלֶד אֶת־חֲנוֹךְ וַיְהִי

of Nod, east of Eden. **17** And Cain knew his wife, and she conceived and bore Enoch. And he was

בֹּנֶה עִיר וַיִּקְרָא שֵׁם הָעִיר כְּשֵׁם בְּנוֹ חֲנוֹךְ: יח וַיִּוָּלֵד לַחֲנוֹךְ אֶת־עִירָד

the builder of a city, and he called the name of the city like the name of his son Enoch. **18** Born to Enoch was Irad,

סַגִּי חוֹבִי מִלְּמִשְׁבָּק: יד הָא תָרִיכְתָּא יָתִי יוֹמָא דֵין מֵעַל אַפֵּי אַרְעָא וּמִן קֳדָמָךְ לֵית אֶפְשָׁר לְאִטַּמָּרָא וְאֵהֵי מְטַלְטַל וְגָלֵי בְּאַרְעָא וִיהֵי כָל דְּיִשְׁכְּחִנַּנִי יִקְטְלִנָּנִי: טו וַאֲמַר לֵהּ יְיָ לְכֵן כָּל קָטִיל קַיִן לְשַׁבְעָא דָרִין יִתְפְּרַע מִנֵּהּ וְשַׁוִּי יְיָ לְקַיִן אָתָא בְּדִיל דְּלָא לְמִקְטַל יָתֵהּ כָּל דְּיִשְׁכְּחִנֵּהּ: טז וּנְפַק קַיִן מִן קֳדָם יְיָ וִיתִיב בְּאַרְעָא גָּלֵי וּמְטַלְטַל דַּהֲוַת עֲבִידָא עֲלוֹהִי מִלְּקַדְמִין כְּגִינְתָּא (נ״א דְגִינְתָּא) דְעֵדֶן: יז וִידַע קַיִן יָת אִתְּתֵהּ וְעַדִּיאַת וִילִידַת יָת חֲנוֹךְ וַהֲוָה בָּנֵי קַרְתָּא וּקְרָא שְׁמָא דְקַרְתָּא כְּשׁוּם בְּרֵהּ חֲנוֹךְ: יח וְאִתְיְלִיד לַחֲנוֹךְ יָת עִירָד

רש״י

לך רשות לדור במקום אחד (אונקלוס): (יג) **גדול עוני מנשוא.** בתמיה, אתה טוען עליונים ותחתונים ועווני אי אפשר לטעון (ב״ר כב:יא): (טו) **לכן כל הורג קין.** זה אחד מן המקראות שקצרו דבריהם ורמזו ולא פירשו. לכן כל הורג קין לשון גערה, כה יעשה לו, כך וכך עונשו, ולא פירש עונשו: **שבעתים יקם.** איני רוצה להנקם מקין עכשיו, לסוף שבעה דורות אני נוקם נקמתי ממנו שיעמוד למך מבני בניו ויהרגהו. וסוף המקרא שאמר שבעתים יוקם והיא נקמת הבל מקין למדנו שתחלת מקרא לשון גערה היא שלא תהא בריה מזיקתו. וכיוצא בו ויאמר דוד כל מכה יבוסי ויגע בצנור (שמואל ב ה:ח) ולא פירש מה יעשה לו. אבל דבר הכתוב ברמז, כל מכה יבוסי ויגע בצנור, ויקרב אל השער ויכבשנו, ואת העורים וגו׳ (שם), וגם אותם יכה על אשר אמרו העור והפסח לא יבא [דוד] אל תוך הבית, המכה את אלו אני אעשנו ראש ושר. כאן קצר דבריו, ובדברי הימים (א יא:ו) פירש יהיה לראש ולשר: **וישם ה׳ לקין אות.** חקק לו אות משמו במצחו (תרגום יונתן): (טז) **ויצא קין.** יצא בהכנעה כגונב דעת העליונה (ב״ר כב:יג): **בארץ נוד.** בארץ שכל הגולים נדים שם: **קדמת עדן.** שם גלה אביו כשגורש מגן עדן שנאמר וישכן מקדם לגן עדן (לעיל ג:כד) לשמור את שמירת דרך מבוא הגן, שיש ללמוד שהיה אדם שם. ומצינו רוח מזרחית קולטת בכל מקום את הרוצחים, שנאמר אז יבדיל משה וגו׳ מזרחה שמש (דברים ד:מא; ב״ר כא:ט). דבר אחר בארץ נוד כל מקום שהולך היתה הארץ מזדעזעת תחתיו והבריות אומרים סורו מעליו זהו שהרג את אחיו (תנחומא ט): (יז) **ויהי.** קין **בנה עיר ויקרא שם העיר** לזכר **בנו חנוך** (ב״ר כג:א):

gravity of his sin, but arguing that the terms of his exile amounted to a death sentence. God accepted his plea.

15. **שִׁבְעָתַיִם יֻקָּם** — *[Who after] seven generations will be punished.* Translation follows *Rashi,* who interprets this as "an abbreviated verse with an implied clause: *Whoever slays Cain will be punished.* As for Cain himself, only *after seven generations will I execute My vengeance upon him,* when Lamech, one of his descendants, will arise and slay him."

16. **בְּאֶרֶץ־נוֹד** — *In the land of Nod*. The word נוד means *wandering*, so that Cain was banished to a place where exiles wander . . . to the *east of Eden,* where his father had been exiled when he was driven out of the Garden [cf. 3:24]. Notably, the eastern region always forms a place of refuge for murderers, for the cities of refuge that Moses later set aside were also to the east, *"the place of sunrise"* [cf. *Deut.* 4:41] (*Rashi*).

17-26. The descendants of Cain. To illustrate God's attribute of patience, the Torah enumerates Cain's many descendants to show that God did not punish him until he had seen many generations of offspring (*Ramban).*

17. **וַיֵּדַע קַיִן אֶת־אִשְׁתּוֹ** — *And Cain knew his wife.* Alone and banished from his parents, Cain strove to have children with whom he could associate (*Abarbanel*). The Torah calls him *the builder of a city,* implying that this describes his personality. Cut off from the earth, from God, and from his fellow men, Cain was left only with his own intelligence and talent, which he utilized to build cities. Urban life, unlike rural life, cultivates sophisticated skills in its practitioners. The following verses list those skills (*R' Hirsch*).

וְעִירָד יָלַד אֶת־מְחוּיָאֵל וּמְחִיָּיאֵל יָלַד אֶת־
‹ begot ‹ and Mehujael ‹‹ Mehujael, ‹ begot ‹ and Irad

מְתוּשָׁאֵל וּמְתוּשָׁאֵל יָלַד אֶת־לָמֶךְ׃ חמישי יט וַיִּקַּח־לוֹ
‹‹ to himself ‹ And he took 19 ‹‹ Lamech. ‹ begot ‹ and Methushael ‹‹ Methushael,

לֶמֶךְ שְׁתֵּי נָשִׁים שֵׁם הָאַחַת עָדָה וְשֵׁם הַשֵּׁנִית
‹ of the second ‹ and the name ‹ was Adah, ‹ of the [first] one ‹ The name ‹‹ wives: ‹ two ‹‹ – did Lamech –

צִלָּה׃ כ וַתֵּלֶד עָדָה אֶת־יָבָל הוּא הָיָה אֲבִי יֹשֵׁב
‹ of those who dwell ‹ the fore-runner ‹ was ‹ he ‹‹ Jabal; ‹ And Adah bore 20 ‹‹ was Zillah.

אֹהֶל וּמִקְנֶה׃ כא וְשֵׁם אָחִיו יוּבָל הוּא הָיָה אֲבִי
‹ the fore-runner ‹ was ‹ he ‹‹ was Jubal; ‹ of his brother ‹ The name 21 ‹‹ and [raise] cattle. ‹ in tents

כָּל־תֹּפֵשׂ כִּנּוֹר וְעוּגָב׃ כב וְצִלָּה גַם־הִוא יָלְדָה אֶת־תּוּבַל קַיִן לֹטֵשׁ
‹ who sharpened ‹‹ Tubal-cain, ‹ bore ‹‹ – she too – ‹‹ And Zillah 22 ‹‹ and flute. ‹ the harp ‹ who handle ‹ of all

כָּל־חֹרֵשׁ נְחֹשֶׁת וּבַרְזֶל וַאֲחוֹת תּוּבַל־קַיִן נַעֲמָה׃ ששי כג וַיֹּאמֶר לֶמֶךְ לְנָשָׁיו
‹‹ to his wives, ‹ And Lamech said 23 ‹‹ was Naamah. ‹ of Tubal-cain ‹ And the sister ‹‹ and iron. ‹ of copper ‹ cutting implements ‹ all

עָדָה וְצִלָּה שְׁמַעַן קוֹלִי נְשֵׁי לֶמֶךְ הַאְזֵנָּה אִמְרָתִי כִּי אִישׁ הָרַגְתִּי
‹ have I slain ‹ a man ‹ For ‹‹ to my speech: ‹ listen ‹‹ of Lemech, ‹ wives ‹‹ my voice; ‹ hear you ‹‹ and Zillah, ‹ Adah

וְעִירָד אוֹלִיד יָת מְחוּיָאֵל וּמְחִיָּיאֵל אוֹלִיד יָת מְתוּשָׁאֵל וּמְתוּשָׁאֵל אוֹלִיד יָת לָמֶךְ׃ יט וּנְסִיב לֵהּ לֶמֶךְ תַּרְתֵּין נְשִׁין שׁוּם חֲדָא עָדָה וְשׁוּם תִּנְיֵתָא צִלָּה׃ כ וִילִידַת עָדָה יָת יָבָל הוּא הֲוָה רַבְּהוֹן דְּכָל דְּיָתְבֵי מַשְׁכְּנִין וּמָרֵי בְעִיר׃ כא וְשׁוּם אֲחוּהִי יוּבָל הוּא הֲוָה רַבְּהוֹן דְּכָל דִּמְנַגֵּן עַל פּוּם נִבְלָא יָדְעֵי זְמַר כִּנּוֹרָא וְאַבּוּבָא׃ כב וְצִלָּה אַף הִיא יְלִידַת יָת תּוּבַל קַיִן רַבְּהוֹן דְּכָל יָדְעֵי עֲבִידַת נְחָשָׁא וּפַרְזְלָא וַאֲחָתֵהּ דְּתוּבַל קַיִן נַעֲמָה׃ כג וַאֲמַר לֶמֶךְ לִנְשׁוֹהִי עָדָה וְצִלָּה שְׁמַעַן קָלִי נְשֵׁי לֶמֶךְ אָצֵיתָא לְמֵימְרִי לָא גַבְרָא קְטָלִית דִּבְדִילֵהּ

רש"י

(יח) ועירד ילד. יש מקום שהוא אומר בזכר הוליד ויש מקום שהוא אומר ילד, שהלידה משמשת שתי לשונות, לידת האשה, נייסטר"א בלע"ז, וזריעת תולדות האיש, איינגדרי"ר בלע"ז. כשהוא אומר הוליד בלשון הפעיל מדבר בלידת האשה, פלוני הוליד את אשתו בן או בת. כשהוא אומר ילד מדבר בזריעת האיש: **(יט) ויקח לו למך.** לא היה לו לפרש כל זה אלא ללמדנו מסוף הענין שקיים הקב"ה הבטחתו שאמר שבעתים יקם קין. עמד למך לאחר שהוליד בנים ועשה דור שביעי והרג את קין, זהו שאמר כי איש הרגתי לפצעי וגו' (להלן פסוק כג; תנחומא יא): **שתי נשים.** כך היה דרכן של דור המבול, אחת לפריה ורביה ואחת לתשמיש. זו שהיא לתשמיש משקה כוס של עקרין כדי שתעקר ומקושטת ככלה ומאכילה מעדנים, וחברתה נזופה כאלמנה. וזהו שפירש איוב (כד:כא) רועה עקרה לא תלד ואלמנה לא ייטיב, כמו שמפורש באגדת חלק (שם ליתא, והוא בב"ר כג:ב): **עדה.** היא של פריה ורביה, ועל שם שמגונה עליו ומוסרת מאצלו [ס"א ממאכלו]. עדה תרגום של סורה (שם): **צלה.** היא של תשמיש, על שם שיושבת תמיד בצלו. דברי אגדה הם בבראשית רבה (שם): **(כ) אבי ישב אהל ומקנה.** הוא היה הראשון לרועי בהמות במדברות ויושב אהלים חדש כאן וחדש כאן בשביל מרעה לצאנו, וכשכלה המרעה במקום זה הולך ותוקע אהלו במקום אחר. ומ"א, בונה בתים לעבודת כוכבים, כמה דאת אמר סמל הקנאה המקנה (יחזקאל ח:ג), וכן אחיו תופש כנור ועוגב (פסוק כא) לזמר לעבודת כוכבים (ב"ר שם ג): **(כב) תובל קין.** תובל אומנתו של קין. תובל ל' תבלין, תיבל והתקין אומנתו של קין לעשות כלי זיין לרוצחים (שם): **לטש כל חרש נחשת וברזל.** מחדד אומנות נחשת וברזל כמו ילטוש עיניו לי (איוב טז:ט). חורש אינו לשון פֹּעֶל אלא ל' פּוֹעֵל, שהרי נקוד קמץ קטן וטעמו למטה, כלומר מחדד ומצחצח כל כלי אומנות נחשת וברזל: **נעמה.** היא אשתו של נח (ב"ר שם): **(כג) שמען קולי.** שהיו נשיו פורשות ממנו מתשמיש לפי שהרג את קין ואת תובל קין בנו, שהיה למך סומא ותובל קין מושכו, וראה את קין ונדמה לו כחיה ואמר לאביו למשוך בקשת והרגו, וכיון שידע שהוא קין זקנו הכה כף אל כף וספק את בנו ביניהם והרגו, והיו נשיו פורשות ממנו והוא מפייסן (תנחומא שם; ילק"ש לח): **שמען קולי.** להשמע לי לתשמיש, **וכי איש אשר הרגתי**

19. שְׁתֵּי נָשִׁים — *Two wives.* Such was the practice of the generation of the Flood. They would take two wives, one to bear children and the other for pleasure. The latter was meant not to have children and would be pampered like a bride, while the former would be bereft of companionship, and left mourning like a widow throughout her life [cf. comm. to *Job* 24:21] (*Rashi; Midrash*).

21. כִּנּוֹר וְעוּגָב — *The harp and flute.* Jubal was the originator of the art of music (*Radak*).

22. נַעֲמָה — *Naamah.* Her name, which means *lovely*, is mentioned because she was the wife of Noah, and her deeds were lovely and pleasant (*Rashi*).

23-24. Lamech's plea. Lamech was blind and his son Tubal-cain used to lead him. One day, Tubal cain saw Cain and, mistaking him for an animal, he bade his father to shoot an arrow, which killed Cain. When Lamech realized he had killed

לְפִצְעִי וְיֶלֶד לְחַבֻּרָתִי: כד כִּי שִׁבְעָתַיִם יֻקַּם־קָיִן

‹‹ did Cain suffer vengeance, ‹ [if] at seven [generations] ‹ For **24** *‹‹ by my bruise. ‹ and a child ‹ by my wound*

וְלֶמֶךְ שִׁבְעִים וְשִׁבְעָה: כה וַיֵּדַע אָדָם עוֹד אֶת־אִשְׁתּוֹ

‹‹ his wife, ‹ again ‹ Adam knew **25** ‹‹ *at seventy-seven!* ‹ *[then] Lamech*

וַתֵּלֶד בֵּן וַתִּקְרָא אֶת־שְׁמוֹ שֵׁת כִּי שָׁת־לִי אֱלֹהִים

‹ *has God* ‹ *to me* ‹ *provided* ‹‹ because: ‹‹ Seth, ‹ his name ‹ and she called ‹ a son ‹ and she bore

זֶרַע אַחֵר תַּחַת הֶבֶל כִּי הֲרָגוֹ קָיִן: כו וּלְשֵׁת גַּם־

‹ – also ‹‹ And to Seth **26** ‹‹ *had Cain.* ‹ *killed him* ‹ *for* ‹‹ *of Abel,* ‹ *in place* ‹ *another,* ‹ *a child,*

הוּא יֻלַּד־בֵּן וַיִּקְרָא אֶת־שְׁמוֹ אֱנוֹשׁ אָז הוּחַל לִקְרֹא בְּשֵׁם יְהוָה: ס

‹‹ of HASHEM. ‹ in the Name ‹ to call ‹ it became profaned ‹ Then ‹‹ Enosh. ‹ his name ‹ and he called ‹‹ a son, ‹ was born ‹‹ to him –

[ה] א זֶה סֵפֶר תּוֹלְדֹת אָדָם בְּיוֹם בְּרֹא אֱלֹהִים אָדָם בִּדְמוּת אֱלֹהִים

‹ of God ‹ in the likeness ‹‹ of Man; ‹ by God ‹ of the creating ‹ – on the day ‹‹ of Adam ‹ of the descendants ‹ the account ‹ This is **1** [5]

אֲנָא סָבִיל חוֹבִין וְאַף לָא עוּלֵימָא
חֲבִילִית דִּבְדִילֵהּ יִשְׁתֵּיצֵי זַרְעִי:
כד אֲרֵי לְשַׁבְעָא דָרִין אִיתְלִין לְקָיִן
הֲלָא לְלֶמֶךְ בְּרֵהּ שַׁבְעִין וְשַׁבְעָא:
כה וִידַע אָדָם עוֹד יָת אִתְּתֵהּ
וִילִידַת בַּר וּקְרַת יָת שְׁמֵהּ שֵׁת אֲרֵי
אֲמָרַת (נ״א אֲמַר) יְהַב לִי יְיָ בַּר
אָחֳרָן חֲלָף הֶבֶל דִּקְטָלֵהּ קָיִן:
כו וּלְשֵׁת אַף הוּא אִתְיְלִיד בַּר וּקְרָא
יָת שְׁמֵהּ אֱנוֹשׁ בְּכֵן בְּיוֹמוֹהִי חָלוּ
בְּנֵי אֱנָשָׁא מִלְּצַלָּאָה בִּשְׁמָא דַייָ:
א דֵּין סְפַר תּוּלְדַת אָדָם בְּיוֹמָא
דִּבְרָא יְיָ אָדָם בִּדְמוּת אֱלֹהִים

רש״י

לפצעי הוא נהרג, וכי אני פצעתיו מזיד שיהא הפצע קרוי על שמי. **וילד** אשר הרגתי **לחבורתי** נהרג, כלומר ע״י חבורתי, בתמיה, והלא שוגג אני ולא מזיד, לא זהו פצעי ולא זו חבורתי (שם ושם): **פצע.** מכת חרב או חץ, נברדור״א בלע״ז: (כד) **כי שבעתים יקם קין.** קין שהרג מזיד נתלה לו עד שבעה דורות, אני שהרגתי שוגג לא כל שכן שיתלה לי שביעיות הרבה (ילק״ש שם): **שבעים ושבעה.** לשון רבוי שביעיות אחז לו. כך דרש ר׳ תנחומא (שם). ומדרש ב״ר (כג:ד) לא הרג למך כלום, ונשיו פורשות ממנו משקיימו פריה ורביה לפי שנגזרה גזרה לכלות זרעו של קין לאחר שבעה דורות. אמרו, מה אנו יולדות לבהלה, למחר המבול בא ושוטף את הכל. והוא אומר להן וכי איש הרגתי לפצעי, וכי אני הרגתי את הבל שהיה איש בקומה וילד בשנים שיהא זרעי כלה באותו עון, ומה קין שהרג נתלה לו שבעה דורות, אני שלא הרגתי לא כל שכן שיתלו לי שביעיות הרבה. וזהו ק״ו של שטות, אם כן אין הקדוש ברוך הוא גובה את חובו ומקיים את דבורו: (כה) **וידע אדם וגו׳.** בא לו למך אצל אדם הראשון וקבל על נשיו. אמר להם, וכי עליכם לדקדק על גזירתו של מקום, אתם עשו מצותכם והוא יעשה את שלו. אמרו לו קשוט עצמך תחלה, והלא פרשת מאשתך זה מאה ושלשים שנה משנקנסה מיתה על ידך. מיד **וידע אדם עוד.** ומהו עוד, ללמד שנתוספה לו תאוה על תאותו. בב״ר (שם ה): (כו) **אז הוחל.** [לשון חולין (שם ו)] לקרא את שמות האדם ואת שמות העצבים בשמו של הקב״ה לעשותן אלילים ולקרותן אלהות (שם ז; תנחומא נח יח; תרגום יונתן; „אמין כח״ לס׳ יוה״כ): (א) **זה ספר תולדת אדם.** זו היא ספירת תולדות אדם. ומדרשי אגדה יש רבים: **ביום ברא וגו׳.** מגיד שביום שנברא הוליד (ב״ר כד:ז):

Cain, he beat his hands together in grief and accidently struck his son, killing him, too. This angered his wives who refused to live with him, and he tried to appease them. He demanded that they obey him and come back, for, he asked, since he had not killed intentionally, could he be considered a murderer? As to their fears that God would punish him, he contended, "If the punishment of Cain, an intentional murderer, was delayed until the seventh generation, surely my punishment will be deferred many times seven because I killed accidently!" He used the number *seventy-seven* to denote many times seven [i.e., a long period, not meaning exactly seventy-seven] (*Rashi*).

26. The generation of Enosh introduced idolatry, which was to become the blight of humanity for thousands of years. By ascribing Godlike qualities to man and lifeless objects, they created the abominable situation in which *it became profaned to call in the Name of HASHEM (Rashi).*

Rambam (Hil. Avodas Kochavim 1:1-2) explains how the grievous misconception of idol worship began and developed. Very briefly, he says that it began when people felt that they should honor the heavenly bodies as God's emissaries to the world, just as it is proper to honor the ministers of a ruler. Eventually, this trend spread and people became more and more corrupted, until worshipers forgot about God and assumed that all powers were vested in whatever representation they chose to worship.

5.

⤞ The genealogy of mankind.

A new narrative begins, enumerating the generations from Adam to Noah. The genealogy begins with Seth, for it was through him that the human race survived. Abel died without issue, and Cain's descendants perished in the Flood (*Radak; Chizkuni*).

Ramban explains why the people of that era lived such long lives. As God's handiwork, Adam was physically perfect and so were his children. As such it was natural for them to live a long time. After the Flood, however, a deterioration of the atmosphere caused a gradual shortening of life until it would appear that in the times of the Patriarchs, people lived a normal life

עָשָׂה אֹתוֹ: ב זָכָר וּנְקֵבָה בְּרָאָם וַיְבָרֶךְ אֹתָם
‹ them ‹ He blessed ‹‹ He created them. ‹ and female ‹ Male 2 ‹‹ him. ‹ He made

וַיִּקְרָא אֶת־שְׁמָם אָדָם בְּיוֹם הִבָּרְאָם: ג וַיְחִי אָדָם
‹ And Adam lived 3 ‹‹ they were created. ‹ on the day ‹ Man ‹ their name ‹ and called

שְׁלֹשִׁים וּמְאַת שָׁנָה וַיּוֹלֶד בִּדְמוּתוֹ כְּצַלְמוֹ וַיִּקְרָא
‹ and he called ‹‹ according to his image, ‹ in his likeness ‹ then he begot ‹‹ years, ‹ and one hundred ‹ thirty

אֶת־שְׁמוֹ שֵׁת: ד וַיִּהְיוּ יְמֵי־אָדָם אַחֲרֵי הוֹלִידוֹ
‹ his begetting ‹ after ‹ of Adam ‹ – the days ‹‹ And they were 4 ‹‹ Seth. ‹ his name

אֶת־שֵׁת שְׁמֹנֶה מֵאֹת שָׁנָה וַיּוֹלֶד בָּנִים וּבָנוֹת:
‹‹ and daughters. ‹ sons ‹ and he begot ‹‹ years, ‹ hundred ‹ eight ‹ Seth –

ה וַיִּהְיוּ כָּל־יְמֵי אָדָם אֲשֶׁר־חַי תְּשַׁע מֵאוֹת שָׁנָה וּשְׁלֹשִׁים שָׁנָה וַיָּמֹת:
‹‹ and he died. ‹‹ years; ‹ and thirty ‹ years ‹ hundred ‹ nine ‹‹ he lived – ‹ that ‹ of Adam ‹ the days ‹ – all ‹‹ And they were 5

ס ו וַיְחִי־שֵׁת חָמֵשׁ שָׁנִים וּמְאַת שָׁנָה וַיּוֹלֶד אֶת־אֱנוֹשׁ: ז וַיְחִי־שֵׁת
‹ And Seth lived 7 ‹‹ Enosh. ‹ and he begot ‹ years ‹ and one hundred ‹ years ‹ five ‹ Seth lived 6

אַחֲרֵי הוֹלִידוֹ אֶת־אֱנוֹשׁ שֶׁבַע שָׁנִים וּשְׁמֹנֶה מֵאוֹת שָׁנָה וַיּוֹלֶד בָּנִים
‹ sons ‹ and he begot ‹‹ years, ‹ hundred ‹ and eight ‹ years ‹ seven ‹ Enosh ‹ his begetting ‹ after

וּבָנוֹת: ח וַיִּהְיוּ כָּל־יְמֵי־שֵׁת שְׁתֵּים עֶשְׂרֵה שָׁנָה וּתְשַׁע מֵאוֹת שָׁנָה
‹‹ years; ‹ hundred ‹ and nine ‹ years ‹ twelve ‹‹ of Seth – ‹ the days ‹ – all ‹‹ And they were 8 ‹‹ and daughters.

וַיָּמֹת: ס ט וַיְחִי אֱנוֹשׁ תִּשְׁעִים שָׁנָה וַיּוֹלֶד אֶת־קֵינָן: י וַיְחִי אֱנוֹשׁ אַחֲרֵי
‹ after ‹ And Enosh lived 10 ‹‹ Kenan. ‹ and he begot ‹ years, ‹ ninety ‹ Enosh lived 9 ‹‹ and he died.

הוֹלִידוֹ אֶת־קֵינָן חֲמֵשׁ עֶשְׂרֵה שָׁנָה וּשְׁמֹנֶה מֵאוֹת שָׁנָה וַיּוֹלֶד בָּנִים
‹ sons ‹ and he begot ‹ years, ‹ hundred ‹ and eight ‹ years ‹ fifteen ‹ Kenan ‹ his begetting

וּבָנוֹת: יא וַיִּהְיוּ כָּל־יְמֵי אֱנוֹשׁ חָמֵשׁ שָׁנִים וּתְשַׁע מֵאוֹת שָׁנָה וַיָּמֹת:
‹‹ and he died. ‹‹ years; ‹ hundred ‹ and nine ‹ years ‹ five ‹‹ of Enosh – ‹ the days ‹ – all ‹‹ And they were 11 ‹‹ and daughters.

עֲבַד יָתֵהּ: ב דְּכַר וְנוּקְבָא בְּרָאנוּן וּבָרִיךְ יָתְהוֹן וּקְרָא יָת שְׁמְהוֹן אָדָם בְּיוֹמָא דְאִתְבְּרִיאוּ: ג וַחֲיָא אָדָם מְאָה וּתְלָתִין שְׁנִין וְאוֹלִיד בִּדְמוּתֵהּ דְּדָמֵי לֵהּ וּקְרָא יָת שְׁמֵהּ שֵׁת: ד וַהֲווֹ יוֹמֵי אָדָם בָּתַר דְּאוֹלִיד יָת שֵׁת תְּמָנֵי מְאָה שְׁנִין וְאוֹלִיד בְּנִין וּבְנָן: ה וַהֲווֹ כָּל יוֹמֵי אָדָם דִּי חֲיָא תְּשַׁע מְאָה וּתְלָתִין שְׁנִין וּמִית: ו וַחֲיָא שֵׁת מְאָה וַחֲמֵשׁ שְׁנִין וְאוֹלִיד יָת אֱנוֹשׁ: ז וַחֲיָא שֵׁת בָּתַר דְּאוֹלִיד יָת אֱנוֹשׁ תְּמָנֵי מְאָה וּשְׁבַע שְׁנִין וְאוֹלִיד בְּנִין וּבְנָן: ח וַהֲווֹ כָּל יוֹמֵי שֵׁת תְּשַׁע מְאָה וְתַרְתָּא עַשְׂרֵי שְׁנִין וּמִית: ט וַחֲיָא אֱנוֹשׁ תִּשְׁעִין שְׁנִין וְאוֹלִיד יָת קֵינָן: י וַחֲיָא אֱנוֹשׁ בָּתַר דְּאוֹלִיד יָת קֵינָן תְּמָנֵי מְאָה וַחֲמֵשׁ עַשְׂרֵי שְׁנִין וְאוֹלִיד בְּנִין וּבְנָן: יא וַהֲווֹ כָּל יוֹמֵי אֱנוֹשׁ תְּשַׁע מְאָה וַחֲמֵשׁ שְׁנִין וּמִית:

רש"י

(ג) **שלשים ומאת שנה.** עד כאן פירש מן האשה (שם ו; עירובין יח:):

span of seventy and eighty years, while only the most righteous lived longer.

2. זָכָר וּנְקֵבָה בְּרָאָם — *Male and female He created them.* The Talmud comments that a man without a wife is not a man, for it is said, *Male and female He created them . . . and called their name Man* [only when a man is united with his wife can he be called *Man*] (*Yevamos* 63a).

3. בִּדְמוּתוֹ כְּצַלְמוֹ — *In his likeness according to his image.* The verse mentions this to indicate that God gave Adam, who himself was created in God's likeness, the capacity to repro-

ס יב וַיְחִי קֵינָן שִׁבְעִים שָׁנָה וַיּוֹלֶד אֶת־מַהֲלַלְאֵל׃
« Mahalalel. ‹ and he begot « years, ‹ seventy ‹ Kenan lived 12

יג וַיְחִי קֵינָן אַחֲרֵי הוֹלִידוֹ אֶת־מַהֲלַלְאֵל אַרְבָּעִים
‹ forty ‹ Mahalalel ‹ his begetting ‹ after ‹ And Kenan lived 13

שָׁנָה וּשְׁמֹנֶה מֵאוֹת שָׁנָה וַיּוֹלֶד בָּנִים וּבָנוֹת׃
« and daughters. ‹ sons ‹ and he begot « years, ‹ hundred ‹ and eight ‹ years

יד וַיִּהְיוּ כָּל־יְמֵי קֵינָן עֶשֶׂר שָׁנִים וּתְשַׁע מֵאוֹת
‹ hundred ‹ and nine ‹ years ‹ ten « of Kenan — ‹ the days ‹ — all « And they were 14

שָׁנָה וַיָּמֹת׃ ס טו וַיְחִי מַהֲלַלְאֵל חָמֵשׁ שָׁנִים
‹ years ‹ five ‹ Mahalalel lived 15 « and he died. « years;

וְשִׁשִּׁים שָׁנָה וַיּוֹלֶד אֶת־יָרֶד׃ טז וַיְחִי מַהֲלַלְאֵל
‹ And Mahalalel lived 16 « Jared. ‹ and he begot « years, ‹ and sixty

אַחֲרֵי הוֹלִידוֹ אֶת־יֶרֶד שְׁלֹשִׁים שָׁנָה וּשְׁמֹנֶה מֵאוֹת שָׁנָה וַיּוֹלֶד בָּנִים
‹ sons ‹ and he begot « years, ‹ hundred ‹ and eight ‹ years ‹ thirty ‹ Jared ‹ his begetting ‹ after

וּבָנוֹת׃ יז וַיִּהְיוּ כָּל־יְמֵי מַהֲלַלְאֵל חָמֵשׁ וְתִשְׁעִים שָׁנָה וּשְׁמֹנֶה מֵאוֹת
‹ hundred ‹ and eight ‹ years ‹ ninety-five « of Mahalalel — ‹ the days ‹ — all « And they were 17 « and daughters.

שָׁנָה וַיָּמֹת׃ ס יח וַיְחִי־יֶרֶד שְׁתַּיִם וְשִׁשִּׁים שָׁנָה וּמְאַת שָׁנָה וַיּוֹלֶד
‹ and he begot « years, ‹ and one hundred ‹ years ‹ sixty-two ‹ Jared lived 18 « and he died. « years;

אֶת־חֲנוֹךְ׃ יט וַיְחִי־יֶרֶד אַחֲרֵי הוֹלִידוֹ אֶת־חֲנוֹךְ שְׁמֹנֶה מֵאוֹת שָׁנָה
« years, ‹ hundred ‹ eight ‹ Enoch ‹ his begetting ‹ after ‹ And Jared lived 19 « Enoch.

וַיּוֹלֶד בָּנִים וּבָנוֹת׃ כ וַיִּהְיוּ כָּל־יְמֵי־יֶרֶד שְׁתַּיִם וְשִׁשִּׁים שָׁנָה וּתְשַׁע
‹ and nine ‹ years ‹ sixty-two « of Jared — ‹ the days ‹ — all « And they were 20 « and daughters. ‹ sons ‹ and he begot

מֵאוֹת שָׁנָה וַיָּמֹת׃ ס כא וַיְחִי חֲנוֹךְ חָמֵשׁ וְשִׁשִּׁים שָׁנָה וַיּוֹלֶד אֶת־מְתוּשָׁלַח׃
« Methuselah. ‹ and he begot ‹ years, ‹ sixty-five ‹ Enoch lived 21 « and he died. « years; ‹ hundred

יב וַחֲיָא קֵינָן שַׁבְעִין שְׁנִין וְאוֹלִיד יָת
מַהֲלַלְאֵל: יג וַחֲיָא קֵינָן בָּתַר דְּאוֹלִיד
יָת מַהֲלַלְאֵל תַּמְנֵי מְאָה וְאַרְבְּעִין
שְׁנִין וְאוֹלִיד בְּנִין וּבְנָן: יד וַהֲווֹ כָּל יוֹמֵי
קֵינָן תְּשַׁע מְאָה וַעֲשַׂר שְׁנִין וּמִית:
טו וַחֲיָא מַהֲלַלְאֵל שִׁתִּין וַחֲמֵשׁ שְׁנִין
וְאוֹלִיד יָת יָרֶד: טז וַחֲיָא מַהֲלַלְאֵל
בָּתַר דְּאוֹלִיד יָת יֶרֶד תַּמְנֵי מְאָה
וּתְלָתִין שְׁנִין וְאוֹלִיד בְּנִין וּבְנָן: יז וַהֲווֹ
כָּל יוֹמֵי מַהֲלַלְאֵל תַּמְנֵי מְאָה
וְתִשְׁעִין וַחֲמֵשׁ שְׁנִין וּמִית: יח וַחֲיָא
יֶרֶד מְאָה וְשִׁתִּין וְתַרְתֵּין שְׁנִין
וְאוֹלִיד יָת חֲנוֹךְ: יט וַחֲיָא יֶרֶד בָּתַר
דְּאוֹלִיד יָת חֲנוֹךְ תַּמְנֵי מְאָה
שְׁנִין וְאוֹלִיד בְּנִין וּבְנָן: כ וַהֲווֹ כָּל
יוֹמֵי יֶרֶד תְּשַׁע מְאָה וְשִׁתִּין וְתַרְתֵּין
שְׁנִין וּמִית: כא וַחֲיָא חֲנוֹךְ שִׁתִּין
וַחֲמֵשׁ שְׁנִין וְאוֹלִיד יָת מְתוּשָׁלַח:

---

duce offspring who were also in this noble likeness. This is not mentioned concerning Cain or Abel because, since their seed perished, the Torah did not wish to prolong the descriptions of them (*Ibn Ezra; Ramban*).

The ten generations from Adam to Noah

אָדָם — *Adam:* died in the year 930 from Creation;

שֵׁת — *Seth:* born in the year 130 from Creation; died in 1042.

After his time, people begin to do evil.

אֱנוֹשׁ — *Enosh:* 235-1140;

קֵינָן — *Kenan:* 325-1235;

מַהֲלַלְאֵל — *Mahalalel:* 395-1290;

יֶרֶד — *Jared*: 460-1422;

חֲנוֹךְ — *Enoch:* 622-987;

מְתוּשֶׁלַח — *Methuselah:* 687-1656;

לֶמֶךְ — *Lamech:* 874-1651;

נֹחַ — *Noah:* 1056-2006.

Thus, Noah was born 126 years after Adam died; Lamech was the farthest descendant Adam lived to see.

כב וַיִּתְהַלֵּךְ חֲנוֹךְ אֶת־הָאֱלֹהִים אַחֲרֵי הוֹלִידוֹ
< his begetting < after < God < with < And Enoch walked 22

אֶת־מְתוּשֶׁלַח שְׁלֹשׁ מֵאוֹת שָׁנָה וַיּוֹלֶד בָּנִים
< sons < and he begot << years; < hundred < [for] three < Methuselah

וּבָנוֹת: כג וַיְהִי כָּל־יְמֵי חֲנוֹךְ חָמֵשׁ וְשִׁשִּׁים
< [were] sixty-five < of Enoch < the days < [that] all < And it was 23 << and daughters.

שָׁנָה וּשְׁלֹשׁ מֵאוֹת שָׁנָה: כד וַיִּתְהַלֵּךְ חֲנוֹךְ אֶת־
< with < And Enoch walked 24 << years. < hundred < and three < years

הָאֱלֹהִים וְאֵינֶנּוּ כִּי־לָקַח אֹתוֹ אֱלֹהִים: ס שביעי
<< — did God. << him < He took < for << then he was no more, << God;

כה וַיְחִי מְתוּשֶׁלַח שֶׁבַע וּשְׁמֹנִים שָׁנָה וּמְאַת שָׁנָה
<< years, < and one hundred < years < eighty-seven < Methuselah lived 25

וַיּוֹלֶד אֶת־לָמֶךְ: כו וַיְחִי מְתוּשֶׁלַח אַחֲרֵי הוֹלִידוֹ אֶת־לֶמֶךְ שְׁתַּיִם
< two < Lamech < his begetting < after < And Methuselah lived 26 << Lamech. < and he begot

וּשְׁמוֹנִים שָׁנָה וּשְׁבַע מֵאוֹת שָׁנָה וַיּוֹלֶד בָּנִים וּבָנוֹת: כז וַיִּהְיוּ כָּל־יְמֵי
< the days < — all << And they were 27 << and daughters. < sons < and he begot << years, < hundred < and seven < years < and eighty

מְתוּשֶׁלַח תֵּשַׁע וְשִׁשִּׁים שָׁנָה וּתְשַׁע מֵאוֹת שָׁנָה וַיָּמֹת: ס כח וַיְחִי־לֶמֶךְ
< Lamech lived 28 << and he died. << years; < hundred < and nine < years < sixty-nine << of Methuselah —

שְׁתַּיִם וּשְׁמֹנִים שָׁנָה וּמְאַת שָׁנָה וַיּוֹלֶד בֵּן: כט וַיִּקְרָא אֶת־שְׁמוֹ נֹחַ
< Noah, < his name < And he called 29 << a son. < and he begot << years, < and one hundred < years < eighty-two

לֵאמֹר *זֶה יְנַחֲמֵנוּ מִמַּעֲשֵׂנוּ וּמֵעִצְּבוֹן יָדֵינוּ מִן־הָאֲדָמָה אֲשֶׁר אֵרְרָהּ
<< He cursed it < which < the ground < from < of our hands, < and from the toil < from our work < will provide us relief < This one << saying,

* הקורא יטעים הגרשים קודם התלישא

כב וְהַלִּיךְ חֲנוֹךְ בְּדַחַלְתָּא דַייָ בָּתַר דְּאוֹלִיד יָת מְתוּשֶׁלַח תְּלָת מְאָה שְׁנִין וְאוֹלִיד בְּנִין וּבְנָן: כג וַהֲוָה כָּל יוֹמֵי חֲנוֹךְ תְּלָת מְאָה וְשִׁתִּין וַחֲמֵשׁ שְׁנִין: כד וְהַלִּיךְ חֲנוֹךְ בְּדַחַלְתָּא דַייָ וְלֵיתוֹהִי אֲרֵי (לָא) אֲמֵית יָתֵהּ יְיָ: כה וַחֲיָא מְתוּשֶׁלַח מְאָה וּתְמָנָן וּשְׁבַע שְׁנִין וְאוֹלִיד יָת לָמֶךְ: כו וַחֲיָא מְתוּשֶׁלַח בָּתַר דְּאוֹלִיד יָת לֶמֶךְ שְׁבַע מְאָה וּתְמָנָן וְתַרְתֵּין שְׁנִין וְאוֹלִיד בְּנִין וּבְנָן: כז וַהֲווֹ כָּל יוֹמֵי מְתוּשֶׁלַח תְּשַׁע מְאָה וְשִׁתִּין וּתְשַׁע שְׁנִין וּמִית: כח וַחֲיָא לֶמֶךְ מְאָה וּתְמָנָן וְתַרְתֵּין שְׁנִין וְאוֹלִיד בָּר: כט וּקְרָא יָת שְׁמֵהּ נֹחַ לְמֵימָר דֵּין יְנַחֲמִנָּנָא מֵעוֹבָדָנָא וּמִלֵּאוּת יְדָנָא מִן אַרְעָא דִּי לַטְטַהּ

רש"י

(כד) **ויתהלך חנוך.** צדיק היה וקל [ס"א וקבל] בדעתו לשוב להרשיע, לפיכך מיהר הקב"ה וסילקו והמיתו קודם זמנו, וזהו ששינה הכתוב במיתתו לכתוב **ואיננו** בעולם למלאות שנותיו **כי לקח אתו** לפני זמנו, כמו הנני לוקח ממך את מחמד עיניך (יחזקאל כד:טז; ב"ר כה:א): (כח) **ויולד בן.** שממנו נבנה העולם (תנחומא יא): (כט) **זה ינחמנו.** ינח ממנו את **עצבון ידינו.** עד שלא בא נח לא היה להם כלי מחרישה והוא הכין להם, והיתה הארץ מוציאה קוצים ודרדרים כשזורעים חטים מקללתו של אדם הראשון (שם) ובימי נח נחה, וזהו ינחמנו ינח ממנו, ואם לא תפרשהו כך אין טעם הלשון נופל על השם ואתה צריך לקרות שמו מנחם (ב"ר כה:ב):

24. Although Enoch was a righteous man, he was liable to go astray. To avert this, God cut his life short, as implied by the expression *he was no more,* rather than *he died* — i.e., *he was no more* in the world to complete his allotted years (*Rashi*). *Targum Yonasan* paraphrases the verse as follows: And Enoch served in truth before God, and behold, he was not with the sojourners of earth, for he was withdrawn and he ascended to heaven by the word of God.

29. **זֶה יְנַחֲמֵנוּ** — *This one will provide us relief.* Our rendering follows *Rashi* who relates נֹחַ, *Noah,* to the root נוּחַ, *rest, ease, relief:* i.e., *"He will provide us relief . . . from the toil of our hands."* This was said [prophetically] in reference to the invention of

יהוה: ל וַיְחִי־לֶמֶךְ אַחֲרֵי הוֹלִידוֹ אֶת־נֹחַ

< Noah < his begetting < after < Lamech lived 30 << — *did* HASHEM.

חָמֵשׁ וְתִשְׁעִים שָׁנָה וַחֲמֵשׁ מֵאֹת שָׁנָה וַיּוֹלֶד

< and he begot << years, < hundred < and five < years < ninety-five

בָּנִים וּבָנוֹת: לא וַיְהִי כָּל־יְמֵי־לֶמֶךְ שֶׁבַע וְשִׁבְעִים

< seventy-seven << of Lamech — < the days < — all << And they were 31 << and daughters. < sons

שָׁנָה וּשְׁבַע מֵאוֹת שָׁנָה וַיָּמֹת: ס לב וַיְהִי־נֹחַ

< And [when] Noah was 32 << and he died. << years; < hundred < and seven < years

בֶּן־חֲמֵשׁ מֵאוֹת שָׁנָה וַיּוֹלֶד נֹחַ אֶת־שֵׁם אֶת־חָם

< Ham, < Shem, < Noah begot << years, < hundred < of five < of the age

וְאֶת־יָפֶת: [ו] א וַיְהִי כִּי־הֵחֵל הָאָדָם לָרֹב עַל־פְּנֵי הָאֲדָמָה וּבָנוֹת יֻלְּדוּ

< were born < and daughters < of the ground < the face < upon < to increase < Man began < when < And it came to pass 1 [6] << and Japheth.

לָהֶם: ב וַיִּרְאוּ בְנֵי־הָאֱלֹהִים אֶת־בְּנוֹת הָאָדָם כִּי טֹבֹת הֵנָּה וַיִּקְחוּ לָהֶם

< for themselves < and they took << they were good, < that < of Man < of the daughters << of the rulers — < — the sons << they saw 2 << to them,

נָשִׁים מִכֹּל אֲשֶׁר בָּחָרוּ: ג וַיֹּאמֶר יהוה לֹא־יָדוֹן רוּחִי בָאָדָם לְעֹלָם

<< *forever,* < *concerning Man* << *— My spirit —* << *It shall not contend* << And HASHEM said, 3 << they chose. < that < from all < wives

יְיָ: ל וַחֲיָא לֶמֶךְ בָּתַר דְּאוֹלִיד יָת נֹחַ חֲמֵשׁ מְאָה וְתִשְׁעִין וַחֲמֵשׁ שְׁנִין וְאוֹלִיד בְּנִין וּבְנָן: לא וַהֲווֹ כָּל יוֹמֵי לֶמֶךְ שְׁבַע מְאָה וְשַׁבְעִין וּשְׁבַע שְׁנִין וּמִית: לב וַהֲוָה נֹחַ בַּר חֲמֵשׁ מְאָה שְׁנִין וְאוֹלִיד נֹחַ יָת שֵׁם יָת חָם וְיָת יָפֶת: א וַהֲוָה כַּד שְׁרִיאוּ בְּנֵי אֲנָשָׁא לְמִסְגֵּי עַל אַפֵּי אַרְעָא וּבְנָתָא אִתְיְלִידוּ לְהוֹן: ב וַחֲזוֹ בְּנֵי רַבְרְבַיָּא יָת בְּנַת אֲנָשָׁא אֲרֵי שַׁפִּירָן אִנִּין וּנְסִיבוּ לְהוֹן נְשִׁין מִכֹּל דִּי אִתְרְעִיאוּ: ג וַאֲמַר יְיָ לָא יִתְקַיַּם דָּרָא בִּישָׁא הָדֵין קֳדָמַי לְעָלָם

רש"י

(לב) **בן חמש מאות שנה.** א"ר יודן מה טעם כל הדורות הולידו לק' שנה [ולמאתים שנה] וזה לת"ק. אמר הקב"ה, אם רשעים הם יאבדו במים ורע לצדיק זה [ס"א לזרע של צדיק זה], ואם צדיקים הם אטריח עליו לעשות תיבות הרבה, כבש את מעינו ולא הוליד עד ת"ק שנה כדי שלא יהא יפת הגדול שבבניו ראוי לעונשין לפני המבול דכתיב כי הנער בן מאה שנה ימות (ישעיה סה:כ) ראוי לעונש לעתיד, וכן לפני מתן תורה (ב"ר כו:ב): **את שם את חם ואת יפת.** והלא יפת הגדול הוא, אלא בתחלה אתה דורש את שהוא צדיק ונולד כשהוא מהול ושאברהם יצא ממנו כו' (שם ג): (ב) **בני האלהים.** בני השרים והשופטים (ב"ר כו:ה). [דבר אחר בני האלהים הם השרים ההולכים בשליחותו של מקום אף הם היו מתערבין בהם (פדר"א כב; דב"ר סוף פ"א; ילק"ש מד).] כל אלהים שבמקרא לשון מרות, וזה יוכיח ואתה תהיה לו לאלהים (שמות ד:טז) ראה נתתיך אלהים (שם ז:א): **כי טבת הנה.** א"ר יודן טבת כתיב [חסר ו', שלא היו, אלא] כשהיו מטיבין אותה מקושטת ליכנס לחופה היה גדול נכנס ובועלה תחלה (ב"ר כו:ה): **מכל אשר בחרו.** אף בעולת בעל, אף הזכר והבהמה (ב"ר שם): (ג) **לא ידון רוחי באדם.** לא יתרעם ויריב רוחי עלי בשביל האדם: **לעולם.** לאורך ימים. הנה רוחי נידון בקרבי אם להשחית ואם לרחם, לא יהיה מדון זה ברוחי לעולם, כלומר לאורך ימים:

farming tools, which was attributed to Noah. Until his time, in consequence of the curse decreed upon Adam (3:18), the earth produced thorns and thistles when one planted wheat. In Noah's days this ceased.

6.

1-8. Prelude to the Flood.

1. **וַיְהִי** — *And it came to pass.* The Talmud notes that where the term וַיְהִי, *and it came to pass,* occurs in Scripture, it often presages trouble. In this case, our chapter begins the account of mankind's quickening descent into the abyss (*Megillah* 10b).

2. **בְּנֵי־הָאֱלֹהִים** — *The sons of the rulers*. These were the sons of the princes and judges, for *elohim* always implies rulership [cf. notes to 1:1], as in *Exodus* 4:16: *and you shall be his* אֱלֹהִים, *master* (*Rashi*). *The daughters of man* were the daughters of the general populace (*R' Saadiah Gaon*); the multitude, the lower classes (*Rambam, Moreh* 1:14), who did not have the power to resist their superiors (*Radak*). Thus, the Torah begins the narrative of the tragedy by speaking of the subjugation of the weak by the powerful.

According to many commentators, בְּנֵי הָאֱלֹהִים, literally, *the sons of God*, are the God-fearing descendants of Seth, while the *daughters of Man* (implying less spiritual people) are the iniquitous descendants of Cain. The result of such marriages was that Seth's righteous offspring were enticed by the proponents of a godless, depraved culture, and suffered the fate of destruction with all of mankind — except for Noah and his family.

3. **לֹא־יָדוֹן רוּחִי . . .** — *It shall not contend — My spirit.* Seeing that mankind had not lived up to His aspirations, God

בְּשַׁגָּם הוּא בָשָׂר וְהָיוּ יָמָיו מֵאָה וְעֶשְׂרִים שָׁנָה:
« years. ‹ and twenty ‹ one hundred ‹ his days shall be «[but] flesh; ‹ he is ‹ in that additionally

ד הַנְּפִלִים הָיוּ בָאָרֶץ בַּיָּמִים הָהֵם וְגַם אַחֲרֵי־כֵן
4 The Nephilim ‹ were ‹ on the earth ‹ in those days « —and also ‹ after ‹ that, «

אֲשֶׁר יָבֹאוּ בְּנֵי הָאֱלֹהִים אֶל־בְּנוֹת הָאָדָם וְיָלְדוּ
‹ and they would bear « of man— ‹ the daughters ‹ with ‹ of the rulers ‹ —the sons « they would mate ‹ when

לָהֶם הֵמָּה הַגִּבֹּרִים אֲשֶׁר מֵעוֹלָם אַנְשֵׁי הַשֵּׁם:
« of renown. ‹ were men ‹ from old, ‹ that, ‹ the mighty ‹ They were « to them.

5 פ מפטיר ה וַיַּרְא יהוה כִּי רַבָּה רָעַת הָאָדָם בָּאָרֶץ
« upon the earth, ‹ of Man ‹ was the wickedness ‹ great ‹ that ‹ HASHEM saw

וְכָל־יֵצֶר מַחְשְׁבֹת לִבּוֹ רַק רַע כָּל־הַיּוֹם: 6 ו וַיִּנָּחֶם יהוה כִּי־עָשָׂה
‹ He made ‹ that ‹ And HASHEM regretted 6 « day long. ‹ all ‹ evil ‹ was totally ‹ of his heart ‹ of the thoughts ‹ product ‹ and [that] every

אֶת־הָאָדָם בָּאָרֶץ וַיִּתְעַצֵּב אֶל־לִבּוֹ: 7 ז וַיֹּאמֶר יהוה אֶמְחֶה אֶת־הָאָדָם
‹ Man ‹ I will obliterate « And HASHEM said, 7 « His heart. ‹ in ‹ and He was saddened « on earth, ‹ Man

בְּדִיל דְּאִנּוּן בִּשְׂרָא וְעוֹבָדֵיהוֹן בִּישַׁיָּא אַרְכָּא יְהִיבַת לְהוֹן מְאָה וְעֶשְׂרִין שְׁנִין אִם יְתוּבוּן: ד גִּבָּרַיָּא הֲווֹ בְאַרְעָא בְּיוֹמַיָּא הָאִנּוּן וְאַף בָּתַר כֵּן דִּי עָלִין בְּנֵי רַבְרְבַיָּא לְוַת בְּנַת אֲנָשָׁא וִילִידָן לְהוֹן אִנּוּן גִּבָּרַיָּא דִּי מֵעָלְמָא אֱנָשִׁין דִּשְׁמָא: ה וַחֲזָא יְיָ אֲרֵי סְגִיאַת בִּישַׁת אֱנָשָׁא בְּאַרְעָא וְכָל יִצְרָא מַחְשְׁבַת לִבֵּהּ לְחוֹד בִּישׁ כָּל יוֹמָא: ו וְתָב יְיָ בְּמֵימְרֵהּ אֲרֵי עֲבַד יָת אֱנָשָׁא בְּאַרְעָא וַאֲמַר בְּמֵימְרֵהּ לְמִתְבַּר תָּקְפְּהוֹן כִּרְעוּתֵהּ: ז וַאֲמַר יְיָ אֶמְחֵי יָת אֱנָשָׁא

רש"י

בְּשַׁגָּם הוא בשר. כמו בְּשֶׁגַּם, כלומר בשביל שגם זאת בו שהוא בשר, ואעפ"כ אינו נכנע לפני, ומה אם יהיה אש או דבר קשה. כיוצא בו עד שקמתי דבורה (שופטים ה:ז) כמו שֶׁקַּמְתִּי. וכן שאתה מדבר עמי (שם ו:יז) כמו שֶׁאַתָּה. אף בְּשַׁגָּם כמו בְּשֶׁגַּם: **והיו ימיו וגו'.** עד ק"ך שנה אאריך להם אפי ואם לא ישובו אביא עליהם מבול (אונקלוס; תרגום יונתן). וא"ת משנולד יפת עד המבול אינו אלא מאה שנה. אין מוקדם ומאוחר בתורה, כבר היתה הגזרה גזורה עשרים שנה קודם שהוליד נח תולדות, וכן מצינו בסדר עולם (פרק כח). יש מדרשי אגדה רבים בלא ידון אבל זה הוא לאמות פשוטו: **(ד) הנפילים.** ע"ש שנפלו והפילו את העולם (ב"ר שם ז) ובלשון עברי ל' ענקים הוא (פדר"א שם): **בימים ההם.** בימי דור אנוש ובני קין (שם): **וגם אחרי כן.** אע"פ שראו באבדן של דור אנוש שעלה אוקיינוס והציף שליש העולם לא נכנע דור המבול ללמוד מהם (ב"ר שם; תנחומא נח יח): **אשר יבאו.** היו יולדות ענקים כמותם (ב"ר שם): **הגבורים.** למרוד במקום (תנחומא יב): **אנשי השם.** אותן שנקבו בשמות, עירד, מחויאל, מתושאל, שנקבו ע"ש אבדן, שנמוחו והותשו. ד"א אנשי שממון, ששממו את העולם (ב"ר שם): **(ו) וינחם ה' כי עשה.** נחמה היתה לפניו שבראו בתחתונים, שאילו היה מן העליונים היה ממרידן (ב"ר כז:ד): **ויתעצב.** האדם. **אל לבו.** של מקום, עלה במחשבתו של מקום להעציבו, וזהו תרגום אונקלוס. ד"א, וינחם, נהפכה מחשבתו של מקום ממדת רחמים למדת הדין (ב"ר לג:ג) עלה במחשבה לפניו מה לעשות באדם שעשה בארץ. וכן כל לשון ניחום שבמקרא לשון נמלך מה לעשות, ובן אדם ויתנחם (במדבר כג:יט) ועל עבדיו יתנחם (דברים לב:לו) וינחם ה' על הרעה (שמות לב:יד) נחמתי כי המלכתי (שמואל א טו:יא), כולם לשון מחשבה אחרת הם: **ויתעצב אל לבו.** נתאבל על אבדן מעשה ידיו (ב"ר סוף פכ"ז), כמו נעצב המלך על בנו (שמואל ב יט:ג), וזו כתבתי לתשובת המינים. גוי [ס"א אפיקורס] אחד שאל את רבי יהושע בן קרחה, אמר לו אין אתם מודים שהקב"ה רואה את הנולד. אמר לו הן. אמר לו והא כתיב ויתעצב אל לבו. אמר לו נולד לך בן זכר מימיך. אמר לו הן. אמר לו ומה עשית. אמר לו שמחתי ושימחתי את הכל. אמר לו ולא היית יודע שסופו למות. אמר לו בשעת חדותא חדותא בשעת אבלא אבלא. אמר לו כך מעשה הקב"ה, אע"פ שגלוי לפניו שסופן לחטוא ולאבדן לא נמנע מלבראן (ב"ר כז:ד) בשביל הצדיקים העתידים לעמוד מהם (שם ח:ד): **(ז) ויאמר ה' אמחה את האדם.** הוא עפר ואביא עליו

resolved that He would not wait much longer, debating with Himself, as it were, whether to destroy it because of its sins, or to show mercy (*Rashi*), because *he is [but] flesh* and cannot survive without compassion (*Sforno*).

Man is unworthy that God's spirit should reside in him, since he is but flesh like the other creatures, and his soul is drawn to the flesh rather than to God's spirit (*R' Bachya*).

מֵאָה וְעֶשְׂרִים שָׁנָה — *One hundred and twenty years.* God would wait 120 years before bringing the Flood, so that mankind would have ample opportunity to repent (*Rashi, Ramban*). Others interpret that the human life span would gradually decrease until it would be a maximum of 120 years (*Ibn Ezra*).

4. הַנְּפִלִים — *The Nephilim.* They were giants — the same race that terrified Moses' spies (*Numbers* 13:33). They were given this title from the root נפל, *to fall*, because they fell and caused others to fall (*Rashi*), through their egregious sinfulness (*Gur Aryeh*). Alternatively, they were so called because the hearts of those who saw them fell in amazement at their size (*Ibn Ezra*).

6. וַיִּנָּחֶם ה׳ — *And HASHEM regretted.* In a penetrating discourse on the concept of God's regret and sadness, *Akeidas Yitzchak* explains that this "sadness" does not contradict the principle that God knows the future. As an example, he cites the case of

אֲשֶׁר־בָּרָ֙אתִי֙ מֵעַל֙ פְּנֵ֣י הָֽאֲדָמָ֔ה מֵֽאָדָם֙ עַד־

whom ‹ *I created* ‹ *from upon* ‹ *the face* ‹ *of the earth;* ‹‹ *from man* ‹ *to* ‹

בְּהֵמָ֔ה עַד־רֶ֖מֶשׂ וְעַד־ע֣וֹף הַשָּׁמָ֑יִם כִּ֥י נִחַ֖מְתִּי כִּ֥י

animal, ‹ *to* ‹ *creeping things,* ‹ *and to* ‹ *birds* ‹ *of the sky;* ‹ *for* ‹ *I regret* ‹ *that* ‹

עֲשִׂיתִֽם׃ ח וְנֹ֕חַ מָ֥צָא חֵ֖ן בְּעֵינֵ֥י יְהוָֽה׃ פפפ

I made them. ‹‹ **8** But Noah ‹ found ‹ favor ‹ in the eyes ‹ of HASHEM. ‹‹

קמ"ו פסוקים. אמצי"ה סימן. יחזקיה"ו סימן.

דִּי בְרֵאתִי מֵעַל אַפֵּי אַרְעָא מֵאֱנָשָׁא עַד בְּעִירָא עַד רִחֲשָׁא וְעַד עוֹפָא דִשְׁמַיָּא אֲרֵי תָבִית בְּמֵימְרִי אֲרֵי עֲבַדְתִּנּוּן: ח וְנֹחַ אַשְׁכַּח רַחֲמִין קֳדָם יְיָ:

THE HAFTARAH FOR BEREISHIS APPEARS ON PAGE 322.

When Erev Rosh Chodesh Cheshvan coincides with Bereishis, the regular Haftarah is replaced with the reading for Shabbas Erev Rosh Chodesh, page 349.

רש"י

מים ואמחה אותו, לכך נאמר לשון מחוי (ב"ר כח:ב; תנחומא ישן נח ד): **מאדם עד בהמה.** אף הם השחיתו דרכם (ב"ר שם ח). ד"א הכל נברא בשביל האדם וכיון שהוא כלה מה צורך באלו (שם ו; סנהדרין קח.): **כי נחמתי כי עשיתם.** חשבתי מה לעשות על אשר עשיתים:

someone who plants a sapling and nurtures it proudly, protecting it from harm as it grows to maturity, when he will cut it down for lumber. When that time comes, he feels sad that he must chop down a tree for which he worked so hard, even though he knew from the start that he would be doing so eventually. In this sense, the Torah borrows human terms to describe God as "being saddened."

8. וְנֹחַ מָצָא חֵן — *But Noah found favor.* God's *favor* was needed in order to save Noah's family, otherwise only he would have been spared. Although Noah himself was righteous, he did not try to influence the rest of his generation to know God and to repent. Since he did not attempt to help others, his merit would have been insufficient to save others. If a righteous person attempts to make others righteous, God may spare them for his sake, because there is hope he can influence them to repent (*Sforno*).

קמ"ו פסוקים. אמצי"ה סימן. יחזקיה"ו סימן — This Masoretic note means: There are 146 verses in the *Sidrah,* numerically corresponding to [the names of the two kings of Judah,] אֲמַצְיָה, *Amaziah,* and יְחִזְקִיָּהוּ, *Hezekiah*.

Besides having names with similar *gematria* (numerical value), these two kings' lives paralleled one another in many ways: Each succeeded his father to the throne at the age of twenty-five; each is described with the phrase וַיַּעַשׂ הַיָּשָׁר בְּעֵינֵי ה׳, *He did what was proper in the eyes of HASHEM;* each was attacked in the fourteenth year of his reign — *Amaziah* by enemies, *Hezekiah* by a near-fatal illness; and each ruled for twenty-nine years.

Moreover, their names are nearly synonymous as their respective roots אמץ and חזק both indicate *power* or *strength.* Thus אֲמַצְיָה means *power of God,* and יְחִזְקִיָּהוּ means *God is my strength.* It is this last similarity that seems to be the point of the Masoretic note; God's creation of the world *ex nihilo* and His subsequent active role in the unfolding of the history of mankind (as seen through His involvement with Adam and Eve, Cain and Tubal-cain, Lamech and Noah) — the subject matter of the *Sidrah* — attest to God's power in general [אֲמַצְיָה] and His involvement with each individual [יְחִזְקִיָּהוּ] (*Aramez Badavar;* see also Masoretic note at end of *Sidrah Mikeitz*).

PARASHAS NOACH / פרשת נח

ט אֵלֶּה תּוֹלְדֹת נֹחַ נֹחַ אִישׁ צַדִּיק תָּמִים הָיָה
9 These are < the offspring < of << Noah, Noah < a righteous man, < perfect < was he
בְּדֹרֹתָיו אֶת־הָאֱלֹהִים הִתְהַלֶּךְ־נֹחַ׃ י וַיּוֹלֶד נֹחַ
in his generations; << with < God < did Noah walk. << 10 Noah begot <
שְׁלֹשָׁה בָנִים אֶת־שֵׁם אֶת־חָם וְאֶת־יָפֶת׃ יא וַתִּשָּׁחֵת הָאָרֶץ לִפְנֵי
three < sons: << Shem, < Ham, < and Japheth. << 11 [Now] the earth had become corrupt < before <
הָאֱלֹהִים וַתִּמָּלֵא הָאָרֶץ חָמָס׃ יב וַיַּרְא אֱלֹהִים אֶת־הָאָרֶץ וְהִנֵּה
God; << and the earth had become filled < with robbery. << 12 And God saw < the earth < and indeed <

אונקלוס

ט אִלֵּין תּוּלְדַת נֹחַ נֹחַ גְּבַר זַכַּאי שְׁלִים הֲוָה בְּדָרוֹהִי בְּדַחַלְתָא דַייָ הַלִּיךְ נֹחַ: י וְאוֹלִיד נֹחַ תְּלָתָא בְנִין יָת שֵׁם יָת חָם וְיָת יָפֶת: יא וְאִתְחַבָּלַת אַרְעָא קֳדָם יְיָ וְאִתְמְלִיאַת אַרְעָא חֲטוֹפִין: יב וַחֲזָא יְיָ יָת אַרְעָא וְהָא

רש"י

(ט) **אלה תולדת נח נח איש צדיק.** הואיל והזכירו ספר בשבחו, שנאמר זכר צדיק לברכה (משלי י:ז; פס"ר יב (מז.)). ד"א, ללמדך שעיקר תולדותיהם של צדיקים מעשים טובים (תנחומא ב; ב"ר ל:ו): **בדרתיו.** יש מרבותינו דורשים אותו לשבח, כל שכן שאילו היה בדור צדיקים היה צדיק יותר. ויש שדורשים אותו לגנאי, לפי דורו היה צדיק, ואילו היה בדורו של אברהם לא היה נחשב לכלום (תנחומא ה; ב"ר שם ט): **את האלהים התהלך נח.** ובאברהם הוא אומר התהלך לפני (להלן יז:א). נח היה צריך סעד לתומכו, אבל אברהם היה מתחזק [ומהלך] בצדקו מאליו (שם ושם י): **התהלך.** לשון עבר. וזהו שמושו של ל' [ס"א ה'] [בל' כבד] משמשת להבא ולשעבר בלשון אחד. קום התהלך (להלן יג:יז) להבא, התהלך נח לשעבר. התפלל בעד עבדיך (שמואל א יב:יט) להבא. ובא והתפלל אל הבית הזה (מלכים א ח:מב) לשון עבר, אלא שהוי"ו שבראשו הופכו להבא: (יא) **ותשחת.** לשון ערוה וע"ז, כמו פן תשחיתון (דברים ד:טז) כי השחית כל בשר וגו' (פסוק יב; סנהדרין נז.): **ותמלא הארץ חמס.** גזל

PARASHAS NOACH

9-10. Noah. The ten generations from Adam to Noah had ended in failure; mankind had stumbled into a downward spiral until God resolved that all the inhabitants of the earth would be wiped out, with the exception of Noah and his family, and enough animals to replenish the earth after the destruction. Like Adam, the father of the entire human race, Noah would become the father of mankind after the Flood. Therefore, although the Torah had listed him previously as the last link in the genealogy of his predecessors, it mentions him again now, since he and his children were to become the new ancestors of mankind (*Abarbanel*).

9. נֹחַ אִישׁ צַדִּיק — *Noah was a righteous man.* The verse began to introduce the list of Noah's *offspring,* but once he was mentioned, Scripture praised him as a righteous man. According to the Midrash, the Torah means to teach that the primary "offspring" of the righteous are their good deeds, for the worthwhile things that a person does are his primary legacy (*Rashi*).

R' Moshe Feinstein comments homiletically on why the Torah likens a person's good deeds to his offspring. A person should *love* good deeds, the way he loves his own children, and he should perform them out of love, not just duty. A person should never disparage a good deed as being insignificant, just as he does not fail to love a child who lacks outstanding ability. And a person should work hard to perfect his deeds, just as he spares no effort to help his children.

Ibn Ezra and *B'chor Shor* render תולדת as *the history,* so that the primary subject of the chapter is not his family, but his life story as it relates to the Flood and its aftermath.

בְּדֹרֹתָיו — *In his generations.* There are different interpretations of this phrase: Some Sages maintain that it is in his praise: Noah was righteous even in his corrupt generation; how much more righteous would he have been had he lived in a truly righteous generation — if he had had the companionship and inspiration of Abraham! According to others, however, it is critical of him — only *in* **his** *generations,* by comparison with his extremely wicked contemporaries, did Noah stand out as a righteous man; but had he lived in the time of Abraham he would have been insignificant (*Rashi*). Accordingly, the righteous of each generation must be judged in terms of their own time (*Sefer HaParshiyos*).

It is true that Noah was not nearly as great as Abraham, but it is fair to say that he would have been far greater had he not been surrounded by corrupt and immoral people.

אֶת־הָאֱלֹהִים — *With God.* He feared only God, and was not enticed by astrology, and surely not by idolatry. He walked in the path God showed him, for he was a prophet (*Ramban*).

10. שְׁלֹשָׁה בָנִים — *Three sons.* They are not named in the order of their birth. Japheth was the eldest, but Shem is mentioned first because Scripture enumerates them according to wisdom, not age (*Sanhedrin* 69b). Once the Torah mentions Shem, it names Ham who was next in line; otherwise all three would be listed out of order (*Ramban*). Though they had been named above (5:32), the Torah mentions them after telling of Noah's righteousness to indicate that he inculcated such behavior into his children, as well (*Radak*).

11-12. The behavior of people deteriorated. At first they

נִשְׁחָתָה כִּי־הִשְׁחִית כָּל־בָּשָׂר אֶת־דַּרְכּוֹ עַל־
< upon < its way < flesh < [had] all < corrupted < for << it was corrupted,

הָאָרֶץ: פ יג וַיֹּאמֶר אֱלֹהִים לְנֹחַ קֵץ כָּל־בָּשָׂר בָּא
< has come < flesh < of all < The end << to Noah: < God said **13** << the earth.

לְפָנַי כִּי־מָלְאָה הָאָרֶץ חָמָס מִפְּנֵיהֶם וְהִנְנִי
< and indeed, I am [set] << through them; < with robbery < is the earth < filled < for << before Me,

מַשְׁחִיתָם אֶת־הָאָרֶץ: יד עֲשֵׂה לְךָ תֵּבַת עֲצֵי־גֹפֶר קִנִּים תַּעֲשֶׂה
< shall you make < with compartments << of gopher wood; < an Ark < for yourself < Make **14** << from the earth. < to destroy them

אֶת־הַתֵּבָה וְכָפַרְתָּ אֹתָהּ מִבַּיִת וּמִחוּץ בַּכֹּפֶר: טו וְזֶה אֲשֶׁר תַּעֲשֶׂה
< you should make < how < This is **15** << with pitch. < and out < inside < it < and you shall cover << the Ark,

אֹתָהּ שְׁלֹשׁ מֵאוֹת אַמָּה אֹרֶךְ הַתֵּבָה חֲמִשִּׁים אַמָּה רָחְבָּהּ וּשְׁלֹשִׁים
< and thirty << its width; < cubits < fifty << of the Ark; < the length < cubits < hundred < — three << it

אִתְחַבָּלַת אֲרֵי חַבִּילוּ כָּל בִּסְרָא אֱנַשׁ יָת אָרְחֵהּ עַל אַרְעָא: יג וַאֲמַר יְיָ לְנֹחַ קִצָּא דְכָל בִּסְרָא עֲלַת לִקֳדָמַי אֲרֵי אִתְמְלִיאַת אַרְעָא חֲטוֹפִין מִן קֳדָם עוֹבָדֵיהוֹן בִּישַׁיָּא וְהָא אֲנָא מְחַבֵּלְהוֹן עִם אַרְעָא: יד עִבֵד לָךְ תֵּבוֹתָא דְאָעִין דְּקַדְרוֹם מְדוֹרִין תַּעְבֵּד יָת תֵּבוֹתָא וְתַחֲפֵי יָתַהּ מִגָּו וּמִבָּרָא בְּכֻפְרָא: טו וְדֵין דִּי תַעְבֵּד יָתַהּ תְּלַת מְאָה אַמִּין אָרְכָּא דְתֵבוֹתָא חַמְשִׁין אַמִּין פְּתָיַהּ וּתְלָתִין

רש"י

[שנאמר ומן החמס אשר בכפיהם (יונה ג:ח)]: **(יב) כי השחית כל בשר.** אפילו בהמה חיה ועוף נזקקין לשאינן מינן (ב"ר כח:ח; תנחומא יב; סנהדרין קח.): **(יג) קץ כל בשר.** כל מקום שאתה מוצא זנות, אנדרלמוסיא באה לעולם והורגת טובים ורעים (ב"ר כו:ה; תנחומא ראה ג): **כי מלאה הארץ חמס.** לא נחתם גזר דינם אלא על הגזל (סנהדרין שם; תנחומא ד; ב"ר לא:ג־ד): **את הארץ.** כמו מן הארץ, ודומה לו כצאתי את העיר (שמות ט:כט) מן העיר. חלה את רגליו (מלכים א טו:כג) מן רגליו. ד"א את הארץ, עם הארץ (אונקלוס; תרגום יונתן) שאף שלשה טפחים של עומק המחרישה נמוחו (ב"ר לא:ז) ונטשטשו: **(יד) עשה לך תבת.** הרבה ריוח והצלה לפניו, ולמה הטריחו בבנין זה. כדי שיראוהו אנשי דור המבול עוסק בה ק"כ שנה ושואלין אותו מה זאת לך, והוא אומר להם עתיד הקב"ה להביא מבול לעולם, אולי ישובו (תנחומא ה; ב"ר ל:ז; תנחומא ישן בראשית לז): **עצי גפר.** כך שמו (סנהדרין קח:) [וכך מתרגם אעין דקדרום (עי' ר"ה כג.)]. ולמה ממין זה, ע"ש גפרית שנגזר עליהם להמחות בו (ב"ר כז:ג; סנהדרין שם): **קנים.** [מדורים] מדורים לכל בהמה וחיה (אונקלוס; פדר"א כד; ב"ר לא:ט): **בכפר.** זפת בלשון ארמי, ומצינו בתלמוד כופרא (שבת סז.). בתיבתו של משה ע"י שהיו המים תשים דיה בחומר מבפנים וזפת מבחוץ, ועוד, כדי שלא יריח אותו צדיק ריח רע של זפת, אבל כאן מפני חוזק המים

were *corrupt* — being guilty of immorality and idolatry — and they sinned covertly, *before God.* Later, *the earth had become filled with robbery* — which was obvious to all. Then the entire earth *was corrupted,* because man is the essence of the world, and his corruption infects all of Creation (*Zohar*). Such is the progression of sin. It begins in private, when people still have a sense of right and wrong. But once people develop the habit of sinning, they gradually lose their shame, and immoral behavior becomes the accepted — even the required — norm. In Noah's time, the immoral sexual conduct of the people extended to animals, as well, until they too cohabited with other species.

The Midrash teaches that they stole from one another in petty ways that were not subject to the authority of the courts. Though this is not the gravest kind of sin, it is morally damaging in the extreme, because thievery within the letter of the law weakens the conscience and corrupts the social fabric (*R' Hirsch*).

13-22. The decree. God decreed that a generation that behaved so immorally had forfeited its right to exist, but even then, He extended mercy to them. God could have saved Noah in many ways. Why then did He burden him with the task of constructing an Ark for, as the Sages teach, one hundred twenty years? So that when the curious would see him cutting down lumber and working on the Ark for so long, they would ask him why. He would answer, "God is about to bring a Flood on the world because of your sins," and they would thus be inspired to repent . . . But instead of seizing the opportunity, Noah's contemporaries scoffed at him (*Rashi*).

14. עֲשֵׂה לְךָ — *Make for yourself.* Noah was to build the Ark himself (*Abarbanel*). Homiletically, he was told, "Make an Ark to symbolize your own behavior. You remained aloof from your compatriots, instead of chastising them and trying to save them by improving their conduct. Now, you will isolate yourself in an Ark with beasts and animals" (*Alshich*). Noah's failure to try and influence his generation is why the Flood is called מֵי נֹחַ, *waters of Noah* (*Isaiah* 54:9), implying that he was responsible for the Flood (*Zohar*).

15. Even according to the smallest estimate of 18 inches per cubit, the dimensions of the Ark were 450 x 75 x 45 feet = 1,518,750 cubic feet. Each of its three stories had 33,750 square feet of floor space for a total of 101,250 square feet.

אַמָּה קוֹמָתָהּ: טז צֹהַר ׀ תַּעֲשֶׂה לַתֵּבָה וְאֶל־אַמָּה

< a cubit < and to << for the Ark, < shall you make < A window 16 << its height. < cubits

תְּכַלֶּנָּה מִלְמַעְלָה וּפֶתַח הַתֵּבָה בְּצִדָּהּ תָּשִׂים

<< you shall put; < in its side < of the Ark < The entrance << at the top. < you shall finish it

תַּחְתִּיִּם שְׁנִיִּם וּשְׁלִשִׁים תַּעֲשֶׂהָ: יז וַאֲנִי הִנְנִי מֵבִיא

< to bring <— indeed, I am about << And as for Me 17 << you shall make it. < and third [decks] < second, < with bottom,

אֶת־הַמַּבּוּל מַיִם עַל־הָאָרֶץ לְשַׁחֵת כָּל־בָּשָׂר

<< flesh, < all < to destroy << the earth, < upon < of water < the Flood

אֲשֶׁר־בּוֹ רוּחַ חַיִּים מִתַּחַת הַשָּׁמָיִם כֹּל אֲשֶׁר־בָּאָרֶץ יִגְוָע:

<<shall perish. <in the earth < that is < everything << the heavens; < from under << of life, < a breath < in which there is

יח וַהֲקִמֹתִי אֶת־בְּרִיתִי אִתָּךְ וּבָאתָ אֶל־הַתֵּבָה אַתָּה וּבָנֶיךָ וְאִשְׁתְּךָ

< and your wife, < and your sons, < — you, << the Ark < into < and you shall enter << with you, < My covenant < But I will establish 18

וּנְשֵׁי־בָנֶיךָ אִתָּךְ: יט וּמִכָּל־הָחַי מִכָּל־בָּשָׂר שְׁנַיִם מִכֹּל תָּבִיא אֶל־

< into < shall you bring < of each < two < flesh, < of all < that lives, < And from all 19 << with you. < of your sons < and the wives

הַתֵּבָה לְהַחֲיֹת אִתָּךְ זָכָר וּנְקֵבָה יִהְיוּ: כ מֵהָעוֹף לְמִינֵהוּ וּמִן־

< and from < according to its kind, < From [each] bird 20 << shall they be. < and female < male << with you; < to keep alive < the Ark

אַמִּין רוּמַהּ: טז נְהוֹר תַּעְבֵּד לְתֵבוּתָא וּלְאַמְּתָא תְּשַׁכְלְלִנַּהּ מִלְעֵלָּא וְתַרְעָא דְתֵבוּתָא בְּסִטְרַהּ תְּשַׁוֵּי מְדוֹרִין אַרְעִין תִּנְיָנִין וּתְלִיתָאִין תַּעְבְּדִנַּהּ: יז וַאֲנָא הָא אֲנָא מַיְתֵי יָת טוֹפָנָא מַיָּא עַל אַרְעָא לְחַבָּלָא כָּל בִּסְרָא דִּי בֵהּ רוּחָא דְחַיֵּי מִתְּחוֹת שְׁמַיָּא כֹּל דִּי בְאַרְעָא יְמוּת: יח וְאָקֵים יָת קְיָמִי עִמָּךְ וְתֵיעוֹל לְתֵבוּתָא אַתְּ וּבְנָיךְ וְאִתְּתָךְ וּנְשֵׁי בְנָיךְ עִמָּךְ: יט וּמִכָּל דְּחַי מִכָּל בִּסְרָא תְּרֵין מִכֹּלָּא תָּעֵיל לְתֵבוּתָא לְקַיָּמָא עִמָּךְ דְּכַר וְנוּקְבָא יְהוֹן: כ מֵעוֹפָא לִזְנוֹהִי וּמִן

רש"י

זפתה מבית ומחוץ (ב"ר לא:ט; סוטה יב.): (טז) **צהר.** י"א חלון, וי"א אבן טובה המאירה להם (ב"ר שם יא): **ואל אמה תכלנה מלמעלה.** כסויה משופע ועולה עד שהוא קצר מלמעלה ועומד על אמה, כדי שיזובו המים למטה מכאן ומכאן: **בצדה תשים.** שלא יפלו הגשמים בה: **תחתים שנים ושלשים.** שלש עליות זו על גב זו. עליונים לאדם, אמצעים למדור [בהמה חיה ועופות], תחתיים לזבל (סנהדרין שם): (יז) **ואני הנני מביא.** הנני מוכן להסכים עם אותם שזרזוני ואמרו לפני כבר מה אנוש כי תזכרנו (תהלים ח:ה; ב"ר שם יב): **מבול.** שבלה את הכל, שבלבל את הכל, שהוביל את הכל מן הגבוה לנמוך. וזהו לשון אונקלוס שתרגם טופנא, שהציף את הכל והביאם לבבל שהיא עמוקה (פסחים פז:). לכך נקראת שנער שננערו שם כל מתי מבול [ס"א מימי מבול] (שבת קיג:; זבחים קיג:): (יח) **והקמתי את בריתי.** ברית היה צריך על הפירות שלא ירקבו ויטפשו, ושלא יהרגוהו רשעים שבדור (ב"ר שם): **אתה ובניך ואשתך.** האנשים לבד והנשים לבד, מכאן שנאסרו בתשמיש המטה (שם): (יט) **ומכל החי.** אפי' שדים (שם יג): **שנים מכל.** מכל מין ומין [ס"א מן הפחות] שבהם לא פחתו משנים, אחד זכר ואחד נקבה: (כ) **מהעוף למינהו.** אותן שדבקו במיניהם ולא השחיתו דרכם. ומאליהם באו, וכל שהתיבה קולטתו הכניס בה (סנהדרין קח:; תנחומא יב):

16. צֹהַר — *A window.* Some say it was a skylight — according to most commentators, it was the window Noah opened after the Flood (8:6) — and some say it was a luminous precious stone [or one that refracted the outside light (*Chizkuni*)] to illuminate the interior (*Rashi*).

וְאֶל־אַמָּה — *And to a cubit.* The Ark's roof sloped upward to a cubit, so that the rain would run off (*Rashi*).

18. בְּרִיתִי — *My covenant.* This is a promise that the year's supply of food in the Ark would not spoil (*Rashi*); or it refers to the covenant after the Flood (9:8-17), in which God pledged not to destroy the world again through a flood (*Sforno*).

19. שְׁנַיִם מִכֹּל — *Two of each.* As the following verse explains, these animals were to be one male and one female, so that the species could be replenished after the Flood. In the case of the kosher species that could be used for offerings, Noah was later commanded to bring seven pairs (7:2), so that he could bring offerings of gratitude and commitment after returning to dry land.

There were many huge beasts, such as elephants, and so many species of all sizes that even ten such arks could not have held them all, along with one year's provisions. It was a miracle that the small Ark could contain them. Even though the same miracle could have taken place in a smaller ark, thus sparing Noah the hard physical labor of building such a huge one, nevertheless, God wanted it to be so large in order to make the miracle less obvious, because people should try to reduce their reliance on miracles as much as

הַבְּהֵמָה֙ לְמִינָהּ מִכֹּל רֶמֶשׂ הָאֲדָמָה לְמִינֵהוּ
<< according to its kind, < on the ground < thing that creeps < and from every < according to its kind, < [each] animal

שְׁנַיִם מִכֹּל יָבֹאוּ אֵלֶיךָ לְהַחֲיוֹת׃ כא וְאַתָּה
< And as for you, **21** << to keep alive. < to you < shall come < of every [one] < two

קַח־לְךָ מִכָּל־מַאֲכָל֙ אֲשֶׁר יֵאָכֵל וְאָסַפְתָּ אֵלֶיךָ
<< to yourself, < and gather [it] in < is eaten < that < food < of every < for yourself < take

וְהָיָה לְךָ וְלָהֶם לְאָכְלָה׃ כב וַיַּעַשׂ נֹחַ כְּכֹל אֲשֶׁר
< that < according to everything < Noah did **22** << as food. < and for them < for you < that it shall be

צִוָּה אֹתוֹ אֱלֹהִים כֵּן עָשָׂה׃ שני – [ז] א וַיֹּאמֶר יהוה֙ לְנֹחַ בֹּא־אַתָּה
<— you << Come << to Noah, < [Then] HASHEM said **1** [7] << he did. < so << God commanded him,

וְכָל־בֵּיתְךָ אֶל־הַתֵּבָה כִּי־אֹתְךָ רָאִיתִי צַדִּיק לְפָנַי בַּדּוֹר הַזֶּה׃
<< in this generation. < before Me < [to be] righteous < that I have seen < it is you < for << the Ark, < into << your household — < and all

ב מִכֹּל ׀ הַבְּהֵמָה הַטְּהוֹרָה תִּקַּח־לְךָ שִׁבְעָה שִׁבְעָה אִישׁ וְאִשְׁתּוֹ
<< with its mate, < a male << seven [pairs] of each, < unto you < take < that is clean < animal < Of every **2**

וּמִן־הַבְּהֵמָה אֲשֶׁר לֹא טְהֹרָה הִוא שְׁנַיִם אִישׁ וְאִשְׁתּוֹ׃ ג גַּם מֵעוֹף
< of the birds < also, **3** << with its mate; < a male << two, << are not clean, < that < the animals < and of

הַשָּׁמַיִם שִׁבְעָה שִׁבְעָה זָכָר וּנְקֵבָה לְחַיּוֹת זֶרַע עַל־פְּנֵי כָל־הָאָרֶץ׃
<< the earth. < of all < the face < upon < offspring < to keep alive << and female, < male << [by] seven, < seven << of the heavens,

בְּעִירָא לִזְנַהּ וּמִכֹּל רִחֲשָׁא דְאַרְעָא לִזְנוֹהִי תְּרֵין מִכֹּלָּא יֵעֲלוּן לְוָתָךְ לְקַיָּמָא: כא וְאַתְּ סַב לָךְ מִכָּל מֵיכַל דְּמִתְאֲכֵל וְתִכְנוֹשׁ לְוָתָךְ וִיהֵי לָךְ וּלְהוֹן לְמֵיכָל: כב וַעֲבַד נֹחַ כְּכֹל דִּי פַקִּיד יָתֵהּ יְיָ כֵּן עֲבָד: א וַאֲמַר יְיָ לְנֹחַ עוֹל אַתְּ וְכָל אֱנָשׁ בֵּיתָךְ לְתֵבוֹתָא אֲרֵי יָתָךְ חֲזֵתִי זַכַּאי קֳדָמַי בְּדָרָא הָדֵין: ב מִכֹּל בְּעִירָא דַכְיָא תִּסַּב לָךְ שַׁבְעָא שַׁבְעָא דְּכַר וְנוּקְבָא וּמִן בְּעִירָא דִּי לָא (אִיתָהָא) דַכְיָא הִיא תְּרֵין דְּכַר וְנוּקְבָא: ג אַף מֵעוֹפָא דִשְׁמַיָּא שַׁבְעָא שַׁבְעָא דְּכַר וְנוּקְבָא לְקַיָּמָא זַרְעָא עַל אַפֵּי כָל אַרְעָא:

רש"י

(כב) **ויעש נח.** זה בנין התיבה (ב"ר שם יד): (א) **ראיתי צדיק.** ולא נאמר צדיק תמים. מכאן שאומרים מקצת שבחו של אדם בפניו וכולו שלא בפניו (שם לב:ג): (ב) **הטהורה.** העתידה להיות טהורה לישראל (זבחים קטז.) למדנו שלמד נח תורה (ב"ר כו:א): **שבעה שבעה.** זכר ונקבה (אונקלוס; ב"ר לב:ד) כדי שיקריב מהם קרבן בצאתו (שם לד:ט; תנחומא ויקהל ו): (ג) **גם מעוף השמים וגו'.** בטהורים הכתוב מדבר, ולמד סתום מן המפורש:

possible (*Rambam*).

The animals came to Noah of their own accord, and he led them past the Ark. The Ark accepted only those which had not been involved in the sexual perversion that was one of the causes of the generation's downfall (*Rashi; Sanhedrin* 108b).

21. אֲשֶׁר יֵאָכֵל — *That is eaten.* The Midrash records that the greater part of the provisions consisted of pressed figs and greens for the various animals. Noah also stored seeds for future planting after the Flood.

7.

1-10. The final call. With the Flood to begin *in seven days,* God bid Noah to enter the Ark with his family. In addition to the one pair from each species that he had been commanded previously to bring, he was now told to bring seven pairs of the animals that the Torah would later declare to be *clean,* i.e., kosher, so that he would be able to use them as offerings when he left the Ark (*Rashi*). They would also provide him with a supply of livestock for food, in anticipation of God's removal of the prohibition against eating meat [9:3] (*Radak*).

Up to now, the *Sidrah* had spoken of *Elohim,* which indicates God's Attribute of Justice. Here He is called HASHEM, which indicates God's Attribute of Mercy, for He is saving Noah from the Flood, and, in addition, He is saving Noah's entire family and possessions, which, on their own merits, did not deserve to be saved (*Sforno*). The Name HASHEM is also an indication that Noah's future offerings would be accepted, since the chapters dealing with offerings use only the Name HASHEM (*Ramban*).

ד כִּי֩ לְיָמִ֨ים ע֜וֹד שִׁבְעָ֗ה אָֽנֹכִי֙ מַמְטִ֣יר עַל־הָאָ֔רֶץ

4 For ‹ in seven more days ‹ I ‹ will send rain ‹ upon ‹ the earth, ‹‹

אַרְבָּעִ֣ים י֔וֹם וְאַרְבָּעִ֖ים לָ֑יְלָה וּמָחִ֗יתִי אֶֽת־כָּל־

forty ‹ days ‹ and forty ‹ nights, ‹‹ and I will blot out ‹ all ‹

הַיְקוּם֙ אֲשֶׁ֣ר עָשִׂ֔יתִי מֵעַ֖ל פְּנֵ֥י הָאֲדָמָֽה׃

existence ‹ that ‹ I have made, ‹‹ from upon ‹ the face ‹ of the ground. ‹‹

ה וַיַּ֖עַשׂ נֹ֑חַ כְּכֹ֥ל אֲשֶׁר־צִוָּ֖הוּ יהוה׃ ו וְנֹ֗חַ בֶּן־

5 And Noah did ‹ according to everything ‹ that ‹ HASHEM had commanded him. ‹‹ 6 Noah ‹ was of the age ‹

שֵׁ֥שׁ מֵא֖וֹת שָׁנָ֑ה וְהַמַּבּ֣וּל הָיָ֔ה מַ֖יִם עַל־הָאָֽרֶץ׃

of six ‹ hundred ‹ years ‹ when the Flood ‹ was ‹ water ‹ upon ‹ the earth. ‹‹

ז וַיָּ֣בֹא נֹ֗חַ וּ֠בָנָיו וְאִשְׁתּ֧וֹ וּנְשֵֽׁי־בָנָ֛יו אִתּ֖וֹ אֶל־הַתֵּבָ֑ה מִפְּנֵ֖י מֵ֥י הַמַּבּֽוּל׃

7 Noah entered ‹‹ with his sons, — [together] ‹ his wife, ‹ and the wives ‹ of his sons ‹ with him — ‹‹ into ‹ the Ark ‹ because of ‹ the waters ‹ of the Flood. ‹‹

ח מִן־הַבְּהֵמָה֙ הַטְּהוֹרָ֔ה וּמִן־הַ֨בְּהֵמָ֔ה אֲשֶׁ֥ר אֵינֶ֖נָּה טְהֹרָ֑ה וּמִ֨ן־הָע֔וֹף

8 Of ‹ the animals ‹ that are clean, ‹‹ of ‹ the animals ‹ that ‹ are not ‹ clean, ‹‹ of ‹ the birds, ‹‹

וְכֹ֥ל אֲשֶׁר־רֹמֵ֖שׂ עַל־הָאֲדָמָֽה׃ ט שְׁנַ֨יִם שְׁנַ֜יִם בָּ֧אוּ אֶל־נֹ֛חַ אֶל־הַתֵּבָ֖ה

and [of] every thing ‹ that ‹ creeps ‹ upon ‹ the ground, ‹‹ 9 two ‹ [by] two ‹ they came ‹ to ‹ Noah ‹ into ‹ the Ark, ‹‹

זָכָ֣ר וּנְקֵבָ֑ה כַּֽאֲשֶׁ֛ר צִוָּ֥ה אֱלֹהִ֖ים אֶת־נֹֽחַ׃ י וַיְהִ֖י לְשִׁבְעַ֣ת הַיָּמִ֑ים וּמֵ֣י

male ‹ and female, ‹‹ as ‹ God had commanded ‹ Noah. ‹‹ 10 And it came to pass ‹ after the seven-day period ‹ that the waters ‹

ד אֲרֵי לִזְמַן יוֹמִין עוֹד שַׁבְעָא אֲנָא מָחֵית מִטְרָא עַל אַרְעָא אַרְבְּעִין יְמָמִין וְאַרְבְּעִן לֵילָוָן וְאֶמְחֵי יָת כָּל יְקוּמָא דִי עֲבָדִית מֵעַל אַפֵּי אַרְעָא: ה וַעֲבַד נֹחַ כְּכֹל דִּי פַקְדֵהּ יְיָ: ו וְנֹחַ בַּר שִׁית מְאָה שְׁנִין וְטוֹפָנָא הֲוָה מַיָּא עַל אַרְעָא: ז וְעַל נֹחַ וּבְנוֹהִי וְאִתְּתֵהּ וּנְשֵׁי בְנוֹהִי עִמֵּהּ לְתֵבוֹתָא מִן קֳדָם מֵי טוֹפָנָא: ח מִן בְּעִירָא דַּכְיָא וּמִן בְּעִירָא דִּי לֵיתָהָא דַּכְיָא וּמִן עוֹפָא וְכֹל דִּי רָחֵשׁ עַל אַרְעָא: ט תְּרֵין תְּרֵין עַלּוּ לְוַת נֹחַ לְתֵבוֹתָא דְּכַר וְנוּקְבָא כְּמָא דִי פַקִּיד יְיָ יָת נֹחַ: י וַהֲוָה לִזְמַן שִׁבְעַת יוֹמִין וּמֵי

רש"י

(ד) **כי לימים עוד שבעה.** אלו שבעת ימי אבלו של מתושלח הצדיק, שחס הקב"ה על כבודו ועכב את הפורענות (ב"ר לב:ז; סנהדרין שם). לא וחשוב שנותיו של מתושלח ותמצא שהם כלים בשנת ת"ר שנה לחיי נח: **כי לימים עוד שבעה.** מהו עוד, זמן אחר זמן, זה נוסף על ק"כ שנה (סנהדרין שם): **ארבעים יום.** כנגד יצירת הולד, שקלקלו להטריח ליוצרם לצור צורת ממזרים (ב"ר לב:ה): (ה) **ויעש נח.** זה ביאתו לתיבה (שם): (ז) **נח ובניו.** האנשים לבד והנשים לבד, לפי שנאסרו בתשמיש המטה מפני שהעולם שרוי בצער (תנחומא יא): **מפני מי המבול.** אף נח מקטני אמנה היה, מאמין ואינו מאמין שיבא המבול, ולא נכנס לתיבה עד שדחקוהו המים (שם ו): (ט) **באו אל נח.** מאליהן (ב"ר לב:ח; תנחומא יב; זבחים קטז.): **שנים שנים.** כלם הושוו במנין זה, מן הפחות היו שנים:

4. כִּי לְיָמִים עוֹד שִׁבְעָה — *For in seven more days.* After the original period that God allotted the people for repentance, His mercy decreed that He give them seven additional days. Alternatively, these were the seven days of mourning for Methuselah, who had just died and in whose honor God delayed the Flood (*Rashi*).

7. נֹחַ וּבָנָיו — *Noah . . . with his sons.* The men and women are listed separately because marital intimacy was forbidden at a time when the whole world was in distress (*Rashi*).

מִפְּנֵי מֵי הַמַּבּוּל — *Because of the waters of the Flood.* The implication is that Noah and his family entered the Ark only when the rising water forced them to seek refuge. Indeed, the Midrash comments that his faith was less than perfect, for if the water had not reached his ankles, he would not have entered (*Rashi*; *Midrash*). He may have thought that God, in His mercy, would relent, or that the people would repent at the last minute. Nevertheless, the verse implies a criticism of his reluctance, for man should not allow his calculations to stand in the way of his compliance with God's command (*Me'am Loez*).

8. אֲשֶׁר אֵינֶנָּה טְהֹרָה — *That are not clean.* By using this long expression instead of the single word הַטְּמֵאָה, *unclean*, the Torah teaches a moral lesson: One should never utter a gross expression, for the Torah, which stresses brevity, added several extra letters to the Hebrew text of our verse to avoid using the unseemly expression *unclean* (*Pesachim* 3a).

9. שְׁנַיִם שְׁנַיִם — *Two [by] two.* There were at least *two* from every species (*Rashi*); but there were seven pairs of clean an-

הַמַּבּוּל הָיוּ עַל־הָאָרֶץ׃ יא בִּשְׁנַת שֵׁשׁ־מֵאוֹת שָׁנָה

< year < hundredth < the six < In the year [that was] **11** << the earth. < upon < were < of the Flood

לְחַיֵּי־נֹחַ בַּחֹדֶשׁ הַשֵּׁנִי בְּשִׁבְעָה־עָשָׂר יוֹם

< day < on the seventeenth << in the second month, << of Noah, < of the life

לַחֹדֶשׁ בַּיּוֹם הַזֶּה נִבְקְעוּ כָּל־מַעְיְנוֹת תְּהוֹם רַבָּה

<< that is great; < of the deep < the fountains < [did] all < burst forth < on that day << of the month,

וַאֲרֻבֹּת הַשָּׁמַיִם נִפְתָּחוּ׃ יב וַיְהִי הַגֶּשֶׁם עַל־הָאָרֶץ אַרְבָּעִים יוֹם

< days < forty < the earth < upon < And the rain was **12** << were opened. < of the heavens < and the windows

וְאַרְבָּעִים לָיְלָה׃ יג בְּעֶצֶם הַיּוֹם הַזֶּה בָּא נֹחַ וְשֵׁם־וְחָם וָיֶפֶת בְּנֵי־נֹחַ

<< of Noah, < the sons < and Japheth, < Ham, < [with] Shem, < Noah came, < of that day < In the midst **13** << nights. < and forty

טוֹפָנָא הֲווֹ עַל אַרְעָא: יא בִּשְׁנַת שִׁית מְאָה שְׁנִין לְחַיֵּי נֹחַ בְּיַרְחָא תִּנְיָנָא בְּשִׁבְעַת עַשְׂרָא יוֹמָא לְיַרְחָא בְּיוֹמָא הָדֵין אִתְבְּזָעוּ כָּל מַבּוּעֵי תְּהוֹמָא רַבָּא וְכַוֵּי שְׁמַיָּא אִתְפַּתָּחוּ: יב וַהֲוָה מִטְרָא נָחֵת עַל אַרְעָא אַרְבְּעִין יְמָמִין וְאַרְבְּעִין לֵילָוָן: יג בִּכְרַן יוֹמָא הָדֵין עַל נֹחַ וְשֵׁם וְחָם וָיֶפֶת בְּנֵי נֹחַ

רש"י

(יא) **בחודש השני.** רבי אליעזר אומר זה מרחשון, ר' יהושע אומר זה אייר (סדר עולם פ"ב; ראש השנה יא:): **נבקעו.** להוציא מימיהן: **תהום רבה.** מדה כנגד מדה, הם חטאו ברבה רעת האדם (לעיל ו:ה) ולקו בתהום רבה (סנהדרין קח.): (יב) **ויהי הגשם על הארץ.** ולהלן (פסוק יז) הוא אומר ויהי המבול, אלא כשהורידן הורידן ברחמים שאם יחזרו יהיו גשמי ברכה, וכשלא חזרו היו למבול (עי' ב"ר לא:יב; מכילתא בשלח שירה פ"ה): **ארבעים יום וגו'.** אין יום ראשון מן המנין לפי שאין לילו עמו, שהרי כתיב ביום הזה נבקעו כל מעינות. נמצאו ארבעים יום כלים בכ"ח בכסלו לר' אליעזר, שהחדשים נמנין כסדרן אחד מלא ואחד חסר, הרי י"ב ממרחשון וכ"ח מכסליו: (יג) **בעצם היום הזה.** למדך הכתוב שהיו בני דורו אומרים אילו אנו רואים אותו נכנס לתיבה אנו שוברין אותה והורגין אותו. אמר הקב"ה, אני מכניסו לעיני כלם, ונראה דבר מי יקום (ספרי האזינו שלז; ב"ר לב:ח):

imals (*Mizrachi*).

R' Yaakov Kamenetsky notes that this verse states that the unclean animals *came to Noah* on their own, instinctively, but verse 2 implies that the clean animals did not come, for Noah had to *take* them. The unclean animals were in the Ark only to preserve their species, but the clean animals had the additional purpose of being offerings after the Flood was over. [For God to have sent these animals to Noah without any effort on his part would have diminished the significance of his offerings. A person's free-willed offering is an expression of his gratitude or an effort to increase his closeness to God. Consequently, it is his *own* desire and his *own* exertions that give value to the offering.]

כַּאֲשֶׁר צִוָּה אֱלֹהִים — *As God had commanded.* The Torah sums up verses 5-9 by praising Noah, who had scrupulously followed every directive of God in bringing his family and the multitude of animals into the Ark (*Ramban*).

10-24. The Flood inundates the world. In the six hundredth year of Noah's life — the year 1656 from Creation (*Seder Olam*) — the deluge began. Now Scripture gives the exact date and the details of the events as they happened.

The Torah states that the Flood began in the *second month,* which *Rashi* interprets as the month of Marcheshvan, the second month of the year counting from Rosh Hashanah. This follows the Talmudic view of Rabbi Eliezer; Rabbi Yehoshua maintains that it is the month of Iyar, the second month from Nissan (*Rosh Hashanah* 11b). From the time of the Exodus,all the months of the Torah are numbered from Nissan, in honor of the Exodus, which took Israel from servitude and began its mission as the recipient of the Torah at Sinai.

11. בִּשְׁנַת שֵׁשׁ־מֵאוֹת שָׁנָה — *In the . . . six hundredth year.* The *Zohar* states that this verse, which speaks of a deluge emanating from above and below, alludes to the potential of a great flood of spiritual growth that was destined for that year. It would have been the year when the Written and Oral Torahs were given, but mankind failed dismally and was undeserving of the opportunity. *Zohar* adds that the same opportunity would come to the world during the sixth century of the sixth millennium: the years 5500-5600 (1739-40 to 1839-40). Indeed, that century saw an unusual flowering of Torah accomplishment, and also a secular explosion of thought and achievement, such as the American and French Revolutions, the Industrial Revolution, and an explosion of political and economic thought. Had Israel and society as a whole been more worthy, there is no telling how much more spiritual growth there could have been.

12. Noting that in verse 17 the narrative mentions *Flood,* while here it refers to *rain, Rashi* explains that the precipitation began gently, so that — had the people repented at the last minute — it still could have been transformed into a rain of blessing. Only when they refused did it become a Flood.

וְאֵ֣שֶׁת נֹ֗חַ וּשְׁלֹ֧שֶׁת נְשֵֽׁי־בָנָ֛יו אִתָּ֖ם אֶל־הַתֵּבָֽה׃

« the Ark ‹ into ‹ with them, ‹ of his sons ‹ wives ‹ and the three ‹ of Noah, ‹ with the wife

יד הֵ֜מָּה וְכָל־הַֽחַיָּ֣ה לְמִינָ֗הּ וְכָל־הַבְּהֵמָה֙ לְמִינָ֔הּ

14 « after its kind, ‹ animal ‹ every « after its kind, ‹ beast ‹ and every ‹ — they

וְכָל־הָרֶ֛מֶשׂ הָֽרֹמֵ֥שׂ עַל־הָאָ֖רֶץ לְמִינֵ֑הוּ וְכָל־

‹ and every « after its kind, ‹ the earth ‹ on ‹ that creeps ‹ creeping thing ‹ every

הָע֣וֹף לְמִינֵ֔הוּ כֹּ֖ל צִפּ֥וֹר כָּל־כָּנָֽף׃ טו וַיָּבֹ֥אוּ אֶל־נֹ֖חַ

‹ Noah ‹ to ‹ They came 15 « of wing. ‹ of any kind ‹ bird ‹ every « after its kind, ‹ bird

אֶל־הַתֵּבָ֑ה שְׁנַ֤יִם שְׁנַ֙יִם֙ מִכָּל־הַבָּשָׂ֔ר אֲשֶׁר־בּ֖וֹ

‹ in which there was ‹ flesh ‹ of all ‹ [by] two ‹ two « the Ark; ‹ into

ר֥וּחַ חַיִּֽים׃ טז וְהַבָּאִ֗ים זָכָ֨ר וּנְקֵבָ֤ה מִכָּל־בָּשָׂר֙ בָּ֔אוּ כַּאֲשֶׁ֛ר

‹ as « did they come, ‹ flesh ‹ of all ‹ and female ‹ male « [Thus] they that came, 16 « of life. ‹ a breath

צִוָּ֥ה אֹת֖וֹ אֱלֹהִ֑ים וַיִּסְגֹּ֥ר יְהוָ֖ה בַּעֲדֽוֹ׃ שלישי — יז וַיְהִ֧י הַמַּבּ֛וּל אַרְבָּעִ֥ים

‹ forty ‹ [When] the Flood was 17 « on his behalf. ‹ And HASHEM shut [it] « God had commanded him.

י֖וֹם עַל־הָאָ֑רֶץ וַיִּרְבּ֣וּ הַמַּ֗יִם וַיִּשְׂאוּ֙ אֶת־הַתֵּבָ֔ה וַתָּ֖רָם מֵעַ֥ל הָאָֽרֶץ׃

« the earth. ‹ above ‹ so that it was lifted ‹ the Ark ‹ and raised ‹ the waters increased « the earth, ‹ on ‹ days

יח וַיִּגְבְּר֥וּ הַמַּ֛יִם וַיִּרְבּ֥וּ מְאֹ֖ד עַל־הָאָ֑רֶץ וַתֵּ֥לֶךְ הַתֵּבָ֖ה עַל־פְּנֵ֥י הַמָּֽיִם׃

« of the waters. ‹ the surface ‹ upon ‹ and the Ark moved about « the earth, ‹ upon ‹ and increased greatly ‹ The waters strengthened 18

יט וְהַמַּ֗יִם גָּ֥בְר֛וּ מְאֹ֥ד מְאֹ֖ד עַל־הָאָ֑רֶץ וַיְכֻסּ֗וּ כָּל־הֶֽהָרִים֙ הַגְּבֹהִ֔ים

« which are high ‹ the mountains ‹ all ‹ covered were « the earth, ‹ upon ‹ exceedingly much ‹ strengthened ‹ The waters 19

וְאִתַּת נֹחַ וּתְלָתָא נְשֵׁי בְנוֹהִי עִמְּהוֹן לְתֵבוֹתָא: יד אִנּוּן וְכָל חַיְתָא לִזְנַהּ וְכָל בְּעִירָא לִזְנַהּ וְכָל רִחֲשָׁא דְּרָחֵשׁ עַל אַרְעָא לִזְנוֹהִי וְכָל עוֹפָא לִזְנוֹהִי כֹּל צִפַּר כָּל דְּפָרַח: טו וְעַלוּ עִם נֹחַ לְתֵבוֹתָא תְּרֵין תְּרֵין מִכָּל בִּשְׂרָא דִּי בֵהּ רוּחָא דְחַיֵּי: טז וְעָלַיָּא דְּכַר וְנוּקְבָא מִכָּל בִּשְׂרָא עַלוּ כְּמָא דִי פַקִּיד יָתֵהּ יְיָ וַאֲגֵן יְיָ (בְּמֵימְרֵהּ) עֲלוֹהִי: יז וַהֲוָה טוֹפָנָא אַרְבְּעִין יוֹמִין עַל אַרְעָא וּסְגִיאוּ מַיָּא וּנְטָלוּ יָת תֵּבוֹתָא וְאִתְּרָמַת מֵעַל אַרְעָא: יח וּתְקִיפוּ מַיָּא וּסְגִיאוּ לַחֲדָא עַל אַרְעָא וּמְהַלְּכָא תֵבוֹתָא עַל אַפֵּי מַיָּא: יט וּמַיָּא תְּקִיפוּ לַחֲדָא לַחֲדָא עַל אַרְעָא וְאִתְחֲפִיאוּ כָּל טוּרַיָּא רָמַיָּא

רש"י

(יד) **צפור כל כנף.** דבוק הוא, לפור של כל מין כנף, לרבות חגבים (חולין קלט:) [כנף זה לשון נולה, כמו ושסע אותו בכנפיו (ויקרא א:יז) שאפי' נולתה עולה. אף כאן, לפור כל מין מראית נולה]: (טז) **ויסגור ה' בעדו.** הגין עליו שלא שברוה. הקיף התיבה דובים ואריות (ב"ר לב:ח) והיו הורגין בהם (תנחומא ישן י). ופשוטו של מקרא, סגר כנגדו מן המים, וכן כל בעד שבמקרא לשון כנגד הוא. בעד כל רחם (להלן כ:יח) בעדך ובעד בניך (מלכים ב ד:ד) עור בעד עור (איוב ב:ד) מגן בעדי (תהלים ג:ד) התפלל בעד עבדיך (שמואל א יב:יט) כנגד עבדיך: (יז) **ותרם מעל הארץ.** משוקעת היתה במים אחת עשרה אמה כספינה טעונה שמשוקעת מקלתה במים, ומקראות שלפניו יוכיחו (ב"ר לב:ט): (יח) **ויגברו.** מאליהן:

15. Here we find man in his loftiest state, for the entire world comes *to Noah;* it was because of him that they were all saved and preserved (*R' Hirsch*). The verse stresses that they came in matched pairs — not one species was missing — which was a miracle! (*Ibn Caspi*) . . . Such precision would have been impossible by natural means (*R' Bachya*).

17-19. The ravages of the Flood. First the waters lifted the Ark; then they became increasingly violent and tossed it aimlessly about (*Radak*). Verse 19 uses the word מְאֹד, *very*, twice after it has already been used in verse 18, to emphasize the powerful surge of the waters; it could not possibly have been stronger (*Ibn Ezra*). The Sages add that the waters were scalding hot (*Sanhedrin* 108b). The Torah uses derivatives of the expression גְּבוּרָה, literally, *strength,* twice in verses 18-19, which also indicates the great abundance of the waters, which uprooted trees and swept away buildings (*Ramban*).

אֲשֶׁר־תַּחַת כָּל־הַשָּׁמָיִם: כ חֲמֵשׁ עֶשְׂרֵה אַמָּה
< cubits < Fifteen **20** « heavens. < the entire < under < that are

מִלְמַעְלָה גָּבְרוּ הַמָּיִם וַיְכֻסּוּ הֶהָרִים: כא וַיִּגְוַע
< Perished **21** « the mountains. < and covered were < did the waters strengthen, < upward

כָּל־בָּשָׂר ׀ הָרֹמֵשׂ עַל־הָאָרֶץ בָּעוֹף וּבַבְּהֵמָה
< among the animals, < – among the birds, « the earth < upon < that moves < flesh < [had] all

וּבַחַיָּה וּבְכָל־הַשֶּׁרֶץ הַשֹּׁרֵץ עַל־הָאָרֶץ וְכֹל
< and all « the earth, < upon < that crawl < the crawling things < and among all < among the beasts,

הָאָדָם: כב כֹּל אֲשֶׁר נִשְׁמַת־רוּחַ חַיִּים בְּאַפָּיו מִכֹּל אֲשֶׁר בֶּחָרָבָה מֵתוּ:
« died. < on dry land, < that was < of everything « in its nostrils, < of life, < of the spirit < the breath < that there was < Every-thing **22** « mankind.

כג *וַיִּמַח אֶת־כָּל־הַיְקוּם ׀ אֲשֶׁר ׀ עַל־פְּנֵי הָאֲדָמָה מֵאָדָם עַד־בְּהֵמָה
< animal < to < – from man « of the ground < the face < on < that was < existence < all < And He blotted out **23**

עַד־רֶמֶשׂ וְעַד־עוֹף הַשָּׁמַיִם וַיִּמָּחוּ מִן־הָאָרֶץ וַיִּשָּׁאֶר אַךְ־נֹחַ
< Noah, < was only < Left surviving « the earth. < from < and they were blotted out « of the heavens; < bird < and to < creeping thing < to

וַאֲשֶׁר אִתּוֹ בַּתֵּבָה: כד וַיִּגְבְּרוּ הַמַּיִם עַל־הָאָרֶץ חֲמִשִּׁים וּמְאַת יוֹם:
« days. < one hundred and fifty < the earth < on < And the waters strengthened **24** « in the Ark. < with him < and those

[ח] א וַיִּזְכֹּר אֱלֹהִים אֶת־נֹחַ וְאֵת כָּל־הַחַיָּה וְאֶת־כָּל־הַבְּהֵמָה אֲשֶׁר
< that were < the animals < and all < the beasts < and all < Noah < God remembered **1** **[8]**

דִּי תְחוֹת כָּל שְׁמַיָּא: כ חֲמֵשׁ עַשְׂרֵי
אַמִּין מִלְעֵלָּא תְּקִיפוּ מַיָּא וְאִתְחֲפִיאוּ
טוּרַיָּא: כא וּמִית כָּל בִּשְׂרָא דְּרָחֵשׁ עַל
אַרְעָא בְּעוֹפָא וּבִבְעִירָא וּבְחַיְתָא
וּבְכָל רִחְשָׁא דְּרָחֵשׁ עַל אַרְעָא וְכֹל
אֱנָשָׁא: כב כֹּל דִּי נִשְׁמְתָא רוּחָא דְּחַיִּין
בְּאַנְפּוֹהִי מִכֹּל דִּי בְּיַבֶּשְׁתָּא מִיתוּ:
כג וּמְחָא יָת כָּל יְקוּמָא דִּי עַל אַפֵּי
אַרְעָא מֵאֱנָשָׁא עַד בְּעִירָא עַד רִחְשָׁא
וְעַד עוֹפָא דִשְׁמַיָּא וְאִתְמְחִיאוּ מִן
אַרְעָא וְאִשְׁתְּאַר בְּרַם נֹחַ וְדִי עִמֵּהּ
בְּתֵיבוּתָא: כד וּתְקִיפוּ מַיָּא עַל אַרְעָא
מְאָה וְחַמְשִׁין יוֹמִין: א וּדְכִיר יְיָ יָת
נֹחַ וְיָת כָּל חַיְתָא וְיָת כָּל בְּעִירָא דִּי

* מ' רפה

רש"י

(כ) **חמש עשרה אמה מלמעלה.** למעלה של גובה כל ההרים, לאחר שהושוו המים לראשי ההרים (יומא עו.): (כב) **נשמת רוח חיים.** נשמה של רוח חיים: **אשר בחרבה.** ולא דגים שבים (סנהדרין קח.; זבחים קיג:; ב"ר לב:יא): (כג) **וימח.** לשון ויפעל הוא ואינו לשון ויפעל והוא מגזרת ויפן ויבן. כל תיבה שסופה ה"א, כגון בנה, מחה, קנה, כשהוא נותן וא"ו יו"ד בראשה נקוד בחירק תחת היו"ד: **אך נח.** לבד נח זהו פשוטו. ומדרש אגדה גונח וכוהה [ס"א וכוחה] דם מטורח הבהמות והחיות (סנהדרין קח:; תנחומא ישן יד; ברייתא דל"ב מדות מדה ג). וי"א שאיחר מזונות לארי והכישו ועליו נאמר הן צדיק בארץ ישלם (משלי יא:לא; תנחומא ט): (א) **ויזכור אלהים.** זה השם מדת הדין הוא, ונהפכה למדת רחמים על ידי תפלת הצדיקים (סוכה יד.; תנחומא יא). ורשעתן של רשעים הופכת מדת רחמים למדת

20. *Haamek Davar* suggests that Mt. Ararat was the world's highest mountain at the time of the Flood, and the waters rose to 15 cubits above it. The numerous mountains that are now far higher than Ararat came into being or bulged up to their present height as a result of the upheavals of the Flood.

Thus, even those who climbed to the highest mountain peaks to escape the violent waters found nowhere else to flee and drowned (*Rosh*). In addition, the upheaval of those months of intense heat and turmoil caused a great shifting and turning of geological strata and a deep burial of animal remains. Thus the attempt to date the earth and fossils is futile (*Malbim*), for no one can know how much the heat and water pressure affected the geology of the planet and the animal and plant remains.

21-22. The verses mention only land creatures, implying that God spared the fish, because they did not participate in Man's sins (*Mizrachi*).

8.

1-8. The waters recede. This chapter recounts the onset of God's mercy, as the water began to recede and the earth slowly reached the stage where Noah could begin to resettle the earth and resume normal life again.

1. וַיִּזְכֹּר אֱלֹהִים — *God remembered*. To say that God "remembered" implies that forgetfulness is possible for Him, which is clearly an absurdity. The Torah uses this term, like many

אִתּוֹ בַּתֵּבָה וַיַּעֲבֵר אֱלֹהִים רוּחַ עַל־הָאָרֶץ
«the earth, ‹ over ‹ a spirit ‹ and God caused to pass « in the Ark; ‹ with him

וַיָּשֹׁכּוּ הַמָּיִם: ב וַיִּסָּכְרוּ מַעְיְנֹת תְּהוֹם וַאֲרֻבֹּת
‹ and the windows ‹ of the deep ‹ the fountains ‹ And closed were 2 « and the waters subsided.

הַשָּׁמָיִם וַיִּכָּלֵא הַגֶּשֶׁם מִן־הַשָּׁמָיִם: ג וַיָּשֻׁבוּ הַמַּיִם
‹ The waters [then] receded 3 « the heavens. ‹ from ‹ the rain ‹ and restrained was « of the heavens;

מֵעַל הָאָרֶץ הָלוֹךְ וָשׁוֹב וַיַּחְסְרוּ הַמַּיִם מִקְצֵה
‹ at the end ‹ and the waters diminished « receding, ‹ continuously « the earth, ‹ from upon

חֲמִשִּׁים וּמְאַת יוֹם: ד וַתָּנַח הַתֵּבָה בַּחֹדֶשׁ הַשְּׁבִיעִי בְּשִׁבְעָה־עָשָׂר יוֹם
‹ day ‹ on the seventeenth ‹ in the seventh month, ‹ And the Ark came to rest 4 « days. ‹ of one hundred and fifty

לַחֹדֶשׁ עַל הָרֵי אֲרָרָט: ה וְהַמַּיִם הָיוּ הָלוֹךְ וְחָסוֹר עַד הַחֹדֶשׁ הָעֲשִׂירִי
« the tenth month. ‹ until ‹ diminishing, ‹ continuously ‹ were ‹ The waters 5 « of Ararat. ‹ the mountains ‹ upon « of the month,

בָּעֲשִׂירִי בְּאֶחָד לַחֹדֶשׁ נִרְאוּ רָאשֵׁי הֶהָרִים: ו וַיְהִי מִקֵּץ אַרְבָּעִים יוֹם
‹ days, ‹ of forty ‹ at the end ‹ And it came to pass 6 « of the mountains. ‹ the tops ‹ visible were « of the month, ‹ on the first ‹ In the tenth [month],

עִמֵּהּ בְּתֵבוּתָא וְאַעְבַּר יְיָ רוּחָא
עַל אַרְעָא וְנָחוּ מַיָּא: ב וְאִסְתְּכַרוּ
מַבּוּעֵי תְהוֹמָא וְכַוֵּי שְׁמַיָּא וְאִתְכְּלִי
מִטְרָא מִן שְׁמַיָּא: ג וְתָבוּ מַיָּא מֵעַל
אַרְעָא אָזְלִין וְתָיְבִין וַחֲסָרוּ מַיָּא
מִסּוֹף מְאָה וְחַמְשִׁין יוֹמִין: ד וְנָחַת
תֵּבוּתָא בְּיַרְחָא שְׁבִיעָאָה בְּשִׁבְעַת
עֲשַׂר יוֹמָא לְיַרְחָא עַל טוּרֵי קַרְדוּ:
ה וּמַיָּא הֲווֹ אָזְלִין וְחָסְרִין עַד
יַרְחָא עֲשִׂירָאָה בַּעֲשִׂירָאָה בְּחַד
לְיַרְחָא אִתְחֲזִיאוּ רֵישֵׁי טוּרַיָּא:
ו וַהֲוָה מִסּוֹף אַרְבְּעִין יוֹמִין

רש"י

הדין, שנאמר וירא ה' כי רבה רעת האדם וגו' ויאמר ה' אמחה (לעיל ו:ה,ז) והוא שם מדת הרחמים (ב"ר לג:ג): **ויזכור אלהים את נח וגו'.** מה זכר להם לבהמות, זכות שלא השחיתו דרכם קודם לכן (תנחומא ישן יא) ושלא שמשו בתיבה (תנחומא יא־יב): **ויעבר אלהים רוח.** רוח תנחומין והנחה עברה לפניו (תרגום יונתן): **על הארץ.** על עסקי הארץ: **וישכו.** כמו וחמת המלך שככה (אסתר ז:י), לשון הנחת חמה (סנהדרין קח:; תנחומא ישן יב): (ב) **ויסכרו מעינות.** כשנפתחו כתיב כל מעינות (לעיל ז:יא) וכאן אין כתיב כל, לפי שנשתיירו מהם אותן שיש בהם צורך לעולם, כגון חמי טבריא וכיוצא בהן (ב"ר לג:ד; סנהדרין קח.): **ויכלא.** וימנע (תרגום יונתן) כמו לא תכלא רחמיך (תהלים מ:יב) לא יכלה ממך (להלן כג:ו): (ג) **מקצה חמשים ומאת יום.** התחילו לחסור, והוא אחד בסיון. כיצד, בכ"ז בכסליו פסקו הגשמים, הרי ג' מכסליו, וכ"ט מטבת, הרי ל"ב, ושבט ואדר וניסן ואייר קי"ח, הרי ק"נ (סדר עולם פ"ד; ב"ר שם ז): (ד) **בחדש השביעי.** סיון, והוא שביעי לכסליו שבו פסקו הגשמים (שם ושם): **בשבעה עשר יום.** מכאן אתה למד שהיתה התיבה משוקעת במים י"א אמה. שהרי כתיב בעשירי באחד לחדש נראו ראשי ההרים, זה אב שהוא עשירי [למרחשון] לירידת גשמים, והם היו גבוהים על ההרים חמש עשרה אמה. וחסרו מיום אחד בסיון עד אחד באב חמש עשרה אמה לששים יום הרי אמה לד' ימים. נמצא שבי"ו בסיון לא חסרו המים אלא ד' אמות, ונחה התיבה ליום המחרת, למדת שהיתה משוקעת י"א אמה במים שעל ראשי ההרים (שם ושם): (ה) **בעשירי וגו' נראו ראשי ההרים.** זה אב שהוא עשירי למרחשון שהתחיל הגשם. וא"ת הוא אלול, ועשירי לכסליו שפסק הגשם, כשם שאתה אומר בחדש השביעי סיון והוא שביעי להפסקה, אי אפשר לומר כן. על כרחך שביעי אי אתה מונה אלא להפסקה, שהרי לא כלו ארבעים של ירידת גשמים ומאה וחמשים של תגבורת המים עד אחד בסיון, ואם אתה אומר שביעי לירידה אין זה סיון. והעשירי אי אפשר למנות אלא לירידה, שאם אתה אומר להפסקה והוא אלול אי אתה מוצא בראשון באחד לחדש חרבו המים מעל הארץ (להלן ח:יג) שהרי מקץ ארבעים יום משנראו ראשי ההרים שלח את העורב (ערוך ע' קל (ז); פדר"א פכ"ג) וכ"א יום הוחיל בשליחות היונה (סדר עולם שם; ב"ר שם ו) הרי ששים יום משנראו ראשי ההרים עד שחרבו פני האדמה. וא"ת באלול נראו נמצא שחרבו במרחשון והוא קורא אותו ראשון ואין זה אלא תשרי שהוא ראשון לבריאת עולם (סדר עולם שם) ולרבי יהושע הוא ניסן: (ו) **מקץ ארבעים יום.** משנראו ראשי ההרים (ערוך שם):

others, to make it easier for us to understand the course of events: God's wisdom had decreed that up to this point He should ignore the plight of His creatures, as if He had forgotten them. Now, when He was ready to show them mercy, it was as if He had remembered. The commentators state that Noah earned this mercy because he fed and cared for the animals during all the months in the Ark (*Midrash*).

— God "remembered" that the animals that were permitted to enter the Ark had not previously perverted their way, and that they had refrained from mating in the Ark (*Rashi*).

— He noted that Noah was a perfectly righteous man, and there was a Divine covenant to save him. Concerning the animals, God *remembered* His plan that the earth should continue with the same species as before (*Ramban*).

רוּחַ — *A spirit*. The translation follows *Rashi* and many commentators. *Ramban* and others render *wind.* This *spirit* or *wind* caused the waters to stop their seething, boiling fury, and, as in verse 2, it sealed the sources of the water, so that the Flood could begin to recede.

3-6. On the first of Sivan — the seventh month and 150 days from 27 Kislev when the rain ended — the water began to

וַיִּפְתַּח נֹחַ אֶת־חַלּוֹן הַתֵּבָה אֲשֶׁר עָשָׂה: ז וַיְשַׁלַּח
‹ He sent out 7 « he had made. ‹ which ‹ of the Ark ‹ the window ‹ that Noah opened

אֶת־הָעֹרֵב וַיֵּצֵא יָצוֹא וָשׁוֹב עַד־יְבֹשֶׁת הַמַּיִם
‹ of the waters ‹ the drying ‹ until ‹ and returning — ‹ — going forth « and it went ‹ the raven,

מֵעַל הָאָרֶץ: ח וַיְשַׁלַּח אֶת־הַיּוֹנָה מֵאִתּוֹ
‹ from him ‹ the dove ‹ [Then] he sent out 8 « the earth. ‹ from upon

לִרְאוֹת הֲקַלּוּ הַמַּיִם מֵעַל פְּנֵי הָאֲדָמָה:
« of the ground. ‹ the face ‹ from upon ‹ whether the waters had subsided ‹ to see

ט וְלֹא־מָצְאָה הַיּוֹנָה מָנוֹחַ לְכַף־רַגְלָהּ וַתָּשָׁב אֵלָיו אֶל־הַתֵּבָה כִּי
‹ for « the Ark, ‹ to ‹ to him ‹ and it returned « of its foot, ‹ for the sole ‹ a resting place ‹ But the dove could not find 9

מַיִם עַל־פְּנֵי כָל־הָאָרֶץ וַיִּשְׁלַח יָדוֹ וַיִּקָּחֶהָ וַיָּבֵא אֹתָהּ אֵלָיו אֶל־
‹ into ‹ to him ‹ it ‹ and brought ‹ and took it, ‹ his hand, ‹ So he put forth « the earth. ‹ of all ‹ the surface ‹ was upon ‹ water

הַתֵּבָה: י וַיָּחֶל עוֹד שִׁבְעַת יָמִים אֲחֵרִים וַיֹּסֶף שַׁלַּח אֶת־הַיּוֹנָה מִן־
‹ from ‹ the dove ‹ sent out ‹ and again « that were additional, ‹ days ‹ [for] seven ‹ again ‹ He waited 10 « the Ark.

הַתֵּבָה: יא וַתָּבֹא אֵלָיו הַיּוֹנָה לְעֵת עֶרֶב וְהִנֵּה עֲלֵה־זַיִת טָרָף בְּפִיהָ
« with its bill! ‹ plucked ‹ from an olive tree ‹ a leaf « — and behold! « of the evening ‹ toward the time ‹ the dove ‹ Back to him came 11 « the Ark.

וּפְתַח נֹחַ יָת כַּוַּת תֵּבוֹתָא דִּי עֲבָד: ז וְשַׁלַּח יָת עוֹרְבָא וּנְפַק מִפַּק וְתַיִב עַד דְּיַבִּישׁוּ מַיָּא מֵעַל אַרְעָא: ח וְשַׁלַּח יָת יוֹנָה מִלְּוָתֵהּ לְמֵיחֲזֵי הֲקַלִּיאוּ מַיָּא מֵעַל אַפֵּי אַרְעָא: ט וְלָא אַשְׁכַּחַת יוֹנָה מְנָח לְפַרְסַת רַגְלַהּ וְתָבַת לְוָתֵהּ לְתֵבוֹתָא אֲרֵי מַיָּא עַל אַפֵּי כָל אַרְעָא וְאוֹשִׁיט יְדֵהּ וְנַסְבַהּ וְאָעֵיל יָתַהּ לְוָתֵהּ לְתֵבוֹתָא: י וְאוֹרִיךְ עוֹד שִׁבְעָא יוֹמִין אָחֳרָנִין וְאוֹסֵיף שַׁלַּח יָת יוֹנָה מִן תֵּבוֹתָא: יא וַאֲתַת לְוָתֵהּ יוֹנָה לְעִדַּן רַמְשָׁא וְהָא טְרַף זֵיתָא תְּבִיר נָחִית בְּפוּמַהּ

רש"י

את חלון התבה אשר עשה. לנהר, ולא זה פתח התיבה העשוי לביאה ויציאה (ב"ר שם ה): **(ז) יצוא ושוב.** הולך ומקיף סביבות התיבה ולא הלך בשליחותו שהיה חושדו על בת זוגו, וכמו ששנינו באגדת חלק (סנהדרין קח:): **עד יבשת המים.** פשוטו כמשמעו. אבל מדרש אגדה, מוכן היה העורב לשליחות אחרת בעצירת גשמים בימי אליהו, שנאמר והעורבים מביאים לו לחם ובשר (מלכים א יז:ו; ב"ר שם): **(ח) וישלח את היונה.** לסוף ז' ימים שהרי כתיב ויחל עוד ז' ימים אחרים (פסוק י) מכלל זה אתה למד שאף בראשונה הוחיל ז' ימים (סדר עולם שם; ב"ר שם ו): **וישלח.** אין זה ל' שליחות אלא ל' שלוח, שלחה ללכת לדרכה ובזו יראה אם קלו המים, שאם תמצא מנוח לא תשוב אליו (ב"ר שם): **(י) ויחל.** לשון המתנה, וכן לי שמעו ויחלו (איוב כט:כא) והרבה יש במקרא: **(יא) טרף בפיה.** אומר אני שזכר היה לכן קוראו פעמים לשון זכר ופעמים לשון נקבה, לפי שכל יונה שבמקרא לשון נקבה, כמו כיוני הגאיות כלם הומות (יחזקאל ז:טז) כיונה פותה (הושע ז:יא): **טרף.** חטף. ומדרש אגדה ל' מזון

recede, and on the 17th of Sivan, the bottom of the Ark rested on the mountains of Ararat. It was not until the tenth month from the *beginning* of the rain that the mountaintops became visible. Forty days after that, Noah opened the skylight of the Ark to learn when it would be possible to leave the Ark and begin to re-establish normal life on earth.

7. Sending forth the raven. Noah wanted to test whether the air was still too moist for the raven to tolerate. It was, for the raven kept circling back and forth (*Sforno*). Moreover, the raven returned with nothing in its mouth, indicating that vegetation had not yet begun to grow.

Ravens feed on carrion of man and beast. Noah reasoned that if the raven would bring some back, it would be proof that the water had descended enough for the raven to have found some carrion on the ground (*Radak*).

The raven continually flew to and fro until Noah left the Ark when the earth dried (*Ibn Ezra*).

8-12. The dove. Seven days after sending the raven, Noah set the dove free; if it would find a resting place it would not return to him (*Rashi*). Although the mountaintops were already visible, the bird would not consider them a *resting place* because they were denuded of trees, so that the dove could not build a nest (*Ramban*), or because the land was still saturated from the long Flood (*Sforno*).

9. וַיִּשְׁלַח יָדוֹ וַיִּקָּחֶהָ — *So he put forth his hand, and took it.* Noah's compassion teaches us that one should treat an unsuccessful messenger as well as a successful one, if the failure was not his fault (*Haamek Davar*).

11. וַתָּבֹא אֵלָיו הַיּוֹנָה — *Back to him came the dove.* By saying that the dove came back to *him,* the Torah implies that it

וַיֵּדַע נֹחַ כִּי־קַלּוּ הַמַּיִם מֵעַל הָאָרֶץ׃ יב וַיִּיָּחֶל עוֹד
‹ again ‹ Then he waited 12 « the earth. ‹ from upon ‹ the waters had subsided ‹ that ‹ And Noah knew

שִׁבְעַת יָמִים אֲחֵרִים וַיְשַׁלַּח אֶת־הַיּוֹנָה וְלֹא־
‹ and not « the dove; ‹ and sent out ‹ that were additional ‹ days ‹ [for] seven

יָסְפָה שׁוּב־אֵלָיו עוֹד׃ יג וַיְהִי בְּאַחַת וְשֵׁשׁ־מֵאוֹת
‹ in the six hundredth and first ‹ And it came to pass 13 « any more. ‹ to him ‹ return ‹ again did it

שָׁנָה בָּרִאשׁוֹן בְּאֶחָד לַחֹדֶשׁ חָרְבוּ הַמַּיִם מֵעַל
‹ from upon ‹ the waters dried « of the month, ‹ on the first ‹ in the first [month], « year,

הָאָרֶץ וַיָּסַר נֹחַ אֶת־מִכְסֵה הַתֵּבָה וַיַּרְא וְהִנֵּה חָרְבוּ פְּנֵי הָאֲדָמָה׃
« of the ground. ‹ the surface ‹ dried had ‹ — and behold! « and he looked « of the Ark, ‹ the covering ‹ Noah removed « the earth;

יד וּבַחֹדֶשׁ הַשֵּׁנִי בְּשִׁבְעָה וְעֶשְׂרִים יוֹם לַחֹדֶשׁ יָבְשָׁה הָאָרֶץ׃ ס
« was the earth. ‹ [fully] dried ‹ of the month, ‹ day ‹ on the twenty-seventh « And in the second month, 14

רביעי – טו וַיְדַבֵּר אֱלֹהִים אֶל־נֹחַ לֵאמֹר׃ טז צֵא מִן־הַתֵּבָה אַתָּה וְאִשְׁתְּךָ
‹ and your wife, ‹ you « the Ark: ‹ from ‹ Go forth 16 « saying, ‹ Noah, ‹ to ‹ God spoke 15

וּבָנֶיךָ וּנְשֵׁי־בָנֶיךָ אִתָּךְ׃ יז כָּל־הַחַיָּה אֲשֶׁר־אִתְּךָ מִכָּל־בָּשָׂר בָּעוֹף
‹ of birds, « flesh, ‹ of all ‹ with you ‹ that is ‹ living being ‹ Every 17 *« with you. ‹ of your sons ‹ and the wives ‹ your sons,*

וִידַע נֹחַ אֲרֵי קַלִּיאוּ מַיָּא מֵעַל אַרְעָא: יב וְאוֹרִיךְ עוֹד שִׁבְעָא יוֹמִין אָחֳרָנִין וְשַׁלַּח יָת יוֹנָה וְלָא אוֹסֵיפַת לְמִתּוּב לְוָתֵהּ עוֹד: יג וַהֲוָה בְּשִׁית מְאָה וְחַד שְׁנִין בְּקַדְמָאָה בְּחַד לְיַרְחָא נְגוּבוּ מַיָּא מֵעַל אַרְעָא וְאַעְדִּי נֹחַ יָת חוּפָאָה דְּתֵיבוּתָא וַחֲזָא וְהָא נְגוּבוּ אַפֵּי אַרְעָא: יד וּבְיַרְחָא תִּנְיָנָא בְּעַשְׂרִין וְשַׁבְעָא יוֹמָא לְיַרְחָא יַבִּישַׁת אַרְעָא: טו וּמַלִּיל יְיָ עִם נֹחַ לְמֵימָר: טז פּוּק מִן תֵּיבוּתָא אַתְּ וְאִתְּתָךְ וּבְנָיךְ וּנְשֵׁי בְנָיךְ עִמָּךְ: יז כָּל חַיְתָא דְּעִמָּךְ מִכָּל בִּשְׂרָא בְּעוֹפָא

רש"י

ודרשו בפיה ל' מאמר אמרה יהיו מזונותי מרורין כזית בידו של הקב"ה ולא מתוקין כדבש בידי בשר ודם (פדר"א שם; סנהדרין שם; עירובין יח:): **(יב) וייחל.** הוא ל' ויחל אלא שזה ל' ויפעל וזה ל' ויתפעל, ויחל וימתן, וייחל ויתמתן: **(יג) בראשון.** לר' אליעזר הוא תשרי ולרבי יהושע הוא ניסן (סדר עולם שם; ר"ה יא:): **חרבו.** נעשה כמין טיט שקרמו פניה של מעלה (סדר עולם שם; ב"ר לג:ז): **(יד) בשבעה ועשרים.** וירידתן בחדש השני בי"ז בחדש, אלו י"א ימים שהחמה יתירה על הלבנה, שמשפט דור המבול שנה תמימה היה (עדיות ב:י; סדר עולם שם; ב"ר שם): **יבשה.** נעשה גריד כהלכתה (ס"ע שם; ב"ר שם): **(טז) אתה ואשתך וגו'.** איש ואשתו. כאן

meant to come back to Noah, in fulfillment of its mission to bring back a sign of God's response.The bird did not come back merely to return to its nest or because it was tired (see *Haamek Davar).*

By bringing back a bitter olive leaf in its mouth, the dove was saying symbolically, "Better that my food be bitter but from God's hand, than sweet as honey but dependent on mortal man" (*Rashi*). R' Hirsch elaborates: For a full year, the dove could not earn its own food; hunger forced it to rely on Noah's kindness. Then it found a bitter leaf that it would ordinarily not eat — and carried it back to Noah, preaching the lesson of the Sages, that even the bitterest food eaten in freedom is better than the sweetest food given in servitude.

13. The earth dries. The earth's surface had dried, but it was not yet firm enough to walk upon (*Rashi*). Thus, Noah waited for God's command before leaving the Ark (*Midrash; Radak*).

14. From 17 Marcheshvan, when the rains began, to 27 Marcheshvan of the following year, when Noah was finally able to leave the Ark, was a full solar year, making 365 days that the earth was uninhabitable (*Rashi*).

16. The command to leave the Ark. In telling Noah that the Ark would save him, God used the Name *HASHEM* (7:1), which denotes mercy. Here, in telling him to return to the world, He uses the Name *Elohim,* and uses it throughout the narrative. In addition to its familiar connotation of God as Judge, it also refers to Him as God Who dominates nature and uses it to carry out His ends. Just as judgment proceeds along clearly defined rules, so too nature has its clearly defined laws, within which God guides the world, unless He chooses to override them and perform a miracle. The Name *Elohim* refers to this aspect of God's total mastery, for it describes Him as "the Mighty One Who wields authority over the beings above and below" (*Tur Orach Chaim* 5) and the בַּעַל הַיְכֹלֶת, *the Omnipotent One* (*Shulchan Aruch*, ibid.). Here, when God called upon Noah to leave the Ark and build the world anew, He appeared as the God Who created and preserves the natural world, and Who would rejuvenate the universe that had lain virtually dormant for a year (*Haamek Davar*). Regarding this

וּבַבְּהֵמָה וּבְכָל־הָרֶמֶשׂ הָרֹמֵשׂ עַל־הָאָרֶץ
« the earth ‹ on ‹ that creep ‹ creeping things ‹ and of all ‹ of animals,

°הַיְצֵא [°הוצא כ׳] אִתָּךְ וְשָׁרְצוּ בָאָרֶץ וּפָרוּ וְרָבוּ
‹ and multiply ‹ and be fruitful ‹ on the earth ‹ and let them be prolific « with you, ‹ — order [them] out

עַל־הָאָרֶץ: יח וַיֵּצֵא־נֹחַ וּבָנָיו וְאִשְׁתּוֹ וּנְשֵׁי־בָנָיו
‹ of his sons ‹ and the wives ‹ his wife, ‹ and his sons, « So Noah went forth, **18** « *the earth.* ‹ on

אִתּוֹ: יט כָּל־הַחַיָּה כָּל־הָרֶמֶשׂ וְכָל־הָעוֹף כֹּל
‹ everything ‹ bird, ‹ and every ‹ creeping thing, ‹ every ‹ living being, ‹ Every **19** « with him.

רוֹמֵשׂ עַל־הָאָרֶץ לְמִשְׁפְּחֹתֵיהֶם יָצְאוּ מִן־הַתֵּבָה: כ וַיִּבֶן נֹחַ מִזְבֵּחַ
‹ an altar ‹ [Then] Noah built **20** « the Ark. ‹ of ‹ came out ‹ by their families « the earth, ‹ on ‹ that moves

לַיהוָה וַיִּקַּח מִכֹּל ׀ הַבְּהֵמָה הַטְּהֹרָה וּמִכֹּל הָעוֹף הַטָּהֹר וַיַּעַל עֹלֹת
‹ burnt-offerings ‹ and offered ‹ that is clean, ‹ bird ‹ and of every ‹ that is clean ‹ animal ‹ of every ‹ and he took ‹ to HASHEM

בַּמִּזְבֵּחַ: כא וַיָּרַח יהוה אֶת־רֵיחַ הַנִּיחֹחַ וַיֹּאמֶר יהוה אֶל־לִבּוֹ לֹא אֹסִף
‹ *I will not continue* « His heart: ‹ in ‹ and HASHEM said « that was pleasing, ‹ the aroma ‹ HASHEM smelled **21** « on the altar.

וּבִבְעִירָא וּבְכָל רִחֲשָׁא דְּרָחֵשׁ עַל אַרְעָא אַפֵּיק עִמָּךְ וְיִתְיַלְּדוּן בְּאַרְעָא וְיִפְשׁוּן וְיִסְגּוּן עַל אַרְעָא: יח וּנְפַק נֹחַ וּבְנוֹהִי וְאִתְּתֵהּ וּנְשֵׁי בְנוֹהִי עִמֵּהּ: יט כָּל חַיְתָא כָּל רִחֲשָׁא וְכָל עוֹפָא כֹּל דְּרָחֵשׁ עַל אַרְעָא לְזַרְעֲיָתְהוֹן נְפַקוּ מִן תֵּיבוּתָא: כ וּבְנָא נֹחַ מַדְבְּחָא קֳדָם יְיָ וּנְסֵיב מִכֹּל בְּעִירָא דַכְיָא וּמִכֹּל עוֹפָא דְּכֵי וְאַסֵּיק עֲלָוָן בְּמַדְבְּחָא: כא וְקַבֵּיל יְיָ בְּרַעֲוָא יָת קוּרְבָּנֵהּ וַאֲמַר יְיָ בְּמֵימְרֵהּ לָא אוֹסֵף

רש"י

התיר להם תשמיש המטה (ב"ר לד:ז): **(יז) הוצא.** הוצא כתיב היצא קרי (שם ח). היצא אמור להם שיצאו. הוצא אם אינם רוצים לצאת הוציאם אתה: **ושרצו בארץ.** ולא בתבה, מגיד שאף הבהמה והעוף נאסרו בתשמיש (שם; תנחומא ישן יז): **(יט) למשפחתיהם.** קבלו עליהם על מנת לידבק במינן (מדרש אגדה): **(כ) מכל הבהמה הטהורה.** אמר, לא צוה לי הקדוש ברוך הוא להכנים מאלו ז' ז' אלא כדי להקריב קרבן מהם (ב"ר לד:ט):

definition of the Name *Elohim*, commentators note that its numerical value equals that of הַטֶּבַע, *the nature*, indicating that He controls all natural phenomena.

17. הַיְצֵא — *Order [them] out.* The *k'siv* (Masoretic spelling) is הוצא, while the *k'ri* (Masoretic pronunciation) is הַיְצֵא. *Rashi* explains the duality: הַיְצֵא means *order them out,* i.e., tell them to leave on their own; while הוצא means *force them out*, in the event they refuse to leave.

בָּאָרֶץ — *On the earth.* Only back on earth were the animals to be fruitful and multiply, but in the Ark, all sexual activity was forbidden (*Rashi*). The next verse, by mentioning the males and females separately, suggests that the prohibition was still in force, even after the end of the Flood's ravages. *Gur Aryeh* (to 7:17) explains that Noah, fearing another flood, decided to refrain from marital life, saying, "Am I to go out and beget children for a curse?" (*Midrash),* until God promised that He would not bring another flood.

20. Noah brings an offering. Noah thought: God saved me from the waters of the Flood and brought me forth from the prison [of the Ark]. Am I not obliged to bring Him an offering and an elevation-offering? (*Pirkei d'Rabbi Eliezer*). He understood that the reason God had him take seven pairs of clean animals was so that they would be available should he wish to bring offerings.

In connection with offerings, God is always called *HASHEM,* the Name signifying the Attribute of Mercy. This proves that offerings are directed toward the Merciful God Who desires *life,* not death and suffering. The purpose of the sacrificial service is to bring about a person's closeness and dedication to Godliness. The non-Jewish, blasphemous view of sacrifices as an appeasement of a "vengeful God of nature" could never be connected with the Name *HASHEM* (*R' Hirsch*).

Rambam (*Hil. Beis HaBechirah* 2:2) comments: There was a tradition that the altars of David and Solomon, of Abraham (where he bound Isaac, in 22:2), of Noah, of Cain and Abel, and of Adam were all at the same place: Mount Moriah, the site of the Temple in Jerusalem.

20-21. For details concerning offerings, their names, and terminology, see the Book of *Leviticus.*

21. אֶל־לִבּוֹ — *In His heart.* When Scripture uses this term, it means that God kept the resolution private and did not reveal it to a prophet, meaning Noah, at that time. When He directed Moses to write the Torah, however, God revealed to him that Noah's offering was accepted and that, as a result, God resolved not to bring another deluge upon the entire world (*Ramban*).

לְקַלֵּל עוֹד אֶת־הָאֲדָמָה בַּעֲבוּר הָאָדָם כִּי יֵצֶר

to curse › again › the ground › because of › man, » since › the thoughts

לֵב הָאָדָם רַע מִנְּעֻרָיו וְלֹא־אֹסִף עוֹד לְהַכּוֹת

of the heart › of man › are evil › from his youth; » nor › will I continue › again › to smite

22 אֶת־כָּל־חַי כַּאֲשֶׁר עָשִׂיתִי: כב עֹד כָּל־יְמֵי הָאָרֶץ

every › living being, › as › I have done. » 22 Continuously, › all › the days › of the earth, »

זֶרַע וְקָצִיר וְקֹר וָחֹם וְקַיִץ וָחֹרֶף וְיוֹם וָלַיְלָה לֹא יִשְׁבֹּתוּ:

seedtime › and harvest, › cold › and heat, › summer › and winter, › day › and night, › shall not cease. »

[9] 1 [ט] א וַיְבָרֶךְ אֱלֹהִים אֶת־נֹחַ וְאֶת־בָּנָיו וַיֹּאמֶר לָהֶם פְּרוּ וּרְבוּ וּמִלְאוּ

[9] 1 God blessed › Noah › and his sons, › and He said › to them, » Be fruitful › and multiply › and fill ›

2 אֶת־הָאָרֶץ: ב וּמוֹרַאֲכֶם וְחִתְּכֶם יִהְיֶה עַל כָּל־חַיַּת הָאָרֶץ וְעַל כָּל־עוֹף

the land. » 2 Fear of you › and dread of you › shall be › upon › every › beast › of the earth › and upon › every › bird ›

לְמֵילַט עוֹד יָת אַרְעָא בְּדִיל חוֹבֵי אֱנָשָׁא אֲרֵי יִצְרָא לִבָּא דֶאֱנָשָׁא בִּישׁ מִזְּעִירֵהּ וְלָא אוֹסֵף עוֹד לְמִמְחֵי יָת כָּל דְּחַי כְּמָא דִי עֲבָדִית: כב עוֹד כָּל יוֹמֵי אַרְעָא זְרוֹעָא וַחֲצָדָא וְקוֹרָא וְחוֹמָא וְקַיְטָא וְסִתְוָא וִימָם וְלֵילְיָא לָא יִבְטְלוּן: א וּבָרִיךְ יְיָ יָת נֹחַ וְיָת בְּנוֹהִי וַאֲמַר לְהוֹן פּוּשׁוּ וּסְגוּ וּמְלוּ יָת אַרְעָא: ב וְדַחֲלַתְכוֹן וְאֵימַתְכוֹן תְּהֵי עַל כָּל חֵיוַת אַרְעָא וְעַל כָּל עוֹפָא

רש"י

(כא) **מנעריו.** מנעריו כתיב, משננער לצאת ממעי אמו ניתן בו יצר הרע (ב"ר לד:י; ירושלמי ברכות ג:ה): **לא אסף [וגו'] ולא אסף.** כפל הדבר לשבועה. הוא שכתוב אשר נשבעתי מעבור מי נח (ישעיה נד:ט) ולא מצינו בה שבועה אלא זו שכפל דבריו, והיא שבועה. וכן דרשו חכמים במסכת שבועות (לו.): (כב) **עד כל ימי הארץ וגו' לא ישבתו.** ו' עתים הללו שני חדשים לכל אחד ואחד, כמו ששנינו חצי תשרי ומרחשון וחצי כסליו זרע, חצי כסליו וטבת וחצי שבט קור [ס"א חורף] וכו' בב"מ (קו:) [ס"א עוד כל ימי כלומר תמיד, כמו עוד טומאתו בו]: **קר.** קשה מחורף: **חרף.** עת זרע שעורים וקטניות החריפין להתבשל מהר, [קור] הוא חצי שבט ואדר וחצי ניסן: **קציר.** חצי ניסן ואייר וחצי סיון: **קיץ.** הוא זמן לקיטת תאנים וזמן שמייבשים אותן בשדות, ושמו קיץ, כמו והלחם והקיץ לאכול הנערים (שמואל ב טז:ב): **חם.** הוא סוף ימות החמה חצי אב ואלול וחצי תשרי שהעולם חם ביותר כמו ששנינו במסכת יומא (כט.) שלהי קייטא קשי מקייטא: **ויום ולילה לא ישבתו.** מכלל ששבתו כל ימות המבול שלא שמשו המזלות ולא ניכר בין יום ובין לילה (ב"ר לד:יא): **לא ישבתו.** לא יפסקו כל אלה מלהתנהג כסדרן: (ב) **וחתכם.** ואימתכם (אונקלוס), כמו תראו חתת (איוב ו:כא). ואגדה, ל'

רַע מִנְּעֻרָיו — *Are evil from his youth.* Man receives the Evil Inclination from birth before he has the wisdom and maturity to combat it [meaning that man's animal instincts are inborn, while the intellect and spiritual desire for self-improvement must be inculcated and developed with time and maturity]. Thus, while individuals are responsible for their sins, mankind as a whole should not be wiped out totally because of sin. God will punish people in other, less drastic ways (*Ramban; Abarbanel*).

22. God guaranteed that as long as this world continues to exist, the natural cycle of the seasons will not cease, which implies that this cycle had been in abeyance during the Flood. The *Chofetz Chaim* used to say that if someone were to ask him how he could be sure that the sun would rise the next morning or that winter would give way to spring and summer, he would reply that in this verse God assured that all of this would go on continuously. Nonbelievers require statistics and studies; for believers, the greatest of all proofs is God's promise. Or, as the *Chofetz Chaim* and others have said in similar contexts, "For believers there are no questions; for nonbelievers there are no answers."

9.

1-15. Rebuilding a ruined world. Above, the Torah recorded Noah's offerings as his personal token of devotion to God, and it recorded God's resolve that the world would continue. Now, these two resolutions are translated into the combination blessing and charge that God conferred upon Noah and his progeny.

The world had benefited from God's blessing to Adam (1:28) until the Generation of the Flood abrogated it with their corruption. When Noah left the Ark, God renewed the blessing of prolific procreation by repeating it to Noah and his sons (*Tanchuma Yashan; Ibn Caspi*).

1. פְּרוּ וּרְבוּ — *Be fruitful and multiply.* These words would be repeated in verse 7. Here it is a *blessing* that the human race would be prolific; in verse 7 it is the *commandment* to beget children (*Rashi*). When Noah left the Ark and saw the world destroyed, with only four human couples still alive, he was dismayed and fearful. God allayed his concern by giving him this blessing that the world would become repopulated (*Abarbanel*).

2. . . . וּמוֹרַאֲכֶם — *Fear of you . . .* Lest Noah be afraid that the few surviving people would be in constant danger from the hordes of animals in the world, God assured him that He had implanted in animals an instinctive fear of human beings (*Abarbanel*).

הַשָּׁמָיִם בְּכֹל אֲשֶׁר תִּרְמֹשׂ הָאֲדָמָה וּבְכָל־דְּגֵי

‹ the fish ‹ and in all ‹ the earth ‹ moves on ‹ that ‹ in everything ‹‹ of the heavens,

הַיָּם בְּיֶדְכֶם נִתָּנוּ: ג כָּל־רֶמֶשׂ אֲשֶׁר הוּא־חַי לָכֶם

‹ for you ‹‹ lives, ‹ that ‹ moving thing ‹ Every 3 ‹‹ they are given. ‹ in your hand ‹‹ of the sea;

יִהְיֶה לְאָכְלָה כְּיֶרֶק עֵשֶׂב נָתַתִּי לָכֶם אֶת־כֹּל:

‹‹ everything. ‹ you ‹ I have given ‹ herbage ‹ like the green ‹‹ for food; ‹ shall be

ד אַךְ־בָּשָׂר בְּנַפְשׁוֹ דָמוֹ לֹא תֹאכֵלוּ: ה וְאַךְ אֶת־דִּמְכֶם לְנַפְשֹׁתֵיכֶם

‹ which belongs to your souls ‹ your blood ‹ However, 5 ‹‹ you shall not eat. ‹ [in] its blood, ‹ with its soul ‹‹ flesh; ‹ But 4

אֶדְרֹשׁ מִיַּד כָּל־חַיָּה אֶדְרְשֶׁנּוּ וּמִיַּד הָאָדָם מִיַּד אִישׁ אָחִיו אֶדְרֹשׁ

‹ I will demand ‹ [for that of] his brother ‹ every man ‹ of ‹‹ man, ‹ but of ‹‹ will I demand it; ‹ beast ‹ every ‹ of ‹‹ I will demand,

דִּשְׁמַיָּא בְּכֹל דִּי תַרְחִישׁ אַרְעָא
וּבְכָל נוּנֵי יַמָּא בִּידְכוֹן יְהוֹן מְסִירִין:
ג כָּל רִחֲשָׁא דִּי הוּא חַי לְכוֹן יְהֵי
לְמֵיכַל כִּירוֹק עִשְׂבָּא יְהָבִית לְכוֹן
יָת כֹּלָּא: ד בְּרַם בִּשְׂרָא בְּנַפְשֵׁהּ דְּמֵהּ
לָא תֵיכְלוּן: ה וּבְרַם יָת דִּמְכוֹן
לְנַפְשָׁתֵיכוֹן אֶתְבַּע מִיַּד כָּל חַיְתָא
אֶתְבְּעִנֵּהּ וּמִיַּד אֱנָשָׁא מִיַּד גְּבַר
דְּיֵשׁוֹד יָת דְּמָא דַאֲחוּהִי אֶתְבַּע

רש"י

חיות, שכל זמן שתינוק בן יומו חי אין אתה צריך לשומרו מן העכברים, עוג מלך הבשן מת צריך לשומרו מן העכברים, שנא' ומוראכם וחתכם יהיה, אימתי יהיה מוראכם על החיות כל זמן שאתם חיים (ב"ר שם יב; שבת קנא:). (ג) **לכם יהיה לאכלה.** שלא הרשיתי לאדם הראשון בשר אלא ירק עשב, ולכם, **כירק עשב** שהפקרתי לאדם הראשון **נתתי לכם את כל** (סנהדרין נט:): (ד) **בשר בנפשו.** אסר להם אבר מן החי, כלומר, כל זמן שנפשו בו לא תאכלו הבשר (שם נז.): **בנפשו דמו.** בעוד נפשו בו. בשר בנפשו לא תאכלו, הרי אבר מן החי, ואף דמו [בנפשו] לא תאכלו, הרי דם מן החי (שם נט.): (ה) **ואך את דמכם.** אע"פ שהתרתי לכם נטילת נשמה בבהמה, את דמכם אדרוש מהשופך דם עצמו (ב"ק צא:): **לנפשותיכם.** אף החונק עצמו (ב"ר שם יג) אע"פ שלא יצא ממנו דם: **מיד כל חיה.** [לפי שחטאו דור המבול והופקרו למאכל חיות רעות לשלוט בהן (מדרש אגדה) שנאמר נמשל כבהמות נדמו (תהלים מט:יג; שבת קנא:), לפיכך הוצרך] להזהיר עליהם את החיות (מדרש אגדה; תרגום יונתן): **ומיד האדם.** מיד ההורג במזיד ואין עדים אני אדרוש (שם ושם): **מיד איש אחיו.** שהוא אוהב לו כאח והרגו שוגג אני אדרוש, אם לא יגלה ויבקש על עונו לימחל, שאף השוגג צריך כפרה (סנהדרין לז:; מכות ב:, ח:, יא:; שבועות ז:-ח.) ואם אין עדים לחייבו גלות והוא אינו נכנע הקב"ה דורש ממנו, כמו שדרשו רבותינו והאלהים אנה לידו (שמות

The *Zohar* explains that in man's ideal state, the *image of God* in which he was created would be sufficient to frighten animals, which are an infinitely lower order of life. But when the generation of the Flood degraded itself and sank to the level of animals, it forfeited this aura. Now God restored that blessing. This concept means that as long as man is true to his Godly image, he need not fear beasts, but if he descends from his calling, after the fashion of the Generation of the Flood, he must indeed fear the beasts of the wild.

3. God now gave Noah and his descendants a right that had never been given to Adam or his progeny: permission to eat meat. Noah was given the right to eat meat, just as God had given Adam the right to eat vegetation, because (a) had it not been for the righteousness of Noah, no life would have survived the Flood; and, (b) he had toiled over the animals and attended to their needs in the Ark. Of him was it said, *You shall eat the toil of your hands* (*Psalms* 128:2). Thus, Noah had acquired rights over them (*Or HaChaim*).

4. . . . אַךְ־בָּשָׂר בְּנַפְשׁוֹ — *But flesh; with its soul . . .* This commandment limits the permission to eat meat. It is forbidden to eat אֵבֶר מִן הַחַי, *a limb taken from a living animal.* Accordingly, the verse states that flesh is prohibited while life is still in the animal, and that this prohibition applies to its blood, as well (*Rashi*).

5. The Torah places another limitation on man's right to take a life. God states that He will demand an accounting from one who spills his own blood, for a human being's life belongs not to him but to God. Though Noah had been granted authority over animal life, he had no right to commit suicide; only God has the right to end life (*Bava Kamma* 91b; *Rashi*).

מִיַּד כָּל־חַיָּה — *Of every beast.* Beasts, too, are forbidden to kill people (*Rashi*), and if they do, they will be killed through Divine means (*Ran,* cited by *Abarbanel*). Alternatively, this passage refers to a person who turns over another to be killed by wild beasts (*Bereishis Rabbah* 34:13, *Rambam, Hil. Rotzeiach* 2:3). Alternatively, the verse refers to murder, and warns that God will not permit a murderer to go unpunished. He will be hunted down by wild animals or by *the hand of man* (*Ramban*).

וּמִיַּד הָאָדָם — *But of man . . .* The verse gives other examples of bloodshed that God will not condone: someone who contrives to kill without witnesses, so that he is beyond the reach of the courts; or someone who kills *his brother,* i.e., someone he loves so very much that the death had to have been accidental or unintentional. In such a case, too, the killer may well have a degree of responsibility due to his failure to exercise proper vigilance. Whenever a life is taken, God will inflict whatever punishment is merited according to the degree of the crime or the carelessness that led to the death.

אֶת־נֶפֶשׁ הָאָדָם: ו שֹׁפֵךְ דַּם הָאָדָם בָּאָדָם דָּמוֹ
< shall his blood < by man << of man, < the blood < Whoever sheds 6 << of man. < the soul

יִשָּׁפֵךְ כִּי בְּצֶלֶם אֱלֹהִים עָשָׂה אֶת־הָאָדָם:
<< man. < He made < of God < in the image < for << be shed;

ז וְאַתֶּם פְּרוּ וּרְבוּ שִׁרְצוּ בָאָרֶץ וּרְבוּ־בָהּ: ס
<< on it. < and multiply < on the earth < be prolific << and multiply; < be fruitful << And you, 7

חמישי – ח וַיֹּאמֶר אֱלֹהִים אֶל־נֹחַ וְאֶל־בָּנָיו אִתּוֹ
< with him < his sons < and to < Noah < to < And God said 8

לֵאמֹר: ט וַאֲנִי הִנְנִי מֵקִים אֶת־בְּרִיתִי אִתְּכֶם וְאֶת־זַרְעֲכֶם אַחֲרֵיכֶם:
<< after you, < your offspring < and with < with you < My covenant < establish < indeed, I << And as for Me, 9 << saying:

י וְאֵת כָּל־נֶפֶשׁ הַחַיָּה אֲשֶׁר אִתְּכֶם בָּעוֹף בַּבְּהֵמָה וּבְכָל־חַיַּת הָאָרֶץ
< of the land < beast < and with every < with the animals, < — with the birds, << with you < that is < that is living < being < every < and with 10

אִתְּכֶם מִכֹּל יֹצְאֵי הַתֵּבָה לְכֹל חַיַּת הָאָרֶץ: יא וַהֲקִמֹתִי אֶת־בְּרִיתִי
< My covenant < And I will confirm 11 << of the land. < beast < to every << the Ark; < that exited < — of all << [that is] with you

אִתְּכֶם וְלֹא־יִכָּרֵת כָּל־בָּשָׂר עוֹד מִמֵּי הַמַּבּוּל וְלֹא־יִהְיֶה עוֹד מַבּוּל
< a flood < again < shall there be < and never << of the flood, < by the waters < again < flesh < all < shall be cut off < Never << with you:

יָת נַפְשָׁא דֶאֱנָשָׁא: ו דְּיֵשׁוֹד דְּמָא דֶאֱנָשָׁא בְּסַהֲדִין עַל מֵימַר דַּיָּנַיָּא דְּמֵהּ יִתְּשַׁד אֲרֵי בְּצַלְמָא דַייָ עֲבַד יָת אֱנָשָׁא: ז וְאַתּוּן פּוּשׁוּ וּסְגוּ אִתְיְלִידוּ בְּאַרְעָא וּסְגוּ בַהּ: ח וַאֲמַר יְיָ לְנֹחַ וְלִבְנוֹהִי עִמֵּהּ לְמֵימָר: ט וַאֲנָא הָא אֲנָא מֵקִים יָת קְיָמִי עִמְּכוֹן וְעִם בְּנֵיכוֹן בַּתְרֵיכוֹן: י וְעִם כָּל נַפְשָׁא חַיְתָא דְּעִמְּכוֹן בְּעוֹפָא בִּבְעִירָא וּבְכָל חֵיוַת אַרְעָא דְּעִמְּכוֹן מִכֹּל נַפְקֵי תֵבוֹתָא לְכֹל חֵיוַת אַרְעָא: יא וְאָקֵם יָת קְיָמִי עִמְּכוֹן וְלָא יִשְׁתֵּיצֵי כָּל בִּשְׂרָא עוֹד מִמֵּי טוֹפָנָא וְלָא יְהֵי עוֹד טוֹפָנָא

רש"י

כא:יג) במס' מכות (י:) הקדוש ברוך הוא מזמנן לפונדק אחד וכו': (ו) **באדם דמו ישפך.** אם יש עדים המיתוהו אתם, למה, **כי בצלם אלהים וגו'** (אונקלוס): **עשה את האדם.** זה מקרא חסר וצריך להיות עשה העושה את האדם, וכן הרבה במקרא: (ז) **ואתם פרו ורבו.** לפי פשוטו הראשונה (לעיל פסוק א) לברכה (עי' כתובות ה.) וכאן לצווי (סנהדרין נט.־נט:). ולפי מדרשו להקיש מי שאינו עוסק בפריה ורביה לשופך דמים (ב"ר שם יד; יבמות סג:): (ט) **ואני הנני.** מסכים אני עמך (עי' ב"ר לד:יב). שהיה נח דואג לעסוק בפריה ורביה עד שהבטיחו הקב"ה שלא לשחת העולם עוד (תנחומא יא) וכן [עשה] באחרונה אמר לו הנני מסכים לעשות קיום וחיזוק ברית להבטחתי, ואתן לך אות (שם ואילך ג): (י) [**חית הארץ אתכם.** הם המתהלכים עם הבריות: **מכל יצאי התיבה.** להביא שקצים ורמשים:] **חית הארץ.** להביא המזיקין, שאינן בכלל החיה אשר אתכם, שאין הילוכן עם הבריות: (יא) **והקמתי.** אעשה קיום לבריתי. ומהו קיומו, אות הקשת, כמו שמסיים והולך:

6. This verse refers to murder that was committed in such a way that it incurs the death penalty of the courts.

8-17. The rainbow; sign of the covenant. God established a covenant with Noah and his descendants, and all living beings, until the end of time. This covenant would be signified forever by the rainbow. After a rainstorm, which could have been a harbinger of another deluge like that in Noah's time, the appearance of the rainbow will be a reminder of God's pledge never again to wash away all of mankind in a flood. According to *Ibn Ezra,* it was then that God created the atmospheric conditions that would cause a rainbow to be seen after a rainstorm. Most other commentators disagree, maintaining that the rainbow, which had existed since Creation, would henceforth be designated as a sign that a deluge like Noah's would never recur. *R' Hirsch* states that it is the eternal sign that, no matter how bleak the future may seem, God will lead mankind to its ultimate goal.

That the rainbow is a phenomenon that is predictable and explainable in natural terms is no contradiction to its status as a Divinely ordained sign. The new moon, too, symbolizes the power of renewal that God assigned to the Jewish people, even though its appearance could be calculated to the split second for hundreds of years; indeed, this predictability is the basis of the current Jewish calendar, which was promulgated in the 4th century C.E. Nevertheless, God utilized the natural phenomena of His world as reminders of His covenant, for the very laws of nature should recall to thinking people that there is a God of nature.

11. וְלֹא־יִכָּרֵת כָּל־בָּשָׂר עוֹד — *Never shall be cut off all flesh again.* Part of the world's population may be destroyed, but never again will the *entire* world be destroyed by a flood or any other catastrophe (*Sforno, Or HaChaim*), even if the peo-

לְשַׁחֵת הָאָרֶץ: יב וַיֹּאמֶר אֱלֹהִים זֹאת אוֹת־

< is the sign < This << And God said, 12 *<< the earth. < to destroy*

הַבְּרִית אֲשֶׁר־אֲנִי נֹתֵן בֵּינִי וּבֵינֵיכֶם וּבֵין כָּל־נֶפֶשׁ

< being < every < and between < and you, < between Me < give < I < that < of the covenant

חַיָּה אֲשֶׁר אִתְּכֶם לְדֹרֹת עוֹלָם: יג אֶת־קַשְׁתִּי

< My rainbow 13 *<< forever: < to generations < with you, < that is < that is living*

נָתַתִּי בֶּעָנָן וְהָיְתָה לְאוֹת בְּרִית בֵּינִי וּבֵין הָאָרֶץ:

<< the earth. < and between < between Me < of the covenant < a sign < and it shall be << in the cloud, < I have set

יד וְהָיָה בְּעַנְנִי עָנָן עַל־הָאָרֶץ וְנִרְאֲתָה הַקֶּשֶׁת

<< – the bow – << and it will be seen << the earth, < over < a cloud < when I place << And it shall happen, 14

בֶּעָנָן: טו וְזָכַרְתִּי אֶת־בְּרִיתִי אֲשֶׁר בֵּינִי וּבֵינֵיכֶם וּבֵין כָּל־נֶפֶשׁ חַיָּה

< that is living < being < every < and between < and you < between Me < which is < My covenant < I will remember 15 *<< in the cloud,*

בְּכָל־בָּשָׂר וְלֹא־יִהְיֶה עוֹד הַמַּיִם לְמַבּוּל לְשַׁחֵת כָּל־בָּשָׂר:

<< flesh. < all < to destroy < become a flood < [that] the waters < again < and it shall never be << flesh, < among all

טז וְהָיְתָה הַקֶּשֶׁת בֶּעָנָן וּרְאִיתִיהָ לִזְכֹּר בְּרִית עוֹלָם בֵּין אֱלֹהִים וּבֵין

< and between < God < between < that is everlasting < the covenant < to remember < and I will look upon it << in the cloud, < And the bow shall be 16

כָּל־נֶפֶשׁ חַיָּה בְּכָל־בָּשָׂר אֲשֶׁר עַל־הָאָרֶץ: יז וַיֹּאמֶר אֱלֹהִים אֶל־נֹחַ

<< Noah, < to < And God said 17 *<< the earth. < on < that is < flesh < among all < that is living < being < every*

זֹאת אוֹת־הַבְּרִית אֲשֶׁר הֲקִמֹתִי בֵּינִי וּבֵין כָּל־בָּשָׂר אֲשֶׁר עַל־הָאָרֶץ:

<< the earth. < upon < that is < flesh < all < and between < between Me < I have confirmed < that < of the covenant < the sign < This is

לְחַבָּלָא אַרְעָא: יב וַאֲמַר יְיָ דָּא אָת
קְיָם דִּי אֲנָא יָהֵב בֵּין מֵימְרִי וּבֵינֵיכוֹן
וּבֵין כָּל נַפְשָׁא חַיְתָא דִּי עִמְּכוֹן לְדָרֵי
עָלְמָא: יג יָת קַשְׁתִּי יְהָבִית בַּעֲנָנָא
וּתְהֵי לְאָת קְיָם בֵּין מֵימְרִי וּבֵין
אַרְעָא: יד וַהֲוָה בַּעֲנָנוּתִי עֲנָנָא עַל
אַרְעָא וְתִתְחֲזֵי קַשְׁתָּא בַּעֲנָנָא:
טו וְדָכִירְנָא יָת קְיָמִי דִּי בֵין מֵימְרִי
וּבֵינֵיכוֹן וּבֵין כָּל נַפְשָׁא חַיְתָא בְּכָל
בִּשְׂרָא וְלָא יְהֵי עוֹד מַיָּא לְטוֹפָנָא
לְחַבָּלָא כָּל בִּשְׂרָא: טז וּתְהֵי קַשְׁתָּא
בַּעֲנָנָא וְאֶחֱזִנַּהּ לְמִדְכַּר קְיָם עָלַם בֵּין
מֵימְרָא דַייָ וּבֵין כָּל נַפְשָׁא חַיְתָא
בְּכָל בִּשְׂרָא דִּי עַל אַרְעָא: יז וַאֲמַר יְיָ
לְנֹחַ דָּא אָת קְיָם דִּי אֲקֵמִית בֵּין
מֵימְרִי וּבֵין כָּל בִּשְׂרָא דִּי עַל אַרְעָא:

רש"י

(יב) **לדרת עולם.** נכתב חסר, שיש דורות שלא הוצרכו לאות לפי שצדיקים גמורים היו, כמו דורו של חזקיהו מלך יהודה ודורו של רבי שמעון בן יוחאי (ב"ר לה:ב): (יד) **בענני ענן.** כשתעלה במחשבה לפני להביא חשך ואבדון לעולם: (טו) **בין אלהים ובין כל נפש חיה.** בין מדת הדין של מעלה וביניכם. שהיה לו לכתוב ביני ובין כל נפש חיה (שם ג), אלא זהו מדרשו, כשתבא מדת הדין לקטרג [עליכם לחייב אתכם] אני רואה את האות ונזכר: (יז) **זאת אות הברית.** הראהו הקשת ואמר לו הרי האות שאמרתי:

ple are sinful (*Chizkuni*). The Egyptians erred in this regard. They thought that they could drown the Jewish babies without fear of God's measure-for-measure retribution, because He had sworn never to bring another flood. But they did not realize that only the *entire world* would not be flooded; therefore, the Egyptian army could be drowned at the splitting of the sea.

12. לְדֹרֹת עוֹלָם — *To generations forever.* The word דֹרֹת is spelled without the two customary *vavs* [דורות], implying that it would not be necessary for the rainbow to appear in every generation. In periods of exceptional righteousness, such as during the reign of King Hezekiah and the time of R' Shimon bar Yochai, the reassurance of a rainbow was not needed (*Rashi, Mizrachi*).

13. לְאוֹת בְּרִית — *A sign of the covenant.* One who sees a rainbow recites the blessing: *Blessed are You,* Hashem, *our God, King of the universe,* זוֹכֵר הַבְּרִית וְנֶאֱמָן בִּבְרִיתוֹ וְקַיָּם בְּמַאֲמָרוֹ, *Who remembers His covenant, is trustworthy in His covenant, and fulfills His word (Orach Chaim* 229:1).

17. זֹאת אוֹת־הַבְּרִית — *This is the sign of the covenant.* When you see it, it should remind you of the Flood, and you must bestir yourselves to rouse people to repent (*Sforno*).

פ ששי – יח וַיִּהְיוּ בְנֵי־נֹחַ הַיֹּצְאִים מִן־הַתֵּבָה שֵׁם
18 And they were — the sons of Noah — who came out — of the Ark — Shem,
וְחָם וָיָפֶת וְחָם הוּא אֲבִי כְנָעַן: יט שְׁלֹשָׁה אֵלֶּה
Ham, and Japheth; and Ham — he is — the father of Canaan. 19 These three
בְּנֵי־נֹחַ וּמֵאֵלֶּה נָפְצָה כָל־הָאָרֶץ: כ וַיָּחֶל נֹחַ
[were] the sons of Noah, and from these was spread out the whole world. 20 Noah debased himself
אִישׁ הָאֲדָמָה וַיִּטַּע כָּרֶם: כא וַיֵּשְׁתְּ מִן־הַיַּיִן וַיִּשְׁכָּר וַיִּתְגַּל בְּתוֹךְ
— the man of the earth — and he planted a vineyard. 21 He drank of the wine and became drunk, and he uncovered himself within
אָהֳלֹה: כב וַיַּרְא חָם אֲבִי כְנַעַן אֵת עֶרְוַת אָבִיו וַיַּגֵּד לִשְׁנֵי־אֶחָיו בַּחוּץ:
his tent. 22 Ham saw — the father of Canaan — the nakedness of his father, and he told his two brothers outside.
כג וַיִּקַּח שֵׁם וָיֶפֶת אֶת־הַשִּׂמְלָה וַיָּשִׂימוּ עַל־שְׁכֶם שְׁנֵיהֶם וַיֵּלְכוּ
23 And Shem took with Japheth a garment, and they laid it upon the shoulders of the two of them, and they walked

יח וַהֲווֹ בְנֵי נֹחַ דִּי נְפָקוּ מִן תֵּבוֹתָא שֵׁם וְחָם וָיֶפֶת וְחָם הוּא אֲבוּהִי דִכְנָעַן: יט תְּלָתָא אִלֵּין בְּנֵי נֹחַ וּמֵאִלֵּין אִתְבַּדָּרוּ כָּל אַרְעָא: כ וְשָׁרֵי נֹחַ גְּבַר פָּלַח בְּאַרְעָא וּנְצִיב כַּרְמָא: כא וּשְׁתִי מִן חַמְרָא וּרְוִי וְאִתְגְּלִי בְּגוֹ מַשְׁכְּנֵהּ: כב וַחֲזָא חָם אֲבוּהִי דִכְנַעַן יָת עֶרְיַת אֲבוּהִי וְחַוִּי לִתְרֵין אֲחוֹהִי בְּשׁוּקָא: כג וּנְסֵיב שֵׁם וָיֶפֶת יָת כְּסוּתָא וְשַׁוִּיאוּ עַל כְּתַף תַּרְוֵיהוֹן וַאֲזָלוּ

רש"י

(יח) וחם הוא אבי כנען. למה הולרך לומר כאן. לפי שהפרשה עסוקה ובאה בשכרותו של נח שקלקל בה חם, ועל ידו נתקלל כנען, ועדיין לא כתב תולדות חם ולא ידענו שכנען בנו, לפיכך הולרך לומר כאן וחם הוא אבי כנען: **(כ) ויחל.** עשה עלמו חולין, שהיה לו לעסוק תחלה בנטיעה אחרת (ב"ר לו:ג): **איש האדמה.** אדוני האדמה, כמו איש נעמי (רות א:ג): **ויטע כרם.** כשנכנס לתיבה הכניס עמו זמורות ויחורי תאנים (ב"ר שם): **(כא) אהלה.** אהלה כתיב, רמז לעשרת השבטים שנקראו על שם שומרון שנקראת אהלה, שגלו על עסקי היין, שנאמר השותים במזרקי יין (עמוס ו:ו; ב"ר לו:ד; תנחומא ישן כ): **ויתגל.** לשון ויתפעל: **(כב) וירא חם אבי כנען.** יש מרבותינו אומרים כנען ראה והגיד לאביו, לכך הוזכר על הדבר ונתקלל (תנחומא טו; ב"ר שם ז): **וירא את ערות אביו.** יש מרבותינו אומרים סרסו, וי"א רבעו (סנהדרין ע.): **(כג) ויקח שם ויפת.** אין כתיב ויקחו אלא ויקח, לימד על שם שנתאמץ במלוה יותר מיפת, לכך זכו בניו לטלית של ליצית, ויפת זכה לקבורה לבניו, שנ'

18-27. The intoxication and shame of Noah. The Torah records a shameful event where Noah was humiliated and that resulted in the blessings and curse that influence the trend of history to this very day. Even the greatest people can become degraded if they lose control of themselves, and through the different reactions of his sons and grandson, it shows that crisis brings out the true character of people.

18-19. Noah's sons are mentioned twice in these verses, to stress that one righteous father produced three such radically different sons! Nevertheless, all three — even Ham — were worthy of being saved from the Flood (*R' Hirsch*). *Sforno* adds that God gave His blessing of fruitfulness to all of them as sons of Noah, even the wicked Ham, so that from the three of them the entire world was populated.

The ancients divided three continents: Asia was taken by Shem; Africa by Ham; and Europe by Japheth (*Abarbanel*).

20. וַיָּחֶל נֹחַ — *Noah debased himself.* The translation follows *Rashi*. Noah *debased himself* by craving wine so much that he planted a vineyard before any other trees. Other commentators render this phrase as *Noah began*: Noah was the first one to plant vineyards rather than individual grapevines, so great was his craving for wine.

אִישׁ הָאֲדָמָה — *The man of the earth.* The word אִישׁ implies mastery; Noah was the "master" because the earth had been saved thanks to him (*Rashi*). Alternatively, Noah is associated with the earth because he was skilled at working it (*Ibn Ezra*), or because he devoted himself to cultivating the earth, rather than to building cities (*Ramban*).

22. וַיַּרְא חָם אֲבִי כְנַעַן — *Ham saw — the father of Canaan.* Noah's intoxication caused him to become uncovered, and Ham gazed at him disrespectfully. *R' Hirsch* explains the term עֶרְוָה as shame, not nakedness: Ham enjoyed the sight of his father's dishevelment and drunkenness.

Canaan is associated with the event because he had a part in disgracing Noah. Some of the Sages say that he was the one who saw Noah and ran to tell his father (*Rashi*). According to *Sforno,* Ham gazed at — but did not protest — the indignity that Canaan had perpetrated upon Noah [for according to *Pirkei d'Rabbi Eliezer,* Canaan castrated Noah]. Others maintain that it was Ham who did so (*Rashi).*

Whatever Canaan did to precipitate or aggravate the situation, Ham's conduct was disgraceful, for he entered the tent and leered at Noah's debasement, and then, instead of averting his gaze and covering his father, as his brothers did, he went derisively to tell his brothers.

23. וַיִּקַּח שֵׁם — *And Shem took.* The verb is in the singular

אֲחֹרַנִּית וַיְכַסּוּ אֵת עֶרְוַת אֲבִיהֶם וּפְנֵיהֶם

< their faces << of their father; < the nakedness < and they covered < backward,

אֲחֹרַנִּית וְעֶרְוַת אֲבִיהֶם לֹא רָאוּ: כד וַיִּיקֶץ נֹחַ

< Noah awoke 24 << they saw not. < of their father < and the nakedness < were turned backward,

מִיֵּינוֹ וַיֵּדַע אֵת אֲשֶׁר־עָשָׂה לוֹ בְּנוֹ הַקָּטָן:

<< [by] his small son. < to him < was done < which < that < and he realized < from his wine

כה וַיֹּאמֶר אָרוּר כְּנָעַן עֶבֶד עֲבָדִים יִהְיֶה לְאֶחָיו: כו וַיֹּאמֶר בָּרוּךְ יהוה

< *is* HASHEM, < *Blessed* << And he said, 26 << *to his brothers.* < *shall he be* < *of slaves* < *a slave* << *is Canaan;* < *Cursed* << And he said, 25

אֱלֹהֵי שֵׁם וִיהִי כְנַעַן עֶבֶד לָמוֹ: כז יַפְתְּ אֱלֹהִים לְיֶפֶת וְיִשְׁכֹּן בְּאָהֳלֵי־

< *in the tents* < *but he will dwell* < *Japheth,* < *May God extend* 27 << *to them.* < *be a slave* < *Canaan* < *and let* << *of Shem;* < *the God*

מְחַזְּרִין וַחֲפִיאוּ יָת עֶרְיְתָא דַאֲבוּהוֹן וְאַפֵּיהוֹן מְחַזְּרִין וְעֶרְיְתָא דַאֲבוּהוֹן לָא חֲזוֹ: כד וְאִתְּעַר נֹחַ מֵחַמְרֵהּ וִידַע יָת דִּי עֲבַד לֵהּ בְּרֵהּ זְעֵירָא: כה וַאֲמַר לִיט כְּנָעַן עֶבֶד פָּלַח עַבְדִין יְהֵי לַאֲחוֹהִי: כו וַאֲמַר בְּרִיךְ יְיָ אֱלָהֵהּ דְּשֵׁם וִיהֵי כְּנַעַן עַבְדָּא לְהוֹן: כז יַפְתֵּי יְיָ לְיֶפֶת וְיַשְׁרֵי שְׁכִינְתֵּהּ בְּמַשְׁכְּנֵהּ

רש"י

אתן לגוג מקום שם קבר (יחזקאל לט:יא). והם שבזה את אביו נאמר בזרעו כן ינהג מלך אשור את שבי מצרים ואת גלות כוש נערים וזקנים ערום ויחף וחשופי שת וגו' (ישעיה כ:ד; תנחומא טו; ב"ר שם ו): **ופניהם אחרנית.** למה נאמר פעם שניה, מלמד שכשקרבו אצלו והוצרכו להפוך עצמם לכסותו הפכו פניהם אחורנית: **(כד) בנו הקטן.** הפסול (ב"ר שם ז) והבזוי, כמו הנה קטן נתתיך בגוים בזוי באדם (ירמיה מט:טו): **(כה) ארור כנען.** אתה גרמת לי שלא אוליד בן רביעי אחר לשמשני, ארור בנך רביעי להיות משמש את זרעם של אלו הגדולים שהוטל עליהם טורח עבודתי מעתה (ב"ר שם). ומה ראה חם שסרסו, אמר להם לאחיו, אדם הראשון שני בנים היו לו והרג זה את זה בשביל ירושת העולם (שם כב:ז) ואבינו יש לו ג' בנים ועודנו מבקש בן רביעי (שם לו:ה): **(כו) ברוך ה' אלהי שם.** שעתיד לשמור הבטחתו לזרעו לתת להם את ארץ כנען: **ויהי.** להם כנען למס עובד: **(כז) יפת אלהים ליפת.** מתורגם יפתי, ירחיב (אונקלוס דברים יב:כ): **וישכן באהלי שם.** ישרה שכינתו בישראל

because only Shem took the initiative in this meritorious deed, then Japheth joined him. Therefore, the descendants of Shem (i.e., Jews) were rewarded with the *mitzvah* of fringed garments [*tzitzis*]; those of Japheth with burial in *Eretz Yisrael* [*Ezekiel* 39:11]; those of Ham were eventually *led away by the king of Assyria . . . naked and barefoot* [*Isaiah* 20:4] *(Midrash; Rashi*).

Shem and Japheth draped the garment over their shoulders and walked in backward, averting their gaze; and even when they had to turn around to cover Noah, they looked away (*Rashi*).

24. Although Ham was not the youngest, he is called *small,* because he was *unfit and despicable (Rashi*).

25-27. Noah foretells the destiny of his sons. *R' Hirsch* calls these verses the most far-reaching prophecy ever uttered, for in it Noah encapsulated the entire course of human history.

25. אָרוּר כְּנָעַן — *Cursed is Canaan.* Ham sinned and Canaan is cursed! R' Yehudah explains that God had already blessed Noah and his sons, and there cannot be a curse where a blessing had been given. Therefore Noah cursed his grandson, who, as noted above, was deeply involved in the humiliating incident. R' Nechemiah follows the view cited above that Canaan bore responsibility because he instigated the tragedy (*Midrash*).

Noah foresaw that Canaan's descendants would always be wicked and morally degraded; thus we find the Patriarchs scrupulously avoiding marriage with the accursed Canaanites (*Radak*).

עֶבֶד עֲבָדִים — *A slave of slaves.* The phrase is meant literally, that Canaanites would be enslaved even by people who are themselves subjugated (*Sforno*), or it is a figure of speech meaning that they would be "the lowliest of slaves" (*Ralbag*).

Indisputably, many descendants of Shem and Japheth, too, have been sold into slavery, while not every Canaanite is or was a slave. The curse is that from birth the Canaanites will be steeped in the culture of slavery and not seriously desire freedom. The descendants of Shem and Japheth, however, will have a nobler spirit; they will always crave freedom, even if they are enslaved (*Haamek Davar*).

26. בָּרוּךְ ה' — *Blessed is* HASHEM . . . Noah did not bless Shem directly, but his blessing indicated the nature and striving of Shem. The standard-bearers of Shem would be Israel, for whom the primary goal of life is to serve God and increase His glory in the world. Consequently, when God is blessed, they, too, are exalted.

Though Israel is HASHEM's most devoted servant, He is the universal God, not only Shem's. He is called the God of Shem in the sense that He is called the God of Abraham, Isaac, and Jacob, in that He is especially revealed in their history and because they are the ones who recognized and proclaimed His greatness (*R' Hirsch*).

27. This seminal verse charts the relationship between the two critical factors of human intellect and spirituality. Japheth was blessed with beauty and sensitivity; Shem was blessed with holiness and the Divine Presence. Of the many nations descending from both, the blessing of Japheth took root in ancient Greece and the culture it spawned, while the

שֵׁם וִיהִי כְנַעַן עֶבֶד לָמוֹ: כח וַיְחִי־נֹחַ אַחַר
‹ after ‹ Noah lived 28 « to them. ‹ be a slave ‹ Canaan ‹ may « of Shem;

הַמַּבּוּל שְׁלֹשׁ מֵאוֹת שָׁנָה וַחֲמִשִּׁים שָׁנָה:
« years. ‹ and fifty ‹ years ‹ hundred ‹ three ‹ the Flood

כט וַיְהִי כָּל־יְמֵי־נֹחַ תְּשַׁע מֵאוֹת שָׁנָה וַחֲמִשִּׁים
‹ and fifty ‹ years ‹ hundred ‹ nine « of Noah – ‹ the days ‹ – all « And they were 29

שָׁנָה וַיָּמֹת: פ [י] א וְאֵלֶּה תּוֹלְדֹת בְּנֵי־נֹחַ שֵׁם חָם
‹ Ham, ‹ Shem, « of Noah: ‹ of the sons ‹ the descendants ‹ These are 1 [10] « and he died. « years;

וָיָפֶת וַיִּוָּלְדוּ לָהֶם בָּנִים אַחַר הַמַּבּוּל: ב בְּנֵי יֶפֶת
‹ of Japheth: ‹ The sons 2 « the Flood. ‹ after ‹ sons ‹ to them ‹ there were born « and Japheth;

גֹּמֶר וּמָגוֹג וּמָדַי וְיָוָן וְתֻבָל וּמֶשֶׁךְ וְתִירָס: ג וּבְנֵי גֹּמֶר אַשְׁכְּנַז וְרִיפַת
‹ Riphath, ‹ Ashkenaz, « of Gomer: ‹ The sons 3 « and Tiras. ‹ Meshech, ‹ Tubal, ‹ Javan, ‹ Madai, ‹ Magog, ‹ Gomer,

וְתֹגַרְמָה: ד וּבְנֵי יָוָן אֱלִישָׁה וְתַרְשִׁישׁ כִּתִּים וְדֹדָנִים: ה מֵאֵלֶּה נִפְרְדוּ
‹ were separated ‹ From these 5 « and the Dodanim. ‹ the Kittim « and Tarshish, ‹ Elishah ‹ of Javan: ‹ The sons 4 « and Togarmah.

אִיֵּי הַגּוֹיִם בְּאַרְצֹתָם אִישׁ לִלְשֹׁנוֹ לְמִשְׁפְּחֹתָם בְּגוֹיֵהֶם: ו וּבְנֵי חָם כּוּשׁ
‹ Cush, « of Ham: ‹ The sons 6 « in their nations. ‹ by their families, ‹ according to its language, ‹ – each « in their lands ‹ of the nations ‹ the islands

וּמִצְרַיִם וּפוּט וּכְנָעַן: ז וּבְנֵי כוּשׁ סְבָא וַחֲוִילָה וְסַבְתָּה וְרַעְמָה וְסַבְתְּכָא
« and Sabteca. ‹ Raamah, ‹ Sabtah, ‹ Havilah, ‹ Seba, « of Cush: ‹ The sons 7 « and Canaan. ‹ Put, ‹ Mizraim,

דְשֵׁם וִיהֵי כְנַעַן עַבְדָּא לְהוֹן: כח וַחֲיָא נֹחַ בָּתַר טוֹפָנָא תְּלַת מְאָה וְחַמְשִׁין שְׁנִין: כט וַהֲווֹ כָּל יוֹמֵי נֹחַ תְּשַׁע מְאָה וְחַמְשִׁין שְׁנִין וּמִית: א וְאִלֵּין תּוּלְדַת בְּנֵי נֹחַ שֵׁם חָם וָיֶפֶת וְאִתְיְלִידוּ לְהוֹן בְּנִין בָּתַר טוֹפָנָא: ב בְּנֵי יֶפֶת גּוֹמֶר וּמָגוֹג וּמָדַי וְיָוָן וְתוּבָל וּמֶשֶׁךְ וְתִירָס: ג וּבְנֵי גּוֹמֶר אַשְׁכְּנַז וְרִיפַת וְתוֹגַרְמָה: ד וּבְנֵי יָוָן אֱלִישָׁה וְתַרְשִׁישׁ כִּתִּים וְדֹדָנִים: ה מֵאִלֵּין אִתְפְּרָשׁוּ נַגְוָת עַמְמַיָּא בְּאַרְעֲהוֹן גְּבַר לְלִישָׁנֵהּ לְזַרְעֲיָתְהוֹן בְּעַמְמֵיהוֹן: ו וּבְנֵי חָם כּוּשׁ וּמִצְרַיִם וּפוּט וּכְנָעַן: ז וּבְנֵי כוּשׁ סְבָא וַחֲוִילָה וְסַבְתָּה וְרַעְמָה וְסַבְתְּכָא

רש"י

(אונקלוס). ומדרש חכמים, אע"פ שיפת אלהים ליפת, שכנה כורש שהיה מבני יפת בית שני, לא שרתה בו שכינה, והיכן שרתה, במקדש ראשון שבנה שלמה שהיה מבני שם (יומא י.): ויהי כנען עבד למו. אף משיגלו בני שם ימכרו להם עבדים מבני כנען: (ב) ותירס. זו פרס (שם):

28-29. Noah's death. Noah was born in the year 1056 from Creation, the Flood occurred in 1656, and he died in 2006, ten years after the Dispersion (Chapter 11). Abraham was born in 1948; thus he knew Noah and was 58 years old when Noah died. It is fascinating that from Adam to Abraham, there was a word-of-mouth tradition spanning only four people: Adam, Lamech, Noah, and Abraham [see Time Line, p. 59]. Similarly, Moses, through whom the Torah was given, saw Kohath, who saw Jacob, who saw Abraham. Accordingly, there were not more than seven people who carried the tradition firsthand from Adam to the generation that received the Torah (*Abarbanel*).

blessing of Shem rested on Israel and its immersion in Torah and *mitzvos.* Noah's blessing states that Japheth's gift is important and beautiful, but only if it is placed at the service of the spiritual truths represented by Shem; otherwise it can be not only dissipated but harmful. As *R' Hirsch* puts it, "The seeker of beauty, the artist, is open to external stimuli. He is sensitive and easily moved . . . But the tragedies of history — past and ongoing — bear eloquent testimony to the ongoing truth that perceptions of beauty are not enough. Without an external ideal which controls and directs both the perceptions and expressions of beauty, man descends to immoral unethical hedonism . . . He can build temples of passion and call them tents of a new godliness, golden calves and deify them as the purpose of existence . . ." Such is the beauty of Japheth if it is divorced from the tents of Shem. Together, they are the perfection Noah envisioned; separate, they are the tragedy that fills the history of the world.

10.

☙ The descendants of Noah; the seventy nations.

The Talmudic tradition that there are seventy primary nations is based upon the ensuing list of Noah's descendants

וּבְנֵי רַעְמָה שְׁבָא וּדְדָן׃ ח וְכוּשׁ יָלַד אֶת־נִמְרֹד
« Nimrod. ‹ begot ‹ And Cush **8** « and Dedan. ‹ Sheba « of Raamah: ‹ The sons

הוּא הֵחֵל לִהְיוֹת גִּבֹּר בָּאָרֶץ׃ ט הוּא־הָיָה
‹ was ‹ He **9** « on earth. ‹ a mighty man ‹ to be ‹ was the first ‹ He

גִבֹּר־צַיִד לִפְנֵי יְהֹוָה עַל־כֵּן יֵאָמַר כְּנִמְרֹד גִּבּוֹר
‹ a *mighty* ‹ *Like Nimrod* « it is said: ‹ therefore « HASHEM; ‹ before ‹ hunter ‹ a mighty

צַיִד לִפְנֵי יְהֹוָה׃ י וַתְּהִי רֵאשִׁית מַמְלַכְתּוֹ בָּבֶל
‹ [was] Babel, ‹ of his kingdom ‹ [that] the beginning ‹ It was **10** « *HASHEM.* ‹ *before* ‹ *hunter*

וְאֶרֶךְ וְאַכַּד וְכַלְנֵה בְּאֶרֶץ שִׁנְעָר׃ יא מִן־
‹ From **11** « of Shinar. ‹ in the land ‹ and Calneh ‹ Accad, ‹ Erech,

הָאָרֶץ הַהִוא יָצָא אַשּׁוּר וַיִּבֶן אֶת־נִינְוֵה
‹ Nineveh, ‹ and built ‹ Ashur ‹ went forth ‹ that land

וְאֶת־רְחֹבֹת עִיר וְאֶת־כָּלַח׃ יב וְאֶת־רֶסֶן בֵּין נִינְוֵה וּבֵין כָּלַח הִוא
‹ that is « Calah, ‹ and between ‹ Nineveh ‹ between ‹ and Resen **12** ‹ Calah, ‹ Rehovoth-ir,

הָעִיר הַגְּדֹלָה׃ יג וּמִצְרַיִם יָלַד אֶת־לוּדִים וְאֶת־עֲנָמִים וְאֶת־לְהָבִים
‹ Lehabim, ‹ Anamim, ‹ Ludim, ‹ begot ‹ And Mizraim **13** « that is great. ‹ the city

וְאֶת־נַפְתֻּחִים׃ יד וְאֶת־פַּתְרֻסִים וְאֶת־כַּסְלֻחִים אֲשֶׁר יָצְאוּ מִשָּׁם
‹ from there ‹ came forth ‹ that « and Casluhim, ‹ Pathrusim, **14** ‹ Naphtuhim,

פְּלִשְׁתִּים וְאֶת־כַּפְתֹּרִים׃ ס טו וּכְנַעַן יָלַד אֶת־צִידֹן בְּכֹרוֹ וְאֶת־חֵת׃
« and Heth; ‹ his firstborn, ‹ Zidon ‹ begot ‹ Canaan **15** « and the Caphtorim. ‹ both the Philistines

טז וְאֶת־הַיְבוּסִי וְאֶת־הָאֱמֹרִי וְאֵת הַגִּרְגָּשִׁי׃ יז וְאֶת־הַחִוִּי וְאֶת־הַעַרְקִי
‹ the Arkite, ‹ the Hivite, **17** ‹ the Girgashite, ‹ the Amorite, ‹ and the Jebusite, **16**

וּבְנֵי רַעְמָה שְׁבָא וּדְדָן׃ ח וְכוּשׁ אוֹלִיד יָת נִמְרֹד הוּא שָׁרֵי לְמֶהֱוֵי גִּבַּר (תַּקִּיף) בְּאַרְעָא׃ ט הוּא הֲוָה גִּבַּר תַּקִּיף קֳדָם יְיָ עַל כֵּן יִתְאֲמַר כְּנִמְרֹד גִּבַּר תַּקִּיף קֳדָם יְיָ׃ י וַהֲוָה רֵישׁ מַלְכוּתֵהּ בָּבֶל וְאֶרֶךְ וְאַכַּד וְכַלְנֵה בְּאַרְעָא דְבָבֶל׃ יא מִן אַרְעָא (נ״א עֵיצָה) הַהִיא נְפַק אֲתוּרָאָה וּבְנָא יָת נִינְוֵה וְיָת רְחֹבֹת (נ״א רְחוֹבֵי) קַרְתָּא וְיָת כָּלַח׃ יב וְיָת רֶסֶן בֵּין נִינְוֵה וּבֵין כָּלַח הִיא קַרְתָּא רַבְּתָא׃ יג וּמִצְרַיִם אוֹלִיד יָת לוּדָאֵי וְיָת עֲנָמָאֵי וְיָת לְהָבָאֵי וְיָת נַפְתּוּחָאֵי׃ יד וְיָת פַּתְרוּסָאֵי וְיָת כַּסְלוּחָאֵי דִּי נְפָקוּ מִתַּמָּן פְּלִשְׁתָּאֵי וְיָת קַפּוּטְקָאֵי׃ טו וּכְנַעַן אוֹלִיד יָת צִידוֹן בָּכְרֵהּ וְיָת חֵת׃ טז וְיָת יְבוּסָאֵי וְיָת אֱמוֹרָאֵי וְיָת גִּרְגָּשָׁאֵי׃ יז וְיָת חִוָּאֵי וְיָת עַרְקָאֵי

רש״י

(ח) להיות גבר. להמריד כל העולם על הקדוש ברוך הוא בעצת דור הפלגה (עירובין נג.; חולין פט.): **(ט) גבר ציד.** צד דעתן של בריות בפיו ומטען למרוד במקום (ב״ר לז:ב; תרגום ירושלמי): **לפני ה׳.** מתכוין להקניטו על פניו (ת״כ בחוקותי פרשתא ב:ג): **על כן יאמר.** על כל אדם מרשיע בעזות פנים, יודע רבונו ומתכוין למרוד בו, יאמר, זה כנמרוד גבור ציד (שם): **(יא) מן הארץ.** כיון שראה אשור את בניו שומעין לנמרוד ומורדין במקום לבנות המגדל, יצא מתוכם (ב״ר שם ד; אונקלוס כ״א, ועי׳ תרגום יונתן): **(יב) העיר הגדלה.** היא נינוה, שנא׳ ונינוה היתה עיר גדולה לאלהים (יונה ג:ג; ב״ר שם): **(יג) להבים.** שפניהם דומים ללהב: **(יד) פתרסים ואת כסלחים אשר יצאו משם פלשתים.** משניהם יצאו שהיו פתרוסים וכסלוחים מחליפין משכב נשותיהם אלו לאלו ויצאו מהם פלשתים [וכפתורים] (ב״ר שם):

(*R' Bachya*). For a complete commentary on the identity of these nations in modern terms, see ArtScroll's *Bereishis,* vol. I, pp. 308-332.

8-10. Nimrod. Before Nimrod there were neither wars nor reigning monarchs. He subjugated the Babylonians until they crowned him (v. 10), after which he went to Assyria and built great cities (*Radak; Ramban*). The Torah calls him *a mighty hunter,* which *Rashi* and most commentators interpret figuratively: Nimrod ensnared men with his words and incited them to rebel against God. He was the forerunner of the hypocrite who drapes himself in robes of piety in order to deceive the masses (*R' Hirsch*). His first conquest, which laid the basis for his subsequent empire-building, was Babel, which became the center of Nebuchadnezzar's Babylonian Empire. It was one of the greatest cities of the ancient world.

וְאֶת־הַסִּינִי׃ יח וְאֶת־הָאַרְוָדִי וְאֶת־הַצְּמָרִי
the Sinite, 18 the Arvadite, the Zemarite,

וְאֶת־הַחֲמָתִי וְאַחַר נָפֹצוּ מִשְׁפְּחוֹת הַכְּנַעֲנִי׃
and the Hamathite. Afterward, branched out [did] the families of the Canaanites.

יט וַיְהִי גְּבוּל הַכְּנַעֲנִי מִצִּידֹן בֹּאֲכָה גְרָרָה
19 And it was [extended] – the boundary of the Canaanite – from Zidon going toward Gerar,

עַד־עַזָּה בֹּאֲכָה סְדֹמָה וַעֲמֹרָה וְאַדְמָה וּצְבֹיִם
as far as Gaza; going toward Sodom, Gomorrah, Admah, and Zeboiim,

עַד־לָשַׁע׃ כ אֵלֶּה בְנֵי־חָם לְמִשְׁפְּחֹתָם לִלְשֹׁנֹתָם בְּאַרְצֹתָם בְּגוֹיֵהֶם׃
as far as Lasha. 20 These are the children of Ham, by their families, by their languages, in their lands, in their nations.

ס כא וּלְשֵׁם יֻלַּד גַּם־הוּא אֲבִי כָּל־בְּנֵי־עֵבֶר אֲחִי יֶפֶת הַגָּדוֹל׃
21 And to Shem, were born also to him; [he was] the ancestor of all those who lived on the other side; the brother of Japheth the elder.

כב בְּנֵי שֵׁם עֵילָם וְאַשּׁוּר וְאַרְפַּכְשַׁד וְלוּד וַאֲרָם׃ כג וּבְנֵי אֲרָם עוּץ
22 The sons of Shem: Elam, Ashur, Arpachshad, Lud, and Aram. 23 The sons of Aram: Uz,

וְחוּל וְגֶתֶר וָמַשׁ׃ כד וְאַרְפַּכְשַׁד יָלַד אֶת־שָׁלַח וְשֶׁלַח יָלַד אֶת־עֵבֶר׃
Hul, Gether, and Mash. 24 Arpachshad begot Shelah, and Shelah begot Eber.

וְיָת אַנְתּוֹסָאֵי׃ יח וְיָת אַרְוָדָאֵי וְיָת צְמָרָאֵי וְיָת חֲמָתָאֵי וּבָתַר כֵּן אִתְבַּדָּרוּ זַרְעֲיַת כְּנַעֲנָאֵי׃ יט וַהֲוָה תְּחוּם כְּנַעֲנָאֵי מִצִּידוֹן מָטֵי לִגְרָר עַד עַזָּה מָטֵי לִסְדוֹם וַעֲמוֹרָה וְאַדְמָה וּצְבוֹיִם עַד לָשַׁע׃ כ אִלֵּין בְּנֵי חָם לְזַרְעֲיָתְהוֹן לְלִישָּׁנְהוֹן בְּאַרְעָתְהוֹן בְּעַמְמֵיהוֹן׃ כא וּלְשֵׁם אִתְיְלִיד אַף הוּא אֲבוּהוֹן דְּכָל בְּנֵי עֵבֶר אֲחוּהִי דְּיֶפֶת רַבָּא׃ כב בְּנֵי שֵׁם עֵילָם וְאַשּׁוּר וְאַרְפַּכְשַׁד וְלוּד וַאֲרָם׃ כג וּבְנֵי אֲרָם עוּץ וְחוּל וְגֶתֶר וָמַשׁ׃ כד וְאַרְפַּכְשַׁד אוֹלִיד יָת שָׁלַח וְשֶׁלַח אוֹלִיד יָת עֵבֶר׃

רש"י

(יח) **ואחר נפצו.** מאלה נפוצו משפחות הרבה: (יט) **גבול.** סוף ארצו. כל גבול ל' סוף וקצה: **באכה.** שם דבר. [ול"נ, כאדם האומר לחבירו גבול זה מגיע עד אשר תבא לגבול פלוני]: (כ) **ללשנתם בארצתם.** אע"פ שנחלקו ללשונות וארצות, כלם בני חם הם: (כא) **אבי כל בני עבר** הנהר, היה שֵׁם: **אחי יפת הגדול.** איני יודע אם יפת הגדול אם שם. כשהוא אומר שם בן מאת שנה וגו' שנתים אחר המבול (להלן יא:י) הוי אומר יפת הגדול (ב"ר שם ז), שהרי בן ת"ק שנה היה נח כשהתחיל להוליד והמבול היה בשנת שש מאות שנה לנח, נמצא שהגדול בבניו היה בן מאה שנה, ושם לא הגיע למאה עד שנתים אחר המבול: **אחי יפת.** ולא אחי חם, שאלו שניהם כבדו את אביהם וזה בזהו (עי' תרגום יונתן):

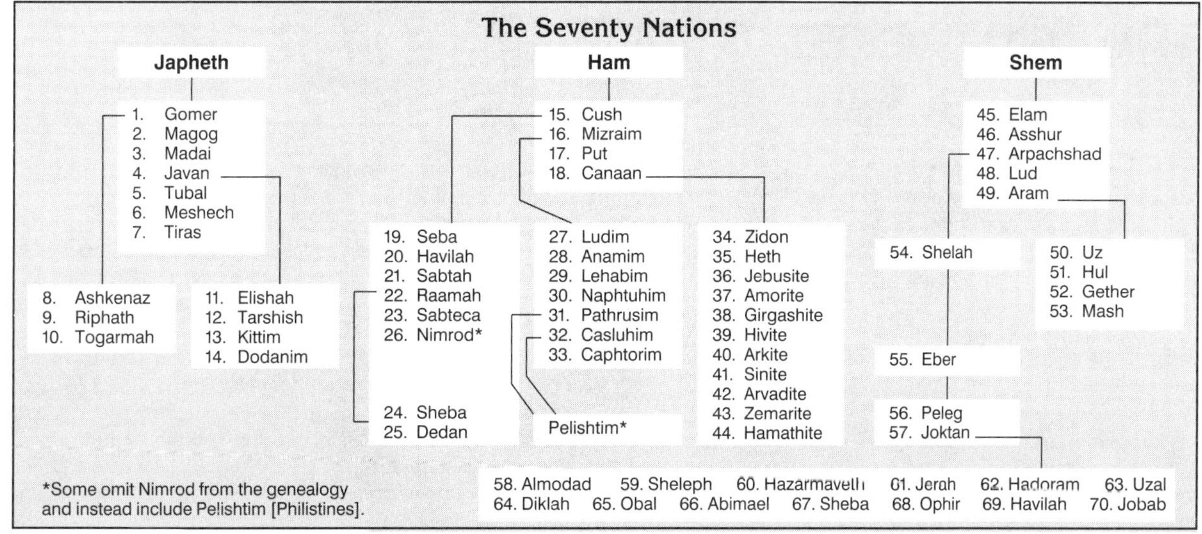

כה וּלְעֵבֶר יֻלַּד שְׁנֵי בָנִים שֵׁם הָאֶחָד פֶּלֶג כִּי

‹ for ‹‹ was Peleg, ‹ of the [first] one ‹ The name ‹‹ sons: ‹ two ‹ were born ‹ And to Eber 25

בְיָמָיו נִפְלְגָה הָאָרֶץ וְשֵׁם אָחִיו יָקְטָן: כו וְיָקְטָן

‹ Joktan 26 ‹‹ was Joktan. ‹ of his brother ‹ and the name ‹‹ was the earth; ‹ divided ‹ in his days

יָלַד אֶת־אַלְמוֹדָד וְאֶת־שָׁלֶף וְאֶת־חֲצַרְמָוֶת

‹ Hazarmaveth, ‹ Sheleph, ‹ Almodad, ‹ begot

וְאֶת־יָרַח: כז וְאֶת־הֲדוֹרָם וְאֶת־אוּזָל וְאֶת־דִּקְלָה:

‹ Diklah, ‹ Uzal, ‹ Hadoram, 27 ‹ Jerah,

כח וְאֶת־עוֹבָל וְאֶת־אֲבִימָאֵל וְאֶת־שְׁבָא:

‹ Sheba, ‹ Abimael, ‹ Obal, 28

כט וְאֶת־אוֹפִר וְאֶת־חֲוִילָה וְאֶת־יוֹבָב כָּל־אֵלֶּה

‹ these ‹ all ‹‹ and Jobab; ‹ Havilah, ‹ Ophir, 29

כה וּלְעֵבֶר אִתְיְלִידוּ תְּרֵין בְּנִין שׁוּם חַד פֶּלֶג אֲרֵי בְּיוֹמוֹהִי אִתְפְּלִיגַת אַרְעָא וְשׁוּם אֲחוּהִי יָקְטָן: כו וְיָקְטָן אוֹלִיד יָת אַלְמוֹדָד וְיָת שָׁלֶף וְיָת חֲצַרְמָוֶת וְיָת יָרַח: כז וְיָת הֲדוֹרָם וְיָת אוּזָל וְיָת דִּקְלָה: כח וְיָת עוֹבָל וְיָת אֲבִימָאֵל וְיָת שְׁבָא: כט וְיָת אוֹפִר וְיָת חֲוִילָה וְיָת יוֹבָב כָּל אִלֵּין בְּנֵי יָקְטָן: ל וַהֲוָה מוֹתְבָנְהוֹן מִמֵּשָׁא מָטֵי לִסְפַר טוּר מָדִינְחָא: לא אִלֵּין בְּנֵי שֵׁם לְזַרְעֲיָתְהוֹן לְלִישָׁנֵיהוֹן לְאַרְעָתְהוֹן לְעַמְמֵיהוֹן: לב אִלֵּין זַרְעֲיַת בְּנֵי נֹחַ לְתוֹלְדָתְהוֹן בְּעַמְמֵיהוֹן וּמֵאִלֵּין אִתַּפְרָשׁוּ עַמְמַיָּא בְּאַרְעָא בָּתַר טוֹפָנָא: א וַהֲוָה כָל אַרְעָא לִישָׁן חָד וּמַמְלַל חָד: ב וַהֲוָה בְּמִטַּלְהוֹן בְּקַדְמֵיתָא וְאַשְׁכָּחוּ בִקְעֲתָא בְּאַרְעָא דְבָבֶל וִיתִיבוּ תַמָּן: ג וַאֲמָרוּ

בְּנֵי יָקְטָן: ל וַיְהִי מוֹשָׁבָם מִמֵּשָׁא בֹּאֲכָה סְפָרָה הַר הַקֶּדֶם: לא אֵלֶּה

‹ These are 31 ‹‹ to the east. ‹ the mountain ‹ Sephar, ‹ going toward ‹ [extended] from Mesha ‹ Their dwelling place was 30 ‹‹ of Joktan. ‹ were the sons

בְנֵי־שֵׁם לְמִשְׁפְּחֹתָם לִלְשֹׁנֹתָם בְּאַרְצֹתָם לְגוֹיֵהֶם: לב אֵלֶּה מִשְׁפְּחֹת

‹ the families ‹ These are 32 ‹‹ by their nations. ‹ in their lands, ‹ by their languages, ‹ according to their families, ‹ of Shem ‹ the children

בְּנֵי־נֹחַ לְתוֹלְדֹתָם בְּגוֹיֵהֶם וּמֵאֵלֶּה נִפְרְדוּ הַגּוֹיִם בָּאָרֶץ אַחַר הַמַּבּוּל:

‹‹ the Flood. ‹ after ‹ on the earth ‹ the nations ‹ were separated ‹ and from these ‹‹ in their nations; ‹ according to their descendants, ‹ of Noah, ‹ of the children

פ שביעי — [יא] א וַיְהִי כָל־הָאָרֶץ שָׂפָה אֶחָת וּדְבָרִים אֲחָדִים: ב וַיְהִי

‹ And it came to pass 2 ‹‹ that were in common. ‹ and of purposes ‹ was of one language ‹ earth ‹ [that] the whole ‹ And it was 1 [11]

בְּנָסְעָם מִקֶּדֶם וַיִּמְצְאוּ בִקְעָה בְּאֶרֶץ שִׁנְעָר וַיֵּשְׁבוּ שָׁם: ג וַיֹּאמְרוּ

‹ They said 3 ‹‹ there. ‹ and settled ‹ of Shinar ‹ in the land ‹ a valley ‹ they found ‹‹ from the east, ‹ when they migrated

רש"י

(כה) **נפלגה.** נתבלבלו הלשונות ונפוצו מן הבקעה ונתפלגו בכל העולם. למדנו שהיה עבר נביא, שקרא שם בנו ע"ש העתיד (ב"ר שם). ושנינו בסדר עולם (פרק א) שבסוף ימיו נתפלגו, שא"ת בתחלת ימיו, הרי יקטן אחיו לעיר ממנו והוליד כמה משפחות קודם לכן, שנא' ויקטן ילד וגו'. וא"כ ויהי כל הארץ וגו'. וא"ת באמצע ימיו, לא בא הכתוב לסתום אלא לפרש, הא למדת שבשנת מות פלג נתפלגו: **יקטן.** שהיה ענו ומקטין עצמו (ב"ר שם) לכך זכה להעמיד כל המשפחות הללו: (כו) **חצרמות.** ע"ש מקומו. דברי אגדה (שם):

(א) **שפה אחת.** לשון הקודש (תנחומא יט; תרגום יונתן; ירושלמי מגילה א:ט): **ודברים אחדים.** באו בעצה אחת ואמרו, לא כל הימנו שיבור לו את העליונים, נעלה לרקיע ונעשה עמו מלחמה. ד"א, על יחידו של עולם (תנחומא ישן כד). ד"א, ודברים אחדים [ס"א דברים חדים], אמרו אחת לאלף ותרנ"ו שנים הרקיע מתמוטט כשם שעשה בימי המבול, בואו ונעשה לו סמוכות. ב"ר (לח:ו): (ב) **בנסעם מקדם.** שהיו יושבים שם, כדכתיב למעלה (י:ל) ויהי מושבם וגו' הר הקדם, ונסעו משם לתור להם

11.

1-9. The Tower of Babel and the Dispersion. *Rambam* in *Moreh Nevuchim* states that a fundamental principle of the Torah is that the universe was created *ex nihilo,* and Adam was the forerunner of the human race. Since the human race was later dispersed over all the earth, and divided into different families speaking very dissimilar languages, people might come to doubt that they could all have originated

אִישׁ אֶל־רֵעֵהוּ הָבָה נִלְבְּנָה לְבֵנִים וְנִשְׂרְפָה
‹ and burn ‹ bricks ‹ let us make ‹ Come, «his companion, ‹ to ‹ [each] man

לִשְׂרֵפָה וַתְּהִי לָהֶם הַלְּבֵנָה לְאָבֶן וְהַחֵמָר הָיָה
‹ served ‹ and the bitumen « as stone, « — the brick — « them ‹ And it served « *[them] in fire.*

לָהֶם לַחֹמֶר׃ ד וַיֹּאמְרוּ הָבָה ׀ נִבְנֶה־לָּנוּ עִיר
« *a city,* ‹ *us* ‹ *let us build* ‹ *Come,* « And they said, 4 « as mortar. ‹ them

וּמִגְדָּל וְרֹאשׁוֹ בַשָּׁמַיִם וְנַעֲשֶׂה־לָּנוּ שֵׁם פֶּן־
‹ *lest* « *a name,* ‹ *for ourselves* ‹ *and let us make* « *in the heavens,* ‹ *with its top* ‹ *and a tower*

נָפוּץ עַל־פְּנֵי כָל־הָאָרֶץ׃ ה וַיֵּרֶד יהוה לִרְאֹת אֶת־הָעִיר וְאֶת־הַמִּגְדָּל
‹ and the tower ‹ the city ‹ to look at ‹ HASHEM descended 5 « *earth.* ‹ *of the whole* ‹ *the face* ‹ *across* ‹ *we be dispersed*

אֲשֶׁר בָּנוּ בְּנֵי הָאָדָם׃ ו וַיֹּאמֶר יהוה הֵן עַם אֶחָד וְשָׂפָה אַחַת לְכֻלָּם
« *for all,* ‹ *with one language* ‹ *they are one people* ‹ *Indeed,* « HASHEM said, 6 « of man. ‹ [by] the sons ‹ was built ‹ which

וְזֶה הַחִלָּם לַעֲשׂוֹת וְעַתָּה לֹא־יִבָּצֵר מֵהֶם כֹּל אֲשֶׁר יָזְמוּ לַעֲשׂוֹת׃
« *to do?* ‹ *they proposed* ‹ *that* ‹ *— all* « *from them* ‹ *be withheld* ‹ *should [it] not* ‹ *And now,* « *to do!* ‹ *they begin* ‹ *and this*

גְּבַר לְחַבְרֵהּ הָבוּ נִרְמֵי לִבְנִין וְנִשְׂרְפִנּוּן בְּנוּרָא (יְקֵדְתָּא) וַהֲוַת לְהוֹן לִבְנְתָא לְאַבְנָא וְחֵימָרָא הֲוַת לְהוֹן לְשִׁיעַ׃ ד וַאֲמָרוּ הָבוּ נִבְנֵי לָנָא קַרְתָּא וּמַגְדְּלָא וְרֵישֵׁהּ מָטֵי עַד צֵית שְׁמַיָּא וְנַעְבֵּיד לָנָא שׁוּם דִּילְמָא נִתְבַּדַּר עַל אַפֵּי כָל אַרְעָא׃ ה וְאִתְגְּלִי יְיָ לְאִתְפְּרָעָא עַל עוֹבָדֵי קַרְתָּא וּמַגְדְּלָא דִּי בְנוֹ בְּנֵי אֲנָשָׁא׃ ו וַאֲמַר יְיָ הָא עַמָּא חַד וְלִישָּׁן חַד לְכָלְּהוֹן וְדֵין דְּשָׁרִיוּ לְמֶעְבַּד וּכְעַן לָא יִתְמְנַע מִנְּהוֹן כֹּל דִּי חַשִּׁיבוּ לְמֶעְבַּד׃

רש"י

מקום להחזיק את כלם, ולא מצאו אלא שנער (ב"ר שם ז): (ג) **איש אל רעהו.** אומה לאומה, מצרים לכוש (שם ח) וכוש לפוט ופוט לכנען (תנחומא יח): **הבה.** הזמינו עצמכם. כל הבה לשון הזמנה הוא, שמכינים עצמן ומתחברים למלאכה או לעצה או למשא. הבה, הזמינו, אפרליי"ר בלעז: **לבנים.** שאין אבנים בבבל (במ"ר יד:ג) שהיא בקעה: **ונשרפה לשרפה.** כך עושין הלבנים שקורים טיול"ש בלע"ז, שורפים אותם בכבשן: **לחמר.** לטוח הקיר: (ד) **פן נפוץ.** שלא יביא עלינו שום מכה להפיצנו מכאן: (ה) **וירד ה' לראות.** לא הוצרך לכך אלא בא ללמד לדיינים שלא ירשיעו הנידון עד שיראו ויבינו. מדרש רבי תנחומא (שם): **בני האדם.** אלא בני מי, שמא בני חמורים וגמלים, אלא בני אדם הראשון שכפר [ס"א שכפה] את הטובה ואמר האשה אשר נתתה עמדי (לעיל ג:יב) אף אלו כפ[ר]ו בטובה למרוד במי שהשפיעם טובה ומלטם מן המבול: (ו) **הן עם אחד.** כל טובה זו יש עמהן שעם אחד הם **ושפה אחת לכולם,** ודבר זה החלו לעשות: **החלם.** כמו אמרם, עשותם, להתחיל הם לעשות: **לא יבצר מהם וגו' לעשות.** בתמיה. יבצר ל' מניעה כתרגומו, ודומה לו יבצור רוח נגידים (תהלים עו:יג):

from one person. Therefore the Torah records the genealogy of the nations, why they were dispersed, and the cause of the formation of their different languages.

The year of the following narrative is 1996 from Creation, 340 years after the Flood. Noah and his children were still alive at the time, and Abraham, 48 years old, had already recognized his Creator (*Seder Olam*). All the national families were concentrated in present-day Iraq [בָּבֶל] and they all spoke *one language,* the Holy Tongue (*Rashi*), the language with which the world was created (*Mizrachi*).

All the ingredients for greatness were there: The nations were united, they were in a central location, they spoke the Holy Tongue, and — if they desired guidance in achieving holiness — they had Noah, Shem, and Abraham among them. Instead, as happens so often in human history, they chose to ignore their spiritual advantages and turn to their opportunities for self-aggrandizement and power. It seems ludicrous that people who had firsthand evidence of the Flood could have found grounds to rationalize a way of bypassing God's control of events, but such is man's capacity for self-deception that he can negate reality and build substance around a vacuum.

According to the Sages, Nimrod was the primary force behind this rebellion. He planned to build a tower ascending to Heaven and, from it, wage war against God. But though the Midrashim perceive sinister and idolatrous motives in this plan, the verses do not reveal the evil motives of the conspirators. As for the memory of the Flood — which should have frightened them from confronting God — the builders of the tower rationalized that such an upheaval occurs only once every 1656 years, so that they had nothing to fear from Divine intervention for another 1316 years, by which time they would have waged their "war" against God and won.

5. וַיֵּרֶד ה' — *HASHEM descended.* This is an obvious anthropomorphism [the figurative assignment of human characteristics to God]. When God wishes to examine the deeds of lowly

ז הבה נרדה ונבלה שם שפתם אשר לא ישמעו
< there should be no understanding < that << their language, < there < and confuse < let us descend < Come, 7
איש שפת רעהו: ח ויפץ יהוה אתם משם על־פני
< the face < over < from there < them < And HASHEM dispersed 8 << of his companion. < of the language < [by] one person
כל־הארץ ויחדלו לבנת העיר: ט על־כן קרא
< [they] called < that reason < For 9 << the city. < building < and they stopped << earth; < of the whole
שמה בבל כי־שם בלל יהוה שפת כל־הארץ ומשם הפיצם יהוה
< HASHEM dispersed them < and from there << earth, < of the whole < the language < that HASHEM confused < it was there < because << Babel, < its name
על־פני כל־הארץ: פ י אלה תולדת שם שם בן־מאת שנה ויולד
< when he begot < years < of one hundred < was of the age < Shem << of Shem: < are the descendants < These 10 << earth. < of the whole < the face < over
את־ארפכשד שנתים אחר המבול: יא ויחי־שם אחרי הולידו
< his begetting < after < And Shem lived 11 << the Flood. < after < two years << Arpachshad,

ז הָבוּ נִתְגְּלֵי וּנְבַלְבֵּל תַּמָּן לִישָׁנְהוֹן דִּי לָא יִשְׁמְעוּן גְּבַר (נ״א אֱנָשׁ) לִישַׁן חַבְרֵהּ: ח וּבַדַּר יְיָ יָתְהוֹן מִתַּמָּן עַל אַפֵּי כָל אַרְעָא וּמְנָעוּ לְמִבְנֵי (נ״א וְאִתְמְנָעוּ מִלְּמִבְנֵי) קַרְתָּא: ט עַל כֵּן קְרָא שְׁמַהּ בָּבֶל אֲרֵי תַמָּן בַּלְבֵּל יְיָ לִישַׁן כָּל אַרְעָא וּמִתַּמָּן בַּדָּרִנּוּן יְיָ עַל אַפֵּי כָּל אַרְעָא: י אִלֵּין תּוֹלְדַת שֵׁם שֵׁם בַּר מְאָה שְׁנִין וְאוֹלִיד יָת אַרְפַּכְשָׁד תַּרְתֵּין שְׁנִין בָּתַר טוֹפָנָא: יא וַחֲיָא שֵׁם בָּתַר דְּאוֹלִיד

רש״י

(ז) **הבה נרדה.** בבית דינו נמלך מענותנותו יתירה (ב״ר ח:ח; סנהדרין לח:): **הבה.** מדה כנגד מדה. הם אמרו הבה נבנה, והוא כנגדם מדד ואמר הבה נרדה (תנחומא ישן כה): **ונבלה.** ונבלבל (אונקלוס). נו״ן משמש בלשון רבים וה״א אחרונה יתירה כה״א של נרדה: **לא ישמעו.** זה שואל לבינה וזה מביא טיט, וזה עומד עליו ופוצע את מוחו (ב״ר לח:י): (ח) **ויפץ ה׳ אותם משם.** בעוה״ז (סנהדרין קז:). מה שאמרו פן נפוץ נתקיים עליהם, הוא שאמר שלמה מגורת רשע היא תבואנו (משלי י:כד; תנחומא שם): (ט) **ומשם הפיצם.** למד שאין להם חלק לעוה״ב (סנהדרין שם). וכי איזו קשה, של דור המבול או של דור הפלגה. אלו לא פשטו יד בעיקר להלחם בו ואלו פשטו יד בעיקר להלחם בו, ואלו נשטפו, ואלו לא נאבדו מן העולם. אלא שדור המבול היו גזלנים והיתה מריבה ביניהם, לכך נאבדו, ואלו היו נוהגים אהבה וריעות ביניהם, שנא׳ שפה אחת ודברים אחדים. למדת ששנאוי המחלוקת וגדול השלום (ב״ר לח:ו): (י) **שם בן מאת שנה. כשהוליד את ארפכשד שנתים אחר המבול** (תרגום יונתן):

man, Scripture calls it *descent (Radak)*. From God's "descent" to observe conditions among the sinners of Babel, the Midrash derives that a judge must not condemn the accused until he has investigated the case fully.

It may be that the actual construction of the city and tower were not sins, but that they would have led to sins that the Torah does not spell out. That is why the next verse speaks of what they *propose* to do (*HaK'sav V'HaKabbalah*). Indeed, *Malbim* contends that the actual sins that may have been committed were secondary. The primary importance of the incident was that it resulted in the dispersion of the families and the formation of a multitude of languages. As explained by *Rambam* [see introduction to this chapter], this is why the Torah recorded the event.

7. הָבָה נֵרְדָה — *Come, let us descend.* The plural indicates that God deliberated with His Celestial Court (*Rashi*). God does not need the advice of the angels, of course, but He consulted, as it were, to set an example that people should show courtesy to others by involving them in discussions, and that it is unwise for people to take decisions upon themselves without consulting others.

7-8. Since their unity had led them to this course of action and made its success possible, Hashem said that He would destroy their unity (*Akeidas Yitzchak*). *Ramban* notes Kabbalistically that this generation attempted to "mutilate the shoots," i.e., disrupt the unity between Hashem and His Creation; therefore an appropriate "measure for measure" punishment was dispersion, which would disrupt *their* unity.

What they had feared when they said, *lest we be dispersed* [v. 4], now actually happened (*Rashi*).

9. *Rashi* queries: Whose sin was greater — the generation of the Flood, which did not plan a rebellion against God, or the generation of the Dispersion, which did? The former, who were robbers and contended with one another, were utterly destroyed in the Flood, while the latter, who dwelt amicably in brotherly love toward one another, were spared despite their blasphemies. This demonstrates how hateful is strife and how great is peace!

10-32. The ten generations from Noah to Abraham. "There were ten generations from Noah to Abraham. This demonstrates how patient God is, for all the generations kept provoking Him, until the Patriarch Abraham came and received the reward of them all" (*Avos* 5:2). The cycle was repeated. There had been ten generations from Adam to Noah, giving mankind the opportunity to fulfill its responsi-

אֶת־אַרְפַּכְשָׁד חֲמֵשׁ מֵאוֹת שָׁנָה וַיּוֹלֶד בָּנִים
< sons < and he begot << years, < hundred < five < Arpachshad

וּבָנוֹת: ס יב וְאַרְפַּכְשַׁד חַי חָמֵשׁ וּשְׁלֹשִׁים שָׁנָה
< years < thirty-five < lived < Arpachshad 12 << and daughters.

וַיּוֹלֶד אֶת־שָׁלַח: יג וַיְחִי אַרְפַּכְשַׁד אַחֲרֵי הוֹלִידוֹ
< his begetting < after < And Arpachshad lived 13 << Shelah. < and then he begot

אֶת־שֶׁלַח שָׁלֹשׁ שָׁנִים וְאַרְבַּע מֵאוֹת שָׁנָה וַיּוֹלֶד
< and he begot << years, < hundred < and four < years < three < Shelah;

בָּנִים וּבָנוֹת: ס יד וְשֶׁלַח חַי שְׁלֹשִׁים שָׁנָה וַיּוֹלֶד
< and then he begot < years < thirty < lived < Shelah 14 << and daughters. < sons

אֶת־עֵבֶר: טו וַיְחִי־שֶׁלַח אַחֲרֵי הוֹלִידוֹ אֶת־עֵבֶר
< Eber, < his begetting < after < And Shelah lived 15 << Eber.

שָׁלֹשׁ שָׁנִים וְאַרְבַּע מֵאוֹת שָׁנָה וַיּוֹלֶד בָּנִים
< sons < and he begot << years, < hundred < and four < years < three

וּבָנוֹת: ס טז וַיְחִי־עֵבֶר אַרְבַּע וּשְׁלֹשִׁים שָׁנָה וַיּוֹלֶד אֶת־פָּלֶג:
<< Peleg. < and then he begot < years < thirty-four < Eber lived 16 << and daughters.

יז וַיְחִי־עֵבֶר אַחֲרֵי הוֹלִידוֹ אֶת־פֶּלֶג שְׁלֹשִׁים שָׁנָה וְאַרְבַּע מֵאוֹת שָׁנָה
<< years, < hundred < and four < years < thirty < Peleg < his begetting < after < And Eber lived 17

וַיּוֹלֶד בָּנִים וּבָנוֹת: ס יח וַיְחִי־פֶלֶג שְׁלֹשִׁים שָׁנָה וַיּוֹלֶד אֶת־רְעוּ:
<< Reu. < and then he begot < years, < thirty < Peleg lived 18 << and daughters. < sons < and he begot

יט וַיְחִי־פֶלֶג אַחֲרֵי הוֹלִידוֹ אֶת־רְעוּ תֵּשַׁע שָׁנִים וּמָאתַיִם שָׁנָה וַיּוֹלֶד
< and he begot << years, < and two hundred < years < nine < Reu < his begetting < after < And Peleg lived 19

בָּנִים וּבָנוֹת: ס כ וַיְחִי רְעוּ שְׁתַּיִם וּשְׁלֹשִׁים שָׁנָה וַיּוֹלֶד אֶת־שְׂרוּג:
<< Serug. < and then he begot < years, < thirty-two < Reu lived 20 << and daughters. < sons

כא וַיְחִי רְעוּ אַחֲרֵי הוֹלִידוֹ אֶת־שְׂרוּג שֶׁבַע שָׁנִים וּמָאתַיִם שָׁנָה וַיּוֹלֶד
< and he begot << years, < and two hundred < years < seven < Serug < his begetting < after < And Reu lived 21

יָת אַרְפַּכְשַׁד חֲמֵשׁ מְאָה שְׁנִין
וְאוֹלִיד בְּנִין וּבְנָן: יב וְאַרְפַּכְשַׁד חֲיָא
תְּלָתִין וַחֲמֵשׁ שְׁנִין וְאוֹלִיד יָת
שָׁלַח: יג וַחֲיָא אַרְפַּכְשַׁד בָּתַר
דְּאוֹלִיד יָת שֶׁלַח אַרְבַּע מְאָה
וּתְלָת שְׁנִין וְאוֹלִיד בְּנִין וּבְנָן:
יד וְשֶׁלַח חֲיָא תְּלָתִין שְׁנִין וְאוֹלִיד
יָת עֵבֶר: טו וַחֲיָא שֶׁלַח בָּתַר דְּאוֹלִיד
יָת עֵבֶר אַרְבַּע מְאָה וּתְלָת שְׁנִין
וְאוֹלִיד בְּנִין וּבְנָן: טז וַחֲיָא עֵבֶר
תְּלָתִין וְאַרְבַּע שְׁנִין וְאוֹלִיד יָת פֶּלֶג:
יז וַחֲיָא עֵבֶר בָּתַר דְּאוֹלִיד יָת
פֶּלֶג אַרְבַּע מְאָה וּתְלָתִין שְׁנִין
וְאוֹלִיד בְּנִין וּבְנָן: יח וַחֲיָא פֶּלֶג
תְּלָתִין שְׁנִין וְאוֹלִיד יָת רְעוּ: יט וַחֲיָא
פֶּלֶג בָּתַר דְּאוֹלִיד יָת רְעוּ מָאתָן
וּתְשַׁע שְׁנִין וְאוֹלִיד בְּנִין וּבְנָן: כ וַחֲיָא
רְעוּ תְּלָתִין וְתַרְתֵּין שְׁנִין וְאוֹלִיד יָת
שְׂרוּג: כא וַחֲיָא רְעוּ בָּתַר דְּאוֹלִיד יָת
שְׂרוּג מָאתָן וּשְׁבַע שְׁנִין וְאוֹלִיד

---

bility to carry out the plan of Creation. They failed, and the Flood wiped them away. Then the mission of humanity fell to Noah and his offspring. The next ten generations failed as well, but this time Abraham was able to prevent destruction. So great was he and so concerned with helping others that he was able to save the world. Simultaneously, he assumed the role that had previously been that of the entire race: He and his offspring would be the people of God and bear the primary responsibility for bringing the Divine plan to fruition. The children of Noah would be left with the seven universal commandments, but Abraham's would accept the Torah with its 613 commandments.

19. With Peleg, the human life span shortened dramatically. His father lived for 464 years, while he died at only 239. Since the Torah notes that the Dispersion took place in Peleg's time (10:25), *Sforno* (ibid.) conjectures that the cause of this change was that the people were suddenly cast into unfamiliar climates, and this sapped their vitality.

בָּנִים וּבָנוֹת: ס כב וַיְחִי שְׂרוּג שְׁלֹשִׁים שָׁנָה וַיּוֹלֶד
sons and daughters. 22 Serug lived thirty years, and then he begot

אֶת־נָחוֹר: כג וַיְחִי שְׂרוּג אַחֲרֵי הוֹלִידוֹ אֶת־נָחוֹר
Nahor. 23 And Serug lived after his begetting Nahor

מָאתַיִם שָׁנָה וַיּוֹלֶד בָּנִים וּבָנוֹת: ס כד וַיְחִי נָחוֹר
two hundred years, and he begot sons and daughters. 24 Nahor lived

תֵּשַׁע וְעֶשְׂרִים שָׁנָה וַיּוֹלֶד אֶת־תָּרַח: כה וַיְחִי נָחוֹר
twenty-nine years, and then he begot Terah. 25 And Nahor lived

אַחֲרֵי הוֹלִידוֹ אֶת־תֶּרַח תְּשַׁע־עֶשְׂרֵה שָׁנָה
after his begetting Terah, nineteen years

וּמְאַת שָׁנָה וַיּוֹלֶד בָּנִים וּבָנוֹת: ס כו וַיְחִי־תֶרַח שִׁבְעִים שָׁנָה וַיּוֹלֶד
and one hundred years, and he begot sons and daughters. 26 Terah lived seventy years, and then he begot

אֶת־אַבְרָם אֶת־נָחוֹר וְאֶת־הָרָן: כז וְאֵלֶּה תּוֹלְדֹת תֶּרַח תֶּרַח הוֹלִיד
Abram, Nahor, and Haran. 27 Now these are the descendants of Terah: Terah begot

אֶת־אַבְרָם אֶת־נָחוֹר וְאֶת־הָרָן וְהָרָן הוֹלִיד אֶת־לוֹט: כח וַיָּמָת הָרָן
Abram, Nahor, and Haran; and Haran begot Lot. 28 Haran died

עַל־פְּנֵי תֶּרַח אָבִיו בְּאֶרֶץ מוֹלַדְתּוֹ בְּאוּר כַּשְׂדִּים: מפטיר – כט וַיִּקַּח אַבְרָם
in the lifetime of Terah his father, in the land of his birth, in Ur Kasdim. 29 And Abram took

בְּנִין וּבְנָן: כב וַחֲיָא שְׂרוּג תְּלָתִין
שְׁנִין וְאוֹלִיד יָת נָחוֹר: כג וַחֲיָא
שְׂרוּג בָּתַר דְּאוֹלִיד יָת נָחוֹר מָאתָן
שְׁנִין וְאוֹלִיד בְּנִין וּבְנָן: כד וַחֲיָא
נָחוֹר עַשְׂרִין וּתְשַׁע שְׁנִין וְאוֹלִיד
יָת תָּרַח: כה וַחֲיָא נָחוֹר בָּתַר דְּאוֹלִיד
יָת תֶּרַח מְאָה וּתְשַׁע עֲשַׂר שְׁנִין
וְאוֹלִיד בְּנִין וּבְנָן: כו וַחֲיָא תֶרַח
שִׁבְעִין שְׁנִין וְאוֹלִיד יָת אַבְרָם
יָת נָחוֹר וְיָת הָרָן: כז וְאִלֵּין תּוּלְדָת
תֶּרַח תֶּרַח אוֹלִיד יָת אַבְרָם
יָת נָחוֹר וְיָת הָרָן וְהָרָן אוֹלִיד
יָת לוֹט: כח וּמִית הָרָן עַל אַפֵּי
תֶּרַח אֲבוּהִי בְּאַרַע יַלָּדוּתֵהּ
בְּאוּרָא דְכַסְדָּאֵי: כט וּנְסִיב אַבְרָם

רש"י

(כח) **על פני תרח אביו.** בחיי אביו (תנחומא אחרי ז). ומ"א אומר, ע"י אביו מת, שקבל תרח על אברם בנו לפני נמרוד על שכתת את צלמיו, והשליכו לכבשן האש, והרן יושב ואומר בלבו, אם אברם נוצח אני משלו, ואם נמרוד נוצח אני משלו. וכשניצל אברם אמרו לו להרן משל מי אתה, אמר להם הרן משל אברם אני. השליכוהו לכבשן האש ונשרף וזהו אור כשדים (ב"ר שם יג). ומנחם פירש אור בקעה, וכן באורים כבדו ה' (ישעיה כד:יד), וכן מאורת צפעוני (שם יא:ח). כל חור ובקע עמוק קרוי אור:

26. Birth of Abraham. In a real sense, Creation now begins anew, for it was Abraham who would bear the burden of holiness in the world. His name signified this. At first he was Abram, a contraction of אַב אֲרָם, *father [i.e., teacher] of Aram,* for he began as a leader of only his own nation, but ultimately he became a father to the whole world [see 17:5] (*Rashi*).

The Talmud [*Bava Basra* 91a] records that Abraham's mother was Amathlai, daughter of Karnebo.

27. תֶּרַח תֶּרַח — *Terah: Terah*. The Midrash notes that anyone whose name is repeated has a share in the World to Come. But Terah was an idolater! This indicates that he ultimately repented and earned a share in the World to Come!

28. וַיָּמָת הָרָן עַל־פְּנֵי תֶּרַח – *Haran died in the lifetime* [lit., *in the presence*] *of Terah his father.* The translation follows *Rashi.* According to *Midrash Tanchuma,* Terah saw him die.

Rashi adds that, Midrashically, the phrase signifies that Haran died מִפְּנֵי, *because of,* Terah. Terah, who was a manufacturer and seller of idols, complained to Nimrod that Abraham had smashed his wares, so Nimrod had Abraham thrown into a fiery furnace. Haran was challenged to choose between Abraham and Nimrod. He did not know with whom to side, and decided to join whoever emerged victorious. When Abraham was miraculously saved from the fire, Haran sided with him, whereupon Haran was thrown into the furnace. Since Haran was willing to defy Nimrod not because of his belief but because he expected a miracle, he was unworthy of one; thus he died in *Ur Kasdim,* literally the *fire* of the land of Kasdim [Chaldea].

29. וַיִּקַּח אַבְרָם — *And Abram took.* When Haran died, his brothers, Abraham and Nahor, married his daughters to carry on his memory and to assuage Terah's grief (*Imrei Shefer*).

וְנָחוֹר לָהֶם נָשִׁים שֵׁם אֵשֶׁת־אַבְרָם שָׂרָי וְשֵׁם

as did Nahor › for themselves › wives; »the name › of the wife › of Abram › was Sarai. » and the name ›

אֵשֶׁת־נָחוֹר מִלְכָּה בַּת־הָרָן אֲבִי־מִלְכָּה וַאֲבִי

of the wife › of Nahor › was Milcah, › the daughter › of Haran, › the father › of Milcah › and the father ›

30 יִסְכָּה: ל וַתְּהִי שָׂרַי עֲקָרָה אֵין לָהּ וָלָד:

of Iscah. » 30 And Sarai was › barren, » she had no › child. »

31 לא וַיִּקַּח תֶּרַח אֶת־אַבְרָם בְּנוֹ וְאֶת־לוֹט בֶּן־הָרָן

31 Terah took › Abram › his son, › and Lot › the son › of Haran, »

בֶּן־בְּנוֹ וְאֵת שָׂרַי כַּלָּתוֹ אֵשֶׁת אַבְרָם בְּנוֹ וַיֵּצְאוּ אִתָּם מֵאוּר כַּשְׂדִּים

his grandson, » and Sarai › his daughter-in-law, › the wife › of Abram › his son, » and they departed › with them › from Ur › Kasdim ›

32 לָלֶכֶת אַרְצָה כְּנַעַן וַיָּבֹאוּ עַד־חָרָן וַיֵּשְׁבוּ שָׁם: לב וַיִּהְיוּ יְמֵי־תֶרַח חָמֵשׁ

to go › toward the land › of Canaan; » they arrived › at › Haran › and they settled › there. » 32 And they were » the days — › of Terah — » five ›

שָׁנִים וּמָאתַיִם שָׁנָה וַיָּמָת תֶּרַח בְּחָרָן: פפפ קנ"ג פסוקים. בצלא"ל סימן. אב"י יסכ"ה לו"ט סימן.

years › and two hundred › years, » and Terah died › in Haran. »

THE HAFTARAH FOR NOACH APPEARS ON PAGE 324.

When Rosh Chodesh Cheshvan coincides with Noach, the regular Maftir and Haftarah are replaced with the readings for Shabbas Rosh Chodesh: Maftir, page 325 (28:9-15); Haftarah, page 352.

וְנָחוֹר לְהוֹן נְשִׁין שׁוּם אִתַּת אַבְרָם שָׂרַי וְשׁוּם אִתַּת נָחוֹר מִלְכָּה בַּת הָרָן אֲבוּהָא דְמִלְכָּה וַאֲבוּהָא דְיִסְכָּה: ל וַהֲוָת שָׂרַי עֲקָרָה לֵית לַהּ וְלָד: לא וּדְבַר תֶּרַח יָת אַבְרָם בְּרֵהּ וְיָת לוֹט בַּר הָרָן בַּר בְּרֵהּ וְיָת שָׂרַי כַּלְּתֵהּ אִתַּת אַבְרָם בְּרֵהּ וּנְפַקוּ עִמְּהוֹן מֵאוּרָא דְכַסְדָּאֵי לְמֵיזַל לְאַרְעָא דִכְנַעַן וַאֲתוֹ עַד חָרָן וִיתִיבוּ תַמָּן: לב וַהֲווֹ יוֹמֵי תֶרַח מָאתַן וַחֲמֵשׁ שְׁנִין וּמִית תֶּרַח בְּחָרָן:

רש"י

(כט) **יסכה.** זו שרה, על שם שסוכה ברוח הקודש, ושהכל סוכין ביפיה (מגילה יד.) [ס"א כמו שנאמר ויראו אותה שרי פרעה (להלן יב:טו)]. ועוד, יסכה הוא לשון נסיכות, כמו שרה לשון שררה (ברכות יג.): (לא) **ויצאו אתם.** ויצאו תרח ואברם עם לוט ושרי: (לב) **וימת תרח בחרן.** לאחר שיצא אברם מחרן ובא לארץ כנען והיה שם יותר משׁשים שנה, שהרי כתיב ואברם בן חמש שנים ושבעים שנה בצאתו מחרן (להלן יב:ד) ותרח בן שבעים שנה היה כשנולד אברם, הרי קמ"ה לתרח כשיצא אברם מחרן, עדיין נשארו משנותיו הרבה. ולמה הקדים הכתוב מיתתו של תרח ליציאתו של אברם, שלא יהא הדבר מפורסם לכל ויאמרו לא קיים אברם את כבוד אביו שהניחו זקן והלך לו, לפיכך קראו הכ' מת, [ועוד] שהרשעים אף בחייהם קרוים מתים והצדיקים אף במיתתן קרוים חיים, שנאמר ובניהו בן יהוידע בן איש חי (שמואל ב כג:כ; ב"ר לט:ז; ברכות יח.-יח:): **בחרן.** הנו"ן הפוכה, לומר לך עד אברם חרון אף של מקום בעולם (ספרי האזינו שיח):

שָׂרָי — *Sarai.* Her name was later changed to Sarah [17:15]. Just as Abram's change of name signified a new and greater role for him, so did Sarai's.

יִסְכָּה — *Iscah*. Iscah was Sarah. *Maharal* comments on Sarai's two names. A woman has two missions in life, the first from birth as an individual, and the second when she marries and is elevated to a higher, joint mission with her husband. Thus Iscah is the name indicating her personal greatness and Sarai/Sarah, the name indicating her Abrahamitic mission, is used exclusively from the time of her marriage.

32. וַיָּמָת תֶּרַח — *And Terah died.* Based on various verses, *Rashi* comments that Terah died more than 60 years after Abraham's departure from Haran. Nevertheless, Terah's death is recorded here to avoid the public implication that Abraham disrespectfully abandoned his father in his old age. In another sense, the report of Terah's death is accurate. The Sages teach that even while alive, the wicked are called dead; and the righteous, even when dead, are called alive. Thus, in the spiritual sense, the wicked Terah was truly "dead."

Ramban comments that it is common for the Torah to record a father's death before proceeding with the narrative of the son, even though the death occurred many years later, for the Torah records a person's death when his role is over. Thus, Noah's death was recorded above, even though he was still alive at the time of the Dispersion.

In a deeper sense, *Maharal* explains that Abraham was uniquely absolved from the commandment to honor his father because the commandment to him to leave his family and go to *Eretz Yisrael* (12:1) inaugurated a new sort of existence on earth. Abraham had ceased to be part of his biological family, for the mantle of chosenness had been placed upon him. In this sense, his previous family and homeland had gone out of his life, as if Terah had died.

קנ"ג פסוקים. בצלא"ל סימן. אב"י יסכ"ה לו"ט סימן. — This

THE SEVEN NOAHIDE LAWS — שֶׁבַע מִצְוֹות בְּנֵי נֹחַ (*Sanhedrin 56a; Rambam, Hil. Melachim 9:1*)		
1	IDOLATRY	עֲבוֹדָה זָרָה
2	"BLESSING" THE DIVINE NAME	בִּרְכַּת הַשֵּׁם
3	MURDER	שְׁפִיכוּת דָּמִים
4	SEXUAL TRANGRESSIONS	גִּלּוּי עֲרָיוֹת
5	THEFT (AND CIVIL LAW)	גָּזֵל
6	COURTS SYSTEM	דִּינִים
7	EATING A LIMB TORN FROM A LIVE ANIMAL	אֵבֶר מִן הַחַי

CHRONOLOGY/TIME LINE — ADAM TO JACOB

NAME	YEARS	BORN-DIED
ADAM	930	1-930
SETH	912	130-1042
ENOSH	905	235-1140
KENAN	910	325-1235
MAHALALEL	895	395-1290
YERED	962	460-1422
ENOCH	365	622-987
METHUSELAH	969	687-1656
LAMECH	777	874-1651
NOAH	950	1056-2006
SHEM	600	1558-2158
ARPACHSHAD	438	1658-2096
SHELAH	433	1693-2126
EBER	464	1723-2187
PELEG	239	1757-1996
REU	239	1787-2026
SERUG	230	1819-2049
NAHOR	148	1849-1997
TERAH	205	1878-2083
ABRAHAM	175	1948-2123
ISAAC	180	2048-2228
JACOB	147	2108-2255

Time line: 100 200 300 400 500 600 700 800 900 1000 1100 1200 1300 1400 1500 1600 1700 1800 1900 2000 2100 2200

1656 — THE FLOOD

1996 — THE DISPERSION

Masoretic note means: There are 153 verses in the *Sidrah*, numerically corresponding to mnemonics, בְּצַלְאֵל, *Bezalel,* and אֲבִי יִסְכָּה לוֹט, *father of Iscah,* [and] *Lot*.

The name בְּצַלְאֵל alludes to the *Sidrah* of *Noach* in two ways: (a) The name בְּצַלְאֵל is compounded of בְּצַל אֵל, *in the protective shelter of God,* an allusion to Noah and his family in the Ark (*R' David Feinstein*); and (b) just as Noah was ordered to build a תֵּבָה, *Ark,* to house his family and thus preserve humanity from the ravages of the flood, so was Bezalel son of Uri instructed to build a תֵּבָה, *Ark,* to house the Tablets of the Ten Commandments.

The mnemonic אֲבִי יִסְכָּה לוֹט refers to Abraham's brother Haran who is identified at the end of the *Sidrah* as *the father of Iscah and Lot.* Haran died as a young man leaving three children, Lot, Milcah and Iscah (also called Sarai). After Haran's death, his brother Nahor married Milcah and Abraham married Iscah (Sarai). Lot also attached himself to Abraham's family and joined them in their journey to Caanan. Thus the expression *the father of Iscah and Lot* may additionally be an allusion to Abraham who, if not their father, nevertheless cared for them. If so, it is an apt mnemonic for the *Sidrah* of *Noach,* for at this point the Torah's narration of the story of mankind in general becomes the story of Abraham and his descendants *(Aramez Badavar).*

PARASHAS LECH LECHA / פרשת לך לך

[יב] א וַיֹּאמֶר יהוה אֶל־אַבְרָם לֶךְ־לְךָ מֵאַרְצְךָ
[12] 1 HASHEM said < to < Abram, << Go < for yourself < from your land,
וּמִמּוֹלַדְתְּךָ וּמִבֵּית אָבִיךָ אֶל־הָאָרֶץ אֲשֶׁר אַרְאֶךָּ:
from your relatives, < and from the house < of your father < to < the land < that < I will show you. <<
ב וְאֶעֶשְׂךָ לְגוֹי גָּדוֹל וַאֲבָרֶכְךָ וַאֲגַדְּלָה שְׁמֶךָ וֶהְיֵה בְּרָכָה: ג וַאֲבָרְכָה
2 And I will make you < into a nation < that is great; << I will bless you, < and make great < your name, << and you shall be < a blessing. << 3 I will bless <

אונקלוס

א וַאֲמַר יְיָ לְאַבְרָם אִיזֵיל לָךְ מֵאַרְעָךְ וּמִיַּלָּדוּתָךְ וּמִבֵּית אֲבוּךְ לְאַרְעָא דִּי אַחֲזִנָּךְ: ב וְאֶעְבְּדִנָּךְ לְעַם סַגִּי וַאֲבָרְכִנָּךְ וַאֲרַבֵּי שְׁמָךְ וּתְהֵא מְבָרָךְ: ג וַאֲבָרֵךְ

רש"י

(א) **לך לך.** להנאתך ולטובתך. שם אעשך לגוי גדול, וכאן אי אתה זוכה לבנים (ראש השנה טז:), ועוד, שאודיע טבעך בעולם (תנחומא ג): (ב) **ואעשך לגוי גדול.** לפי שהדרך גורמת לשלשה דברים, ממעטת פריה ורביה, וממעטת את הממון, וממעטת את השם, לכך הוזקק לשלש ברכות הללו, שהבטיחו על הבנים ועל הממון ועל השם [ס"א וזהו ואגדלה שמך, הריני מוסיף אות על שמך, שעד עכשיו שמך אברם, מכאן ואילך אברהם, ואברהם עולה רמ"ח, כנגד אבריו של אדם (ב"ר לט:יא): **ואברכך.** בממון. ב"ר (שם): **והיה ברכה.** הברכות נתונות בידך. עד עכשיו היו בידי, ברכתי את אדם ואת נח ואותך, ומעכשיו אתה תברך את אשר תחפוץ (שם). ד"א, ואעשך לגוי גדול, זה שאומרים אלהי

PARASHAS LECH LECHA

12.

◆§ A new creation.

This *Sidrah* begins a new birth of mankind: the story of Abraham and his descendants. The first 2,000 years from Creation were the Era of Desolation. Adam had fallen, Abel had been murdered, idolatry had been introduced to the world, ten dismal generations had been washed away by the Deluge, and the ten generations from Noah had failed [see *Avos* 5:2]. Abraham was born in the year 1948 from Creation. In the year 2,000 — four years after the Dispersion and six years before the death of Noah — he started to influence disciples to serve Hashem. With the emergence of Abraham, the Era of Desolation had come to an end and the Era of Torah had begun (*Avodah Zarah* 9a).

With Abraham there began a profound change in the spiritual nature of mankind. The plan of Creation was for all human beings to have an equal share in fulfilling the Divine mission and for the Torah to be given to all mankind. But after twenty generations of failure, the privilege of being God's Chosen People was earned by Abraham and his offspring. They would receive the Torah and they would be in the vanguard of perfecting the world and bringing all people to accept the sovereignty of the One God [see *Avos*, ibid.; *Derech Hashem*].

◆§ The concept of trial.

Abraham did not win his new status by default; he had to prove his greatness by passing ten tests of faith (*Avos* 5:4). The first trial mentioned in Scripture is in the first passage of this *Sidrah,* the command that Abraham give up his entire past and follow God's lead to a new land. By definition, a Heavenly test is one that forces a person to choose between God's will and his own nature or understanding of what is right. Clearly, it would be no challenge to Abraham, who was the epitome of kindness, to be asked to help the needy, but it would be a supreme test of faith for him to desert his aged father and homeland or to give his cherished, beloved son as an offering [see Chapter 22]. Thus, Abraham was tested by being forced to subordinate his wishes and wisdom to those of God. By doing so, he demonstrated his conviction that man's highest goal is to accept the Divine wisdom as the sole truth.

Since God knows all future events and how every person will respond to any given situation, why was it necessary to test Abraham? According to *Rambam* (*Moreh Nevuchim* 3:24) the trials were meant to display to the *world* how a great man obeys God. Thus, when Abraham set precedents in faithful obedience, his performance under extreme pressure became a lesson for the rest of humanity.

Ramban explains the concept of trial differently. Of course the outcome is never in doubt to God, for He knows that the person being tested will persevere. To the contrary, a just God does not impose trials that are beyond the capacity of the individual — God tests only righteous people who will do His will, not the wicked who will disobey. Thus, all the Torah's trials are for the benefit of those being tested. But that is known only to God. The person being tested has free choice, and he must find the strength and wisdom to choose correctly. If he does, then he has translated his potential into action and made himself a greater person, for actual deed far outweighs mere potential in the Heavenly scales of judgment, and he can therefore be rewarded for what he *did*, rather than for what he was merely *capable* of doing. [For a list of Abraham's ten trials, see introduction to Ch. 22.]

◆§ Abraham comes to Canaan.

God's command that Abraham and Sarah sever all ties with their past and loved ones — when they were 75 and 65 years old — was one of the ten trials, for it is never easy for a person to start life over again, especially when he has achieved status and prosperity. By bringing him to *Eretz Yisrael* and promising that the Land would become the heritage of his family, God was establishing the Land as the eternal patrimony of the Jewish

מְבָרְכֶיךָ וּמְקַלֶּלְךָ אָאֹר וְנִבְרְכוּ בְךָ כֹּל מִשְׁפְּחֹת

‹ the families ‹ all ‹ through you ‹ and they will be blessed ‹‹ I will curse; ‹ and the one who curses you ‹‹ those who bless you,

הָאֲדָמָה: ד וַיֵּלֶךְ אַבְרָם כַּאֲשֶׁר דִּבֶּר אֵלָיו יְהֹוָה

‹‹ HASHEM, ‹to him ‹ had spoken ‹ as ‹ So Abram went 4 ‹‹ of the earth.

וַיֵּלֶךְ אִתּוֹ לוֹט וְאַבְרָם בֶּן־חָמֵשׁ שָׁנִים וְשִׁבְעִים

‹ and seventy ‹ years ‹ of five ‹ was of the age ‹ and Abram ‹‹ Lot; ‹ and with him went

שָׁנָה בְּצֵאתוֹ מֵחָרָן: ה וַיִּקַּח אַבְרָם אֶת־שָׂרַי אִשְׁתּוֹ וְאֶת־לוֹט בֶּן־אָחִיו

‹ of his brother, ‹ the son ‹ and Lot, ‹ his wife ‹ Sarai ‹ Abram took 5 ‹‹ from Haran. ‹ when he went forth ‹ years

וְאֶת־כָּל־רְכוּשָׁם אֲשֶׁר רָכָשׁוּ וְאֶת־הַנֶּפֶשׁ אֲשֶׁר־עָשׂוּ בְחָרָן וַיֵּצְאוּ

‹ and they went forth ‹‹ in Haran; ‹ they made ‹ that ‹ and the souls ‹ they had amassed, ‹ that ‹ their possessions ‹ and all

מְבָרְכָיךְ וּמְלַטְטָךְ אֵלוּט וְיִתְבָּרְכוּן בְּדִילָךְ כֹּל זַרְעֲיַת אַרְעָא: ד וַאֲזַל אַבְרָם כְּמָא דִי מַלִּיל עִמֵּהּ יְיָ וַאֲזַל עִמֵּהּ לוֹט וְאַבְרָם בַּר שִׁבְעִין וַחֲמֵשׁ שְׁנִין בְּמִפְּקֵהּ מֵחָרָן: ה וּדְבַר אַבְרָם יָת שָׂרַי אִתְּתֵהּ וְיָת לוֹט בַּר אֲחוּהִי וְיָת כָּל קִנְיָנְהוֹן דִּי קְנוֹ וְיָת נַפְשָׁתָא דְּשַׁעְבִּידוּ לְאוֹרַיְתָא בְּחָרָן וּנְפָקוּ

רש"י

אברהם. ואברכך, זה שאומרים אלהי יצחק. ואגדלה שמך, זה שאומרים אלהי יעקב. יכול יהיו חותמין בכולן, ת"ל והיה ברכה, בך חותמין ולא בהם (פסחים קיז:): **מארצך [וממולדתך]**. והלא כבר יצא משם עם אביו ובא עד חרן. אלא כך אמר לו, התרחק עוד משם וצא מבית אביך: **אשר אראך**. לא גלה לו הארץ מיד, כדי לחבבה בעיניו ולתת לו שכר על כל דבור ודבור. כיוצא בו, את בנך את יחידך אשר אהבת את יצחק. כיוצא בו, על אחד ההרים אשר אמר אליך (להלן כב:ב). כיוצא בו, וקרא אליה את הקריאה אשר אנכי דובר אליך (יונה ג:ב; ב"ר שם ט): (ג) **ונברכו בך**. יש אגדות רבות, וזהו פשוטו, אדם אומר לבנו תהא כאברהם. וכן כל ונברכו בך שבמקרא, וזה מוכיח, בך יברך ישראל לאמר ישימך אלהים כאפרים וכמנשה (להלן מח:כ): (ה) **אשר עשו בחרן**. שהכניסום תחת כנפי השכינה. אברהם מגייר את האנשים ושרה מגיירת הנשים, ומעלה עליהם הכתוב כאילו עשאום (ב"ר שם יד, פד:ד; סנהדרין לט:). ופשוטו של מקרא, עבדים ושפחות שקנו להם, כמו עשה את כל הכבד הזה (להלן לא:א) לשון קנין. וישראל עושה חיל (במדבר

God kept him in suspense and thereby made the destination more beloved in his eyes, and also enabled him to be rewarded for every step he took (*Rashi*).

The Torah expresses Abraham's test in ascending degrees of difficulty. It is hard for someone to leave his homeland, even harder to leave his extended family, and hardest of all to leave his parents (*Ramban*).

2. **וְהָיֵה בְּרָכָה** — *And you shall be a blessing.* You will have the power to bless whomever you wish (*Rashi*). *Ramban* interprets: You will be the standard by which people will bless themselves. This idea is further expanded in the next verse, which states that not only will the Canaanites bless themselves by Abraham, but *all the families of the earth* will do so.

4. Lot's father was Haran, Abraham's brother, who had died in the flames of Ur Kasdim [see notes to 11:28]. Abraham then undertook the responsibility of raising the orphaned Lot (*Chizkuni*).

Some commentators note that God had not bidden Abraham to take Lot with him and that Lot's later behavior showed that he should not have done so. *Zohar Chadash* explains that Abraham took him because he foresaw that David and the Messiah would descend from Lot; and because Haran had died in support of Abraham, Abraham felt that he had to be compassionate to his son.

5. **הַנֶּפֶשׁ אֲשֶׁר־עָשׂוּ** — *The souls that they made.* The *souls* refer to those whom they had converted to faith in Hashem, for Abraham converted the men and Sarah the women. According to

people. There was a further symbolism. Though Abraham and Sarah had many disciples, they were essentially alone; they could never blend into whatever culture surrounded them. Abraham was called an *Ivri,* from the word עֵבֶר, *the [other] side*. Literally this means that he came to Canaan from the other side of the Euphrates, but the Sages interpret the title in a deeper sense, too. He was on one side of a moral and spiritual divide, and the rest of the world was on the other. Righteous people must be ready to endure such isolation; popularity is pleasant but it is also a snare, because the natural desire to win the approval of others can easily lead people to bend their principles. Abraham and Sarah were now given the challenge of moving to the *other side* — not only of their native river, but of anyone who preferred not to acknowledge the sovereignty of God.

At this point in his life, the Patriarch's name was Abram and the Matriarch's was Sarai; their names were not changed to Abra**ham** and Sara**h** until vs. 17:5 and 15, twenty-four years after they left for Canaan. Nevertheless, in the notes we refer to them by their familiar names of Abraham and Sarah, as do the commentators.

1. **לֶךְ־לְךָ** — *Go for yourself*. The seemingly superfluous לְךָ, *for yourself,* means "go for your own benefit and for your own good." And what is this benefit and good? The following verses explain: *I will make you into a nation that is great,* for here you will not merit the privilege of having children and there you will, and there you will become famous [so that you will be able to carry out your spiritual mission]. By not specifying Abraham's destination, saying only *to the land that I will show you*,

לָלֶכֶת אַרְצָה כְּנַעַן וַיָּבֹאוּ אַרְצָה כְּנָעַן׃ ו וַיַּעֲבֹר
to go › to the land › of Canaan, » and they came › to the land › of Canaan. » 6 Pass ›

אַבְרָם בָּאָרֶץ עַד מְקוֹם שְׁכֶם עַד אֵלוֹן מוֹרֶה
did Abram › into the land › as far as › the site › of Shechem, › as far as › the plain › of Moreh, »

וְהַכְּנַעֲנִי אָז בָּאָרֶץ׃ ז וַיֵּרָא יהוה אֶל־אַבְרָם וַיֹּאמֶר
and the Canaanite › then › was in the land. » 7 HASHEM appeared › to › Abram › and He said, »

לְזַרְעֲךָ אֶתֵּן אֶת־הָאָרֶץ הַזֹּאת וַיִּבֶן שָׁם מִזְבֵּחַ
To your offspring › I will give › this land. » So he built › there › an altar ›

לַיהוה הַנִּרְאֶה אֵלָיו׃ ח וַיַּעְתֵּק מִשָּׁם הָהָרָה מִקֶּדֶם לְבֵית־אֵל וַיֵּט
to HASHEM › Who appeared › to him. » 8 He relocated › from there › to the mountain › east › of Beth-el › and pitched ›

אָהֳלֹה בֵּית־אֵל מִיָּם וְהָעַי מִקֶּדֶם וַיִּבֶן־שָׁם מִזְבֵּחַ לַיהוה וַיִּקְרָא
his tent, » [with] Beth-el › on the west › and Ai › on the east; » and he built › there › an altar › to HASHEM › and he called out ›

בְּשֵׁם יהוה׃ ט וַיִּסַּע אַבְרָם הָלוֹךְ וְנָסוֹעַ הַנֶּגְבָּה׃ פ י וַיְהִי רָעָב בָּאָרֶץ
in the Name › of HASHEM. » 9 Then Abram journeyed [on], › continuing › to journey › toward the South. » 10 There was › a famine › in the land, »

לְמֵיזַל לְאַרְעָא דִכְנָעַן וַאֲתוֹ לְאַרְעָא
דִכְנָעַן: ו וַעֲבַר אַבְרָם בְּאַרְעָא עַד
אֲתַר שְׁכֶם עַד מֵישַׁר מוֹרֶה וּכְנַעֲנָאָה
בְּכֵן בְּאַרְעָא: ז וְאִתְגְּלִי יְיָ לְאַבְרָם
וַאֲמַר לִבְנָיךְ אֶתֵּן יָת אַרְעָא הָדָא
וּבְנָא תַמָּן מַדְבְּחָא קֳדָם יְיָ דְּאִתְגְּלִי
לֵהּ: ח וְאִסְתַּלַּק מִתַּמָּן לְטוּרָא
מִמַּדְנַח לְבֵית אֵל וּפְרַס מַשְׁכְּנֵהּ בֵּית
אֵל מִמַּעַרְבָא וְעַי מִמַּדִינְחָא וּבְנָא
תַמָּן מַדְבְּחָא קֳדָם יְיָ וְצַלִּי בִּשְׁמָא
דַייָ: ט וּנְטַל אַבְרָם אָזֵיל וְנָטֵל
לְדָרוֹמָא: י וַהֲוָה כַפְנָא בְּאַרְעָא

רש"י

כד:יח) לשון קונה וכונס: (ו) **ויעבור אברם בארץ.** נכנס בתוכה: **עד מקום שכם.** להתפלל על בני יעקב כשיבאו להלחם בשכם (מדרש אגדה; ב"ר לט:טו): **אלון מורה.** היא שכם (סוטה לב.), הראהו הר גריזים והר עיבל, ששם קבלו ישראל שבועת התורה (מדרש אגדה): **והכנעני אז בארץ.** היה הולך וכובש את א"י מזרעו של שם, שבחלקו של שם נפלה כשחלק נח את הארץ לבניו, שנאמר ומלכי צדק מלך שלם (להלן יד:יח) לפיכך, ויאמר אל אברם לזרעך אתן את הארץ הזאת (פסוק ז), עתיד אני להחזירה לבניך, שהם מזרעו של שם (מדרש אגדה; ת"כ סוף קדושים): (ז) **ויבן שם מזבח.** על בשורת הזרע ועל בשורת ארץ ישראל (ב"ר לט:טו־טז): (ח) **ויעתק משם.** אהלו: **מקדם לבית אל.** במזרחה של בית אל, נמצאת בית אל במערבו, הוא שנא' **בית אל מים: אהלה.** אהלה כתיב, בתחלה נטה את אהל אשתו ואח"כ את שלו (שם טו): **ויבן שם מזבח.** נתנבא שעתידין בניו להכשל שם על עון עכן, והתפלל שם עליהם (שם טז): (ט) **הלוך ונסוע.** לפרקים יושב כאן חדש או יותר, ונוסע משם ונוטה אהלו במקום אחר, וכל מסעיו **הנגבה**, ללכת לדרומה של ארץ ישראל, והיא לצד ירושלים, שהיא בחלקו של יהודה, שנטלו בדרומה של ארץ ישראל הר המוריה שהיא נחלתו. [ב"ר] (שם): (י) **רעב בארץ.** באותה הארץ לבדה, לנסותו אם יהרהר אחר דבריו של הקב"ה שאמר לו ללכת אל ארץ כנען ועכשיו משיאו לצאת ממנה (תנחומא ה):

the simple meaning, however, it refers to the servants they had acquired (*Rashi*), who agreed unanimously to accompany Abraham on his mission (*Radak*).

6. Deeds of the Patriarchs, portents for the children. *Ramban* states a fundamental principle in understanding the Torah's narrative concerning the Patriarchs: כָּל מַה שֶּׁאֵירַע לְאָבוֹת סִימָן לְבָנִים, *Whatever happened to the Patriarchs is a portent for the children*. The Torah relates at length such incidents as their journeys, digging of wells, etc., because they serve as lessons for the future. Thus, Abraham's stopover in Shechem — in addition to his prayers for Jacob's sons who would one day fight against Shechem — was a portent that Shechem would be the first place to be conquered by Jews [34:25], nearly three hundred years before Israel gained full possession of the land. Then he encamped between Beth-el and Ai, the latter being the first place conquered by Joshua. [According to *Rashi*, at the *Plain of Moreh* God showed Abraham Mount Gerizim and Mount Ebal where, immediately after their arrival in the Land, his descendants would take an oath to observe the Torah.] The story of the Patriarchs is replete with such symbolic acts in order to couple the particular Divine decree with a physical deed, following the principle that whenever a prophecy is clothed in a symbolic act, the decree becomes permanent and unalterable.

7. וַיֵּרָא ה׳ — *HASHEM appeared.* God is not physical, so the means by which He "speaks" and makes Himself "visible" to people is an eternal mystery. Nevertheless, the Torah tells us that He *appeared* in a way that was tangible to Abraham (*R' Hirsch*). In gratitude for the promise of children and the Land, Abraham built an altar to God (*Rashi*).

8. Abraham built a second altar at which he *called out in the Name of HASHEM.* According to *Rashi* this means that he prayed at the site where his descendants would face possible catastro-

וַיֵּרֶד אַבְרָם מִצְרַיְמָה לָגוּר שָׁם כִּי־כָבֵד הָרָעָב

and Abram descended ‹ to Egypt ‹ to sojourn ‹ there, ‹ for ‹ severe ‹ was the famine ‹

בָּאָרֶץ׃ יא וַיְהִי כַּאֲשֶׁר הִקְרִיב לָבוֹא מִצְרָיְמָה

in the land. « 11 And it occurred, ‹ as ‹ he drew close ‹ to entering ‹ into Egypt, «

וַיֹּאמֶר אֶל־שָׂרַי אִשְׁתּוֹ הִנֵּה־נָא יָדַעְתִּי כִּי אִשָּׁה

he said ‹ to ‹ Sarai ‹ his wife, « *Indeed* ‹ *now* ‹ *I have known* ‹ *that* ‹ *a woman* ‹

יְפַת־מַרְאֶה אָתְּ׃ יב וְהָיָה כִּי־יִרְאוּ אֹתָךְ הַמִּצְרִים

of beautiful ‹ *appearance* ‹ *are you.* « 12 *And it shall be,* ‹ *when* ‹ *they will see* ‹ *you* « *— the Egyptians —* «

וְאָמְרוּ אִשְׁתּוֹ זֹאת וְהָרְגוּ אֹתִי וְאֹתָךְ יְחַיּוּ׃ יג אִמְרִי־נָא אֲחֹתִי אָתְּ

and they will say, « *'His wife* ‹ *this is!';* « *then they will kill* ‹ *me,* ‹ *while you* ‹ *they will keep alive.* « 13 *Say,* ‹ *please,* ‹ *that my sister* ‹ *you are,* «

לְמַעַן יִיטַב־לִי בַעֲבוּרֵךְ וְחָיְתָה נַפְשִׁי בִּגְלָלֵךְ׃ שני יד וַיְהִי כְּבוֹא אַבְרָם

so that ‹ *it may go well* ‹ *with me* ‹ *for your sake,* « *and remain alive* ‹ *may my soul* ‹ *on account of you.* « 14 But it happened, ‹ at the entry ‹ of Abram ‹

מִצְרָיְמָה וַיִּרְאוּ הַמִּצְרִים אֶת־הָאִשָּׁה כִּי־יָפָה הִוא מְאֹד׃ טו וַיִּרְאוּ אֹתָהּ

into Egypt, « the Egyptians saw ‹ the woman « — that she ‹ was beautiful ‹ to the utmost. « 15 [When] see ‹ her ‹

שָׂרֵי פַרְעֹה וַיְהַלְלוּ אֹתָהּ אֶל־פַּרְעֹה וַתֻּקַּח הָאִשָּׁה בֵּית פַּרְעֹה׃

did the officials ‹ of Pharaoh, ‹ they praised ‹ her ‹ [as worthy] for ‹ Pharaoh, « and the woman was taken ‹ to the palace ‹ of Pharaoh. «

וּנְחַת אַבְרָם לְמִצְרַיִם לְאִתּוֹתָבָא תַּמָּן אֲרֵי תַקִּיף כַּפְנָא בְּאַרְעָא׃ יא וַהֲוָה כַּד קְרֵיב לְמֵיעַל לְמִצְרָיִם וַאֲמַר לְשָׂרַי אִתְּתֵהּ הָא כְעַן יְדָעִית אֲרֵי אִתְּתָא שַׁפִּירַת חֵיזוּ אָתְּ׃ יב וִיהֵי כַּד (נ"א אֲרֵי) יֶחֱזוּן יָתִיךְ מִצְרָאֵי וְיֵימְרוּן אִתְּתֵהּ דָּא וְיִקְטְלוּן יָתִי וְיָתִיךְ יְקַיְּמוּן׃ יג אִמְרִי כְעַן אֲחָתִי אָתְּ בְּדִיל דְּיוֹטִיב לִי בְּדִילָךְ וְתִתְקַיַּם נַפְשִׁי בְּפִתְגָּמָיְכִי׃ יד וַהֲוָה כַּד עַל אַבְרָם לְמִצְרָיִם וַחֲזוֹ מִצְרָאֵי יָת אִתְּתָא אֲרֵי שַׁפִּירְתָא הִיא לַחֲדָא׃ טו וַחֲזוֹ יָתַהּ רַבְרְבֵי פַרְעֹה וְשַׁבַּחוּ יָתַהּ לְפַרְעֹה וְאִדַּבָּרַת אִתְּתָא לְבֵית פַּרְעֹה׃

רש"י

(יא) הנה נא ידעתי. מדרש אגדה, עד עכשיו לא הכיר בה מתוך צניעות שבשניהם, ועכשיו הכיר בה על ידי מעשה (שם). ד"א, מנהג העולם שע"י טורח הדרך אדם מתבזה, וזאת עמדה ביופיה (ב"ר מ:ד). ופשוטו של מקרא, **הנה נא,** הגיעה השעה שיש לדאוג על יפיך. **ידעתי** זה ימים רבים **כי אשה יפת מראה את,** ועכשיו אנו באים בין אנשים שחורים ומכוערים אחיהם של כושים ולא הורגלו באשה יפה (שם). ודומה לו הנה נא אדני סורו נא (להלן יט:ב): **(יג) למען ייטב לי בעבורך.** יתנו לי מתנות: **(יד) ויהי כבוא אברם מצרימה.** היה לו לומר כבואם מצרימה, אלא למד שהטמין אותה בתיבה, וע"י שתבעו את המכס פתחו וראו אותה (ב"ר שם ה; תנחומא שם): **(טו) ויהללו אתה אל פרעה.** הללוה ביניהם לומר הגונה זו למלך (תנחומא שם):

phe because of the sin of Achan (see *Joshua* ch. 7). Others comment that, having arrived in *Eretz Yisrael,* Abraham *called out in the Name of HASHEM* in the sense that he preached the unity of God and sought to draw converts to Him.

10-20. Abraham in Egypt. This is another test of Abraham's faith. Immediately after he settled in the new homeland where God had promised him every manner of blessing, there was a famine. Though this seemed to be a direct contradiction of God's glowing promises, Abraham's faith did not waver. This event foreshadowed Jacob's descent to Egypt because of a famine (*Midrash*).

In view of Sarah's great beauty, this test was especially difficult because the Egyptians were notorious for their immorality. Now Abraham and Sarah would be at the mercy of the Egyptians, who might lust after her and kill him (*Abarbanel*). Knowing that he and Sarah would be in grave danger in Egypt if they came as man and wife, Abraham claimed that she was his sister. Could Abraham have told an outright lie, to say she was his sister if she really was his niece?! (11:29). The Sages explain that a man often refers to his relative as his sister (*Midrash HaGadol*). Though Abraham thought that this ruse would protect Sarah as well as himself, *Ramban* comments that it was a "great sin" for him to put her in danger. [Nor was the ruse effective against Pharaoh — the only person who did not need to negotiate for Abraham's "sister," and who would not be so publicly immoral as to kill Abraham to take his wife.]

13. לְמַעַן יִיטַב־לִי בַעֲבוּרֵךְ — *So that it may go well with me for your sake.* I.e., they will give me gifts (*Rashi*). The sense of

טז וּלְאַבְרָם הֵיטִיב בַּעֲבוּרָהּ וַיְהִי־לוֹ צֹאן־וּבָקָר
16 And for Abram ‹ it went well ‹ for her sake, ‹‹ and there belonged ‹ to him ‹ sheep, ‹ cattle,

וַחֲמֹרִים וַעֲבָדִים וּשְׁפָחֹת וַאֲתֹנֹת וּגְמַלִּים׃
donkeys, ‹ slaves, ‹ and maidservants, ‹ female donkeys, ‹ and camels. ‹‹

יז וַיְנַגַּע יְהוָה ׀ אֶת־פַּרְעֹה נְגָעִים גְּדֹלִים וְאֶת־
17 But HASHEM afflicted ‹ Pharaoh ‹ [with] plagues ‹ that were severe, ‹ along with

בֵּיתוֹ עַל־דְּבַר שָׂרַי אֵשֶׁת אַבְרָם׃ יח וַיִּקְרָא פַרְעֹה
his household, ‹‹ over ‹ the matter ‹ of Sarai, ‹ the wife ‹ of Abram. ‹‹ 18 Pharaoh called ‹

לְאַבְרָם וַיֹּאמֶר מַה־זֹּאת עָשִׂיתָ לִּי לָמָּה לֹא־הִגַּדְתָּ לִּי כִּי אִשְׁתְּךָ
Abram ‹ and he said, ‹‹ What ‹ is this ‹ you have done ‹ to me? ‹‹ Why ‹ did you not tell ‹ me ‹ that ‹ your wife ‹

הִוא׃ יט לָמָה אָמַרְתָּ אֲחֹתִי הִוא וָאֶקַּח אֹתָהּ לִי לְאִשָּׁה וְעַתָּה הִנֵּה
is she? ‹‹ 19 Why ‹ did you say, ‹ 'My sister ‹ is she,' ‹‹ [so that] I took ‹ her ‹ for me ‹ as a wife? ‹‹ Now, ‹ here is ‹

אִשְׁתְּךָ קַח וָלֵךְ׃ כ וַיְצַו עָלָיו פַּרְעֹה אֲנָשִׁים וַיְשַׁלְּחוּ אֹתוֹ וְאֶת־אִשְׁתּוֹ
your wife; ‹‹ take [her] ‹ and go! ‹‹ 20 And command ‹ concerning him ‹ did Pharaoh ‹ [to his] men, ‹‹ and they sent away ‹ him ‹ and his wife ‹

טז וּלְאַבְרָם אוֹטִיב בְּדִילַהּ וַהֲווֹ לֵהּ
עָאן וְתוֹרִין וַחֲמָרִין וְעַבְדִין
וְאַמְהָן וְאַתְנָן וְגַמְלִין׃ יז וְאַיְתִי
יְיָ עַל פַּרְעֹה מַכְתָּשִׁין רַבְרְבִין
וְעַל אֱנָשׁ בֵּיתֵהּ עַל עֵיסַק שָׂרַי
אִתַּת אַבְרָם׃ יח וּקְרָא פַרְעֹה לְאַבְרָם
וַאֲמַר מָה דָא עֲבַדְתְּ לִי לְמָא
לָא חַוֵּיתָא לִי אֲרֵי אִתְּתָךְ הִיא׃
יט לְמָא אֲמַרְתְּ אֲחָתִי הִיא וּדְבָרִית
יָתַהּ לִי לְאִנְתּוּ וּכְעַן הָא אִתְּתָךְ
דְּבַר וְאִזֵיל׃ כ וּפַקֵּיד עֲלוֹהִי פַּרְעֹה
גּוּבְרִין וְאַלְוִיאוּ יָתֵהּ וְיָת אִתְּתֵהּ

רש"י

(טז) ולאברם היטיב. פרעה בעבורה [נתן לו מתנות]: **(יז) וינגע ה' וגו'.** במכת ראתן לקה, שהתשמיש קשה לו (ב"ר מא:ב): **ואת ביתו.** כתרגומו ועל אינש ביתיה [ומדרשו לרבות כותליו עמודיו וכליו (תנחומא שם)]: **על דבר שרי.** על פי דבורה, אומרת למלאך הך והוא מכה (ב"ר שם; תנחומא שם):

(יט) קח ולך. ולא כאבימלך שאמר לו הנה ארצי לפניך (להלן כ:טו) אלא אמר לו לך ואל תעמוד, שהמצרים שטופי זמה הם, שנא' וזרמת סוסים זרמתם (יחזקאל כג:כ; מדרש אגדה): **(כ) ויצו עליו.** על אודותיו לשלחו ולשמרו: **וישלחו.** כתרגומו ואלויאו:

Abraham's statement was that if the nobles of Egypt were to shower him with gifts to win his "sister's" hand, the masses would be afraid to harm him, and Sarah's safety would be assured (*Gur Aryeh*). But his plan did not succeed, for Sarah's exceptional beauty brought about a different turn of events (*Ran*).

16. . . . וַיְהִי־לוֹ — *And there belonged to him.* In sharp contrast to his later behavior toward the king of Sodom, from whom he was entitled to monetary compensation but vehemently refused to accept anything (14:23), Abraham *did* accept lavish gifts from Pharaoh. In the context of Abraham's claim that Sarah was his sister and the implication that he would allow her to marry a suitable person, Abraham had no choice: Had he refused gifts, he would have aroused Pharaoh's suspicions (*Abarbanel*).

17. וַיְנַגַּע ה' — *But HASHEM afflicted.* God smote Pharaoh and his household with a debilitating skin disease that made cohabitation impossible, thus assuring that Sarah's chastity would be safeguarded (*Rashi; Gur Aryeh*). The verse mentions that she was the wife of Abraham because it was in his merit, too, that God punished Pharaoh (*Ramban*).

18-19. וַיִּקְרָא פַרְעֹה לְאַבְרָם — *Pharaoh called Abram.* Although Pharaoh suspected that his affliction was because of Sarah, he could not be certain she was Abraham's wife. He made the accusation in order to draw the truth from Abraham. When Abraham did not respond, Pharaoh realized that his suspicion was correct, so he ordered Abraham to take his wife and leave (*Ramban*). By asking, *"Why did you not tell* **me**?" Pharaoh implied that even if Abraham distrusted the morality of the Egyptian masses, he surely could have confided in Pharaoh! *Rashi* notes that unlike Abimelech (20:15), who invited Abraham to settle in his country after a similar abduction of Sarah, Pharaoh told Abraham to leave Egypt, because he knew that Abraham and Sarah could not be safe anywhere in his immoral country.

20. וַיְשַׁלְּחוּ — *And they sent away.* Pharaoh hastened to rid himself of the cause of his Divine affliction, but, not wishing to incur God's further wrath by mistreating Abraham and Sarah, he sent them away in honor, guaranteeing that no evil would befall them.

וְאֶת־כָּל־אֲשֶׁר־לוֹ׃ [יג] א וַיַּעַל אַבְרָם מִמִּצְרַיִם

« from Egypt, ‹ And Abram went up 1 [13] « his. ‹ that was ‹ and all

הוּא וְאִשְׁתּוֹ וְכָל־אֲשֶׁר־לוֹ וְלוֹט עִמּוֹ הַנֶּגְבָּה׃

« toward the South [of Canaan]. « with him, ‹ and Lot « his, ‹ that was ‹ and all ‹ and his wife ‹ he

ב וְאַבְרָם כָּבֵד מְאֹד בַּמִּקְנֶה בַּכֶּסֶף וּבַזָּהָב׃ ג וַיֵּלֶךְ

‹ He went 3 « and with gold. ‹ with silver, ‹ with livestock, ‹ to the utmost ‹ was laden ‹ Now Abram 2

לְמַסָּעָיו מִנֶּגֶב וְעַד־בֵּית־אֵל עַד־הַמָּקוֹם אֲשֶׁר־

‹ where ‹ the site ‹ until « Beth-el, ‹ until ‹ from the south ‹ on his journeys

הָיָה שָׁם אָהֳלֹה בַּתְּחִלָּה בֵּין בֵּית־אֵל וּבֵין הָעָי׃ ד אֶל־מְקוֹם הַמִּזְבֵּחַ

‹ of the altar ‹ the site ‹ to 4 « Ai, ‹ and between ‹ Beth-el ‹ between « [was] at first, ‹ his tent ‹ there ‹ it was

אֲשֶׁר־עָשָׂה שָׁם בָּרִאשֹׁנָה וַיִּקְרָא שָׁם אַבְרָם בְּשֵׁם יהוה׃ שלישי — ה וְגַם־

‹ Also 5 « of HASHEM. ‹ in the Name « — did Abram — « there ‹ and call out « at first; ‹ there ‹ he had made ‹ which

לְלוֹט הַהֹלֵךְ אֶת־אַבְרָם הָיָה צֹאן־וּבָקָר וְאֹהָלִים׃ ו וְלֹא־נָשָׂא אֹתָם

‹ them [both] ‹ Not able to support 6 « and tents. ‹ cattle, ‹ sheep, ‹ there were ‹ Abram ‹ with ‹ who went ‹ to Lot

הָאָרֶץ לָשֶׁבֶת יַחְדָּו כִּי־הָיָה רְכוּשָׁם רָב וְלֹא יָכְלוּ לָשֶׁבֶת יַחְדָּו׃

« together. ‹ to dwell ‹ and they were not able ‹ [too] extensive ‹ their possessions were ‹ for « together, ‹ [to enable them] to dwell ‹ was the land

וְיָת כָּל דִּי לֵהּ׃ א וּסְלִיק אַבְרָם מִמִּצְרַיִם הוּא וְאִתְּתֵהּ וְכָל דִּי לֵהּ וְלוֹט עִמֵּהּ לְדָרוֹמָא׃ ב וְאַבְרָם תַּקִּיף לַחֲדָא בִּבְעִירָא בְּכַסְפָּא וּבְדַהֲבָא׃ ג וַאֲזַל לְמַטְלָנוֹהִי מִדָּרוֹמָא וְעַד בֵּית אֵל עַד אַתְרָא דִּי פְרַס תַּמָּן מַשְׁכְּנֵהּ בְּקַדְמֵיתָא בֵּין בֵּית אֵל וּבֵין עָי׃ ד לַאֲתַר מַדְבְּחָא דִּי עֲבַד תַּמָּן בְּקַדְמֵיתָא וְצַלִּי תַמָּן אַבְרָם בִּשְׁמָא דַייָ׃ ה וְאַף לְלוֹט דְּאָזֵיל עִם אַבְרָם הֲוָה עָאן וְתוֹרִין וּמַשְׁכְּנִין׃ ו וְלָא סוֹבָרַת יָתְהוֹן אַרְעָא לְמִיתַב כַּחֲדָא אֲרֵי הֲוָה קִנְיָנְהוֹן סַגִּי וְלָא יְכִילוּ לְמִיתַב כַּחֲדָא׃

רש"י

(א) ויעל אברם וגו' הנגבה. לבא לדרומה של ארץ ישראל. כמו שאמר למעלה (יב:ט) הלוך ונסוע הנגבה, להר המוריה. ומכל מקום כשהוא הולך ממצרים לארץ כנען מדרום לצפון הוא מהלך, שארץ מצרים בדרומה של ארץ ישראל, כמו שמוכיח במסעות ובגבולי הארץ: **(ב) כבד מאד.** טעון משאות: **(ג) וילך למסעיו.** כשחזר ממצרים לארץ כנען היה הולך ולן באכסניות שלן בהם בהליכתו למצרים (ב"ר מא:ג), למדך דרך ארץ שלא ישנה אדם מאכסניא שלו (ערכין טז:). ד"א, בחזרתו פרע הקפותיו (ב"ר שם): **מנגב.** ארץ מצרים בדרומה של ארץ כנען: **(ד) אשר עשה שם בראשונה.** ואשר קרא שם אברהם בשם ה'. וגם יש לומר ויקרא שם עכשיו בשם ה': **(ה) ההלך את אברם.** מי גרם שהיה לו זאת, הליכתו עם אברם (שם; ב"ק צג.): **(ו) ולא נשא אותם.** לא היתה יכולה להספיק מרעה למקניהם. ולשון קצר הוא וצריך להוסיף עליו, [כמו] ולא

13.

1-6. The return to Eretz Yisrael.

1. **וַיַּעַל אַבְרָם** — *And Abram went up.* Although it is literally true that Abraham *ascended* because the terrain of *Eretz Yisrael* is higher than that of Egypt, the *Zohar* perceives in the verb the additional indication that Abraham *ascended spiritually* from the "lower degrees" of Egypt. He left a place of spiritual pollution and returned to his former, higher condition.

To signify this resumption of his mission of proclaiming God's Name, Abraham returned to the altar where he had declared his devotion when he first arrived in the Land (v. 4).

3. **לְמַסָּעָיו** — *On his journeys.* The implication is that these *journeys* were part of a known itinerary, implying that Abraham lodged in the same places where he stayed on his way to Egypt. The Sages (*Arachin* 16b) comment that the Torah mentions this insignificant detail to teach proper etiquette. One should not change his customary lodgings unless he has suffered harassment and anguish there. Otherwise, one discredits himself [as he will be considered hard to please or disreputable], or he will give the impression that his lodgings were unsatisfactory, thus harming his host's reputation. Alternatively, Abraham went to the same places to pay the bills he had incurred on his trip to Egypt (*Rashi*).

The teachers of *mussar* (ethics) derive a lesson in frugality from Abraham's behavior. On the way to Egypt he was not yet as wealthy, so he must have used inexpensive accommodations. On the way back, though he was much wealthier, he did not waste money on unnecessary luxury.

6-9. Abraham and Lot part ways. The lust for wealth brings out the worst in people. Abraham resisted it completely, but Lot allowed it to warp his judgment until, as the succeeding passages indicate, it destroyed nearly all of his family.

7 וַיְהִי־רִיב בֵּין רֹעֵי מִקְנֵה־אַבְרָם וּבֵין רֹעֵי

< the herdsmen < and between < of Abram, < of the livestock < the herdsmen < between < a quarrel < And there was 7

מִקְנֵה־לוֹט וְהַכְּנַעֲנִי וְהַפְּרִזִּי אָז יֹשֵׁב בָּאָרֶץ׃

« in the land. < were dwelling < at that time < and the Perizzite < – and the Canaanite « of Lot < of the livestock

8 וַיֹּאמֶר אַבְרָם אֶל־לוֹט אַל־נָא תְהִי מְרִיבָה בֵּינִי

< *between me* < *strife* < *be* < *please,* < *Let there not,* « Lot: < to < And Abram said 8

וּבֵינֶךָ וּבֵין רֹעַי וּבֵין רֹעֶיךָ כִּי־אֲנָשִׁים אַחִים

< *who are brothers* < *men* < *for* « *your herdsmen,* < *and between* < *my herdsmen* < *and between* « *and between you,*

אֲנָחְנוּ׃ 9 הֲלֹא כָל־הָאָרֶץ לְפָנֶיךָ הִפָּרֶד נָא מֵעָלָי אִם־הַשְּׂמֹאל וְאֵימִנָה

« *then I will go right,* < *[you go] left* < *If* « *from me:* < *please,* < *Separate,* « *before you?* < *the land* < *all* < *Is not* 9 « *we are.*

וְאִם־הַיָּמִין וְאַשְׂמְאִילָה׃ 10 וַיִּשָּׂא־לוֹט אֶת־עֵינָיו וַיַּרְא אֶת־כָּל־כִּכַּר

< plain < the entire < and saw < his eyes < And Lot raised 10 « *then I will go left.* < *[you go] right* < *and if*

הַיַּרְדֵּן כִּי כֻלָּהּ מַשְׁקֶה לִפְנֵי | שַׁחֵת יהוה אֶת־סְדֹם וְאֶת־עֲמֹרָה

« and Gomorrah < Sodom < HASHEM destroyed < – before « [was] well irrigated < all of it < that < of the Jordan

ז וַהֲוַת מַצּוּתָא בֵּין רָעֵי בְעִירָא דְאַבְרָם וּבֵין רָעֵי בְעִירָא דְלוֹט וּכְנַעֲנָאָה וּפְרִזָּאָה בְּכֵן יָתִיב בְּאַרְעָא: ח וַאֲמַר אַבְרָם לְלוֹט לָא כְעַן תְּהֵי מַצּוּתָא בֵּינִי וּבֵינָךְ וּבֵין רַעֲוָתִי וּבֵין רַעֲוָתָךְ אֲרֵי גוּבְרִין אַחִין אֲנָחְנָא: ט הֲלָא כָל אַרְעָא קֳדָמָךְ אִיתַּפְרֵשׁ כְּעַן מִלְוָתִי אִם אַתְּ לְצִפּוּנָא אֲנָא לְדָרוֹמָא וְאִם אַתְּ לְדָרוֹמָא אֲנָא לְצִפּוּנָא: י וּזְקַף לוֹט יָת עֵינוֹהִי וַחֲזָא יָת כָּל מֵישַׁר יַרְדְּנָא אֲרֵי כֻלַּהּ בֵּית שַׁקְיָא קֳדָם חַבָּלוּת יְיָ יָת סְדוֹם וְיָת עֲמֹרָא

רש"י

נשא אותם מרעה הארץ, לפיכך כתב ולא נשא בלשון זכר: (ז) **ויהי ריב.** לפי שהיו רועיו של לוט רשעים ומרעים בהמתם בשדות אחרים, ורועי אברם מוכיחים אותם על הגזל, והם אומרים נתנה הארץ לאברם, ולו אין יורש ולוט [בן אחיו] יורשו, ואין זה גזל, והכתוב אומר **והכנעני והפרזי אז יושב בארץ,** ולא זכה בה אברם עדיין (ב"ר שם ה): (ח) **אנשים אחים.** קרובים. ומדרש אגדה, דומין בקלסתר פנים (שם ו): (ט) **אם השמאל ואימנה.** בכל אשר תשב [ס"א אשב] לא אתרחק ממך ואעמוד לך למגן ולעזר. וסוף דבר הוצרך לו, שנא' וישמע אברם כי נשבה אחיו וגו' (להלן יד:יד): **ואימנה.** אימין את עצמי כמו ואשמאילה אשמאיל את עצמי. וא"ת היה לו לינקד וְאֵימִנָה. כך מצינו במקום אחר, אם אש לְהֵמִין (שמואל ב יד:יט) ואין נקוד לְהַיְמִין: (י) **כי כלה משקה.** ארץ נחלי מים: **לפני שחת ה' את סדום ואת עמורה.** היה אותו מישור:

7. וַיְהִי־רִיב — *And there was a quarrel.* Lot's dishonest shepherds grazed their flocks on other people's pastures. When Abraham's shepherds rebuked them for this, they responded that God had promised the land to Abraham, and since he was childless, Lot was his heir and the land was his. However, the verse specifically negates this contention by emphasizing that the Canaanites and Perizzites were still in the land; Abraham had not yet become the legitimate owner (*Rashi*).

8. אַל־נָא תְהִי מְרִיבָה — *Let there not, please, be strife.* Abraham wanted peace, but understood that the only way to avoid strife was for him to separate from Lot. So, too, in the future, God in His wisdom decreed that Israel was not to be friendly with Lot's descendants (see *Midrash* to *Numbers* 21:5), for anyone who tried to show them mercy would suffer humiliation and war. The Torah loves peace and Abraham exemplified peace, but any person who seeks peace in opposition to the wisdom of the Torah courts disaster (*R' Aharon Kotler*).

9. אִם הַשְּׂמֹאל וְאֵימִנָה — *If [you go] left then I will go right.* Directions are given assuming that one is facing east, with *right* being south and *left* being north. קֶדֶם, *in front,* refers to the east, and אָחוֹר, *behind,* refers to the west (see *Sforno*). Thus when Abraham told Lot to go either to the right or the left he assumed that Lot would continue grazing his flocks in the central mountain range of *Eretz Yisrael.* When Lot chose to go to the east, he was choosing to give up Abraham's way of life.

10-13. Lot chooses money over morality. Seeing that the two could not continue to be together, Abraham gave Lot the first choice of where to live. Lot chose the richest part of the country, even though it was also the cruelest and most corrupt. Perhaps he thought that he could enjoy the Sodomites' wealth without being affected by their evil. He was wrong.

10. כִּי כֻלָּהּ מַשְׁקֶה — *That all of it [was] well irrigated.* The Jordan Valley is similar to the Nile valley in that a river, which is not dependent on rain, constantly flows down the center of the valley and provides water for irrigation. Lot chose the "Egyptian" way of life where he would not have to look for God's help for his income. As Pharaoh exclaimed: *Who is HASHEM that I should heed His voice?* (*Exodus* 5:2), since the Nile was his god. (See *Ramban, Deuteronomy* 11:10; see also Yehuda Feliks, *Animals and Plants of the Torah.*)

כְּגַן־יהוה כְּאֶרֶץ מִצְרַיִם בֹּאֲכָה צֹעַר׃ יא וַיִּבְחַר־

like the garden — of HASHEM, — like the land — of Egypt, — coming toward — Zoar. 11 — And he chose

לוֹ לוֹט אֵת כָּל־כִּכַּר הַיַּרְדֵּן וַיִּסַּע לוֹט מִקֶּדֶם

for himself — did Lot — the whole — plain — of the Jordan, — and Lot journeyed — from the east;

וַיִּפָּרְדוּ אִישׁ מֵעַל אָחִיו׃ יב אַבְרָם יָשַׁב בְּאֶרֶץ־

and [thus] they parted, — one person — from near — his brother. 12 — Abram — dwelled — in the land

כְּנָעַן וְלוֹט יָשַׁב בְּעָרֵי הַכִּכָּר וַיֶּאֱהַל עַד־סְדֹם׃

of Canaan, — while Lot — dwelled — in the cities — of the plain — and he pitched tents — as far as — Sodom.

יג וְאַנְשֵׁי סְדֹם רָעִים וְחַטָּאִים לַיהוה מְאֹד׃ יד וַיהוה אָמַר אֶל־אַבְרָם

13 Now the people — of Sodom — were wicked — and sinners — toward HASHEM, — exceedingly. 14 — HASHEM — said — to — Abram

אַחֲרֵי הִפָּרֶד־לוֹט מֵעִמּוֹ שָׂא נָא עֵינֶיךָ וּרְאֵה מִן־הַמָּקוֹם אֲשֶׁר־אַתָּה

after — the parting — of Lot — from him, — Raise — now — your eyes — and see — from — the place — where — you are

שָׁם צָפֹנָה וָנֶגְבָּה וָקֵדְמָה וָיָמָּה׃ טו כִּי אֶת־כָּל־הָאָרֶץ אֲשֶׁר־אַתָּה

there: — northward, — southward, — eastward, — and westward. 15 *For — all — the land — that — you*

רֹאֶה לְךָ אֶתְּנֶנָּה וּלְזַרְעֲךָ עַד־עוֹלָם׃ טז וְשַׂמְתִּי אֶת־זַרְעֲךָ כַּעֲפַר הָאָרֶץ

see, — to you — will I give it, — and to your descendants — for — ever. 16 *I will make — your offspring — as the dust — of the earth*

כְּגִינְתָא דַייָ כְּאַרְעָא דְמִצְרַיִם מָטֵי לְצֹעַר׃ יא וּבְחַר לֵהּ לוֹט יָת כָּל מֵישַׁר יַרְדְּנָא וּנְטַל לוֹט מִלְּקַדְמִין וְאִתְפָּרָשׁוּ גַּבְרָא מֵעַל אֲחוּהִי׃ יב אַבְרָם יְתֵב בְּאַרְעָא דִכְנָעַן וְלוֹט יְתֵב בְּקִרְוֵי מֵישְׁרָא וּפְרַס עַד סְדוֹם׃ יג וְאֱנָשֵׁי דִסְדוֹם בִּישִׁין בְּמָמוֹנְהוֹן וְחַיָּבִין בְּגְוִיָּתְהוֹן קֳדָם יְיָ לַחֲדָא׃ יד וַייָ אֲמַר לְאַבְרָם בָּתַר דְּאִתְפָּרֵשׁ לוֹט מֵעִמֵּהּ זְקוֹף כְּעַן עֵינָךְ וַחֲזֵי מִן אַתְרָא דִּי אַתְּ תַּמָּן לְצִפּוּנָא וּלְדָרוֹמָא וּלְמָדִינְחָא וּלְמַעַרְבָא׃ טו אֲרֵי יָת כָּל אַרְעָא דִּי אַתְּ חָזֵי לָךְ אֶתְּנִנַּהּ וְלִבְנָיךְ עַד עָלָם׃ טז וְאֲשַׁוִּי יָת בְּנָךְ סַגִּיאִין כְּעַפְרָא דְאַרְעָא

רש"י

כגן ה'. לאילנות (ספרי עקב לח; ב"ר שם ז): **בארץ מצרים.** לזרעים (שם ושם): **באכה צער.** עד צוער. ומ"א דורשו לגנאי על שהיו שטופי זמה בחר לו לוט בשכונתם. במסכת הוריות (י:; ב"ר שם; תנחומא וירא יב): **(יא) ככר.** מישור, כתרגומו: **מקדם.** נסע מאצל אברם [ממזרחו] והלך לו למערבו של אברם, נמצא נוסע ממזרח למערב. ומדרש אגדה הסיע עצמו מקדמונו של עולם, אמר אי אפשי לא באברם ולא באלהיו (ב"ר שם, ועי' ב"ר לח:ז): **(יב) ויאהל.** נטה אהלים לרועיו ולמקנהו **עד סדום:** **(יג) ואנשי סדום רעים.** ואעפ"כ לא נמנע לוט מלשכון עמהם. ורבותינו למדו מכאן שם רשעים ירקב (משלי י:ז; יומא לח:; לקח טוב): **רעים.** בגופם: **וחטאים.** בממונם: **לה' מאד.** יודעים רבונם ומתכוונים למרוד בו (סנהדרין קט.; תורת כהנים בחקתי ב:ח): **(יד) אחרי הפרד לוט.** כל זמן שהרשע עמו היה הדבור פורש ממנו (תנחומא וילא י) [לפי שאמר לו הקב"ה לך לך ולא עם לוט (ב"ר מא:ח)]: **(טז) [ושמתי את זרעך כעפר הארץ.** שיהו מפוזרין בכל העולם כעפר המפוזר (שם ט). ועוד שאם אין עפר אין בעולם אילנות ותבואה, כך אם אין ישראל אין העולם מתקיים, שנאמר והתברכו בזרעך (להלן כו:ד; ב"ר שם). אבל לימות

11. מִקֶּדֶם — *From the east.* Since the word קֶדֶם can also be understood as the *ancient one,* Lot separated himself מִקַּדְמוֹנוֹ שֶׁל עוֹלָם, *from [God,] the Ancient One of the World,* saying: "I want neither Abraham nor his God!" (*Midrash; Rashi*).

וַיִּפָּרְדוּ — *And [thus] they parted.* Though Lot contained the spiritual sparks that were to produce Ruth, the ancestress of King David, he *parted from Abram.* In time the rift between their progeny would become so absolute that his male descendants from Ammon and Moab would be prohibited from entering the congregation of Israel [*Deut.* 23:4] (*Pesikta Zutresa*).

14-18. The repetition of the promise. After Lot's departure, God repeated His promise to Abraham (12:7), to emphasize that the Land had been given exclusively to him and his descendants, not to Lot.

15. לְךָ אֶתְּנֶנָּה — *To you will I give it.* Take possession of the Land, so that you can bequeath it to your descendants, for, in the legal sense, *Eretz Yisrael* is a legacy from the Patriarchs (*Bava Basra* 119b). In the plain meaning, God was assuring Abraham that even then the inhabitants of Canaan would honor him as if he were already a ruler (*Ramban, Sforno*).

עַד־עוֹלָם — *For ever.* God did not say that Jews would always *possess* the Land — for during the long centuries of exile they certainly did not — but that the nation of Israel and the Land of Israel would always be destined for each other, just as it was given to Abraham, though he never took legal possession of it in his lifetime (*R' Hirsch*).

16. כַּעֲפַר הָאָרֶץ — *As the dust of the earth.* Just as dust outlives all who tread upon it, so God promised Abraham that his off-

אֲשֶׁר ׀ אִם־יוּכַל אִישׁ לִמְנוֹת אֶת־עֲפַר הָאָרֶץ
so that < if < it is possible < for a person < to count < the dust < of the earth, «

גַּם זַרְעֲךָ יִמָּנֶה׃ יז קוּם הִתְהַלֵּךְ בָּאָרֶץ לְאָרְכָּהּ
[then,] too, < your offspring < will be counted. « 17 Arise, < walk about < in the land < through its length <

וּלְרָחְבָּהּ כִּי לְךָ אֶתְּנֶנָּה׃ יח וַיֶּאֱהַל אַבְרָם וַיָּבֹא
and through its breadth! « For < to you < I will give it. « 18 And Abram pitched [his] tents < and came <

וַיֵּשֶׁב בְּאֵלֹנֵי מַמְרֵא אֲשֶׁר בְּחֶבְרוֹן וַיִּבֶן־שָׁם מִזְבֵּחַ
and dwelled < in the plains < of Mamre < which are < in Hebron; « and he built < there < an altar <

לַיהוָה׃ פ רביעי [יד] א וַיְהִי בִּימֵי אַמְרָפֶל מֶלֶךְ־שִׁנְעָר אַרְיוֹךְ מֶלֶךְ
to HASHEM. « [14] 1 And it happened < in the days < of Amraphel, < King < of Shinar; < Arioch, < King <

אֶלָּסָר כְּדָרְלָעֹמֶר מֶלֶךְ עֵילָם וְתִדְעָל מֶלֶךְ גּוֹיִם׃ ב עָשׂוּ מִלְחָמָה אֶת־
of Ellasar; < Chedorlaomer, < King < of Elam, < and Tidal, < King < of Goiim, « 2 [that these] made < war < on <

בֶּרַע מֶלֶךְ סְדֹם וְאֶת־בִּרְשַׁע מֶלֶךְ עֲמֹרָה שִׁנְאָב ׀ מֶלֶךְ אַדְמָה וְשֶׁמְאֵבֶר
Bera, < King < of Sodom; < on < Birsha, < King < of Gomorrah; < Shinab, < King < of Admah; < Shemeber, <

כְּמָא דִּי לָא אֶפְשַׁר לִגְבַר לְמִמְנֵי יָת עַפְרָא דְאַרְעָא אַף בְּנָיךְ לָא יִתְמְנוּן׃ יז קוּם הַלִּיךְ בְּאַרְעָא לְאָרְכַּהּ וּלְפִתְיַהּ אֲרֵי לָךְ אֶתְנִנַּהּ׃ יח וּפְרַס אַבְרָם וַאֲתָא וִיתֵב בְּמֵישְׁרֵי מַמְרֵא דִּי בְחֶבְרוֹן וּבְנָא תַמָּן מַדְבְּחָא קֳדָם יְיָ׃ א וַהֲוָה בְּיוֹמֵי אַמְרָפֶל מַלְכָּא דְבָבֶל אַרְיוֹךְ מַלְכָּא דְאֶלָּסָר כְּדָרְלָעֹמֶר מַלְכָּא דְעֵילָם וְתִדְעָל מַלְכָּא דְעַמְמֵי׃ ב סְדָרוּ (נ"א עֲבַדוּ) קְרָבָא עִם בֶּרַע מַלְכָּא דִסְדֹם וְעִם בִּרְשַׁע מַלְכָּא דַעֲמֹרָה שִׁנְאָב מַלְכָּא דְאַדְמָה וְשֶׁמְאֵבֶר

רש"י

המשיח משולין כחול שמקהה שיני הכל כן יפלו ויקהו כל העולם, שנאמר ולו יקהת עמים (להלן מט:י; ב"ר לט:ח; במ"ר ב:יג:) **אשר אם יוכל איש.** כשם שאי אפשר לעפר להמנות כך זרעך לא ימנה: (יח) **ממרא.** שם אדם (ב"ר מב:ח): [**באלני ממרא.** שמרד בע"ז:] **אשר בחברון.** שחבר את עצמו להקב"ה:] (א) **אמרפל.** הוא נמרוד שאמר לאברהם פול לתוך כבשן האש (עירובין נג.; תנחומא ו): **מלך גוים.** מקום יש ששמו גוים, על שם שנתקבצו שמה מכמה גוים ומקומות והמליכו איש עליהם ושמו תדעל (ב"ר מב:ד): (ב) **ברע.** רע לשמים ורע לבריות: **ברשע.** שנתעלה ברשעו: **שנאב.** שונא אביו שבשמים: **שמאבר.** שם אבר לעוף ולקפוץ

spring would outlive all the nations that would persecute them (*Midrash*).

17. This is both a promise and a command: a *promise* of God's protection while Abraham roamed freely through the Land; and a *command* that he walk through it to symbolize that he was taking possession of God's gift (*Ramban*).

18. As he had done before, Abraham expressed his gratitude for God's prophecy by erecting an altar (*Abarbanel*).

14.

☙ The War of the Kings.

This chapter reveals a new side of Abraham's nature: his physical courage in battle. Lot, happily settled in Sodom, became the victim of a war involving the major kingdoms of the region. Although Abraham was hopelessly outnumbered, he mobilized his disciples and went into battle to rescue Lot. Miraculously, he triumphed and, in a further demonstration of his noble character, he refused to accept any spoils, though he was entitled to them by the international law of the day. However, he would not deprive his allies of their rightful share. Thereby he proved his own integrity in two ways: By refusing personal gain he showed that he had acted only to save his nephew, but not for himself, and he showed that he would not deprive others of their entitlements in order to prove his own righteousness.

1. . . . אַמְרָפֶל — *Amraphel . . .* The Sages (*Eruvin* 53a) identify *Amraphel* as Nimrod, who reigned over Shinar [Babylon], and who had ordered that Abraham be thrown into the furnace because of his refusal to accept idol worship. The Midrash identifies *Chedorlaomer* as Elam, son of Shem son of Noah. Although, as indicated in verse 5, Chedorlaomer was the leader of this alliance, Amraphel is mentioned first because he was the senior of the four kings. For twelve years, Chedorlaomer and his allies dominated the region and a wide array of lesser kings paid tribute to them (v. 4). Then, for a period of thirteen years, five vassal kings rebelled (ibid.), until the alliance asserted its authority, crushing the revolt and taking spoils, not only from the rebel kingdoms, but from others, as well — from anyone they suspected of sympathizing with the rebels (vs. 5-6).

מֶלֶךְ °צְבוֹיִם [°צביים כ׳] וּמֶלֶךְ בֶּלַע הִיא־צֹעַר׃

« Zoar. < which is < of Bela, < and the King « of Zeboiim; < King

ג כָּל־אֵלֶּה חָבְרוּ אֶל־עֵמֶק הַשִּׂדִּים הוּא יָם הַמֶּלַח׃

« of Salt. < the Sea < that is [now] < of Siddim, < the Valley < at < had joined < these < All 3

ד שְׁתֵּים עֶשְׂרֵה שָׁנָה עָבְדוּ אֶת־כְּדָרְלָעֹמֶר

< Chedorlaomer, < they served < years < Twelve 4

וּשְׁלֹשׁ־עֶשְׂרֵה שָׁנָה מָרָדוּ׃ ה וּבְאַרְבַּע עֶשְׂרֵה

< And in the fourteenth 5 « they rebelled. < years < and thirteen

שָׁנָה בָּא כְדָרְלָעֹמֶר וְהַמְּלָכִים אֲשֶׁר אִתּוֹ וַיַּכּוּ

< and struck < with him < who were < and the kings < Chedorlaomer < came < year,

אֶת־רְפָאִים בְּעַשְׁתְּרֹת קַרְנַיִם וְאֶת־הַזּוּזִים בְּהָם וְאֵת הָאֵימִים

< the Emim < in Ham, < the Zuzim < at Ashteroth-karnaim, < the Rephaim

בְּשָׁוֵה קִרְיָתָיִם׃ ו וְאֶת־הַחֹרִי בְּהַרְרָם שֵׂעִיר עַד אֵיל פָּארָן אֲשֶׁר

< which is < of Paran < the plain < as far as < of Seir, < in their mountain < and the Horites 6 « at Shaveh-kiriathaim;

עַל־הַמִּדְבָּר׃ ז וַיָּשֻׁבוּ וַיָּבֹאוּ אֶל־עֵין מִשְׁפָּט הִוא קָדֵשׁ וַיַּכּוּ אֶת־כָּל־

< all < they struck « Kadesh; < which is « En-mishpat, < to < and they came < And [then] they turned back 7 « the desert. < next to

שְׂדֵה הָעֲמָלֵקִי וְגַם אֶת־הָאֱמֹרִי הַיֹּשֵׁב בְּחַצְצֹן תָּמָר׃ ח וַיֵּצֵא מֶלֶךְ־סְדֹם

< of Sodom < did the King < And go forth 8 « in Hazazon-tamar. < who dwell < the Amorites < and also « of the Amalekites; < the fields

וּמֶלֶךְ עֲמֹרָה וּמֶלֶךְ אַדְמָה וּמֶלֶךְ °צְבוֹיִם [°צביים כ׳] וּמֶלֶךְ בֶּלַע

< of Bela, < and the King < of Zeboiim, < the King < of Admah, < the King < of Gomorrah, < and the King

מַלְכָּא דִצְבוֹיִם וּמַלְכָּא דְבֶלַע הִיא צֹעַר: ג כָּל אִלֵּין אִתְכְּנָשׁוּ לְמֵישַׁר חַקְלַיָּא הוּא אֲתַר יַמָּא דְמִלְחָא: ד תַּרְתֵּי עֲשַׂר שְׁנִין פְּלָחוּ יָת כְּדָרְלָעֹמֶר וּתְלָת עֶשְׂרֵי שְׁנִין מְרָדוּ: ה וּבְאַרְבַּע עֶשְׂרֵי שְׁנִין אֲתָא כְדָרְלָעֹמֶר וּמַלְכַיָּא דִי עִמֵּהּ וּמְחוֹ יָת גִּבָּרַיָּא דִי בְעַשְׁתְּרוֹת קַרְנַיִם וְיָת תַּקִּיפַיָּא דִבְהֶמְתָּא וְיָת אֵימְתָנֵי דִבְשָׁוֵה קִרְיָתָיִם: ו וְיָת חוֹרָאֵי דִי בְטוּרְהוֹן דְשֵׂעִיר עַד מֵישַׁר פָּארָן דִי סְמִיךְ עַל מַדְבְּרָא: ז וְתָבוּ וַאֲתוֹ לְמֵישַׁר פְּלוּג דִינָא הִיא רְקָם וּמְחוֹ יָת כָּל חֲקַל עֲמַלְקָאָה וְאַף יָת אֱמוֹרָאָה דְיָתֵיב בְּעֵין גֶּדִי: ח וּנְפַק מַלְכָּא דִסְדוֹם וּמַלְכָּא דַעֲמוֹרָה וּמַלְכָּא דְאַדְמָה וּמַלְכָּא דִצְבוֹיִם וּמַלְכָּא דְבֶלַע

רש"י

ולמרוד בהקב"ה (תנחומא ח): **בלע.** שם העיר (ב"ר שם ה): (ג) **עמק השדים.** כך שמו, על שם שהיו בו שדות הרבה (אונקלוס): **הוא ים המלח.** לאחר זמן נמשך הים לתוכו ונעשה ים המלח. ומדרש אגדה אומר שנתבקעו הצורים סביבותיו ונמשכו יאורים לתוכו (ב"ר שם): (ד) **שתים עשרה שנה עבדו.** חמשה מלכים הללו את כדרלעומר: (ה) **ובארבע עשרה שנה.** למרדן (שם): **בא כדרלעומר.** לפי שהוא היה בעל המעשה נכנס בעובי הקורה (שם): **והמלכים וגו׳.** אלו שלשה מלכים: **זוזים.** הם זמזומים (דברים ב:כ): (ו) **בהררם.** בהר שלהם (אונקלוס): **איל פארן.** כתרגומו מישר. ואומר אני שאין איל לשון מישור אלא מישור של פארן איל שמו. ושל ממרא אלוני שמו. ושל ירדן ככר שמו. ושל שטים אבל שמו אבל השטים (דברים לג:מט). וכן בעל גד (יהושע יא:יז) בעל שמו. וכולן מתורגמין מישר, וכל אחד שמו עליו: **על המדבר.** אצל המדבר, כמו ועליו מטה מנשה (במדבר ב:כ): (ז) **עין משפט הוא קדש.** ע"ש העתיד, שעתידין משה ואהרן להשפט שם על עסקי אותו העין, והם מי מריבה (תנחומא ח). [ואונקלוס תרגמו כפשוטו, מקום שהיו בני המדינה מתקבצים שם לכל משפט]: **שדה העמלקי.** עדיין לא נולד עמלק, ונקרא על שם העתיד (ב"ר מב:ז; תנחומא ח): **בחצצן תמר.** הוא עין גדי, מקרא מלא בדברי הימים (ב כ:ב) ביהושפט:

7. וַיָּשֻׁבוּ — *And [then] they turned back.* Having terrorized the southern kingdoms, the four kings turned back northward to their real goal, the conquest of the rebel kingdoms.

8-10. Sodom is defeated. This was the key battle of the rebellion. With his four allies, the king of Sodom took the initiative in attacking Chedorlaomer's invading force (*Haamek Davar*). To give themselves the advantage, the five kings chose a battlefield that could be defended by an outnumbered army with the advantage of familiarity with the terrain. Had they been brave and able fighters, they would have won, but the kings of Sodom and Gomorrah were soft and decadent. Not only were they routed, they fled in such panic that they fell into the very pits that they had relied on to give them the upper hand (*R' Hirsch*).

הִוא־צֹעַר וַיַּעַרְכוּ אִתָּם מִלְחָמָה בְּעֵמֶק הַשִּׂדִּים׃
which is Zoar, and they engaged them in battle in the Valley of Siddim:

9 ט אֵת כְּדָרְלָעֹמֶר מֶלֶךְ עֵילָם וְתִדְעָל מֶלֶךְ גּוֹיִם
With Chedorlaomer, King of Elam, Tidal, King of Goiim,

וְאַמְרָפֶל מֶלֶךְ שִׁנְעָר וְאַרְיוֹךְ מֶלֶךְ אֶלָּסָר אַרְבָּעָה
Amraphel, King of Shinar, and Arioch, King of Ellasar — four

מְלָכִים אֶת־הַחֲמִשָּׁה׃ י וְעֵמֶק הַשִּׂדִּים בֶּאֱרֹת
kings against the five. 10 And [now,] the Valley of Siddim was [full of] pits

בֶּאֱרֹת חֵמָר וַיָּנֻסוּ מֶלֶךְ־סְדֹם וַעֲמֹרָה וַיִּפְּלוּ־
and pits of tar. They fled — the kings of Sodom and Gomorrah — and they fell

שָׁמָּה וְהַנִּשְׁאָרִים הֶרָה נָּסוּ׃ יא וַיִּקְחוּ אֶת־כָּל־רְכֻשׁ סְדֹם וַעֲמֹרָה
there [while] the rest to a mountain fled. 11 They seized all the possessions of Sodom and Gomorrah

וְאֶת־כָּל־אָכְלָם וַיֵּלֵכוּ׃ יב וַיִּקְחוּ אֶת־לוֹט וְאֶת־רְכֻשׁוֹ בֶּן־אֲחִי אַבְרָם
and all their food and they went [away]. 12 And they seized Lot and his possessions — the son of the brother of Abram —

וַיֵּלֵכוּ וְהוּא יֹשֵׁב בִּסְדֹם׃ יג וַיָּבֹא הַפָּלִיט וַיַּגֵּד לְאַבְרָם הָעִבְרִי וְהוּא
and they went [away]; for he was residing in Sodom. 13 Then there came the fugitive and he told Abram, the Ivri, who [now] was

הִיא צוֹעַר וְסַדָּרוּ עִמְּהוֹן קְרָבָא בְּמֵישַׁר חַקְלַיָּא: ט עִם כְּדָרְלָעֹמֶר מַלְכָּא דְעֵילָם וְתִדְעָל מַלְכָּא דְעַמְמִין וְאַמְרָפֶל מַלְכָּא דְבָבֶל וְאַרְיוֹךְ מַלְכָּא דְאֶלָּסָר אַרְבְּעָה מַלְכִין לָקֳבֵיל חַמְשָׁא: י וּמֵישַׁר חַקְלַיָּא בֵּירִין בֵּירִין מַסְּקָן חֵימָרָא וַעֲרָקוּ מַלְכָּא דִסְדוֹם וַעֲמוֹרָה וּנְפָלוּ תַמָּן וּדְאִשְׁתְּאָרוּ לְטוּרָא עֲרָקוּ: יא וּשְׁבוֹ יָת כָּל קִנְיָנָא דִסְדוֹם וַעֲמוֹרָה וְיָת כָּל מֵיכָלְהוֹן וַאֲזָלוּ: יב וּשְׁבוֹ יָת לוֹט וְיָת קִנְיָנֵהּ בַּר אֲחוּהִי דְאַבְרָם וַאֲזָלוּ וְהוּא יָתֵב בִּסְדוֹם: יג וַאֲתָא מְשֵׁיזָבָא וְחַוִּי לְאַבְרָם עִבְרָאָה וְהוּא

רש"י

(ט) **ארבעה מלכים וגו׳.** ואעפ"כ נצחו המועטים, להודיעך שגבורים היו, ואעפ"כ לא נמנע אברהם מלרדוף אחריהם: (י) **בארות בארות חמר.** בארות הרבה היו שם שנוטלים משם אדמה לטיט של בנין (אונקלוס). ומ"א שהיה הטיט [מוגבל] בהם, ונעשה נס למלך סדום שילא משם. לפי שהיו באומות מקלתן שלא היו מאמינים שניצול אברהם מאור כשדים מכבשן האש, וכיון שילא זה מן החמר האמינו באברהם למפרע (ב"ר שם): **הרה נסו.** להר נסו. הרה כמו להר. כל תיבה שצריכה למ"ד בתחלתה הטיל לה ה"א בסופה. ויש חילוק בין הרה לההרה, שה"א שבסוף התיבה עומדת במקום למ"ד שבראשה, אבל אינה עומדת במקום למ"ד ונקודה [ס"א לנקוד] פתח תחתיה, והרי הרה כמו לְהַר או כמו אל הר ואינו מפרש לאיזה הר אלא שכל א׳ נס באשר מצא הר תחלה. וכשהוא נותן ה"א בראשה לכתוב ההרה או המדברה פתרונו כמו אל ההר או כמו להר, ומשמע לאותו הר הידוע ומפורש בפרשה: (יב) **והוא יושב בסדום.** מי גרם לו זאת, ישיבתו בסדום (שם): (יג) **ויבא הפליט.** לפי פשוטו זה עוג שפלט מן המלחמה, והוא שכתוב כי רק עוג נשאר מיתר הרפאים (דברים ג:יא) וזהו נשאר, שלא הרגוהו אמרפל וחביריו כשהכו את הרפאים בעשתרות קרנים. תנחומא (חקת כה). ומדרש ב"ר, זה עוג שפלט מדור המבול, וזהו מיתר הרפאים, שנאמר הנפילים היו בארץ וגו׳ (לעיל ו:ד). ומתכוין שיהרג אברם וישא את שרה (ב"ר שם ח): **העברי.** שבא מעבר הנהר (שם):

12. Lot taken captive. The Midrash notes that the invaders took Lot captive because of his relationship to Abraham. They put him in a cage and boasted, "We have captured Abram's nephew!" As the verse implies, he deserved his fate *for he was residing in Sodom*, having chosen of his own free will to leave Abraham and associate with wicked people (*Yafeh To'ar*).

Zohar explains that Abraham was a target of the kings, because he weaned people away from idolatry and taught them to serve God. Also, God incited them to this course so that Abraham would defeat them and thereby become so respected that people would be attracted to his teachings.

13. הַפָּלִיט — *The fugitive.* The Midrash identifies him as the giant Og, king of Bashan, the only *fugitive* who survived the Flood. In the plain meaning, he is called a fugitive because he had just escaped the battle of the Rephaim, who had been conquered by the four kings [see *Deut.* 3:11].

The Midrash notes that Og hoped to incite Abraham to go to war to rescue Lot, confident that he would be killed in the battle, and Og would then be able to take Sarah as his queen (*Rashi*). God rewards for good and punishes for evil: For his good deed of informing Abraham, Og was rewarded with exceptionally long life; for his wicked motive, however, he ultimately fell into the hands of Abraham's descendants.

הָעִבְרִי — *The Ivri*. For the reason for this name, see introduction to Chapter 12. Alternatively, the name means that he was a descendant of Eber. Only Abraham's descendants are called

שֹׁכֵן בְּאֵלֹנֵי מַמְרֵא הָאֱמֹרִי אֲחִי אֶשְׁכֹּל וַאֲחִי

< and the brother < of Eshcol < the brother << the Amorite, < of Mamre, < in the plains < dwelling

עָנֵר וְהֵם בַּעֲלֵי בְרִית־אַבְרָם: יד וַיִּשְׁמַע אַבְרָם

< And [when] Abram heard **14** << [with] Abram. < of a covenant < members < they being << of Aner,

כִּי נִשְׁבָּה אָחִיו וַיָּרֶק אֶת־חֲנִיכָיו יְלִידֵי בֵיתוֹ

<< in his house < who had been born < his disciples < he armed << was his brother, < taken captive < that

שְׁמֹנָה עָשָׂר וּשְׁלֹשׁ מֵאוֹת וַיִּרְדֹּף עַד־דָּן: טו וַיֵּחָלֵק

< And [his forces] were split **15** << Dan. < as far as < and he pursued [them] << hundred — < and three < — eighteen

עֲלֵיהֶם ׀ לַיְלָה הוּא וַעֲבָדָיו וַיַּכֵּם וַיִּרְדְּפֵם עַד־חוֹבָה אֲשֶׁר מִשְּׂמֹאל

< to the north < which is < Hobah < as far as << and he pursued them << and he struck them; << with his servants < — he << [at] night < against them

לְדַמָּשֶׂק: טז וַיָּשֶׁב אֵת כָּל־הָרְכֻשׁ וְגַם אֶת־לוֹט אָחִיו וּרְכֻשׁוֹ הֵשִׁיב

<< he brought back, < and his possessions < his brother < Lot < and also << the possessions; < all < He brought back **16** << of Damascus.

וְגַם אֶת־הַנָּשִׁים וְאֶת־הָעָם: יז וַיֵּצֵא מֶלֶךְ־סְדֹם לִקְרָאתוֹ אַחֲרֵי שׁוּבוֹ

< his return < after < to meet him < The King of Sodom went out **17** << and the people. < the women < and also

שָׁרֵי בְּמֵישְׁרֵי מַמְרֵא אֱמוֹרָאָה אֲחוּהִי
דְאֶשְׁכּוֹל וַאֲחוּהִי דְעָנֵר וְאִנּוּן אֱנָשֵׁי
קְיָמֵהּ דְּאַבְרָם: יד וּשְׁמַע אַבְרָם אֲרֵי
אִשְׁתְּבִי אֲחוּהִי וְזָרֵיז יָת עוּלֵימוֹהִי
יְלִידֵי בֵיתֵהּ תְּלָת מְאָה וְתַמְנֵי עֲסַר
וּרְדַף עַד דָּן: טו וְאִתְפְּלֵג עֲלֵיהוֹן
לֵילְיָא הוּא וְעַבְדוֹהִי וּמְחוֹנוּן וּרְדָפִנּוּן
עַד חוֹבָה דִּי מִצִּפּוּנָא לְדַמָּשֶׂק:
טז וַאֲתֵיב יָת כָּל קִנְיָנָא וְאַף יָת
לוֹט בַּר אֲחוּהִי וְקִנְיָנֵהּ אֲתֵיב
וְאַף יָת נְשַׁיָּא וְיָת עַמָּא: יז וּנְפַק
מַלְכָּא דִסְדוֹם לְקַדָּמוּתֵהּ בָּתַר דְּתָב

רש"י

בעלי ברית אברם. שכרתו עמו ברית [ד"א, שהשיאו לו עצה על המילה (שם) כמו שמפורש במקום אחר (ברש"י תחלת וירא)]: **(יד) וירק.** כתרגומו וזריז. וכן והריקותי אחריכם חרב (ויקרא כו:לג) אזדיין בחרבי עליכם. וכן אריק חרבי (שמות טו:ט). וכן והרק חנית וסגור (תהלים לה:ג): **חניכיו.** [חניכו כתיב [ס"א קרי] זה אליעזר שחנכו למצות, [ס"א שחינך אותו למצות] והוא לשון התחלת כניסת האדם או כלי לאומנות שהוא עתיד לעמוד בה. וכן חנוך לנער (משלי כב:ו) חנוכת המזבח (במדבר ז:יא) חנוכת הבית (תהלים ל:א). ובלע"ז קורין לו איניציי"ר: **שמונה עשר וגו'.** רבותינו אמרו אליעזר לבדו היה והוא מנין גימטריא של שמו (ב"ר מג:ב; נדרים לב.): **עד דן.** שם תשש כחו, שראה שעתידין בניו להעמיד שם עגל (סנהדרין צו.): **(טו) ויחלק עליהם.** לפי פשוטו סרס המקרא, ויחלק הוא ועבדיו עליהם לילה, כדרך הרודפים שמתפלגים אחר הנרדפים כשבורחים זה לכאן וזה לכאן: **לילה.** כלומר אחר שחשכה לא נמנע מלרדפם. ומ"א, שנחלק הלילה, ובחציו הראשון נעשה לו נס, וחציו השני נשמר ובא לו לחצות לילה של מצרים (ב"ר שם): **עד חובה.** אין מקום ששמו חובה, ודן קורא חובה ע"ש עבודת כוכבים שעתידה להיות שם (תנחומא יג):

"Ivrim" for they alone spoke Hebrew, Eber's language. Eber's other descendants spoke Aramaic, and are called Arameans (*Radak*).

14-16. Abraham saves Lot.

14. וַיָּרֶק אֶת־חֲנִיכָיו — *He armed his disciples.* Abraham armed the disciples he had educated in the service of Hashem. The Sages fault him for using Torah scholars to wage war, and maintain that this was one of the reasons his descendants were consigned to Egyptian servitude (*Nedarim* 32a).

The Talmud offers a Midrashic interpretation that the 318 warriors whom Abraham mobilized consisted of one person, Abraham's loyal servant Eliezer. He was equivalent to 318 people, as indicated by the numerical value of his name (ibid.).

יְלִידֵי בֵיתוֹ — *Who had been born in his house.* Abraham and Sarah had converted many disciples, but the ones who were most receptive to their teachings were those who had been in their household from birth. Lot, however, had formed his attitudes and character before he came under Abraham's tutelage, and Abraham could only refine him, not transform him (*R' Hirsch*).

עַד־דָּן — *As far as Dan.* At Dan, in the north of *Eretz Yisrael,* Abraham's strength ebbed because he foresaw prophetically that his descendants would set up a calf there as an idol [*I Kings* 12:29] (*Rashi*). This is one of many instances in the Torah where future events have an effect on current history. The sense of this phenomenon is that the potential for the future is contained in the present; if there was idolatry in Abraham's offspring, it indicated an insufficiency in *him*.

15. מִשְּׂמֹאל — *To the north.* See commentary to 13:9.

16. וְגַם אֶת־לוֹט — *And also Lot.* First the Torah lists the lesser accomplishment, that Abraham was able to retrieve and return all the property that had been looted by the marauders. Then it relates the greater triumph — the one that was Abraham's goal — the rescue of Lot, even though one would have expected the defeated kings to avenge themselves against Abraham by killing his nephew (*Or HaChaim*).

מֵהַכּוֹת אֶת־כְּדָרְלָעֹמֶר וְאֶת־הַמְּלָכִים אֲשֶׁר אִתּוֹ

«with him, ‹ that were ‹ and the kings ‹ Chedorlaomer ‹ from striking

אֶל־עֵמֶק שָׁוֵה הוּא עֵמֶק הַמֶּלֶךְ: יח וּמַלְכִּי־צֶדֶק

‹ [Meanwhile] Malchizedek, 18 « of the king. ‹ the valley ‹ which is ‹ of Shaveh ‹ the Valley ‹ to

מֶלֶךְ שָׁלֵם הוֹצִיא לֶחֶם וָיָיִן וְהוּא כֹהֵן לְאֵל

‹ unto God, ‹ a priest ‹ he was « and wine; ‹ bread ‹ brought out ‹ of Salem, ‹ King

עֶלְיוֹן: יט וַיְבָרְכֵהוּ וַיֹּאמַר בָּרוּךְ אַבְרָם לְאֵל

‹ *to God,* ‹ *Abram* ‹ *Blessed is* « and said: ‹ He blessed him 19 « the Most High.

עֶלְיוֹן קֹנֵה שָׁמַיִם וָאָרֶץ: כ וּבָרוּךְ אֵל עֶלְיוֹן

‹ *the Most High,* ‹ *God,* ‹ *and blessed is* 20 « *and earth;* ‹ *of heaven* ‹ *Maker* « *the Most High,*

אֲשֶׁר־מִגֵּן צָרֶיךָ בְּיָדֶךָ וַיִּתֶּן־לוֹ מַעֲשֵׂר מִכֹּל: חמישי כא וַיֹּאמֶר מֶלֶךְ־סְדֹם

‹ The King of Sodom said 21 « of everything. ‹ a tenth ‹ And he [Abram] gave him « *into your hand.* ‹ *your foes* ‹ *has delivered* ‹ *Who*

אֶל־אַבְרָם תֶּן־לִי הַנֶּפֶשׁ וְהָרְכֻשׁ קַח־לָךְ: כב וַיֹּאמֶר אַבְרָם אֶל־מֶלֶךְ

‹ the King ‹ to ‹ Abram said 22 « *for yourself.* ‹ *take* ‹ *but the possessions* ‹ *the people,* ‹ *me* ‹ *Give* « Abram: ‹ to

סְדֹם הֲרִמֹתִי יָדִי אֶל־יהוה אֵל עֶלְיוֹן קֹנֵה שָׁמַיִם וָאָרֶץ: כג אִם־מִחוּט

‹ *from a thread* ‹ *if [I take]* 23 « *and earth,* ‹ *of heaven* ‹ *Maker* « *the Most High,* ‹ *God,* ‹ *Hashem,* ‹ *to* ‹ *my hand* ‹ *I lift up* « of Sodom:

מִלְּמִמְחֵי יָת כְּדָרְלָעוֹמֶר וְיָת מַלְכַיָּא דִּי עִמֵּהּ לְמֵישַׁר מַפְנָא הוּא אֲתַר בֵּית רֵיסָא דְמַלְכָּא: יח וּמַלְכִּי צֶדֶק מַלְכָּא דִירוּשְׁלֶם אַפֵּיק לְחֵם וַחֲמַר וְהוּא מְשַׁמֵּשׁ קֳדָם אֵל עִלָּאָה: יט וּבָרְכֵהּ וַאֲמַר בְּרִיךְ אַבְרָם לְאֵל עִלָּאָה דִּקְנְיָנֵהּ שְׁמַיָּא וְאַרְעָא: כ וּבְרִיךְ אֵל עִלָּאָה דִּמְסַר סָנְאָיךְ בִּידָךְ וִיהַב לֵהּ חַד מִן עַסְרָא מִכֹּלָּא: כא וַאֲמַר מַלְכָּא דִסְדוֹם לְאַבְרָם הַב לִי נַפְשָׁתָא וְקִנְיָנָא (סַב) דְּבַר לָךְ: כב וַאֲמַר אַבְרָם לְמַלְכָּא דִסְדוֹם אֲרֵימִית יְדִי בִּצְלוֹ קֳדָם יְיָ (קֳדָם) אֵל עִלָּאָה דִּקְנְיָנֵהּ שְׁמַיָּא וְאַרְעָא: כג אִם מִחוּטָא

רש"י

(יז) **עמק שוה.** כך שמו כתרגומו, למישר מפנא, פנוי מאילנות ומכל מכשול: **עמק המלך.** בית ריסא דמלכא (אונקלוס). בית רים א' שהוא שלשים קנים שהיה מיוחד למלך לצחק שם. ומ"א, עמק שהושוו שם כל האומות והמליכו את אברם עליהם לנשיא אלהים ולקצין (ב"ר שם): (יח) **ומלכי צדק.** מ"א, הוא שם בן נח (נדרים לב:; תרגום יונתן): **לחם ויין.** כך עושים ליגיעי מלחמה, והראה לו שאין בלבו עליו על שהרג את בניו (תנחומא טו). ומ"א, רמז לו על המנחות ועל הנסכים שיקריבו שם בניו (ב"ר שם): (יט) **קנה שמים וארץ.** כמו עושה שמים וארץ, על ידי עשייתו קנאן להיות שלו: (כ) **אשר מגן.** אשר הסגיר (אונקלוס). וכן אמגנך ישראל (הושע יא:ח): **ויתן לו.** אברם (ב"ר מג:ח; מד:ז; פס"ר כה (קכז:)): **מעשר מכל.** אשר לו, לפי שהיה כהן: (כא) **תן לי הנפש.** מן השבי שלי שהצלת, החזר לי הגופים לבדם: (כב) **הרמתי ידי.** לשון שבועה, מרים אני את ידי לאל עליון (ב"ר מג:ט; תרגום יונתן). וכן בי נשבעתי (להלן כב:טז) נשבע אני. וכן נתתי כסף השדה קח ממני (שם כג:יג) נותן אני לך כסף השדה וקחהו ממני:

18. וּמַלְכִּי־צֶדֶק — *[Meanwhile] Malchizedek*. After meeting Abraham at the Valley of Shaveh, the king of Sodom escorted him to the city of Salem [= Jerusalem] where they were met by Malchizedek, whom the Sages identify as Shem, son of Noah. He was called Malchizedek because he was the king [מֶלֶךְ] of the future site of the Temple, the home of righteousness [צֶדֶק]. As the most honored of Noah's children, Shem was made the priest of God in Jerusalem (*Ramban*).

כֹּהֵן לְאֵל עֶלְיוֹן — *A priest unto God, the Most High.* Unlike the priests of the other nations who served angels, Malchizedek served Hashem (*Ramban*).

19. The Sages derive that Malchizedek did not pass on the priesthood to his heirs; it was stripped from him and given to Abraham (*Nedarim* 32b). Even though Abraham himself was a descendant of Malchizedek — Shem — he won the priesthood through personal merit, not through inheritance (*Ran*, ibid.).

20. וּבָרוּךְ אֵל — *And blessed is God.* How can a human being bless God, as if man is capable of giving Him something He lacks? A blessing is an acknowledgment that God is the Source of all good (*Chinuch* §430). When used to bless God, the word for blessing, *berachah*, is derived from בְּרֵכָה, *a spring,* meaning that God is like a never-ending spring, that provides a constant flow of blessing to His creatures. Thus, when we "bless" God, we are acknowledging His majesty (*Rashba*; *Nefesh HaChaim*).

מַעֲשֵׂר מִכֹּל — *A tenth of everything.* By giving tithes to Malchizedek, Abraham symbolized that his descendants would give *maaser* [tithes] to the Levites (*Ramban*).

21-23. Abraham declines the king's offer. Seeing Abraham's magnanimity to Malchizedek, the king of Sodom is emboldened to make an audacious request. Though Abraham, as the victor, was entitled to keep all the spoils of the war, the

וְעַד שְׂרוֹךְ־נַעַל וְאִם־אֶקַּח מִכָּל־אֲשֶׁר־לָךְ

« yours! ‹ that is ‹ from anything ‹ I take ‹ and if « of a shoe; ‹ a lace ‹ to

וְלֹא תֹאמַר אֲנִי הֶעֱשַׁרְתִּי אֶת־אַבְרָם: כד בִּלְעָדַי

« Aside from me! 24 « who made Abram rich.' ‹ 'It is I « [So that] you shall not say,

רַק אֲשֶׁר אָכְלוּ הַנְּעָרִים וְחֵלֶק הָאֲנָשִׁים אֲשֶׁר

‹ who ‹ of the men ‹ and the share « the young men consumed ‹ that which ‹ Only

הָלְכוּ אִתִּי עָנֵר אֶשְׁכֹּל וּמַמְרֵא הֵם יִקְחוּ חֶלְקָם: ס [טו] א אַחַר ׀

‹ After 1 [15] « their portion. ‹ will take ‹ — they « and Mamre ‹ Eshcol, ‹ Aner, « with me: ‹ went

הַדְּבָרִים הָאֵלֶּה הָיָה דְבַר־יְהוָה אֶל־אַבְרָם בַּמַּחֲזֶה לֵאמֹר אַל־תִּירָא

« fear, ‹ Do not « saying, ‹ in a vision, ‹ Abram ‹ to ‹ of HASHEM ‹ the word ‹ there came « these matters,

אַבְרָם אָנֹכִי מָגֵן לָךְ שְׂכָרְךָ הַרְבֵּה מְאֹד: ב וַיֹּאמֶר אַבְרָם אֲדֹנָי יֱהוִה

« HASHEM/ELOHIM: ‹ O Lord, « And Abram said, 2 « is very great. ‹ your reward « for you; ‹ a shield ‹ I am « Abram,

וְעַד עַרְקַת מְסָנָא וְאִם אֶסַּב מִכָּל דִּי לָךְ וְלָא תֵימַר אֲנָא עַתָּרִית יָת אַבְרָם: כד לְחוֹד (בַּר) מִדַּאֲכַלוּ עוּלֵמַיָּא וְחֻלָק גֻּבְרַיָּא דִּי אֲזָלוּ עִמִּי עָנֵר אֶשְׁכֹּל וּמַמְרֵא אִנּוּן יְקַבְּלוּן חֻלָקְהוֹן: א בָּתַר פִּתְגָּמַיָּא הָאִלֵּין הֲוָה פִּתְגָּמָא דַּייָ עִם אַבְרָם בִּנְבוּאָה לְמֵימָר לָא תִדְחַל אַבְרָם מֵימְרִי תְּקוֹף לָךְ אַגְרָךְ סַגִּי לַחֲדָא: ב וַאֲמַר אַבְרָם יְיָ אֱלֹהִים

רש"י

(כג) **אם מחוט ועד שרוך נעל.** אעכב לעצמי מן השבי: **ואם אקח מכל אשר לך.** ואי"ת לתת לי שכר מבית גנזיך לא אקח: **ולא תאמר וגו'.** שהקב"ה הבטיחני לעשרני, שנאמר ואברכך וגו' (לעיל יב:ב; תנחומא יג): (כד) **הנערים.** עבדי **אשר הלכו אתי ועוד ענר אשכול וממרא וגו'.** אע"פ שעבדי נכנסו למלחמה, שנאמר הוא ועבדיו ויכם, וענר וחביריו ישבו על הכלים לשמור, אפילו הכי הם יקחו חלקם. וממנו למד דוד, שאמר כחלק היורד במלחמה וכחלק היושב על הכלים יחדיו יחלוקו (שמואל א ל:כד). ולכך נאמר ויהי מהיום ההוא ומעלה וישימה לחוק ומשפט (שם כה), ולא נאמר והלאה, לפי שכבר ניתן החוק בימי אברהם (ב"ר מג:ט): (א) **אחר הדברים האלה.** כ"מ שנאמר אחר, סמוך, אחרי, מופלג (ב"ר מד:ה). אחר הדברים האלה, אחר שנעשה לו נס זה שהרג את המלכים והיה דואג ואומר שמא קבלתי שכר על כל צדקותי, לכך אמר לו המקום **אל תירא אברם** (שם ד; תרגום יונתן): **אנכי מגן לך.** מן העונש, שלא תענש על כל אותן נפשות שהרגת (ב"ר שם; פדר"א פכ"ז). ומה שאתה דואג על קבול שכרך, שכרך הרבה מאד (ב"ר שם). [יש לי לתת לך שכר הרבה יותר ממה שראה לתת לך מלך סדום, לפי שבטחת בי (תנחומא יג). וראיה לדבר בדברי הימים (ב כה:ט) ויאמר אמציהו לאיש האלהים וגו':]

king asked that all his subjects be returned to him, while Abraham would keep the wealth. To show devotion to God, however, Abraham rejected any personal gain from his victory, human and material. He vowed, "Even the most insignificant spoils of my victories will I not retain — thus have I vowed to HASHEM" (*Ibn Caspi*). I decline all personal gains so that you will not go about boasting that it was you, rather than God, who made me rich (*Rashi*). That he returned the spoils was praiseworthy, but the Sages maintain that in returning the people, he erred, because he thereby prevented them from being taught the way of God (*Nedarim* 32a).

15.

1-6. God's reassurance to Abraham. *Do not fear, Abram.* It is axiomatic that God treats a person according to what his deeds have earned him, and that his store of merit becomes depleted if God changes the course of nature for his benefit. Apprehensive, therefore, that all his merits had been consumed by the miracle of his victory over the kings, Abraham feared that he could no longer expect Divine assistance in the future, and that he might be punished for having slain enemy soldiers in the fray (*Rashi*). Moreover, the successors to the defeated kings might collect even greater armies and stage a reprisal attack on him (*Ramban*). Consequently, God appeared to Abraham and reassured him.

1. אָנֹכִי מָגֵן לָךְ — *I am a shield for you.* You need not fear punishment, nor need you fear for the future (*Rashi*). This assurance is immortalized in the *Amidah/Shemoneh Esrei* prayer, the first blessing of which describes God as *Shield of Abraham.* It is God's promise that the inner spark of Abraham's heritage will never be extinguished from the Jewish people.

2. אֲדֹנָי ה' — *O Lord, HASHEM/ELOHIM*. This is an unusual combination of Divine Names. Abraham addressed God as *Lord,* indicating complete obedience and acknowledgment of His mastery, and the Sages comment that he was the first person ever to refer to God as *Adon* [Master] (*Berachos* 7b). The second Name in our verse, *HASHEM/ELOHIM,* is spelled like the Four-letter Name, but vowelized and pronounced *Elohim*. This usage combines the Names that refer respectively to mercy and judgment. By this combination, Abraham was saying that God is merciful even in judgment (*Rashi, Deuteronomy* 3:24, according to *Mizrachi*). As *R' Hirsch* explains, even God's imposition of harsh judgment is, in essence, merciful, because in His wisdom He knows when harsh judgment is necessary to lay the foundation of a brighter future.

מַה־תִּתֶּן־לִי וְאָנֹכִי הוֹלֵךְ עֲרִירִי וּבֶן־מֶשֶׁק בֵּיתִי
Of what [value] | is that which You give me | [as long as] I | go | childless, | and the one who | manages | my household
הוּא דַּמֶּשֶׂק אֱלִיעֶזֶר: ג וַיֹּאמֶר אַבְרָם הֵן לִי
is | Eliezer of Damascus? | 3 [Then] Abram said, | Indeed, | to me
לֹא נָתַתָּה זָרַע וְהִנֵּה בֶן־בֵּיתִי יוֹרֵשׁ אֹתִי: ד וְהִנֵּה
You have not given | offspring; | and indeed, | the one | over my household | inherits | me. | 4 Suddenly,
דְבַר־יהוה אֵלָיו לֵאמֹר לֹא יִירָשְׁךָ זֶה כִּי־אִם
the word | of Hashem | [came] to him, | saying: | Not inherit you | will this one. | But | rather
אֲשֶׁר יֵצֵא מִמֵּעֶיךָ הוּא יִירָשֶׁךָ: ה וַיּוֹצֵא אֹתוֹ הַחוּצָה וַיֹּאמֶר הַבֶּט־נָא
he that | shall come forth | from within you, | he | will inherit you. | 5 And He took | him | outside, | and He said, | Gaze, | now,
הַשָּׁמַיְמָה וּסְפֹר הַכּוֹכָבִים אִם־תּוּכַל לִסְפֹּר אֹתָם וַיֹּאמֶר לוֹ כֹּה יִהְיֶה
toward the Heavens, | and count | the stars | — if | you are able | to count | them! | And He said | to him, | So | shall be
זַרְעֶךָ: ו וְהֶאֱמִן בַּיהוה וַיַּחְשְׁבֶהָ לּוֹ צְדָקָה: ששי ז וַיֹּאמֶר אֵלָיו אֲנִי יהוה
your offspring! | 6 And he trusted | in Hashem, | and He reckoned it | to him | as righteousness. | 7 He said | to him, | I am | Hashem

מַה תִּתֵּן לִי וַאֲנָא אָזֵל בְּלָא וְלָד
וּבַר פַּרְנָסָא הָדֵין דִּבְבֵיתִי הוּא
דַּמַּשְׂקָאָה אֱלִיעֶזֶר: ג וַאֲמַר אַבְרָם
הָא לִי לָא יְהַבְתְּ וְלָד וְהָא בַר בֵּיתִי
יָרֵית יָתִי: ד וְהָא פִתְגָּמָא דַייָ עִמֵּהּ
לְמֵימַר לָא יִרְתִנָּךְ דֵּין אֱלָהֵן בַּר
דְּתוֹלִיד הוּא יִרְתִנָּךְ: ה וְאַפֵּיק יָתֵהּ
לְבָרָא וַאֲמַר אִסְתְּכֵי כְּעַן לְצֵית
שְׁמַיָּא וּמְנֵי כוֹכְבַיָּא אִם תִּכּוֹל
לְמִמְנֵי יָתְהוֹן וַאֲמַר לֵהּ כְּדֵין יְהוֹן
בְּנָיךְ: ו וְהֵימִין בְּמֵימְרָא דַייָ
וְחַשְׁבַהּ לֵהּ לְזָכוּ: ז וַאֲמַר לֵהּ אֲנָא יְיָ

רש"י

(ב) **הולך ערירי.** מנחם בן סרוק פירשו לשון יורש, וחבר לו ער ועונה (מלאכי ב:יב). ערירי בלא יורש, כאשר תאמר ובכל תבואתי תשרש (איוב לא:יב) תעקר שרשיה, כך לשון ערירי חסר בנים, ובלע"ז דישאנפנטי"ש. ולי נראה ער ועונה מגזרת ולבי ער (שה"ש ה:ב; שבת נה:), וערירי לשון חורבן, וכן ערו ערו (תהלים קלז:ז), וכן ערות יסוד (חבקוק ג:יג), וכן ערער תתערער (ירמיה נא:נח), וכן כי ארזה ערה (צפניה ב:יד): **ובן משק ביתי.** כתרגומו, שכל ביתי ניזון על פיו, כמו ועל פיך ישק (להלן מא:מ), אפוטרופס שלי, ואילו היה לי בן היה בני ממונה על שלי: **דמשק.** לפי התרגום, מדמשק היה. ולפי מדרש אגדה, שרדף המלכים עד דמשק (ב"ר שם). ובגמרא שלנו דרשו נוטריקון, דולה ומשקה מתורת רבו לאחרים (יומא כח:): (ג) **הן לי לא נתת זרע.** ומה תועלת בכל אשר תתן לי (תרגום יונתן): (ה) **ויוצא אתו החוצה.** לפי פשוטו, הוציאו מאהלו לחוץ לראות הכוכבים. ולפי מדרשו, אמר לו צא מאצטגנינות שלך, שראית במזלות שאינך עתיד להעמיד בן, אברם אין לו בן אבל אברהם יש לו בן. וכן שרי לא תלד אבל שרה תלד. אני קורא לכם שם אחר וישתנה המזל (נדרים לב.; ב"ר שם י). ד"א, הוציאו מחללו של עולם והגביהו למעלה מן הכוכבים, וזהו לשון הבטה, מלמעלה למטה (ב"ר שם יב): (ו) **והאמן בה'.** לא שאל לו אות על זאת, אבל על ירושת הארץ שאל לו אות ואמר לו במה אדע (להלן פסוק ח; נדרים שם; פס"ר מז (קנ.)): **ויחשבה לו צדקה.** הקב"ה חשבה לאברם לזכות ולצדקה על האמונה שהאמין בו. ד"א, במה אדע, לא שאל לו אות, אלא אמר לפניו הודיעני באיזה זכות יתקיימו בה. אמר לו הקב"ה, בזכות הקרבנות (ב"ר שם; תענית כז:):

וְאָנֹכִי הוֹלֵךְ עֲרִירִי — *[As long as] I go childless.* Of what avail will Your gifts be to me? Since I am childless, whatever You give me will be inherited by others (*B'chor Shor*). Abraham's plaint was based on his undiluted commitment to the propagation of faith in God and allegiance to His teachings. He foresaw that none of his many disciples would remain completely true to that creed; even his own nephew had deserted it. Consequently, if he were to remain childless, all of God's blessings would be in vain (*Akeidas Yitzchak*).

5. הַחוּצָה — *Outside.* The Midrash interprets that God took Abraham outside the realm of reason and nature. Abraham knew that he and Sarah could not have children together, but God told him now that the Jewish people transcend the laws of nature, which are symbolized by the stars and constellations. Thus, even though he and Sarah were naturally incapable of having children together, they were superior to the stars and would have children, if such was God's design. This vision also symbolized to Abraham that just as no one can conquer the stars, so will no nation ever succeed in exterminating Israel (*Pesikta Zutresa*).

Furthermore, God indicated that when Israel does God's Will, they are above all others — like the stars; when they disobey His will, they are trampled by all — like the dust of the earth [cf. 13:16; 28:14] (*Megillah* 16a).

6. וְהֶאֱמִן בַּה' — *And he trusted in HASHEM.* This unswerving faith had been part of Abraham for a long time. Had the meaning been that he *began* to trust from that moment on, the Hebrew would have read וַיַּאֲמֵן בַּה' (*Ibn Caspi*).

וַיַּחְשְׁבֶהָ לּוֹ צְדָקָה — *And He reckoned it to him as righteousness.* God considered Abraham's faith as an act of righteousness (*Rashi*). *Ramban* understands this phrase differently: Abraham's faith had been established so clearly and so often that

אֲשֶׁר הוֹצֵאתִיךָ מֵאוּר כַּשְׂדִּים לָתֶת לְךָ

< to you < to give < *Kasdim* < *of Ur* < *brought you out* < *Who*

אֶת־הָאָרֶץ הַזֹּאת לְרִשְׁתָּהּ: ח וַיֹּאמַר אֲדֹנָי יֱהֹוִה

<< HASHEM/ ELOHIM: < My Lord, < And he said, **8** << *to inherit it.* < *this land*

בַּמָּה אֵדַע כִּי אִירָשֶׁנָּה: ט וַיֹּאמֶר אֵלָיו קְחָה לִי

<< to Me: < Take < to him, < And He said **9** << *I am to inherit it?* < *that* < *shall I know* < *Whereby*

עֶגְלָה מְשֻׁלֶּשֶׁת וְעֵז מְשֻׁלֶּשֶׁת וְאַיִל מְשֻׁלָּשׁ וְתֹר וְגוֹזָל: י וַיִּקַּח־לוֹ

< to Him < And he took **10** << *and a young dove.* < *a turtle-dove,* << *triple,* < *rams,* << *triple,* < *goats,* << *triple,* < *heifers,*

אֶת־כָּל־אֵלֶּה וַיְבַתֵּר אֹתָם בַּתָּוֶךְ וַיִּתֵּן אִישׁ־בִּתְרוֹ לִקְרַאת רֵעֵהוּ

<< its counterpart. < facing < of the pieces < each one < and he placed << in the middle, < them < then he divided << these; < all

וְאֶת־הַצִּפֹּר לֹא בָתָר: יא וַיֵּרֶד הָעַיִט עַל־הַפְּגָרִים וַיַּשֵּׁב אֹתָם אַבְרָם:

<< did Abram. < and drive them away << the carcasses, < upon < did birds of prey < Descend **11** << he did not divide. < the birds < [But] of

דִּי אַפֵּקְתָּךְ מֵאוּרָא דְכַשְׂדָּאֵי לְמִתַּן לָךְ יָת אַרְעָא הָדָא לְמֵירְתַהּ: ח וַאֲמָר יְיָ אֱלֹהִים בְּמָא אִדַּע אֲרֵי אֵירְתִנַּהּ: ט וַאֲמַר לֵהּ קָרֵב קֳדָמַי עֶגְלָא תִלְתָּא וְעִזָּא תִלְתָּא וּדְכַר תִּלְתָּא (נ״א עִגְלִין תְּלָתָא וְעִזִּין תְּלָת וְדִכְרִין תְּלָתָא) וְשַׁפְנִינָא וּבַר יוֹנָא: י וְקָרֵב קֳדָמוֹהִי יָת כָּל אִלֵּין וּפַלִּיג יָתְהוֹן בְּשָׁוֶה וִיהַב פַּלְגַיָּא פַּלּוּג לָקֳבֵל חַבְרֵהּ וְיָת עוֹפָא לָא פַלִּיג: יא וּנְחַת עוֹפָא עַל פַּגְלַיָּא וְאַפְרַח יָתְהוֹן אַבְרָם:

רש״י

(ט) **עגלה משלשת.** ג׳ עגלים, רמז לג׳ פרים, פר יום הכפורים ופר העלם דבר של צבור ועגלה ערופה (ב״ר שם): **ועז משלשת.** רמז לשעיר הנעשה בפנים ושעירי מוספין של מועד ושעירת חטאת יחיד (שם): **ואיל משולש.** אשם ודאי ואשם תלוי וכבשה של חטאת יחיד (שם): **ותור וגוזל.** תור ובן יונה (שם): (י) **ויבתר אתם.** חלק כל אחד לב׳ חלקים. ואין המקרא יוצא מידי פשוטו, לפי שהיה כורת עמו ברית לשמור הבטחתו להוריש לבניו את הארץ, כדכתיב ביום ההוא כרת ה׳ את אברם ברית לאמר וגו׳ (להלן פסוק יח), ודרך כורתי ברית לחלק בהמה ולעבור בין בתריה, כמה שנאמר להלן העוברים בין בתרי העגל (ירמיה לד:יט), אף כאן תנור עשן ולפיד אש אשר עבר בין הגזרים הוא שלוחו של שכינה שהוא אש: **ואת הצפר לא בתר.** לפי שהאומות נמשלו לפרים ואילים ושעירים, שנאמר סבבוני פרים רבים וגו׳ (תהלים כב:יג), ואומר האיל אשר ראית בעל הקרנים מלכי מדי ופרס (דניאל ח:כ), ואומר הצפיר השעיר מלך יון (שם פסוק כא). וישראל נמשלו [בתורים ובני יונה, תור שנאמר אל תתן לחית נפש תורך (תהלים עד:יט)] לבני יונה, שנאמר יונתי בחגוי הסלע (שיר השירים ב:יד), לפיכך בתר הבהמות, רמז שיהיו האומות כלים והולכים, ואת הצפור לא בתר, רמז שיהיו ישראל קיימין לעולם (פדר״א פכ״ח): (יא) **העיט.** הוא עוף, על שם שהוא עט ושואף אל הנבלות לטוש עלי אוכל. כמו ותעט אל השלל (שמואל א טו:יט): **על הפגרים.** על הבתרים: [ס״א **הפגרים.** מתרגמינן פגליא, אלא מתוך שהורגלו לתרגם איש בתרו ויהב פלגיא נתחלף להם תיבת פגליא לפלגיא ותרגמו הפגרים פלגיא, וכל המתרגם כן טועה לפי שאין להקיש בתרים לפגרים, שבתרים תרגומו פלגיא ופגרים תרגומו פגליא לשון פגול, כמו פגול הוא (ויקרא יט:ז) לשון פגר:] **וישב.** לשון נשיבה והפרחה,

his belief in God's promise now could hardly have been remarkable. Instead, he explains, it was *Abraham* who reckoned God's promise of children as a manifestation of righteous kindness, for God had made the promise unconditionally, without regard to Abraham's future merit.

8. בַּמָּה אֵדַע — *Whereby shall I know*. Abraham thought that the promise of the Land was conditional on the righteousness of himself and his offspring, and he feared that he was not worthy to receive it and that his descendants might sin and become unworthy to retain it (*Rashi; Mizrachi; Gur Aryeh; Maharzu*).

By the use of animals to seal the covenant (v. 9), God was answering, "You and your descendants will merit the Land because of the sacrifices you are about to offer, and the Temple offerings that will be a means of atonement for your children." But Abraham persisted that if the Temple would be destroyed, what merit would Israel have then? God answered that when the Jewish people recite the order of the sacrificial service, as it is contained in the daily prayers, God would consider it as if they had actually brought the offerings (*Megillah* 31b).

9. קְחָה לִי — *Take to Me.* God commanded Abraham to take the animals and perform the following ritual in order to seal the covenant and give it the status of an irrevocable oath (*Sforno*). For even though the *merit* of the Patriarchs may have dissipated over the generations, a *covenant* is irrevocable. The reasons for these particular animals and that there be three of each are discussed in ArtScroll's *Bereishis,* vol. I, pp. 519-21.

10. בַּתָּוֶךְ — *In the middle.* Abraham cut the animals into two parts. In the plain sense, the passing between the severed parts constituted the accepted ritual in those days of those who enter a covenant. The smoking furnace and fire (v.17) were emissaries of the Divine Presence, as if the *Shechinah* was joining Abraham in passing between the parts, to symbolize God's participation in the covenant (*Rashi*).

However, Abraham did not cut up the birds, because sacrificial birds are not dissected (*Ramban*). Also, since the birds symbolized Israel (*Song of Songs* 2:14), they were left whole to symbolize that Israel would live forever (*Rashi*).

11. וַיֵּרֶד הָעַיִט — *Descend did birds of prey.* The symbolism is described in different ways. King David would seek to destroy the enemy nations, but God would "drive him away," pending

יב וַיְהִי הַשֶּׁמֶשׁ לָבוֹא וְתַרְדֵּמָה נָפְלָה עַל־אַבְרָם
<< Abram; < upon < fell < a deep sleep < was about to set, < as the sun < And it happened, 12

וְהִנֵּה אֵימָה חֲשֵׁכָה גְדֹלָה נֹפֶלֶת עָלָיו׃ יג וַיֹּאמֶר
< And He said 13 << upon him. < was falling < that was great < a darkness << a fear, < and then

לְאַבְרָם יָדֹעַ תֵּדַע כִּי־גֵר ׀ יִהְיֶה זַרְעֲךָ בְּאֶרֶץ
< in a land < shall your offspring be < aliens < that < Know with certainty < to Abram,

לֹא לָהֶם וַעֲבָדוּם וְעִנּוּ אֹתָם אַרְבַּע מֵאוֹת שָׁנָה׃ יד וְגַם אֶת־הַגּוֹי אֲשֶׁר
< that < the nation < But also 14 << years. < hundred < — four << them < and they will oppress < — and they will enslave them, << their own < not

יַעֲבֹדוּ דָּן אָנֹכִי וְאַחֲרֵי־כֵן יֵצְאוּ בִּרְכֻשׁ גָּדוֹל׃ טו וְאַתָּה תָּבוֹא אֶל־
< to < you shall come << As for you: 15 << that is great. < with wealth < they will leave < that < and after << I shall judge, < they will serve,

אֲבֹתֶיךָ בְּשָׁלוֹם תִּקָּבֵר בְּשֵׂיבָה טוֹבָה׃ טז וְדוֹר רְבִיעִי יָשׁוּבוּ הֵנָּה כִּי
< for << here, < shall return < And the fourth generation 16 << that is good. < in an old age < you shall be buried << in peace; < your ancestors

יב וַהֲוָה שִׁמְשָׁא לְמֵיעַל וְשִׁנְתָא נְפָלַת עַל אַבְרָם וְהָא אֵימָא קְבַל סַגִּי נְפָלַת עֲלוֹהִי: יג וַאֲמַר לְאַבְרָם מִדַּע תִּדַּע אֲרֵי דַיָּרִין יְהוֹן בְּנָיךְ בְּאַרְעָא דְּלָא דִילְהוֹן וְיִפְלְחוּן בְּהוֹן וִיעַנּוּן יָתְהוֹן אַרְבַּע מְאָה שְׁנִין: יד וְאַף יָת עַמָּא דִּי יִפְלְחוּן בְּהוֹן דָּיִין אֲנָא וּבָתַר כֵּן יִפְּקוּן בְּקִנְיָנָא סַגִּי: טו וְאַתְּ תֵּיעוֹל לְוַת אֲבָהָתָךְ בִּשְׁלָם תִּתְקְבַר בְּסֵיבוּ טָבָא: טז וְדָרָא רְבִיעָאָה יְתוּבוּן הָכָא אֲרֵי

רש"י

כמו ישב רוחו (תהלים קמז:יח). רמז שיבא דוד בן ישי לכלותם ואין מניחים אותו מן השמים עד שיבוא מלך המשיח (פדר"א שם): **(יב) והנה אימה חשכה גדולה וגו'.** רמז לצרות וחשך של גליות (שם; ב"ר מד:יז): **(יג) כי גר יהיה זרעך.** משנולד יצחק עד שיצאו ישראל ממצרים ד' מאות שנה. כיצד, יצחק בן ששים שנה כשנולד יעקב, ויעקב כשירד למצרים אמר ימי שני מגורי שלשים ומאת שנה (להלן מז:ט), הרי ק"ץ. ובמצרים היו מאתים ועשר כמנין רד"ו הרי ת' שנה. וא"ת במצרים היו ד' מאות, הרי קהת מיורדי מצרים היה, צא וחשוב שנותיו של קהת (שמות ו:יח) ושל עמרם (שם פסוק כ) ושמנים של משה שהיה כשיצאו ישראל ממצרים, אין אתה מוצא אלא שלש מאות וחמשים, ואתה צריך להוציא מהם כל השנים שחי קהת אחר לידת עמרם ושחי עמרם אחר לידת משה (סדר עולם רבה פ"ג): **בארץ לא להם.** ולא נאמר בארץ מצרים אלא לא להם משנולד יצחק ויגר אברם וגו' (להלן כא:לד), ויגר [ס"א וישב] יצחק בגרר (שם כו:ו), [ס"א ובילחק גור בארץ הזאת (שם כו:ג),] ויעקב גר בארץ חם (תהלים קה:כג), לגור בארץ באנו (להלן מז:ד): **(יד) וגם את הגוי.** וגם לרבות הארבע מלכיות (ב"ר מד:יט) שאף הם כלים על ששעבדו את ישראל (פדר"א פכ"ח, פל"ה): **דן אנכי.** בעשר מכות (ב"ר מד:כ): **ברכוש גדול.** בממון גדול כמו שנא' וינצלו את מצרים (שמות יב:לו; ברכות ט.-ט:): **(טו) ואתה תבא.** ולא תראה כל אלה: **אל אבותיך.** אביו עובד כוכבים והוא מבשרו שיבא אליו, ללמדך שעשה תרח תשובה (ב"ר לח:יב): **תקבר בשיבה טובה.** בשרו שיעשה ישמעאל תשובה בימיו (שם), ולא יצא עשו לתרבות רעה בימיו, ולפיכך מת ה' שנים קודם זמנו ובו ביום מרד עשו (שם סג:יב): **(טז) ודור רביעי ישובו הנה.** לאחר שיגלו למצרים יהיו שם ג' דורות

the coming of Messiah (*Rashi*). Or, the birds represent the nations, which would try to exterminate Israel (*Radak*), or prevent it from serving God (*Ramban*), but God or the descendants of Abraham would drive them away (ibid.).

12. אֵימָה — *A fear.* During the good tidings above, Abraham did not experience fear, but now that he was about to be told about the bitter exiles, God symbolized those times to Abraham by casting sleep, fear, and darkness upon him (*Radak*). The Midrash finds an allusion to Israel's progressively intensifying subjugations under the Four Monarchies: *Fear* represented Babylon; *darkness* was Media-Persia; *great* darkness was Greece [the Syrian-Greeks of Antiochus, who persecuted Israel prior to the miracle of Chanukah]; and *fell upon* was the crushing present exile initiated by Rome. All of them ruled Israel in *Eretz Yisrael*; Babylon destroyed the First Temple and Rome the Second, and the others dominated the Land during parts of the Second Temple era. Thus, God warned Abraham that Israel might be subjugated and/or exiled by these four powers — but only if Israel sinned (*Ramban*).

13-14. Egyptian exile and redemption. The exiles of the Four Monarchies would be conditional on Israel's deeds, and even if they came about, they would be far in the future. But, God now told Abraham, there would be an exile that had to take place and that would begin relatively soon.

13. גֵר יִהְיֶה זַרְעֲךָ — *Aliens shall your offspring be.* There would be 400 years of alien status, which would include the 210 years of literal exile in Egypt, and also the 22 years that Jacob spent with Laban in Haran [see *Vayeitzei*]. The *servitude* mentioned in this prophecy took place during the last 116 years of the Egyptian servitude, the last 86 years of which were a time of harsh *oppression*, when Pharaoh intensified the suffering of the Jews. The calculation of the 400 years would begin with the birth of Isaac; since he never had the permanent home or the prestige and honor enjoyed by Abraham, he and his offspring were considered aliens, even during the years that they lived in *Eretz Yisrael*. After those 400 years, Abraham's offspring would be able to take possession of the Land.

14. הַגּוֹי אֲשֶׁר יַעֲבֹדוּ — *The nation that they will serve.* Just as I will cause your offspring to suffer, so will I punish the oppressors for the violence they will do to the Israelites (*Ramban*).

לָא שְׁלִים חוֹבָא דֶאֱמוֹרָאָה עַד כְּעַן:
יז וַהֲוָה שִׁמְשָׁא עֲלַת וְקִבְלָא הֲוָה וְהָא
תַנּוּר דִּתְנַן וּבְעוּר דְּאֶשָּׁתָא דִּי עֲדָא
בֵּין פַּלְגַיָּא הָאִלֵּין: יח בְּיוֹמָא הַהוּא
גְּזַר יְיָ עִם אַבְרָם קְיָם לְמֵימַר לִבְנָיךְ
יְהָבִית יָת אַרְעָא הָדָא מִן נַהֲרָא
דְמִצְרַיִם וְעַד נַהֲרָא רַבָּא נַהֲרָא פְרָת:
יט יָת שַׁלְמָאֵי וְיָת קְנִזָּאֵי וְיָת
קַדְמוֹנָאֵי: כ וְיָת חִתָּאֵי וְיָת פְּרִזָּאֵי
וְיָת גִּבָּרַיָּא: כא וְיָת אֱמוֹרָאֵי וְיָת
כְּנַעֲנָאֵי וְיָת גִּרְגָּשָׁאֵי וְיָת יְבוּסָאֵי:
א וְשָׂרַי אִתַּת אַבְרָם לָא יְלִידַת
לֵהּ וְלַהּ אַמְתָא מִצְרֵיתָא וּשְׁמַהּ

לֹא־שָׁלֵם עֲוֺן הָאֱמֹרִי עַד־הֵנָּה: יז וַיְהִי הַשֶּׁמֶשׁ
‹ that the sun ‹ Then it was 17 « then. ‹ until ‹ of the Amorite ‹ will [be] the iniquity ‹ complete ‹ not [yet]

בָּאָה וַעֲלָטָה הָיָה וְהִנֵּה תַנּוּר עָשָׁן וְלַפִּיד אֵשׁ
‹ of fire ‹ and a torch ‹ of smoke ‹ a furnace « and there it was, « was there, ‹ and a thick darkness ‹ set,

אֲשֶׁר עָבַר בֵּין הַגְּזָרִים הָאֵלֶּה: יח בַּיּוֹם הַהוּא
‹ On that day 18 « these pieces. ‹ between ‹ passed ‹ that

כָּרַת יְהוָה אֶת־אַבְרָם בְּרִית לֵאמֹר לְזַרְעֲךָ נָתַתִּי
‹ have I given ‹ To your descendants « saying, ‹ a covenant, ‹ Abram ‹ with ‹ HASHEM made

אֶת־הָאָרֶץ הַזֹּאת מִנְּהַר מִצְרַיִם עַד־הַנָּהָר הַגָּדֹל נְהַר־פְּרָת:
« the Euphrates River: « that is great, ‹ the river ‹ to ‹ of Egypt ‹ from the river « this land,

יט אֶת־הַקֵּינִי וְאֶת־הַקְּנִזִּי וְאֵת הַקַּדְמֹנִי: כ וְאֶת־הַחִתִּי וְאֶת־הַפְּרִזִּי
‹ the Perizzite, ‹ the Hittite, 20 « and the Kadmonite; ‹ the Kenizzite, ‹ [the lands of] the Kennite, 19

וְאֶת־הָרְפָאִים: כא וְאֶת־הָאֱמֹרִי וְאֶת־הַכְּנַעֲנִי וְאֶת־הַגִּרְגָּשִׁי וְאֶת־הַיְבוּסִי:
« and the Jebusite. ‹ the Girgashite, ‹ the Canaanite, ‹ the Amorite, 21 « and the Rephaim;

ס [טז] א וְשָׂרַי אֵשֶׁת אַבְרָם לֹא יָלְדָה לוֹ וְלָהּ שִׁפְחָה מִצְרִית וּשְׁמָהּ
‹ whose name ‹ who was Egyptian ‹ a maidservant ‹ She had « to him. ‹ borne [a child] ‹ had not ‹ of Abram, ‹ the wife ‹ And Sarai, 1 [16]

רש"י

והרביעי ישובו לארץ הזאת (תרגום יונתן; עדיות ב:ט וכפי' הרמב"ס), לפי שבארץ כנען היה מדבר עמו וכרת ברית זו, כדכתיב לתת לך את הארץ הזאת לרשתה (לעיל פסוק ז). וכן היה, ירד יעקב למצרים, צא וחשוב דורותיו, יהודה פרץ וחצרון, וכלב בן חצרון מבאי הארץ היה (סוטה יא:; סנהדרין סט:): **כי לא שלם עון האמורי.** להיות משתלם מארצו עד אותו זמן, שאין הקב"ה נפרע מאומה עד שתתמלא סאתה, שנא' בסאסאה בשלחה תריבנה (ישעיה כז:ח; סוטה ט.): **(יז) ויהי השמש באה.** כמו ויהי הם מריקים שקיהם (להלן מב:לה) ויהי הם קוברים איש (מלכים ב יג:כא), כלומר, ויהי דבר זה: **השמש באה.** שקעה: **ועלטה היה.** חשך היום: **והנה תנור עשן וגו'.** רמז לו שיפלו המלכיות בגיהנם (פדר"א פכ"ח): **באה.** טעמו למעלה, לכך הוא מבואר שבאה כבר. ואם היה טעמו למטה באל"ף היה מבואר כשהיא שוקעת, ואי אפשר לומר כן, שהרי כבר כתוב ויהי השמש לבא (לעיל פסוק יב) והעברת תנור עשן לאחר מכאן היתה, נמצא שכבר שקעה. וזה חילוק בכל תיבה לשון נקבה שיסודה שתי אותיות, כמו בא, קם, שב, כשהטעם למעלה לשון עבר הוא, כגון זה, וכגון ורחל באה (להלן כט:ט) קמה אלומתי (שם לז:ז) הנה שבה יבמתך (רות א:טו). וכשהטעם למטה הוא לשון הווה, דבר שנעשה עכשיו והולך, כמו באה עם הצאן (להלן כט:ו) בערב היא באה ובבקר היא שבה (אסתר ב:יד): **(יח) לזרעך נתתי.** אמירתו של הקב"ה כאילו היא עשויה (ב"ר מד:כב): **עד הנהר הגדל נהר פרת.** לפי שהוא דבוק לארץ ישראל קוראהו גדול, אע"פ שהוא מאוחר בארבעה נהרות היוצאים מעדן, שנא' והנהר הרביעי הוא פרת (לעיל ב:יד). משל הדיוט, עבד מלך מלך, הדבק לשחור וישתחוו לך (ספרי דברים ו; שבועות מז:ב): **(יט) את הקיני.** עשר אומות יש כאן ולא נתן להם אלא שבעה גוים. והשלשה אדום ומואב ועמון, והם קיני קניזי קדמוני, עתידים להיות ירושה לעתיד, שנאמר אדום ומואב משלוח ידם ובני עמון משמעתם (ישעיה יא:יד; ב"ר מד:כג): **(כ) ואת הרפאים.** ארץ עוג, שנאמר בה ההוא יקרא ארץ רפאים (דברים ג:יג): **(א) שפחה מצרית.** בת פרעה היתה, כשראה נסים שנעשו לשרה

The word *also* indicates that the Four Monarchies — all the nations that will persecute Israel throughout its history — will not escape punishment for their cruelty (*Rashi*).

17. The ratification of the Covenant. The furnace and fire symbolized that the Divine Presence was there to seal the covenant, and the smoking furnace also symbolized Gehinnom, into which the Four Monarchies would descend (*Rashi*). Alternatively, they symbolized the intense darkness and the fire that would be present at the Revelation at Sinai [*Exodus* 19:18] (*Moreh Nevuchim*).

19-21. The Torah lists the ten nations whose territories comprise God's gift to Abraham's descendants . *Rashi* notes that only the last seven were conquered by Joshua, but the lands of the first three — the Kennites, Kennizites, and Kadmonites — would belong to Edom, Moab, and Ammon; they will not belong to Israel until Messianic times [see *Isaiah* 11:14].

16.

⁂ The birth of Ishmael.

Despite their spiritual riches and Godly assurances, Abraham and Sarah were still heartbroken at their barrenness, for without heirs they would not be able to continue the mission of bringing God's teachings to mankind. Recognizing that it was

הָגָר׃ ב וַתֹּאמֶר שָׂרַי אֶל־אַבְרָם הִנֵּה־נָא עֲצָרַנִי

was Hagar. 2 And Sarai said — to — Abram, — Indeed, — now, — restrained me

יהוה מִלֶּדֶת בֹּא־נָא אֶל־שִׁפְחָתִי אוּלַי אִבָּנֶה

HASHEM has — from giving birth; — come, — now, — to — my maidservant, — perhaps — I will be built up

מִמֶּנָּה וַיִּשְׁמַע אַבְרָם לְקוֹל שָׂרָי׃ ג וַתִּקַּח שָׂרַי

through her. — And Abram acceded — to the voice — of Sarai. 3 And she took — Sarai —

אֵשֶׁת־אַבְרָם אֶת־הָגָר הַמִּצְרִית שִׁפְחָתָהּ מִקֵּץ

the wife of Abram — Hagar — the Egyptian, — her maidservant — at the end

עֶשֶׂר שָׁנִים לְשֶׁבֶת אַבְרָם בְּאֶרֶץ כְּנָעַן וַתִּתֵּן אֹתָהּ לְאַבְרָם אִישָׁהּ

of ten — years — of the dwelling — of Abram — in the land — of Canaan — and she gave — her — to Abram — her husband,

לוֹ לְאִשָּׁה׃ ד וַיָּבֹא אֶל־הָגָר וַתַּהַר וַתֵּרֶא כִּי הָרָתָה וַתֵּקַל גְּבִרְתָּהּ

to him — as a wife. 4 And he came — to — Hagar — and she conceived; — [and when] she saw — that — she had conceived, — she belittled — her mistress

בְּעֵינֶיהָ׃ ה וַתֹּאמֶר שָׂרַי אֶל־אַבְרָם חֲמָסִי עָלֶיךָ אָנֹכִי נָתַתִּי שִׁפְחָתִי

in her eyes. 5 And [so] Sarai said — to — Abram, — The injustice done to me — is due to you! — It was I — who gave — my maidservant

בְּחֵיקֶךָ וַתֵּרֶא כִּי הָרָתָה וָאֵקַל בְּעֵינֶיהָ יִשְׁפֹּט יהוה בֵּינִי *וּבֵינֶיךָ׃

into your bosom, — and when she saw — that — she had conceived, — I was belittled — in her eyes. — Let HASHEM judge — between me — and between you!

ו וַיֹּאמֶר אַבְרָם אֶל־שָׂרַי הִנֵּה שִׁפְחָתֵךְ בְּיָדֵךְ עֲשִׂי־לָהּ הַטּוֹב בְּעֵינָיִךְ

6 Abram said — to — Sarai, — Here is — your maidservant — in your hand; — do — to her — as is fit — in your eyes.

*נקוד על י׳ בתרא

הָגָר׃ ב וַאֲמַרַת שָׂרַי לְאַבְרָם הָא כְּעַן מַנְעַנִי יְיָ מִלְּמֵילַד עוּל כְּעַן לְוַת אַמְתִי מָאִים אִתְבְּנֵי מִנַּהּ וְקַבִּיל אַבְרָם לְמֵימַר שָׂרָי׃ ג וּדְבָרַת שָׂרַי אִתַּת אַבְרָם יָת הָגָר מִצְרֵיתָא אַמְתַהּ מִסּוֹף עֲשַׂר שְׁנִין לְמִתַּב אַבְרָם בְּאַרְעָא דִכְנָעַן וִיהָבַת יָתַהּ לְאַבְרָם בַּעְלַהּ לֵהּ לְאִנְתּוּ׃ ד וְעַל לְוַת הָגָר וְעַדִּיאַת וַחֲזַת אֲרֵי עַדִּיאַת וּקְלַת רִבּוֹנְתַּהּ בְּעֵינָהָא׃ ה וַאֲמַרַת שָׂרַי לְאַבְרָם דִּין לִי עֲלָךְ אֲנָא יְהָבִית אַמְתִי לָךְ וַחֲזַת אֲרֵי עַדִּיאַת וְקַלִּית בְּעֵינָהָא יְדוּן יְיָ בֵּינִי וּבֵינָךְ׃ ו וַאֲמַר אַבְרָם לְשָׂרַי הָא אַמְתִיךְ בִּידִיךְ עֲבִידִי לַהּ כִּדְתַקִּין בְּעֵינָיְכִי

רש״י

אמר מוטב שתהא בתי שפחה בבית זה ולא גבירה בבית אחר (ב״ר מה:א): **(ב) אולי אבנה ממנה.** לימד על מי שאין לו בנים שאינו בנוי אלא הרוס (שם ב): **אבנה ממנה.** בזכות שאכניס צרתי לתוך ביתי (שם עא:ז). [כמו שאמר נתן אלהים שכרי אשר נתתי שפחתי לאישי (להלן ל:יח)]: **לקול שרי.** לרוח הקדש שבה (ב״ר מה:ב): **(ג) ותקח שרי,** לקחתה בדברים, אשריך שזכית לידבק בגוף קדוש כזה (שם ג): **מקץ עשר שנים.** מועד הקבוע לאשה ששהתה י׳ שנים ולא ילדה לבעלה חייב לישא אחרת (יבמות סד.; ב״ר שם): **לשבת אברם וגו׳.** מגיד שאין ישיבת חוצה לארץ עולה מן המנין, לפי שלא נאמר לו ואעשך לגוי גדול (לעיל יב:ב) עד שבא לארץ ישראל (יבמות שם; ב״ר שם): **(ד) ויבא אל הגר ותהר.** מביאה ראשונה (ב״ר שם ד): **ותקל גברתה בעיניה.** אמרה, שרה זו אין סתרה כגלויה, מראה עצמה כאילו היא צדקת ואינה צדקת, שלא זכתה להריון כל השנים הללו, ואני נתעברתי מביאה ראשונה (שם): **(ה) חמסי עליך.** חמס העשוי לי עליך אני מטילה העונש. כשהתפללת להקב״ה מה תתן לי ואנכי הולך ערירי (לעיל טו:ב) לא התפללת אלא עליך, והיה לך להתפלל על שנינו והייתי אני נפקדת עמך. ועוד, דבריך אתה חומס ממני, שאתה שומע בזיוני ושותק (ב״ר שם ה): **אנכי נתתי שפחתי וגו׳ ביני וביניך.** כל ביניך שבמקרא חסר וזה מלא, קרי ביה ובניך, שהכניסה עין הרע בעיבורה של הגר והפילה עוברה. הוא שהמלאך אומר להגר הנך הרה (להלן פסוק יא), והלא כבר הרתה והוא מבשר לה שתהר, אלא מלמד שהפילה הריון הראשון (ב״ר שם):

she who was infertile, Sarah suggested that Abraham marry her maidservant Hagar, and, if a son were born, Sarah would raise him, so that he would be considered her adopted child.

Hagar was a daughter of Pharaoh. After seeing the miracles that were wrought on Sarah's behalf when she was abducted and taken to his palace, he gave Hagar to her, saying, "Better that she be a servant in their house than a princess in someone else's." So it was that Hagar, an Egyptian princess, became Abraham's wife and bore him Ishmael (*Midrash; Rashi*).

6. שִׁפְחָתֵךְ בְּיָדֵךְ — *Your maidservant in your hand.* To me she is

וַתְּעַנֶּהָ שָׂרַי וַתִּבְרַח מִפָּנֶיהָ: ז וַיִּמְצָאָהּ מַלְאַךְ
And Sarai dealt harshly with her, so [Hagar] fled from before her. 7 Find her did an angel

יהוה עַל־עֵין הַמַּיִם בַּמִּדְבָּר עַל־הָעַיִן בְּדֶרֶךְ שׁוּר:
of HASHEM by the spring of water in the desert, by the spring on the road to Shur.

ח וַיֹּאמַר הָגָר שִׁפְחַת שָׂרַי אֵי־מִזֶּה בָאת וְאָנָה
8 And he said, Hagar, maidservant of Sarai, where is this place from which you have come and where

תֵלֵכִי וַתֹּאמֶר מִפְּנֵי שָׂרַי גְּבִרְתִּי אָנֹכִי בֹּרַחַת:
are you going? And she said, From before Sarai my mistress I am running away.

ט וַיֹּאמֶר לָהּ מַלְאַךְ יהוה שׁוּבִי אֶל־גְּבִרְתֵּךְ
9 And say to her did an angel of HASHEM, Return to your mistress,

וְהִתְעַנִּי תַּחַת יָדֶיהָ: י וַיֹּאמֶר לָהּ מַלְאַךְ יהוה הַרְבָּה אַרְבֶּה אֶת־זַרְעֵךְ
and allow yourself to be dealt with harshly under her hands. 10 And say to her did an angel of HASHEM, I will greatly increase your offspring,

וְלֹא יִסָּפֵר מֵרֹב: יא וַיֹּאמֶר לָהּ מַלְאַךְ יהוה הִנָּךְ הָרָה וְיֹלַדְתְּ בֵּן וְקָרָאת
and they will not be counted because of [their] multitude. 11 And say to her did an angel of HASHEM, Indeed, you will conceive, and you will give birth to a son; you shall call

שְׁמוֹ יִשְׁמָעֵאל כִּי־שָׁמַע יהוה אֶל־עָנְיֵךְ: יב וְהוּא יִהְיֶה פֶּרֶא אָדָם יָדוֹ
his name Ishmael, for HASHEM has listened to your [cries from] your affliction. 12 And he shall be a wild-ass of a man: his hand

בַּכֹּל וְיַד כֹּל בּוֹ וְעַל־פְּנֵי כָל־אֶחָיו יִשְׁכֹּן: יג וַתִּקְרָא שֵׁם־יהוה הַדֹּבֵר
against all, and the hand of all against him; and in the face of all his brothers shall he dwell. 13 And she called the Name of HASHEM Who spoke

וְעַנִּיתַהּ שָׂרַי וְעָרְקַת מִקֳּדָמָהָא: ז וְאַשְׁכְּחַהּ מַלְאֲכָא דַייָ עַל עֵינָא דְמַיָּא בְּמַדְבְּרָא עַל עֵינָא בְּאָרְחָא דְחַגְרָא: ח וַאֲמַר הָגָר אַמְתָא דְשָׂרַי מְנָן אַתְּ אָתְיָא וּלְאָן אַתְּ אָזְלָא וַאֲמַרַת מִן קֳדָם שָׂרַי רִבּוֹנְתִּי אֲנָא עָרְקָא (נ״א עֲרָקַת): ט וַאֲמַר לַהּ מַלְאֲכָא דַייָ תּוּבִי לְוַת רִבּוֹנְתִּךְ וְאִשְׁתַּעְבְּדִי תְּחוֹת יְדָהָא: י וַאֲמַר לַהּ מַלְאֲכָא דַייָ אַסְגָּאָה אַסְגֵּי יָת בְּנָיְכִי וְלָא יִתְמְנוּן מִסְּגֵי: יא וַאֲמַר לַהּ מַלְאֲכָא דַייָ הָא אַתְּ מְעַדְיָא וּתְלִידִי בַּר וְתִקְרִי שְׁמֵהּ יִשְׁמָעֵאל אֲרֵי קַבִּיל יְיָ צְלוֹתִיךְ: יב וְהוּא יְהֵא מָרוֹד בְּאֱנָשָׁא הוּא יְהֵא צְרִיךְ לְכֹלָּא וִידָא דְכָל בְּנֵי אֲנָשָׁא יְהוֹן צְרִיכִין לֵהּ וְעַל אַפֵּי כָל אֲחוֹהִי יִשְׁרֵי: יג וְצַלִּיאַת בִּשְׁמָא דַייָ דְּמִתְמַלֵּל

רש״י

(ו) ותענה שרי. היתה משעבדת בה בקושי (שם ו): **(ח) אי מזה באת.** מהיכן באת. יודע היה, אלא ליתן לה פתח ליכנס עמה בדברים. ולשון אי מזה, איה המקום שתאמר עליו מזה אני באה: **(ט) ויאמר לה מלאך ה׳ וגו׳.** על כל אמירה היה שלוח לה מלאך אחר, לכך נאמר מלאך בכל אמירה ואמירה (שם ז): **(יא) הנך הרה.** כשתשובי תהרי, כמו הנך הרה (שופטים יג:ז) דאשת מנוח: **וילדת בן.** כמו ויולדת. ודומה לו ישבת בלבנון מקוננת בארזים (ירמיה כב:כג): **וקראת שמו.** צווי הוא. כמו שאומר לזכר וקראת את שמו יצחק (להלן יז:יט): **(יב) פרא אדם.** אוהב מדברות לצוד חיות. כמו שכתוב וישב במדבר ויהי רובה קשת (שם כא:כ; ב״ר שם ט; פדר״א פ״ל): **ידו בכל.** לסטים (תנחומא שמות א): **ויד כל בו.** הכל שונאין אותו ומתגרין בו: **ועל פני כל אחיו ישכון.** שיהיה זרעו גדול:

a wife; I have no right to treat her unkindly. But to you she is a servant; if she mistreated you, do what you feel is right (*Radak; Haamek Davar*). Sarah's intent was not malicious, but to force Hagar to cease her insulting demeanor. But instead of acknowledging Sarah's superior position, Hagar fled (*Abarbanel; Sforno*).

8. שִׁפְחַת שָׂרַי — *Maidservant of Sarai.* By addressing Hagar as *maidservant*, the angel reminded her of her subservience to her mistress. Hagar acknowledged this status by referring to Sarah [next verse] as *my mistress* (*Chizkuni*).

11-12. הִנָּךְ הָרָה — *Indeed, you will conceive.* Hagar had already been pregnant, but she had miscarried. Now the angel promised her that if she showed Sarah the proper respect, she would have a son destined for power and material greatness. He would be an untamed brigand, a hated plunderer, and warrior (*Rashi*). *Onkelos* translates the description of Ishmael in the economic sense: He would be dependent on other nations, and they, in turn, would be dependent on him.

אֵלֶיהָ אַתָּה אֵל רֳאִי כִּי אָמְרָה הֲגַם הֲלֹם רָאִיתִי

< could I have seen < here < Even < she said, < for < of Vision, < the God < You are << to her,

אַחֲרֵי רֹאִי׃ יד עַל־כֵּן קָרָא לַבְּאֵר בְּאֵר לַחַי רֹאִי

<< Appearing to Me. < of the Living One < The Well < the well < he called < this reason < For 14 << having seen? < after

הִנֵּה בֵין־קָדֵשׁ וּבֵין בָּרֶד׃ טו וַתֵּלֶד הָגָר לְאַבְרָם

< to Abram < Hagar bore 15 << Bered. < and between < Kadesh < between < There it is

בֵּן וַיִּקְרָא אַבְרָם שֶׁם־בְּנוֹ אֲשֶׁר־יָלְדָה הָגָר

< Hagar bore < that < of his son < the name < and Abram called < a son

יִשְׁמָעֵאל׃ טז וְאַבְרָם בֶּן־שְׁמֹנִים שָׁנָה וְשֵׁשׁ שָׁנִים בְּלֶדֶת־הָגָר

< when Hagar gave birth < years < and six < years < of eighty < was of the age < And Abram 16 << Ishmael.

אֶת־יִשְׁמָעֵאל לְאַבְרָם׃ ס [יז] א וַיְהִי אַבְרָם בֶּן־תִּשְׁעִים שָׁנָה וְתֵשַׁע

< and nine < years < of ninety < was of the age < Abram < It was when 1 [17] << to Abram. < Ishmael < to

שָׁנִים וַיֵּרָא יהוה אֶל־אַבְרָם וַיֹּאמֶר אֵלָיו אֲנִי־אֵל שַׁדַּי הִתְהַלֵּךְ לְפָנַי

< before Me < walk << Shaddai; < El < I am << to him, < and said < Abram < to < HASHEM appeared << years,

עִמַּהּ אֲמַרַת אַתְּ הוּא אֱלָהָא דְחָזֵי כֹלָּא אֲרֵי אֲמֶרֶת הַבְרַם הָכָא (נ״א הַאַף אֲנָא) שָׁרֵתִי חָזְיָא בָּתַר דְּאִתְגְּלִי לִי: יד עַל כֵּן קְרָא לְבֵירָא בֵּירָא דְמַלְאַךְ קַיָּמָא אִתַּחֲזִי עֲלַהּ הָא (הִיא) בֵּין רְקָם וּבֵין חַגְרָא: טו וִילִידַת הָגָר לְאַבְרָם בָּר וּקְרָא אַבְרָם שׁוּם בְּרֵהּ דִּי לִידַת הָגָר יִשְׁמָעֵאל: טז וְאַבְרָם בַּר תְּמָנַן וְשִׁת שְׁנִין כַּד יְלִידַת הָגָר יָת יִשְׁמָעֵאל לְאַבְרָם: א וַהֲוָה אַבְרָם בַּר תִּשְׁעִין וּתְשַׁע שְׁנִין וְאִתְגְּלִי יְיָ לְאַבְרָם וַאֲמַר לֵהּ אֲנָא אֵל שַׁדַּי פְּלַח קֳדָמַי

רש״י

(יג) **אתה אל ראי.** נקוד חטף קמ״ץ מפני שהוא שם דבר, אלוה הראיה, שרואה בעלבון של עלובין (ב״ר מה:י) [ס״א ד״א, אתה אל ראי ומשמע שהוא רואה הכל ואין שום דבר רואה אותו (תרגום יונתן)]: **הגם הלם.** ל׳ תימה, וכי סבורה הייתי שאף הלום במדברות ראיתי שלוחיו של מקום **אחרי ראי** אותם בביתו של אברהם [ששם הייתי רגילה לראות מלאכים]. ותדע שהיתה רגילה לראות, שהרי מנוח ראה את המלאך פעם אחת ואמר מות נמות (שופטים יג:כב), וזו ראתה ארבעה זה אחר זה ולא חרדה (מגילה יז:; ב״ר שם ז): (יד) **באר לחי רואי.** כתרגומו, בירא דמלאך קימא אתחזי עלה: (טו) **ויקרא אברם שם וגו׳.** אע״פ שלא שמע אברם דברי המלאך שאמר וקראת שמו ישמעאל, שרתה רוח הקודש עליו וקראו ישמעאל (מדרש אגדה): [(טז) **ואברם בן שמונים וגו׳.** לשבחו של ישמעאל נכתב, להודיעך שהי׳ בן י״ג שנה כשנמול ולא עכב (שם:)] (א) **אני אל שדי.** אני הוא שיש די באלהותי לכל בריה. ולפיכך **התהלך לפני** ואהיה לך לאלוה ולפטרון. וכן כל מקום שהוא במקרא פירושו כך, די שלו [ס״א די יש לו] והכל לפי הענין (ב״ר מו:ג): **התהלך לפני.** כתרגומו, פלח קדמי, הדבק בעבודתי:

13. **אֵל רֳאִי** — *The God of Vision,* Who sees the humiliation and misery of the afflicted (*Rashi*). Although an angel, not God, had spoken to her, she understood that he was God's emissary. She went on to exclaim that though it was common for angels to be seen in Abraham's house, now she had even seen one here in the desert!

14. **בְּאֵר לַחַי רֹאִי** — *The Well of the Living One Appearing to Me,* or the well at which the everlasting angel appeared to me (*Targum*). This well was a place of prayer in the future; see 24:62.

17.

The covenant of circumcision: new names and a new destiny.

The year was 2047 from Creation; Abraham was 99 years old, Sarah 89, and Ishmael 13. At this advanced age Abraham was given the commandment of circumcision, one of his ten trials. Despite his age and the difficulty of performing the hitherto unknown operation, he did not hesitate to comply. The commandment was given prior to Isaac's conception: (a) so that he would be conceived in holiness; and (b) in order to emphasize the miracle that Abraham could have a child even though his organ had been weakened (*Radak*). *Michtav MeEliyahu* explains the magnitude of the test: the public would regard circumcision as bizarre, causing people to shun him, and it would thus seriously contradict his lifelong method of bringing people close to God. Thus Abraham was challenged to accept a commandment that opposed his concept of how to serve God.

1. **אֵל שַׁדַּי** — *El Shaddai.* This Name depicts God literally as שֶׁדַּי, *Who is sufficient* in granting His mercies, and Who has *sufficient* power to give whatever is necessary (*Rashi* to 43:14).

הִתְהַלֵּךְ לְפָנַי — *Walk before Me,* serve Me, by observing the *mitzvah* of circumcision, *and as a result of this, you will become perfect* (*Rashi*).

By removing some of his skin through circumcision — an apparent contradiction to *physical* perfection — man would become *perfect*, because this slight diminution of an organ would be the symbol of his covenant with God. Such closeness can be achieved only through man's own efforts; had he been born that way, the lack of a foreskin would be meaningless

וֶהְיֵה תָמִים: ב וְאֶתְּנָה בְרִיתִי בֵּינִי וּבֵינֶךָ וְאַרְבֶּה
‹ and I will increase « and between you, ‹ between Me ‹ My covenant ‹ I will set 2 « perfect. ‹ and be

אוֹתְךָ בִּמְאֹד מְאֹד: ג וַיִּפֹּל אַבְרָם עַל־פָּנָיו וַיְדַבֵּר
‹ and speak « his face, ‹ upon ‹ And Abram fell 3 « most exceedingly. ‹ you

אִתּוֹ אֱלֹהִים לֵאמֹר: ד אֲנִי הִנֵּה בְרִיתִי אִתָּךְ וְהָיִיתָ
‹ You shall be « with you: ‹ My covenant ‹ this is « As for Me, 4 « saying, ‹ did God ‹ with him

לְאַב הֲמוֹן גּוֹיִם: ה וְלֹא־יִקָּרֵא עוֹד אֶת־שִׁמְךָ אַבְרָם
« Abram, ‹ shall your name ‹ any longer ‹ be called ‹ not 5 « of nations; ‹ of a multitude ‹ a father

וְהָיָה שִׁמְךָ אַבְרָהָם כִּי אַב־הֲמוֹן גּוֹיִם נְתַתִּיךָ: ו וְהִפְרֵתִי אֹתְךָ
‹ I will make you fruitful 6 « have I made you; ‹ of nations ‹ of a multitude ‹ the father ‹ for « Abraham, ‹ that your name is ‹ but it shall be

בִּמְאֹד מְאֹד וּנְתַתִּיךָ לְגוֹיִם וּמְלָכִים מִמְּךָ יֵצֵאוּ: שביעי ז וַהֲקִמֹתִי
‹ I will establish 7 « shall be descended. ‹ from you ‹ and kings « nations; ‹ and I will make of you « most exceedingly

אֶת־בְּרִיתִי בֵּינִי וּבֵינֶךָ וּבֵין זַרְעֲךָ אַחֲרֶיךָ לְדֹרֹתָם לִבְרִית עוֹלָם לִהְיוֹת
‹ to be « that is everlasting, ‹ as a covenant ‹ throughout their generations, « after you, ‹ your offspring ‹ and between ‹ and between you ‹ between Me ‹ My covenant

לְךָ לֵאלֹהִים וּלְזַרְעֲךָ אַחֲרֶיךָ: ח וְנָתַתִּי לְךָ וּלְזַרְעֲךָ אַחֲרֶיךָ אֵת ׀ אֶרֶץ
‹ the land ‹ after you ‹ and to your offspring ‹ to you ‹ And I will give 8 « after you. ‹ and to your offspring ‹ a God ‹ unto you

מְגֻרֶיךָ אֵת כָּל־אֶרֶץ כְּנַעַן לַאֲחֻזַּת עוֹלָם וְהָיִיתִי לָהֶם לֵאלֹהִים:
« a God. ‹ unto them ‹ and I shall be « that is everlasting; ‹ as a possession « of Canaan — ‹ of the land ‹ — the whole « of your sojourns

וֶהֱוֵי שְׁלִים: ב וְאֶתֵּן קְיָמִי בֵּין מֵימְרִי
וּבֵינָךְ וְאַסְגֵּי יָתָךְ לַחֲדָא לַחֲדָא: ג וּנְפַל
אַבְרָם עַל אַפּוֹהִי וּמַלִּיל עִמֵּהּ יְיָ
לְמֵימָר: ד אֲנָא הָא (גְזַר) קְיָמִי עִמָּךְ
וּתְהֵי לְאַב סְגִי עַמְמִין: ה וְלָא יִתְקְרֵי
עוֹד יָת שְׁמָךְ אַבְרָם וִיהֵי שְׁמָךְ אַבְרָהָם
אֲרֵי אַב סְגִי עַמְמִין יְהָבְתָּךְ: ו וְאַפֵּישׁ
יָתָךְ לַחֲדָא לַחֲדָא וְאֶתְּנִנָּךְ לְעַמְמִין
וּמַלְכִין דְּשַׁלִּיטִין בְּעַמְמַיָּא מִנָּךְ יִפְקוּן:
ז וַאֲקִים יָת קְיָמִי בֵּין מֵימְרִי וּבֵינָךְ וּבֵין
בְּנָיךְ בַּתְרָךְ לְדָרֵיהוֹן לִקְיָם עָלָם
לְמֶהֱוֵי לָךְ לֶאֱלָהָא וְלִבְנָיךְ בַּתְרָךְ:
ח וְאֶתֵּן לָךְ וְלִבְנָיךְ בַּתְרָךְ יָת אַרְעָא
תּוֹתָבוּתָךְ יָת כָּל אַרְעָא דִכְנַעַן
לְאַחֲסָנַת עָלָם וְאֶהֱוֵי לְהוֹן לֶאֱלָהָא:

רש"י

והיה תמים. אף זה לווי אחר לווי, היה שלם בכל נסיונותי. ולפי מדרשו, התהלך לפני במלות מילה ובדבר הזה תהיה תמים, שכל זמן שהערלה בך אתה בעל מום לפני (ב"ר שם ד). ד"א, והיה תמים, [עכשיו אתה חסר ה' איברים, ב' עינים ב' אזנים וראש הגויה.] אוסיף לך אות על שמך ויהיו מנין אותיותיך רמ"ח כמנין איבריך (תנחומא טז; נדרים לב:): **(ב) ואתנה בריתי.** ברית של אהבה וברית הארץ להורישה לך ע"י מלוה זו (ב"ר שם ט): **(ג) ויפל אברם על פניו.** ממורא השכינה, שעד שלא מל לא היה בו כח לעמוד ורוה"ק נצבת עליו, וזהו שנאמר בבלעם נופל וגלוי עינים (במדבר כד:ד). בברייתא דר"א מצאתי כן (פדר"א פכ"ט): **(ה) כי אב המון גוים.** ל' נוטריקון של שמו (ב"ר שם ז). ורי"ש שהיתה בו בתחלה, שלא היה אב אלא לארם שהוא מקומו ועכשיו אב לכל העולם (ברכות יג.), לא זזה ממקומה. שאף יו"ד של שרי נתרעמה על השכינה עד שהוסיפה ליהושע, שנאמר ויקרא משה להושע בן נון יהושע (במדבר יג:טז; סנהדרין קז.; ב"ר מז:א): **(ו) ונתתיך לגוים.** ישראל ואדום, שהרי ישמעאל כבר היה לו ולא היה מבשרו עליו: **(ז) והקמותי את בריתי.** ומה היא הברית, **להיות לך לאלהים:** **(ח) לאחוזת עולם.** ושם אהיה [ס"א **והייתי**] **להם לאלהים** (ב"ר

(*Radak*). Closeness to God through his own efforts is Man's ultimate perfection. [See below 9-14.]

5. God changed Abram's name to *Abraham*, a contraction representing his new status as *av hamon* — father of a multitude — whereas the name Avram represented his former status as only *av Aram* — father of Aram, his native country.

Abraham's new description as *father of a multitude of nations* was not rhetorical; it has halachic implications that shed light on its deeper meaning. In explaining how converts who bring their first fruits to the Temple can recite the required formula thanking God for the Land He swore to give *our* fathers (*Deuteronomy* 26:3) — though converts do not descend from the Patriarchs — *Rambam* states: All converts are considered descendants of Abraham because the Torah calls him *the father of . . . nations*, and therefore a convert can be called a son of Abraham (*Rambam,* Commentary to Mishnah *Bikkurim* 1:4). This means that the spiritual mission of mankind, which began with Adam, was now transferred to Abraham.

ט וַיֹּאמֶר אֱלֹהִים אֶל־אַבְרָהָם וְאַתָּה אֶת־בְּרִיתִי
‹ My covenant ‹ And as for you, « Abraham, ‹ to ‹ God said 9
תִשְׁמֹר אַתָּה וְזַרְעֲךָ אַחֲרֶיךָ לְדֹרֹתָם: י זֹאת
‹ This is 10 « throughout their generations. ‹ after you ‹ and your offspring ‹ – you « shall you keep
בְּרִיתִי אֲשֶׁר תִּשְׁמְרוּ בֵּינִי וּבֵינֵיכֶם וּבֵין זַרְעֲךָ
‹ your offspring ‹ and between ‹ and between you ‹ between Me ‹ you shall keep ‹ which ‹ My covenant
אַחֲרֶיךָ הִמּוֹל לָכֶם כָּל־זָכָר: יא וּנְמַלְתֶּם אֵת בְּשַׂר עָרְלַתְכֶם וְהָיָה
‹ and that shall be « of your foreskin, ‹ the flesh ‹ You shall circumcise 11 « male. ‹ every ‹ among you ‹ To circumcise « after you:
לְאוֹת בְּרִית בֵּינִי וּבֵינֵיכֶם: יב וּבֶן־שְׁמֹנַת יָמִים יִמּוֹל לָכֶם כָּל־זָכָר
‹ male ‹ every ‹ among you ‹ circumcised shall be ‹ days ‹ of eight ‹ At the age 12 « and between you. ‹ between Me ‹ of the covenant ‹ the sign
לְדֹרֹתֵיכֶם יְלִיד בָּיִת וּמִקְנַת־כֶּסֶף מִכֹּל בֶּן־נֵכָר אֲשֶׁר לֹא מִזַּרְעֲךָ הוּא:
« is he. ‹ of your offspring, ‹ not ‹ who, ‹ outsider ‹ from any ‹ with money ‹ and he that is purchased ‹ in the household ‹ – he that is born « throughout your generations

ט וַאֲמַר יְיָ לְאַבְרָהָם וְאַתְּ יָת קְיָמִי תִּטָּר אַתְּ וּבְנָיךְ בַּתְרָךְ לְדָרֵיהוֹן: י דָּא קְיָמִי דִּי תִטְּרוּן בֵּין מֵימְרִי וּבֵינֵיכוֹן וּבֵין בְּנָיךְ בַּתְרָךְ מִגְזַר לְכוֹן כָּל דְּכוּרָא: יא וְתִגְזְרוּן יָת בִּשְׂרָא דְעָרְלַתְכוֹן וּתְהֵי (נ״א וִיהֵי) לְאָת קְיָם בֵּין מֵימְרִי וּבֵינֵיכוֹן: יב וּבַר תְּמַנְיָא יוֹמִין יִתְגְּזַר (נ״א יִגְזַר) לְכוֹן כָּל דְּכוּרָא לְדָרָתֵיכוֹן יְלִידֵי בֵיתָא וּזְבִינֵי כַסְפָּא מִכֹּל בַּר עַמְמִין דִּי לָא מִבְּנָךְ הוּא:

רש"י

מו:ט) אבל [בן ישראל] הדר בחוצה לארץ כמי שאין לו אלוה (כתובות קי:): **(ט) ואתה.** וי"ו זו מוסיף על ענין ראשון. אני הנה בריתי אתך ואתה היה זהיר לשמרו, ומה היא שמירתו, זאת בריתי אשר תשמרו וגו' המול לכם וגו' (ב"ר מו:ט): **(י) ביני וביניכם וגו'.** אותם של עכשיו: **ובין זרעך אחריך.** העתידין להולד אחריך: **המול.** כמו להמול כמו שאתה אומר עשות כמו לעשות: **(יא) ונמלתם.** כמו ומלתם, והנו"ן בו יתירה ליסוד הנופל [בו] לפרקים, כמו נ' של נושך ונ' של נושא. ונמלתם כמו ונשאתם (להלן מה:יט). אבל יִמּוֹל לשון יִפָּעֵל, כמו יֵעָשֶׂה, יֵאָכֵל: **(יב) יליד בית.** שילדתו השפחה בבית: **ומקנת כסף.** שקנאו משנולד: **(יג) המול ימול יליד ביתך.** כאן כפל עליו ולא אמר לח' ימים, ללמדך שיש יליד בית נמול לאחד [ס"א לאחר שמנה ימים], כמו שמפורש במסכת שבת (קלה:): **(יד) וערל זכר.** כאן למד שהמילה באותו

9-14. The covenant of circumcision. From the sequence of this chapter, it is clear that the blessings of children and possession of the Land depended on circumcision, a connection that is also implied in the second blessing of the Blessing after Meals. The symbolic significance of this commandment is indicated by the name of the flesh that is removed in performance of the commandment — עָרְלָה [*orlah*], commonly translated as *foreskin,* but more accurately, as it is used in Scripture, *a barrier* standing in the way of a beneficial result. For example, the sinful habits that predispose a person not to change his lifestyle are called the *orlah* of the heart (*Leviticus* 26:41; *Jeremiah* 9:25; *Ezekiel* 44:7). Thus, although this concept is beyond human understanding, circumcision is a means to help the Jew ennoble himself and return to the spiritual state of Adam before his sin. As the Sages teach, Adam was born circumcised, but after his sin his foreskin was extended and covered the organ (*Sanhedrin* 38b), as a symbol that he had created a barrier between himself and holiness.

By removing the superfluous skin covering the organ of continuity, circumcision teaches that man must eliminate the natural barriers blocking his advancement. But circumcision's capacity to accomplish this is not a logical outcome of the physical act; to the contrary, it is metaphysical. This aspect of circumcision is symbolized by the commandment that it be done on the eighth day of a boy's life. As *Maharal* teaches, the natural order of Creation involves cycles of seven, such as the seven days of the week and the seven years of the *Shemittah* agricultural cycle. The number eight represents the concept that one can rise above limitations of nature. By commanding Israel to circumcise its male children on the *eighth* day, God taught that the Jew's ability to remove the barriers to his spiritual ascent transcends the natural order of life. Nevertheless, God gives man the ability to do it — and since he can, he must.

10. בְּרִיתִי — *My covenant.* Here circumcision is called the *covenant*, but in the next verse it is called the *sign* of the covenant, implying that the actual covenant is something else. *R' Hirsch* sees in this a fundamental Jewish principle. A commandment consists of two parts: the physical act and its underlying moral or spiritual teaching — and neither is complete without the other. Just as it is not enough to perform the commanded deeds if they are denuded of intellectual and moral content, so it is not enough to philosophize on the commandments and seek moral improvement without actually performing the commandments. Hence, the physical act is the covenant, but it is also a *sign* of the covenant's deeper meaning.

12. יְלִיד בָּיִת — *He that is born in the household . . .* A master is required to circumcise his non-Jewish slave, whether he was born to the Jewish owner from a maidservant or was *purchased with money* after he was born (*Rashi*).

יג הִמּ֣וֹל ׀ יִמּ֗וֹל יְלִ֥יד בֵּֽיתְךָ֖ וּמִקְנַ֣ת כַּסְפֶּ֑ךָ וְהָיְתָ֧ה

< Thus shall be << with your money. < and he that is purchased < in your household < he that is born < Surely circumcised shall be 13

בְרִיתִ֛י בִּבְשַׂרְכֶ֖ם לִבְרִ֥ית עוֹלָֽם׃ יד וְעָרֵ֣ל ׀ זָכָ֗ר אֲשֶׁ֤ר

< who < male < An uncircumcised 14 << that is everlasting. < for a covenant < in your flesh < My covenant

לֹֽא־יִמּוֹל֙ אֶת־בְּשַׂ֣ר עָרְלָת֔וֹ וְנִכְרְתָ֛ה הַנֶּ֥פֶשׁ הַהִ֖וא

< that soul < — cut off shall be << of his foreskin < the flesh < circumcise < will not

מֵעַמֶּ֑יהָ אֶת־בְּרִיתִ֖י הֵפַֽר׃ טו וַיֹּ֤אמֶר אֱלֹהִים֙ אֶל־

< to < And God said 15 << he has breached. < My covenant << from its people;

יג אִתְגַּזָּרָא יִתְגַּזְּרוּן (נ"א מִגְזַר יִגְזַר)
יְלִיד בֵּיתָךְ וּזְבִינֵי כַסְפָּךְ וּתְהֵי (נ"א
וִיהֵי) קְיָמִי בִּבְשַׂרְכוֹן לִקְיָם עָלָם:
יד וְעָרֵל דִּכוּרָא דִּי לָא יִגְזַר יָת בְּשַׂר
עָרְלְתֵהּ וְיִשְׁתֵּיצֵי אֱנָשָׁא הַהוּא
מֵעַמֵּיהּ יָת קְיָמִי אַשְׁנִי: טו וַאֲמַר יְיָ
לְאַבְרָהָם שָׂרַי אִתְּתָךְ לָא תִקְרֵי יָת
שְׁמַהּ שָׂרָי אֲרֵי שָׂרָה שְׁמַהּ: טז וַאֲבָרֵךְ
יָתַהּ וְאַף אֶתֵּן מִנַּהּ לָךְ בָּר וַאֲבָרְכִנַּהּ
וּתְהֵי לִכְנִשַׁת עַמְמִין מַלְכִין דְּשַׁלִּיטִין
בְּעַמְמַיָּא מִנַּהּ יְהוֹן: יז וּנְפַל אַבְרָהָם
עַל אַפּוֹהִי וַחֲדִי וַאֲמַר בְּלִבֵּהּ הַלְּבַר
מְאָה שְׁנִין יְהֵי וְלַד וְאִם שָׂרָה הֲבַת
תִּשְׁעִין שְׁנִין תְּלִיד: יח וַאֲמַר אַבְרָהָם

אַבְרָהָ֔ם שָׂרַ֣י אִשְׁתְּךָ֔ לֹא־תִקְרָ֥א אֶת־שְׁמָ֖הּ שָׂרָ֑י כִּ֥י שָׂרָ֖ה שְׁמָֽהּ׃

<< is her name. < Sarah < for << Sarai, < her name < call < Do not << your wife: < [As for] Sarai << Abraham,

טז וּבֵרַכְתִּ֣י אֹתָ֔הּ וְגַ֨ם נָתַ֧תִּי מִמֶּ֛נָּה לְךָ֖ בֵּ֑ן וּבֵרַכְתִּ֙יהָ֙ וְהָֽיְתָ֣ה לְגוֹיִ֔ם מַלְכֵ֥י

< kings << to nations; < and she shall give rise < I will bless her << a son; < to you < through her < I will give < moreover, < her; < I will bless 16

עַמִּ֖ים מִמֶּ֥נָּה יִהְיֽוּ׃ יז וַיִּפֹּ֧ל אַבְרָהָ֛ם עַל־פָּנָ֖יו וַיִּצְחָ֑ק וַיֹּ֣אמֶר בְּלִבּ֗וֹ הַלְּבֶ֤ן

< Can it be that to one of the age < in his heart, < and he said << and he laughed; < his face < upon < And Abraham fell 17 << will arise. < from her < of peoples

מֵאָֽה־שָׁנָה֙ יִוָּלֵ֔ד וְאִם־שָׂרָ֔ה הֲבַת־תִּשְׁעִ֥ים שָׁנָ֖ה תֵּלֵֽד׃ יח וַיֹּ֥אמֶר אַבְרָהָ֖ם

< And Abraham said 18 << shall give birth? << years — < of ninety < — who is of the age << Sarah < And can it be that << [a child] shall be born? < years < of one hundred

רש"י

מקום שהוא ניכר בין זכר לנקבה (שם קח.): **אשר לא ימול.** משיגיע לכלל עונשין (שבת קלג:) **ונכרתה,** אבל אביו אין ענוש עליו כרת (יבמות ע:) אבל עובר בעשה (קידושין כט.): **ונכרתה הנפש.** הולך ערירי (יבמות נה.) ומת קודם זמנו (מו"ק כח.): (טו) **לא תקרא את שמה שרי.** דמשמע שרי לי ולא לאחרים. **כי שרה שמה,** שתהא שרה על כל (ברכות יג.): (טז) **וברכתי אתה.** ומה היא הברכה, שחזרה לנערותה, שנאמר היתה לי עדנה (להלן יח:יב; ב"ר מז:ב): **וברכתיה.** בהנקת שדים (ב"ר שם) כשנצרכה לכך ביום משתה של יצחק, שהיו מרננים עליהם שהביאו אסופי מן השוק ואומרים בננו הוא, והביאה כל אחת בנה עמה ומניקתה לא הביאה, והיא הניקה את כולם. הוא שנאמר היניקה בנים שרה (להלן כא:ז). ב"ר (נג:ט) רמזו במקרא: (יז) **ויפל אברהם על פניו ויצחק.** זה ת"א לשון שמחה וחדי, ושל שרה לשון מחוך (להלן יח:יב). למדת שאברהם האמין ושמח, ושרה לא האמינה ולגלגה. וזהו שהקפיד הקב"ה על שרה (שם יג) ולא הקפיד על אברהם: **הלבן.** יש תמיהות שהן קיימות, כמו הנגלה נגליתי (שמואל א ב:כז), הרואה אתה (שם ב טו:כז). אף זו היא קיימת, וכך אמר בלבו, הנעשה חסד זה לאחר מה שהקב"ה עושה לי: **ואם שרה הבת תשעים שנה.** היתה כדאי לילד. ואף על פי שדורות הראשונים היו מולידים בני ת"ק שנה, בימי אברהם נתמעטו השנים כבר ובא תשות כח לעולם, ולא ולמד

14. **וְנִכְרְתָה** — *Cut off shall be.* An adult who intentionally remains uncircumcised suffers כָּרֵת, *spiritual excision.* Excision means that the soul loses its share in the World to Come, and the violator may die childless and prematurely. [See commentary to *Leviticus* 7:20.]

15-22. The promise to Sarah. Previously, the covenant was solely with Abraham. Now Sarah was made an equal party in this covenantal promise. And just as Abraham's new role was signified by a change of name, so was Sarah's (*R' Hirsch*). The word *Sarai* means *my* princess, implying that she owed her greatness to her status as Abraham's wife. Henceforth, she would be called only *Sarah*, which signifies that she is a "*princess* to all the nations of the world."

As the story of the Patriarchs and Matriarchs unfolds, we see that infertility was common among them, but that prayer and Divine intervention resulted in the emergence of the nation. This was God's way of proving that the Jewish people are not a natural phenomenon; without miracles we could not have existed, nor could we continue to exist.

17. **וַיִּצְחָק** — *And he laughed.* Abraham laughed out of sheer joy at the news that Sarah would bear a son. *Onkelos* renders וַחֲדִי, *and he rejoiced*. In the case of Sarah, however [see 18:12], *Onkelos* renders וְחַיְכַת, *she laughed,* a translation that is supported by the context of that passage. Abraham had faith and *rejoiced,* while Sarah was skeptical and *laughed*; hence, God was angry with Sarah but not with Abraham (*Rashi*).

אֶל־הָאֱלֹהִים לוּ יִשְׁמָעֵאל יִחְיֶה לְפָנֶיךָ׃

<< before You! < might live < Ishmael < If only << God, < to

יט וַיֹּאמֶר אֱלֹהִים אֲבָל שָׂרָה אִשְׁתְּךָ יֹלֶדֶת לְךָ

< you < will bear < your wife < Sarah < In truth, << God said, 19

בֵּן וְקָרָאתָ אֶת־שְׁמוֹ יִצְחָק וַהֲקִמֹתִי אֶת־בְּרִיתִי

< My covenant < and I will establish << Isaac; < his name < and you shall call << a son,

אִתּוֹ לִבְרִית עוֹלָם לְזַרְעוֹ אַחֲרָיו׃ כ וּלְיִשְׁמָעֵאל

< But regarding Ishmael 20 << after him. < for his offspring < that is everlasting < as a covenant < with him

שְׁמַעְתִּיךָ הִנֵּה ׀ בֵּרַכְתִּי אֹתוֹ וְהִפְרֵיתִי אֹתוֹ

<< I will make him fruitful, << him, < I have blessed < Indeed << I have heard you:

וְהִרְבֵּיתִי אֹתוֹ בִּמְאֹד מְאֹד שְׁנֵים־עָשָׂר נְשִׂיאִם

< princes < twelve << most exceedingly; < him < and I will increase

יוֹלִיד וּנְתַתִּיו לְגוֹי גָּדוֹל׃ כא וְאֶת־בְּרִיתִי אָקִים אֶת־יִצְחָק אֲשֶׁר תֵּלֵד

< bear < whom < Isaac < with < I will establish < But My covenant 21 << that is great. < into a nation < and I will make him << will he beget,

לְךָ שָׂרָה לַמּוֹעֵד הַזֶּה בַּשָּׁנָה הָאַחֶרֶת׃ כב וַיְכַל לְדַבֵּר אִתּוֹ וַיַּעַל אֱלֹהִים

< and God ascended << with him, < speaking < And He finished 22 << that follows. < in the year < at this time < will Sarah < to you

מֵעַל אַבְרָהָם׃ כג וַיִּקַּח אַבְרָהָם אֶת־יִשְׁמָעֵאל בְּנוֹ וְאֵת כָּל־יְלִידֵי בֵיתוֹ

< in his household < those [servants] born < and all < his son, Ishmael < Then Abraham took 23 << Abraham. < from upon

וְאֵת כָּל־מִקְנַת כַּסְפּוֹ כָּל־זָכָר בְּאַנְשֵׁי בֵּית אַבְרָהָם וַיָּמָל אֶת־בְּשַׂר

< the flesh < and he circumcised << of Abraham — < of the house < among the people < the males < — all << with his money < those he had purchased < and all

קֳדָם יְיָ לְוַי יִשְׁמָעֵאל יִתְקַיַּם קֳדָמָךְ׃ יט וַאֲמַר יְיָ בְּקוּשְׁטָא שָׂרָה אִתְּתָךְ תְּלִיד לָךְ בָּר וְתִקְרֵי יָת שְׁמֵהּ יִצְחָק וַאֲקֵים יָת קְיָמִי עִמֵּהּ לִקְיָם עָלָם לִבְנוֹהִי בַתְרוֹהִי׃ כ וּלְיִשְׁמָעֵאל קַבֵּלִית צְלוֹתָךְ הָא בָּרֵכִית יָתֵהּ וְאַפֵּשׁ יָתֵהּ וְאַסְגֵּי יָתֵהּ לַחֲדָא לַחֲדָא תְּרֵין עֲשַׂר רַבְרְבַיָּא יוֹלִיד וְאֶתְנִנֵּהּ לְעַם סַגִּי׃ כא וְיָת קְיָמִי אֲקִים עִם יִצְחָק דִּי תְלִיד לָךְ שָׂרָה לְזִמְנָא הָדֵין בְּשַׁתָּא אָחֳרַנְתָּא׃ כב וְשֵׁצִי לְמַלָּלָא עִמֵּהּ וְאִסְתַּלַּק יְקָרָא דַייָ מֵעִלָּווֹהִי דְּאַבְרָהָם׃ כג וּדְבַר אַבְרָהָם יָת יִשְׁמָעֵאל בְּרֵהּ וְיָת כָּל יְלִידֵי בֵיתֵהּ וְיָת כָּל זְבִינֵי כַסְפֵּהּ כָּל דְּכוּרָא בֶּאֱנָשֵׁי בֵּית אַבְרָהָם וּגְזַר יָת בִּשְׂרָא

רש"י

מעשרה דורות שמנח ועד אברהם שמהרו תולדותיהם בני שלשים ובני שבעים (פדר"א פכ"ב): **(יח) לו ישמעאל יחיה.** הלואי שיחיה ישמעאל, איני כדאי לקבל מתן שכר כזה (ב"ר מז:ד): **יחיה לפניך.** יחיה ביראתך (תרגום יונתן) כמו התהלך לפני (לעיל פסוק א) פלח קדמי: **(יט) אבל.** לשון אמתת דברים (אונקלוס; תרגום יונתן), וכן אבל אשמים אנחנו (להלן מב:כא) אבל בן אין לה (מלכים ב ד:יד): **וקראת את שמו יצחק.** על שם הצחוק (מדרש חז"י). וי"א על שם עשרה נסיונות ול' שנה של שרה וח' ימים שנימול וק' שנה של אברהם (פדר"א לב; ב"ר נג:ז): [**והקימותי את בריתי.** למה נאמר, והרי כבר כתיב ואתה את בריתי תשמור אתה וזרעך וגו', אלא לפי שאומר והקימותי וגו', יכול בני ישמעאל ובני קטורה בכלל הקיום, ת"ל והקימותי את בריתי אתו, ולא עם אחרים (עי' סנהדרין נט:): **ואת בריתי אקים את יצחק.** למה נאמר, אלא למד שהיה קדוש מבטן (עי' שבת קלז:). ד"א, אמר רבי אבא מכאן למד ק"ו בן הגבירה מבן האמה. כתיב הנה ברכתי אותו והרביתי אותו והפריתי אותו, זה ישמעאל, וק"ו ואת בריתי אקים את יצחק (ב"ר מז:ה):] **את בריתי.** ברית המילה תהא מסורה לזרעו של יצחק (סנהדרין שם): **(כ) שנים עשר נשיאים.** כעננים יכלו, כמו נשיאים ורוח (משלי כה:יד; ב"ר שם): **(כב) מעל אברהם.** לשון נקיה הוא כלפי שכינה. ולמדנו שהצדיקים מרכבתו של מקום (ב"ר שם ו, ועי' סט:ג):

18. לוּ יִשְׁמָעֵאל יִחְיֶה לְפָנֶיךָ — *If only Ishmael might live before You.* Abraham's response was twofold: (a) I am unworthy of so great a reward as to have a son now; (b) it will suffice for me if only Ishmael lived righteously before You (*Rashi*). *Ramban* maintains that Abraham feared that the birth of his true heir might signal Ishmael's death, so that this response constitutes a literal prayer for his life.

20. נְשִׂיאִם — *Princes.* The Torah uses this word because it can also be translated as *clouds*, to allude to the fact that Ishmael's offspring will enjoy a period of ascendancy, but ultimately they will dissipate like clouds (*Rashi*).

"We see from the prophecy in this verse that 2337 years elapsed before the Arabs, Ishmael's descendants, became a great nation [with the rise of Islam in the seventh cen-

עָרְלָתָם בְּעֶצֶם הַיּוֹם הַזֶּה כַּאֲשֶׁר דִּבֶּר אִתּוֹ אֱלֹהִים׃

« God had spoken with him. ‹ as ‹ of that day ‹ in the midst ‹ of their foreskin

מפטיר כד וְאַבְרָהָם בֶּן־תִּשְׁעִים וָתֵשַׁע שָׁנָה בְּהִמֹּלוֹ

‹ at his circumcising ‹ years ‹ and nine ‹ of ninety ‹ was of the age ‹ Abraham 24

בְּשַׂר עָרְלָתוֹ׃ כה וְיִשְׁמָעֵאל בְּנוֹ בֶּן־שְׁלֹשׁ עֶשְׂרֵה

‹ of thirteen ‹ was of the age ‹ his son ‹ and Ishmael 25 « of his foreskin; ‹ the flesh

שָׁנָה בְּהִמֹּלוֹ אֵת בְּשַׂר עָרְלָתוֹ׃ כו בְּעֶצֶם הַיּוֹם הַזֶּה נִמּוֹל אַבְרָהָם

‹ was Abraham circumcised ‹ of that day ‹ In the midst 26 « of his foreskin. ‹ of the flesh ‹ when he was circumcised ‹ years

וְיִשְׁמָעֵאל בְּנוֹ׃ כז וְכָל־אַנְשֵׁי בֵיתוֹ יְלִיד בָּיִת וּמִקְנַת־כֶּסֶף מֵאֵת

‹ from ‹ for money ‹ and he who was purchased ‹ in his household ‹ he who was born « of his household, ‹ the men ‹ and all 27 « his son, ‹ with Ishmael

בֶּן־נֵכָר נִמֹּלוּ אִתּוֹ׃ פפפ

« with him. ‹ were circumcised « an outsider,

קכ״ו פסוקים. נמל״ו סימן. מכנדב״י סימן.

דְעָרְלָתְהוֹן בִּכְרַן יוֹמָא הָדֵין
כְּמָא דִּי מַלִּיל עִמֵּהּ יְיָ׃ כד וְאַבְרָהָם
בַּר תִּשְׁעִין וּתְשַׁע שְׁנִין כַּד גְּזַר
בִּשְׂרָא דְעָרְלְתֵהּ׃ כה וְיִשְׁמָעֵאל
בְּרֵהּ בַּר תְּלָת עַשְׂרֵי שְׁנִין כַּד גְּזַר
יָת בִּשְׂרָא דְעָרְלְתֵהּ׃ כו בִּכְרַן יוֹמָא
הָדֵין אִתְגְּזַר (נ״א גְּזַר) אַבְרָהָם
וְיִשְׁמָעֵאל בְּרֵהּ׃ כז וְכָל אֱנָשֵׁי בֵיתֵהּ
יְלִידֵי בֵיתָא וּזְבִינֵי כַסְפָּא מִן בַּר
עַמְמִין אִתְגְּזָרוּ (נ״א גְּזָרוּ) עִמֵּהּ׃

THE HAFTARAH FOR LECH LECHA APPEARS ON PAGE 326.

רש״י

(כג) **בעצם היום.** בו ביום שנצטוה, ביום ולא בלילה, לא נתיירא לא מן הגוים ולא מן הליצנים, ושלא יהיו אויביו [ס״א אוהביו] ובני דורו אומרים אילו ראינוהו לא הנחנוהו למול ולקיים מצותו של מקום (ב״ר מז:ט): **וימל.** לשון ויפעל: (כד) **בהמלו.** בְּהִפָּעֲלוֹ כמו בהבראם (לעיל ב:ד) [נטל אברהם סכין ואחז בערלתו ורצה לחתוך והיה מתירא, שהיה זקן, מה עשה הקב״ה, שלח ידו ואחז עמו, שנא׳ וכרות עמו הברית (נחמיה ט:ח) לו לא נאמר אלא עמו. ב״ר (מט:ב)]: (כה) **בהמלו את בשר ערלתו.** באברהם לא נאמר את, לפי שלא היה חסר אלא חתוך בשר, שכבר נתמעך על ידי תשמיש, אבל ישמעאל שהיה ילד הוזקק לחתוך ערלה ולפרוע המילה, לכך נאמר בו את (ב״ר מז:ח): (כו) **בעצם היום.** שמלאו לאברהם צ״ט שנה ולישמעאל י״ג שנים **נמול אברהם וישמעאל בנו:**

tury C.E.] . . . . Throughout this period, Ishmael hoped anxiously, until finally the promise was fulfilled and they dominated the world. We, the descendants of Isaac, for whom the fulfillment of the promises made to us is delayed due to our sins . . . should *surely* anticipate the fulfillment of God's promises and not despair" (*R' Bachya* citing *R' Chananel*).

קכ״ו פסוקים. נמל״ו סימן. מכנדב״י סימן. — This Masoretic note means: There are 126 verses in the *Sidrah*, numerically corresponding to the mnemonic נִמֹּל״וּ [= 126 = "they were circumcised"] and also to מַכְנַדְבַ״י (see *Ezra* 10:40).

נַדְבַי resembles נָדִיב and נָדִיב is interpreted in the Talmud (*Chagigah* 3a) and Midrash to *Song of Songs* 7:2 as a reference to Abraham (see ArtScroll comm. there). The meaning of מַךְ may be derived from *Sotah* 10b where the same word is given two meanings with regard to David: (a) He was humble and self-effacing [מַךְ = *a poor person*]; and (b) he was born circumcised [מַכָּה = מַךְ, *a wound*]. Either interpretation can be applied to Abraham, who was humble and who circumcised himself (*R' David Feinstein*).

PARASHAS VAYEIRA / פרשת וירא

[יח] א וַיֵּרָ֤א אֵלָיו֙ יְהֹוָ֔ה בְּאֵלֹנֵ֖י מַמְרֵ֑א וְה֛וּא יֹשֵׁ֥ב

‹ was sitting ‹ while he ‹‹ of Mamre, ‹ in the plains ‹ did HASHEM ‹ to him ‹ Appeared **1** [18]

פֶּֽתַח־הָאֹ֖הֶל כְּחֹ֥ם הַיּֽוֹם׃ ב וַיִּשָּׂ֤א עֵינָיו֙ וַיַּ֔רְא וְהִנֵּה֙

‹‹ There were ‹‹ and saw: ‹ his eyes ‹ He lifted **2** ‹‹ of the day. ‹ in the heat ‹ of the tent ‹ [at the] entrance

שְׁלֹשָׁ֣ה אֲנָשִׁ֔ים נִצָּבִ֖ים עָלָ֑יו וַיַּ֗רְא וַיָּ֤רָץ לִקְרָאתָם֙ מִפֶּ֣תַח הָאֹ֔הֶל

‹‹ of the tent, ‹ from the entrance ‹ toward them ‹ and so he ran ‹‹ He perceived, ‹‹ over him. ‹ standing ‹ men ‹ three

וַיִּשְׁתַּ֖חוּ אָֽרְצָה׃ ג וַיֹּאמַ֑ר אֲדֹנָ֗י אִם־נָ֨א מָצָ֤אתִי חֵן֙ בְּעֵינֶ֔יךָ אַל־נָ֥א

‹ please, ‹ do not, ‹‹ in Your eyes, ‹ favor ‹ I have found ‹ now ‹ if ‹‹ O Lord, ‹‹ And he said, **3** ‹‹ to the ground. ‹ and bowed

אונקלוס

א וְאִתְגְּלִי לֵהּ יְיָ בְּמֵישְׁרֵי מַמְרֵא וְהוּא יָתֵב בִּתְרַע מַשְׁכְּנָא כְּמֵיחַם יוֹמָא: ב וּזְקַף עֵינוֹהִי וַחֲזָא וְהָא תְּלָתָא גֻבְרִין (נ״א גַבְרִין) קָיְמִין עִלָּווֹהִי וַחֲזָא וּרְהַט לְקַדָּמוּתְהוֹן מִתְּרַע מַשְׁכְּנָא וּסְגִיד עַל אַרְעָא: ג וַאֲמַר יְיָ אִם כְּעַן אַשְׁכָּחִית רַחֲמִין קֳדָמָךְ (נ״א בְּעֵינָיךְ) לָא כְעַן

רש״י

(א) **וירא אליו.** לבקר את החולה (סוטה יד.; תנחומא ישן א) [אמר רבי חמא בר חנינא יום שלישי למילתו היה, ובא הקב״ה ושאל בשלומו (ב״מ פו:)]: **באלוני ממרא.** הוא שנתן לו עצה על המילה, לפיכך נגלה אליו בחלקו (תנחומא ג; ב״ר מב:ח): **ישב.** ישב כתיב, בקש לעמוד, א״ל הקב״ה שב ואני אעמוד, ואתה סימן לבניך, שעתיד אני להתיצב בעדת הדיינין והן יושבין, שנא׳ אלהים נצב בעדת אל (תהלים פב:א; ב״ר מח:ז; שבועות לה:): **פתח האהל.** לראות אם יש עובר ושב ויכניסם בביתו (ב״מ פו:): **כחם היום.** הוציא הקב״ה חמה מנרתיקה שלא להטריחו באורחים, ולפי שראהו מצטער שלא היו אורחים באים הביא מלאכים עליו בדמות אנשים (שם): (ב) **והנה שלשה אנשים.** אחד לבשר את שרה ואחד להפוך את סדום ואחד לרפאות את אברהם, שאין מלאך אחד עושה שתי שליחיות (ב״ר נ:ב). תדע לך שכן, כל הפרשה הוא מזכירן בלשון רבים, ויאכלו (פסוק ח) ויאמרו אליו (פסוק ט), ובבשורה נאמר ויאמר שוב אשוב אליך (פסוק י) ובהפיכת סדום הוא אומר כי לא אוכל לעשות דבר (להלן יט:כב) לבלתי הפכי (שם כא). ורפאל שרפא את אברהם הלך משם להציל את לוט, הוא שנאמר ויהי כהוציאם אותם החוצה ויאמר המלט על נפשך (שם יז) למדת שהאחד היה מציל (ב״מ פו:): **נצבים עליו.** לפניו (תרגום יונתן) [כמו ועליו מטה מנשה (במדבר ב:כ)], אבל לשון נקיה הוא כלפי המלאכים: **וירא.** מהו וירא וירא שני פעמים, הראשון כמשמעו, והשני לשון הבנה. נסתכל שהיו נצבים במקום אחד והבין שלא היו רוצים להטריחו, [ואף על פי שיודעים היו שילא לקראתם עמדו במקומם לכבודו, להראותו שלא רצו להטריחו,] וקדם הוא ורץ לקראתם. [בבבא מציעא (פו:), כתיב נצבים עליו וכתיב וירץ לקראתם, כד חזיוהו דהוה שרי ואסר פירשו הימנו, מיד וירץ לקראתם]: (ג) **ויאמר אדני אם נא וגו׳.** לגדול שבהם אמר, וקראם כולם אדונים, ולגדול אמר אל נא תעבור, וכיון שלא יעבור הוא יעמדו חביריו עמו, ובלשון זה הוא חול. ד״א, קדש (שבועות לה:) והיה אומר להקב״ה

PARASHAS VAYEIRA

18.

1-8. Visiting the sick and hospitality to strangers. As if to show what it was about Abraham that made him so uniquely worthy to be the spiritual father of all mankind, the Torah relates what he did on the third day after his circumcision, when the wound is most painful and the patient most weakened. God visited him to show him honor for having carried out the commandment and to acknowledge that he had thereby elevated himself to a new spiritual plateau. *Or HaChaim* explains that when people carry out great deeds, God shows Himself to them as a token of tribute, as He did here and as He would do in the Wilderness when the Jewish people erected the Tabernacle as a home for the *Shechinah*. Thus, God's visit to Abraham was to demonstrate that he had become a "chariot of the Divine Presence" (see *Bereishis Rabbah* 82:6), meaning that even his physical being had become pure enough to be a resting place for God, as it were.

To spare Abraham the physical strain of caring for guests, God brought a heat wave so that no wayfarers were up and about that day. But Abraham longed for guests, because a *tzaddik* is never content with past accomplishments; he seeks to serve God at all times. In Abraham's case, his manner of service was through being kind to people, thereby drawing them into his orbit so that he could inspire them with his example to learn about and serve God. In response, God sent him three angels in the guise of people, and Abraham ran to invite them in and serve them personally, despite his age and illness. He also pressed Ishmael into service, for education of the young must be practical; theoretical preaching about kindness will fail to achieve the desired result unless it is accompanied by *acts* of kindness.

2. שְׁלֹשָׁה אֲנָשִׁים — *Three men.* As is apparent from the rest of the narrative, they were actually angels in the "guise" of men. God sent three different angels because, in the words of the Midrash, "one angel does not perform two missions." In this case the three angels were Michael, who informed Abraham that Sarah would have a son [v. 14]; Gabriel, who overturned Sodom [19:25]; and Raphael, who healed Abraham and saved Lot *(Rashi* as explained by *Gur Aryeh*). The last two tasks, healing Abraham and saving Lot, constituted a single mission because they were for the sake of rescue.

וַיַּרְא . . . וַיַּרְא — *And saw . . . He perceived.* The word is repeated because two things happened. First Abraham saw them coming. Then they stopped at a distance and he *perceived* that the reason they did so was to indicate that they did not wish to trouble him. In response, he ignored his pain and dashed toward them to invite them in (*Rashi*).

3. אֲדֹנָי — *O Lord.* According to most interpretations, the word אֲדֹנָי in this passage is sacred, referring to God. In taking leave

תַּעֲבֹר מֵעַל עַבְדֶּךָ: ד יֻקַּח־נָא מְעַט־מַיִם וְרַחֲצוּ

< and wash < of water < a small amount < now < Let be brought 4 << Your servant. < from < go away

רַגְלֵיכֶם וְהִשָּׁעֲנוּ תַּחַת הָעֵץ: ה וְאֶקְחָה פַת־לֶחֶם

< of bread < a piece < I will bring 5 << the tree. < beneath < and recline < your feet,

וְסַעֲדוּ לִבְּכֶם אַחַר תַּעֲבֹרוּ כִּי־עַל־כֵּן עֲבַרְתֶּם

< you have passed < that [purpose] < for < — since << go on < afterwards << your heart, < that you may sustain

עַל־עַבְדְּכֶם וַיֹּאמְרוּ כֵּן תַּעֲשֶׂה כַּאֲשֶׁר דִּבַּרְתָּ:

<< you have said. < just as < shall you do, < So << They said, << your servant. < by

ו וַיְמַהֵר אַבְרָהָם הָאֹהֱלָה אֶל־שָׂרָה וַיֹּאמֶר מַהֲרִי שְׁלֹשׁ סְאִים קֶמַח

< of meal, < se'ahs < [Sift] three << Hurry! << and said, < Sarah < to < to the tent < [Then] Abraham hastened 6

סֹלֶת לוּשִׁי וַעֲשִׂי עֻגוֹת: ז וְאֶל־הַבָּקָר רָץ אַבְרָהָם וַיִּקַּח בֶּן־בָּקָר רַךְ

< tender << a calf, < he took << Abraham, < ran < the cattle < [Then] to 7 << cakes! < and make < Knead << [yielding] fine flour!

וָטוֹב וַיִּתֵּן אֶל־הַנַּעַר וַיְמַהֵר לַעֲשׂוֹת אֹתוֹ: ח וַיִּקַּח חֶמְאָה וְחָלָב

< and milk < cream < He took 8 << it. < to prepare < and he hurried < the youth < to < and he gave [it] << and good,

וּבֶן־הַבָּקָר אֲשֶׁר עָשָׂה וַיִּתֵּן לִפְנֵיהֶם וְהוּא עֹמֵד עֲלֵיהֶם תַּחַת הָעֵץ

< the tree < beneath < by them < stood < and he << before them; < and he placed [these] << [the youth] had prepared, < which < and the calf

תִּעבַּר מֵעַל עַבְדָּךְ: ד יִסְּבוּן כְּעַן זְעֵיר מַיָּא וְאַסְחוּ רַגְלֵיכוֹן וְאִסְתְּמִיכוּ תְּחוֹת אִילָנָא: ה וְאֶסַּב פִּתָּא דְלַחְמָא וּסְעִידוּ לִבְּכוֹן בָּתַר כֵּן תִּעְבְּרוּן אֲרֵי עַל כֵּן עֲבַרְתּוּן עַל עַבְדְּכוֹן וַאֲמָרוּ כֵּן תַּעְבֵּד כְּמָא דִי מַלֶּלְתָּא: ו וְאוֹחִי אַבְרָהָם לְמַשְׁכְּנָא לְוַת שָׂרָה וַאֲמַר אוֹחָא תְּלָת סְאִין קִמְחָא דְסָלְתָּא לוּשִׁי וְעִבִידִי גְרִיצָן: ז וּלְוַת תּוֹרֵי רְהַט אַבְרָהָם וּדְבַר בַּר תּוֹרֵי רַכִּיךְ וְטַב וִיהַב לְעוּלֵמָא וְאוֹחִי לְמֶעְבַּד יָתֵהּ: ח וּנְסִיב שְׁמַן וַחֲלָב וּבַר תּוֹרֵי דִּי עֲבַד וִיהַב קֳדָמֵיהוֹן וְהוּא מְשַׁמֵּשׁ עִלָּוֵיהוֹן תְּחוֹת אִילָנָא

רש"י

להמתין לו עד שירוץ ויכנים את האורחים (שבת קכז.). ואע"פ שכתוב אחר וירץ לקראתם, האמירה קודם לכן היתה. ודרך המקראות לדבר כן, כמו שפירשתי אצל לא ידון רוחי באדם (לעיל ו:ג) שנכתב אחר ויולד נח (שם ה:לב), וא"א לומר כן אא"כ קדמה גזרת ק"ך שנה [ס"א קדמה הגזירה כ' שנים]. ושתי הלשונות בב"ר (מח:י, ט, מט:ז; ועי' ויק"ר יא:ה): (ד) **יקח נא.** על ידי שליח, והקב"ה שלם לבניו ע"י שליח, שנאמר וירם משה את ידו ויך את הסלע (במדבר כ:יא; ב"מ שם): **ורחצו רגליכם.** כסבור שהם ערביים שמשתחוים לאבק רגליהם (ב"מ שם) והקפיד שלא להכניס עבודה זרה לביתו. אבל לוט שלא הקפיד הקדים לינה לרחיצה, שנאמר ולינו ורחצו רגליכם (להלן יט:ב; ב"ר נ:ד): **תחת העץ.** תחת האילן (אונקלוס): (ה) [**וסעדו לבכם.** בתורה בנביאים ובכתובים מצינו דפתא סעדתא דלבא. בתורה וסעדו לבכם. בנביאים סעד לבך פת לחם (שופטים יט:ה). בכתובים ולחם לבב אנוש יסעד (תהלים קד:טו). א"ר חמא לבבכם אין כתיב כאן אלא לבכם, מגיד שאין יצה"ר שולט במלאכים. בראשית רבה (מח:יא):] **אחר תעבורו.** אחר כן תלכו: **כי על כן עברתם.** כי הדבר הזה אני מבקש מכם מאחר שעברתם עלי לכבודי: **כי על כן.** כמו על אשר, וכן כל כי על כן שבמקרא. כי על כן באו בצל קורתי (להלן יט:ח) כי על כן ראיתי פניך (להלן לג:י) כי על כן לא נתתיה (שם לח:כו) כי על כן ידעת חנותנו (במדבר י:לא): (ו) **קמח סלת.** סלת לעוגות. קמח לעמילן של טבחים לכסות את הקדירה [ו]לשאוב את הזוהמא (עי' ב"מ שם, פסחים מב:): (ז) **בן בקר רך וטוב.** ג' פרים היו, כדי להאכילן ג' לשונות בחרדל (ב"מ שם): **אל הנער.** זה ישמעאל, לחנכו במצות (ב"ר שם יג): (ח) **ויקח חמאה וגו'.** ולחם לא הביא, לפי שפירסה שרה נדה, שחזר לה אורח כנשים אותו היום ונטמאת העיסה (ב"ר שם יד; ב"מ פז.): **חמאה.** שומן החלב שקולטין מעל פניו: **ובן הבקר אשר עשה.** אשר תקן, קמא קמא שתיקן אמטי ואייתי קמייהו (ב"מ פו:):

from God, Abraham implored Him *not to go away from Your servant,* but wait while he attended to his guests. Abraham's action shows that "hospitality to wayfarers is greater than receiving the Divine Presence" (*Shevuos* 35b; *Shabbos* 127a).

4. וְרַחֲצוּ רַגְלֵיכֶם — *And wash your feet.* At this point, Abraham did not know they were angels — he thought they were Arabs who worship the dust of their feet, and he would not allow an object of idolatry to come into his house (*Rashi*).

5. פַּת־לֶחֶם — *A piece of bread.* From this understated, modest description of the sumptuous meal he was about to serve, the Talmud derives that "the righteous say little and do much" (*Bava Metzia* 87a).

כֵּן תַּעֲשֶׂה — *So shall you do.* Do as you said, give us nothing more than a morsel (*Ibn Ezra).* As you said, let us but recline under the tree to refresh ourselves and be on our way (*Ramban*). In order not to detain them, Abraham ran to Sarah's tent and asked her to hurry (*Sforno*).

7. רָץ אַבְרָהָם — *Ran Abraham. Ramban* emphasizes how this portrays Abraham's great desire to show hospitality. Though he had many servants eager to serve him, and he was old and weak from his circumcision, he ran *personally* to choose the animals for the meat.

8. First Abraham served the dairy items, for they required little preparation. Only after his guests had slaked their thirst and

וַיֹּאכֵלוּ׃ ט וַיֹּאמְרוּ *אֵלָיו אַיֵּה שָׂרָה אִשְׁתֶּךָ וַיֹּאמֶר

‹And he said, ‹‹ your wife? ‹ Sarah ‹ Where is ‹‹ to him, ‹ They said 9 ‹‹ and they ate.

הִנֵּה בָאֹהֶל׃ י וַיֹּאמֶר שׁוֹב אָשׁוּב אֵלֶיךָ כָּעֵת

‹ at this time [next year] ‹ to you ‹ I will surely return ‹‹ And he said, 10 ‹‹ in the tent! ‹ [She is] there

חַיָּה וְהִנֵּה־בֵן לְשָׂרָה אִשְׁתֶּךָ וְשָׂרָה שֹׁמַעַת פֶּתַח

‹ at the entrance ‹ could hear ‹ And Sarah ‹‹ your wife. ‹ to Sarah ‹ a son ‹ and there will be ‹‹ alive [and well],

הָאֹהֶל וְהוּא אַחֲרָיו׃ יא וְאַבְרָהָם וְשָׂרָה זְקֵנִים בָּאִים בַּיָּמִים חָדַל לִהְיוֹת

‹ to be ‹ there ceased ‹‹ with [their] days; ‹ coming ‹‹ were old, ‹ and Sarah ‹ And Abraham 11 ‹‹ behind him. ‹ which was ‹ of the tent

לְשָׂרָה אֹרַח כַּנָּשִׁים׃ יב וַתִּצְחַק שָׂרָה בְּקִרְבָּהּ לֵאמֹר אַחֲרֵי בְלֹתִי

‹ I have withered ‹ After ‹‹ saying, ‹ within herself, ‹ And Sarah laughed 12 ‹‹ like [other] women. ‹ the cycle ‹ with Sarah

הָיְתָה־לִּי עֶדְנָה וַאדֹנִי זָקֵן׃ יג וַיֹּאמֶר יהוה אֶל־אַבְרָהָם לָמָּה זֶּה

‹ is it ‹ Why ‹‹ Abraham, ‹ to ‹ And [then] HASHEM said 13 ‹‹ is old! ‹ And my husband ‹‹ delicate skin? ‹ for me ‹ shall there [again] be

* נקוד על אי"ו

וַאֲכָלוּ׃ ט וַאֲמָרוּ לֵהּ אָן שָׂרָה אִתְּתָךְ וַאֲמַר הָא בְּמַשְׁכְּנָא׃ י וַאֲמַר מִתַּב אִתּוּב לְוָתָךְ כְּעִדָּן דְּאַתּוּן קַיָּמִין וְהָא בַר לְשָׂרָה אִתְּתָךְ וְשָׂרָה שְׁמַעַת בִּתְרַע מַשְׁכְּנָא וְהוּא אֲחוֹרוֹהִי׃ יא וְאַבְרָהָם וְשָׂרָה סִיבוּ עַלוּ בְּיוֹמִין פְּסַק מִלְּמֶהֱוֵי לְשָׂרָה אוֹרַח כִּנְשַׁיָּא׃ יב וְחַיְכַת שָׂרָה בִּמְעָהָא לְמֵימָר בָּתַר דְּסֵיבִית הֲוַת לִי עוּלֵימוּ וְרִבּוֹנִי סִיב׃ יג וַאֲמַר יְיָ לְאַבְרָהָם לְמָא דְנָן

רש"י

ויאכלו. נראו כמו שאכלו, מכאן שלא ישנה אדם מן המנהג (שם): **(ט) ויאמרו אליו.** נקוד על אי"ו [שבאליו], ותניא ר' שמעון בן אלעזר אומר כל מקום שהכתב רבה על הנקודה אתה דורש הכתב, וכאן הנקודה רבה על הכתב ואתה דורש הנקודה, שאף לשרה שאלו איו אברהם, למדנו שישאל אדם באכסניא שלו לאיש על האשה ולאשה על האיש (ב"ר מח:טו) [בבבא מציעא (פז.) איתא, יודעין היו מלאכי השרת שרה אמנו היכן היתה, אלא להודיע שצנועה היתה כדי לחבבה על בעלה אמר רבי יוסי בר חנינא, כדי לשגר לה כוס של ברכה]: **הנה באהל.** צנועה היא: **(י) כעת חיה.** כעת הזאת לשנה הבאה, ופסח היה, ולפסח הבא נולד יצחק (סדר עולם פ"ה) מדלא קרינן כָּעֵת אלא כְּעֵת: **כעת חיה.** כעת הזאת שתהא חיה לכם, שתהיו כלכם שלמים וקיימים (אונקלוס): **שוב אשוב.** לא בשרו המלאך שישוב אליו, אלא בשליחותו של מקום אמר לו, כמו ויאמר לה מלאך ה' הרבה ארבה (לעיל טז:י) והוא אין בידו להרבות, אלא בשליחותו של מקום, אף כאן בשליחותו של מקום אמר לו כן [אלישע אמר לשונמית למועד הזה כעת חיה את חובקת בן. ותאמר, אל אדני איש האלהים, אל תכזב בשפחתך (מלכים ב ד:טז), אותן המלאכים שבשרו את שרה אמרו למועד אשוב. אמר לה אלישע, אותן המלאכים שהם חיים וקיימים לעולם אמרו למועד אשוב, אבל אני בשר ודם שהיום חי ומחר מת, בין חי ובין מת למועד הזה וגו' (ב"ר נג:ב)]: **והוא אחריו.** הפתח היה אחר המלאך (מדרש אגדה): **(יא) חדל להיות.** פסק ממנה (ב"ר מח:טז): **אורח כנשים.** אורח נדות: **(יב) בקרבה.** מסתכלת במעיה ואומרת אפשר הקרבים הללו טעונין ולד, השדים הללו שצמקו מושכין חלב. תנחומא (שופטים יח): **עדנה.** צחות בשר (ב"מ פז.), ול' משנה משיר את

hunger did he bring out the full meal that consisted of calves' meat (*Daas Zekeinim*).

וַיֹּאכֵלוּ — *And they ate.* Angels do not eat in the human sense; they only appeared to eat. This teaches that one should not deviate from the local custom (*Rashi*).

9-15. The promise of a son is revealed to Sarah. Previously, the prophecy of a son had been given only to Abraham. Now it would be conveyed to Sarah as well. The angels began by inquiring after her whereabouts, although everyone knew she was in the tent. This was to draw attention to her modesty and so endear her even more to her husband (*Rashi*). In the plain sense, *Sforno* comments that since their mission was to inform her of the prophecy, they had to be sure she could hear them. The commentators explain that the angel spoke in the first person as if it was in his power to grant her a child — because he was acting as God's emissary.

11. בָּאִים בַּיָּמִים — *Coming with [their] days. Zohar* comments that each day in a person's life carries with it its own challenge and mission. What is to be accomplished today cannot be postponed to tomorrow, because tomorrow has its own set of things to do. In the normal course of events, people go through life with their "spiritual calendars" marred by countless days and hours that were wasted or, even worse, misused. But the greatest people, such as Abraham and Sarah, come through life with all their days intact, all of them utilized properly and purposefully. This is signified by בָּאִים בַּיָּמִים, *coming with [their] days*: They reached their old age with a rich harvest of days that truly mattered.

12. וַתִּצְחַק שָׂרָה — *And Sarah laughed* in disbelief because she thought that the guest's statement was simply a courteous, but meaningless blessing, not a prophecy from God. In view of her advanced age, she thought that such a miraculous rejuvenation would be as great a miracle as the resurrection of the dead, which only God Himself could accomplish (*Radak; Sforno*).

Although Sarah did not know this truly was a message from God Himself, God was angered at her reaction, for a person of her great stature should have had faith that the miracle of birth *could* happen.

עֶדְנָה — *Delicate skin.* In the literal sense, this is simply a simile

צָחֲקָה שָׂרָה לֵאמֹר הַאַף אֻמְנָם אֵלֵד וַאֲנִי

that Sarah laughed, saying: 'Is it so that in truth I shall bear [a child], though I

זָקַנְתִּי: יד הֲיִפָּלֵא מֵיהוָה דָּבָר לַמּוֹעֵד אָשׁוּב אֵלֶיךָ

have aged?' **14** *Is there beyond the capability of* H*ASHEM* *anything?! At the appointed time I will return to you*

כָּעֵת חַיָּה וּלְשָׂרָה בֵן: שני טו וַתְּכַחֵשׁ שָׂרָה | לֵאמֹר

at this time [next year] alive [and well], and to Sarah there will be a son. **15** Sarah denied [it], saying,

לֹא צָחַקְתִּי כִּי | יָרֵאָה וַיֹּאמֶר | לֹא כִּי צָחָקְתְּ: טז וַיָּקֻמוּ מִשָּׁם הָאֲנָשִׁים

I did not laugh, for she was frightened. But he said, *No, indeed you laughed.* **16** They got up from there — the men —

וַיַּשְׁקִפוּ עַל־פְּנֵי סְדֹם וְאַבְרָהָם הֹלֵךְ עִמָּם לְשַׁלְּחָם: יז וַיהוָה אָמָר

and gazed down upon the face of Sodom, while Abraham was walking with them to send them [on their way]. **17** And HASHEM said,

הַמְכַסֶּה אֲנִי מֵאַבְרָהָם אֲשֶׁר אֲנִי עֹשֶׂה: יח וְאַבְרָהָם הָיוֹ יִהְיֶה לְגוֹי

Am I concealing from Abraham what I [am about to] do? **18** *But Abraham is surely to become a nation,*

חַיְכַת שָׂרָה לְמֵימַר הַבְרַם בְּקוּשְׁטָא אוֹלִיד וַאֲנָא סֵיבִית: יד הֲיִתְכַּסֵּי מִן קֳדָם יְיָ פִּתְגָּמָא לִזְמַן אֵתוּב לְוָתָךְ כְּעִדָּן דְּאַתּוּן קַיָּמִין וּלְשָׂרָה בָר: טו וְכַדִּיבַת שָׂרָה לְמֵימָר לָא חַיְכִית אֲרֵי דְחֵלַת וַאֲמַר לָא בְּרָם חַיָּכְתְּ: טז וְקָמוּ מִתַּמָּן גֻּבְרַיָּא וְאִסְתְּכִיאוּ עַל אַפֵּי סְדוֹם וְאַבְרָהָם אָזֵל עִמְּהוֹן לְאַלְוָאֵיהוֹן: יז וַייָ אֲמַר הַמְכַסֵּי אֲנָא מֵאַבְרָהָם דִּי אֲנָא עָבֵד: יח וְאַבְרָהָם מֶהֱוֵי יְהֱוֵי לְעַם

רש"י

השער ומעדן את הבשר (מנחות פו.). ד"א, לשון עידן, זמן וסת נדות (ב"ר מח:יז): **(יג) האף אמנם.** הגם אמת אלד: **ואני זקנתי.** שינה הכתוב מפני השלום, שהרי היא אמרה ואדני זקן (ב"מ שם; ב"ר שם יח): **(יד) היפלא.** כתרגומו, היתכסי, וכי שום דבר מופלא ומופרד ומכוסה ממני מלעשות כרצוני: **למועד.** לאותו מועד המיוחד שקבעתי לך אתמול, למועד הזה בשנה האחרת: **(טו) כי יראה וגו' כי צחקת.** כי הראשון משמש לשון דהא, שנותן טעם לדבר, ותכחש שרה לפי שיראה. והשני משמש בלשון אלא, ויאמר לא כדבריך הוא, אלא צחקת. שאמרו רבותינו כי משמש בד' לשונות, אי, דלמא, אלא, דהא (ראש השנה ג.; גיטין צ.): **(טז) וישקפו.** כל השקפה שבמקרא לרעה חוץ מהשקיפה ממעון קדשך (דברים כו:טו), שגדול כח מתנות עניים שהופך מדת הרוגז לרחמים (שמות רבה מא:א): **לשלחם.** ללוותם, כסבור אורחים הם (מדרש אגדה): **(יז) המכסה אני.** בתמיה: **אשר אני עושה.** בסדום. לא יפה לי לעשות דבר זה שלא מדעתו. אני נתתי לו את הארץ הזאת, וחמשה כרכין הללו שלו הן, שנא' גבול הכנעני מצידון באכה סדומה ועמורה וגו' (לעיל י:יט; ב"ר מט:ב; תנחומא ה; תרגום ירושלמי). קראתי אותו אברהם [ס"א אביהם] אב המון גוים (לעיל יז:ה), ואשמיד את הבנים ולא אודיע לאב (ב"ר שם) שהוא אוהבי (תנחומא שם; תרגום יונתן): **(יח) ואברהם היו יהיה.** מ"א, זכר צדיק לברכה (משלי י:ז),

for the return of youthfulness that would enable her to give birth. According to the Midrashic interpretation, her menses resumed for the first time in many years, signifying that she could give birth *(Rashi)*.

13. וַאֲנִי זָקַנְתִּי — *Though I have aged.* Her actual words in verse 12 were וַאדֹנִי זָקֵן, *my husband is old,* but for the sake of peace between husband and wife, God now changed the uncomplimentary reference from her husband to herself (*Rashi*).

16-21. Abraham learns about Sodom's destruction. The angels had left Abraham and were on their way to destroy Sodom and rescue Lot, but God delayed the destruction until Abraham had an opportunity to intercede in its behalf. The Torah explains God's reason: "Since Abraham is destined to become a great and mighty nation, and he will teach his values of kindness and justice to future generations, it is appropriate that I tell him what I plan to do. Otherwise people will wonder, 'How could God have hidden this from him?' or 'How could Abraham have been so callous that he failed to pray for his neighbors?' Furthermore, if there is legitimate cause to pardon the Sodomites, Abraham will beseech Me to do so. But if they are completely guilty, even he will want the judgment against them to be carried out" (*Ramban*). Alternatively, God wanted Abraham to know that the opportunity for repentance is always open to sinners (*Sforno*).

❧ The contrast between Israel and Sodom.

The implication of verse 19 is that the seed of Sodom's wickedness lay in its failure to abide by the principles that Abraham would inculcate in his offspring. The cruelties of Sodom have become part of the language as the epitome of selfishness, callousness and depravity (see Ch. 19), but the root of their evil was greed. To discourage undesirable newcomers, the Sodomites institutionalized state cruelty, so that it became a crime to feed a starving person or offer alms to a beggar. Even the sexual perversion for which Sodom is notorious was employed to keep visitors away. According to one opinion of the Sages, this cruelty stemmed from an attitude of, "What is mine is mine and what is yours is yours" (*Avos* 5:10), or, in the popular idiom, "Neither a lender nor a borrower be." Such selfishness descends to cruelty and perversion — and a metropolis that elevates such behavior to a legitimate way of life forfeits its right to exist.

גָּדוֹל וְעָצוּם וְנִבְרְכוּ־בוֹ כֹּל גּוֹיֵי הָאָרֶץ: יט כִּי

great and mighty, and they will be blessed through him — all the nations of the earth? 19 For

יְדַעְתִּיו לְמַעַן אֲשֶׁר יְצַוֶּה אֶת־בָּנָיו וְאֶת־בֵּיתוֹ

I have known him [well] because of the fact that he will always command his children and his household

אַחֲרָיו וְשָׁמְרוּ דֶּרֶךְ יהוה לַעֲשׂוֹת צְדָקָה וּמִשְׁפָּט

after him, so that they will keep the way of HASHEM, to do charity and justice,

לְמַעַן הָבִיא יהוה עַל־אַבְרָהָם אֵת אֲשֶׁר־דִּבֶּר

in order that HASHEM may then bring upon Abraham that which He had spoken

עָלָיו: כ וַיֹּאמֶר יהוה זַעֲקַת סְדֹם וַעֲמֹרָה כִּי־רָבָּה וְחַטָּאתָם כִּי כָבְדָה

regarding him. 20 So HASHEM said, The outcry of Sodom and Gomorrah — because it has become great, and their sin — because it has been grave

מְאֹד: כא אֵרְדָה־נָּא וְאֶרְאֶה הַכְּצַעֲקָתָהּ הַבָּאָה אֵלַי עָשׂוּ | כָּלָה וְאִם־

exceedingly, 21 I will descend now and I will see: If in accordance with its outcry which has come to Me they have acted — then destruction! And if

לֹא אֵדָעָה: כב וַיִּפְנוּ מִשָּׁם הָאֲנָשִׁים וַיֵּלְכוּ סְדֹמָה וְאַבְרָהָם עוֹדֶנּוּ עֹמֵד

not, I will know. 22 They turned from there — the men, and they went toward Sodom, with Abraham still standing

סַגִּי וְתַקִּיף וְיִתְבָּרְכוּן בְּדִילֵהּ כֹּל עַמְמֵי אַרְעָא: יט אֲרֵי גְּלֵי קֳדָמַי (נ״א יְדַעְתִּנֵּהּ) בְּדִיל דִּי יְפַקֵּד יָת בְּנוֹהִי וְיָת אֱנַשׁ בֵּיתֵהּ בַּתְרוֹהִי וְיִטְּרוּן אָרְחָן דְּתַקְּנָן קֳדָם יְיָ לְמֶעְבַּד צְדַקְתָּא וְדִינָא בְּדִיל דְּיַיְתִי יְיָ עַל אַבְרָהָם יָת דִּי מַלֵּל עֲלוֹהִי: כ וַאֲמַר יְיָ קְבֵלַת דִּסְדוֹם וַעֲמוֹרָה אֲרֵי סְגִיאַת וְחוֹבָתְהוֹן אֲרֵי תְקִיפַת לַחֲדָא: כא אִתְגְּלֵי כְעַן וְאֶדּוּן הַכִּקְבִלְתְּהוֹן דְּעָלַת לִקֳדָמַי עֲבָדוּ אֶעְבֵּד עִמְּהוֹן גְּמִירָא (אִם לָא תָיְבִין) וְאִם תָּיְבִין לָא אֶתְפְּרָע: כב וְאִתְפְּנִיאוּ מִתַּמָּן גֻּבְרַיָּא וַאֲזָלוּ לִסְדוֹם וְאַבְרָהָם עַד כְּעַן מְשַׁמֵּשׁ

רש״י

הואיל והזכירו ברכו (יומא לח:; ב״ר מט:א). ופשוטו, וכי ממנו אני מעלים, והרי הוא חביב לפני להיות לגוי גדול ולהתברך בו כל גויי הארץ: **(יט) כי ידעתיו.** [אברי ידעתיה, כתרגומו,] לשון חבה, כמו מודע לאישה (רות ב:א) הלא בועז מודעתנו (שם ג:ב) ואדעך בשם (שמות לג:יז). ואמנם עיקר לשון כולם אינו אלא לשון ידיעה, שהמחבב את האדם מקרבו אצלו ויודעו ומכירו. ולמה ידעתיו, למען אשר יצוה, לפי שהוא מצוה את בניו עלי לשמור דרכי. ואם תפרשהו כתרגומו, יודע אני בו שיצוה את בניו וגו׳, אין למען נופל על הלשון: **יצוה.** לשון הווה, כמו ככה יעשה איוב (איוב א:ה): **למען הביא.** כך הוא מצוה לבניו, שמרו דרך ה׳ כדי שיביא ה׳ על אברהם וגו׳. על בית אברהם לא נאמר אלא על אברהם, למדנו, כל המעמיד בן צדיק כאילו אינו מת (ב״ר שם ד): **(כ) ויאמר ה׳.** אל אברהם, שעשה כאשר אמר שלא יכסה ממנו: **כי רבה.** כל רבה שבמקרא הטעם למטה בבי״ת לפי שהן מתורגמין גדולה או גדלה והולכת (שם ה, כז:ג), אבל זה טעמו למעלה ברי״ש לפי שמתורגם גדלה כבר, כמו שפירשתי ויהי השמש באה (לעיל טו:יז) הנה שבה יבמתך (רות א:טו): **(כא) ארדה נא.** למד לדיינים שלא יפסקו דיני נפשות אלא בראיה, הכל כמו שפרשתי בפרשת הפלגה (לעיל יא:ה). ד״א, ארדה נא לסוף מעשיהם (מדרש אגדה): **הכצעקתה.** של מדינה (תרגום ירושלמי): **הבאה אלי עשו.** וכן עומדים במרדם, **כלה** אני עושה בהם, **ואם לא** יעמדו במרדם, **אדעה** מה אעשה, להפרע מהן ביסורין, ולא אכלה אותן (ב״ר שם ו). וכיוצא בו מצינו במקום אחר, ועתה הורד עדיך מעליך ואדעה מה אעשה לך (שמות לג:ה). ולפיכך יש הפסק נקודת פסיק בין עשו לכלה כדי להפריד תיבה מחברתה. ורבותינו דרשו, הכצעקתה, צעקת ריבה אחת שהרגוה במיתה משונה על שנתנה מזון לעני, כמפורש בחלק (סנהדרין קט:): **(כב) ויפנו משם.** ממקום שאברהם ליווס שם: **ואברהם עודנו עומד לפני ה׳.** והלא לא הלך לעמוד לפניו, אלא הקב״ה בא אצלו

19. God loves Abraham. The word יְדַעְתִּיו refers to *knowledge*, but the Torah often uses love as its secondary meaning, for one who loves another brings him close and seeks to know him well (*Rashi*). The verse goes on to explain that God loved Abraham because he would always convey God's teachings to his offspring. One reveals his values by what he teaches his children, for to preach morality but not inculcate it in one's own family reveals that the preaching is less than sincere. In summing up the greatness of Abraham and the reason he was entitled to a role in the Divine conduct of the world, God said that it was because of what he would teach his children.

The Israelite nation is distinguished by being compassionate, shy, and benevolent. The last of these traits is derived from our text: *to do charity (Yevamos* 79a). Citing our verse, *Rambam* in his code rules *(Hil. Matanos Aniyim* 10:1): We must therefore practice the commandment of charity more than any other, because it is the characteristic of the true descendant of Abraham.

21. וְאִם־לֹא אֵדָעָה — *And if not, I will know*. If they do not persist in their rebellious ways [but repent (*Onkelos*)], *I will know* what to do. I will punish them, but not destroy them entirely (*Rashi*).

22-33. Abraham intercedes for Sodom. The angels had already arrived in Sodom to carry out its destruction, but Abraham prayed for its survival, in line with the teaching of the Sages (*Berachos* 10a) that even if a sharp sword is upon one's neck, he should not desist from prayer (*Sforno*). Abraham's prayer was twofold. He argued that the Attribute of Justice must be tem-

לִפְנֵי יְהֹוָה: כג וַיִּגַּשׁ אַבְרָהָם וַיֹּאמַר הַאַף תִּסְפֶּה
‹ that You will destroy ‹ Will it also be « and he said, ‹ Abraham came forward **23** « HASHEM. ‹ before

צַדִּיק עִם־רָשָׁע: כד אוּלַי יֵשׁ חֲמִשִּׁים צַדִּיקִם
‹ righteous people ‹ fifty ‹ there are ‹ Perhaps **24** « the wicked? ‹ along with ‹ the righteous

בְּתוֹךְ הָעִיר הַאַף תִּסְפֶּה וְלֹא־תִשָּׂא לַמָּקוֹם לְמַעַן
‹ for the sake of ‹ the place ‹ spare ‹ and not ‹ that You will destroy ‹ Will it also be « of the city? ‹ in the midst

חֲמִשִּׁים הַצַּדִּיקִם אֲשֶׁר בְּקִרְבָּהּ: כה חָלִלָה לְּךָ
‹ to You ‹ It would be sacrilegious **25** « within it? ‹ who are ‹ righteous people ‹ the fifty

מֵעֲשֹׂת | כַּדָּבָר הַזֶּה לְהָמִית צַדִּיק עִם־רָשָׁע וְהָיָה כַצַּדִּיק כָּרָשָׁע
« so to the wicked. ‹ just as to the righteous ‹ that it will be « the wicked; ‹ along with ‹ the righteous ‹ to kill « as this, ‹ such a thing ‹ to have done

חָלִלָה לָּךְ הֲשֹׁפֵט כָּל־הָאָרֶץ לֹא יַעֲשֶׂה מִשְׁפָּט: כו וַיֹּאמֶר יְהֹוָה אִם־
‹ If « And HASHEM said, **26** « justice? ‹ will not do ‹ the earth ‹ of all ‹ Shall it be that the Judge « to You! ‹ It would be sacrilegious

אֶמְצָא בִסְדֹם חֲמִשִּׁים צַדִּיקִם בְּתוֹךְ הָעִיר וְנָשָׂאתִי לְכָל־הַמָּקוֹם
‹ place ‹ the entire ‹ then I would spare « of the city, ‹ in the midst ‹ righteous people ‹ fifty ‹ in Sodom ‹ I find

בַּעֲבוּרָם: כז וַיַּעַן אַבְרָהָם וַיֹּאמַר הִנֵּה־נָא הוֹאַלְתִּי לְדַבֵּר אֶל־אֲדֹנָי
‹ my Lord ‹ to ‹ to speak ‹ I desired ‹ now, ‹ Indeed, « and said, ‹ Abraham responded **27** « for their sake.

בִּצְלוֹ קֳדָם יְיָ: כג וּקְרֵב אַבְרָהָם וַאֲמָר הֲבִרְגַז תְּשֵׁיצֵי זַכָּאי עִם חַיָּיב: כד מָאִים אִית חַמְשִׁין זַכָּאִין בְּגוֹ קַרְתָּא הֲבִרְגַז תְּשֵׁיצֵי וְלָא תִשְׁבּוֹק לְאַתְרָא בְּדִיל חַמְשִׁין זַכָּאִין דִּי בְגַוַּהּ: כה קוּשְׁטָא אִנּוּן דִּינָךְ מִלְּמֶעְבַּד כְּפִתְגָּמָא הָדֵין לְקַטָּלָא זַכָּאָה עִם חַיָּבָא וִיהֵי זַכָּאָה כְּחַיָּבָא קוּשְׁטָא אִנּוּן דִּינָךְ דְּדָיִן (נ״א הֲדַיַּן) כָּל אַרְעָא לָא (נ״א בְּרַם) יַעְבֵּד דִּינָא: כו וַאֲמַר יְיָ אִם אַשְׁכַּח בִּסְדוֹם חַמְשִׁין זַכָּאִין בְּגוֹ קַרְתָּא וְאֶשְׁבּוֹק לְכָל אַתְרָא בְּדִילְהוֹן: כז וַאֲתֵיב אַבְרָהָם וַאֲמַר הָא כְעַן שָׁרֵיתִי לְמַלָּלָא קֳדָם יְיָ

רש״י

ואמר לו זעקת סדום ועמורה כי רבה, והיה לו לכתוב וה׳ עודנו עומד על אברהם, אלא תיקון סופרים הוא זה (ב״ר שם ז): **(כג) ויגש אברהם.** מלינו הגשה למלחמה, ויגש יואב וגו׳ (דברי הימים א יט:יד). הגשה לפיוס, ויגש אליו יהודה (להלן מד:יח). והגשה לתפלה, ויגש אליהו הנביא (מלכים א יח:לו). ולכל אלה נכנס אברהם, לדבר קשות ולפיוס ולתפלה (ב״ר שם ח): **האף תספה.** הגם תספה. ולתרגום של אונקלוס שתרגומו לשון רוגז כך פירושו, האף ישיאך שתספה לדיק עם רשע (שם; תנחומא ח): **(כד) אולי יש חמשים צדיקים.** עשרה לדיקים לכל כרך וכרך כי חמשה מקומות יש (תרגום יונתן). וא״ת לא ילילו הלדיקים את הרשעים, למה תמית הלדיקים (ב״ר שם): **(כה) חלילה לך.** חולין הוא לך (ע״ז ד.; תרגום יונתן), יאמרו כך היא אומנותו, שוטף הכל, לדיקים ורשעים. כך עשית לדור המבול ולדור הפלגה (תנחומא שם): **כדבר הזה.** לא הוא ולא כיולא בו (שם; ב״ר שם ט): **חלילה לך.** לעולם הבא (תנחומא ישן יא): **השופט כל הארץ.** נקוד בחט״ף פתח ה״א של השופט, לשון תמיה, וכי מי שהוא שופט **לא יעשה משפט** אמת (ב״ר שם): **(כו) אם אמצא בסדום וגו׳ לכל המקום.** לכל הכרכים. לפי שסדום היתה מטרפולין וחשובה מכולם תלה בה הכתוב:

pered by Mercy, so that if there were ten truly righteous people in any of the five condemned cities, that entire city should be spared. Barring that, he asked that at the very least, the righteous people themselves should be saved. In response, God said that He would indeed exercise mercy (*Ramban*), but there was no one except for Lot who deserved to be saved.

R' Moshe Feinstein explained why Abraham pleaded so strenuously for people who were so notorious for their wickedness. Ordinarily people preach kindness, but they become outraged and hate those who dispute their values. Abraham, on the other hand, felt no animosity toward evildoers; he wanted only for them to change for the better. Therefore he felt that if there was a nucleus of ten good people in a city, there was hope that they could influence the others by teaching and example.

24. **חֲמִשִּׁים צַדִּיקִם** — *Fifty righteous people.* A total of five cities were condemned, all of them mentioned in 14:2. Sodom and Gomorrah were the most prominent. Less significant were Admah and Zeboiim; Zoar was the smallest of the group. Abraham mentioned fifty — a quorum of ten righteous people [see v. 26] for each city (*Rashi*).

27. **הִנֵּה־נָא הוֹאַלְתִּי** — *Indeed, now, I desired. . .* In the previous verse, God had acquiesced to Abraham's petition, but now Abraham begged His indulgence to continue his pleas. Suspecting that his first request would be unavailing because the fifty righteous men would not be found in Sodom, but encouraged by God's receptiveness, Abraham asked for permission to petition further.

וְאָנֹכִי עָפָר וָאֵפֶר׃ כח אוּלַי יַחְסְרוּן חֲמִשִּׁים

although I am > [but] dust > and ash. >> 28 Perhaps > there shall be lacking > [from] the fifty >

הַצַּדִּיקִם חֲמִשָּׁה הֲתַשְׁחִית בַּחֲמִשָּׁה אֶת־כָּל־

righteous people > five? >> Would You destroy > because of the five > the entire >

הָעִיר וַיֹּאמֶר לֹא אַשְׁחִית אִם־אֶמְצָא שָׁם

city? >> And He said, >> I will not destroy > if > I find > there >

אַרְבָּעִים וַחֲמִשָּׁה׃ כט וַיֹּסֶף עוֹד לְדַבֵּר אֵלָיו וַיֹּאמַר

forty-five. >> 29 He continued > further > to speak > to Him > and he said, >>

אוּלַי יִמָּצְאוּן שָׁם אַרְבָּעִים וַיֹּאמֶר לֹא אֶעֱשֶׂה

Perhaps > there would be found > there > forty? >> And He said, > I will not act >

בַּעֲבוּר הָאַרְבָּעִים׃ ל וַיֹּאמֶר אַל־נָא יִחַר לַאדֹנָי

for the sake > of the forty. >> 30 And he said, > Let not > now > my Lord be angered >

וַאֲדַבֵּרָה אוּלַי יִמָּצְאוּן שָׁם שְׁלֹשִׁים וַיֹּאמֶר לֹא אֶעֱשֶׂה אִם־אֶמְצָא

and I will speak: >> Perhaps > there would be found > there > thirty? >> And He said, >> I will not act > if > I find >

שָׁם שְׁלֹשִׁים׃ לא וַיֹּאמֶר הִנֵּה־נָא הוֹאַלְתִּי לְדַבֵּר אֶל־אֲדֹנָי אוּלַי יִמָּצְאוּן

there > thirty. >> 31 So he said, >> Indeed, > now, > I desired > to speak > to > my Lord: >> Perhaps > there would be found >

שָׁם עֶשְׂרִים וַיֹּאמֶר לֹא אַשְׁחִית בַּעֲבוּר הָעֶשְׂרִים׃ לב וַיֹּאמֶר אַל־נָא

there > twenty? >> And He said, >> I will not destroy > for the sake > of the twenty. >> 32 So he said, >> Let not > now >

יִחַר לַאדֹנָי וַאֲדַבְּרָה אַךְ־הַפַּעַם אוּלַי יִמָּצְאוּן שָׁם עֲשָׂרָה וַיֹּאמֶר

my Lord be angered > and I will speak > just > this one time [more]: >> Perhaps > there would be found > there > ten? >> And He said, >>

לֹא אַשְׁחִית בַּעֲבוּר הָעֲשָׂרָה׃ לג וַיֵּלֶךְ יהוה כַּאֲשֶׁר כִּלָּה לְדַבֵּר אֶל־

I will not destroy > for the sake > of the ten. >> 33 HASHEM departed > when > He finished > speaking > to >

וַאֲנָא עָפָר וּקְטָם׃ כח מָאִים יַחְסְרוּן חַמְשִׁין זַכָּאִין חַמְשָׁא הַתְחַבֵּל בְּחַמְשָׁא יָת כָּל קַרְתָּא וַאֲמַר לָא אֲחַבֵּל אִם אַשְׁכַּח תַּמָּן אַרְבְּעִין וְחַמְשָׁא׃ כט וְאוֹסֵיף עוֹד לְמַלָּלָא קֳדָמוֹהִי וַאֲמַר מָאִים יִשְׁתַּכְּחוּן תַּמָּן אַרְבְּעִין וַאֲמַר לָא אֶעְבֵּד גְּמִירָא בְּדִיל אַרְבְּעִין׃ ל וַאֲמַר לָא כְעַן יִתְקֵף קֳדָם (נ״א רוּגְזָא דַ)יְיָ וַאֲמַלֵּל מָאִים יִשְׁתַּכְּחוּן תַּמָּן תְּלָתִין וַאֲמַר לָא אֶעְבֵּד גְּמִירָא אִם אַשְׁכַּח תַּמָּן תְּלָתִין׃ לא וַאֲמַר הָא כְעַן שָׁרֵיתִי לְמַלָּלָא קֳדָם יְיָ מָאִים יִשְׁתַּכְּחוּן תַּמָּן עֶשְׂרִין וַאֲמַר לָא אֲחַבֵּל בְּדִיל עֶשְׂרִין׃ לב וַאֲמַר לָא כְעַן יִתְקֵף קֳדָם (נ״א רוּגְזָא דַ)יְיָ וַאֲמַלֵּל בְּרַם זִמְנָא הָדָא מָאִים יִשְׁתַּכְּחוּן תַּמָּן עַשְׂרָא וַאֲמַר לָא אֲחַבֵּל בְּדִיל עַשְׂרָא׃ לג וְאִסְתַּלַּק יְקָרָא דַייָ כַּד שֵׁצִי לְמַלָּלָא עִם

רש״י

(כז) ואנכי עפר ואפר. וכבר הייתי ראוי להיות עפר על ידי המלכים ואפר ע״י נמרוד לולי רחמיך אשר עמדו לי (ב״ר שם יא): **(כח) התשחית בחמשה.** והרי הן ט׳ לכל כרך, ואתה צדיקו של עולם תצטרף עמהם (ב״ר מט:ט): **(כט) אולי ימצאון שם ארבעים.** וימלטו ד׳ הכרכים, וכן שלשים יצילו ג׳ מהם או עשרים יצילו ב׳ מהם או עשרה יצילו אחד מהם (תרגום יונתן): **(לא) הואלתי.** רציתי, כמו ויואל משה (שמות ב:כא): **(לב) אולי ימצאון שם עשרה.** על פחות לא ביקש. אמר, דור המבול היו ח׳, נח ובניו ונשיהם, ולא הצילו על דורן (ב״ר מט:יג). ועל ט׳ ע״י צירוף כבר בקש ולא מצא: **(לג) וילך ה׳ וגו׳.** כיון שנשתתק הסניגור הלך לו הדיין (שם יד):

28. בַּחֲמִשָּׁה — *Because of the five.* Would You destroy the entire area because five people would be lacking from the total of fifty? (*Ibn Ezra*). There would still be nine for each city, and You, O Righteous One of the Universe, could be added to them, making a total of the required ten for each place! (*Midrash; Rashi*).

29-32. Abraham now pleaded for a new concession. Up to now, the complex of five cities had been treated as a single unit. Now Abraham prayed that the cities be judged separately, so that a group of ten in one of the cities would save that city, even if it was not sufficient to rescue the others. Since the merit of a large group of people is greater than that of a smaller one, Abraham asked first for salvation for the sake of forty, and then thirty, twenty, and finally ten (*Rashi*, according to *Ramban* and *R' Bachya*). *Ramban*, however, holds that Abraham was still praying for all five cities. His plea was that the successively smaller numbers of righteous people should be sufficient to save them all.

אַבְרָהָם וְאַבְרָהָם שָׁב לִמְקֹמוֹ: שלישי **[יט]** א וַיָּבֹאוּ

« They came **1** [19] « to his place. ‹ returned ‹ and Abraham « Abraham,

שְׁנֵי הַמַּלְאָכִים סְדֹמָה בָּעֶרֶב וְלוֹט יֹשֵׁב בְּשַׁעַר־

‹ at the gate ‹ was sitting ‹ and Lot ‹ in the evening ‹ to Sodom « angels — ‹ — the two

סְדֹם וַיַּרְא־לוֹט וַיָּקָם לִקְרָאתָם וַיִּשְׁתַּחוּ אַפַּיִם

‹ [with his] face ‹ and he bowed, ‹ to meet them ‹ and he stood up ‹ and Lot saw [them] « of Sodom;

אָרְצָה: ב וַיֹּאמֶר הִנֶּה נָּא־אֲדֹנַי סוּרוּ נָא אֶל־בֵּית

‹ *the house* ‹ *to* ‹ *please,* ‹ *turn aside,* « *my lords;* ‹ *now,* ‹ *Indeed* « And he said, **2** « to the ground.

עַבְדְּכֶם וְלִינוּ וְרַחֲצוּ רַגְלֵיכֶם וְהִשְׁכַּמְתֶּם וַהֲלַכְתֶּם לְדַרְכְּכֶם וַיֹּאמְרוּ

« And they said, « *on your way!* ‹ *and you will go* ‹ *then wake up early* « *your feet,* ‹ *and wash* ‹ *spend the night* « *of your servant;*

לֹּא* כִּי בָרְחוֹב נָלִין: ג וַיִּפְצַר־בָּם מְאֹד וַיָּסֻרוּ אֵלָיו וַיָּבֹאוּ אֶל־בֵּיתוֹ

« his house; ‹ to ‹ and came ‹ toward him ‹ so they turned « very much, ‹ them ‹ And he implored **3** « *we will spend the night.* ‹ *in the square* ‹ *rather* ‹ *No,*

וַיַּעַשׂ לָהֶם מִשְׁתֶּה וּמַצּוֹת אָפָה וַיֹּאכֵלוּ: ד טֶרֶם יִשְׁכָּבוּ וְאַנְשֵׁי הָעִיר

« of the city, ‹ the people ‹ they had lain down, ‹ Before **4** « and they ate. « he baked, ‹ and matzos ‹ a feast ‹ for them ‹ he made

* ל' דגושה

אַבְרָהָם וְאַבְרָהָם תָּב לְאַתְרֵהּ: א וְעַלּוּ תְּרֵין מַלְאָכַיָּא לִסְדוֹם בְּרַמְשָׁא וְלוֹט יָתֵב בְּתַרְעָא (נ״א בִּתְרַע) דִסְדוֹם וַחֲזָא לוֹט וְקָם לְקַדָּמוּתְהוֹן וּסְגִיד עַל אַפּוֹהִי עַל אַרְעָא: ב וַאֲמַר בְּבָעוּ כְעַן רִבּוֹנַי זוּרוּ כְעַן לְבֵית עַבְדְּכוֹן וּבִיתוּ וְאַסְחוּ רַגְלֵיכוֹן וּתְקַדְּמוּן וּתְהָכוּן לְאָרְחֲכוֹן וַאֲמָרוּ לָא אֱלָהֵן בִּרְחוֹבָא נְבִית: ג וְאַתְקֵיף בְּהוֹן לַחֲדָא וְזָרוּ לְוָתֵהּ וְעַלּוּ לְבֵיתֵהּ וַעֲבַד לְהוֹן מִשְׁתְּיָא וּפַטִּיר אֲפָא לְהוֹן וַאֲכָלוּ: ד עַד לָא שְׁכִיבוּ וְאֱנָשֵׁי קַרְתָּא

רש"י

ואברהם שב למקומו. נסתלק הדיין נסתלק הסניגור, והקטיגור מקטרג, לפיכך ויבואו שני המלאכים סדומה, להשחית (שם): **(א) שני המלאכים.** אחד להשחית את סדום ואחד להציל את לוט, הוא אותו שבא לרפאות את אברהם. והשלישי שבא לבשר את שרה כיון שעשה שליחותו נסתלק לו (ב"ר נ:ב; תנחומא ח): **המלאכים.** ולהלן קראם אנשים, כשהיתה שכינה עמהם קראם אנשים. ד"א, אצל אברהם שכחו גדול והיו המלאכים תדירין אצלו כאנשים קראם אנשים, ואצל לוט קראם מלאכים (ב"ר שם; תנחומא ישן כ): **בערב.** וכי כל כך שהו המלאכים מחברון לסדום, אלא מלאכי רחמים היו וממתינים שמא יוכל אברהם ללמד עליהם סנגוריא (ב"ר שם א): **ולוט ישב בשער סדום.** ישב כתיב, אותו היום מינוהו שופט עליהם [ס"א על השופטים] (ב"ר נ:ג): **וירא לוט וגו'.** מבית אברהם למד לחזר על האורחים (שם ד; תנחומא ישן טו): **(ב) הנה נא אדני.** הנה נא אתם אדונים לי אחר שעברתם עלי. ד"א, הנה נא, צריכים אתם לתת לב על הרשעים הללו שלא יכירו בכם, וזו היא עצה נכונה, **סורו נא,** עקמו את הדרך לביתי דרך עקלתון, שלא יכירו שאתם נכנסים שם, לכך נאמר סורו. בראשית רבה (שם): **ולינו ורחצו רגליכם.** וכי דרכן של בני אדם ללון תחלה ואח"כ לרחוץ. ועוד, שהרי אברהם אמר להם תחלה רחצו רגליכם. אלא כך אמר לוט, אם [כש]יבואו אנשי סדום ויראו שכבר רחצו רגליהם, יעלילו עלי ויאמרו כבר עברו שני ימים או שלשה שבאו לביתך ולא הודעתנו, לפיכך אמר מוטב שיתעכבו כאן באבק רגליהם שיהיו נראין כמו שבאו עכשיו, לפיכך אמר לינו תחלה ואחר כך רחצו (שם): **ויאמרו לא.** ולאברהם אמרו כן תעשה, מכאן שמסרבין לקטן ואין מסרבין לגדול (ב"מ פז.; ב"ר שם; תנחומא יא): **כי ברחוב נלין.** הרי כי משמש בלשון אלא, שאמרו לא נסור אל ביתך אלא ברחובה של עיר נלין: **(ג) ויסרו אליו.** עקמו את הדרך לצד ביתו (ב"ר שם): **ומצות אפה.** פסח היה (ב"ר מח:יב; סדר עולם פ"ה; קדושתא ובכן

19.

1-22. Sodom is destroyed and Lot is saved. Lot showed that his years with Abraham had ennobled him so much that he had remained righteous in Sodom, even heroically so. Despite the mortal danger of being hospitable to visitors in the cruel environment of Sodom, Lot took the "men" into his home.

1. שְׁנֵי הַמַּלְאָכִים — *The two angels.* Here the two visitors are called *angels,* but when they came to Abraham, they were called *men* (18:2). When they came to Abraham, God was with them, making them seem no more significant than ordinary mortals. Alternatively, in the presence of Abraham, to whom angels were commonplace, they were called men, not so in the presence of Lot, who was overawed by them (*Rashi*).

2. וְלִינוּ וְרַחֲצוּ רַגְלֵיכֶם — *Spend the night and wash your feet.* Surely Lot should have *first* washed their feet as Abraham did (18:4), and *then* invited them to spend the night. However, Lot feared that if the visitors were discovered in his house with clean feet, the Sodomites would accuse him of having harbored them for several days without reporting it, but if their feet were unwashed, it would appear that they had just arrived *(Rashi)*.

Out of politeness, the angels refused Lot's initial invitation, and accepted only when he insisted (*Ramban*). It may be that they refused in order to test Lot, and give him the opportunity to prove that he was deserving of salvation because he had still retained the moral teachings of Abraham.

3. וּמַצּוֹת — *Matzos.* The angels came on 15 Nissan, the date that would later become Passover (*Rashi*).

4-5. Hearing about the audacious visitors who had the temerity

אַנְשֵׁי סְדֹם֙ נָסַ֣בּוּ עַל־הַבַּ֔יִת מִנַּ֖עַר וְעַד־זָקֵ֑ן
<< old, < to < from young << the house, < about < surrounded << of Sodom, < the people

כָּל־הָעָ֖ם מִקָּצֶֽה׃ ה וַיִּקְרְא֤וּ אֶל־לוֹט֙ וַיֹּ֣אמְרוּ ל֔וֹ
<< to him, < and they said < Lot < to < And they called 5 << from one end [to the other]. < of the people < all

אַיֵּ֧ה הָאֲנָשִׁ֛ים אֲשֶׁר־בָּ֥אוּ אֵלֶ֖יךָ הַלָּ֑יְלָה הוֹצִיאֵ֣ם
< Bring them out << tonight? < to you < came < who < the men < Where are

אֵלֵ֔ינוּ וְנֵדְעָ֖ה אֹתָֽם׃ ו וַיֵּצֵ֧א אֲלֵהֶ֛ם ל֖וֹט הַפֶּ֑תְחָה
<< to the entrance, << — did Lot — << to them < He went out 6 << them. < that we may know < to us

וְהַדֶּ֖לֶת סָגַ֥ר אַחֲרָֽיו׃ ז וַיֹּאמַ֑ר אַל־נָ֥א אַחַ֖י תָּרֵֽעוּ׃
<< act wickedly. < my brothers, < I beg you, < Do not, << And he said, 7 << behind him. < he shut << and the door,

ח הִנֵּה־נָ֨א לִ֜י שְׁתֵּ֣י בָנ֗וֹת אֲשֶׁ֤ר לֹא־יָדְעוּ֙ אִ֔ישׁ אוֹצִֽיאָה־נָּ֤א אֶתְהֶן֙
< them < now < I shall bring out << a man. < have never known < who < daughters < two < I have < now, < Indeed, 8

אֲלֵיכֶ֔ם וַעֲשׂ֣וּ לָהֶ֔ן כַּטּ֖וֹב בְּעֵינֵיכֶ֑ם רַק֩ לָאֲנָשִׁ֨ים הָאֵל֜ אַל־תַּעֲשׂ֣וּ דָבָ֔ר
<< anything, < do < do not < to these men < but << in your eyes; < as is good < to them < and you may do << to you

כִּֽי־עַל־כֵּ֥ן בָּ֖אוּ בְּצֵ֥ל קֹרָתִֽי׃ ט וַיֹּאמְר֣וּ ׀ גֶּשׁ־הָ֗לְאָה וַיֹּֽאמְרוּ֙ הָאֶחָ֤ד
< This fellow << Then they said, << away! < Move << And they said, 9 << of my roof. < under the shadow < they have come < for this reason < because

בָּֽא־לָגוּר֙ וַיִּשְׁפֹּ֣ט שָׁפ֔וֹט עַתָּ֕ה נָרַ֥ע לְךָ֖ מֵהֶ֑ם וַיִּפְצְר֨וּ בָאִ֤ישׁ בְּלוֹט֙ מְאֹ֔ד
<< exceedingly, < upon Lot, < upon the man, < They put pressure << than [we will treat] them! < we will treat you worse < Now << and attempts to act as a judge? < to sojourn < came

אֱנָשֵׁי סְדוֹם אַקִּיפוּ עַל בֵּיתָא מֵעוּלֵימָא וְעַד סָבָא כָּל עַמָּא מִסּוֹפֵהּ: ה וּקְרוֹ לְלוֹט וַאֲמָרוּ לֵהּ אָן גֻּבְרַיָּא דִּי אֲתוֹ לְוָתָךְ לֵילְיָא אַפֵּקִנּוּן לְוָתָנָא וְנִדַּע יָתְהוֹן: ו וּנְפַק לְוָתְהוֹן לוֹט לִתַרְעָא וְדָשָׁא אֲחַד בַּתְרוֹהִי: ז וַאֲמַר בְּבָעוּ כְעַן אַחַי לָא תַבְאִישׁוּן: ח הָא כְעַן לִי תַּרְתֵּין בְּנָן דִּי לָא יְדָעֲנוּן גְּבַר אַפֵּק כְּעַן יָתְהֶן לְוָתְכוֹן וְעִיבִידוּ לְהֵין כִּדְתַקִּין בְּעֵינֵיכוֹן לְחוֹד לְגֻבְרַיָּא הָאִלֵּין לָא תַעְבְּדוּן מִדַּעַם אֲרֵי עַל כֵּן עַלּוּ בִּטְלַל שֵׁרוּתִי: ט וַאֲמָרוּ קְרֵב לְהַלָּא וַאֲמָרוּ חַד אֲתָא לְאִתּוֹתָבָא וְהָא דָיֵין דִּינָא כְּעַן נַבְאֵשׁ לָךְ מִדִּילְהוֹן וּתְקִיפוּ בְּגַבְרָא בְלוֹט לַחֲדָא

רש"י

ואמרתם זבח פסח): (ד) **טרם ישכבו ואנשי העיר אנשי סדום.** כך נדרש בב"ר (נ:ה), טרם ישכבו ואנשי העיר היו בפיהם של מלאכים, שהיו שואלים ללוט מה טיבם ומעשיהם, והוא אומר להם רובם רשעים. עודם מדברים בהם ואנשי סדום וגו'. ופשוטו של מקרא, ואנשי העיר אנשי רשע נסבו על הבית. ועל שהיו רשעים נקראים אנשי סדום, כמ"ש הכתוב ואנשי סדום רעים וחטאים (לעיל יג:יג; ב"ר מא:ז): **כל העם מקצה.** מקצה העיר עד הקצה, שאין אחד מוחה בידם, שאפי' צדיק אחד אין בהם (ב"ר נ:ה): (ה) **ונדעה אותם.** במשכב זכר, כמו אשר לא ידעו איש (ב"ר נ:ה): (ח) **האל.** כמו האלה: **כי על כן באו.** כי הטובה הזאת תעשו לכבודי על אשר באו **בצל קורתי,** [תרגום] בטלל שרותי (אונקלוס), תרגום של קורה שרותא: (ט) **ויאמרו גש הלאה.** קרב להלאה (שם; ב"ר שם ז) כלומר, התקרב לצדדין ותתרחק ממנו, וכן כל הלאה שבמקרא לשון רחוק כמו זרה הלאה (במדבר יז:ב) הנה הלאי ממך והלאה (ש"א כ:כב). גש הלאה, המשך להלן, בלשון לע"ז טריטידנו"ש. ודבר נזיפה הוא (ילק"ש ויגש קנא) לומר, אין אנו חוששין לך. ודומה לו, קרב אליך אל תגש בי (ישעיה סה:ה), וכן גשה לי ואשבה (שם מט:כ), המשך לצדדין בעבורי ואשב אצלך. אתה מליץ על האורחים, איך מלאך לבך (ב"ר שם). על שאמר להם על הבנות אמרו לו גש הלאה, לשון נחת, ועל שהיה מליץ על האורחים אמרו: **האחד בא לגור.** אדם נכרי יחידי אתה בינינו שבאת לגור: **וישפט שפוט.** שנעשית

to spend a night in their city, hordes of Sodomites converged on Lot's home — without even a single voice of protest — demanding that the guests be turned over to them. When the Sodomites said that they wanted to *know them,* they meant that they wanted to sodomize them (*Rashi, Ibn Ezra*).

7-8. Lot was a perplexing hero. On the one hand, he risked his safety, if not his life, to defend the angels. On the other hand, incredibly, he offered his own children to the crazed mob. Usually a man will fight to the death for the honor of his wife and daughters, yet this man offered his daughters to be dishonored! Said the Holy One, Blessed is He, to him: "By your life! It is for *yourself* that you keep them," because the end was that the drunken Lot lived with his daughters and they conceived by him [v. 36] (*Tanchuma*).

9. וַיִּשְׁפֹּט שָׁפוֹט — *And attempts to act as a judge.* It is difficult to discern in Lot's words where he was judging them. However, in line with the Midrash quoted by *Rashi* (v. 1) that Lot was appointed that day to be a judge, Lot was claiming the right of sanctuary for the men within his home — as was the custom for the courts and the home of the judge. Therefore they were rebelling against his status as judge by demanding the men be turned over to them (*Maasei Hashem*).

וַיִּגְּשׁוּ לִשְׁבֹּר הַדָּלֶת: י וַיִּשְׁלְחוּ הָאֲנָשִׁים אֶת־יָדָם

and they approached › to break › the door. » 10 The men stretched out › their hand ›

וַיָּבִיאוּ אֶת־לוֹט אֲלֵיהֶם הַבָּיְתָה וְאֶת־הַדֶּלֶת

and brought › Lot › to them › into the house, » and the door ›

סָגָרוּ: יא וְאֶת־הָאֲנָשִׁים אֲשֶׁר־פֶּתַח הַבַּיִת הִכּוּ

they closed. » 11 And the men › who were › at the entrance › of the house › they struck ›

בַּסַּנְוֵרִים מִקָּטֹן וְעַד־גָּדוֹל וַיִּלְאוּ לִמְצֹא הַפָּתַח:

with blindness, › from the small › up to › the great; › and they were not able › to find › the entrance. »

יב וַיֹּאמְרוּ הָאֲנָשִׁים אֶל־לוֹט עֹד מִי־לְךָ פֹה חָתָן

12 Then the men said › to › Lot, » In addition, » whom › do you have › here » — son-in-law, ›

וּבָנֶיךָ וּבְנֹתֶיךָ וְכֹל אֲשֶׁר־לְךָ בָּעִיר הוֹצֵא מִן־הַמָּקוֹם: יג כִּי־

your sons, › or your daughters? — » *all* › *that* › *you have* › *in the city* › *remove* › *from* › *the place,* » 13 *for* ›

מַשְׁחִתִים אֲנַחְנוּ אֶת־הַמָּקוֹם הַזֶּה כִּי־גָדְלָה צַעֲקָתָם אֶת־פְּנֵי יהוה

we are [about] to destroy » *this place;* » *for* › *grown great* › *has their outcry* › *before* › *the Face* › *of* HASHEM, »

וַיְשַׁלְּחֵנוּ יהוה לְשַׁחֲתָהּ: יד וַיֵּצֵא לוֹט וַיְדַבֵּר ׀ אֶל־חֲתָנָיו ׀ לֹקְחֵי בְנֹתָיו

so HASHEM *has sent us* › *to destroy it.* » 14 So Lot went out › and spoke › to › his sons-in-law, » [and] the betrothed › of his daughters, »

וַיֹּאמֶר קוּמוּ צְּאוּ* מִן־הַמָּקוֹם הַזֶּה כִּי־מַשְׁחִית יהוה אֶת־הָעִיר וַיְהִי

and he said, › *Get up* › *and go out* › *from* › *this place,* » *for* › HASHEM *is [about] to destroy* › *the city!* » [But] he seemed ›

כִמְצַחֵק בְּעֵינֵי חֲתָנָיו: טו וּכְמוֹ הַשַּׁחַר עָלָה וַיָּאִיצוּ הַמַּלְאָכִים בְּלוֹט

like a jester › in the eyes › of his sons-in-law. » 15 And at the time › the dawn › was breaking, › the angels pressured › Lot ›

* צ' דגושה

וּקְרִיבוּ לְמִתְּבַר דָּשָׁא: י וְאוֹשִׁיטוּ
גֻּבְרַיָּא יָת יְדֵיהוֹן וְאַיְתִיאוּ יָת לוֹט
לְוָתְהוֹן לְבֵיתָא וְיָת דָּשָׁא אֲחָדוּ:
יא וְיָת גֻּבְרַיָּא דְבִתְרַע בֵּיתָא מְחוֹ
בְּשַׁבְרִירַיָּא מִזְּעֵירָא וְעַד רַבָּא וּלְאִיוּ
לְאַשְׁכָּחָא תַרְעָא: יב וַאֲמָרוּ גֻבְרַיָּא
לְלוֹט עוֹד מָן לָךְ הָכָא חַתְנָא וּבְנָיךְ
וּבְנָתָךְ וְכֹל דִּי לָךְ בְּקַרְתָּא אַפֵּיק מִן
אַתְרָא: יג אֲרֵי מְחַבְּלִין אֲנַחְנָא יָת
אַתְרָא הָדֵין אֲרֵי סְגִיאַת קְבִלְתְּהוֹן
קֳדָם יְיָ וְשַׁלְּחָנָא יְיָ לְחַבָּלוּתַהּ:
יד וּנְפַק לוֹט וּמַלִּיל עִם חַתְנוֹהִי נָסְבֵי
בְנָתֵהּ וַאֲמַר קוּמוּ פּוּקוּ מִן אַתְרָא
הָדֵין אֲרֵי מְחַבֵּל יְיָ יָת קַרְתָּא וַהֲוָה
כִּמְחָיֵיךְ בְּעֵינֵי חַתְנוֹהִי: טו וּכְמִסַּק
צַפְרָא הֲוָה וּדְחִיקוּ מַלְאֲכַיָּא בְּלוֹט

רש"י

מוכיח אותנו (שם ג; סדר א"ר פל"א): **דלת.** הסובבת לנעול ולפתוח: **(יא) פתח.** הוא החלל שבו נכנסין ויוצאין: **בסנורים.** מכת עורון (פדר"א כה): **מקטן ועד גדול.** הקטנים התחילו בעבירה תחלה שנאמר מנער ועד זקן (לעיל פסוק ד) לפיכך התחילה הפורענות מהם (ב"ר שם ח): **(יב) עוד מי לך פה.** פשוטו של מקרא, מי יש לך עוד בעיר הזאת חוץ מאשתך ובנותיך שבבית: **חתן ובניך ובנתיך.** אם יש לך חתן או בנים ובנות הוצא מן המקום: **ובניך.** בני בנותיך הנשואות. ומ"א, עוד, מאחר שעושין נבלה כזאת מי לך פתחון פה ללמד סנגוריא עליהם, שכל הלילה היה מלין עליהם טובות. קרי ביה מי לך פֶּה (שם ה): **(יד) חתניו.** שתי בנות נשואות היו לו בעיר: **לקחי בנותיו.** שאותן שבבית ארוסות להם (ב"ר שם ט): **(טו) ויאיצו.** כתרגומו, ודחיקו, מהרוהו:

11. וַיִּלְאוּ — *And they were not able.* How degenerate! Though stricken with blindness, they persisted in their evil plan, still seeking the door and vainly trying to enter (*Alshich; Sforno*).

13. מַשְׁחִתִים אֲנַחְנוּ — *We are [about] to destroy.* Other very wicked nations were not punished as severely as Sodom. But Sodom was in *Eretz Yisrael* which, as God's heritage, could not tolerate such abominations in its midst. . . . Also, God wished to make Sodom an example to the Children of Israel who were to inherit it [see *Deut.* 29:17-24] (*Ramban*).

14. וַיְהִי כִמְצַחֵק — *[But] he seemed like a jester.* Mockery makes serious discussion impossible, because every attempt to prove one's point is turned aside with a contemptuous joke. As the Sages have observed, "One jest repulses a hundred rebukes."

15-26. Lot is saved. By their impudence, Lot's sons-in law

לֵאמֹר קוּם קַח אֶת־אִשְׁתְּךָ וְאֶת־שְׁתֵּי בְנֹתֶיךָ
< your daughters < and both < your wife < – take < Get up << saying:

הַנִּמְצָאֹת פֶּן־תִּסָּפֶה בַּעֲוֺן הָעִיר: טז וַיִּתְמַהְמָהּ ׀
<< Still he delayed; 16 << of the city! < because of the iniquity < you be obliterated < lest << who are present,

וַיַּחֲזִיקוּ הָאֲנָשִׁים בְּיָדוֹ וּבְיַד־אִשְׁתּוֹ וּבְיַד שְׁתֵּי
< of both < and the hand < of his wife, < and the hand < – by his [Lot's] hand, << so the men grasped [them]

בְנֹתָיו בְּחֶמְלַת יהוה עָלָיו וַיֹּצִאֻהוּ וַיַּנִּחֻהוּ מִחוּץ
< outside < and left him < and they took him out << on him; < of HASHEM < in the mercy << his daughters –

לָעִיר: יז וַיְהִי כְהוֹצִיאָם אֹתָם הַחוּצָה וַיֹּאמֶר
<< that he said: < outside < them < as they took < And it was 17 << the city.

הִמָּלֵט עַל־נַפְשֶׁךָ אַל־תַּבִּיט אַחֲרֶיךָ וְאַל־תַּעֲמֹד בְּכָל־הַכִּכָּר הָהָרָה
< to the mountain < the plain; < [anywhere] in all < stop < and do not < behind you < look < Do not << your life! < for < Flee

הִמָּלֵט פֶּן־תִּסָּפֶה: יח וַיֹּאמֶר לוֹט אֲלֵהֶם אַל־נָא אֲדֹנָי: יט הִנֵּה־נָא
< now, < Indeed, 19 << O Lord. < please! < No, << to them: < Lot said 18 << you be obliterated. < lest < flee

מָצָא עַבְדְּךָ חֵן בְּעֵינֶיךָ וַתַּגְדֵּל חַסְדְּךָ אֲשֶׁר עָשִׂיתָ עִמָּדִי לְהַחֲיוֹת
< to save < with me < You did < which < Your kindness < and You magnified << in Your eyes, < favor < Your servant has found

לְמֵימָר קוּם דְּבַר יָת אִתְּתָךְ וְיָת תַּרְתֵּין בְּנָתָךְ דְּאִשְׁתְּכַחַן מְהֵימְנַן עִמָּךְ דִּילְמָא תִלְקֵי בְּחוֹבֵי קַרְתָּא: טז וְאִתְעַכַּב וְאַתְקִיפוּ גֻּבְרַיָּא בִּידֵהּ וּבִידָא דְאִתְּתֵהּ וּבְיַד תַּרְתֵּין בְּנָתֵהּ כִּרְחַם (נ״א בִּדְחַס; נ״א כַּד חָס) יְיָ עֲלוֹהִי וְאַפְּקוּהִי וְאַשְׁרוּהִי מִבָּרָא לְקַרְתָּא: יז וַהֲוָה כַּד אַפִּיקוּ יָתְהוֹן לְבָרָא וַאֲמַר חוּס עַל נַפְשָׁךְ לָא תִסְתְּכֵי לַאֲחוֹרָךְ וְלָא תְקוּם בְּכָל מֵישְׁרָא לְטוּרָא אִשְׁתֵּזֵב דִּלְמָא תִלְקֵי: יח וַאֲמַר לוֹט לְוָתְהוֹן בְּבָעוּ כְעַן רִבּוֹנָי (נ״א יְיָ): יט הָא כְעַן אַשְׁכַּח עַבְדָּךְ רַחֲמִין קֳדָמָךְ וְאַסְגֵּיתָא טֵיבוּתָךְ דִּי עֲבַדְתָּ עִמִּי לְקַיָּמָא

רש״י

הנמצאות. המזומנות לך בבית להצילם. ומ״א יש, וזה ישובו של מקרא: **תספה.** תהיה כלה. עד תום כל הדור (דברים ב:יד) מתורגם עד דסף כל דרא: (טז) **ויתמהמה.** כדי להציל את ממונו (ב״ר שם יא): **ויחזיקו.** אחד מהם היה שליח להצילו וחברו להפוך את סדום, לכך נאמר ויאמר המלט ולא נאמר ויאמרו (שם): (יז) **המלט על נפשך.** דייך להציל נפשות, אל תחוס על הממון (תוספתא סנהדרין יד:א): **אל תביט אחריך.** אתה הרשעת עמהם (תנחומא יד) ובזכות אברהם אתה ניצול (פס״ר ג (י.); ב״ר שם) אינך כדאי לראות בפורענותם ואתה ניצול: **בכל הככר.** ככר הירדן: **ההרה המלט.** אצל אברהם ברח (שם ושם) שהוא יושב בהר, שנא׳ ויעתק משם ההרה (לעיל יב:ח), ואף עכשיו היה יושב שם, שנאמר עד המקום אשר היה שם אהלה בתחלה (שם יג:ג). אע״פ שכתוב ויאהל אברם וגו׳ (שם יח), אהלים הרבה היו לו ונמשכו עד חברון: **המלט.** ל׳ השמטה. וכן כל אמלטה שבמקרא, אשמולי״ר בלע״ז, וכן והמליטה זכר (ישעיה סו:ז) שנשמט העובר מן הרחם. כלפור נמלטה (תהלים קכד:ז) לא יכלו מלט משא (ישעיה מו:ב) להשמיט משא הרעי שבנקביהם: (יח) **אל נא אדני.** רבותינו אמרו שם זה קדש, שנאמר בו להחיות את נפשי, מי שיש בידו להמית ולהחיות (שבועות לה:). ותרגומו בבעו כען ה׳: **אל נא.** אל

had lost their chance to be saved, so the angels insisted that Lot hurry and take his wife and single daughters, for if he delayed, the lethal downpour would begin and it would be too late for him. This illustrates a common principle of God's conduct, one that is often encountered in history: Someone who is totally righteous — an Abraham, for example — may be saved by miracles even when everything around him is crashing down. Less righteous people may be granted an opportunity to save themselves from impending doom, but once the destruction begins, they will be caught up in the general carnage. Thus, Lot deserved to leave Sodom, whether in his own merit or Abraham's — or, as the Midrash teaches, because "two precious treasures" would descend from him: Ruth, the ancestress of King David, and Naamah the Ammonite, who would marry King Solomon; these two righteous descendants of Lot would become the mothers of the Davidic dynasty and the King Messiah. However, he could be saved only before the upheaval began, but not from its midst. Furthermore, neither he nor the others in his entourage were entitled to witness the fate of the other Sodomites and still remain unscathed. Thus, when Lot's wife turned around to see the horrors that her fellows were suffering, she, too, died.

18-20. Lot begs for a concession. Lot was afraid that if he was required to flee to the mountain indicated by the angel, he would die from the rigors of the flight, since it was too far for him. He pleaded that one of the five towns be spared, at least for a short time, so that he could take refuge there.

18. אַל־נָא אֲדֹנָי — *No, please! O Lord.* Following the Talmud (*Shevuos* 35b), *Rashi* explains that Lot first addressed the angel, asking him not to insist on the trek to the mountain. Then Lot

אֶת־נַפְשִׁי וְאָנֹכִי לֹא אוּכַל לְהִמָּלֵט הָהָרָה פֶּן־
‹ lest ‹ to the mountain, ‹ to flee ‹ am not able ‹ but I ‹‹ my life;
תִּדְבָּקַנִי הָרָעָה וָמַתִּי: כ הִנֵּה־נָא הָעִיר הַזֹּאת
‹ this city ‹‹ now, ‹ There it is, 20 ‹‹ and I die. ‹ by the destruction ‹ I be overtaken
קְרֹבָה לָנוּס שָׁמָּה וְהִוא מִצְעָר אִמָּלְטָה נָּא שָׁמָּה
‹‹ there. ‹ please, ‹ I shall flee, ‹‹ small; ‹ and it is ‹‹ there, ‹ to escape ‹ is near [enough]
הֲלֹא מִצְעָר הִוא וּתְחִי נַפְשִׁי: רביעי כא וַיֹּאמֶר אֵלָיו
‹‹ to him: ‹ And He said 21 ‹‹ shall my soul. ‹ — and survive ‹ it is? ‹ that small ‹ Is it not so

יָת נַפְשִׁי וַאֲנָא לֵית אֲנָא יָכִיל לְאִשְׁתֵּזָבָא לְטוּרָא דִּילְמָא תְּעַרְעִנַּנִי בִּשְׁתָּא וְאֵימוּת: כ הָא כְעַן קַרְתָּא הָדָא קְרִיבָא לְמֵעֲרוֹק לְתַמָּן וְהִיא זְעֵירָא אִשְׁתֵּזֵב כְּעַן תַּמָּן הֲלָא זְעֵירָא הִיא וְתִתְקַיַּם נַפְשִׁי: כא וַאֲמַר לֵהּ הָא נְסֵיבִית אַפָּךְ אַף לְפִתְגָּמָא הָדֵין בְּדִיל דְּלָא לְמֶהְפַּךְ יָת קַרְתָּא דְּבְעֵיתָא עֲלַהּ: כב אוֹחִי לְאִשְׁתֵּזְבָא תַּמָּן אֲרֵי לָא אִכּוֹל לְמֶעְבַּד פִּתְגָּמָא עַד מֵיתָךְ לְתַמָּן עַל כֵּן קְרָא שְׁמָא דְקַרְתָּא צוֹעַר: כג שִׁמְשָׁא נְפַק עַל אַרְעָא וְלוֹט עַל לְצוֹעַר: כד וַייָ אַמְטַר עַל סְדוֹם וְעַל עֲמוֹרָה גָּפְרֵיתָא וְאֶשָּׁתָא מִן

הִנֵּה נָשָׂאתִי פָנֶיךָ גַּם לַדָּבָר הַזֶּה לְבִלְתִּי הָפְכִּי אֶת־הָעִיר אֲשֶׁר
‹ about which ‹ the city ‹ my overturning ‹ to preclude ‹‹ regarding this matter, ‹ even ‹ you favor ‹ I have shown ‹ Indeed,
דִּבַּרְתָּ: כב מַהֵר הִמָּלֵט שָׁמָּה כִּי לֹא אוּכַל לַעֲשׂוֹת דָּבָר עַד־בֹּאֲךָ שָׁמָּה
‹‹ there. ‹ your arrival ‹ until ‹ anything ‹ to do ‹ I am not able ‹ for ‹‹ there, ‹ flee ‹ Hurry, 22 ‹‹ you have spoken.
עַל־כֵּן קָרָא שֵׁם־הָעִיר צוֹעַר: כג הַשֶּׁמֶשׁ יָצָא עַל־הָאָרֶץ וְלוֹט בָּא
‹ arrived ‹ and Lot ‹ the earth ‹ upon ‹ rose ‹ The sun 23 ‹‹ Zoar. ‹ of the city ‹ the name ‹ he called ‹ Therefore
צֹעֲרָה: כד וַיהוָה הִמְטִיר עַל־סְדֹם וְעַל־עֲמֹרָה גָּפְרִית וָאֵשׁ מֵאֵת
‹ from ‹ and fire ‹ sulfur ‹ Gomorrah ‹ and upon ‹ Sodom ‹ upon ‹ had caused to rain ‹ Now HASHEM 24 ‹‹ at Zoar.

רש"י

תאמרו אלי להמלט ההרה: **נא.** לשון בקשה: **(יט) פן תדבקני הרעה.** כשהייתי אצל אנשי סדום היה הקב"ה רואה מעשי ומעשי בני העיר והייתי נראה צדיק וכדאי להנצל, וכשאבא אצל צדיק אני כרשע. וכן אמרה הצרפית לאליהו, באת אלי להזכיר את עוני (מלכים א יז:יח) עד שלא באת אצלי היה הקב"ה רואה מעשי ומעשי עמי ואני צדקת ביניהם, ומשבאת אצלי, לפי מעשיך אני רשעה (ב"ר נ:יא): **(כ) העיר הזאת קרובה.** קרובה ישיבתה, נתיישבה מקרוב, לפיכך לא נתמלאה סאתה עדיין (שבת י:). ומה היא קריבתה, מדור הפלגה, שנתפלגו האנשים והתחילו להתיישב איש איש במקומו, והיא היתה בשנת מות פלג, ומשם עד כאן נ"ב שנה, שפלג מת בשנת מ"ח לאברהם. כיצד, פלג חי אחרי הולידו את רעו ר"ט שנה, צא מהם ל"ב כשנולד שרוג ומשרוג עד שנולד נחור ל' הרי ס"ב, ומנחור עד שנולד תרח כ"ט הרי צ"א, ומשם עד שנולד אברהם ע' הרי קס"א, תן להם מ"ח הרי ר"ט, ואותה שנה היתה שנת הפלגה. וכשנחרבה סדום היה אברהם בן צ"ט שנה, הרי מדור הפלגה עד כאן נ"ב שנה. וצוער איחרה ישיבתה אחר ישיבת סדום וחברותיה שנה אחת, הוא שנאמר **אמלטה נא,** נא בגימטריא נ"א (שם): **הלא מצער היא.** והלא עוונותיה מועטין ויכול אתה להניחה: **ותחי נפשי.** בה. זהו מדרשו (שם). ופשוטו של מקרא, הלא עיר קטנה היא ואנשים בה מעט אין לך להקפיד אם תניחנה ותחי נפשי בה (שם): **(כא) גם לדבר הזה.** לא דייך שאתה ניצול אלא אף כל העיר אציל בגללך: **הפכי.** הופך אני כמו עד בואי (להלן מח:ה) אחרי רואי (לעיל טז:יג) מדי דברי בו (ירמיה לא:יט): **(כב) כי לא אוכל לעשות.** זה עונשן של מלאכים על שאמרו כי משחיתים אנחנו (לעיל פסוק יג) ותלו הדבר בעצמן (ב"ר נ:ט) לפיכך לא זזו משם עד שהוזקקו לומר שאין הדבר ברשותן: **כי לא אוכל.** לשון יחיד. מכאן אתה למד שהאחד הופך והאחד מציל, שאין ב' מלאכים נשלחים לדבר אחד (שם ב): **על כן קרא שם העיר צוער.** על שם והיא מצער: **(כד) וה' המטיר.** כל מקום שנאמר וה', הוא ובית דינו (שם נא:ב): **המטיר על סדום.** בעלות השחר, כמ"ש וכמו השחר עלה (לעיל פסוק טו). שעה שהלבנה עומדת ברקיע עם החמה לפי שהיו מהם עובדין לחמה ומהם ללבנה, אמר הקב"ה, אם אפרע מהם ביום יהיו עובדי לבנה אומרים אילו היה בלילה שהלבנה מושלת לא היינו חרבין, ואם אפרע מהם בלילה יהיו עובדי החמה אומרים אילו היה ביום כשהחמה מושלת לא היינו חרבין, לכך כתיב וכמו השחר עלה, ונפרע מהם בשעה שהחמה והלבנה מושלים (ב"ר נ:יב): **המטיר וגו' גפרית ואש.** בתחלה מטר ונעשה

addressed God, with the plea given in the next two verses.

20. **קְרֹבָה לָנוּס שָׁמָּה** — *Is near [enough] to escape there.* In the plain sense, Lot was speaking of the distance to the town relative to the mountain, as noted above. *Rashi*, however, explains *near* as referring to *nearness* in time, meaning that the town — which would later be named Zoar — had been populated more recently than the other four Sodomite cities, so that its measure of sin is not yet full. Since it had not sinned as much as the other towns, it could be spared from destruction for the time being, and Lot could take refuge there.

22. **מַהֵר** — *Hurry.* The angel told Lot that God had agreed to his request, but that the *upheaval*, the total destruction, could not begin before Lot's safe arrival in Zoar; the sulfur and fire, however, had begun descending at dawn (*Gur Aryeh*).

צוֹעַר — *Zoar.* The city was named Zoar, meaning *small*, because Lot referred to it as a *small* city [מִצְעָר, v. 20], and because its

יהוה מִן־הַשָּׁמָיִם: כה וַיַּהֲפֹךְ אֶת־הֶעָרִים הָאֵל

< these cities < He overturned 25 « heaven. < out of < HASHEM,

וְאֵת כָּל־הַכִּכָּר וְאֵת כָּל־יֹשְׁבֵי הֶעָרִים וְצֶמַח

< and the vegetation < of the cities < the inhabitants < all < with « plain, < and the entire

הָאֲדָמָה: כו וַתַּבֵּט אִשְׁתּוֹ מֵאַחֲרָיו וַתְּהִי נְצִיב

< a pillar < and she became < behind him < His wife looked 26 « of the soil.

מֶלַח: כז וַיַּשְׁכֵּם אַבְרָהָם בַּבֹּקֶר אֶל־הַמָּקוֹם אֲשֶׁר־

< that < the place < to < in the morning < Abraham arose early 27 « of salt.

עָמַד שָׁם אֶת־פְּנֵי יהוה: כח וַיַּשְׁקֵף עַל־פְּנֵי סְדֹם

< of Sodom < the face < upon < And he gazed down 28 « of HASHEM. < the Presence < before < there < he had stood

וַעֲמֹרָה וְעַל כָּל־פְּנֵי אֶרֶץ הַכִּכָּר וַיַּרְא וְהִנֵּה עָלָה קִיטֹר הָאָרֶץ כְּקִיטֹר

< like the smoke < of the earth < the smoke < there rose < — and indeed! « and he saw « of the plain; < of the land < surface < the entire < and upon < and Gomorrah

הַכִּבְשָׁן: כט וַיְהִי בְּשַׁחֵת אֱלֹהִים אֶת־עָרֵי הַכִּכָּר וַיִּזְכֹּר אֱלֹהִים

< that God remembered < of the plain < the cities < when God destroyed < And so it was 29 « of a kiln.

אֶת־אַבְרָהָם וַיְשַׁלַּח אֶת־לוֹט מִתּוֹךְ הַהֲפֵכָה בַּהֲפֹךְ אֶת־הֶעָרִים

< of the cities < in the overturning < the upheaval < from amidst < Lot < so He sent « Abraham;

אֲשֶׁר־יָשַׁב בָּהֵן לוֹט: ל וַיַּעַל לוֹט מִצּוֹעַר וַיֵּשֶׁב בָּהָר וּשְׁתֵּי בְנֹתָיו

< and his two daughters « on the mountain, < and settled < from Zoar < Now Lot went up 30 « Lot. < in them < had lived < that

קֳדָם יְיָ מִן שְׁמַיָּא: כה וַהֲפַךְ יָת קִרְוַיָּא הָאִלֵּין וְיָת כָּל מֵישְׁרָא וְיָת כָּל יָתְבֵי קִרְוַיָּא וְצִמְחָא דְאַרְעָא: כו וְאִסְתְּכִיאַת אִתְּתֵהּ מִבַּתְרוֹהִי וַהֲוַת קָמָא דְמִלְחָא: כז וְאַקְדֵּים אַבְרָהָם בְּצַפְרָא לְאַתְרָא דִּי שַׁמֵּשׁ תַּמָּן בִּצְלוֹ קֳדָם יְיָ: כח וְאִסְתְּכִי עַל אַפֵּי סְדוֹם וַעֲמוֹרָה וְעַל כָּל אַפֵּי אַרְעָא דְמֵישְׁרָא וַחֲזָא וְהָא סְלִיק תְּנָנָא דְאַרְעָא כִּתְנָנָא דְאַתּוּנָא: כט וַהֲוָה בְּחַבָּלוּת (נ״א כַּד חֲבַל) יְיָ יָת קִרְוֵי מֵישְׁרָא וּדְכִיר יְיָ יָת אַבְרָהָם וְשַׁלַּח יָת לוֹט מִגּוֹ הֲפֶכְתָּא כַּד הֲפַךְ יָת קִרְוַיָּא דִּי הֲוָה יָתֵב בְּהֵן לוֹט: ל וּסְלֵק לוֹט מִצּוֹעַר וִיתֵב בְּטוּרָא וְתַרְתֵּין בְּנָתֵהּ

רש״י

גפרית ואש (מכילתא בשלח שירה פ״ה): **מאת ה׳.** דרך המקראות לדבר כן, כמו נשי למך (לעיל ד:כג) ולא אמר נשיי, וכן אמר דוד קחו עמכם את עבדי אדוניכם (מלכים א א:לג) ולא אמר את עבדיי, וכן אמר אחשורוש בשם המלך (אסתר ח:ח) ולא אמר בשמי. אף כאן אמר מאת ד׳ ולא אמר מאתו (סנהדרין לח:; ב״ר נא:ב): **מן השמים.** הוא שאמר הכתוב כי בם ידין עמים וגו׳ (איוב לו:לא). כשבא ליסר הבריות מביא עליהם אש מן השמים כמו שעשה לסדום, וכשבא להוריד המן [מן השמים], הנני ממטיר לכם לחם מן השמים (שמות טז:ד; תנחומא ישן בשלח כ; תנחומא י): **(כה) ויהפך את הערים וגו׳.** ארבעתן יושבות בסלע אחד והפכן מלמעלה למטה, שנאמר בחלמיש שלח ידו וגו׳ (איוב כח:ט; ב״ר נא:ד): **(כו) ותבט אשתו מאחריו.** מאחריו של לוט: **ותהי נציב מלח.** במלח חטאה ובמלח לקתה (ב״ר נא:ה). אמר לה תני מעט מלח לאורחים הללו. אמרה לו אף המנהג הרע הזה אתה בא להנהיג במקום הזה (שם נ:ד): **(כח) קיטור.** תימור של עשן, טורק״א בלע״ז: **הכבשן.** חפירה ששורפין בה את האבנים לסיד, וכן כל כבשן שבתורה: **(כט) ויזכור אלהים את אברהם.** מהו זכירתו של אברהם, על לוט נזכר, שהיה לוט יודע ששרה אשתו של אברהם, ושמע שאמר אברהם במצרים על שרה אחותי היא (לעיל יב:יט) ולא גלה הדבר שהיה חס עליו, לפיכך חס הקב״ה עליו (ב״ר נא:ו):

salvation was due to its smaller size and lesser iniquity. Its original name was *Bela*, as in 14:2 (*Rashi*).

24. מֵאֵת ה׳ מִן־הַשָּׁמָיִם — *From* HASHEM, *out of heaven*. This emphasizes that the *sulfur and fire* were not natural, earthly phenomena, but were Divinely originated visitations, without any natural cause (*Sforno*). The use of HASHEM, the Name of Mercy, implies that the people of Sodom had fallen to such depths of depravity that it was an act of mercy to remove them from the earth.

26. וַתַּבֵּט אִשְׁתּוֹ — *His wife peered*. She died because she turned around to look at the destruction, and, as explained above [v. 17], she was not worthy enough to see others being destroyed and be spared herself. *Ramban* cites a view that she turned around in the hope that her married daughters were following. *Tur* points out that the death of Lot's wife was a necessary precondition to the following episode, for if she had been alive, her daughters would not have conceived through Lot.

27-29. When Abraham had concluded his pleading for Sodom, God did not tell him what the outcome would be; therefore, he arose in the morning to see what had happened (*Daas Sofrim*). In this passage, the Torah states clearly that Lot had been spared only for the sake of Abraham (*Ran*).

עִמּוֹ כִּי יָרֵא לָשֶׁבֶת בְּצוֹעַר וַיֵּשֶׁב בַּמְּעָרָה הוּא

< he << in the cave, < he dwelt << in Zoar; < to dwell < he was afraid < for << with him,

וּשְׁתֵּי בְנֹתָיו: לא וַתֹּאמֶר הַבְּכִירָה אֶל־הַצְּעִירָה

<< the younger, < to < The older one said **31** << with his two daughters.

אָבִינוּ זָקֵן וְאִישׁ אֵין בָּאָרֶץ לָבוֹא עָלֵינוּ כְּדֶרֶךְ

< in the manner < unto us < to come < in the land < and there is no man < is old < Our father

כָּל־הָאָרֶץ: לב לְכָה נַשְׁקֶה אֶת־אָבִינוּ יַיִן וְנִשְׁכְּבָה

< and lie < wine, < to our father, < let us give drink < Come, **32** *<< the earth. < of all*

עִמּוֹ וּנְחַיֶּה מֵאָבִינוּ זָרַע: לג וַתַּשְׁקֶיןָ אֶת־אֲבִיהֶן

< to their father, < So they gave drink **33** *<< to offspring. < through our father < so that we may give life << with him,*

יַיִן בַּלַּיְלָה הוּא וַתָּבֹא הַבְּכִירָה וַתִּשְׁכַּב אֶת־אָבִיהָ וְלֹא־יָדַע בְּשִׁכְבָהּ

< of her lying down < and he was not aware << her father, < with < and lay < and the older one came < on that night; < wine,

*וּבְקוּמָהּ: לד וַיְהִי מִמָּחֳרָת וַתֹּאמֶר הַבְּכִירָה אֶל־הַצְּעִירָה הֵן־שָׁכַבְתִּי

< I lay < Indeed, << the younger, < to < that the older one said < on the next day < And it was **34** << and of her getting up.

אֶמֶשׁ אֶת־אָבִי נַשְׁקֶנּוּ יַיִן גַּם־הַלַּיְלָה וּבֹאִי שִׁכְבִי עִמּוֹ וּנְחַיֶּה מֵאָבִינוּ

< through our father < so that we may give life < with him < lie < and you come << tonight, < also < wine < let us give drink to him, << my father; < with < last night

* נקוד על ו' בתרא

עִמֵּהּ אֲרֵי דְחֵיל לְמִתַּב בְּצוֹעַר וִיתֵב בִּמְעַרְתָּא הוּא וְתַרְתֵּין בְּנָתֵהּ: לא וַאֲמֶרֶת רַבְּתָא לִזְעֶרְתָּא אֲבוּנָא סִיב וּגְבַר לֵית בְּאַרְעָא לְמֵיעַל עֲלָנָא כְּאוֹרַח כָּל אַרְעָא: לב אִיתָא נַשְׁקֵי יָת אֲבוּנָא חַמְרָא וְנִשְׁכּוּב עִמֵּהּ וּנְקַיֵּם מֵאֲבוּנָא בְּנִין: לג וְאַשְׁקִיאָה יָת אֲבוּהֶן חַמְרָא בְּלֵילְיָא הוּא וְעַלַּת רַבְּתָא וּשְׁכִיבָא עִם אֲבוּהָא וְלָא יְדַע בְּמִשְׁכְּבַהּ וּבְקִימַהּ: לד וַהֲוָה בְּיוֹמָא דְבַתְרוֹהִי וַאֲמֶרֶת רַבְּתָא לִזְעֶרְתָּא הָא שְׁכֵיבִית רַמְשָׁא עִם אַבָּא נַשְׁקִנֵּהּ חַמְרָא אַף בְּלֵילְיָא וְעוּלִי שְׁכִיבִי עִמֵּהּ וּנְקַיֵּם מֵאֲבוּנָא

רש"י

(ל) **כי ירא לשבת בצוער.** לפי שהיתה קרובה לסדום: (לא) **אבינו זקן.** ואם לא עכשיו אימתי, שמא ימות או יפסוק מלהוליד: **ואיש אין בארץ.** סבורות היו שכל העולם נחרב כמו בדור המבול (שם ח): (לג) **ותשקין וגו'.** יין נזדמן להם במערה להוציא מהן שני אומות (שם; ספרי עקב מג; מכילתא בשלח שירה פ"ב): **ותשכב את אביה.** ובצעירה כתיב ותשכב עמו. לצעירה לפי שלא פתחה בזנות אלא אחותה לימדתה, חיסך עליה הכתוב ולא פירש גנותה, אבל בכירה שפתחה בזנות פרסמה הכתוב במפורש (תנחומא בלק יז). **ובקומה** של בכירה נקוד, הרי כאילו לא נכתב, לומר שבקומה ידע, ואעפ"כ לא נשמר ליל שני מלשתות (נזיר כג.). [א"ר לוי, כל מי

31-38. Lot's daughters: Moab and Ammon — the roots of Jewish monarchy. [This theme is treated at length in the *Overview* to the ArtScroll edition of *Ruth*.] Lot's daughters were modest, righteous women whose actions were nobly motivated. Thinking that the rest of the world had been destroyed in the upheaval of Sodom — and that even Zoar had been spared only while they were there — they felt that it was their responsibility to save the human race by bearing children, even though the only living male was their own father. The Torah does not label their actions as incestuous because they sincerely thought there was no other way to insure the propagation of the species. Because their intentions were pure, they merited that among their descendants would be Ruth, ancestress of David, and Naamah, queen of Solomon and mother of Rehoboam, his successor and the next link in the Davidic chain (*R' Bachya*). Lot, however, was not comparable to his daughters; his intentions were not at all sincere. Even though he was intoxicated and unaware of what he was doing the first night, he knew in the morning what had happened [see v. 33] — but allowed himself to become intoxicated again, knowing full well what the result would be (*Rashi*).

31. **אָבִינוּ זָקֵן** — *Our father is old.* And if not now, when? He may die or become impotent (*Rashi*).

לָבוֹא עָלֵינוּ — *To come unto us.* Almost everywhere that this phrase is used it employs the preposition אל, *to,* and not על, *on*. (See for instance *Genesis* 16:4; 29:21,23,30; 30:4,16; 38:2,8,9, 16,18.) The only other use of על, *on,* occurs in the commandment of *Yibum,* the levirate marriage (*Deuteronomy* 25:5). The motivation of Lot's daughters was similar to that of Tamar (*Genesis* 38:14) and Ruth who are also associated with *Yibum*. (See *Horayos* 11a, and *Ramban*, *Bereishis* 38:8.)

33. **וּבְקוּמָהּ** — *And of her getting up.* In the Torah scroll, this word has a dot over it, a traditional method of drawing attention to a special interpretation. It indicates that though he was not aware *of her lying down,* he was well aware of *her getting up.* Nevertheless, he was not more vigilant on the second night than he was on the first (*Rashi; Midrash*), an indication of his own lechery.

זָרַע: לה וַתַּשְׁקֶיןָ גַּם בַּלַּיְלָה הַהוּא אֶת־אֲבִיהֶן יָיִן
« wine; ‹ to their father, ‹ that night ‹ also ‹ So they gave drink 35 « *to offspring.*

וַתָּקָם הַצְּעִירָה וַתִּשְׁכַּב עִמּוֹ וְלֹא־יָדַע בְּשִׁכְבָהּ
‹ of her lying down ‹ and he was not aware ‹ with him, ‹ and lay ‹ and the younger one got up

וּבְקֻמָהּ: לו וַתַּהֲרֶיןָ שְׁתֵּי בְנוֹת־לוֹט מֵאֲבִיהֶן:
« from their father. « of Lot — ‹ daughters ‹ — the two « And [thus] they conceived 36 « and of her getting up.

לז וַתֵּלֶד הַבְּכִירָה בֵּן וַתִּקְרָא שְׁמוֹ מוֹאָב הוּא
‹ he is « Moab; ‹ his name ‹ and she called ‹ to a son ‹ The older gave birth 37

אֲבִי־מוֹאָב עַד־הַיּוֹם: לח וְהַצְּעִירָה גַם־הִוא יָלְדָה
‹ gave birth « she — ‹ — also « And the younger one 38 « this day. ‹ until ‹ of Moab ‹ the ancestor

בֵּן וַתִּקְרָא שְׁמוֹ בֶּן־עַמִּי הוּא אֲבִי בְנֵי־עַמּוֹן עַד־הַיּוֹם: ס [כ] א וַיִּסַּע
‹ He journeyed 1 [20] « this day. ‹ until ‹ of Ammon ‹ of the people ‹ the ancestor ‹ he is « Ben-ammi; ‹ his name ‹ and she called ‹ to a son

מִשָּׁם אַבְרָהָם אַרְצָה הַנֶּגֶב וַיֵּשֶׁב בֵּין־קָדֵשׁ וּבֵין שׁוּר וַיָּגָר בִּגְרָר:
« in Gerar. ‹ and he sojourned « Shur, ‹ and between ‹ Kadesh ‹ between ‹ and he settled ‹ of the south, ‹ to the land ‹ Abraham did, ‹ from there,

ב וַיֹּאמֶר אַבְרָהָם אֶל־שָׂרָה אִשְׁתּוֹ אֲחֹתִי הִוא וַיִּשְׁלַח אֲבִימֶלֶךְ מֶלֶךְ
‹ King ‹ — Abimelech, « so he sent « *is she;* ‹ *My sister* « his wife, ‹ Sarah ‹ of ‹ Abraham said 2

גְּרָר וַיִּקַּח אֶת־שָׂרָה: ג וַיָּבֹא אֱלֹהִים אֶל־אֲבִימֶלֶךְ בַּחֲלוֹם הַלָּיְלָה
‹ of the night ‹ in a dream ‹ Abimelech ‹ to ‹ And God came 3 « Sarah. ‹ and took « of Gerar —

בְּנִין: לה וְאַשְׁקִיאָה אַף בְּלֵילְיָא הַהוּא יָת אֲבוּהֶן חַמְרָא וְקָמַת זְעֶרְתָּא וּשְׁכֵיבַת עִמֵּהּ וְלָא יְדַע בְּמִשְׁכְּבַהּ וּבְקִימַהּ: לו וְעַדִּיאָה תַּרְתֵּין בְּנַת לוֹט מֵאֲבוּהֶן: לז וִילִידַת רַבְּתָא בַּר וּקְרַת שְׁמֵהּ מוֹאָב הוּא אֲבוּהוֹן דְּמוֹאָבָא עַד יוֹמָא דֵין: לח וּזְעֶרְתָּא אַף הִיא יְלִידַת בַּר וּקְרַת שְׁמֵהּ בַּר עַמִּי הוּא אֲבוּהוֹן דִּבְנֵי עַמּוֹן עַד יוֹמָא דֵין: א וּנְטַל מִתַּמָּן אַבְרָהָם לְאַרְעָא דָרוֹמָא וִיתֵב בֵּין רְקָם וּבֵין חַגְרָא וְאִתּוֹתַב בִּגְרָר: ב וַאֲמַר אַבְרָהָם עַל שָׂרָה אִתְּתֵהּ אֲחָתִי הִיא וּשְׁלַח אֲבִימֶלֶךְ מַלְכָּא דִגְרָר וּדְבַר יָת שָׂרָה: ג וַאֲתָא מֵימַר מִן קֳדָם יְיָ לְוַת אֲבִימֶלֶךְ בְּחֶלְמָא דְלֵילְיָא

רש"י

שהוא להוט אחר בולמוס של עריות לסוף מאכילין אותו מבשרו (ב"ר שם ט; תנחומא יב)]: (לו) ותהרין וגו'. אע"פ שאין האשה מתעברת מביאה ראשונה, אלו שלטו בעצמן והוציאו ערותן [ס"א עדותן (ערוך, ערך ג')] [לחוץ] ונתעברו מביאה ראשונה (ב"ר שם): (לז) מואב. זו שלא היתה צנועה פירשה שמאביה הוא, אבל צעירה קראתו בלשון נקיה [בן עמי], וקבלה שכר בימי משה, שנאמר בבני עמון אל תתגר בם (דברים ב:יט) כלל, ובמואב לא הזהיר אלא שלא ילחמו בם אבל לצערן התיר לו [ס"א להם] (ב"ר שם יח; ב"ק לח:): (א) ויסע משם אברהם. כשראה שחרבו הכרכים ופסקו העוברים והשבים נסע לו משם (ב"ר נב:ג). ד"א, להתרחק מלוט שיצא עליו שם רע שבא על בנותיו (שם ד): (ב) ויאמר אברהם. כאן לא נטל רשות, אלא על כרחה שלא בטובתה, לפי שכבר לוקחה לבית פרעה ע"י כן (שם): אל שרה אשתו. על שרה

37-38. The Sages (*Horayos* 10b) note a difference between the two daughters. The elder was so shameless that she gave her son a name that clearly suggested his disgraceful parentage: The name Moab is derived from מֵאָב, *from father.* The younger one, however, gave her son a name that means *son of my people,* thus modestly concealing his father. She was rewarded in Moses' time, when God commanded the Jewish people not to provoke Ammon even without waging war (*Rashi*).

20.

Sarah is abducted by Abimelech.

Kadesh and Shur were large cities in the Philistine part of Canaan. Abraham chose to live there because the area was heavily populated and would provide him the opportunity to spread his belief in God (*Sforno*). *Radak* suggests that he settled in Philistia to establish his presence — and thus the future claim of his offspring — in another part of *Eretz Yisrael.*

2. אֲחֹתִי הִוא — *My sister is she.* Abraham did not ask Sarah's permission to use this ruse, because she would have refused due to her previous abduction by Pharaoh (*Gur Aryeh*). On the other hand, he did not expect an abduction to take place in Gerar if the people thought she was his sister. They would have tried to convince her "brother" to give her in marriage, but would not have taken her by force. Consequently he did not feel he was endangering her.

וַיִּקַּח אֶת־שָׂרָה — *And took Sarah.* Abimelech planned to marry her. That her beauty was so great at the age of 90 that a king

וַיֹּאמֶר לוֹ הִנְּךָ מֵת עַל־הָאִשָּׁה אֲשֶׁר־לָקַחְתָּ

«you have taken; < whom < the woman < because of < to die < Indeed you are «to him, < and said

וְהִוא בְּעֻלַת בָּעַל: ד וַאֲבִימֶלֶךְ לֹא קָרַב אֵלֶיהָ

« her; < come near < had not < But Abimelech **4** *« of a husband. < the mate < and [moreover] she is*

וַיֹּאמַר אֲדֹנָי הֲגוֹי גַּם־צַדִּיק תַּהֲרֹג: ה הֲלֹא הוּא

< he himself < Did not **5** *« You will slay? < it is righteous < even though < Is it so that a nation « My Lord, «* and [so] he said,

אָמַר־לִי אֲחֹתִי הִוא וְהִיא־גַם־הִוא אָמְרָה אָחִי

< 'My brother « said: < she herself < even, < And she, « is she'? < 'My sister « me: < tell

הוּא בְּתָם־לְבָבִי וּבְנִקְיֹן כַּפַּי עָשִׂיתִי זֹאת: ו וַיֹּאמֶר אֵלָיו הָאֱלֹהִים

< God did, *<* to him, *<* And He said **6** *« this. < have I done < of my hands <* and the cleanness *< of my heart < In the innocence « is he!'*

בַּחֲלֹם גַּם אָנֹכִי יָדַעְתִּי כִּי בְתָם־לְבָבְךָ עָשִׂיתָ זֹּאת וָאֶחְשֹׂךְ גַּם־אָנֹכִי

< I— < —even « and I *prevented « this, < that you did < of your heart < it was in the innocence < that « knew, < I < Also «* in the dream,

אוֹתְךָ מֵחֲטוֹ־לִי עַל־כֵּן לֹא־נְתַתִּיךָ לִנְגֹּעַ אֵלֶיהָ: ז וְעַתָּה הָשֵׁב אֵשֶׁת־

< the wife < return < But now, 7 *« her. < to touch < I did not allow you < that reason < for « against Me; < from sinning < you*

וַאֲמַר לֵהּ הָא אַתְּ מִית עַל עֵיסַק אִתְּתָא דִי דְבַרְתָּא וְהִיא אִתַּת גְּבָר: ד וַאֲבִימֶלֶךְ לָא קְרֵב לְוָתַהּ וַאֲמַר יְיָ הַעַם אַף זַכַּאי תִקְטוֹל: ה הֲלָא הוּא אֲמַר לִי אֲחָתִי הִיא וְהִיא אַף הִיא אֲמַרַת אָחִי הוּא בְּקַשִׁיטוּת לִבִּי וּבְזַכָּאוּת יְדַי עֲבָדִית דָּא: ו וַאֲמַר לֵהּ מֵימַר מִן קֳדָם יְיָ בְּחֶלְמָא אַף קֳדָמַי גְּלֵי אֲרֵי בְּקַשִׁיטוּת לִבָּךְ עֲבַדְתָּ דָּא וּמְנָעִית אַף אֲנָא יָתָךְ מִלְּמֶחֱטֵי קֳדָמַי עַל כֵּן לָא שְׁבַקְתָּךְ לְמִקְרַב לְוָתַהּ: ז וּכְעַן אֲתֵיב אִתַּת

רש"י

אשתו, וכיוצא בו אל הלקח ארון וגו' ואל מות חמיה (שמואל א ד:כא) שניהם בלשון על: (ד) **לא קרב אליה.** המלאך מנעו (ב"ר נב:יג) כמו שנאמר לא נתתיך לנגוע אליה: **הגוי גם צדיק תהרוג.** אף אם הוא צדיק תהרגנו, שמא כך דרכך לאבד האומות חנם. כך עשית לדור המבול [ולדור הפלגה], אף [הם] אני אומר שהרגתם על לא דבר כמו שאתה אומר להרגני (שם ו): (ה) **גם היא.** לרבות עבדים וגמלים וחמרים, את כולם שאלתי ואמרו לי אחיה הוא (שם): **בתם לבבי.** שלא דמיתי לחטוא (שם): **ובנקיון כפי.** נקי אני מן החטא, שלא נגעתי בה (שם): (ו) **ידעתי כי בתם לבבך וגו'.** אמת שלא דמית מתחלה לחטוא, אבל נקיות כפים אין כאן [הדא אמרה משמוש ידים יש כאן] (שם): **לא נתתיך.** לא ממך היה שלא נגעת בה, אלא חשכתי אני אותך מחטוא ולא נתתי לך כח, וכן ולא נתנו אלהים (להלן לא:ז), וכן לא נתנה אביה לבוא (שופטים טו:א; ב"ר שם ז): (ז) **השב אשת האיש.** ואל תהא סבור שמא תתגנה בעיניו ולא יקבלנה, או ישנאך ולא יתפלל עליך. [א"ל אבימלך ומי מפייסו שלא נגעתי בה. א"ל:]

desired her may be because she had become youthful again so that she could bear a child (*Ramban*). Alternatively, he wished to marry into the august family of Abraham (*Ran*).

3. It is astounding that God appeared to Abimelech to warn him, since prophecy is given only to people of the highest spiritual caliber. To protect the honor of the righteous, however, God appears even to heathens, provided that they are people of some stature. In the case of Sarah's abduction in Egypt, Pharaoh was completely unworthy, so God punished him without giving him the benefit of a prophetic warning (*Radak*).

4. לֹא קָרַב אֵלֶיהָ — *Had not come near her. Come near* is a euphemism for intimacy. To prevent Abimelech from forcing Sarah to live with him, he was punished with impotence (*Rashi*).

הֲגוֹי גַּם־צַדִּיק תַּהֲרֹג — *Is it so that a nation even though it is righteous You will slay?* If it is Your practice to destroy nations without cause, then I must assume that You destroyed the generations of the Flood and of the Dispersion without just cause, just as You now do to me! (*Rashi*; cf. *Rashi* to 18:25: חָלִלָה לְּךָ).

Abimelech was indignant at the suggestion that he had done something wrong, because, in comparison with the bestiality of Sodom, Abraham and Sarah were treated hospitably in Gerar. He saw even her abduction in a positive light, for Abimelech was doing her the honor of making her his queen (*R' Hirsch*).

Abimelech felt that since his intentions were good, he was blameless. Judaism rejects this view. Good intentions do not purify a wrong deed. Its measure is whether it complies with God's will; if it is wrong in His eyes, then good intentions do not give it sanction. A person in Abimelech's position has the further obligation to set an example of appropriate behavior — is it right that even an unmarried woman must fear the whim of every prince? (*R' Hirsch*).

6. וָאֶחְשֹׂךְ — *I prevented.* Rav Aibu said: It is like a warrior riding at full speed, who reined in his horse to avoid hitting a child. Whom do we praise, the horse or the rider? Surely the rider! So, too, God told Abimelech that he deserved no credit for not harming Sarah; it was God who stayed his hand (*Midrash*).

הָאִישׁ֙ כִּֽי־נָבִ֣יא ה֔וּא וְיִתְפַּלֵּ֥ל בַּֽעַדְךָ֖ וֶֽחְיֵ֑ה וְאִם־
‹ but if « and you will live; ‹ for you ‹ and he will pray « is he, ‹ a prophet ‹ for ‹ of the man

אֵֽינְךָ֣ מֵשִׁ֗יב דַּ֚ע כִּי־מ֣וֹת תָּמ֔וּת אַתָּ֖ה וְכָל־אֲשֶׁר־
‹ that is ‹ and all ‹ you « you shall surely die — ‹ that ‹ know « return [her], ‹ you do not

לָֽךְ׃ ח וַיַּשְׁכֵּ֨ם אֲבִימֶ֜לֶךְ בַּבֹּ֗קֶר וַיִּקְרָא֙ לְכָל־עֲבָדָ֔יו
‹ his servants ‹ to all ‹ he called « in the morning; ‹ Abimelech arose early 8 « yours.

וַיְדַבֵּ֛ר אֶת־כָּל־הַדְּבָרִ֥ים הָאֵ֖לֶּה בְּאָזְנֵיהֶ֑ם וַיִּֽירְא֥וּ
‹ and frightened « in their ears, ‹ of these things ‹ all ‹ and he spoke

הָאֲנָשִׁ֖ים מְאֹֽד׃ ט וַיִּקְרָ֨א אֲבִימֶ֜לֶךְ לְאַבְרָהָ֗ם
‹ to Abraham ‹ And [then] Abimelech called 9 « exceedingly. ‹ were the people

וַיֹּ֨אמֶר ל֜וֹ מֶֽה־עָשִׂ֤יתָ לָּ֙נוּ֙ וּמֶֽה־חָטָ֣אתִי לָ֔ךְ כִּֽי־הֵבֵ֧אתָ עָלַ֛י וְעַל־
‹ and upon ‹ upon me ‹ you brought ‹ that ‹ against you ‹ have I sinned ‹ How « to us? ‹ have you done ‹ What « to him, ‹ and said

מַמְלַכְתִּ֖י חֲטָאָ֣ה גְדֹלָ֑ה מַעֲשִׂים֙ אֲשֶׁ֣ר לֹא־יֵעָשׂ֔וּ עָשִׂ֖יתָ עִמָּדִֽי׃
« unto me! ‹ have you done ‹ ought not to be done ‹ that ‹ Deeds « that is so great? ‹ a sin ‹ my kingdom

י וַיֹּ֥אמֶר אֲבִימֶ֖לֶךְ אֶל־אַבְרָהָ֑ם מָ֣ה רָאִ֔יתָ כִּ֥י עָשִׂ֖יתָ אֶת־הַדָּבָ֥ר הַזֶּֽה׃
« [as] this? ‹ such a thing ‹ you did ‹ that ‹ did you see ‹ What « Abraham, ‹ to ‹ And Abimelech said 10

יא וַיֹּ֙אמֶר֙ אַבְרָהָ֔ם כִּ֣י אָמַ֗רְתִּי רַ֚ק אֵין־יִרְאַ֣ת אֱלֹהִ֔ים בַּמָּק֖וֹם הַזֶּ֑ה
« in this place, ‹ of God ‹ fear ‹ there is no ‹ 'It is solely that « I said, ‹ Because « And Abraham said, 11

וַהֲרָג֖וּנִי עַל־דְּבַ֥ר אִשְׁתִּֽי׃ יב וְגַם־אָמְנָ֗ה אֲחֹתִ֤י בַת־אָבִי֙ ה֔וא אַ֖ךְ לֹ֣א
‹ not ‹ though « is she, ‹ of my father ‹ the daughter ‹ my sister, ‹ indeed, ‹ Moreover, 12 « of my wife.' ‹ account ‹ on ‹ and they will slay me

גַּבְרָא אֲרֵי נְבִיָּא הוּא וִיצַלֵּי עֲלָךְ וּתְחֵי וְאִם לֵיתָךְ מָתִיב דַּע אֲרֵי מֵימַת תְּמוּת אַתְּ וְכָל דִּי לָךְ: ח וְאַקְדֵּים אֲבִימֶלֶךְ בְּצַפְרָא וּקְרָא לְכָל עַבְדּוֹהִי וּמַלִּיל יָת כָּל פִּתְגָּמַיָּא הָאִלֵּין קֳדָמֵיהוֹן וּדְחִילוּ גּוּבְרַיָּא לַחֲדָא: ט וּקְרָא אֲבִימֶלֶךְ לְאַבְרָהָם וַאֲמַר לֵהּ מָא עֲבַדְתָּ לָנָא וּמָא חָבִית (נ״א חָטֵית) לָךְ אֲרֵי אַיְתֵיתָא עֲלַי וְעַל מַלְכוּתִי חוֹבָא רַבָּא עוֹבָדִין דִּי לָא כָשְׁרִין לְאִתְעֲבָדָא עֲבַדְתָּ עִמִּי: י וַאֲמַר אֲבִימֶלֶךְ לְאַבְרָהָם מָא חֲזֵיתָ אֲרֵי עֲבַדְתָּ יָת פִּתְגָּמָא הָדֵין: יא וַאֲמַר אַבְרָהָם אֲרֵי אֲמָרִית לְחוֹד לֵית דַּחַלְתָּא דַיְיָ בְּאַתְרָא הָדֵין וְיִקְטְלֻנַּנִי עַל עֵיסַק אִתְּתִי: יב וּבְרַם בְּקוּשְׁטָא אֲחָתִי בַּת אַבָּא הִיא בְּרַם לָא

רש״י

כי נביא הוא. ויודע שלא נגעת בה, לפיכך ויתפלל בעדך (ב״ר שם ח): **(ט) מעשים אשר לא יעשו.** מכה אשר לא הורגלה לבא על בריה באה לנו על ידך, עצירת כל נקבים, של זרע ושל קטנים ורעי ואזנים וחוטם (שם יג; פס״ר מב (קעו:, קעח.); ב״ק צב.): **(יא) רק אין יראת אלהים.** אכסנאי שבא לעיר, על עסקי אכילה ושתיה שואלין אותו או על עסקי אשתו שואלין אותו, אשתך היא או אחותך היא (ב״ק שם): **(יב) אחותי בת אבי היא.** ובת אב מותרת לבן נח שאין אבות לגוי (יבמות צח.; תנחומא ישן כו). וכדי לאמת דבריו השיבו כן. ואם תאמר, והלא בת אחיו היתה (סנהדרין נח:). בני בנים הרי הן כבנים (יבמות סב:) והרי היא בתו של תרח. וכך הוא אומר ללוט כי

7. **כִּי־נָבִיא הוּא** — *For a prophet is he.* Not that a prophet's wife should be treated differently than a commoner's. Rather, because Abraham is a prophet, he knows that you did not touch her, and therefore *he will pray for you and you will live* (*Rashi*).

9. **מַעֲשִׂים אֲשֶׁר לֹא־יֵעָשׂוּ** — *Deeds that ought not to be done.* "It is wrong for a man like you to cause harm to innocent people by claiming that your wife is your sister" (*Radak, Sforno*).

10-11. Abimelech's questions in verse 9 were merely rhetorical, and required no answer. Now, however, he demanded to know why Abraham deceived him (*Radak*).

12. **. . . . וְגַם** — *Moreover. . . .* Even where one is compelled to dissemble, he should remain as close to truth as possible. Therefore, having explained why he was afraid to tell the truth, Abraham maintained that even *in the literal sense*, his claim of being Sarah's brother — though misleading — was not untrue [see below]. Nor had he said explicitly that Sarah was *not* his wife; he merely emphasized that she was his sister (*Malbim*).

Although Sarah was his *brother's* daughter, not his *father's*, so that she was not his sister in the literal sense, Abraham's statement was justified since "grandchildren are considered as children"; thus he could call Sarah his sister in the accepted figura-

בַּת־אִמִּי וַתְּהִי־לִי לְאִשָּׁה: יג וַיְהִי כַּאֲשֶׁר הִתְעוּ אֹתִי
< He caused me to wander, < when << And so it was, 13 << a wife. < to me < and she was << of my mother; < the daughter

אֱלֹהִים מִבֵּית אָבִי וָאֹמַר לָהּ זֶה חַסְדֵּךְ אֲשֶׁר
< which < your kindness < 'Let this be << to her, < I said << of my father, < from the house << God did,

תַּעֲשִׂי עִמָּדִי אֶל כָּל־הַמָּקוֹם אֲשֶׁר נָבוֹא שָׁמָּה
<< there, < we come < that < such a place < any < – at << for me < you shall do

אִמְרִי־לִי אָחִי הוּא: יד וַיִּקַּח אֲבִימֶלֶךְ צֹאן וּבָקָר
< and cattle < sheep < So Abimelech took 14 << is he.' < My brother << of me: < say

וַעֲבָדִים וּשְׁפָחֹת וַיִּתֵּן לְאַבְרָהָם וַיָּשֶׁב לוֹ
< to him < and he returned << to Abraham; < and gave [them] < and maidservants < and slaves

בַּת אִמָּא וַהֲוַת לִי לְאִנְתּוּ: יג וַהֲוָה כַּד
טָעוּ עַמְמַיָּא בָּתַר עוֹבָדֵי יְדֵיהוֹן יָתִי
קָרִיב יְיָ לְדַחַלְתֵּהּ מִבֵּית אַבָּא
וַאֲמָרִית לַהּ דֵּין (נ״א דָּא) טִיבוּתִיךְ דִּי
תַעְבְּדִי עִמִּי לְכָל אַתְרָא דִּי נְהָךְ
לְתַמָּן אֱמָרִי עֲלַי אָחִי הוּא: יד וּדְבַר
אֲבִימֶלֶךְ עָאן וְתוֹרִין וְעַבְדִין וְאַמְהָן
וִיהַב לְאַבְרָהָם וַאֲתֵיב לֵהּ יָת שָׂרָה
אִתְּתֵהּ: טו וַאֲמַר אֲבִימֶלֶךְ הָא אַרְעִי
קֳדָמָךְ בִּדְתַקִּין בְּעֵינָיךְ תִּיב:
טז וּלְשָׂרָה אֲמַר הָא יְהָבִית אֶלֶף
סַלְעִין דִּכְסַף לְאָחִיךְ הָא הוּא לִיךְ
כְּסוּת דִּיקָר (עַיְנִין) חֲלַף דִּשְׁלָחִית
דְּבַרְתִּיךְ וַחֲזֵית יָתִיךְ וְיָת כָּל דְּעִמָּךְ
וְעַל (נ״א הֲלָא עַל) כָּל מָה דַּאֲמָרַת
וְאִתּוֹכָחַת: יז וְצַלִּי אַבְרָהָם קֳדָם

אֵת שָׂרָה אִשְׁתּוֹ: טו וַיֹּאמֶר אֲבִימֶלֶךְ הִנֵּה אַרְצִי לְפָנֶיךָ בַּטּוֹב בְּעֵינֶיךָ
< in your eyes < in [the place that] is good << before you: < my land < Here is << And Abimelech said, 15 << his wife. < Sarah

שֵׁב: טז וּלְשָׂרָה אָמַר הִנֵּה נָתַתִּי אֶלֶף כֶּסֶף לְאָחִיךְ הִנֵּה הוּא־לָךְ
< for you < It is << Indeed! << to your brother. < pieces of silver < a thousand < I have given < Indeed, << he said, < And to Sarah 16 << settle.

כְּסוּת עֵינַיִם לְכֹל אֲשֶׁר אִתָּךְ וְאֵת כֹּל וְנֹכָחַת: יז וַיִּתְפַּלֵּל אַבְרָהָם אֶל־
< to < Abraham prayed 17 << you will be vindicated. < all < and with << with you; < who are < for all < of the eyes < a covering

רש״י

אנשים אחים אנחנו (לעיל יג:ח; פדר״א לו): **אך לא בת אמי.** הרן מאם אחרת היה: (יג) **ויהי כאשר התעו אותי וגו׳.** אונקלוס תרגם מה שתרגם. ויש ליישב עוד דבר דבור על אפניו. כשהוציאני הקב״ה מבית אבי להיות משוטט ונד ממקום למקום ידעתי שאעבור במקום רשעים, **ואומר לה זה חסדך: כאשר התעו.** לשון רבים, ואל תתמה, כי הרבה מקומות לשון אלהות ולשון מרות קרוי ל׳ רבים. אשר הלכו אלהים (שמואל ב ז:כג) אלהים חיים (דברים ה:כג) אלהים קדושים (יהושע כד:יט), וכל לשון אלהים ל׳ רבים. וכן ויקח אדני יוסף (להלן לט:כ) אדוני האדונים (דברים י:יז) אדוני הארץ (להלן מב:לג) וכן בעליו עמו (שמות כב:יד) והועד בבעליו (שם כא:כט). וא״ת, מהו ל׳ התעו. כל הגולה ממקומו ואינו מיושב קרוי תועה, כמו ותלך ותתע (להלן כא:יד) תעיתי כשה אובד (תהלים קיט:קעו) יתעו לבלי אוכל (איוב לח:מא) ילאו ויתעו לבקש אכלם: **אמרי לי.** עלי, (אונקלוס), וכן וישאלו אנשי המקום לאשתו (להלן כו:ז) על אשתו, וכן ואמר פרעה לבני ישראל (שמות יד:ג) כמו על בני ישראל, פן יאמרו לי אשה הרגתהו (שופטים ט:נד): (יד) **ויתן לאברהם.** כדי שיתפייס ויתפלל עליו (פס״ר מב (קעז.)): (טו) **הנה ארצי לפניך.** אבל פרעה א״ל הנה אשתך קח ולך (לעיל יב:יט), לפי שנתירא, שהמצרים שטופי זמה (מדרש אגדה לעיל יב:יט): (טז) **ולשרה אמר.** אבימלך לכבודה, כדי לפייסה, הנה עשיתי לך כבוד זה, **נתתי** ממון **לאחיך,** שאמרת עליו אחי הוא, **הנה** הממון והכבוד הזה **לך כסות עינים: לכל אשר אתך.** יכסו עיניהם שלא יקילוך. שאילו השיבותיך ריקנית יש להם לומר לאחר שנתעלל בה החזירה, עכשיו שהוצרכתי לבזבז ממון ולפייסך יהיו יודעים שעל כרחי השיבותיך, וע״י נס: **ואת כל.** ועם כל באי עולם: **ונכחת.** יהא לך פתחון פה להתוכח ולהראות

tive sense of the word (*Rashi*).

13. This was Abraham's third justification: Since God had commanded him to become a wanderer, he resorted to this plan whenever they came to a new place; it does not imply low esteem for Abimelech and his subjects (*Malbim*).

14-18. Abimelech appeases Abraham and Sarah. Abimelech knew that he had to appease both Abraham and Sarah, because he would not be healed unless Abraham prayed for him, and only Sarah could forgive him for the harm and humiliation he had caused her, so he gave them gifts, humbled himself, and assured them that they could feel secure in his land. In this latter respect, the contrast between Philistia and Egypt is glaring. The Egyptians were an immoral, licentious people, so that Pharaoh could not invite Abraham and Sarah to settle in his country. He ordered them out for their own protection — and his, because if they were harmed, he would suffer Divine punishment. Abimelech, however, had no such fears. Furthermore, by inviting Abraham to remain, Abimelech was demonstrating to all that he had not violated Sarah, for a woman with whom the king had been intimate would never be permitted to return to a commoner husband in the king's own land (*Abarbanel*).

16. **כְּסוּת עֵינַיִם** — *A covering of the eyes.* Abimelech referred to his gift to Sarah as *A covering of the eyes,* a diversion of attention from her, for it served as a vindication of her conduct and would

הָאֱלֹהִים וַיִּרְפָּא אֱלֹהִים אֶת־אֲבִימֶלֶךְ וְאֶת־אִשְׁתּוֹ
God, » and God healed ‹ Abimelech, ‹ his wife, ‹
וְאַמְהֹתָיו וַיֵּלֵדוּ: יח כִּי־עָצֹר עָצַר יהוה בְּעַד
and his maids, ‹ and they were able to procreate; » 18 for ‹ completely restrained ‹ had HASHEM ‹ the opening ‹
כָּל־רֶחֶם לְבֵית אֲבִימֶלֶךְ עַל־דְּבַר שָׂרָה אֵשֶׁת
of every ‹ womb ‹ of the household ‹ of Abimelech, ‹ on ‹ account ‹ of Sarah, ‹ the wife ‹
אַבְרָהָם: ס [כא] א וַיהוה פָּקַד אֶת־שָׂרָה כַּאֲשֶׁר
of Abraham. » [21] 1 HASHEM ‹ remembered ‹ Sarah ‹ as ‹
אָמָר וַיַּעַשׂ יהוה לְשָׂרָה כַּאֲשֶׁר דִּבֵּר: ב וַתַּהַר וַתֵּלֶד שָׂרָה לְאַבְרָהָם
He had said; » and HASHEM did ‹ for Sarah ‹ as ‹ He had spoken. » 2 Conceived ‹ and she bore, » Sarah did, » unto Abraham ‹
בֵּן לִזְקֻנָיו לַמּוֹעֵד אֲשֶׁר־דִּבֶּר אֹתוֹ אֱלֹהִים: ג וַיִּקְרָא אַבְרָהָם אֶת־שֶׁם־
a son, » in his old age, » at the appointed time ‹ that ‹ He spoke ‹ of it, ‹ God did. » 3 Abraham called ‹ the name ‹
בְּנוֹ הַנּוֹלַד־לוֹ אֲשֶׁר־יָלְדָה־לּוֹ שָׂרָה יִצְחָק: ד וַיָּמָל אַבְרָהָם אֶת־יִצְחָק
of his son ‹ who was born ‹ to him » — who ‹ was borne ‹ to him ‹ by Sarah — » Isaac. » 4 Abraham circumcised ‹ Isaac ‹

יְיָ וְאַסִּי יְיָ יָת אֲבִימֶלֶךְ וְיָת אִתְּתֵהּ וְאַמְהָתֵהּ וְאִתְרְוָחוּ: יח אֲרֵי מֵיחַד אֲחַד יְיָ בְּאַפֵּי כָל פְּתַח וַלְדָא לְבֵית אֲבִימֶלֶךְ עַל עֵיסַק שָׂרָה אִתַּת אַבְרָהָם: א וַייָ דְּכִיר יָת שָׂרָה כְּמָא דִּי אֲמַר וַעֲבַד יְיָ לְשָׂרָה כְּמָא דִּי מַלִּיל: ב וְעַדִּיאַת וִילִידַת שָׂרָה לְאַבְרָהָם בַּר לְסִיבְתוֹהִי לִזְמַן דִּי מַלִּיל יָתֵהּ יְיָ: ג וּקְרָא אַבְרָהָם יָת שׁוּם בְּרֵהּ דְּאִתְיְלִיד לֵהּ דִּילִידַת לֵהּ שָׂרָה יִצְחָק: ד וּגְזַר אַבְרָהָם יָת יִצְחָק

רש"י

דברים נכרים הללו. ול' הוכחה בכל מקום ברור דברים, ובלע"ז אשפרובי"ר. ואונקלוס תרגם בפנים אחרים, ולשון המקרא כך הוא נופל על התרגום, הנה הוא לך כסות של כבוד על העינים שלי ששלטו בך ובכל אשר אתך, ועל כן תרגמו וחזית יתך וית כל דעמך. ויש מדרש אגדה, אבל ישוב לשון המקרא פירשתי: **(יז) וילדו.** כתרגומו, ואתרוחו, נפתחו נקביהם והוליאו, והיא לידה שלהם: **(יח) בעד כל רחם.** כנגד כל פתח: **על דבר שרה.** ע"פ דבורה של שרה (ב"ר נב:יג): **(א) וה' פקד את שרה וגו'.** סמך פרשה זו לכאן ללמדך שכל המבקש רחמים על חבירו והוא צריך לאותו דבר הוא נענה תחלה, שנאמר ויתפלל וגו' וסמיך ליה וה' פקד את שרה, שפקדה כבר קודם שריפא את אבימלך (בבא קמא צב.): **כאשר אמר.** בהריון: **כאשר דבר.** בלידה. והיכן היא אמירה והיכן הוא דבור. אמירה ויאמר אלהים אבל שרה אשתך וגו' (לעיל יז:יט). דבור היה דבר ה' אל אברם בברית בין הבתרים (לעיל טו:א) ושם נאמר לא יירשך זה וגו' (שם ד) והביא היורש משרה (מכילתא בא פי"ג): **ויעש ה' לשרה כאשר דבר.** לאברהם: **(ב) [לזקוניו.** שהיה זיו איקונין שלו דומה לו (ב"ר נג:ו): **למועד אשר דבר.** ר' יודן ורבי חמא. רבי יודן אומר מלמד שנולד לט' חדשים, שלא יאמרו מביתו של אבימלך הוא. ר' חמא אומר לשבעה חדשים (שם:)] **למועד אשר דבר אתו.** דמליל יתיה (אונקלוס), את המועד אשר דבר וקבע, כשא"ל למועד אשוב אליך (לעיל יח:יד) שרט לו שריטה בכותל, אמר לו כשתגיע חמה לשריטה זו בשנה האחרת תלד (תנחומא ישן לו):

prevent people from looking at her contemptuously.

17-18. The punishment for the abduction of Sarah was that the bodily orifices of all Abimelech's people became closed. They could not relieve themselves or give birth until Abraham prayed for them.

21.

1-8. Isaac's birth. The prophecies to Abraham and Sarah, and their joint longings to build the future for which God had created the world, finally found fulfillment with the birth of Sarah's son. Moreover, the manner in which it happened — that a woman who was infertile even in her youth had a child at the age of 90 — established the miraculous nature of God's Chosen People. God could just as easily have given a child to Sarah in her prime, but that would not have demonstrated Divine intervention.

וַה' פָּקַד אֶת־שָׂרָה — *HASHEM remembered Sarah.* The chapter before this concluded with Abraham's prayer that the women of Abimelech's court be able to conceive. As soon as he prayed for them, Sarah herself conceived. This teaches that "Someone who prays on behalf of another when he himself has need of that same thing, he is answered first" (*Rashi*).

The proximity also teaches that the key to conception is in God's hand. He withheld it from Abimelech and his servants and gave it to Sarah, as His wisdom dictated (*R' Bachya*).

According to tradition, Sarah conceived on the first day of Rosh Hashanah. Therefore, this narrative is the Torah reading of that day, so that it will inspire people to follow Sarah's example of righteousness and prayer.

3. יִצְחָק — *Isaac.* This name — which God had commanded Abraham to give (17:19) — is derived from the word צחק, *laughter*, for by all the laws of nature the very idea of his birth was "laughable" (*R' Hirsch*). The laughter memorialized in this name, however, is the joy of Abraham, not the original skepticism of Sarah; God would not have chosen this name if it had

בְּנוֹ בֶּן־שְׁמֹנַת יָמִים כַּאֲשֶׁר צִוָּה אֹתוֹ אֱלֹהִים׃

« God did. ‹ to him ‹ He commanded ‹ as « days, ‹ of eight ‹ at the age « his son

חמישי ה וְאַבְרָהָם בֶּן־מְאַת שָׁנָה בְּהִוָּלֶד לוֹ אֵת יִצְחָק

‹ was Isaac ‹ to him ‹ when born « years ‹ of one hundred ‹ was at the age ‹ And Abraham 5

בְּנוֹ׃ ו וַתֹּאמֶר שָׂרָה צְחֹק עָשָׂה לִי אֱלֹהִים כָּל־

‹ *who-ever* ‹‹ *— has God;* ‹‹ *for me* ‹ *He has made* ‹ *Laughter* ‹ Sarah said, 6 « his son.

הַשֹּׁמֵעַ יִצְחַק־לִי׃ ז וַתֹּאמֶר מִי מִלֵּל לְאַבְרָהָם

‹‹ *to Abraham,* ‹ *is the One Who said* ‹ *Who* ‹‹ And she said, 7 « *for me.* ‹ *will laugh* ‹ *hears*

הֵינִיקָה בָנִים שָׂרָה כִּי־יָלַדְתִּי בֵן לִזְקֻנָיו׃ ח וַיִּגְדַּל הַיֶּלֶד וַיִּגָּמַל וַיַּעַשׂ

‹ And make ‹‹ and he was weaned; ‹ The child grew 8 « *in his old age!* ‹ *a son* ‹ *I have borne* ‹ *For* ‹‹ *would Sarah be'?* ‹ *of children* ‹ *'A wet nurse*

אַבְרָהָם מִשְׁתֶּה גָדוֹל בְּיוֹם הִגָּמֵל אֶת־יִצְחָק׃ ט וַתֵּרֶא שָׂרָה אֶת־בֶּן־

‹ the son ‹ Sarah saw 9 « of Isaac. ‹ of the weaning ‹ on the day ‹ a great banquet ‹ did Abraham

הָגָר הַמִּצְרִית אֲשֶׁר־יָלְדָה לְאַבְרָהָם מְצַחֵק׃ י וַתֹּאמֶר לְאַבְרָהָם גָּרֵשׁ

‹ *Drive out* ‹‹ to Abraham, ‹ So she said 10 « mocking. ‹‹ to Abraham, ‹ she had borne ‹ whom ‹‹ the Egyptian, ‹ of Hagar

הָאָמָה הַזֹּאת וְאֶת־בְּנָהּ כִּי לֹא יִירַשׁ בֶּן־הָאָמָה הַזֹּאת עִם־בְּנִי עִם־

‹ *with* ‹ *my son,* ‹ *with* ‹‹ *of that slave woman —* ‹ *— the son* ‹‹ *inherit* ‹ *he shall not* ‹ *for* ‹‹ *and her son,* ‹ *this slavewoman*

בְּרֵהּ בַּר תְּמַנְיָא יוֹמִין כְּמָא דִי
פַּקִּיד יָתֵהּ יְיָ׃ ה וְאַבְרָהָם בַּר מְאָה
שְׁנִין כַּד אִתְיְלִיד לֵהּ יָת יִצְחָק בְּרֵהּ׃
ו וַאֲמֶרֶת שָׂרָה חֶדְוָא עֲבַד לִי יְיָ כָּל
דִּשְׁמַע יֶחְדֵי לִי׃ ז וַאֲמֶרֶת מָאן מְהֵימָן
דַּאֲמַר לְאַבְרָהָם וְקַיֵּים דְּתוֹנִיק בְּנִין
שָׂרָה אֲרֵי יְלֵידִית בַּר לְסִיבְתוֹהִי׃
ח וּרְבָא רַבְיָא וְאִתְחֲסִיל וַעֲבַד
אַבְרָהָם מִשְׁתְּיָא רַבָּא בְּיוֹמָא
דְּאִתְחֲסִיל יָת יִצְחָק׃ ט וַחֲזַת שָׂרָה
יָת בַּר הָגָר מִצְרֵיתָא דִּילִידַת
לְאַבְרָהָם מְחַיֵּיךְ׃ י וַאֲמֶרֶת לְאַבְרָהָם
תָּרֵךְ אַמְתָא הָדָא וְיָת בְּרַהּ אֲרֵי לָא
יֵרַת בַּר אַמְתָא הָדָא עִם בְּרִי עִם

רש"י

(ו) **יצחק לי.** ישמח עלי (אונקלוס). ומדרש אגדה, הרבה עקרות נפקדו עמה, הרבה חולים נתרפאו בו ביום, הרבה תפלות נענו עמה ורב שחוק היה בעולם (ב"ר שם ח): (ז) **מי מלל לאברהם.** לשון שבח וחשיבות [כמו מי פעל ועשה (ישעיה מא:ד) מי ברא אלה (שם מ:כו)]. ראו מה הוא ומי הוא שומר הבטחתו, הקב"ה מבטיח ועושה: **מלל.** שינה הכתוב ולא אמר דבר, גימטריא שלו ק', כלומר לסוף מאה לאברהם (ב"ר נג:ט): **היניקה בנים שרה.** ומהו בנים לשון רבים, ביום המשתה הביאו השרות בניהן עמהן והיניקה אותם, שהיו אומרות לא ילדה שרה, אלא אסופי הביאו מן השוק (ב"מ פז.): (ח) **ויגמל.** לסוף כ"ד חודש (ב"ר שם י; כתובות ס.): **משתה גדול.** שהיו שם גדולי הדור, שם ועבר ואבימלך (תנחומא ישן וישלח כג): (ט) **מצחק.** לשון עבודת כוכבים, כמו שנאמר ויקומו לצחק (שמות לב:ו; ב"ר נג:יא). ד"א, ל' גילוי עריות, כמה דתימא לצחק בי (להלן לט:יז). ד"א, ל' רציחה, כמ"ד יקומו נא הנערים וישחקו לפנינו וגו' (שמואל ב ב:יד)]: (י) **עם בני וגו'.** [מתשובת שרה כי לא יירש בן האמה הזאת עם בני אתה למד] שהיה מריב עם יצחק על הירושה ואומר אני בכור ונוטל פי שנים, ויוצאים לשדה ונוטל קשתו ויורה בו

represented derision (*R' Bachya*). In verse 6, Sarah herself said that all who heard of this great event would take part in her *joy*, thus ratifying this implication of the name.

Isaac's primary character trait was גְּבוּרָה, or introspective strength of character and self-restraint, a concept that would seem to contradict his name. However, in order to be truly strong, one must be able to laugh at the world and its seemingly insuperable obstacles (*R' Gedaliah Schorr*).

7. מִי מִלֵּל — *Who is the One Who said.* Sarah exclaimed, "Who but God could have done this?" (*Rashi*).

8. מִשְׁתֶּה גָּדוֹל — *A great banquet.* It was "*great*" because the great men of the generation attended: Shem, Eber, and Abimelech (*Tanchuma; Rashi*). According to *Tosafos (Shabbos* 130a), this feast took place at Isaac's *circumcision*. In this view, the word הִגָּמֵל is homiletically rendered as two words ה״ג, *on the eighth day*, מָל, *he circumcised,* Isaac, since the numerical value of the letters ה and ג is eight [5 + 3]. According to *R' Bachya*, Abraham made this great feast when Isaac began to study the Torah.

9. מְצַחֵק — *Mocking* [or: *playing; making sport*]. This term expresses what Sarah saw that convinced her that Ishmael could not remain in the household. Scripture uses this verb to denote the three cardinal sins: idolatry [*Exodus* 32:6]; adultery [39:17]; and murder [*II Samuel* 2:14]. Thus Ishmael's behavior proved that he had become thoroughly corrupt and evil, and he had to be sent away (*Rashi*).

10. כִּי לֹא יִירַשׁ — *For he shall not inherit. HaKsav V'HaKabbalah* discerns Sarah's intent by noting her use of the word יִירַשׁ, *shall inherit,* rather than its synonym יִנְחַל. The subtle difference

יִצְחָק: יא וַיֵּרַע הַדָּבָר מְאֹד בְּעֵינֵי אַבְרָהָם עַל אוֹדֹת

‹ regarding «‹ of Abraham, ‹ in the eyes ‹ greatly ‹ was the matter ‹ Distressing 11 « Isaac!

בְּנוֹ: יב וַיֹּאמֶר אֱלֹהִים אֶל־אַבְרָהָם אַל־יֵרַע

‹ be distressing ‹ Let it not « Abraham, ‹ to ‹ So God said 12 « his son.

בְּעֵינֶיךָ עַל־הַנַּעַר וְעַל־אֲמָתֶךָ כֹּל אֲשֶׁר תֹּאמַר

‹ she tells ‹ that ‹ all « your slave woman; ‹ or over ‹ the youth ‹ over ‹ in your eyes

אֵלֶיךָ שָׂרָה שְׁמַע בְּקֹלָהּ כִּי בְיִצְחָק יִקָּרֵא לְךָ זָרַע:

« offspring. ‹ your ‹ will they be considered ‹ [only] through Isaac ‹ for « her voice, ‹ heed « — Sarah — « you

יג וְגַם אֶת־בֶּן־הָאָמָה לְגוֹי אֲשִׂימֶנּוּ כִּי זַרְעֲךָ הוּא: יד וַיַּשְׁכֵּם אַבְרָהָם ׀

‹ So Abraham awoke early 14 « is he. ‹ your offspring ‹ for « I will make him, ‹ into a nation ‹ of the slave woman ‹ the son ‹ But also 13

בַּבֹּקֶר וַיִּקַּח־לֶחֶם וְחֵמַת מַיִם וַיִּתֵּן אֶל־הָגָר שָׂם עַל־שִׁכְמָהּ וְאֶת־הַיֶּלֶד

« the boy, ‹ along with ‹ her shoulder ‹ on ‹ he placed [them] « Hagar; ‹ to ‹ and gave [them] « of water, ‹ and a skin bottle ‹ bread ‹ and he took « in the morning,

וַיְשַׁלְּחֶהָ וַתֵּלֶךְ וַתֵּתַע בְּמִדְבַּר בְּאֵר שָׁבַע: טו וַיִּכְלוּ הַמַּיִם מִן־הַחֵמֶת

« the skin bottle, ‹ from ‹ was the water ‹ When finished 15 « of Beer Sheba. ‹ in the desert ‹ and she strayed ‹ she departed, « and he sent her off;

יִצְחָק: יא וּבְאֵישׁ פִּתְגָּמָא לַחֲדָא בְּעֵינֵי אַבְרָהָם עַל עֵיסַק בְּרֵהּ: יב וַאֲמַר יְיָ לְאַבְרָהָם לָא יַבְאֵשׁ בְּעֵינָיךְ עַל עוּלֵימָא וְעַל אַמְתָךְ כֹּל דִּי תֵימַר לָךְ שָׂרָה קַבֵּל מִנַּהּ אֲרֵי בְיִצְחָק יִתְקְרוּן לָךְ בְּנִין: יג וְאַף יָת בַּר אַמְתָא לְעַם אֲשַׁוְּנֵהּ אֲרֵי בְנָךְ הוּא: יד וְאַקְדֵּים אַבְרָהָם בְּצַפְרָא וּנְסִיב לַחְמָא וְרָקְבָא דְמַיָּא וִיהַב לְהָגָר שַׁוִּי עַל כַּתְפַּהּ וְיָת רַבְיָא וְשַׁלְּחַהּ וַאֲזָלַת וְתָעַת בְּמַדְבְּרָא (נ״א בְּמַדְבַּר) בְּאֵר שָׁבַע: טו וּשְׁלִימוּ מַיָּא מִן רָקְבָא

רש״י

חלים, כמה דלת למר כמתלהלה היורה זקים וגו' ולמר הלל משחק לני (משלי כו:יח־יט; ב״ר שם): **עם בני עם יצחק.** מכיון שהול בני לפי' לם לינו הגון כילחק, לו הגון כילחק לפי' לינו בני לין זה כדלי לירש עמו, ק״ו עם בני עם ילחק, שםתיהן בו (שם): **(יא) על אודות בנו.** ששמע שילל לתרבות רעה (תנחומל שמות ל; שמות רבה ל:ל). ופשוטו, על שלומרת לו לשלחו: **(יב) שמע בקלה.** [בקול רוה״ק שבה (עי' רש״י לעיל טז:ב)] למדנו שהיה לברהם טפל לשרה בנביאות (שם ושם): **(יד) לחם וחמת מים.** ולל כסף וזהב, לפי שהיה שונלו על שילל לתרבות רעה (שם ושם): **ואת הילד.** לף הילד שם על שכמה, שהכניסה בו שרה עין רעה ולחזתו חמה ולל יכול לילך ברגליו (ב״ר שם יג): **ותלך ותתע.** חזרה לגלולי בית לביה (פדר״ל פ״ל): **(טו) ויכלו המים.** לפי שדרך חולים לשתות הרבה (ב״ר שם יג):

between the roots ירש and נחל explains what concerned Sarah. The verb נחל is used when an inheritance is divided among more than one heir, as in בְּיוֹם הַנְחִילוֹ אֶת־בָּנָיו, *the day when he will cause his sons to inherit* (*Deut.* 21:16); and עַל־פִּי הַגּוֹרָל תֵּחָלֵק, *According to the lot will its inheritance be divided* (*Num.* 26:56). The word ירש, however, indicates an inheritance taken by a single heir as in וְהִנֵּה בֶן־בֵּיתִי יוֹרֵשׁ אֹתִי, *and indeed the one in charge of my house inherits me* (15:3). [The expression is also used when a group of people inherits jointly.] Thus, Sarah's use of the words יירש indicates her fear. A division of the inheritance would not have concerned her, but she feared that Ishmael's superior physical prowess and his seniority would enable him to seize the *entire* inheritance for himself. Furthermore, any relationship with wicked people would have been harmful to Isaac and his children, as Abraham had recognized when he decided that he could not remain together with Lot.

11. עַל אוֹדֹת בְּנוֹ — *Regarding his son*. Abraham was distressed since Ishmael's behavior showed that he had fallen into evil ways [*Shemos Rabbah* 1]. The plain meaning is Abraham was upset because Sarah demanded that he drive him away (*Rashi*).

Presumably Abraham noticed the same things about Ishmael that Sarah did, but he must have felt that he should not let Ishmael leave the wholesome influence of his home. If Hagar had corrupted the boy in Abraham's home, surely it would be much worse if she were the sole influence over him (*R' Hirsch*).

14. וַיַּשְׁכֵּם — *Awoke early.* Just as Abraham awoke early to perform the commandment of circumcision, with alacrity and without delay, so he did now, and he would do so on his way to the *Akeidah* (22:3). Once he learned that the expulsion of Hagar and Ishmael was God's will, Abraham complied at once.

וַתֵּתַע — *And strayed.* Once Hagar was in the desert and away from Abraham's control (*Zohar Chadash, Ruth* 82a), she *strayed* back to the idolatry of her father's house (*Rashi*).

15-21. Ishmael is saved. The blessing that Ishmael would be a great nation was placed in jeopardy when he was near death in the desert, but he was saved through a miracle.

15. וַיִּכְלוּ הַמַּיִם — *When finished was the water.* Undoubtedly Abraham gave them enough water for the trip, but Ishmael became

וַתַּשְׁלֵךְ אֶת־הַיֶּלֶד תַּחַת אַחַד הַשִּׂיחִם: טז וַתֵּלֶךְ

< She went **16** << of the trees. < one < beneath < the boy < she cast off

וַתֵּשֶׁב לָהּ מִנֶּגֶד הַרְחֵק כִּמְטַחֲוֵי קֶשֶׁת כִּי אָמְרָה

<< she said, < for << of the bow, < of some shots < at a distance << opposite [him], < herself < and sat down

אַל־אֶרְאֶה בְּמוֹת הַיָּלֶד וַתֵּשֶׁב מִנֶּגֶד וַתִּשָּׂא

< she lifted << opposite [him]; < and she sat << *of the child;* < *the death* < *see* < *Let me not*

אֶת־קֹלָהּ וַתֵּבְךְּ: יז וַיִּשְׁמַע אֱלֹהִים אֶת־קוֹל הַנַּעַר

<< of the youth, < the cry < God heard **17** << and she wept. < her voice,

וַיִּקְרָא מַלְאַךְ אֱלֹהִים ׀ אֶל־הָגָר מִן־הַשָּׁמַיִם

< heaven < from < Hagar < to << of God — < — did an angel << and call

וַיֹּאמֶר לָהּ מַה־לָּךְ הָגָר אַל־תִּירְאִי כִּי־שָׁמַע אֱלֹהִים אֶל־קוֹל הַנַּעַר

<< *of the youth,* < *the cry* < *God has heard* < *for* << *fear,* < *Do not* << *Hagar?* < *[troubles]* < *What* << *to you,* < *and said her,*

בַּאֲשֶׁר הוּא־שָׁם: יח קוּמִי שְׂאִי אֶת־הַנַּעַר וְהַחֲזִיקִי אֶת־יָדֵךְ בּוֹ כִּי־

< *for* << *upon him,* < *your hand* < *with* < *and take hold* < *the youth,* < *lift up* < *Arise,* **18** << *there.* < *he is* < *as*

לְגוֹי גָּדוֹל אֲשִׂימֶנּוּ: יט וַיִּפְקַח אֱלֹהִים אֶת־עֵינֶיהָ וַתֵּרֶא בְּאֵר מַיִם וַתֵּלֶךְ

< she went << of water; < a well < and she perceived < her eyes < Then God opened **19** << *I will make him.* < *into a great nation*

וַתְּמַלֵּא אֶת־הַחֵמֶת מַיִם וַתַּשְׁקְ אֶת־הַנָּעַר: כ וַיְהִי אֱלֹהִים אֶת־הַנַּעַר

< the youth, < with < God was **20** << to the youth. < and she gave drink << with water, < the skin bottle < and she filled

וּרְמַת יָת רַבְיָא תְּחוֹת חַד מִן אִילָנַיָּא: טז וַאֲזַלַת וִיתִיבַת לַהּ מִקֳּבֵל אַרְחֵיקַת (נ״א אַרְחִיק) כְּמֵיגַד קַשְׁתָּא אֲרֵי אֲמֶרֶת לָא אֶחֱזֵי בְּמוֹתָא דְרַבְיָא וִיתִיבַת מִקֳּבֵל וַאֲרִימַת יָת קָלַהּ וּבְכָת: יז וּשְׁמִיעַ קֳדָם יְיָ יָת קָלֵהּ דְּרַבְיָא וּקְרָא מַלְאֲכָא דַייָ לְהָגָר מִן שְׁמַיָּא וַאֲמַר לַהּ מָא לִיךְ הָגָר לָא תִדְחֲלִי אֲרֵי שְׁמִיעַ קֳדָם יְיָ יָת קָלֵהּ דְּרַבְיָא בַּאֲתַר דְּהוּא תַמָּן: יח קוּמִי טוּלִי יָת רַבְיָא וְאַתְקִיפִי יָת יְדֵךְ בֵּהּ אֲרֵי לְעַם סַגִּי אֲשַׁוְּנֵהּ: יט וּגְלָא יְיָ יָת עֵינָהָא וַחֲזַת בֵּירָא דְמַיָּא וַאֲזַלַת וּמְלַת יָת רָקְבָּא מַיָּא וְאַשְׁקִיאַת יָת רַבְיָא: כ וַהֲוָה מֵימְרָא דַייָ בְּסַעֲדֵהּ דְּרַבְיָא

רש״י

(טז) **מנגד.** מרחוק: **במטחוי קשת.** כשתי טיחות (שם). והוא לשון יריית חץ, בלשון משנה, שהטיח באשתו (סנהדרין מו.) על שם שהזרע יורה כחץ. וא״ת, היה לו לכתוב כמטחי קשת, משפט הוי״ו ליכנס לכאן, כמו בחגוי הסלע (שיר השירים ב:יד) מגזרת והיתה אדמת יהודה למצרים לחגא (ישעיה יט:יז), ומגזרת יחוגו וינועו כשכור (תהלים קז:כז), וכן קצוי ארץ (שם סה:ו) מגזרת קצה: **ותשב מנגד.** כיון שקרב למות הוסיפה להתרחק: (יז) **את קול הנער.** מכאן שיפה תפלת החולה מתפלת אחרים עליו, והיא קודמת להתקבל (ב״ר שם יד): **באשר הוא שם.** לפי מעשים שהוא עושה עכשיו הוא נדון, ולא לפי מה שהוא עתיד לעשות (ר״ה השנה טז:). לפי שהיו מלאכי השרת מקטרגים ואומרים, רבש״ע, מי שעתיד זרעו להמית בניך בצמא אתה מעלה לו באר. והוא משיבם, עכשיו מה הוא, צדיק או רשע. אמרו לו, צדיק. אמר להם, לפי מעשיו של עכשיו אני דנו, וזהו באשר הוא שם (ב״ר שם). והיכן המית את ישראל בצמא, כשהגלם נבוכדנצר, שנאמר משא בערב וגו׳ לקראת צמא התיו מים וגו׳ (ישעיה כא:יג-יד). כשהיו מוליכין אותם אצל ערביים היו ישראל אומרים לשבאים, בבקשה מכם, הוליכונו אצל בני דודנו ישמעאל וירחמו עלינו, שנא׳ אורחות דדנים (שם). [אל תקרי דדנים אלא דודים.] ואלו יוצאים לקראתם ומביאין להם בשר ודג מלוח ונודות נפוחים. כסבורים ישראל שמלאים מים, וכשמכניסו לתוך פיו ופותחו, הרוח נכנס בגופו ומת (תנחומא יתרו ה; איכ״ר ב:ד):

ill and thirsty, so he drank copiously (*Rashi*). Alternatively, they became lost in the desert and used up the water (*Rashbam*).

16. **אַל־אֶרְאֶה** — *Let me not see.* Her behavior was disgraceful and indicative of her flawed character. Rather than comfort her child in his dying moments, she thought only of herself and the discomfort she would feel in the presence of his agony. Therefore, God heard *his* cry, not hers. Her loud weeping was selfish and therefore valueless (*R' Hirsch*).

17. **בַּאֲשֶׁר הוּא־שָׁם** — *As he is there.* According to the Midrash [see also *Rosh Hashanah* 16b], the angels pleaded with God not to perform a miracle for Ishmael, because in the future his offspring would persecute and murder Jews, but God responded that He would judge Ishmael only according to his present deeds and not according to what would happen in the future (*Rashi*).

19. **וַיִּפְקַח אֱלֹהִים אֶת־עֵינֶיהָ** — *Then God opened her eyes.* The Torah does not say that a well was created miraculously; the verse implies that her eyes were opened and she saw a well that had been there all along. This teaches that God always provides what we need, but we must be ready to open our eyes and see it (*Midrash*).

וַיִּגְדָּל וַיֵּשֶׁב בַּמִּדְבָּר וַיְהִי רֹבֶה קַשָּׁת: כא וַיֵּשֶׁב

‹ He dwelled 21 « an archer. ‹ a shooter [of arrows], ‹ and became ‹ in the desert ‹ he dwelled « and he grew up;

בְּמִדְבַּר פָּארָן וַתִּקַּח־לוֹ אִמּוֹ אִשָּׁה מֵאֶרֶץ מִצְרָיִם:

« of Egypt. ‹ from the land ‹ a wife ‹ his mother did, ‹ for him « and take ‹ of Paran, ‹ in the desert

פ ששי כב וַיְהִי בָּעֵת הַהִוא וַיֹּאמֶר אֲבִימֶלֶךְ וּפִיכֹל

‹ and Phicol, ‹ — Abimelech « that they said ‹ at that time ‹ It happened 22

שַׂר־צְבָאוֹ אֶל־אַבְרָהָם לֵאמֹר אֱלֹהִים עִמְּךָ בְּכֹל

‹ in all ‹ is with you ‹ God « saying, « Abraham, ‹ to « of his legion — ‹ general

אֲשֶׁר־אַתָּה עֹשֶׂה: כג וְעַתָּה הִשָּׁבְעָה לִּי בֵאלֹהִים

‹ by God ‹ to me ‹ swear ‹ So now 23 « do. ‹ you ‹ that

הֵנָּה אִם־תִּשְׁקֹר לִי וּלְנִינִי וּלְנֶכְדִּי כַּחֶסֶד אֲשֶׁר־

‹ that ‹ according to the kindness « nor with my grandchild; ‹ nor with my descendant ‹ with me ‹ deal falsely ‹ that you will not « here,

עָשִׂיתִי עִמְּךָ תַּעֲשֶׂה עִמָּדִי וְעִם־הָאָרֶץ אֲשֶׁר־גַּרְתָּה בָּהּ: כד וַיֹּאמֶר אַבְרָהָם

« Abraham said, 24 « in it. ‹ you have sojourned ‹ which ‹ the land, ‹ and with « with me, ‹ you shall do ‹ with you, ‹ I have done

אָנֹכִי אִשָּׁבֵעַ: כה וְהוֹכִחַ אַבְרָהָם אֶת־אֲבִימֶלֶךְ עַל־אֹדוֹת בְּאֵר הַמָּיִם

‹ of water ‹ to the well ‹ regard ‹ in ‹ with Abimelech ‹ Then Abraham disputed 25 « will swear. ‹ I

אֲשֶׁר גָּזְלוּ עַבְדֵי אֲבִימֶלֶךְ: כו וַיֹּאמֶר אֲבִימֶלֶךְ לֹא יָדַעְתִּי מִי עָשָׂה

‹ did ‹ who ‹ I do not know « Abimelech, ‹ Said 26 « of Abimelech did. ‹ — the servants « they seized ‹ that

אֶת־הַדָּבָר הַזֶּה וְגַם־אַתָּה לֹא־הִגַּדְתָּ לִּי וְגַם אָנֹכִי לֹא שָׁמַעְתִּי בִּלְתִּי

‹ except for ‹ heard [of it] ‹ have not ‹ I myself ‹ and moreover « me, ‹ told ‹ have never ‹ you ‹ furthermore, « this thing;

הַיּוֹם: כז וַיִּקַּח אַבְרָהָם צֹאן וּבָקָר וַיִּתֵּן לַאֲבִימֶלֶךְ וַיִּכְרְתוּ שְׁנֵיהֶם בְּרִית:

« a covenant. « — the two of them — « and they established « to Abimelech; ‹ and gave [them] ‹ and cattle ‹ sheep ‹ Abraham took 27 « today.

וּרְבָא וִיתֵב בְּמַדְבְּרָא וַהֲוָה רָבֵי קַשְׁתָּא: כא וִיתֵב בְּמַדְבְּרָא דְפָארָן וּנְסִיבַת לֵהּ אִמֵּהּ אִתְּתָא מֵאַרְעָא דְמִצְרָיִם: כב וַהֲוָה בְּעִדָּנָא הַהִיא וַאֲמַר אֲבִימֶלֶךְ וּפִיכֹל רַב חֵילֵהּ לְאַבְרָהָם לְמֵימַר מֵימְרָא דַייָ בְּסַעֲדָךְ בְּכֹל דִּי אַתְּ עָבֵד: כג וּכְעַן קַיֵּם לִי בְּמֵימְרָא דַייָ הָכָא דְּלָא תְשַׁקַּר בִּי וּבִבְרִי וּבְבַר בְּרִי כְּטִיבוּתָא דִּי עֲבָדִית עִמָּךְ תַּעְבֵּד עִמִּי וְעִם אַרְעָא דְּאִתּוֹתַבְתָּא בַהּ: כד וַאֲמַר אַבְרָהָם אֲנָא אֲקַיֵּם: כה וְאוֹכַח אַבְרָהָם יָת אֲבִימֶלֶךְ עַל עֵיסַק בֵּירָא דְמַיָּא דִּי אַנִּיסוּ עַבְדֵי אֲבִימֶלֶךְ: כו וַאֲמַר אֲבִימֶלֶךְ לָא יְדָעִית מָאן עֲבַד יָת פִּתְגָּמָא הָדֵין וְאַף אַתְּ לָא חַוֵּיתָ לִי וְאַף אֲנָא לָא שְׁמָעִית אֶלָּהֵן יוֹמָא דֵין: כז וּדְבַר אַבְרָהָם עָאן וְתוֹרִין וִיהַב לַאֲבִימֶלֶךְ וּגְזָרוּ תַרְוֵיהוֹן קְיָם:

רש"י

(כ) **רובה קַשָּׁת.** יורה חלים בקשת (פדר"א ל): **קַשָּׁת.** על שם האומנות, כמו חַמָּר, גַּמָּל, צַיָּד, לפיכך השי"ן מודגשת. היה יושב במדבר ומלסטס את העוברים, הוא שנאמר ידו בכל וגו' (לעיל טז:יב; תנחומא שמות ה; ב"ר נג:ח): **(כא) מארץ מצרים.** ממקום גדוליה, שנאמר ולה שפחה מצרית וגו' (לעיל טז:א). היינו דאמרי אינשי, זרוק חוטרא לאוירא אעיקריה קאי (ב"ר נג:טו): **(כב) אלהים עמך.** לפי שראו שיצא משכונת סדום לשלום, ועם המלכים נלחם ונפלו בידו, ונפקדה אשתו לזקוניו (ב"ר נד:ב): **(כג) ולניני ולנכדי.** עד כאן רחמי האב על הבן (שם): **כחסד אשר עשיתי עמך תעשה עמדי.** שאמרתי לך הנה ארצי לפניך (לעיל כ:טו; ב"ר שם): **(כה) והוכח.** נתוכח עמו

22-34. The alliance with Abimelech. These events occurred at the time of Isaac's birth. Knowing of all the miracles that God had done for Abraham, Abimelech came to seal a covenant with him (*Rashbam*). Abimelech stressed that he sought this treaty of friendship not because of Abraham's wealth or power, but because *God is with you in all that you do* (*Sforno*).

23. הִשָּׁבְעָה לִּי — *Swear to me.* While Abimelech demanded an oath of Abraham, he did not offer nor did Abraham request a reciprocal oath from him. Historically, the word of Abraham's descendants has been good, while the assurances made to them have been broken at will. Abraham and Abimelech both knew the worthlessness of such oaths (*R' Hirsch*).

כח וַיַּצֵּב אַבְרָהָם אֶת־שֶׁבַע כִּבְשֹׂת הַצֹּאן לְבַדְּהֶן׃

« by themselves. ‹ of the flock ‹ ewes ‹ seven ‹ Abraham set aside **28**

כט וַיֹּאמֶר אֲבִימֶלֶךְ אֶל־אַבְרָהָם מָה הֵנָּה שֶׁבַע

‹ *— the seven* « *are they* ‹ *What* « Abraham, ‹ to ‹ Abimelech said **29**

כְּבָשֹׂת הָאֵלֶּה אֲשֶׁר הִצַּבְתָּ לְבַדָּנָה׃ ל וַיֹּאמֶר כִּי

‹ *Because* « And he replied, **30** « *by themselves?* ‹ *you have set aside* ‹ *that* « *these —* ‹ *ewes,*

אֶת־שֶׁבַע כְּבָשֹׂת תִּקַּח מִיָּדִי בַּעֲבוּר תִּהְיֶה־לִּי

‹ *for me* ‹ *it may be* ‹ *so that* « *from my hand,* ‹ *you are to take* ‹ *ewes* ‹ *the seven*

לְעֵדָה כִּי חָפַרְתִּי אֶת־הַבְּאֵר הַזֹּאת׃ לא עַל־כֵּן קָרָא

‹ he called ‹ Therefore **31** « *this well.* ‹ *I dug* ‹ *that* ‹ *as testimony*

לַמָּקוֹם הַהוּא בְּאֵר שָׁבַע כִּי שָׁם נִשְׁבְּעוּ שְׁנֵיהֶם׃ לב וַיִּכְרְתוּ בְרִית בִּבְאֵר

‹ at Beer ‹ a covenant ‹ Thus, they established **32** « the two of them. ‹ they took an oath, ‹ there ‹ because « Beer Sheba, ‹ that place

שָׁבַע וַיָּקָם אֲבִימֶלֶךְ וּפִיכֹל שַׂר־צְבָאוֹ וַיָּשֻׁבוּ אֶל־אֶרֶץ פְּלִשְׁתִּים׃ לג וַיִּטַּע

‹ [Abraham] planted **33** « of the Philistines. ‹ the land ‹ to ‹ and they returned « of his legion, ‹ the general ‹ with Phicol, ‹ Abimelech arose « Sheba.

אֶשֶׁל בִּבְאֵר שָׁבַע וַיִּקְרָא־שָׁם בְּשֵׁם יהוה אֵל עוֹלָם׃ לד וַיָּגָר אַבְרָהָם

‹ And Abraham sojourned **34** « of the Universe. ‹ God ‹ of HASHEM, ‹ the Name ‹ there ‹ and he proclaimed « in Beer Sheba, ‹ an *eshel*

בְּאֶרֶץ פְּלִשְׁתִּים יָמִים רַבִּים׃ פ שביעי **[כב]** א וַיְהִי אַחַר הַדְּבָרִים הָאֵלֶּה

‹ these things ‹ after ‹ And it was **1** [22] « many years. ‹ of the Philistines ‹ in the land

כח וַאֲקִים אַבְרָהָם יָת שְׁבַע חוּרְפַּן דְּעָאן בִּלְחוֹדֵיהֶן׃ כט וַאֲמַר אֲבִימֶלֶךְ לְאַבְרָהָם מָה אִנּוּן שְׁבַע חוּרְפַּן אִלֵּין דַּאֲקֵמְתָּא בִּלְחוֹדֵיהֶן׃ ל וַאֲמַר אֲרֵי יָת שְׁבַע חוּרְפַּן תְּקַבֵּל מִן יְדִי בְּדִיל דִּתְהֵי לִי לְסַהֲדוּ אֲרֵי חֲפָרִית יָת בֵּירָא הָדֵין (נ״א הָדָא)׃ לא עַל כֵּן קְרָא לְאַתְרָא הַהוּא בְּאֵר שָׁבַע אֲרֵי תַמָּן קַיָּמוּ תַּרְוֵיהוֹן׃ לב וּגְזָרוּ קְיָם בִּבְאֵר שָׁבַע וְקָם אֲבִימֶלֶךְ וּפִיכֹל רַב חֵילֵהּ וְתָבוּ לַאֲרַע פְּלִשְׁתָּאֵי׃ לג וּנְצִיב נִצְבָּא (נ״א אִילָנָא) בִּבְאֵר שָׁבַע וְצַלִּי תַמָּן בִּשְׁמָא דַּייָ אֱלָהָא דְעָלְמָא׃ לד וְאִתּוֹתַב אַבְרָהָם בַּאֲרַע פְּלִשְׁתָּאֵי יוֹמִין סַגִּיאִין׃ א וַהֲוָה בָּתַר פִּתְגָמַיָּא הָאִלֵּין

רש״י

על כך (תרגום יונתן): **(ל) בעבור תהיה לי.** זאת: **לעדה.** לשון עדות של נקבה, כמו ועדה המצבה (להלן לא:נב): **כי חפרתי את הבאר.** מריבים היו עליה רועי אבימלך ואומרים אנחנו חפרנוה. אמרו ביניהם, כל מי שיתראה על הבאר ויעלו המים לקראתו שלו הוא, ועלו לקראת אברהם (ב״ר שם ה): **(לג) אשל.** רב ושמואל, חד אמר פרדס להביא ממנו פירות לאורחים בסעודה, וחד אמר פונדק לאכסניא ובו כל מיני מאכל [ס״א פירות]. ומצינו לשון נטיעה באהלים שנאמר ויטע אהלי אפדנו (דניאל יא:מה; ב״ר נד:ו; סוטה י.): **ויקרא שם וגו׳.** על ידי אותו אשל נקרא שמו של הקב״ה אלוה לכל העולם. לאחר שאוכלין ושותין אומר להם, ברכו למי שאכלתם משלו. סבורים אתם שמשלי אכלתם, משל מי שאמר והיה העולם אכלתם (סוטה י:): **(לד) ימים רבים.** מרובים על של חברון. בחברון עשה כ״ה שנה וכאן כ״ו, שהרי בן ע״ה שנה היה בצאתו מחרן, אותה שנה ויבא וישב באלוני ממרא (לעיל יג:יח). שלא מצינו קודם לכן שנתיישב אלא שם, שבכל מקומותיו היה כאורח, חונה ונוסע והולך, שנאמר ויעבור אברם (שם יב:ו) ויעתק משם (שם ח) ויהי רעב וירד אברם מצרימה (שם י). ובמצרים לא עשה אלא שלשה חדשים, שהרי שלחו פרעה מיד. וילך למסעיו (שם יג:ג) עד ויבא וישב באלוני ממרא אשר בחברון (שם יח), ושם ישב עד שנהפכה סדום. מיד, ויסע משם אברהם (שם כ:א) מפני בושה של לוט, ובא לארץ פלשתים, ובן צ״ט שנה היה, שהרי בשלישי למילתו באו אצלו המלאכים. הרי כ״ה שנה, וכאן כתיב ימים רבים, מרובים על הראשונים, ולא בא הכתוב לסתום אלא לפרש, ואם היו מרובים עליהם שתי שנים או יותר היה מפרשם, וע״כ אינם יתרים יותר משנה, הרי כ״ו שנה. מיד יצא משם וחזר לחברון, ואותה שנה קדמה לפני עקידתו של יצחק י״ב שנים. כך שנויה בסדר עולם (פ״א; ב״ר נד:ו): **(א) אחר הדברים האלה.** יש מרבותינו אומרים אחר דבריו של שטן, שהיה מקטרג ואומר מכל סעודה שעשה אברהם לא הקריב לפניך פר א׳ או איל א׳. אמר לו, כלום עשה

30. כִּי. . .תִּקַּח — *Because . . . you are to take.* Abraham wanted Abimelech to accept the gift as a token of his acknowledgment of Abraham's right to the well. This is similar to the ancient mode of acquisition of property through a symbolic barter effected by removing one's shoe and giving it to the other party [see notes to *Ruth* 4:7] (*Sforno*).

33. אֶשֶׁל — *An eshel.* The Talmudic Sages Rav and Shmuel differ as to the meaning of *eshel.* Rav understands it to mean that Abraham planted an *orchard,* whose fruits he served to wayfarers, while Shmuel interprets [figuratively] that it was an *inn for lodging*, in which he maintained a supply of fruit for wayfarers (*Rashi*). According to the figurative interpretation, אֶשֶׁל is an acrostic of the words אֲכִילָה, *eating;* שְׁתִיָּה, *drinking;* and לְוָיָה, *escorting* — the three basic services a host should provide his guests (*Rashi* to *Sotah* 10a).

34. The verse does not read וַיֵּשֶׁב אַבְרָהָם, *and Abraham settled,*

וְהָאֱלֹהִ֔ים נִסָּ֖ה אֶת־אַבְרָהָ֑ם וַיֹּ֣אמֶר אֵלָ֔יו אַבְרָהָ֖ם

‹‹ Abraham, ‹ to him, ‹ He said ‹‹ Abraham. ‹ tested ‹ that God

וַיֹּ֥אמֶר הִנֵּֽנִי׃ ב וַיֹּ֡אמֶר קַח־נָ֠א אֶת־בִּנְךָ֙ אֶת־יְחִֽידְךָ֤ אֲשֶׁר־אָהַ֙בְתָּ֙

‹‹ you love ‹ whom ‹ your only one, ‹ your son, ‹ please, ‹ Take, ‹ And He said, 2 ‹‹ Here I am. ‹ and he replied,

וַיְיָ נַסִּי יָת אַבְרָהָם וַאֲמַר לֵהּ אַבְרָהָם וַאֲמַר הָא אֲנָא: ב וַאֲמַר דְּבַר כְּעַן יָת בְּרָךְ יָת יְחִידָךְ דִּי רְחַמְתְּ

רש"י

אלא בשביל בנו, אילו הייתי אומר לו זבח אותו לפני לא היה מעכב. וי"א אחר דבריו של ישמעאל, שהיה מתפאר על יצחק שמל בן י"ג שנה ולא מיחה. אמר לו יצחק, באבר אחד אתה מיירא(ני), אילו אמר לי הקב"ה זבח עצמך לפני לא הייתי מעכב (סנהדרין פט:; ב"ר נה:ד): **הנני.** כך היא ענייתם של חסידים, לשון ענוה הוא ולשון זימון (תנחומא כב): **(ב) קח נא.** אין נא אלא לשון בקשה, אמר לו בבקשה ממך עמוד לי בזה הנסיון, שלא יאמרו הראשונות לא היה בהן ממש (שם; סנהדרין שם): **את בנך.** אמר לו שני בנים

which would imply *permanent residence*. Rather it uses the term וַיָּגָר, *sojourned,* as a גֵּר, *alien*. For, as *Rashi* points out (15:13), Abraham's years in the land of the Philistines after the birth of Isaac were reckoned as part of the 400 years during which his descendants were to be *aliens in a land not their own*.

22.

◆§ The tenth trial: The Akeidah/Binding of Isaac on the altar

This section epitomizes the Jew's determination to serve God no matter how difficult the circumstances, the very reason for Israel's existence (*Abarbanel*). This test was especially difficult because Abraham could not rationalize that Isaac deserved to die for having somehow been found unworthy or for becoming evil. This was decidedly not the case. Isaac's greatness was not only unchallenged, it was ratified by God when He identified Isaac as Abraham's only son, whom he loved (v. 2), implying that Isaac was still worthy of his exalted status. Moreover, human sacrifice is viewed as the antithesis of the *gemilas chesed,* lovingkindness, that had been a central doctrine of Abraham's service of God. Thus, his act of sacrificing Isaac would be seen by all as a refutation of Abraham's lifework. If so, Abraham's taking Isaac's life represented unquestioned obedience to God. Whether or not he could bring himself to do that was the test.

According to the accepted chronology, Isaac was 37 at the *Akeidah*. This is derived as follows: Sarah was 90 at his birth, and 127 at her death. Since she died when she heard that her son had been taken to be slaughtered (see introductory note to Ch. 23), he was 37 years old then.

Pesikta Rabbasi teaches that the *Akeidah* took place on Rosh Hashanah. Therefore it is the Torah reading for the second day of Rosh Hashanah, and the prayers of that day are filled with references to this supreme act. In return for Abraham's superhuman dedication to God, he was given the promise of Jewish survival and triumph that sustains us to this day.

For a discussion of the concept of trial, see the introduction to Chapter 12.

◆§ A List of the Ten Trials

The Sages state clearly that Abraham was tested ten times (*Avos* 5:3); however, there are several versions of what the tests were. Following are the lists of tests given by *Rashi* and *Rambam* in their commentaries to the above Mishnah:

Rashi

1. Abraham hid underground for thirteen years from King Nimrod, who wanted to kill him.
2. Nimrod flung Abraham into a burning furnace.
3. Abraham was commanded to leave his family and homeland.
4. Almost as soon as he arrived in Canaan, he was forced to leave to escape a famine.
5. Sarah was kidnaped by Pharaoh's officials.
6. The kings captured Lot, and Abraham was forced to go to war to rescue him.
7. God told Abraham that his offspring would suffer under four monarchies.
8. At an advanced age, he was commanded to circumcise himself and his son.
9. He was commanded to drive away Ishmael and Hagar.
10. He was commanded to sacrifice Isaac.

Rambam

1. Abraham's exile from his family and homeland.
2. The hunger in Canaan after God had assured him that he would become a great nation there.
3. The corruption in Egypt that resulted in Sarah's abduction.
4. The war with the four kings.
5. His marriage to Hagar after having despaired that Sarah would ever give birth.
6. The commandment of circumcision.
7. Abimelech's abduction of Sarah.
8. Driving away Hagar after she had given birth.
9. The very distasteful command to drive away Ishmael.
10. The binding of Isaac on the altar.

1. וְהָאֱלֹהִים נִסָּה — *That God tested.* This is the only one of Abraham's Ten Trials that the Torah explicitly calls a test, because the others were carried to completion as he understood them — Abraham actually left his homeland, sent away Ishmael, and so on — but this one remained nothing more than a test, because God did not permit Abraham to slaughter Isaac (*Abarbanel*).

The Midrash renders נִסָּה in the sense of *elevated,* like a נֵס, *banner,* that flies high above an army or ship. Hence the verse would be rendered: And God *exalted* Abraham, trial upon trial, greatness after greatness. Abraham could achieve nothing higher, and after these events we do not find God addressing Abraham again, for he had achieved the zenith of his potential.

2. קַח־נָא — *Take, please.* Since Abraham was 137 and Isaac was 37, there was no way Abraham could force Isaac to go. Rather, he was to take him by persuasion to do the will of God (*Zohar*).

God pleaded with Abraham to withstand this test, because otherwise people would say that his earlier sacrifices were without substance (*Rashi*).

בִּנְךָ — *Your son.* God did not immediately reveal to Abraham the clear identity of the intended offering. The Talmud records the conversation, as follows:

אֶת־יִצְחָק וְלֶךְ־לְךָ אֶל־אֶרֶץ הַמֹּרִיָּה וְהַעֲלֵהוּ

— Isaac — and get yourself to the land of Moriah; and bring him up

שָׁם לְעֹלָה עַל אַחַד הֶהָרִים אֲשֶׁר אֹמַר אֵלֶיךָ׃

there as an offering, upon one of the mountains which I shall indicate to you.

ג וַיַּשְׁכֵּם אַבְרָהָם בַּבֹּקֶר וַיַּחֲבֹשׁ אֶת־חֲמֹרוֹ וַיִּקַּח

3 Abraham rose early in the morning, and he saddled his donkey; he took

אֶת־שְׁנֵי נְעָרָיו אִתּוֹ וְאֵת יִצְחָק בְּנוֹ וַיְבַקַּע עֲצֵי עֹלָה וַיָּקָם וַיֵּלֶךְ

his two servants with him, and Isaac, his son. He split the wood for the offering, then he rose and went

אֶל־הַמָּקוֹם אֲשֶׁר־אָמַר־לוֹ הָאֱלֹהִים׃ ד בַּיּוֹם הַשְּׁלִישִׁי וַיִּשָּׂא אַבְרָהָם

toward the place which God indicated to him. 4 On the third day Abraham raised

יָת יִצְחָק וְאִיזֵיל לָךְ לְאַרְעָא פּוּלְחָנָא
וְאַסְקֵהּ (קֳדָמַי) תַּמָּן לַעֲלָתָא עַל
חַד (מִן) טוּרַיָּא דִּי אֵימָר לָךְ׃
ג וְאַקְדֵּים אַבְרָהָם בְּצַפְרָא וְזָרֵז יָת
חֲמָרֵהּ וּדְבַר יָת תְּרֵין עוּלֵימוֹהִי עִמֵּהּ
וְיָת יִצְחָק בְּרֵהּ וְצַלַּח אָעֵי דַעֲלָתָא
וְקָם וַאֲזַל לְאַתְרָא דִּי אֲמַר לֵהּ יְיָ׃
ד בְּיוֹמָא תְלִיתָאָה וּזְקַף אַבְרָהָם

רש"י

יש לי. אמר לו את יחידך. אמר לו זה יחיד לאמו וזה יחיד לאמו. אמר לו אשר אהבת. אמר לו שניהם אני אוהב. אמר לו את יצחק. ולמה לא גילה לו מתחלה, שלא לערבבו פתאום ותזוח דעתו עליו ותטרף. וכדי לחבב עליו את המצוה וליתן לו שכר על כל דבור ודבור (שם ושם;ב"ר שם ז): **ארץ המוריה.** ירושלים. וכן בדברי הימים (ב ג:א) לבנות את בית ה' בירושלים בהר המורי'. ורבותינו ז"ל פירשו על שם שמשם הוראה יוצאה לישראל (תענית טז.; ב"ר נה:ז). ואונקלוס תרגמו על שם עבודת הקטרת, שיש בו מור, נרד ושאר בשמים (ב"ר שם): **והעלהו** [**שם**]. לא אמר לו שחטהו, לפי שלא היה חפץ הקדוש ב"ה לשחטו אלא להעלותו להר [על מנת] לעשותו עולה, ומשהעלהו אמר לו הורידהו (ב"ר נו:ח): **אחד ההרים.** הקב"ה מתהא הצדיקים [ס"א משהא לצדיקים] ואח"כ מגלה להם, וכל זה כדי להרבות שכרן. וכן אל הארץ אשר אראך (לעיל יב:א), וכן ביונה (ג:ב) וקרא עליה את הקריאה (ב"ר נה:ז): (ג) **וישכם.** נזדרז למצוה (פסחים ד.; תנחומא שם): **ויחבש.** הוא בעצמו, ולא צוה לאחד מעבדיו, שהאהבה מקלקלת השורה (ב"ר שם ח): **את שני נעריו.** ישמעאל ואליעזר, שאין אדם חשוב רשאי לצאת לדרך בלא ב' אנשים, שאם יצטרך האחד לנקביו ויתרחק יהיה השני עמו (שם; ויק"ר כו:ז; תנחומא בלק ח): **ויבקע.** תרגומו וצלח, כמו וצלחו הירדן (שמואל ב יט:יח), לשון ביקוע, פינדר"א בלע"ז: (ד) **ביום השלישי.** למה איחר מלהראותו מיד, כדי שלא יאמרו הממו וערבבו פתאום וטרף דעתו, ואילו היה לו שהות להמלך אל לבו לא היה עושה (תנחומא כב):

God said, "Take your son."
"But I have *two* sons. Which should I take?"
"אֶת־יְחִידְךָ, *Your only one!"*
"But each of them is the only son of his mother."
"אֲשֶׁר־אָהַבְתָּ, *Whom you love!"* God answered.
"But I love them both."
"אֶת־יִצְחָק, I mean *Isaac,"* God replied.

There were two reasons why God did not say directly, "Take Isaac." First, He wanted to avoid giving a sudden command, lest Abraham be accused of complying in a state of disoriented confusion. [This is also a reason for having him travel for three days of reflection before carrying out the injunction.] Additionally, the slow unfolding of the offering's identity was to make the commandment more precious to Abraham, by arousing his curiosity and rewarding him for complying with every word of the command (*Sanhedrin* 89b; *Rashi*).

הַמֹּרִיָּה — *Moriah,* Jerusalem. The Sages explained that Jerusalem was so named because הוֹרָאָה, *teaching,* went forth from it to the world. *Onkelos* renders: *to the land of Divine Service.* Apparently he takes the word *Moriah* as derived from מוֹר, *myrrh*, one of the spices in the Temple incense mixture (*Rashi*).

וְהַעֲלֵהוּ — *Bring him up.* God did not say, "slaughter him," because He did not intend for Isaac to be slaughtered, but only that he be *brought up* to the mountain and be *prepared* as a burnt-offering. Once Abraham had complied literally and *brought him up,* God told him not to slaughter Isaac [v. 12]. This resolves the apparent contradiction between God's original command that Isaac be brought as an offering and His later order that he remain unharmed. Abraham had been commanded to *bring him up*, which he did, but not to actually slaughter him (*Rashi*).

In thinking that he was to slaughter Isaac, Abraham did not misunderstand God's first command, because the general rule is that once an animal is designated as an offering, the entire sacrificial service must be performed. For example, if someone were to sanctify an animal, he could not discharge his obligation merely by placing it on an altar and then taking it down. Only God could tell Abraham that Isaac was to be "brought up" but not slaughtered (*R' Chaim Soloveitchik).*

3. וַיַּשְׁכֵּם . . . וַיַּחֲבֹשׁ — *Rose early . . . and he saddled*. Excruciating though it must have been for him, Abraham did not delay. He woke up early in the morning and, ignoring his personal dignity, saddled the donkey personally instead of having it done by a servant. This demonstrates that the zealous hasten to perform their religious duty — which is why it is customary to perform circumcisions early in the morning, if possible (*Pesachim* 4a), and that love [of God] causes one to ignore the normal rules of personal conduct (*Sanhedrin* 105b). Some have noted as a tribute to Abraham's great presence of mind and equanimity that he was able to sleep that night.

שְׁנֵי נְעָרָיו — *His two young men.* Abraham took Eliezer and Ishmael, who had come to visit him (*Midrash*).

אֶת־עֵינָיו וַיַּרְא אֶת־הַמָּקוֹם מֵרָחֹק׃ ה וַיֹּאמֶר
his eyes, and perceived the place from afar. 5 Said

אַבְרָהָם אֶל־נְעָרָיו שְׁבוּ־לָכֶם פֹּה עִם־הַחֲמוֹר
Abraham to his young men, Stay [by] yourselves here with the donkey,

וַאֲנִי וְהַנַּעַר נֵלְכָה עַד־כֹּה וְנִשְׁתַּחֲוֶה וְנָשׁוּבָה
[while] I and the lad will go until there; we will prostrate ourselves and we will return

אֲלֵיכֶם׃ ו וַיִּקַּח אַבְרָהָם אֶת־עֲצֵי הָעֹלָה וַיָּשֶׂם עַל־
to you. 6 Abraham took the wood of the offering, and placed it on

יִצְחָק בְּנוֹ וַיִּקַּח בְּיָדוֹ אֶת־הָאֵשׁ וְאֶת־הַמַּאֲכֶלֶת
Isaac, his son. He took in his hand the fire and the knife,

וַיֵּלְכוּ שְׁנֵיהֶם יַחְדָּו׃ ז וַיֹּאמֶר יִצְחָק אֶל־אַבְרָהָם אָבִיו וַיֹּאמֶר אָבִי
and they went, the two of them together. 7 [Then] Isaac spoke to Abraham his father, and he said: My father!

וַיֹּאמֶר הִנֶּנִּי בְנִי וַיֹּאמֶר הִנֵּה הָאֵשׁ וְהָעֵצִים וְאַיֵּה הַשֶּׂה לְעֹלָה׃ ח וַיֹּאמֶר
And he said, Here I am, my son. And he said, Here are the fire and the wood, but where is the lamb for the offering? 8 Said

אַבְרָהָם אֱלֹהִים יִרְאֶה־לּוֹ הַשֶּׂה לְעֹלָה בְּנִי וַיֵּלְכוּ שְׁנֵיהֶם יַחְדָּו׃ ט וַיָּבֹאוּ
Abraham: God will seek out for Himself the lamb for the offering, my son. And they went, the two of them together. 9 They arrived

אֶל־הַמָּקוֹם אֲשֶׁר אָמַר־לוֹ הָאֱלֹהִים וַיִּבֶן שָׁם אַבְרָהָם אֶת־הַמִּזְבֵּחַ
at the place that God had indicated to him, and he built, there, Abraham did, the altar

יָת עֵינוֹהִי וַחֲזָא יָת אַתְרָא מֵרָחִיק: ה וַאֲמַר אַבְרָהָם לְעוּלֵימוֹהִי אוֹרִיכוּ לְכוֹן הָכָא עִם חֲמָרָא וַאֲנָא וְעוּלֵימָא נִתְמְטֵי עַד כָּא וְנִסְגּוּד וּנְתוּב לְוַתְכוֹן: ו וּנְסֵיב אַבְרָהָם יָת אָעֵי דַעֲלָתָא וְשַׁוִּי עַל יִצְחָק בְּרֵהּ וּנְסֵיב בִּידֵהּ יָת אֶשָּׁתָא וְיָת סַכִּינָא וַאֲזָלוּ תַּרְוֵיהוֹן כַּחֲדָא: ז וַאֲמַר יִצְחָק לְאַבְרָהָם אֲבוּהִי וַאֲמַר אַבָּא וַאֲמַר הָא אֲנָא בְרִי וַאֲמַר הָא אֶשָּׁתָא וְאָעַיָּא וְאָן אִימְרָא לַעֲלָתָא: ח וַאֲמַר אַבְרָהָם קֳדָם יְיָ גְּלֵי לֵהּ אִימְרָא לַעֲלָתָא בְּרִי וַאֲזָלוּ תַּרְוֵיהוֹן כַּחֲדָא: ט וַאֲתוֹ לְאַתְרָא דִּי אֲמַר לֵהּ יְיָ וּבְנָא תַמָּן אַבְרָהָם יָת מַדְבְּחָא

רש"י

וירא את המקום. ראה ענן קשור על ההר (שם כג; ב"ר נו:א): **(ה) עד כה.** כלומר, דרך מועט למקום אשר לפנינו. ומדרש אגדה, אראה היכן הוא מה שאמר לי המקום כה יהיה זרעך (לעיל טו:ה; שם ושם): **ונשובה.** נתנבא שישובו שניהם (שם ושם; מועד קטן יח.): **(ו) המאכלת.** סכין על שם שאוכלת את הבשר, כמה דתימא וחרבי תאכל בשר (דברים לב:מב), ושמכשרת בשר לאכילה. דבר אחר, זאת נקראת מאכלת, על שם שישראל אוכלים מתן שכרה (ב"ר שם ג): **וילכו שניהם יחדו.** אברהם שהיה יודע שהולך לשחוט את בנו היה הולך ברצון ושמחה כיצחק שלא היה מרגיש בדבר: **(ח) יראה לו השה.** כלומר יראה ויבחר לו השה (תרגום יונתן) ואם אין שה, **לעולה בני.** ואע"פ שהבין יצחק שהוא הולך להשחט, **וילכו שניהם יחדו,** בלב שוה (ב"ר שם ד; תרגום ירושלמי):

4. וַיַּרְא אֶת־הַמָּקוֹם מֵרָחֹק — *And perceived the place from afar.* Abraham saw a cloud hovering over the mountain and recognized it as signifying God's Presence (*Pirkei D'Rabbi Eliezer*). He said, "Isaac, my son, do you see what I see?" "Yes," Isaac said, and Abraham understood that Isaac had the degree of spiritual insight that made him worthy to be an offering.

He then turned to the two attendants and asked, "Do you see what I see?" They did not. Noting this, Abraham put them in the same category as his donkey (next verse) and said, in effect, "The donkey sees nothing and you see nothing, therefore, *stay here with the donkey.*"

5. וְנָשׁוּבָה — *And we will return.* The word is in the plural even though, since Abraham planned to sacrifice Isaac, he should have said, "and *I* will return to you." [Unwittingly] he prophesied that *both* of them would return (*Rashi*).

6. וַיֵּלְכוּ שְׁנֵיהֶם יַחְדָּו — *And they went, the two of them together,* in complete harmony. Abraham who knew that he was going to slay his son went with the same alacrity as Isaac who thought that he was joining his father in offering an animal. In verse 8, this phrase is repeated. By then, Isaac knew that he would be the offering, yet the two of them still walked together, with the same attitude and common purpose (*Rashi*), a tribute to them both.

7-8. וְאַיֵּה הַשֶּׂה — *But where is the lamb*. Until now Isaac did not know the true purpose of the journey, but as they walked toward the mountain with no animal in sight, he suspected the nature of the test, and he asked this probing question. Abraham answered

וַיַּעֲרֹךְ אֶת־הָעֵצִים וַיַּעֲקֹד אֶת־יִצְחָק בְּנוֹ וַיָּשֶׂם

‹ and he placed ‹ his son, ‹ Isaac, ‹ then he bound « the wood; ‹ and he arranged

אֹתוֹ עַל־הַמִּזְבֵּחַ מִמַּעַל לָעֵצִים: י וַיִּשְׁלַח אַבְרָהָם

‹ Abraham sent forth 10 « the wood. ‹ atop ‹ the altar ‹ on ‹ him

אֶת־יָדוֹ וַיִּקַּח אֶת־הַמַּאֲכֶלֶת לִשְׁחֹט אֶת־בְּנוֹ:

« his son. ‹ to slaughter ‹ the knife ‹ and took ‹ his hand

יא וַיִּקְרָא אֵלָיו מַלְאַךְ יהוה מִן־הַשָּׁמַיִם וַיֹּאמֶר

‹ and he said, « heaven, ‹ from ‹ of HASHEM ‹ an angel ‹ to him ‹ And there called 11

וְסַדַּר יָת אָעַיָּא וַעֲקַד יָת יִצְחָק בְּרֵהּ וְשַׁוִּי יָתֵהּ עַל מַדְבְּחָא עֵיל מִן אָעַיָּא: י וְאוֹשִׁיט אַבְרָהָם יָת יְדֵהּ וּנְסֵיב יָת סַכִּינָא לְמִיכַּס יָת בְּרֵהּ: יא וּקְרָא לֵהּ מַלְאֲכָא דַייָ מִן שְׁמַיָּא וַאֲמַר אַבְרָהָם אַבְרָהָם וַאֲמַר הָא אֲנָא: יב וַאֲמַר לָא תוֹשֵׁיט יְדָךְ לְעוּלֵימָא וְלָא תַעְבֵּד לֵהּ מִדָּעַם אֲרֵי כְעַן יְדַעְנָא (נ״א יְדָעִית) אֲרֵי דְחֲלָא דַייָ אַתְּ וְלָא מְנַעְתָּ יָת בְּרָךְ יָת יְחִידָךְ מִנִּי: יג וּזְקַף אַבְרָהָם יָת עֵינוֹהִי בָּתַר אִלֵּין וַחֲזָא וְהָא דִכְרָא

אַבְרָהָם | אַבְרָהָם וַיֹּאמֶר הִנֵּנִי: יב וַיֹּאמֶר אַל־תִּשְׁלַח יָדְךָ אֶל־הַנַּעַר וְאַל־

‹ *nor* ‹ *the lad* ‹ *against* ‹ *your hand* ‹ *send forth* ‹ *Do not* « And he said, 12 « *Here I am.* ‹ And he said, « *Abraham!* ‹ *Abraham!*

תַּעַשׂ לוֹ מְאוּמָה כִּי | עַתָּה יָדַעְתִּי כִּי־יְרֵא אֱלֹהִים אַתָּה וְלֹא חָשַׂכְתָּ

‹ *withheld* ‹ *since you have not* « *are you,* ‹ *of God* ‹ *a fearer* ‹ *that* ‹ *I know* ‹ *now* ‹ *for* « *anything,* ‹ *to him* ‹ *do*

אֶת־בִּנְךָ אֶת־יְחִידְךָ מִמֶּנִּי: יג וַיִּשָּׂא אַבְרָהָם אֶת־עֵינָיו וַיַּרְא וְהִנֵּה־אַיִל

« a ram! ‹ and there was « and saw, ‹ his eyes ‹ Abraham raised 13 « *from Me.* ‹ *your only one,* ‹ *your son,*

רש״י

(ט) **ויעקד.** ידיו ורגליו מאחוריו. הידים והרגלים ביחד היא עקידה (שבת נד.). והוא לשון עקודים (להלן ל:לט) שהיו קרסוליהם לבנים, מקום שעוקדים אותן בו היה ניכר (תרגום יונתן להלן ל:לט): (יא) **אברהם אברהם.** לשון חבה הוא, שכופל את שמו (ב״ר שם ז; ת״כ ויקרא א:א): (יב) **אל תשלח.** לשחוט. אמר לו א״כ לחנם באתי לכאן, אעשה בו חבלה ואוציא ממנו מעט דם. א״ל אל תעש לו מאומה, אל תעש בו מום (ב״ר שם): [**כי עתה ידעתי.** א״ר אבא, א״ל אברהם, אפרש לפניך את שיחתי. אתמול אמרת לי כי ביצחק יקרא לך זרע, וחזרת ואמרת קח נא את בנך, עכשיו אתה אומר לי אל תשלח ידך אל הנער. אמר לו הקב״ה, לא אחלל בריתי ומוצא שפתי לא אשנה (תהלים פט:לה). כשאמרתי לך קח, מוצא שפתי לא אשנה, לא אמרתי לך שחטהו אלא העלהו. אסקתיה, אחתיה (ב״ר שם ח):] **כי עתה ידעתי.** מעתה יש לי מה להשיב לשטן (סנהדרין פט:) ולאומות התמהים מה היא חיבתי אצלך. יש לי פתחון פה עכשיו, שרואים כי ירא אלהים אתה (תנחומא ישן מו, בחוקותי ז): (יג) **והנה איל.** מוכן היה

delicately, "*God will seek out for Himself the lamb,* but if there is no lamb, then you, *my son*, *will be the offering*." Then Isaac understood (*Rashi*). The much younger Isaac could have resisted or fled easily, but he walked on together with Abraham.

9. וַיַּעֲקֹד אֶת־יִצְחָק — *He bound Isaac.* Why did Abraham tie him? And could he bind a 37-year-old man without his consent? Isaac said: "Father, I am a vigorous young man and you are old. I fear that when I see the slaughtering knife in your hand I will instinctively jerk and possibly injure you. I might also injure myself and thus become unfit for the sacrifice. Or an involuntary movement by me might prevent you from performing the ritual slaughter properly. Therefore, bind me well, so that at the final moment I will not be deficient in filial honor and respect, and thereby not fulfill the commandment properly." Thereupon, Abraham immediately *bound Isaac, his son (Midrash)*.

10. וַיִּקַּח אֶת־הַמַּאֲכֶלֶת — *And took the knife.* The Sages depict movingly the intensity of the emotion that enveloped the participants. Abraham felt a mixture of joy in fulfilling God's will, but also sadness that his beloved son was about to die. As he reached for the knife, tears streamed from his eyes and fell into Isaac's. Yet he rejoiced to do God's will (*Midrash*).

Abraham looked at Isaac, and Isaac looked up at the angels on high. Isaac saw them, but Abraham did not (*Targum Yonasan*). The angels wept, too, as it were, and their tears fell into Isaac's eyes (*Rashi* to 27:1). The angels appealed, "Master of the Universe . . . was Abraham not hospitable to strangers, and did he not lead them into Your service by proclaiming You as the source of all blessing? Did not Sarah's menses return in Abraham's merit that she might give birth to Isaac? Will the promises made to Abraham regarding his offspring now be broken? Lo! the knife is at his throat. How long will You wait?" (*Pirkei D'Rabbi Eliezer*).

11. אַבְרָהָם אַבְרָהָם — *Abraham! Abraham!* The repetition of the name expressed love (*Rashi*), and urgency (*Midrash*).

13. וַיִּשָּׂא אַבְרָהָם אֶת־עֵינָיו — *Abraham raised his eyes,* to see if there was an animal he could offer in place of Isaac (*Radak*).

Abraham wanted to dedicate the lives of all his descendants, just as he had been ready to offer the life of his son. The "binding" of Isaac represented total submission to God's will; now Abraham sought to make this dedication eternal by bringing an offering in Isaac's place. Thus, the daily Temple offerings were a

אַחַר נֶאֱחַז בַּסְּבַךְ בְּקַרְנָיו וַיֵּלֶךְ אַבְרָהָם וַיִּקַּח
‹ and he took ‹ Abraham went ‹‹ by its horns. ‹ in the thicket ‹ caught ‹ —afterward,

אֶת־הָאַיִל וַיַּעֲלֵהוּ לְעֹלָה תַּחַת בְּנוֹ: יד וַיִּקְרָא
‹ He called 14 ‹‹ of his son. ‹ instead ‹ as an offering ‹ and he brought it ‹ the ram

אַבְרָהָם שֵׁם־הַמָּקוֹם הַהוּא יהוה ׀ יִרְאֶה אֲשֶׁר
‹ as ‹‹ *Yireh,* ‹ *HASHEM* ‹ of that site ‹ the name ‹ did Abraham

יֵאָמֵר הַיּוֹם בְּהַר יהוה יֵרָאֶה: טו וַיִּקְרָא מַלְאַךְ יהוה
‹ An angel of HASHEM called 15 ‹‹ *He will be seen.* ‹ *of HASHEM* ‹ *On the mountain* ‹‹ this day: ‹ it is said

אֶל־אַבְרָהָם שֵׁנִית מִן־הַשָּׁמָיִם: טז וַיֹּאמֶר בִּי
‹ *By Myself* ‹ and he said, 16 ‹‹ heaven ‹ from ‹ a second time ‹ Abraham ‹ to

נִשְׁבַּעְתִּי נְאֻם־יהוה כִּי יַעַן אֲשֶׁר עָשִׂיתָ אֶת־הַדָּבָר הַזֶּה וְלֹא חָשַׂכְתָּ
‹ *withheld* ‹ *and have not* ‹ *this thing* ‹ *you have done* ‹ *since* ‹ *that* ‹‹ *of HASHEM —* ‹ *— the word* ‹‹ *I swear*

אֶת־בִּנְךָ אֶת־יְחִידֶךָ: יז כִּי־בָרֵךְ אֲבָרֶכְךָ וְהַרְבָּה אַרְבֶּה אֶת־זַרְעֲךָ כְּכוֹכְבֵי
‹ *like the stars* ‹ *your offspring* ‹ *shall I increase* ‹ *and greatly* ‹ *I shall surely bless you* ‹ *that* 17 ‹‹ *your only one,* ‹ *your son,*

הַשָּׁמַיִם וְכַחוֹל אֲשֶׁר עַל־שְׂפַת הַיָּם וְיִרַשׁ זַרְעֲךָ אֵת שַׁעַר אֹיְבָיו:
‹‹ *of his enemies;* ‹ *the gates* ‹ *will your offspring* ‹ *and inherit* ‹‹ *of the sea;* ‹ *the shore* ‹ *is on* ‹ *that* ‹ *and like the sand* ‹ *of the heavens*

בָּתַר אֲחִיד בְּאִילָנָא בְּקַרְנוֹהִי וַאֲזַל אַבְרָהָם וּנְסֵיב יָת דִּכְרָא וְאַסְקֵהּ לַעֲלָתָא חֲלַף בְּרֵהּ: יד וּפְלַח וְצַלִּי אַבְרָהָם תַּמָּן בְּאַתְרָא הַהוּא וַאֲמַר קֳדָם יְיָ הָכָא יְהוֹן פָּלְחִין דָּרַיָּא בְּכֵן יִתְאֲמַר בְּיוֹמָא הָדֵין בְּטוּרָא הָדֵין אַבְרָהָם קֳדָם יְיָ פְּלַח: טו וּקְרָא מַלְאֲכָא דַיְיָ לְאַבְרָהָם תִּנְיָנוּת מִן שְׁמַיָּא: טז וַאֲמַר בְּמֵימְרִי קַיֵּמִית אֲמַר יְיָ אֲרֵי חֲלָף דִּי עֲבַדְתָּא יָת פִּתְגָּמָא הָדֵין וְלָא מְנַעְתָּא יָת בְּרָךְ יָת יְחִידָךְ: יז אֲרֵי בָרָכָא אֲבָרְכִנָּךְ וְאַסְגָּאָה אַסְגֵּי יָת בְּנָיךְ כְּכוֹכְבֵי שְׁמַיָּא וּכְחָלָא דִּי עַל כֵּיף יַמָּא וְיִרְתוּן בְּנָיךְ יָת קִרְוֵי סַנְאֵיהוֹן:

רש"י

לכך משעת ימי בראשית (אבות ה:ו): **אחר.** אחרי שאמר לו המלאך אל תשלח ידך ראהו כשהוא נאחז, והוא שמתרגמינן וזקף אברהם עינוהי בתר אלין. [ס"א, לפי האגדה, אחר כל דברי המלאך והשכינה ואחר טענותיו של אברהם]: **בסבך.** אילן (אונקלוס): **בקרניו.** שהיה רץ אצל אברהם והשטן סובכו ומערבבו באילנות [כדי לעכבו] (פדר"א פל"א): **תחת בנו.** מאחר שכתוב ויעלהו לעולה לא חסר המקרא כלום, ומהו תחת בנו, על כל עבודה שעשה ממנו היה מתפלל ואומר יה"ר שתהא זו כאילו היא עשויה בבני. כאילו בני שחוט, כאילו דמו זרוק, כאילו בני מופשט, כאילו הוא נקטר ונעשה דשן (ב"ר נו:ט; תנחומא שלח יד): **(יד) ה' יראה.** פשוטו כתרגומו, ה' יבחר ויראה לו את המקום הזה להשרות בו שכינתו ולהקריב כאן קרבנות: **אשר יאמר היום.** שיאמרו לימי הדורות עליו בהר זה יראה הקב"ה לעמו: **היום.** הימים העתידין, כמו עד היום הזה שבכל המקרא, שכל הדורות הבאים הקוראים את המקרא הזה אומרים עד היום הזה על היום שעומדים בו (סוטה מו:). ומ"א, ה' יראה עקידה זו לסלוח לישראל בכל שנה ולהצילם מן הפורענות, כדי שיאמר היום הזה בכל דורות הבאים בהר ה' יראה אפרו של יצחק צבור ועומד לכפרה (תנחומא כג; ירושלמי תענית ב:ה): **(יז) ברך אברכך.** אחת לאב ואחת לבן (ב"ר נו:יא): **והרבה ארבה.** אחת לאב ואחת לבן (שם):

national continuation of the *Akeidah* (*R' Hirsch*).

אַחַר נֶאֱחַז — *Afterward, caught.* After the preceding events, when the angel had told Abraham not to harm the lad, *he saw a ram caught in the thicket* (*Rashi*).

14. ה׳ יִרְאֶה — *HASHEM Yireh* [i.e., "*HASHEM will see*"]. The original name of the place was *Shalem*, the name given it by Shem, son of Noah — whom the Sages identify with Malchizedek, king of Jerusalem. After the *Akeidah,* Abraham called it *Yireh.* In deference to both Shem and Abraham, God synthesized both names and called it *Yerushalayim* (*Midrash*).

15. שֵׁנִית — *A second time.* Having sacrificed the ram and named the mountain, Abraham had turned this epochal event into the standard of behavior for his descendants. Only then did the angel reappear to announce the great blessing that lay in store (*R' Hirsch*).

16. בִּי נִשְׁבַּעְתִּי — *By Myself I swear.* Just as I am eternal, so My oath is eternal (*Radak*). God had already promised Abraham that his offspring would be as numerous as the stars (15:5) and the dust (13:16); now He assured Abraham that they would prevail over their enemies. Thus even if they were to sin grievously, they would never be completely destroyed or fall into the hands of their enemies permanently. Accordingly, this was a solemn assurance of Israel's ultimate redemption (*Ramban*).

17. כְּכוֹכְבֵי הַשָּׁמַיִם — *Like the stars of the heavens.* When Israel complies with God's will, they resemble the stars of the heavens; then no nation can dominate them. But when they flout His will, they resemble the sand of the seashore — trampled by every tyrannical foot (*Midrash Or HaAfelah*).

18 וְהִתְבָּרְכוּ בְזַרְעֲךָ כֹּל גּוֹיֵי הָאָרֶץ עֵקֶב אֲשֶׁר

18 and bless themselves / by your offspring / will all / the nations / of the earth, / because / you have

שָׁמַעְתָּ בְּקֹלִי׃ יט וַיָּשָׁב אַבְרָהָם אֶל־נְעָרָיו וַיָּקֻמוּ

listened / to My voice. / 19 Abraham returned / to / his young men, / and they rose

וַיֵּלְכוּ יַחְדָּו אֶל־בְּאֵר שָׁבַע וַיֵּשֶׁב אַבְרָהָם בִּבְאֵר

and went / together / to / Beer Sheba, / and Abraham stayed / at Beer

שָׁבַע׃ פ מפטיר כ וַיְהִי אַחֲרֵי הַדְּבָרִים הָאֵלֶּה וַיֻּגַּד

Sheba. / 20 It happened / after / these things, / that it was told

לְאַבְרָהָם לֵאמֹר הִנֵּה יָלְדָה מִלְכָּה גַם־הִוא בָּנִים

to Abraham, / saying: / Behold, / Milcah has given birth / —also / she— / children, / to

לְנָחוֹר אָחִיךָ׃ כא אֶת־עוּץ בְּכֹרוֹ וְאֶת־בּוּז אָחִיו וְאֶת־קְמוּאֵל אֲבִי אֲרָם׃

unto Nahor, / your brother: / 21 Uz, / his firstborn, / Buz, / his brother; / Kemuel, / the father / of Aram;

כב וְאֶת־כֶּשֶׂד וְאֶת־חֲזוֹ וְאֶת־פִּלְדָּשׁ וְאֶת־יִדְלָף וְאֵת בְּתוּאֵל׃ כג וּבְתוּאֵל

22 and Chesed, / Hazo, / Pildash, / Jidlaph, / and Bethuel. / 23 And Bethuel

יָלַד אֶת־רִבְקָה שְׁמֹנָה אֵלֶּה יָלְדָה מִלְכָּה לְנָחוֹר אֲחִי אַבְרָהָם׃

begot / Rebecca; / these eight / Milcah bore / to Nahor, / the brother / of Abraham.

כד וּפִילַגְשׁוֹ וּשְׁמָהּ רְאוּמָה וַתֵּלֶד גַּם־הִוא אֶת־טֶבַח וְאֶת־גַּחַם

24 And his concubine, / whose name / was Reumah, / she gave birth / —also / she— / to Tebah, / Gaham,

וְאֶת־תַּחַשׁ וְאֶת־מַעֲכָה׃ פפפ קמ"ז פסוקים. אמנו"ן סימן.

Tahash / and Maachah.

יח וְיִתְבָּרְכוּן בְּדִיל בְּנָךְ כֹּל עַמְמַיָּא דְאַרְעָא חֲלָף דִּי קַבֵּלְתָּא בְּמֵימְרִי׃ יט וְתַב אַבְרָהָם לְעוּלֵימוֹהִי וְקָמוּ וַאֲזָלוּ כַּחֲדָא לִבְאֵר שָׁבַע וִיתֵיב אַבְרָהָם בִּבְאֵר שָׁבַע׃ כ וַהֲוָה בָּתַר פִּתְגָמַיָּא הָאִלֵּין וְאִתְחֲוָא לְאַבְרָהָם לְמֵימָר הָא יְלֵידַת מִלְכָּה אַף הִיא בְּנִין לְנָחוֹר אָחוּךְ׃ כא יָת עוּץ בּוּכְרֵהּ וְיָת בּוּז אָחוּהִי וְיָת קְמוּאֵל אֲבוּהִי דַאֲרָם׃ כב וְיָת כֶּשֶׂד וְיָת חֲזוֹ וְיָת פִּלְדָּשׁ וְיָת יִדְלָף וְיָת בְּתוּאֵל׃ כג וּבְתוּאֵל אוֹלִיד יָת רִבְקָה תְּמַנְיָא אִלֵּין יְלֵידַת מִלְכָּה לְנָחוֹר אֲחוּהִי דְאַבְרָהָם׃ כד וּלְחֵנָתֵהּ וּשְׁמַהּ רְאוּמָה וִילֵידַת אַף הִיא יָת טֶבַח וְיָת גַּחַם וְיָת תַּחַשׁ וְיָת מַעֲכָה׃

THE HAFTARAH FOR VAYEIRA APPEARS ON PAGE 328.

רש"י

(יט) וישב אברהם בבאר שבע. לא ישיבה ממש, שהרי בחברון היה יושב, י"ב שנים לפני עקידתו של יצחק יצא מבאר שבע והלך לו לחברון, כמו שנא' ויגר אברהם בארץ פלשתים ימים רבים (לעיל כא:לד) מרובים משל חברון הראשונים, והם כ"ו שנה כמו שפירשנו למעלה (כא:לד): **(כ) אחרי הדברים האלה ויוגד וגו'.** בשובו מהר המוריה היה אברהם מהרהר ואומר אילו היה בני שחוט כבר היה הולך בלא בנים, היה לי להשיאו אשה מבנות ענר אשכול וממרא. בשרו הקב"ה שנולדה רבקה בת זוגו, וזהו הדברים האלה, הרהורי דברים שהיו ע"י עקידה (ב"ר נז:ג): **גם היא.** אף היא השוותה משפחותיה למשפחות אברהם י"ב. מה אברהם י"ב שבטים, שילאו מיעקב ח' בני הגבירות וד' בני שפחות, אף אלו ח' בני גבירות וד' בני פלגש (שם): **(כג) ובתואל ילד את רבקה.** כל היחוסין הללו לא נכתבו אלא בשביל פסוק זה (שם):

18. וְהִתְבָּרְכוּ בְזַרְעֲךָ — *And bless themselves by your offspring.* The nations will pray to God: "Bless us as You have blessed the offspring of Abraham" (*Radak*).

20-23. The birth of Rebecca. The birth of Rebecca at this time is another instance of the Divine Providence with which the story of the Patriarchs is replete. Isaac, who had gained the status of a "perfect offering," did not now have to marry a debauched Canaanite woman. To accentuate this fact, the Torah did not mention the genealogy of Nahor's family until now.

קמ"ז פסוקים. אמנו"ן סימן — This Masoretic note means: The *Sidrah* contains 147 verses, numerically corresponding to the mnemonic אַמְנוֹן [= 147].

This is apparently a reference to the profound אֱמוּנָה, *faithfulness*, of Abraham, which is the primary theme of the *Sidrah*. This faithfulness reached its zenith when he was commanded to sacrifice the son through whom his every future promise was to have been fulfilled. Yet his faith in God was so complete that he complied unhesitatingly (*R' David Feinstein*).

PARASHAS CHAYEI SARAH / פרשת חיי שרה

[כג] א וַיִּהְיוּ֙ חַיֵּי שָׂרָה מֵאָה שָׁנָה וְעֶשְׂרִים

< and twenty < years, < one hundred << of Sarah – < – the lifetime << And they were 1 23

שָׁנָה וְשֶׁבַע שָׁנִים שְׁנֵי חַיֵּי שָׂרָה׃ ב וַתָּמָת שָׂרָה

< Sarah died 2 << of Sarah. < of the lifetime < the years << years; < and seven < years,

בְּקִרְיַת אַרְבַּע הִוא חֶבְרוֹן בְּאֶרֶץ כְּנָעַן וַיָּבֹא֙ אַבְרָהָם לִסְפֹּד לְשָׂרָה

< Sarah < to eulogize < and Abraham came << of Canaan; < in the land < Hebron < which is < in Kiriath-arba

וְלִבְכֹּתָהּ׃* ג וַיָּקָם֙ אַבְרָהָם מֵעַל פְּנֵי מֵתוֹ וַיְדַבֵּר אֶל־בְּנֵי־חֵת לֵאמֹר׃

<< saying: < of Heth, < the Sons < to < and spoke < of his dead, < the face < from upon < Abraham rose up 3 << and to weep for her.

* כ׳ זעירא

אונקלוס

א וַהֲווֹ חַיֵּי שָׂרָה מְאָה וְעֶשְׂרִין וּשְׁבַע שְׁנִין שְׁנֵי חַיֵּי שָׂרָה: ב וּמִיתַת שָׂרָה בְּקִרְיַת אַרְבַּע הִיא חֶבְרוֹן בְּאַרְעָא דִכְנָעַן וַאֲתָא אַבְרָהָם לְמִסְפְּדַהּ לְשָׂרָה וּלְמִבְכְּיַהּ: ג וְקָם אַבְרָהָם מֵעַל אַפֵּי מִיתֵהּ וּמַלֵּיל עִם בְּנֵי חִתָּאָה לְמֵימָר:

רש״י

(א) ויהיו חיי שרה מאה שנה ועשרים שנה ושבע שנים. לכך נכתב שנה בכל כלל וכלל, לומר לך שכל אחד נדרש לעצמו. בת ק׳ כבת כ׳ לחטא, מה בת כ׳ לא חטאה, שהרי אינה בת עונשין, אף בת ק׳ בלא חטא, ובת כ׳ כבת ז׳ ליופי (ב״ר נח:א): **שני חיי שרה.** כלן שוין לטובה: **(ב) בקרית ארבע.** על שם ארבעה ענקים שהיו שם, אחימן ששי ותלמי ואביהם (ב״ר נח:ד). דבר אחר, על שם ארבעה זוגות שנקברו שם איש ואשתו, אדם וחוה. אברהם ושרה, יצחק ורבקה, יעקב ולאה (פדר״א פ״כ): **ויבא אברהם.** מבאר שבע: **לספוד לשרה ולבכתה.** ונסמכה מיתת שרה לעקידת יצחק, לפי שע״י בשורת העקידה שנזדמן בנה לשחיטה וכמעט שלא נשחט, פרחה

PARASHAS CHAYEI SARAH

23.

The *Sidrah* shows Jewish respect for the dead and concern for the future. These are essential concepts in Judaism; we neither reject what has gone before nor neglect what lies ahead. The narrative begins with the death of Sarah and Abraham's intense desire to give her a proper burial in a place worthy of her greatness. To acquire the fitting burial plot, he was forced to negotiate with the transparently greedy Ephron and gladly paid an exorbitant price. That accomplished, Abraham looked ahead and turned to the responsibility of finding the proper wife for Isaac.

⇐§ Sarah's life span, and purchase of a burial site.

The Sages teach that the narratives of Sarah's death and the *Akeidah* follow each other to indicate that she died as a result of that event. She was told by Satan that Abraham had actually slaughtered Isaac, and she cried out in grief and died (*Targum Yonasan*). This explains why Abraham and Isaac were not present at her death.

R' Yaakov Kamenetsky explained that this cannot mean that Sarah died "accidentally" before her time, because, in connection with Sarah's life span, the Sages teach that Isaac had to anticipate his own possible death when he came to within five years of the age at which she died (see comm. to 27:2). This dictum could not have applied to Sarah if her death was not natural. Rather, the sense of the *Targum Yonasan* is that Sarah's time had come in any case, but that the immediate cause of death was the news of the *Akeidah*. Some commentators say that her last breath came with the proud knowledge that she had succeeded in raising a son who was willing to give up even his life in the service of God.

In addition, the Torah records the birth of Rebecca before the death of Sarah in line with the tradition that a righteous person is not taken from the world until his or her successor has been born, as implied by the verse (*Ecclesiastes* 1:5), *The sun rises and the sun sets (Sforno, Baal HaTurim).*

1. . . . מֵאָה שָׁנָה — *One hundred years, twenty years, and seven years. Rashi* explains that the repetition of *years* divides Sarah's life into three periods, each with its own uniqueness [and each period shared the particular characteristic of its neighbor]. At a hundred she was as sinless as a 20-year-old, for until the age of 20, a person does not suffer Heavenly punishment. And at 20 she still had the wholesome beauty of a 7-year-old, who does not use cosmetics and whose beauty is natural (*Chizkuni*). *R' Moshe Feinstein* commented that a child's beauty is pure and is never used to tempt others to go astray. Part of Sarah's greatness was that, despite her breathtaking beauty as an adult, all who saw her recognized her purity and innocence.

2. בְּקִרְיַת אַרְבַּע — *In Kiriath-arba* [lit., *the City of Four*]. The city was so named because four giants lived there (see *Numbers* 13:22); or the name was given prophetically because four illustrious couples would be buried there: Adam and Eve, Abraham and Sarah, Isaac and Rebecca, and Jacob and Leah (*Rashi*).

לִסְפֹּד לְשָׂרָה וְלִבְכֹּתָהּ — *To eulogize Sarah and to weep for her.* The nuances of the phrase denote that Abraham eulogized his beloved wife by emphasizing the noble traits that had become associated with her name, for the name Sarah represented her as the princess of all mankind [see comm. to 17:15] (*Kli Yakar).*

The word וְלִבְכֹּתָהּ is written with a small כ to suggest that the full extent of his weeping was kept private. His grief was infinite, but the full measure of his pain was concealed in his heart and the privacy of his home (*R' Hirsch*).

3. Abraham turned from his tears to provide for Sarah's burial. To purchase a grave site, he needed the cooperation of the de-

ד גֵּר־וְתוֹשָׁב אָנֹכִי עִמָּכֶם תְּנוּ לִי אֲחֻזַּת־קֶבֶר

‹ for a burial site ‹ legal possession [of land] ‹ me ‹ grant ‹‹ among you; ‹ am I ‹ and a resident ‹ An alien 4

עִמָּכֶם וְאֶקְבְּרָה מֵתִי מִלְּפָנָי: ה וַיַּעֲנוּ בְנֵי־חֵת

‹ And the Sons of Heth answered 5 ‹‹ from before me. ‹ my dead ‹ then I will bury ‹ with you,

אֶת־אַבְרָהָם לֵאמֹר לוֹ: ו שְׁמָעֵנוּ | אֲדֹנִי נְשִׂיא

‹ A prince ‹‹ my lord: ‹ Hear us, 6 ‹‹ to him: ‹ saying ‹ Abraham,

אֱלֹהִים אַתָּה בְּתוֹכֵנוּ בְּמִבְחַר קְבָרֵינוּ קְבֹר

‹ bury ‹ of our burial places ‹ in the choicest ‹‹ in our midst; ‹ are you ‹ of God

אֶת־מֵתֶךָ אִישׁ מִמֶּנּוּ אֶת־קִבְרוֹ לֹא־יִכְלֶה מִמְּךָ

‹ from you, ‹ will not withhold ‹ his burial place ‹ of us ‹ [each] man ‹‹ your dead,

מִקְּבֹר מֵתֶךָ: ז וַיָּקָם אַבְרָהָם וַיִּשְׁתַּחוּ לְעַם־הָאָרֶץ לִבְנֵי־חֵת: ח וַיְדַבֵּר

‹ He spoke 8 ‹‹ of Heth. ‹ to the Sons ‹ of the land, ‹ to the [representatives] of the people ‹ and bowed ‹ [Then] Abraham rose up 7 ‹‹ your dead. ‹ from burying

אִתָּם לֵאמֹר אִם־יֵשׁ אֶת־נַפְשְׁכֶם לִקְבֹּר אֶת־מֵתִי מִלְּפָנַי שְׁמָעוּנִי

‹ heed me, ‹‹ from before me, ‹ my dead ‹ to bury ‹ your soul [the will] ‹ within ‹ [you] have ‹ If ‹‹ saying: ‹ with them

וּפִגְעוּ־לִי בְּעֶפְרוֹן בֶּן־צֹחַר: ט וְיִתֶּן־לִי אֶת־מְעָרַת הַמַּכְפֵּלָה אֲשֶׁר־לוֹ

‹‹ his, ‹ which is ‹ of Machpelah ‹ the Cave ‹ to me ‹ Let him grant 9 ‹‹ of Zohar. ‹ son ‹ with Ephron ‹ for me ‹ and intercede

אֲשֶׁר בִּקְצֵה שָׂדֵהוּ בְּכֶסֶף מָלֵא יִתְּנֶנָּה לִּי בְּתוֹכְכֶם לַאֲחֻזַּת־קָבֶר:

‹‹ for a burial site. ‹ as [land] legally possessed ‹ in your midst, ‹ to me ‹ let him grant it ‹ in full ‹ for [its] price ‹‹ of his field; ‹ on the edge ‹ which is

ד דַּיָּר וְתוֹתַב אֲנָא עִמְּכוֹן הָבוּ לִי אַחְסָנַת קְבוּרָא עִמְּכוֹן וְאֶקְבַּר מִיתִי מִן קֳדָמָי: ה וְאָתִיבוּ בְנֵי חִתָּאָה יָת אַבְרָהָם לְמֵימַר לֵהּ: ו קַבֵּל מִנָּנָא רִבּוֹנָנָא רַב קֳדָם יְיָ אַתְּ בֵּינָנָא בִּשְׁפַר קִבְרָנָא קְבַר יָת מִיתָךְ אֱנָשׁ מִנָּנָא יָת קִבְרֵהּ לָא יִכְלֵי (נ״א יִמְנַע) מִנָּךְ מִלְּמִקְבַּר מִיתָךְ: ז וְקָם אַבְרָהָם וּסְגִיד לְעַמָּא דְאַרְעָא לִבְנֵי חִתָּאָה: ח וּמַלֵּיל עִמְּהוֹן לְמֵימַר אִם אִית רַעֲוָא (בְ)נַפְשְׁכוֹן לְמִקְבַּר יָת מִיתִי מִן קֳדָמַי קַבִּילוּ מִנִּי וּבְעוּ לִי מִן עֶפְרוֹן בַּר צוֹחַר: ט וְיִתֶּן לִי יָת מְעָרַת כָּפֶלְתָּא דִּי לֵהּ דִּי בִּסְטַר חַקְלֵהּ בִּכְסַף שְׁלִים יִתְנִנַּהּ לִי בֵּינֵיכוֹן לְאַחְסָנַת קְבוּרָא:

רש״י

נשמתה ממנה ומתה (תנחומא סוף וירא; פדר״א פל״ב): (ד) **גר ותושב אנכי עמכם.** גר מארץ אחרת ונתישבתי עמכם. ומדרש אגדה, אם תרצו הריני גר, ואם לאו אהיה תושב ואטלנה מן הדין, שאמר לי הקב״ה לזרעך אתן את הארץ הזאת (לעיל יב:ז; ב״ר נח:ו): **אחזת קבר.** אחוזת קרקע לבית הקברות: (ו) **לא יכלה.** לא ימנע (אונקלוס), כמו לא תכלא רחמיך (תהלים מ:יב), וכמו ויכלא הגשם (לעיל ח:ב): (ח) **נפשכם.** רצונכם: **ופגעו לי.** לשון בקשה, כמו אל תפגעי בי (רות א:טז): (ט) **המכפלה.** בית ועלייה על גביו. ד״א, שכפולה בזוגות (עירובין נג.): **בכסף מלא.** שלם, [ס״א אשלם] כל שוויה, וכן דוד אמר לארונה בכסף מלא (דברי הימים א כא:כד):

scendants of Heth, the son of Canaan (10:15), who were the leaders of the region.

4. גֵּר־וְתוֹשָׁב — *An alien and a resident*, I am both an *alien* from another land and a *resident* who has settled among you (*Rashi*).

Abraham expressed the dual role that every Jew must play. On the one hand, he is a *resident* of his country, and as such he must work and pray for its welfare, as Jeremiah urged his people on the threshold of exile (*Jeremiah* 29:7). But on the other hand, the Jew in this world is always an *alien*, for his allegiance is to God and his goals are set forth by the Torah. A Jew must always be ready to be a lonely alien, resisting the culture that surrounds him and maintaining his unique responsibility (*R' Yosef Dov Soloveitchik*).

7-9. Abraham bowed in gratitude for their generous response and entreated further, specifying which plot he wanted.

Since it would have been unseemly for the rich and distinguished Ephron to sell his ancestral inheritance, Abraham did not approach him directly with an offer to buy the field. Instead, he asked the people of the city to entreat Ephron dignifiedly on his behalf. Abraham asked for it as a "gift," to indicate that even though he was ready to pay handsomely for the plot, he would still consider it a gift (*Ramban*).

9. מְעָרַת הַמַּכְפֵּלָה — *The Cave of Machpelah.* The word *machpelah* means *double*. The cave was so called either because it contained two chambers, an upper and a lower level, or on account of the זוגות, *couples*, who were [to be] buried there (*Rashi*).

י וְעֶפְרוֹן יֹשֵׁב בְּתוֹךְ בְּנֵי־חֵת וַיַּעַן עֶפְרוֹן הַחִתִּי
< and Ephron the Hittite responded << of Heth; < of the Sons < in the midst < was sitting < Now, Ephron 10

אֶת־אַבְרָהָם בְּאָזְנֵי בְנֵי־חֵת לְכֹל בָּאֵי שַׁעַר־עִירוֹ
< of his city, < to the gate < who come < for all < of Heth, < of the Sons < within earshot < to Abraham

לֵאמֹר: יא לֹא־אֲדֹנִי שְׁמָעֵנִי הַשָּׂדֶה נָתַתִּי לָךְ
< *you,* < *I have granted* < *The field* << *hear me!* << *my lord;* < *No,* 11 << saying:

וְהַמְּעָרָה אֲשֶׁר־בּוֹ לְךָ נְתַתִּיהָ לְעֵינֵי בְנֵי־עַמִּי
< *of my people* < *of the sons* < *before the eyes* << *I have granted it;* < *to you* << *is in it,* < *that* < *and as for the cave*

נְתַתִּיהָ לָּךְ קְבֹר מֵתֶךָ: יב וַיִּשְׁתַּחוּ אַבְרָהָם לִפְנֵי עַם־הָאָרֶץ: יג וַיְדַבֵּר
< He spoke 13 << of the land. < the [representatives] of the people < before < Abraham bowed 12 << *your dead.* < *bury* < *to you;* < *have I granted it*

אֶל־עֶפְרוֹן בְּאָזְנֵי עַם־הָאָרֶץ לֵאמֹר אַךְ אִם־אַתָּה לוּ שְׁמָעֵנִי נָתַתִּי
<< *'I have granted' [you said];* << *hear me!* < *would only* < *you* < *if* < *Rather,* << saying: < of the land < of the [representatives] of the people < within earshot < Ephron < to

כֶּסֶף הַשָּׂדֶה קַח מִמֶּנִּי וְאֶקְבְּרָה אֶת־מֵתִי שָׁמָּה: יד וַיַּעַן עֶפְרוֹן
< And Ephron replied 14 << *there.* < *my dead* < *then I will bury* < *from me,* < *take* < *of the field* < *[rather] the price*

אֶת־אַבְרָהָם לֵאמֹר לוֹ: טו אֲדֹנִי שְׁמָעֵנִי אֶרֶץ אַרְבַּע מֵאֹת שֶׁקֶל־כֶּסֶף
<< *of silver —* < *shekels* < *hundred* < *[worth] four* < *Land* << *hear me!* < *My lord,* 15 << to him: < saying < to Abraham,

י וְעֶפְרוֹן יָתֵב בְּגוֹ בְּנֵי חִתָּאָה וַאֲתֵיב עֶפְרוֹן חִתָּאָה יָת אַבְרָהָם קֳדָם בְּנֵי חִתָּאָה לְכָל עָלֵי תְּרַע קַרְתֵּהּ לְמֵימָר: יא לָא רִבּוֹנִי קַבֵּיל מִנִּי חַקְלָא יְהָבִית לָךְ וּמְעַרְתָּא דִּי בֵהּ לָךְ יְהָבִיתַהּ לְעֵינֵי בְנֵי עַמִּי יְהָבִיתַהּ לָךְ קְבַר מִיתָךְ: יב וּסְגִיד אַבְרָהָם קֳדָם עַמָּא דְאַרְעָא: יג וּמַלִּיל עִם עֶפְרוֹן קֳדָם עַמָּא דְאַרְעָא לְמֵימָר בְּרַם אִם אַתְּ עָבֵד לִי טִיבוּ קַבֵּל מִנִּי אֶתֵּן כַּסְפָּא דְמֵי חַקְלָא סַב מִנִּי וְאֶקְבַּר יָת מִיתִי תַּמָּן: יד וַאֲתֵיב עֶפְרוֹן יָת אַבְרָהָם לְמֵימַר לֵהּ: טו רִבּוֹנִי קַבֵּל מִנִּי אַרְעָא שַׁוְיָא אַרְבַּע מְאָה סִלְעִין דִּכְסַף

רש"י

(י) **ועפרון ישב.** כתיב חסר, אותו היום מנוהו שוטר עליהם, מפני חשיבותו של אברהם שהיה צריך לו עלה לגדולה (ב"ר נח:ז): **לכל באי שער עירו.** שכולן בטלו ממלאכתן ובאו לגמול חסד לשרה (שם): (יא) **לא אדני.** לא תקנה אותה בדמים: **נתתי לך.** הרי היא כמו שנתתיה לך: (יג) **אך אם אתה לו שמעני.** אתה אומר לי לשמוע לך וליקח בחנם, אני אי אפשי בכך. אך אם אתה לו שמעני, הלואי ותשמעני: **נתתי.** דוני"ש בלע"ז, מוכן הוא אצלי והלואי נתתי לך כבר:

11. לֹא־אֲדֹנִי — *No, my lord*, you need not purchase it (*Rashi*). Unctuously, Ephron implied that he would be honored to give the entire field as a gift.

Abraham was interested only in acquiring the cave itself; he was content that the adjacent field remain Ephron's. Ephron, on the other hand — by way of magnanimity or trickery — offered to give him the field as well as the cave, for it would be unbecoming for Abraham to own the cave as a sepulcher, while the field belonged to another. Abraham rejoiced at Ephron's offer not to divide the property and he purchased the entire parcel for the full price Ephron suggested (*Ramban*).

As the later verses reveal, Ephron's public generosity was a sham. He not only had no intention of making a gift, he hypocritically implied to Abraham that he expected an outrageously high price for the plot. As the Sages put it, the righteous say little but do much [see commentary to 18:5], but the wicked promise much and perform not even a little. They would offer to anoint with oil from an empty flask.

לְעֵינֵי בְנֵי־עַמִּי — *Before the eyes of the sons of my people.* Ephron implied, "Abraham, surely you understand that I must make this generous offer while my people are looking on, but I cannot be expected to give away a valuable property free of charge" (*Haamek Davar*).

13. נָתַתִּי — *I have granted.* The *Pesikta Zutresa* comments, from here we see that the word of the righteous is equivalent to their action, for it does not state *I will grant* but *I have granted*.

Chizkuni notes that in Abraham's response, the word נָתַתִּי is separated from the rest of the phrase by a disjunctive cantellation [*Azlah Geireish*] and is thus not part of the rest of the phase כֶּסֶף הַשָּׂדֶה, *the price of the field.* Rather the word נָתַתִּי should be seen as a rhetorical response to Ephron's offer in verse 11: הַשָּׂדֶה נָתַתִּי לָךְ, *the field I have granted you.* Abraham is telling Ephron, *You said* נָתַתִּי, *that you have granted me the field as a gift, but I say* כֶּסֶף הַשָּׂדֶה קַח מִמֶּנִּי, *the price of the field take from me.*

בֵּינִי וּבֵינְךָ מַה־הִוא וְאֶת־מֵתְךָ קְבֹר: טז וַיִּשְׁמַע

< And listen **16** << bury. < And your dead << is it? < what < and < between
between you, me

אַבְרָהָם אֶל־עֶפְרוֹן וַיִּשְׁקֹל אַבְרָהָם לְעֶפְרֹן

< to Ephron < and Abraham weighed out << Ephron, < to < did Abraham

אֶת־הַכֶּסֶף אֲשֶׁר דִּבֶּר בְּאָזְנֵי בְנֵי־חֵת אַרְבַּע מֵאוֹת

< hundred < four << of < of the < within < he had < which < the money
Heth, Sons earshot specified

שֶׁקֶל כֶּסֶף עֹבֵר לַסֹּחֵר: שני יז וַיָּקָם ׀ שְׂדֵה עֶפְרוֹן

< of Ephron < the << And it was **17** << to [any] < that passes < of < shekels
field established — merchant. over silver

אֲשֶׁר בַּמַּכְפֵּלָה אֲשֶׁר לִפְנֵי מַמְרֵא הַשָּׂדֶה

< the field << Mamre, < before < which is < in Machpelah, < that is

וְהַמְּעָרָה אֲשֶׁר־בּוֹ וְכָל־הָעֵץ אֲשֶׁר בַּשָּׂדֶה אֲשֶׁר בְּכָל־גְּבֻלוֹ סָבִיב:

<< around < its bound- < within < that << in the field, < that were < the trees < and all < within < that is < and the cave
[it] — aries all were it

יח לְאַבְרָהָם לְמִקְנָה לְעֵינֵי בְנֵי־חֵת בְּכֹל בָּאֵי שַׁעַר־עִירוֹ: יט וְאַחֲרֵי־כֵן

< this < And after **19** << of his < to the < who < among < of < of the < before < as a < for Abraham **18**
city. gate came all Heth, Sons the eyes purchase

קָבַר אַבְרָהָם אֶת־שָׂרָה אִשְׁתּוֹ אֶל־מְעָרַת שְׂדֵה הַמַּכְפֵּלָה עַל־פְּנֵי

< facing < of Machpelah < of the field < the cave < in < his wife < Sarah < Abraham buried

מַמְרֵא הִוא חֶבְרוֹן בְּאֶרֶץ כְּנָעַן: כ וַיָּקָם הַשָּׂדֶה וְהַמְּעָרָה אֲשֶׁר־בּוֹ

<< was < that < and the cave < the field << [Thus] was **20** << of < in the land < Hebron, < which is < Mamre,
in it, established, Canaan.

לְאַבְרָהָם לַאֲחֻזַּת־קָבֶר מֵאֵת בְּנֵי־חֵת: [כד] א וְאַבְרָהָם זָקֵן בָּא בַּיָּמִים

<< with < coming << was < And Abraham **1** **24** << of < the < from < for a < as [land] legal- < for Abraham
[his] days, old, Heth. Sons burial site, ly possessed

בֵּינָא וּבֵינָךְ מַה הִיא וְיָת מִיתָךְ קְבַר: טז וְקַבֵּל אַבְרָהָם מִן עֶפְרוֹן וּתְקַל אַבְרָהָם לְעֶפְרוֹן יָת כַּסְפָּא דְּמַלֵּיל קֳדָם בְּנֵי חִתָּאָה אַרְבַּע מְאָה סִלְעִין דִּכְסַף מִתְקַבַּל סְחוֹרָא (נ״א דְּמִתְקַבַּל (בְּ)סְחוֹרְתָא) בְּכָל מְדִינְתָא: יז וְקָם חֲקַל עֶפְרוֹן דִּי בִּכְפֶלְתָּא דִּי קֳדָם מַמְרֵא חַקְלָא וּמְעַרְתָּא דִּי בֵהּ וְכָל אִילָנֵי דִּי בְחַקְלָא דִּי בְּכָל תְּחוּמֵהּ סְחוֹר סְחוֹר: יח לְאַבְרָהָם לִזְבִינוֹהִי לְעֵינֵי בְּנֵי חִתָּאָה בְּכֹל עָלֵי תְּרַע קַרְתֵּהּ: יט וּבָתַר כֵּן קְבַר אַבְרָהָם יָת שָׂרָה אִתְּתֵהּ לִמְעַרְתָּא חֲקַל כָּפֶלְתָּא עַל אַפֵּי מַמְרֵא הִיא חֶבְרוֹן בְּאַרְעָא דִּכְנָעַן: כ וְקָם חַקְלָא וּמְעַרְתָּא דִּי בֵהּ לְאַבְרָהָם לְאַחְסָנַת קְבוּרָא מִן בְּנֵי חִתָּאָה: א וְאַבְרָהָם סִיב עַל בְּיוֹמִין

רש״י

(טו) **ביני ובינך.** בין שני אוהבים כמותו מה היא חשובה לכלום, אלא הנח את המכר ואת מתך קבור: (טז) **וישקל אברהם לעפרן.** חסר וי״ו, לפי שאמר הרבה ואפילו מעט לא עשה, שנטל ממנו שקלים גדולים שהן קנטרין, שנאמר עובר לסוחר, שמתקבלים בשקל בכל מקום ויש מקום ששקליהן גדולים שהן קנטרין, צנטינאר״ש בלע״ז (ב״ר נח:ז; ב״מ פז.): (יז) **ויקם שדה עפרון.** תקומה היתה לו שיצאה מיד הדיוט ליד מלך (ב״ר נח:ח). ופשוטו של מקרא ויקם השדה והמערה אשר בו וכל העץ לאברהם למקנה וגו׳: (יח) **בכל באי שער עירו.** בקרב כולם ובמעמד כולם הקנהו לו:

15. בֵּינִי וּבֵינְךָ מַה־הִוא — *Between me and between you, what is it?* After naming an exorbitant price, Ephron made light of it, saying, "Between such friends as us, of what significance is 400 silver *shekels*?" (*Rashi*).

This illustrates Abraham's love for Sarah. He chose the finest burial site for her and did not haggle over the price. As the Midrash states, this is one of three places where Scripture attests to the Jews' uncontestable possession of the Holy Land. For the Cave of Machpelah, the site of the Temple, and the Tomb of Joseph were all purchased without bargaining and were paid for with unquestionably legal tender.

17. וַיָּקָם — *And it was established* [lit., *rose*]. The Midrash interprets the word in the literal sense: The property became *elevated,* because it passed from the possession of a commoner, Ephron, to that of a king, Abraham.

19. Although it is clear that these events took place *in the land of Canaan,* the verse mentions that Sarah was buried there to emphasize that burial anywhere in the Land is meritorious (*Haamek Davar*).

וַיהוָה בֵּרַךְ אֶת־אַבְרָהָם בַּכֹּל׃ ב וַיֹּאמֶר אַבְרָהָם

< And Abraham said 2 « with everything. < Abraham < had blessed < and HASHEM

אֶל־עַבְדּוֹ זְקַן בֵּיתוֹ הַמֹּשֵׁל בְּכָל־אֲשֶׁר־לוֹ שִׂים־

< Place « was his: < that < all < who controlled < of his household < the elder < his servant, < to

נָא יָדְךָ תַּחַת יְרֵכִי׃ ג וְאַשְׁבִּיעֲךָ בַּיהוָה אֱלֹהֵי

< God < by HASHEM, < And I will have you swear 3 « my thigh. < under < your hand < now

הַשָּׁמַיִם וֵאלֹהֵי הָאָרֶץ אֲשֶׁר לֹא־תִקַּח אִשָּׁה לִבְנִי מִבְּנוֹת הַכְּנַעֲנִי

< of the Canaanites, < from the daughters < for my son < a wife < you not take < that < of the earth, < and God < of the heaven

אֲשֶׁר אָנֹכִי יוֹשֵׁב בְּקִרְבּוֹ׃ ד כִּי אֶל־אַרְצִי וְאֶל־מוֹלַדְתִּי תֵּלֵךְ וְלָקַחְתָּ

< and you shall take < shall you go < my relatives < and to < my land < to < Rather, 4 « in their midst. < dwell < I < that

וַייָ בָּרִיךְ יָת אַבְרָהָם בְּכֹלָּא: ב וַאֲמַר אַבְרָהָם לְעַבְדֵּהּ סָבָא דְבֵיתֵהּ דְּשַׁלִּיט בְּכָל דִּי לֵהּ שַׁוִּי כְעַן יְדָךְ תְּחוֹת יַרְכִּי: ג וַאֲקַיֵּם עֲלָךְ בְּמֵימְרָא דַייָ אֱלָהָא דִשְׁמַיָּא וֶאֱלָהָא דְאַרְעָא דִּי לָא תִסַּב אִתְּתָא לִבְרִי מִבְּנָת כְּנַעֲנָאֵי דִּי אֲנָא יָתֵב בֵּינֵיהוֹן: ד אֱלָהֵן לְאַרְעִי וּלְיַלָּדוּתִי תֵּיזִיל וְתִסַּב

רש״י

(א) **ברך את אברהם בכל.** בכל עולה בגימטריא בן (תנחומא ישן ו) ומאחר שהיה לו בן היה צריך להשיאו אשה (תנחומא נח יב): (ב) **זקן ביתו.** לפי שהוא דבוק, נקוד זָקֵן: **תחת ירכי.** לפי שהנשבע צריך שיטול בידו חפץ של מצוה כגון ספר תורה או תפילין (שבועות לח:), והמילה היתה מצוה ראשונה לו ובאה לו ע״י צער והיתה חביבה

24.

1-10. The mission to find a wife for Isaac. Abraham's own productive life was coming to an end. Isaac was 37 years old when Sarah died, and Abraham was troubled by the thought that had Isaac been slaughtered at the *Akeidah*, he would have left no children to succeed him. Therefore, Abraham now took it upon himself to provide for the future by finding a wife for Isaac. But Isaac's mate had to be a worthy successor to his mother; she had to be the next Sarah of the Jewish people, a woman who would be not only a wife and mother, but a Matriarch. To find such a woman, Abraham turned toward his ancestral home, to his and Sarah's family. And to make the selection, he dispatched Eliezer. More than a trusted servant, Eliezer was the "rosh yeshivah" of Abraham's household, the one who taught the disciples and exemplified Abraham's way of life. Only such a person had the stature and understanding to be worthy of the heavenly assistance needed to chart the next epoch in the development of the Jewish people.

1. בַּכֹּל — *With everything.* God had given Abraham everything — riches, possessions, honor, longevity, and children. The one thing he lacked was to see his son have children to inherit his status and honor (*Ramban*).

Rashi notes that the numerical value of this word, 52, is the same as that of בֵּן, *son*, for all of Abraham's good fortune was worthless to him as long as he had no heir, as he had said to God (15:2), *What can You give me, seeing that I am childless? (Akeidas Yitzchak).*

2. עַבְדּוֹ זְקַן בֵּיתוֹ — *His servant, the elder of his household.* Even sixty years before, Eliezer had been Abraham's most trusted servant (see 15:2); now he is not only the senior servant, but the *elder of his household* (*R' Hoffmann*).

תַּחַת יְרֵכִי — *Under my thigh. Thigh* is a euphemism for the male organ; offspring, too, are described as יוֹצְאֵי יְרֵךְ, lit., *coming out of the [father's] thigh* (46:26; *Exodus* 1:5).

Rashi explains why Abraham chose it for use in certifying the oath. One who takes an oath must place his hand on some sacred object, such as a Torah scroll or *tefillin* [see *Shevuos* 38b]. Because circumcision was the first precept given to Abraham, and because he fulfilled it through much pain, it was particularly precious to him, so Abraham asked Eliezer to take his oath upon it. *Targum Yonasan* renders similarly. *Tanchuma Yashan* explains that the reason the Patriarchs cherished the mitzvah of circumcision is that they knew that through it their descendants would be saved from *Gehinnom.* It is therefore appropriate to invoke that *mitzvah* before the quest for the woman who together with Isaac would forge the next link in Jewish identity.

3. וְאַשְׁבִּיעֲךָ — *And I will have you swear.* In view of his advanced age, Abraham feared that he might die before Eliezer's return. Accordingly, the oath assured Abraham that his plan would be carried out even in his absence, because he knew that Isaac would follow Eliezer's counsel (*Ramban* to v. 1).

Although he did not doubt Eliezer's loyalty, Abraham recognized that human beings have enormous reservoirs of strength to draw upon in times of crisis — but only if they are determined to persevere. By imposing the oath, Abraham guaranteed that Eliezer would persist in his mission, even if it seemed to have limited chances of success (*Shem MiShmuel).*

מִבְּנוֹת הַכְּנַעֲנִי — *From the daughters of the Canaanites.* The rejection of the Canaanites could not have been based on their idol worship, because Abraham's family in Charan worshiped idols, as well. Rather, Abraham was motivated by the moral degeneracy of the Canaanites. Idolatry is an intellectual perversion, and

אִשָּׁה לִבְנִי לְיִצְחָק: ה וַיֹּאמֶר אֵלָיו הָעֶבֶד אוּלַי

‹ Perhaps « did the servant: ‹ to him ‹ Say **5** *« for Isaac. ‹ for my son ‹ a wife*

לֹא־תֹאבֶה הָאִשָּׁה לָלֶכֶת אַחֲרַי אֶל־הָאָרֶץ הַזֹּאת

« this land; ‹ to ‹ after me ‹ to follow « the woman shall not wish

הֶהָשֵׁב אָשִׁיב אֶת־בִּנְךָ אֶל־הָאָרֶץ אֲשֶׁר־יָצָאתָ

‹ you departed ‹ that ‹ the land ‹ to ‹ your son ‹ shall I take back

מִשָּׁם: ו וַיֹּאמֶר אֵלָיו אַבְרָהָם הִשָּׁמֶר לְךָ פֶּן־

‹ lest ‹ yourself ‹ Guard « did Abraham, ‹ to him ‹ Say **6** *« from there?*

תָּשִׁיב אֶת־בְּנִי שָׁמָּה: ז יהוה | אֱלֹהֵי הַשָּׁמַיִם אֲשֶׁר

‹ Who ‹ of the heaven, ‹ God ‹ HASHEM, **7** *« to there. ‹ my son ‹ you return*

לְקָחַנִי מִבֵּית אָבִי וּמֵאֶרֶץ מוֹלַדְתִּי וַאֲשֶׁר דִּבֶּר־

‹ spoke ‹ and Who « of my birth, ‹ and from the land ‹ of my father ‹ from the house ‹ took me

לִי וַאֲשֶׁר נִשְׁבַּע־לִי לֵאמֹר לְזַרְעֲךָ אֶתֵּן אֶת־הָאָרֶץ הַזֹּאת הוּא יִשְׁלַח

‹ will send ‹ He « this land' — ‹ will I give ‹ 'To your offspring « saying, ‹ to me ‹ swore ‹ and Who ‹ concerning me,

מַלְאָכוֹ לְפָנֶיךָ וְלָקַחְתָּ אִשָּׁה לִבְנִי מִשָּׁם: ח וְאִם־לֹא תֹאבֶה הָאִשָּׁה

« the woman will not wish ‹ But if **8** *« from there. ‹ for my son ‹ a wife ‹ and you will take « before you, ‹ His angel*

לָלֶכֶת אַחֲרֶיךָ וְנִקִּיתָ מִשְּׁבֻעָתִי זֹאת רַק אֶת־בְּנִי לֹא תָשֵׁב שָׁמָּה:

« to there. ‹ return ‹ do not ‹ my son ‹ However, « from this oath of mine. ‹ you shall then be released ‹ after you, ‹ to follow

ט וַיָּשֶׂם הָעֶבֶד אֶת־יָדוֹ תַּחַת יֶרֶךְ אַבְרָהָם אֲדֹנָיו וַיִּשָּׁבַע לוֹ עַל־

‹ regarding ‹ to him ‹ and he swore ‹ his master ‹ of Abraham ‹ the thigh ‹ under ‹ his hand ‹ So the servant placed **9**

הַדָּבָר הַזֶּה: שלישי י וַיִּקַּח הָעֶבֶד עֲשָׂרָה גְמַלִּים מִגְּמַלֵּי אֲדֹנָיו וַיֵּלֶךְ

‹ and he went « of his master, ‹ from the camels ‹ camels ‹ ten ‹ Then the servant took **10** *« this matter.*

אִתְּתָא לִבְרִי לְיִצְחָק: ה וַאֲמַר לֵהּ
עַבְדָּא מָאִים לָא תֵיבֵי אִתְּתָא לְמֵיתֵי
בַּתְרַי לְאַרְעָא הָדָא הַאֲתָבָא אָתֵיב
יָת בְּרָךְ לְאַרְעָא דִּי נְפַקְתָּא מִתַּמָּן:
ו וַאֲמַר לֵהּ אַבְרָהָם אִסְתַּמַּר לָךְ
דִּילְמָא תָתֵיב יָת בְּרִי תַּמָּן: ז יְיָ
אֱלָהָא דִשְׁמַיָּא דִּי דַבְּרַנִי מִבֵּית אַבָּא
וּמֵאֲרַע יַלְדוּתִי וְדִי מַלִּיל לִי וְדִי קַיֵּים
לִי לְמֵימַר לִבְרָךְ אֶתֵּן יָת אַרְעָא
הָדָא הוּא יִשְׁלַח מַלְאֲכֵהּ קֳדָמָךְ
וְתִסַּב אִתְּתָא לִבְרִי מִתַּמָּן: ח וְאִם לָא
תֵיבֵי אִתְּתָא לְמֵיתֵי בַּתְרָךְ וּתְהֵי
זַכָּאָה מִמּוֹמָתִי דָּא לְחוֹד יָת בְּרִי לָא
תָתֵב לְתַמָּן: ט וְשַׁוִּי עַבְדָּא יָת יְדֵהּ
תְּחוֹת יַרְכָּא דְאַבְרָהָם רִבּוֹנֵהּ וְקַיֵּים
לֵהּ עַל פִּתְגָּמָא הָדֵין: י וּדְבַר עַבְדָּא
עַשְׂרָא גַמְלִין מִגַּמְלֵי רִבּוֹנֵהּ וַאֲזַל

רש"י

עליו, ונטלה (ב"ר נט:ח): **(ז) ה' אלהי השמים אשר לקחני מבית אבי.** ולא אמר ואלהי הארץ, ולמעלה (פסוק ג) הוא אומר ואשביעך בה' אלהי השמים ואלהי הארץ. א"ל, עכשיו הוא אלהי השמים ואלהי הארץ שהרגלתיו בפי הבריות, אבל כשלקחני מבית אבי היה אלהי השמים ולא אלהי הארץ, שלא היו באי עולם מכירים בו ושמו לא היה רגיל בארץ (ב"ר שם ח; ספרי האזינו שיג): **מבית אבי.** מחרן: **ומארץ מולדתי.** מאור כשדים: **ואשר דבר לי.** לצרכי, כמו אשר דבר עלי (מלכים א ב:ד). וכן כל לי ולו ולהם הסמוכים אצל דבור מפורשים בלשון על, ותרגום שלהם עלי עלוהי עליהון, שאין נופל אצל דיבור לשון לי ולו ולהם, אלא אלי אליו אליהם, ותרגום שלהם עמי עמיה עמהון. אבל אצל אמירה נופל לשון לי ולו ולהם: **ואשר נשבע לי.** בין הבתרים (ב"ר שם י; ילק"ש קז): **(ח) ונקית משבעתי וגו'.** וקח לו אשה מבנות ענר אשכול וממרא: **רק את בני וגו'.** רק מיעוט הוא, בני אינו חוזר אבל יעקב בן בני סופו לחזור (ב"ר שם): **(י) מגמלי אדניו.** נכרין היו משאר גמלים, שהיו יוצאין זמומין

as such it can be remedied, but a lack of morality, ethics, and modesty affects a person's entire nature, and disqualifies a woman from being the mate of an Isaac (*R' Hirsch*, based on *Drashos HaRan*).

5-9. Eliezer did not doubt that he would find a suitable mate who would consent to marry Isaac, but he was afraid that she might not want to leave her family to go with him — hence his question as to whether Isaac could go to Haran (*R' Hoffmann*). Abraham refused because he would not let Isaac lose the special sanctity with which he had been invested when he was brought as an עוֹלָה תְמִימָה, *an offering completely devoted* to God (*Pesikta Zutresa*); thus he emphasized that Isaac was on no account to

וְכָל־טוּב אֲדֹנָיו בְּיָדוֹ וַיָּקָם וַיֵּלֶךְ אֶל־אֲרַם נַהֲרַיִם

Aram Naharaim · to · and went · and got up · in his hand · of his master · of the wealth · with all [manner]

אֶל־עִיר נָחוֹר׃ יא וַיַּבְרֵךְ הַגְּמַלִּים מִחוּץ לָעִיר אֶל־

toward · the city · outside · He made the camels kneel down · 11 · of Nahor. · the city · to

בְּאֵר הַמָּיִם לְעֵת עֶרֶב לְעֵת צֵאת הַשֹּׁאֲבֹת׃

of the women who draw water. · for the going out · at the time · of evening, · at the time · of water · a well

יב וַיֹּאמַר ׀ יהוה אֱלֹהֵי אֲדֹנִי אַבְרָהָם הַקְרֵה־נָא

please, · cause it to happen, · Abraham, · of my master · God · HASHEM, · And he said, 12

לְפָנַי הַיּוֹם וַעֲשֵׂה־חֶסֶד עִם אֲדֹנִי אַבְרָהָם׃ יג הִנֵּה אָנֹכִי נִצָּב עַל־עֵין

the spring · by · am standing · I · Indeed, 13 · Abraham. · my master · with · kindness · that You do · today · before me

הַמָּיִם וּבְנוֹת אַנְשֵׁי הָעִיר יֹצְאֹת לִשְׁאֹב מָיִם׃ יד וְהָיָה הַנַּעֲרָ אֲשֶׁר אֹמַר

I shall say · that · that the girl · Let it be · 14 · water. · to draw · go out · of the town · of the people · and the daughters · of water

אֵלֶיהָ הַטִּי־נָא כַדֵּךְ וְאֶשְׁתֶּה וְאָמְרָה שְׁתֵה וְגַם־גְּמַלֶּיךָ אַשְׁקֶה אֹתָהּ

her · will I water,' · your camels · and even · 'Drink, · and she replies, · so I may drink,' · your jug · please, · 'Tilt, · to her,

הֹכַחְתָּ לְעַבְדְּךָ לְיִצְחָק וּבָהּ אֵדַע כִּי־עָשִׂיתָ חֶסֶד עִם־אֲדֹנִי׃

my master. · with · kindness · You have done · that · [let] me know · and through her · for Isaac; · for Your servant, · will You have designated

וְכָל שְׁפַר רִבּוֹנֵהּ בִּידֵהּ וְקָם וַאֲזַל לַאֲרָם דִּי עַל פְּרַת לְקַרְתָּא דְנָחוֹר: יא וְאַשְׁרֵי גַמְלַיָּא מִבָּרָא לְקַרְתָּא עִם בֵּירָא דְמַיָּא לְעִדַּן רַמְשָׁא לְעִדַּן דְּנָפְקָן מַלְיָתָא: יב וַאֲמַר יְיָ אֱלָהֵהּ דְּרִבּוֹנִי אַבְרָהָם זַמִּין כְּעַן קֳדָמַי יוֹמָא דֵין וְעִבַד טִיבוּ עִם רִבּוֹנִי אַבְרָהָם: יג הָא אֲנָא קָאֵם עַל עֵינָא דְמַיָּא וּבְנָת אֱנָשֵׁי קַרְתָּא נָפְקָן לְמִמְלֵי מַיָּא: יד וִיהֵי עוּלֶמְתָּא דִּי אֵימַר לַהּ אַרְכִינִי כְעַן קוּלְתִיךְ וְאֶשְׁתֵּי וְתֵימַר אִשְׁתְּ וְאַף גַּמְלָיךְ אַשְׁקֵי יָתַהּ זַמֶּנְתָּא לְעַבְדָּךְ לְיִצְחָק וּבַהּ אִידַע אֲרֵי עֲבַדְתָּ טִיבוּ עִם רִבּוֹנִי:

רש"י

מפני הגזל שלא ירעו בשדות אחרים (שם יח): **וכל טוב אדניו בידו.** שטר מתנה כתב ליצחק על כל אשר לו, כדי שיקפצו לשלוח לו בתם (שם): **ארם נהרים.** בין שתי נהרות יושבת: **(יא) ויברך הגמלים.** הרביצם (שם): **(יד) אתה הוכחת.** ראויה היא לו, שתהא גומלת חסדים וכדאי היא ליכנס בביתו של אברהם (עי' יבמות עט.). ולשון הוכחת בררת, אפרובי"ר בלע"ז: **ובה אדע.** לשון תחינה, הודע לי בה **כי עשית חסד.** אם תהיה ממשפחתו והוגנת לו אדע כי עשית חסד: **(טז) בתולה.** ממקום

leave the Land that God had promised to his descendants (*Radak*). While refusing this permission, Abraham assured Eliezer that God would bless his mission with success.

10. אֲרַם נַהֲרַיִם — *Aram Naharaim* [lit., *Aram of the pair of rivers*]. The country was so called because it was situated between two rivers [the Euphrates and the Tigris] (*Rashi*).

11-14. Eliezer's criteria. Eliezer was not interested in a *wealthy* girl for Isaac. He preferred someone of modest means, the kind who would go to draw water herself, not have servants do it for her (*Malbim*).

13. נִצָּב עַל־עֵין הַמָּיִם — *Am standing by the spring of water.* Eliezer wanted to see how the girl would behave at the well where the girl would be natural and act in accordance with her own character. At home, however, her behavior might well reflect the constraints of her family's orders or expectations (*Chizkuni*).

14. וְאָמְרָה שְׁתֵה וְגַם־גְּמַלֶּיךָ אַשְׁקֶה — *And she replies, 'Drink, and even your camels will I water.'* Thus, her response will go *beyond* my request, and she will offer all that is needed (*Sforno*).

Ordinarily it is forbidden to base one's actions on omens, such as Eliezer's request that a girl's behavior would be a sign for him. This prohibition, however, applies only to omens unrelated to the choice being made, such as saying that if the sun shines tomorrow it is a sign that I should marry this woman. In Eliezer's case, his omen was appropriate to his mission: Since the Matriarch of Israel had to be a woman of kindness and sensitivity, Eliezer was looking not for omens but for proof of her qualifications (*Ran, Chullin* 95b). In this regard, R' Yitzchok Zev Soloveitchik noted that even though Eliezer was to see a miracle performed for Rebecca (see v. 16), that did not suffice for him. The test of a mother of the Jewish people had to be kindness, not miracles.

טו וַיְהִי־הוּא טֶרֶם כִּלָּה לְדַבֵּר וְהִנֵּה רִבְקָה יֹצֵאת
15 And so it was, before he had finished speaking that all of a sudden Rebecca was going out
אֲשֶׁר יֻלְּדָה לִבְתוּאֵל בֶּן־מִלְכָּה אֵשֶׁת נָחוֹר אֲחִי
who — [she] had been born to Bethuel the son of Milcah the wife of Nahor, brother
אַבְרָהָם וְכַדָּהּ עַל־שִׁכְמָהּ: טז וְהַנַּעֲרָ טֹבַת מַרְאֶה
of Abraham — with her jug upon her shoulder. **16** Now the girl was of good appearance,
מְאֹד בְּתוּלָה וְאִישׁ לֹא יְדָעָהּ וַתֵּרֶד הָעַיְנָה
exceedingly; a virgin and a man had not known her. She descended to the spring,
וַתְּמַלֵּא כַדָּהּ וַתָּעַל: יז וַיָּרָץ הָעֶבֶד לִקְרָאתָהּ וַיֹּאמֶר הַגְמִיאִינִי נָא
she filled her jug and she ascended. **17** The servant ran toward her, and said, *Give me to swallow, please,*
מְעַט־מַיִם מִכַּדֵּךְ: יח וַתֹּאמֶר שְׁתֵה אֲדֹנִי וַתְּמַהֵר וַתֹּרֶד כַּדָּהּ עַל־יָדָהּ
a little water from your jug. **18** She said, *Drink, my lord,* and she hurried and she lowered her jug upon her hand
וַתַּשְׁקֵהוּ: יט וַתְּכַל לְהַשְׁקֹתוֹ וַתֹּאמֶר גַּם לִגְמַלֶּיךָ אֶשְׁאָב עַד אִם־כִּלּוּ
and gave him to drink. **19** [When] she finished giving him to drink, she said, *Even for your camels I will draw [water] until when they have finished*
לִשְׁתֹּת: כ וַתְּמַהֵר וַתְּעַר כַּדָּהּ אֶל־הַשֹּׁקֶת וַתָּרָץ עוֹד אֶל־הַבְּאֵר לִשְׁאֹב
drinking. **20** So she hurried and poured out her jug into the trough and ran again to the well to draw [water];

טו וַהֲוָה הוּא עַד לָא שֵׁיצִי לְמַלָּלָא וְהָא
רִבְקָה נְפָקַת דְּאִתְיְלִידַת לִבְתוּאֵל בַּר
מִלְכָּה אִתַּת נָחוֹר אֲחוּהִי דְאַבְרָהָם
וְקוּלְתַהּ עַל כַּתְפַּהּ: טז וְעוּלֶמְתָּא
שַׁפִּירַת חֵיזוּ (נ״א שַׁפִּירָא לְמֶחֱזֵי)
לַחֲדָא בְּתֻלְתָּא וּגְבַר לָא יַדְעַהּ וּנְחָתַת
לְעֵינָא וּמְלַת קוּלְתַהּ וּסְלֵקַת: יז וּרְהַט
עַבְדָּא לְקַדָּמוּתַהּ וַאֲמַר אַשְׁקִינִי (נ״א
אַטְעֲמִנִי) כְּעַן זְעֵיר מַיָּא מִקּוּלְתִיךְ:
יח וַאֲמֶרֶת אִשְׁתְּ רִבּוֹנִי וְאוֹחִיאַת
וַאֲחֵיתַת קוּלְתַהּ עַל יְדַהּ וְאַשְׁקְתֵהּ:
יט וְשֵׁיצִיאַת לְאַשְׁקָיוּתֵהּ וַאֲמֶרֶת אַף
לְגַמְלָיךְ אַמְלֵי עַד דִּי סַפְּקוּן לְמִשְׁתֵּי:
כ וְאוֹחִיאַת וּנְפָצַת קוּלְתַהּ לְבֵית
שַׁקְיָא וּרְהָטַת עוֹד לְבֵירָא לְמִמְלֵי

רש"י

בתולים: **ואיש לא ידעה.** שלא כדרכה. לפי שבנות הכנענים היו משמרות מקום בתוליהן ומפקירות עצמן ממקום אחר, העיד על זו שנקייה מכל (ב"ר ס:ה): **(יז) וירץ העבד לקראתה.** לפי שראה שעלו המים לקראתה (שם): **הגמיאיני נא.** לשון גמיעה (שבת עז.), הומי"ר בלע"ז: **(יח) ותרד כדה.** מעל שכמה: **(יט) עד אם כלו.** הרי אם משמש בלשון אשר: **אם כלו.** ת"א די ספקון, שזו היא גמר שתייתן כששתו די ספוקן: **(כ) ותער.** לשון נפילה (אונקלוס). והרבה יש בלשון משנה, המערה מכלי אל כלי (עבודה זרה עב.). ובמקרא יש לו דומה, אל תער נפשי (תהלים קמא:ח) אשר הערה למות נפשו (ישעיה נג:יב): **השקת.** אבן חלולה ששותים בה הגמלים:

15. So swift was the Divine response to Eliezer's petition that while he was still in the midst of his supplication, Providence had already caused Rebecca to leave her house and go to the well.

16. וַתְּמַלֵּא כַדָּהּ וַתָּעַל — *She filled her jug and she ascended.* Unlike the other girls at the well, who wasted their time in idle chatter and gossip, Rebecca did her task quickly and without delay (*Minchah Belulah*).

The Midrash interprets the "ascent" of this phrase as a reference not to Rebecca, but to the water, rendering *she filled her jug and it [the water] ascended to meet her.* So great was her virtue that a miracle happened when she came to the well.

18. Rebecca is equal to the test. Rebecca acted in a most exalted manner: She lowered the jug herself to spare Eliezer the effort, and וַתַּשְׁקֵהוּ, she actually brought the jug near his mouth, so he would not even have to hold it. Furthermore, she did not say at this point that she would water the camels as well, because if Eliezer had known, he might want to drink too quickly or too little, to spare her the extra effort. So she let him think that all she would do was give him a bit of water (*Or HaChaim*).

19. גַּם לִגְמַלֶּיךָ אֶשְׁאָב — *Even for your camels I will draw [water].* Now the miracle of the ascending water stopped; she had to draw all the water for the camels through sheer physical exertion, and this was the great proof of her kindness (*Ramban*). The translator of *R' Hirsch*'s commentary notes that in their first drink, ten camels would consume at least 140 gallons of water! Rebecca's undertaking such a strenuous task so eagerly for a total stranger is a supreme indication of her sterling character.

20. וַתָּרָץ עוֹד אֶל־הַבְּאֵר — *And ran again to the well.* Rebecca runs eagerly when she performs an act of kindness, as Abraham did when he was providing for *his* guests (see 18:7), a further sign of her suitability to join Abraham's household.

וַתִּשְׁאַב לְכָל־גְּמַלָּיו: כא וְהָאִישׁ מִשְׁתָּאֵה לָהּ
and she drew [water] < for all < his camels. « 21 The man < was astonished < at her, «
מַחֲרִישׁ לָדַעַת הַהִצְלִיחַ יהוה דַּרְכּוֹ אִם־לֹא:
maintaining silence < to know < whether HASHEM had made successful < his journey < or < not. «
כב וַיְהִי כַּאֲשֶׁר כִּלּוּ הַגְּמַלִּים לִשְׁתּוֹת וַיִּקַּח הָאִישׁ
22 And it was, < when < the camels had finished < drinking, « the man took <
נֶזֶם זָהָב בֶּקַע מִשְׁקָלוֹ וּשְׁנֵי צְמִידִים עַל־יָדֶיהָ
a nose ring < of gold, « a *beka* < was its weight, « and two < bracelets < on [to wear] < her hands, «
עֲשָׂרָה זָהָב מִשְׁקָלָם: כג וַיֹּאמֶר בַּת־מִי אַתְּ הַגִּידִי נָא לִי הֲיֵשׁ בֵּית־
ten < gold [shekels] < was their weight. « 23 And he said, « The daughter < of whom < are you? « Inform me please. « Is there < in the house <
אָבִיךְ מָקוֹם לָנוּ לָלִין: כד וַתֹּאמֶר אֵלָיו בַּת־בְּתוּאֵל אָנֹכִי בֶּן־מִלְכָּה
of your father < *place* < *for us* < *to spend the night?* « 24 She said < to him, « The daughter < *of Bethuel* < am I, « the son < *of Milcah* <
אֲשֶׁר יָלְדָה לְנָחוֹר: כה וַתֹּאמֶר אֵלָיו גַּם־תֶּבֶן גַּם־מִסְפּוֹא רַב עִמָּנוּ גַּם־
whom < she bore < to Nahor. « 25 And she said < to him, « *Even* < *straw* < *[and] even* < *fodder* < *is plentiful* < *with us* < *as well as* <
מָקוֹם לָלוּן: כו וַיִּקֹּד הָאִישׁ וַיִּשְׁתַּחוּ לַיהוה: רביעי כז וַיֹּאמֶר בָּרוּךְ יהוה
place < *to spend the night.* « 26 Bow [his head] low < did the man < and he prostrated himself < to HASHEM. « 27 He said, « *Blessed* < *is HASHEM,* <

וּמְלַת לְכָל גַּמְלוֹהִי: כא וְגַבְרָא שָׁהֵי בַהּ מִסְתַּכֵּל שָׁתִיק לְמֵידַע הַאַצְלַח יְיָ אָרְחֵהּ אִם לָא: כב וַהֲוָה כַּד סַפִּיקוּ גַמְלַיָּא לְמִשְׁתֵּי וּנְסֵיב גַּבְרָא קָדָשָׁא דְדַהֲבָא תִּקְלָא מַתְקְלֵהּ וּתְרֵין שֵׁירִין עַל יְדָהָא מַתְקַל עֲשַׂר סִלְעִין דְּדַהֲבָא מַתְקַלְהוֹן: כג וַאֲמַר בַּת מָן אַתְּ חַוִּי כְעַן לִי הַאִית בֵּית אֲבוּךְ אֲתַר כָּשַׁר לָנָא לִמְבָת: כד וַאֲמֶרֶת לֵהּ בַּת בְּתוּאֵל אֲנָא בַּר מִלְכָּה דִּילֵידַת לְנָחוֹר: כה וַאֲמֶרֶת לֵהּ אַף תִּבְנָא אַף כִּסָּתָא סַגִּי עִמָּנָא אַף אֲתַר כָּשַׁר לִמְבָת: כו וּכְרַע גַּבְרָא וּסְגִיד קֳדָם יְיָ: כז וַאֲמַר בְּרִיךְ יְיָ

רש"י

(כא) משתאה. לשון שאיה, כמו שאו ערים, תשאה שממה (שם ו:יא): **משתאה.** משתומם ומתבהל על שראה דברו קרוב להצליח, אבל אינו יודע אם ממשפחת אברהם היא אם לאו. ואל תתמה בתי"ו של משתאה, שאין לך תיבה שתחלת יסודה שי"ן ומדברת בלשון מתפעל שאין תי"ו מפרידה בין שתי אותיות של עיקר היסוד, כגון משתאה [מגזרת שאה], משתולל (ישעיה נט:טו) מגזרת שולל, וישתומם (שם טז) מגזרת שממה, וישתמר חקות עמרי (מיכה ו:טז) מגזרת וישמר, אף כאן משתאה מגזרת תשאה. וכשם שאתה מוצא לשון משומם באדם נבהל ונאלם ובעל מחשבות, כמו על יומו נשמו אחרונים (איוב יח:כ) שומו שמים (ירמיה ב:יב) אשתומם כשעה חדא (דניאל ד:טז), כך תפרש לשון שאייה באדם בהול ובעל מחשבות. ואונקלוס תרגם לשון שהייה, וגברא שהי, שוהה ועומד במקום אחד לראות ההצליח ה' דרכו. ואין לתרגם שתי, שהרי אינו לשון שתיה, שאין אל"ף נופלת בלשון שתיה: **משתאה לה.** משתומם עליה, כמו אמרי לי אחי הוא (לעיל כ:יג), וכמו וישאלו אנשי המקום לאשתו (להלן כו:ז): **(כב) בקע.** רמז לשקלי ישראל בקע לגלגלת (תרגום יונתן): **ושני צמידים.** רמז לשני לוחות מצומדות (ב"ר ס:ו): **עשרה זהב משקלם.** רמז לעשרת הדברות שבהן (שם): **(כג) ויאמר בת מי את.** לאחר שנתן לה שאלה, לפי שהיה בטוח בזכותו של אברהם שהצליח הקב"ה דרכו (ברב"ת): **ללין.** לינה אחת, לין שם דבר. והיא אמרה [גם מקום] ללון, כמה לינות (ב"ר שם): **(כד) בת בתואל.** השיבתו על ראשון ראשון ועל אחרון אחרון (כלה רבתי פ"ד): **(כה) מספוא.** כל מאכל הגמלים קרוי מספוא, כגון עצה (שבת עו.)

21. מִשְׁתָּאֵה לָהּ — *Was astonished at her.* Eliezer was amazed at the immediate fulfillment of his prayer, which surpassed all his expectations (*R' Hirsch*) . . . and he waited to learn whether she was of Abraham's family (*Rashi*).

Although courtesy dictated that he try to stop her from exerting herself so much on his behalf, he remained silent, because he realized that God might be showing him that his mission was successful (*Sforno*).

22. So confident was Eliezer that God had intervened to show him Isaac's future bride that he presented her with these lavish gifts even before asking her who she was. The gifts, which he had prepared beforehand, alluded to the destiny of her future offspring. The *beka* is a half-*shekel,* which symbolized the amount that every Jew would contribute for the Sanctuary every year; the two bracelets symbolized the two Tablets of the Law; and their weight of ten *shekels* symbolized the Ten Commandments (*Rashi*).

25. In keeping with her previous display of giving more than Eliezer asked of her, she responded to his request for personal lodging by saying that she would provide for his camels, as well.

27. בָּרוּךְ ה' — *Blessed is* HASHEM. Eliezer's expression of gratitude revealed his own stature as Abraham's prime disciple and

אֱלֹהֵי אֲדֹנִי אַבְרָהָם אֲשֶׁר לֹא־עָזַב חַסְדּוֹ וַאֲמִתּוֹ

‹ and His truth ‹ His kindness ‹ has not withheld ‹ Who ‹‹ Abraham, ‹ of my master ‹ God

מֵעִם אֲדֹנִי אָנֹכִי בַּדֶּרֶךְ נָחַנִי יהוה בֵּית אֲחֵי אֲדֹנִי׃

‹‹ of my master. ‹ of the brothers ‹ [to] the house ‹‹ has HASHEM guided me, ‹ on the [right] path ‹‹ As for me, ‹‹ my master. ‹ from

כח וַתָּרָץ הַנַּעֲרָ וַתַּגֵּד לְבֵית אִמָּהּ כַּדְּבָרִים הָאֵלֶּה׃

‹‹ according to these events ‹ of her mother ‹ to the household ‹ and related ‹ The girl ran **28**

כט וּלְרִבְקָה אָח וּשְׁמוֹ לָבָן וַיָּרָץ לָבָן אֶל־הָאִישׁ

‹‹ the man, ‹ to ‹ Laban ran ‹‹ was Laban: ‹ whose name ‹ a brother ‹ Rebecca had **29**

הַחוּצָה אֶל־הָעָיִן׃ ל וַיְהִי ׀ כִּרְאֹת אֶת־הַנֶּזֶם

‹ the nose ring, ‹ [that] when he saw ‹ [For] it was **30** ‹‹ the spring. ‹ to ‹ outside

וְאֶת־הַצְּמִדִים עַל־יְדֵי אֲחֹתוֹ וּכְשָׁמְעוֹ אֶת־דִּבְרֵי רִבְקָה אֲחֹתוֹ לֵאמֹר

‹‹ saying, ‹ his sister ‹ of Rebecca ‹ the words ‹ and when he heard ‹‹ of his sister, ‹ the hands ‹ on ‹ and the bracelets

כֹּה־דִבֶּר אֵלַי הָאִישׁ וַיָּבֹא אֶל־הָאִישׁ וְהִנֵּה עֹמֵד עַל־הַגְּמַלִּים עַל־

‹ by ‹ the camels ‹ by ‹ he was [still] standing ‹ and indeed, ‹ the man, ‹ to ‹ he came ‹‹ — *the man,* ‹‹ *to me* ‹ *did he speak* ‹ *Thus*

הָעָיִן׃ לא וַיֹּאמֶר בּוֹא בְּרוּךְ יהוה לָמָּה תַעֲמֹד בַּחוּץ וְאָנֹכִי פִּנִּיתִי הַבַּיִת

‹ the house, ‹ have cleared ‹ *when I* ‹ *outside* ‹ *should you stand* ‹ *Why* ‹‹ *of* HASHEM*!* ‹ *you who are blessed* ‹ *Come,* ‹ He said, **31** ‹‹ the spring.

וּמָקוֹם לַגְּמַלִּים׃ לב וַיָּבֹא הָאִישׁ הַבַּיְתָה וַיְפַתַּח הַגְּמַלִּים וַיִּתֵּן תֶּבֶן

‹ straw ‹ He gave ‹‹ the camels. ‹ and unharnessed ‹ to the house, ‹ So the man came **32** ‹‹ *for the camels?* ‹ *and place*

אֱלָהָא דְרִבּוֹנִי אַבְרָהָם דִּי לָא מְנַע טִיבוּתֵהּ וְקוּשְׁטֵהּ מִן רִבּוֹנִי אֲנָא בְּאוֹרַח תַּקְנָא דַּבְּרַנִי יְיָ לְבֵית אֲחֵי רִבּוֹנִי׃ כח וּרְהָטַת עוּלֶמְתָּא וְחַוִּיאַת לְבֵית אִמַּהּ כְּפִתְגָּמַיָּא הָאִלֵּין׃ כט וּלְרִבְקָה אֲחָא וּשְׁמֵהּ לָבָן וּרְהַט לָבָן לְגַבְרָא לְבָרָא לְעֵינָא׃ ל וַהֲוָה כַּד חֲזָא יָת קָדָשָׁא וְיָת שֵׁירַיָּא עַל יְדֵי אֲחָתֵהּ וְכַד שְׁמַע יָת פִּתְגָּמֵי רִבְקָה אֲחָתֵהּ לְמֵימַר כְּדֵין מַלִּיל עִמִּי גַּבְרָא וַאֲתָא לְוַת גַּבְרָא וְהָא קָאֵם עִלָּוֵי גַּמְלַיָּא עַל עֵינָא׃ לא וַאֲמַר עוּל בְּרִיכָא דַייָ לְמָא אַתְּ קָאֵם בְּבָרָא וַאֲנָא פַּנֵּיתִי בֵיתָא וַאֲתַר כְּשַׁר לְגַמְלַיָּא׃ לב וְעַל גַּבְרָא לְבֵיתָא וּשְׁרָא גַּמְלַיָּא וִיהַב תִּבְנָא

רש"י

ושעורים (סוטה ט.): **(כז) בדרך.** דרך המזומן [ס"א המיומן], דרך הישר (אונקלוס), באותו דרך שהייתי לריך. וכן כל בי"ת ולמ"ד וה"א המשמשים בראש התיבה ונקודים בפת"ח מדברים בדבר הפשוט שנזכר כבר במקום אחר או שהוא מבורר וניכר באיזו הוא מדבר: **(כח) לבית אמה.** דרך הנשים היתה להיות להן בית לישב בו למלאכתן, ואין הבת מגדת אלא לאמה (ב"ר ס:ז): **(כט) וירץ.** למה רץ ועל מה רץ, ויהי כראות את הנזם, אמר, עשיר הוא זה, ונתן עיניו בממון: **(ל) [עמד] על הגמלים.** לשמרן, כמו והוא עומד עליהם (לעיל יח:ח) לשמשם: **(לא) פניתי הבית.** מעבודת כוכבים (ב"ר שם): **(לב) ויפתח.** התיר זמם שלהם, שהיה סותם את פיהם שלא ירעו בדרך

the master of his household. Everything that had happened, he ascribed to the grace of God, and made clear that it was not in his merit, but in Abraham's. *Haamek Davar* comments that he refers to the *God of my master Abraham,* because Abraham was the first to proclaim Him.

Perceptively, Eliezer speaks of *kindness and truth,* because it is important for the two to come together. Kindness alone can be harmful, because it can cause someone to give in to the wishes of the one he loves, even in cases where it is wrong. Therefore, truth must regulate kindness to prevent it from going astray *(R' Hirsch).*

אָנֹכִי — *As for me.* Although I am but Abraham's *servant*, far away from him and his land, God has guided me and brought me directly to my destination (*Da'as Sofrim*).

28-31. Laban. The Torah introduces us to Rebecca's family, where it seems that her father played little role, and her brother, Laban, was dominant. In those days, the women had separate houses where they did their work, and since a daughter naturally confides only in her mother, Rebecca ran and told her mother about her encounter at the well. Once the family heard the news, Laban took charge. From the profound influence he exercised in the household it would appear that he was either the only son or the oldest (*R' Hoffmann*).

Following the Midrashic perspective, *Rashi* interprets Laban's

וּמִסְפּוֹא֙ לַגְּמַלִּ֔ים וּמַ֙יִם֙ לִרְחֹ֣ץ רַגְלָ֔יו וְרַגְלֵ֥י

and fodder < for the camels, >> and water < to bathe < his feet < and the feet <

הָאֲנָשִׁ֖ים אֲשֶׁ֥ר אִתּֽוֹ׃ לג °וַיּוּשַׂ֣ם [°ויישם כ׳] לְפָנָיו֙

of the men < who were < with him. >> 33 [Food] was placed < before him <

לֶֽאֱכֹ֔ל וַיֹּ֕אמֶר לֹ֣א אֹכַ֔ל עַ֥ד אִם־דִּבַּ֖רְתִּי דְּבָרָ֑י

to eat, >> but he said, >> I will not eat < until then < that < I have spoken < my words. >>

וַיֹּ֖אמֶר דַּבֵּֽר׃ לד וַיֹּאמַ֑ר עֶ֥בֶד אַבְרָהָ֖ם אָנֹֽכִי׃ לה וַֽיהוה

And he said, >> Speak. >> 34 Then he said, >> A servant < of Abraham < am I. >> 35 And HASHEM <

בֵּרַ֧ךְ אֶת־אֲדֹנִ֛י מְאֹ֖ד וַיִּגְדָּ֑ל וַיִּתֶּן־ל֞וֹ צֹ֤אן וּבָקָר֙ וְכֶ֣סֶף וְזָהָ֔ב וַעֲבָדִם֙

has blessed < my master < greatly, < and he became great; >> He has given < him < sheep < and cattle, < silver < and gold, < slaves <

וּשְׁפָחֹ֔ת וּגְמַלִּ֖ים וַחֲמֹרִֽים׃ לו וַתֵּ֡לֶד שָׂרָה֩ אֵ֨שֶׁת אֲדֹנִ֥י בֵן֙ לַֽאדֹנִ֔י אַחֲרֵ֖י

and maidservants, < camels < and donkeys. >> 36 Give birth < did Sarah, < wife < of my master, < [to] a son < to my master < after <

זִקְנָתָ֑הּ וַיִּתֶּן־ל֖וֹ אֶת־כָּל־אֲשֶׁר־לֽוֹ׃ לז וַיַּשְׁבִּעֵ֥נִי אֲדֹנִ֖י לֵאמֹ֑ר לֹֽא־תִקַּ֤ח

she had grown old, >> and he gave < him < all < that < he possesses. >> 37 And my master had me take an oath < saying, >> 'Do not < take <

אִשָּׁה֙ לִבְנִ֔י מִבְּנוֹת֙ הַֽכְּנַעֲנִ֔י אֲשֶׁ֥ר אָנֹכִ֖י יֹשֵׁ֥ב בְּאַרְצֽוֹ׃ לח אִם־לֹ֧א

a wife < for my son < from the daughters < of the Canaanites < that < I < dwell < in their land. >> 38 Unless <

וְכִסָּתָא לְגַמְלַיָּא וּמַיָּא לְאַסְחָאָה רַגְלוֹהִי וְרַגְלֵי גֻּבְרַיָּא דִּי עִמֵּהּ: לג וְשַׁוִּיאוּ קֳדָמוֹהִי לְמֵיכָל וַאֲמַר לָא אֵיכוּל עַד דַּאֲמַלֵּל פִּתְגָּמָי וַאֲמַר מַלֵּל: לד וַאֲמַר עַבְדָּא דְאַבְרָהָם אֲנָא: לה וַיָי בָּרִיךְ יָת רִבּוֹנִי לַחֲדָא וּרְבָא וִיהַב לֵהּ עָאן וְתוֹרִין וּכְסַף וּדְהַב וְעַבְדִּין וְאַמְהָן וְגַמְלִין וַחֲמָרִין: לו וִילֵידַת שָׂרָה אִתַּת רִבּוֹנִי בַר לְרִבּוֹנִי בָּתַר דְּסֵיבַת וִיהַב לֵהּ יָת כָּל דִּי לֵהּ: לז וְקַיֵּים עֲלַי רִבּוֹנִי לְמֵימָר לָא תִסַּב אִתְּתָא לִבְרִי מִבְּנַת כְּנַעֲנָאֵי דִּי אֲנָא יָתֵב בְּאַרְעֲהוֹן: לח אֱלָהֵן

רש"י

בשדות אחרים (ב"ר ס:ח): (לג) עד אם דברתי. הרי אם משמש בלשון אשר ובלשון כי, כמו עד כי יבא שילה (להלן מט:י). וזהו שאמרו חז"ל כי משמש בד' לשונות, והאחד אי, והוא אם (ר"ה ג.): (לו) ויתן לו את כל אשר לו. שטר מתנה הראה להם (פדר"א פט"ז): (לז) לא תקח אשה לבני מבנות הכנעני. אם לא תלך תחלה אל

character as motivated by greed. This follows the principle of the Sages — and indeed, the approach that people generally take in dealing with others — that wicked people should be assumed to act wickedly, even when their actions seem to be virtuous. Conversely, people who are known to be righteous should always be given the benefit of the doubt, even when they seem to be acting improperly. Thus, upon hearing that the stranger was the servant of Abraham and that he was dispensing such lavish gifts, Laban assumed that he surely had gifts for the rest of the family — and if Eliezer had given Rebecca, a mere child, such extravagant gifts, just imagine what lay in store for Laban! Therefore, without showing his father the least courtesy, Laban dashed to the waiting servant and sanctimoniously tried to ingratiate himself with the wealthy and generous Eliezer.

Ramban, however, interprets Laban's character in the context of this passage as *basically* straightforward and honorable, since nothing up to this point in the narrative suggests otherwise.

33-39. The recapitulation. Eliezer allowed Laban to provide for the camels and the servants who accompanied him, but he refused to eat anything himself until he had completed his mission by securing the family's consent for the marriage. Eliezer repeated the whole story in order to convince them that God willed this marriage, thus delicately suggesting that it was not in their power to prevent it (*Radak*). That he did so is to be expected; what *is* surprising is that the Torah, which is so sparing of words, records Eliezer's entire recapitulation. The Sages exclaimed: יָפָה שִׂיחָתָן שֶׁל עַבְדֵי אָבוֹת לִפְנֵי הַמָּקוֹם מִתּוֹרָתָן שֶׁל בְּנֵיהֶם, *The ordinary conversation of the Patriarchs' servants is more pleasing before God than even the teachings of their children,* for Eliezer's full account of his journey is recorded in the Torah, whereas many important halachic principles can be derived only from textual allusions. From Eliezer's subtle changes in recounting the episode, the expositors have perceived both great ethical messages and his own wisdom.

37. וַיַּשְׁבִּעֵנִי אֲדֹנִי — *And my master had me take an oath.* I am here only because of the oath; there is no shortage of women in my country, but my master rejects them (*Radak; Sforno*). His mention of the oath was also to explain why he could not eat with them. Since he had taken an oath, he had to set everything aside until he had fulfilled his commitment (*Akeidas Yitzchak*).

אֶל־בֵּית־אָבִי תֵּלֵךְ וְאֶל־מִשְׁפַּחְתִּי וְלָקַחְתָּ אִשָּׁה
‹ a wife ‹ and you shall take « my family, ‹ and to ‹ you go, ‹ of my father ‹ the house ‹ to

לִבְנִי: לט וָאֹמַר אֶל־אֲדֹנִי אֻלַי לֹא־תֵלֵךְ הָאִשָּׁה
« the woman will not follow ‹ 'Perhaps « my master, ‹ to ‹ And I said **39** *« for my son.'*

אַחֲרָי: מ וַיֹּאמֶר אֵלָי יהוה אֲשֶׁר־הִתְהַלַּכְתִּי לְפָנָיו
‹ before Him, ‹ I have walked ‹ Whom « 'HASHEM, « to me, ‹ He replied **40** *« after me?'*

יִשְׁלַח מַלְאָכוֹ אִתָּךְ וְהִצְלִיחַ דַּרְכֶּךָ וְלָקַחְתָּ
‹ and you will take « your journey, ‹ and will make successful ‹ with you ‹ His angel ‹ will send

אִשָּׁה לִבְנִי מִמִּשְׁפַּחְתִּי וּמִבֵּית אָבִי: מא אָז תִּנָּקֶה
‹ will you be released ‹ Then **41** *« of my father. ‹ and from the house ‹ from my family ‹ for my son ‹ a wife*

מֵאָלָתִי כִּי תָבוֹא אֶל־מִשְׁפַּחְתִּי וְאִם־לֹא יִתְּנוּ לָךְ וְהָיִיתָ נָקִי מֵאָלָתִי:
« from my oath.' ‹ released ‹ then, you shall be « to you, ‹ they will not give [her] ‹ and if ‹ my family; ‹ to ‹ you have come ‹ when ‹ from my oath

מב וָאָבֹא הַיּוֹם אֶל־הָעָיִן וָאֹמַר יהוה אֱלֹהֵי אֲדֹנִי אַבְרָהָם אִם־יֶשְׁךָ־נָּא
‹ please, ‹ You have [the desire], ‹ if « Abraham, ‹ of my master ‹ God ‹ 'HASHEM, « and I said, ‹ the spring ‹ to ‹ today ‹ I came **42**

מַצְלִיחַ דַּרְכִּי אֲשֶׁר אָנֹכִי הֹלֵךְ עָלֶיהָ: מג הִנֵּה אָנֹכִי נִצָּב עַל־עֵין הַמָּיִם
‹ of water; ‹ the spring ‹ by ‹ am standing ‹ I ‹ Indeed, **43** *« upon: ‹ go ‹ I ‹ that ‹ my path ‹ to make successful*

וְהָיָה הָעַלְמָה הַיֹּצֵאת לִשְׁאֹב וְאָמַרְתִּי אֵלֶיהָ הַשְׁקִינִי־נָא מְעַט־מַיִם
‹ water ‹ a little ‹ please, ‹ "Give me to drink, « to her, ‹ and I shall say ‹ to draw [water] ‹ who comes out ‹ that the young woman ‹ let it be

לְבֵית אַבָּא תֵּיזִיל וּלְזַרְעִיתִי וְתִסַּב אִתְּתָא לִבְרִי: לט וַאֲמָרִית לְרִבּוֹנִי מָאִים לָא תֵיזִיל אִתְּתָא בַּתְרָי: מ וַאֲמַר לִי יְיָ דִּי פְלָחִית קֳדָמוֹהִי יִשְׁלַח מַלְאֲכֵהּ עִמָּךְ וְיַצְלַח אָרְחָךְ וְתִסַּב אִתְּתָא לִבְרִי מִזַּרְעִיתִי וּמִבֵּית אַבָּא: מא בְּכֵן תְּהֵי זַכַּי (נ״א זַכָּא) מִמּוֹמָתִי אֲרֵי תְהַךְ לְזַרְעִיתִי וְאִם לָא יִתְּנוּן לָךְ וּתְהֵי זַכַּי מִמּוֹמָתִי: מב וְאָתִית (נ״א וַאֲתֵיתִי) יוֹמָא דֵין לְעֵינָא וַאֲמָרִית יְיָ אֱלָהָא דְרִבּוֹנִי אַבְרָהָם אִם אִית כְּעַן רַעֲוָא קֳדָמָךְ לְאַצְלָחָא אָרְחִי דִּי אֲנָא אָזֵל עֲלַהּ: מג הָא אֲנָא קָאֵם עַל עֵינָא דְמַיָּא וּתְהֵי עוּלֶמְתָּא דְּתִפּוֹק לְמִמְלֵי וְאֵימַר לַהּ אַשְׁקִינִי כְעַן זְעֵיר מַיָּא

רש״י

בית אבי ולא תאבה ללכת אחריך (קדושין סא:): **(לט) אלי לא תלך האשה.** אלי כתיב, בת היתה לו לאליעזר, והיה מחזר למצוא עילה שיאמר [לו] אברהם לפנות אליו להשיאו בתו. אמר לו אברהם בני ברוך ואתה ארור ואין ארור מדבק בברוך (ב״ר נט:ט): **(מב) ואבא היום.** היום יצאתי והיום באתי. מכאן שקפלה לו הארץ (סנהדרין צה.; ב״ר שם יא). אמר רבי אחא, יפה שיחתן של עבדי אבות לפני המקום מתורתן של בנים, שהרי פרשה של אליעזר כפולה בתורה, והרבה גופי תורה לא נתנו אלא ברמיזה (ב״ר ס:ח):

39. **אֻלַי** — *Perhaps.* Normally the word is spelled אוּלַי, with a ו. As it is spelled here, it could be read as אֵלַי, *to me.* By using this spelling, the Torah conveys Eliezer's personal hope: He was anxious to marry his own daughter to Isaac; thus, when he asked Abraham the logical question about what to do if the woman would not go with him, he was not simply *asking*, but *hoping* she would not, and that Isaac would come "*to me*." But Abraham answered: "My son is blessed [22:18] and you [as a Canaanite] are accursed. The accursed cannot unite with the blessed" (*Rashi*). But why didn't the Torah insert this spelling with its implied meaning in verse 5, when Eliezer asked the question? The *Kotzker Rebbe* explains that Eliezer, to the best of his own personal knowledge, was sincere; it was only subconsciously that he wanted his trip to Haran to end in failure. Only now, when he had found Rebecca and reflected back to his conversation with Abraham, did he recognize what his true motive had been.

41. Another departure from the original version of the narrative: Eliezer did not use Abraham's term שְׁבוּעָה for *oath* [see v. 8]. He substituted the stronger term אָלָה, *imprecation,* an oath reinforced by a curse, for he wanted to impress them with the seriousness of Abraham's intention (*Ibn Ezra*).

He also did not repeat Abraham's command that he not permit Isaac to go to his family's land (v. 8), for they might take that as a disparaging comment on their homeland (*Abarbanel).*

43. In verse 16, Eliezer used the word נַעֲרָ, *girl*. Here he tactfully said עַלְמָה, a more specific word that denotes a young woman in the vigor of her youth, thus implying that Rebecca had passed a very exacting test (*Malbim*).

מִכַּדֵּךְ: מד וְאָמְרָה אֵלַי גַּם־אַתָּה שְׁתֵה וְגַם לִגְמַלֶּיךָ

< for your camels < and also < may drink < you <“Certainly << me, < and she will answer 44 << from your jug,”

אֶשְׁאָב הִוא הָאִשָּׁה אֲשֶׁר־הֹכִיחַ יהוה לְבֶן־אֲדֹנִי:

<< of my master.’ < for the son < HASHEM has designated < whom < shall be the woman < she < I will draw [water],”

מה אֲנִי טֶרֶם אֲכַלֶּה לְדַבֵּר אֶל־לִבִּי וְהִנֵּה רִבְקָה

< Rebecca < of a sudden < my heart, < to < speaking < I had finished < [even] before << And I, 45

יֹצֵאת וְכַדָּהּ עַל־שִׁכְמָהּ וַתֵּרֶד הָעַיְנָה וַתִּשְׁאָב

<< and drew [water]. < to the spring < and she descended << her shoulder, < upon < with her jug < was going out

וָאֹמַר אֵלֶיהָ הַשְׁקִינִי נָא: מו וַתְּמַהֵר וַתּוֹרֶד כַּדָּהּ

< her jug < and she lowered < She hurried 46 << please.’ < ‘Give me to drink, < to her, < Then I said

מֵעָלֶיהָ וַתֹּאמֶר שְׁתֵה וְגַם־גְּמַלֶּיךָ אַשְׁקֶה וָאֵשְׁתְּ וְגַם הַגְּמַלִּים הִשְׁקָתָה:

<< she gave to drink. < the camels < and also < So I drank << I will give to drink.’ < your camels < and also < ‘Drink, << and she said, < from upon herself

מז וָאֶשְׁאַל אֹתָהּ וָאֹמַר בַּת־מִי אַתְּ וַתֹּאמֶר בַּת־בְּתוּאֵל בֶּן־נָחוֹר

< of Nahor, < son < of Bethuel, < ‘The daughter < And she said, << are you?’ < of whom < ‘The daughter << and I said, < her < Then I questioned 47

אֲשֶׁר יָלְדָה־לּוֹ מִלְכָּה וָאָשִׂם הַנֶּזֶם עַל־אַפָּהּ וְהַצְּמִידִים עַל־יָדֶיהָ:

<< her hands. < on < and the bracelets < her nose < on < the ring < And I placed << [by] Milcah.’ < to him < was born < who

מח וָאֶקֹּד וָאֶשְׁתַּחֲוֶה לַיהוה וָאֲבָרֵךְ אֶת־יהוה אֱלֹהֵי אֲדֹנִי אַבְרָהָם

<< Abraham, < of my master < God < HASHEM, < and I blessed << to HASHEM < and prostrated myself < Then I bowed [my head] low 48

אֲשֶׁר הִנְחַנִי בְּדֶרֶךְ אֱמֶת לָקַחַת אֶת־בַּת־אֲחִי אֲדֹנִי לִבְנוֹ: מט וְעַתָּה

< And now, 49 << for his son. < of my master < of the brother < the daughter < to take < of truth < on the path < guided me < Who

אִם־יֶשְׁכֶם עֹשִׂים חֶסֶד וֶאֱמֶת אֶת־אֲדֹנִי הַגִּידוּ לִי וְאִם־לֹא הַגִּידוּ לִי

<< me, < tell < not, < and if << me; < tell << my master, < with < and truth < kindness < you have [the intention] to do < if

מִקּוּלְתִּיךְ: מד וְתֵימַר לִי אַף אַתְּ אִשְׁתְּ וְאַף לְגַמְלָיךְ אַמְלֵי הִיא אִתְּתָא דְּזַמִּין יְיָ לְבַר רִבּוֹנִי: מה אֲנָא עַד לָא שֵׁיצִיתִי לְמַלָּלָא עִם לִבִּי וְהָא רִבְקָה נְפָקַת וְקוּלְתַהּ עַל כַּתְפַּהּ וּנְחָתַת לְעֵינָא וּמְלָת וַאֲמָרִית לַהּ אַשְׁקִינִי כְעַן: מו וְאוֹחִיאַת וַאֲחִיתַת קוּלְתַהּ מִנַּהּ וַאֲמֶרֶת אִשְׁתְּ וְאַף גַּמְלָיךְ אַשְׁקֵי וּשְׁתֵיתִי וְאַף גַּמְלַיָּא אַשְׁקִיאַת: מז וּשְׁאֵלִית יָתַהּ וַאֲמָרִית בַּת מָן אַתְּ וַאֲמֶרֶת בַּת בְּתוּאֵל בַּר נָחוֹר דִּילֵידַת לֵהּ מִלְכָּה וְשַׁוֵּיתִי קָדָשָׁא עַל אַפַּהּ וְשֵׁירַיָּא עַל יְדָהָא: מח וּכְרָעִית וּסְגָדִית קֳדָם יְיָ וּבָרֵכִית יָת יְיָ אֱלָהֵהּ דְּרִבּוֹנִי אַבְרָהָם דְּדַבְּרַנִי בְּאוֹרַח קְשׁוֹט לְמִסַּב יָת בַּת אֲחוּהִי דְרִבּוֹנִי לִבְרֵהּ: מט וּכְעַן אִם אִיתֵיכוֹן עָבְדִין טִיבוּ וּקְשׁוֹט עִם רִבּוֹנִי חַווֹ לִי וְאִם לָא חַווֹ לִי

רש"י

(מד) **גם אתה.** גם, לרבות אנשים שעמו: **הכיח.** בירר והודיע, וכן כל הוכחה שבמקרא בירור דבר: (מה) **טרם אכלה.** טרם שאני מכלה. וכן כל לשון הווה פעמים שהוא מדבר בלשון עבר, ויכול לכתוב טרם כליתי, ופעמים שמדבר בלשון עתיד, כמו כי אמר איוב (איוב א:ה) הרי לשון עבר, ככה יעשה איוב (שם) הרי לשון עתיד, ופירוש שניהם לשון הווה, כי אומר היה איוב אולי חטאו בני וגו' (שם) והיה עושה כך: (מז) **ואשאל ואשם.** שנה הסדר, שהרי הוא תחלה נתן ואח"כ שאל. אלא שלא יתפשוהו

47. וָאֶשְׁאַל אֹתָהּ — *Then I questioned her.* Actually Eliezer gave her the jewelry before asking her who she was. Here he changed the sequence because they would have said, "How could you have given her gifts before you knew who she was?" (*Rashi*).

49. חֶסֶד — *Kindness* denotes an intention to do something that is not obligated, while אֱמֶת, *truth,* means to give permanence to the *kindness* (*Ibn Ezra*).

According to *Sforno*: The *kindness* would be to Abraham, in

וְאֶפְנֶה עַל־יָמִין אוֹ עַל־שְׂמֹאל: נ וַיַּעַן לָבָן וּבְתוּאֵל

‹ Then Laban and Bethuel answered **50** « the left. ‹ to ‹ or ‹ the right ‹ to ‹ and then I will turn

וַיֹּאמְרוּ מֵיְהוָה יָצָא הַדָּבָר לֹא נוּכַל דַּבֵּר אֵלֶיךָ

‹ to you ‹ to say ‹ We are not able « the matter! ‹ has gone forth ‹ From HASHEM « and they said,

רַע אוֹ־טוֹב: נא הִנֵּה־רִבְקָה לְפָנֶיךָ קַח וָלֵךְ וּתְהִי

‹ and let her be « and go, ‹ take [her] « before you; ‹ Rebecca ‹ Here is **51** « good. ‹ or ‹ bad

אִשָּׁה לְבֶן־אֲדֹנֶיךָ כַּאֲשֶׁר דִּבֶּר יהוה: נב וַיְהִי

‹ And it was, **52** « HASHEM has spoken. ‹ as ‹ of your master ‹ to the son ‹ a wife

כַּאֲשֶׁר שָׁמַע עֶבֶד אַבְרָהָם אֶת־דִּבְרֵיהֶם וַיִּשְׁתַּחוּ אַרְצָה לַיהוה:

« to HASHEM. ‹ to the ground ‹ he prostrated himself « their words, « of Abraham — ‹ — the servant « he heard ‹ when

חמישי נג וַיּוֹצֵא הָעֶבֶד כְּלֵי־כֶסֶף וּכְלֵי זָהָב וּבְגָדִים וַיִּתֵּן לְרִבְקָה וּמִגְדָּנֹת

‹ and delicious fruits « to Rebecca; ‹ and he gave [them] ‹ and garments, ‹ of gold, ‹ and objects ‹ of silver ‹ objects ‹ The servant brought out **53**

נָתַן לְאָחִיהָ וּלְאִמָּהּ: נד וַיֹּאכְלוּ וַיִּשְׁתּוּ הוּא וְהָאֲנָשִׁים אֲשֶׁר־עִמּוֹ

« with him, ‹ who were ‹ and the men ‹ he « and they drank, ‹ They ate **54** « and her mother. ‹ to her brother ‹ he gave

וַיָּלִינוּ וַיָּקוּמוּ בַבֹּקֶר וַיֹּאמֶר שַׁלְּחֻנִי לַאדֹנִי: נה וַיֹּאמֶר אָחִיהָ וְאִמָּהּ

« Her brother and her mother said, **55** « to my master. ‹ Send me « he said, ‹ in the morning, ‹ [when] they arose « and they spent the night;

וְאִתְפְּנֵי עַל יַמִּינָא אוֹ עַל שְׂמָאלָא: נ וַאֲתֵיב לָבָן וּבְתוּאֵל וַאֲמַרוּ מִן קֳדָם יְיָ נְפַק פִּתְגָּמָא לֵית אֲנַחְנָא יָכְלִין לְמַלָּלָא עִמָּךְ בִּישׁ אוֹ טָב: נא הָא רִבְקָה קֳדָמָךְ דְּבַר וְאִיזֵיל וּתְהֵי אִתְּתָא לְבַר רִבּוֹנָךְ כְּמָא דִּי מַלֵּיל יְיָ: נב וַהֲוָה כַּד שְׁמַע עַבְדָּא דְאַבְרָהָם יָת פִּתְגָּמֵיהוֹן וּסְגֵיד עַל אַרְעָא קֳדָם יְיָ: נג וְאַפֵּק עַבְדָּא מָנִין דִּכְסַף וּמָנִין דִּדְהַב וּלְבוּשִׁין וִיהַב לְרִבְקָה וּמִגְדָּנִין יְהַב לַאֲחוּהָא וּלְאִמַּהּ: נד וַאֲכַלוּ וּשְׁתִיאוּ הוּא וְגוּבְרַיָּא דִּי עִמֵּהּ וּבִיתוּ וְקָמוּ בְצַפְרָא וַאֲמַר שַׁלְּחוּנִי לְוַת רִבּוֹנִי: נה וַאֲמַר אֲחוּהָא וְאִמַּהּ

רש"י

בדבריו ויאמרו היאך נתת לה ועדיין אינך יודע מי היא: (מט) **על ימין.** מבנות ישמעאל: **על שמאל.** מבנות לוט שהיה יושב לשמאלו של אברהם. ב"ר (שם ט): (נ) **ויען לבן ובתואל.** רשע היה וקפץ להשיב לפני אביו (פסיקתא זוטרתא): **לא נוכל דבר אליך.** למאן בדבר הזה, לא ע"י תשובת דבר רע ולא ע"י תשובת דבר הגון, לפי שניכר שמה' יצא הדבר לפי דבריך שזימנה לך: (נב) **וישתחו ארצה.** מכאן שמודים על בשורה טובה (ב"ר ס:ו): (נג) **ומגדנות.** לשון מגדים, שהביא עמו מיני פירות (שם יא) של א"י: (נד) **וילינו.** כל לינה שבמקרא לינת לילה [א'] (ב"מ קי:): (נה) **ויאמר אחיה ואמה.** ובתואל היכן היה. הוא היה רוצה לעכב ובא מלאך והמיתו (ב"ר שם יב): **ימים.** שנה (כתובות נז:) כמו ימים תהיה גאולתו (ויקרא כה:כט), שכך נותנין לבתולה זמן י"ב חדש לפרנס את עצמה בתכשיטים (כתובות נז:; ב"ר שם יב):

that they would yield to his wishes by sending Rebecca so far away. The *truth* would be to Rebecca, because it was for her benefit that she marry Isaac.

50. מֵה' יָצָא הַדָּבָר — *From* HASHEM *has gone forth the matter.* The Sages see this response as a proof that God ordains a man's proper mate (*Moed Katan* 18b). Even though the comment was made by Laban and Bethuel, the Torah would not have quoted these words unless they were true (*Rashba).*

In his great impudence, Laban hastened to speak up before his father, an indication of his wickedness (*Rashi*).

רַע אוֹ־טוֹב — *Bad or good.* Since the match is obviously God's wish, we have no right to say bad, to reject it, or say good, i.e., affirm it. Therefore, *Here is Rebecca before you, take [her] and go* (v. 51) — you do not need our permission (*Sforno).*

R' Bachya observes that Laban's character is reflected in the precedence he gave to the mention of "bad."

51. כַּאֲשֶׁר דִּבֶּר ה' — *As* HASHEM *has spoken.* Nowhere in the chapter did God speak explicitly. However, God "speaks" through His control of events, and the entire narrative shows that He wanted Rebecca to become Isaac's wife (*Ramban).*

53. וַיִּתֵּן לְרִבְקָה — *And he gave [them] to Rebecca.* Now that the family had agreed to the match, Eliezer acted as Isaac's agent to marry her, and the gifts served the function of the ring customarily used nowadays. The earlier gifts that Eliezer had given Rebecca at the well were meant only for the purpose of betrothal, because it is not permitted to marry a woman without consent (*Lekach Tov).*

לְאָחִיהָ וּלְאִמָּהּ — *To her brother and her mother.* Where was her father Bethuel? The entire family had expected extravagant gifts from Eliezer. Disappointed that he had given them only fruit (*Alshich),* Bethuel tried to renege on his agreement, or to poison Eliezer, so God sent an angel to kill him (*Midrash; Rashi*).

תֵּשֵׁב הַנַּעֲרָ אִתָּנוּ יָמִים אוֹ עָשׂוֹר אַחַר תֵּלֵךְ:

« she will go. ‹ after that «ten [months]; ‹ or ‹ a year ‹ with us ‹ Let the girl remain

נו וַיֹּאמֶר אֲלֵהֶם אַל־תְּאַחֲרוּ אֹתִי וַיהוָה הִצְלִיחַ

‹ made successful ‹ in that HASHEM ‹ me ‹ delay ‹ Do not « to them, ‹ He said 56

דַּרְכִּי שַׁלְּחוּנִי וְאֵלְכָה לַאדֹנִי: נז וַיֹּאמְרוּ נִקְרָא

‹ Let us call « And they said, 57 « to my master. ‹ and I will go ‹ Send me, « my path.

לַנַּעֲרָ וְנִשְׁאֲלָה אֶת־פִּיהָ: נח וַיִּקְרְאוּ לְרִבְקָה

‹ for Rebecca ‹ They called 58 « what she says. ‹ and ask ‹ for the girl

וַיֹּאמְרוּ אֵלֶיהָ הֲתֵלְכִי עִם־הָאִישׁ הַזֶּה וַתֹּאמֶר

‹ And she said, « this man? ‹ with ‹ Will you go « to her, ‹ and they said

אֵלֵךְ: נט וַיְשַׁלְּחוּ אֶת־רִבְקָה אֲחֹתָם וְאֶת־מֵנִקְתָּהּ וְאֶת־עֶבֶד אַבְרָהָם

‹ of Abraham ‹ [along with] the servant « and her nurse, ‹ their sister, ‹ Rebecca ‹ So they sent off 59 « I will go.

וְאֶת־אֲנָשָׁיו: ס וַיְבָרְכוּ אֶת־רִבְקָה וַיֹּאמְרוּ לָהּ אֲחֹתֵנוּ אַתְּ הֲיִי לְאַלְפֵי

‹ thousands ‹ come to be ‹ may you ‹ Our sister, « to her, ‹ and they said ‹ Rebecca ‹ They blessed 60 « and his men.

רְבָבָה וְיִירַשׁ זַרְעֵךְ אֵת שַׁעַר שֹׂנְאָיו: סא וַתָּקָם רִבְקָה וְנַעֲרֹתֶיהָ

« with her maidens; ‹ Then Rebecca arose 61 « of its foes. ‹ the gate ‹ may your offspring ‹ and inherit « of myriads,

וַתִּרְכַּבְנָה עַל־הַגְּמַלִּים וַתֵּלַכְנָה אַחֲרֵי הָאִישׁ וַיִּקַּח הָעֶבֶד אֶת־רִבְקָה

‹ Rebecca ‹ the servant took « the man; ‹ after ‹ and they went ‹ the camels ‹ upon ‹ they rode

תֵּתֵיב עוּלֶמְתָּא עִמָּנָא עִדַּן בְּעִדַּן אוֹ עַסְרָא יַרְחִין בָּתַר כֵּן תֵּיזִיל: נו וַאֲמַר לְהוֹן לָא תְאַחֲרוּן יָתִי וַייָ אַצְלַח אָרְחִי שַׁלְּחוּנִי וְאֵיהַךְ לְוַת רִבּוֹנִי: נז וַאֲמַרוּ נִקְרֵי לְעוּלֶמְתָּא וְנִשְׁמַע מַה דְּהִיא אָמְרָה: נח וּקְרוֹ לְרִבְקָה וַאֲמַרוּ לַהּ הֲתֵיזְלִי עִם גַּבְרָא הָדֵין וַאֲמֶרֶת אֵיזִיל: נט וְאַלְוִיאוּ (נ״א וְשַׁלַּחוּ) יָת רִבְקָה אֲחַתְהוֹן וְיָת מֵנִקְתַּהּ וְיָת עַבְדָּא דְאַבְרָהָם וְיָת גַּבְרוֹהִי: ס וּבָרִיכוּ יָת רִבְקָה וַאֲמַרוּ לַהּ אֲחָתָנָא אַתְּ הֲוִי לְאַלְפִין וּלְרִבְוָן וְיִרְתוּן בְּנַיְכִי יָת קִרְוֵי סַנְאֵיהוֹן: סא וְקָמַת רִבְקָה וְעוּלֶמְתָהָא וּרְכִיבָא עַל גַּמְלַיָּא וַאֲזַלָא בָּתַר גַּבְרָא וּדְבַר עַבְדָּא יָת רִבְקָה

רש״י

או עשור. י' חדשים (אונקלוס). וא"ת ימים ממש, אין דרך המבקשים לבקש דבר מועט ואם לא תרצה תן לנו מרובה מזה (כתובות נז:): **(נז) ונשאלה את פיה.** [מכאן] שאין משיאין את האשה אלא מדעתה (ב"ר שם): **(נח) ותאמר אלך.** מעצמי, ואף אם אינכם רוצים (שם): [(ס) **את היי לאלפי רבבה.** את וזרעך תקבלו אותה ברכה שנאמר לאברהם בהר המוריה והרבה ארבה את זרעך וגו' (לעיל כב:יז), יהי רצון שיהא אותו הזרע ממך ולא מאשה אחרת:]

55. יָמִים אוֹ עָשׂוֹר — *A year or ten* [*months*]. This was the period of time generally given to a young bride to prepare for her marriage (*Kesubos* 57b). Ostensibly, therefore, Laban and his mother were making a customary and reasonable request, but, like Bethuel, they intended to break the engagement. Knowing or suspecting this, Eliezer would not consider any delay. "Since everything has gone so smoothly and God guided my mission so speedily, it is obvious that He wishes me to return to my master without delay" (*Abarbanel*).

57. וְנִשְׁאֲלָה אֶת־פִּיהָ — *And ask what she says.* From this we learn that a girl should be given in marriage only with her consent [*Midrash*; see *Kiddushin* 41a] (*Rashi*). According to *Rashbam,* this was another ploy to delay the marriage. Laban and his mother argued that only she had a right to say that she was willing to forgo her twelve-month period of preparation. She replied very emphatically; according to *Rashi* she said that she would go even without their consent.

59. וַיְשַׁלְּחוּ — *So they sent off.* Whether, as *Rashi* would interpret, they gave permission reluctantly to avoid her threatened defiance, or as *Radak* and *Rambam* interpret, they graciously acquiesced to her wishes, once Rebecca expressed her intention, they no longer hindered her. Immediately, they arranged a procession and blessed her. However, *Abarbanel* observes, no one from the family accompanied her, probably as an expression of their displeasure.

וְאֶת־מֵנִקְתָּהּ — *And her nurse.* According to the most common Rabbinic chronology, the nurse was sent along because Rebecca was but three years old at the time, so that she would have needed someone to care for her. *Ibn Ezra*, however, comments that she was older, but it was customary for the *nurse* of a girl's infancy to remain with her as her servant throughout her life.

60. שַׁעַר שֹׂנְאָיו — *The gate of its foes.* In the simple meaning of the term, they wished that her offspring would always be victorious in battle. *Haamek Davar*, however, comments that the

וַיֵּלַךְ׃ סב וְיִצְחָק בָּא מִבּוֹא בְּאֵר לַחַי רֹאִי וְהוּא

‹ for he ‹‹ [to] Be'er-lahai-ro'i, ‹ from having gone ‹ came ‹ Now Isaac 62 ‹‹ and he went.

יוֹשֵׁב בְּאֶרֶץ הַנֶּגֶב׃ סג וַיֵּצֵא יִצְחָק לָשׂוּחַ בַּשָּׂדֶה

‹ in the field ‹ to pray ‹ Isaac went out 63 ‹‹ of the south. ‹ in the land ‹ dwelt

לִפְנוֹת עָרֶב וַיִּשָּׂא עֵינָיו וַיַּרְא וְהִנֵּה גְמַלִּים בָּאִים׃

‹‹ coming. ‹ camels ‹ there were ‹‹ and saw: ‹ his eyes ‹ and he raised ‹ evening ‹ toward

סד וַתִּשָּׂא רִבְקָה אֶת־עֵינֶיהָ וַתֵּרֶא אֶת־יִצְחָק

‹‹ Isaac; ‹ and saw ‹ her eyes ‹ And Rebecca raised 64

וַתִּפֹּל מֵעַל הַגָּמָל׃ סה וַתֹּאמֶר אֶל־הָעֶבֶד מִי־הָאִישׁ הַלָּזֶה הַהֹלֵךְ

‹ *who is walking* ‹ *that man* ‹ *Who is* ‹‹ the servant, ‹ to ‹ And she said 65 ‹‹ the camel. ‹ from upon ‹ she fell

בַּשָּׂדֶה לִקְרָאתֵנוּ וַיֹּאמֶר הָעֶבֶד הוּא אֲדֹנִי וַתִּקַּח הַצָּעִיף וַתִּתְכָּס׃

‹‹ and covered herself. ‹ the veil ‹ She then took ‹‹ *my master.* ‹ *He is* ‹‹ And the servant said, ‹‹ *toward us?* ‹ *in the field*

וַאֲזַל׃ סב וְיִצְחָק אֲתָא מִמֵּתוֹהִי (נ״א עַל בְּמֵיתוֹהִי) מְבֵּירָא דְמַלְאַךְ קַיָּמָא אִתְחֲזִי עֲלַהּ וְהוּא יָתֵב בְּאַרַע דָּרוֹמָא׃ סג וּנְפַק יִצְחָק לְצַלָּאָה בְחַקְלָא לְמִפְנֵי רַמְשָׁא וּזְקַף עֵינוֹהִי וַחֲזָא וְהָא גַמְלַיָּא אָתָן׃ סד וּזְקָפַת רִבְקָה יָת עֵינָהָא וַחֲזַת יָת יִצְחָק וְאִתְרְכִינַת מֵעַל גַּמְלָא׃ סה וַאֲמֶרֶת לְעַבְדָּא מָן גַּבְרָא דֵיכִי דִּמְהַלֵּךְ בְּחַקְלָא לְקַדָּמוּתָנָא וַאֲמַר עַבְדָּא הוּא רִבּוֹנִי וּנְסֵיבַת עֵיפָא וְאִתְכַּסִּיאַת׃

רש״י

(סב) **מבוא באר לחי רואי.** שהלך להביא הגר לאברהם אביו שישאנה (ב״ר שם יד): **יושב בארץ הנגב.** קרוב לאותו באר שנאמר ויסע משם אברהם ארצה הנגב וישב בין קדש ובין שור (לעיל כ:א), ושם היה הבאר, שנא' הנה בין קדש ובין ברד (שם טז:יד): (סג) **לשוח.** לשון תפלה, כמו ישפך שיחו (תהלים קב:א; ברכות כו:; ב״ר ס:יד): (סד) **ותרא את יצחק.** ראתה אותו הדור ותוהא [ס״א ונתביישה ס״א ותמהה] מפניו (ב״ר ס:טו): **ותפל.** השמיטה עצמה לארץ, כתרגומו ואתרכינת, הטתה עצמה לארץ ולא הגיעה עד הקרקע, כמו הטי נא כדך (לעיל פסוק יד) ארכיני, ויט שמים (שמואל ב כב:י) וארכין, ל' מוטה לארץ. ודומה לו, כי יפול לא יוטל (תהלים לז:כד) כלומר, אם יטה לארץ לא יגיע עד הקרקע (ב״ר שם): (סה) **ותתכס.** לשון ותתפעל, כמו ותקבר (להלן לה:ח) ותשבר (ש״א ד:יח):

Torah often uses the word *gate* to refer to the judges and counselors who convene at the gate of a city. Thus they blessed Rebecca that her descendants should achieve such a reputation for integrity and wisdom that even their enemies would seek their advice.

62-67. Isaac and Rebecca. The brief passage describing the meeting and marriage of Isaac and Rebecca is touching and reflective of basic principles of Judaism and Jewish marriage. It begins with Isaac walking back home from praying at a place that recalled God's mercy to the previous generation, for Jews cleave to their past and the God Who guided it. Isaac and Rebecca "met," but not by chance. She displayed the personal modesty that has always been one of the glories of Jewish women and she recognized intuitively that the stranger she had just encountered was a holy person. Finally, Isaac brought her to his mother's tent, and there it became apparent that she was a fitting successor to Sarah, for the holy presence of Sarah returned to the tent of her son. It was then that Isaac loved her (v. 67), for the Jewish home is a temple and its priestess is the wife and mother whose spirit infuses it. Isaac could love only a mate who could be his companion in creating the Chosen People. In Rebecca he found her.

62. בָּא מִבּוֹא — *Came from having gone. HaK'sav VehaKabbalah* suggests an alternate reading of the verse, based on the cantellation *[Zakef Katan]* which separates the first two words from the following place name: *Now Isaac came [to] Be'er-lahai-ro'i because of the [imminent] coming* of his prospective wife, desiring to come to greet her, even if he was precluded from leaving Israel to find her.

בְּאֵר לַחַי רֹאִי — *Be'er-lahai-ro'i.* This was the propitious site where Hagar's prayers had once been answered, and it was there that Isaac had gone to pray. Even before he prayed, his needs were answered, and his bride was already approaching, in the manner of [*Isaiah* 65:24] טֶרֶם יִקְרָאוּ וַאֲנִי אֶעֱנֶה, *before they call I will answer* (*Sforno*).

Rashi cites the Midrash that Isaac had gone to Be'er-lahai-ro'i to bring Hagar back as a wife for Abraham. This follows the tradition that Keturah (25:1), Abraham's second wife, was Hagar.

63. לָשׂוּחַ בַּשָּׂדֶה לִפְנוֹת עָרֶב — *To pray in the field toward evening.* From this description that Isaac prayed before nightfall, the Talmud (*Berachos* 26b) and Midrash derive the tradition that Isaac instituted the *Minchah* [afternoon] prayer. That Abraham instituted the *Shacharis* [morning] prayer is derived from 19:27; and that Jacob instituted the *Maariv* [evening] prayer is derived from 28:11.

64. וַתִּפֹּל מֵעַל הַגָּמָל — *She fell from upon the camel.* While most commentators translate literally that she *fell*, meaning that she alighted quickly from the camel and stood modestly, *Rashi* explains that overawed by the dignified appearance of the approaching man, Rebecca modestly inclined herself to one side, while still mounted on the camel, in order to turn her face from him. [Then, upon hearing that he was Isaac, she veiled herself (*Ramban*).]

סו וַיְסַפֵּר הָעֶבֶד לְיִצְחָק אֵת כָּל־הַדְּבָרִים אֲשֶׁר
‹ that ‹ the things ‹ all ‹ Isaac ‹ The servant told 66

עָשָׂה: סז וַיְבִאֶהָ יִצְחָק הָאֹהֱלָה שָׂרָה אִמּוֹ וַיִּקַּח
‹ he took [in marriage] « his mother; ‹ [of] Sarah ‹ into the tent ‹ And Isaac brought her 67 « he had done.

אֶת־רִבְקָה וַתְּהִי־לוֹ לְאִשָּׁה וַיֶּאֱהָבֶהָ וַיִּנָּחֵם יִצְחָק
‹ and [thus] Isaac was consoled « and he loved her; ‹ [his] wife, ‹ to him ‹ she became « Rebecca,

אַחֲרֵי אִמּוֹ: פ ששי [כה] א וַיֹּסֶף אַבְרָהָם וַיִּקַּח אִשָּׁה
‹ a wife ‹ took ‹ Abraham once again 1 [25] « his mother. ‹ after

וּשְׁמָהּ קְטוּרָה: ב וַתֵּלֶד לוֹ אֶת־זִמְרָן וְאֶת־יָקְשָׁן
‹ Jokshan, ‹ Zimran, ‹ him ‹ She bore 2 « Keturah. ‹ whose name was

וְאֶת־מְדָן וְאֶת־מִדְיָן וְאֶת־יִשְׁבָּק וְאֶת־שׁוּחַ: ג וְיָקְשָׁן יָלַד אֶת־שְׁבָא
‹ Sheba ‹ begot ‹ Jokshan 3 « and Shuah. ‹ Ishbak, ‹ Midian, ‹ Medan,

וְאֶת־דְּדָן וּבְנֵי דְדָן הָיוּ אַשּׁוּרִם וּלְטוּשִׁם וּלְאֻמִּים: ד וּבְנֵי מִדְיָן עֵיפָה
‹ Ephah, « of Midian: ‹ And the children 4 « and Leummim. ‹ Letushim, ‹ Asshurim, ‹ were ‹ of Dedan ‹ and the children ‹ and Dedan,

וָעֵפֶר וַחֲנֹךְ וַאֲבִידָע וְאֶלְדָּעָה כָּל־אֵלֶּה בְּנֵי קְטוּרָה: ה וַיִּתֵּן אַבְרָהָם
‹ Abraham gave 5 « of Keturah. ‹ were the children ‹ these ‹ all ‹ and Eldaah; ‹ Abida, ‹ Hanoch, ‹ Epher,

אֶת־כָּל־אֲשֶׁר־לוֹ לְיִצְחָק: ו וְלִבְנֵי הַפִּילַגְשִׁים אֲשֶׁר לְאַבְרָהָם
« to Abraham, ‹ who were ‹ of the concubines ‹ But to the children 6 « to Isaac. ‹ he had ‹ that ‹ all

סו וְאִשְׁתָּעִי עַבְדָּא לְיִצְחָק יָת כָּל פִּתְגָּמַיָּא דִּי עֲבָד: סז וְאַעֲלַהּ יִצְחָק לְמַשְׁכְּנָא וַחֲזָא וְהָא תַקְנִין עוֹבָדָהָא כְּעוֹבָדֵי שָׂרָה אִמֵּהּ וּנְסֵיב יָת רִבְקָה וַהֲוַת לֵהּ לְאִנְתּוּ וְרַחֲמַהּ וְאִתְנְחֵם יִצְחָק בָּתַר דְּמִיתַת אִמֵּהּ: א וְאוֹסֵיף אַבְרָהָם וּנְסֵיב אִתְּתָא וּשְׁמַהּ קְטוּרָה: ב וִילֵידַת לֵהּ יָת זִמְרָן וְיָת יָקְשָׁן וְיָת מְדָן וְיָת מִדְיָן וְיָת יִשְׁבָּק וְיָת שׁוּחַ: ג וְיָקְשָׁן אוֹלִיד יָת שְׁבָא וְיָת דְּדָן וּבְנֵי דְדָן הֲווֹ לְמַשְׁרְיָן וְלִשְׁכוּנִין וּלְנַגְוָן: ד וּבְנֵי מִדְיָן עֵיפָה וָעֵפֶר וַחֲנוֹךְ וַאֲבִידָע וְאֶלְדָּעָה כָּל אִלֵּין בְּנֵי קְטוּרָה: ה וִיהַב אַבְרָהָם יָת כָּל דִּי לֵהּ לְיִצְחָק: ו וְלִבְנֵי לְחֵינָתָא דִּי לְאַבְרָהָם

רש"י

(סו) **ויספר העבד.** גלה לו נסים שנעשו לו, שקפצה לו הארץ ושנזדמנה לו רבקה בתפלתו (ב"ר שם): (סז) **האהלה שרה אמו.** ויביאה האהלה והרי היא שרה אמו, כלומר, ונעשית דוגמת שרה אמו. שכל זמן ששרה קיימת היה נר דלוק מע"ש לע"ש וברכה מצויה בעיסה וענן קשור על האהל, ומשמתה פסקו, וכשבאת רבקה חזרו. ב"ר (שם טז): **אחרי אמו.** דרך ארץ, כל זמן שאמו של אדם קיימת כרוך הוא אצלה, ומשמתה הוא מתנחם באשתו (פדר"א פל"ב): (א) **קטורה.** זו הגר, ונקראת קטורה על שם שנאים מעשיה כקטרת. ושקשרה פתחה, שלא נזדווגה לאדם מיום שפירשה מאברהם (תנחומא ח; ב"ר סא:ד): (ג) **אשורם ולטושם.** שם ראשי אומות (ב"ר שם ה). ותרגום של אונקלוס אין לי ליישבו עם לשון המקרא [שפירש למשרין לשון מחנה. וא"ת שאינו כן מפני האל"ף שאינה יסודית. הרי לנו תיבות שאין בראשם אל"ף ונתוספה אל"ף בראשם, כמו אומת אכך (עמוס ו:ז) שהוא מן נכה רגלים (שמואל ב ד:ד). וכמו אסוך שמן (מלכים ב ד:ב) שהוא מן ורחצת וסכת (רות ג:ג): **ולטושם.** הם בעלי אהלים המתפזרים אנה ואנה ונוסעים איש באהלי אפדנו. וכן הוא אומר והנה נטושים ע"פ כל הארץ (שמואל א ל:טז). שכן למ"ד ונו"ן מתחלפות זו בזו]: (ה) **ויתן אברהם וגו'.** אמר ר' נחמיה ברכה דיאתיקי [שלו] נתן לו. שאמר לו הקב"ה לאברהם והיה ברכה (לעיל יב:ב) הברכות מסורות בידך לברך את מי שתרצה, ואברהם מסרן ליצחק (ב"ר סא:ו): (ו) **הפילגשים.** חסר כתיב שלא היתה אלא פלגש אחת, היא הגר היא קטורה (שם ד). נשים בכתובה, פלגשים בלא כתובה, כדאמרי' בסנהדרין (כא.) בנשים ופלגשים דדוד:

67. הָאֹהֱלָה שָׂרָה אִמּוֹ — *Into the tent [of] Sarah his mother.* As long as Sarah was alive, a lamp burned in her tent from one Sabbath eve to the next, her dough was blessed, and a cloud [signifying the Divine Presence; see *Exodus* 40:34] hung over her tent. When Sarah died, these blessings ceased, but when Rebecca entered the tent, they resumed. Thus the Midrash renders the verse: *He brought her into the tent — she was Sarah, his mother* (*Rashi*). This proved to Isaac that Rebecca was the worthy successor of Sarah.

First he brought her into Sarah's tent. When he observed that her actions were like those of Sarah, he married her (*Malbim*).

וַיִּנָּחֵם יִצְחָק אַחֲרֵי אִמּוֹ — *And [thus] Isaac was consoled after his mother.* He found consolation only through his love for his wife. This love was inspired by her righteousness and the aptness of her deeds, the only criteria upon which the Torah bases the love between husband and wife (*Ramban*). [Since Isaac was 37 years old when his mother died (17:17 and 23:1), and he was 40 when he married Rebecca (25:20), we see that he mourned for his mother for three years.]

25.

1. קְטוּרָה — *Keturah.* Abraham remarried Hagar, who was given this name since her deeds were as pleasant as incense

נָתַן אַבְרָהָם מַתָּנֹת וַיְשַׁלְּחֵם מֵעַל יִצְחָק בְּנוֹ

< his son, < Isaac < from near < then he sent them away « gifts; < Abraham gave

בְּעוֹדֶנּוּ חַי קֵדְמָה אֶל־אֶרֶץ קֶדֶם: ז וְאֵלֶּה יְמֵי

< are the days < Now these 7 « of the east. < the land < to < eastward « alive, < while he was still

שְׁנֵי־חַיֵּי אַבְרָהָם אֲשֶׁר־חָי מְאַת שָׁנָה וְשִׁבְעִים

< and seventy < years, < one hundred « he lived: < which < of Abraham < of the life < of the years

שָׁנָה וְחָמֵשׁ שָׁנִים: ח וַיִּגְוַע וַיָּמָת אַבְרָהָם בְּשֵׂיבָה

< at an old age < did Abraham < and die < And expire **8** « years. < and five < years,

טוֹבָה זָקֵן וְשָׂבֵעַ וַיֵּאָסֶף אֶל־עַמָּיו: ט וַיִּקְבְּרוּ אֹתוֹ יִצְחָק וְיִשְׁמָעֵאל

< and Ishmael < —Isaac « him < They buried **9** « his people. < to < and he was gathered « and content, < mature < that was good,

בָּנָיו אֶל־מְעָרַת הַמַּכְפֵּלָה אֶל־שְׂדֵה עֶפְרֹן בֶּן־צֹחַר הַחִתִּי אֲשֶׁר

< which is < the Hittite, < of Zohar < the son < of Ephron < the field < in < of Machpelah, < the cave < in « his sons —

עַל־פְּנֵי מַמְרֵא: י הַשָּׂדֶה אֲשֶׁר־קָנָה אַבְרָהָם מֵאֵת בְּנֵי־חֵת שָׁמָּה קֻבַּר

< was buried < there « of Heth, < the Sons < from < Abraham had bought < that < The field **10** « Mamre. < facing

אַבְרָהָם וְשָׂרָה אִשְׁתּוֹ: יא וַיְהִי אַחֲרֵי מוֹת אַבְרָהָם וַיְבָרֶךְ אֱלֹהִים

< [that] God blessed < of Abraham < the death < after < And it was **11** « his wife. < and Sarah < Abraham,

אֶת־יִצְחָק בְּנוֹ וַיֵּשֶׁב יִצְחָק עִם־בְּאֵר לַחַי רֹאִי: פ שביעי יב וְאֵלֶּה תֹּלְדֹת

< are the descendants < These **12** « Be'er-lahai-ro'i. < near < and Isaac settled « his son, < Isaac

יְהַב אַבְרָהָם מַתְּנָן וְשַׁלְּחִנּוּן מֵעַל
יִצְחָק בְּרֵהּ עַד דְּהוּא קַיָּם קִידוּמָא
לַאֲרַע מָדִינְחָא: ז וְאִלֵּין יוֹמֵי שְׁנֵי חַיֵּי
אַבְרָהָם דַּחֲיָא מְאָה וְשַׁבְעִין וְחָמֵשׁ
שְׁנִין: ח וְאִתְנְגִיד וּמִית אַבְרָהָם בְּסֵיבוּ
טָבָא סִיב וּשְׂבַע יוֹמִין (נ״א וּשְׂבַע)
וְאִתְכְּנֵישׁ לְעַמֵּהּ: ט וּקְבַרוּ יָתֵהּ יִצְחָק
וְיִשְׁמָעֵאל בְּנוֹהִי בִּמְעָרַת כְּפֶלְתָּא
לַחֲקַל עֶפְרוֹן בַּר צֹחַר חִתָּאָה דִּי עַל
אַפֵּי מַמְרֵא: י חַקְלָא דִּי זְבַן אַבְרָהָם
מִן בְּנֵי חִתָּאָה תַּמָּן אִתְקְבַר אַבְרָהָם
וְשָׂרָה אִתְּתֵהּ: יא וַהֲוָה בָּתַר דְּמִית
אַבְרָהָם וּבָרִיךְ יְיָ יָת יִצְחָק בְּרֵהּ
וִיתֵב יִצְחָק עִם בֵּירָא דְּמַלְאַךְ
קַיָּמָא אִתַּחְזֵי עֲלַהּ: יב וְאִלֵּין תּוֹלְדַת

רש"י

[**נתן אברהם מתנת.** פירשו רבותינו, שם טומאה מסר להם (שם לח.). ד"א, מה שניתן לו על אודות שרה ושאר מתנות שנתנו לו, הכל נתן להם, שלא רצה ליהנות מהם:] (ז) **מאת שנה ושבעים שנה וחמש שנים.** בן ק' כבן ע' [לכח], ובן ע' כבן ה' בלא חטא: (ט) **יצחק וישמעאל.** מכאן שעשה ישמעאל תשובה והוליך את יצחק לפניו (בבא בתרא טז:) והיא שיבה טובה שנאמרה באברהם (ב"ר לח:יב): (יא) **ויהי אחרי מות אברהם ויברך וגו'.** נחמו תנחומי אבלים (סוטה יד.). ד"א, אע"פ שמסר הקדוש ברוך הוא את הברכות לאברהם נתיירא לברך את יצחק, מפני שצפה את עשו יוצא ממנו, אמר, יבא בעל הברכות ויברך את אשר ייטב בעיניו. ובא הקב"ה וברכו

[*ketores*], and because she remained chaste [*keturah* is Aramaic for *tied*] even after she was separated from Abraham (*Midrash; Rashi*).

Ramban explains that at this point in his life, Abraham felt no need to find a wife from among his family in Haran. That was required of Isaac — as it would be again later of Jacob — because the covenant of Israel would be fulfilled through him.

7. אֲשֶׁר־חָי — *Which he lived.* Abraham had lived his life *fully;* not one day was wasted. He died in the year 2123 (*Seder Olam*).

9. יִצְחָק וְיִשְׁמָעֵאל בָּנָיו — *Isaac and Ishmael his sons.* Since the older Ishmael gave precedence to his younger brother — unlike Esau, who forced himself ahead of Jacob at the burial of Isaac [35:29] (*Mizrachi*) — we infer that he repented (*Rashi*).

11. וַיְבָרֶךְ אֱלֹהִים אֶת־יִצְחָק בְּנוֹ — *[That] God blessed Isaac his son.* That God blessed Isaac after Abraham's death implies that the blessing and the death were related (*Nachalas Yaakov*). Therefore the Sages infer that God blessed him by comforting him in his mourning. Alternatively, God conferred upon Isaac the blessings that He had given to Abraham (*Rashi).*

12-18. Ishmael's genealogy. In the simple sense, Ishmael's descendants are enumerated in deference to Abraham (*Radak*) [hence the appellation: *son of Abraham*] and to inform us that the seed of the righteous shall be blessed.

יִשְׁמָעֵאל בֶּן־אַבְרָהָם אֲשֶׁר יָלְדָה הָגָר הַמִּצְרִית

< the Egyptian, < — Hagar << she bore < whom << of Abraham, < son < of Ishmael,

שִׁפְחַת שָׂרָה לְאַבְרָהָם: יג וְאֵלֶּה שְׁמוֹת בְּנֵי יִשְׁמָעֵאל

< of Ishmael < of the sons < are the names < These 13 << to Abraham. << of Sarah — < the maidservant

בִּשְׁמֹתָם לְתוֹלְדֹתָם בְּכֹר יִשְׁמָעֵאל נְבָיֹת וְקֵדָר

< Kedar, << Nebaioth, < of Ishmael < the firstborn << in order of their birth: < by their names,

וְאַדְבְּאֵל וּמִבְשָׂם: יד וּמִשְׁמָע וְדוּמָה וּמַשָּׂא: טו חֲדַד

< Hadad 15 << and Massa; < Dumah, < Mishma, 14 << and Mibsam; < Adbe'el,

וְתֵימָא יְטוּר נָפִישׁ וָקֵדְמָה: מפטיר טז אֵלֶּה הֵם בְּנֵי

< the sons < are < These 16 << and Kedmah. < Naphish, < Jetur, < and Tema;

יִשְׁמָעֵאל וְאֵלֶּה שְׁמֹתָם בְּחַצְרֵיהֶם וּבְטִירֹתָם שְׁנֵים־עָשָׂר נְשִׂיאִם

< chieftains < twelve << and in their strongholds, < in their open cities < are their names < and these < of Ishmael

לְאֻמֹּתָם: יז וְאֵלֶּה שְׁנֵי חַיֵּי יִשְׁמָעֵאל מְאַת שָׁנָה וּשְׁלֹשִׁים שָׁנָה וְשֶׁבַע

< and seven < years < and thirty < years < one hundred << of Ishmael: < of the life < the years < These were 17 << for their nations.

שָׁנִים וַיִּגְוַע וַיָּמָת וַיֵּאָסֶף אֶל־עַמָּיו: יח וַיִּשְׁכְּנוּ מֵחֲוִילָה עַד־שׁוּר אֲשֶׁר

< which is < Shur < to < from Havilah < They dwelt 18 << his people. < to < and was gathered < and he died < he expired << years,

עַל־פְּנֵי מִצְרַיִם בֹּאֲכָה אַשּׁוּרָה עַל־פְּנֵי כָל־אֶחָיו נָפָל: פפפ

<< he dwelt. < his brothers < all < over << Assyria; < toward < Egypt < facing

ק"ה פסוקים. יהויד"ע סימן.

THE HAFTARAH FOR CHAYEI SARAH APPEARS ON PAGE 332.

יִשְׁמָעֵאל בַּר אַבְרָהָם דִּי יְלֵידַת הָגָר מִצְרֵתָא אַמְתָא דְשָׂרָה לְאַבְרָהָם: יג וְאִלֵּין שְׁמָהַת בְּנֵי יִשְׁמָעֵאל בִּשְׁמָהַתְהוֹן לְתוּלְדָתְהוֹן בּוּכְרָא דְיִשְׁמָעֵאל נְבָיוֹת וְקֵדָר וְאַדְבְּאֵל וּמִבְשָׂם: יד וּמִשְׁמָע וְדוּמָה וּמַשָּׂא: טו חֲדַד וְתֵימָא יְטוּר נָפִישׁ וָקֵדְמָה: טז אִלֵּין אִנּוּן בְּנֵי יִשְׁמָעֵאל וְאִלֵּין שְׁמָהַתְהוֹן בְּפַצְחֵיהוֹן וּבִכְרַכֵּיהוֹן תְּרֵין עֲסַר רַבְרְבִין לְאֻמֵּיהוֹן: יז וְאִלֵּין שְׁנֵי חַיֵּי יִשְׁמָעֵאל מְאָה וּתְלָתִין וּשְׁבַע שְׁנִין וְאִתְנְגִיד וּמִית וְאִתְכְּנִישׁ לְעַמֵּהּ: יח וּשְׁרוֹ מֵחֲוִילָה עַד חַגְרָא דִּי עַל אַפֵּי מִצְרַיִם מָטֵי לְאָתוּר עַל אַפֵּי כָל אֲחוּהִי שְׁרָא:

רש"י

(תנחומא לך לך ד; ב"ר סא:ו): (יג) **בשמותם לתולדתם.** סדר לידתן זה אחר זה: (טז) **בחצריהם.** כרכים שאין להם חומה. ותרגומו בפצחיהון שהם מפוצחים, לשון פתיחה, כמו פצחו ורננו (תהלים צח:ד): (יז) **ואלה שני חיי ישמעאל וגו'.** אמר רבי חייא בר אבא למה נמנו שנותיו של ישמעאל כדי לייחס בהם שנותיו של יעקב. משנותיו של ישמעאל למדנו ששמש יעקב בבית עבר י"ד שנה כשפירש מאביו קודם שבא אצל לבן. שהרי כשפירש יעקב מאביו מת ישמעאל שנא' וילך עשו אל ישמעאל וגו' (להלן כח:ט) כמו שמפורש בסוף מגלה נקראת (טז:־יז.; יבמות סד.): **ויגוע.** לא נאמרה גויעה [ואסיפה] אלא בצדיקים (בבא בתרא טז:): (יח) **נפל.** שכן (אונקלוס). כמו ומדין ועמלק וכל בני קדם נופלים בעמק (שופטים ז:יב). כאן הוא אומר לשון נפילה ולהלן אומר על פני כל אחיו ישכון (לעיל טז:יב). עד שלא מת אברהם, ישכון. משמת אברהם, נפל (ב"ר סב:ה):

13. *Nebaioth,* the firstborn, and *Kedar,* the second son, are the most important of the Ishmaelite tribes. They are mentioned together in *Isaiah* 60:7. One of Esau's wives was Mahalath, the sister of Nebaioth [28:9].

16. *These are the sons of Ishmael.* As is customary in Scripture, the subject is closed with a general statement summing up the matter, the closing summary also being used as a means of further clarification (*Radak*): *And these are their names in their open cities and in their strongholds* [fortified cities (*Radak*)]. Whether they took up residence in *open cities* [denoting, according to *R' Hoffmann*, the circular *encampments* of nomadic tribes] or in *strongholds,* they lived in security and honor. All those bearing these tribal names, regardless of where they lived, were descendants of Ishmael (cf. *Radak*).

17. Ishmael's age is given because it assists in dating the various events that occurred in Jacob's life (*Rashi* [*Yevamos* 64a]).

18. The sense of this passage is that God fulfilled the promise to Hagar in 16:12: *over all his brothers shall he dwell.* As *Rashi* explains there, the blessing meant that Ishmael's descendants would be so numerous that they would have to expand beyond their own borders into those of their brothers.

ק"ה פסוקים. יהויד"ע סימן — This Masoretic note means: There are 105 verses in *Chayei Sarah,* numerically corresponding to the mnemonic יְהוֹיָדָ"ע [= יָהּ יוֹדִיעַ, *God makes known*]. This implies that God made His will known through Eliezer (*R' David Feinstein*).

PARASHAS TOLDOS / פרשת תולדות

אונקלוס

יט וְאִלֵּין תּוֹלְדַת יִצְחָק בַּר אַבְרָהָם אַבְרָהָם אוֹלִיד יָת יִצְחָק: כ וַהֲוָה יִצְחָק בַּר אַרְבְּעִין שְׁנִין כַּד נְסֵיב יָת רִבְקָה בַּת בְּתוּאֵל אֲרַמָּאָה מִפַּדַּן אֲרָם אֲחָתֵהּ דְּלָבָן אֲרַמָּאָה לֵהּ לְאִנְתּוּ: כא וְצַלִּי יִצְחָק קֳדָם יְיָ לָקֳבֵל

19 וְאֵלֶּה תּוֹלְדֹת יִצְחָק בֶּן־אַבְרָהָם אַבְרָהָם
‹ — Abraham ‹‹ of Abraham ‹ son ‹ of Isaac ‹ are the descendants ‹ And these 19

הוֹלִיד אֶת־יִצְחָק: 20 וַיְהִי יִצְחָק בֶּן־אַרְבָּעִים
‹ of forty ‹ of the age ‹ And Isaac was 20 ‹‹ Isaac. ‹ begot

שָׁנָה בְּקַחְתּוֹ אֶת־רִבְקָה בַּת־בְּתוּאֵל הָאֲרַמִּי
‹ the Aramean ‹ of Bethuel ‹ daughter ‹ Rebecca, ‹ when he took ‹ years

מִפַּדַּן אֲרָם אֲחוֹת לָבָן הָאֲרַמִּי לוֹ לְאִשָּׁה: 21 וַיֶּעְתַּר יִצְחָק לַיהוה לְנֹכַח
‹ opposite ‹ HASHEM ‹ Isaac entreated 21 ‹‹ as a wife. ‹ for himself ‹ the Aramean, ‹ of Laban ‹ sister ‹ from Paddan-aram,

רש"י

(יט) **ואלה תולדות יצחק.** יעקב ועשו האמורים בפרשה: **אברהם הוליד את יצחק.** [לאחר שקרא הקב"ה שמו אברהם אח"כ הוליד את יצחק (אגדת בראשית לז). ד"א] ע"י שכתב הכתוב יצחק בן אברהם הוזקק לומר אברהם הוליד את יצחק. לפי שהיו ליצני הדור אומרים מאבימלך נתעברה שרה, שהרי כמה שנים שהתה עם אברהם ולא נתעברה הימנו. מה עשה הקב"ה, צר קלסתר פניו של יצחק דומה לאברהם והעידו הכל אברהם הוליד את יצחק. וזהו שכתב כאן, יצחק בן אברהם היה, שהרי עדות יש שאברהם הוליד את יצחק (שם; תנחומא א; ב"מ פז.): (כ) **בן ארבעים שנה.** שהרי כשבא אברהם מהר המוריה נתבשר שנולדה רבקה, ויצחק היה בן ל"ז שנה שהרי בו בפרק מתה שרה, ומשנולד יצחק עד העקידה שמתה שרה ל"ז שנה כי בת צ' היתה כשנולד יצחק ובת קכ"ז כשמתה שנא' ויהיו חיי שרה וגו' הרי ליצחק ל"ז שנים. ובו בפרק נולדה רבקה המתין לה עד שתהא ראויה לביאה ג' שנים (נדה מד:) ונשאה (סדר עולם פ"א, ועי' ילק"ש קי ויבמות סא: תוד"ה אין; סוף מס' סופרים): **בת בתואל מפדן ארם אחות לבן.** וכי עדיין לא נכתב שהיא בת בתואל ואחות לבן ומפדן ארם, אלא להגיד שבחה, שהיתה בת רשע ואחות רשע ומקומה אנשי רשע ולא למדה ממעשיהם (ב"ר סג:ד): **מפדן ארם.** על שם ששני ארם היו ארם נהרים וארם צובה קורא אותו פדן, [לשון] צמד בקר (שמואל א יא:ז) תרגום פדן תורין. ויש פותרין פדן ארם כמו שדה ארם (הושע יב:יג), שבלשון ישמעאל קורין לשדה פדן: (כא) **ויעתר.** הרבה והפציר בתפלה:

PARASHAS TOLDOS

Each of the Patriarchs maintained a yeshivah in which he taught about the existence of God and His will. Abraham's academy had hundreds if not thousands of students — Isaac had an academy of one. His lone student was Jacob, whom he trained and appointed to teach others (*Rambam, Hil. Avodah Zarah* 1:2-3). This provides a clue to the way in which Isaac's role diverged from that of Abraham. Abraham could accept everyone into his orbit; Isaac could not.

The Torah devotes much less space to Isaac's life than to the lives of Abraham and Jacob. On the one hand, Isaac seems to be but a bridge between his father and his son; on the other hand, he had the task of drawing the line between good and evil — as represented by Jacob and Esau — because the emerging nation of Israel could not be a mixture of good and evil. In contrast to Abraham whose primary characteristic was *chesed,* kindness, Isaac's was *gevurah*, strength. One requires strength to differentiate between good and evil — and then to purge the bad and nurture the good. Isaac and Rebecca produced two sons; one became the personification of righteousness and the other the personification of wickedness, and it was the lot of the parents to make the distinction so that the nation of Israel would be pure.

Lest one think that Isaac discarded Abraham's way in favor of his own, the Torah stresses at the very beginning of the *Sidrah* that Isaac was the *son of Abraham — Abraham begot Isaac.* In the Jewish scheme of life, kindness and strength must go together. Kindness not tempered by strength can lead to self-indulgence and hedonism; strength without kindness can lead to selfishness and cruelty.

19-23. Rebecca's barrenness and pregnancy. The Sages note that the Matriarchs Sarah, Rebecca, and Rachel were barren. The commentators explain that their experiences prove that the emergence of Israel is a miracle, for each new generation was a gift of God to a mother who could not have given birth naturally. Their experience is a demonstration of the dictum that God desires the prayers of the righteous (*Yevamos* 64a), whose pleas for Heavenly mercy and attempts at self-improvement show how human beings can raise themselves to spiritual heights.

19. יִצְחָק בֶּן־אַבְרָהָם — *Isaac son of Abraham . . .* The Torah stresses that Abraham and Isaac were father and son. The cynics of that generation had been saying that Sarah must have become pregnant by Abimelech, since she and Abraham had been married for many decades without a child, but she had given birth only after being taken by the Philistine king. Therefore God made Isaac's features so undeniably similar to Abraham's that even the scoffers had to admit that אַבְרָהָם הוֹלִיד אֶת יִצְחָק, "it was indeed *Abraham who gave birth to Isaac!*" (*Tanchuma; Rashi*).

21. וַיֶּעְתַּר יִצְחָק — *Isaac entreated.* The root עתר denotes abundance; thus, the sense of the verse is that Isaac prayed abundantly for Rebecca and she simultaneously prayed on her own behalf. He was *opposite* her in the sense that he stood in one corner and she stood in the other one as they both prayed (*Rashi*).

He knew that *he* would have children, because God had promised that Abraham's destiny would be fulfilled through

אִשְׁתּוֹ כִּי עֲקָרָה הִוא וַיֵּעָתֶר לוֹ יהוה וַתַּהַר
< and conceive << –did Hashem, << by him < Allow Himself to be entreated << was she. < barren < because < his wife,

רִבְקָה אִשְׁתּוֹ: כב וַיִּתְרֹצְצוּ הַבָּנִים בְּקִרְבָּהּ וַתֹּאמֶר
<< and she said, << within her, < did the children < Struggle 22 << his wife. < did Rebecca

אִם־כֵּן לָמָּה זֶּה אָנֹכִי וַתֵּלֶךְ לִדְרֹשׁ אֶת־יהוה:
<< of Hashem. < to inquire < And she went << *am I?* < *thus* < *why* < *so,* < *If*

כג וַיֹּאמֶר יהוה לָהּ שְׁנֵי °גוֹיִם [°גיים כ׳] בְּבִטְנֵךְ וּשְׁנֵי לְאֻמִּים מִמֵּעַיִךְ
< *from your insides* < *kingdoms* < *and two* << *are in your womb;* < *nations* < *Two* << *to her:* < And Hashem said 23

יִפָּרֵדוּ וּלְאֹם מִלְאֹם יֶאֱמָץ וְרַב יַעֲבֹד צָעִיר: כד וַיִּמְלְאוּ יָמֶיהָ לָלֶדֶת
<< to give birth, < were her days < Completed 24 << *the younger.* < *shall serve* < *and the elder* << *will be mighty;* < *[more] than the [other] kingdom* < *and one kingdom* << *shall be separated;*

אִתְּתֵהּ אֲרֵי עֲקָרָה הִיא וְקַבֵּל צְלוֹתֵהּ יְיָ וְעַדִּיאַת רִבְקָה אִתְּתֵהּ: כב וְדַחֲקִין בְּנַיָּא בִּמְעָהָא וַאֲמֶרֶת אִם כֵּן לְמָא דְנָן אֲנָא וַאֲזָלַת לְמִתְבַּע אוּלְפַן מִן קֳדָם יְיָ: כג וַאֲמַר יְיָ לַהּ תְּרֵין עַמְמִין בִּמְעַיְכִי וְתַרְתֵּין מַלְכְוָן מִמֵּעַיְכִי יִתְפָּרְשָׁן וּמַלְכוּ מִמַּלְכוּ יִתְקַף וְרַבָּא יִשְׁתַּעְבֵּיד לִזְעִירָא: כד וּשְׁלִימוּ יוֹמָהָא לְמֵילַד

רש״י

ויעתר לו. נתפלר [ונתפייס] ונתפתה לו. ואומר אני, כל לשון עתר לשון הפלרה ורבוי הוא. וכן ועתר ענן הקטורת (יחזקאל ח:יא) מרבית עלית העשן, וכן והעתרתם עלי דבריכם (שם לה:יג), וכן ונעתרות נשיקות שונא (משלי כז:ו) דומות למרובות והנס למשא, אנקריש״א בלע״ז: **לנכח אשתו.** זה עומד בזוית זו ומתפלל וזו עומדת בזוית זו ומתפללת (ב״ר שם ה, ועי׳ תענית כג:): **ויעתר לו.** לו ולא לה, שאין דומה תפלת צדיק בן רשע לתפלת צדיק בן צדיק, לפיכך לו ולא לה (יבמות סד.): **(כב) ויתרוצצו.** על כרחך המקרא הזה אומר דרשני, שסתם מה היא רציה זו וכתב אם כן למה זה אנכי. רבותינו דרשוהו לשון ריצה, כשהיתה עוברת על פתחי תורה של שם ועבר יעקב רץ ומפרכס לצאת, עוברת על פתחי ע״ז עשו מפרכס לצאת (ב״ר שם ו). ד״א, מתרוצצים זה עם זה ומריבים בנחלת שני עולמות (ילק״ש קי): **ותאמר אם כן.** גדול צער העבור: **למה זה אנכי.** מתאוה ומתפללת על הריון: **ותלך לדרש.** לבית מדרשו של שם (תרגום יונתן) [ועבר] (ב״ר שם): **לדרש את ה׳.** שיגיד לה [ס״א להגיד] מה תהא בסופה (אונקלוס): **(כג) ויאמר ה׳ לה.** ע״י שליח. לשם נאמר ברוח הקדש והוא אמר לה (ב״ר שם ז): **שני גוים בבטנך.** גיים כתיב, אלו אנטונינוס ורבי שלא פסקו מעל שולחנם לא צנון ולא חזרת לא בימות החמה ולא בימות הגשמים (עבודה זרה יא.): **ושני לאמים.** אין לאום אלא מלכות (שם ב:): **ממעיך יפרדו.** מן המעים הם נפרדים, זה לרשעו וזה לתומו: **מלאם יאמץ.** לא ישוו בגדולה, כשזה קם זה נופל, וכן הוא אומר אמלאה החרבה (יחזקאל כו:ב) לא נתמלאה צור אלא מחרבנה של ירושלים (מגילה ו.): **(כד) וימלאו ימיה.** אבל בתמר כתיב ויהי בעת לדתה (להלן לח:כז), שלא מלאו ימיה כי לז׳ חדשים ילדתם (ב״ר סג:ח):

Isaac's offspring (17:19), but he begged God that the blessing be realized through the worthy woman who stood opposite him (*Sforno*).

לוֹ — *By him.* The implication of the masculine singular form is that God responded to Isaac's prayer, rather than Rebecca's. There is no comparison between the prayer of a righteous child of a righteous person and that of a righteous child of a wicked person (*Rashi*). Although it is much more difficult — and therefore meritorious — for the product of an evil family to become righteous, Isaac's achievement was even more unique than Rebecca's. It would have been easy for him to become a carbon copy of his father — surely as great a role model as had ever lived — but Isaac did not content himself with that. He forged his own path toward the service of God, and the merit of such an accomplishment is awesome.

22. וַיִּתְרֹצְצוּ הַבָּנִים — *Struggle did the children.* The Rabbis explain that וַיִּתְרֹצְצוּ is derived from the root רוץ, *to run:* When Rebecca passed the Torah academy of Shem and Eber, Jacob "ran" and struggled to come forth; and when she passed a temple of idol worship, Esau "ran" and struggled to come forth (*Midrash*). *Gur Aryeh* explains that this embryonic Jacob-Esau struggle was not influenced by their personal Good and Evil Inclinations, for they are not present before birth. Rather, Jacob and Esau represented cosmic forces in Creation, forces that transcended the normal course of personality development, and that existed even before birth.

לִדְרֹשׁ אֶת־ה׳ — *To inquire of Hashem. Haamek Davar* explains that there are two types of prophets. The first is a person with whom Hashem communicates with a specific message, such as Abraham at the Covenant of the Pieces and regarding the destruction of Sodom. The second is one who is able to discern through the Divine spirit hidden facts and phenomena. Such a prophet is also called a רוֹאֶה, *Seer,* as in *I Samuel* 9:9. Rebecca thus went to a prophet of the second type, and not to Isaac who was of the first type, in order to interpret the mystery of her womb.

As indicated by the next verse, Hashem conveyed the significance of her frightening symptoms only to *her* and not to Isaac. Since God did not reveal this prophecy to Isaac, Rebecca felt that she did not have the right to do so, even years later when she conspired to win Isaac's blessings for Jacob over Esau. *Chizkuni* explains that this is why Isaac could not imagine Esau to be a sinner.

23. וַיֹּאמֶר ה׳ לָהּ — *And Hashem said to her.* Through the prophet, God conveyed to her that the unborn infants represented two nations and two conflicting ideologies — Israel and Edom — and that their struggle in the womb symbolized the future rivalries between them, which would end with the younger prevailing over the older (*R' Hoffmann*). Thus, the turmoil within her was due to the irreconcilable conflict between

וְהִנֵּה תוֹמִם בְּבִטְנָהּ: כה וַיֵּצֵא הָרִאשׁוֹן אַדְמוֹנִי

« red, ‹ The first one emerged **25** « in her womb. ‹ there were twins ‹ and indeed

כֻּלּוֹ כְּאַדֶּרֶת שֵׂעָר וַיִּקְרְאוּ שְׁמוֹ עֵשָׂו: כו וְאַחֲרֵי־

‹ After **26** « Esau. ‹ his name ‹ so they called « that is hairy; ‹ like a mantle ‹ entirely

כֵן יָצָא אָחִיו וְיָדוֹ אֹחֶזֶת בַּעֲקֵב עֵשָׂו וַיִּקְרָא שְׁמוֹ יַעֲקֹב וְיִצְחָק בֶּן־

‹ was of the age ‹ and Isaac « Jacob; ‹ his name ‹ so he called « of Esau; ‹ onto the heel ‹ grasping ‹ with his hand ‹ his brother ‹ emerged ‹ that

שִׁשִּׁים שָׁנָה בְּלֶדֶת אֹתָם: כז וַיִּגְדְּלוּ הַנְּעָרִים וַיְהִי עֵשָׂו אִישׁ יֹדֵעַ צַיִד

‹ hunting, ‹ who knows ‹ a man ‹ and Esau became ‹ The youths grew up **27** « them. ‹ when she bore ‹ years ‹ of sixty

וְהָא תְיוּמִין בִּמְעָהָא: כה וּנְפַק קַדְמָאָה סְמוֹק כֻּלֵּהּ כִּגְלִים (נ״א כִּכְלָן) דִּשְׂעָר וּקְרוֹ שְׁמֵהּ עֵשָׂו: כו וּבָתַר כֵּן נְפַק אֲחוּהִי וִידֵהּ אֲחִידָא בְּעִקְבָא דְעֵשָׂו וּקְרָא שְׁמֵהּ יַעֲקֹב וְיִצְחָק בַּר שִׁתִּין שְׁנִין כַּד יְלִידַת יָתְהוֹן: כז וּרְבִיוּ עוּלֵמַיָּא וַהֲוָה עֵשָׂו גְּבַר נַחְשִׁירְכָן

רש״י

והנה תומם. חסר, ובתמר תאומים, מלא, לפי ששניהם צדיקים, אבל כאן אחד צדיק ואחד רשע (שם): **(כה) אדמוני.** סימן הוא שיהא שופך דמים (שם): **כלו כאדרת שער.** מלא שער כטלית של צמר המלאה שער, פלוקיד״א בלע״ז: **ויקראו שמו עשו.** הכל קראו לו כן, לפי שהיה נעשה ונגמר בשערו כבן שנים הרבה (תרגום יונתן): **(כו) ואחרי כן יצא אחיו וגו׳.** שמעתי מדרש אגדה הדורשו לפי פשוטו. בדין היה אוחז בו לעכבו, יעקב נוצר מטיפה ראשונה ועשו מן השנייה. צא ולמד משפופרת שפיה קצרה, תן בה שתי אבנים זו תחת זו, הנכנסת ראשונה תצא אחרונה והנכנסת אחרונה תצא ראשונה. נמצא עשו הנוצר באחרונה יצא ראשון, ויעקב שנוצר ראשונה יצא אחרון, ויעקב בא לעכבו שיהא ראשון ללידה כראשון ליצירה ויפטור את רחמה ויטול את הבכורה מן הדין (ב״ר שם): **בעקב עשו.** סימן שאין זה מספיק לגמור מלכותו עד שזה עומד ונוטלה הימנו (פדר״א פל״ב; ילק״ש קי): **ויקרא שמו יעקב.** הקב״ה [אמר אתם קריתון לבכורכם שם אף אני אקרא לבני בכורי שם הה״ד ויקרא שמו יעקב] (ב״ר שם; תנחומא שמות ד). ד״א, אביו קרא לו יעקב על שם אחיזת העקב: **בן ששים שנה.** י׳ שנים משנשאה עד שנעשית בת י״ג שנה וראויה להריון, וי׳ שנים הללו ציפה והמתין לה כמו שעשה אביו לשרה (לעיל טז:ג). כיון שלא נתעברה ידע שהיא עקרה והתפלל עליה. ושפחה לא רצה לישא, לפי שנתקדש בהר המוריה להיות עולה תמימה (ב״ר סד:ג): **(כז) ויגדלו הנערים ויהי עשו.** כל זמן שהיו קטנים לא היו ניכרים במעשיהם ואין אדם מדקדק בהם מה טיבם. כיון שנעשו בני י״ג שנה זה פירש לבתי מדרשות וזה פירש לע״ז (ב״ר סג:י): **יודע ציד.** לצוד ולרמות את אביו בפיו, ושואלו, אבא, היאך מעשרין את המלח ואת התבן. כסבור אביו שהוא מדקדק במצות (שם):

the two nations that was already taking shape (*Mizrachi*).

The Sages teach that the two of them will never be mighty simultaneously; when one falls, the other will rise (*Megillah* 6a). History has demonstrated this prophecy in practice. Two regimes, one espousing morality and justice and the other standing for license and barbarity, cannot long coexist. They must always be in conflict until one comes to dominate the other, whether through victory on the battlefield or in the contest for men's minds.

25. וַיֵּצֵא הָרִאשׁוֹן אַדְמוֹנִי — *The first one emerged red.* His complexion was ruddy and he was as hairy as a woolen garment. The redness of his complexion portended his murderous nature (*Rashi*), since there is no other reason for the Torah to have mentioned it (*Mizrachi*).

The young King David, too, was ruddy, and Samuel feared that this might indicate a tendency toward bloodshed on his part. But God reassured him, saying that David had *beautiful eyes* (*I Samuel* 16:12), meaning that he would kill only upon the ruling of the Sanhedrin, which acts as the *eyes* of the nation, whereas Esau would kill whenever the mood moved him (*Midrash*).

All character traits, even the basest, can be used for good. Man must harness his nature and not let his nature harness him. David and Esau had similar personalities, but David utilized it for good and became one of the greatest people who ever lived. Esau let his nature run rampant, and became the eternal symbol of evil and cruelty.

עֵשָׂו — *Esau.* The name means *completely developed*. "They" — everyone — called him that, because he had as much hair as a child several years older (*Rashi*).

26. וְאַחֲרֵי־כֵן יָצָא אָחִיו — *After that emerged his brother.* The verse goes on to say that Jacob grasped Esau's heel, indicating that he was trying to prevent Esau from being born first. *Rashi* cites the Midrash that Jacob was justified in trying to be the firstborn because he had been conceived before Esau, so that Jacob should legitimately have been born first.

Pachad Yitzchak explains that the contention between Jacob and Esau was over who would assume the spiritual mission of Abraham and Isaac. Since Jacob was conceived first, he was the *spiritual* firstborn and therefore *entitled* to the blessings. In the strictly legal sense, however — relating to shares in an inheritance and other legal privileges of the firstborn — the determining factor is birth, not conception. Thus, the later efforts of Jacob and Rebecca to secure the blessing for Jacob must be understood in the light of Jacob's spiritual superiority.

By grasping Esau's heel, the infant Jacob portended that Esau's period of dominion will barely be complete before Jacob wrests it from him (*Rashi*), so that Jacob's ascendancy will come on the heels of Esau's.

יַעֲקֹב — *Jacob.* In contrast to Esau, who was named by everyone present, "*he*" named him Jacob, but the Torah does not specify who gave the name. Either God commanded Isaac to give the name, or Isaac gave it on his own. The name is a play on the word *ekev*, meaning heel, because Jacob grasped Esau's heel (*Rashi*).

איש שדה ויעקב איש תם ישב אהלים:
a man of the field; but Jacob was a man who is wholesome, dwelling in tents.

כח ויאהב יצחק את־עשו כי־ציד בפיו ורבקה
28 Isaac loved Esau for [he put] game in his mouth; but Rebecca

אהבת את־יעקב: כט ויזד יעקב נזיד ויבא עשו
loves Jacob. 29 Jacob stewed a stew, and Esau came in

מן־השדה והוא עיף: ל ויאמר עשו אל־יעקב
from the field, and he was exhausted. 30 Esau said to Jacob,

הלעיטני נא מן־האדם האדם הזה כי עיף אנכי על־כן קרא־שמו
Pour into me, now, some of that very red stuff for exhausted am I. (Because of this he called his name

אדום: לא ויאמר יעקב מכרה כיום את־בכרתך לי: לב ויאמר עשו
Edom.) 31 Jacob said, *Sell, as this day, your birthright to me.* 32 And Esau said,

גְּבַר נָפֵק לְחַקְלָא וְיַעֲקֹב גְּבַר שְׁלִים מְשַׁמֵּשׁ בֵּית אוּלְפָנָא: כח וּרְחֵם יִצְחָק יָת עֵשָׂו אֲרֵי מִצֵּידֵהּ הֲוָה אָכִיל וְרִבְקָה רְחֵימַת יָת יַעֲקֹב: כט וּבַשִּׁיל יַעֲקֹב תַּבְשִׁילָא וַאֲתָא (נ״א וְעַל) עֵשָׂו מִן חַקְלָא וְהוּא מְשַׁלְהֵי: ל וַאֲמַר עֵשָׂו לְיַעֲקֹב אַטְעֵמְנִי כְעַן מִן סִמּוֹקָא סִמּוֹקָא הָדֵין אֲרֵי מְשַׁלְהֵי אֲנָא עַל כֵּן קְרָא שְׁמֵהּ אֱדוֹם: לא וַאֲמַר יַעֲקֹב זַבִּין כְּיוֹם דִּלְהֵן יָת בְּכֵרוּתָךְ לִי: לב וַאֲמַר עֵשָׂו

רש״י

איש שדה. כמשמעו אדם בטל, וצודה בקשתו חיות ועופות: **תם.** אינו בקי בכל אלה אלא כלבו כן פיו. מי שאינו חריף לרמות קרוי תם: **ישב אהלים.** אהלו של שם ואהלו של עבר (ב״ר סג): (כח) [**כי ציד**] **בפיו.** כתרגומו, בפיו של יצחק. ומדרשו, בפיו של עשו, שהיה צד אותו ומרמהו בדבריו (תנחומא ח): (כט) **ויזד.** לשון בישול, כתרגומו: **והוא עיף.** ברציחה, כמה דתימא כי עיפה נפשי להורגים (ירמיה ד:לא; ב״ר סג:יב): (ל) **הלעיטני.** אפתח פי ושפוך הרבה לתוכה, כמו ששנינו אין אובסין את הגמל אבל מלעיטין אותו (שבת קנה:; ב״ר שם): **מן האדם האדם.** עדשים אדומות. ואותו היום מת אברהם (ב״ר יא) שלא יראה את עשו בן בנו יוצא לתרבות רעה ואין זו שיבה טובה שהבטיחו הקב״ה, לפיכך קצר הקב״ה ה׳ שנים משנותיו, שיצחק חי ק״פ שנה וזה קע״ה שנה, ובישל יעקב עדשים להברות את האבל (שם יב). ולמה עדשים, שדומות לגלגל, שהאבלות גלגל החוזר בעולם (בבא בתרא טז:). [ועוד מה עדשים אין להם פה כך האבל אין לו פה שאסור לדבר (שם; ב״ר שם יד). ולפיכך המנהג להברות את האבל בתחלת מאכלו ביצים, שהם עגולים ואין להם פה כך אבל אין לו פה, כדאמרינן במועד קטן (כא:) אבל כל שלשה ימים הראשונים אינו משיב שלום לכל אדם וכ״ש שאינו שואל בתחלה, מג׳ ועד ז׳ משיב ואינו שואל וכו׳]: (לא) **מכרה כיום.** כתרגומו, כיום דילהן, כיום שהוא ברור כך מכור לי מכירה ברורה: **בכרתך.** לפי שהעבודה בבכורות אמר יעקב אין רשע זה כדאי שיקריב להקב״ה (ב״ר שם:יג):

27-28. The personalities emerge. Until they grew up — reached bar-mitzvah age — they were relatively similar to one another (*Sifsei Chachamim*). From the age of 13, the essential differences became apparent, with Esau turning to idols and Jacob going to the study hall. Esau became a hunter, but not only in the literal sense. He became adept at trapping his father by asking questions that would make him appear to be unusually pious. He would ask, for example, how tithes should be taken from salt and straw [although he knew full well that they were not subject to tithes]. And he gained his father's love by serving him conscientiously; for example, by hunting *game* to put *in his mouth,* so that Isaac could eat fresh and tasty meat. Jacob, however, was morally wholesome, saying what he thought and never being duplicitous, and spending all his time in the study tents of Shem and Eber (*Rashi).*

29-34. Sale of the birthright. Jacob's intense desire to "purchase" the birthright becomes more understandable in view of the circumstances in which Jacob was cooking the lentil stew. The Sages teach that Abraham died that day and Jacob was preparing the stew as the traditional mourner's meal for his father (*Bava Basra* 16b) — and on that very day, Esau's sinfulness became public knowledge. This made the birthright even more precious to Jacob, because the spiritual mission of Abraham's family was brought to mind and because Esau's unsuitability for it became so blatantly obvious.

The Midrash teaches that since the sacrificial service was performed by the firstborn in those days, Jacob said, "Shall this wicked man stand and bring the offerings!" Therefore he strove mightily to obtain the birthright.

30. הלעיטני נא — *Pour into me,* נא, *now.* Although the word is usually translated as *please,* it is often translated as *now* (See *Genesis* 12:11, *Rashi* and *Ibn Ezra*). *Me'am Loez* cites an interpretation by *Ahavas Zion* that the word נא here means *raw,* as in the verse regarding the pascal lamb (*Exodus* 12:9). Thus Esau, apparently seeing that the stew was still cooking, asked that it be poured down his throat נא, *raw*.

אדום — *Edom.* The word *Edom* means red. Esau was ruddy and sold his birthright for the sake of red food. Thus, the name Edom is a term of contempt (*Rashbam*).

31. כיום — *As this day.* The sale must be binding and certain, just as this day is certain — make the sale as clear as day (*Rashi*).

הִנֵּ֤ה אָֽנֹכִי֙ הוֹלֵ֣ךְ לָמ֔וּת וְלָמָּה־זֶּ֥ה לִ֖י בְּכֹרָֽה׃

< is a birthright? < to me < so of what use << to die, < about < I am < Indeed,

לג וַיֹּ֣אמֶר יַעֲקֹ֗ב הִשָּׁ֤בְעָה לִּי֙ כַּיּ֔וֹם וַיִּשָּׁבַ֖ע ל֑וֹ וַיִּמְכֹּ֥ר

< and so he sold << to him; < and he swore < as this day < to me < Swear < Jacob said, 33

אֶת־בְּכֹרָת֖וֹ לְיַעֲקֹֽב׃ לד וְיַעֲקֹ֞ב נָתַ֣ן לְעֵשָׂ֗ו לֶ֚חֶם

< bread < to Esau < gave < Jacob 34 << to Jacob. < his birthright

וּנְזִ֣יד עֲדָשִׁ֔ים וַיֹּ֣אכַל וַיֵּ֔שְׁתְּ וַיָּ֖קָם וַיֵּלַ֑ךְ וַיִּ֥בֶז עֵשָׂ֖ו

< [thus,] Esau spurned << and he left; < and he got up, < and he drank, < and he ate < of lentils, < and stew

אֶת־הַבְּכֹרָֽה׃ פ [כו] א וַיְהִ֤י רָעָב֙ בָּאָ֔רֶץ מִלְּבַד֙ הָרָעָ֣ב הָרִאשׁ֔וֹן אֲשֶׁ֥ר

< that < that was earlier < the famine < aside from << in the land, < a famine < There was 1 26 << the birthright.

הָיָ֖ה בִּימֵ֣י אַבְרָהָ֑ם וַיֵּ֧לֶךְ יִצְחָ֛ק אֶל־אֲבִימֶּ֥לֶךְ מֶֽלֶךְ־פְּלִשְׁתִּ֖ים גְּרָֽרָה׃

<< to Gerar. < of the Philistines, < King < Abimelech, < to < and Isaac went << of Abraham; < in the days < was

ב וַיֵּרָ֤א אֵלָיו֙ יְהוָ֔ה וַיֹּ֖אמֶר אַל־תֵּרֵ֣ד מִצְרָ֑יְמָה שְׁכֹ֣ן בָּאָ֔רֶץ אֲשֶׁ֖ר אֹמַ֥ר

< I shall tell < that < in the Land < dwell << to Egypt; < descend < Do not << and said, < did HASHEM < to him < Appear 2

אֵלֶֽיךָ׃ ג גּ֚וּר בָּאָ֣רֶץ הַזֹּ֔את וְאֶהְיֶ֥ה עִמְּךָ֖ וַאֲבָרְכֶ֑ךָּ כִּֽי־לְךָ֣ וּֽלְזַרְעֲךָ֗ אֶתֵּן֙

< will I give < and your offspring < to you < for << and I will bless you; < with you < and I will be < in this Land < Sojourn 3 << you.

הָא אֲנָא אָזֵל לִמְמָת וּלְמָה דְּנָן לִי בְּכֵרוּתָא: לג וַאֲמַר יַעֲקֹב קַיֵּם לִי כְּיוֹם דִּלְהֵן וְקַיֵּים לֵהּ וְזַבִּין יָת בְּכֵרוּתֵהּ לְיַעֲקֹב: לד וְיַעֲקֹב יְהַב לְעֵשָׂו לְחֵם וְתַבְשִׁיל דִּטְלוֹפְחִין וַאֲכַל וּשְׁתִי וְקָם וַאֲזַל וְשָׁט עֵשָׂו יָת בְּכֵרוּתָא: א וַהֲוָה כַפְנָא בְּאַרְעָא בַּר מִכַּפְנָא קַדְמָאָה דִּי הֲוָה בְּיוֹמֵי דְאַבְרָהָם וַאֲזַל יִצְחָק לְוַת אֲבִימֶלֶךְ מַלְכָּא דִפְלִשְׁתָּאֵי לִגְרָר: ב וְאִתְגְּלִי לֵהּ יְיָ וַאֲמַר לָא תֵחוֹת לְמִצְרָיִם שְׁרֵי בְּאַרְעָא דִּי אֵימַר לָךְ: ג דּוּר בְּאַרְעָא הָדָא וִיהֵי מֵימְרִי בְּסַעְדָּךְ וְאֶבָרְכִנָּךְ אֲרֵי לָךְ וְלִבְנָיךְ אֶתֵּן

רש"י

(לב) הנה אנכי הולך למות. [מתנודדת והולכת היא הבכורה, שלא תהא כל עת העבודה בבכורות כי שבט לוי יטול אותה. ועוד] אמר עשו מה טיבה של עבודה זו. א"ל, כמה אזהרות ועונשין ומיתות תלוין בה, כאותה ששנינו אלו הן שבמיתה שתויי יין ופרועי ראש (סנהדרין כב:). אמר, אני הולך למות על ידה, אם כן מה חפץ לי בה: **(לד) ויבז עשו.** העיד הכתוב על רשעו שביזה עבודתו של מקום: **(ב) אל תרד מצרימה.** שהיה דעתו לרדת למצרים כמו שירד אביו בימי הרעב, אמר לו אל תרד מצרימה, שאתה עולה תמימה ואין חוצה לארץ כדאי לך (ב"ר סד:ג; תנחומא ישן ו):

32. **אָנֹכִי הוֹלֵךְ לָמוּת** — *I am about to die.* Esau thought he would very likely die as a result of performing the sacrificial service improperly, since some such breaches are punishable by death (*Rashi*); or, as a hunter, he was subject to constant danger and could not look forward to a long life (*Ramban*).

34. **וּנְזִיד עֲדָשִׁים** — *And stew of lentils.* The food Jacob was cooking is not identified until after the sale, to emphasize Esau's grossness: For what did he give up his precious birthright? — for a pot of beans! (*R' Bachya*).

וַיִּבֶז עֵשָׂו אֶת־הַבְּכֹרָה — *[Thus,] Esau spurned the birthright.* This sums up the transaction. Esau was neither duped nor defrauded. He sold the birthright because he held it in contempt. It had no value to him when he was famished and it remained meaningless after he was gorged.

26.

1-12. A famine forces Isaac to Philistia. In a repetition of Abraham's experience, Isaac was faced with a famine that forced him to leave his home. Verse 2, in which God commanded him not to go to Egypt but to remain in the Land, implies that he was planning to go there, as his father had done. So he went to Philistia, the central part of the Land along the Mediterranean coast. *Ramban* comments that in line with the famous principle that the experiences of the Patriarchs foreshadowed the future of their descendants, Isaac's sojourn in Philistia portended the Babylonian Exile, just as Abraham's earlier descent to Egypt had portended the Egyptian Exile. In Babylonia the Jews were treated relatively well and even rose to prominence, just as Isaac, though imperiled, was not mistreated and was even honored by Abimelech. At the same time, in another episode that seems familiar in the light of Jewish history, when Isaac became *too* successful, he aroused the jealousy of the masses and was forced to leave the country.

2. **אַל־תֵּרֵד מִצְרָיְמָה** — *Do not descend to Egypt*, for you are an עוֹלָה תְמִימָה, *unblemished offering,* and it does not befit you to reside outside the Land (*Rashi*). *Mizrachi* explains that when Isaac was placed on the altar of the *Akeidah,* he became tantamount to an offering that is completely consumed on the Altar.

אֶת־כָּל־הָאֲרָצֹת הָאֵל וַהֲקִמֹתִי אֶת־הַשְּׁבֻעָה
all < these lands, << and I will establish < the oath <

אֲשֶׁר נִשְׁבַּעְתִּי לְאַבְרָהָם אָבִיךָ: ד וְהִרְבֵּיתִי
that < I swore < to Abraham < your father: << 4 'I will increase <

אֶת־זַרְעֲךָ כְּכוֹכְבֵי הַשָּׁמַיִם וְנָתַתִּי לְזַרְעֲךָ
your offspring < like the stars < of the heavens; << and I will give < to your offspring <

אֵת כָּל־הָאֲרָצֹת הָאֵל וְהִתְבָּרְכוּ בְזַרְעֲךָ כֹּל גּוֹיֵי
all < these lands; << and they shall bless themselves < by your offspring << — all < the nations <

הָאָרֶץ: ה עֵקֶב אֲשֶׁר־שָׁמַע אַבְרָהָם בְּקֹלִי וַיִּשְׁמֹר מִשְׁמַרְתִּי מִצְוֹתַי
of the earth.' << 5 Because < Abraham listened < to My voice, < and he observed < My safeguards, < My commandments, <

חֻקּוֹתַי וְתוֹרֹתָי: שני ו וַיֵּשֶׁב יִצְחָק בִּגְרָר: ז וַיִּשְׁאֲלוּ אַנְשֵׁי הַמָּקוֹם לְאִשְׁתּוֹ
My decrees, < and My teachings. << 6 So Isaac settled < in Gerar. << 7 [When] they asked << — the men < of the place — << concerning his wife, <

וַיֹּאמֶר אֲחֹתִי הִוא כִּי יָרֵא לֵאמֹר אִשְׁתִּי פֶּן־יַהַרְגֻנִי אַנְשֵׁי הַמָּקוֹם
he said, << My sister < is she << — for < he was afraid < to say < my wife, << lest < they kill me << — the men < of the place — <<

יָת כָּל אַרְעָתָא הָאִלֵּין וְאָקֵים יָת קְיָמָא דִּי קַיֵּמִית לְאַבְרָהָם אֲבוּךְ: ד וְאַסְגֵּי יָת בְּנָיךְ סַגִּיאִין כְּכוֹכְבֵי שְׁמַיָּא וְאֶתֵּן לִבְנָיךְ יָת כָּל אַרְעָתָא הָאִלֵּין וְיִתְבָּרְכוּן בְּדִיל בְּנָיךְ כֹּל עַמְמֵי אַרְעָא: ה חֲלָף דִּי קַבִּיל אַבְרָהָם בְּמֵימְרִי וּנְטַר מַטְּרַת מֵימְרִי פִּקּוֹדַי קְיָמַי וְאוֹרָיָתָי: ו וִיתֵב יִצְחָק בִּגְרָר: ז וּשְׁאִילוּ אֱנָשֵׁי אַתְרָא לְאִתְּתֵהּ (נ״א עַל עֵיסַק אִתְּתֵהּ) וַאֲמַר אֲחָתִי הִיא אֲרֵי דְחֵיל לְמֵימַר אִתְּתִי דִלְמָא יִקְטְלֻנַּנִי אֱנָשֵׁי אַתְרָא

רש״י

(ג) **האל.** כמו האלה: (ד) **והתברכו בזרעך.** אדם אומר לבנו יהא זרעך כזרעו של יצחק, וכן בכל המקרא, וזה אב לכולן, בך יברך ישראל לאמר ישמך וגו' (להלן מח:כ). ואף לענין הקללה מצינו כן, והיתה האשה לאלה (במדבר ה:כז) שהמקלל שונאו אומר תהא כפלונית. וכן והנחתם שמכם לשבועה לבחירי (ישעיה סה:טו), שהנשבע אומר אהא כפלוני אם עשיתי כך וכך (ספרי נשא יח): (ה) **שמע אברהם בקולי.** כשנסיתי אותו (פדר״א פל״א): **וישמור משמרתי.** גזרות להרחקה על אזהרות שבתורה, כגון שניות לעריות ושבות לשבת (יבמות כא.): **מצותי.** דברים שאילו לא נכתבו ראויין הם להצטוות, כגון גזל ושפיכות דמים (יומא סז:): **חקותי.** דברים שיצר הרע ואומות העולם משיבין עליהם, כגון אכילת חזיר ולבישת שעטנז, שאין טעם בדבר אלא גזירת המלך וחקותיו על עבדיו (שם): **ותורתי.** להביא תורה שבעל פה הלכה למשה מסיני (שם כח:;ב״ר סד:ד): (ז) **לאשתו.** על אשתו, כמו אמרי לי אחי הוא (לעיל כ:יג):

Just as such an offering may not be removed from the Temple Courtyard, so was Isaac forbidden from leaving the sacred soil of the Land.

3. **וַהֲקִמֹתִי אֶת־הַשְּׁבֻעָה** — *And I will establish the oath*. This was not a promise that God would *fulfill* the oath, for it is inconceivable that God would not keep His word. Rather, God recognized Isaac's own merit by reiterating His oath to Abraham and giving it the status of a *new oath* to Isaac, for each of the Patriarchs in his own right was worthy of the promise (*Ramban*).

5. The gift of the Land is attributed to Abraham's loyalty in obeying the word of God. The verse speaks of four categories of commandments, which *Rashi* explains as follows:

❑ מִשְׁמַרְתִּי, *My safeguards,* are Rabbinic enactments that serve as barriers against infringement of Biblical prohibitions.

❑ מִצְוֹתַי, *My commandments,* are laws that man's moral sense would have dictated.

❑ חֻקּוֹתַי, *My decrees,* are laws that reason cannot explain, and which are thus, as it were, *royal decrees* that God enacts on His subjects.

❑ וְתוֹרֹתָי, *and My teachings*, in the plural, are the Written Torah and the Oral Torah. The latter includes rules and interpretations transmitted to Moses at Sinai.

The consensus of Rabbinic opinion is that Abraham arrived at a knowledge of the *entire Torah* through Divine Inspiration and observed it voluntarily. This explains how our verse can praise Abraham for observing Rabbinic ordinances (*Ramban*).

In a novel interpretation, *R' Hirsch* derives the word Torah from הרה, *conceive.* Just as an embryo grows from a seed that is implanted at conception, so too God's teachings plant a seed, so to speak, which develops in the recipient to an ever-greater consciousness of good. Similarly, *Tur* comments that the Oral Torah is the subject of the term in the second of the Torah blessings: חַיֵּי עוֹלָם נָטַע בְּתוֹכֵנוּ, [*God*] *implanted eternal life within us,* because the Oral Law is like a sapling that is planted and then grows to produce its own fruit.

6-16. Isaac in Gerar. Because of his covenant with Abraham, Abimelech showed Isaac no malice; it was the *residents* who inquired about the identity of Rebecca. Knowing that they could spirit a wife away from her husband and murder him on some pretext, Isaac reverted to Abraham's ruse, by identifying his wife as his sister (*Ramban* to v. 1 and 12:11).

עַל־רִבְקָה כִּי־טוֹבַת מַרְאֶה הִוא: ח וַיְהִי כִּי אָרְכוּ־
< they lengthened < as < And it came to pass, **8** << *is she!* < *appearance* < *of good* < *for* < *Rebecca* < *because of*

לוֹ שָׁם הַיָּמִים וַיַּשְׁקֵף אֲבִימֶלֶךְ מֶלֶךְ פְּלִשְׁתִּים
< of the Philistines < King < did Abimelech < [that] gaze down << — his days — << there < for him

בְּעַד הַחַלּוֹן וַיַּרְא וְהִנֵּה יִצְחָק מְצַחֵק אֵת רִבְקָה
< Rebecca < with < was sporting < Isaac << — indeed! << and saw < the window < through

אִשְׁתּוֹ: ט וַיִּקְרָא אֲבִימֶלֶךְ לְיִצְחָק וַיֹּאמֶר אַךְ הִנֵּה
<< *indeed!* < *But* << and said, < to Isaac < And Abimelech called **9** << his wife.

אִשְׁתְּךָ הִוא וְאֵיךְ אָמַרְתָּ אֲחֹתִי הִוא וַיֹּאמֶר
< Say << *she is?'* < *'My sister* << *could you say,* < *How* << *she is!* < *Your wife*

אֵלָיו יִצְחָק כִּי אָמַרְתִּי פֶּן־אָמוּת עָלֶיהָ: י וַיֹּאמֶר אֲבִימֶלֶךְ מַה־זֹּאת
< *is this* < *What* << Abimelech said, **10** << *because of her.'* < *I would die* < *'Lest* << *I said,* < *Because* << did Isaac, < to him

עָשִׂיתָ לָּנוּ כִּמְעַט שָׁכַב אַחַד הָעָם אֶת־אִשְׁתֶּךָ וְהֵבֵאתָ עָלֵינוּ אָשָׁם:
<< *guilt!* < *upon us* < *and you would have brought* << *your wife,* < *with* << *of the people —* < *— one* << *has he lain* < *Nearly* << *to us?* < *[that] you have done*

יא וַיְצַו אֲבִימֶלֶךְ אֶת־כָּל־הָעָם לֵאמֹר הַנֹּגֵעַ בָּאִישׁ הַזֶּה וּבְאִשְׁתּוֹ
< *and his wife* < *this man* < *Whoever touches* << saying, < the people < all < Abimelech then commanded **11**

מוֹת יוּמָת: יב וַיִּזְרַע יִצְחָק בָּאָרֶץ הַהִוא וַיִּמְצָא בַּשָּׁנָה הַהִוא מֵאָה
< one hundred < in that year < and he brought in << in that land, < Isaac sowed **12** << *shall surely be put to death.*

שְׁעָרִים וַיְבָרְכֵהוּ יהוה: שלישי יג וַיִּגְדַּל הָאִישׁ וַיֵּלֶךְ הָלוֹךְ וְגָדֵל עַד כִּי־
< then that < until < becoming greater < continually < and went on << And the man grew great **13** << [for] HASHEM had blessed him. << times [what was estimated];

עַל רִבְקָה אֲרֵי שַׁפִּירַת חֵיזוּ הִיא: ח וַהֲוָה כַּד סְגִיאוּ לֵהּ תַּמָּן יוֹמַיָּא וְאִסְתְּכִי אֲבִימֶלֶךְ מַלְכָּא דִפְלִשְׁתָּאֵי מִן חֲרַכָּא וַחֲזָא וְהָא יִצְחָק מְחַיֵּךְ עִם רִבְקָה אִתְּתֵהּ: ט וּקְרָא אֲבִימֶלֶךְ לְיִצְחָק וַאֲמַר בְּרַם הָא אִתְּתָךְ הִיא וְאֶכְדֵּין אֲמַרְתָּ אֲחָתִי הִיא וַאֲמַר לֵהּ יִצְחָק אֲרֵי אֲמָרִית דִּלְמָא אֵימוּת עֲלַהּ: י וַאֲמַר אֲבִימֶלֶךְ מָה דָא עֲבַדְתָּ לָנָא כִּזְעֵיר פּוֹן שְׁכִיב דִּמְיַחַד בְּעַמָּא עִם אִתְּתָךְ וְאַיְתֵיתָא עֲלָנָא חוֹבָא: יא וּפַקִּיד אֲבִימֶלֶךְ יָת כָּל עַמָּא לְמֵימָר דְּיַנְזֵק בְּגַבְרָא הָדֵין וּבְאִתְּתֵהּ אִתְקְטָלָא יִתְקְטֵל: יב וּזְרַע יִצְחָק בְּאַרְעָא הַהִיא וְאַשְׁכַּח בְּשַׁתָּא הַהִיא עַל חַד מְאָה בִּדְשַׁעֲרוּהִי וּבָרְכֵהּ יְיָ: יג וּרְבָא גַּבְרָא וַאֲזַל אָזֵל (נ״א סָגֵי) וְרָבֵי עַד דִּי

רש״י

(ח) **כי ארכו.** אמר, מעתה אין לי לדאוג מאחר שלא אנסוה עד עכשיו, ולא נזהר להיות נשמר (ב״ר סד:ה): **וישקף אבימלך וגו׳.** שראהו משמש מטתו (שם): (י) **אחד העם.** המיוחד בעם (אונקלוס) זה המלך (תרגום יונתן): **והבאת עלינו אשם.** אם שכב כבר הבאת אשם עלינו: (יב) **בארץ ההיא.** אע״פ שאינה חשובה כא״י עצמה, כארץ שבעה גוים: **בשנה ההיא.** אע״פ שאינה כתקנה, שהיתה שנת רעבון: **בארץ ההיא בשנה ההיא.** שניהם למה. לומר שהארץ קשה והשנה קשה (ב״ר סד:ו): **מאה שערים.** שאמדוה כמה ראויה לעשות ועשתה על אחת שאמדוה מאה. ורבותינו אמרו, אומד זה למעשרות היה (ב״ר שם):

10. אַחַד הָעָם — *One of the people.* This term also has the connotation of the *most distinguished one* of the people: the king himself! This explains Abimelech's emotional outburst at Isaac, for his complaint was an implied admission that he himself had coveted Rebecca and was on the verge of taking her for himself. Not only would that have brought great guilt upon him, it would have brought great suffering upon him and his subjects — as he knew from the experience of Sarah.

As king, Abimelech contended, I would certainly not be expected first to seek your consent, since it would be an honor for one to give his sister in marriage to the king (*Sforno*).

11. וַיְצַו אֲבִימֶלֶךְ — *Abimelech then commanded.* Realizing that no husband of a beautiful woman was safe in his land, Abimelech found it necessary to assure Isaac's safety by issuing a royal decree on his behalf. What a vindication of Isaac's initial apprehensions when entering this godless country!

12. מֵאָה שְׁעָרִים — *One hundred times [what was estimated].* According to our Rabbis, Isaac was scrupulous to determine the quantity of his crop in order to establish how much he was required to give as tithes (*Rashi*).

גָּדַל מְאֹד: יד וַיְהִי־לוֹ מִקְנֵה־צֹאן וּמִקְנֵה בָקָר

‹ of cattle, ‹ and herds ‹ of sheep ‹ flocks ‹ He possessed 14 « exceedingly. ‹ he was great

וַעֲבֻדָּה רַבָּה וַיְקַנְאוּ אֹתוֹ פְּלִשְׁתִּים: טו וְכָל־

‹ And all 15 « did the Philistines. ‹ him ‹ and envy « and much enterprise;

הַבְּאֵרֹת אֲשֶׁר חָפְרוּ עַבְדֵי אָבִיו בִּימֵי אַבְרָהָם

‹ of Abraham ‹ in the days « of his father — ‹ — the servants « they had dug ‹ that ‹ the wells

אָבִיו סִתְּמוּם פְּלִשְׁתִּים וַיְמַלְאוּם עָפָר:

« with earth. ‹ and they filled them « did the Philistines, ‹ stop them up « his father,

טז וַיֹּאמֶר אֲבִימֶלֶךְ אֶל־יִצְחָק לֵךְ מֵעִמָּנוּ כִּי־

‹ *for* ‹ *from us* ‹ *Go away* « Isaac, ‹ to ‹ And Abimelech said 16

עָצַמְתָּ מִמֶּנּוּ מְאֹד: יז וַיֵּלֶךְ מִשָּׁם יִצְחָק וַיִּחַן בְּנַחַל־גְּרָר וַיֵּשֶׁב שָׁם:

« there. ‹ and dwelled ‹ of Gerar, ‹ in the valley ‹ and he encamped « Isaac did, « from there, ‹ So he went 17 « *exceedingly!* ‹ *than we* ‹ *you have become more mighty*

יח וַיָּשָׁב יִצְחָק וַיַּחְפֹּר | אֶת־בְּאֵרֹת הַמַּיִם אֲשֶׁר חָפְרוּ בִּימֵי אַבְרָהָם

‹ of Abraham ‹ in the days ‹ they had dug ‹ that ‹ of water ‹ the wells ‹ and dug ‹ And Isaac went back 18

אָבִיו וַיְסַתְּמוּם פְּלִשְׁתִּים אַחֲרֵי מוֹת אַבְרָהָם וַיִּקְרָא לָהֶן שֵׁמוֹת כַּשֵּׁמֹת

‹ like the names ‹ names ‹ them ‹ and he called « of Abraham; ‹ the death ‹ after ‹ and that the Philistines had stopped them up ‹ his father

אֲשֶׁר־קָרָא לָהֶן אָבִיו: יט וַיַּחְפְּרוּ עַבְדֵי־יִצְחָק בַּנָּחַל וַיִּמְצְאוּ־שָׁם בְּאֵר

‹ a well ‹ there ‹ and they found ‹ in the valley « of Isaac — ‹ — the servants « And they dug 19 « [by] his father. ‹ them ‹ had [been] called ‹ that

רְבָא לַחֲדָא: יד וַהֲוָה לֵהּ גֵּיתֵי עָנָא וְגֵיתֵי תוֹרִין וּפָלְחָנָא (נ״א וַעֲבוּדָה) סַגִּיָא וְקַנִּיאוּ בֵהּ פְּלִשְׁתָּאֵי: טו וְכָל בֵּירִין דִּי חֲפָרוּ עַבְדֵי אֲבוּהִי בְּיוֹמֵי אַבְרָהָם אֲבוּהִי טַמּוֹנוּן פְּלִשְׁתָּאֵי וּמְלוֹנוּן עַפְרָא: טז וַאֲמַר אֲבִימֶלֶךְ לְיִצְחָק אִזֵיל מֵעִמָּנָא אֲרֵי תְקֵפְתָּא מִנָּנָא לַחֲדָא: יז וַאֲזַל מִתַּמָּן יִצְחָק וּשְׁרָא בְּנַחֲלָא דִגְרָר וִיתֵב תַּמָּן: יח וְתָב יִצְחָק וַחֲפַר יָת בֵּירֵי דְמַיָּא דִּי חֲפָרוּ בְּיוֹמֵי אַבְרָהָם אֲבוּהִי וְטַמּוֹנוּן פְּלִשְׁתָּאֵי בָּתַר דְּמִית אַבְרָהָם וּקְרָא לְהֵין שְׁמָהָן כִּשְׁמָהָן דִּי הֲוָה קָרֵי לְהֵין אֲבוּהִי: יט וַחֲפָרוּ עַבְדֵי יִצְחָק בְּנַחֲלָא וְאַשְׁכָּחוּ תַמָּן בֵּירָא

רש״י

(יג) **כי גדל מאד.** שהיו אומרים, זבל פרדותיו של יצחק ולא כספו וזהבו של אבימלך (שם ז): (יד) **ועבדה רבה.** פעולה רבה, בלשון לע״ז אובריי״א. עֲבוֹדָה משמע עבודה אחת, עֲבֻדָּה משמע פעולה רבה: (טו) **סתמום פלשתים.** מפני שאמרו תקלה הם לנו מפני הגייסות הבאות עלינו (תוספתא סוטה י:ב). [ומתרגמינן] טמונון פלשתאי, לשון סתימה, ובלשון משנה מטמטם את הלב (פסחים מב.): (יז) **בנחל גרר.** רחוק מן העיר: (יח) **וישב ויחפר.** הבארות

14. וַיְקַנְאוּ אֹתוֹ פְּלִשְׁתִּים — *And envy him did the Philistines.* Since the verse says that they envied *him* — not that they envied his *wealth* — *R' Hirsch* infers that the envy was directed at him, personally. The Philistines felt threatened by Isaac's success.

15. סִתְּמוּם פְּלִשְׁתִּים — *Stop them up did the Philistines.* By doing so, the Philistines violated Abimelech's covenant with Abraham [21:27] (*Midrash HaGadol*). They claimed that these wells could become a menace because of marauding troops (*Rashi*), because in a country where water was in short supply, such wells might attract robbers, or an invading army could use them as its water supply. Accordingly, there was a valid reason to stop up the wells. Nevertheless, the incident shows the difference between the status of Abraham and that of Isaac. While Abraham was alive, the natives' respect for the *prince of God* prevented them from tampering with his wells (v.18), but when the wells reverted to Isaac, the Philistines acted with impunity (*R' Hirsch*).

16. כִּי־עָצַמְתָּ מִמֶּנּוּ מְאֹד — *For you have become more mighty than we exceedingly.* Though I am king, I do not have as many possessions as you. It is a disgrace to us that you should be wealthier than the king! (*Ramban*). The *Midrash* (*Bamidbar Rabbah* 18:21) states that the double forms of the five letters מנצפ״ך, *mem, nun, tzadi, pei,* and *caf,* were established by the *Tzufim,* the prophets. Each one of the letters is associated with a verse that encapsulates a prophetic view of Jewish destiny. The verse for the letter *mem* is לֵךְ מֵעִמָּנוּ כִּי עָצַמְתָּ מִמֶּנּוּ מְאֹד, *Go away from us for you have become more mighty than we exceedingly,* with its proliferation of *mems.* The prophecy is that our success will engender the jealousy of the nations, leading to our banishment. Also, as *Haamek Davar* explains, this foreshadowed the pales of settlement of future exiles when Jewish residency rights were restricted.

18. שֵׁמוֹת כַּשֵּׁמֹת — *Names like the names.* In doing so, Isaac was motivated by respect for his father. Thus the Torah teaches that

מַיִם חַיִּים׃ כ וַיָּרִיבוּ רֹעֵי גְרָר עִם־רֹעֵי יִצְחָק
‹ of Isaac ‹ the herdsmen ‹ with « of Gerar — ‹ — the herdsmen « And they quarreled **20** « of spring water.

לֵאמֹר לָנוּ הַמָּיִם וַיִּקְרָא שֵׁם־הַבְּאֵר עֵשֶׂק
‹ Esek ‹ of that well ‹ the name ‹ so he called « *is the water,* ‹ *Ours* « saying,

כִּי הִתְעַשְּׂקוּ עִמּוֹ׃ כא וַיַּחְפְּרוּ בְּאֵר אַחֶרֶת וַיָּרִיבוּ
‹ and they quarreled « another well, ‹ Then they dug **21** « with him. ‹ they contended ‹ because

גַּם־עָלֶיהָ וַיִּקְרָא שְׁמָהּ שִׂטְנָה׃ כב וַיַּעְתֵּק מִשָּׁם
‹ from there ‹ He relocated **22** « Sitnah. ‹ its name ‹ so he called « over that; ‹ also

וַיַּחְפֹּר בְּאֵר אַחֶרֶת וְלֹא רָבוּ עָלֶיהָ וַיִּקְרָא שְׁמָהּ
‹ its name ‹ so he called « over it, ‹ they did not quarrel « another well; ‹ and dug

רְחֹבוֹת וַיֹּאמֶר כִּי־עַתָּה הִרְחִיב יהוה לָנוּ וּפָרִינוּ בָאָרֶץ׃ רביעי כג וַיַּעַל
‹ He went up **23** « *in the land.* ‹ *and we can be fruitful* ‹ *to us,* ‹ *Hashem has granted ample space* ‹ *now* ‹ *For* « and he said, « Rehoboth,

מִשָּׁם בְּאֵר שָׁבַע׃ כד וַיֵּרָא אֵלָיו יהוה בַּלַּיְלָה הַהוּא וַיֹּאמֶר אָנֹכִי אֱלֹהֵי
‹ *the God* ‹ *I am* « and said, ‹ that night ‹ did Hashem ‹ to him ‹ Appear **24** « to Beer Sheba. ‹ from there

אַבְרָהָם אָבִיךָ אַל־תִּירָא כִּי־אִתְּךָ אָנֹכִי וּבֵרַכְתִּיךָ וְהִרְבֵּיתִי אֶת־זַרְעֲךָ
‹ *your offspring* ‹ *and I will increase* ‹ *I will bless you* « *am I;* ‹ *with you* ‹ *for* ‹ *Fear not,* « *your father:* ‹ *of Abraham*

בַּעֲבוּר אַבְרָהָם עַבְדִּי׃ כה וַיִּבֶן שָׁם מִזְבֵּחַ וַיִּקְרָא בְּשֵׁם יהוה וַיֶּט־שָׁם
‹ there ‹ and he pitched « of Hashem, ‹ the Name ‹ and invoked « an altar, ‹ there ‹ He built **25** « *my servant.* ‹ *Abraham* ‹ *because of*

מַיָּא נָבְעִין׃ כ וּנְצוֹ רַעֲוָתָא דִגְרָר עִם רַעֲוָתָא דְיִצְחָק לְמֵימַר דִּי לָנָא מַיָּא וּקְרָא שְׁמָא דְבֵירָא עִסְקָא אֲרֵי אִתְעַסִּיקוּ עִמֵּהּ׃ כא וַחֲפָרוּ בֵּירָא אָחֳרִי וּנְצוֹ אַף עֲלַהּ וּקְרָא שְׁמַהּ שִׂטְנָה׃ כב וְאִסְתַּלַּק מִתַּמָּן נַחֲפַר בֵּירָא אָחֳרִי וְלָא נְצוֹ עֲלַהּ וּקְרָא שְׁמַהּ רְחֹבוֹת וַאֲמַר אֲרֵי כְעַן אַפְתֵּי יְיָ לָנָא וְנִיפּוּשׁ (נ״א וְיַפְשִׁנָּנָא) בְּאַרְעָא׃ כג וְאִסְתַּלַּק מִתַּמָּן בְּאֵר שָׁבַע׃ כד וְאִתְגְּלִי לֵהּ יְיָ בְּלֵילְיָא הַהוּא וַאֲמַר אֲנָא אֱלָהֵהּ דְּאַבְרָהָם אֲבוּךְ לָא תִדְחַל אֲרֵי בְסַעְדָּךְ מֵימְרִי וַאֲבָרֵכִנָּךְ וְאַסְגֵּי יָת בְּנָיךְ בְּדִיל אַבְרָהָם עַבְדִּי׃ כה וּבְנָא תַמָּן מַדְבְּחָא וְצַלִּי בִּשְׁמָא דַיְיָ וּפָרַס תַּמָּן

רש״י

אשר חפרו בימי אברהם אביו, ופלשתים סתמום קודם שנסע יצחק מגרר, חזר וחפרן: (כ) עשק. ערעור (עי׳ ב״מ יד.): כי התעשקו עמו. נתעשקו עמו עליה במריבה וערעור: (כא) שטנה. נויישמנ״ט: (כב) ופרינו בארץ. כתרגומו, וניפוש בארעא:

one should not deviate unnecessarily from his father's way (*R' Bachya*).

19-22. The prophetic dispute over the wells. The commentators note that there must be reasons why the Torah relates the seemingly trivial incidents of the wells in such detail. Following the thesis that the experiences of the Patriarchs are signposts of Jewish history, the three wells of this passage correspond to the three Temples, the two that were destroyed, and the eternal one yet to be built. The first well, named *Esek,* or *contention*, alludes to the First Temple, which fell victim to the strife of the nations that finally destroyed it. The second well, *Sitnah*, or *enmity,* a harsher name than *Esek,* alludes to the Second Temple period, when the enmity of Israel's enemies was longer lasting and more virulent. The third well, *Rehoboth,* or *spaciousness*, alludes to the future Temple, the era when strife and enmity will be things of the past (*Ramban*).

20. לָנוּ הַמָּיִם — *Ours is the water.* "The well is located in the valley and draws from our own water supply; hence, it is ours." But in verse 19, the Torah testified to the contrary, since it was *spring water,* meaning that it had its own underground source and did not drain water from Philistine streams or rivers (*Ramban*).

22. וַיַּחְפֹּר — *And [he] dug.* This time Isaac himself presided over the digging, or perhaps he even dug the first clod to initiate the venture. It was in his merit that this venture was not opposed (*Haamek Davar*).

23-25. God assures Isaac. After the conflict with the Philistines, Isaac was afraid that they would launch an attack and try to kill him (*Ramban*), or that he would continue to lose assets because of their enmity (*Sforno*). In response, God appeared to him and promised him protection.

25. וַיִּבֶן שָׁם מִזְבֵּחַ — *He built there an altar.* As Abraham had done (12:7, 13:18), Isaac brought an offering to thank God for His

אָהֳלוֹ וַיִּכְרוּ־שָׁם עַבְדֵי־יִצְחָק בְּאֵר: כו וַאֲבִימֶלֶךְ
‹ Abimelech 26 « a well. « of Isaac — ‹ — the servants « there ‹ they dug « his tent;
הָלַךְ אֵלָיו מִגְּרָר וַאֲחֻזַּת מֵרֵעֵהוּ וּפִיכֹל שַׂר־
‹ general ‹ and Phicol, ‹ of his friends ‹ with a group ‹ from Gerar ‹ to him ‹ went
צְבָאוֹ: כז וַיֹּאמֶר אֲלֵהֶם יִצְחָק מַדּוּעַ בָּאתֶם
‹ have you come ‹ Why « did Isaac, ‹ to them ‹ Say 27 « of his legion.
אֵלָי וְאַתֶּם שְׂנֵאתֶם אֹתִי וַתְּשַׁלְּחוּנִי מֵאִתְּכֶם:
« from you! ‹ and drove me away ‹ me ‹ hate ‹ [For] you ‹ to me?
כח וַיֹּאמְרוּ רָאוֹ רָאִינוּ כִּי־הָיָה יהוה ׀ עִמָּךְ וַנֹּאמֶר
« so we said, « with you, ‹ HASHEM has been ‹ that ‹ We have seen repeatedly « And they said, 28
תְּהִי נָא אָלָה בֵּינוֹתֵינוּ בֵּינֵינוּ וּבֵינֶךָ וְנִכְרְתָה בְרִית עִמָּךְ: כט אִם־תַּעֲשֵׂה
‹ you do ‹ If 29 « with you: ‹ a covenant ‹ and let us make « and between you, ‹ between us « between ourselves, ‹ an oath ‹ now ‹ 'Let there be
עִמָּנוּ רָעָה כַּאֲשֶׁר לֹא נְגַעֲנוּךָ וְכַאֲשֶׁר עָשִׂינוּ עִמְּךָ רַק־טוֹב וַנְּשַׁלֵּחֲךָ
‹ and we sent you away « good, ‹ only ‹ with you ‹ we have done ‹ and just as ‹ we have not touched you, ‹ Just as « evil . . . ! ‹ with us
בְּשָׁלוֹם אַתָּה עַתָּה בְּרוּךְ יהוה: חמישי ל וַיַּעַשׂ לָהֶם מִשְׁתֶּה וַיֹּאכְלוּ וַיִּשְׁתּוּ:
« and they drank. ‹ and they ate ‹ a feast ‹ for them ‹ He made 30 « of HASHEM!' ‹ the blessed one ‹ now ‹ — You are « in peace

מַשְׁכְּנֵהּ וּכְרוֹ תַמָּן עַבְדֵי יִצְחָק בֵּירָא: כו וַאֲבִימֶלֶךְ אֲזַל לְוָתֵהּ מִגְּרָר וְסִיעַת מֵרַחֲמוֹהִי וּפִיכֹל רַב חֵילֵהּ: כז וַאֲמַר לְהוֹן יִצְחָק מָא דֵין אֲתֵיתוֹן לְוָתִי וְאַתּוּן סְנֵאתוּן יָתִי וְשַׁלַּחְתּוּנִי מִלְּוָתְכוֹן: כח וַאֲמָרוּ מֶחֱזָא חֲזֵינָא אֲרֵי הֲוָה מֵימְרָא דַייָ בְּסַעְדָּךְ וַאֲמַרְנָא תִּתְקַיַּם כְּעַן מוֹמָתָא דַהֲוָת בֵּין אֲבָהָתָנָא בֵּינָנָא וּבֵינָךְ וְנִגְזַר קְיָם עִמָּךְ: כט אִם תַּעְבֵּד עִמָּנָא בִּישָׁא כְּמָא דִי לָא אַנְזֵיקְנָךְ וּכְמָא דִי עֲבַדְנָא עִמָּךְ לְחוֹד טַב וְשַׁלַּחְנָךְ בִּשְׁלָם אַתְּ כְּעַן בְּרִיכָא דַייָ: ל וַעֲבַד לְהוֹן מִשְׁתְּיָא וַאֲכָלוּ וּשְׁתִיאוּ:

רש"י

(כו) ואחזת מרעהו. כתרגומו וסיעת מרחמוהי (ב"ר סד:ט) סיעת מאוהביו. ויש פותרין מרעהו מ' מיסוד התיבה, כמו שלשים מרעים (שופטים יד:יא) דשמשון. כדי שתהיה תיבת ואחזת דבוקה. אבל אין דרך ארץ לדבר על המלכות כן, סיעת אוהביו, שאם כן כל סיעת אוהביו הוליך עמו ולא היה לו אלא סיעה אחת של אוהבים. לכן יש לפותרו כלשון הראשון. ואל תתמה על תי"ו של ואחזת ואף על פי שאין התיבה סמוכה, יש דוגמתה במקרא, עזרת מצר (תהלים ס:יג) ושכורת ולא מיין (ישעיה נא:כא): **אחזת.** לשון קבוצה ואגודה, שנאחזין יחד: **(כח) ראו ראינו.** ראו באביך ראינו בך (ב"ר שם י): **תהי נא אלה בינותינו וגו'.** האלה אשר בינותינו מימי אביך תהי גם עתה בינינו ובינך (אונקלוס): **(כט) לא נגענוך.** כשאמרנו לך לך מעמנו (לעיל פסוק טז): **אתה.** גם אתה [עתה] עשה לנו כמו כן:

parts of the Land, but he did not build an altar then, because he did not wish to inflame his neighbors by publicizing such a promise. Now, however, the promise that he would be blessed and fruitful was no threat to them (*Meshech Chochmah).*

26-33. Abimelech reaffirms the treaty. *Targum Yonasan* explains Abimelech's sudden change of heart: "When Isaac left Gerar the wells dried up and the trees bore no fruit. They felt that this befell them because they had driven him away, so Abimelech went to Isaac from Gerar . . ."

27. מַדּוּעַ בָּאתֶם אֵלָי — *Why have you come to me?* Isaac's apparent lack of graciousness is quite understandable. Abimelech had ignored his treaty with Abraham, thus showing that he and his people did not honor their commitments. What, then, was the purpose of this new visit? (*Abarbanel*). Abimelech responded by saying that he wanted not merely to reaffirm the previous covenant, but to strengthen it. He said that the oath *between ourselves* from Abraham's time, should now be formally extended to apply *between us and between you.* Furthermore, he wanted it to take the form of an אָלָה, which implies not merely an oath, but one that includes a curse against anyone who violates it.

29. אִם־תַּעֲשֵׂה עִמָּנוּ רָעָה — *If you do with us evil . . . !* In all such cases, the Torah leaves the threatened consequences to the imagination. Thus, since the oath is strengthened by a curse, it is as if Abimelech were saying: *"If you do with us evil* — then may God take terrible retribution against you" (*Ramban*).

רַק־טוֹב — *Only good.* We have protected you by warning the people against interfering with you (*Ramban*).

How glaring is their omission of any reference to the herdsmen who quarreled over the wells, or stopped up Abraham's wells! Perhaps in their perverted way, they rationalized, as have anti-Semites through the ages, that their acts of harassment were justifiable, or that Isaac should be grateful that they took out their wrath against his wells and not against his person.

אַתָּה עַתָּה בְּרוּךְ ה' — *You are now the blessed one of* HASHEM. Now we call upon you, who are blessed of HASHEM, to reciprocate our kindness by entering into a treaty with us (*Rashi, Rashbam*).

לא וַיַּשְׁכִּימוּ בַבֹּקֶר וַיִּשָּׁבְעוּ אִישׁ לְאָחִיו וַיְשַׁלְּחֵם

31 They awoke early ‹ in the morning ‹ and they swore ‹ [each] man ‹ to his brother; ‹‹ then sent them off ‹

יִצְחָק וַיֵּלְכוּ מֵאִתּוֹ בְּשָׁלוֹם: לב וַיְהִי | בַּיּוֹם הַהוּא

did Isaac ‹ and they departed ‹ from him ‹ in peace. ‹‹ **32** And it was ‹ on that very day ‹

וַיָּבֹאוּ עַבְדֵי יִצְחָק וַיַּגִּדוּ לוֹ עַל־אֹדוֹת הַבְּאֵר

that they came ‹‹ — the servants ‹ of Isaac — ‹‹ and told ‹ him ‹ all about ‹ the well ‹

אֲשֶׁר חָפָרוּ וַיֹּאמְרוּ לוֹ מָצָאנוּ מָיִם: לג וַיִּקְרָא אֹתָהּ

that ‹ they had dug, ‹‹ and they said ‹ to him, ‹‹ *We have found* ‹ *water!* ‹‹ **33** And he called ‹ it ‹

שִׁבְעָה עַל־כֵּן שֵׁם־הָעִיר בְּאֵר שֶׁבַע עַד הַיּוֹם הַזֶּה: ס לד וַיְהִי עֵשָׂו בֶּן־

Shibah; ‹‹ therefore, ‹ the name ‹ of the city ‹ is Beer Sheba ‹ until ‹ this very day. ‹‹ **34** And when Esau was ‹ of the age ‹

אַרְבָּעִים שָׁנָה וַיִּקַּח אִשָּׁה אֶת־יְהוּדִית בַּת־בְּאֵרִי הַחִתִּי וְאֶת־בָּשְׂמַת

of forty ‹ years, ‹‹ he took ‹ [as] a wife ‹ Judith ‹ daughter ‹ of Beeri ‹ the Hittite, ‹ and Basemath ‹

בַּת־אֵילֹן הַחִתִּי: לה וַתִּהְיֶיןָ מֹרַת רוּחַ לְיִצְחָק וּלְרִבְקָה: ס [כז] א וַיְהִי

daughter ‹ of Elon ‹ the Hittite; ‹‹ **35** and they were ‹ of rebellious ‹ spirit ‹ to Isaac ‹ and to Rebecca. ‹‹ **27** **1** And it was, ‹

לא וְאַקְדִּימוּ בְצַפְרָא וְקַיִּימוּ גְּבַר לַאֲחוּהִי וְשַׁלְּחִנּוּן יִצְחָק וַאֲזָלוּ מִנֵּיהּ בִּשְׁלָם: לב וַהֲוָה בְּיוֹמָא הַהוּא וַאֲתוֹ עַבְדֵי יִצְחָק וְחַוִּיאוּ לֵהּ עַל עֵיסַק בֵּירָא דִּי חֲפָרוּ וַאֲמָרוּ לֵהּ אַשְׁכַּחְנָא מַיָּא: לג וּקְרָא יָתַהּ שִׁבְעָה עַל כֵּן שְׁמָא דְקַרְתָּא בֵּאֵרָא דְשֶׁבַע (נ״א בְּאֵר שֶׁבַע) עַד יוֹמָא הָדֵין: לד וַהֲוָה עֵשָׂו בַּר אַרְבְּעִין שְׁנִין וּנְסִיב אִתְּתָא יָת יְהוּדִית בַּת בְּאֵרִי חִתָּאָה וְיָת בָּשְׂמַת בַּת אֵילוֹן חִתָּאָה: לה וַהֲוָאָה מְסָרְבָן וּמַרְגְּזָן עַל מֵימַר יִצְחָק וְרִבְקָה: א וַהֲוָה

רש״י

(לג) **שבעה.** ע״ש הברית (תנחומא ישן ויצא ט): (לד) **בן ארבעים שנה.** עשו היה נמשל לחזיר, שנא׳ יכרסמנה חזיר מיער (תהלים פ:יד). החזיר הזה כשהוא שוכב פושט טלפיו לומר ראו שאני טהור, כך אלו גוזלים וחומסים ומראים עצמם כשרים. כל מ׳ שנה היה עשו צד נשים מתחת יד בעליהן ומענה אותם, כשהיה בן מ׳ אמר אבא בן מ׳ שנה נשא אשה אף אני כן (ב״ר סה:א): (לה) **מורת רוח.** לשון המראת רוח, כמו ממרים הייתם (דברים ט:כד), כל מעשיהן היו להכעיס ולעצבון **ליצחק ולרבקה,** שהיו

32. בַּיּוֹם הַהוּא — *On that very day.* While Abimelech was still there, Isaac's servants came with this news of God's beneficence, so that the Philistine delegation would be impressed and stand in awe of Isaac (*Radak*).

33. בְּאֵר שֶׁבַע — *Beer Sheba*. The name of the city commemorates two occurrences: the בְּאֵר, *well,* and the שְׁבוּעָה, *oath* (*Ramban*). They named the well *Shivah* — which means *seven* as well as *oath* — to commemorate the *seven* ewes that Abraham had given to Abimelech (21:28-31), as well as the oath (*Ibn Ezra*).

עַד הַיּוֹם הַזֶּה — *Until this very day,* the days of Moses, when the Torah was given. Throughout Scripture, *until this day* means until the time of the scribe who recorded the matter (*Rashbam* to 19:37).

34-35. Esau marries. *Rashi* cites the Midrash: Esau is compared to a swine that, when it lies down, stretches out its cloven hooves, as if to say, "See, I am a kosher animal!" Similarly, the descendants of Esau rob and extort while they pretend to be honorable . . . So it was with Esau. Until he was 40, he had been living immorally, snatching married women from their husbands and violating them, but when he became 40, he said hypocritically that he would follow the example of his father who married at that age.

Unlike his father, however, Esau married Hittite women; his passions were unbridled and he chose to marry into a nation that matched his evil nature. With these marriages, Esau set the seal on his complete unfitness to carry on the mission of Abraham. In a home ruled by two Hittite women, the Abrahamitic ideal lies buried (*R' Hirsch*).

27.

This chapter is one of the most crucial and mystifying in the Torah — crucial because the decision about which son was to receive the Patriarchal blessings would determine who would be God's Chosen People, so that the eternal destinies of Jacob and Esau and their offspring were in the balance. And mystifying because it is hard to fathom how the righteous Isaac could be so adamant in choosing Esau and why Rebecca would resort to such a blatant deception to secure the blessings for Jacob. The commentators offer many interpretations; our commentary will draw upon several of those themes.

1-4. Isaac's decision to bless Esau. As the firstborn, Esau had the presumptive right to the blessings, and Isaac would not have had the right to deny them to him unless there was compelling cause. Clearly, despite Esau's marriage to Hittite women, Isaac was unaware of the *degree* of Esau's sinfulness,

כִּי־זָקֵן יִצְחָק וַתִּכְהֶיןָ עֵינָיו מֵרְאֹת וַיִּקְרָא
< that he called << from seeing, < were his eyes < and weakened < Isaac had become old < when

אֶת־עֵשָׂו ׀ בְּנוֹ הַגָּדֹל וַיֹּאמֶר אֵלָיו בְּנִי וַיֹּאמֶר
< And he said << My son. << to him, < and said < who was older, < his son < Esau,

אֵלָיו הִנֵּנִי: ב וַיֹּאמֶר הִנֵּה־נָא זָקַנְתִּי לֹא יָדַעְתִּי
< I do not know << I have aged; < now, < Indeed, << And he said, 2 << Here I am. << to him,

יוֹם מוֹתִי: ג וְעַתָּה שָׂא־נָא כֵלֶיךָ תֶּלְיְךָ וְקַשְׁתֶּךָ וְצֵא הַשָּׂדֶה וְצוּדָה
< and hunt < [to] the field < and go out << and your bow — < — your sword << your gear < please, < take, < Now 3 << of my death. < the day

לִּי °צָיִד [°צידה כ']: ד וַעֲשֵׂה־לִי מַטְעַמִּים כַּאֲשֶׁר אָהַבְתִּי וְהָבִיאָה
< and bring << I like < as < delicacies < for me < Then make 4 << game. < for me

לִּי וְאֹכֵלָה בַּעֲבוּר תְּבָרֶכְךָ נַפְשִׁי בְּטֶרֶם אָמוּת: ה וְרִבְקָה שֹׁמַעַת
< was listening < And Rebecca 5 << I die. < before < my soul may bless you < so that << and I will eat, < to me

כַּד סִיב יִצְחָק וְכַהֲן עֵינוֹהִי מִלְּמֶחֱזֵי וּקְרָא יָת עֵשָׂו בְּרֵהּ רַבָּא וַאֲמַר לֵהּ בְּרִי וַאֲמַר לֵהּ הָא אֲנָא: ב וַאֲמַר הָא כְעַן סֵיבִית לֵית אֲנָא יָדַע יוֹמָא דְאֵימוּת: ג וּכְעַן סַב כְּעַן זֵינָךְ סַיְפָךְ וְקַשְׁתָּךְ וּפוּק לְחַקְלָא וְצוּד לִי צֵידָא: ד וַעֲבֵיד לִי תַבְשִׁילִין כְּמָא דִי רְחֵימִית וְאָעֵיל לִי וְאֵיכוּל בְּדִיל דִּי תְבָרְכִנָּךְ נַפְשִׁי עַד לָא אֵימוּת: ה וְרִבְקָה שְׁמַעַת

רש"י

(א) **ותכהין.** בעשנן של אלו [שהיו מעשנות ומקטירות לע"ז] (תנחומא ח; פס"ר יב; פיוט לפ' זכור). ד"א, כשנעקד ע"ג המזבח והיה אביו רוצה לשחטו, באותה שעה נפתחו השמים וראו מלאכי השרת והיו בוכים, וירדו דמעותיהם ונפלו על עיניו לפיכך כהו עיניו (ב"ר שם י). דבר אחר, כדי שיטול יעקב את הברכות (תנחומא שם): (ב) **לא ידעתי יום מותי.** א"ר יהושע בן קרחה, אם מגיע אדם לפרק אבותיו ידאג חמש שנים לפניהן וחמש שנים לאחר כן. ויצחק היה בן קכ"ג, אמר, שמא לפרק אמי אני מגיע והיא בת קכ"ז מתה, והריני בן ה' שנים סמוך לפרקה. לפיכך לא ידעתי יום מותי, שמא לפרק אמי שמא לפרק אבא (ב"ר שם יב): (ג) **שא נא.** לשון השחזה, כלותה שנינו אין משחיזין את הסכין אבל משיאה על גבי חברתה (ביצה כח.). חדד סכינך ושחוט יפה, שלא תאכילני נבלה (ב"ר סה:יג): **תליך.** חרבך שדרך לתלותה: **וצודה לי [ציד].** מן ההפקר, ולא מן הגזל (שם):

and Rebecca had not felt authorized to tell him about the prophecy given her at the beginning of the *Sidrah.* Also, Isaac felt that it was Esau who needed blessings to arm him in his struggle against an inborn nature that tended toward bloodshed and other cardinal sins, whereas Jacob had the inner strength to grow and be holy without the assistance of the blessings.

It seems also, as will be seen below, that Isaac planned to bestow two sets of blessings, one for Esau and one for Jacob, each set suited to the needs and nature of its intended recipient. He also felt, according to some, that the two brothers should both be parts of God's nation: Jacob with the higher calling of Torah scholarship and spiritual ascendancy, and Esau with material success that he would use to support and assist Jacob. Had Esau been worthy, this could have happened, just as the tribe of Zebulun undertook to engage in commerce to support the Torah scholarship of Issachar, and in the time of the Mishnah, the wealthy Azariah supported his scholarly brother Shimon. Rebecca, however, guided by Divine inspiration, knew that Esau was not entitled even to this.

1. וַתִּכְהֶיןָ עֵינָיו מֵרְאֹת — *And weakened were his eyes from seeing.* Isaac was 123 years old then.

Rashi offers three reasons for Isaac's failing eyesight:
(a) From the smoke of the incense that Esau's wives offered to their idols. Further, God caused him this blindness to spare him from continuing to see idol worship in his household (*Tanchuma*). (b) When Isaac lay bound on the altar at the *Akeidah,* the ministering angels wept over him. Their tears fell into his eyes and dimmed them (*Bereishis Rabbah*). (3) Providence caused his blindness so that Jacob might receive the blessing [without Isaac realizing whom he was blessing] (*Tanchuma*).

2. הִנֵּה־נָא זָקַנְתִּי — *Indeed, now, I have aged.* And I wish to bestow the blessings while I am still alive (*Rashbam*). A blessing is more efficacious when a person is near death, because the soul is freer of its physical bonds (*Sforno*).

At the age of 123, Isaac had come within five years of the age at which his mother died, 127, and the Sages teach that one should begin to think that he might not exceed the age of whichever parent died first (*Midrash*).

3-4. Isaac wanted Esau to earn the blessing by performing the commandment of honoring his father. Isaac sent Esau out to the field to hunt, so as to make the task more arduous and therefore the *mitzvah* more meritorious (*Alshich*).

5-17. Rebecca's scheme. Having been told before the twins were born that the younger would be the superior one, Rebecca knew that the blessings had to go to Jacob. She also knew from that prophecy that the two could not coexist — because when one would rise the other would fall — so that any plan Isaac might have to enlist them in joint service of God could not succeed — but she had not felt authorized to convey this knowledge to Isaac. Her only alternative was to deceive Isaac into giving the blessings to Jacob.

בְּדַבֵּר יִצְחָק אֶל־עֵשָׂו בְּנוֹ וַיֵּלֶךְ עֵשָׂו הַשָּׂדֶה לָצוּד
< to hunt < [to] the field < and Esau went << his son; < Esau < to < as Isaac spoke

צַיִד לְהָבִיא: ו וְרִבְקָה אָמְרָה אֶל־יַעֲקֹב בְּנָהּ
< her son, < Jacob < to < said < Now Rebecca 6 << to bring. < game

לֵאמֹר הִנֵּה שָׁמַעְתִּי אֶת־אָבִיךָ מְדַבֵּר אֶל־עֵשָׂו
< *Esau* < *to* < *speaking* < *your father* < *I heard* < *Indeed* << *saying,*

אָחִיךָ לֵאמֹר: ז הָבִיאָה לִּי צַיִד וַעֲשֵׂה־לִי
< *for me* < *and make* < *some game* < *me* < *'Bring* 7 << *saying,* < *your brother*

מַטְעַמִּים וְאֹכֵלָה וַאֲבָרֶכְכָה לִפְנֵי יהוה לִפְנֵי
< *before* < *of* HASHEM < *in the presence* < *and I will bless you* << *and I will eat,* < *delicacies*

מוֹתִי: ח וְעַתָּה בְנִי שְׁמַע בְּקֹלִי לַאֲשֶׁר אֲנִי מְצַוָּה אֹתָךְ: ט לֶךְ־נָא אֶל־
< *to* < *now* < *Go* 9 << *you.* < *command* < *I* < *to that which* < *my voice* < *heed* < *my son,* < *So now,* 8 << *my death.'*

הַצֹּאן וְקַח־לִי מִשָּׁם שְׁנֵי גְּדָיֵי עִזִּים טֹבִים וְאֶעֱשֶׂה אֹתָם מַטְעַמִּים
< *[into] delicacies* < *them* < *and I will make* << *that are choice,* < *of the goats* < *young kids* < *two* < *from there* << *me* < *and bring* < *the flock*

לְאָבִיךָ כַּאֲשֶׁר אָהֵב: י וְהֵבֵאתָ לְאָבִיךָ וְאָכָל בַּעֲבֻר אֲשֶׁר יְבָרֶכְךָ לִפְנֵי
< *before* < *he may bless you* < *that* < *in order* << *and he shall eat,* < *to your father* < *Then you should bring [them]* 10 << *he likes.* < *as* < *for your father,*

מוֹתוֹ: יא וַיֹּאמֶר יַעֲקֹב אֶל־רִבְקָה אִמּוֹ הֵן עֵשָׂו אָחִי אִישׁ שָׂעִר וְאָנֹכִי
< *and I* < *who is hairy* < *is a man* < *my brother* < *Esau* < *Indeed* << *his mother,* << *Rebecca,* < *to* < *Jacob said* 11 << *his death.*

אִישׁ חָלָק: יב אוּלַי יְמֻשֵּׁנִי אָבִי וְהָיִיתִי בְעֵינָיו כִּמְתַעְתֵּעַ וְהֵבֵאתִי עָלַי
< *upon myself* < *I will [thus] bring* << *as a scoffer;* < *in his eyes* < *and I shall be* < *my father will touch me* < *Perhaps* 12 << *who is smooth skinned.* < *am a man*

כַּד מַלִּיל יִצְחָק לְוַת עֵשָׂו בְּרֵהּ וַאֲזַל
עֵשָׂו לְחַקְלָא לְמֵיצַד צֵידָא לְאַיְתָאָה:
ו וְרִבְקָה אֲמֶרֶת לְוַת יַעֲקֹב בְּרַהּ לְמֵימַר
הָא שְׁמָעִית מִן אֲבוּךְ מְמַלֵּל עִם עֵשָׂו
אָחוּךְ לְמֵימָר: ז אַיְתִי לִי צֵידָא וְעִבֵיד
לִי תַבְשִׁילִין וְאֵיכוּל וַאֲבָרְכִנָּךְ קֳדָם יְיָ
קֳדָם מוֹתִי: ח וּכְעַן בְּרִי קַבֵּל מִנִּי לְמָא
דִי אֲנָא מְפַקְּדָא יָתָךְ: ט אִזֵיל כְּעַן לְוַת
עָנָא וְסַב לִי מִתַּמָּן תְּרֵין גַּדְיֵי (בְּנֵי) עִזִּין
טָבָן וְאֶעְבֵד יָתְהוֹן תַּבְשִׁילִין לְאָבוּךְ
כְּמָא דִי רְחֵם: י וְתַיְתֵי (נ״א וְתָעֵיל)
לְאָבוּךְ וְיֵיכוּל בְּדִיל דִי יְבָרְכִנָּךְ קֳדָם
מוֹתֵהּ: יא וַאֲמַר יַעֲקֹב לְרִבְקָה אִמֵּהּ הָא
עֵשָׂו אָחִי גְּבַר שַׂעֲרָן וַאֲנָא גְּבַר שְׁעִיעַ:
יב מָאִים יְמַשְׁמְשִׁנַּנִי אַבָּא וְאֵהֵי בְעֵינוֹהִי
כְּמִתְלָעֵב וְאֵהֵי (נ״א וָאֱהִי) מַיְתֵי עֲלַי

רש"י

(ה) **לצוד ציד להביא.** מהו להביא. אם לא ימצא ציד יביא מן הגזל (שם): [(ז) **לפני ה'.** ברשותו, שיסכים על ידי:] (ט) **וקח לי.** משלי הם ואינם גזל, שכך כתב לה יצחק בכתובתה ליטול שני גדיי עזים בכל יום (שם יד): [**שני גדיי עזים.** וכי שני גדיי עזים היה מאכלו של יצחק. אלא פסח היה, האחד הקריב לפסחו והאחד עשה מטעמים. בפרקי דרבי אליעזר (פל"ב): **באשר אהב.** כי טעם הגדי כטעם הצבי:] (יא) **איש שער.** בעל שער: (יב) **ימשני.** כמו ממשש בצהרים (דברים כח:כט):

For Jacob, this was the ultimate test, his personal *Akeidah* — a test of awesome proportions — because, as the Sages derive from Scripture, Jacob personified truth and he was to receive the blessings that would be ratified by God Whose very seal is "Truth." But his mother was commanding him to secure those blessings by perpetrating a falsehood against his father. For Jacob to behave in such a way was totally foreign to his nature. Thus, both brothers were to engage in difficult tasks to earn the blessings: Esau was at the hunt risking his life, and Jacob was at home risking his soul, his spiritual essence.

7. **לִפְנֵי ה'** — *In the presence of* HASHEM. Rebecca added these words to impress upon Jacob the immensity of his father's blessing, because the prophetic spirit would descend upon him while he uttered the benedictions (*Radak*) . . . And such blessings would be irrevocable. Accordingly, if Esau were to receive them, they would remain with his descendants forever and Jacob would never be able to stand against him (*Ramban*).[Alternatively, Rebecca may have added these words so that Jacob would fear that the blessing of Abraham — to carry forward the creation of the Nation of Israel and to inherit the Land of Israel — was included in the blessing Isaac would give to Esau. However, Isaac did not give that blessing to Jacob masquerading as Esau, but to Jacob on his own right (28:4).]

12. **אוּלַי יְמֻשֵּׁנִי אָבִי** — *Perhaps my father will touch me.* "Even if

קְלָלָה וְלֹא בְרָכָה: יג וַתֹּאמֶר לוֹ אִמּוֹ עָלַי קִלְלָתְךָ
< your curse, < On me shall be «< did his mother, < to him < Then say 13 « a blessing. < and not < a curse

בְּנִי אַךְ שְׁמַע בְּקֹלִי וְלֵךְ קַח־לִי: יד וַיֵּלֶךְ וַיִּקַּח
< got [them], < So he went, 14 « for me. < get [them] < and go < to my voice < listen < just « my son;

וַיָּבֵא לְאִמּוֹ וַתַּעַשׂ אִמּוֹ מַטְעַמִּים כַּאֲשֶׁר
< as < delicacies < and his mother made « to his mother, < and brought [them]

אָהֵב אָבִיו: טו וַתִּקַּח רִבְקָה אֶת־בִּגְדֵי עֵשָׂו בְּנָהּ
< her son < of Esau < the garments < Rebecca [then] took 15 « his father liked.

הַגָּדֹל הַחֲמֻדֹת אֲשֶׁר אִתָּהּ בַּבָּיִת וַתַּלְבֵּשׁ אֶת־יַעֲקֹב בְּנָהּ הַקָּטָן:
« who was younger. < her son < Jacob < and she clothed « in the house, < with her < that were < that were precious < who was older

טז וְאֵת עֹרֹת גְּדָיֵי הָעִזִּים הִלְבִּישָׁה עַל־יָדָיו וְעַל חֶלְקַת צַוָּארָיו: יז וַתִּתֵּן
< She put 17 « of his neck. < the smooth-skinned part < and over < his arms < over < she covered < of the goats < of the young kids < the skins < With 16

אֶת־הַמַּטְעַמִּים וְאֶת־הַלֶּחֶם אֲשֶׁר עָשָׂתָה בְּיַד יַעֲקֹב בְּנָהּ: יח וַיָּבֹא
< And he came 18 « her son. < of Jacob < into the hand < she had made < which < and the bread < the delicacies

אֶל־אָבִיו וַיֹּאמֶר אָבִי וַיֹּאמֶר הִנֶּנִּי מִי אַתָּה בְּנִי: יט וַיֹּאמֶר יַעֲקֹב
< Jacob said 19 « my son? < are you, < who « Here I am; « and he said, < Father, « and said, < his father < to

לְוָטִין וְלָא בִרְכָן: יג וַאֲמַרַת לֵהּ אִמֵּהּ עֲלַי אִתְאֲמַר בִּנְבוּאָה דְּלָא יֵיתוֹן לְוָטַיָּא עֲלָךְ בְּרִי בְּרַם קַבֵּל מִנִּי וְאִזֵיל סַב לִי: יד וַאֲזַל וּנְסִיב וְאַיְתֵי לְאִמֵּהּ וַעֲבָדַת אִמֵּהּ תַּבְשִׁילִין כְּמָא דִי רְחֵם אֲבוּהִי: טו וּנְסִיבַת רִבְקָה יָת לְבוּשֵׁי עֵשָׂו בְּרַהּ רַבָּא דְּכְיָתָא דִי עִמַּהּ בְּבֵיתָא וְאַלְבִּישַׁת יָת יַעֲקֹב בְּרַהּ זְעֵירָא: טז וְיָת מַשְׁכֵי דְגַדְיֵי (בְּנֵי) עִזֵּי אַלְבִּישַׁת עַל יְדוֹהִי וְעַל שְׁעִיעוּת צַוְרֵיהּ: יז וִיהָבַת יָת תַּבְשִׁילַיָּא וְיָת לַחְמָא דִי עֲבָדַת בִּידָא דְיַעֲקֹב בְּרַהּ: יח וְעַל לְוַת אֲבוּהִי וַאֲמַר אַבָּא וַאֲמַר הָא אֲנָא מָן אַתְּ בְּרִי: יט וַאֲמַר יַעֲקֹב

רש"י

(טו) החמדות. הנקיות, כתרגומו, דכייתא. דבר אחר, שחמד אותן מן נמרוד (ב"ר סה:טז): אשר אתה בבית. והלא כמה נשים היו לו והוא מפקיד אצל אמו. אלא שהיה בקי

Father were to have no reason to be suspicious, but will caress me affectionately, he will realize that I am smooth skinned." It is noteworthy that Jacob was not afraid that his voice would be recognized. Perhaps they had similar voices [see on v. 22], or Jacob could imitate Esau's (*Ramban*).

13. עָלַי קִלְלָתְךָ — *On me shall be your curse.* I take full responsibility. Rebecca had no fear that there would be a curse, for she had complete confidence in the prophecy that *the elder shall serve the younger* [25:23] (*Rashbam*).

She said, "Have no fear that he will curse you. If he does, may it come on me, not you," for it is the way of women (*Ibn Ezra*) to be compassionate and ready to suffer to protect their children (*Yohel Or*).

14. וַיֵּלֶךְ . . . וַיָּבֵא — *So he went . . . and brought.* Since the blessings were precious to Jacob, he should have hurried to bring the delicacies to his father, just as Abraham had run to greet his guests (18:2). So, too, there are frequent references to haste in the narrative of Eliezer and Rebecca. Our verse implies otherwise, however. Jacob did not apply himself enthusiastically to this scheme, carrying out his mother's request only reluctantly (*HaK'sav V'HaKabbalah*).

15. בִּגְדֵי עֵשָׂו . . . הַחֲמֻדֹת — *The garments of Esau . . . that were precious.* They were the *precious garments* that Esau stole from the great hunter Nimrod (*Rashi*). Esau, renowned for his great filial devotion, would always wear these precious garments while he served his father (*Rashbam*). Alternatively, *Esau's clean garments,* following *Onkelos.*

18-27. Jacob comes to Isaac. The Midrash states that Jacob came to Isaac with head bowed and in tears, so unhappy was he that he had to use deception, even though it was to gain what was truly his.

It is noteworthy that even when he was forced to deceive Isaac, Jacob stayed as close to the truth as possible. As the commentary will show, he tried to use ambiguous language so that he could mislead Isaac without lying directly. In translation, some of the interpretations seem very strained, but the Hebrew allows for such interpretations quite easily.

18. וַיֹּאמֶר אָבִי — *And said, "Father."* Jacob did not begin a conversation until the next verse. Here he merely called out "Father" to test whether Isaac would recognize his voice. If so, Jacob would have abandoned the scheme and acted as if he had come to visit (*Alshich*).

אֶל־אָבִיו אָנֹכִי עֵשָׂו בְּכֹרֶךָ עָשִׂיתִי כַּאֲשֶׁר דִּבַּרְתָּ
< *you told* < as < *I have done* << *your firstborn;* < Esau << *It is I,* << his father, < to

אֵלָי קוּם־נָא שְׁבָה וְאָכְלָה מִצֵּידִי בַּעֲבוּר תְּבָרְכַנִּי
< *bless me,* < *so that* < *of my game* < *and eat* < *sit* << *please,* < *rise up,* << *me;*

נַפְשֶׁךָ׃ כ וַיֹּאמֶר יִצְחָק אֶל־בְּנוֹ מַה־זֶּה מִהַרְתָּ
< *that you* < *is it* < *How* << his son, < to < Isaac said **20** << *may*
were so quick *your soul.*

לִמְצֹא בְּנִי וַיֹּאמֶר כִּי הִקְרָה יהוה אֱלֹהֶיךָ לְפָנָי׃
<< *before* < *your God,* < *did* < *make it* < *Because* << And he << *my* << *to find,*
me. HASHEM, *happen* said, *son?*

כא וַיֹּאמֶר יִצְחָק אֶל־יַעֲקֹב גְּשָׁה־נָּא וַאֲמֻשְׁךָ בְּנִי
<< *my* < *so I can* < *please,* < *Come* << Jacob, < to < And Isaac said **21**
son; *touch you,* *close,*

לַאֲבוּהִי אֲנָא עֵשָׂו בּוּכְרָךְ עֲבָדִית כְּמָא דִי מַלֶּלְתָּא עִמִּי (נ״א לִי) קוּם כְּעַן אִסְתְּחַר וְתֵיכוּל מִצֵּידִי בְּדִיל דִּי תְּבָרְכִנַּנִי נַפְשָׁךְ׃ כ וַאֲמַר יִצְחָק לִבְרֵהּ מָא דֵין אוֹחֵיתָא לְאַשְׁכָּחָא בְּרִי וַאֲמַר אֲרֵי זַמִּין יְיָ אֱלָהָךְ קֳדָמָי׃ כא וַאֲמַר יִצְחָק לְיַעֲקֹב קְרֵיב כְּעַן וְאֶמְשְׁנָּךְ בְּרִי הַאַתְּ דֵין בְּרִי עֵשָׂו אִם לָא׃ כב וּקְרֵיב יַעֲקֹב לְוַת יִצְחָק אֲבוּהִי וּמָשְׁיֵהּ וַאֲמַר קָלָא (דְ)יַעֲקֹב וִידַיָּא יְדֵי (נ״א יְדוֹהִי דְ)עֵשָׂו׃ כג וְלָא אִשְׁתְּמוֹדְעֵהּ אֲרֵי הֲוָאָה יְדוֹהִי כִּידֵי עֵשָׂו אֲחוּהִי שְׂעִירָן (נ״א שַׂעֲרָנִין) וּבָרְכֵהּ׃ כד וַאֲמַר אַתְּ דֵין בְּרִי עֵשָׂו וַאֲמַר (הָא) אֲנָא׃ כה וַאֲמַר קָרֵיב קֳדָמַי וְאֵיכוּל מִצֵּידָא דִבְרִי בְּדִיל דִּי תְּבָרְכִנָּךְ נַפְשִׁי וְקָרֵיב

הַאַתָּה זֶה בְּנִי עֵשָׂו אִם־לֹא׃ כב וַיִּגַּשׁ יַעֲקֹב אֶל־יִצְחָק אָבִיו וַיְמֻשֵּׁהוּ
<< and he < his < Isaac < to < So Jacob drew close **22** << *not?* < *or* < Esau < *my* < *indeed,* < *are you,*
touched him. father son

וַיֹּאמֶר הַקֹּל קוֹל יַעֲקֹב וְהַיָּדַיִם יְדֵי עֵשָׂו׃ כג וְלֹא הִכִּירוֹ כִּי־הָיוּ יָדָיו
<< his hands < because < For he did not **23** << *of* < *are the* < *but the* << *of* < *is the* < *The* << He then
were recognize him *Esau.* *hands* *hands* *Jacob,* *voice* *voice* said,

כִּידֵי עֵשָׂו אָחִיו שְׂעִרֹת וַיְבָרְכֵהוּ׃ כד וַיֹּאמֶר אַתָּה זֶה בְּנִי עֵשָׂו וַיֹּאמֶר
<< And he << *Esau?* < *my* < *indeed,* < *Are you,* < He said, **24** << so he << hairy; << his < of < —like
said, *son* blessed him. brother— Esau the hands

אָנִי׃ כה וַיֹּאמֶר הַגִּשָׁה לִּי וְאֹכְלָה מִצֵּיד בְּנִי לְמַעַן תְּבָרֶכְךָ נַפְשִׁי וַיַּגֶּשׁ־
< So he << *may my* < *bless you* < *so that* << *of my* < *of the* < *and let* < *to me* < *Bring it* << He said, **25** << *I am.*
brought it close *soul.* *son,* *game* *me eat* *close*

רש״י

במעשיהן ותופשן (שם): **(יט) אנכי עשו בכרך.** אנכי הוא המביא לך, ועשו הוא בכורך (תנחומא ישן י): **עשיתי.** כמה דברים **כאשר דברת אלי: שבה.** לשון מיסב על השלחן, לכך מתורגם אסתחר: **(כא) גשה נא ואמשך.** אמר יצחק בלבו, אין דרך עשו להיות שם שמים שגור בפיו, וזה אמר כי הקרה ה' אלהיך (ב"ר סה:יט): **(כב) קול יעקב.** שמדבר בלשון תחנונים, קום נא, אבל עשו בלשון קנטוריא דבר, יקום אבי (תנחומא יא): **(כד) ויאמר אני.** לא אמר אני עשו אלא אני (ברב"ת):

19. אָנֹכִי עֵשָׂו בְּכֹרֶךָ — *It is I, Esau your firstborn. Rashi* explains: אָנֹכִי, *It is I* who bring this to you; עֵשָׂו בְּכֹרֶךָ, *Esau* (however) *is your firstborn.*

עָשִׂיתִי כַּאֲשֶׁר דִּבַּרְתָּ אֵלָי — *I have done as you told me.* Continuing the interpretation that Jacob used ambiguous language when necessary: *I have done* on many occasions . . . *as you told me* (*Rashi*).

מִצֵּידִי — *Of my game.* This word is sometimes used even for food that was not hunted (*R' Chananel*).

20. מִהַרְתָּ — *You were so quick.* Isaac had specifically asked Esau to take his weapons and *go out to the field* in order to make the task more arduous and hence the *mitzvah* greater (v. 3). The quick return made him apprehensive that "Esau" had not carried out the mission as bidden.

Isaac understood Jacob's reply to mean, "I had planned to hunt far away, but *God made it happen* that game appeared before me near home, where there is usually none to be found." This "coincidence" was a sure sign that it was arranged by God, Who obviously did so in Isaac's merit (*Malbim*).

21. גְּשָׁה־נָּא — *Come close, please.* Jacob's mention of God's Name (v. 20) made Isaac suspicious, since he knew that it was not characteristic of Esau to speak that way (*Rashi*). Isaac thought that Esau was so pious that he avoided the use of God's Name since he was often in unclean places, or because he was afraid he might pronounce it without proper concentration (*Ramban*).

22. הַקֹּל קוֹל יַעֲקֹב וְהַיָּדַיִם יְדֵי עֵשָׂו — *The voice is the voice of Jacob, but the hands are the hands of Esau.* Isaac could not have meant the *sound* of the voice, since the Sages comment that Jacob and Esau sounded so alike that Isaac could not tell them apart.

לוֹ וַיֹּאכַל וַיָּבֵא לוֹ יַיִן וַיֵּשְׁתְּ: כו וַיֹּאמֶר אֵלָיו יִצְחָק
‹— Isaac «to him ‹ Then he said 26 « and he drank. ‹ wine ‹ him ‹ and he brought « and he ate, ‹ to him

אָבִיו גְּשָׁה־נָּא וּשְׁקָה־לִּי בְּנִי: כז וַיִּגַּשׁ וַיִּשַּׁק־לוֹ
«him; ‹ and kissed ‹ So he drew close 27 « my son. ‹ me, ‹ and kiss ‹ please, ‹ Come close, « his father —

וַיָּרַח אֶת־רֵיחַ בְּגָדָיו וַיְבָרְכֵהוּ וַיֹּאמֶר רְאֵה רֵיחַ
‹ the fragrance ‹ See, « he said, « and blessed him; ‹ of his garments ‹ the fragrance ‹ he smelled

בְּנִי כְּרֵיחַ שָׂדֶה אֲשֶׁר בֵּרְכוֹ יהוה: ששי כח וְיִתֶּן־לְךָ הָאֱלֹהִים מִטַּל
‹ of the dew ‹ may God, ‹ to you, ‹ And give 28 « HASHEM had blessed it. ‹ which ‹ of a field ‹ is like the fragrance ‹ of my son

הַשָּׁמַיִם וּמִשְׁמַנֵּי הָאָרֶץ וְרֹב דָּגָן וְתִירֹשׁ: כט יַעַבְדוּךָ עַמִּים
«will peoples, ‹ Serve you 29 « and wine. ‹ grain ‹ and abundant ‹ of the earth, ‹ and the fatness ‹ of the heavens

לֵהּ וַאֲכַל וְאַיְתִי (נ״א וְאָעֵיל) לֵהּ חַמְרָא וּשְׁתִי: כו וַאֲמַר לֵהּ יִצְחָק אֲבוּהִי קְרֵיב כְּעַן וּנְשַׁק לִי (נ״א וְשַׁק לִי) בְּרִי: כז וּקְרֵיב וּנְשַׁק לֵהּ וַאֲרַח יָת רֵיחָא דִלְבוּשׁוֹהִי וּבָרְכֵהּ וַאֲמַר חֲזֵי רֵיחָא דִבְרִי כְּרֵיחָא דְחַקְלָא דִּי בָרְכֵהּ יְיָ: כח וְיִתֵּן לָךְ יְיָ מִטַּלָּא דִשְׁמַיָּא וּמִטּוּבָא דְאַרְעָא וּסְגִיאוּת (נ״א וְסַגְיוּת) עִיבוּר וַחֲמָר: כט יִפְלְחֻנָּךְ עַמְמִין

רש״י

(כז) וירח וגו׳. והלא אין ריח רע יותר משטף העזים, אלא מלמד שנכנס עמו ריח גן עדן (ב״ר סה:כב): כריח שדה אשר ברכו ה׳. שנתן בו ריח טוב, וזהו שדה תפוחים. כך דרשו רז״ל (תענית כט:): (כח) ויתן לך. יתן ויחזור ויתן (ב״ר סו:ג). ולפי פשוטו מוסב לענין הראשון, ראה ריח בני שנתן לו הקב״ה כריח שדה וגו׳ ועוד יתן לך מטל השמים וגו׳: מטל השמים. כמשמעו, ומ״א יש להרבה פנים. [ד״א, מהו האלהים, בדין. אם ראוי לך יתן לך ואם לאו לא יתן לך, אבל לעשו אמר משמני הארץ יהיה מושבך (להלן פס׳ לט), בין צדיק בין רשע יתן לך. וממנו למד שלמה כשעשה הבית סידר תפלתו, ישראל שהוא בעל אמונה ומצדיק עליו הדין לא יקרא עליך תגר, לפיכך ונתת לאיש ככל דרכיו אשר תדע את לבבו (מלכים א ח:לט), אבל נכרי מחוסר אמנה, לפיכך אמר אתה תשמע השמים וגו׳ ועשית ככל אשר יקרא אליך הנכרי (שם פסוק

Rather, his statement that the *voice is Jacob's voice* refers to Jacob's manner of speaking, inasmuch as Jacob spoke gently and invoked the Name of Heaven (*Rashi*).

26. וּשְׁקָה־לִּי — *And kiss me.* Kabbalistically, a kiss brings about the deep spiritual intimacy that Isaac wished to arouse in order to cause the *Shechinah* to alight upon him, preparatory to his giving the blessings (*Alshich*).

27. רֵיחַ בְּגָדָיו — *The fragrance of his garments.* But the pungent smell of washed goatskin is most offensive! This teaches that the fragrance of the Garden of Eden entered the room with Jacob, and it was *this* fragrance that Isaac smelled (*Rashi*).

How did Isaac know what the fragrance of Gan Eden was if he had not smelled it previously? Indeed Abraham's actions at the *Akeidah* had also brought the fragrance of Gan Eden to Isaac! But how can we equate the Gan Eden fragrance that accompanied Jacob's claiming *I am Esau your firstborn* with the fragrance that accompanied Abraham's willingness to sacrifice his son at God's command?

Chesed, kindness, is the hallmark of Abraham's lifework, as *Emes,* truth, is the essence of Jacob's, as it says, *Grant truth to Jacob, kindness to Abraham* (*Micah* 7:20). (See commentary 27:5-17.) For Abraham, the *Akeidah* was the antithesis of the kindness to which he had dedicated his life. All the people he had brought to the service of Hashem through kindness were now likely to reject Abraham and his God, for there is nothing as barbaric as killing one's own child. Yet Abraham was willing to sacrifice all that to fulfill Hashem's will. Similarly, Jacob, for whom truth was the pillar of his life, was willing to lie when the future of God's chosen people was at risk. This ability to give up the personal, spiritual value as dear to Abraham and Jacob as life itself, in order to fulfill the will of God, twice brought Isaac the whiff of Gan Eden (*R' Chaim Yaakov Goldvicht).*

28-29. The blessing. Since the Divine Presence was resting upon him, Isaac knew that the person standing before him was worthy of the blessings.

28. וְיִתֶּן־לְךָ הָאֱלֹהִים — *And give to you, may God.* Since this verse begins the text of the blessings, which is a new topic, the conjunction ו, meaning *and,* seems to be superfluous. Consequently, *Rashi* cites the Midrash that states that it refers to a continuous, repetitive action: May God give you the following blessing over and over again, without stop.

The definite article — *the* God (הָאֱלֹהִים) — accentuates that the reference is specifically to God in His role as *Elohim,* the Dispenser of Strict Justice, in contrast with the name ה׳, HASHEM, which depicts Him in His role as Dispenser of Mercy. Thus, Isaac said that God would give Jacob this blessing only if he were justifiably worthy of it, but not otherwise. But to Esau, however, Isaac stated unconditionally [v. 39]: *of the fatness of the earth shall be your dwelling* — whether you deserve it or not (*Rashi,* following *Midrash Tanchuma*).

The above Midrash may seem difficult, since, in the plain meaning of the passage, Isaac thought that he was blessing Esau, who was hardly righteous enough to deserve the blessings in terms of strict justice. Accordingly, we must say that these words were placed into Isaac's mouth by Divine inspiration.

דָּגָן וְתִירֹשׁ — *Grain and wine.* In addition to their literal meaning, grain refers to the necessities of life, and wine to its pleasures. In Torah study, too, there are grain and wine: the essential knowl-

°וְיִשְׁתַּחֲוּ [°וישתחו כ׳] לְךָ לְאֻמִּים הֱוֵה גְבִיר

< a lord < be << will kingdoms; < to you < and bow down

לְאַחֶיךָ וְיִשְׁתַּחֲווּ לְךָ בְּנֵי אִמֶּךָ אֹרְרֶיךָ אָרוּר

<< are cursed, < those who curse you << of your mother; < will the sons < to you < and bow down << to your brothers,

וּמְבָרְכֶיךָ בָּרוּךְ: ל וַיְהִי כַּאֲשֶׁר כִּלָּה יִצְחָק לְבָרֵךְ

< blessing < Isaac had finished < when < And it was, **30** << are blessed. < and those who bless you

אֶת־יַעֲקֹב וַיְהִי אַךְ יָצֹא יָצָא יַעֲקֹב מֵאֵת פְּנֵי

< the presence < from being in < had Jacob made his exit, < that scarcely < and it was << Jacob,

יִצְחָק אָבִיו וְעֵשָׂו אָחִיו בָּא מִצֵּידוֹ: לא וַיַּעַשׂ גַּם־הוּא מַטְעַמִּים וַיָּבֵא

< and brought [them] < delicacies << he— < —also << He made **31** << from his hunt. < came back < his brother < that Esau << his father, < of Isaac

לְאָבִיו וַיֹּאמֶר לְאָבִיו יָקֻם אָבִי וְיֹאכַל מִצֵּיד בְּנוֹ בַּעֲבֻר תְּבָרְכַנִּי

< bless me < so that << of his son, < of the game < and he should eat << —my father— << He should rise << to his father, < he said << to his father;

נַפְשֶׁךָ: לב וַיֹּאמֶר לוֹ יִצְחָק אָבִיו מִי־אָתָּה וַיֹּאמֶר אֲנִי בִּנְךָ בְּכֹרְךָ עֵשָׂו:

<< Esau. < your firstborn, < your son, < I am < And he said, << are you? < Who << his father— < —Isaac << to him < He said **32** << shall your soul.

לג וַיֶּחֱרַד יִצְחָק חֲרָדָה גְּדֹלָה עַד־מְאֹד וַיֹּאמֶר מִי־אֵפוֹא הוּא הַצָּד־

< —the one who hunted << is he < [and] where < Who [is he] << and said, < an extreme, < to < that was great < a trembling < Then Isaac trembled **33**

וְיִשְׁתַּעְבְּדוּן לָךְ מַלְכְּוָן הֱוֵי רַב לַאֲחָיךְ
וְיִסְגְּדוּן לָךְ בְּנֵי אִמָּךְ לִיטָיךְ יְהוֹן
לִיטִין וּבָרִיכָךְ יְהוֹן בְּרִיכִין: ל וַהֲוָה
כַּד שֵׁיצִי יִצְחָק לְבָרָכָא יָת יַעֲקֹב
וַהֲוָה בְּרַם מִפַּק נְפַק יַעֲקֹב מִלְוַת אַפֵּי
יִצְחָק אֲבוּהִי וְעֵשָׂו אֲחוּהִי אֲתָא (נ״א
עַל) מִצֵּידֵהּ: לא וַעֲבַד אַף הוּא
תַּבְשִׁילִין וְאַיְתִי לְוַת אֲבוּהִי וַאֲמַר
לַאֲבוּהִי יְקוּם אַבָּא וְיֵיכוּל מִצֵּידָא
דִבְרֵהּ בְּדִיל דִּי תְבָרְכִנַּנִי נַפְשָׁךְ:
לב וַאֲמַר לֵהּ יִצְחָק אֲבוּהִי מָן אַתְּ
וַאֲמַר אֲנָא בְּרָךְ בּוּכְרָךְ עֵשָׂו:
לג וּתְוָה יִצְחָק תְּוְהָא רַבָּא עַד
לַחֲדָא וַאֲמַר מָן הוּא דֵיכִי דְּצָד

רש״י

מג) בין ראוי בין שאינו ראוי תן לו כדי שלא יקרא עליך תגר, (תנחומא ישן יד)]: (כט) **בני אמך.** ויעקב אמר ליהודה בני אביך (להלן מט:ח), לפי שהיו לו בנים מכמה אמהות, וכאן שלא נשא אלא אשה אחת אמר בני אמך (ב"ר שם ד): **ארריך ארור ומברכיך ברוך.** ובבלעם הוא אומר מברכיך ברוך ואורריך ארור (במדבר כד:ט). הצדיקים תחלתם יסורי' וסופן שלוה ואורריהם ומצעריהם קודמים למברכיהם, לפיכך יצחק הקדים קללת אוררים לברכת מברכים. והרשעים תחלתן שלוה וסופן יסורין, לפיכך בלעם הקדים ברכה לקללה (ב"ר שם): **(ל) יצא יצא.** זה יוצא וזה בא (תנחומא יא; ב"ר שם ה): **(לג) ויחרד.** כתרגומו, ותוה, לשון תמיה. ומדרשו, ראה גיהנם פתוחה מתחתיו (תנחומא שם; ב"ר סז:ב): **מי אפוא.** לשון לעצמו, משמש עם כמה דברים. [ד"א,] איפוא, איה פה, מי הוא ואיפוא הוא הצד ציד:

edge of the text and law, and the homiletical interpretations that give spice to learning.

29. According to the view that Isaac still thought he was blessing Esau, this verse says clearly that Isaac wanted Jacob to be Esau's vassal. *Sforno* explains that it was for Jacob's benefit that Isaac blessed Esau with mastery. Isaac did not want Jacob to be encumbered by material responsibilities which would hinder his spiritual development, nor did he want him to have too much material wealth and power, lest he become corrupted by it. Thus Jacob would have inherited *Eretz Yisrael* and been free to serve God, while Esau would rule the land and provide for its inhabitants. That Isaac meant for Jacob to inherit the Land and have the spiritual blessings of Abraham is clear from 28:4. There, when he knew he was blessing Jacob, he specified both the blessings and the Land (*Sforno*).

30-40. Esau arrives for his blessings. Esau arrived immediately after Jacob had secured the blessings, and he felt both rage and anguish. Correctly, he assumed that Isaac must have had a blessing in reserve, and begged that he, too, be blessed.

31. The commentators compare Esau's tone and content as he addressed Isaac with Jacob's. The contrast is stark.

33. וַיֶּחֱרַד יִצְחָק — *Then Isaac trembled.* Isaac perceived Gehinnom open beneath Esau (*Rashi*), which was in sharp contrast to the fragrance of Eden that had accompanied Jacob into Isaac's chamber.

The presence of Gehinnom with Esau made Isaac realize that he had been deceived all along — Esau was truly evil. This made Isaac fear that the vision of Gehinnom proved that he, Isaac, would be punished for having allowed himself to be so grievously misled (*Pesikta d'Rav Kahana*).

צַיִד וַיָּבֵא לִי וָאֹכַל מִכֹּל בְּטֶרֶם תָּבוֹא וָאֲבָרְכֵהוּ

<< and I blessed him? << you came, < before < from all < and I ate < to me, < and brought [it] < game,

גַּם־בָּרוּךְ יִהְיֶה: לד כִּשְׁמֹעַ עֵשָׂו אֶת־דִּבְרֵי אָבִיו

<< of his father, < the words < When Esau heard 34 << shall he remain! < blessed < Indeed,

וַיִּצְעַק צְעָקָה גְּדֹלָה וּמָרָה עַד־מְאֹד וַיֹּאמֶר

< and he said << an extreme, < to < and bitter < that was great < a cry < he cried out

לְאָבִיו בָּרְכֵנִי גַם־אָנִי אָבִי: לה וַיֹּאמֶר בָּא אָחִיךָ

< Your brother came << He said, 35 << my father! << me, < also << Bless me, < to his father,

בְּמִרְמָה וַיִּקַּח בִּרְכָתֶךָ: לו וַיֹּאמֶר הֲכִי קָרָא שְׁמוֹ

< his name < [they] called < Is it because << He said, 36 << your blessing. < and he took < with cleverness

יַעֲקֹב וַיַּעְקְבֵנִי זֶה פַעֲמַיִם אֶת־בְּכֹרָתִי לָקָח וְהִנֵּה עַתָּה לָקַח בִּרְכָתִי

<< my blessing! < he took away < now < and indeed, < he took away < My birthright << two times? < these < that he outwitted me < Jacob

וַיֹּאמַר הֲלֹא־אָצַלְתָּ לִּי בְּרָכָה: לז וַיַּעַן יִצְחָק וַיֹּאמֶר לְעֵשָׂו הֵן גְּבִיר

< a lord < Indeed, < to Esau, < and said < Isaac answered, 37 << a blessing? < for me < Have you not set aside << Then he said,

שַׂמְתִּיו לָךְ וְאֶת־כָּל־אֶחָיו נָתַתִּי לוֹ לַעֲבָדִים וְדָגָן וְתִירֹשׁ סְמַכְתִּיו

<< have I supported him, < and wine < [through] grain << as servants; < him < have I given < his brothers < and all << over you, < have I placed him

וּלְכָה אֵפוֹא מָה אֶעֱשֶׂה בְּנִי: לח וַיֹּאמֶר עֵשָׂו אֶל־אָבִיו הַבְרָכָה אַחַת

< Could it be that [but] one blessing << his father, < to < And Esau said 38 << my son? << can I do, < — what << [from] where < and for you,

הִוא־לְךָ אָבִי בָּרְכֵנִי גַם־אָנִי אָבִי וַיִּשָּׂא עֵשָׂו קֹלוֹ וַיֵּבְךְּ: לט וַיַּעַן יִצְחָק

< did Isaac, < So he answered, 39 << and wept. < his voice < And Esau raised << my father! << me — < — also << Bless me, < my father? < from you, < there is

צֵידָא וְאָעֵיל לִי וַאֲכָלִית מִכֹּלָא עַד לָא תֵעוֹל וּבָרֵכִיתֵהּ אַף בְּרִיךְ יְהֵי: לד כַּד שְׁמַע עֵשָׂו יָת פִּתְגָמֵי אֲבוּהִי וּצְוַח צְוָחָא רַבָּא וּמְרִירָא עַד לַחֲדָא וַאֲמַר לַאֲבוּהִי בָּרֵכְנִי אַף אֲנָא אַבָּא: לה וַאֲמַר עַל אָחוּךְ בְּחָכְמְתָא וְקַבֵּיל בִּרְכְּתָךְ: לו וַאֲמַר יָאוּת קְרָא שְׁמֵהּ יַעֲקֹב וְחַכְּמַנִי (נ״א וְכָמַנִי) דְּנָן תַּרְתֵּין זִמְנִין יָת בְּכֵירוּתִי נְסִיב וְהָא כְעַן קַבֵּיל בִּרְכְּתִי וַאֲמַר הֲלָא שְׁבַקְתָּ לִי בִּרְכְּתָא: לז וַאֲתֵיב יִצְחָק וַאֲמַר לְעֵשָׂו הָא רַב שַׁוִּיתֵהּ לָךְ (נ״א עֲלָוָךְ) וְיָת כָּל אֲחוֹהִי לֵהּ לְעַבְדִּין וְעִיבוּר וַחֲמָר סְעַדְתֵּהּ וְלָךְ הָכָא מָה אֶעְבֵּד בְּרִי: לח וַאֲמַר עֵשָׂו לַאֲבוּהִי הֲבִרְכְּתָא חֲדָא הִיא לָךְ אַבָּא בָּרֵךְ לִי אַף אֲנָא אַבָּא וַאֲרִים עֵשָׂו קָלֵהּ וּבְכָא: לט וַאֲתֵיב יִצְחָק

רש״י

ואכל מכל. מכל טעמים שבקשתי לטעום טעמתי בו (ב״ר סס): **גם ברוך יהיה.** שלא תאמר אילולי שרימה יעקב לאביו לא נטל את הברכות, לכך הסכים וברכו מדעתו (שם): **(לה) במרמה.** בחכמה (אונקלוס; ב״ר שם ד): **(לו) הכי קרא שמו.** לשון תימה הוא, כמו הכי אחי אתה (להלן כט:טו). שמא לכך נקרא שמו יעקב ע״ש סופו, שהיה עתיד לעקבני. תנחומא (ישן כג) למה חרד יצחק. אמר, שמא עון יש בי שברכתי קטן לפני גדול ושניתי סדר היחס. התחיל עשו מצעק ויעקבני זה פעמים. אמר לו אביו מה עשה לך. אמר לו את בכרתי לקח. אמר, בכך הייתי מצר וחרד שמא עברתי על שורת הדין, עכשיו לבכור ברכתי, גם ברוך יהיה: **ויעקבני.** כתרגומו וכמני ארבני. וארב (דברים יט:יא) וכמן [ס״א ויכמון]. ויש מתרגמין וחכמני, נתחכם לי: **אצלת.** לשון הפרשה כמו ויאצל (במדבר יא:כה) [ס״א ויצל (להלן לא:ט)]: **(לז) הן גביר.** ברכה זו שביעית היא והוא עושה אותה ראשונה. אלא אמר לו, מה תועלת לך בברכה, אם תקנה נכסים שלו הם, שהרי גביר שמתיו לך ומה שקנה עבד קנה רבו (ב״ר סז:ה): **ולכה אפוא מה אעשה.** איה [אי]פה אבקש מה לעשות לך: **(לח) הברכה אחת.** ה״א זו משמשת לשון תימה כמו הבמחנים (במדבר יג:יט)

36. יַעֲקֹב וַיַּעְקְבֵנִי — *Jacob that he outwitted me* . . . Esau made a play on words. Jacob's name came from the word עָקֵב, *heel,* because he was holding onto Esau's heel when they were born (25:26). But it can also be rendered *outwit* (*Rashi*), or *deceit* (*Radak*).

הֲלֹא־אָצַלְתָּ לִּי בְּרָכָה — *Have you not set aside for me a blessing?* Even though you had originally intended to bestow your *superior* blessing upon me, you certainly did not intend to leave my brother without any blessing. Therefore, give me the blessing you had intended for Jacob (*Sforno*).

38. וַיֵּבְךְּ — *And wept.* Esau produced but a few tears . . . But see how much peace and tranquility God bestowed upon Esau for those tears! (*Tanchuma*). For we will remain under Esau's power until we repent and shed tears that can outweigh his (*Zohar*).

אָבִיו וַיֹּאמֶר אֵלָיו הִנֵּה מִשְׁמַנֵּי הָאָרֶץ יִהְיֶה

< shall be < of the earth < the fatness < Indeed, << to him: < and he said < his father,

מוֹשָׁבֶךָ וּמִטַּל הַשָּׁמַיִם מֵעָל: * מ וְעַל־חַרְבְּךָ תִחְיֶה

<< shall you live, < your sword < By 40 *<< from above. < of the heavens < and of the dew < your dwelling*

וְאֶת־אָחִיךָ תַּעֲבֹד וְהָיָה כַּאֲשֶׁר תָּרִיד וּפָרַקְתָּ

< you may cast off << you are [validly] aggrieved, < that when < [yet] it shall be << you shall serve; < but your brother

עֻלּוֹ מֵעַל צַוָּארֶךָ: מא וַיִּשְׂטֹם עֵשָׂו אֶת־יַעֲקֹב עַל־

< because of < toward Jacob < Now Esau harbored hatred **41** *<< your neck. < from upon < his yoke*

הַבְּרָכָה אֲשֶׁר בֵּרְכוֹ אָבִיו וַיֹּאמֶר עֵשָׂו בְּלִבּוֹ יִקְרְבוּ יְמֵי אֵבֶל אָבִי

<< for my father, < of mourning < will the days < Draw near << in his heart, < and Esau said << his father had blessed him; < with which < the blessing

וְאַהַרְגָה אֶת־יַעֲקֹב אָחִי: מב וַיֻּגַּד לְרִבְקָה אֶת־דִּבְרֵי עֵשָׂו בְּנָהּ הַגָּדֹל

<< who was older, < her son < of Esau, < [were] the words < to Rebecca < Told **42** *<< my brother. < Jacob < then I will kill*

וַתִּשְׁלַח וַתִּקְרָא לְיַעֲקֹב בְּנָהּ הַקָּטָן וַתֹּאמֶר אֵלָיו הִנֵּה עֵשָׂו אָחִיךָ

< your brother < Esau < Indeed, << to him, < and she said < who was younger < her son < for Jacob < and called < and she sent

* חצי הספר בפסוקים

אֲבוּהִי וַאֲמַר לֵהּ הָא מִטּוּבָא דְאַרְעָא יְהֵא מוֹתְבָךְ וּמִטַּלָּא דִשְׁמַיָּא מִלְּעֵלָּא: מ וְעַל חַרְבָּךְ תֵּיחֵי וְיָת אָחוּךְ תִּפְלָח וִיהֵי כַּד יַעְבְּרוּן בְּנוֹהִי עַל פִּתְגָּמֵי אוֹרַיְתָא וְתַעְדֵּי נִירֵהּ מֵעַל צַוְּרָךְ: מא וּנְטַר עֵשָׂו דְּבָבוּ לְיַעֲקֹב עַל בִּרְכְתָא דִּי בָרְכֵהּ אֲבוּהִי וַאֲמַר עֵשָׂו בְּלִבֵּהּ יִקְרְבוּן יוֹמֵי אֶבְלֵהּ דְּאַבָּא וְאֶקְטוֹל יָת יַעֲקֹב אָחִי: מב וְאִתְחַוָּא לְרִבְקָה יָת פִּתְגָּמֵי עֵשָׂו בְּרַהּ רַבָּא וּשְׁלַחַת וּקְרַת לְיַעֲקֹב בְּרַהּ זְעֵירָא וַאֲמֶרֶת לֵהּ הָא עֵשָׂו אָחוּךְ

רש"י

השמנה היא (שם כ) הכמות נבא (שמואל ב ג:לג): **(לט) משמני הארץ וגו'.** זו איטליא"ה של יון (ב"ר שם ו): **(מ) ועל חרבך.** כמו בחרבך. יש על שהוא במקום אות ב', כמו עמדתם על חרבכם (יחזקאל לג:כו) בחרבכם. על צבאתם (שמות ו:כו) בצבאתם: **והיה כאשר תריד.** לשון צער, כמו אריד בשיחי (תהלים נה:ג). כלומר, כשיעברו ישראל על התורה ויהיה לך פתחון פה להצטער על הברכות שנטל, **ופרקת עלו וגו'** (אונקלוס; ב"ר שם ז): **(מא) יקרבו ימי אבל אבי.** כמשמעו, שלא אצער את אבא (ב"ר שם ח). ומ"א לכמה פנים יש: **(מב) ויגד לרבקה.** ברוח הקודש הוגד לה מה שעשו מהרהר בלבו (ב"ר שם ט):

39. **מִשְׁמַנֵּי הָאָרֶץ** — *Of the fatness of the earth.* This blessing does not conflict with Jacob's, since God's natural blessing is abundant enough for *both* of them. Furthermore, since Jacob was Abraham's heir, he would realize his blessing in *Eretz Yisrael,* while Esau would realize his in another land (*Ramban*).

Unlike the blessing he gave Jacob (v. 28), Isaac did not say that *God* would grant Esau's blessing, which would have implied that it would be given under Divine providence and guidance. Rather, it would come in the *normal* course of nature (*R' Hirsch*).

40. **וְעַל־חַרְבְּךָ תִחְיֶה** — *By your sword shall you live.* The implication was not that Esau would be forced to become a brigand and plunder with his sword, for he was blessed with sustenance from the *fatness of the earth and the dew of the heavens.* Rather, the blessing was that he would be victorious in war and survive his battles (*Ramban*). Since the Roman Empire, conqueror of the world, was descended from Esau, the fulfillment of this blessing is obvious (*Abarbanel*).

כַּאֲשֶׁר תָּרִיד — *That when you are [validly] aggrieved.* If Israel ever transgresses the Torah, and is thus undeserving of dominion, you will have a right to be *aggrieved* that he has taken the blessings; then *you may cast off his yoke from upon your neck* (*Rashi*).

This is in consonance with the prophecy given Rebecca while she was pregnant: Her two sons would not be able to coexist; when one ascended, the other would decline (25:23).

41-45. Esau's hatred of Jacob. The eternal rivalry between the brothers became intensified with Esau's determination to kill Jacob when the opportune time came. It was a resolve that his descendants would attempt to carry out time after time to this very day, but, as the Pesach *Haggadah* declares, the Holy One, Blessed is He, rescues us from their hand.

Esau's filial devotion to his father was intact and he did not wish to cause him grief (*Rashi*). Perhaps he feared that Isaac would curse him if he harmed Jacob, and the blessing would then turn into a curse (*Ramban*). Nevertheless, Rebecca feared for Jacob's life, even while Isaac was still alive. Perhaps she knew that Jacob's daily proximity would inflame Esau so much that he might lose control of himself and kill Jacob. Although Esau implied that he would not carry out his intention until Isaac died, Rebecca could not be sure when that would happen, so she ordered Jacob to flee before it was too late (*Or HaChaim*).

42. **וַיֻּגַּד לְרִבְקָה** — *Told to Rebecca.* Esau's intention was revealed to her by רוּחַ הַקֹּדֶשׁ, *Divine Inspiration* (*Rashi*).

מִתְנַחֵם לְךָ לְהָרְגֶךָ: מג וְעַתָּה בְנִי שְׁמַע בְּקֹלִי וְקוּם
< and arise, < to my voice; < listen < my son, < So now, 43 << to kill you. < regarding you < is consoling himself

בְּרַח־לְךָ אֶל־לָבָן אָחִי חָרָנָה: מד וְיָשַׁבְתָּ עִמּוֹ
< with him < And you should dwell 44 << to Haran. << my brother, < Laban < to < for yourself < flee

יָמִים אֲחָדִים עַד אֲשֶׁר־תָּשׁוּב חֲמַת אָחִיךָ: מה עַד־
< Until 45 << of your brother. < — the wrath << it should subside < when < until << for a few years

שׁוּב אַף־אָחִיךָ מִמְּךָ וְשָׁכַח אֵת אֲשֶׁר־עָשִׂיתָ
< you have done < which < that < and he forgets << from upon you, < of your brother < of the anger < the subsiding

לּוֹ וְשָׁלַחְתִּי וּלְקַחְתִּיךָ מִשָּׁם לָמָה אֶשְׁכַּל גַּם־שְׁנֵיכֶם יוֹם אֶחָד:
<< [on] one day? < of both of you < also < should I be bereft < Why << from there. < and bring you < then I will send << to him;

מו וַתֹּאמֶר רִבְקָה אֶל־יִצְחָק קַצְתִּי* בְחַיַּי מִפְּנֵי בְּנוֹת חֵת אִם־לֹקֵחַ יַעֲקֹב
< Jacob takes < if << of Heth; < the daughters < on account of < with my life < I am disgusted << Isaac, < to < Rebecca said 46

אִשָּׁה מִבְּנוֹת־חֵת כָּאֵלֶּה מִבְּנוֹת הָאָרֶץ לָמָּה לִּי חַיִּים: [כח] א וַיִּקְרָא
< So call 1 28 << life? < do I need < why < of the land, < of the daughters < like these, < of Heth < from the daughters < a wife

יִצְחָק אֶל־יַעֲקֹב וַיְבָרֶךְ אֹתוֹ וַיְצַוֵּהוּ וַיֹּאמֶר לוֹ לֹא־תִקַּח אִשָּׁה מִבְּנוֹת
< from the daughters < a wife < take < Do not << to him, < and he said < and he instructed him << him; < and blessed < Jacob < to < did Isaac

כְּנָעַן: ב קוּם לֵךְ פַּדֶּנָה אֲרָם בֵּיתָה בְתוּאֵל אֲבִי אִמֶּךָ וְקַח־לְךָ מִשָּׁם
< from there < for yourself < and take << of your mother, < the father < of Bethuel < to the house < to Paddan-aram, < go < Arise, 2 << of Canaan.

* ק' זעירא

כָּמֵן לָךְ לְמִקְטְלָךְ: מג וּכְעַן בְּרִי קַבֵּל מִנִּי וְקוּם אִיזֵל לָךְ לְוָת לָבָן אָחִי לְחָרָן: מד וְתֵתֵיב עִמֵּהּ יוֹמִין זְעֵירִין עַד דִּיתוּב רוּגְזָא דְאָחוּךְ: מה עַד תּוּב רוּגְזָא דְאָחוּךְ מִנָּךְ וְיִנְשֵׁי יָת דִּי עֲבַדְתְּ לֵהּ וְאֶשְׁלַח וְאֶדְבְּרִנָּךְ מִתַּמָּן לְמָא אֶתְכַּל אַף תַּרְוֵיכוֹן יוֹמָא חָד: מו וַאֲמֶרֶת רִבְקָה לְיִצְחָק עָקִית בְּחַיַּי מִן קֳדָם בְּנַת חִתָּאָה אִם נְסִיב יַעֲקֹב אִתְּתָא מִבְּנַת חִתָּאָה כְּאִלֵּין מִבְּנַת אַרְעָא לְמָא לִי חַיִּין: א וּקְרָא יִצְחָק לְיַעֲקֹב וּבָרִיךְ יָתֵהּ וּפַקְדֵהּ וַאֲמַר לֵהּ לָא תִסַּב אִתְּתָא מִבְּנַת כְּנָעַן: ב קוּם אִיזֵל לְפַדַּן אֲרָם לְבֵית בְּתוּאֵל אֲבוּהָא דְאִמָּךְ וְסַב לָךְ מִתַּמָּן

רש"י

מתנחם לך. נחם על האחוה לחשוב מחשבה אחרת להתנכר לך ולהרגך. ומ"א, כבר אתה מת בעיניו ושתה עליך כוס של תנחומים (שם). ולפי פשוטו לשון תנחומים, מתנחם הוא על הברכות בהריגתך (תנחומא ישן ויצא א): **(מד) אחדים.** מועטים (אונקלוס): **(מה) למה אשכל.** אהיה שכולה משניכם. לימד על הקובר את בניו שקרוי שכול, וכן ביעקב אמר כאשר שכלתי שכלתי (להלן מג:יד): **גם שניכם.** אם יקום עליך ואתה תהרגנו יעמדו בניו ויהרגוך. ורוח הקדש נזרקה בה ונתנבאה שביום אחד ימותו, כמו שמפורש בפ' המקנא לאשתו (סוטה יג.): **(מו) קצתי בחיי.** מאסתי בחיי: **(ב) פדנה.** כמו לפדן: **ביתה בתואל.** לבית בתואל. כל תיבה שצריכה למ"ד בתחלתה הטיל לה

44-45. יָמִים אֲחָדִים — *A few years.* The Midrash notes that Rebecca had innocently hoped that Esau's anger would subside after a while, but she was mistaken. Instead, *Edom's . . . anger tore perpetually and he kept his wrath forever (Amos* 1:11). Jacob was in exile for over twenty years, and she never saw him again.

45. אֶשְׁכַּל גַּם־שְׁנֵיכֶם — *Should I be bereft also of both of you.* This was an unintentional prophecy that they would die on the same day. The Talmud (*Sotah* 13a) states that, figuratively, such was the case (*Rashi*), for Esau died and was buried on the day Jacob was brought to burial in the Cave of Machpelah. *Chizkuni* suggests that Rebecca is referring to Isaac and Jacob, since Esau planned to kill Jacob immediately after the death of his father.

46. בְּנוֹת חֵת — *The daughters of Heth,* Esau's wives. She did not wish to tell Isaac that Jacob's life was in danger, so she referred to the unsuitability of the Hittite women (*Rashbam*).

28.

1-5. The admonition against marrying a Canaanite; the Abrahamitic blessing is conveyed to Jacob.

1. וַיְבָרֶךְ אֹתוֹ — *And blessed him.* This *blessing* is the one given further in v. 3 (*Radak*). Earlier, Isaac had been tricked into blessing Jacob; now he ratified the blessing of his own free will.

אִשָּׁה מִבְּנוֹת לָבָן אֲחִי אִמֶּךָ: ג וְאֵל שַׁדַּי יְבָרֵךְ

‹ bless ‹ Shaddai ‹ And may El **3** « of your mother. ‹ the brother ‹ of Laban ‹ from the daughters ‹ a wife

אֹתְךָ וְיַפְרְךָ וְיַרְבֶּךָ וְהָיִיתָ לִקְהַל עַמִּים: ד וְיִתֶּן־

‹ May He grant **4** « of peoples. ‹ a congregation ‹ and may you become « and make you numerous, ‹ make you fruitful ‹ you,

לְךָ אֶת־בִּרְכַּת אַבְרָהָם לְךָ וּלְזַרְעֲךָ אִתָּךְ לְרִשְׁתְּךָ

‹ that you may possess « with you, ‹ and to your offspring ‹ to you ‹ of Abraham, ‹ the blessing ‹ to you

אֶת־אֶרֶץ מְגֻרֶיךָ אֲשֶׁר־נָתַן אֱלֹהִים לְאַבְרָהָם:

« to Abraham. ‹ God gave ‹ that ‹ of your sojourning ‹ the land

שביעי ה וַיִּשְׁלַח יִצְחָק אֶת־יַעֲקֹב וַיֵּלֶךְ פַּדֶּנָה אֲרָם אֶל־לָבָן בֶּן־בְּתוּאֵל

‹ of Bethuel ‹ the son ‹ Laban ‹ to « toward Paddan-aram, ‹ and he went ‹ Jacob ‹ So Isaac sent away **5**

הָאֲרַמִּי אֲחִי רִבְקָה אֵם יַעֲקֹב וְעֵשָׂו: ו וַיַּרְא עֵשָׂו כִּי־בֵרַךְ יִצְחָק

‹ Isaac had blessed ‹ that ‹ When Esau saw **6** « and Esau. ‹ of Jacob ‹ mother ‹ of Rebecca, ‹ brother ‹ the Aramean,

אֶת־יַעֲקֹב וְשִׁלַּח אֹתוֹ פַּדֶּנָה אֲרָם לָקַחַת־לוֹ מִשָּׁם אִשָּׁה בְּבָרְכוֹ אֹתוֹ

‹ him ‹ as he blessed « a wife, ‹ from there ‹ himself ‹ to take ‹ to Paddan-aram ‹ and had sent him away ‹ Jacob

וַיְצַו עָלָיו לֵאמֹר לֹא־תִקַּח אִשָּׁה מִבְּנוֹת כְּנָעַן: מפטיר ז וַיִּשְׁמַע יַעֲקֹב אֶל־

‹ to ‹ and that Jacob listened **7** « of Canaan; ‹ from the daughters ‹ a wife ‹ You shall not take « saying, ‹ him ‹ he commanded

אִתְּתָא מִבְּנַת לָבָן אֲחוּהָא דְאִמָּךְ: ג וְאֵל שַׁדַּי יְבָרֵךְ יָתָךְ וְיַפְשָׁךְ וְיַסְגְּנָךְ וּתְהֵי לִכְנִשַׁת שִׁבְטִין: ד וְיִתֵּן לָךְ יָת בִּרְכְתָא דְאַבְרָהָם לָךְ וְלִבְנָיךְ עִמָּךְ לְמֵירְתָךְ יָת אֲרַע תּוֹתָבוּתָךְ דִּי יְהַב יְיָ לְאַבְרָהָם: ה וּשְׁלַח יִצְחָק יָת יַעֲקֹב וַאֲזַל לְפַדַּן אֲרָם לְוַת לָבָן בַּר בְּתוּאֵל אֲרַמָּאָה אֲחוּהָא דְרִבְקָה אִמֵּהּ דְּיַעֲקֹב וְעֵשָׂו: ו וַחֲזָא עֵשָׂו אֲרֵי בָרִיךְ יִצְחָק יָת יַעֲקֹב וְשַׁלַּח יָתֵהּ לְפַדַּן אֲרָם לְמִסַּב לֵהּ מִתַּמָּן אִתְּתָא כַּד בָּרִיךְ יָתֵהּ וּפַקִּיד עֲלוֹהִי לְמֵימַר לָא תִסַּב אִתְּתָא מִבְּנַת כְּנָעַן: ז וְקַבִּיל יַעֲקֹב מִן

רש"י

ה"א בסופה (יבמות יג:): (ג) **ואל שדי.** מי שדי בברכותיו למתברכין מפיו **יברך אותך:** (ד) **את ברכת אברהם.** שאמר לו ואעשך לגוי גדול (לעיל יב:ב). והתברכו בזרעך (שם כב:יח). יהיו אותן ברכות [ה]אמורות לך [ס"א בשבילך], ממך יצא אותו הגוי ואותו הזרע המבורך: (ה) **אם יעקב ועשו.** איני יודע מה מלמדנו: (ז) **וישמע יעקב.** מחובר לענין שלמעלה, וירא עשו כי ברך יצחק וגו' וכי שלח אותו פדנה ארם וכי שמע יעקב אל אביו והלך פדנה ארם וכי רעות בנות כנען, והלך גם הוא אל ישמעאל:

3-4. **אֵל שַׁדַּי** — *El Shaddai.* Isaac blessed Jacob wholeheartedly, specifically giving him the Abrahamitic blessings, which meant that the destiny of Israel would be carried only by his offspring.

Jacob's nation would be *a congregation of peoples* in the sense that it would comprise many distinct tribes [*peoples*] with different characteristics and missions, but all would be united as parts of the same *congregation* (*R' Hirsch*).

Haamek Davar points out that more than a blessing, Isaac was actually prophesying that on his return, Jacob would receive this very blessing from God as El Shaddai (see 35:11).

4. **אֶרֶץ מְגֻרֶיךָ** — *The land of your sojourning.* This blessing is to be understood in conjunction with the earlier one (27:28). Isaac specified that those earlier blessings of prosperity should be fulfilled in the land that was promised to Abraham, while Esau's blessings would be fulfilled elsewhere (*Ramban* to 27:39).

For the first time Isaac said explicitly that he was granting Jacob the "blessing of Abraham." The Patriarchs did not function as individuals; their mission in life required the partnership of a wife worthy to be a Jewish Matriarch. This is clear in the relationship of Abraham and Sarah. So, too, only after Isaac married Rebecca did Abraham give him "everything" he had, which included all his blessings (see *Rashi* to 25:5). Only now, when Jacob was going to find his proper match, could Isaac confer upon him the blessing of Abraham (*R' Yosef Dov Soloveitchik*).

5. There is no mention here of Isaac sending wealth along with Jacob, as would be expected. *Ramban* (25:34) conjectures that Isaac was afraid that if Jacob went with great wealth, he would become a target for his enemies.

The Midrash, however, comments that Isaac did indeed send considerable gifts with Jacob, but at the outset of his journey, Eliphaz, son of Esau, robbed him of his fortune.

אֵם יַעֲקֹב וְעֵשָׂו — *Mother of Jacob and Esau.* The verse repeats the obvious to imply that even though Esau had the same genealogy as Jacob and it would have been just as logical for his parents to ask him to seek his mate in Haran, they did not do so because the heir of Abraham was Jacob, not Esau (*Ramban*). Or, it was as the loving mother of *both* that she wanted Jacob sent away, in order to avert bloodshed between them (*Tur*).

6-9. Esau marries the daughter of Ishmael.

6. **וַיַּרְא עֵשָׂו** — *When Esau saw* that in his second blessing to Jacob, Isaac conferred upon him the Abrahamitic gift of *Eretz*

אָבִיו וְאֶל־אִמּוֹ וַיֵּלֶךְ פַּדֶּנָה אֲרָם: ח וַיַּרְא עֵשָׂו

his father › and to › his mother › and went › to Paddan-aram; »
8 then Esau saw ›

כִּי רָעוֹת בְּנוֹת כְּנָעַן בְּעֵינֵי יִצְחָק אָבִיו:

that › evil › were the daughters › of Canaan › in the eyes › of Isaac, › his father. »

ט וַיֵּלֶךְ עֵשָׂו אֶל־יִשְׁמָעֵאל וַיִּקַּח אֶת־מָחֲלַת ׀ בַּת־יִשְׁמָעֵאל בֶּן־

9 So Esau went › to › Ishmael › and took › Mahalath, › the daughter › of Ishmael › son ›

אַבְרָהָם אֲחוֹת נְבָיוֹת עַל־נָשָׁיו לוֹ לְאִשָּׁה: ססס ק״ו פסוקים. על״ו סימן.

of Abraham, › sister › of Nebaioth, » in addition to » his wives, » for himself › as a wife. »

אֲבוּהִי וּמִן אִמֵּהּ וַאֲזַל לְפַדַּן אֲרָם: ח וַחֲזָא עֵשָׂו אֲרֵי בִישָׁא בְּנַת כְּנָעַן בְּעֵינֵי יִצְחָק אֲבוּהִי: ט וַאֲזַל עֵשָׂו לְוַת יִשְׁמָעֵאל וּנְסִיב יָת מַחֲלַת בַּת יִשְׁמָעֵאל בַּר אַבְרָהָם אֲחָתֵהּ דִּנְבָיוֹת עַל נְשׁוֹהִי לֵהּ לְאִנְתּוּ:

THE HAFTARAH FOR TOLDOS APPEARS ON PAGE 335.
When Erev Rosh Chodesh Kislev coincides with Toldos, the regular Haftarah is replaced with the Haftarah for Shabbas Erev Rosh Chodesh, page 349.

רש״י

(ט) אחות נביות. ממשמע שנאמר בת ישמעאל איני יודע שהיא אחות נביות. אלא למדנו שמת ישמעאל משיעדה לעשו קודם נשואיה, והשיאה נביות אחיה. ולמדנו שהיה יעקב באותו הפרק בן ס״ג שנים. שהרי ישמעאל בן ע״ד שנים היה כשנולד יעקב. שי״ד שנה היה גדול ישמעאל מיצחק ויצחק בן ס׳ שנה בלדת אותם, הרי ע״ד. ושנותיו היו קל״ז, שנא׳ ואלה שני חיי ישמעאל וגו׳ (לעיל כה:יז), נמצא יעקב כשמת ישמעאל בן ס״ג שנים היה. ולמדנו מכאן שנטמן בבית עבר י״ד שנה ואח״כ הלך לחרן. שהרי לא שהה בבית לבן לפני לידתו של יוסף אלא י״ד שנה, שנא׳ עבדתיך י״ד שנה בשתי בנותיך ושש שנים בצאנך (להלן לא:מא), ושכר הצאן משנולד יוסף היה, שנא׳ ויהי כאשר ילדה רחל את יוסף וגו׳ (שם ל:כה). ויוסף בן ל׳ שנה היה כשמלך, ומשם עד שירד יעקב למצרים ט׳ שנים, ז׳ של שובע וב׳ של רעב, ויעקב אמר לפרעה ימי שני מגורי שלשים ומאת שנה (שם מז:ט). צא וחשוב י״ד שנה שלפני לידת יוסף ול׳ של יוסף וט׳ משמלך עד שבא יעקב הרי נ״ג. וכשפירש מאביו היה בן ס״ג, הרי קט״ז, והוא אומר שלשים ומאת שנה, הרי חסרים י״ד שנים. הא למדת שאחר שקבל הברכות נטמן בבית עבר י״ד שנים [אבל לא נענש עליהם בזכות התורה, שהרי לא פירש יוסף מאביו אלא כ״ב שנה, דהיינו מי״ז עד ל״ט, כנגד כ״ב שפירש יעקב מאביו ולא כבדו. והם כ׳ שנים בבית לבן ושתי שנים ששהה בדרך, כדכתיב ויבן לו בית ולמקנהו עשה סכות (להלן לג:יז) ופי׳ רז״ל מזה הפסוק ששהה י״ח חדשים בדרך, דבית הוא בימות הגשמים וסוכות הוא בימות החמה. ולחשבון הפסוקים שחשבנו לעיל משפירש מאביו עד שירד למצרים שהיה בן ק״ל שנים שם אנו מוצאים עוד י״ד שנים. אלא ודאי נטמן בבית עבר בהליכתו לבית לבן, ללמוד תורה ממנו, ובשביל זכות התורה לא נענש עליהם ולא פירש יוסף ממנו אלא כ״ב שנה, מדה כנגד מדה] (מגילה טז:-יז.): **על נשיו.** הוסיף רשעה על רשעתו שלא גרש את הראשונות (ב״ר סז:יג):

For twenty-three years Esau had permitted the behavior of his Canaanite wives to cause anguish to his parents, yet it seems to have dawned on him only now. Instead of divorcing them, however, he merely took another wife *in addition* to them (*R' Hirsch*).

ק״ו פסוקים. על״ו סימן — This Masoretic note means: There are 106 verses in the *Sidrah,* numerically corresponding to the mnemonic עלי״ו [*they* (i.e., Isaac and Jacob) *ascended*].

This alludes to the primary themes of the *Sidrah*: the *ascendancy* of Isaac as a result of his experiences in Gerar (see 26:4,13, and 28) and the *ascendancy* of Jacob, thanks to the birthright and the blessings (*R' David Feinstein*).

Yisrael, he assumed that he had been stripped of this blessing because he had wed Hittite women. Therefore, he now took a daughter of Ishmael in the hope that he would ingratiate himself with Isaac and regain the blessing of the Land (*Rashbam*).

9. אֲחוֹת נְבָיוֹת — *Sister of Nebaioth.* Citing *Megillah* 17a, *Rashi* notes that the apparently superfluous description *sister of Nebaioth* is added to imply the tradition that Ishmael died immediately after he designated his daughter as Esau's bride. Nebaioth is mentioned because it was he who actually gave her in marriage.

PARASHAS VAYEITZEI / פרשת ויצא

י וַיֵּצֵא יַעֲקֹב מִבְּאֵר שָׁבַע וַיֵּלֶךְ חָרָנָה: יא וַיִּפְגַּע
10 Jacob departed < from Beer-sheba < and he went < toward Haran. » 11 He encountered <
בַּמָּקוֹם וַיָּלֶן שָׁם כִּי־בָא הַשֶּׁמֶשׁ וַיִּקַּח מֵאַבְנֵי
the place < and spent the night < there < because < the sun had set; « he took < from the stones <
הַמָּקוֹם וַיָּשֶׂם מְרַאֲשֹׁתָיו וַיִּשְׁכַּב בַּמָּקוֹם הַהוּא: יב וַיַּחֲלֹם וְהִנֵּה סֻלָּם
of the place » he placed [them] < around his head, < and he lay down < in that place. » 12 And he dreamed, < and there appeared < a ladder <

אונקלוס

י וּנְפַק יַעֲקֹב מִבְּאֵרָא דְשָׁבַע וַאֲזַל לְחָרָן: יא וַעֲרַע בְּאַתְרָא וּבָת תַּמָּן אֲרֵי עַל שִׁמְשָׁא וּנְסִיב מֵאַבְנֵי אַתְרָא וְשַׁוִּי אִסָּדוֹהִי וּשְׁכִיב בְּאַתְרָא הַהוּא: יב וַחֲלַם וְהָא סוּלָמָא

רש"י

(י) **ויצא יעקב.** על ידי שבשביל שרעות בנות כנען בעיני יצחק אביו הלך עשו אל ישמעאל הפסיק הענין בפרשתו של יעקב וכתב וירא עשו כי ברך וגו', ומשגמר חזר לענין הראשון: **ויצא.** לא היה צריך לכתוב אלא וילך יעקב חרנה, ולמה הזכיר יציאתו, אלא מגיד שיציאת צדיק מן המקום עושה רושם, שבזמן שהצדיק בעיר הוא הודה הוא זיוה הוא הדרה, יצא משם פנה הודה פנה זיוה פנה הדרה. וכן ותצא מן המקום (רות א:ז) האמור בנעמי ורות (ב"ר סח:ו): **וילך חרנה.** יצא ללכת לחרן (שם ח): (יא) **ויפגע במקום.** לא הזכיר הכתוב באיזה מקום, אלא במקום הנזכר במקום אחר, הוא הר המוריה שנאמר בו וירא את המקום מרחוק (לעיל כב:ד; פסחים פח.): **ויפגע.** כמו ופגע ביריחו (יהושע טז:ז) ופגע בדבשת (שם יט:יא; אונקלוס). ורבותינו פירשו לשון תפלה, כמו ואל תפגע בי (ירמיה ז:טז), ולמדנו שתקן תפלת ערבית (ברכות כו:; ב"ר שם ט). ושינה הכתוב ולא כתב ויתפלל ללמדך שקפצה לו הארץ, כמו שמפורש בפ' גיד הנשה (חולין צא:): **כי בא השמש.** היה לו לכתוב ויבא השמש וילן שם, כי בא השמש משמע ששקעה לו חמה פתאום, שלא בעונתה, כדי שילין שם (שם; ב"ר שם י): **וישם מראשתיו.** עשאן כמין מרזב סביב לראשו שירא מפני חיות רעות (ב"ר שם יא). התחילו מריבות זו עם זו, זאת אומרת עלי יניח צדיק את ראשו וזאת אומרת עלי יניח, מיד עשאן הקב"ה אבן אחת, וזהו שנא' ויקח את האבן אשר שם מראשותיו (להלן פסוק יח; חולין שם): **וישכב במקום ההוא.** לשון מעוט. באותו מקום שכב, אבל י"ד שנים ששמש בבית [ס"א את] עבר לא שכב בלילה, שהיה עוסק בתורה (ב"ר שם):

PARASHAS VAYEITZEI

10-22. Jacob's flight and his vision at Moriah. Jacob had left his parents to begin a personal exile that, unknown to him at the time, would include twenty years in the home of Laban, a mendacious rogue, who, as the Passover *Haggadah* says, attempted to uproot the Jewish people. Before going to Haran, Jacob spent fourteen years at the academy of Shem and Eber, a fact that the Sages deduce from the chronology of the period. Surely, as great a man as Jacob did not need more years of study to become a scholar. He went there for a different reason.

R' Yaakov Kamenetsky explained that the first sixty-three years of his life he studied Torah with his father, in an atmosphere insulated from the corruption of Canaan. Now he would be living in Haran, among people who were Laban's comrades in dishonesty. To survive spiritually in such an environment, he needed the Torah of Shem and Eber, for they too, had been forced to cope with corrosive surroundings. Shem had lived in the generation of the Flood and Eber had lived with those who built the Tower of Babel. Jacob's fourteen years in their tutelage made it possible for him to emerge spiritually unscathed from his personal exile. That was his personal preparation for the coming ordeal. Then, God prepared him further with the vision of the angels and the Divine promise with which our *Sidrah* begins. God's promise sustained him, but it was his own efforts that earned him the prophecy.

10. וַיֵּצֵא יַעֲקֹב מִבְּאֵר שָׁבַע — *Jacob departed from Beer-sheba.* For the purposes of the narrative, it would have been sufficient to say merely he *went to Haran*. Therefore the Sages infer that Jacob's departure from Beer-sheba had a significance of its own: "A righteous person's departure from a place leaves a void. As long as he lives in a city, he constitutes its glory, its splendor, and its beauty; when he departs, its glory, splendor, and beauty depart with him" (*Rashi*).

11. בַּמָּקוֹם הַהוּא — *In that place.* This was Mount Moriah, the site where Abraham bound Isaac on the altar and where the Temple would later stand. The Sages interpret the term וַיִּפְגַּע, which usually means *encountered*, to have the less common meaning *prayed*, so that Jacob's primary encounter was not with a geographical location, but with God. Since the verse states that this took place just before he retired for the night, the Sages credit Jacob with instituting עַרְבִית, *the Evening Prayer* (*Rashi*).

וַיִּקַּח מֵאַבְנֵי — *He took from the stones.* Midrashically, the Sages render that he took several stones. The stones began quarreling, each one saying, "Upon *me* shall this righteous man rest his head." Thereupon God combined them all into one stone. That is why verse 18 reads: *and [he] took* **the** *stone*, in the singular (*Rashi*).

The Sages teach that the stones symbolized the nation that Jacob would soon begin to establish. There were twelve stones which coalesced into one. They represented the twelve tribes — each of them unique and with its own separate mission — but all of them united in a single nation.

Alternately, there were three stones (*Bereishis Rabbah* 68:11) representing the *Yichud Shem,* or Divine essences of Abraham, Isaac, and Jacob that were merged. This prefigures the Kabbalistic concept of the merging of Abraham's attribute of *chesed*/kindness, with the *gevurah*/strength attribute of Isaac, to form the attribute of Jacob, *emes*/truth (*R' Chaim Yaakov Goldvicht*).

12. Symbolism of Jacob's dream. The dreams mentioned in Scripture are vehicles of prophecy; otherwise the Torah —

מֻצָּב אַרְצָה וְרֹאשׁוֹ מַגִּיעַ הַשָּׁמָיְמָה וְהִנֵּה מַלְאֲכֵי

‹ angels ‹ and there appeared ‹‹ heavenward; ‹ was reaching ‹ and its top ‹ earthward ‹ that was set

אֱלֹהִים עֹלִים וְיֹרְדִים בּוֹ: יג וְהִנֵּה יהוה נִצָּב עָלָיו

‹‹ over him, ‹ was standing ‹ HASHEM ‹‹ And then 13 ‹‹ on it. ‹ and descending ‹ ascending ‹ of God

וַיֹּאמַר אֲנִי יהוה אֱלֹהֵי אַבְרָהָם אָבִיךָ וֵאלֹהֵי

‹ and God ‹ your father ‹ of Abraham ‹ God ‹ HASHEM, ‹ I am ‹‹ and He said,

יִצְחָק הָאָרֶץ אֲשֶׁר אַתָּה שֹׁכֵב עָלֶיהָ לְךָ אֶתְּנֶנָּה

‹ will I give it ‹ to you ‹‹ upon, ‹ are lying ‹ you ‹ which ‹ the ground ‹‹ of Isaac;

וּלְזַרְעֶךָ: יד וְהָיָה זַרְעֲךָ כַּעֲפַר הָאָרֶץ וּפָרַצְתָּ יָמָּה וָקֵדְמָה וְצָפֹנָה וָנֶגְבָּה

‹‹ and southward; ‹ and northward, ‹ and eastward, ‹ westward, ‹ and you shall burst forth ‹‹ of the earth, ‹ as the dust ‹ Your offspring shall be 14 ‹‹ and to your descendants.

וְנִבְרְכוּ בְךָ כָּל־מִשְׁפְּחֹת הָאֲדָמָה וּבְזַרְעֶךָ: טו וְהִנֵּה אָנֹכִי עִמָּךְ

‹‹ with you; ‹ I am ‹ Indeed, 15 ‹‹ and through your offspring. ‹ of the earth ‹ the families ‹ all ‹ through you ‹ and will be blessed

נָעִיץ בְּאַרְעָא וְרֵישֵׁהּ מָטֵי עַד צֵית שְׁמַיָּא וְהָא מַלְאֲכַיָּא דַייָ סָלְקִין וְנָחֲתִין בֵּהּ: יג וְהָא יְקָרָא דַייָ מְעַתַּד עִלָּווֹהִי וַאֲמַר אֲנָא יְיָ אֱלָהֵהּ דְּאַבְרָהָם אֲבוּךְ וֵאלָהֵהּ דְּיִצְחָק אַרְעָא דִּי אַתְּ שָׁרֵי עֲלַהּ לָךְ אֶתְּנִנַּהּ וְלִבְנָיךְ: יד וִיהוֹן בְּנָיךְ סַגִּיאִין כְּעַפְרָא דְאַרְעָא וְתִתְקֵף לְמַעַרְבָא וּלְמָדִינְחָא וּלְצִפּוּנָא וּלְדָרוֹמָא וְיִתְבָּרְכוּן בְּדִילָךְ כָּל זַרְעֲיַת אַרְעָא וּבְדִיל בְּנָיךְ: טו וְהָא מֵימְרִי בְּסַעְדָּךְ

רש"י

(יב) עולים ויורדים. עולים תחלה ואח"כ יורדים. מלאכים שליווהו בארץ אין יוצאים חוצה לארץ, ועלו לרקיע, וירדו מלאכי חוצה לארץ ללוותו (שם יב): **(יג) נצב עליו.** לשמרו (שם סט:ג): **ואלהי יצחק.** אע"פ שלא מצינו במקרא שייחד הקב"ה שמו על הצדיקים בחייהם לכתוב אלהי פלוני, משום שנא' הן בקדושיו לא יאמין (איוב טו:טו), כאן ייחד שמו על יצחק, לפי שכהו עיניו וכלוא בבית והרי הוא כמת, ויצר הרע פסק ממנו. תנחומא (תולדות ז): **שכב עליה.** קיפל הקב"ה כל א"י תחתיו, רמז לו שתהא נוחה ליכבש לבניו [כד' אמות שזה מקומו של אדם] (חולין שם): **(יד) ופרצת.** וחזקת (אונקלוס), כמו וכן יפרוץ (שמות א:יב): **(טו) אנכי עמך.** לפי שהיה ירא מעשו

which uses words very sparingly — would not cite them. Jacob's dream at Mount Moriah symbolized the future of the Jewish people and man's ability to connect himself to God's master plan. Among the many interpretations of the dream are these:

□ **Mount Sinai.** The ladder alludes to Sinai, since the words סִינַי and סֻלָּם both have the numerical value of 130; the angels represent Moses and Aaron; and God stood atop the ladder just as He stood atop Sinai to give the Torah (*Midrash*). Accordingly, the Torah, given at Sinai and taught by sages such as Moses and Aaron, is the bridge from heaven to earth.

□ **The Four Kingdoms.** Jacob was shown the guardian angels of the Four Kingdoms that would *ascend* to dominate Israel. Jacob saw each angel climbing a number of rungs corresponding to the years of its dominion, and then descending, as its reign ended: Babylon's angel climbed 70 rungs and then went down; Media's angel 52; Greece's 130 — but the angel of Edom/Esau kept climbing indefinitely, symbolizing the current exile, which seems to be endless. Jacob was frightened, until God assured him (v. 15) that he would receive Divine protection and eventually return to the Land (*Vayikra Rabbah* 29:2; *Rambam* citing *Pirkei d'Rabbi Eliezer*).

□ **The Land's greatness.** Jacob was shown that the angels that protected him in *Eretz Yisrael* were going back up to heaven and were being replaced by lesser angels, which would escort him while he was outside the Land. This process was reversed when he returned to the Land (32:2) and the angels of the Land returned to him. This vision instilled in him a recognition of the great holiness of the Land and a desire to return to it (*Rashi*, according to *Abarbanel*). By speaking of angels ascending and being replaced by others, the Torah indicates that God extends His protection to His righteous ones, though the angels are unseen by anyone, perhaps even by those they escort.

□ **Jacob's uniqueness.** The angels, which are God's agents in carrying out His guidance of earthly affairs, constantly go up to heaven to receive His commands and then come back to earth to carry them out, as it were. Jacob and the Jewish nation, however, are under the direct guidance of God, Who is atop the ladder (*Ramban*; *Ibn Ezra*).

13. אֲשֶׁר אַתָּה שֹׁכֵב עָלֶיהָ — *Which you are lying upon,* the entire land of Canaan. God folded the entire country under Jacob, so that, in effect, he lay on all of the Land (*Chullin* 91b). Since the exact site of Jacob's dream was the future Holy of Holies of the Temple, this symbolized that every bit of the Land was to be infused with holiness. Similarly, a Jew can never be content with an occasional visit to the Temple or study hall; every area of his life should be hallowed (*Sfas Emes*).

14. כַּעֲפַר הָאָרֶץ — *As the dust of the earth. Sforno* connects this phrase with the following one, rendering: Only after your offspring shall have become as degraded *as the dust of the earth* [see *Isaiah* 51:23] *shall they burst forth westward, and eastward, and northward, and southward.* As the Sages have taught, God's future salvation will come only after Israel has experi-

וּשְׁמַרְתִּיךָ בְּכֹל אֲשֶׁר־תֵּלֵךְ וַהֲשִׁבֹתִיךָ אֶל־
I will guard you < in all [places] < that < you go, << and I will return you < to <

הָאֲדָמָה הַזֹּאת כִּי לֹא אֶעֱזָבְךָ עַד אֲשֶׁר
this soil; << for < I will not leave you < until < then <

אִם־עָשִׂיתִי אֵת אֲשֶׁר־דִּבַּרְתִּי לָךְ: טז וַיִּיקַץ יַעֲקֹב
when < I will have done < that < which < I have spoken < concerning you. << 16 Jacob awoke <

מִשְּׁנָתוֹ וַיֹּאמֶר אָכֵן יֵשׁ יהוה בַּמָּקוֹם הַזֶּה וְאָנֹכִי
from his sleep << and said, < Surely < HASHEM is present < in this place < and I <

לֹא יָדַעְתִּי: יז וַיִּירָא וַיֹּאמַר מַה־נּוֹרָא הַמָּקוֹם הַזֶּה
did not < know! << 17 And he became frightened < and said, << How < awesome < is this place! <<

אֵין זֶה כִּי אִם־בֵּית אֱלֹהִים וְזֶה שַׁעַר הַשָּׁמָיִם: יח וַיַּשְׁכֵּם יַעֲקֹב בַּבֹּקֶר
This is none < other than < the house < of God < and this is < the gate < of the heavens! << 18 Jacob arose early < in the morning <

וַיִּקַּח אֶת־הָאֶבֶן אֲשֶׁר־שָׂם מְרַאֲשֹׁתָיו וַיָּשֶׂם אֹתָהּ מַצֵּבָה וַיִּצֹק שֶׁמֶן
and he took < the stone < that < he placed < around his head < and set < it [up] < as a monument; << and he poured < oil <

עַל־רֹאשָׁהּ: יט וַיִּקְרָא אֶת־שֵׁם־הַמָּקוֹם הַהוּא בֵּית־אֵל וְאוּלָם לוּז שֵׁם־
on < its top. << 19 And he called < the name < of that place < Beth-el; << however, < Luz < was the name <

וְאֶטְרִנָּךְ בְּכָל אֲתַר דִּי תְהַךְ וַאֲתִיבִנָּךְ
לְאַרְעָא הָדָא אֲרֵי לָא אֶשְׁבְּקִנָּךְ
עַד דִּי אֶעְבֵּד יָת דִּי מַלֵּלִית לָךְ:
טז וְאִתְּעַר יַעֲקֹב מִשִּׁנְתֵּהּ וַאֲמַר
בְּקוּשְׁטָא (אִית) יְקָרָא דַייָ שָׁרֵי
בְּאַתְרָא הָדֵין וַאֲנָא לָא הֲוֵיתִי יָדַע:
יז וּדְחִיל וַאֲמַר מָה דְּחִילוּ אַתְרָא
הָדֵין לֵית דֵּין אֲתַר הֶדְיוֹט אֱלָהֵן
אֲתַר דְּרַעֲוָא בֵהּ מִן קֳדָם יְיָ וְדֵין תְּרַע
קֳבֵל שְׁמַיָּא: יח וְאַקְדֵּים יַעֲקֹב בְּצַפְרָא
וּנְסִיב יָת אַבְנָא דִּי שַׁוִּי אִסָּדוֹהִי
וְשַׁוִּי יָתַהּ קָמָא וַאֲרִיק מִשְׁחָא עַל
רֵישַׁהּ: יט וּקְרָא יָת שְׁמָא דְאַתְרָא
הַהוּא בֵּית אֵל וּבְרַם לוּז שְׁמָא

רש"י

ומלבן (ב"ר סח:ח; תנחומא ישן ג, וישלח י): **עד אשר אם עשיתי.** אם משמש בלשון כי: **דברתי לך.** לצרכך ועליך. מה שהבטחתי לאברהם על זרעו לך הבטחתי ולא לעשו, שלא אמרתי לו כי יצחק יקרא לך זרע אלא כי ביצחק (לעיל כא:יב) ולא כל יצחק (נדרים לא.). וכן כל לי ולך ולו ולהם הסמוכים אצל דבור משמשים לשון על, וזה יוכיח, שהרי עם יעקב לא דבר קודם לכן: **(טז) ואנכי לא ידעתי.** שאם ידעתי לא ישנתי במקום קדוש כזה (מדרש אגדה; ברב"ת; ירושלמי מגילה ג:ג): **(יז) כי אם בית אלהים.** א"ר אלעזר בשם רבי יוסי בן זמרא, הסולם הזה עומד בבאר שבע ואמצע שפועו מגיע כנגד בית המקדש. שבאר שבע עומד בדרומה של יהודה, וירושלים בצפונה בגבול שבין יהודה ובנימין, ובית אל היה בצפון של נחלת בנימין בגבול שבין בנימין ובין בני יוסף. נמצא סולם שרגליו בבאר שבע וראשו בבית אל מגיע אמצע שפועו נגד ירושלים (ב"ר סט:ז). וכלפי שאמרו רבותינו שאמר הקב"ה צדיק זה בא לבית מלוני ויפטר בלא לינה (חולין צא:), ועוד אמרו, יעקב קראו לירושלים בית אל (פסחים פח.), וזו לוז היא ולא ירושלים, ומהיכן למדו לומר כן. אומר אני שנעקר הר המוריה ובא לכאן, וזו היא קפיצת הארץ האמורה בשחיטת חולין (צא:), שבא בית המקדש לקראתו עד בית אל, וזהו ויפגע במקום. וא"ת, וכשעבר יעקב על בית המקדש מדוע לא עכבו שם. איהו לא יהיב לביה להתפלל במקום שהתפללו אבותיו ומן השמים יעכבוהו, איהו עד חרן אזל, כדאמרינן בפרק גיד הנשה (שם), וקרא מוכיח, וילך חרנה. כי מטא לחרן אמר, אפשר שעברתי על מקום שהתפללו אבותי ולא התפללתי בו. יהב דעתיה למהדר, וחזר עד בית אל וקפצה לו הארץ. [בית אל לא זה הוא הסמוך לעי, אלא לירושלים, ועל שם שהיתה עיר האלהים קראה בית אל. והוא הר המוריה שהתפלל בו אברהם, והוא השדה שהתפלל בו יצחק. וכן אמרו בגמרא, לכו ונעלה וגו' (ישעיה ב:ג) לא כאברהם שקראו הר, ולא כיצחק שקראו שדה, אלא כיעקב שקראו בית אל (פסחים פח.)]: **מה נורא.** תרגום מה דחילו אתרא הדין. דחילו שם דבר הוא, כמו סוכלתנו, וכסו למלבש: **וזה שער השמים.** מקום תפלה לעלות תפלתם [ס"א תפלות] השמימה. ומדרשו, שבית המקדש של מעלה מכוון כנגד בית המקדש של מטה (ב"ר סט:ז; תרגום יונתן; ירושלמי ברכות ד:ה):

enced much degradation. [See *Overview* to ArtScroll *Daniel*.]

15. אֵת אֲשֶׁר־דִּבַּרְתִּי לָךְ — *That which I have spoken concerning you.* "Do not fear Esau or Laban, because I am with you and will not leave you until I have completed what I promised regarding you. I promised Abraham to give this land to his offspring (12:7), but it is only through you — not through Esau — that this promise will be fulfilled" (*Rashi*).

16. וַיִּיקַץ יַעֲקֹב — *Jacob awoke.* He understood clearly that his dream was a prophecy, for when prophets are shown a vision, they recognize it to be a communication from God (*Moreh Nevuchim*).

17. בֵּית־אֱלֹהִים — *The house of God.* This is not an ordinary place, but a sanctuary of God's Name, a place suitable for prayer (*Targum Yonasan*). Furthermore, it is *the gate of the heavens,* meaning that it is the site from which man's prayers go up to God. Midrashically, the Heavenly Temple corresponds to the earthly Temple, so that Jacob was at the place that is the most propitious for prayer and service (*Rashi*).

הָעִיר לָרִאשֹׁנָה׃ כ וַיִּדַּר יַעֲקֹב נֶדֶר לֵאמֹר אִם־

‹ If ‹‹ saying, ‹ a vow, ‹ Then Jacob vowed 20 ‹‹ originally. ‹ of the city

יִהְיֶה אֱלֹהִים עִמָּדִי וּשְׁמָרַנִי בַּדֶּרֶךְ הַזֶּה אֲשֶׁר

‹ that ‹ on this way ‹ and He will guard me ‹‹ with me, ‹ God will be

אָנֹכִי הוֹלֵךְ וְנָתַן־לִי לֶחֶם לֶאֱכֹל וּבֶגֶד לִלְבֹּשׁ׃

‹‹ to wear; ‹ and clothes ‹ to eat ‹ bread ‹ me ‹ and He will give ‹‹ am going; ‹ I

21 כא וְשַׁבְתִּי בְשָׁלוֹם אֶל־בֵּית אָבִי וְהָיָה יהוה לִי

‹ to me ‹ and HASHEM will be ‹‹ of my father, ‹ the house ‹ to ‹ in peace ‹ and I will return

לֵאלֹהִים׃ כב וְהָאֶבֶן הַזֹּאת אֲשֶׁר־שַׂמְתִּי מַצֵּבָה יִהְיֶה בֵּית אֱלֹהִים וְכֹל

‹ and all ‹‹ of God, ‹ a house ‹ shall become ‹ as a monument ‹ I have set up ‹ which ‹ — then this stone 22 ‹‹ a God

אֲשֶׁר תִּתֶּן־לִי עַשֵּׂר אֲעַשְּׂרֶנּוּ לָךְ׃ שני [כט] א וַיִּשָּׂא יַעֲקֹב רַגְלָיו וַיֵּלֶךְ

‹ and went ‹ his feet ‹ So Jacob lifted 1 29 ‹‹ to You. ‹ I shall repeatedly tithe it ‹ me ‹ You will give ‹ that

דְּקַרְתָּא בְּקַדְמֵיתָא׃ כ וְקַיֵּים יַעֲקֹב קְיָם לְמֵימָר אִם יְהֵא מֵימְרָא דַייָ בְּסַעְדִּי וְיִטְּרִנַּנִי בְּאָרְחָא הָדֵין דִּי אֲנָא אָזֵל וְיִתֶּן לִי לַחְמָא (נ״א לְחֵם) לְמֵיכַל וּכְסוּ לְמִלְבָּשׁ׃ כא וְאֵיתוּב בִּשְׁלָם לְבֵית אַבָּא וִיהֵא מֵימְרָא דַייָ לִי לֶאֱלָהָא׃ כב וְאַבְנָא הָדָא דִּי שַׁוֵּיתִי קָמָא תְּהֵי דִּי אֱהֵי פָּלַח עֲלַהּ (מִן) קֳדָם יְיָ וְכֹל דִּי תִּתֶּן לִי חַד מִן עַסְרָא אַפְרְשִׁנֵּהּ קֳדָמָךְ׃ א וּנְטַל יַעֲקֹב רַגְלוֹהִי (נ״א רִיגְלוֹהִי) וַאֲזַל

רש״י

(כ) **אם יהיה אלהים עמדי.** אם ישמור לי הבטחות הללו שהבטיחני להיות עמדי, כמו שאמר לי והנה אנכי עמך (לעיל פסוק טו; ב״ר ע:ד): **ושמרני.** כמו שאמר לי ושמרתיך בכל אשר תלך (לעיל שם; ב״ר סט:ו): **ונתן לי לחם לאכול.** כמו שאמר כי לא אעזבך (שם ושם), והמבקש לחם הוא קרוי נעזב, שנאמר ולא ראיתי צדיק נעזב וזרעו מבקש לחם (תהלים לז:כה; ב״ר שם): (**כא**) **ושבתי.** כמו שאמר לי והשיבותיך אל האדמה (לעיל שם): **בשלום.** שלם מן החטא, שלא אלמד מדרכי לבן: **והיה ה׳ לי לאלהים.** שיחול שמו עלי מתחלה ועד סוף, שלא ימצא פסול בזרעי (ספרי ואתחנן לא), כמ״ש אשר דברתי לך (לעיל שם), והבטחה זו הבטיח לאברהם, שנאמר להיות לך לאלהים ולזרעך אחריך (שם יז:ז) [זרעך מיוחס שלא ימצא בו שום פסול]: (**כב**) **והאבן הזאת.** כך מפורש וי״ו זו של והאבן, אם תעשה לי את אלה ואף אני אעשה זאת: **והאבן הזאת אשר שמתי מצבה וגו׳.** כתרגומו אהי פלח עלה קדם ה׳. וכן עשה בשובו מפדן ארם כשאמר לו קום עלה בית אל (להלן לה:א), מה נאמר שם, ויצב יעקב מצבה וגו׳ ויסך עליה נסך (שם יד): (**א**) **וישא יעקב רגליו.** משנתבשר בשורה טובה שהובטח בשמירה נשא לבו את רגליו ונעשה

20. וַיִּדַּר יַעֲקֹב נֶדֶר לֵאמֹר — *Then Jacob vowed a vow, saying.* The word *saying* usually means that the statement was to be repeated to others, but in this case there was no one to whom Jacob could have repeated his vow. Accordingly, the Midrash derives that Jacob was "speaking" to future generations, as it were. He meant to set an example that in time of danger or distress, one should vow to perform good deeds, which will be a source of merit to rescue one from trouble.

אִם־יִהְיֶה אֱלֹהִים עִמָּדִי — *If God will be with me.* The "*if*" does not imply doubt that God would keep His word. Rather, Jacob feared that he might sin and forfeit God's protection (*Ramban*).

לֶחֶם לֶאֱכֹל וּבֶגֶד לִלְבֹּשׁ — *Bread to eat and clothes to wear,* so that poverty will not cause me to act against my own sense of propriety and God's will (*Sforno*). The righteous ask only for necessities; they have no need for luxuries (*Radak*).

21. וְהָיָה ה׳ לִי לֵאלֹהִים — *And HASHEM will be to me a God.* This is one of the conditions made by Jacob which, if carried out by God, would require him to fulfill his vow of the next verse. Jacob was beseeching God to rest His Name upon him and his offspring, so that there would be no blemish in his posterity, as God had promised to Abraham [17:7] (*Rashi*). *Gur Aryeh* explains that Jacob's statement cannot be understood as a promise of loyalty to God, because such an interpretation would imply that if God did not fulfill Jacob's requests, he would *not* accept HASHEM as his God. Clearly, Jacob would never say such a thing.

Ramban, however, holds that this was indeed part of Jacob's promise, meaning that if God permitted him to return safely, he would be able to serve God properly. As the Sages teach, "He who dwells outside *Eretz Yisrael* is like one who has no God" (*Kesubos* 110b) — so dramatic is the difference in holiness between the Land and the rest of the world.

22. עַשֵּׂר אֲעַשְּׂרֶנּוּ לָךְ — *I shall repeatedly tithe it to You.* Jacob's tithe included not only a tenth of earnings, but also his pledge to dedicate a tenth of his children to God's service. Specifically, this was the tribe of Levi, which was consecrated to serve God, and to whom Jacob imparted the esoteric teachings and wisdom of the Torah (*Bereishis Rabbah* 70:7).

That Jacob eventually set aside a tithe from his possessions is mentioned by *Rashi* in 32:14 and *Ibn Ezra* in 35:14. *R' Moshe Feinstein* stated that a Jew should tithe not only his possessions, but should also contribute time to the service of worthy causes.

29.

1-12. Jacob meets Rachel at the well.

Again, a well becomes the place where a mate is found for a major figure in Jewish history. At a well, Eliezer found Rebecca, and later Moses met Zipporah at a well. Also, as the stories of

אַרְצָה בְנֵי־קֶדֶם: ב וַיַּרְא וְהִנֵּה בְאֵר בַּשָּׂדֶה וְהִנֵּה־

< And there were «in the field! < a well < [that] there was < He saw **2** « of the east. < of the people < toward the land

שָׁם שְׁלֹשָׁה עֶדְרֵי־צֹאן רֹבְצִים עָלֶיהָ כִּי מִן־

< from < for « beside it, < lying < of flocks < droves < three < there

הַבְּאֵר הַהִוא יַשְׁקוּ הָעֲדָרִים וְהָאֶבֶן גְּדֹלָה עַל־

< over < was large < and the stone « the droves, < they would water < that well

פִּי הַבְּאֵר: ג וְנֶאֶסְפוּ־שָׁמָּה כָל־הָעֲדָרִים וְגָלְלוּ

< they would roll « the droves, < were all < there < [When] assembled **3** « of the well. < the opening

אֶת־הָאֶבֶן מֵעַל פִּי הַבְּאֵר וְהִשְׁקוּ אֶת־הַצֹּאן וְהֵשִׁיבוּ אֶת־הָאֶבֶן עַל־

< over < the stone < then they would return « the flocks; < and they would water « of the well < the mouth < from upon < the stone

פִּי הַבְּאֵר לִמְקֹמָהּ: ד וַיֹּאמֶר לָהֶם יַעֲקֹב אַחַי מֵאַיִן אַתֶּם וַיֹּאמְרוּ מֵחָרָן

< *From Haran* « And they said, « *are you?* < *from where* < *My brothers,* « did Jacob, « to them, < He said **4** « to its place. < of the well < the opening

אֲנָחְנוּ: ה וַיֹּאמֶר לָהֶם הַיְדַעְתֶּם אֶת־לָבָן בֶּן־נָחוֹר וַיֹּאמְרוּ יָדָעְנוּ: ו וַיֹּאמֶר

< Then he said **6** « *We know.* « And they said, « *of Nahor?* < *the son* < *Laban* < *Do you know* « to them, < He said **5** « *are we.*

לָהֶם הֲשָׁלוֹם לוֹ וַיֹּאמְרוּ שָׁלוֹם וְהִנֵּה רָחֵל בִּתּוֹ בָּאָה עִם־הַצֹּאן:

« *the flock!* < *with* < *is coming* < *his daughter* < *Rachel* < *and here* « *It is well;* « They said, « *with him?* < *Is it well* « to them,

לַאֲרַע בְּנֵי מָדִינְחָא: ב וַחֲזָא וְהָא בֵירָא בְּחַקְלָא וְהָא תַמָּן תְּלָתָא עֶדְרִין דְּעָן רְבְעִין עֲלַהּ אֲרֵי מִן בֵּירָא הַהִיא מַשְׁקַן עֲדָרַיָּא וְאַבְנָא רַבְּתָא עַל פּוּמָא דְבֵירָא: ג וּמִתְכַּנְשִׁין לְתַמָּן כָּל עֲדָרַיָּא וּמְגַנְדְּרִין יָת אַבְנָא מֵעַל פּוּמָא דְבֵירָא וּמַשְׁקַן יָת עָנָא וּמְתִיבִין יָת אַבְנָא עַל פּוּמָא דְבֵירָא לְאַתְרַהּ: ד וַאֲמַר לְהוֹן יַעֲקֹב אַחַי מְנָן אַתּוּן וַאֲמָרוּ מֵחָרָן אֲנָחְנָא: ה וַאֲמַר לְהוֹן הַיְדַעְתּוּן יָת לָבָן בַּר נָחוֹר וַאֲמָרוּ יָדְעְנָא: ו וַאֲמַר לְהוֹן הַשְׁלָם לֵהּ וַאֲמָרוּ שְׁלָם וְהָא רָחֵל בְּרַתֵּהּ אָתְיָא עִם עָנָא:

רש"י

קל ללכת. כך מפורש בבראשית רבה (ע:ח): (ב) **ישקו העדרים.** משקים הרועים את העדרים, והמקרא דבר בלשון קצרה: (ג) **ונאספו.** רגילים היו להאסף, לפי שהיתה האבן גדולה: **וגללו.** וגוללין, ותרגומו ומגנדרין. כל לשון הווה משתנה לדבר בלשון עתיד ובל' עבר, לפי שכל דבר ההוה תמיד כבר היה ועתיד להיות: **והשיבו.** תרגומו ומתיבין: (ו) **באה עם הצאן.** הטעם באל"ף, ותרגומו אתיא. ורחל באה הטעם למעלה בבי"ת, ותרגומו אתת. הראשון לשון עושה והשני לשון עשתה:

Abraham and Isaac have shown, wells were important in symbolic ways. Commentators note that wisdom is symbolized by the water below the ground; it is buried and hidden, but it is accessible to those who understand that it is vital to life and worthy of the intense effort needed to bring it to the surface. Women, too, represent wisdom: *Wisdom of women builds her home (Proverbs* 14:1), as when Abraham hesitated to send away Hagar and Ishmael at Sarah's insistence and God told him to do everything she asked of him (21:12). It is understandable, therefore, that the human symbols of wisdom were associated with the earthly symbols of wisdom.

1. וַיִּשָּׂא יַעֲקֹב רַגְלָיו — *So Jacob lifted his feet.* At the good tidings of the prophecy assuring him of God's protection, his heart *lifted his feet* and he felt very light as he continued on his way (*Rashi*).

2. . . . וְהִנֵּה בְאֵר — *There was a well . . .!* The Torah narrates this incident at length to illustrate how those who trust in God shall renew their strength [*Isaiah* 40:31]. For though Jacob was weary from his long journey, he was able to roll away the stone unassisted, a task that usually required the combined effort of all the shepherds, as they explained to him in verse 8 (*Ramban*).

In the plain meaning, their reason for putting such a heavy boulder over the well was to protect the scarce water or to prevent children or objects from falling into the well. *R' Hirsch* comments, however, that it gives us an insight into the base character of the Arameans. No one trusted another or allowed anyone a possible advantage. There was a selfish fear that someone might get a bit more than his share of water, so they made it impossible for anyone to get water unless others were present to monitor his use of the well.

5. לָבָן בֶּן־נָחוֹר — *Laban the son* [descendant] *of Nahor*. Laban was Nahor's *grandson;* his father was Bethuel.

6. הֲשָׁלוֹם לוֹ — *Is it well with him?* Jacob's sensitivity prompted him to ask about Laban's personal circumstances. Since he was about to visit Laban, he wanted to know how best to approach him (*Sforno*).

Realizing that Jacob wanted to know more about Laban's per-

7 וַיֹּאמֶר הֵן עוֹד הַיּוֹם גָּדוֹל לֹא־עֵת הֵאָסֵף הַמִּקְנֶה
He said, Indeed, yet the day is long; it is not time to bring in the livestock;
הַשְׁקוּ הַצֹּאן וּלְכוּ רְעוּ׃ 8 וַיֹּאמְרוּ לֹא נוּכַל עַד
water the flocks and go and graze. 8 But they said, We are not able to, until
אֲשֶׁר יֵאָסְפוּ כָּל־הָעֲדָרִים וְגָלְלוּ אֶת־הָאֶבֶן מֵעַל
when are gathered all the droves, and they will roll the stone from upon
פִּי הַבְּאֵר וְהִשְׁקִינוּ הַצֹּאן׃ 9 עוֹדֶנּוּ מְדַבֵּר עִמָּם
the opening of the well; then we will water the flocks. 9 He was still speaking with them,
וְרָחֵל ׀ בָּאָה עִם־הַצֹּאן אֲשֶׁר לְאָבִיהָ כִּי רֹעָה הִוא׃ 10 וַיְהִי כַּאֲשֶׁר
when Rachel arrived with the flock that belonged to her father, for a shepherdess was she. 10 And it was, when
רָאָה יַעֲקֹב אֶת־רָחֵל בַּת־לָבָן אֲחִי אִמּוֹ וְאֶת־צֹאן לָבָן אֲחִי אִמּוֹ
Jacob saw Rachel, daughter of Laban, brother of his mother, and the flock of Laban, brother of his mother,
וַיִּגַּשׁ יַעֲקֹב וַיָּגֶל אֶת־הָאֶבֶן מֵעַל פִּי הַבְּאֵר וַיַּשְׁקְ אֶת־צֹאן לָבָן אֲחִי
Jacob came forward and rolled the stone from upon the opening of the well and he watered the flock of Laban, brother
אִמּוֹ׃ 11 וַיִּשַּׁק יַעֲקֹב לְרָחֵל וַיִּשָּׂא אֶת־קֹלוֹ וַיֵּבְךְּ׃ 12 וַיַּגֵּד יַעֲקֹב לְרָחֵל
of his mother. 11 Then Jacob kissed Rachel; and he raised his voice and he wept. 12 Jacob told Rachel

ז וַאֲמַר הָא עוֹד יוֹמָא סַגִּי לָא עִדַּן לְמִכְנַשׁ בְּעִיר אַשְׁקוּ עָנָא וְאֱזִילוּ רְעוּ׃ ח וַאֲמָרוּ לָא נִכּוֹל עַד דִּי יִתְכַּנְּשׁוּן (נ״א מִתְכַּנְּשִׁין) כָּל עֲדָרַיָּא וִיגַנְדְּרוּן (נ״א וּמְגַנְדְּרִין) יָת אַבְנָא מֵעַל פּוּמָא דְבֵירָא וְנַשְׁקֵי עָנָא׃ ט עַד דְּהוּא מְמַלֵּל עִמְּהוֹן וְרָחֵל אֲתָת עִם עָנָא דִּי לַאֲבוּהָא אֲרֵי רָעִיתָא הִיא׃ י וַהֲוָה כַּד חֲזָא יַעֲקֹב יָת רָחֵל בַּת לָבָן אֲחוּהָא דְאִמֵּהּ וְיָת עָנָא דְלָבָן אֲחוּהָא דְאִמֵּהּ וּקְרֵב יַעֲקֹב וְגַנְדַּר יָת אַבְנָא מֵעַל פּוּמָא דְבֵירָא וְאַשְׁקֵי יָת עָנָא דְלָבָן אֲחוּהָא דְאִמֵּהּ׃ יא וּנְשַׁק יַעֲקֹב לְרָחֵל וַאֲרֵים יָת קָלֵהּ וּבְכָא׃ יב וְחַוִּי יַעֲקֹב לְרָחֵל אֲרֵי

רש״י

(ז) **הן עוד היום גדול.** לפי שראה אותם רובצים כסבור שרוצים לאסוף המקנה הביתה ולא ירעו עוד. אמר להם הן עוד היום גדול, כלומר, אם שכירי יום אתם לא השלמתם פעולת היום, ואם הבהמות שלכם אעפ״כ לא עת האסף המקנה וגו׳ (ב״ר ע:יא): (ח) **לא נוכל.** להשקות, לפי שהאבן גדולה: **וגללו.** זה מתורגם ויגנדרון, לפי שהוא לשון עתיד: (י) **ויגש יעקב ויגל.** כאדם שמעביר את הפקק מעל פי צלוחית, להודיעך שכחו גדול (ב״ר ע:יב): (יא) **ויבך.** לפי שצפה ברוח הקודש שאינה נכנסת עמו לקבורה (שם). ד״א, לפי שבא בידים ריקניות. אמר, אליעזר עבד אבי אבא היו בידיו נזמים וצמידים ומגדנות, ואני אין בידי כלום (שם). לפי שרדף אליפז בן עשו במצות אביו אחריו להורגו, והשיגו, ולפי שגדל אליפז בחיקו של יצחק (דברים רבה ב:כ) משך ידו. א״ל, מה אעשה לצווי של אבא. אמר לו יעקב, טול מה שבידי, והעני חשוב כמת (ברב״ת):

sonal life than they could tell him, they pointed out his daughter, as if to say: *"Look, his daughter is coming* — perhaps you should ask her your questions directly" (*Haamek Davar*).

9. כִּי רֹעָה הִוא — *For a shepherdess was she.* Rachel was Laban's only shepherd. Leah did not share this chore, either because the sun might have been harmful to her weak eyes [see v. 17], or because she was older, and Laban was afraid to let her mingle with the shepherds. Rachel, however, was still too young to arouse the interest of the shepherd boys (*Ramban*).

That Rachel came leading all of Laban's sheep indicates that the flock was small. Indeed, Laban became prosperous only after Jacob began working for him [see 30:30]. Even so, Rachel must have been a skilled shepherdess to tend even a small flock by herself at such a young age (*Or HaChaim*).

11. וַיֵּבְךְּ — *And he wept.* Jacob wept because he foresaw that Rachel would not be buried with him in the Cave of Machpelah. Another reason he wept was because he had come empty-handed. He thought: "Eliezer, who was only my grandfather's *servant*, came for my mother laden with riches, while I come here destitute." Isaac had given Jacob money and gifts when he sent him to Haran, but Esau had ordered his son Eliphaz to ambush Jacob and kill him. Eliphaz pursued and found Jacob, but, having been raised by Isaac, he could not bring himself to kill. Eliphaz asked Jacob, "What about my father's command?" Jacob told him that he could be in technical compliance with Esau's order by taking away all of the wealth that Isaac had sent, and thus impoverishing him, Jacob, for the Sages say that a poor person is tantamount to a dead man. Eliphaz complied. Thus, when Jacob met Rachel, he had nothing to give her (*Rashi* citing Midrash).

כִּי אֲחִי אָבִיהָ הוּא וְכִי בֶן־רִבְקָה הוּא וַתָּרָץ
‹ then she ran «‹ was he; ‹ of Rebecca ‹ a son ‹ and that «‹ was he, ‹ of her father ‹ a relative ‹ that

וַתַּגֵּד לְאָבִיהָ: יג וַיְהִי כִשְׁמֹעַ לָבָן אֶת־שֵׁמַע
‹ the news ‹ when Laban heard ‹ And it was, 13 « her father. ‹ and told

יַעֲקֹב בֶּן־אֲחֹתוֹ וַיָּרָץ לִקְרָאתוֹ וַיְחַבֶּק־לוֹ וַיְנַשֶּׁק־
‹ kissed ‹ him, ‹ hugged ‹ toward him, ‹ he ran «‹ his sister, ‹ son of ‹ of Jacob,

לוֹ וַיְבִיאֵהוּ אֶל־בֵּיתוֹ וַיְסַפֵּר לְלָבָן אֵת כָּל־
‹ all ‹ to Laban ‹ he recounted «‹ his house; ‹ to ‹ and brought him ‹ him,

הַדְּבָרִים הָאֵלֶּה: יד וַיֹּאמֶר לוֹ לָבָן אַךְ עַצְמִי וּבְשָׂרִי אָתָּה וַיֵּשֶׁב עִמּוֹ
‹ with him ‹ And he stayed «‹ *you are!* ‹ *and my flesh* ‹ *my bone* ‹ *Nevertheless,* «‹ did ‹ to him ‹ Then say Laban, 14 « these events.

חֹדֶשׁ יָמִים: טו וַיֹּאמֶר לָבָן לְיַעֲקֹב הֲכִי־אָחִי אַתָּה וַעֲבַדְתַּנִי חִנָּם
«‹ *for nothing?* ‹ *should you serve me* ‹ *you are,* ‹ *my relative* ‹ *Just because* «‹ to Jacob, ‹ Then Laban said 15 « of days. ‹ a month

הַגִּידָה לִּי מַה־מַּשְׂכֻּרְתֶּךָ: טז וּלְלָבָן שְׁתֵּי בָנוֹת שֵׁם הַגְּדֹלָה לֵאָה וְשֵׁם
‹ and the name ‹ was Leah ‹ of the older one ‹ The name «‹ daughters. ‹ two ‹ (Laban had 16 « *are your wages?* ‹ *What* «‹ *me:* ‹ *Tell*

הַקְּטַנָּה רָחֵל: יז וְעֵינֵי לֵאָה רַכּוֹת וְרָחֵל הָיְתָה יְפַת־תֹּאַר וִיפַת מַרְאֶה:
«‹ of appearance.) ‹ and beautiful ‹ of form ‹ beautiful ‹ was ‹ while Rachel «‹ were soft, ‹ of Leah ‹ The eyes 17 « was Rachel. ‹ of the younger one

בַּר אֲחַת (נ״א אֲרֵי אֲחִי) דַאֲבוּהָא הוּא וַאֲרֵי בַּר רִבְקָה הוּא וּרְהָטַת וְחַוִּיאַת לַאֲבוּהָא: יג וַהֲוָה כַּד שְׁמַע לָבָן יָת שֵׁמַע יַעֲקֹב בַּר אֲחָתֵהּ וּרְהַט לְקַדָּמוּתֵהּ וְגַפֵּף לֵהּ וְנַשִּׁיק לֵהּ וְאַעֲלֵהּ לְבֵיתֵהּ וְאִשְׁתָּעִי לְלָבָן יָת כָּל פִּתְגָּמַיָּא הָאִלֵּין: יד וַאֲמַר לֵהּ לָבָן בְּרַם קָרִיבִי וּבִשְׂרִי אַתְּ וִיתֵיב עִמֵּהּ יְרַח יוֹמִין: טו וַאֲמַר לָבָן לְיַעֲקֹב הֲמִדְּאָחִי אַתְּ וְתִפְלְחִנַּנִי מַגָּן חַוִּי לִי מָה אַגְרָךְ: טז וּלְלָבָן תַּרְתֵּין בְּנָן שׁוּם רַבְּתָא לֵאָה וְשׁוּם זְעֶרְתָּא רָחֵל: יז וְעֵינֵי לֵאָה יָאֲיָן וְרָחֵל הֲוַת שַׁפִּירָא בְרֵיוָא וְיָאָה בְחֶזְוָא:

רש״י

(יב) **כי אחי אביה הוא.** קרוב לאביה, כמו אנשים אחים אנחנו (לעיל יג:ח; פדר״א פל״ו). ומדרשו, אם לרמאות הוא בא גם אני אחיו ברמאות, ואם אדם כשר הוא גם אני בן רבקה אחותו הכשרה (ב״ר שם יג; ב״ב קכג.): **ותגד לאביה.** לפי שאמה מתה ולא היה לה להגיד אלא לו (ב״ר שם): (יג) **וירץ לקראתו.** כסבור ממון הוא טעון, שהרי עבד הבית בא לכאן בעשרה גמלים טעונים (שם): **ויחבק [לו].** כשלא ראה עמו כלום אמר שמא זהובים הביא והנם בחיקו (שם): **וינשק לו.** אמר שמא מרגליות הביא והם בפיו (שם): **ויספר ללבן.** שלא בא אלא מתוך אונס אחיו, ושנטלו ממונו ממנו (ב״ר ע:יג): (יד) **אך עצמי ובשרי.** מעתה אין לי לאספך הביתה הואיל ואין בידך כלום, אלא מפני קורבה אטפל בך חדש ימים (שם יד) וכן עשה, ואף זו לא לחנם, שהיה רועה צאנו: (טו) **הכי אחי אתה.** לשון תימה. וכי בשביל שאחי אתה תעבדני חנם: **ועבדתני.** כמו ותעבדני (אונקלוס). וכן כל תיבה שהיא לשון עבר הוסף וי״ו בראשה והיא הופכת התיבה להבא: (יז) **רכות.** שהיתה סבורה לעלות בגורלו של עשו ובוכה,

12. כִּי אֲחִי אָבִיהָ הוּא — *That a relative* [lit., *brother*] *of her father was he.* In addition to the plain meaning that Jacob introduced himself to Rachel as her relative, *Rashi* cites the Midrashic interpretation. He intimated that should Laban try to cheat him, he could defend himself by being Laban's *brother* in deceit; but if Laban dealt honorably, Jacob would act with all of the integrity expected of a son of Rebecca. *Or HaChaim* elaborates that Jacob was surely not threatening to match Laban's thievery. Rather, he meant to say that he would defend himself strenuously, but only within the law.

13. וַיָּרָץ לִקְרָאתוֹ — *He ran toward him.* The greedy Laban came running at the very mention of Jacob's name, confident that Jacob must be laden with wealth and precious gifts. If a mere servant, Eliezer, had come with ten richly laden camels (24:10), surely Isaac's heir must be enormously wealthy (*Rashi*).

Seeing that Jacob was empty-handed, Laban thought that he might have money hidden on his person. He therefore *embraced* him, to feel surreptitiously whether he had any hidden treasures (*Rashi* based on Midrash).

14. אַךְ עַצְמִי וּבְשָׂרִי אָתָּה — *Nevertheless, my bone and my flesh you are!* The expression *nevertheless* indicates it is not the desired course. Indeed, in Laban's mind, if Jacob had no money, then he was not worthy of hospitality; *nevertheless* Laban "magnanimously" put family loyalty ahead of his usual avarice and invited him to stay for a month as a guest. As indicated by the next verse, Jacob worked even during that time, and Laban realized that he was a valuable commodity, so he invited Jacob to negotiate terms of permanent employment *(Rashi).*

17. וְעֵינֵי לֵאָה רַכּוֹת — *The eyes of Leah were soft,* because she wept constantly in prayer that she would not have to marry Esau. People used to say that since Rebecca has two sons and Laban two daughters, the elder daughter would be married to

שלישי יח וַיֶּאֱהַב יַעֲקֹב אֶת־רָחֵל וַיֹּאמֶר אֶעֱבָדְךָ שֶׁבַע
18 Jacob loved < Rachel, < so he said, << I will work for you < seven <

שָׁנִים בְּרָחֵל בִּתְּךָ הַקְּטַנָּה: יט וַיֹּאמֶר לָבָן טוֹב
years < for Rachel < your daughter < who is younger. << 19 Laban said, << It is better <

תִּתִּי אֹתָהּ לָךְ מִתִּתִּי אֹתָהּ לְאִישׁ אַחֵר שְׁבָה
that I give < her < to you < than that I give < her < to another man; << reside <

עִמָּדִי: כ וַיַּעֲבֹד יַעֲקֹב בְּרָחֵל שֶׁבַע שָׁנִים וַיִּהְיוּ
with me. << 20 So Jacob worked < for Rachel < seven < years, << and they were <

בְעֵינָיו כְּיָמִים אֲחָדִים בְּאַהֲבָתוֹ אֹתָהּ: כא וַיֹּאמֶר יַעֲקֹב אֶל־לָבָן הָבָה
in his eyes < like a few days < because of his love < for her. << 21 Jacob said < to < Laban, << Give over <

אֶת־אִשְׁתִּי כִּי מָלְאוּ יָמַי וְאָבוֹאָה אֵלֶיהָ: כב וַיֶּאֱסֹף לָבָן אֶת־כָּל־אַנְשֵׁי
my wife < for < fulfilled < are my [stipulated] days, << and I will come < to her. << 22 So Laban gathered < all < the people <

הַמָּקוֹם וַיַּעַשׂ מִשְׁתֶּה: כג וַיְהִי בָעֶרֶב וַיִּקַּח אֶת־לֵאָה בִתּוֹ וַיָּבֵא אֹתָהּ
of the place < and he made < a feast. << 23 And it was < in the evening, << [that] he took < Leah < his daughter < and brought < her <

יח וּרְחֵים יַעֲקֹב יָת רָחֵל וַאֲמַר אֶפְלְחִנָּךְ שְׁבַע שְׁנִין בְּרָחֵל בְּרַתָּךְ זְעֶרְתָּא: יט וַאֲמַר לָבָן טַב דְּאֶתֵּן יָתַהּ לָךְ מִדְּאֶתֵּן יָתַהּ לִגְבַר אָחֳרָן תִּיב עִמִּי: כ וּפְלַח יַעֲקֹב בְּרָחֵל שְׁבַע שְׁנִין וַהֲווֹ בְעֵינוֹהִי כְּיוֹמִין זְעִירִין בִּדְרַחֲמֵהּ יָתַהּ: כא וַאֲמַר יַעֲקֹב לְלָבָן הַב יָת אִתְּתִי אֲרֵי אַשְׁלֵמִית יוֹמֵי פָלְחָנִי וְאֵעוֹל לְוָתַהּ: כב וּכְנַשׁ לָבָן יָת כָּל אֱנָשֵׁי אַתְרָא וַעֲבַד מִשְׁתְּיָא: כג וַהֲוָה בְרַמְשָׁא וּדְבַר יָת לֵאָה בְרַתֵּהּ וְאָעֵל יָתַהּ לְוָתֵהּ

רש"י

שהיו הכל אומרים שני בנים לרבקה ושתי בנות ללבן הגדולה לגדול והקטנה לקטן (ב"ר סם טז; ב"ב קכג.): [**תאר**. הוא לורת הפרלוף, לשון יתארהו בשרד (ישעיה מד:יג), קונפ"אש בלע"ז: **מראה**. הוא זיו קלסתר:] (**יח**) **אעבדך שבע שנים**. הם ימים אחדים שאמרה לו אמו, וישבת עמו ימים אחדים (לעיל כז:מד). ותדע שכן הוא, שהרי כתיב ויהיו בעיניו כימים אחדים (ב"ר שם יז): **ברחל בתך הקטנה**. כל הסימנים הללו למה. לפי שהיה יודע בו שהוא רמאי. אמר לו אעבדך ברחל. ושמא תאמר רחל אחרת מן השוק, ת"ל בתך. ושמא תאמר אחליף ללאה שמה ואקרא שמה רחל, ת"ל הקטנה. ואעפ"כ לא הועיל, שהרי רמהו (שם): (**כא**) **מלאו ימי**. שאמרה לי אמי. ועוד, מלאו ימי, שהרי אני בן פ"ד שנה, ואימתי אעמיד י"ב שבטים. וזהו שאמר ואבואה אליה, והלא קל שבקלים אינו אומר כן, אלא להוליד תולדות אמר כך (שם יח):

the elder son, while the younger daughter was destined to marry the younger son (*Rashi*).

Great is prayer, for Leah's prayer brought about annulment of the decree that she marry Esau, and even allowed her to be the first to marry Jacob and have children with him (*Midrash*).

18. אֶעֱבָדְךָ שֶׁבַע שָׁנִים — *I will work for you seven years.* In response to Laban's wish to negotiate monetary terms, Jacob said, "Do you think I came here for your money? My wish is to *marry Rachel your younger daughter* and begin the sacred task of building Israel!" (*Chasam Sofer*).

בְּרָחֵל בִּתְּךָ הַקְּטַנָּה — *For Rachel your daughter who is younger.* This term has become the idiom for terms spelled out as clearly as possible. Knowing of Laban's proclivity for twisting the truth, Jacob specified as carefully as he could who his bride was to be: not just any girl named Rachel and not just any daughter of Laban. But all his precautions were to no avail (*Rashi*).

19. טוֹב תִּתִּי — *It is better that I give.* Laban did not agree to Jacob's request for Rachel. His statement is a value judgment that it would be better for her to marry Jacob than another man, but makes no commitment.

20. בְּאַהֲבָתוֹ אֹתָהּ — *Because of his love for her.* Only his great love for Rachel permitted Jacob to consider seven long years as if they were only a few days; for Rachel's sake they were a trivial price to pay (*Mizrachi*).

21. הָבָה אֶת־אִשְׁתִּי — *Give over my wife.* After seven years, Laban said nothing; Jacob was forced to approach Laban to remind him of the arrangement (*Ralbag*).

Jacob's expression *and I will come to her* would have been vulgar in a lesser person. Jacob's only intent was that he was already 84 years old and he had to begin his mission of bringing the twelve tribes into the world. His concern was to serve God, not physical pleasure (*Rashi*).

22-25. Laban substitutes Leah for Rachel. Living up to his reputation as a deceitful rogue, Laban substituted Leah for Rachel on the wedding night. Jacob and Rachel expected Laban to attempt such a deception, and they prepared against it by arranging a secret signal between them. Seeing that they were about to substitute her sister Leah for her, however, Rachel confided the sign to her sister so that Leah would not be put to shame. Laban "magnanimously" presented the bride with Zilpah as a maidservant, but this was part of his ruse. Zilpah was the younger of two maids in the household, and it was assumed that

אֵלָיו וַיָּבֹא אֵלֶיהָ׃ כד וַיִּתֵּן לָבָן לָהּ אֶת־זִלְפָּה

< Zilpah < to her < — And Laban gave 24 << to her. < and he came << to him;

שִׁפְחָתוֹ לְלֵאָה בִתּוֹ שִׁפְחָה׃ כה וַיְהִי בַבֹּקֶר וְהִנֵּה־

< that here < in the morning, < And it was, 25 << as a maid-servant. < his daughter < — to Leah << his maidservant

הִוא לֵאָה וַיֹּאמֶר אֶל־לָבָן מַה־זֹּאת עָשִׂיתָ לִּי

<< to me? < you have done < is this < What << Laban, < to < So he said << was Leah! < she

וְעַל לְוָתַהּ׃ כד וִיהַב לָבָן לַהּ יָת זִלְפָּה אַמְתַהּ לְלֵאָה בְרַתֵּהּ לְאַמְהוּ׃ כה וַהֲוָה בְצַפְרָא וְהָא הִיא לֵאָה וַאֲמַר לְלָבָן מָה דָא עֲבַדְתָּ לִי הֲלָא בְרָחֵל פְּלָחִית עִמָּךְ וּלְמָא שַׁקַּרְתָּ בִּי׃ כו וַאֲמַר לָבָן לָא מִתְעֲבֵד כְּדֵין בְּאַתְרָנָא לְמִתַּן זְעֶרְתָּא קֳדָם רַבְּתָא׃ כז אַשְׁלִים שְׁבוּעֲתָא דְדָא וְנִתֵּן לָךְ אַף יָת דָּא בְּפָלְחָנָא דִי תִפְלַח עִמִּי עוֹד שְׁבַע שְׁנִין אָחֳרָנִין׃

הֲלֹא בְרָחֵל עָבַדְתִּי עִמָּךְ וְלָמָּה רִמִּיתָנִי׃ כו וַיֹּאמֶר לָבָן לֹא־יֵעָשֶׂה

< It is not done << Laban said, 26 << have you deceived me? < Why << for you? < that I worked < for Rachel < Was it not

כֵן בִּמְקוֹמֵנוּ לָתֵת הַצְּעִירָה לִפְנֵי הַבְּכִירָה׃ כז מַלֵּא שְׁבֻעַ זֹאת וְנִתְּנָה

< and we will give < of this one < the week < Complete 27 << the elder. < before < the younger < to give << in our place, < so

לְךָ גַּם־אֶת־זֹאת בַּעֲבֹדָה אֲשֶׁר תַּעֲבֹד עִמָּדִי עוֹד שֶׁבַע־שָׁנִים אֲחֵרוֹת׃

<< additional. < years < seven < another < for me < you will perform < which < for the work < this [other] one, < also < to you

רש"י

(כה) **ויהי בבקר והנה היא לאה,** אבל בלילה לא היתה לאה. לפי שמסר יעקב סימנים לרחל. וכשראתה רחל שמכניסין לו לאה אמרה עכשיו תכלם אחותי, עמדה ומסרה לה אותן סימנים (מגילה יג:; ב"ב קכג.): (כז) **מלא שבע זאת.** דבוק הוא, שהרי נקוד בחטף. שבוע של זאת (אונקלוס) והן שבעת ימי המשתה. בגמ' ירושלמית במ"ק (א:ז). [וא"א לומר שבוע ממש, שאם כן היה צריך לינקד בפתח הסי"ן. ועוד, ששבוע לשון זכר, כדכתיב שבעה שבועות תספר לך (דברים טז:ט). לפיכך אין משמע שבוע אלא שבעה, שטיי"א בלע"ז]: **ונתנה לך.** לשון רבים כמו ונשרפה, נרדה ונבלה (לעיל יא:ג,ז) אף זו לשון ונתן (אונקלוס): **ונתנה וגו' גם את זאת.** מיד [לאחר שבעת ימי המשתה],

she would become the maidservant of the younger sister, while Bilhah, the older maid, would become the servant of Leah. Thus, by presenting Zilpah to the bride, Laban fortified the deception that she was Rachel (*Rashi* from *Megillah* 13b).

All of Laban's machinations, however, could not have succeeded had not God wanted them to, for it is illogical to believe that Jacob could not have detected something amiss until the morning. Despite Rachel's incredible unselfishness and Laban's equally incredible dishonesty, the marriage to Leah took place unimpeded because God's plan required that Jacob and Leah become husband and wife — in fact, in a real sense, she became his primary wife, because she had as many sons as Jacob's three other wives combined, and she, not Rachel, was buried with Jacob in the Cave of Machpelah. On the wedding night, Jacob's acute spiritual antenna recognized that he was with the partner who was destined for him, and that is why he detected nothing wrong (*R' Aharon Kotler).*

Michtav MeEliyahu explains the respective roles of the two sisters. Rachel was Jacob's intended mate for *this* world; Leah was his intended mate for the higher world of the spirit. Rachel was the wife of *Jacob* and Leah was the wife of *Israel* — the name signifying his higher spiritual role of the future. It is illustrative of this concept that Rachel produced Joseph, who would save his family from famine, but Leah produced Levi and Judah, the tribes of priesthood and the Davidic, Messianic monarchy. Because his destiny was to *become* Israel, he had to marry Leah, and God arranged for him to do so, contrary to his perceptions at that moment. The Midrash declares, "Jacob dedicated his entire being to work [for Laban] only because of Rachel." Rachel — the "beautiful" one who attracted the notice of people occupied with the activity of the material world — represents the mission of elevating and ultimately conquering *this* world.

26. לֹא־יֵעָשֶׂה כֵן בִּמְקוֹמֵנוּ לָתֵת הַצְּעִירָה לִפְנֵי הַבְּכִירָה — *It is not done so in our place to give the younger before the elder.* Our citizenry will not permit it (*Ramban);* the people would not allow me to keep my word (*Sforno*). Ever the rogue, Laban justified his wicked act by shifting responsibility. He portrayed himself as having been forced to do so, because the community, or some vague influential body, compelled him to act in this way (*R' Hoffmann*).

But why did Laban weaken the moral justification for his action by limiting the rule of marrying the older before the younger to בִּמְקוֹמֵנוּ, *in our place*? And why did he describe Leah and Rachel as בְּכִירָה and צְעִירָה, instead of גְּדֹלָה and קְטַנָּה as they are described everywhere else? Although both sets of words are translated as *older* and *younger,* the usage here of בְּכִירָה and צְעִירָה invokes the term for *firstborn,* בְּכוֹר [and alludes to the word for blessing, בְּרָכָה]. Thus Laban is delivering a barbed rebuke to Jacob: In your place you transform the younger, the צָעִיר, into בְּכוֹר, the older, as you stole Esau's birthright blessing. But here, we don't change the birth order (*R' Eliezer Ashkenazi*).

27. שְׁבֻעַ זֹאת — *The week of this one.* Laban promised that as soon as the seven days of Leah's wedding feast were over, Jacob could marry Rachel and *then* "pay" for her by working for an-

כח וַיַּעַשׂ יַעֲקֹב כֵּן וַיְמַלֵּא שְׁבֻעַ זֹאת וַיִּתֶּן־לוֹ

28 And Jacob did / so / and he completed / the week / for this one; / and he gave him

אֶת־רָחֵל בִּתּוֹ לוֹ לְאִשָּׁה: כט וַיִּתֵּן לָבָן לְרָחֵל בִּתּוֹ

Rachel, / his daughter, / to him / as a wife. 29 And Laban gave / to Rachel / his daughter

אֶת־בִּלְהָה שִׁפְחָתוֹ לָהּ לְשִׁפְחָה: ל וַיָּבֹא גַּם אֶל־

Bilhah / his maidservant / – to her / as a maidservant. 30 He came / also / to

רָחֵל וַיֶּאֱהַב גַּם־אֶת־רָחֵל מִלֵּאָה וַיַּעֲבֹד עִמּוֹ עוֹד

Rachel / and he loved / also / Rachel / [but] more than Leah; / and he worked / for him / another

שֶׁבַע־שָׁנִים אֲחֵרוֹת: לא וַיַּרְא יהוה כִּי־שְׂנוּאָה לֵאָה וַיִּפְתַּח אֶת־רַחְמָהּ

seven / years / additional. 31 HASHEM saw / that / unloved / was Leah, / so He opened / her womb;

וְרָחֵל עֲקָרָה: לב וַתַּהַר לֵאָה וַתֵּלֶד בֵּן וַתִּקְרָא שְׁמוֹ רְאוּבֵן כִּי אָמְרָה

but Rachel / [remained] barren. 32 Leah conceived / and bore / a son, / and she called / his name / Reuben, / as / she had declared,

כִּי־רָאָה יהוה בְּעָנְיִי כִּי עַתָּה יֶאֱהָבַנִי אִישִׁי: לג וַתַּהַר עוֹד וַתֵּלֶד בֵּן

Because / HASHEM has discerned / my humiliation, / for / now / love me / will my husband. 33 And she conceived / again / and bore / a son

וַתֹּאמֶר כִּי־שָׁמַע יהוה כִּי־שְׂנוּאָה אָנֹכִי וַיִּתֶּן־לִי גַּם־אֶת־זֶה וַתִּקְרָא

and she declared, / *Because / HASHEM has heard / that / unloved / am I, / He has given / me / also / this one,* / and she called

כח וַעֲבַד יַעֲקֹב כֵּן וְאַשְׁלֵם שְׁבוּעֲתָא דְדָא וִיהַב לֵהּ יָת רָחֵל בְּרַתֵּהּ לֵהּ לְאִנְתּוּ: כט וִיהַב לָבָן לְרָחֵל בְּרַתֵּהּ יָת בִּלְהָה אַמְתֵהּ לַהּ לְאַמְהוּ: ל וְעַל אַף לְוָת רָחֵל וּרְחֵים אַף יָת רָחֵל מִלֵּאָה וּפְלַח עִמֵּהּ עוֹד שְׁבַע שְׁנִין אָחֳרָנִין: לא וַחֲזָא יְיָ אֲרֵי שְׂנִיאֲתָא לֵאָה וִיהַב לַהּ עִדּוּי וְרָחֵל עַקְרָא: לב וְעַדִּיאַת לֵאָה וִילִידַת בָּר וּקְרַת שְׁמֵהּ רְאוּבֵן אֲרֵי אֲמֶרֶת אֲרֵי גְלֵי קֳדָם יְיָ עֲלְבּוֹנִי אֲרֵי כְעַן יְרַחֲמִנַּנִי בַעְלִי: לג וְעַדִּיאַת עוֹד וִילִידַת בָּר וַאֲמֶרֶת אֲרֵי שְׁמִיעַ קֳדָם יְיָ אֲרֵי שְׂנִיאֲתָא אֲנָא וִיהַב לִי אַף יָת דֵּין וּקְרַת

רש"י

ותעבוד לאחר נשואיה: (ל) **עוד שבע שנים אחרות.** הקישן לראשונות, מה ראשונות באמונה אף האחרונות באמונה, ואע"פ שברמאות בא עליו (ב"ר ע:כ): (לב) **ותקרא שמו ראובן.** רבותינו פירשו, אמרה, ראו מה בין בני לבן חמי שמכר הבכורה ליעקב, וזה לא מכרה ליוסף ולא ערער עליו, ולא עוד שלא ערער

other seven years (*Rashi*). The Torah included Laban's sanctimonious statement to allude to the rule that two celebrations should not be mixed (*Yerushalmi Moed Katan* 1:7).

Ramban suggests that the שְׁבֻעַ, the *set of seven,* does not refer to the week of wedding celebrations, but to the original seven years of service. According to *Ramban,* the wedding took place before the full seven years had passed. Laban is now insisting that the initial period in payment for Leah must be completed before he would give Rachel to him and begin the second seven-year period.

31-35. Leah bears four sons. The Sages taught that the Matriarchs were barren, because God desires the prayers of the righteous (*Yevamos* 64a). Presumably, Leah would be included in that dictum, yet she began to give birth as soon as she was married! A clue to this anomaly can be found in the use of God's Names in this chapter and the next. In the case of Leah, the Torah states that *HASHEM* — the Name signifying Mercy — saw her plight (v. 31). But when Rachel complained to Jacob about *her* barrenness, he told her that not he, but *ELOHIM* — the Name signifying Judgment — had deprived her of children. The implication is that Leah had children only because her predicament, as the less-favored wife, caused God to have mercy on her. Otherwise, Judgment would have dictated that she, like Sarah, Rebecca, and Rachel, would have been barren until her prayers succeeded in changing her nature (*R' Hoffmann*).

31. כִּי־שְׂנוּאָה לֵאָה — *That unloved* [lit., *hated*] *was Leah. Ramban* cites *Radak* that Jacob surely loved Leah, but that his greater love for Rachel made her seem unloved — or even hated — by comparison.

32. רְאוּבֵן — *Reuben* [lit., *see, a son*]. The Torah explains Leah's reason for giving this name to her newborn son: In His mercy, *HASHEM* had seen her plight as the secondary wife, and He had given her the first of Jacob's sons, so that he would feel an upsurge of love for her. *Sforno* comments that Jacob must have resented her complicity in Laban's plot to deceive him at the time of the wedding. Now, however, that God had ratified her conduct by giving her the first child, Jacob would surely realize that she had acted properly.

שְׁמוֹ שִׁמְעוֹן: לד וַתַּהַר עוֹד וַתֵּלֶד בֵּן וַתֹּאמֶר עַתָּה

< *Now,* << and she declared, < a son < and bore < again < And she conceived **34** << Simeon. < his name

הַפַּעַם יִלָּוֶה אִישִׁי אֵלַי כִּי־יָלַדְתִּי לוֹ שְׁלֹשָׁה בָנִים

<< *sons;* < *three* < *him* < *I have borne* < *for* < *with me* < *will my husband* < *join* < *this time*

עַל־כֵּן קָרָא־שְׁמוֹ לֵוִי: לה וַתַּהַר עוֹד וַתֵּלֶד בֵּן

< a son < and bore < again < And she conceived **35** << Levi. < his name < He called < therefore

וַתֹּאמֶר הַפַּעַם אוֹדֶה אֶת־יהוה עַל־כֵּן קָרְאָה שְׁמוֹ יְהוּדָה וַתַּעֲמֹד

< then she stopped << Judah; < his name < she called < therefore << *HASHEM;* < *let me gratefully praise* < *This time* << and she declared,

מִלֶּדֶת: [ל] א וַתֵּרֶא רָחֵל כִּי לֹא יָלְדָה לְיַעֲקֹב וַתְּקַנֵּא רָחֵל בַּאֲחֹתָהּ

<< of her sister; < so Rachel became envious < to Jacob, < she had not borne [children] < that < Rachel saw **1** **30** << giving birth.

וַתֹּאמֶר אֶל־יַעֲקֹב הָבָה־לִּי בָנִים וְאִם־אַיִן מֵתָה אָנֹכִי: ב וַיִּחַר־אַף

< did the anger < Flare up **2** << *am I.* < *dead* < *not,* <— *and if* << *children* < *me* < *Give* << Jacob, < to < she said

שְׁמֵהּ שִׁמְעוֹן: לד וְעַדִּיאַת עוֹד וִילֵידַת בָּר וַאֲמֶרֶת הָדָא זִמְנָא יִתְחַבַּר לִי בַעְלִי אֲרֵי יְלֵידִית לֵהּ תְּלָתָא בְנִין עַל כֵּן קְרָא שְׁמֵהּ לֵוִי: לה וְעַדִּיאַת עוֹד וִילֵידַת בָּר וַאֲמֶרֶת הָדָא זִמְנָא אוֹדֶה קֳדָם יְיָ עַל כֵּן קְרַת שְׁמֵהּ יְהוּדָה וְקָמַת מִלְּמֵילַד: א וַחֲזַת רָחֵל אֲרֵי לָא יְלֵידַת לְיַעֲקֹב וְקַנִּיאַת רָחֵל בַּאֲחָתַהּ וַאֲמֶרֶת לְיַעֲקֹב הַב לִי בְנִין וְאִם לָא מֵיתָא אֲנָא: ב וּתְקֵיף רוּגְזָא

רש"י

עליו אלא שבקש להוציאו מן הבור (ברכות ז:): **(לד) הפעם ילוה אישי.** לפי שהאמהות נביאות היו ויודעות שי"ב שבטים יוצאים מיעקב וד' נשים ישא, אמרה, מעתה אין לו פתחון פה עלי שהרי נטלתי כל חלקי בבנים (ברב"ת; תנחומא ט): **על כן.** כל מי שנאמר בו על כן מרובה באוכלוסין, חוץ מלוי, שאהרן היה מכלה בהם (ב"ר עא:ד): **קרא שמו לוי.** בכולם כתיב ותקרא, [שהיא] קראה, וזה כתב בו קרא. ויש מ"א באלה הדברים רבה ששלח הקב"ה גבריאל והביאו לפניו וקרא לו שם זה, ונתן לו כ"ד מתנות כהונה, ועל שם שלוהו במתנות קראו לוי (עי' ברב"ת; ופדר"א פל"ז): **(לה) הפעם אודה.** שנטלתי יותר מחלקי מעתה יש לי להודות (ב"ר שם): **(א) ותקנא רחל באחתה.** קנאה במעשיה הטובים. אמרה, אלולי שצדקה ממני לא זכתה לבנים (ב"ר שם:ו): **הבה לי.** וכי כך עשה אביך לאמך והלא התפלל עליה (ב"ר עא:ז): **מתה אנכי.** מכאן למי שאין לו בנים שחשוב כמת (ב"ר עא:ו; נדרים סד:):

34. יִלָּוֶה אִישִׁי אֵלַי — *Join will my husband with me.* Until now I could hold one child in each hand. Now that there are three, Jacob must lend his hand (*Daas Sofrim).*

לֵוִי — *Levi.* The Matriarchs were prophetesses and knew that Jacob was to beget twelve tribes by four wives. Once Leah had three sons, she said, "Now my husband will have no cause for complaint against me, for I have given him my full share of children" (*Rashi*).

35. יְהוּדָה — *Judah.* This word contains the letters of God's Ineffable Name, as well as the root that means "thankfulness" and "praise" (*Sforno*); thus, the name has the connotation of thanks to God. She was especially grateful now, because, as the mother of one-third of Jacob's twelve sons, she had been granted more than her rightful share (*Rashi*).

Chiddushei HaRim notes that Jews have come to be called *Yehudim*, after Judah, because it is a Jewish characteristic always to be grateful to God, with the attitude that He has given us more than our rightful share.

30.

1-8. Rachel is fulfilled through Bilhah. Rachel longed for children, but in vain. She begged Jacob to help her, to no avail. Finally, she chose to follow the course of Sarah, who asked Abraham to marry her servant Hagar in the expectation that she would raise Hagar's children and be fulfilled vicariously.

1-2. וַתְּקַנֵּא רָחֵל — *So Rachel became envious.* Ordinarily, envy is not a commendable trait, but there are exceptions. The Sages teach that envy of another's Torah achievements leads one to study more and results in an increase in knowledge. Here, too, Rachel was certain that Leah had earned the privilege of having so many children because of her superior righteousness. Such envy is wholesome (*Rashi*).

מֵתָה אָנֹכִי — *Dead am I.* "If you do not pray and gain children for me, I will remain childless and be regarded as dead," or, alternatively, knowing how much Jacob loved her, Rachel sought to frighten him by saying she would die from grief. The Midrash adds that she also held up the example of Isaac who prayed for Rebecca. But her tactic backfired, for Jacob was angered by this threat and by her implication that it was in his power to give or withhold children. He replied, " Why do you complain to me? Am I to blame for your condition? *Instead of God am I Who has withheld from you fruit of the womb*? Moreover, *I* am not the barren one — it is from *you* that God withheld children, not from me; as for the comparison with Isaac, his prayer could be effective because he had no children, but I already have children."

The Sages say that God took Jacob to task for his insensitivity to Rachel: God said to him, "Is this the way to answer an ag-

יַעֲקֹב בְּרָחֵל וַיֹּאמֶר הֲתַחַת אֱלֹהִים אָנֹכִי אֲשֶׁר־
< Who << am I, < of God < In the place of << and he said, < at Rachel, < of Jacob

מָנַע מִמֵּךְ פְּרִי־בָטֶן׃ ג וַתֹּאמֶר הִנֵּה אֲמָתִי בִלְהָה
<< Bilhah, < my maid < Here is << She said, 3 << of the womb? < fruit < from you < has withheld

בֹּא אֵלֶיהָ וְתֵלֵד עַל־בִּרְכַּי וְאִבָּנֶה גַם־אָנֹכִי
<< I— < —also << and I may be built up < my knees < upon < that she may give birth < to her, < come

מִמֶּנָּה׃ ד וַתִּתֶּן־לוֹ אֶת־בִּלְהָה שִׁפְחָתָהּ לְאִשָּׁה
<< as a wife, < her maidservant < Bilhah < him < So she gave 4 << through her.

וַיָּבֹא אֵלֶיהָ יַעֲקֹב׃ ה וַתַּהַר בִּלְהָה וַתֵּלֶד לְיַעֲקֹב
< to Jacob < and bore < Bilhah conceived 5 << did Jacob. << to her, < and he came

בֵּן׃ ו וַתֹּאמֶר רָחֵל דָּנַנִּי אֱלֹהִים וְגַם שָׁמַע בְּקֹלִי וַיִּתֶּן־לִי בֵּן עַל־כֵּן
< Therefore << a son. < me < and He has given < my voice < He has heard < and also < has God, < Judged me << Then Rachel said, 6 << a son.

קָרְאָה שְׁמוֹ דָּן׃ ז וַתַּהַר עוֹד וַתֵּלֶד בִּלְהָה שִׁפְחַת רָחֵל בֵּן שֵׁנִי לְיַעֲקֹב׃
<< to Jacob. < a second son << of Rachel— < the maidservant < —Bilhah, << and bore < again < She conceived 7 << Dan. < his name < she called

ח וַתֹּאמֶר רָחֵל נַפְתּוּלֵי אֱלֹהִים ׀ נִפְתַּלְתִּי עִם־אֲחֹתִי גַּם־יָכֹלְתִּי וַתִּקְרָא
< And she called << have I prevailed! < [and] also < my sister, < to [equal] < have I maneuvered < that are sacred < Schemes < And Rachel said, 8

שְׁמוֹ נַפְתָּלִי׃ ט וַתֵּרֶא לֵאָה כִּי עָמְדָה מִלֶּדֶת וַתִּקַּח אֶת־זִלְפָּה שִׁפְחָתָהּ
< her maidservant < Zilpah < she took << giving birth, < she had stopped < that < [When] Leah saw 9 << Naphtali. < his name

דְּיַעֲקֹב בְּרָחֵל וַאֲמַר הָא מִנִּי (נ״א הֲמִנִּי) אַתְּ בָּעְיָא הֲלָא מִן קֳדָם יְיָ תִּבְעִין דִּי מְנַע מִנִּיךְ וַלְדָּא דִמְעִין׃ ג וַאֲמֶרֶת הָא אַמְתִי בִלְהָה עוּל לְוָתַהּ וּתְלִיד וַאֲנָא אֲרַבֵּי וְאֶתְבְּנֵי אַף אֲנָא מִנַּהּ׃ ד וִיהָבַת לֵהּ יָת בִּלְהָה אַמְתַהּ לְאִנְתּוּ וְעַל לְוָתַהּ יַעֲקֹב׃ ה וְעַדִּיאַת בִּלְהָה וִילִידַת לְיַעֲקֹב בָּר׃ ו וַאֲמֶרֶת רָחֵל דָּנַנִּי יְיָ וְאַף קַבִּיל צְלוֹתִי וִיהַב לִי בָּר עַל כֵּן קְרַת שְׁמֵהּ דָּן׃ ז וְעַדִּיאַת עוֹד וִילִידַת בִּלְהָה אַמְתָא דְרָחֵל בָּר תִּנְיָן לְיַעֲקֹב׃ ח וַאֲמֶרֶת רָחֵל קַבִּיל יְיָ בָּעוּתִי בְּאִתְחַנָּנוּתִי בִּצְלוֹתִי חֲמֵידִית דִּיהֵי לִי וְלַד כַּאֲחָתִי אַף אִתְיְהִיב לִי וּקְרַת שְׁמֵהּ נַפְתָּלִי׃ ט וַחֲזַת לֵאָה אֲרֵי קָמַת מִלְּמֵילַד וּדְבָרַת יָת זִלְפָּה אַמְתַהּ

רש״י

(ב) **התחת.** וכי במקומו אני: **אשר מנע ממך.** את אומרת שאעשה כאבא אני איני כאבא. אבא לא היו לו בנים אני יש לי בנים. ממך מנע ולא ממני (ב״ר שם ז): (ג) **על ברכי.** כתרגומו ואנא ארבי: **ואבנה גם אנכי.** מהו גם. אמרה לו זקנך אברהם היו לו בנים מהגר וחגר מתניו כנגד שרה. אמר לה זקנתי הכניסה צרתה לביתה. אמרה לו אם הדבר הזה מעכב הנה אמתי [בלהה] **ואבנה גם אנכי ממנה** כְּשָׂרָה (שם): (ו) **דנני אלהים.** דנני וחייבני וזכני (שם): (ח) **נפתולי אלהים.** מנחם בן סרוק פירשו במחברת צמיד פתיל (במדבר יט:טו), חבורים מאת המקום נתחברתי עם אחותי לזכות לבנים. ואני מפרשו לשון עקש ופתלתול (דברים לב:ה), נתעקשתי והפצרתי פצירות ונפתולים הרבה למקום להיות שוה לאחותי: **גם יכלתי.** הסכים על ידי. ואונקלוס תרגם לשון תפלה, כלומר, בקשות החביבות לפניו נתקבלתי ונעתרתי כאחותי. **נפתלתי,** נתקבלה תפלתי. ומ״א יש רבים בלשון נוטריקון (ב״ר עא:ח):

grieved person? By your life, your children [by your other wives] are destined to stand humbly before her son Joseph!" Undoubtedly, however, Jacob *did* pray for her, but he admonished her for wrongfully implying that a *tzaddik* has the power to coerce God, as it were, to respond to his wish (*Ramban*).

There was a positive result of Jacob's displeasure. Rachel prayed fervently on her own behalf, and, after unselfishly giving her maidservant Bilhah to Jacob, she was eventually blessed with children of her own. Those children, the Torah states, were in response to *her* prayers (*Sforno* to v. 22).

6. דָּנַנִּי אֱלֹהִים — *Judged me has God.* Rachel said that at first God had judged her and found her wanting, so she remained barren, but then He judged her again *and heard* her *voice*, giving her a son through Bilhah (*Midrash*).

8. . . . נַפְתּוּלֵי אֱלֹהִים — *Schemes that are sacred . . .* "I have attempted every possible scheme to influence God to grant me children as He did my sister" (*Rashi*).

9-13. Leah follows suit. Knowing prophetically that Jacob was destined to have twelve sons, and seeing that she had stopped giving birth, Leah gave her own maidservant Zilpah to Jacob as a wife. She did not have the motivation of the barren Rachel, but both righteous sisters had one thing in common: Each wanted to have the greatest possible share in laying the foundation for God's Chosen People.

וַתִּתֶּן אֹתָהּ לְיַעֲקֹב לְאִשָּׁה: י וַתֵּלֶד זִלְפָּה שִׁפְחַת
< — the maidservant << Zilpah bore 10 << as a wife. < to Jacob < her < and she gave

לֵאָה לְיַעֲקֹב בֵּן: יא וַתֹּאמֶר לֵאָה °בָּא גָד [°בגד כ׳]
<< — good luck! << It has come << And Leah declared, 11 << a son. < to Jacob << of Leah —

וַתִּקְרָא אֶת־שְׁמוֹ גָּד: יב וַתֵּלֶד זִלְפָּה שִׁפְחַת לֵאָה
<< of Leah — < — the maidservant << Zilpah bore 12 << Gad. < his name < So she called

בֵּן שֵׁנִי לְיַעֲקֹב: יג וַתֹּאמֶר לֵאָה בְּאָשְׁרִי כִּי אִשְּׁרוּנִי
< deemed me fortunate < For << In my good fortune! << Leah declared, 13 << to Jacob. < a second son

בָּנוֹת וַתִּקְרָא אֶת־שְׁמוֹ אָשֵׁר: רביעי יד וַיֵּלֶךְ רְאוּבֵן בִּימֵי קְצִיר־חִטִּים
<< of wheat; < of the harvest < in the days < Reuben went [out] 14 << Asher. < his name < So she called < have women!

וַיִּמְצָא דוּדָאִים בַּשָּׂדֶה וַיָּבֵא אֹתָם אֶל־לֵאָה אִמּוֹ וַתֹּאמֶר רָחֵל אֶל־
< to < Rachel said << his mother; < Leah < to < them < and brought < in the field < *dudaim* < and he found

לֵאָה תְּנִי־נָא לִי מִדּוּדָאֵי בְּנֵךְ: טו וַתֹּאמֶר לָהּ הַמְעַט קַחְתֵּךְ אֶת־אִישִׁי
<< *my husband?* < *that you took* < *Was it not enough* < *to her,* < [Then] she said 15 << *of your son.* < *some of the dudaim* < *to me* < *Please give* << Leah,

וְלָקַחַת גַּם אֶת־דּוּדָאֵי בְּנִי וַתֹּאמֶר רָחֵל לָכֵן יִשְׁכַּב עִמָּךְ הַלָּיְלָה
< *tonight* < *with you* < *he shall lie* < *Therefore,* << Rachel said, << *of my son!* < *the dudaim* < *even* < — *And [you want now] to take*

וִיהָבַת יָתַהּ לְיַעֲקֹב לְאִנְתּוּ: י וִילִידַת זִלְפָּה אַמְתָא דְלֵאָה לְיַעֲקֹב בָּר: יא וַאֲמֶרֶת לֵאָה אֲתָא גָד וּקְרַת יָת שְׁמֵהּ גָּד: יב וִילִידַת זִלְפָּה אַמְתָא דְלֵאָה בָּר תִּנְיָן לְיַעֲקֹב: יג וַאֲמֶרֶת לֵאָה תֻּשְׁבַּחְתָּא הֲוָת לִי אֲרֵי בְכֵן יְשַׁבְּחֻנַּנִי נְשַׁיָּא וּקְרַת יָת שְׁמֵהּ אָשֵׁר: יד וַאֲזַל רְאוּבֵן בְּיוֹמֵי חֲצַד חִטִּין וְאַשְׁכַּח יַבְרוּחִין בְּחַקְלָא וְאַיְתִי יָתְהוֹן לְלֵאָה אִמֵּהּ וַאֲמֶרֶת רָחֵל לְלֵאָה הָבִי כְעַן לִי מִיַּבְרוּחֵי דִבְרִיךְ: טו וַאֲמֶרֶת לַהּ הַזְעֵיר דִּדְבַרְתְּ יָת בַּעְלִי וְתִסְבִין (נ״א וּלְמִסַּב) אַף יָת יַבְרוּחֵי דִבְרִי וַאֲמֶרֶת רָחֵל בְּכֵן יִשְׁכּוּב עִמָּךְ בְּלֵילְיָא

רש״י

(י) **ותלד זלפה.** בכולן נאמר הריון חוץ מזלפה, לפי שהיתה בחורה מכולן ותינוקת בשנים ואין הריון ניכר בה (ב״ר עא:ט). וכדי לרמות [ל]יעקב נתנה לבן ללאה, שלא יבין שמכניסין לו את לאה שכך מנהגן ליתן שפחה הגדולה לגדולה והקטנה לקטנה: (יא) **בא גד.** בא מזל טוב (תרגום יונתן), כמו גד גדי וסנוק לא (שבת סז:), ודומה לו העורכים לגד שלחן (ישעיה סה:יא). ומדרש אגדה, שנולד מהול, כמו גדו אילנא (דניאל ד:יא; מדרש אגדה). ולא ידעתי על מה נכתב תיבה אחת. [דבר אחר, למה נקראת תיבה אחת, בגד כמו בגדת בי כשנאת אל שפחתי, כאיש שבגד באשת נעורים]: (יד) **בימי קציר חטים.** להגיד שבחן של שבטים, שעת הקציר היה ולא פשט ידו בגזל להביא חטים ושעורים אלא דבר הפקר שאין אדם מקפיד בו (ב״ר עב:ב; ועי׳ סנהדרין לט:): **דודאים.** סיגלי, ועשב הוא, ובלשון ישמעאל יסמי״ן (סנהדרין שם): (טו) **ולקחת גם את דודאי בני.** בתמיה, ולעשות עוד זאת ליקח גם את דודאי בני. ותרגומו ולמיסב: **לכן ישכב עמך הלילה.** שלי היתה שכיבת לילה זו ואני נותנה לך תחת דודאי בנך. ולפי שזלזלה במשכב

11. **בָּא גָד** — *It has come — good luck!* The phrase is written (כְּתִיב) in the Torah as a single word, בָּגָד, but pronounced (קְרִי) as if it were two words, בָּא גָד. *Rashi* interprets גָד as מַזָּל טוֹב, *good luck.* The spelling בָּגָד, as a single word, implies betrayal [בָּגַד, *to betray*] because it is a betrayal in a sense for a husband to take another wife (*Rashi*).

14-16. The dudaim. The incident of the *dudaim* is one of the most puzzling in the Torah. What were they? Why were they so important to Rachel, Leah, and Reuben? Why does the Torah relate the puzzling episode? Regarding other verses, it is *axiomatic* that human intelligence is capable of only a superficial understanding of God's word; regarding the verses of the *dudaim,* it is *obvious* beyond doubt that the episode is filled with mysteries of the Torah.

14. **דוּדָאִים** — *Dudaim.* The commentators suggest many possible translations of this word, among which are jasmine, violets, mandrakes, and baskets of figs. Some of these items were reputed to induce fertility and others were fragrant and capable of inducing good feelings.

According to *Sforno,* Reuben *deliberately* sought the *dudaim,* because they were believed to have fertility-inducing powers, and he knew that his mother Leah longed to have more children.

15. *Sforno* explains Leah's reaction to Rachel's request: [He was my husband before he was yours. Once I was already married to him] you should never have consented to become my rival-wife.

יִשְׁכַּב עִמָּךְ הַלָּיְלָה — *He shall lie with you tonight.* Rachel and Leah each had her own room, and Jacob alternated between them. That night, Jacob was to have stayed with Rachel, but she ceded

תַּחַת דּוּדָאֵי בְּנֵךְ: טז וַיָּבֹא יַעֲקֹב מִן־הַשָּׂדֶה בָּעֶרֶב

in exchange for | the dudaim | of your son. | 16 When Jacob came | from | the field | in the evening,

וַתֵּצֵא לֵאָה לִקְרָאתוֹ וַתֹּאמֶר אֵלַי תָּבוֹא

Leah went out | toward him | and said, | To me | you must come

כִּי שָׂכֹר שְׂכַרְתִּיךָ בְּדוּדָאֵי בְּנִי וַיִּשְׁכַּב עִמָּהּ

for | I have surely hired you | with the dudaim | of my son. | So he lay | with her

בַּלַּיְלָה הוּא: יז וַיִּשְׁמַע אֱלֹהִים אֶל־לֵאָה וַתַּהַר

that night. | 17 | God listened | to | Leah; | and she conceived

וַתֵּלֶד לְיַעֲקֹב בֵּן חֲמִישִׁי: יח וַתֹּאמֶר לֵאָה נָתַן אֱלֹהִים שְׂכָרִי אֲשֶׁר־

and bore | to Jacob | a fifth son. | 18 And Leah declared, | God has granted | my reward | that

נָתַתִּי שִׁפְחָתִי לְאִישִׁי וַתִּקְרָא שְׁמוֹ יִשָּׂשכָר: יט וַתַּהַר עוֹד לֵאָה וַתֵּלֶד

I gave | my maidservant | to my husband. | So she called | his name | Issachar. | 19 Then she conceived | again, | Leah did, | and she bore

בֵּן־שִׁשִּׁי לְיַעֲקֹב: כ וַתֹּאמֶר לֵאָה זְבָדַנִי אֱלֹהִים ׀ אֹתִי זֵבֶד טוֹב הַפַּעַם

a sixth son | to Jacob. | 20 Leah said, | God has endowed | me | [with] an endowment | that is good; | this time,

יִזְבְּלֵנִי אִישִׁי כִּי־יָלַדְתִּי לוֹ שִׁשָּׁה בָנִים וַתִּקְרָא אֶת־שְׁמוֹ זְבֻלוּן:

make his permanent home with me | will my husband, | for | I have borne | him | six | sons. | So she called | his name | Zebulun.

חֲלַף יַבְרוּחֵי דִבְרִיךְ: טז וַאֲתָא (נ״א וְעַל) יַעֲקֹב מִן חַקְלָא בְּרַמְשָׁא וּנְפָקַת לֵאָה לְקַדָּמוּתֵהּ וַאֲמֶרֶת לְוָתִי תֵּיעוֹל אֲרֵי מֵיגַר אֲגַרְתִּיךְ בְּיַבְרוּחֵי דִבְרִי וּשְׁכִיב עִמַּהּ בְּלֵילְיָא הוּא: יז וְקַבִּיל יְיָ צְלוֹתַהּ דְּלֵאָה וְעַדִּיאַת וִילִידַת לְיַעֲקֹב בַּר חֲמִישָׁאי: יח וַאֲמֶרֶת לֵאָה יְהַב יְיָ אַגְרִי דִּי יְהָבִית אַמְתִי לְבַעְלִי וּקְרַת שְׁמֵהּ יִשָּׂשכָר: יט וְעַדִּיאַת עוֹד לֵאָה וִילִידַת בַּר שְׁתִיתָאי לְיַעֲקֹב: כ וַאֲמֶרֶת לֵאָה יְהַב יְיָ יָתַהּ לִי חֲלַק טַב הָדָא זִמְנָא יְהֵי מְדוֹרֵהּ דְּבַעְלִי לְוָתִי אֲרֵי יְלֵידִית לֵהּ שִׁתָּא בְנִין וּקְרַת יָת שְׁמֵהּ זְבוּלֻן:

רש״י

הצדיק לא זכתה להקבר עמו (ב״ר עב:ג): (טז) **שכר שכרתיך.** נתתי לרחל שכרה: **בלילה הוא.** הקב״ה סייעו [ס״א סייע לה] שיצא משם יששכר (נדה לא.): (יז) **וישמע אלהים אל לאה.** שהיתה מתאוה ומחזרת להרבות שבטים (ב״ר שם ה): (כ) **זבד טוב.** כתרגומו: **יזבלני.** לשון בית זבול (מלכים א ח:יג). הירבידיירי״א בלע״ז, בית מדור. מעתה לא תהא עיקר דירתו אלא עמי (אונקלוס) שיש לי בנים כנגד כל נשיו (עי׳ פירש״י לעיל כט:לד-לה):

the privilege to Leah in exchange for the *dudaim*. Because Rachel made light of being with that righteous man, she was not privileged to be buried — to lie in eternal repose — with him (*Rashi*). It would have been demeaning for both sisters to be buried with Jacob, because the Torah would later forbid the marriage of two sisters to the same man. In choosing between two supremely righteous women, a lapse as relatively minor as Rachel's in this instance was enough to tip the scales in Leah's favor (*Gur Aryeh*).

16. וַתֵּצֵא לֵאָה — *Leah went out.* The Sages viewed this unfavorably, as an immodest act, and because of it, the Midrash describes Leah critically as a יַצְאָנִית, "one who is fond of going out." See *Rashi* to 34:1.

17-21. Leah's last three children. Despite Leah's impropriety (v. 16), God recognized that her motive was a pure and overpowering desire to serve God by participating in the building of His people (*Or HaChaim*), and He rewarded her with more children.

17. וַיִּשְׁמַע אֱלֹהִים — *God listened.* The Torah stresses that God responded to her prayers, not that there was some magical power in the *dudaim*. Children are a gift of God (*Radak*).

18. יִשָּׂשכָר — *Issachar.* The double ש in Issachar refers to a double שָׂכָר, which means both *hire* and *reward.* Leah *hired* Jacob with her son's *dudaim* (v. 16), and she was *rewarded* for her prayers and pure intent (*Rashbam*). But since the first of these connotations is uncomplimentary, one ש is not pronounced. Thus the name is pronounced *Yissachar* and not *Yissas'char*, as it is spelled (*Daas Zekeinim*).

20. זְבָדַנִי אֱלֹהִים — *God has endowed me.* God was generous to me, because my actions in the affair of the *dudaim* were only for His honor (*Sforno*).

יִזְבְּלֵנִי אִישִׁי — *Make his permanent home with me will my husband.* The word זְבוּל, meaning *abode*, became the basis for Zebulun's name, because now that Leah had given birth to half of the sons Jacob was destined to have, she felt that she would surely gain the company of her righteous husband.

כא וְאַחַר יָלְדָה בַּת וַתִּקְרָא אֶת־שְׁמָהּ דִּינָה׃

« Dinah. < her name < and she called « a daughter < she bore < And afterward, 21

כב וַיִּזְכֹּר אֱלֹהִים אֶת־רָחֵל וַיִּשְׁמַע אֵלֶיהָ אֱלֹהִים

« did God < to her < and listen < Rachel; < God remembered 22

וַיִּפְתַּח אֶת־רַחְמָהּ׃ כג וַתַּהַר וַתֵּלֶד בֵּן וַתֹּאמֶר

« and she said, « a son, < and she bore < She conceived 23 « her womb. < and He opened

אָסַף אֱלֹהִים אֶת־חֶרְפָּתִי׃ כד וַתִּקְרָא אֶת־שְׁמוֹ

< his name < So she called 24 « my disgrace. < God has taken away

יוֹסֵף לֵאמֹר יֹסֵף יהוה לִי בֵּן אַחֵר׃ כה וַיְהִי כַּאֲשֶׁר יָלְדָה רָחֵל אֶת־יוֹסֵף

« to Joseph, < Rachel had given birth < when < And it was, 25 « another son. < for me < may HASHEM < Add on « saying, « Joseph,

וַיֹּאמֶר יַעֲקֹב אֶל־לָבָן שַׁלְּחֵנִי וְאֵלְכָה אֶל־מְקוֹמִי וּלְאַרְצִי׃ כו תְּנָה

< Give [me] 26 « and to my land. < my place < to < and I will go < Send me « Laban, < to < Jacob said

אֶת־נָשַׁי וְאֶת־יְלָדַי אֲשֶׁר עָבַדְתִּי אֹתְךָ בָּהֵן וְאֵלֵכָה כִּי אַתָּה יָדַעְתָּ

< know < you < for « and I will go; < for them, < for you < I have worked < whom < and my children < my wives

כא וּבָתַר כֵּן יְלִידַת בַּת וּקְרַת יָת
שְׁמַהּ דִּינָה׃ כב וְעַל דּוּכְרָנָא דְרָחֵל
קֳדָם יְיָ וְקַבִּיל צְלוֹתַהּ יְיָ וִיהַב
לַהּ עִדּוּי׃ כג וְעַדִּיאַת וִילִידַת בָּר
וַאֲמֶרֶת כְּנַשׁ יְיָ יָת חִסּוּדִי׃ כד וּקְרַת
יָת שְׁמֵהּ יוֹסֵף לְמֵימָר יוֹסֵף יְיָ לִי
בַּר אָחֳרָן׃ כה וַהֲוָה כַּד יְלִידַת
רָחֵל יָת יוֹסֵף וַאֲמַר יַעֲקֹב לְלָבָן
שַׁלְּחַנִי וְאֵיהַךְ לְאַתְרִי וּלְאַרְעִי׃
כו הַב יָת נְשַׁי וְיָת בְּנַי דִּי פְלָחִית
יָתָךְ בְּהוֹן וְאֵהָךְ אֲרֵי אַתְּ יְדַעְתָּ

רש"י

(כא) **דינה.** פירשו רבותינו שדנה לאה דין בעצמה, אם זה זכר לא תהא רחל אחותי כאחת השפחות, והתפללה עליו ונהפך לנקבה (ברכות ס.; תנחומא ח): (כב) **ויזכור אלהים את רחל.** זכר לה שמסרה סימניה לאחותה (ב"ב קכג.; ב"ר עג:ד). ושהיתה מצירה שלא תעלה בגורלו של עשו שמא יגרשנה יעקב לפי שאין לה בנים (תנחומא ישן כ), ואף עשו הרשע כך עלה בלבו כששמע שאין לה בנים, הוא שייסד הפייט (בקרובות ליום א' דר"ה שחרית) האדמון כשט שלא חלה, לצה לקחתה לו ונתבהלה: (כג) **אסף.** הכניסה במקום שלא תראה. וכן אסף חרפתנו (ישעיה ד:א) ולא יאסף הביתה (שמות ט:יט) אספו נגהם (יואל ד:טו) וירחך לא יאסף (ישעיה ס:כ) לא יטמן: **חרפתי.** שהייתי לחרפה שאני עקרה, והיו אומרים עלי שאעלה לחלקו של עשו הרשע (תנחומא ישן שם). ומדרש אגדה, כל זמן שאין לאשה בן אין לה במי לתלות סרחונה, משיש לה בן תולה בו. מי שבר כלי זה, בנך. מי אכל תאנים אלו, בנך (ב"ר שם ה): (כד) **יסף ה' לי בן אחר.** יודעת היתה בנבואה שאין יעקב עתיד להעמיד אלא שנים עשר שבטים. אמרה, יהי רצון שאותו שהוא עתיד להעמיד יהא ממני, לכך לא נתפללה אלא על בן אחר (שם עג:ו): (כה) **כאשר ילדה רחל את יוסף.** משנולד שטנו של עשו, שנאמר והיה בית יעקב אש ובית יוסף להבה ובית עשו לקש (עובדיה א:יח), אש בלא להבה אינו שולט למרחוק, משנולד יוסף בטח יעקב בהקב"ה ורצה לשוב (תנחומא ישן כג; ב"ר עג:ז; ב"ב קכג:): (כו) **תנה את נשי וגו'.** איני רוצה לצאת כי אם ברשות (עי' תנחומא ישן כד):

21. דִּינָה — *Dinah*. *Rashi,* citing *Berachos* 60a, comments that the name comes from דִּין, *judgment*, for Leah passed judgment on herself. She reasoned, "Jacob is destined to beget twelve tribes. I have already borne six, and each of the handmaids has borne two, making a total of ten. If the child I am carrying is a male, then Rachel will not even be equal to one of the handmaids." In order to spare Rachel from such humiliation, Leah prayed for a miracle — that the fetus be changed to a female.

22-24. Rachel conceives; the birth of Joseph. God's desire for the prayers of the righteous had been sated, and He gave Rachel her first child. This auspicious event took place on Rosh Hashanah, the Day of Remembrance (*Rosh Hashanah* 11a).

23-24. אָסַף . . . יוֹסֵף — *[God] has taken away . . . Add on may [HASHEM]*. The name Joseph is a play on two concepts: that the birth of a son had removed her disgrace and that, knowing that Jacob would have one more son, Rachel wanted the name to embody a prayer that she become the mother of that son. Her choice of God's Names in these ideas is significant. Her disgrace had been removed by Elohim — the God of *Judgment* — for she recognized the elements that had moved God to answer her prayers. But her request for the future was a plea for mercy — to HASHEM, the Name of Mercy — for the righteous never place full reliance on themselves; she knew that she was dependent on God's mercy.

Rashi cites the Midrash that one aspect of her *disgrace* was that a childless woman is blamed for anything that goes wrong or breaks in the home, but when there is a baby, the blame is placed on him. *R' Gedaliah Schorr* explained that this seemingly strange comment testifies to completeness of God's blessing. In Rachel's case, for example, not only was the blessing of a child of vital importance to her because it gave her a share in the destiny of the Jewish people, God's goodness extended even to such trivial matters as diverting blame for the breakage of a dish.

25-36. Jacob wishes to leave, but concludes an employment contract with Laban. According to the Midrash, although Jacob's fourteen years of service for his wives had ended and he was theoretically free to leave at any time, he waited until after

אֶת־עֲבֹדָתִ֖י אֲשֶׁ֥ר עֲבַדְתִּֽיךָ׃ כז וַיֹּ֤אמֶר אֵלָיו֙ לָבָ֔ן

my work ‹ that ‹ I worked for you. « 27 But he said ‹ to him « Laban did, «

אִם־נָ֛א מָצָ֥אתִי חֵ֖ן בְּעֵינֶ֑יךָ נִחַ֕שְׁתִּי וַיְבָרְכֵ֥נִי יְהוָ֖ה

If ‹ now ‹ I have found ‹ favor ‹ in your eyes! « I have learned by divination — ‹ [that] HASHEM has blessed me ‹

בִּגְלָלֶֽךָ׃ חמישי כח וַיֹּאמַ֑ר נָקְבָ֧ה שְׂכָרְךָ֛ עָלַ֖י וְאֶתֵּֽנָה׃

on account of you. « 28 And he said, « Specify ‹ your wage ‹ to me ‹ and I will give it. «

כט וַיֹּ֣אמֶר אֵלָ֔יו אַתָּ֣ה יָדַ֔עְתָּ אֵ֖ת אֲשֶׁ֣ר עֲבַדְתִּ֑יךָ

29 But he said ‹ to him, ‹ You ‹ know ‹ the manner ‹ in which ‹ I worked for you, «

וְאֵ֛ת אֲשֶׁר־הָיָ֥ה מִקְנְךָ֖ אִתִּֽי׃ ל כִּ֡י מְעַט֩ אֲשֶׁר־הָיָ֨ה לְךָ֤ לְפָנַי֙ וַיִּפְרֹ֣ץ לָרֹ֔ב

and the way ‹ in which ‹ your livestock were ‹ with me. « 30 For ‹ the little ‹ that ‹ you had ‹ before I [came] ‹ has burst forth ‹ to abundance, «

וַיְבָ֧רֶךְ יְהוָ֛ה אֹתְךָ֖ לְרַגְלִ֑י וְעַתָּ֗ה מָתַ֛י אֶֽעֱשֶׂ֥ה גַם־אָנֹכִ֖י לְבֵיתִֽי׃ לא וַיֹּ֖אמֶר

[as] HASHEM has blessed ‹ you ‹ with my coming; « and now, ‹ when ‹ will I do [something] « — myself as well — « for my house? « 31 He said, ‹

מָ֣ה אֶתֶּן־לָ֑ךְ וַיֹּ֤אמֶר יַעֲקֹב֙ לֹא־תִתֶּן־לִ֣י מְא֔וּמָה אִם־תַּֽעֲשֶׂה־לִּי֙

What ‹ shall I give ‹ you? « And Jacob said, « You shall not give ‹ me ‹ anything; « if ‹ you will do ‹ for me ‹

הַדָּבָ֣ר הַזֶּ֔ה אָשׁ֖וּבָה אֶרְעֶ֥ה צֹֽאנְךָ֖ אֶשְׁמֹֽר׃ לב אֶֽעֱבֹ֨ר בְּכָל־צֹֽאנְךָ֜ הַיּ֗וֹם

this thing, « I will return ‹ I will pasture ‹ your flocks ‹ and I will guard [them]: « 32 I will pass ‹ through all ‹ your flocks ‹ today. «

יָת פָּלְחָנִי דִּפְלַחְתָּךְ: כז וַאֲמַר לֵהּ לָבָן אִם כְּעַן אַשְׁכַּחִית רַחֲמִין קֳדָמָךְ נַסֵּיתִי וּבָרְכַנִי יְיָ בְּדִילָךְ: כח וַאֲמַר פָּרֵישׁ אַגְרָךְ עֲלַי וְאֶתֵּן: כט וַאֲמַר לֵהּ אַתְּ יְדַעְתָּ יָת דִּי פְלַחְתָּךְ וְיָת דִּי הֲוָה בְעִירָךְ עִמִּי: ל אֲרֵי זְעֵיר דִּי הֲוָה לָךְ קֳדָמַי וּתְקֵיף לְמִסְגֵּי וּבָרִיךְ יְיָ יָתָךְ בְּדִילִי וּכְעַן אֵימָתַי אֶעְבֵּד אַף אֲנָא לְבֵיתִי: לא וַאֲמַר מָא אֶתֵּן לָךְ וַאֲמַר יַעֲקֹב לָא תִתֶּן לִי מִדַּעַם אִם תַּעְבֶּד לִי פִּתְגָּמָא הָדֵין אֶתוּב אֶרְעֵי עָנָךְ אֶטָּר: לב אֶעְבַּר בְּכָל עָנָךְ יוֹמָא דֵין

רש"י

(כז) **נחשתי.** מנחש הייתי, נסיתי בנחוש שלי שעל ידך באה לי ברכה. כשבאת לכאן לא היו לי בנים, שנאמר והנה רחל בתו באה עם הצאן (לעיל כט:ו), אפשר יש לו בנים והוא שולח בתו אצל הרועים, ועכשיו היו לו בנים, שנאמר וישמע את דברי בני לבן (להלן לא:א; תנחומא שמות טז): (כח) **נקבה שכרך.** כתרגומו, פריש אגרך: (כט) **ואת אשר היה מקנך אתי.** את חשבון מעוט מקנך שבא לידי מתחלה כמה היו: (ל) **לרגלי.** עם רגלי, בשביל ביאת רגלי באת אצלך הברכה. כמו העם אשר ברגליך (שמות יא:ח) לעם אשר ברגלי (שופטים ח:ה) הבאים עמי (ב"ר עג:ח): **גם אנכי לביתי.** לצורך ביתי (תרגום יונתן). עכשיו אין עושין לצרכי אלא בניי,

the birth of Joseph, because he knew prophetically that through the merit of the tribe of Joseph, God would enable him to conquer Esau. Once Joseph was born, Jacob was ready to risk Esau's wrath and safely return home. Out of courtesy, he asked Laban for permission to leave. Laban, however, was reluctant to part with Jacob who, as he admitted — probably with reluctance — was serving him well, and in whose merit God had blessed him.

27. אִם־נָא מָצָאתִי חֵן — *If now I have found favor.* "If you love me — as a relative should — you would not desert me" (*Sforno*). Laban went on to say that he had divined through occult means that he had become a wealthy man — and been blessed with sons (*Rashi*) — only because of Jacob's presence.

28-30. Laban had hoped the pious Jacob would be flattered by this acknowledgment of Heavenly intervention, and declare himself willing to remain without pay. But when Jacob remained silent, Laban realized that he would have to offer an inducement. Accordingly, he asked Jacob to stipulate his terms (*R' Hirsch*).

31. מָה אֶתֶּן־לָךְ — *What shall I give you.* Laban pressed further, asking Jacob to spell out what he wanted to be paid to compensate him for what he could expect to earn if he were to work for himself (*Sforno*).

Jacob consented to remain and he proposed an arrangement by which, in the natural order of events, he would gain little. Knowing Laban's larcenous and conniving nature, Jacob knew that Laban would balk at paying him what he was worth, but would jump at a ridiculous arrangement under which Jacob would be fortunate to earn more than a pittance.

לֹא־תִתֶּן־לִי מְאוּמָה — *You shall not give me anything* of the flocks you now possess. Whatever you profited from my past work is yours, because I worked solely for the right to marry your daughters. My wage for *continuing* to tend your flocks will come from

הָסֵר מִשָּׁם כָּל־שֶׂה ׀ נָקֹד וְטָלוּא וְכָל־שֶׂה־
‹ lamb ‹ every «or spotted, ‹speckled ‹ lamb ‹ every ‹ from there ‹ Remove

חוּם בַּכְּשָׂבִים וְטָלוּא וְנָקֹד בָּעִזִּים וְהָיָה שְׂכָרִי׃
« my wage. ‹ – that will be « among the goats ‹ or speckled ‹ and the spotted « among the sheep, ‹ brownish

לג וְעָנְתָה־בִּי צִדְקָתִי בְּיוֹם מָחָר כִּי־תָבוֹא עַל־
‹regarding ‹ it will come ‹when « of the morrow, ‹ on the day ‹ shall my integrity ‹ for me ‹ Testify **33**

שְׂכָרִי לְפָנֶיךָ כֹּל אֲשֶׁר־אֵינֶנּוּ נָקֹד וְטָלוּא בָּעִזִּים
« among the goats, ‹ or spotted ‹ speckled ‹ is not ‹ that ‹ any « before you; ‹ my wage

וְחוּם בַּכְּשָׂבִים גָּנוּב הוּא אִתִּי׃ לד וַיֹּאמֶר לָבָן הֵן לוּ יְהִי כִדְבָרֶךָ׃
« according to your words. ‹ it will be ‹ If only « Yes! ‹ And Laban said, **34** « [if] in my possession. ‹ it is, ‹ stolen « among the sheep, ‹ or [that is not] brownish

לה וַיָּסַר בַּיּוֹם הַהוּא אֶת־הַתְּיָשִׁים הָעֲקֻדִּים וְהַטְּלֻאִים וְאֵת כָּל־הָעִזִּים
‹ the goats ‹ and all « and the spotted ones, ‹ that were ringed ‹ the he-goats ‹ on that day ‹ So he removed **35**

הַנְּקֻדּוֹת וְהַטְּלֻאֹת כֹּל אֲשֶׁר־לָבָן בּוֹ וְכָל־חוּם בַּכְּשָׂבִים וַיִּתֵּן בְּיַד־בָּנָיו׃
« of his sons. ‹ into the hand ‹ – and he gave [them over] « among the sheep ‹ the brownish ones ‹ and all « in it, ‹ [had] white ‹ that ‹ – every one « and that were spotted ‹ that were speckled

לו וַיָּשֶׂם דֶּרֶךְ שְׁלֹשֶׁת יָמִים בֵּינוֹ וּבֵין יַעֲקֹב וְיַעֲקֹב רֹעֶה אֶת־צֹאן לָבָן
‹ of Laban ‹ the flocks ‹ was tending ‹ and Jacob « Jacob; ‹ and between ‹ between himself ‹ days ‹ of three ‹ a journey ‹ And he put **36**

הַעֲדֵי (נ״א אַעְדִּי) מִתַּמָּן כָּל אִמַּר נְמוֹר וּרְקוֹעַ וְכָל אִמַּר שְׁחוּם בְּאִמְּרַיָּא וּרְקוֹעַ וּנְמוֹר בְּעִזַּיָּא וִיהֵי אַגְרִי: לג וְתַסְהֵד בִּי זָכוּתִי בְּיוֹם דִּמְחָר אֲרֵי תֵיעוֹל עַל אַגְרִי קֳדָמָךְ כֹּל דִּי לֵיתוֹהִי נְמוֹר וּרְקוֹעַ בְּעִזַּיָּא וּשְׁחוּם בְּאִמְּרַיָּא גְּנוּבָא הוּא עִמִּי: לד וַאֲמַר לָבָן בְּרַם לְוַי יְהֵי כְפִתְגָּמָךְ: לה וְאַעְדִּי בְּיוֹמָא הַהוּא יָת תְּיָשַׁיָּא רְגוֹלַיָּא וּרְקוֹעַיָּא וְיָת כָּל עִזַּיָּא נְמוֹרַיָּא וּרְקוֹעַיָּא כֹּל דִּי חִוָּר בֵּהּ וְכָל שְׁחוּם בְּאִמְּרַיָּא וִיהַב בְּיַד בְּנוֹהִי: לו וְשַׁוִּי מַהֲלַךְ תְּלָתָא יוֹמִין בֵּינוֹהִי וּבֵין יַעֲקֹב וְיַעֲקֹב רָעֵי יָת עָנָא דְלָבָן

רש״י

וצריך אני להיות עושה גם אני עמהם לסמכן, וזהו גם (ב״ר שם): **(לב) נקד.** מנומר בחברבורות דקות כמו נקודות, פויינטור״א בלע״ז: **טלוא.** לשון טלאי, חברבורות רחבות: **חום.** שחום (אונקלוס) דומה לאדום, רו״ש בלע״ז. לשון משנה, שחמתית ונמלאת לבנה (בבא בתרא פג.) לענין התבואה: **והיה שכרי.** אותן שיוולדו מכאן ולהבא נקודים וטלואים בעזים ושחומים בכשבים יהיו שלי, ואותן שישנן עכשיו הפרש מהם והפקידם ביד בניך, שלא תאמר לי על הנולדים מעתה אלו היו שם מתחלה, ועוד, שלא תאמר לי ע״י הזכרים שהם נקודים וטלואים תלדנה הנקבות דוגמתן מכאן ואילך: **(לג) וענתה בי וגו׳.** אם תחשדני שאני נוטל משלך כלום תענה בי צדקתי, כי תבוא צדקתי ותעיד על שכרי לפניך שלא תמצא בעדרי כי אם נקודים וטלואים, וכל שתמצא בהן שאינו נקוד או טלוא או חום בידוע שגנבתיו לך ובגניבה הוא שרוי אצלי: **(לד) הן.** ל׳ קבלת דברים (תרגום יונתן): **לו יהי כדברך.** הלואי שתחפוץ בכך (שם ואונקלוס): **(לה) ויסר.** לבן ביום ההוא וגו׳: **התישים.** עזים זכרים: **כל אשר לבן בו.** כל אשר היתה בו חברבורת לבנה (תרגום יונתן): **ויתן.** לבן ביד בניו:

those unnaturally colored animals that will be born *in the future* (*Rashbam*).

Although the commentators differ as to the precise interpretation of *every* detail of Jacob's proposition, his arrangement was basically as follows: From the flocks in Jacob's care, Laban would remove all animals of unusual color, leaving the normally colored ones with Jacob. Of the animals to be born from the flocks he would be tending, Jacob would keep only the abnormally colored ones. Since such animals are freakish, and since Jacob added that existing animals of unusual colors should be removed from the flocks so that heredity would not contribute to such future births, the arrangement would be entirely to Laban's advantage.

33. וְעָנְתָה־בִּי צִדְקָתִי — *Testify for me shall my integrity.* Should you ever suspect me of taking animals that are not due me, an investigation of my flocks will verify my integrity (*Rashi*), for if any normally colored animal is in my possession, you may assume that it was stolen from you.

34. Laban assumed that the pure white and pure black animals left with Jacob would bear only a trifling percentage of discolored young. Small wonder that he accepted the proposed arrangement without hesitation.

35-36. Laban's new deceit. As an additional precaution, Laban kept a large distance between the flocks he separated and the flocks he left with Jacob, lest the animals mingle and mate.

הַנּוֹתָרֶת: לז וַיִּקַּח־לוֹ יַעֲקֹב מַקַּל לִבְנֶה לַח וְלוּז

< and of hazel < that was moist, < of poplar < a rod << did Jacob, < for himself < Then take 37 << that were left.

וְעַרְמוֹן וַיְפַצֵּל בָּהֵן פְּצָלוֹת לְבָנוֹת מַחְשֹׂף הַלָּבָן

< the white < that revealed < that were white, < peelings < in them < He peeled << and of chestnut.

אֲשֶׁר עַל־הַמַּקְלוֹת: לח וַיַּצֵּג אֶת־הַמַּקְלוֹת אֲשֶׁר

< which < the rods < And he set up 38 << the rods. < on < that was

פִּצֵּל בָּרְהָטִים בְּשִׁקֲתוֹת הַמָּיִם אֲשֶׁר תָּבֹאןָ הַצֹּאן

< the sheep < would come < to which < for watering < – in the receptacles << in the running streams < he had peeled,

לִשְׁתּוֹת לְנֹכַח הַצֹּאן וַיֵּחַמְנָה בְּבֹאָן לִשְׁתּוֹת: לט וַיֶּחֱמוּ הַצֹּאן אֶל־

< from < Then the sheep became aroused 39 << to drink. < when they would come < so they would become aroused << the sheep, < facing << to drink –

הַמַּקְלוֹת וַתֵּלַדְןָ הַצֹּאן עֲקֻדִּים נְקֻדִּים וּטְלֻאִים: מ וְהַכְּשָׂבִים

< The lambs 40 << and spotted ones. < speckled ones, < to ringed ones, < and the sheep gave birth << [seeing] the rods

הִפְרִיד יַעֲקֹב וַיִּתֵּן פְּנֵי הַצֹּאן אֶל־עָקֹד וְכָל־חוּם בְּצֹאן לָבָן וַיָּשֶׁת

< He set up << of Laban. < among the flocks < the brownish ones < and all < the ringed ones < toward < of the flocks < the face < and he positioned < Jacob segregated

דְּאִשְׁתָּאֲרַן: לז וּנְסֵיב לֵהּ יַעֲקֹב חוּטְרִין דִּלְבָן רַטִּיבִין וּדְלוּז וְדִדְלוּף וְקַלִּיף בְּהוֹן קִלְפִין חִוָּרִין קְלוּף חִוָּר דִּי עַל חוּטְרַיָּא: לח וּדְעִיץ יָת חוּטְרַיָּא דִּי קַלִּיף בְּרַהֲטַיָּא אֲתַר בֵּית שָׁקְיָא דְמַיָּא אֲתַר דְּאָתָן (נ״א דְּאָתְיָן) עָנָא לְמִשְׁתֵּי לְקִבְלֵיהוֹן דְּעָנָא וּמִתְיַחֲמָן בְּמֵיתֵיהוֹן לְמִשְׁתֵּי: לט וּמִתְיַחֲמָן עָנָא לְחוּטְרַיָּא וִילִידָא עָנָא רְגוֹלִין נְמוֹרִין וּרְקוֹעִין: מ וְאִמְּרַיָּא אַפְרֵשׁ יַעֲקֹב וִיהַב בְּרֵישׁ עָנָא כָּל דִּרְגוֹל וְכָל דִּשְׁחוּם בְּעָנָא דְלָבָן וְשַׁוִּי

רש״י

(לו) הנותרת. הרעועות שבהן, החולות והעקרות שאינן אלא שיריים, אותן מסר לו (תנחומא ישן כד; ב״ר עג:ט): (לז) מקל לבנה. עץ הוא ושמו לבנה (אונקלוס), כמא דתימא תחת אלון ולבנה (הושע ד:יג). ואומר אני, הוא שקורין טרינבל״א שהוא לבן: לח. כשהוא רטוב: ולוז. ועוד לקח מקל לוז, עץ שגדלין בו אגוזים דקים, קולדר״י בלע״ז: וערמון. קשטניי״ר בלע״ז: פצלות. קלופים קלופים, שהיה עושהו מנומר: מחשף הלבן. גלוי לובן [ס״א לבן] של מקל. כשהיה קולפו היה נראה ונגלה לובן שלו במקום הקלוף (תרגום יונתן): (לח) ויצג. תרגומו ודעיץ. לשון תחיבה ונעילה הוא בלשון ארמי. והרבה יש בתלמוד דלה ושלפה (שבת כ:) דץ ביה מידי (חולין לג:). דלה כמו דעלה, אלא שמקצר את לשונו: ברהטים. במרוצות המים. [בשקתות.] בבריכות העשויות בארץ להשקות שם הצאן: אשר תבאן וגו׳. ברהטים אשר תבאן הצאן לשתות, שם הציג המקלות לנכח הצאן (אונקלוס): ויחמנה וגו׳. הבהמה רואה את המקלות והיא נרתעת לאחוריה והזכר רובעה ויולדת כיוצא בו. רבי אושעיא אומר, המים נעשין זרע במעיהן ולא היו צריכות לזכר, וזהו ויחמנה בבואן לשתות (ב״ר עג:י): (לט) אל המקלות. אל מראות המקלות (שם): עקדים. משונים במקום

All of this would seem to have been Laban's right, because anyone is entitled to protect his interests in a business arrangement. In practice, however, the deceitful Laban did not keep his bargain. The full extent of his duplicity is impossible to fathom, but a reading of Jacob's outrage when he had had his fill of Laban's thievery reveals how much he suffered at Laban's hands.

37-38. Citing *II Samuel* 22:27, *with the trustworthy, act trustingly; and with the crooked, act perversely*, the Talmud (*Megillah* 13b) teaches that while it is never permitted to steal or lie, one must protect himself against thieves and connivers. Consequently, Jacob resorted to several devices to outwit his uncle and retain what was rightfully his under the original terms of the arrangement. He placed colored rods in front of the flocks at the time they conceived, so that they would bear lambs having the same markings as the rods they were facing. *R' Bachya* and others comment that Jacob did not adopt this course until instructed to do so by an angel (see 31:10-12).

38. When the female animals would see the rods in their watering troughs, they would become startled and recoil backward. At that moment the males would mount them, and they would later give birth to lambs having the same markings as the rod they were facing (*Rashi*).

R' Bachya observes that this concept contains an important lesson. If imagination is a determining factor in the nature of unborn lambs, as this verse indicates, then how much more important will it be when sensitive, thinking human beings procreate! Therefore, when husband and wife unite, they must purge their minds of all impure thoughts and every element which is foreign or which concerns third parties. The degree of their moral and spiritual purity will affect the souls of their children (*R' Munk*).

40-42. In the course of attempting to influence the birth of the animals to his advantage, Jacob separated the flocks, making the newborn spotted ones lead the monochrome ones, so the latter would be influenced by the leaders and bear similar offspring. He did not apply these measures indiscriminately. For maximum advantage, he set up the peeled rods only when the early-bearing sturdier members of the flocks were about to mate, thus securing the hardiest animals for himself.

לוֹ עֲדָרִים֙ לְבַדּ֔וֹ וְלֹ֥א שָׁתָ֖ם עַל־צֹ֥אן לָבָֽן׃

for himself < droves < separately, << and he did not place them < with < the flocks < of Laban. <<

מא וְהָיָ֗ה בְּכָל־יַחֵם֮ הַצֹּ֣אן הַמְקֻשָּׁרוֹת֒ וְשָׂ֨ם יַעֲקֹ֧ב

41 And it would be < whenever < that < it was arousal [time] < for the flocks < that were early bearing, << Jacob would place <

אֶת־הַמַּקְל֛וֹת לְעֵינֵ֥י הַצֹּ֖אן בָּרְהָטִ֑ים לְיַחְמֵ֖נָּה

the rods < before the eyes < of the sheep < in the running streams, << to arouse them <

בַּמַּקְלֽוֹת׃ מב וּבְהַעֲטִ֥יף הַצֹּ֖אן לֹ֣א יָשִׂ֑ים וְהָיָ֤ה

from the rods. << 42 But when the flocks were late bearing, << he would not place [them]; << thus were <

הָעֲטֻפִים֙ לְלָבָ֔ן וְהַקְּשֻׁרִ֖ים לְיַעֲקֹֽב׃ מג וַיִּפְרֹ֥ץ הָאִ֖ישׁ מְאֹ֣ד מְאֹ֑ד וַֽיְהִי־ל֗וֹ

the late-bearing ones < to Laban < and the early-bearing ones < to Jacob. << 43 The man burst forth in [his prosperity] < extraordinarily, << and he had <

צֹ֣אן רַבּ֔וֹת וּשְׁפָחוֹת֙ וַעֲבָדִ֔ים וּגְמַלִּ֖ים וַחֲמֹרִֽים׃ [לא] א וַיִּשְׁמַ֗ע

flocks < that were multiplying, < maidservants < and servants, < camels < and donkeys. << 31 1 Then he heard <

אֶת־דִּבְרֵ֤י בְנֵֽי־לָבָן֙ לֵאמֹ֔ר לָקַ֣ח יַעֲקֹ֔ב אֵ֖ת כָּל־אֲשֶׁ֣ר לְאָבִ֑ינוּ וּמֵאֲשֶׁ֣ר

the words < of the sons < of Laban < saying, << *Jacob has taken* < *all* < *that* < *belonged to our father,* << *and from that which* <

לְאָבִ֔ינוּ עָשָׂ֕ה אֵ֥ת כָּל־הַכָּבֹ֖ד הַזֶּֽה׃ ב וַיַּ֥רְא יַעֲקֹ֖ב אֶת־פְּנֵ֣י לָבָ֑ן וְהִנֵּ֛ה

belonged to our father < *he amassed* < *all* < *this wealth.* << 2 Jacob discerned < the countenance < of Laban < and indeed <

אֵינֶ֥נּוּ עִמּ֖וֹ כִּתְמ֥וֹל שִׁלְשֽׁוֹם׃ ג וַיֹּ֤אמֶר יהוה֙ אֶל־יַעֲקֹ֔ב שׁ֛וּב אֶל־אֶ֥רֶץ

it was not < with him < as yesterday < and the day before. << 3 And HASHEM said < to < Jacob, << *Return* < *to* < *the land* <

לֵהּ עֶדְרִין בִּלְחוֹדוֹהִי וְלָא עָרֵבִנּוּן עִם
עָנָא דְלָבָן: מא וַהֲוֵי בְּכָל עִדַּן
דְּמִתְיַחֲמָן עָנָא מְבַכְּרָתָא וּמְשַׁוֵּי
יַעֲקֹב יָת חוּטְרַיָּא קֳדָם עָנָא בִּרְהָטַיָּא
לְיַחָמוּתְהוֹן בְּחוּטְרַיָּא: מב וּבְלַקִּישׁוּת
עָנָא לָא מְשַׁוֵּי וִיהוֹן לַקִּישַׁיָּא לְלָבָן
וּבַכִּירַיָּא לְיַעֲקֹב: מג וּתְקֵיף גַּבְרָא
לַחֲדָא לַחֲדָא וַהֲוָה לֵהּ עָן סַגִּיאָן
וְאַמְהָן וְעַבְדִין וְגַמְלִין וַחֲמָרִין:
א וּשְׁמַע יָת פִּתְגָּמֵי בְנֵי לָבָן לְמֵימַר
נְסִיב יַעֲקֹב יָת כָּל דִּי לַאֲבוּנָא וּמִדִּי
לַאֲבוּנָא קְנָא יָת כָּל נִכְסַיָּא הָדֵין:
ב וַחֲזָא יַעֲקֹב יָת סְבַר אַפֵּי לָבָן וְהָא
לֵיתוֹהִי עִמֵּהּ כְּמֵאתְמַלֵּי וּמִדְּקַמּוֹהִי:
ג וַאֲמַר יְיָ לְיַעֲקֹב תּוּב לְאַרְעָא

רש"י

עקידתן, הם קרסולי ידיהם ורגליהם (תרגום יונתן): **(מ) והכשבים הפריד יעקב.** הנולדים עקודים ונקודים הבדיל והפריש לעצמן ועשה אותן עדר עדר לבדו, והוליך אותו העדר העקוד לפני הצאן. ופני הצאן ההולכות אחריהם צופות אליהם. זהו שנאמר **ויתן פני הצאן אל עקוד,** שהיו פני הצאן אל העקודים, **ואל כל חום** שמצא **בצאן לבן, וישת לו עדרים,** כמו שפירשתי: **(מא) המקשרות.** כתרגומו, הבכירות, ואין לו עד במקרא. ומנחם חברו עם אחיתפל בקושרים (שמואל ב טו:לא) ויהי הקשר אמיץ (שם יב), אותן המתקשרות יחד למהר עבורן: **(מב) ובהעטיף.** לשון איחור, כתרגומו, [ובלקישות.] ומנחם חברו עם המחלצות והמעטפות (ישעיה ג:כב) לשון עטיפת כסות, כלומר, מתעטפות בעורן וצמרן ואינן מתאוות להתייחם ע"י הזכרים: **(מג) צאן רבות.** פרות ורבות [יותר] משאר צאן: **ושפחות ועבדים.** מכר צאנו בדמים יקרים ולוקח לו כל אלה (תנחומא ישן כד): **(א) עשה.** כנס, כמו ויעש חיל ויך את עמלק (שמואל א יד:מח):

31.

1-3. The decision to flee. After twenty years of labor in Haran, Jacob left with his family to return to *Eretz Yisrael.* The decision was precipitated by the clear perception that Laban's family was resentful of Jacob's success. Like Pharaoh and Abimelech before them — and countless others since — they were convinced that the Jew was an interloper, and that whatever he achieved was at their expense. In a prophecy, God instructed Jacob to leave and, with sensitive concern for their feelings, the Patriarch informed his wives and sought their consent, which they gave wholeheartedly.

1-2. וַיִּשְׁמַע אֶת־דִּבְרֵי בְנֵי־לָבָן — *Then he heard the words of the sons of Laban.* Jacob heard the angry slanderous remarks against him, caused by their jealousy of his success (*Sforno*). Regarding Laban, the Torah does not quote him, but verse 2 states that his face showed Jacob that all was not well. The crafty Laban's displeasure was more internalized than that of his brash sons, but he could not completely conceal his frustration. A

אֲבוֹתֶיךָ וּלְמוֹלַדְתֶּךָ וְאֶהְיֶה עִמָּךְ׃ ד וַיִּשְׁלַח יַעֲקֹב

‹ Jacob sent 4 « with you. ‹ and I will be « and to your birthplace, ‹ of your fathers

וַיִּקְרָא לְרָחֵל וּלְלֵאָה הַשָּׂדֶה אֶל־צֹאנוֹ׃ ה וַיֹּאמֶר

‹ And he said 5 « his flock. ‹ to « to the field, ‹ and Leah ‹ Rachel ‹ and called

לָהֶן רֹאֶה אָנֹכִי אֶת־פְּנֵי אֲבִיכֶן כִּי־אֵינֶנּוּ אֵלַי

‹ toward me ‹ it is not ‹ that ‹ of your father ‹ the countenance ‹ do I ‹ discern ‹ to them,

כִּתְמֹל שִׁלְשֹׁם וֵאלֹהֵי אָבִי הָיָה עִמָּדִי׃ ו וְאַתֵּנָה

‹ Now you 6 « with me. ‹ was ‹ of my father ‹ but the God « and the day before; ‹ as yesterday

יְדַעְתֶּן כִּי בְּכָל־כֹּחִי עָבַדְתִּי אֶת־אֲבִיכֶן׃ ז וַאֲבִיכֶן הֵתֶל בִּי וְהֶחֱלִף

‹ and changed ‹ me ‹ mocked ‹ Yet your father 7 « your father. ‹ I served ‹ my strength ‹ with all ‹ that ‹ have known

אֶת־מַשְׂכֻּרְתִּי עֲשֶׂרֶת מֹנִים וְלֹא־נְתָנוֹ אֱלֹהִים לְהָרַע עִמָּדִי׃ ח אִם־

‹ If 8 « to me. ‹ to do harm « did God — « but not permit him « times; ‹ ten ‹ my wage

כֹּה יֹאמַר נְקֻדִּים יִהְיֶה שְׂכָרֶךָ וְיָלְדוּ כָל־הַצֹּאן נְקֻדִּים וְאִם־כֹּה יֹאמַר

« he would say: ‹ thus ‹ and if « speckled ones; « the flock — ‹ — all « then they would bear « your wages,' ‹ shall be ‹ 'Speckled ones « he would say: ‹ thus

עֲקֻדִּים יִהְיֶה שְׂכָרֶךָ וְיָלְדוּ כָל־הַצֹּאן עֲקֻדִּים׃ ט וַיַּצֵּל אֱלֹהִים אֶת־מִקְנֵה

‹ the livestock ‹ Thus, God salvaged 9 « ringed ones « the flock ‹ — all « then they would bear « your wages,' ‹ shall be ‹ 'Ringed ones

אֲבִיכֶם וַיִּתֶּן־לִי׃ י וַיְהִי בְּעֵת יַחֵם הַצֹּאן וָאֶשָּׂא עֵינַי וָאֵרֶא בַּחֲלוֹם

« in a dream ‹ and saw ‹ my eyes ‹ that I raised ‹ the sheep were ready for mating ‹ at the time ‹ And it happened 10 « to me. ‹ and gave [them] ‹ of your father

דַאֲבָהָתָךְ וּלְיַלָּדוּתָךְ וִיהֵי מֵימְרִי
בְּסַעְדָּךְ: ד וּשְׁלַח יַעֲקֹב וּקְרָא לְרָחֵל
וּלְלֵאָה לְחַקְלָא לְוַת עָנֵהּ: ה וַאֲמַר לְהֵין
חָזֵי אֲנָא יָת סְבַר אַפֵּי אֲבוּכֶן אֲרֵי לֵיתוֹהִי
עִמִּי כְּמֵאִתְמַלֵּי וּמִדְּקַמּוֹהִי וֵאלָהֵהּ
דְּאַבָּא הֲוָה מֵימְרֵהּ בְּסַעְדִּי: ו וְאַתִּין
יְדַעְתִּין אֲרֵי בְּכָל חֵילִי פְּלָחִית יָת
אֲבוּכֶן: ז וַאֲבוּכֶן שַׁקַּר בִּי וְאַשְׁנִי יָת אַגְרִי
עֲשַׂר זִמְנִין וְלָא שַׁבְקֵהּ יְיָ לְאַבְאָשָׁא עִמִּי:
ח אִם כְּדֵין הֲוָה אֲמַר נְמוֹרִין יְהֵא אַגְרָךְ
וִילִידָן כָּל עָנָא נְמוֹרִין וְאִם כְּדֵין הֲוָה
אֲמַר רְגוֹלִין יְהֵא אַגְרָךְ וִילִידָן כָּל עָנָא
רְגוֹלִין: ט וְאַפְרֵשׁ יְיָ יָת גֵּיתֵי דַאֲבוּכוֹן
וִיהַב לִי: י וַהֲוָה בְּעִדַּן דְּאִתְיַחֲמָא
עָנָא וּזְקָפִית עֵינַי וַחֲזֵית בְּחֶלְמָא

רש"י

(ג) **שוב אל ארץ אבותיך.** ושם אהיה עמך, אבל בעודך מחובר לטמא אי אפשר להשרות שכינתי עליך (פדר"א פל"ו; תנחומא י): (ד) **ויקרא לרחל וללאה.** לרחל תחלה ואח"כ ללאה, שהיא היתה עיקר הבית, שבשבילה נזדווג יעקב עם לבן. ואף בניה של לאה מודים בדבר, שהרי בועז ובית דינו משבט יהודה אומרים כרחל וכלאה אשר בנו שתיהם וגו' (רות ד:יא) הקדימו רחל ללאה (ב"ר עא:ב; רות רבה ז:יג): (ז) **עשרת מנים.** אין מונים פחות מעשרה (ב"ר עד:ג). מונים. לשון סכום כלל החשבון, והן

man's face mirrors his feelings (*Akeidas Yitzchak*).

3. וְאֶהְיֶה עִמָּךְ — *And I will be with you.* When you return home, *I will be with you,* but as long as you remain here with the unclean Laban, My Presence will not rest on you (*Rashi*). This removal of God's protection, as evidenced by the displeasure of Laban and his sons, was designed to provoke Jacob to leave Haran and return to *Eretz Yisrael* (*Malbim*).

4-16. Jacob wins the consent of his wives. Jacob's first step was to summon his wives and explain his position to them. Knowing how difficult it is for people, especially women, to uproot themselves from their home, Jacob tried to convince Rachel and Leah of their wicked father's dishonesty, and to impress upon them the necessity of an expedient departure, since only God's protection had prevented Laban from harming him until now (*Tzror HaMor*).

7. וְהֶחֱלִף אֶת־מַשְׂכֻּרְתִּי עֲשֶׂרֶת מֹנִים — *And changed my wage ten times. R' Munk* notes that the Torah specifies only one example of Laban's deceit [see 30:35]; however, as *Ramban* emphasizes in a comment that is fundamental to a proper understanding of the narrative, there must have been many such instances which the Torah does not enumerate. This is evidenced by Jacob's direct reproach to Laban regarding Laban's pattern of constant duplicity, as well as regular, unilateral changes of his wage (vs. 36 ff), a reproach that Laban did not deny. Further, one can persecute by stealing and one can persecute by failing to acknowledge another's honest service. As *Ibn Caspi* comments, Jacob

וְהִנֵּה הָעַתֻּדִים הָעֹלִים עַל־הַצֹּאן עֲקֻדִּים נְקֻדִּים

‹ speckled, ‹ were ringed, ‹ the sheep ‹ that mounted ‹ the he-goats ‹ —And indeed

וּבְרֻדִּים׃ יא וַיֹּאמֶר אֵלַי מַלְאַךְ הָאֱלֹהִים בַּחֲלוֹם

‹‹ in the dream, ‹‹ of God— ‹ —an angel ‹‹ to me ‹ And he said **11** *‹‹ and checkered.*

יַעֲקֹב וָאֹמַר הִנֵּנִי׃ יב וַיֹּאמֶר שָׂא־נָא עֵינֶיךָ וּרְאֵה

‹ and see ‹ your eyes ‹ now ‘Raise ‹ And he said, **12** *‹‹ ‘Here I am.’ ‹‹ And I said, ‹‹ ‘Jacob!’*

כָּל־הָעַתֻּדִים הָעֹלִים עַל־הַצֹּאן עֲקֻדִּים נְקֻדִּים

‹ speckled, ‹ are ringed, ‹ the sheep ‹ that are mounting ‹ the he-goats ‹ that all

וּבְרֻדִּים כִּי רָאִיתִי אֵת כָּל־אֲשֶׁר לָבָן עֹשֶׂה לָּךְ׃

‹‹ to you. ‹ is doing ‹ Laban ‹ that ‹ all ‹ I have seen ‹ for ‹‹ and checkered,

וְהָא תְיָשַׁיָּא דְּסָלְקִין עַל עָנָא רְגוֹלִין נְמוֹרִין וּפַצִּיחִין׃ יא וַאֲמַר לִי מַלְאָכָא דַייָ בְּחֶלְמָא יַעֲקֹב וַאֲמָרִית הָא אֲנָא׃ יב וַאֲמַר זְקוֹף כְּעַן עֵינָךְ וַחֲזֵי כָּל תְּיָשַׁיָּא דְּסָלְקִין עַל עָנָא רְגוֹלִין נְמוֹרִין וּפַצִּיחִין אֲרֵי גְלֵי קֳדָמַי יָת כָּל דִּי לָבָן עָבֵד לָךְ׃ יג אֲנָא אֱלָהָא דְּאִתְגְּלֵיתִי עֲלָךְ בְּבֵית אֵל דִּי מְשַׁחְתָּא תַמָּן קָמָא דִּי קַיֵּמְתָּא קֳדָמַי תַּמָּן קְיָם כְּעַן קוּם פּוּק מִן אַרְעָא הָדָא וְתוּב לְאַרְעָא דְיַלָּדוּתָךְ׃ יד וַאֲתִיבַת רָחֵל וְלֵאָה וַאֲמָרָא לֵהּ הַעַד (כְּעַן) לָנָא חֲלָק וְאַחֲסָנָא בְּבֵית אֲבוּנָא׃ טו הֲלָא נוּכְרָאִין אִתְחֲשַׁבְנָא לֵהּ אֲרֵי זַבְּנָנָא וַאֲכַל אַף מֵיכַל יָת כַּסְפָּנָא׃ טז אֲרֵי כָל עוּתְרָא דִּי אַפְרֵשׁ יְיָ מֵאֲבוּנָא לָנָא הוּא וְלִבְנָנָא וּכְעַן

יג אָנֹכִי הָאֵל בֵּית־אֵל אֲשֶׁר מָשַׁחְתָּ שָּׁם מַצֵּבָה אֲשֶׁר נָדַרְתָּ לִּי שָׁם

‹ there ‹ to Me ‹ you vowed ‹ [and] where ‹ a monument ‹ there ‹ you anointed ‹ where ‹ of Beth-el ‹ the God ‹ I am **13**

נֶדֶר עַתָּה קוּם צֵא מִן־הָאָרֶץ הַזֹּאת וְשׁוּב אֶל־אֶרֶץ מוֹלַדְתֶּךָ׃

‹‹ of your birth.’ ‹ the land ‹ to ‹ and return ‹ this land ‹ from ‹ go out ‹ —arise, ‹ Now ‹‹ a vow.

יד וַתַּעַן רָחֵל וְלֵאָה וַתֹּאמַרְנָה לוֹ הַעוֹד לָנוּ חֵלֶק וְנַחֲלָה בְּבֵית אָבִינוּ׃

‹‹ of our father? ‹ in the house ‹ and an inheritance ‹ a share ‹ for us ‹ Is there still ‹‹ to him, ‹ and said ‹ Then Rachel and Leah replied **14**

טו הֲלוֹא נָכְרִיּוֹת נֶחְשַׁבְנוּ לוֹ כִּי מְכָרָנוּ וַיֹּאכַל גַּם־אָכוֹל אֶת־כַּסְפֵּנוּ׃

‹‹ our money! ‹ and even totally consumed ‹ he has sold us ‹ For ‹‹ by him? ‹ we are considered ‹ as strangers ‹ Is it not that **15**

טז כִּי כָל־הָעֹשֶׁר אֲשֶׁר הִצִּיל אֱלֹהִים מֵאָבִינוּ לָנוּ הוּא וּלְבָנֵינוּ וְעַתָּה

‹ so now, ‹‹ and to our children; ‹ it belongs ‹ to us ‹ from our father ‹ God has salvaged ‹ that ‹ the wealth ‹ all ‹ Rather, **16**

רש"י

עשיריות. למדנו שהחליף תנאו מאה פעמים (ב"ר עג:ג): (י) **והנה העתדים.** אע"פ שהבדילם לבן כולם שלא יתעברו הצאן דוגמתן, היו המלאכים מביאין אותן מעדר המסור ביד בני לבן לעדר שביד יעקב (שם עג:י): **וברדים.** כתרגומו, ופציחין, פיי"ר בלע"ז. חוט של לבן מקיף את גופן סביב, וחברבורת שלו פתוחה ומפולשת מזו אל זו [ס"א מזן אל זן], ואין לי להביא עד מן המקרא: (יג) **האל בית אל.** כמו אל בית אל ה"א יתירה. ודרך מקראות לדבר כן, כמו כי אתם באים אל הארץ כנען (במדבר לד:ב): **משחת שם.** לשון רבוי וגדולה (תרגום יונתן) כש[נמשח למלכות, כך ויצק שמן על ראשה (לעיל כח:יח) להיות משוחה למזבח (תנחומא וישלח ח): **אשר נדרת לי.** וצריך אתה לשלמו (שם) שאמרת יהיה בית אלהים (שם כב) שתקריב שם קרבנות (פדר"א פל"ב): (יד) **העוד לנו.** למה נעכב על ידך מלשוב, כלום אנו מייחלות לירש מנכסי אבינו כלום בין הזכרים: (טו) **הלוא נכריות נחשבנו לו.** אפילו בשעה שדרך בני אדם לתת נדוניא לבנותיו, בשעת נשואין, נהג עמנו כנכריות, כי מכרנו לך [שעבדת אותו בנו י"ד שנה ולא נתנו לך אלא] בשכר הפעולה: **את כספנו.** שעכב דמי שכר פעולתך: (טז) **כי כל העשר.** כי זה משמש בלשון אלא. כלומר משל אבינו אין לנו כלום אלא מה שהציל הקב"ה מאבינו שלנו הוא: **הציל.** לשון הפריש (אונקלוס). וכן כל לשון הצלה שבמקרא לשון הפרשה, שמפרישו מן הרעה ומן האויב:

began this point by speaking of his own superhuman dedication to his job, *yet your father mocked me,* meaning that instead of showing appreciation, Laban took advantage of him.

12. **וּרְאֵה כָּל־הָעַתֻּדִים הָעֹלִים** — *And see that all the he-goats that are mounting . . .* Ordinarily it is forbidden to watch animals in the act of mating (*Avodah Zarah* 2:2), so Jacob realized that there must have been some practical reason why the angel told him to do so. He inferred from this that a miracle was about to occur and he should therefore peel the rods in order to conceal God's miraculous intervention (*R' Bachya*).

13. As God's emissary, the angel spoke in the first person, describing himself as *the God of Beth-el* — the God Who appeared to you in Beth-el [see 28:13] (*Radak*), and Who promised you My protection, assuring you that I would bring you back to

כֹּל אֲשֶׁר אָמַר אֱלֹהִים אֵלֶיךָ עֲשֵׂה: יז וַיָּקָם יַעֲקֹב
< Jacob arose 17 << do. << to you, < God has said < that < everything

וַיִּשָּׂא אֶת־בָּנָיו וְאֶת־נָשָׁיו עַל־הַגְּמַלִּים: יח וַיִּנְהַג
< He led 18 << the camels. < onto < and his wives < his children < and lifted

אֶת־כָּל־מִקְנֵהוּ וְאֶת־כָּל־רְכֻשׁוֹ אֲשֶׁר רָכָשׁ מִקְנֵה
< – the purchase << he had amassed < which < his wealth < and all < his livestock < all

קִנְיָנוֹ אֲשֶׁר רָכַשׁ בְּפַדַּן אֲרָם לָבוֹא אֶל־יִצְחָק
< Isaac < to < – to go << in Paddan-aram < he had amassed < which < of his acquired property

אָבִיו אַרְצָה כְּנָעַן: יט וְלָבָן הָלַךְ לִגְזֹז אֶת־צֹאנוֹ וַתִּגְנֹב רָחֵל
< and Rachel stole << his sheep, < to shear < had gone < And Laban 19 << of Canaan. < to the land << his father,

אֶת־הַתְּרָפִים אֲשֶׁר לְאָבִיהָ: כ וַיִּגְנֹב יַעֲקֹב אֶת־לֵב לָבָן הָאֲרַמִּי עַל־
< by < the Aramean < of Laban < the heart < Jacob stole 20 << belonged to her father. < that < the *teraphim*

בְּלִי הִגִּיד לוֹ כִּי בֹרֵחַ הוּא: כא וַיִּבְרַח הוּא וְכָל־אֲשֶׁר־לוֹ וַיָּקָם וַיַּעֲבֹר
< and he crossed < and he rose up, << he had – < that < and everything < – he << Thus he fled 21 << he was fleeing. < that < him < telling < not

אֶת־הַנָּהָר וַיָּשֶׂם אֶת־פָּנָיו הַר הַגִּלְעָד: כב וַיֻּגַּד לְלָבָן בַּיּוֹם הַשְּׁלִישִׁי
< on the third day < to Laban < It was told 22 << Gilead. < [toward] Mount < his face < and he set << the river,

כֹּל דִּי אֲמַר יְיָ לָךְ עֲבֵד: יז וְקָם יַעֲקֹב וּנְטַל יָת בְּנוֹהִי וְיָת נְשׁוֹהִי עַל גַּמְלַיָּא: יח וּדְבַר יָת כָּל גֵּיתֵיהּ וְיָת כָּל קִנְיָנֵהּ דִּי קְנָא גֵּיתֵי קִנְיָנֵהּ דִּי קְנָא בְּפַדַּן אֲרָם לְמֵיעַל לְוַת יִצְחָק אֲבוּהִי לְאַרְעָא דִכְנָעַן: יט וְלָבָן אֲזַל לְמִגַּז יָת עָנֵהּ וְכַסִּיאַת (נ״א וּנְסִיבַת) רָחֵל יָת צַלְמָנַיָּא דִּי לַאֲבוּהָא: כ וְכַסִּי יַעֲקֹב מִן (לִבָּא דְ)לָבָן אֲרַמָּאָה עַל דְּלָא חַוִּי לֵהּ אֲרֵי אָזֵל הוּא: כא וַאֲזַל הוּא וְכָל דִּי לֵהּ וְקָם וַעֲבַר יָת פְּרָת וְשַׁוִּי יָת אַפּוֹהִי לְטוּרָא דְגִלְעָד: כב וְאִתְחַוָּא לְלָבָן בְּיוֹמָא תְלִיתָאָה

רש"י

(יז) את בניו ואת נשיו. הקדים זכרים לנקבות, ועשו הקדים נקבות לזכרים, שנאמר ויקח עשו את נשיו ואת בניו וגו' (להלן לו:ו; ב"ר עד:ה): **(יח) מקנה קנינו.** מה שקנה מצאנו, עבדים ושפחות וגמלים וחמורים (ב"ר שם): **(יט) לגזז את צאנו.** שנתן ביד בניו דרך שלשת ימים בינו ובין יעקב: **ותגנב רחל את התרפים.** להפריש את אביה מעבודת כוכבים נתכוונה (ב"ר עד:ה): **(כב) ביום השלישי.** שהרי דרך שלשת ימים היה ביניהם:

that land (*Malbim*).

Jacob's account included two dreams. The first described the miracle of the flocks,which occurred at the beginning of his six-year service; the second was the command to leave Laban, which was given the night before this meeting in the field (*Ramban*).

17-21. Jacob's flight. Jacob purposely left in a grand manner — leading his flocks and systematically gathering all his wealth — so as not to arouse the suspicions of Laban's people. Anyone who saw him leaving so openly would assume that he was departing with Laban's full knowledge and consent. Had he gone stealthily, he would have been stamped as a fugitive (*Abarbanel*).

17. אֶת־בָּנָיו וְאֶת־נָשָׁיו — *His children and his wives.* In the case of Esau, the order is reversed: He *took his wives and his sons* (36:6), because Esau married only to satisfy his personal lusts; his children were always secondary. To Jacob, however, his primary responsibility was to bring the Jewish people into being (*Gur Aryeh*).

19. וַתִּגְנֹב רָחֵל אֶת־הַתְּרָפִים אֲשֶׁר לְאָבִיהָ — *And Rachel stole the teraphim that belonged to her father.* The *teraphim* were idols, and Rachel took them to keep Laban from idol worship (*Rashi*). The Torah records this episode because her intentions were noble (*Midrash*).

Ramban derives the word from the root רפה, *weak* [see *Exodus* 5:17], alluding to the "weakness" of their prognostications. The *Zohar* relates the word to תרף and תורפה, denoting *obscenity.* Many consider them to have been household gods, supposed to be the protectors of the home, similar to the later Roman Penates, which were consulted as oracles (*R' Hirsch*).

20-21. וַיִּגְנֹב יַעֲקֹב אֶת־לֵב — *Jacob stole the heart.* The "deceit" was that Jacob did not reveal that he knew of the displeasure of Laban and his sons. This lulled Laban into feeling secure that Jacob had no thought of leaving; otherwise Laban would have taken steps to prevent Jacob's possible departure (*Sforno*).

Jacob assumed that God would prevent Laban from learning of his departure. As has often happened in Jewish history, however, God did not act as people wanted Him to. Laban pursued

כִּי בָרַח יַעֲקֹב: כג וַיִּקַּח אֶת־אֶחָיו עִמּוֹ וַיִּרְדֹּף

< and he chased < with him < his brethren < So he took **23** « Jacob had fled. < that

אַחֲרָיו דֶּרֶךְ שִׁבְעַת יָמִים וַיַּדְבֵּק אֹתוֹ בְּהַר

< on Mount < with him < and he caught up « days, < of seven < a journey < after him

הַגִּלְעָד: כד וַיָּבֹא אֱלֹהִים אֶל־לָבָן הָאֲרַמִּי בַּחֲלֹם

< in a dream < the Aramean < Laban < to < But God had come **24** « Gilead.

הַלָּיְלָה וַיֹּאמֶר לוֹ הִשָּׁמֶר לְךָ פֶּן־תְּדַבֵּר עִם־יַעֲקֹב

< *Jacob* < *with* < *you speak* < *lest* < *yourself* < *Guard* « to him, < and said < of the night

מִטּוֹב עַד־רָע: כה וַיַּשֵּׂג לָבָן אֶת־יַעֲקֹב וְיַעֲקֹב

< Jacob « Jacob. < Laban overtook **25** « *bad.* < *to* < *from good*

תָּקַע אֶת־אָהֳלוֹ בָּהָר וְלָבָן תָּקַע אֶת־אֶחָיו בְּהַר הַגִּלְעָד: כו וַיֹּאמֶר לָבָן

< Laban said **26** « Gilead. < on Mount < his brethren < had stationed < while Laban « on the mountain, < his tent < had pitched

לְיַעֲקֹב מֶה עָשִׂיתָ וַתִּגְנֹב אֶת־לְבָבִי וַתְּנַהֵג אֶת־בְּנֹתַי כִּשְׁבֻיוֹת חָרֶב:

« *of the sword?* < *like captives* < *my daughters* < *and that you have led away* « *my heart,* < *that you have stolen* < *have you done* < *What* « to Jacob,

כז לָמָּה נַחְבֵּאתָ לִבְרֹחַ וַתִּגְנֹב אֹתִי וְלֹא־הִגַּדְתָּ לִּי וָאֲשַׁלֵּחֲךָ בְּשִׂמְחָה

< *with happiness,* < *— for I would have sent you off* « *me* < *And you did not tell* « *me?* < *and you deceived* « *to flee,* < *have you been stealthy* < *Why* **27**

אֲרֵי אֲזַל יַעֲקֹב: כג וּדְבַר יָת אֲחוּהִי עִמֵּהּ וּרְדַף בַּתְרוֹהִי מַהֲלַךְ שִׁבְעַת יוֹמִין וְאַדְבֵּק יָתֵהּ בְּטוּרָא דְגִלְעָד: כד וַאֲתָא מֵימַר מִן קֳדָם יְיָ לְוַת לָבָן אֲרַמָּאָה בְּחֶלְמָא דְלֵילְיָא וַאֲמַר לֵהּ אִסְתַּמַּר לָךְ דִּילְמָא תְמַלֵּיל עִם יַעֲקֹב מִטַּב עַד בִּישׁ: כה וְאַדְבֵּיק לָבָן יָת יַעֲקֹב וְיַעֲקֹב פְּרַס יָת מַשְׁכְּנֵהּ בְּטוּרָא וְלָבָן אַשְׁרֵי עִם אֲחוּהִי בְּטוּרָא דְגִלְעָד: כו וַאֲמַר לָבָן לְיַעֲקֹב מָה עֲבַדְתָּ וְכַסֵּיתָא מִנִּי וְדַבַּרְתָּ יָת בְּנָתַי כִּשְׁבִיּוֹת חַרְבָּא: כז לְמָא אִטְמַרְתָּ לְמֵיזַל וְכַסֵּיתָא מִנִּי וְלָא חַוֵּיתָא לִי וַאֲשַׁלְּחִנָּךְ פּוֹן בְּחֶדְוָא

רש"י

(כג) את אחיו. קרוביו: **דרך שבעת ימים.** כל אותן ג' ימים שהלך המגיד להגיד ללבן הלך יעקב לדרכו, נמצא יעקב רחוק מלבן ששה ימים, ובשביעי השיגו לבן. למדנו שכל מה שהלך יעקב בשבעה ימים הלך לבן ביום אחד [שנא' וירדוף אחריו דרך שבעת ימים, ולא נאמר וירדוף אחריו ז' ימים] (ב"ר שם ו): **(כד) מטוב עד רע.** כל טובתן של רשעים רעה היא אצל הצדיקים (יבמות קג:): **(כו) כשביות חרב.** כל חיל הבא למלחמה קרוי חרב: **(כז) ותגנב אותי.** גנבת את דעתי (תרגום יונתן):

and caught him — but God saved Jacob through other means. God's protection, too, is a common thread in Jewish history (*Haamek Davar*).

23-24. Laban's pursuit and God's warning. When Laban set out in pursuit, he intended to kill Jacob, and the Torah speaks of him as if he had actually done so, as the verse quoted in the *Haggadah* states, *An Aramean was the destroyer of my father (Deuteronomy* 26:5). For the gentile nations, God reckons evil intentions as if they had carried them out (*Rashi*), because their general performance justifies the assumption that they would have done so if they had had the opportunity.

24. וַיָּבֹא אֱלֹהִים אֶל־לָבָן הָאֲרַמִּי — *But God had come to Laban the Aramean.* Before Laban caught up with Jacob, God *had already* come to Laban. There are many such verses (*Ibn Ezra*) that are not in strict chronological sequence, but that supply more detailed information about an earlier incident. They are placed later in the narrative in order not to break the continuity of the story.

Though Laban was a cheat and his companions were idolaters, God came to him in a prophetic dream in honor of the righteous Jacob (*Ramban*), just as He had once come to Abimelech, in honor of Abraham (*Radak*).

מִטּוֹב עַד־רָע — *From good to bad.* God warned Laban not to speak [even of doing good] to Jacob, because the good of the wicked is bad to the righteous. Righteous people despise any benefits they may derive from the wicked; their benefits are not truly good (*Rashi*).

According to *Ramban,* God told Laban not to offer Jacob anything *good* in order to entice him to return, or to threaten him with harm if he failed to do so.

25-43. The confrontation of Jacob and Laban. In verse 23, Laban merely overtook Jacob, but now, in the morning, they met in a face-to-face confrontation (*Lekach Tov*).

26. Typical of charlatans, Laban tries to put Jacob on the defensive, accusing *him* of chicanery for having stolen away with his daughters, as if they were prisoners of war. Portraying himself as the aggrieved father, he speaks of his daughters before mentioning Jacob's flight or the theft of his *teraphim* (*Haamek Davar*).

וּבְשִׁרִים בְּתֹף וּבְכִנּוֹר: כח וְלֹא נְטַשְׁתַּנִי לְנַשֵּׁק

with songs, with drum, and with lyre! 28 And you did not [even] allow me to kiss

לְבָנַי וְלִבְנֹתָי עַתָּה הִסְכַּלְתָּ עֲשׂוֹ: כט יֶשׁ־לְאֵל יָדִי

my [grand]sons and my daughters; now you have been foolish to act [so]. 29 There is in the power of my hand

לַעֲשׂוֹת עִמָּכֶם רָע וֵאלֹהֵי אֲבִיכֶם אֶמֶשׁ ׀ אָמַר

[the ability] to do to all of you harm; but the God of your father last night said

אֵלַי לֵאמֹר הִשָּׁמֶר לְךָ מִדַּבֵּר עִם־יַעֲקֹב מִטּוֹב

to me, saying, 'Guard yourself from speaking with Jacob from good

עַד־רָע: ל וְעַתָּה הָלֹךְ הָלַכְתָּ כִּי־נִכְסֹף נִכְסַפְתָּה

to bad.' 30 Now — you have certainly left because you longed greatly

לְבֵית אָבִיךָ לָמָּה גָנַבְתָּ אֶת־אֱלֹהָי: לא וַיַּעַן יַעֲקֹב וַיֹּאמֶר לְלָבָן כִּי

for the house of your father; but why did you steal my gods? 31 Jacob answered and said to Laban, Because

יָרֵאתִי כִּי אָמַרְתִּי פֶּן־תִּגְזֹל אֶת־בְּנוֹתֶיךָ מֵעִמִּי: לב עִם אֲשֶׁר תִּמְצָא

I was afraid, for I said, for fear that you might steal your daughters from me. 32 With whomever you find

אֶת־אֱלֹהֶיךָ לֹא יִחְיֶה נֶגֶד אַחֵינוּ הַכֶּר־לְךָ מָה עִמָּדִי וְקַח־לָךְ:

your gods, he shall not live; in the presence of our brethren identify for yourself what is with me and take [it] for yourself.

וְלֹא־יָדַע יַעֲקֹב כִּי רָחֵל גְּנָבָתַם: לג וַיָּבֹא לָבָן בְּאֹהֶל־יַעֲקֹב ׀ וּבְאֹהֶל

(Now he did not know — Jacob — that Rachel had stolen them.) 33 Laban came into the tent of Jacob, and into the tent

וּבְתוּשְׁבְּחָן בְּתוּפִּין וּבְכִנָּרִין: כח וְלָא שְׁבַקְתַּנִי לְנַשָּׁקָא לִבְנַי וְלִבְנָתַי כְּעַן אַסְכָּלְתָּא לְמֶעְבָּד: כט אִית חֵילָא בִידִי לְמֶעְבַּד עִמְּכוֹן בִּישׁ וֵאלָהָא דַאֲבוּכוֹן בְּרַמְשָׁא אֲמַר לִי לְמֵימַר אִסְתַּמַּר לָךְ מִלְּמַלָּלָא עִם יַעֲקֹב מִטַּב עַד בִּישׁ: ל וּכְעַן מֵיזַל אֲזַלְתָּ אֲרֵי חַמָּדָא חַמֶּדְתָּא לְבֵית אֲבוּךְ לְמָא נְסַבְתָּא יָת דַּחַלְתִּי: לא וַאֲתֵיב יַעֲקֹב וַאֲמַר לְלָבָן אֲרֵי דְחֵילִית אֲרֵי אֲמָרִית דִּילְמָא תָנֵיס יָת בְּנָתָךְ מִנִּי: לב עִם (נ״א אֲתַר) דִּי תַשְׁכַּח יָת דַּחַלְתָּךְ לָא יִתְקַיַּם קֳדָם אֲחָנָא אִשְׁתְּמוֹדַע לָךְ מָא דְעִמִּי וְסַב לָךְ וְלָא יְדַע יַעֲקֹב אֲרֵי רָחֵל נְסֵיבַתְנוּן: לג וְעַל לָבָן בְּמַשְׁכְּנָא דְיַעֲקֹב וּבְמַשְׁכְּנָא

רש״י

(כט) **יש לאל ידי.** יש כח וחיל בידי לעשות עמכם רע (אונקלוס) וכל אל שהוא לשון קדש על שם עוזו ורוב אוניס הוא: (ל) **נכספתה.** חמדת (אונקלוס). והרבה יש במקרא, נכספה וגם כלתה נפשי (תהלים פד:ג), למעשה ידיך תכסוף (איוב יד:טו): (לא) **כי יראתי וגו'.** השיבו על ראשון ראשון, שאמר לו ותנהג את בנותי וגו' (לעיל פסוק כו; אדר״נ לז): (לב) **לא יחיה.** ומאותה קללה מתה רחל בדרך (ב״ר שם ז, ט): **מה עמדי.** משלך (תרגום יונתן): (לג) **באהל יעקב.** הוא אהל רחל (ב״ר שם ט) שהיה יעקב תדיר אצלה, וכן הוא אומר בני רחל אשת יעקב (להלן מו:יט) ובכולן לא נאמר אשת יעקב (ב״ר עג:ב):

29-30. Continuing his diatribe, the "innocent, well-meaning, victimized father and grandfather" says that Jacob deserved to be dealt with very severely, but that he, Laban, would desist from that course only because God had come to Jacob's defense — but that did not absolve Jacob from responsibility for the heinous crime of stealing the *teraphim!* A misguided desire for independence from his loving father-in-law did not give Jacob the right to steal such precious possessions!

When Jacob's sons heard their grandfather speaking of his "gods," they exclaimed, "We are ashamed of you, Grandfather, that in your old age you can refer to them as your gods!" (*Midrash*).

31-32. To Laban's personal abuse, Jacob did not respond in kind; he was calm and understated. As for the *teraphim,* Jacob invited Laban to search for them. Unaware that Rachel had stolen them, Jacob pronounced a curse on anyone among his company who had them, a curse that came true with Rachel's premature death. For, as the Sages teach, even an unintentional curse that escapes the lips of the righteous comes about (*Rashi*).

By saying *Now he did not know — Jacob — that Rachel had stolen them,* the Torah testifies that Jacob uttered the imprecation because he suspected that an idolatrous servant had stolen the *teraphim* to worship them in secret. Had he had even the

לֵאָה וּבְאֹהֶל שְׁתֵּי הָאֲמָהֹת וְלֹא מָצָא וַיֵּצֵא

of Leah, › and into the tent › of the two › maidservants, » but he did not find [anything]. » [Then] he left ›

מֵאֹהֶל לֵאָה וַיָּבֹא בְּאֹהֶל רָחֵל: לד וְרָחֵל לָקְחָה

the tent › of Leah, › and he came › into the tent › of Rachel. » 34 Now Rachel › had taken ›

אֶת־הַתְּרָפִים וַתְּשִׂמֵם בְּכַר הַגָּמָל וַתֵּשֶׁב עֲלֵיהֶם

the *teraphim,* › and put them › into the saddle cushion › of the camel › and sat › on them. »

וַיְמַשֵּׁשׁ לָבָן אֶת־כָּל־הָאֹהֶל וְלֹא מָצָא: לה וַתֹּאמֶר

Laban rummaged › through the whole › tent, » but he did not find [anything]. » 35 She said ›

אֶל־אָבִיהָ אַל־יִחַר בְּעֵינֵי אֲדֹנִי כִּי לוֹא אוּכַל

to › her father, › *Let it not cause anger* › *in the eyes* › *of my lord* › *that* › *I cannot* ›

לָקוּם מִפָּנֶיךָ כִּי־דֶרֶךְ נָשִׁים לִי וַיְחַפֵּשׂ וְלֹא מָצָא אֶת־הַתְּרָפִים:

rise up › *before you,* » *for* › *the way* › *of women* › *is upon me.* » Thus he searched › but did not find › the *teraphim.* »

לו וַיִּחַר לְיַעֲקֹב וַיָּרֶב בְּלָבָן וַיַּעַן יַעֲקֹב וַיֹּאמֶר לְלָבָן מַה־פִּשְׁעִי מַה

36 Then Jacob became angered › and he argued › with Laban; » Jacob responded › and said › to Laban, » *What* › *is my transgression?* » *What* ›

חַטָּאתִי כִּי דָלַקְתָּ אַחֲרָי: לז כִּי־מִשַּׁשְׁתָּ אֶת־כָּל־כֵּלַי מַה־מָּצָאתָ

is my sin › *that* › *you have hotly pursued* › *me?* » 37 *When* › *you rummaged* › *through all* › *my utensils,* » *what* › *did you find* ›

מִכֹּל כְּלֵי־בֵיתֶךָ שִׂים כֹּה נֶגֶד אַחַי וְאַחֶיךָ וְיוֹכִיחוּ בֵּין שְׁנֵינוּ: לח זֶה

of all › *the utensils* › *of your house?* » *Set it* › *here* › *before* › *my brethren* › *and your brethren,* » *and let them decide* › *between* › *the two of us.* » 38 *These* ›

דְלֵאָה וּבְמַשְׁכְּנָא דְתַרְתֵּין לְחֵינָתָא
וְלָא אַשְׁכַּח וּנְפַק מִמַּשְׁכְּנָא דְלֵאָה
וְעַל בְּמַשְׁכְּנָא דְרָחֵל: לד וְרָחֵל
נְסִיבַת יָת צַלְמָנַיָּא וְשַׁוְיָתְנוּן
בַּעֲבִיטָא דְגַמְלָא וִיתִיבַת עֲלֵיהוֹן
וּמַשִּׁישׁ לָבָן יָת כָּל מַשְׁכְּנָא וְלָא
אַשְׁכַּח: לה וַאֲמֶרֶת לַאֲבוּהָא לָא
יִתְקֵף בְּעֵינֵי רִבּוֹנִי אֲרֵי לָא אִכּוּל
לְמֵיקַם מִן קֳדָמָךְ אֲרֵי אֹרַח נְשִׁין לִי
וּבְלַשׁ וְלָא אַשְׁכַּח יָת צַלְמָנַיָּא:
לו וּתְקֵיף לְיַעֲקֹב וּנְצָא עִם לָבָן וַאֲתֵיב
יַעֲקֹב וַאֲמַר לְלָבָן מַה חוֹבִי מַה
סוּרְחָנִי אֲרֵי רְדַפְתָּא בַּתְרָי: לז אֲרֵי
מַשִּׁשְׁתָּא יָת כָּל מָנַי מָה אַשְׁכַּחְתָּא
מִכֹּל מָנֵי בֵיתָךְ שַׁוִּי הָכָא קֳדָם אַחַי
וְאַחָיךְ וְיוֹכִיחוּן בֵּין תַּרְוָנָא: לח דְּנַן

רש"י

ויבא באהל רחל. כשילא מאהל לאה חזר לו לאהל רחל קודם שחפש באהל האמהות [ס"א השפחות], וכל כך למה, לפי שהיה מכיר בה שהיא משמשנית (שם עד:ט): **(לד) בכר הגמל.** לשון כרים וכסתות, כתרגומו, בעביטא דגמלא, והיא מרדעת העשויה כמין כר. ובטירובין (טז.) הקיפוה בעביטין, והן עביטי גמלים (כלים כג:ב), בשטי"ל בלע"ז: **(לו) דלקת.** רדפת (אונקלוס), כמו על ההרים דלקונו (איכה ד:יט), וכמו מדלוק אחרי פלשתים (שמואל א יז:נג): **(לז) ויוכיחו.** ויבררו עם מי הדין, אפרובי"ר בלע"ז:

slightest notion that *Rachel* had stolen them, he would: (a) not have denied it so boldly; and (b) never have uttered a curse. He would have known that she had no desire to worship idols, but that her motive was to wean her father from idolatry (*Akeidas Yitzchak; Sforno; Alshich*).

Because of her utter contempt for Laban's "gods," Rachel placed them beneath her (*Zohar*). In the plain sense of the verse, however, she simply wanted to hide them. And she knew that if she explained to Laban that the *way of women* was upon her (v. 35), he would not trouble her to rise.

36. The Torah does not record whether or not Laban searched through the belongings of his grandchildren and the servants. Perhaps he did; or possibly Laban felt that only Jacob or his wives would have the audacity to enter his tent and steal his "gods." Nevertheless, when Laban had finished ransacking Jacob's belongings and failed to find the *teraphim,* the outraged Patriarch — who had painfully maintained his silence all these years — could contain himself no longer.

וַיִּחַר לְיַעֲקֹב — *Then Jacob became angered.* Originally, Jacob had invited the search. Now, however, that Laban had turned up nothing, Jacob suspected that Laban's charge was merely a pretext to enable him to make a general search. This is what angered him.

עֶשְׂרִים שָׁנָה אָנֹכִי עִמָּךְ רְחֵלֶיךָ וְעִזֶּיךָ לֹא

< never < and your she-goats < your ewes << with you, < I have been < years < twenty

שִׁכֵּלוּ וְאֵילֵי צֹאנְךָ לֹא אָכָלְתִּי: לט טְרֵפָה לֹא־

< I never < That which was mangled [by a beast] 39 << I did not eat. < of your flock < and the rams << miscarried,

הֵבֵאתִי אֵלֶיךָ אָנֹכִי אֲחַטֶּנָּה מִיָּדִי תְּבַקְשֶׁנָּה

<< you would demand it, < from my hand < would bear the loss, < — I myself << to you < brought

גְּנֻבְתִי יוֹם וּגְנֻבְתִי לָיְלָה: מ הָיִיתִי בַיּוֹם אֲכָלַנִי

< I was consumed < By day << [This is how] I was: 40 << by night. < or stolen < by day < whether it was stolen

חֹרֶב וָקֶרַח בַּלָּיְלָה וַתִּדַּד שְׁנָתִי מֵעֵינָי: מא זֶה־לִּי עֶשְׂרִים שָׁנָה בְּבֵיתֶךָ

<< in your household: < years < twenty < to me < This is 41 << from my eyes. < did my sleep < drift away << by night; < and frost < by scorching heat,

עֲבַדְתִּיךָ אַרְבַּע־עֶשְׂרֵה שָׁנָה בִּשְׁתֵּי בְנֹתֶיךָ וְשֵׁשׁ שָׁנִים בְּצֹאנֶךָ וַתַּחֲלֵף

< and you changed << for your flocks; < years < and six < daughters, < for your two < years < fourteen < I served you

אֶת־מַשְׂכֻּרְתִּי עֲשֶׂרֶת מֹנִים: מב לוּלֵי אֱלֹהֵי אָבִי אֱלֹהֵי אַבְרָהָם וּפַחַד

< and the Fear < of Abraham < — the God << of my father < for the God < Were it not 42 << times. < ten < my wage

יִצְחָק הָיָה לִי כִּי עַתָּה רֵיקָם שִׁלַּחְתָּנִי אֶת־עָנְיִי וְאֶת־יְגִיעַ כַּפַּי

< of my hands < and the toil < my suffering << you would have sent me away; < empty [handed] < now < certainly << with me, < Who was << of Isaac —

עֶסְרִין שְׁנִין אֲנָא עִמָּךְ רְחֵלָיךְ וְעִזָּיךְ לָא אַתְכִּילוּ וְדִכְרֵי עָנָךְ לָא אֲכָלִית: לט דִּתְבִירָא לָא אַיְתֵיתִי לָךְ דַּהֲוָה (נ״א דַּהֲוַת) שָׁגְיָא מִמִּנְיָנָא מִנִּי אַתְּ בָּעֵי לַהּ נְטָרִית בִּימָמָא וּנְטָרִית בְּלֵילְיָא: מ הֲוֵיתִי בִימָמָא אֲכַלְנִי שַׁרְבָא וּגְלִידָא (הֲוָה) נָחֵית עֲלַי בְּלֵילְיָא וְנַדַּת שִׁנְתִּי מֵעֵינָי: מא דְּנַן לִי עֶסְרִין שְׁנִין בְּבֵיתָךְ פְּלַחְתָּךְ אַרְבַּע עֶסְרֵי שְׁנִין בְּתַרְתֵּין בְּנָתָךְ וְשִׁית שְׁנִין בְּעָנָךְ וְאַשְׁנֵיתָא יָת אַגְרִי עֲשַׂר זִמְנִין: מב אִילוּלָא פּוֹן אֱלָהֵהּ דְּאַבָּא אֱלָהֵהּ דְּאַבְרָהָם וּדְדָחִיל (לֵהּ) יִצְחָק הֲוָה בְּסַעְדִּי אֲרֵי כְעַן רֵיקָן שַׁלַּחְתָּנִי יָת עַמְלִי וְיָת לֵיאוּת יְדַי

רש״י

(לח) **לא שכלו.** לא הפילו עיבורים, כמו רחם משכיל (הושע ט:יד) תפלט פרתו ולא תשכל (איוב כא:י): **ואילי צאנך.** מכאן אמרו איל בן יומו קרוי איל, שאל״כ מה שבחו, אילים לא אכל אבל כבשים אכל, א״כ גזלן הוא (ב״ק סה.): **(לט) טרפה.** ע״י ארי וזאב (אונקלוס; תרגום יונתן): **אנכי אחטנה.** לשון קולע באבן אל השערה ולא יחטיא (שופטים כ:טז) אני ובני שלמה חטאים (מלכים א א:כא) חסרים. אנכי אחסרנה, אם חסרה חסרה לי, שמידי תבקשנה: **אנכי אחטנה.** תרגומו דהות שגיא ממניא, שהיתה נפקדת ומחוסרת, כמו ולא נפקד ממנו איש (במדבר לא:מט) תרגומו ולא שגא: **גנבתי יום וגנבתי לילה.** גנובת יום או גנובת לילה, הכל שלמתי (תרגום יונתן וירושלמי): **גנבתי.** כמו רבתי בגוים שרתי במדינות (איכה א:א) מלאתי משפט (ישעיה א:כא) אוהבתי לדוש (הושע י:יא): **(מ) אכלני חרב.** לשון אש אוכלה (דברים ד:כד): **וקרח.** כמו משליך קרחו (תהלים קמז:יז) תרגומו גלידא: **שנתי.** לשון שינה: **(מא) ותחלף את משכרתי.** היית משנה תנאי שבינינו מנקוד לטלוא ומעקודים לברודים (לעיל פסוקים ז־ח): **(מב) ופחד יצחק.** לא רצה לומר אלהי יצחק, שאין הקב״ה מייחד שמו על הצדיקים בחייהם. ואע״פ שאמר לו בצאתו מבאר שבע אני ה׳ אלהי אברהם אביך ואלהי יצחק (לעיל כח:יג), בשביל שכהו עיניו והרי הוא כמת (תנחומא תולדות ז), ויעקב נתיירא לומר ואלהי, ואמר ופחד:

38. זֶה עֶשְׂרִים שָׁנָה — *These twenty years . . .* Indignantly, Jacob defended himself, by recounting the hardships he endured in Laban's service. Given Jacob's consistent honesty and devotion, therefore, Laban's suspicion that he would steal his gods — or *anything* of his, for that matter — was wholly unjustified (*Haamek Davar*).

"Had I been dishonest, you would have discovered it by now, for no one can conceal dishonesty for twenty years. Furthermore, these years were spent with *you*, the ultimate rogue; no one could better sniff out chicanery than you!" (*Or HaChaim*).

לֹא שִׁכֵּלוּ — *Never miscarried.* Jacob always made sure the sheep had enough water and pasture, so that miscarriages did not happen (*Rashbam*). Likewise, Jacob continued, he paid for animals that been attacked and mangled by beasts of prey, even though a shepherd is exempt from such damages (*Nachalas Yaakov*). Alternatively, Jacob's care was so exemplary that his flocks were never attacked (*R' Bachya*).

41. עֲבַדְתִּיךָ אַרְבַּע־עֶשְׂרֵה שָׁנָה בִּשְׁתֵּי בְנֹתֶיךָ — *I served you fourteen years for your two daughters.* Bitterly, Jacob alluded to Laban's trickery, which caused him to work *fourteen* years for *two* wives instead of *seven* years for Rachel, as he had originally proposed. In consideration of Leah's feelings, however, Jacob was not explicit (*R' Hoffmann*).

42. וּפַחַד יִצְחָק — *And the Fear of Isaac.* This appellation for God

רָאָה אֱלֹהִים וַיּוֹכַח אָמֶשׁ: שביעי מג וַיַּעַן לָבָן וַיֹּאמֶר

< and said < Then Laban replied **43** « last night. < so He admonished [you] « God saw,

אֶל־יַעֲקֹב הַבָּנוֹת בְּנֹתַי וְהַבָּנִים בָּנַי וְהַצֹּאן צֹאנִי

« are my sheep, < and the sheep < are my sons < the sons < are my daughters, < The daughters « Jacob, < to

וְכֹל אֲשֶׁר־אַתָּה רֹאֶה לִי־הוּא וְלִבְנֹתַי מָה־אֶעֱשֶׂה

< could I do <— what « Yet to my daughters « it is. < mine < see < you < that < and all

לָאֵלֶּה הַיּוֹם אוֹ לִבְנֵיהֶן אֲשֶׁר יָלָדוּ: מד וְעַתָּה

< So now, **44** « they have borne! < whom < to their sons < or « today, < to these

גְּלִי קֳדָם יְיָ וְאוֹכַח בְּרַמְשָׁא: מג וַאֲתֵיב לָבָן וַאֲמַר לְיַעֲקֹב בְּנָתָא בְנָתַי וּבְנַיָּא בְנַי וְעָנָא עָנִי וְכֹל דִּי אַתְּ חָזֵי דִּילִי הוּא וְלִבְנָתַי מָה אֶעְבֵּד לְאִלֵּין יוֹמָא דֵין אוֹ לִבְנֵיהֶן דִּי יְלִידָא: מד וּכְעַן אֱתָא נִגְזַר קְיָם אֲנָא וְאַתְּ וִיהֵי לְסָהִיד בֵּינִי וּבֵינָךְ: מה וּנְסִיב יַעֲקֹב אַבְנָא וּזְקָפַהּ קָמָא: מו וַאֲמַר יַעֲקֹב לַאֲחוֹהִי לְקוֹטוּ אַבְנִין וּנְסִיבוּ אַבְנִין וַעֲבָדוּ דְּגוֹרָא וַאֲכָלוּ תַמָּן עַל דְּגוֹרָא: מז וּקְרָא לֵהּ לָבָן יְגַר שַׂהֲדוּתָא וְיַעֲקֹב קְרָא לֵהּ גַּלְעֵד: מח וַאֲמַר לָבָן דְּגוֹרָא הָדֵין סָהִיד בֵּינִי וּבֵינָךְ יוֹמָא דֵין עַל כֵּן

לְכָה נִכְרְתָה בְרִית אֲנִי וָאָתָּה וְהָיָה לְעֵד בֵּינִי וּבֵינֶךָ: מה וַיִּקַּח יַעֲקֹב

< Then Jacob took **45** « and between you. < between me < a witness < and He shall be « and you, < I « a covenant, < let us make < come,

אָבֶן וַיְרִימֶהָ מַצֵּבָה: מו וַיֹּאמֶר יַעֲקֹב לְאֶחָיו לִקְטוּ אֲבָנִים וַיִּקְחוּ אֲבָנִים

< stones < So they took « stones! < Gather « to his brethren, < And Jacob said **46** « as a monument. < and raised it up < a stone

וַיַּעֲשׂוּ־גָל וַיֹּאכְלוּ שָׁם עַל־הַגָּל: מז וַיִּקְרָא־לוֹ לָבָן יְגַר שָׂהֲדוּתָא וְיַעֲקֹב

< but Jacob « Jegar-sahadutha; « Laban did, « it, < And he called **47** « the mound. < on < there < and they ate « a mound, < and made

קָרָא לוֹ גַּלְעֵד: מח וַיֹּאמֶר לָבָן הַגַּל הַזֶּה עֵד בֵּינִי וּבֵינְךָ הַיּוֹם עַל־כֵּן

< therefore « today; < and between you < between me < is a witness < This mound < And Laban said, **48** « Galeed. < it < called

רש"י

ויוכח. לשון תוכחה הוא ולא לשון הוכחה (תרגום יונתן): **(מג) מה אעשה לאלה.** איך תעלה על לבי להרע להן: **(מד) והיה לעד.** הקב"ה: **(מו) לאחיו.** הם בניו שהיו לו אחים נגשים לצרה ולמלחמה עליו (ב"ר עד:יג): **(מז) יגר שהדותא.** תרגומו של גלעד (תרגום יונתן): **גלעד.** גל עד:

refers to the fear that Isaac experienced when he was on the *Akeidah* and he felt the knife on his throat. This fear was instinctive, but Isaac conquered it and dedicated himself to God, and Jacob credited this merit with defending him against Laban's machinations (*R' Hirsch*).

עָנְיִי וְאֶת־יְגִיעַ כַּפַּי — *My suffering and the toil of my hands.* God perceived that whatever I achieved was by great toil, so He pitied and vindicated me accordingly.

43. הַבָּנוֹת בְּנֹתַי — *The daughters are my daughters. . .* Laban's arrogance is astounding. He began his diatribe against Jacob with protestations of aggrieved innocence and victimization. But as soon as Jacob exposed his false pretensions, he blurted out his true feelings.

44-54. Laban proposes a treaty. His fulminations ended, Laban resumed his self-righteousness and demanded that Jacob promise not to mistreat his family, as if thirteen years had not proven that he was a model husband and father. The agreement included two parts: (1) Jacob would not mistreat Laban's daughters (vs. 48-50); and (2) neither party would pass a designated landmark with hostile intentions (vs. 51-53).

46. לְאֶחָיו — *To his brethren,* Jacob's sons who stood by him in trouble and battle, like *brethren* (*Rashi*). Jacob could not have been speaking to Laban's companions: first, because he had no right to issue orders to them; and second, because a company that was ready to kill him at Laban's orders could hardly be called "brethren" (*Gur Aryeh*).

וַיֹּאכְלוּ שָׁם — *And they ate there.* A meal was part of the ceremony of the covenant, signaling the mutual acceptance of the pact (*Radak* to 26:30).

47. Jacob and Laban both gave it the same name, but Jacob used Hebrew, because he would not abandon the sacred tongue (*Sforno*), and Laban used Aramaic. The name means *the mound is a witness* (*Rashi*). The place was formally given that name in the next verse.

קָרָא־שְׁמ֖וֹ גַּלְעֵֽד׃ מט וְהַמִּצְפָּה֙ אֲשֶׁ֣ר אָמַ֔ר יִ֥צֶף יהוָ֖ה

he called its name Galeed. 49 And as for the Mizpah — because he said, May HASHEM keep watch

בֵּינִ֣י וּבֵינֶ֑ךָ כִּ֥י נִסָּתֵ֖ר אִ֥ישׁ מֵרֵעֵֽהוּ׃ נ אִם־תְּעַנֶּ֣ה

between me and between you when we are hidden, one from his friend. 50 If you will ill-treat

אֶת־בְּנֹתַ֗י וְאִם־תִּקַּ֤ח נָשִׁים֙ עַל־בְּנֹתַ֔י אֵ֥ין אִ֖ישׁ

my daughters or if you will take wives in addition to my daughters — [though] no man

עִמָּ֑נוּ רְאֵ֕ה אֱלֹהִ֥ים עֵ֖ד בֵּינִ֥י וּבֵינֶֽךָ׃ נא וַיֹּ֥אמֶר לָבָ֖ן

may be among us — but see! God is a witness between me and between you. 51 And Laban said

לְיַעֲקֹ֑ב הִנֵּ֣ה ׀ הַגַּ֣ל הַזֶּ֗ה וְהִנֵּה֙ הַמַּצֵּבָ֔ה אֲשֶׁ֥ר יָרִ֖יתִי בֵּינִ֥י וּבֵינֶֽךָ׃ נב עֵ֚ד

to Jacob, Here is this mound, and here is the monument which I have cast between me and between you. 52 A witness

הַגַּ֣ל הַזֶּ֔ה וְעֵדָ֖ה הַמַּצֵּבָ֑ה אִם־אָ֗נִי לֹֽא־אֶעֱבֹ֤ר אֵלֶ֙יךָ֙ אֶת־הַגַּ֣ל הַזֶּ֔ה וְאִם־

shall this mound be and a witness shall the monument be that I may not cross over toward you [beyond] this mound, and that

אַ֠תָּ֠ה לֹֽא־תַעֲבֹ֨ר אֵלַ֜י אֶת־הַגַּ֥ל הַזֶּ֛ה וְאֶת־הַמַּצֵּבָ֥ה הַזֹּ֖את לְרָעָֽה׃

you may not cross over to me [beyond] this mound and this monument, for evil.

נג אֱלֹהֵ֨י אַבְרָהָ֜ם וֵֽאלֹהֵ֤י נָחוֹר֙ יִשְׁפְּט֣וּ בֵינֵ֔ינוּ *אֱלֹהֵ֖י אֲבִיהֶ֑ם

53 The God of Abraham and the god of Nahor should judge between us — the god of their father.

וַיִּשָּׁבַ֣ע יַעֲקֹ֔ב בְּפַ֖חַד אָבִ֥יו יִצְחָֽק׃ נד וַיִּזְבַּ֨ח יַעֲקֹ֥ב זֶ֙בַח֙ בָּהָ֔ר וַיִּקְרָ֥א

And Jacob swore by the Fear of his father Isaac. 54 Then Jacob slaughtered a feast on the mountain, and called

* חול

קְרָא שְׁמֵהּ גַּלְעֵד: מט וְסָכוּתָא דִּי אֲמַר יִסֶךְ מֵימְרָא דַייָ בֵּינִי וּבֵינָךְ אֲרֵי נִתְכַּסֵי גְּבַר מֵחַבְרֵהּ: נ אִם תְּעַנֵּי יָת בְּנָתַי וְאִם תִּסַב נְשִׁין עַל בְּנָתַי לֵית אֱנַשׁ עִמָּנָא חֲזֵי מֵימְרָא דַייָ סָהִיד בֵּינִי וּבֵינָךְ: נא וַאֲמַר לָבָן לְיַעֲקֹב הָא דְּגוֹרָא הָדֵין וְהָא קַמְתָא דִּי אֲקֵימִית בֵּינִי וּבֵינָךְ: נב סָהִיד דְּגוֹרָא הָדֵין וְסָהֲדָא קָמָא אִם אֲנָא לָא אֶעְבַּר לְוָתָךְ יָת דְּגוֹרָא הָדֵין וְאִם אַתְּ לָא תִעְבַּר לְוָתִי יָת דְּגוֹרָא הָדֵין וְיָת קַמְתָא הָדָא לְבִישׁוּ: נג אֱלָהֵהּ דְּאַבְרָהָם וֵאלָהֵהּ דְּנָחוֹר יְדוּנוּן בֵּינָנָא אֱלָהֵהּ דַּאֲבוּהוֹן וְקַיֵּים יַעֲקֹב בִּדְדָחִיל לֵהּ אֲבוּהִי יִצְחָק: נד וּנְכֵס יַעֲקֹב נִכְסָתָא בְּטוּרָא וּקְרָא

רש"י

(מט) והמצפה אשר אמר וגו'. והמצפה אשר בהר הגלעד, כמ"ש ויעבר את מצפה גלעד (שופטים יא:כט), למה נקראת שמה מצפה, לפי שאמר כל אחד מהם לחברו יצף ה' ביני ובינך אם תעבור את הברית: כי נסתר. ולא נראה איש את רעהו: (נ) בנתי בנתי. ב' פעמים, אף בלהה וזלפה בנותיו היו מפלגש (ב"ר עד:יג; פדר"א פל"ו): אם תענה את בנתי. למנוע מהן עונת תשמיש (יומא עז.): (נא) יריתי. כמו ירה בים (שמות טו:ד). כזה שהוא יורה החץ [ס"א החנית] (ב"ר שם טו): (נב) אם אני. הרי אם משמש בל' אשר, כמו עד אם דברתי דברי (לעיל כד:לג) ופירושו עד אשר דברתי דברי: לרעה. לרעה אי אתה עובר אבל אתה עובר לפרקמטיא (ב"ר שם): (נג) אלהי אברהם. קדש: ואלהי נחור. חול: אלהי אביהם. חול (מסכת סופרים ד:ה): (נד) ויזבח יעקב זבח. שחט בהמות

49. **וְהַמִּצְפָּה** — *And as for the Mizpah* [= watchtower]. According to *Rashi*, as explained by *Ramban*, the *watchtower* was a high, conspicuous structure on the mountain; it was *not* the mound or pillar. Thus, our passage is elliptic: It explains that the structure was called *Mizpah, Watchtower,* because . . . (see *Judges* 11:29).

52. **עֵד הַגַּל הַזֶּה** — *A witness shall this mound be.* These landmarks will serve as reminders of our pact (*Ibn Caspi*). They went on to stipulate that the pact prohibited them only to cross the landmark for unfriendly purposes, but they could certainly cross it to trade with one another (*Rashi*).

53. **אֱלֹהֵי אֲבִיהֶם** — *The god of their father.* Laban referred to the god of Terah, the father of both Abraham and Nahor.

The Pesach *Haggadah* states that Laban wished to uproot everything — but the commentators wonder where we find Laban attempting such far-reaching destruction. *R' Yaakov Kamenetsky* finds it in this verse. Laban "benevolently" wanted to find common ground with Jacob in the god of their forefathers, but for Jacob to acknowledge the existence of any god other than HASHEM would uproot the very basis of the Jewish people. Jacob took his oath only by the *Dread of his father Isaac,* making clear that he owed allegiance only to HASHEM, for all ties to

לְאֶחָיו לֶאֱכָל־לָחֶם וַיֹּאכְלוּ לֶחֶם וַיָּלִינוּ בָּהָר׃

to his brethren ‹ to eat ‹ a meal; ‹‹ and they ate ‹ a meal ‹ and they spent the night ‹ on the mountain. ‹‹

מפטיר **[לב]** 32 א 1 וַיַּשְׁכֵּם לָבָן בַּבֹּקֶר וַיְנַשֵּׁק לְבָנָיו

And Laban awoke early ‹ in the morning; ‹‹ he kissed ‹ his sons ‹

וְלִבְנוֹתָיו וַיְבָרֶךְ אֶתְהֶם וַיֵּלֶךְ וַיָּשָׁב לָבָן לִמְקֹמוֹ׃ ב 2 וְיַעֲקֹב הָלַךְ לְדַרְכּוֹ

and his daughters ‹ and he blessed ‹ them; ‹‹ then Laban went and returned ‹ to his place. ‹‹ 2 Jacob ‹ went ‹ on his way, ‹‹

וַיִּפְגְּעוּ־בוֹ מַלְאֲכֵי אֱלֹהִים׃ ג 3 וַיֹּאמֶר יַעֲקֹב כַּאֲשֶׁר רָאָם מַחֲנֵה אֱלֹהִים

and encounter ‹ him ‹ did angels ‹ of God. ‹‹ 3 Jacob said ‹ when ‹ he saw them, ‹‹ A camp ‹ *of God* ‹

זֶה וַיִּקְרָא שֵׁם־הַמָּקוֹם הַהוּא מַחֲנָיִם׃ **פפפ** קמ״ח פסוקים. חלק״י סימן. מחני״ם סימן.

is this! ‹‹ So he called ‹ the name ‹ of that place ‹ Mahanaim. ‹‹

לַאֲחוּהִי לְמֵיכַל לַחְמָא וַאֲכָלוּ לַחְמָא וּבִיתוּ בְּטוּרָא׃ א וְאַקְדֵּים לָבָן בְּצַפְרָא וּנְשַׁק לִבְנוֹהִי וְלִבְנָתֵהּ וּבָרִיךְ יָתְהֵן וַאֲזַל וְתָב לָבָן לְאַתְרֵהּ׃ ב וְיַעֲקֹב אֲזַל לְאָרְחֵהּ וַעֲרָעוּ בֵהּ מַלְאֲכַיָּא דַייָ׃ ג וַאֲמַר יַעֲקֹב כַּד חֲזָנוּן מַשְׁרִיתָא מִן קֳדָם יְיָ דֵּין וּקְרָא שְׁמָא דְאַתְרָא הַהוּא מַחֲנָיִם׃

THE HAFTARAH FOR VAYEITZEI APPEARS ON PAGE 337.

רש״י

למשתה: **לאחיו.** לאוהביו שעם לבן (תרגום יונתן): **לאכל לחם.** כל דבר מאכל קרוי לחם, כמו עבד לחם רב (דניאל ה:א) נשחיתה עץ בלחמו (ירמיה יא:יט): **(ב) ויפגעו בו מלאכי אלהים.** מלאכים של ארץ ישראל באו לקראתו ללוותו לארץ (תנחומא וישלח ג): **(ג) מחנים.** שתי מחנות של חוצה לארץ שבאו עמו עד כאן, ושל ארץ ישראל שבאו לקראתו (שם):

Terah's family had long since been severed. Jews owe their loyalty only to the God of the Patriarchs.

54. וַיִּקְרָא לְאֶחָיו — *And called to his brethren.* Now that the pact had been concluded, Jacob referred to Laban's companions as his brethren [see v. 23] (*Rashi*), and invited them all to share a meal so that they would part on good terms (*Ramban*).

32.

1. וַיְבָרֶךְ אֶתְהֶם — *And blessed them.* Although the Sages have taught that even the blessing of a common person should not be denigrated, Scripture has a deeper purpose in mentioning that Laban blessed his daughters and grandsons. It means to teach how effective a blessing can be when it is conferred with total sincerity, for Laban was surely sincere in blessing his own daughters and their children (*Sforno*).

2. מַלְאֲכֵי אֱלֹהִים — *Angels of God.* They were angels who minister in *Eretz Yisrael*. They came to meet him to accompany Jacob to the Holy Land, replacing the angels that had been with him outside the Land. This reversed the changing of the angelic guard that took place when he left *Eretz Yisrael* to go to Haran [28:12] (*Midrash; Rashi*).

3. מַחֲנֵה אֱלֹהִים — *A camp of God.* Jacob meant to assure those with him: "These are not the troops of Esau or Laban coming to attack us; they are camps of holy angels which God sent to protect us from our enemies" (*Targum Yonasan*).

מַחֲנָיִם — *Mahanaim* [lit., *a pair of camps*]. There were two camps of angels: those who ministered outside the Holy Land who had accompanied him, and those of the Holy Land who now came to meet him (*Tanchuma; Rashi*).

Ramban suggests that the plural refers to Jacob's camp on earth and the camp of angels on high. The title implies that both camps are equal, because they both exist only to bless God and assert His unity.

◆§ קמ״ח פסוקים. חלק״י סימן. מחני״ם סימן — This Masoretic note means: There are 148 verses in the *Sidrah,* numerically corresponding to the mnemonics מַחֲנַיִ״ם, *two camps,* and חֶלְקִ״י, *my portion,* each of which totals 148.

The Jewish people are referred to as God's חֵלֶק, *portion,* as in כִּי חֵלֶק ה׳ עַמּוֹ, *HASHEM'S portion is His people* [*Deuteronomy* 32:9]. Thus the birth of eleven of the twelve tribes, as described in this *Sidrah,* constitutes the nation that God describes as חֶלְקִי, *My portion.* Additionally, the final word of the *Sidrah* is מַחֲנָיִם, *Machanaim* [lit., *a pair of camps*], the name Jacob gave to the place. It also alludes to Jacob's abundant, flourishing growth, a condition which he was to describe in 32:11 as having grown into שְׁנֵי מַחֲנוֹת, *two camps* (*R' David Feinstein*).

PARASHAS VAYISHLACH / פרשת וישלח

ד וַיִּשְׁלַ֨ח יַעֲקֹ֤ב מַלְאָכִים֙ לְפָנָ֔יו אֶל־עֵשָׂ֖ו אָחִ֑יו
4 Then Jacob sent > messengers > before him > to > Esau > his brother

אַ֥רְצָה שֵׂעִ֖יר שְׂדֵ֥ה אֱדֽוֹם׃ ה וַיְצַ֤ו אֹתָם֙ לֵאמֹ֔ר כֹּ֣ה
to the land > of Seir, > the field > of Edom. >> 5 He commanded > them, > saying: >> Thus >

תֹאמְר֔וּן לַֽאדֹנִ֖י לְעֵשָׂ֑ו כֹּ֤ה אָמַר֙ עַבְדְּךָ֣ יַעֲקֹ֔ב עִם־לָבָ֣ן גַּ֔רְתִּי וָאֵחַ֖ר
shall you say, > 'To my lord, > to Esau, >> so > said > your servant > Jacob: >> With > Laban > have I sojourned, >> and I have lingered >

עַד־עָֽתָּה׃ ו וַֽיְהִי־לִי֙ שׁ֣וֹר וַחֲמ֔וֹר צֹ֖אן וְעֶ֣בֶד וְשִׁפְחָ֑ה וָֽאֶשְׁלְחָה֙ לְהַגִּ֣יד
until > now. >> 6 I have [acquired] > oxen > and donkeys, > sheep, > servants, > and maidservants, >> and I am sending > to tell >

אונקלוס

ד וּשְׁלַח יַעֲקֹב אִזְגַּדִּין קֳדָמוֹהִי לְוַת עֵשָׂו אֲחוּהִי לְאַרְעָא דְשֵׂעִיר לַחֲקַל אֱדוֹם: ה וּפַקִּיד יָתְהוֹן לְמֵימַר כִּדְנַן תֵּימְרוּן לְרִבּוֹנִי לְעֵשָׂו כִּדְנַן אֲמַר עַבְדָּךְ יַעֲקֹב עִם לָבָן דָּרִית וְאוֹחָרִית עַד כְּעָן: ו וַהֲוָה לִי תּוֹרִין וַחֲמָרִין עָן וְעַבְדִּין וְאַמְהָן וּשְׁלָחִית לְחַוָּאָה

רש"י

(ד) **וישלח יעקב מלאכים.** מלאכים ממש (ב"ר עה:ד): **ארצה שעיר.** לארץ שעיר, כל תיבה שצריכה למ"ד בתחלתה הטיל לה הכתוב ה"א בסופה (יבמות יג:): (ה) **גרתי.** לא נעשיתי שר וחשוב אלא גר. אינך כדאי לשנוא אותי על ברכות אביך שברכני הוה גביר לאחיך (לעיל כז:כט), שהרי לא נתקיימה בי (תנחומא ישן ה). [ד"א, גרתי בגימטריא תרי"ג (ברב"ת), כלומר, עם לבן הרשע גרתי ותרי"ג מצות שמרתי ולא למדתי ממעשיו הרעים:] (ו) **ויהי לי שור וחמור.** אבא אמר לי מטל השמים ומשמני הארץ (לעיל כז:כח), זו אינה לא מן השמים ולא מן הארץ (תנחומא ישן ה): **שור וחמור.** דרך ארץ לומר על שוורים הרבה שור. אדם אומר לחבירו בלילה, קרא התרנגול, ואינו אומר קראו התרנגולים (שם): **ואשלחה להגיד לאדני.** להודיע שאני בא אליך:

PARASHAS VAYISHLACH

4-7. Esau advances to attack Jacob. After he had received the Patriarchal blessings from Isaac, Jacob had been sent away from home to protect him against Esau's threatened vengeance. Now, thirty-four years later — including fourteen years of study in the academy of Shem and Eber and twenty years with Laban — Esau's hatred remained implacable and, as Jacob advanced toward *Eretz Yisrael* with his family and entourage, Esau advanced toward him with an imposing, frightening army, determined to carry out his old, but still-fresh threat.

According to the *Zohar*, Jacob took the initiative in seeking a reconciliation while Isaac was still alive, because, given Esau's great respect for his father, it seemed logical that he would make peace with Jacob to avoid saddening their father. *Ramban* notes that Jacob could not avoid this potentially dangerous confrontation because the direct route to his parents' home in the south of the Land took him through Esau's habitat of Edom. However, according to the Midrash, Jacob should have taken a roundabout route to avoid Edom, for the Sages fault him for "taking the dog [Esau] by the ears . . . Esau was going about his business and you send messengers to say, 'So said your servant Jacob!' "

The confrontation between the brothers is recorded to illustrate how God protected His servant from the hand of a stronger enemy. Furthermore, it shows that Jacob did not rely on his own righteousness, but strove mightily to ensure his safety through *practical* measures. Indeed, our Sages saw in this chapter the textbook of Jewish behavior in this exile, and, accordingly, we should follow his example by making a threefold preparation in our struggles with Esau's descendants: prayer, gifts [= appeasement], and battle, as will be noted in the commentary (*Ramban*). Indeed, the Midrash (*Bereishis Rabbah* 78:15) records that in Talmudic times the rabbis who had to intervene with the Romans to counteract oppressive decrees would study this chapter before they went. Once, R' Yannai failed to do so, and his trip was a dismal failure. Obviously he remembered the narrative, but, just as obviously, when men of his caliber study it to find guidance regarding specific situations, they see messages and nuances that escape others.

4. מַלְאָכִים — *Messengers.* According to *Rashi* and another view in the Midrash, he sent real angels, in order to both impress and terrify Esau. This teaches that righteous people are greater than angels, for when Jacob had need of emissaries, he had the right to summon angels to do his bidding (*Tanchuma).* The reason for the greater stature of human beings is that angels are created with a particular degree of holiness, and they remain forever static. Human beings, however, achieve their standing through their own striving, and they can grow constantly.

אַרְצָה שֵׂעִיר — *To the land of Seir,* the mountainous region from the Dead Sea southward toward the Gulf of Aqaba.

5. וַיְצַו אֹתָם לֵאמֹר — *He commanded them, saying.* Jacob wanted his messengers to deliver the message verbatim, including the fact that in his conversations with them he had referred to Esau as "my lord" and to himself as Esau's "servant." This was part of Jacob's tactful approach, because thereby Esau would realize that Jacob truly held him in great esteem (*Or HaChaim*).

עִם־לָבָן גַּרְתִּי — *With Laban I have sojourned.* The verb גַּרְתִּי, *lodged*, implies staying as a *stranger* [from גֵּר = *alien*]. Thus Ja-

לַאדֹנִ֔י לִמְצֹא־חֵ֖ן בְּעֵינֶֽיךָ׃ ז וַיָּשֻׁ֙בוּ֙ הַמַּלְאָכִ֔ים

‹ The messengers returned 7 « in your eyes.' ‹ favor ‹ to find ‹ my lord

אֶֽל־יַעֲקֹ֖ב לֵאמֹ֑ר בָּ֤אנוּ אֶל־אָחִ֙יךָ֙ אֶל־עֵשָׂ֔ו וְגַם֙

‹ more-over, « Esau; ‹ to ‹ your brother, ‹ to ‹ We came ‹ saying, ‹ Jacob, ‹ to

הֹלֵ֣ךְ לִקְרָֽאתְךָ֔ וְאַרְבַּע־מֵא֥וֹת אִ֖ישׁ עִמּֽוֹ׃ ח וַיִּירָ֧א יַעֲקֹ֛ב מְאֹ֖ד וַיֵּ֣צֶר ל֑וֹ

« him. ‹ and it distressed « exceedingly, ‹ Jacob became frightened 8 « are with him. ‹ men ‹ hundred ‹ and four ‹ toward you, ‹ he is coming

לְרִבּוֹנִי לְאַשְׁכָּחָא רַחֲמִין בְּעֵינָךְ:
ז וְתָבוּ אִזְגַּדַּיָּא לְוַת יַעֲקֹב לְמֵימָר
אֲתֵינָא לְוַת אָחוּךְ לְוַת עֵשָׂו וְאַף
אָזֵיל לְקַדָּמוּתָךְ וְאַרְבַּע מְאָה גוּבְרִין
עִמֵּהּ: ח וּדְחֵיל יַעֲקֹב לַחֲדָא וַעֲקַת לֵהּ

רש"י

למצא חן בעיניך. שאני שלם עמך ומבקש אהבתך: **(ז) באנו אל אחיך אל עשו.** שהיית אומר אחי הוא (ב"ר שם ד) אבל הוא נוהג עמך כעשו הרשע, עודנו בשנאתו (תנחומא ישן ו; ב"ר שם ז): **(ח) ויירא ויצר.** ויירא שמא ייהרג, ויצר לו אם יהרוג הוא את אחרים (תנחומא ד; ב"ר עו:ב):

cob meant to tell Esau, "I have not become a great prince nor have I achieved status . . . I remained merely an alien. Therefore, you need not hate me for having received Father's blessing [27:29], since it has clearly not been fulfilled."

Midrashically, the numerical value of גַּרְתִּי equals תרי״ג, 613. Thus Jacob implied to Esau, "Though *I have sojourned with Laban,* I have observed the 613 Divine Commandments, and have not learned from his evil ways" (*Rashi*). This was a message to Esau that he should not trifle with Jacob, for his righteousness was still intact.

7. בָּאנוּ אֶל־אָחִיךָ אֶל־עֵשָׂו — *We came to your brother, to Esau.* This was part of their report on Esau's intentions. "We came to the person whom you regard as a *brother*, but he behaves toward you as a wicked *Esau* — he still harbors hatred" (*Rashi*).

8-21. Battle, prayer, and tribute. Jacob prepared for the confrontation in three ways: He readied himself and his camp for a battle to the death, he threw himself upon God's mercy through prayer, and he sent a lavish tribute to appease Esau's anger. On the surface, these courses of action convey contradictory messages; aggression and servility seem to be irreconcilable characteristics. Total faith in God would seem to rule out either form of reliance on human effort [see Faith and Trust, 40:15]. Of course, one can view such a combination of approaches pragmatically; people routinely adopt tactics without being troubled by a lack of sincerity — if it works, do it! But Jacob was the embodiment of truth; it is inconceivable that he would adopt insincere charades.

That Jacob could dedicate himself with conviction to contradictory courses of action is testimony to his self-discipline. He could cast his lot with God, yet not fail to make the necessary human responses to a crisis; he could recognize an element of justice in Esau's hurt at losing the blessings, yet prepare for an attack as if there were no defense but his own strong arms. This chapter teaches that Israel in exile must always be able to recognize and act upon the varying and sometimes conflicting elements in any situation.

☙ Jacob's fear

On the surface it would seem that Jacob's fear of Esau (v. 8) betrayed a lack of faith in God's promise of protection when he went to Haran (28:15), a promise that God reiterated when He commanded Jacob to return to *Eretz Yisrael* (31:3). *Rashi* (v. 11), however, explains that the righteous are never sure of themselves, and that is why Jacob was afraid that he might have sinned in the interim and thereby forfeited his right to the Godly shield from harm. Although Jacob did not know of any specific sins, he feared that there might have been some. The Midrash suggests that he was distressed by the very fact that he was afraid, for such fear indicated a lack of trust in God's promise.

Others comment that the sin that concerned him was his approach to Esau, his archenemy, for, as noted above, the Midrash cites that as an error. He might have felt that he was at fault in sealing a covenant with Laban, or it may have been his failure to honor his parents for twenty years that troubled him. The *Zohar* comments that God instilled this fear in Jacob so that he would be forced to pray, for God craves the prayers of the righteous.

Rambam (Yesodei HaTorah 10:4) discusses the rule of the Sages that God never withdraws a prophecy to do good (*Berachos* 7a); if so, how could Jacob have doubted the Divine promise to protect him? *Rambam* explains that this dictum applies only to a public prophecy, but not one given privately to an individual, like God's promise to Jacob; such a prophecy is subject to the continued worthiness of the recipient.

R' Hirsch notes the contrast between Jacob's confidence during his years with Laban and his fear at this time. Jacob knew that Esau had felt personally injured by Jacob, and this might influence God to take pity on Esau.

8-9. Military preparations. Jacob divided his people in such a manner that each camp had some of his men, maidservants, and cattle, but he kept his wives and children together. His strategy was to station the family camp in the rear, so that the other one would be a buffer between them and Esau (*Abarbanel*).

8. וַיִּירָא . . . וַיֵּצֶר — *Became frightened . . . and it distressed.* In the plain sense, Jacob was apprehensive at the news that Esau was coming with a sizable army to attack him (*Ramban*). He was *frightened* that *he* would be killed, and he was *distressed* that, in defending himself and his family, he might kill others (*Rashi*). *Distress* is a stronger emotion than *fear.* The prospect that he might be forced to kill was more disturbing to Jacob than the possibility that he might be killed (*Ralbag*).

וַיַּחַץ אֶת־הָעָם אֲשֶׁר־אִתּוֹ וְאֶת־הַצֹּאן וְאֶת־הַבָּקָר

So he divided the people who were with him, and the flock, and the cattle,

וְהַגְּמַלִּים לִשְׁנֵי מַחֲנוֹת: ט וַיֹּאמֶר אִם־יָבוֹא עֵשָׂו

and the camels — into two camps. 9 For he said, If Esau comes

אֶל־הַמַּחֲנֶה הָאַחַת וְהִכָּהוּ וְהָיָה הַמַּחֲנֶה הַנִּשְׁאָר

to the one camp and strikes it, then it will be [that] the camp that remains

לִפְלֵיטָה: י וַיֹּאמֶר יַעֲקֹב אֱלֹהֵי אָבִי אַבְרָהָם

may escape. 10 Then Jacob said, God of my father Abraham

וֵאלֹהֵי אָבִי יִצְחָק יהוה הָאֹמֵר אֵלַי שׁוּב לְאַרְצְךָ וּלְמוֹלַדְתְּךָ וְאֵיטִיבָה

and God of my father Isaac; HASHEM Who said to me, 'Return to your land and to your birthplace and I will do good

עִמָּךְ: יא קָטֹנְתִּי מִכֹּל הַחֲסָדִים וּמִכָּל־הָאֱמֶת אֲשֶׁר עָשִׂיתָ אֶת־עַבְדֶּךָ

with you' — 11 I am unworthy of all the kindnesses and of all the truth that You have done with Your servant;

כִּי בְמַקְלִי עָבַרְתִּי אֶת־הַיַּרְדֵּן הַזֶּה וְעַתָּה הָיִיתִי לִשְׁנֵי מַחֲנוֹת:

for with my staff I crossed this Jordan and now I have become two camps.

וּפַלֵּיג יָת עַמָּא דִּי עִמֵּהּ וְיָת עָנָא וְיָת תּוֹרֵי וְגַמְלַיָּא לִתְרֵין מַשְׁרְיָן: ט וַאֲמַר אִם יֵיתֵי עֵשָׂו לְמַשְׁרִיתָא חֲדָא וְיִמְחִנֵּהּ וִיהֵי (נ״א וְיִמְחִנַּהּ וּתְהֵי) מַשְׁרִיתָא דְּיִשְׁתָּאֲרָא לְשֵׁיזָבָא: י וַאֲמַר יַעֲקֹב אֱלָהֵהּ דְּאַבָּא אַבְרָהָם וֵאלָהֵהּ דְּאַבָּא יִצְחָק יְיָ דִּי אֲמַר לִי תּוּב לְאַרְעָךְ וּלְיַלָּדוּתָךְ וְאוֹטֵיב עִמָּךְ: יא זְעֵירָן זַכְוָתִי מִכֹּל חִסְדִּין וּמִכָּל טַבְוָן דִּי עֲבַדְתָּ עִם עַבְדָּךְ אֲרֵי יְחִידִי עֲבָרִית יָת יַרְדְּנָא הָדֵין וּכְעַן הֲוֵיתִי לִתְרֵין (נ״א לְתַרְתֵּין) מַשְׁרְיָן:

רש״י

(ט) **המחנה האחת והכהו.** מחנה משמש לשון זכר ולשון נקבה. אם תחנה עלי מחנה (תהלים כז:ג) הרי לשון נקבה, המחנה הזה (להלן לג:ח) לשון זכר. וכן יש שאר דברים משמשים לשון זכר ולשון נקבה. השמש יצא על הארץ (לעיל יט:כג), מקצה השמים מוצאו (תהלים יט:ז) הרי לשון זכר, והשמש זרחה על המים (מלכים ב ג:כב) הרי לשון נקבה. וכן רוח, והנה רוח גדולה באה (איוב א:יט) הרי לשון נקבה, ויגע בארבע פנות הבית (שם) הרי לשון זכר, ורוח גדולה וחזק מפרק הרים (מלכים א יט:יא) הרי לשון זכר ולשון נקבה. וכן אש, ואש יצאה מאת ה' (במדבר טז:לה) לשון נקבה, אש לוהט (תהלים קד:ד) לשון זכר: **והיה המחנה הנשאר לפליטה.** על כרחו, כי אלחם עמו. התקין עצמו לשלשה דברים, לדורון לתפלה ולמלחמה. לדורון, ותעבור המנחה על פניו (להלן פסוק כב). לתפלה, אלהי אבי אברהם (פסוק י). למלחמה, והיה המחנה הנשאר לפליטה (תנחומא ישן ו): (י) **ואלהי אבי יצחק.** ולהלן הוא אומר ופחד יצחק (לעיל לא:מב, ועי' רש"י שם). ועוד מהו שחזר והזכיר שם המיוחד, היה לו לכתוב האומר אלי שוב לארצך וגו'. אלא כך אמר יעקב לפני הקב"ה, שתי הבטחות הבטחתני, אחת בצאתי מבית אבי מבאר שבע, שאמרת לי אני ה' אלהי אברהם אביך ואלהי יצחק (כח:יג) ושם אמרת לי ושמרתיך בכל אשר תלך (שם טו), ובבית לבן אמרת לי שוב אל ארץ אבותיך ולמולדתך ואהיה עמך (לא:ג), ושם נגלית אלי בשם המיוחד לבדו, שנאמר ויאמר ה' אל יעקב שוב אל ארץ אבותיך וגו' (שם). בשתי הבטחות האלו אני בא לפניך: (יא) **קטנתי מכל החסדים.** נתמעטו זכיותי ע"י החסדים והאמת שעשית עמי (תענית כ:; שבת לב.). לכך אני ירא, שמא משהבטחתני נתלכלכתי בחטא ויגרום לי להמסר ביד עשו (תנחומא בשלח כח; ברכות ד.; במ"ר יט:לב): **ומכל האמת.** אמתת דבריך שאמרת לי כל ההבטחות שהבטחתני: **כי במקלי.** לא היה עמי לא כסף ולא זהב ולא מקנה אלא מקלי לבדו. ומדרש אגדה נתן מקלו בירדן ונבקע הירדן (תנחומא ישן ויצא ג):

9. הַמַּחֲנֶה הַנִּשְׁאָר לִפְלֵיטָה — *The camp that remains may escape.* While Esau's force was fighting Jacob and the first camp, the other camp, with Jacob's family, would flee to safety. *Ramban* comments on what Jacob's strategy portended for the future of Israel. Various countries will decree the extermination or the crippling of the Jewish people, but the nation will always survive, because Jews in other countries will be treated benevolently and thus insure the survival of the nation.

10-13. Prayer. This was the second component of Jacob's three-pronged strategy, for he knew that without God's help, all of man's plans and exertions are in vain.

11. קָטֹנְתִּי — *I am unworthy.* According to *Ramban,* Jacob, in his humility, declared that he had never been worthy of all the kindnesses God had done him. *Rashi,* however, translates *I have been diminished.* My merits have been diminished by all the *kindnesses* You have shown me, and that is why I am afraid. Since Your promise to me, I may have become soiled by sin and not deserve to be delivered from Esau's hands.

Kindnesses are benefits that God confers without having first promised them; *truth* refers to the kindnesses He does in fulfillment of earlier promises.

Jacob knew that he was being escorted by angels now just as he had been when he left *Eretz Yisrael* to journey to Laban. Obviously, therefore, he was still righteous. Why was he afraid? This shows that even good people can be judged and punished for not having achieved their full potential. Of this, Jacob was frightened. Perhaps he had failed to grow as much as he could have. Similarly, the Torah demands that one not merely study, but *exert* himself in his Torah study. And if one fails to do so, it is tantamount to not learning (see *Leviticus* 26:3,15). This is a challenge to every Jew to strive to live up to his potential (*R' Moshe Feinstein*).

יב הַצִּילֵנִי נָא מִיַּד אָחִי מִיַּד עֵשָׂו כִּי־יָרֵא אָנֹכִי

‹ *I fear* ‹ *for* ‹‹ *of Esau,* ‹ *from the hand* ‹ *of my brother,* ‹ *from the hand* ‹ *please,* ‹ *Rescue me,* **12**

אֹתוֹ פֶּן־יָבוֹא וְהִכַּנִי אֵם עַל־בָּנִים׃ יג וְאַתָּה אָמַרְתָּ

‹‹ *had said,* ‹ *And You* **13** ‹‹ *children.* ‹ *with* ‹ *[as well as] mother* ‹‹ *and strike me,* ‹ *he come* ‹ *lest* ‹‹ *him,*

הֵיטֵב אֵיטִיב עִמָּךְ וְשַׂמְתִּי אֶת־זַרְעֲךָ כְּחוֹל הַיָּם

‹ *of the sea* ‹ *like the sand* ‹ *your offspring* ‹ *and I will make* ‹ *with you* ‹ *'I will surely do good*

אֲשֶׁר לֹא־יִסָּפֵר מֵרֹב׃ שני יד וַיָּלֶן שָׁם בַּלַּיְלָה הַהוּא

‹‹ *that night,* ‹ *there* ‹ *He spent the night* **14** ‹‹ *because it is too numerous.'* ‹ *be counted* ‹ *cannot* ‹ *which*

יב שֵׁזְבִנִי כְעַן מִידָא דְאָחִי מִידָא
דְעֵשָׂו אֲרֵי דָחֵל אֲנָא מִנֵּהּ דִּילְמָא
יֵיתֵי וְיִמְחִנַּנִי אִמָּא עַל בְּנַיָּא׃ יג וְאַתְּ
אֲמַרְתָּ אוֹטָבָא אוֹטֵיב עִמָּךְ וַאֲשַׁוֵּי יָת
בְּנָיךְ סַגִּיאִין כְּחָלָא דְיַמָּא דִּי לָא
יִתְמְנוּן מִסְּגֵי׃ יד וּבָת תַּמָּן בְּלֵילְיָא
הַהוּא וּנְסֵיב מִן דְּאַיְתִי בִידֵהּ
תִּקְרֻבְתָּא לְעֵשָׂו אֲחוּהִי׃ טו עִזֵּי מָאתָן
וּתְיָשַׁיָּא עֶסְרִין רְחֵלִין מָאתָן וְדִכְרִין
עֶסְרִין׃ טז גַּמְלֵי מֵינְקָתָא וּבְנֵיהוֹן
תְּלָתִין תּוֹרְתָא אַרְבְּעִין וְתוֹרֵי עַסְרָא
אַתְנָן עֶסְרִין וְעִירֵי עַסְרָא׃ יז וִיהַב בְּיַד
עַבְדּוֹהִי עֶדְרָא עֶדְרָא בִּלְחוֹדוֹהִי
וַאֲמַר לְעַבְדוֹהִי עִבָּרוּ קֳדָמַי

וַיִּקַּח מִן־הַבָּא בְיָדוֹ מִנְחָה לְעֵשָׂו אָחִיו׃ טו עִזִּים מָאתַיִם וּתְיָשִׁים

‹ *and he-goats,* ‹‹ *two hundred,* ‹ *She-goats,* **15** ‹‹ *his brother:* ‹ *to Esau* ‹ *a tribute* ‹ *in his hand,* ‹ *that which had come* ‹ *from* ‹ *then he took,*

עֶשְׂרִים רְחֵלִים מָאתַיִם וְאֵילִים עֶשְׂרִים׃ טז גְּמַלִּים מֵינִיקוֹת וּבְנֵיהֶם

‹ *with their colts,* ‹ *that are nursing* ‹ *she-camels* **16** ‹‹ *twenty;* ‹ *and rams,* ‹‹ *two hundred,* ‹ *ewes,* ‹‹ *twenty;*

שְׁלֹשִׁים פָּרוֹת אַרְבָּעִים וּפָרִים עֲשָׂרָה אֲתֹנֹת עֶשְׂרִים וַעְיָרִם עֲשָׂרָה׃

‹‹ *ten.* ‹ *and he-donkeys,* ‹‹ *twenty,* ‹ *she-donkeys,* ‹‹ *ten;* ‹ *and bulls,* ‹‹ *forty,* ‹ *cows,* ‹‹ *thirty;*

יז וַיִּתֵּן בְּיַד־עֲבָדָיו עֵדֶר עֵדֶר לְבַדּוֹ וַיֹּאמֶר אֶל־עֲבָדָיו עִבְרוּ לְפָנַי

‹ *before me* ‹ *Pass on* ‹‹ *his servants,* ‹ *to* ‹ *and he said* ‹‹ *separately,* ‹ *each drove* ‹ *of his servants* ‹ *in the hand* ‹ *He put* **17**

רש"י

(יב) **מיד אחי מיד עשו.** מיד אחי שאין נוהג עמי כאח אלא כעשו הרשע: (יג) **היטב איטיב.** היטב בזכותך, איטיב בזכות אבותיך (ב"ר עו:ז): **ושמתי את זרעך כחול הים.** והיכן א"ל כן, והלא לא א"ל אלא והיה זרעך כעפר הארץ (לעיל כח:יד). אלא שא"ל כי לא אעזבך עד אשר אם עשיתי את אשר דברתי לך (שם טו, וע"י רש"י שם), ולאברהם אמר הרבה ארבה את זרעך ככוכבי השמים וכחול אשר על שפת הים (שם כב:יז; ברב"א): (יד) **הבא בידו.** ברשותו, וכן ויקח את כל ארצו מידו (במדבר כא:כו; מכילתא משפטים נזיקין פ"ה). ומ"א, מן הבא בידו, אבנים טובות ומרגליות שאדם צר בצרור ונושאם בידו (תנחומא ישן יא). [דבר אחר, מן הבא בידו, מן החולין, שנטל מעשר, כמה דאת אמר עשר אעשרנו לך (לעיל כח:כב), והדר לקח מנחה (פס"ז, ועי' פדר"א פל"ז)]: (טו) **עזים מאתים ותישים עשרים.** מאתים עזים צריכות עשרים תישים, וכן כולם הזכרים כדי צורך הנקבות. ובב"ר (שם) דורש מכאן לעונה האמורה בתורה. הטיילים בכל יום, הפועלים שתים בשבת, החמרים אחת בשבת, הגמלים אחת לשלשים יום. הספנים אחת לששה חדשים (כתובות סא:). ואיני יודע לכוין המדרש הזה בכוון, אך נראה בעיני שלמדנו מכאן שאין העונה שוה בכל אדם אלא לפי טורח המוטל עליו, שמצינו כאן שמסר לכל תיש עשר עזים וכן לכל איל, לפי שהם פנויים ממלאכה דרכן להרבות תשמיש ולעבר עשר נקבות, ובהמה משנתעברה אינה מקבלת זכר. ופרים שעוסקין במלאכה לא מסר לזכר אלא ארבע נקבות, ולחמור שהולך בדרך רחוקה שתי נקבות לזכר, ולגמלים שהולכים דרך יותר רחוקה נקבה אחת לזכר (ירושלמי כתובות ה:ז): (טז) **גמלים מיניקות שלשים.** ובניהם עמהם. ומדרש אגדה, ובניהם בנאיהם, זכר כנגד נקבה, ולפי שצנוע בתשמיש לא פרסמו הכתוב (ב"ר שם): **ועירים.** חמורים זכרים (שם): (יז) **עדר עדר לבדו.** כל מין ומין לעצמו (שם ח): **עברו לפני.** דרך יום או פחות ואני אבוא אחריכם:

14-22. The tribute. To show his good will and subservience, Jacob sent a lavish series of tributes to Esau in the hope of assuaging his wrath. Jacob thus set a pattern for future generations that would confront Esau's oppression. When Israel is powerless to fight its enemies, instead of asserting that its cause is just, it must appease its enemies in terms that they, in their greed, can comprehend. Jacob spent the night in his camp, hoping for a prophetic vision — but none came. *Radak* comments that by not appearing to him, God was implying to Jacob that even the most righteous people should not rely on God's miracles, but should make all rational preparations.

15-16. As a skilled shepherd (*Ibn Ezra*), Jacob sent sufficient males for the needs of the females (*Rashi*).

17. **עֵדֶר עֵדֶר לְבַדּוֹ** — *Each drove separately.* He instructed his servants to keep a distance between the various droves, so that the greedy Esau would see animals coming toward him from clear across the horizon. This would make the gift seem even larger and more impressive (*Rashi*).

וְרֶ֣וַח תָּשִׂ֔ימוּ בֵּ֥ין עֵ֖דֶר וּבֵ֥ין עֵֽדֶר׃ יח וַיְצַ֥ו

< He instructed 18 « drove. < and between < drove < between < you should leave < and a space

אֶת־הָרִאשׁ֖וֹן לֵאמֹ֑ר כִּ֣י יִֽפְגָשְׁךָ֞ עֵשָׂ֣ו אָחִ֗י וּשְׁאֵֽלְךָ֙

< and asks you, « my brother — < — Esau « he meets you < When « saying, < the first one,

לֵאמֹ֔ר לְמִי־אַ֙תָּה֙ וְאָ֣נָה תֵלֵ֔ךְ וּלְמִ֖י אֵ֥לֶּה לְפָנֶֽיךָ׃

« that are before you?' — < are these < and whose « are you going, < where « are you, < 'Whose « saying,

יט וְאָמַרְתָּ֙ לְעַבְדְּךָ֣ לְיַעֲקֹ֔ב מִנְחָ֥ה הִוא֙ שְׁלוּחָ֔ה

< sent < it is < A tribute « to Jacob. < 'To your servant « You shall say, 19

לַאדֹנִ֖י לְעֵשָׂ֑ו וְהִנֵּ֥ה גַם־ה֖וּא אַחֲרֵֽינוּ׃ כ וַיְצַ֞ו גַּ֣ם

< also < He instructed 20 « behind us.' < he, as well, is < and indeed « to Esau, < to my lord,

אֶת־הַשֵּׁנִ֗י גַּ֚ם אֶת־הַשְּׁלִישִׁ֔י גַּ֚ם אֶת־כָּל־הַהֹ֣לְכִ֔ים אַחֲרֵ֥י הָעֲדָרִ֖ים

< the droves, < after < who went < all < also < the third, < also < the second,

לֵאמֹ֑ר כַּדָּבָ֤ר הַזֶּה֙ תְּדַבְּר֣וּן אֶל־עֵשָׂ֔ו בְּמֹצַאֲכֶ֖ם אֹתֽוֹ׃ כא וַאֲמַרְתֶּ֕ם גַּ֗ם

< 'Moreover « And you shall say, 21 « him. < when you find < Esau < to < shall you speak < like this < In a manner « saying,

הִנֵּ֛ה עַבְדְּךָ֥ יַעֲקֹ֖ב אַחֲרֵ֑ינוּ כִּֽי־אָמַ֞ר אֲכַפְּרָ֣ה פָנָ֗יו בַּמִּנְחָה֙ הַהֹלֶ֣כֶת לְפָנָ֔י

« before me, < that goes < with the tribute < his [angry] face < I will appease < he said, < (For « is behind us.' < Jacob < your servant < — indeed

וְאַחֲרֵי־כֵן֙ אֶרְאֶ֣ה פָנָ֔יו אוּלַ֖י יִשָּׂ֥א פָנָֽי׃ כב וַתַּעֲבֹ֥ר הַמִּנְחָ֖ה עַל־פָּנָ֑יו וְה֛וּא

< while he < before him < So the tribute passed on 22 « my face [in forgiveness].) < he will lift up < perhaps « his face; < I will see < that < and after

וּרְוָחָא תְּשַׁוּוֹן בֵּין עֶדְרָא וּבֵין עֶדְרָא׃ יח וּפַקֵּד יָת קַדְמָאָה לְמֵימָר אֲרֵי יְעַרְעִנָּךְ עֵשָׂו אָחִי וּשְׁאֵלִנָּךְ לְמֵימָר לְמָן אַתְּ (נ״א דְּמַאן אַתְּ) וּלְאָן אַתְּ אָזֵל וּלְמָן אִלֵּין דְּקֳדָמָךְ׃ יט וְתֵימַר לְעַבְדָּךְ לְיַעֲקֹב (נ״א דְּעַבְדָּךְ דְּיַעֲקֹב) תִּקְרֻבְתָּא הִיא דִּמְשַׁלְּחָא לְרִבּוֹנִי לְעֵשָׂו וְהָא אַף הוּא אָתֵי בַתְרָנָא׃ כ וּפַקִּיד אַף יָת תִּנְיָנָא אַף יָת תְּלִיתָאָה אַף יָת כָּל דְּאָזְלִין בָּתַר עֲדָרַיָּא לְמֵימָר כְּפִתְגָּמָא הָדֵין תְּמַלְּלוּן עִם עֵשָׂו כַּד תַּשְׁכְּחוּן יָתֵהּ׃ כא וְתֵימְרוּן אַף הָא עַבְדָּךְ יַעֲקֹב אָתֵי בַתְרָנָא אֲרֵי אֲמַר אֲנִחֶנֵּהּ לְרוּגְזֵהּ בְּתִקְרֻבְתָּא דְּאָזְלָא לָקֳדָמַי וּבָתַר כֵּן אֶחֱזֵי אַפּוֹהִי מָאִים יִסַּב אַפָּי׃ כב וַעֲבָרַת תִּקְרֻבְתָּא עַל אַפּוֹהִי וְהוּא

רש"י

ורוח תשימו. עדר לפני חברו מלא עין, כדי להשביע עינו של אותו רשע ולתווהו על רבוי הדורון (שם): **(יח) למי אתה.** של מי אתה, מי שולחך, ותרגום דמאן את: **ולמי אלה לפניך.** [ואלה שלפניך של מי הם,] למי המנחה הזאת שלוחה. למ"ד משמשת בראש התיבה במקום של. כמו וכל אשר אתה רואה לי הוא (לעיל לא:מג) שלי הוא. לה' הארץ ומלואה (תהלים כד:א) של ה': **(יט) ואמרת לעבדך ליעקב.** על ראשון ראשון ועל אחרון אחרון. ששאלת למי אתה, לעבדך ליעקב אני, ותרגומו דעבדך דיעקב. וששאלת ולמי אלה לפניך. מנחה היא שלוחה וגו': **והנה גם הוא [אחרינו].** יעקב: **(כא) אכפרה פניו.** אבטל רוגזו. וכן וכפר בריתכם את מות (ישעיה כח:יח) לא תוכלי כפרה (שם מז:יא). ונראה בעיני שכל כפרה שאצל עון וחטא ואצל פנים כולן לשון קנוח והעברה הן, ולשון ארמי הוא, והרבה בתלמוד, וכפר ידיה (ב"מ כד.) בעי לכפורי ידיה בההוא גברא (גיטין נו.). וגם בלשון המקרא נקראים המזרקים של קדש כפורי זהב (עזרא א:י) על שם שהכהן מקנח ידיו בהן בשפת המזרק (זבחים צג:): **(כב) על פניו.** כמו לפניו,

18. . . . **לְמִי־אַתָּה** — *Whose are you . . .* Homiletically, Esau's questions fell into two categories (a) *Whose are you?* — to whom are you loyal? And *Where are you going?* — What is your goal in life? Jacob's servants — and his progeny throughout history — reply that they are and will always remain dedicated to the ideals of Jacob. (b) *Whose are these that are before you?* Are you willing to contribute your possessions to the benefit of society? To this, Jacob said that the answer is yes — Jews pay taxes and strive for the betterment of the lands where they live. But this loyalty is predicated upon the unyielding recognition that *he himself is behind us.* Though we are loyal citizens, we never forget that we remain servants of Jacob's ideals (*R' Yosef Dov Soloveitchik*).

20. בְּמֹצַאֲכֶם אֹתוֹ — *When you find him.* Thus shall you speak to Esau whenever you encounter him *throughout history* (*R' Munk*).

21. כִּי־אָמַר אֲכַפְּרָה פָנָיו — (*For he said, "I will appease his [angry] face"*) According to *Rashi, Rashbam,* and *Ibn Ezra*, this phrase was not part of Jacob's instructions to the messengers, but a parenthetical explanation of his motives in sending the tribute. Accordingly, the word *said* should be understood as *he said to himself*. *Ramban*, however, maintains that this phrase *did* form part of Jacob's instructions to the emissaries. They were to tell Esau that Jacob had sent the gifts to appease him.

לָן בַּלַּיְלָה־הַהוּא בַּמַּחֲנֶה׃ כג וַיָּקָם ׀ בַּלַּיְלָה הוּא

spent > that night > in the camp. » 23 But he got up > that night >

וַיִּקַּח אֶת־שְׁתֵּי נָשָׁיו וְאֶת־שְׁתֵּי שִׁפְחֹתָיו

and he took > his two wives, > his two handmaids, >

וְאֶת־אַחַד עָשָׂר יְלָדָיו וַיַּעֲבֹר אֵת מַעֲבַר יַבֹּק׃

and his eleven sons > and he crossed over > the ford > of the Jabbok. »

כד וַיִּקָּחֵם וַיַּעֲבִרֵם אֶת־הַנָּחַל וַיַּעֲבֵר אֶת־אֲשֶׁר־לוֹ׃ כה וַיִּוָּתֵר יַעֲקֹב לְבַדּוֹ

24 Then he took them > and brought them across > the stream, » then he brought across > that > which was > his. » 25 Left alone > was Jacob > by himself, »

וַיֵּאָבֵק אִישׁ עִמּוֹ עַד עֲלוֹת הַשָּׁחַר׃ כו וַיַּרְא כִּי לֹא יָכֹל לוֹ וַיִּגַּע

and a man wrestled > with him > until > the rise > of the dawn. » 26 When he saw > that > he could not overcome > him » he struck [Jacob], >

בָּת בְּלֵילְיָא הַהוּא בְּמַשְׁרִיתָא׃ כג וְקָם בְּלֵילְיָא הוּא וּנְסִיב יָת תַּרְתֵּין נְשׁוֹהִי וְיָת תַּרְתֵּין לְחֵינָתֵהּ וְיָת חַד עֲסַר בְּנוֹהִי וַעֲבַר יָת מַעֲבַר יוּבְקָא׃ כד וּדְבָרִנּוּן וְעַבָּרִנּוּן יָת נַחֲלָא וְאַעְבַּר יָת דִּי לֵהּ׃ כה וְאִשְׁתְּאַר יַעֲקֹב בִּלְחוֹדוֹהִי וְאִשְׁתַּדֵּל גַּבְרָא עִמֵּהּ עַד דִּסְלֵק צַפְרָא׃ כו וַחֲזָא אֲרֵי לָא יָכִיל לֵהּ וּקְרֵב

רש"י

וכן חמס ושוד ישמע בה על פני תמיד (ירמיה ו:ז), וכן המכעיסים אותי על פני (ישעיה סה:ג). ומדרש אגדה, על פניו, אף הוא שרוי בכעס שהיה צריך לכל זה (ב"ר עו:ח): (כג) **ואת אחד עשר ילדיו.** ודינה היכן היתה, נתנה בתיבה ונעל בפניה שלא יתן בה עשו עיניו. ולכך נענש יעקב שמנעה מאחיו, שמא תחזירנו למוטב, ונפלה ביד שכם (שם ט): **יבק.** שם הנהר: (כד) **את אשר לו.** הבהמה והמטלטלים. עשה עצמו כגשר, נוטל מכאן ומניח כאן (שם): (כה) **ויותר יעקב.** שכח פכים קטנים וחזר עליהם [מכאן שהצדיקים חסים על ממונם, שלא ישלחו ידיהם בגזל] (חולין צא.): **ויאבק איש.** מנחם פי' ויתעפר איש, מל' אבק, שהיו מעלים עפר ברגליהם ע"י

25-32. The struggle with the angel. This confrontation was one of the cosmic events in history. The Rabbis explained that this man was the guardian angel of Esau (*Rashi*), in the guise of a man. The Sages teach that every nation has a Heavenly power, an angel that guides its destiny on earth, and acts as an "intermediary," between the nation and God. Two nations, however, are unique: Israel and Esau. Israel needs no go-between; it is God's own people. And Jacob, because his image is engraved upon God's Throne of Glory, symbolizes man's highest potential. Esau's guardian angel is different from all the others, for just as Esau epitomizes evil, so his angel is the prime spiritual force of evil — Satan himself.

"Satan descends and seduces man [to sin], then he ascends to incite [God, by prosecuting man for his sinfulness], and then he receives permission to take man's life . . . Satan, the Evil Inclination, and the Angel of Death are one and the same" (*Bava Basra* 16a). The angel of Esau *had* to attack Jacob, because, as the last and greatest of the Patriarchs, Jacob symbolized man's struggle to raise himself and the rest of the world with him — and Satan exists to cripple that effort. Thus the battle between Jacob and the "man" was the eternal struggle between good and evil, between man's capacity to perfect himself and Satan's determination to destroy him spiritually.

☙ The prime target.

The *Chofetz Chaim* used to say, "The Evil Inclination doesn't mind if a Jew fasts, prays, and gives charity all day long — provided he does not study Torah!" Abraham represented kindness and Isaac represented service. Kindness and service are two of the three indispensable pillars of the world (*Avos* 1:2), but the third pillar — Torah — is the crucial one for Israel's success in carrying out its mission on earth. Jacob represented Torah — and without it, Israel will fail. That is why Satan did not confront Abraham and Isaac, only Jacob.

Jewish history bears this out all too tragically. In countries where Jews invested heroically in synagogues and charities, but not in institutions of Torah study, they assimilated and nearly disappeared.

25. וַיִּוָּתֵר יַעֲקֹב לְבַדּוֹ — *Left alone was Jacob by himself. Rashi* cites the Talmudic interpretation [*Chullin* 91a] that Jacob had forgotten פַּכִּים קְטַנִּים, *small earthenware pitchers,* and returned to fetch them. From this fact the Sages [ibid.] derive that "to the righteous, their money is dearer to them than their bodies" — the reason for this, as the Talmud explains, is that they scrupulously avoid even a suggestion of dishonesty. Since they earn every penny diligently and honestly, it is dear to them.

Clearly the Sages do not mean that someone should put his life in danger for the sake of even significant sums of money; they mean to stress that Jacob went back for trivial objects because honestly earned wealth has spiritual value to the righteous and should not be treated indifferently. By investing even small pitchers with his zeal for honesty, he turned them into bearers of holiness, and as such, they were as precious as jewels. As the Talmud remarks, a judge should be as scrupulous in deciding the ownership of a penny as of ten thousand dinars.

וַיֵּאָבֵק אִישׁ עִמּוֹ — *And a man wrestled with him.* Just as Jacob was temporarily injured in the struggle but ultimately prevailed, so the Jewish people would suffer losses in the future, but would emerge with even greater victories and blessings (*Sforno*).

עַד עֲלוֹת הַשָּׁחַר — *Until the rise of the dawn.* The angel of evil will fight Jacob's descendants throughout history, until the dawn of salvation (*Lekach Tov*).

26. לֹא יָכֹל לוֹ — *He could not overcome him.* The Midrash per-

בְּכַף־יְרֵכוֹ וַתֵּקַע כַּף־יֶרֶךְ יַעֲקֹב בְּהֵאָבְקוֹ עִמּוֹ׃

« with him. ‹ as he wrestled ‹ of Jacob's hip ‹ the socket ‹ so, dislocated was « of his hip; ‹ the socket

כז וַיֹּאמֶר שַׁלְּחֵנִי כִּי עָלָה הַשָּׁחַר וַיֹּאמֶר לֹא

‹ *I will not* « And [Jacob] said, « *has the dawn.* ‹ *risen* ‹ *for* ‹ *Send me,* « Then [the man] said, 27

אֲשַׁלֵּחֲךָ כִּי אִם־בֵּרַכְתָּנִי׃ כח וַיֹּאמֶר אֵלָיו מַה־

‹ *What* « to him, ‹ He said 28 « *you bless me.* ‹ *if* ‹ *except* ‹ *send you*

שְּׁמֶךָ וַיֹּאמֶר יַעֲקֹב׃ כט וַיֹּאמֶר לֹא יַעֲקֹב יֵאָמֵר

‹ *shall be said* ‹ *'Jacob'* ‹ *Not* « He said, 29 « *Jacob.* ‹ He replied, « *is your name?*

עוֹד שִׁמְךָ כִּי אִם־יִשְׂרָאֵל כִּי־שָׂרִיתָ עִם־אֱלֹהִים וְעִם־אֲנָשִׁים וַתּוּכָל׃

« *and you have overcome.* ‹ *men* ‹ *and with* ‹ *the Divine* ‹ *with* ‹ *you have struggled* ‹ *for* « *Israel,* ‹ *rather* ‹ *but* « *to be your name,* ‹ *any-more*

ל וַיִּשְׁאַל יַעֲקֹב וַיֹּאמֶר הַגִּידָה־נָּא שְׁמֶךָ וַיֹּאמֶר לָמָּה זֶּה תִּשְׁאַל לִשְׁמִי

« *for my name?* ‹ *[that] you ask* ‹ *is it* ‹ *Why* ‹ And he said, « *your name.* ‹ *now,* ‹ *Tell,* « and he said, ‹ Then Jacob asked, 30

וַיְבָרֶךְ אֹתוֹ שָׁם׃ שלישי לא וַיִּקְרָא יַעֲקֹב שֵׁם הַמָּקוֹם פְּנִיאֵל כִּי־רָאִיתִי

‹ *I have seen* ‹ *— For* « Peniel ‹ of the place ‹ the name ‹ So Jacob called 31 « there. ‹ him [Jacob] ‹ And he blessed

בְּפְתֵי יַרְכֵהּ וְזָע פְּתֵי יַרְכָּא דְיַעֲקֹב
בְּאִשְׁתַּדָּלוּתֵהּ עִמֵּהּ׃ כז וַאֲמַר שַׁלְּחַנִי
אֲרֵי סְלֵיק צַפְרָא וַאֲמַר לָא אֲשַׁלְּחִנָּךְ
אֱלָהֵן בָּרֶכְתְּנִי׃ כח וַאֲמַר לֵהּ מָה שְׁמָךְ
וַאֲמַר יַעֲקֹב׃ כט וַאֲמַר לָא יַעֲקֹב
יִתְאֲמַר עוֹד שְׁמָךְ אֱלָהֵן יִשְׂרָאֵל אֲרֵי
רַבְרְבַת קֳדָם יְיָ וְעִם גּוּבְרַיָּא וִיכָלְתָּא׃
ל וּשְׁאֵל יַעֲקֹב וַאֲמַר חַוִּי כְעַן שְׁמָךְ
וַאֲמַר לְמָא דְנַן אַתְּ שָׁאֵל לִשְׁמִי
וּבָרִיךְ יָתֵהּ תַּמָּן׃ לא וּקְרָא יַעֲקֹב
שְׁמָא דְאַתְרָא פְּנִיאֵל אֲרֵי חֲזֵיתִי

רש"י

נעגועס. ולי נראה שהוא לשון ויתקשר, ולשון ארמי הוא, בתר דאביקו ביה (סנהדרין סג:) ואבק ליה מיבק (מנחות מב.) ל' עניבה, שכן דרך שנים שמתעצמים להפיל איש את רעהו שחובקו ואובקו בזרועותיו (חולין שם). ופירשו רז"ל שהוא שרו של עשו (ב"ר עז:ג; תנחומא ח): **(כו) ויגע בכף ירכו.** קולית הירך התקוע בקילבוסת קרוי כף, ע"ש שהבשר שעליה כמין כף של קדירה: **ותקע.** נתקעקעה ממקום מחברתה. ודומה לו פן תקע נפשי ממך (ירמיה ו:ח), לשון הסרה (ב"ר שם). ובמשנה, לקעקע בילתן (ויק"ר כו:ח) לשרש שרשיהן: **(כז) כי עלה השחר.** וצריך אני לומר שירה ביום (ב"ר עח:א; חולין צא:): **ברכתני.** הודה לי על הברכות שברכני אבי, שעשו מערער עליהן: **(כט) לא יעקב.** לא יאמר עוד שהברכות באו לך בעקבה ורמיה כי אם בשררה וגלוי פנים, וסופך שהקב"ה נגלה עליך בבית אל ומחליף שמך ושם הוא מברכך, ואני שם אהיה ואודה לך עליהן. וזה שכתוב וישר אל מלאך ויוכל בכה ויתחנן לו (הושע יב:ה), בכה המלאך ויתחנן לו (חולין צב.). ומה נתחנן לו, בית אל ימצאנו ושם ידבר עמנו (הושע יב:ה), המתן לי עד שידבר עמנו שם. ולא רצה יעקב, ועל כרחו הודה לו עליהן. וזהו ויברך אותו שם, שהיה מתחנן להמתין לו ולא רצה (ב"ר שם ב): **ועם אנשים.** עשו ולבן (פס"ז; ב"ר שם ג, ועי' שם סח:א,ג): **ותוכל.** להם (ב"ר עח:ג): **(ל) למה זה תשאל.** אין לנו שם קבוע, משתנין שמותינו [הכל] לפי מצות עבודת השליחות שאנו משתלחים (ב"ר שם ד):

ceives the angel's crippling blow to the hip as symbolic of a weakening of commitment on the part of financial supporters of Torah education.

27. שַׁלְּחֵנִי — *Send me.* The angel asked to be released because it was his turn to sing God's praises as part of the heavenly chorus, but Jacob insisted on receiving the angel's blessing before he would let go. This blessing by the guardian angel of Esau was an acknowledgment that Jacob was entitled to Isaac's blessings (*Rashi*).

28-29. Rhetorically, the angel asked Jacob his name in order to introduce his statement of blessing. Then the angel declared, "It will no longer be said that you deserve the name *Jacob* — which implies עָקֵב, *heel*, *deceit* — because you obtained the blessings deceitfully, as Esau had charged in 27:36. Instead, Jacob would receive the additional name *Israel,* from שְׂרוּת, *prevailing; superiority*. From then on, it would be acknowledged that he received the blessings because he *prevailed* [שָׂרָה] in an open competition to demonstrate which of the two was more deserving (*Rashi*). The *angel* did not have the authority to rename Jacob, nor was this name-change to take effect immediately. The angel merely revealed to Jacob what *God Himself* would do later (35:10).

30. שְׁמֶךָ — *Your name.* "Knowledge of my name can be of no use to you. I am powerless except for Hashem. Should you summon me, I would not respond nor can I help you in your distress." But the angel blessed him, for he had been commanded to do so, not because he had independent power (*Ramban; Tur*).

31. פְּנִיאֵל — *Peniel* [lit., *face of God*]. In verse 32 the name is given as פְּנוּאֵל, *Penuel.* Both names are identical since the letters א,ה,ו,י are interchangeable (*Radak*).

For Jacob, the name פְּנִיאֵל had a first-person connotation — פָּנַי, *my face* [is toward] אֵל, *God.* But for future generations the place name will signify the imperative; פְּנוּאֵל, *turn to God* (*R' Munk*).

אֱלֹהִים פָּנִים אֶל־פָּנִים וַתִּנָּצֵל נַפְשִׁי׃ לב וַיִּזְרַח־
< Then rise 32 « was my life. < yet saved < face, < to- < face- < the Divine

לוֹ הַשֶּׁמֶשׁ כַּאֲשֶׁר עָבַר אֶת־פְּנוּאֵל וְהוּא צֹלֵעַ עַל־
< on < was limping < and he < Penuel < he passed < as < did the sun < for him

יְרֵכוֹ׃ לג עַל־כֵּן לֹא־יֹאכְלוּ בְנֵי־יִשְׂרָאֵל אֶת־גִּיד
< the sinew < the Children of Israel shall not eat < Therefore 33 « his hip.

הַנָּשֶׁה אֲשֶׁר עַל־כַּף הַיָּרֵךְ עַד הַיּוֹם הַזֶּה כִּי נָגַע
< he struck < because « this day, < until < of the hip < the socket < on < that is < that is displaced

בְּכַף־יֶרֶךְ יַעֲקֹב בְּגִיד הַנָּשֶׁה׃ [לג] א וַיִּשָּׂא יַעֲקֹב
< Jacob raised 1 33 « that is displaced. < on the sinew < of Jacob < of the hip < the socket

עֵינָיו וַיַּרְא וְהִנֵּה עֵשָׂו בָּא וְעִמּוֹ אַרְבַּע מֵאוֹת אִישׁ וַיַּחַץ אֶת־הַיְלָדִים
< the children < so he divided « men — < hundred < [were] four < and with him < coming, < Esau < — there was « and saw < his eyes

עַל־לֵאָה וְעַל־רָחֵל וְעַל שְׁתֵּי הַשְּׁפָחוֹת׃ ב וַיָּשֶׂם אֶת־הַשְּׁפָחוֹת
< the handmaids < He put 2 « handmaids. < the two < and unto < Rachel, < unto < Leah, < unto

וְאֶת־יַלְדֵיהֶן רִאשֹׁנָה וְאֶת־לֵאָה וִילָדֶיהָ אַחֲרֹנִים וְאֶת־רָחֵל
< and Rachel < after [them], < and her children < Leah « first, < and their children

וְאֶת־יוֹסֵף אַחֲרֹנִים׃ ג וְהוּא עָבַר לִפְנֵיהֶם וַיִּשְׁתַּחוּ אַרְצָה שֶׁבַע פְּעָמִים
< times < seven < to the ground < and he bowed < before them < passed < Then he 3 « after [them]. < and Joseph

מַלְאָכַיָּא דַייָ אַפִּין בְּאַפִּין וְאִשְׁתְּזָבַת
נַפְשִׁי׃ לב וּדְנַח לֵהּ שִׁמְשָׁא כַּד עֲבַר
יָת פְּנוּאֵל וְהוּא מַטְלַע עַל יַרְכֵהּ׃
לג עַל כֵּן לָא יֵיכְלוּן בְּנֵי יִשְׂרָאֵל
יָת גִּידָא דְנַשְׁיָא דִּי עַל פְּתֵי יַרְכָּא
עַד יוֹמָא הָדֵין אֲרֵי קְרֵיב בִּפְתֵי
יַרְכָּא דְיַעֲקֹב בְּגִידָא דְנַשְׁיָא׃ א וּזְקַף
יַעֲקֹב עֵינוֹהִי וַחֲזָא וְהָא עֵשָׂו אָתֵי
וְעִמֵּהּ אַרְבַּע מְאָה גֻּבְרִין וּפַלֵּיג
יָת בְּנַיָּא עַל לֵאָה וְעַל רָחֵל וְעַל
תַּרְתֵּין לְחֵינָתָא׃ ב וְשַׁוִּי יָת לְחֵינָתָא
וְיָת בְּנֵיהֶן קַדְמָאִין וְיָת לֵאָה
וּבְנָהָא בַּתְרָאִין וְיָת רָחֵל וְיָת
יוֹסֵף בַּתְרָאִין׃ ג וְהוּא עֲבַר קֳדָמֵיהוֹן
וּסְגִיד עַל אַרְעָא שְׁבַע זִמְנִין

רש"י

(לב) **ויזרח לו השמש.** לשון בני אדם הוא, כשהגענו למקום פלוני האיר לנו השחר. זהו פשוטו. ומ"א, ויזרח לו, לצרכו, לרפאות את צלעתו, כמה דתימא שמש צדקה ומרפא בכנפיה (מלאכי ג:כ; ב"ר שם ה; תנחומא ישן י). ואותן שעות שמיהרה לשקוע בשבילו כשיצא מבאר שבע מיהרה לזרוח בשבילו (ב"ר סח:י; תנחומא ישן שם; סנהדרין צה:): **והוא צלע.** היה צולע כשזרחה השמש: (לג) **גיד הנשה.** ולמה נקרא שמו גיד הנשה. לפי שנשה ממקומו ועלה, והוא לשון קפיצה, וכן נשתה גבורתם (ירמיה נא:ל; חולין צא.), וכן כי נשני אלהים את כל עמלי (להלן מא:נא): [**על כף הירך.** פולפ"א בלע"ז. כל בשר גבוה ותלול ועגול קרוי כף, כמו עד שתתמרך הכף בסימני בגרות (נדה מז:):] (ב) **ואת לאה וילדיה אחרונים.** אחרון אחרון חביב (ב"ר עח:ח): (ג) **עבר לפניהם.** אמר, אם יבא אותו רשע להלחם ילחם בי תחלה (שם):

33.

1-16. The encounter between Jacob and Esau.

1-3. . . . וַיַּחַץ — *Then he divided* . . . Despite the angel's blessing, which assured Jacob that he would prevail against Esau, Jacob did not rely on miracles. *Radak* comments that Jacob kept the children with their own mothers, because maternal love would stimulate the mothers to do the utmost to save their children. And if that was impossible by natural means, they would be the best ones to pray for God's help. Then Jacob placed himself between them and Esau, so that if there were an attack, he would bear the brunt of it and the families could escape. His preparations ended, Jacob confronted Esau, not knowing whether the result would be a bloody battle or a brotherly reconciliation.

33. The prohibition of eating the sinews of an animal's thigh. Two primary tissues are forbidden in the hindquarter: The inner sinew — the sciatic nerve — which branches out from the rear of the spinal column and runs down the inner side of the animal's leg, is forbidden by Torah law. The outer sinew — the common peroneal nerve — which runs across the thigh on the outer side of the animal's leg, is forbidden by the Sages (*Chullin* 91a). Every last trace of these nerves must be removed, and the fat covering the sciatic nerve is removed, as well (ibid. 92b). Additionally, the six nerves which look like strings and certain other veins are removed. The pertinent *halachos* regarding this prohibition are found in *Shulchan Aruch, Yoreh De'ah* §65.

עַד־גִּשְׁתּוֹ עַד־אָחִיו: ד וַיָּרָץ עֵשָׂו לִקְרָאתוֹ וַיְחַבְּקֵהוּ
until ‹ he approached ‹ unto ‹ his brother. 4 ‹‹ Esau ran ‹ toward him ‹ and he embraced him, ‹‹

וַיִּפֹּל עַל־°צַוָּארָיו [°צוארו כ׳] *וַיִּשָּׁקֵהוּ וַיִּבְכּוּ: ה וַיִּשָּׂא
then he fell ‹ upon ‹ his neck ‹ and he kissed him; ‹‹ then they wept. ‹‹ 5 He [Esau] raised ‹

אֶת־עֵינָיו וַיַּרְא אֶת־הַנָּשִׁים וְאֶת־הַיְלָדִים וַיֹּאמֶר
his eyes ‹ and saw ‹ the women ‹ and the children, ‹ and he said, ‹‹

מִי־אֵלֶּה לָּךְ וַיֹּאמַר הַיְלָדִים אֲשֶׁר־חָנַן אֱלֹהִים
Who ‹ are these ‹ to you? ‹‹ He said, ‹‹ The children ‹ whom ‹ God has graciously given ‹

אֶת־עַבְדֶּךָ: רביעי ו וַתִּגַּשְׁןָ הַשְּׁפָחוֹת הֵנָּה וְיַלְדֵיהֶן וַתִּשְׁתַּחֲוֶיןָ: ז וַתִּגַּשׁ
to ‹ your servant. ‹‹ 6 Then approach ‹ did the handmaids ‹‹ — they ‹ and their children — ‹‹ and they bowed down. ‹‹ 7 Then approach ‹

גַּם־לֵאָה וִילָדֶיהָ וַיִּשְׁתַּחֲווּ וְאַחַר נִגַּשׁ יוֹסֵף וְרָחֵל וַיִּשְׁתַּחֲווּ: ח וַיֹּאמֶר
also ‹ did Leah, ‹ and her children ‹ and they bowed down; ‹‹ and afterward, ‹‹ Joseph approached ‹‹ as well as Rachel ‹‹ and they bowed down. ‹‹ 8 And he said, ‹‹

מִי לְךָ כָּל־הַמַּחֲנֶה הַזֶּה אֲשֶׁר פָּגָשְׁתִּי וַיֹּאמֶר לִמְצֹא־חֵן בְּעֵינֵי אֲדֹנִי:
Why did you need ‹ that whole camp ‹ that ‹ I met? ‹‹ He said, ‹‹ To find ‹ favor ‹ in the eyes ‹ of my lord. ‹‹

ט וַיֹּאמֶר עֵשָׂו יֶשׁ־לִי רָב אָחִי יְהִי לְךָ אֲשֶׁר־לָךְ: י וַיֹּאמֶר יַעֲקֹב אַל־נָא
9 Esau said, ‹ I have ‹ a great amount; ‹‹ my brother, ‹ let it ‹ [remain] yours ‹ that which ‹ you have. ‹‹ 10 But Jacob said, ‹‹ No, ‹ I beg of you! ‹

* נקוד על וישקהו

עַד מִקְרְבֵהּ עַד (נ״א לְוַת) אֲחוּהִי: ד וּרְהַט עֵשָׂו לְקַדָּמוּתֵהּ וְגַפְּפֵהּ וּנְפַל עַל צַוְּארֵהּ וְנַשְּׁקֵהּ וּבְכוֹ: ה וּזְקַף יָת עֵינוֹהִי וַחֲזָא יָת נְשַׁיָּא וְיָת בְּנַיָּא וַאֲמַר מָן אִלֵּין לָךְ וַאֲמַר בְּנַיָּא דִּי חָס יְיָ עַל (נ״א חַן יְיָ יָת) עַבְדָּךְ: ו וּקְרִיבַת לְחֵינָתָא אִנִּין וּבְנֵיהֶן וּסְגִידָא: ז וּקְרִיבָא אַף לֵאָה וּבְנָהָא וּסְגִידוּ וּבָתַר כֵּן קְרֵיב יוֹסֵף וְרָחֵל וּסְגִידוּ: ח וַאֲמַר מָן לָךְ כָּל מַשְׁרִיתָא הָדֵין דִּי עֲרָעִית וַאֲמַר לְאַשְׁכָּחָא רַחֲמִין בְּעֵינֵי רִבּוֹנִי: ט וַאֲמַר עֵשָׂו אִית לִי סַגִּי אָחִי אַצְלַח בְּדִילָךְ: י וַאֲמַר יַעֲקֹב בְּבָעוּ

רש״י

(ד) **ויחבקהו.** נתגלגלו רחמיו כשראהו משתחוה כל השתחוואות הללו (שם): **וישקהו.** נקוד עליו. ויש חולקין בדבר הזה בברייתא דספרי (בהעלתך סט), יש שדרשו נקודה זו לומר שלא נשקו בכל לבו. א״ר שמעון בן יוחאי, הלכה היא, בידוע שעשו שונא ליעקב, אלא שנכמרו רחמיו באותה שעה ונשקו בכל לבו: (ה) **מי אלה לך.** מי אלה להיות שלך: (ז) **נגש יוסף ורחל.** בכלן האמהות נגשות לפני הבנים, אבל ברחל יוסף נגש לפניה. אמר, אמי יפת תואר, שמא יתלה בה עיניו אותו רשע, אעמוד כנגדה ואעכבנו מלהסתכל בה. מכאן זכה יוסף לברכת עלי עין (להלן מט:כב; ב״ר עח:י; פס״ר יב): (ח) **מי לך כל המחנה.** מי כל המחנה אשר פגשתי שהוא שלך, כלומר למה הוא לך. פשוטו של מקרא על מוליכי המנחה, ומדרשו, כתות של מלאכים פגע שהיו דוחפין אותו ואת אנשיו ואומרים להם של מי אתם, והם אומרים להם של עשו, והן אומרים הכו הכו. ואלו אומרים הניחו, בנו של יצחק הוא, ולא היו משגיחים עליו. בן בנו של אברהם הוא, ולא היו משגיחים. אחיו של יעקב הוא, אומרים להם א״כ משלנו אתם (ב״ר שם יא): (ט) **יהי לך אשר לך.** כאן הודה לו על הברכות (שם): (י) **אל נא.** אל נא תאמר לי כן (תרגום יונתן):

4. וַיְחַבְּקֵהוּ — *And he embraced him.* Esau's compassion was aroused by Jacob's seven prostrations (*Rashi* from *Midrash*).

וַיִּשָּׁקֵהוּ — *And kissed him.* In the Torah Scroll, there are dots over each letter of this word, an exegetical device that calls attention to hidden allusions. The Sages disagree regarding the significance of the dots in this verse. Some hold that Esau's kisses were insincere; but R' Shimon bar Yochai says that, although it is an immutable rule that Esau hates Jacob, at that moment his mercy was aroused and he kissed Jacob with all his heart (*Rashi*).

וַיִּבְכּוּ — *Then they wept.* Following the above view that Esau was genuinely moved by the sight of Jacob, *R' Hirsch* comments that one cannot cry unless he is genuinely moved, for tears flow from the innermost feelings. Esau's kiss accompanied by tears proved that he was more than a selfish, violent hunter; he, too, was a descendant of Abraham, who was capable of setting aside his sword in favor of humane feelings.

5. Though Esau had asked about the *women* also, Jacob delicately answered only about the *children*. Esau understood from his answer that the women were his wives (*Ramban*).

7. יוֹסֵף וְרָחֵל — *Joseph and Rachel.* In the other groups, the mothers went ahead of their sons, but Joseph stood in front of Rachel to shield her from Esau's covetous gaze, since she was very beautiful (*Rashi*).

9. יְהִי לְךָ אֲשֶׁר־לָךְ — *Let it [remain] yours that which you have.* Esau told Jacob that there was no need to honor him (*Sforno*), but the underlying meaning of the statement was that Esau acquiesced to Jacob's right to Isaac's blessing (*Rashi*).

אִם־נָא מָצָאתִי חֵן בְּעֵינֶיךָ וְלָקַחְתָּ מִנְחָתִי מִיָּדִי

‹‹ from my hand, ‹ my tribute ‹ then you should accept ‹ in your eyes, ‹ favor ‹ I have found ‹ now ‹ If

כִּי עַל־כֵּן רָאִיתִי פָנֶיךָ כִּרְאֹת פְּנֵי אֱלֹהִים

‹‹ of a Divine being, ‹ the face ‹ which is like seeing ‹ your face ‹ of my having seen ‹ the ‹ of ‹ because [gift]

וַתִּרְצֵנִי: יא קַח־נָא אֶת־בִּרְכָתִי אֲשֶׁר הֻבָאת לָךְ:

‹‹ to you, ‹ was brought ‹ which ‹ my gift ‹ please ‹ Accept **11** *‹‹ and [because] you were appeased by me.*

כִּי־חַנַּנִי אֱלֹהִים וְכִי יֶשׁ־לִי־כֹל וַיִּפְצַר־בּוֹ וַיִּקָּח: יב וַיֹּאמֶר נִסְעָה וְנֵלֵכָה

‹ and let us go ‹ Let us travel on ‹ And he said, **12** *‹‹ and he accepted. ‹ him, ‹ He urged ‹‹ everything. ‹ I have ‹ and because ‹ God has been gracious to me, ‹ since*

וְאֵלְכָה לְנֶגְדֶּךָ: יג וַיֹּאמֶר אֵלָיו אֲדֹנִי יֹדֵעַ כִּי־הַיְלָדִים רַכִּים וְהַצֹּאן

‹ and the flock ‹‹ are tender, ‹ the children ‹ that ‹ knows ‹ My lord ‹‹ to him, ‹ But he said **13** *‹‹ alongside you. ‹ – and I will go*

וְהַבָּקָר עָלוֹת עָלָי וּדְפָקוּם יוֹם אֶחָד וָמֵתוּ כָּל־הַצֹּאן: יד יַעֲבָר־נָא אֲדֹנִי

‹ my lord, ‹ please, ‹ Pass, **14** *‹‹ the flock. ‹ – all ‹‹ then they will die ‹ for [even] one day, ‹ if they will be driven hard ‹‹ are my responsibility; ‹ that are nursing ‹ and the cattle*

אִם כְּעַן אַשְׁכַּחִית רַחֲמִין בְּעֵינָךְ תְּקַבֵּל תִּקְרֻבְתִּי מִן יְדִי אֲרֵי עַל כֵּן חֲזִיתִנּוּן לְאַפָּיךְ כְּחֵיזוּ אַפֵּי רַבְרְבַיָּא וְאִתְרְעֵית לִי: יא קַבֵּל כְּעַן יָת תִּקְרֻבְתִּי דְּאִתּוֹתִיאַת לָךְ אֲרֵי רַחִים עֲלַי (קֳדָם) יְיָ וַאֲרֵי אִית לִי כֹּלָּא וּתְקֵיף בֵּהּ וְקַבִּיל: יב וַאֲמַר נִטַּל (נ"א טוּל) וְנֵהָךְ וְאֵיהַךְ לְקָבְלָךְ: יג וַאֲמַר לֵהּ רִבּוֹנִי יָדַע אֲרֵי יָנְקַיָּא רַכִּיכִין וְעָנָא וְתוֹרֵי מֵינִקָתָא עָלָי וּדְחוֹקִנּוּן יוֹמָא חַד וּמִיתוּ כָּל עָנָא: יד יִעְבַּר כְּעַן רִבּוֹנִי

רש"י

אם נא מצאתי חן בעיניך ולקחת מנחתי מידי כי על כן ראיתי פניך וגו'. כי כדאי והגון לך שתקבל מנחתי, על אשר ראיתי פניך והן חשובין לי כראיית פני המלאך, שראיתי שר שלך, ועוד, על שנתרצית לי למחול על סורחני. ולמה הזכיר לו ראיית המלאך, כדי שיתיירא הימנו ויאמר ראה מלאכי[ם] וניצול, איני יכול לו מעתה (סוטה מא:; ב"ר עז:ג): **ותרצני.** נתפייסת לי. וכן כל רצון שבמקרא לשון פיוס, אפיימנ"ט בלע"ז. וכן כי לא לרצון יהיה לכם (ויקרא כב:כ) הקרבנות באות לפייס ולרצות. וכן שפתי צדיק ידעון רצון (משלי י:לב) יודעים לפייס ולרצות: **(יא) ברכתי.** מנחתי, מנחה זו הבאה על ראיית פנים, ולפרקים אינה באה אלא לשאילת שלום. וכל ברכה שהיא לראיית פנים, כגון ויברך יעקב את פרעה (להלן מז:ז), עשו אתי ברכה (מלכים ב יח:לא) דסנחריב, וכן לשאול לו לשלום ולברכו (שמואל ב ח:י) דתועי מלך חמת, כולם לשון ברכת שלום הן, שקורין בלע"ז שלודי"ר [ס"א שלואי"ר], אף זו, ברכתי, מו"ן שלו"ד: **אשר הבאת לך.** לא טרחת בה ואני יגעתי להגיעה עד שבאה לידך (ב"ר עח:יב): **חנני.** נו"ן ראשונה מודגשת לפי שהיא משמשת במקום שתי נוני"ן שהיה לו לומר חננני. שאין חנן בלא שני נוני"ן והשלישית לשימוש כמו עשני זבדני: **יש לי כל.** כל ספוקי. ועשו דבר בלשון גאוה, יש לי רב (לעיל פסוק ט), יותר ויותר מכדי צרכי (תנחומא ג): **(יב) נסעה.** כמו שמעה, סלחה, (דניאל ט:יט) שהוא כמו שמע, סלח, [ס"א כמו שמעה תפלתי (תהלים לט:יג) שלחה הנער (להלן מג:ח)] אף כאן נסעה כמו נסע, והנו"ן יסוד בתיבה. ותרגום של אונקלוס טול ונהך, עשו אמר ליעקב נסע מכאן ונלך: **ואלכה לנגדך.** בשוה לך. טובה זו אעשה לך שאאריך ימי מהלכתי ללכת לאט כאשר אתה צריך. וזהו לנגדך, בשוה לך: **(יג) עלות עלי.** הצאן והבקר שהן עלות מוטלות עלי לנהלן לאט: **עלות.** מגדלות עולליהן, (אונקלוס ותרגום יונתן) לשון עולל ויונק (איכה ב:יא) עול ימים (ישעי' סה:כ) שתי פרות עלות (ש"א ו:י), ובלע"ז אנפנטי"ש: **ודפקום יום אחד.** ואם ידפקום יום אחד ליגעם בדרך במרוצה ומתו כל הצאן: **ודפקום.** כמו קול דודי דופק (שיר השירים ה:ב) נוקש בדלת: **(יד) יעבר נא אדני.** אל נא תאריך ימי הליכתך, עבור כפי דרכך ואף אם תתרחק:

11. יֶשׁ־לִי־כֹל — *I have everything,* everything that I require. This is typical of the righteous, who feel that no matter how much or how little they have in absolute terms, they are content, for they feel that whatever they have is *everything* that they could possibly need. But wicked people like Esau (v. 9) speak boastfully: יֶשׁ־לִי רָב, *I have a great amount,* emphasizing the abundance of their possessions and proclaiming that they have accumulated much more than they could ever need (*Rashi*).

12-13. In their newfound brotherly love, Esau insisted on escorting Jacob, and offered to slow down as much as necessary to keep pace with the slow-moving flocks and family (*Rashi*). Jacob, however, wanted to end the reunion as quickly as possible; whether or not Esau's kisses were sincere [see above, v. 5], the momentary friendship could not be expected to last indefinitely. Obviously, however, Jacob had to cloak his rejection of Esau's offer in diplomatic terms. He protested that he could not allow Esau to inconvenience himself to such an extent, because *the children are tender* — the oldest, Reuben, was only a little more than 12 years old at the time (*Ibn Ezra*). Furthermore, *the flocks will die* (*Rashi*) from fatigue if they are not permitted to go much more slowly than Esau and his troops would normally travel.

Jacob's primary concern was for his young children, but delicacy did not permit him to speak of their possible death, because, as the Sages put it, "a covenant is made with the lips" (*Moed Katan* 18a), meaning that even an unintentional implication, much less an explicit statement, may portend future unpleasant events. Such unintended prognostications often become fulfilled as if they were prophecy.

לִפְנֵי עַבְדּוֹ וַאֲנִי אֶתְנַהֲלָה לְאִטִּי לְרֶגֶל הַמְּלָאכָה

before ‹ his servant; ‹‹ and I ‹ will make my way ‹ at my slow pace, ‹‹ according to the pace ‹ of the livestock ‹

אֲשֶׁר־לְפָנַי וּלְרֶגֶל הַיְלָדִים עַד אֲשֶׁר־אָבֹא אֶל־

that are before me, ‹ and according to the pace ‹ of the children, ‹‹ until ‹ when ‹ I come ‹ to ‹

אֲדֹנִי שֵׂעִירָה: 15 וַיֹּאמֶר עֵשָׂו אַצִּיגָה־נָּא עִמְּךָ מִן־

my lord, ‹ to Seir. ‹‹ 15 Then Esau said, ‹‹ Let me assign ‹ now ‹ to you ‹ from ‹

הָעָם אֲשֶׁר אִתִּי וַיֹּאמֶר לָמָּה זֶּה אֶמְצָא־חֵן בְּעֵינֵי

the people ‹ who are with me. ‹‹ And he said, ‹‹ Why [should you do] this? ‹ Let me [just] find ‹ favor ‹ in the eyes ‹

אֲדֹנִי: 16 וַיָּשָׁב בַּיּוֹם הַהוּא עֵשָׂו לְדַרְכּוֹ שֵׂעִירָה: 17 וְיַעֲקֹב נָסַע סֻכֹּתָה

of my lord! ‹‹ 16 Return ‹ on that day ‹ did Esau ‹ on his way ‹ toward Seir. ‹‹ 17 But Jacob ‹ journeyed ‹ to Succoth ‹

וַיִּבֶן לוֹ בָּיִת וּלְמִקְנֵהוּ עָשָׂה סֻכֹּת עַל־כֵּן קָרָא שֵׁם־הַמָּקוֹם סֻכּוֹת: ס

and built ‹ for himself ‹ a house, ‹‹ and for his livestock ‹ he made ‹ shelters; ‹‹ therefore ‹ he called ‹ the name ‹ of the place ‹ Succoth. ‹‹

18 וַיָּבֹא יַעֲקֹב שָׁלֵם עִיר שְׁכֶם אֲשֶׁר בְּאֶרֶץ כְּנַעַן בְּבֹאוֹ מִפַּדַּן אֲרָם

18 Jacob arrived ‹ whole ‹ [to] the city ‹ of Shechem ‹ which is ‹ in the land ‹ of Canaan, ‹‹ when he came ‹ from Paddan-aram, ‹‹

קֳדָם עַבְדֵּהּ וַאֲנָא אֱדַבַּר בִּנְיָחַ לְרֶגֶל עוּבַדְתָּא דִּי קֳדָמַי וּלְרֶגֶל יָנְקַיָּא עַד דִּי אֵעוּל לְוַת רִבּוֹנִי לְשֵׂעִיר: טו וַאֲמַר עֵשָׂו אֶשְׁבּוֹק כְּעַן עִמָּךְ מִן עַמָּא דִּי עִמִּי וַאֲמַר לְמָא דְנַן אַשְׁכַּח רַחֲמִין בְּעֵינֵי רִבּוֹנִי: טז וְתָב בְּיוֹמָא הַהוּא עֵשָׂו לְאָרְחֵהּ לְשֵׂעִיר: יז וְיַעֲקֹב נְטַל לְסֻכּוֹת וּבְנָא לֵהּ בֵּיתָא וְלִבְעִירֵהּ עֲבַד מְטַלָּן עַל כֵּן קְרָא שְׁמָא דְאַתְרָא סֻכּוֹת: יח וַאֲתָא יַעֲקֹב שְׁלִים קַרְתָּא דִשְׁכֶם דִּי בְּאַרְעָא דִכְנַעַן בְּמֵיתֵהּ מִפַּדַּן דַּאֲרָם

רש"י

אתנהלה. אתנהל, ה"א יתירה, כמו ארדה (לעיל יח:כא) אשמעה (במדבר ט:ח): **לאטי.** לאט שלי, לשון נחת, כמו ההולכים לאט (ישעיה ח:ו) לאט לי לנער (שמואל ב יח:ה). לאטי הלמ"ד מן היסוד ואינה משמשת, אתנהל נחת שלי: **לרגל המלאכה.** לפי צורך הליכת רגלי המלאכה המוטלת עלי [ס"א לפני] להוליך: **ולרגל הילדים.** לפי רגליהם שהם יכולים לילך: **עד אשר אבא אל אדני שעירה.** הרחיב לו הדרך, שלא היה דעתו ללכת אלא עד סוכות. אמר, אם דעתו לעשות לי רעה ימתין עד בואי אצלו (עבודה זרה כה:). והוא לא הלך, ואימתי ילך, בימי המשיח, שנא' ועלו מושיעים בהר ציון לשפוט את הר עשו (עובדיה א:כא; ב"ר שם יד). ומ"א יש לפרשה זו רבים: **(טו) ויאמר למה זה.** תעשה לי טובה זו שאיני צריך לה: **אמצא חן בעיני אדני.** ולא תשלם לי עתה שום גמול: **(טז) וישב ביום ההוא עשו לדרכו.** עשו לבדו, וד' מאות איש שהלכו עמו נשמטו מאצלו אחד אחד. והיכן פרע להם הקב"ה, בימי דוד, שנא' כי אם ארבע מאות איש נער אשר רכבו על הגמלים (שמואל א ל:יז; ב"ר עח:טו): **(יז) ויבן לו בית.** שהה שם י"ח חדש, קיץ וחורף וקיץ. סכות קיץ, בית חורף, סכות קיץ (ב"ר שם טז; מגילה יז.): **(יח) שלם.** שלם בגופו, שנתרפא מצלעתו. שלם בממונו, שלא חסר כלום מכל אותו דורון. שלם בתורתו, שלא שכח תלמודו בבית לבן (שבת לג:; ב"ר עט:ה): **עיר שכם.** כמו לעיר (אונקלוס) וכמוהו עד בואכה בית לחם (רות א:יט): **בבאו מפדן ארם.** כאדם האומר לחבירו יצא פלוני מבין ש[י]ני אריות ובא שלם. אף כאן ויבא שלם מפדן ארם, מלבן ומעשו שנזדווג[ו] לו בדרך:

14. שֵׂעִירָה — *To Seir.* Jacob had no intention of going as far as Seir — indeed, he did not go there — he merely wanted Esau to think he would, so that, in case Esau planned to attack him later, he would be waiting for an encounter that would never take place. [It is axiomatic, however, that Jacob, who was the very epitome of truth, would never utter a blatant falsehood.] The Sages explain that Jacob was alluding to the End of Days, when, as Obadiah (*Obadiah* 1:21) prophesied, Jacob's descendants will come to Mount Seir to render judgment against Esau's descendants *(Rashi)*.

16. Apparently there was a coolness between Jacob and Esau at the parting. It was not accompanied by kissing, as was Jacob's departure from Laban [32:1] (*Haamek Davar*).

17. סֻכּוֹת — *Succoth.* It seems strange that Jacob named the place for animal shelters, rather than for the houses he built for people. *Or HaChaim* suggests that this may have been the first time anyone took the trouble to shelter animals from the sun and cold; until Jacob, shepherds considered livestock to be nothing more than a means for sustenance and profit. Because Jacob here made a public display of compassion for all living creatures, the place was named for that precedent-setting act.

18-20. Jacob arrives in Shechem. Jacob arrived in *Eretz Yisrael* after an absence of nearly twenty-two years. Immediately he purchased a plot of land, to symbolize that he was no longer a transient, but a resident of the land that God had promised to his offspring. There Jacob erected a monument and gave it a name that would always recall the eternal truth that his powerful God is the God of the Jewish nation.

Jacob felt secure only when he reached Shechem because — as the Torah emphasizes — it was in *Eretz Yisrael.* He knew that

וַיִּחַן אֶת־פְּנֵי הָעִיר׃ יט וַיִּקֶן אֶת־חֶלְקַת הַשָּׂדֶה

and he encamped > before > the city. >> 19 He bought > the portion > of the field >

אֲשֶׁר נָטָה־שָׁם אָהֳלוֹ מִיַּד בְּנֵי־חֲמוֹר אֲבִי שְׁכֶם

where > he pitched > there > his tent, >> from the hand > of the children > of Hamor, >> father > of Shechem, >>

בְּמֵאָה קְשִׂיטָה׃ כ וַיַּצֶּב־שָׁם מִזְבֵּחַ וַיִּקְרָא־לוֹ אֵל

for one hundred > kesitahs. >> 20 He set up > there > an altar > and proclaimed > it, >> God, >

אֱלֹהֵי יִשְׂרָאֵל׃ ס חמישי [לד] א וַתֵּצֵא דִינָה בַּת־לֵאָה אֲשֶׁר יָלְדָה לְיַעֲקֹב

the God > of Israel. >> 34 1 Now Dinah went out > — the daughter > of Leah, > who > had borne [her] > to Jacob — >>

לִרְאוֹת בִּבְנוֹת הָאָרֶץ׃ ב וַיַּרְא אֹתָהּ שְׁכֶם בֶּן־חֲמוֹר הַחִוִּי נְשִׂיא הָאָרֶץ

to look over > the daughters > of the land. >> 2 See > her > did Shechem, > son > of Hamor > the Hivvite, > the prince > of the region; >>

וּשְׁרָא לָקֳבֵל (אַפֵּי) קַרְתָּא: יט וּזְבַן יָת אַחְסָנַת חַקְלָא דִּי פְּרַס תַּמָּן מַשְׁכְּנֵהּ מִידָא דִבְנֵי חֲמוֹר אֲבוּהִי דִשְׁכֶם בְּמֵאָה חוּרְפָן: כ וַאֲקֵם תַּמָּן מַדְבְּחָא וּפְלַח עֲלוֹהִי קֳדָם אֵל אֱלָהָא דְיִשְׂרָאֵל: א וּנְפָקַת דִּינָה בַּת לֵאָה דִּי יְלִידַת לְיַעֲקֹב לְמֶחֱזֵי בִּבְנַת אַרְעָא: ב וַחֲזָא יָתַהּ שְׁכֶם בַּר חֲמוֹר חִיוָּאָה רַבָּא דְאַרְעָא

רש"י

[ויחן את פני העיר. ערב שבת היה. בשאלתות דרב אחאי (ב"ר שם ו):] (יט) קשיטה. מעה. אר"ע, כשהלכתי לכרכי הים היו קורין למעה קשיטה (ראש השנה כו.). [ותרגומו חורפן, טובים, חריפים בכל מקום, כגון עובר לסוחר (לעיל כג:טז)]: (כ) ויקרא לו אל אלהי ישראל. לא שהמזבח קרוי אלהי ישראל, אלא על שם שהיה הקב"ה עמו והצילו קרא שם המזבח על שם הנס, להיות שבחו של מקום נזכר בקריאת השם. כלומר, מי שהוא אל, הוא הקב"ה, הוא לאלהים לי ששמי ישראל. וכן מצינו במשה ויקרא שמו ה' נסי (שמות יז:טו) לא שהמזבח קרוי ה', אלא על שם הנס קרא שם המזבח להזכיר שבחו של הקב"ה, ה' הוא נסי. ורבותינו דרשו שהקדוש ברוך הוא קראו ליעקב אל (מגילה יח.), וד"ת כפטיש יפוצץ סלע (ירמיה כג:כט) מתחלקים לכמה טעמים (שבת פח:), ואני ליישב פשוטו של מקרא באתי: (א) **בת לאה.** ולא בת יעקב, אלא ע"ש יציאתה נקראת בת לאה, שאף היא יצאנית היתה שנאמר ותצא לאה לקראתו (לעיל ל:טז) [ועליה משלו המשל כאמה כבתה] (ב"ר פ:א):

Esau would not molest him there, either because Isaac was nearby and the inhabitants stood in awe of him and would protect Jacob, or because the merit of *Eretz Yisrael* would protect him. In contrast, Jacob felt no such security during his sojourn in Succoth. The Midrash points out that as long as he lived there, he kept sending extravagant gifts to Esau in Seir (*Ramban*).

19. וַיִּקֶן — *He bought.* Jacob wanted to establish an inalienable right to the land by means of purchase (*Ramban*). The Midrash notes that this plot became the eventual site of Joseph's sepulcher. It is one of the three places of which the Torah vouches for Israel's ownership, for as our verse tells us, Jacob bought it with uncontested currency. The other two places are the Cave of Machpelah, bought by Abraham, and the site of the Temple, bought by David.

20. מִזְבֵּחַ — *An altar.* Jacob named the altar "God, the God of Israel" [not in the sense that it was a deity (*Sefer HaZikaron*)], because he wanted God's praise to be evoked at every mention of the altar's name. The meaning of the name is: "He Who is *God* — the Holy One, Blessed is He — *is the God* of the person [Jacob] whose name is *Israel*" (*Rashi*).

By erecting the altar and naming it as he did, Jacob fulfilled the vow he had made twenty-two years earlier, before leaving the Land (*Alshich*).

34.

1-4. Dinah's abduction. Jacob had overcome the terrible trials of over twenty years and believed that at last he would find tranquility in *Eretz Yisrael* — as the end of the last chapter indicates — but suddenly he faced an unexpected crisis. His family, which is called on to be a nation of priests and God's standard-bearer on earth, had to experience a moral outrage upon its own flesh and blood right from its beginning. It had to undergo this ordeal so that the world could see in its swift and uncompromising reaction the sacred character of its purity, that it could not tolerate what other nations might consider to be commonplace (*R' Hirsch*).

1. בַּת־לֵאָה — *The daughter of Leah.* Because Dinah *went out* — in contradiction to the code of modesty befitting a daughter of Jacob — she is called the *daughter of Leah* because Leah, too, went out to meet Jacob [see above, 30:16]. With this in mind, the Midrash formulated the proverb, "Like mother like daughter" (*Rashi*). Even though the Sages teach that Dinah was lured out of the house, this implied criticism is valid, for she would not have gone out on her own if she had not been extroverted. She is also called the *daughter of Jacob* (vs. 3,7), because his distinguished reputation [in addition to her great beauty (*Radak*)] influenced Shechem to covet her (*Or HaChaim*).

2. הַחִוִּי — *The Hivvite.* Was he then a Hivvite? — he was an Amorite, as noted in 48:22. Rather, חִוִּי is an Aramaic word meaning *serpentine*. It describes the serpentlike, treacherous manner in which Shechem acted (*Midrash*).

נְשִׂיא — *The prince.* It is to Dinah's credit that she resisted Shechem's blandishments even though he was a prince (*Ramban*). Because of his royal status, no one came to Dinah's aid, despite her screams (*Or HaChaim*).

וַיִּקַּח אֹתָהּ וַיִּשְׁכַּב אֹתָהּ וַיְעַנֶּהָ׃ ג וַתִּדְבַּק נַפְשׁוֹ
‹ was his soul ‹ Attached 3 « and he violated her. ‹ with her, ‹ he lay ‹ her, ‹ he took

בְּדִינָה בַּת־יַעֲקֹב וַיֶּאֱהַב אֶת־הַנַּעֲרָ וַיְדַבֵּר עַל־
‹ upon ‹ and spoke ‹ the maiden ‹ he loved « of Jacob; ‹ daughter ‹ to Dinah,

לֵב הַנַּעֲרָ׃ ד וַיֹּאמֶר שְׁכֶם אֶל־חֲמוֹר אָבִיו לֵאמֹר
« saying, ‹ his father, ‹ Hamor, ‹ to ‹ So Shechem spoke 4 « of the maiden. ‹ the emotions

קַח־לִי אֶת־הַיַּלְדָּה הַזֹּאת לְאִשָּׁה׃ ה וְיַעֲקֹב שָׁמַע
‹ heard ‹ Now Jacob 5 « *for a wife.* ‹ *this girl* ‹ *for me* ‹ *Take*

כִּי טִמֵּא אֶת־דִּינָה בִתּוֹ וּבָנָיו הָיוּ אֶת־מִקְנֵהוּ
‹ his livestock ‹ with ‹ were ‹ but his sons « his daughter, ‹ Dinah, ‹ he had defiled ‹ that

בַּשָּׂדֶה וְהֶחֱרִשׁ יַעֲקֹב עַד־בֹּאָם׃ ו וַיֵּצֵא חֲמוֹר
« Hamor went out 6 « their arrival. ‹ until ‹ so Jacob kept silent « in the field;

אֲבִי־שְׁכֶם אֶל־יַעֲקֹב לְדַבֵּר אִתּוֹ׃ ז וּבְנֵי יַעֲקֹב בָּאוּ מִן־הַשָּׂדֶה כְּשָׁמְעָם
« when they heard; ‹ the field ‹ from ‹ came ‹ of Jacob ‹ And the sons 7 « with him. ‹ to speak ‹ Jacob ‹ to « of Shechem — ‹ — the father

וַיִּתְעַצְּבוּ הָאֲנָשִׁים וַיִּחַר לָהֶם מְאֹד כִּי נְבָלָה עָשָׂה בְיִשְׂרָאֵל לִשְׁכַּב
‹ — to lie « in Israel ‹ had he committed ‹ a disgraceful act ‹ for « exceedingly, ‹ and they were outraged ‹ the men were aggrieved,

אֶת־בַּת־יַעֲקֹב וְכֵן לֹא יֵעָשֶׂה׃ ח וַיְדַבֵּר חֲמוֹר אִתָּם לֵאמֹר שְׁכֶם בְּנִי
« *my son* ‹ *Shechem,* « saying, ‹ with them, ‹ Hamor spoke 8 « be done! ‹ may not ‹ Such a thing « of Jacob. ‹ a daughter ‹ with

חָשְׁקָה נַפְשׁוֹ בְּבִתְּכֶם תְּנוּ נָא אֹתָהּ לוֹ לְאִשָּׁה׃ ט וְהִתְחַתְּנוּ אֹתָנוּ
« *with us;* ‹ *And intermarry* 9 « *as a wife.* ‹ *to him* ‹ *her* ‹ *please* ‹ *Give* « *for your daughter.* ‹ *— his soul longs*

בְּנֹתֵיכֶם תִּתְּנוּ־לָנוּ וְאֶת־בְּנֹתֵינוּ תִּקְחוּ לָכֶם׃ י וְאִתָּנוּ תֵּשֵׁבוּ וְהָאָרֶץ
‹ *the land* « *you shall dwell;* ‹ *And with us* **10** « *for yourselves.* ‹ *take* ‹ *and our daughters* ‹ *to us,* ‹ *give* ‹ *your daughters*

וּדְבַר יָתַהּ וּשְׁכִיב יָתַהּ וְעַנְיַהּ׃ ג וְאִתְרְעִיאַת נַפְשֵׁהּ בְּדִינָה בַּת יַעֲקֹב וּרְחֵים יָת עוּלֶמְתָּא וּמַלִּיל תַּנְחוּמִין עַל לִבָּא דְעוּלֶמְתָּא׃ ד וַאֲמַר שְׁכֶם לַחֲמוֹר אֲבוּהִי לְמֵימָר סַב לִי יָת עוּלֶמְתָּא הָדָא לְאִנְתּוּ׃ ה וְיַעֲקֹב שְׁמַע אֲרֵי סָאֵיב יָת דִּינָה בְרַתֵּהּ וּבְנוֹהִי הֲווֹ עִם גֵּיתוֹהִי בְּחַקְלָא וּשְׁתִיק יַעֲקֹב עַד מֵיתֵיהוֹן׃ ו וּנְפַק חֲמוֹר אֲבוּהִי דִשְׁכֶם לְוַת יַעֲקֹב לְמַלָּלָא עִמֵּהּ׃ ז וּבְנֵי יַעֲקֹב עַלּוּ מִן חַקְלָא כַּד שְׁמָעוּ וְאִתְנְסִיסוּ גֻּבְרַיָּא וּתְקֵיף לְהוֹן לַחֲדָא אֲרֵי קְלָנָא עֲבַד בְּיִשְׂרָאֵל לְמִשְׁכַּב עִם בַּת יַעֲקֹב וְכֵן לָא כָשַׁר לְאִתְעֲבָדָא׃ ח וּמַלִּיל חֲמוֹר עִמְּהוֹן לְמֵימָר שְׁכֶם בְּרִי אִתְרְעִיאַת נַפְשֵׁהּ בִּבְרַתְּכוֹן הָבוּ כְעַן יָתַהּ לֵהּ לְאִנְתּוּ׃ ט וְאִתְחַתְּנוּ בָנָא בְּנָתֵיכוֹן תִּתְּנוּן לָנָא וְיָת בְּנָתָנָא תִּסְּבוּן לְכוֹן׃ י וְעִמָּנָא תִּתְּבוּן וְאַרְעָא

רש״י

(ב) וישכב אותה. כדרכה: ויענה. שלא כדרכה (ב״ר שם ה): (ג) על לב הנערה. דברים המתיישבים על הלב. ראי, אביך בחלקת שדה קטנה כמה ממון בזבז, אני אשאך ותקני העיר וכל שדותיה (ב״ר פ:ז): (ז) וכן לא יעשה. לענות את הבתולות, שהאומות גדרו עצמן מן העריות על ידי המבול (ב״ר שם ו): (ח) חשקה. חפלה:

5-12. Jacob's family learns of the outrage. Jacob's suspicions must have been aroused when Dinah did not return home. Presumably he inquired after her and heard the terrible news that she was being held a prisoner in Shechem's home and had already been violated. *Alshich* comments that if Shechem had not yet assaulted her, Jacob would have risked everything to rescue her, but since it was too late, he waited for his sons to come home so that they could plan their response.

7. וּבְנֵי יַעֲקֹב בָּאוּ — *And the sons of Jacob came.* They arrived at about the same time as Hamor, and did not have the opportunity to consult privately with Jacob (*Rashbam; Malbim*).

Levush explains that *Rashi* understands the verse to stress that Shechem had committed an outrage *in Israel* — a nation that had high standards of morality and viewed such dastardly acts with utter contempt; *such a thing may not be done* — for even the heathen nations had renounced immorality after the

תִּהְיֶה לִפְנֵיכֶם שְׁבוּ וּסְחָרוּהָ וְהֵאָחֲזוּ בָּהּ׃

<< in it. < and acquire property < and trade in it, < —settle << before you < will be

יא וַיֹּאמֶר שְׁכֶם אֶל־אָבִיהָ וְאֶל־אַחֶיהָ אֶמְצָא־חֵן

< favor < Let me find << her brothers, < and to < her father < to < Then Shechem said **11**

בְּעֵינֵיכֶם וַאֲשֶׁר תֹּאמְרוּ אֵלַי אֶתֵּן׃ יב הַרְבּוּ עָלַי

< upon me < Increase **12** *<< — I will give. << me < you tell < and whatever << in your eyes;*

מְאֹד מֹהַר וּמַתָּן וְאֶתְּנָה כַּאֲשֶׁר תֹּאמְרוּ אֵלָי וּתְנוּ־לִי אֶת־הַנַּעֲרָ

< the maiden < me < only give << me; < you tell < whatever < and I will give < and gifts < the marriage contract < exceedingly

לְאִשָּׁה׃ יג וַיַּעֲנוּ בְנֵי־יַעֲקֹב אֶת־שְׁכֶם וְאֶת־חֲמוֹר אָבִיו בְּמִרְמָה וַיְדַבֵּרוּ

<< and they spoke < with cunning < his father, < and Hamor, < Shechem < The sons of Jacob answered **13** << *for a wife.*

אֲשֶׁר טִמֵּא אֵת דִּינָה אֲחֹתָם׃ יד וַיֹּאמְרוּ אֲלֵיהֶם לֹא נוּכַל לַעֲשׂוֹת

< do < We cannot << to them, < They said **14** *<< their sister. < Dinah < he had defiled < — because*

הַדָּבָר הַזֶּה לָתֵת אֶת־אֲחֹתֵנוּ לְאִישׁ אֲשֶׁר־לוֹ עָרְלָה כִּי־חֶרְפָּה הִוא

< it is < a disgrace < for << a foreskin, < who has < to a man < our sister < to give << this thing,

תְּהֵי קֳדָמֵיכוֹן תִּיבוּ וְעִבִידוּ בַהּ סְחוֹרָא
וְאִתְחֲסִינוּ בַהּ׃ יא וַאֲמַר שְׁכֶם לַאֲבוּהָא
וּלְאַחָהָא אַשְׁכַּח רַחֲמִין בְּעֵינֵיכוֹן וְדִי
תֵימְרוּן לִי אֶתֵּן׃ יב אַסְגוֹ עֲלַי לַחֲדָא
מוֹהֲרִין וּמַתְּנָן וְאֶתֵּן כְּמָא דִי תֵימְרוּן לִי
וְהָבוּ לִי יָת עוּלֶמְתָּא לְאִנְתּוּ׃ יג וַאֲתִיבוּ
בְנֵי יַעֲקֹב יָת שְׁכֶם וְיָת חֲמוֹר אֲבוּהִי
בְּחָכְמְתָא וּמַלִּילוּ דִי סָאֵב יָת דִּינָה
אֲחָתְהוֹן׃ יד וַאֲמָרוּ לְהוֹן לָא נִכּוּל
לְמֶעְבַּד פִּתְגָּמָא הָדֵין לְמִתַּן יָת אֲחָתָנָא
לִגְבַר דִּי לֵהּ עָרְלְתָא אֲרֵי חִסוּדָא הִיא

רש"י

(יב) **מהר.** כתובה (ב"ר שם ז; מכילתא משפטים נזיקין ז): (יג) **במרמה.** בחכמה: **אשר טמא.** הכתוב אומר שלא היתה רמיה, שהרי טמא את דינה אחותם (ב"ר שם ח): (יד) **חרפה הוא [לנו].** שמן פסול הוא אצלנו. הבא לחרף חברו אומר לו ערל אתה או בן ערל. חרפה בכל מקום גדוף: (טו) **נאות לכם.** נתרצה לכם, לשון ויאותו הכהנים (מלכים ב יב:ט) [ביהוידע]: **להמל.** להיות נמול. אינו לשון לפעול אלא לשון להפעל:

Flood, since such conduct had been a cause of the Destruction.

Ramban, however, maintains that the Canaanite nations were notorious for their immorality. He interprets *such a thing may not be done* as a reference to *Jewish* standards of morality — Canaanites might condone such high-handed behavior by their nobility, but in Israel, everyone must maintain equally high standards.

13-24. The deception. In order to dispel any notion that Jacob's family could have acquiesced to an intermarriage — even if faced with superior force and certainly not for financial considerations — the Torah says at the outset that the sons answered Shechem and Hamor *with cunning,* meaning that they had no intention of accepting the proposal of Shechem and Hamor (*Haamek Davar*). The Torah (v. 13) justifies their deception by saying parenthetically that they resorted to it only *because he had defiled their sister (Midrash);* they could not sip tea and trade pleasantries with the criminals who now sought to clothe their lust in the respectability of the wedding canopy. But, *Radak* explains, because their response was not truthful, Jacob, the embodiment of truth, remained silent.

Ramban wonders, however, that since Jacob was present, he must have understood what his sons intended and approved, at least tacitly. If so, why was he so angry when they acted as they did (v. 30)? And why did he limit his anger to Simeon and Levi, who carried out the plan? *Ramban* explains that the original intent of the brothers was that the Shechemites would release Dinah because they would never agree to be circumcised. Even if they were to agree, the brothers would be able to seize Dinah and escape while the Shechemite men were ill and weakened. But, in carrying out their massacre, Simeon and Levi acted unilaterally, without Jacob's knowledge.

14-15. לֹא נוּכַל לַעֲשׂוֹת הַדָּבָר הַזֶּה — *We cannot do this thing*. The brothers said that it was beneath their dignity even to discuss money before a question of principle — circumcision — was resolved (*Akeidas Yitzchak*). They argued that marriage to an uncircumcised man would forever disgrace the family (*Ibn Ezra*).

They said, "To us it is a blemish that goes from generation to generation. If one wishes to insult his friend, he says to him: 'You are uncircumcised,' or: 'You are the son of one who is uncircumcised' " (*Rashi*).

They chose circumcision as the means by which to disable the Shechemites in order to inflict injury on the organ that Shechem used to assault Dinah (*Sifsei Kohen*).

לָנוּ: טו אַךְ־בְּזֹאת נֵאוֹת לָכֶם אִם תִּהְיוּ כָמֹנוּ

< like us < you will become < If << to you: < will we acquiesce < on this [condition] < Only 15 << for us.

לְהִמֹּל לָכֶם כָּל־זָכָר: טז וְנָתַנּוּ אֶת־בְּנֹתֵינוּ לָכֶם

< to you, < our daughters < Then we will give 16 << male. < every < among you < to have circumcised

וְאֶת־בְּנֹתֵיכֶם נִקַּח־לָנוּ וְיָשַׁבְנוּ אִתְּכֶם וְהָיִינוּ

< and we will become < with you, < we will dwell << for ourselves; < we will take < and your daughters

לְעַם אֶחָד: יז וְאִם־לֹא תִשְׁמְעוּ אֵלֵינוּ לְהִמּוֹל

<< to be circumcised, < to us < you will not listen < But if 17 << a single people.

וְלָקַחְנוּ אֶת־בִּתֵּנוּ וְהָלָכְנוּ: יח וַיִּיטְבוּ דִבְרֵיהֶם

< did their words [seem] < Good 18 << and go. < our daughter < we will take

בְּעֵינֵי חֲמוֹר וּבְעֵינֵי שְׁכֶם בֶּן־חֲמוֹר: יט וְלֹא־אֵחַר הַנַּעַר לַעֲשׂוֹת

< to do < did the youth < delay < Not 19 << Hamor. < son of < of Shechem, < and in the eyes < of Hamor, < in the eyes

הַדָּבָר כִּי חָפֵץ בְּבַת־יַעֲקֹב וְהוּא נִכְבָּד מִכֹּל בֵּית אָבִיו: כ וַיָּבֹא

<< He came 20 << of his father. < the household < of all < was the most respected < And he << of Jacob. < the daughter < he desired < for << the thing,

חֲמוֹר וּשְׁכֶם בְּנוֹ אֶל־שַׁעַר עִירָם וַיְדַבְּרוּ אֶל־אַנְשֵׁי עִירָם לֵאמֹר:

<< saying, < of their city, < the people < to < and they spoke << of their city < the gate < to << his son — < with Shechem < — Hamor

כא הָאֲנָשִׁים הָאֵלֶּה שְׁלֵמִים הֵם אִתָּנוּ וְיֵשְׁבוּ בָאָרֶץ וְיִסְחֲרוּ אֹתָהּ

<< in it, < and trade < in the land < let them settle << with us; < are they < at peace << These people, 21

וְהָאָרֶץ הִנֵּה רַחֲבַת־יָדַיִם לִפְנֵיהֶם אֶת־בְּנֹתָם נִקַּח־לָנוּ לְנָשִׁים

< as wives < for ourselves < let us take < Their daughters << before them! < of hands < [it has] a breadth < — indeed << for the land

לָנָא: טו בְּרַם בְּדָא נִתְפֵּס לְכוֹן אִם תֶּהֱווֹן כְּוָתָנָא לְמִגְזַר לְכוֹן כָּל דְּכוּרָא: טז וְנִתֵּן יָת בְּנָתָנָא לְכוֹן וְיָת בְּנָתֵיכוֹן נִסַּב לָנָא וְנִתּוּב עִמְּכוֹן וּנְהֵי לְעַמָּא חַד: יז וְאִם לָא תְקַבְּלוּן מִנָּנָא לְמִגְזַר וּנְדַבַּר יָת בְּרַתָּנָא וְנֵזִיל: יח וּשְׁפָרוּ פִתְגָמֵיהוֹן בְּעֵינֵי חֲמוֹר וּבְעֵינֵי שְׁכֶם בַּר חֲמוֹר: יט וְלָא אוֹחַר עוּלֵימָא לְמֶעְבַּד פִּתְגָמָא אֲרֵי אִתְרְעִי בְּבַת יַעֲקֹב וְהוּא יַקִּיר מִכֹּל בֵּית אֲבוּהִי: כ וַאֲתָא חֲמוֹר וּשְׁכֶם בְּרֵהּ לִתְרַע קַרְתְּהוֹן וּמַלִּילוּ עִם אֱנָשֵׁי קַרְתְּהוֹן לְמֵימָר: כא גֻּבְרַיָּא הָאִלֵּין שְׁלָמִין אִנּוּן עִמָּנָא וְיִתִּיבוּן בְּאַרְעָא וְיַעְבְּדוּן בַּהּ סְחוֹרְתָא וְאַרְעָא הָא פְתָיוּת יְדִין קֳדָמֵיהוֹן יָת בְּנָתֵיהוֹן נִסַּב לָנָא לְנְשִׁין

רש"י

(טז) **ונתנו.** נו"ן שנייה מודגשת לפי שהיא משמשת במקום שתי נוני"ן, ונתננו: **ואת בנתיכם נקח לנו.** אתה מוצא בתנאי שאמר חמור ליעקב ובתשובת בני יעקב לחמור שתלו החשיבות בבני יעקב ליקח בנות שכם את שיבחרו להם ובנותיהם יתנו להם לפי דעתם, דכתיב ונתנו את בנותינו, לפי דעתנו, ואת בנותיכם נקח לנו, ככל אשר נחפוץ. וכשדברו חמור ושכם בנו אל יושבי עירם הפכו הדברים, את בנותם נקח לנו לנשים ואת בנותינו נתן להם (להלן פסוק כא) כדי לרצותם שיאותו להמול: (כא) **שלמים.** בשלום ובלב שלם: **והארץ הנה רחבת ידים.** כאדם שידו רחבה ותרנית. כלומר, לא תפסידו כלום, פרקמטיא הרבה באה לכאן ואין לה קונים: (כב) **בהמול.** בהיות נמול:

16. וְיָשַׁבְנוּ אִתְּכֶם וְהָיִינוּ לְעַם אֶחָד — *We will dwell with you, and we will become a single people.* This statement was the source of Jacob's anger when his sons took the lives of the Shechemites (see below). Though Shechem and his people were evil and deserved retribution, Jacob could not countenance a broken word: His sons had no right to break their word. They should have clothed their deception in terms that would not constitute a promise (*Ramban* to v. 13).

19. וְהוּא נִכְבָּד — *And he was the most respected.* As prince of the city, Shechem could have circumcised himself last, but his desire for Dinah was so overpowering that he did not delay; he made himself the example and was circumcised first (*Sforno*). As the next few verses imply, he did so even before his fellow townsmen agreed to the proposal.

20-23. Hamor and Shechem summoned their people to the city gate, the place where — as is clear from many places in Scripture — the courts and decision-making elders would meet. Thus the gate was the place where important proposals like this one would be discussed. Hamor presented the plan in a glamorous and unselfish light. However, he cleverly changed his tune

וְאֶת־בְּנֹתֵינוּ נִתֶּן־לָהֶם: כב אַךְ־בְּזֹאת יֵאֹתוּ לָנוּ

‹‹ with us ‹ will they acquiesce ‹ on this [condition] ‹ Only **22** ‹‹ to them. ‹ let us give ‹ and our daughters

הָאֲנָשִׁים לָשֶׁבֶת אִתָּנוּ לִהְיוֹת לְעַם אֶחָד בְּהִמּוֹל

‹ to have circumcised ‹‹ a single people: ‹ to become ‹ with us ‹ to dwell ‹‹ — those people —

לָנוּ כָּל־זָכָר כַּאֲשֶׁר הֵם נִמֹּלִים: כג מִקְנֵהֶם וְקִנְיָנָם

‹ their possessions, ‹ Their livestock, **23** ‹‹ are circumcised. ‹ they ‹ just as ‹ male ‹ every ‹ among us

וְכָל־בְּהֶמְתָּם הֲלוֹא לָנוּ הֵם אַךְ נֵאוֹתָה לָהֶם וְיֵשְׁבוּ אִתָּנוּ: כד וַיִּשְׁמְעוּ

‹ They listened **24** ‹‹ with us. ‹ and they will dwell ‹ to them ‹ let us acquiesce ‹ Only ‹‹ they will be? ‹ [that] to us ‹ — is it not so ‹‹ their animals ‹ and all

אֶל־חֲמוֹר וְאֶל־שְׁכֶם בְּנוֹ כָּל־יֹצְאֵי שַׁעַר עִירוֹ וַיִּמֹּלוּ כָּל־זָכָר כָּל־

‹ all ‹ male, ‹ — every ‹‹ and they were circumcised ‹‹ of his city, ‹ [through] the gate ‹ who depart ‹ — all ‹‹ his son ‹ Shechem ‹ and to ‹ Hamor ‹ to

יֹצְאֵי שַׁעַר עִירוֹ: כה וַיְהִי בַיּוֹם הַשְּׁלִישִׁי בִּהְיוֹתָם כֹּאֲבִים וַיִּקְחוּ שְׁנֵי־

‹ did two ‹ that take ‹‹ in pain, ‹ when they were ‹ on the third day, ‹ And it came to pass **25** ‹‹ of his city. ‹ [through] the gate ‹ who depart

וְיָת בְּנָתָנָא נִתֵּן לְהוֹן: כב בְּרַם בְּדָא יִתָּפְסוּן לָנָא גוּבְרַיָּא לְמִתַּב עִמָּנָא לְמֶהֱוֵי לְעַמָּא חַד לְמִגְזַר לָנָא כָּל דְּכוּרָא כְּמָא דִּי אִנּוּן גְּזִירִין: כג גֵּיתֵיהוֹן וְקִנְיָנְהוֹן וְכָל בְּעִירְהוֹן הֲלָא לָנָא אִנּוּן בְּרַם נִתְפֵּס לְהוֹן וִיתִיבוּן עִמָּנָא: כד וְקַבִּילוּ מִן חֲמוֹר וּמִן שְׁכֶם בְּרֵהּ כָּל נָפְקֵי תְּרַע קַרְתֵּהּ וּגְזָרוּ כָּל דְּכוּרָא כָּל נָפְקֵי תְּרַע קַרְתֵּהּ: כה וַהֲוָה בְּיוֹמָא תְלִיתָאָה כַּד תְּקִיפוּ עֲלֵיהוֹן כֵּיבֵיהוֹן וּנְסִיבוּ תְּרֵין

רש"י

(כג) אך נאותה להם. לדבר זה ועל ידי כן **ישבו אתנו: (כה) שני בני יעקב.** בניו היו, ואעפ"כ נהגו עצמן **שמעון ולוי,** כשאר אנשים שאינם בניו, שלא נטלו עצה

from the one he had used when he spoke unctuously with Jacob. Then, he had implied that the decision on whether and with whom to intermarry would be up to Jacob's family and that they would have the initiative in their commercial relationships (see v. 9). Now, he said the opposite: The Shechemites would do as *they* pleased in absorbing Jacob's family.

23. הֲלוֹא לָנוּ הֵם — *Is it not so [that] to us they will be?* To induce his people to accept his suggestion, Hamor promised that it would be profitable to them and they would gradually absorb the abundant possessions of Jacob's household. Contrast this with the seeming cordiality of Hamor's invitation to Jacob in verse 10! This is how it always ended: The Jewish stranger came, toiled, and accumulated wealth that ultimately reverted to his hosts (*R' W. Heidenheim*).

24. כָּל־יֹצְאֵי — *All who depart. Chizkuni* infers that all the residents of the city wanted to flee from the decree of circumcision, but no male was allowed to leave the city unless he had been circumcised: *all the males . . . had to submit to circumcision*.

25-31. Simeon and Levi destroy Shechem. As noted above, the brothers intended to rescue Dinah while the Shechemites were weak and ill, but Simeon and Levi acted on their own and carried out a death sentence on all the males of the city. By what right they did so halachically is discussed by the major commentators. Following are three primary lines of reasoning:

☐ *Rambam (Hil. Melachim* Ch. 9) codifies the Seven Noahide Laws that are incumbent on all human beings, and whose violators are subject to the death penalty. One of these laws forbids theft, which includes kidnaping. In taking Dinah against her will, Shechem violated this prohibition. The seventh Noahide law requires all people to enforce this code. By permitting Shechem to act as he did, the people of the city transgressed their responsibility to enforce the laws — so that *they*, like Shechem himself, were liable to the death penalty. Simeon and Levi, therefore, were enforcing the law that had been ignored by the entire Shechemite population.

☐ *Ramban* disagrees with the above on various grounds. He maintains that Simeon and Levi were justified in killing the people because all of them were evil and had violated the Noahide Laws repeatedly in their own right, apart from anything Shechem had done.

☐ *Gur Aryeh* contends that the act of the brothers was entirely unrelated to the Noahide Laws. He suggests that nations that are the victims of aggression have the right to retaliate against their attackers. In this case, the city-state of Shechem committed an act of aggression against the nation of Israel, so that Simeon and Levi had a right to counterattack.

Whatever the interpretation of the legal status of the attack on the city, the other nine brothers apparently refused to take part in the attack, and Jacob was sharply critical of Simeon and Levi.

25. בַיּוֹם הַשְּׁלִישִׁי — *On the third day.* The third day after circumcision is the most painful (*Ibn Ezra*). Alternatively, they waited until the third day since it took until then to circumcise all the males; by the third day, *all* of them were circumcised and in

בְנֵי־יַעֲקֹב שִׁמְעוֹן וְלֵוִי אֲחֵי דִינָה אִישׁ חַרְבּוֹ
‹ his sword ‹ each ‹ of Dinah, ‹ the brothers ‹ and Levi, ‹ Simeon ‹ of Jacob, ‹ of the sons

וַיָּבֹאוּ עַל־הָעִיר בֶּטַח וַיַּהַרְגוּ כָּל־זָכָר׃
« male. ‹ every ‹ and they killed « confidently, ‹ the city ‹ upon ‹ and they came

כו וְאֶת־חֲמוֹר וְאֶת־שְׁכֶם בְּנוֹ הָרְגוּ לְפִי־חָרֶב
« of the sword. ‹ at the point ‹ they killed ‹ his son ‹ and Shechem ‹ And Hamor 26

וַיִּקְחוּ אֶת־דִּינָה מִבֵּית שְׁכֶם וַיֵּצֵאוּ׃ כז בְּנֵי יַעֲקֹב
‹ of Jacob ‹ The sons 27 « and they left. ‹ of Shechem ‹ from the house ‹ Dinah ‹ Then they took

בָּאוּ עַל־הַחֲלָלִים וַיָּבֹזּוּ הָעִיר אֲשֶׁר טִמְּאוּ
‹ had defiled ‹ which ‹ the city ‹ and they plundered ‹ the corpses, ‹ upon ‹ came

אֲחוֹתָם׃ כח אֶת־צֹאנָם וְאֶת־בְּקָרָם וְאֶת־חֲמֹרֵיהֶם וְאֵת אֲשֶׁר־בָּעִיר
‹ was in the town ‹ whatever ‹ their donkeys, ‹ their cattle, ‹ Their flocks, 28 « their sister.

וְאֶת־אֲשֶׁר בַּשָּׂדֶה לָקָחוּ׃ כט וְאֶת־כָּל־חֵילָם וְאֶת־כָּל־טַפָּם וְאֶת־נְשֵׁיהֶם
‹ and their wives ‹ their children, ‹ all ‹ their wealth, ‹ All 29 « they took. ‹ was in the field, ‹ and whatever

שָׁבוּ וַיָּבֹזּוּ וְאֵת כָּל־אֲשֶׁר בַּבָּיִת׃ ל וַיֹּאמֶר יַעֲקֹב אֶל־שִׁמְעוֹן וְאֶל־לֵוִי
‹ Levi, ‹ and to ‹ Simeon ‹ to ‹ Jacob said 30 « in the house. ‹ that was ‹ as well as everything « and they plundered, ‹ they took captive

עֲכַרְתֶּם אֹתִי לְהַבְאִישֵׁנִי בְּיֹשֵׁב הָאָרֶץ בַּכְּנַעֲנִי וּבַפְּרִזִּי וַאֲנִי מְתֵי מִסְפָּר
‹ *[are few] in number* ‹ *people* ‹ *but my* « *and among the Perizzite;* ‹ *among the Canaanite* « *of the land,* ‹ *among the inhabitants* ‹ *making me odious* ‹ *You have caused me anguish,*

בְּנֵי יַעֲקֹב שִׁמְעוֹן וְלֵוִי אֲחֵי דִינָה גְּבַר חַרְבֵּהּ וְעַלּוּ עַל קַרְתָּא דְּיָתְבָא לְרָחֲצָן וּקְטָלוּ כָּל דְּכוּרָא׃ כו וְיָת חֲמוֹר וְיָת שְׁכֶם בְּרֵהּ קְטָלוּ לְפִתְגַּם דְּחָרֶב וּדְבָרוּ יָת דִּינָה מִבֵּית שְׁכֶם וּנְפָקוּ׃ כז בְּנֵי יַעֲקֹב עַלּוּ לְחַלָּצָא קָטִילַיָּא וּבְזוֹ קַרְתָּא דִּי סָאִיבוּ אַחָתְהוֹן׃ כח יָת עָנְהוֹן וְיָת תּוֹרְהוֹן וְיָת חֲמָרֵיהוֹן וְיָת דִּי בְקַרְתָּא וְיָת דִּי בְחַקְלָא בְּזוֹ׃ כט וְיָת כָּל נִכְסֵיהוֹן וְיָת כָּל טַפְלְהוֹן וְיָת נְשֵׁיהוֹן שְׁבוֹ וּבְזוֹ וְיָת כָּל דִּי בְּבֵיתָא׃ ל וַאֲמַר יַעֲקֹב לְשִׁמְעוֹן וּלְלֵוִי עֲכַרְתּוּן יָתִי לְמִתַּן דְּבָבוּ בֵּינָנָא וּבֵין יָתֵב אַרְעָא בִּכְנַעֲנָאָה וּבִפְרִזָּאָה וַאֲנָא עַם דְּמִנְיַן

רש"י

הימנו (ב"ר פ:י): **אחי דינה.** לפי שמסרו עצמן עליה נקראו אחיה (שם): **בטח.** שהיו כואבים. ומדרש אגדה, בטוחים היו על כחו של זקן (שם): **(כז) על החללים.** לפשט את החללים. [וכן ת"א, לחלצא קטיליא]: **(כט) חילם.** ממונם (אונקלוס). וכן עשה לי את החיל הזה (דברים ח:יז) וישראל עושה חיל (במדבר כד:יח) ועזבו לאחרים חילם (תהלים מט:יא): **שבו.** לשון שביה (אונקלוס) לפיכך טעמו מלרע: **(ל) עכרתם.** ל' מים עכורים (ברכות כה:) אין דעתי צלולה עכשיו. ואגדה, צלולה היתה החבית ועכרתם אותה. מסורת היתה ביד כנענים שיפלו ביד בני יעקב אלא שהיו אומרים עד אשר תפרה ונחלת את הארץ (שמות כג:ל) לפיכך היו שותקין (ב"ר שם יב): **מתי מספר.** אנשים מועטים:

pain. Furthermore, the verse does not necessarily mean *physical* pain, but *grief* and *regret* over having submitted to the circumcision (*Daas Zekeinim; Chizkuni*).

איש חרבו — *Each [man took] his sword.* The Midrash notes that Levi was 13 years old at the time. Thus, as *Lekach Tov* points out, it is implied in this Midrashic comment that whenever the Torah uses the term איש, *man,* it refers to a male at least 13 years old. [Cf. *Rashi* to *Nazir* 29b, s.v., ורבי יוסי.]

27. ויבזו העיר — *And they plundered the city. Or HaChaim* maintains that all the brothers participated in taking property. Since the entire city shared responsibility for the attack on Dinah, all the people were responsible to compensate the family for its *humiliation*.

30. Jacob directed his anger only at the two sons who had killed. As explained above, the plunder was justified in the context of the city's crime against Dinah and her family (*Akeidas Yitzchak*).

עֲכַרְתֶּם אֹתִי — *You have caused me anguish.* By their rash violence, Simeon and Levi place Jacob in a potentially vulnerable position should the surrounding Canaanite cities choose to attack him (*Rashi*).

The Canaanites will say that we broke our word after the Shechemites had circumcised themselves (*Sforno*), a particularly galling accusation for Jacob, the paragon of truth. *R' Hirsch* adds that the family's reputation and honor had been crystal clear, until Simeon and Levi besmirched it.

וְנֶאֶסְפוּ עָלַי וְהִכּוּנִי וְנִשְׁמַדְתִּי אֲנִי וּבֵיתִי׃

and should they band together < against me < and attack me, < I will be annihilated << – I < and my household. <<

31 וַיֹּאמְרוּ הַכְזוֹנָה יַעֲשֶׂה אֶת־אֲחוֹתֵנוּ׃ פ

31 And they said, < Can it be that like a harlot < he should treat < our sister? <<

[לה] 1 וַיֹּאמֶר אֱלֹהִים אֶל־יַעֲקֹב קוּם עֲלֵה

35 1 God said < to < Jacob, << Arise < – go up <

בֵית־אֵל וְשֶׁב־שָׁם וַעֲשֵׂה־שָׁם מִזְבֵּחַ לָאֵל הַנִּרְאֶה אֵלֶיךָ בְּבָרְחֲךָ

[to] Beth-el < and dwell < there, << and make < there < an altar < to the God < Who appeared < to you < when you fled <

מִפְּנֵי עֵשָׂו אָחִיךָ׃ 2 וַיֹּאמֶר יַעֲקֹב אֶל־בֵּיתוֹ וְאֶל כָּל־אֲשֶׁר עִמּוֹ

from < Esau < your brother. << 2 Then Jacob said < to < his household < and to < all < who were < with him, <

הָסִרוּ אֶת־אֱלֹהֵי הַנֵּכָר אֲשֶׁר בְּתֹכְכֶם וְהִטַּהֲרוּ וְהַחֲלִיפוּ שִׂמְלֹתֵיכֶם׃

Remove < the alien gods < that are < in your midst; << purify yourselves < and change < your clothes. <<

וְיִתְכַּנְשׁוּן עֲלַי וְיִמְחֲנַנִי וְאֶשְׁתֵּצֵי אֲנָא וֶאֱנַשׁ בֵּיתִי: לא וַאֲמָרוּ הַכְנָפְקַת בָּרָא יִתְעֲבֵד לַאֲחָתָנָא (נ״א יַעְבֵּד יָת אֲחָתָנָא): א וַאֲמַר יְיָ לְיַעֲקֹב קוּם סַק לְבֵית אֵל וְתִיב תַּמָּן וְעִבֵד תַּמָּן מַדְבְּחָא לֵאלָהָא דְּאִתְגְּלִי לָךְ בְּמֵעְרָקָךְ מִן קֳדָם עֵשָׂו אָחוּךְ: ב וַאֲמַר יַעֲקֹב לֶאֱנַשׁ בֵּיתֵהּ וּלְכֹל דִּי עִמֵּהּ אַעְדּוּ יָת טַעֲוַת עַמְמַיָּא דִּי בֵּינֵיכוֹן (נ״א בִּידֵיכוֹן) וְאִדַּכּוּ וְשַׁנּוּ כְּסוּתְכוֹן:

רש״י

(לא) הכזונה. הפקר (שם): **את אחותנו.** ית אחתנא: **(א) קום עלה.** לפי שאחרת בדרך [ס״א נדרך] נענשת ובא לך זאת מבתך (תנחומא ח; ב״ר פא:ב): **(ב) הנכר.** שיש בידכם משלל של שכם: **והטהרו.** מע״ז: **והחליפו שמלתיכם.** שמא יש בידכם כסות של ע״ז (ב״ר שם ג):

31. Simeon and Levi did not respond to Jacob's charge that their act had put the family in danger. Instead, they insisted that there was an overriding issue that they had no right to ignore, no matter what the consequences: "*Can it be that like a harlot he should treat our sister?*" Should we have permitted Shechem, unchecked and unpunished, to treat our sister like a loose woman who has no protector? (*Radak*). As her brothers, we were obligated to defend her honor (*Sforno*).

Most commentators agree that Jacob did not condemn armed resistance under any circumstances; there *are* times when Jews must be ready to fight to defend their self-respect and the honor of their families. Each such instance must be carefully evaluated on its own merits, however, and it was upon such considerations that Jacob criticized what they did.

Jacob remained silent. He did not agree with his sons' contention that their extreme violence was justified, but he stifled his outrage. Only on his deathbed did he curse *their anger* (49:6) — but not them (*R' Hoffmann*).

35.

1-7. Jacob journeys to Beth-el. Nearly twenty-two years earlier, Jacob had vowed that Beth-el would be the site of *God's House* (28:22). Now God commanded him to return there, implying that he must fulfill the vow without delay. Because he had not done so sooner, he had been punished by the abduction of Dinah (*Rashi; Radak*; see also *Vayikra Rabbah* 37:1 and *Tanchuma Vayishlach* 8). Clearly, the commentators explain, God did not make Dinah suffer for Jacob's oversight; people bear responsibility for their *own* sins. The sense of the teaching is that the righteous Patriarch always benefited from Divine protection that prevented enemies and brigands from harming him, just as God warned Laban not to meddle in Jacob's affairs (31:24). Had God not intervened, Laban would indeed have harmed Jacob, as he intended, but because the merit of Jacob and his family was so great, the miracle of God's vision to Laban restrained that wicked charlatan. In the case of Dinah, however, Jacob's failure to promptly carry out his vow caused him to forfeit this Divine aura of protection. As a result, there was no miraculous intercession to protect Dinah from Shechem. A further outgrowth of the incident was that the surrounding cities hated Jacob and his family, frightening them and putting them in jeopardy. But as soon as Jacob went to Beth-el and fulfilled his vow, God cast His fear upon all the cities (v. 5), so that they were no longer a danger to Jacob.

1. לָאֵל הַנִּרְאֶה אֵלֶיךָ — *To the God Who appeared to you.* When Jacob fled from Esau's death threat, God had appeared to him at Beth-el and promised to protect him (28:10-15). Now, he would thank God for having done so, just as one who is saved from a disaster blesses God for performing a miracle on his behalf (*Sforno*).

This Name of God [אֵל] indicates a boundless degree of mercy, surpassing even that indicated by the Tetragrammaton (*Gur Aryeh*, *Exodus* 34:6).

2. הָסִרוּ אֶת־אֱלֹהֵי הַנֵּכָר — *Remove the alien gods* you may have taken from the spoils of Shechem (*Rashi*). For Jacob's family, the ascent to the place where God had revealed Himself to the Patriarch had the same significance as the assembly at Mount Sinai for his descendants. Therefore, Jacob wanted to sanctify them, just as Moses prepared the people for the Revelation at

ג וְנָקוּמָה וְנַעֲלֶה בֵּית־אֵל וְאֶעֱשֶׂה־שָּׁם מִזְבֵּחַ לָאֵל
< to the God < an altar < there < and I will make << [to] Beth-el; < and let us go up < Then let us rise, 3

הָעֹנֶה אֹתִי בְּיוֹם צָרָתִי וַיְהִי עִמָּדִי בַּדֶּרֶךְ אֲשֶׁר
< that < on the road < with me < and was < of my distress, < on the day < me < Who answers

הָלָכְתִּי: ד וַיִּתְּנוּ אֶל־יַעֲקֹב אֵת כָּל־אֱלֹהֵי הַנֵּכָר
< the alien gods < all < Jacob < to < So they gave 4 << I traveled.

אֲשֶׁר בְּיָדָם וְאֶת־הַנְּזָמִים אֲשֶׁר בְּאָזְנֵיהֶם וַיִּטְמֹן
< and bury << in their ears, < that were < and the rings << in their possession, < that were

אֹתָם יַעֲקֹב תַּחַת הָאֵלָה אֲשֶׁר עִם־שְׁכֶם: ה וַיִּסָּעוּ
< They traveled, 5 << Shechem. < near < that was < the terebinth < underneath < did Jacob < them

וַיְהִי | חִתַּת אֱלֹהִים עַל־הֶעָרִים אֲשֶׁר סְבִיבוֹתֵיהֶם וְלֹא רָדְפוּ אַחֲרֵי
< after < so that they did not chase << around them, < that were < the cities < upon < of God < a terror < and there was

בְּנֵי יַעֲקֹב: ו וַיָּבֹא יַעֲקֹב לוּזָה אֲשֶׁר בְּאֶרֶץ כְּנַעַן הִוא בֵּית־אֵל הוּא
< he, < Beth-el — < — it is << of Canaan < in the land < which is < to Luz < Thus Jacob came 6 << of Jacob. < the sons

וְכָל־הָעָם אֲשֶׁר־עִמּוֹ: ז וַיִּבֶן שָׁם מִזְבֵּחַ וַיִּקְרָא לַמָּקוֹם אֵל בֵּית־אֵל
<< El-beth-el, < the place < and he called < an altar < there < And he built 7 << with him. < who were < the people < and all

כִּי שָׁם נִגְלוּ אֵלָיו הָאֱלֹהִים בְּבָרְחוֹ מִפְּנֵי אָחִיו: ח וַתָּמָת דְּבֹרָה מֵינֶקֶת
< — the nurse << Deborah died 8 << his brother. < from < when he fled < was God < to him < that revealed < it was there < for

ג וְנֵקוּם וְנִסַּק לְבֵית אֵל וְאֶעְבֵּד תַּמָּן מַדְבְּחָא לֶאֱלָהָא דְּקַבִּיל צְלוֹתִי בְּיוֹמָא דְעַקְתִי וַהֲוָה מֵימְרֵהּ בְּסַעְדִי בְּאָרְחָא דִי אֲזָלִית: ד וִיהָבוּ לְיַעֲקֹב יָת כָּל טַעֲוַת עַמְמַיָּא דִי בִידֵיהוֹן וְיָת קָדָשַׁיָּא דִי בְאָדְנֵיהוֹן וְטַמַּר יָתְהוֹן יַעֲקֹב תְּחוֹת בְּטְמָא דִי עִם שְׁכֶם: ה וּנְטָלוּ וַהֲוַת דַּחֲלָא דַייָ עַל קִרְוֵי דִי בְסַחֲרָנֵיהוֹן וְלָא רְדָפוּ בָּתַר בְּנֵי יַעֲקֹב: ו וַעַל יַעֲקֹב לְלוּז דִי בְאַרְעָא דִכְנַעַן הִיא בֵּית אֵל הוּא וְכָל עַמָּא דִי עִמֵּהּ: ז וּבְנָא תַמָּן מַדְבְּחָא וּקְרָא לְאַתְרָא אֵל בֵּית אֵל אֲרֵי תַמָּן אִתְגְּלִי לֵהּ יְיָ בְּמֵעַרְקֵהּ מִן קֳדָם אָחוּהִי: ח וּמִיתַת דְּבוֹרָה מֵנִקְתָּא

רש"י

(ד) **האלה.** מין אילן סרק (אונקלוס): **עם שכם.** אצל שכם (תרגום יונתן): (ה) **חתת.** פחד (אונקלוס): (ז) **אל בית אל.** הקב"ה בבית אל, גילוי שכינתו בבית אל. יש תיבה חסרה בי"ת המשמשת בראשה, כמו הנה הוא בית מכיר בן עמיאל (שמואל ב ט:ד) כמו בבית מכיר, בית אביך (להלן לח:יא) כמו בבית אביך: **נגלו אליו האלהים.** במקומות הרבה יש שם אלהות ואדנות בל' רבים, כמו אדני יוסף (להלן לט:כ), אם בעליו עמו (שמות כב:יד), ולא נאמר בעלו, וכן אלהות שהוא ל' שופט ומרות נזכר בל' רבים (שמות כב:ז-ח). אבל אחד מכל שאר השמות לא תמצא בל' רבים (עי' סנהדרין לח:): (ח) **ותמת דבורה.** מה ענין דבורה בבית יעקב. אלא לפי שאמרה רבקה ליעקב ושלחתי ולקחתיך משם (לעיל כז:מה) שלחה דבורה אצלו לפדן ארם לצאת משם, ומתה בדרך. מדברי ר' משה הדרשן למדתיה (ברכ"ת):

Sinai: *he sanctified the people and they washed their garments (Exodus 19:14)* (*R' Hirsch*). The order to change clothes was because some of the clothing taken from Shechem might have been used in idol worship (*Rashi*).

5-6. חִתַּת אֱלֹהִים — *A terror of God.* A casual observer could have assumed that the Canaanites did not attack because Jacob and his camp were a military force to be reckoned with, or perhaps the Canaanites held the Shechemites in disdain and did not care to avenge them, perhaps because they circumcised themselves. If so, then God took no role in this matter. The Torah, however, states that it was a hidden miracle, that what deterred the Canaanites was a *Godly fear*, not a military or political one. Part of this miracle was that *all the people who were with him* arrived safely at Beth-el — no one died in Shechem or on the journey *(Ramban)*.

7. אֵל בֵּית־אֵל — *El-beth-el.* The intent of the name is: God makes His Presence felt in Beth-el (*Rashi*). Jacob had named the place Beth-el twenty-two years before; now he added the Name *El*, to imply, as indicated by the next phrase, that by appearing to him now, God had associated His Presence with the place called Beth-el (*Or HaChaim*).

8. The deaths of Rebecca and Deborah. *Rashi* and *Ramban*

רִבְקָה וַתִּקָּבֵר מִתַּחַת לְבֵית־אֵל תַּחַת הָאַלּוֹן

« the plain; ‹ below ‹ Beth-el, ‹ below ‹ and she was buried « of Rebecca —

וַיִּקְרָא שְׁמוֹ אַלּוֹן בָּכוּת: ט וַיֵּרָא אֱלֹהִים אֶל־

‹ to ‹ And God appeared 9 « Allon-bachuth. ‹ its name ‹ and he called

יַעֲקֹב עוֹד בְּבֹאוֹ מִפַּדַּן אֲרָם וַיְבָרֶךְ אֹתוֹ:

« him. ‹ and He blessed ‹ from Paddan-aram, ‹ when he came ‹ again ‹ Jacob

י וַיֹּאמֶר־לוֹ אֱלֹהִים שִׁמְךָ יַעֲקֹב לֹא־יִקָּרֵא שִׁמְךָ עוֹד יַעֲקֹב כִּי אִם־

‹ *rather* ‹ *but* « *Jacob,* ‹ *anymore [only]* ‹ *your name will not be called* « *is only Jacob;* ‹ *Your name [now]* « Then God said to him, 10

יִשְׂרָאֵל יִהְיֶה שְׁמֶךָ וַיִּקְרָא אֶת־שְׁמוֹ יִשְׂרָאֵל: יא וַיֹּאמֶר לוֹ אֱלֹהִים אֲנִי

‹ *I am* « And God said to him, 11 « Israel. ‹ his name ‹ Thus He called « *your name.* ‹ *shall* [also] *be* ‹ *Israel*

דְרִבְקָה וְאִתְקְבָרַת מִלְּרַע לְבֵית אֵל
בְּשִׁפּוֹלֵי מֵישְׁרָא וּקְרָא שְׁמֵהּ מֵישַׁר
בָּכִיתָא: ט וְאִתְגְּלִי יְיָ לְיַעֲקֹב עוֹד
בְּמֵיתֵהּ מִפַּדַּן אֲרָם וּבָרִיךְ יָתֵהּ:
י וַאֲמַר לֵהּ יְיָ שְׁמָךְ יַעֲקֹב לָא
יִתְקְרֵי שְׁמָךְ עוֹד יַעֲקֹב אֱלָהֵן
יִשְׂרָאֵל יְהֵא שְׁמָךְ וּקְרָא יָת שְׁמֵהּ
יִשְׂרָאֵל: יא וַאֲמַר לֵהּ יְיָ אֲנָא

רש"י

מתחת לבית אל. העיר יושבת בהר ונקברה ברגלי ההר: **תחת האלון.** בשיפולי מישרא (אונקלוס), שהיה מישור מלמעלה בשפוע ההר והקבורה מלמטה. ומישור של בית אל היו קורין לו אלון. ואגדה, נתבשר שם באבל שני, שהוגד לו על אמו שמתה, ואלון בל' יוני אחר [ס"א אבל] (ב"ר פא:ה). ולפיכך העלימו [ס"א ולפי שהעלימו] את יום מותה שלא יקללו הבריות הכרס שיצא ממנו עשו, אף הכתוב לא פרסמה (תנחומא כי תצא ד): (ט) **עוד.** פעם שנית במקום הזה, אחד בלכתו ואחד בשובו (תנחומא ישן כז; ב"ר פב:ג): **ויברך אתו.** ברכת אבלים (ב"ר שם פא:ה): (י) **לא יקרא שמך עוד יעקב.** ל' אדם הבא במארב ועקבה, אלא ל' שר ונגיד (חולין צב.):

discuss the Midrashic tradition that this verse, which mentions only the death of Deborah, is an allusion also to the death of Rebecca. Midrashically this is implied by the name Plain of בָּכוּת, *weeping*, which the Midrash perceives to mean *double weeping* [interpreting the word בָּכוּת as if it were the plural *Bachoth,* בָּכוֹת] — weeping for Rebecca, and weeping for Deborah.

The Torah did not mention Rebecca's death explicitly, because those who attended her decided to bury her secretly, at night, for if she had had the sort of burial she deserved, Esau would have come and people would have spoken disrespectfully of her as the one who gave birth to such a wicked person. Since they kept her death quiet, the Torah, too, only alluded to it (*Rashi* from *Tanchuma*). *Ramban* comments that her death was kept hidden, as it were, because she was buried in tragic circumstances: Isaac was blind and could not leave home to honor her properly, Jacob was absent, and Esau would not come because he hated her for securing the blessings for Jacob. Consequently, she had to be buried by her Hittite neighbors.

Why Deborah was with Jacob at this point is the subject of another dispute between *Rashi* and *Ramban. Rashi* cites *R' Moshe HaDarshan* who states that she was the nurse Laban had given to Rebecca when she left to marry Isaac (24:59). Rebecca — not knowing that Jacob was on the way — had sent Deborah to Haran to tell him that it was finally safe for him to return home, but the aged nurse died on the way home. *Ramban* maintains that it is unlikely that Rebecca would have sent an elderly woman on such a strenuous trip. He suggests that Deborah had returned to Paddan-aram after Rebecca's marriage, but when Jacob left Laban, he took Deborah with him, so that in tribute to his mother Rebecca, he would support her childhood nurse in her old age.

9-15. God blesses and renames Jacob.

9. עוֹד — *Again.* God appeared to Jacob a second time, *after* the weeping had ceased, since the *Shechinah* does not reside where there is sadness (*Sforno*).

וַיְבָרֶךְ אֹתוֹ — *And He blessed him,* upon Rebecca's death, with the blessing of consolation given to mourners (*Rashi*).

10. שִׁמְךָ יַעֲקֹב — *Your name is Jacob.* Although He was about to give Jacob the additional name of Israel, God told him that he would continue to be called Jacob (*Ramban; Sforno).* From that time onward, the name Jacob would be used for matters pertaining to physical and mundane matters, while the name Israel would be used for matters reflecting the spiritual role of the Patriarch and his descendants (*R' Bachya*).

⇐§ Abram/Abraham and Jacob/Israel.

Although both Abraham and Jacob were given new names, there is a basic difference between them, for the Talmud states that anyone who refers to Abraham as Abram is in violation of a negative commandment (*Berachos* 13a), whereas *both* names continue to be used for Jacob. *R' David Feinstein* comments that this difference is implicit in the verses themselves. Our verse begins with the phrase *your name is Jacob*, a clear indication that this was to remain his name, in addition to the new name of Israel. In the case of Abraham, however, there is no such indication.

Or HaChaim explains the reason for the difference. Every name in the Torah represents the soul that God emplaced in that person. Consequently, the name "Jacob" represents his soul, while the name "Israel" represents an enhancement of that soul, which Jacob earned by growing and transcending the mission signified by his original name. Since both manifestations of

אֵל שַׁדַּי פְּרֵה וּרְבֵה גּוֹי וּקְהַל גּוֹיִם יִהְיֶה מִמֶּךָּ
« from you, ‹ shall descend ‹ of nations ‹ and a congregation ‹ a nation « and multiply; ‹ Be fruitful « Shaddai. ‹ El

וּמְלָכִים מֵחֲלָצֶיךָ יֵצֵאוּ: ששי יב וְאֶת־הָאָרֶץ אֲשֶׁר
‹ that ‹ And the land 12 « shall issue. ‹ from your loins ‹ and kings

נָתַתִּי לְאַבְרָהָם וּלְיִצְחָק לְךָ אֶתְּנֶנָּה וּלְזַרְעֲךָ
‹ and to your offspring « I will give it; ‹ to you ‹ and to Isaac, ‹ to Abraham ‹ I gave

אַחֲרֶיךָ אֶתֵּן אֶת־הָאָרֶץ: יג וַיַּעַל מֵעָלָיו אֱלֹהִים
« did God, ‹ from upon him ‹ Then ascend 13 « the land. ‹ I will give ‹ after you

בַּמָּקוֹם אֲשֶׁר־דִּבֶּר אִתּוֹ: יד וַיַּצֵּב יַעֲקֹב מַצֵּבָה בַּמָּקוֹם אֲשֶׁר־דִּבֶּר אִתּוֹ
« with him ‹ [God] spoke ‹ where ‹ at the place ‹ a monument ‹ Jacob had set up 14 « with him. ‹ He had spoken ‹ where ‹ in the place

מַצֶּבֶת אָבֶן וַיַּסֵּךְ עָלֶיהָ נֶסֶךְ וַיִּצֹק עָלֶיהָ שָׁמֶן: טו וַיִּקְרָא יַעֲקֹב אֶת־שֵׁם
‹ the name ‹ Then Jacob called 15 « oil. ‹ upon it ‹ and poured « a libation, ‹ upon it ‹ and he poured « of stone— ‹ —a monument

הַמָּקוֹם אֲשֶׁר דִּבֶּר אִתּוֹ שָׁם אֱלֹהִים בֵּית־אֵל: טז וַיִּסְעוּ מִבֵּית אֵל וַיְהִי־
‹ and there was ‹ from Beth-el ‹ They journeyed 16 « Beth-el. « had God, ‹ there ‹ with him ‹ spoke ‹ where ‹ of the place

אֵל שַׁדַּי פּוּשׁ וּסְגֵי עַם וְכִנְשַׁת שִׁבְטִין יְהֵא (נ״א יְהוֹן) מִנָּךְ וּמַלְכִין דְּשַׁלִּיטִין בְּעַמְמַיָּא מִנָּךְ יִפְּקוּן: יב וְיָת אַרְעָא דִּי יְהָבִית לְאַבְרָהָם וּלְיִצְחָק לָךְ אֶתְּנִנַּהּ וְלִבְנָיךְ בַּתְרָךְ אֶתֵּן יָת אַרְעָא: יג וְאִסְתַּלַּק מֵעִלָּוֹהִי יְקָרָא דַּייָ בְּאַתְרָא דִּי מַלִּיל עִמֵּהּ: יד וַאֲקֵים יַעֲקֹב קָמְתָא בְּאַתְרָא דִּי מַלִּיל עִמֵּהּ קָמַת אַבְנָא וְאַסֵּיךְ עֲלַהּ נִסּוּכִין וַאֲרִיק עֲלַהּ מִשְׁחָא: טו וּקְרָא יַעֲקֹב יָת שְׁמָא דְאַתְרָא דִּי מַלִּיל עִמֵּהּ תַּמָּן יְיָ בֵּית אֵל: טז וּנְטָלוּ מִבֵּית אֵל וַהֲוָה

רש״י

(יא) **אני אל שדי.** שאני כדאי לברך, שהברכות שלי [די למתברכים]: **פרה ורבה.** ע״ש שעדיין לא נולד בנימין ואע״פ שכבר נתעברה ממנו (ב״ר פב:ד): **גוי.** בנימין: **גוים.** מנשה ואפרים שעתידים לצאת מיוסף והם במנין השבטים (שם): **ומלכים.** שאול ואיש בושת שהיו משבט בנימין שעדיין לא נולד (שם). [ופסוק זה דרש אבנר כשהמליך איש בושת, ואף השבטים דרשוהו וקרבו בנימין, דכתיב איש ממנו לא יתן את בתו לבנימין לאשה (שופטים כא:א), וחזרו ואמרו אלמלא היה עולה מן השבטים לא היה הקב״ה אומר ליעקב ומלכים מחלציך יצאו (ב״ר שם; תנחומא ישן כט): **גוי וקהל גוים.** שגוים עתידים בניו ליעשות כמנין הגוים שהם ע׳ אומות. וכן כל הסנהדרין שבעים (תנחומא ישן ל). ד״א, שעתידים בניו להקריב בשעת איסור במות כגוים בימי אליהו (תנחומא שם; שם ה):] (יג) **במקום אשר דבר אתו.** איני יודע מה מלמדנו:

spirituality were present in Jacob/Israel, he was known by both names. In the case of Abraham, however, the original soul of "Abram" continued to be signified in the new name, since the old name was contained in the new one — *Abra***ha***m.* Thus, to use the name Abram would be to negate the existence of the enhanced soul implied by the new name.

11. אֲנִי אֵל שַׁדַּי — *I am El Shaddai.* The Name *El* signifies God's powerful attribute of mercy (see comm. to v. 1). *Shaddai* comes from the word דַּי, *sufficiency,* so that Name has the connotation "The One Who is Sufficient," and it signifies, depending on the context in which the Name is used, that God has sufficient power to bless, for the blessings are His, and He weighs and measures how much blessing one requires or deserves, and conversely, how much suffering one can bear without breaking under the strain (*Rashi* here and to 17:1).

According to *Rashi*, based on the Midrash, the reference to a *nation* alluded to Benjamin, the only son of Jacob who was yet unborn. The plural *congregation of nations* alludes to Joseph's sons Manasseh and Ephraim, who would receive the status of full-fledged tribes (48:5).

12. As part of this pledge of abundant progeny, God reiterated the promise of the Land, since the nation of Israel is associated with the Land (*Malbim*).

13. וַיַּעַל מֵעָלָיו אֱלֹהִים — *Then did ascend from upon him God.* This was not a vision or dream, for the *Shechinah* actually "rested" upon Jacob. This verse is one of the bases for the Sages' expression that the Patriarchs are the "chariots" of God's Presence, meaning that the thoroughly righteous are the bearers of His glory and that it is through them that He displays His sovereignty among human beings (*Ramban*).

16-20. The birth of Benjamin and death of Rachel. At this time Jacob had eleven sons, one short of the total of twelve, which both he and the Matriarchs knew prophetically would be the number of the tribes of Israel. Rachel had been barren for many years. She had seen not only her sister, but the maidservants give birth before her, and she longed for one more son. Now she was finally pregnant. On the way to the home she had never seen and eight years after the birth of her son Joseph, she gave birth to her cherished second son.

עוֹד כִּבְרַת־הָאָרֶץ לָבוֹא אֶפְרָתָה וַתֵּלֶד רָחֵל

still ‹ a small measure ‹ of land ‹ to go ‹ to Ephrath, « when Rachel went into labor ‹

וַתְּקַשׁ בְּלִדְתָּהּ: יז וַיְהִי בְהַקְשֹׁתָהּ בְּלִדְתָּהּ וַתֹּאמֶר

and had difficulty ‹ in her labor. « **17** And it was ‹ when she had difficulty ‹ in her labor ‹ that she said ‹

לָהּ הַמְיַלֶּדֶת אַל־תִּירְאִי כִּי־גַם־זֶה לָךְ בֵּן:

to her, « the midwife did, « Do not ‹ fear, ‹ for ‹ also ‹ this one ‹ is for you ‹ a son. «

יח וַיְהִי בְּצֵאת נַפְשָׁהּ כִּי מֵתָה וַתִּקְרָא שְׁמוֹ בֶּן־אוֹנִי וְאָבִיו קָרָא־לוֹ

18 And it came to pass, ‹ at the departing ‹ of her soul « – for ‹ she died – « that she called ‹ his name ‹ Ben Oni, « but his father ‹ called ‹ him ‹

בִנְיָמִין: יט וַתָּמָת רָחֵל וַתִּקָּבֵר בְּדֶרֶךְ אֶפְרָתָה הִוא בֵּית לָחֶם:

Benjamin. « **19** Thus died ‹ Rachel, « and she was buried ‹ on the road ‹ to Ephrath, ‹ which is ‹ Bethlehem. «

עוֹד כְּרוּבַת אַרְעָא לְמֵיעַל לְאֶפְרָת וִילִידַת רָחֵל וְקַשִׁיאַת בְּמֵילְדַהּ: יז וַהֲוָה בְּקַשְׁיוּתַהּ בְּמֵילְדַהּ וַאֲמֶרֶת לַהּ חָיְתָא לָא תִדְחֲלִי אֲרֵי אַף דֵּין לִיךְ בָּר: יח וַהֲוָה בְּמִפַּק נַפְשַׁהּ אֲרֵי מִיתַת (נ״א מַיְתָא) וּקְרַת שְׁמֵהּ בַּר דְּוָנִי וַאֲבוּהִי קְרָא לֵהּ בִּנְיָמִין: יט וּמִיתַת רָחֵל וְאִתְקְבָרַת בְּאֹרַח אֶפְרָת הִיא בֵּית לָחֶם:

רש״י

(טז) כברת הארץ. מנחם פי׳ ל׳ כביר, רבוי, מהלך רב. ואגדה, בזמן שהארץ חלולה ומנוקבת ככברה, שהניר מצוי, הסתיו עבר והשרב עדיין לא בא (שם ז). ואין זה פשוטו של מקרא, שהרי בנעמן מצינו וילך מאתו כברת ארץ (מלכים ב ה:יט). ואומר אני שהוא שם מדת קרקע כמו מהלך פרסה או יותר, כמו שאתה אומר צמד כרם (ישעיה ה:י), חלקת שדה (לעיל לג:יט), כך במהלך אדם נותן שם מדה [ס״א מדת קרקע כמו מהלך מיל] כברת ארץ: **(יז) כי גם זה.** נוסף לך על יוסף. ורבותינו דרשו, עם כל שבט נולדה תאומה, ועם בנימין נולדה תאומה יתירה (ב״ר שם ח): **(יח) בן אוני.** בן צערי (שם ט): **בנימין.** נראה בעיני לפי שהוא לבדו נולד בארץ כנען שהיא בנגב כשאדם בא מארם נהרים, כמו שנאמר בנגב בארץ כנען (במדבר לג:מ), הלוך ונסוע הנגבה (לעיל יב:ט): **בנימין.** בן ימין. ל׳ צפון וימין אתה בראתם (תהלים פט:יג). לפיכך הוא מלא. [ד״א, בנימין, בן ימים, שנולד לעת זקנתו, ונכתב בנו״ן כמו לקץ הימין (דניאל יב:יג)]:

The Sages observe that a woman's account is examined in heaven when she is in labor. When Rachel improperly stole her father's *teraphim* (31:19) without Jacob's knowledge, he told Laban, *With whomever you find your gods, he shall not live* (31:32). As a result, she was to be punished; but the judgment against her was not carried out until she was in childbirth. The idea that people are judged in times of danger is expressed in the adage, "When the ox is fallen, the knife is sharpened" (*Midrash Lekach Tov*). It may also be that God delayed her death until she could give birth to Benjamin, for otherwise this woman of historic righteousness would have been denied her full share in the building of the nation.

Ramban (*Leviticus* 18:25) sees the timing of Rachel's death as an indication of the great holiness of *Eretz Yisrael*. The Torah would later forbid a man to be married to two sisters, and the Patriarchs observed the Torah before it was given. According to *Ramban*, it was only *outside* of the Land that Jacob would be married to both Rachel and Leah, but in the Land, with its high degree of holiness, he would never have married Rachel after having been married to Leah. Because of Rachel's merit, she did not die *before* they entered the Land, but because of Jacob's merit and the sanctity of the Land, he could not remain married to both of them in *Eretz Yisrael.* Thus, she died only after they entered the Land.

18. בֶּן־אוֹנִי — *Ben Oni*, literally, *Son of My Mourning*, as if to say: His birth caused my death (*Ibn Ezra; Ramban*).

בִּנְיָמִין — *Benjamin. Rashi* offers two interpretations: (a) The name is a contraction of the words בֶּן יָמִין, *son of the right,* that is, *son of the south,* since the south is to the right of someone facing the east (the primary direction in Jewish thought). Thus, the name honors Benjamin as the only one of Jacob's children born in Canaan, which is *south* of Paddan-aram. (b) The word יָמִים, *days,* can be spelled יָמִין as in *Daniel* 12:13. Thus, the name means "son of my days," as if to say that Benjamin was born in Jacob's advanced years.

Ramban comments that Rachel, near death, called him *Ben Oni,* or Son of My Mourning. Jacob wanted to preserve the *form* of the name she gave, but wished to give it an optimistic connotation. So, giving the homonym *Oni* its other translation of *strength*, he named the child *Benjamin* [lit., *son of the right*], i.e., "son of power" or "son of strength," since the right hand is a symbol of strength and success.

19. וַתָּמָת רָחֵל — *Thus died Rachel. Seder Olam* cites a tradition that Rachel was born on the day Jacob received his father's blessing. Since he was 63 then, and 99 when he entered the Land, Rachel died at 36.

בְּדֶרֶךְ אֶפְרָתָה — *On the road to Ephrath.* Rachel's tomb was on the roadside, outside of Bethlehem; in modern times, however, the city has grown until the tomb is now inside it. Instead of bringing Rachel the short distance to Bethlehem, Jacob chose that site because he foresaw that his descendants would pass it on the road to the Babylonian exile. He buried Rachel there so she should pray for them, as it is said concerning that tragic journey (*Jeremiah* 31:14): *Rachel weeping for her children*. Jacob

כ וַיַּצֵּב יַעֲקֹב מַצֵּבָה עַל־קְבֻרָתָהּ הִוא מַצֶּבֶת

20 Jacob set up ‹ a monument ‹ over ‹ her grave; « it is ‹ the monument ‹

קְבֻרַת־רָחֵל עַד־הַיּוֹם: כא וַיִּסַּע יִשְׂרָאֵל וַיֵּט אָהֳלֹה

of the grave ‹ of Rachel ‹ until ‹ today. « 21 Israel journeyed on, « and he pitched ‹ his tent ‹

מֵהָלְאָה לְמִגְדַּל־עֵדֶר: כב וַיְהִי בִּשְׁכֹּן יִשְׂרָאֵל

beyond ‹ Migdal-eder. « 22 And it came to pass, ‹ while Israel dwelt ‹

בָּאָרֶץ הַהִוא וַיֵּלֶךְ רְאוּבֵן וַיִּשְׁכַּב אֶת־בִּלְהָה פִּילֶגֶשׁ אָבִיו וַיִּשְׁמַע

in that land, « that Reuben went ‹ and lay ‹ with ‹ Bilhah, ‹ the concubine ‹ of his father, « and hear ‹

יִשְׂרָאֵל * וַיִּהְיוּ בְנֵי־יַעֲקֹב שְׁנֵים עָשָׂר: כג בְּנֵי לֵאָה בְּכוֹר יַעֲקֹב רְאוּבֵן

did Israel. « And the sons of Jacob were ‹ twelve. « 23 The sons ‹ of Leah: « the firstborn ‹ of Jacob, ‹ Reuben; ‹

כ וַאֲקֵים יַעֲקֹב קָמְתָא עַל קְבֻרְתַּהּ הִיא קָמַת קְבֻרְתָּא דְרָחֵל עַד יוֹמָא דֵין: כא וּנְטַל יִשְׂרָאֵל וּפְרַס מַשְׁכְּנֵהּ מִלְּהַלָּא לְמִגְדְּלָא דְעֵדֶר: כב וַהֲוָה כַּד שְׁרָא יִשְׂרָאֵל בְּאַרְעָא הַהִיא וַאֲזַל רְאוּבֵן וּשְׁכִיב עִם בִּלְהָה לְחֵינָתָא דַאֲבוּהִי וּשְׁמַע יִשְׂרָאֵל וַהֲווֹ בְנֵי יַעֲקֹב תְּרֵי עֲסַר: כג בְּנֵי לֵאָה בּוּכְרָא דְיַעֲקֹב רְאוּבֵן

* פסקא באמצע פסוק

רש"י

(כב) **בשכן ישראל בארץ ההוא.** עד שלא בא לחברון אצל יצחק ארעוהו כל אלה (עי' רש"י לעיל פסוק א): **וישכב.** מתוך שבלבל משכבו מעלה עליו הכתוב כאילו שכבה. ולמה בלבל וחלל יצועיו, שכשמתה רחל נטל יעקב מטתו שהיתה נתונה תדיר באהל רחל ולא בשאר אהלים ונתנה באהל בלהה. בא ראובן ותבע עלבון אמו, אמר, אם אחות אמי היתה צרה לאמי, שפחת אחות אמי תהא צרה לאמי, לכך בלבל (שבת נה:): **ויהיו בני יעקב שנים עשר.** מתחיל לענין ראשון, משנולד בנימין נשלמה המטה ומעתה ראוים להמנות, ומנאן. ורבותינו דרשו, ללמדנו בא שכולם שוין וכולם צדיקים, שלא חטא ראובן (שם): (כג) **בכור יעקב.** אפילו בשעת הקלקלה קראו בכור (ב"ר פב:יא): **בכור יעקב.** בכור לנחלה, בכור לעבודה, בכור למנין. ולא נתנה בכורה ליוסף אלא לענין השבטים, שנעשה לשני שבטים (בבא בתרא קכג.):

set up a monument over her lonely gravesite (v. 20) so that the exiled Jews would recognize it and pray there as they were led into captivity (*Midrash*).

To this very day, Rachel's tomb is a place where men and women shed tears and beg "Mother Rachel" to intercede with God on their behalf.

As a further reason why Jacob chose not to bury her within the city limits, *Ramban* cites *Sifre,* that after Israel occupied the Land, Bethlehem proper would be in the territory of Judah, while the roadside burial site would belong to Rachel's son Benjamin. Nor did Jacob wish to bury her in the Cave of Machpelah because he married her after he was already married to her sister — a marriage of the sort that the Torah would later forbid — and "he would have been embarrassed before his ancestors," had she been with him in the Cave. See also introductory comments to 29:1-12 and 22-25.

22-26. Reuben's error and partial vindication. After Rachel's death, Jacob established his primary residence in the tent of Bilhah, Rachel's maidservant. Reuben considered this an affront to his mother Leah, saying, "If my mother's sister Rachel was my mother's rival, should the *handmaid* of my mother's sister now be my mother's rival?" To defend his mother's honor, Reuben took it upon himself to move Jacob's bed to Leah's tent. This is all that transpired (*Shabbos* 55b); nevertheless, Scripture describes it as starkly as if Reuben had sinned grievously. This follows the dictum that even minor transgressions of great people are judged with the utmost gravity, because their conduct is measured by infinitely higher standards than ours. This is explained at length in the *Overview* to the ArtScroll edition of *Ruth.*

Jacob moved to Bilhah's tent to honor Rachel's memory because he had labored fourteen years for the right to marry her and she had been the mainstay of his household. In tribute to her, he assigned this honor to her loyal maidservant, for even after Bilhah's marriage to Jacob, Bilhah continued to serve Rachel loyally (*Maharsha*). It may also be that Jacob did so because Bilhah was raising the eight-year-old Joseph and the infant Benjamin, who were not only his youngest children, but the only survivors of his most beloved wife.

22. וַיִּשְׁכַּב — *And lay.* As noted above, Reuben did nothing more than tamper with his father's bed, but the Torah describes it as adultery because he interfered with another's right to conduct his married life as he saw fit. The Sages teach that the privacy of the marital relationship is a prerequisite to holiness. Figuratively, therefore, for someone of Reuben's stature, such a deed could be described as an immoral act (*R' David Feinstein*).

שְׁנֵים עָשָׂר — *Twelve.* Although this phrase is written in Torah Scrolls as the beginning of a new paragraph, it is part of verse 22, in which Reuben's transgression is recorded. By combining the very first complete listing of Jacob's twelve sons with Jacob's knowledge of what Reuben had done, the Torah indicates that Jacob did not banish or disinherit Reuben. To the contrary, despite the sin that caused him to lose the privileges of the firstborn (see 49:4), not only was Reuben not rejected, he continued to be listed first among his brothers (*Ramban; Sforno*). Since all twelve sons are grouped together, which implies that they were equally righteous and meritorious, *Sifre* infers that Reuben repented.

23. בְּכוֹר יַעֲקֹב רְאוּבֵן — *The firstborn of Jacob, Reuben.* Although the birthright was later transferred from Reuben to Joseph (see *I Chronicles* 5:1), our verse calls Reuben the firstborn to indicate

וְשִׁמְעוֹן וְלֵוִי וִיהוּדָה וְיִשָּׂשכָר וּזְבֻלֻן: כד בְּנֵי רָחֵל

<< of Rachel: < The sons 24 << and Zebulun. < Issachar; < Judah; < Levi; < Simeon;

יוֹסֵף וּבִנְיָמִן: כה וּבְנֵי בִלְהָה שִׁפְחַת רָחֵל דָּן

< Dan << of Rachel: < maidservant < of Bilhah, < The sons 25 << and Benjamin. < Joseph

וְנַפְתָּלִי: כו וּבְנֵי זִלְפָּה שִׁפְחַת לֵאָה גָּד וְאָשֵׁר אֵלֶּה

< — these are << and Asher < Gad << of Leah: < maidservant < of Zilpah, < And the sons 26 << and Naphtali.

בְּנֵי יַעֲקֹב אֲשֶׁר יֻלַּד־לוֹ בְּפַדַּן אֲרָם: כז וַיָּבֹא יַעֲקֹב אֶל־יִצְחָק אָבִיו

< his father, < Isaac < to < Jacob came 27 << in Paddan-aram. < to him < were born < who < of Jacob, < the sons

מַמְרֵא קִרְיַת הָאַרְבַּע הִוא חֶבְרוֹן אֲשֶׁר־גָּר־שָׁם אַבְרָהָם וְיִצְחָק:

<< and Isaac. < Abraham < there < sojourned < where < Hebron < that is << Kiriath-arba; < [at] Mamre,

כח וַיִּהְיוּ יְמֵי יִצְחָק מְאַת שָׁנָה וּשְׁמֹנִים שָׁנָה: כט וַיִּגְוַע יִצְחָק וַיָּמָת

< and died, < And Isaac expired 29 << years. < and eighty < years < one hundred << of Isaac — < — the days << And they were 28

וַיֵּאָסֶף אֶל־עַמָּיו זָקֵן וּשְׂבַע יָמִים וַיִּקְבְּרוּ אֹתוֹ עֵשָׂו וְיַעֲקֹב בָּנָיו: פ

<< his sons. < and Jacob < — Esau << him < and they buried << of days; < and fulfilled < old << his people, < to < and he was gathered

וְשִׁמְעוֹן וְלֵוִי וִיהוּדָה וְיִשָּׂשכָר וּזְבֻלוּן: כד בְּנֵי רָחֵל יוֹסֵף וּבִנְיָמִן: כה וּבְנֵי בִלְהָה אַמְתָא דְרָחֵל דָּן וְנַפְתָּלִי: כו וּבְנֵי זִלְפָּה אַמְתָא דְלֵאָה גָּד וְאָשֵׁר אִלֵּין בְּנֵי יַעֲקֹב דִּי אִתְיְלִידוּ לֵהּ בְּפַדַּן אֲרָם: כז וַאֲתָא יַעֲקֹב לְוַת יִצְחָק אֲבוּהִי מַמְרֵא קִרְיַת אַרְבַּע הִיא חֶבְרוֹן דִּי דָר תַּמָּן אַבְרָהָם וְיִצְחָק: כח וַהֲווֹ יוֹמֵי יִצְחָק מְאָה וּתְמָנָן שְׁנִין: כט וְאִתְנְגִיד יִצְחָק וּמִית וְאִתְכְּנֵישׁ לְעַמֵּהּ סִיב וּשְׂבַע יוֹמִין וּקְבָרוּ יָתֵהּ עֵשָׂו וְיַעֲקֹב בְּנוֹהִי:

רש"י

(כז) **ממרא.** שם המישור: **קרית ארבע.** שם העיר: **ממרא קרית הארבע.** אל מישור של קרית ארבע. ואם תאמר היה לו לכתוב ממרא הקרית ארבע. כן דרך המקרא בכל דבר ששמו כפול, כגון זה, וכגון בית לחם, אבי עזר, בית אל, אם הוצרך להטיל בו ה"א נותנה בראש התיבה השניה. בית הלחמי (שמואל א טז:א) בעפרת אבי העזרי (שופטים ו:כד) בנה חיאל בית האלי (מלכים א טז:לד): (כט) **ויגוע יצחק.** אין מוקדם ומאוחר בתורה (פסחים ו:). מכירתו של יוסף קדמה למיתתו של יצחק י"ב שנה, שהרי כשנולד יעקב היה יצחק בן ס' שנה, שנאמר ויצחק בן ששים שנה וגו' (לעיל כה:כו) ויצחק מת בשנת ק"כ ליעקב, אם תוציא ששים מק"פ שנה נשארו ק"ך. ויוסף נמכר בן י"ז שנה ואותה שנה שנת מאה ושמונה ליעקב. כיצד, בן ששים ושלש נתברך, י"ד שנה נטמן בבית עבר. הרי שבעים ושבע. וארבע עשרה עבד באשה, ובסוף ארבע עשרה נולד יוסף, שנאמר ויהי כאשר ילדה רחל את יוסף וגו' (לעיל ל:כה), הרי תשעים ואחת, וי"ז עד שלא נמכר יוסף, הרי מאה ושמונה. [עוד מפורש [הוא] מן המקרא, משנמכר יוסף עד שבא יעקב מצרימה כ"ב שנה, שנאמר ויוסף בן שלשים שנה וגו' (להלן מא:מו). וז' שנים שובע ושנתים רעב, הרי כ"ב. וכתיב ימי שני מגורי שלשים ומאת

that he would continue to have certain privileges of his status. Joseph would receive a double share of *Eretz Yisrael* because Jacob would later give his sons Ephraim and Manasseh the status of separate tribes [see below, 48:5]. Reuben, however, would be considered the firstborn in the following ways: (a) regarding the inheritance [for he personally received a double share of Jacob's estate and his tribe would be the first to receive its share of *Eretz Yisrael* (*Yafeh To'ar*)]; (b) regarding the sacrificial service [for before the sin of the Golden Calf the altar service was performed by the firstborn (*Matnos Kehunah*)]; and (c) regarding the census, for the tribe of Reuben was always the first to be counted (*Rashi*).

25-26. **שִׁפְחַת** — *Maidservant.* The Torah refers to Bilhah and Zilpah this way because even after they were freed to marry Jacob, they continued of their own accord to serve Rachel and Leah. However, all of their sons had the same status as the other children (*Haamek Davar*).

27-29. Jacob and Isaac are reunited. One can only imagine the emotions and tears at this reunion. In addition to his twenty years with Laban, Jacob had spent two years en route home, and fourteen years in the academy of Shem and Eber, for a total separation of thirty-six years. He had left as an empty-handed fugitive, and returned with twelve righteous sons and a large camp. But the joy of the reunion was clouded by the absence of Rachel, who had died in the interim. Father and son remained together until Isaac died twenty-one years later; nevertheless, as is customary in Scripture, the Torah records a person's death when his role is over.

27. **גָּר־שָׁם** — *Sojourned there.* The verb indicates that Abraham and Isaac lived in Hebron as גֵּרִים, *aliens.* They were separate and distinct from the rest of the population, living their own private lives as servants of God (*Sh'lah*).

29. **וַיִּגְוַע יִצְחָק** — *And Isaac expired.* In recording Isaac's death here, the Torah does not follow chronological order, for Joseph was sold twelve years before Isaac's death (*Rashi*).

וּשְׂבַע יָמִים — *And fulfilled of days.* Isaac was satisfied with his days; he was fully content with what each day brought him and

[לו] א וְאֵ֗לֶּה תֹּלְד֥וֹת עֵשָׂ֖ו ה֥וּא אֱדֽוֹם׃ ב עֵשָׂ֛ו

36 1 And these ‹ are the descendants ‹ of Esau, ›› he is ‹ Edom. ›› 2 Esau ‹

לָקַ֥ח אֶת־נָשָׁ֖יו מִבְּנ֣וֹת כְּנָ֑עַן אֶת־עָדָ֗ה בַּת־אֵילוֹן֙

had taken ‹ his wives ‹ from the daughters ‹ of Canaan: ›› Adah, ‹ daughter ‹ of Elon ‹

הַֽחִתִּ֔י וְאֶת־אָהֳלִֽיבָמָה֙ בַּת־עֲנָ֔ה בַּת־צִבְע֖וֹן

the Hittite; ›› and Oholibamah, ‹ daughter ‹ of Anah, ‹ daughter ‹ of Zibeon ‹

הַֽחִוִּֽי׃ ג וְאֶת־בָּשְׂמַ֥ת בַּת־יִשְׁמָעֵ֖אל אֲח֥וֹת נְבָיֽוֹת׃ ד וַתֵּ֧לֶד עָדָ֛ה

the Hivvite; ›› 3 and Basemath, ‹ daughter ‹ of Ishmael, ‹ sister ‹ of Nebaioth. ›› 4 Adah bore ‹

לְעֵשָׂ֖ו אֶת־אֱלִיפָ֑ז וּבָ֣שְׂמַ֔ת יָלְדָ֖ה אֶת־רְעוּאֵֽל׃ ה וְאָהֳלִֽיבָמָה֙ יָֽלְדָ֔ה

to Esau ‹ Eliphaz; ›› Basemath ‹ bore ‹ Reuel; ›› 5 and Oholibamah ‹ bore ‹

אֶת־°יְע֥וּשׁ [°יעיש כ׳] וְאֶת־יַעְלָ֖ם וְאֶת־קֹ֑רַח אֵ֚לֶּה בְּנֵ֣י עֵשָׂ֔ו אֲשֶׁ֥ר

Jeush, ‹ Jalam, ‹ and Korah; ‹ these are ‹ the sons ‹ of Esau ‹ who ‹

א וְאִלֵּין תּוּלְדָת עֵשָׂו הוּא אֱדוֹם: ב עֵשָׂו נְסֵיב יָת נְשׁוֹהִי מִבְּנָת כְּנַעַן יָת עָדָה בַּת אֵילוֹן חִתָּאָה וְיָת אָהֳלִיבָמָה בַּת עֲנָה בַּת צִבְעוֹן חִוָּאָה: ג וְיָת בָּשְׂמַת בַּת יִשְׁמָעֵאל אֲחָתֵהּ דִּנְבָיוֹת: ד וִילֵידַת עָדָה לְעֵשָׂו יָת אֱלִיפָז וּבָשְׂמַת יְלֵידַת יָת רְעוּאֵל: ה וְאָהֳלִיבָמָה יְלֵידַת יָת יְעוּשׁ וְיָת יַעְלָם וְיָת קֹרַח אִלֵּין בְּנֵי עֵשָׂו דִּי

רש״י

שנה (להלן מז:ט), נמלא יעקב במכירתו [של יוסף] ק״ח]: (ב) **עדה בת אילון.** היא בשמת בת אילון. ונקראת בשמת ע״ש שהיתה מקטרת בשמים לע״ז (עי׳ רש״י לעיל כו:לה־כז:א): **אהליבמה.** היא יהודית, והוא כינה שמה יהודית לומר שהיא כופרת בע״ז (עי׳ מגילה יג.), כדי להטעות את אביו: **בת ענה בת צבעון.** אם בת ענה לא בת צבעון, ענה בנו של צבעון, שנא׳ ואלה בני צבעון ואיה וענה (להלן פסוק כד). מלמד שבא צבעון על כלתו אשת ענה וילאת אהליבמה מבין שניהם, והודיעך הכתוב שכלן בני ממזרות היו (ב״ר פב:טו; תנחומא וישב א): (ג) **בשמת בת ישמעאל.** ולהלן קורא לה מחלת (לעיל כח:ט). מלינו באגדת מדרש ספר שמואל (פי״ז) ג׳ מוחלים להן עונותיהן, גר שנתגייר, והעולה לגדולה, והנושא אשה. ולמד הטעם מכאן, לכך נקראת מחלת שנמחלו עונותיו: **אחות נביות.** על שם שהוא השיאה לו משמת ישמעאל נקראת על שמו (מגילה יז.): (ה) **ואהליבמה ילדה וגו׳.** קרח זה ממזר היה ובן אליפז היה שבא על אשת אביו [על אהליבמה אשת עשו], שהרי הוא

he had no desire that the future should bring him something new. This is a further example of God's mercy toward the righteous, in that they are content with their lot and desire no luxuries (*Ramban* to 25:8).

36.

⁂ The chronicles of Esau

It is fundamental to a proper understanding of the Scriptural narratives that the Torah is not a history book and that whatever it records must have a halachic or moral purpose. Many important principles of halachah are derived from a seemingly superfluous word or even letter, or from allusions suggested by syntax or construction. Consequently, it is obvious that the Torah would not have devoted an entire chapter to Esau's genealogy unless it contained vital teachings. Indeed, a section of the *Zohar, Idra Rabbah*, is devoted to the mystical exposition of this chapter.

In the literal sense of the verses and from the parallel genealogies in *Chronicles*, it becomes clear that many of Esau's descendants were products of incest and illegitimacy. According to *Mizrachi,* this is reason enough for the chapter. There are other lessons, as well, some of them halachic, which are discussed by the commentators. Furthermore, the Torah teaches us the honor that came to Esau because he was an offspring of Abraham.

1. הוא אֱדוֹם — *He is Edom.* The name — and the fact that it was used throughout his life — gives an insight into Esau's base character. The name was given him as a reference to his gluttony when he sold the birthright for nothing more than red beans (25:30). That greed and depraved set of values characterized him all through his life (*Sforno*).

2. בַּת־עֲנָה בַּת־צִבְעוֹן — *Daughter of Anah, daughter of Zibeon.* As noted above, the Sages and commentators derive from various parts of the chapter that Esau's family was permeated with illegitimacy. Though this commentary cannot deal with those many allusions, this phrase is an illustrative example. The verse implies that Oholibamah was the daughter of two fathers, Anah and Zibeon, an obvious impossibility. Furthermore, verse 24 describes Anah as Zibeon's son. Consequently, our verse implies that Zibeon cohabited with his own daughter-in-law, Anah's wife, and Oholibamah was the product of their adultery. Thus, she and all her offspring were illegitimate (*Rashi*).

3. בָּשְׂמַת בַּת־יִשְׁמָעֵאל — *Basemath, daughter of Ishmael.* In 28:9, which states that this woman married Esau, she is called Mahalath, which implies forgiveness, from the root מחל. From this the Sages derive that one's sins are forgiven on the day of one's marriage (*Rashi*).

4. אֱלִיפָז — *Eliphaz*. There are traditions that Eliphaz, Esau's firstborn, was the most deserving of his children. *Rashi* (29:11) notes that "he had been raised on Isaac's knee, and did not obey his father's command to kill Jacob."

5. קֹרַח — *Korah.* Later (v. 16), Korah was included among the chiefs of *Eliphaz* son of *Adah,* while here he is listed as a son of Esau through *Oholibamah*! This implies that Korah was really the

יֻלְּדוּ־לוֹ בְּאֶרֶץ כְּנָעַן: ו וַיִּקַּח עֵשָׂו אֶת־נָשָׁיו

‹ his wives, ‹ Esau took **6** « of Canaan. ‹ in the land ‹ to him ‹ were born

וְאֶת־בָּנָיו וְאֶת־בְּנֹתָיו וְאֶת־כָּל־נַפְשׁוֹת בֵּיתוֹ

‹ of his household, ‹ the souls ‹ and all ‹ his daughters, ‹ his sons,

וְאֶת־מִקְנֵהוּ וְאֶת־כָּל־בְּהֶמְתּוֹ וְאֵת כָּל־קִנְיָנוֹ

‹ his property ‹ and all ‹ his animals, ‹ and all ‹ his livestock

אֲשֶׁר רָכַשׁ בְּאֶרֶץ כְּנָעַן וַיֵּלֶךְ אֶל־אֶרֶץ מִפְּנֵי

‹ because of ‹ a land ‹ to ‹ and went ‹ of Canaan, ‹ in the land ‹ he had acquired ‹ that

אִתְיְלִידוּ לֵהּ בְּאַרְעָא דִכְנָעַן: ו וּדְבַר עֵשָׂו יָת נְשׁוֹהִי וְיָת בְּנוֹהִי וְיָת בְּנָתֵהּ וְיָת כָּל נַפְשָׁת בֵּיתֵהּ וְיָת גֵּיתוֹהִי וְיָת כָּל בְּעִירֵהּ וְיָת כָּל קִנְיָנֵהּ דִּי קְנָא בְּאַרְעָא דִכְנָעַן וַאֲזַל לְאַרְעָא אוּחֲרֵי מִן קֳדָם יַעֲקֹב אֲחוּהִי: ז אֲרֵי הֲוָה קִנְיָנְהוֹן סַגִּי מִלְּמִתַּב כַּחֲדָא וְלָא יְכִילַת אֲרַע תּוֹתָבוּתְהוֹן לְסוֹבָרָא יָתְהוֹן מִן קֳדָם גֵּיתֵיהוֹן: ח וִיתֵיב עֵשָׂו בְּטוּרָא דְשֵׂעִיר עֵשָׂו הוּא אֱדוֹמָאָה: ט וְאִלֵּין תּוֹלְדַת עֵשָׂו אֲבוּהוֹן דֶּאֱדוֹמָאֵי בְּטוּרָא דְשֵׂעִיר: י אִלֵּין שְׁמָהַת בְּנֵי עֵשָׂו אֱלִיפַז בַּר עָדָה אִתַּת עֵשָׂו רְעוּאֵל בַּר בָּשְׂמַת אִתַּת עֵשָׂו:

יַעֲקֹב אָחִיו: ז כִּי־הָיָה רְכוּשָׁם רָב מִשֶּׁבֶת יַחְדָּו וְלֹא יָכְלָה אֶרֶץ

‹ and the land was not able « together, ‹ [for them] to dwell ‹ [too] great ‹ their possessions were ‹ For **7** « his brother. ‹ Jacob

מְגוּרֵיהֶם לָשֵׂאת אֹתָם מִפְּנֵי מִקְנֵיהֶם: ח וַיֵּשֶׁב עֵשָׂו בְּהַר שֵׂעִיר עֵשָׂו

‹ Esau, « Seir; ‹ on Mount ‹ So Esau settled **8** « their livestock. ‹ because of ‹ them ‹ to support ‹ of their sojourns

הוּא אֱדוֹם: ט וְאֵלֶּה תֹּלְדוֹת עֵשָׂו אֲבִי אֱדוֹם בְּהַר שֵׂעִיר: י אֵלֶּה שְׁמוֹת

‹ the names ‹ These are **10** « Seir. ‹ on Mount ‹ of Edom, ‹ ancestor ‹ of Esau, ‹ the descendants ‹ And these are **9** « Edom. ‹ he is

בְּנֵי־עֵשָׂו אֱלִיפַז בֶּן־עָדָה אֵשֶׁת עֵשָׂו רְעוּאֵל בֶּן־בָּשְׂמַת אֵשֶׁת עֵשָׂו:

« of Esau. ‹ wife ‹ of Basemath, ‹ son ‹ Reuel, « of Esau; ‹ wife ‹ of Adah, ‹ son ‹ Eliphaz, « of Esau: ‹ of the sons

רש"י

מנוי עם אלופי אליפז בסוף הענין (ב"ר שם יב): (ו) **וילך אל ארץ.** לגור באשר ימצא: (ז) **ולא יכלה ארץ מגוריהם.** להספיק מרעה לבהמות שלהם. ומדרש אגדה, **מפני יעקב אחיו,** מפני שטר חוב של גזירת כי גר יהיה זרעך המוטל על זרעו של יצחק. אמר, אלך לי מכאן, אין לי חלק לא במתנה שנתנה לו הארץ הזאת ולא בפרעון השטר, ומפני הבושה שמכר בכורתו (ב"ר שם יג): (ט) **ואלה.** התולדות שהולידו בניו [עכשיו] משהלך לשעיר:

illegitimate child of Eliphaz, Esau's son, through an adulterous union with Oholibamah, his father's wife (*Rashi* from *Midrash*).

בְּאֶרֶץ כְּנָעַן — *In the land of Canaan.* This concludes the list of Esau's offspring who were born in Canaan. Later, the chapter will list those who were born to him afterward in the land of Seir (*R' Hoffman*).

6-8. Esau separates himself from Jacob. In telling of Esau's decision to distance himself from Jacob, the Torah refers to Jacob as Esau's *brother,* implying that the animosity of the past had been erased. The Torah explains that they could not live together because their flocks were too large for the country to support, but the commentators infer that there was an underlying reason why the one who moved away was Esau rather than Jacob. They offer various reasons:

Esau left because he had come to fear the military prowess Jacob's family displayed in Shechem (*Targum Yonasan*); because Jacob, who purchased the birthright, was entitled to Canaan (*Rashbam*); or because Esau wanted no part of the decree (15:13) that the one who lived in Canaan would be subject to a long, hard exile (*Rashi*). *R' Hirsch* comments that despite their "brotherhood," the spiritual and moral gulf between them remained as gaping as ever, and Esau could not tolerate Jacob's proximity. He would have remained if the land could support them both — for Esau's greed overpowered all other considerations — but as it was he found no reason to stay.

6. אֶל־אֶרֶץ — *To a land.* It was an unspecified land; Esau left Canaan for wherever he could find a suitable spot to dwell (*Rashi*).

8. בְּהַר שֵׂעִיר — *On Mount Seir.* He successfully captured the fortified mountain from the original inhabitants, the Horites, descendants of Seir. Esau gained the territory by Divine sanction, as it is written [*Deut.* 2:5]: *because I have given Mount Seir to Esau for a possession.*

עֵשָׂו הוּא אֱדוֹם — *Esau, he is Edom.* Until this point, only Esau *himself* was called Edom, but when he established himself in Seir and had grandchildren there, the entire *nation* came to be

יא וַיִּהְיוּ בְּנֵי אֱלִיפָז תֵּימָן אוֹמָר צְפוֹ וְגַעְתָּם וּקְנַז׃
11 And they were: the sons of Eliphaz — Teman; Omar; Zepho; Gatam; and Kenaz.

יב וְתִמְנַע ׀ הָיְתָה פִילֶגֶשׁ לֶאֱלִיפַז בֶּן־עֵשָׂו וַתֵּלֶד
12 And Timna was a concubine of Eliphaz, son of Esau, and she bore

לֶאֱלִיפַז אֶת־עֲמָלֵק אֵלֶּה בְּנֵי עָדָה אֵשֶׁת עֵשָׂו׃
to Eliphaz Amalek; these are the children of Adah, wife of Esau.

יג וְאֵלֶּה בְּנֵי רְעוּאֵל נַחַת וָזֶרַח שַׁמָּה וּמִזָּה אֵלֶּה
13 And these are the children of Reuel: Nahath and Zerah; Shammah and Mizzah — these

הָיוּ בְּנֵי בָשְׂמַת אֵשֶׁת עֵשָׂו׃ יד וְאֵלֶּה הָיוּ בְּנֵי אָהֳלִיבָמָה בַת־עֲנָה
were the children of Basemath, wife of Esau. 14 And these were the sons of Oholibamah, daughter of Anah,

בַּת־צִבְעוֹן אֵשֶׁת עֵשָׂו וַתֵּלֶד לְעֵשָׂו אֶת־°יְעוּשׁ [°יעיש כ׳] וְאֶת־יַעְלָם
daughter of Zibeon, wife of Esau: She bore to Esau Jeush, and Jalam,

וְאֶת־קֹרַח׃ טו אֵלֶּה אַלּוּפֵי בְנֵי־עֵשָׂו בְּנֵי אֱלִיפַז בְּכוֹר עֵשָׂו אַלּוּף תֵּימָן
and Korah. 15 These are the chiefs of the children of Esau — the children of Eliphaz, firstborn of Esau: Chief Teman,

אַלּוּף אוֹמָר אַלּוּף צְפוֹ אַלּוּף קְנַז׃ טז אַלּוּף קֹרַח אַלּוּף גַּעְתָּם אַלּוּף
Chief Omar, Chief Zepho, Chief Kenaz; 16 Chief Korah, Chief Gatam, Chief

עֲמָלֵק אֵלֶּה אַלּוּפֵי אֱלִיפַז בְּאֶרֶץ אֱדוֹם אֵלֶּה בְּנֵי עָדָה׃ יז וְאֵלֶּה בְּנֵי
Amalek; these are the chiefs of Eliphaz in the land of Edom — these are the children of Adah. 17 And these are the children

רְעוּאֵל בֶּן־עֵשָׂו אַלּוּף נַחַת אַלּוּף זֶרַח אַלּוּף שַׁמָּה אַלּוּף מִזָּה
of Reuel son of Esau: Chief Nahath, Chief Zerah, Chief Shammah, Chief Mizzah;

יא וַהֲווֹ בְּנֵי אֱלִיפָז תֵּימָן אוֹמָר צְפוֹ
וְגַעְתָּם וּקְנַז׃ יב וְתִמְנַע הֲוַת לְחֵינָתָא
לֶאֱלִיפַז בַּר עֵשָׂו וִילִידַת לֶאֱלִיפַז יָת
עֲמָלֵק אִלֵּין בְּנֵי עָדָה אִתַּת עֵשָׂו׃
יג וְאִלֵּין בְּנֵי רְעוּאֵל נַחַת וָזֶרַח שַׁמָּה
וּמִזָּה אִלֵּין הֲווֹ בְּנֵי בָשְׂמַת אִתַּת עֵשָׂו׃
יד וְאִלֵּין הֲווֹ בְּנֵי אָהֳלִיבָמָה בַּת עֲנָה
בַּת צִבְעוֹן אִתַּת עֵשָׂו וִילִידַת לְעֵשָׂו
יָת יְעוּשׁ וְיָת יַעְלָם וְיָת קֹרַח׃ טו אִלֵּין
רַבָּנֵי בְנֵי עֵשָׂו בְּנֵי אֱלִיפַז בּוּכְרָא
דְעֵשָׂו רַבָּא תֵימָן רַבָּא אוֹמָר רַבָּא
צְפוֹ רַבָּא קְנַז׃ טז רַבָּא קֹרַח רַבָּא
גַעְתָּם רַבָּא עֲמָלֵק אִלֵּין רַבָּנֵי דֶאֱלִיפַז
בְּאַרְעָא דֶאֱדוֹם אִלֵּין בְּנֵי עָדָה׃
יז וְאִלֵּין בְּנֵי רְעוּאֵל בַּר עֵשָׂו רַבָּא נַחַת
רַבָּא זֶרַח רַבָּא שַׁמָּה רַבָּא מִזָּה

רש״י

(יב) ותמנע היתה פילגש. להודיע גדולתו של אברהם כמה היו תאבים לידבק בזרעו. תמנע זו בת אלופים היתה, שנא׳ ואחות לוטן תמנע (להלן פסוק כב) ולוטן מאלופי יושבי שעיר היה מן החורים שישבו בה לפנים. אמרה, איני זוכה להנשא לך הלואי שאהיה פילגש (ב״ר פב:יד, ועי׳ סנהדרין צט:). ובדברי הימים (א א:לו) מונה אותה בבניו של אליפז, מלמד שבא על אשתו של שעיר ויצאה תמנע מביניהם, וכשגדלה נעשית פילגשו. וזהו ואחות לוטן תמנע, ולא מנאה עם בני שעיר, שהיתה אחותו מן האם ולא מן האב (תנחומא וישב א): **(טו) אלה אלופי בני עשו.** ראשי משפחות:

called Edom. In the next verse, therefore, he is called *ancestor of Edom* (*Haamek Davar*).

12. וְתִמְנַע הָיְתָה פִּילֶגֶשׁ — *And Timna was a concubine.* She is mentioned [although the wives of Esau's other sons are not (*Ramban*)] to emphasize that Abraham was held in such esteem that people were eager to attach themselves to his descendants. As we see in verse 22, Timna was a descendant of chiefs; she was the sister of Lotan who was one of the chiefs of Seir [and a son of Seir himself (v. 20)], a Horite who lived there from ancient times. Yet she was so anxious to marry a descendant of Abraham that she said to Eliphaz: "If I am unworthy to become your wife, let me at least be your concubine!" (*Rashi*).

Ramban suggests that Timna is mentioned as Amalek's mother to indicate that Amalek — as the child of a concubine — was of lowly birth, not a true heir of Esau, and did not dwell with the other offspring of Esau on Mount Seir. Only the sons of the *true* wives were called Esau's seed, not those of the concubines.

אֵלֶּה אַלּוּפֵי רְעוּאֵל בְּאֶרֶץ אֱדוֹם אֵלֶּה בְּנֵי

‹ the children ‹ — these are ‹‹ of Edom ‹ in the land ‹ of Reuel ‹ the chiefs ‹ these are

בָשְׂמַת אֵשֶׁת עֵשָׂו: יח וְאֵלֶּה בְּנֵי אָהֳלִיבָמָה

‹ of Ohlibamah, ‹ the children ‹ And these are 18 ‹‹ of Esau. ‹ wife ‹ of Basemath,

אֵשֶׁת עֵשָׂו אַלּוּף יְעוּשׁ אַלּוּף יַעְלָם אַלּוּף קֹרַח

‹‹ Korah ‹ Chief ‹ Jalam, ‹ Chief ‹ Jeush, ‹ Chief ‹‹ of Esau: ‹ wife

אֵלֶּה אַלּוּפֵי אָהֳלִיבָמָה בַּת־עֲנָה אֵשֶׁת עֵשָׂו:

‹‹ of Esau. ‹ wife ‹ of Anah, ‹ daughter ‹ of Oholibamah, ‹ the chiefs ‹ — these are

יט אֵלֶּה בְנֵי־עֵשָׂו וְאֵלֶּה אַלּוּפֵיהֶם הוּא אֱדוֹם: פ

‹‹ Edom. ‹ he is ‹‹ their chiefs; ‹ and these are ‹ of Esau, ‹ the children ‹ These are 19

שביעי כ אֵלֶּה בְנֵי־שֵׂעִיר הַחֹרִי יֹשְׁבֵי הָאָרֶץ לוֹטָן וְשׁוֹבָל וְצִבְעוֹן וַעֲנָה:

‹‹ and Anah, ‹ and Zibeon ‹ and Shobal ‹ Lotan ‹‹ of the land: ‹ the inhabitants ‹ the Horite ‹ of Seir ‹ the sons ‹ These are 20

כא וְדִשׁוֹן וְאֵצֶר וְדִישָׁן אֵלֶּה אַלּוּפֵי הַחֹרִי בְּנֵי שֵׂעִיר בְּאֶרֶץ אֱדוֹם:

‹‹ of Edom. ‹ in the land ‹ of Seir ‹ the children ‹ of the Horite, ‹ the chiefs ‹ — these are ‹ and Dishan ‹ and Ezer ‹ and Dishon 21

כב וַיִּהְיוּ בְנֵי־לוֹטָן חֹרִי וְהֵימָם וַאֲחוֹת לוֹטָן תִּמְנָע: כג וְאֵלֶּה בְּנֵי שׁוֹבָל

‹‹ of Shobal: ‹ the sons ‹ These are 23 ‹‹ was Timna. ‹ of Lotan ‹ and the sister ‹ and Hemam; ‹ Hori ‹‹ of Lotan — ‹ the sons ‹‹ And they were: 22

עַלְוָן וּמָנַחַת וְעֵיבָל שְׁפוֹ וְאוֹנָם: כד וְאֵלֶּה בְנֵי־צִבְעוֹן וְאַיָּה וַעֲנָה הוּא

‹ — he is ‹‹ and Anah ‹ Aiah ‹‹ of Zibeon: ‹ the sons ‹ These are 24 ‹‹ and Onam. ‹ Shepho ‹‹ and Ebal; ‹ and Manahath ‹ Alvan

עֲנָה אֲשֶׁר מָצָא אֶת־הַיֵּמִם בַּמִּדְבָּר בִּרְעֹתוֹ אֶת־הַחֲמֹרִים לְצִבְעוֹן

‹ for Zibeon, ‹ the donkeys ‹ while he was pasturing ‹ in the desert ‹ the mules ‹ discovered ‹ who ‹ [the same] Anah

אִלֵּין רַבְּנֵי רְעוּאֵל בְּאַרְעָא (דְ)אֱדוֹם
אִלֵּין בְּנֵי בָשְׂמַת אִתַּת עֵשָׂו: יח וְאִלֵּין
בְּנֵי אָהֳלִיבָמָה אִתַּת עֵשָׂו רַבָּא יְעוּשׁ
רַבָּא יַעְלָם רַבָּא קֹרַח אִלֵּין רַבְּנֵי
אָהֳלִיבָמָה בַּת עֲנָה אִתַּת עֵשָׂו:
יט אִלֵּין בְּנֵי עֵשָׂו וְאִלֵּין רַבְּנֵיהוֹן הוּא
אֱדוֹם: כ אִלֵּין בְּנֵי שֵׂעִיר חוֹרָאָה יָתְבֵי
דְאַרְעָא לוֹטָן וְשׁוֹבָל וְצִבְעוֹן וַעֲנָה:
כא וְדִשׁוֹן וְאֵצֶר וְדִישָׁן אִלֵּין רַבְּנֵי
חוֹרָאָה בְּנֵי שֵׂעִיר בְּאַרְעָא דֶאֱדוֹם:
כב וַהֲווֹ בְּנֵי לוֹטָן חוֹרִי וְהֵימָם וַאֲחָתֵהּ
דְּלוֹטָן תִּמְנָע: כג וְאִלֵּין בְּנֵי שׁוֹבָל
עַלְוָן וּמָנַחַת וְעֵיבָל שְׁפוֹ וְאוֹנָם:
כד וְאִלֵּין בְּנֵי צִבְעוֹן וְאַיָּה וַעֲנָה הוּא
עֲנָה דִּי אַשְׁכַּח יָת גֻּבְרַיָּא בְּמַדְבְּרָא
כַּד הֲוָה רָעֵי יָת חֲמָרַיָּא לְצִבְעוֹן

רש"י

(כ) ישבי הארץ. שהיו יושביה קודם שבא עשו לשם (תרגום יונתן). ורבותינו דרשו שהיו בקיאין בישובה של ארץ, מלא קנה זה לזיתים, מלא קנה זה לגפנים, שהיו טועמין העפר ויודעין אי זו נטיעה ראויה לו (שבת פה.): **(כד) ואיה וענה.** וי"ו יתירה, והוא כמו איה וענה. והרבה יש במקרא, את וקדש וצבא מרמס (דניאל ח:יג), נרדם ורכב וסוס (תהלים עו:ז): **הוא ענה.** האמור למעלה שהוא אחיו של צבעון, וכאן הוא קורא אותו בנו. מלמד שבא צבעון על אמו והוליד את ענה (תנחומא שם; ב"ר שם טו; פסחים נד.): **את הימים.** פרדים. הרביע חמור על סוס נקבה וילדה פרד (עי' ב"ר שם), והוא היה ממזר והביא פסולין לעולם (פסחים שם). ולמה נקרא שמם ימים, שאימתן מוטלת על הבריות, דאמר רבי חנינא מימי לא שאלני אדם על מכת פרדה לבנה וחיה [והלא קא חזינן דחיה, אל תקרי וחיה אלא וחיתה, כי המכה לא תתרפא לעולם] (חולין ז:).

19. הוּא אֱדוֹם — *He is Edom.* In this genealogy lay the roots of Edom, which evolved into Rome, the perpetual enemy of Israel (*Lekach Tov*).

20. בְּנֵי־שֵׂעִיר — *The sons of Seir.* The Seirites, an ancient, populous nation, were the original inhabitants of the land of Seir (see 14:6). Esau's children supplanted them because God gave Seir to them. The Torah does not record how it happened because it was a "hidden miracle," which could have been interpreted as a natural occurrence. [See *Deuteronomy* 2:5; *Ramban* to ibid. 2:10.]

יֹשְׁבֵי הָאָרֶץ — *The inhabitants of the land*. This emphasizes that God is the Master of the world, and He bequeaths it to whomever He desires. The Seirites were *the original inhabitants of Seir,* yet it was God's will that they lose it to Esau's descendants (*Radak*).

24. אֲשֶׁר מָצָא אֶת־הַיֵּמִם בַּמִּדְבָּר — *Who discovered the mules in the desert.* Anah crossbred a donkey with a mare, and the result

אָבִיו: כה וְאֵלֶּה בְנֵי־עֲנָה דִּשֹׁן וְאָהֳלִיבָמָה בַּת־
‹ daughter ‹ and Oholibamah ‹ Dishon ‹‹ of Anah: ‹ the children ‹ These are 25 ‹‹ his father.

עֲנָה: כו וְאֵלֶּה בְּנֵי דִישָׁן חֶמְדָּן וְאֶשְׁבָּן וְיִתְרָן וּכְרָן:
‹‹ and Cheran. ‹ and Ithran ‹ and Eshban ‹ Hemdan ‹ of Dishan: ‹ the sons ‹ These are 26 ‹‹ of Anah.

כז אֵלֶּה בְּנֵי־אֵצֶר בִּלְהָן וְזַעֲוָן וַעֲקָן: כח אֵלֶּה
‹ These are 28 ‹‹ and Akan. ‹ and Zaavan ‹ Bilhan ‹‹ of Ezer: ‹ the sons ‹ These are 27

בְנֵי־דִישָׁן עוּץ וַאֲרָן: כט אֵלֶּה אַלּוּפֵי הַחֹרִי אַלּוּף
‹ Chief ‹‹ of the Horite: ‹ the chiefs ‹ These are 29 ‹‹ and Aran. ‹ Uz ‹‹ of Dishan: ‹ the sons

לוֹטָן אַלּוּף שׁוֹבָל אַלּוּף צִבְעוֹן אַלּוּף עֲנָה: ל אַלּוּף דִּשֹׁן אַלּוּף אֵצֶר
‹ Ezer, ‹ Chief ‹ Dishon, ‹ Chief 30 ‹‹ Anah, ‹ Chief ‹ Zibeon, ‹ Chief ‹ Shobal, ‹ Chief ‹ Lotan,

אַלּוּף דִּישָׁן אֵלֶּה אַלּוּפֵי הַחֹרִי לְאַלֻּפֵיהֶם בְּאֶרֶץ שֵׂעִיר: פ לא וְאֵלֶּה
‹ Now these are 31 ‹‹ of Seir. ‹ in the land ‹ according to their chiefs, ‹ of the Horite, ‹ the chiefs ‹ — these are ‹‹ Dishan ‹ Chief

הַמְּלָכִים אֲשֶׁר מָלְכוּ בְּאֶרֶץ אֱדוֹם לִפְנֵי מְלָךְ־מֶלֶךְ לִבְנֵי יִשְׂרָאֵל:
‹‹ of Israel: ‹ from the Children ‹ a king ‹ there reigned ‹ before ‹ of Edom ‹ in the land ‹ reigned ‹ who ‹ the kings

לב וַיִּמְלֹךְ בֶּאֱדוֹם בֶּלַע בֶּן־בְּעוֹר וְשֵׁם עִירוֹ דִּנְהָבָה: לג וַיָּמָת בָּלַע וַיִּמְלֹךְ
‹ and reign ‹ And Bela died, 33 ‹‹ was Dinhabah. ‹ of his city ‹ and the name ‹‹ of Beor, ‹ son ‹ Bela, ‹‹ in Edom: ‹ He reigned 32

תַּחְתָּיו יוֹבָב בֶּן־זֶרַח מִבָּצְרָה: לד וַיָּמָת יוֹבָב וַיִּמְלֹךְ תַּחְתָּיו חֻשָׁם
‹ did Husham, ‹ after him ‹ and reign ‹ And Jobab died 34 ‹‹ from Bozrah. ‹ of Zerah, ‹ son ‹ did Jobab ‹ after him

אֲבוּהִי: כה וְאִלֵּין בְּנֵי עֲנָה דִּשֹׁן וְאָהֳלִיבָמָה בַּת עֲנָה: כו וְאִלֵּין בְּנֵי דִישָׁן חֶמְדָּן וְאֶשְׁבָּן וְיִתְרָן וּכְרָן: כז אִלֵּין בְּנֵי אֵצֶר בִּלְהָן וְזַעֲוָן וַעֲקָן: כח אִלֵּין בְּנֵי דִישָׁן עוּץ וַאֲרָן: כט אִלֵּין רַבְּנֵי חוֹרָאָה רַבָּא לוֹטָן רַבָּא שׁוֹבָל רַבָּא צִבְעוֹן רַבָּא עֲנָה: ל רַבָּא דִשֹׁן רַבָּא אֵצֶר רַבָּא דִישָׁן אִלֵּין רַבְּנֵי חוֹרָאָה לְרַבְּנֵיהוֹן בְּאַרְעָא דְשֵׂעִיר: לא וְאִלֵּין מַלְכַיָּא דִּי מְלִיכוּ בְּאַרְעָא דֶאֱדוֹם קֳדָם דִּי מְלַךְ מַלְכָּא לִבְנֵי יִשְׂרָאֵל: לב וּמְלַךְ בֶּאֱדוֹם בֶּלַע בַּר בְּעוֹר וְשׁוּם קַרְתֵּהּ דִּנְהָבָה: לג וּמִית בָּלַע וּמְלַךְ תְּחוֹתוֹהִי יוֹבָב בַּר זֶרַח מִבָּצְרָה: לד וּמִית יוֹבָב וּמְלַךְ תְּחוֹתוֹהִי חֻשָׁם

רש"י

(כט) **החרי.** [ו]לא הוזקק לכתוב לנו משפחות החורי אלא מפני תמנע ולהודיע גדולת אברהם כמו שפירשתי למעלה (פסוק יב): **(לא) ואלה המלכים וגו'.** שמנה היו, וכנגדן העמיד יעקב (ב"ר פג:ב) ובטל מלכות עשו בימיהם, ואלו הן, שאול ואיש בשת, דוד ושלמה, רחבעם, אביה, אסא, יהושפט. ובימי יורם בנו כתיב בימיו פשע אדום מתחת יד יהודה וימליכו עליהם מלך (מלכים ב ח:כ). ובימי שאול [ס"א יורם] כתיב, ומלך אין באדום, נצב מלך (מלכים א כב:מח): **(לג) יובב בן זרח מבצרה.** בצרה מערי מואב היא, שנאמר ועל קריות ועל בצרה וגו' (ירמיה מח:כד), ולפי שהעמידה מלך לאדום עתידה ללקוט עמהם, שנא' כי זבח לה' בבצרה

was a mule. Anah himself was illegitimate, for in verse 20 he is called Zibeon's *brother,* and here he is called Zibeon's *son*, indicating that Zibeon committed incest with his own mother. Thus, the illegitimate Anah introduced into the world a "tainted" animal, which was born of an illicit breeding (*Rashi; Pesachim* 54a), thus intimating that "evil begets evil."

29. The Torah lists the Horite chiefs who were overthrown by Esau's offspring in order to show that God honored Isaac by giving his son a heritage that had been the choice of great and powerful kings (*Radak*).

31. The Edomite kings. The Torah lists eight Edomite kings who reigned before the first Jewish king. *Ibn Ezra* cites two interpretations of the period under discussion: (a) The eight Edomite kings reigned up to the time of Moses, who, as the savior and leader of Israel, had the status of a king. (b) The passage is prophetic, giving the names of eight Edomite kings who were destined to reign in *future* years, prior to Saul, the first Jewish king.

Rashi cites this verse as an example of the prophecy given to Rebecca that *the might shall pass from one of them to the other* (25:23), meaning that the two brothers would not both be great simultaneously. Thus, when Esau had kings, Israel had none, and when Israel rose up, Esau declined, and his kings were defeated by Israel. Conversely, for the last 2,000 years Esau's off-

מֵאֶרֶץ הַתֵּימָנִי: לה וַיָּמָת חֻשָׁם וַיִּמְלֹךְ תַּחְתָּיו

< after him < and reign < And Husham died, **35**<< of the Temanites. < of the land

הֲדַד בֶּן־בְּדַד הַמַּכֶּה אֶת־מִדְיָן בִּשְׂדֵה מוֹאָב וְשֵׁם

< and the name << of Moab, < in the field < the Midianites < who defeated << of Bedad, < son < did Hadad

עִירוֹ עֲוִית: לו וַיָּמָת הֲדָד וַיִּמְלֹךְ תַּחְתָּיו שַׂמְלָה

< did Samlah < after him < and reign < And Hadad died, **36**<< was Avith. < of his city

מִמַּשְׂרֵקָה: לז וַיָּמָת שַׂמְלָה וַיִּמְלֹךְ תַּחְתָּיו שָׁאוּל

< did Saul < after him < and reign < And Samlah died, **37** << of Masrekah.

מֵרְחֹבוֹת הַנָּהָר: לח וַיָּמָת שָׁאוּל וַיִּמְלֹךְ תַּחְתָּיו

< after him < and reign < And Saul died, **38** << of Rehoboth-nahar.

בַּעַל חָנָן בֶּן־עַכְבּוֹר: לט וַיָּמָת בַּעַל חָנָן בֶּן־עַכְבּוֹר

<< of Achbor — < son < — Baal-hanan, << He died **39** << of Achbor. < son < did Baal-hanan,

מֵאַרְעָא דָרוֹמָא: לה וּמִית חֻשָׁם וּמְלַךְ תְּחוֹתוֹהִי הֲדַד בַּר בְּדַד דִּקְטִיל יָת מִדְיָנָאֵי בַּחֲקַל מוֹאָב וְשׁוּם קַרְתֵּהּ עֲוִית: לו וּמִית הֲדַד וּמְלַךְ תְּחוֹתוֹהִי שַׂמְלָה מִמַּשְׂרֵקָה: לז וּמִית שַׂמְלָה וּמְלַךְ תְּחוֹתוֹהִי שָׁאוּל מֵרְחוֹבֵי דְעַל פְּרָת: לח וּמִית שָׁאוּל וּמְלַךְ תְּחוֹתוֹהִי בַּעַל חָנָן בַּר עַכְבּוֹר: לט וּמִית בַּעַל חָנָן בַּר עַכְבּוֹר וּמְלַךְ תְּחוֹתוֹהִי הֲדַר וְשׁוּם קַרְתֵּהּ פָּעוּ וְשׁוּם אִתְּתֵהּ מְהֵיטַבְאֵל בַּת מַטְרֵד בַּת מְצָרֵף דַּהֲבָא: מ וְאִלֵּין שְׁמָהַת רַבְּנֵי עֵשָׂו לְזַרְעְיָתְהוֹן לְאַתְרֵיהוֹן בִּשְׁמָהָתְהוֹן רַבָּא תִמְנַע רַבָּא עַלְוָה רַבָּא יְתֵת: מא רַבָּא אָהֳלִיבָמָה רַבָּא אֵלָה רַבָּא פִינֹן: מב רַבָּא קְנַז רַבָּא תֵימָן רַבָּא מִבְצָר: מג רַבָּא

וַיִּמְלֹךְ תַּחְתָּיו הֲדַר וְשֵׁם עִירוֹ פָּעוּ וְשֵׁם אִשְׁתּוֹ מְהֵיטַבְאֵל בַּת־מַטְרֵד

< of Matred, < daughter < was Mehetabel, < of his wife < and the name << was Pau, < of his city < and the name << did Hadar; < after him < and reign

בַּת מֵי זָהָב: מפטיר מ וְאֵלֶּה שְׁמוֹת אַלּוּפֵי עֵשָׂו לְמִשְׁפְּחֹתָם לִמְקֹמֹתָם

< according to their regions, < according to their families, << of Esau, < of the chiefs < the names < Now these are **40** << of Me-zahab. < daughter

בִּשְׁמֹתָם אַלּוּף תִּמְנָע אַלּוּף עַלְוָה אַלּוּף יְתֵת: מא אַלּוּף אָהֳלִיבָמָה

< of Oholibamah; < the chief **41** << of Jetheth; < the chief < of Alvah; < the chief < of Timna; < the chief << by their names:

אַלּוּף אֵלָה אַלּוּף פִּינֹן: מב אַלּוּף קְנַז אַלּוּף תֵּימָן אַלּוּף מִבְצָר: מג אַלּוּף

< the chief **43** << of Mibzar; < the chief < of Teman; < the chief < of Kenaz; < the chief **42** < of Pinon; < the chief < of Elah; < the chief

רש"י

(ישעיה לד:ו; ב"ר סה:ג): **(לה) המכה את מדין בשדה מואב.** שבא מדין על מואב למלחמה והלך מלך אדום לעזור את מואב. ומכאן אנו למדים שהיו מדין ומואב מריבים זה עם זה ובימי בלעם עשו שלום להתקשר על ישראל (ספרי מטות קנז; תנחומא בלק ג; סנהדרין קה.): **(לט) בת מי זהב.** מהו זהב, עשיר היה ואין זהב חשוב בעיניו לכלום (ב"ר סה:ד): **(מ) ואלה שמות אלופי עשו.** שנקראו על שם מדינותיהם לאחר שמת הדר ופסקה מהם מלכות, והראשונים הנזכרים למעלה הם שמות תולדותם. וכן מפורש בדברי הימים (א א:נא) וימת הדד ויהיו אלופי אדום אלוף תמנע וגו':

spring, in their various manifestations, have held sway and the Jewish people have been exiled from their land and former glory. In time to come, however — may it be speedily in our days — the prophetic assurance (*Obadiah* 1:21) will be fulfilled: Saviors will ascend to Mount Zion to render judgment upon [those who trace their greatness to] the mountain of Esau, and the kingdom will be HASHEM'S.

35. When Midian attacked Moab, this Edomite king came to Moab's aid and defeated Midian. From this we learn that Midian and Moab were enemies, but in the time of Balaam they made peace in order to conspire together against Israel (*Rashi*).

40-41. The phrases *according to their regions, by their names* indicate a change in the manner of naming the chiefs. The earlier group of kings (v. 15 ff.) used their own names. After Hadad's death and the end of the Edomite monarchy, the ensuing leaders were known as chieftains of their respective regions. This new procedure is evident from *I Chronicles* 1:51: *And Hadad (= Hadar) died and the chiefs of Edom were: the chief of Timna etc.* (*Rashi*).

✤ For whose sake?

The Midrash concludes its expositions on the *Sidrah* with the following parable: The wheat, the straw, and the stubble engaged in a controversy. The wheat said, "For my sake has the field been sown"; the straw said, "For my sake has the field been

מַגְדִּיאֵל אַלּוּף עִירָם אֵלֶּה ׀ אַלּוּפֵי אֱדוֹם לְמֹשְׁבֹתָם
‹ of Magdiel ‹ and the chief ‹‹ of Iram; ‹ these are ‹ the chiefs ‹ of Edom ‹ by their settlements, ‹

בְּאֶרֶץ אֲחֻזָּתָם הוּא עֵשָׂו אֲבִי אֱדוֹם: פפפ
‹ in the land ‹‹ of their possession ‹ —he is ‹ Esau, ‹ father ‹‹ of Edom.

מַגְדִּיאֵל רַבָּא עִירָם אִלֵּין רַבָּנֵי אֱדוֹם לְמוֹתְבָנְהוֹן בְּאַרְעָא אַחֲסַנְתְּהוֹן הוּא עֵשָׂו אֲבוּהוֹן דֶּאֱדוֹמָאֵי:

קנ״ד פסוקים. קליט״ה סימן.

THE HAFTARAH FOR VAYISHLACH APPEARS ON PAGE 341.

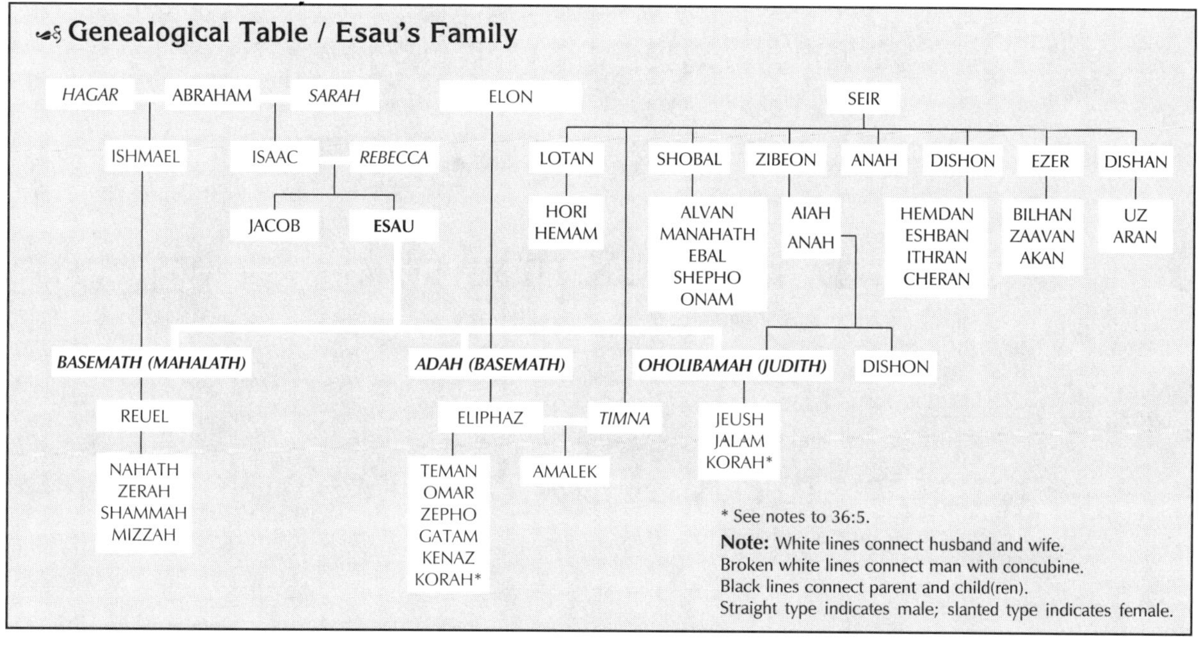

רש״י

(מג) **מגדיאל.** היא רומי (פדר״א פל״ח):

sown"; and the stubble said, "For my sake has the field been sown."

Said the wheat to them, "When the time comes, you will see."

When the harvest season came, the farmer took the stubble and burnt it, scattered the straw, and piled the wheat in a stack, which everyone kissed.

Similarly, Israel and the nations have a controversy, each asserting, "For our sake was the world created." Says Israel, "The hour will come in the Messianic future and you will see how *you shall fan them and the wind shall carry them away (Isaiah* 41:16); but as for Israel — *And you shall rejoice in* H*ASHEM, you shall glory in the Holy One of Israel* (ibid.).

קנ״ד פסוקים. קליט״ה סימן. — This Masoretic note means: There are 154 verses in the *Sidrah*, numerically corresponding to the mnemonic קְלִיטָ״ה [related to מִקְלָט, *refuge, asylum*].

This alludes to the theme of our *Sidrah* which, as expressed by *Ramban* in his introduction to 32:4, is to teach us how to survive in Exile among Esau's descendants (*R' David Feinstein*).

PARASHAS VAYEISHEV / פרשת וישב

[לז] א וַיֵּשֶׁב יַעֲקֹב בְּאֶרֶץ מְגוּרֵי אָבִיו בְּאֶרֶץ
37 1 Jacob settled < in the land < of the sojournings < of his father, << in the land <
כְּנָעַן: ב אֵלֶּה ׀ תֹּלְדוֹת יַעֲקֹב יוֹסֵף בֶּן־שְׁבַע־עֶשְׂרֵה
of Canaan. 2 << These are < the descendants < of Jacob: << Joseph, << at the age < of seventeen <
שָׁנָה הָיָה רֹעֶה אֶת־אֶחָיו בַּצֹּאן וְהוּא נַעַר אֶת־בְּנֵי בִלְהָה וְאֶת־בְּנֵי
years, << was < a shepherd < with < his brothers < by the flock, << but he was < a youth < with < the sons < of Bilhah < and with < the sons <

אונקלוס

א וִיתֵיב יַעֲקֹב בְּאַרְעָא תּוֹתָבוּת אֲבוּהִי בְּאַרְעָא דִּכְנָעַן: ב אִלֵּין תּוֹלְדַת יַעֲקֹב יוֹסֵף בַּר שְׁבַע עֶסְרֵי שְׁנִין (כַּד) הֲוָה רָעֵי עִם אֲחוֹהִי בַּעֲנָא וְהוּא מְרַבֵּי עִם בְּנֵי בִלְהָה וְעִם בְּנֵי

רש"י

(א) וישב יעקב וגו׳. אחר שכתב לך ישובי עשו ותולדותיו בדרך קצרה, שלא היו ספונים וחשובים לפרש היאך נתישבו וסדר מלחמותיהם איך הורישו את החורי (דברים ב:יב), פירש לך ישובי יעקב ותולדותיו בדרך ארוכה כל גלגולי סבתם, לפי שהם חשובים לפני המקום להאריך בהם. וכן אתה מוצא בעשרה דורות שמאדם ועד נח פלוני הוליד פלוני, וכשבא לנח האריך בו. וכן בעשרה דורות שמנח ועד אברהם קצר בהם, ומשהגיע אצל אברהם האריך בו. משל למרגלית שנפלה בין החול אדם ממשמש בחול וכוברו בכברה עד שמוצא את המרגלית ומשמצאה הוא משליך את הצרורות מידו ונוטל המרגלית (תנחומא א; ב"ר לט:י). [ד"א, וישב יעקב, הפשתני הזה נכנסו גמליו טעונים פשתן. הפחמי תמה, אנה יכנס כל הפשתן הזה. היה פיקח אחד משיב לו, ניצוץ אחד יוצא ממפוח שלך ששורף את כולו. כך יעקב ראה כל האלופים הכתובים למעלה, תמה ואמר מי יכול לכבוש את כולן. מה כתיב למטה, אלה תולדות יעקב יוסף (פסוק ב), וכתיב והיה בית יעקב אש ובית יוסף להבה ובית עשו לקש (עובדיה יח) ניצוץ יוצא מיוסף שמכלה ושורף את כולם (תנחומא א; ב"ר פד:ה)]: **(ב) אלה תולדות יעקב.** ואלה של תולדות יעקב, אלה ישוביהם וגלגוליהם עד שבאו לכלל ישוב. סבה ראשונה **יוסף בן שבע עשרה וגו׳,** על ידי זה נתגלגלו וירדו למצרים. זהו אחר ישוב פשוטו של מקרא להיות דבר דבור על אפניו. ומדרש אגדה דורש, תלה הכתוב תולדות יעקב ביוסף מפני כמה דברים. אחת, שכל עצמו של יעקב לא עבד אצל לבן אלא ברחל (ב"ר פד:ה). ושהיה זיו איקונין של יוסף דומה לו (שם ח; תנחומא פקודי יא). וכל מה שאירע ליעקב אירע ליוסף, זה נשטם וזה נשטם, זה אחיו מבקש להרגו וזה אחיו מבקשים להרגו, וכן הרבה בב"ר (שם ו). ועוד נדרש בו, וישב, בקש יעקב לישב בשלוה קפץ עליו רוגזו של יוסף. צדיקים מבקשים לישב בשלוה, אומר הקב"ה, לא דיין לצדיקים מה שמתוקן להם לעולם הבא אלא שמבקשים לישב בשלוה בעולם הזה (עי׳ שם ג; תנ"י מבוא כ"י ג:יג): **והוא נער.** שהיה עושה מעשה נערות, מתקן בשערו, ממשמש בעיניו, כדי שיהיה נראה יפה (ב"ר שם ז): **את בני בלהה.** כלומר רגיל אצל בני בלהה, לפי שהיו אחיו מבזין אותן

PARASHAS VAYEISHEV

37.

1. וַיֵּשֶׁב יַעֲקֹב — *Jacob settled.* From the contrast between words used for Jacob and his father — *settle*, which implies permanency, and *sojourn*, which implies wandering — the Midrash infers that after his long exile and struggles, Jacob wished finally לֵישֵׁב בְּשַׁלְוָה, *to settle down in tranquility,* but the anguish of Joseph's kidnaping pounced upon him. Though the righteous seek tranquility, the Holy One, Blessed is He, says, "Are the righteous not satisfied with what awaits them in the World to Come that they expect to live at ease in This World too?" (*Rashi*).

The sense of the above is not that Jacob and other righteous people are not entitled to tranquility; indeed, Jacob himself spent the last seventeen years of his life in spiritual bliss [see 47:28]. Rather, the sense of the Midrash is that Jacob's mission was not yet complete. He thought that once he had fathered the forebears of the twelve tribes, weathered his exile with Laban, survived his confrontation with Esau, and emerged from the travail of Shechem, he had finished his task of preparing the way for the future of the nation. God saw otherwise. The ensuing events that began upon his arrival in *Eretz Yisrael* paved the way for Israel's descent to Egypt and the momentous miracles that the nation remembers over and over again, especially in the throes of seemingly insuperable oppressions. When Joseph was torn from him and seemed to be dead, Jacob had reason to be sure that his life had ended in failure [see below], but his service of God did not flag. This, too, was part of his service to posterity, for it taught Jews never to surrender to the "inevitable." This is the import of the Sages' teaching that this world is not the place where the righteous can expect tranquility. There is too much to accomplish and too few capable of doing it. Knowing that, the righteous are more than willing to sacrifice a bit of temporary peace for the sake of eternal elevation for their offspring (*R' Gedaliah Schorr).*

בְּאֶרֶץ מְגוּרֵי אָבִיו — *In the land of the sojournings of his father.* In contrast to Esau who preferred to leave his native land in favor of one where he and his heirs would be masters, Jacob chose to live as an alien in the land that had been promised him. This was in fulfillment of God's prophecy to Abraham that his progeny would be aliens (15:13) — and it was a step toward the fulfillment of the rest of that prophecy, that they would go on to inherit the land (*Ramban*). Despite his downtrodden status compared to the lofty level of Esau, Jacob accepted God's will with perfect faith (*Or HaChaim*). Indeed, it would be nearly three centuries and a painful exile before his descendants would become masters of the land that God had promised them, but Jacob's trust was undiminished.

2. נַעַר — *A youth*. That the Torah calls him *a youth* implies that he *acted* immaturely — dressing his hair and adorning his eyes to look handsome (*Rashi*). *Ramban*, however, maintains that it is natural to call Joseph a youth since [with the exception of Benjamin who was still a child] he was the youngest and frailest of the brothers.

אֶת־בְּנֵי בִלְהָה . . . — *With the sons of Bilhah . . .* Except for his

זִלְפָּה נְשֵׁי אָבִיו וַיָּבֵא יוֹסֵף אֶת־דִּבָּתָם רָעָה אֶל־

< to < that were bad < reports about them < and Joseph would bring << of his father; < the wives << of Zilpah,

אֲבִיהֶם: ג וְיִשְׂרָאֵל אָהַב אֶת־יוֹסֵף מִכָּל־בָּנָיו כִּי־

< since < his sons < more than all < Joseph < loved < Now Israel 3 << their father.

בֶן־זְקֻנִים הוּא לוֹ וְעָשָׂה לוֹ כְּתֹנֶת פַּסִּים: ד וַיִּרְאוּ אֶחָיו כִּי־אֹתוֹ

< it was he whom < that << His brothers saw 4 << of fine wool. < a tunic < him < and he made << to him, < was he < of his old age < a son

זִלְפָּה נְשֵׁי אֲבוּהִי וְאַיְתִי יוֹסֵף
יָת דִּבְּהוֹן בִּישָׁא לְוַת אֲבוּהוֹן:
ג וְיִשְׂרָאֵל רְחֵם יָת יוֹסֵף מִכָּל בְּנוֹהִי
אֲרֵי בַר חַכִּים הוּא לֵהּ וַעֲבַד לֵהּ
כִּתּוּנָא דְפַסֵּי: ד וַחֲזוֹ אֲחוֹהִי אֲרֵי יָתֵהּ

רש"י

והוא מקרבן (תנחומא ז): **את דבתם רעה.** כל רעה שהיה רואה באחיו בני לאה היה מגיד לאביו. שהיו אוכלין אבר מן החי ומזלזלין בבני השפחות לקרותן עבדים וחשודים על העריות. ובשלשתן לקה, על אבר מן החי וישחטו שעיר עזים (להלן פסוק לא) במכירתו ולא אכלוהו חי [כדי שילקה בשחיטה]. ועל דבה שספר עליהם שקורין לאחיהם עבדים, לעבד נמכר יוסף (תהלים קה:יז). ועל העריות שספר עליהם, ותשא אשת אדוניו וגו' (להלן לט:ז; ב"ר שם ז; תנחומא ז): **דבתם.** כל לשון דבה פרלרי"ן בלע"ז. כל מה שהיה יכול לדבר בהם רעה היה מספר: **דבה.** ל' דובב שפתי ישנים (שיר השירים ז:י): (ג) **בן זקנים.** שנולד לו לעת זקנתו. ואונקלוס תרגם בר חכים הוא ליה כל מה שלמד משם ועבר מסר לו (ב"ר שם ח). ד"א, שהיה זיו איקונין שלו דומה לו (שם): **פסים.** לשון כלי מלת (שבת יז:), כמו כרפס ותכלת (אסתר א:ו) וכמו כתונת הפסים

work time, Joseph preferred to associate with the sons of Bilhah and Zilpah. Because he held himself aloof from Leah's sons, they came to hate him (*Rashbam*). *Rashi* interprets differently. Leah's sons always slighted the sons of the "maidservants," so Joseph went out of his way to befriend them.

In a radically different interpretation, but one that is similar to a common connotation of the word נַעַר, *Ibn Ezra* comments that the sons of Bilhah and Zilpah took advantage of Joseph and made him their *boy* or *servant*.

נְשֵׁי אָבִיו — *The wives of his father.* In comparison with Rachel and Leah, they were sometimes called maidservants or concubines (see 35:22), but the Torah stresses that they were full-fledged *wives*. Alternatively, they may have assumed the status of *wives* only after Rachel and Leah had both died (*Ramban*).

דִּבָּתָם רָעָה — *Reports about them that were bad.* Whatever misbehavior Joseph noted in Leah's sons, he reported to Jacob. This was one reason they came to hate him. The other reasons are in the following verses. However, as the Midrash explains, Joseph misinterpreted their actions, and they were innocent of his charges (*Rashi*). Although Joseph was sincere in his faulty evaluation, he was at fault because he should have given them the benefit of the doubt and reported all the facts to Jacob, without forming his own negative conclusions (*Mizrachi; Gur Aryeh*).

Based on the context of the verse, however, *Ramban* interprets that it was the sons of Bilhah and Zilpah about whom Joseph brought unpleasant reports to Jacob. This would account for their failure to defend Joseph when Leah's sons conspired to sell him as a slave.

3. The Torah now details an additional cause for the brothers' hatred of Joseph: jealousy over the obvious favoritism Jacob showed him (*Radak*). Indeed, the Sages used this incident as the example for their dictum that a father should not single out one child among his others (*Shabbos* 10b).

Nevertheless, *Zohar* comments differently. Jacob's favoritism was based on Joseph's spiritual and intellectual superiority over his brothers. For the same reason God proclaimed His love for Israel and His hatred of Esau (*Malachi* 1:2,3), and Abraham favored Isaac over Ishmael. Similarly, Jacob favored Joseph. In all these cases, they were expressing the truth that the object of their favor was the authentic guardian of their spiritual heritage, a consideration so important that it overshadowed the danger that others might resent such a preference for one over another (*R' Munk*). *R' Bachya* strengthens this concept by noting that the Torah refers to Jacob here as *Israel*, the name that expresses his higher spiritual nature, thus implying that his choice of Joseph was a function of greatness, not frailty.

בֶּן־זְקֻנִים — *A son of his old age.* Joseph was born in Jacob's old age, which was why he felt greater affection for him (*Rashi*). Although Benjamin was eight years younger than Joseph, Jacob had developed an enduring love for Joseph during those years (*Mizrachi; Gur Aryeh*). [Moreover, when he saw Joseph, Jacob could recall Rachel raising him, while at Benjamin's birth Rachel died.] Alternatively, Joseph was a *wise son to him* [following the Talmudic dictum that the word זָקֵן is a contraction of זֶה שֶׁקָּנָה חָכְמָה, *one who acquired wisdom*]. Whatever Jacob learned in the Academy of Shem and Eber during his fourteen years there he transmitted to Joseph (*Rashi* quoting *Onkelos*).

Before Jacob went to the home of Laban, he studied the Torah of exile at the Academy of Shem and Eber (see introductory comment to 28:10-22). Jacob knew that Joseph was destined to be exiled [although he did not know exactly how and where this would happen], and this was why he singled out Joseph to be taught the lesson of Shem and Eber. It was because of this teaching that Joseph could emerge unscathed from his solitary exile of twenty-two years in Egypt, just as Jacob had been unscathed by his years with Laban (*R' Yaakov Kamenetsky*).

כְּתֹנֶת פַּסִּים — *A tunic of fine wool.* The translation follows *Rashi: a garment of fine wool.* It was a long-sleeved embroidered tunic, made of variously colored strips of fine wool (*Yafeh Toar*).

Such a tunic was a mark of leadership (*Sforno*; see also *II Samuel* 13:18), for after Reuben discredited himself by tampering with Jacob's bed (35:22), Jacob elevated Joseph to the status of the "firstborn," and made him the tunic to symbolize his new position in the family (*Kli Yakar*).

אָהַב אֲבִיהֶם מִכָּל־אֶחָיו וַיִּשְׂנְאוּ אֹתוֹ וְלֹא יָכְלוּ

‹ and they could not ‹‹ him; ‹ so they hated ‹ his brothers ‹ most of all ‹ their father loved

דַּבְּרוֹ לְשָׁלֹם׃ ה וַיַּחֲלֹם יוֹסֵף חֲלוֹם וַיַּגֵּד לְאֶחָיו

‹‹ to his brothers, ‹ and he told [it] ‹ a dream ‹ Joseph dreamt **5** ‹‹ peaceably. ‹ speak with him

וַיּוֹסִפוּ עוֹד שְׂנֹא אֹתוֹ׃ ו וַיֹּאמֶר אֲלֵיהֶם שִׁמְעוּ־נָא

‹ *please,* ‹ *Hear,* ‹‹ to them, ‹ He said **6** ‹‹ him. ‹ to hate ‹ even more ‹ and they continued

הַחֲלוֹם הַזֶּה אֲשֶׁר חָלָמְתִּי׃ ז וְהִנֵּה אֲנַחְנוּ מְאַלְּמִים אֲלֻמִּים בְּתוֹךְ

‹ *in the middle* ‹ *sheaves* ‹ *we were binding* ‹ *I beheld! —* 7 ‹‹ *I dreamt:* ‹ *that* ‹ *this dream*

הַשָּׂדֶה וְהִנֵּה קָמָה אֲלֻמָּתִי וְגַם־נִצָּבָה וְהִנֵּה תְסֻבֶּינָה אֲלֻמֹּתֵיכֶם

‹‹ *— your sheaves did —* ‹‹ *— they surrounded* ‹‹ *then I beheld!* ‹‹ *remained standing;* ‹ *and also* ‹ *did my sheaf* ‹ *rise up* ‹ *then, I beheld! —* ‹‹ *of the field,*

וַתִּשְׁתַּחֲוֶיןָ לַאֲלֻמָּתִי׃ ח וַיֹּאמְרוּ לוֹ אֶחָיו הֲמָלֹךְ תִּמְלֹךְ עָלֵינוּ אִם־

‹ *Would you* ‹‹ *over us?* ‹ *Would you reign as a king* ‹‹ his brothers did, ‹‹ to him, ‹ They said **8** ‹‹ *to my sheaf.* ‹ *and bowed down*

רְחֵם אֲבוּהוֹן מִכָּל אֲחוֹהִי וּסְנוֹ יָתֵהּ
וְלָא צָבָן לְמַלָּלָא עִמֵּהּ לִשְׁלָם׃
ה וַחֲלַם יוֹסֵף חֶלְמָא וְחַוִּי לַאֲחוֹהִי
וְאוֹסִיפוּ עוֹד סְנוֹ יָתֵהּ׃ ו וַאֲמַר לְהוֹן
שְׁמָעוּ כְעַן חֶלְמָא הָדֵין דִּי חֲלֵמִית׃
ז וְהָא אֲנַחְנָא מְאַסְּרִין אֱסָרָן בְּגוֹ
חַקְלָא וְהָא קָמַת אֱסַרְתִּי וְאַף
אִזְדְּקָפַת וְהָא מִסְתַּחֲרָן אֱסָרָתְכוֹן
וְסָגְדָן לֶאֱסַרְתִּי׃ ח וַאֲמָרוּ לֵהּ אֲחוֹהִי
הֲמַלְכוּ אַתְּ מְדַמֵּי לְמִמְלַךְ עֲלָנָא אוֹ

רש"י

(שמואל ב יג:יח) דתמר ואמנון. ומ"א, על שם צרותיו, שנמכר לפוטיפר ולסוחרים ולישמעאלים ולמדינים (ב"ר פד:ח): (ד) **ולא יכלו דברו לשלום.** מתוך גנותם למדנו שבחם שלא דברו אחת בפה ואחת בלב (שם ט): **דברו.** לדבר עמו (אונקלוס): (ז) **מאלמים אלמים.** כתרגומו מאסרין אסרן, עמרין. וכן נושא אלומותיו (תהלים קכו:ו). וכמוהו בלשון משנה והאלומות נוטל ומכריז (בבא מציעא כב:): **קמה אלומתי.** נזקפה: **וגם נצבה.** לעמוד על עמדה בזקיפה (אונקלוס):

4. וְלֹא יָכְלוּ דַּבְּרוֹ לְשָׁלֹם — *And they could not speak to him peaceably.* So great was the brothers' antipathy toward Joseph that they could not carry on a friendly conversation with him even about peaceful matters, topics that were not matters of contention between them (*Ibn Ezra*). Whatever he said they interpreted in a negative, contentious way, even when he tried to be friendly (*R' Hirsch*). But from their ostensibly disgraceful behavior, we see their virtue: They were too honest to pretend love and friendship that they did not truly feel (*Rashi*).

5-11. Joseph's dreams and the intensified hatred. Dreams mentioned in Scripture are generally understood to be vehicles of prophecy. All these dreams came true according to their interpretations.

Joseph's dreams, which were understood as predicting that his brothers would be subservient to him, were taken as Divine revelations that he was to be the leader of the family. As *Sh'lah* puts it, he was to be a spiritual bridge between the exalted level of the Patriarchs and the lesser one of the tribal ancestors. The brothers, however, understood his dreams to be nothing more than nocturnal reflections of his waking fantasies, and they hated him all the more as someone who thought only about selfishly dominating his peers.

Chasam Sofer points out that Joseph's first dream consists of three scenes, each introduced by the word הִנֵּה, *he beheld.* Each scene refers to a different period in Joseph's life. The first scene, describing their collaborative work in the field, ends when the brothers overpowered him in the field — the word מְאַלְּמִים referring not only to the economic content of the dreams but also to strength and fighting; the second scene starts with Joseph rising up on his own — representing his having been in the pit — and reaching a position of authority; and the third scene describes the brothers coming to him for their sustenance. *Chasam Sofer* interprets the word נִצָּבָה, *remained standing,* at the end of the second scene, as a directive to Joseph to be firm with his brothers when they come to him. In contrast to the first dream, the second dream, involving the sun, moon, and the stars, deals with Joseph's spiritual leadership.

5. וַיַּגֵּד לְאֶחָיו — *[Which] he told to his brothers.* Surely Joseph realized that he would inflame his brothers by telling them about his dreams; if so, why did he tell them? The commentators offer various reasons: He was young and not mature enough to realize that he would be inflaming them (*Sforno*). He thought that if he could convince his brothers that his eminence was Divinely decreed, they would stop disliking him (*Chizkuni*). By showing them that they were destined to be dependent on him, he hoped to show them that it was unwise to hate him (*Or HaChaim*). Joseph understood the dreams to be prophecies, and a prophet is forbidden to conceal what he must reveal to others (*Vilna Gaon*).

7. אֲלֻמִּים — *Sheaves.* The symbolism of the *sheaves* implied to Joseph that his brothers would bow to him because of their need for grain. That they *gathered around* indicated that they would

מָשׁוֹל תִּמְשֹׁל בָּנוּ וַיּוֹסִפוּ עוֹד שְׂנֹא אֹתוֹ עַל־
— because of | him | to hate | even more | And they increased | over us? | have dominion as a ruler

חֲלֹמֹתָיו וְעַל־דְּבָרָיו: ט וַיַּחֲלֹם עוֹד חֲלוֹם אַחֵר
another dream, | again | He dreamt | 9 | his words. | and because of | his dreams

וַיְסַפֵּר אֹתוֹ לְאֶחָיו וַיֹּאמֶר הִנֵּה חָלַמְתִּי חֲלוֹם
a dream | *I dreamt* | *Indeed,* | And he said, | to his brothers. | it | and he related

עוֹד וְהִנֵּה הַשֶּׁמֶשׁ וְהַיָּרֵחַ וְאַחַד עָשָׂר כּוֹכָבִים
stars | *and eleven* | *the moon,* | *— the sun,* | *I beheld!* | *again:*

מִשְׁתַּחֲוִים לִי: י וַיְסַפֵּר אֶל־אָבִיו וְאֶל־אֶחָיו וַיִּגְעַר־בּוֹ אָבִיו וַיֹּאמֶר
and he said | did his father, | him | rebuke | his brothers; | and to | his father | to | And he related [it] | 10 | *to me.* | *were bowing down*

לוֹ מָה הַחֲלוֹם הַזֶּה אֲשֶׁר חָלָמְתָּ הֲבוֹא נָבוֹא אֲנִי וְאִמְּךָ וְאַחֶיךָ
and your brothers — | *and your mother* | *— I* | *Are we to come* | *you have dreamt!* | *that* | *is this dream* | *What* | to him,

לְהִשְׁתַּחֲוֹת לְךָ אָרְצָה: יא וַיְקַנְאוּ־בוֹ אֶחָיו וְאָבִיו שָׁמַר אֶת־הַדָּבָר:
the matter [in his mind]. | retained | but his father | were his brothers, | of him | Jealous | 11 | *to the ground?* | *to you* | *to bow down*

שׁוּלְטָן אַתְּ סְבִיר לְמִשְׁלַט בָּנָא וְאוֹסִיפוּ עוֹד סְנוֹ יָתֵהּ עַל חֶלְמוֹהִי וְעַל פִּתְגָמוֹהִי: ט וַחֲלַם עוֹד חֶלְמָא אָחֳרָנָא וְאִשְׁתָּעִי יָתֵהּ לַאֲחוֹהִי וַאֲמַר הָא חֲלֵמִית חֶלְמָא עוֹד וְהָא שִׁמְשָׁא וְסִהֲרָא וְחַד עֲשַׂר כּוֹכְבַיָּא סָגְדָן לִי: י וְאִשְׁתָּעִי לַאֲבוּהִי וְלַאֲחוֹהִי וּנְזַף בֵּהּ אֲבוּהִי וַאֲמַר לֵהּ מָא חֶלְמָא הָדֵין דִּי חֲלֵמְתָּא הֲמֵיתָא נֵיתֵי אֲנָא וְאִמָּךְ וְאַחָיךְ לְמִסְגַּד לָךְ עַל אַרְעָא: יא וְקַנִּיאוּ בֵהּ אֲחוֹהִי וַאֲבוּהִי נְטַר יָת פִּתְגָמָא:

רש"י

(ח) **ועל דבריו.** על דבתם רעה שהיה מביא לאביהם: (י) **ויספר אל אביו ואל אחיו.** לאחר שספר אותו לאחיו חזר וספרו לאביו בפניהם: **ויגער בו.** לפי שהיה מטיל שנאה עליו: **הבוא נבוא.** והלא אמך כבר מתה והוא לא היה יודע שהדברים מגיעין לבלהה שגדלתו כאמו (ב"ר שם יא). ורבותינו למדו מכאן שאין חלום בלא דברים בטלים (ברכות נה.), ויעקב נתכוין להוציא הדבר מלב בניו שלא יקנאוהו, לכך אמר לו הבוא נבוא וגו', כשם שאי אפשר באמך כך השאר הוא בטל: (יא) **שמר את הדבר.** היה ממתין ומצפה מתי יבוא. וכן שומר אמונים (ישעיה כו:ב), וכן לא תשמור על חטאתי (איוב יד:טז) לא תמתין:

surround him like subjects surrounding a king (*Ramban*).

Joseph's sheaf stood up of its own accord in the middle scene of his dream, implying that his rise to power would not be because of his brothers (*Abarbanel*), and it *remained standing*, symbolizing that he would remain in power for a very long time. Indeed, Joseph was viceroy of Egypt for eighty years, the longest reign recorded in Scripture (*Sforno*).

10. . . . הֲבוֹא נָבוֹא — *Are we to come . . .* After scolding Joseph and deriding his dream, Jacob showed that the dream was foolish because it was impossible of fulfillment. Since the *moon* of the dream was a symbol of Rachel, Jacob contended, "Your mother is long dead [so your dream cannot be fulfilled]!" Jacob did not realize, however, that the "moon" referred to Bilhah, who had reared Joseph after Rachel died, or that the dream spoke of a dependence and not a literal bowing.

Rashi, however, notes that Jacob *did* take the dreams seriously, but he spoke strongly against Joseph to remove the jealousy and resentment of the brothers. By ridiculing the dream with respect to *Rachel*, he attempted to reassure them that it had no validity with regard to *them* either.

11. וַיְקַנְאוּ־בוֹ אֶחָיו — *Jealous of him were his brothers.* The plain sense of the verse is that their jealousy continued because Jacob was not successful in minimizing their fears and resentment.

Some commentators, however, see in this jealousy a new element in the brothers' attitude, since up to now the Torah had said that they *hated* Joseph, not that they were jealous. At first they hated him because of Jacob's favoritism, but they were not jealous because he was but a child in their eyes; he was much younger and they saw no reason to take him as a threat to them. But, wise men that they were, when they heard his dreams and realized what they portended, their attitude changed from hatred to jealousy because the source of the dreams had to be Providential — he would indeed become their master, and that provoked them to turn jealous (*R' Bachya*).

✥ Joseph is sent to visit his brothers.

The stage is now set for one of the most perplexing events recorded in the Torah: the near killing of Joseph and his sale into slavery by his brothers. It is axiomatic that the story cannot be understood superficially, for we are not dealing with a band of robbers and murderers who would lightly murder for the sake of a coat; why, then, did the brothers sell Joseph? *Sforno* notes that years later, when the brothers were detained in Egypt and they examined their deeds to find why God had punished them (42:21), they found no cause for remorse in the sale itself. They

שני יב וַיֵּלְכוּ אֶחָיו לִרְעוֹת *אֶת־צֹאן אֲבִיהֶם בִּשְׁכֶם׃

<< in Shechem. < of their father < the sheep < to pasture < Now, his brothers went **12**

יג וַיֹּאמֶר יִשְׂרָאֵל אֶל־יוֹסֵף הֲלוֹא אַחֶיךָ רֹעִים

< *pasturing* < *your brothers* < *Are not* << Joseph, < to < And Israel said **13**

בִּשְׁכֶם לְכָה וְאֶשְׁלָחֲךָ אֲלֵיהֶם וַיֹּאמֶר לוֹ הִנֵּנִי׃

<< *Here I am!* << to him, < He said << *to them.* < *I will send you* < *Go please,* << *in Shechem?*

יד וַיֹּאמֶר לוֹ לֶךְ־נָא רְאֵה אֶת־שְׁלוֹם אַחֶיךָ וְאֶת־שְׁלוֹם הַצֹּאן וַהֲשִׁבֵנִי

< *and bring me back* < *of the sheep,* < *the welfare* < *and about* < *of your brothers* < *the welfare* < *about* < *see* < *please,* < *Go* << to him, < And he said **14**

דָּבָר וַיִּשְׁלָחֵהוּ מֵעֵמֶק חֶבְרוֹן וַיָּבֹא שְׁכֶמָה׃ טו וַיִּמְצָאֵהוּ אִישׁ וְהִנֵּה

<< and there [he] was < A man found him, **15** << to Shechem. < and [Joseph] came < of Hebron, < from the valley < So [Jacob] sent him << *word.*

* נקוד על את

יב וַאֲזָלוּ אֲחוֹהִי לְמִרְעֵי יָת עָנָא
דַאֲבוּהוֹן בִּשְׁכֶם׃ יג וַאֲמַר יִשְׂרָאֵל
לְיוֹסֵף הֲלָא אַחָיךְ רָעָן בִּשְׁכֶם
אֱתָא וְאֶשְׁלְחִנָּךְ לְוָתְהוֹן וַאֲמַר
לֵהּ הָא אֲנָא׃ יד וַאֲמַר לֵהּ אִזֵיל
כְּעַן חֲזֵי יָת שְׁלָמָא דְאַחָיךְ וְיָת
שְׁלָמָא דְעָנָא וַאֲתֵבְנִי פִּתְגָּמָא
וְשַׁלְחֵהּ מִמֵּישַׁר חֶבְרוֹן וַאֲתָא
לִשְׁכֶם׃ טו וְאַשְׁכְּחֵהּ גַּבְרָא וְהָא

רש"י

(יב) **לרעות את צאן.** נקוד על את שלא הלכו אלא לרעות את עצמן (ב"ר פד:יג): (יג) **הנני.** לשון ענוה וזריזות (תנחומא וירא כב). נזדרז למצות אביו ואע"פ שהיה יודע באחיו ששונאין אותו (ב"ר שם): (יד) **מעמק חברון.** והלא חברון בהר שנאמר ויעלו בנגב ויבא עד חברון (במדבר יג:כב). אלא מעצה עמוקה של אותו צדיק הקבור בחברון לקיים מה שנא' לאברהם בין הבתרים כי גר יהיה זרעך (לעיל טו:יג; ב"ר שם; סוטה יא.): **ויבא שכמה.** מקום מוכן לפורענות. שם קלקלו השבטים, שם ענו את דינה, שם נחלקה מלכות בית דוד שנא' וילך רחבעם שכמה (דברי הימים ב י:א; סנהדרין קב.): (טו) **וימצאהו איש.** זה גבריאל, שנאמר והאיש גבריאל (דניאל ט:כא; תנחומא ב):

condemned themselves only for hard-heartedly ignoring Joseph's pleas for mercy. Clearly they considered the act of selling him to have been harsh, but not wrong. Accordingly, in the course of the commentary, we must be alert for hints that will help explain the affair. As a general comment, they felt that Joseph was a threat not so much to them as to the family's destiny. They knew that the weeding-out process that banished Ishmael and Esau from the chosenness of Israel was to be over in their generation. Jacob's offspring were to be perfect — all of them — so that the mission of the Patriarchs could go forward with them. But if Joseph were to bring dissension into the family, he would destroy this potential with untold consequences. If so, then he had to be judged as a traitor and a danger to them all.

13. וַיֹּאמֶר יִשְׂרָאֵל — *And Israel said.* In dispatching Joseph on this fateful mission — which sowed the seeds of the Egyptian exile — he is called *Israel*, reflecting his higher spiritual nature as the architect of the national destiny (*R' Bachya*).

Joseph responded, *Here I am!* Though he knew his brothers hated him, he was humbly ready to do whatever his father asked of him (*Rashi*); thus, he did not respond, "How can I undertake such a mission — they hate me!" (*Ramban*).

14. מֵעֵמֶק חֶבְרוֹן — *From the valley of Hebron.* But Hebron is situated on a *mountain*! Rather, the term מֵעֵמֶק חֶבְרוֹן, *from the "valley" of Hebron,* is to be understood *figuratively:* Jacob's decision to send Joseph to his brothers who sold him into slavery — and what appeared to be his doom — was in fulfillment of עֵצָה עֲמוּקָה, the *profound, deep design* that had been confided to Abraham, who at that time was the only Patriarch who was buried in Hebron. The sense of this *design* was that Joseph's trip would begin the fulfillment of God's prophecy to Abraham (15:13): *Your offspring shall be aliens in a land not their own* (*Midrash; Rashi; Targum Yonasan*). In fact, *Zohar* comments that Jacob took Joseph to the tomb of Abraham and dispatched him from there.

Just as Joseph prayed at the tomb of the Patriarchs to be saved from his ten older brothers, so Caleb came to pray for the strength to resist the conspiracy of the ten spies (*Rashi, Numbers* 13:22). While Joseph represents the beginning of the prophecy to Abraham, Caleb was preparing for its culmination: *And the fourth generation shall return here* (15:16).

Tanchuma Yashan (addition 29, p. 133) explains that Jacob was escorting Joseph from Hebron-on-the-hill until Hebron-of-the-valley. When Joseph told his father to go back, Jacob taught him the laws of *eglah arufah,* the calf whose neck is broken, where the elders must vouch that they had escorted the traveler on his way. *Zohar* (210:b), though, says that it was Joseph who was invoking the basic fact of *eglah arufah* — a corpse is found — hinting to his father that he, Joseph, was likely to end up as that corpse. This may also explain why Jacob could not be comforted, since he felt responsible for Joseph's presumed death (*Bereishis Rabbah* 84:12). As *Rashi* quotes later (45:27), Joseph proved his identity to Jacob by reminding him that they were learning the laws of *eglah arufah* when they parted.

15. אִישׁ — *A man.* This *man* was the angel Gabriel in the likeness of a man (*Targum Yonasan*), whom God sent to lead Joseph to his brothers, to fulfill the prophecy to Abraham (*Ramban*). When Joseph could not find his brothers, he had a perfect excuse to return to Jacob and avoid what he knew would be an unpleasant meeting. Instead, he displayed great loyalty to Jacob by searching for them persistently (*Rashbam*).

תֹעֶה בַּשָּׂדֶה וַיִּשְׁאָלֵהוּ הָאִישׁ לֵאמֹר מַה־תְּבַקֵּשׁ:
—wandering in the field; the man asked him, saying, What do you seek?
טז וַיֹּאמֶר אֶת־אַחַי אָנֹכִי מְבַקֵּשׁ הַגִּידָה־נָּא לִי
16 And he said, My brothers do I seek; tell, please, to me
אֵיפֹה הֵם רֹעִים: יז וַיֹּאמֶר הָאִישׁ נָסְעוּ מִזֶּה כִּי
where they are pasturing. 17 The man said, They have journeyed on from here, for
שָׁמַעְתִּי אֹמְרִים נֵלְכָה דֹּתָיְנָה וַיֵּלֶךְ יוֹסֵף אַחַר
I heard them saying, 'Let us go to Dothan.' So Joseph went after
אֶחָיו וַיִּמְצָאֵם בְּדֹתָן: יח וַיִּרְאוּ אֹתוֹ מֵרָחֹק וּבְטֶרֶם יִקְרַב אֲלֵיהֶם
his brothers and he found them in Dothan. 18 They saw him from afar; and before he would draw near to them,
וַיִּתְנַכְּלוּ אֹתוֹ לַהֲמִיתוֹ: יט וַיֹּאמְרוּ אִישׁ אֶל־אָחִיו הִנֵּה בַּעַל הַחֲלֹמוֹת
they conspired against him to kill him. 19 And they said, a man to his brother, There [he] is! The master of dreams
הַלָּזֶה בָּא: כ וְעַתָּה | לְכוּ וְנַהַרְגֵהוּ וְנַשְׁלִכֵהוּ בְּאַחַד הַבֹּרוֹת וְאָמַרְנוּ
—that one there— is coming! 20 So now, let us go and let us kill him, and we will throw him into one of the pits; and we will say,
חַיָּה רָעָה אֲכָלָתְהוּ וְנִרְאֶה מַה־יִּהְיוּ חֲלֹמֹתָיו: כא וַיִּשְׁמַע רְאוּבֵן וַיַּצִּלֵהוּ
'A beast that is savage devoured him.' Then we shall see what will become of his dreams. 21 Reuben heard, and he rescued him

תָעֵי בְּחַקְלָא וּשְׁאָלֵהּ גַּבְרָא לְמֵימַר מָה אַתְּ בָּעֵי: טז וַאֲמַר יָת אַחַי אֲנָא בָעֵי חַוִּי כְעַן לִי הֵיכָן אִנּוּן רָעָן: יז וַאֲמַר גַּבְרָא נְטָלוּ מִכָּא אֲרֵי שְׁמָעִית דְּאָמְרִין נֵיזֵיל לְדֹתָן וַאֲזַל יוֹסֵף בָּתַר אֲחוֹהִי וְאַשְׁכְּחִנּוּן בְּדֹתָן: יח וַחֲזוֹ יָתֵהּ מֵרָחִיק וְעַד לָא קְרֵיב לְוָתְהוֹן וְחַשִּׁיבוּ עֲלוֹהִי לְמִקְטְלֵהּ: יט וַאֲמָרוּ גְּבַר לַאֲחוּהִי הָא מָרֵי חֶלְמַיָּא דֵיכִי אֲתָא: כ וּכְעַן אִיתוּ וְנִקְטְלִנֵּהּ וְנִרְמִנֵּהּ בַּחֲדָא מִן גֻּבַּיָּא וְנֵימַר חַיְתָא בִישְׁתָּא אֲכַלְתֵּהּ וְנֶחֱזֵי מָא יְהוֹן (נ״א יְהֵי) בְּסוֹף חֶלְמוֹהִי: כא וּשְׁמַע רְאוּבֵן וְשֵׁזְבֵהּ

רש"י

(יז) נסעו מזה. הסיעו עצמן מן האחוה: **נלכה דותינה.** לבקש לך נכלי דתות שימיתוך בהם. ולפי פשוטו שם מקום הוא, ואין מקרא יוצא מידי פשוטו: **(יח) ויתנכלו.** נתמלאו נכלים וערמומיות: **אתו.** כמו אתו עמו כלומר אליו: **(כ) ונראה מה יהיו חלומותיו.** אמר רבי יצחק מקרא זה אומר דרשני, רוח הקדש אומרת כן. הם

17. נָסְעוּ מִזֶּה — *They have journeyed on from here.* They are no longer in this pasture and it is pointless to search for them in this general area (*Sforno*). The Midrash gives a deeper interpretation to these words, which, had Joseph understood, would have frightened him off. The man was saying, "You asked about your *brothers*, but they have gone away from any feelings of brotherhood. Instead, they have gone to Dothan — from the word דָּת, *law* — they are seeking legal grounds to put you to death."

18-24. Reuben saves Joseph. The brothers concluded that they had a right, and even an obligation, to kill Joseph, but his salvation came from an unlikely source. Reuben was the most injured by Joseph inasmuch as Joseph was to assume some of Reuben's rights as firstborn [see 35:22 and *I Chron.* 5:1]; nevertheless, Reuben opposed his brothers. He felt he could not protect Joseph openly against his brothers, so he used the subterfuge of suggesting a "cleaner" way of killing Joseph, in the hope that he would be able to find a way to save him.

18. וַיִּתְנַכְּלוּ אֹתוֹ לַהֲמִיתוֹ — *They conspired against him to kill him.* First they tried to cause his death from a distance by shooting arrows at him, so that they would not kill him with their bare hands (*Tur*). Then they incited dogs against him [reasoning that this would not be considered murder] (*Midrash*). When that, too, failed, they decided to kill him directly (*Ramban*).

Sforno renders this phrase differently: *They regarded him as conspiring against them to kill them.* This explains how the brothers could have contemplated murder. They were convinced that Joseph was the aggressor and they the victims. They were sure that he had come to find fault with them, which he would then report to Jacob in the hope that Jacob would curse them. If so, *he* was the danger to *them*, and they had a right to defend themselves against his "machinations."

20. וְנַשְׁלִכֵהוּ בְּאַחַד הַבֹּרוֹת — *And we will throw him into one of the pits.* Their intention in throwing him into a pit and then looking down at him from its perimeter was to satisfy the image of his dream, since it would seem as if they were bowing down to him. Reuben's admonition: *We will not strike him mortally*! suggested that the image of the dream would be better fulfilled if Joseph were alive at the bottom of the pit (*Chasam Sofer*).

וְנִרְאֶה . . . — *Then we shall see . . .* In the plain meaning, the brothers said this derisively, meaning that Joseph would no

מִיָּדָם וַיֹּאמֶר לֹא נַכֶּנּוּ נָפֶשׁ: כב וַיֹּאמֶר אֲלֵהֶם ׀
from their hand; » he said, » We will not strike him » mortally! » 22 And say » to them »

רְאוּבֵן אַל־תִּשְׁפְּכוּ־דָם הַשְׁלִיכוּ אֹתוֹ אֶל־
did Reuben: » Do not » shed » blood! » Throw » him » into »

הַבּוֹר הַזֶּה אֲשֶׁר בַּמִּדְבָּר וְיָד אַל־תִּשְׁלְחוּ־בוֹ
this pit » which is » in the wilderness, » but a hand » do not » send forth » against him!

לְמַעַן הַצִּיל אֹתוֹ מִיָּדָם לַהֲשִׁיבוֹ אֶל־אָבִיו:
— in order » to rescue » him » from their hand, » to return him » to » his father.

שלישי כג וַיְהִי כַּאֲשֶׁר־בָּא יוֹסֵף אֶל־אֶחָיו וַיַּפְשִׁיטוּ אֶת־יוֹסֵף אֶת־כֻּתָּנְתּוֹ
23 And so it was, » when » Joseph came » to » his brothers » they stripped » Joseph » of his tunic,

אֶת־כְּתֹנֶת הַפַּסִּים אֲשֶׁר עָלָיו: כד וַיִּקָּחֻהוּ וַיַּשְׁלִכוּ אֹתוֹ הַבֹּרָה וְהַבּוֹר
the tunic » of fine wool » that was » on him. » 24 Then they took him » and cast » him » into the pit; » and the pit

רֵק אֵין בּוֹ מָיִם: כה וַיֵּשְׁבוּ לֶאֱכָל־לֶחֶם וַיִּשְׂאוּ עֵינֵיהֶם וַיִּרְאוּ וְהִנֵּה
was empty, » there was not » in it » [any] water. » 25 They sat » to eat » bread; » and they raised » their eyes » and they saw, » there was

מִדֵּיהוֹן וַאֲמַר לָא נִקְטְלִנֵּהּ נְפָשׁ: כב וַאֲמַר לְהוֹן רְאוּבֵן לָא תוֹשְׁדוּן דְּמָא רְמוֹ יָתֵהּ לְגֻבָּא הָדֵין דִּי בְמַדְבְּרָא וִידָא לָא תוֹשְׁטוּן בֵּהּ בְּדִיל לְשֵׁיזָבָא יָתֵהּ מִידֵיהוֹן לַאֲתָבוּתֵהּ לְוָת אֲבוּהִי: כג וַהֲוָה כַּד עַל יוֹסֵף לְוַת אֲחוֹהִי וְאַשְׁלִיחוּ מִן יוֹסֵף יָת כִּתּוּנֵהּ יָת כִּתּוּנָא דְפַסֵּי דִּי עֲלוֹהִי: כד וְנָסְבוּהִי וּרְמוֹ יָתֵהּ לְגֻבָּא וְגֻבָּא רֵיקָא לֵית בֵּהּ מַיָּא: כה וְאַסְחָרוּ לְמֵיכַל לַחְמָא וּזְקָפוּ עֵינֵיהוֹן וַחֲזוֹ וְהָא

רש"י

אומרים נהרגהו, והכתוב מסיים ונראה מה יהיו חלומותיו, נראה דבר מי יקום אם שלכם או שלי. וא"א שיאמרו הם ונראה מה יהיו חלומותיו, שמכיון שיהרגוהו בטלו חלומותיו (תנחומא ישן יג): **(כא) לא נכנו נפש.** מכת נפש זו היא מיתה (אונקלוס): **(כב) למען הציל אתו.** רוח הקדש העידה על ראובן שלא אמר זאת אלא להציל אותו (תנחומא יג) שיבא הוא ויעלנו משם (פדר"א פל"ח). אמר, אני בכור וגדול שבכולן, לא יתלה הסרחון אלא בי (ב"ר פד:טו): **(כג) את כתנתו.** זה חלוק: **את כתנת הפסים.** הוא שהוסיף לו אביו יותר על אחיו (שם טז): **(כד) והבור רק אין בו מים.** ממשמע שנא' והבור רק איני יודע שאין בו מים, מה ת"ל אין בו מים. מים אין בו, אבל

longer cause dissension in the family. Or, they may have meant that their plan would test the truth of Joseph's dreams, for if he were indeed Divinely chosen for leadership, God would not permit the brothers to harm him (*Ramban*). According to the Midrash, God said these words in response to their plan: "You say *let us kill him,* but I say . . . we will see whose plan will prevail, yours or Mine."

21. Reuben did not say, "Do not shed *his* blood" — rather, by insisting that they not shed *any* blood — and not commit murder, he wanted to sound dispassionate and not appear to have any special love for Joseph. Although not recorded in the Torah, there was apparently a prolonged discussion, for Reuben later accused his brothers of not listening to him when he tried to stop them from harming Joseph (42:22), but he was successful only in convincing them not to be guilty of cold-blooded murder, as recorded in verse 22 (*Ramban*).

22. לְמַעַן הַצִּיל אֹתוֹ —*In order to rescue him* [Joseph]. The Torah itself testifies that Reuben's only desire was to return later and rescue Joseph. As the eldest son, he knew Jacob would hold him responsible if anything happened to Joseph (*Rashi*).

24. וַיִּקָּחֻהוּ וַיַּשְׁלִכוּ אֹתוֹ — *Then they took him and cast him.* Although Joseph pleaded with the brothers not to do this to him (42:21), he apparently offered no physical resistance (*Radak*), since he was hopelessly outnumbered.

וְהַבּוֹר רֵק אֵין בּוֹ מָיִם — *And the pit was empty, there was not in it [any] water.* If *the pit was empty,* isn't it obvious that *there was not in it any water*? The redundancy implies that there was no *water* in it — but there *were* serpents and scorpions in it (*Rashi*, *Shabbos* 22a). However, the brothers could not have known that the pit contained lethal creatures, for Reuben, who suggested the plan, intended to save Joseph, not throw him to his death. However, *Zohar* explains that Reuben felt it was sufficient to save Joseph from the brothers, who, in their hatred, willed his death. It requires a much lower level of Divine intervention to save a righteous person from snakes and scorpions than to save him from human enemies, possessors of free will.

25-28. Joseph is sold.

25. וַיֵּשְׁבוּ לֶאֱכָל־לֶחֶם — *They sat to eat bread.* This proves that they had a clear conscience; otherwise they could not have seated themselves comfortably to eat with the entreaties of their brother echoing in their ears (*Sforno*).

Nevertheless, though God is patient, He eventually exacts

אֹרְחַת יִשְׁמְעֵאלִים בָּאָה מִגִּלְעָד וּגְמַלֵּיהֶם
< their camels << from Gilead, < coming < of Ishmaelites < a caravan
נֹשְׂאִים נְכֹאת וּצְרִי וָלֹט הוֹלְכִים לְהוֹרִיד
< to bring [them] down < — traveling << and lotus < balsam, < spices, < bearing
מִצְרָיְמָה: כו וַיֹּאמֶר יְהוּדָה אֶל־אֶחָיו מַה־בֶּצַע
< gain will there be < What << his brothers, < to < Judah said 26 << to Egypt.
כִּי נַהֲרֹג אֶת־אָחִינוּ וְכִסִּינוּ אֶת־דָּמוֹ: כז לְכוּ וְנִמְכְּרֶנּוּ לַיִּשְׁמְעֵאלִים
<< to the Ishmaelites < and let us sell him < Let us go, 27 << his blood? < and cover up < our brother < we kill < if
וְיָדֵנוּ אַל־תְּהִי־בוֹ כִּי־אָחִינוּ בְשָׂרֵנוּ הוּא וַיִּשְׁמְעוּ אֶחָיו: כח וַיַּעַבְרוּ
< Pass by 28 << And his brothers heard. << is he. < our own flesh < our brother, < for << upon him, < be < let it not < — but our hand
אֲנָשִׁים מִדְיָנִים סֹחֲרִים וַיִּמְשְׁכוּ וַיַּעֲלוּ אֶת־יוֹסֵף מִן־הַבּוֹר וַיִּמְכְּרוּ
< and sold < the pit < out of < Joseph < and lifted < they drew << traders; << from Midian, < did men

שְׁיָרַת עֲרָבָאֵי אָתְיָא מִגִּלְעָד
וְגַמְלֵיהוֹן טְעִינִין שְׁעַף וּקְטַף וּלְטוֹם
אָזְלִין לַאֲחָתָא לְמִצְרָיִם: כו וַאֲמַר
יְהוּדָה לַאֲחוֹהִי מָה מָמוֹן מִתַּהֲנֵי
לָנָא אֲרֵי נִקְטוֹל יָת אָחוּנָא וּנְכַסֵּי
עַל דְּמֵהּ: כז אֱתוֹ וּנְזַבְּנִנֵּהּ לַעֲרָבָאֵי
וִידָנָא לָא תְהֵי בֵהּ אֲרֵי אָחוּנָא
בִסְרָנָא הוּא וְקַבִּילוּ מִנֵּהּ אֲחוֹהִי:
כח וַעֲבָרוּ גַבְרֵי מִדְיָנָאֵי תַּגָּרֵי וּנְגִידוּ
וְאַסִּיקוּ יָת יוֹסֵף מִן גֻּבָּא וְזַבִּינוּ

רש״י

נחשים ועקרבים יש בו (שבת כב.): **(כה) ארחת.** כתרגומו שיירת, על שם הולכי אורח: **וגמליהם נשאים וגו׳.** למה פרסם הכתוב את משאם. להודיע מתן שכרן של צדיקים שאין דרכן של ערביים לשאת אלא נפט ועטרן שריחן רע. ולזה נזדמנו בשמים שלא יוזק מריח רע (ב״ר פד:יז; מכילתא בשלח מס׳ ב פ׳ ה): **נכאת.** כל כנוסי בשמים הרבה קרוי נכאת וכן ויראם את כל בית נכתה (מלכים ב כ:יג) מרקחת בשמיו. ואונקלוס תרגם לשון שעוה: **וצרי.** שרף הנוטף מעצי הקטף (כריתות ו.), והוא נטף (שמות ל:לד) הנמנה עם סמני הקטורת: **ולט.** לוטיתא [ס״א לוטס; ס״א לוטוס] שמו בלשון משנה (שביעית ז:ו). ורבותינו פי׳ שרש עשב ושמו אשטרולוזיא״ה במס׳ נדה (ח:):

(כו) מה בצע. מה ממון כתרגומו: **וכסינו את דמו.** ונעלים את מיתתו: **(כז) וישמעו.** וקבילו מניה (אונקלוס), וכל שמיעה שהיא קבלת דברים, כגון זה, וכגון וישמע יעקב אל אביו (לעיל כח:ז) נעשה ונשמע (שמות כד:ז), מתורגם נקבל. וכל שהיא שמיעת האוזן, כגון וישמעו את קול ה׳ אלהים מתהלך בגן (לעיל ג:ח) ורבקה שומעת (שם כז:ה) וישמע ישראל (שם לה:כב) שמעתי את תלונות (שמות טז:יב), כלן מתורגם ושמעו, ושמעת, ושמע, שמיע קדמי: **(כח) ויעברו אנשים מדינים.** זו היא שיירא אחרת, והודיעך הכתוב שנמכר פעמים הרבה: **וימשכו.** בני יעקב **את יוסף מן הבור** וימכרוהו **לישמעאלים** והישמעאלים למדינים והמדינים מכרו אותו

far away from us? (*R' Hirsch*).

27. לְכוּ וְנִמְכְּרֶנּוּ — *Let us go, and let us sell him.* The Ishmaelites are traveling to a distant country, so our deed will never be discovered (*Ramban* v. 25). And by selling him, we will punish him measure for measure: He wanted to become our master; now he will be a slave (*Sforno*).

וַיִּשְׁמְעוּ אֶחָיו — *His brothers heard.* [Where the verb שמע does not refer to hearing with the ear, it usually means that the idea is accepted. However, when no additional verb follows, it may mean that the idea was not accepted. See וַיִּשְׁמַע יִשְׂרָאֵל, *and Israel heard,* regarding the actions of Reuben with Bilhah (35:22). This would support the view of *Rashbam* that the brothers did not sell Joseph, but rather the Midianites did so independently.]

28. אֲנָשִׁים מִדְיָנִים סֹחֲרִים — *Men from Midian, traders.* Verse 25 spoke of an Ishmaelite caravan, this one speaks of Midianites, and verse 36 of Medanites. According to *Rashi*, Joseph was sold several times. Thus our verse states that the brothers lifted Joseph out of the pit and sold him to the Ishmaelites, who in turn sold him to the Midianites — who are called *Medanites* in verse 36. The Midianites then sold him in Egypt. There are several other versions to account for the different names of the slave traders. See ArtScroll *Bereishis*, p. 1650, "Who Sold Joseph?"

punishment. "You sold your brother, then sat down to eat," the Holy One, Blessed is He, said of the tribal ancestors. "There will yet come a time that your descendants will be sold in the midst of a feast!" And so it was many centuries later in Shushan when the king and Haman sat down to drink (*Esther* 3:15), after plotting the extermination of the Jews (*Midrash Tehillim* 10).

26. וַיֹּאמֶר יְהוּדָה — *Judah said.* The Torah names Judah because he saved Joseph's life at this point, just as it named Reuben above — but it refrained from naming those who were guilty of leading the plot against Joseph (*Oznaim LaTorah*).

כִּי נַהֲרֹג . . . — *If we kill . . .* There are various versions of Judah's argument:

❑ Although they would not be killing Joseph directly by leaving him in the pit, it was still homicide, he contended. "Surely, we will be considered murderers, and we will have covered his blood like common killers" (*Ramban*).

❑ What will we gain by letting him die? Revenge must satisfy the avenger's need to punish the wrongdoer, or it must be a deterrent to others. But if we let Joseph die, we will get no satisfaction because we will inevitably grieve over our brutality. And his death will not be a deterrent to other enemies because we will have to conceal his blood to hide our crime (*Sforno*).

❑ How would Joseph's death do us more good than sending him

אֶת־יוֹסֵף לַיִּשְׁמְעֵאלִים בְּעֶשְׂרִים כָּסֶף וַיָּבִיאוּ

‹ and they brought ‹‹ [pieces of] silver; ‹ for twenty ‹ to the Ishmaelites ‹ Joseph

אֶת־יוֹסֵף מִצְרָיְמָה: כט וַיָּשָׁב רְאוּבֵן אֶל־הַבּוֹר

‹‹ the pit ‹ to ‹ Reuben returned **29** ‹‹ to Egypt. ‹ Joseph

וְהִנֵּה אֵין־יוֹסֵף בַּבּוֹר וַיִּקְרַע אֶת־בְּגָדָיו: ל וַיָּשָׁב אֶל־אֶחָיו וַיֹּאמַר הַיֶּלֶד

‹ *The boy* ‹‹ and he said, ‹ his brothers ‹ to ‹ He returned **30** ‹‹ his garments. ‹ So he rent ‹‹ in the pit! ‹ Joseph was not ‹‹ — and [he] beheld —

אֵינֶנּוּ וַאֲנִי אָנָה אֲנִי־בָא: לא וַיִּקְחוּ אֶת־כְּתֹנֶת יוֹסֵף וַיִּשְׁחֲטוּ שְׂעִיר עִזִּים

‹‹ goat, ‹ a male ‹ they slaughtered ‹‹ of Joseph, ‹ the tunic ‹ They took **31** ‹‹ *go?* ‹ *can I* ‹ *— where* ‹‹ *And I* ‹‹ *is not there!*

יָת יוֹסֵף לַעֲרָבָאֵי בְּעֶסְרִין כְּסַף וְאַיְתִיוּ יָת יוֹסֵף לְמִצְרָיִם: כט וְתָב רְאוּבֵן לְגֻבָּא וְהָא לֵית יוֹסֵף בְּגֻבָּא וּבְזַע יָת לְבוּשׁוֹהִי: ל וְתָב לְוַת אֲחוֹהִי וַאֲמַר עוּלֵימָא לֵיתוֹהִי וַאֲנָא לְאָן אֲנָא אָתֵי: לא וּנְסִיבוּ יָת כִּתּוּנָא דְיוֹסֵף וּנְכִיסוּ צְפִיר בַּר עִזֵּי

רש"י

למצרים (תנחומא ישן יג): **(כט) וישב ראובן.** ובמכירתו לא היה שם שהגיע יומו לילך ולשמש את אביו (ב"ר פד:טו). ד"א, עסוק היה בשקו ובתעניתו על שבלבל יצועי אביו (שם יט): **(ל) אנה אני בא.** אנה אברח מצערו של אבא: **(לא) שעיר עזים.** דמו דומה לשל אדם (שם): **הַכֻּתֹּנֶת.** זו שמה, וכשהיא דבוקה לתיבה אחרת כגון כתנת

בְּעֶשְׂרִים כָּסֶף — *For twenty [pieces of] silver.* Because the brothers sold Rachel's firstborn for twenty silver *dinarim*, which is equal to five *shekalim*, we redeem our firstborn sons for that amount, as an atonement for the misdeed of our ancestors. Furthermore, since each brother's share of the twenty pieces of silver came to two *dinarim*, which equals a half-*shekel*, Jews gave a half-*shekel* annually for the Temple's upkeep (*Yerushalmi Shekalim* 2:3).

⁂ The solemn ban against divulging what had occurred.

The brothers proclaimed a חֵרֶם, *solemn ban,* forbidding anyone from divulging to Jacob what had occurred. However, according to *Sefer Chassidim* (ed. *Mekitzei Nirdamim* §1961), the brothers forced Joseph to swear to them directly that he would not attempt to return to Jacob, or even to notify him by word of mouth or letter of his whereabouts without the consent of the brothers. This explains why Joseph did not contact Jacob throughout his twenty-two years in Egypt. He was bound by the oath. Isaac, who was still alive, knew prophetically what had happened, but he was forced to endure Jacob's anguish in silence because of the oath of the brothers. Moreover, *Rashi* cites a Midrash that even God could not comfort Jacob because He was bound by the vow, as it were.

Other commentators explain Joseph's behavior — both his failure to send a message to his father that he was still alive and his harsh treatment of his brothers when they came to Egypt to buy food — as his desire to effect an ultimate reconciliation between himself and his brothers. He provided them the chance to demonstrate their repentance through their protection of Benjamin. Further, by showing them that although he had absolute authority in Egypt and could do to them whatever he wished, he was only interested in their welfare (*Abarbanel, R' Hirsch*).

⁂ Why were the brothers the ones who made Joseph suffer?

The hand of Heaven was at work in the sale of Joseph. The brothers thought he was a menace to them and to the unity and destiny of the family. They thought that they would kill him — and a dead man cannot reign. They thought that they would make him a slave — and a slave cannot reign. But God thought otherwise; Joseph *would* be king, no matter what they did. The Sages teach:

> *Our father Jacob would have had to descend to Egypt in chains and a collar. Said God, "He is My firstborn son, shall I bring him down there in disgrace? . . . Rather, I will lead his son before him and he will be forced to descend after him" (Bereishis Rabbah* 86:2).

But if Joseph *had* to go to Egypt, why did his great and righteous brothers have to be the instruments of his mistreatment?

When people are good, God rewards them by making them the agents of performing good things. And when people are bad, God makes them the agents of bringing about harm (*Shabbos* 32a). But whether people are considered good or bad in God's scale is measured on an individual basis, according to their own potential. Great people are judged more strictly than others because much more is expected of them. What would be overlooked in ordinary people or even praised in inferior ones may fall far short of the mark when it comes to men like Jacob's sons.

It is true that the brothers had reason to dislike Joseph. According to their *own* evaluation of their mission and his deeds, they had reason even to hate him. But their verdict was tainted by jealousy, and because men of their stature had no right to be jealous, God made them the instruments to bring Joseph to Egypt in such a heartless manner. To their lot fell the calumny of having sold their brother into slavery and causing their father twenty-two years of grief. Since it was foreordained that Jacob and his family go to Egypt, Joseph would have gone there anyway, but if his brothers had not fallen short of their ideal, Joseph's and Jacob's tears would not have been on their hands.

Nevertheless, though the brothers did not realize it, their cruel act was for a noble end. Because they were truly righteous people who wanted only to do the right thing, even their misdeed had a good outcome, because thanks to them, Joseph was in Egypt to save the world from famine and lay the foundations for the Exodus and the triumphant journey to Mount Sinai.

31-36. The version told to Jacob. After convincing his brothers to throw Joseph into the pit, from which he hoped to

וַיִּטְבְּלוּ אֶת־הַכֻּתֹּנֶת בַּדָּם׃ לב וַיְשַׁלְּחוּ אֶת־כְּתֹנֶת
and they dipped ‹ the tunic ‹ into the blood. ‹‹ 32 They sent ‹ the tunic ‹
הַפַּסִּים וַיָּבִיאוּ אֶל־אֲבִיהֶם וַיֹּאמְרוּ זֹאת מָצָאנוּ
of fine wool ‹ and they brought [it] ‹ to ‹ their father, ‹‹ and they said, ‹‹ This ‹ we found; ‹‹
הַכֶּר־נָא הַכְּתֹנֶת בִּנְךָ הִוא אִם־לֹא׃ לג וַיַּכִּירָהּ
identify, ‹ please: ‹‹ Whether the tunic ‹ of your son ‹ it is ‹ or ‹ not? ‹‹ 33 He recognized it ‹
וַיֹּאמֶר כְּתֹנֶת בְּנִי חַיָּה רָעָה אֲכָלָתְהוּ טָרֹף טֹרַף יוֹסֵף׃ לד וַיִּקְרַע יַעֲקֹב
and he said, ‹‹ The tunic ‹ of my son! ‹‹ A beast ‹ that is savage ‹ devoured him! ‹‹ Surely torn to pieces ‹‹ was Joseph! ‹‹ 34 Then Jacob rent ‹
שִׂמְלֹתָיו וַיָּשֶׂם שַׂק בְּמָתְנָיו וַיִּתְאַבֵּל עַל־בְּנוֹ יָמִים רַבִּים׃ לה וַיָּקֻמוּ
his garments ‹ and placed ‹ sackcloth ‹ about his waist; ‹‹ and he mourned ‹ for ‹ his son ‹ many days. ‹‹ 35 Arise ‹
כָל־בָּנָיו וְכָל־בְּנֹתָיו לְנַחֲמוֹ וַיְמָאֵן לְהִתְנַחֵם וַיֹּאמֶר כִּי־אֵרֵד אֶל־בְּנִי
did all ‹ his sons ‹ and all ‹ his daughters ‹ to comfort him, ‹‹ but he refused ‹ to be comforted, ‹‹ and he said: ‹‹ For ‹ I will go down ‹ to ‹ my son ‹

וּטְבָלוּ יָת כִּתּוּנָא בִּדְמָא: לב וְשַׁלַּחוּ יָת
כִּתּוּנָא דְפַסֵּי וְאַיְתִיוּ לְוַת אֲבוּהוֹן
וַאֲמָרוּ דָּא אַשְׁכַּחְנָא אִשְׁתְּמוֹדַע כְּעַן
הֲכִתּוּנָא דִבְרָךְ הִיא אִם לָא:
לג וְאִשְׁתְּמוֹדְעַהּ וַאֲמַר כִּתּוּנָא דִבְרִי
חַיְתָא בִישְׁתָא אֲכָלַתֵּהּ מִקְטַל קְטִיל
יוֹסֵף: לד וּבְזַע יַעֲקֹב לְבוּשׁוֹהִי וַאֲסַר
שַׂקָּא בְּחַרְצֵהּ וְאִתְאַבַּל עַל בְּרֵהּ יוֹמִין
סַגִּיאִין: לה וְקָמוּ כָל בְּנוֹהִי וְכָל בְּנָתֵהּ
לְנַחֲמוּתֵהּ וְסָרֵיב לְקַבָּלָא תַנְחוּמִין
וַאֲמַר אֲרֵי אֵחוֹת לְוַת (עַל) בְּרִי

רש"י

יוסף כתנת פסים כתנת בד (ויקרא טז:ד) נקוד כְּתֹנֶת: **(לג) ויאמר כתנת בני.** היא זו: **חיה רעה אכלתהו.** נצנצה בו רוח הקדש, סופו שתתגרה בו אשת פוטיפר (ב"ר שם). ולמה לא גלה לו הקב"ה, לפי שהחרימו וקללו את כל מי שיגלה ושתפו להקב"ה עמהם (תנחומא ב; פדר"א פל"ח). אבל יצחק היה יודע שהוא חי, אמר היאך אגלה והקב"ה אינו רוצה לגלות לו (ב"ר פד:כא): **(לד) ימים רבים.** כ"ב שנה (שם כ), משפירש ממנו עד שירד יעקב למצרים. שנא' יוסף בן שבע עשרה שנה וגו' (לעיל פסוק ב) ובן שלשים שנה היה בעמדו לפני פרעה, ושבע שני השבע ושנתים הרעב כשבא יעקב למצרים הרי כ"ב שנה, כנגד כ"ב שנה שלא קיים יעקב כבוד אב ואם. כ' שנה שהיה בבית לבן, וב' שנה בדרך בשובו מבית לבן שנה וחצי בסכות וששה חדשים בבית אל (מגילה טז:-יז.). וזהו שאמר ללבן זה לי עשרים שנה בביתך (לעיל לא:מא) לי הן ועלי הן, סופי ללקות כנגדן: **(לה) וכל בנתיו.** רבי יהודה אומר אחיות תאומות נולדו עם כל שבט ושבט ונשאום. רבי נחמיה אומר כנעניות היו, אלא מהו וכל בנותיו, כלותיו, שאין אדם נמנע מלקרוא לחתנו בנו ולכלתו בתו (תנחומא ישן י; ב"ר פד:כא): **וימאן להתנחם.** אין אדם מקבל תנחומין על החי וסבור שמת, שעל המת נגזרה גזירה שישתכח מן הלב ולא על החי (ב"ר שם; פסחים נד:): **ארד אל בני.** כמו על בני (אונקלוס). והרבה אל משמשין בלשון על, אל שאול

rescue him, Reuben left and was not present at Joseph's sale. According to one view, it was his turn to be in Beer Sheba to attend Jacob. Alternatively, he did not participate in his brothers' meal and was not present at the sale because he was occupied with fasting and sackcloth in penitence for having moved his father's couch [for the incident with Bilhah; see 35:22] (*Rashi* from *Midrash*).

When he came back to the pit and saw that Joseph had disappeared, he was distraught, saying, in effect, "The boy is missing and I, as the firstborn who will be held responsible for his safety, must flee because of the grief this will cause our father! But where can I go?" (*Maharshal*). Since Reuben *had* tried to save Joseph, he blamed himself for not having pursued his plan aggressively enough (*R' Hirsch*). It is common for generous people to feel they should have given more, and for concerned people to feel they did not do enough.

32. וַיְשַׁלְּחוּ אֶת־כְּתֹנֶת — *They sent the tunic*. The implication is that the brothers sent the tunic to Jacob, but did not present it personally to Jacob. Possibly they felt that since their dislike of Joseph was well known, Jacob would have been suspicious of them and seen through the ruse (*Chizkuni*); or they did not want to be the bearers of evil tidings (*Gur Aryeh*); or they could not bear to witness his grief when he first learned the horrible news (*Oznaim LaTorah*).

34. וַיִּקְרַע יַעֲקֹב שִׂמְלֹתָיו — *Then Jacob rent his garments* in an act of mourning; *and placed sackcloth about his waist* as an act of penitence. For, as *Mahari Weil* writes in his Responsa: If one dispatched an emissary to a dangerous area and that emissary is killed, the sender must undertake acts of penitence (*Malbim*).

יָמִים רַבִּים — *Many days.* Based on *Megillah* 17a, *Rashi* explains that Jacob mourned for all twenty-two years until he was reunited with Joseph.

No child had ever died in the Patriarchal household, because the offspring of the righteous are blessed. Because of this, Jacob mourned for his son so long and refused to be comforted, for he considered Joseph's "death" to be a severe punishment intended for him (*Ramban* to 38:7).

35. וְכָל־בְּנֹתָיו — *And all his daughters.* The Midrash cites two opinions. According to R' Yehudah, a twin girl was born with each of his sons, and they now comforted Jacob. R' Nechemiah maintains that the verse refers to his daughters-in-law, who were like daughters to him (*Rashi*), and his daughter Dinah (*Ramban*).

כַּד אֲבִילָא לִשְׁאוֹל וּבְכָא יָתֵהּ אֲבוּהִי: לו וּמִדְיָנָאֵי זַבִּינוּ יָתֵהּ לְמִצְרַיִם לְפוֹטִיפַר רַבָּא דְפַרְעֹה רַב קָטוֹלַיָּא: א וַהֲוָה בְּעִדָּנָא הַהִיא וּנְחַת יְהוּדָה מִלְוַת אֲחוֹהִי וּסְטָא עַד גַּבְרָא עֲדֻלְמָאָה וּשְׁמֵהּ חִירָה: ב וַחֲזָא תַמָּן יְהוּדָה בַּת גְּבַר תַּגָּרָא וּשְׁמֵהּ שׁוּעַ וּנְסָבַהּ וְעַל לְוָתַהּ: ג וְעַדִּיאַת וִילִידַת בָּר וּקְרָא יָת שְׁמֵהּ עֵר: ד וְעַדִּיאַת עוֹד וִילִידַת בָּר וּקְרַת יָת שְׁמֵהּ אוֹנָן:

אָבֵל שְׁאֹלָה וַיֵּבְךְּ אֹתוֹ אָבִיו: לו וְהַמְּדָנִים מָכְרוּ
< mourning < to the grave. » And weep < for him < did his father. » 36 [Meanwhile] the Medanites < had sold <

אֹתוֹ אֶל־מִצְרָיִם לְפוֹטִיפַר סְרִיס פַּרְעֹה שַׂר
him < to < Egypt, » to Potiphar, < an officer < of Pharaoh, » the Chief <

הַטַּבָּחִים: פ רביעי [לח] א וַיְהִי בָּעֵת הַהִוא
of the Butchers. » 38 1 It was < at that time <

וַיֵּרֶד יְהוּדָה מֵאֵת אֶחָיו וַיֵּט עַד־אִישׁ עֲדֻלָּמִי וּשְׁמוֹ חִירָה: ב וַיַּרְא־שָׁם
that Judah went down < from < his brothers < and turned aside < toward < a man < Adullam < from < whose name < was Hirah. » 2 Saw < there <

יְהוּדָה בַּת־אִישׁ כְּנַעֲנִי וּשְׁמוֹ שׁוּעַ וַיִּקָּחֶהָ וַיָּבֹא אֵלֶיהָ: ג וַתַּהַר וַתֵּלֶד
did Judah < the daughter < of a man < who was a merchant < whose name < was Shua; » he married her < and came < to her. » 3 She conceived < and bore <

בֵּן וַיִּקְרָא אֶת־שְׁמוֹ עֵר: ד וַתַּהַר עוֹד וַתֵּלֶד בֵּן וַתִּקְרָא אֶת־שְׁמוֹ אוֹנָן:
a son < and he called < his name < Er. » 4 She conceived < again < and bore < a son < and she called < his name < Onan. »

רש"י

ואל בית הדמים (שמואל ב כא:א) אל הלקח ארון האלהים ואל מות חמיה ואישה (שם א ד:כא): **אבל שאלה.** כפשוטו לשון קבר הוא, באבלי אקבר ולא אתנחם כל ימי. ומדרשו גיהנם, סימן זה היה מסור בידי מפי הגבורה, אם לא ימות אחד מבני בחיי מובטח אני שאיני רואה גיהנם (תנחומא ויגש ט): **ויבך אתו אביו.** יצחק היה בוכה מפני צרתו של יעקב אבל לא היה מתאבל שהיה יודע שהוא חי (ב"ר פד:כא): **(לו) הטבחים.** שוחטי בהמות המלך: **(א) ויהי בעת ההוא.** למה נסמכה פרשה זו לכאן והפסיק בפרשתו של יוסף, ללמד שהורידוהו אחיו מגדולתו כשראו בצרת אביהם. אמרו, אתה אמרת למכרו, אילו אמרת להשיבו היינו שומעים לך (תנחומא ישן ח; שמות רבה מב:ג): **ויט.** מאת אחיו: **עד איש עדלמי.** נשתתף עמו: **(ב) כנעני.** תגרא (פסחים נ.):

38.

◆§ Judah and Tamar: The roots of the Messiah and the Israelite monarchy.

1. וַיֵּרֶד יְהוּדָה — *Judah went down.* His descent was figurative, in the sense that his brothers *deposed* him from his position of leadership. This narrative interrupts the story of Joseph to teach how Judah's brothers *lowered him in esteem* because of the incident with Joseph, for when they saw their father's intense grief, they blamed Judah for it. "You told us to sell him," they charged. "Had you advised us to send him back to Father, we would have listened!" As a result of their disenchantment with him, Judah moved away from the family and settled in Adullam, where he became the business partner of Hirah (*Rashi*).

Because of Judah's culpability for Jacob's suffering, he was repaid by losing his two oldest sons, so that he would experience the same grief he had caused his father (*Sforno*). Indeed, the Midrash cites R' Yochanan that Judah was punished measure for measure. The brothers, led by Judah, wounded Jacob by showing him the tunic and saying, *"Identify, please,"* and Judah faced public humiliation when Tamar told him in exactly the same words to identify the proof of their tryst (below, v. 25).

2. בַּת־אִישׁ כְּנַעֲנִי — *The daughter of a man who was a merchant.* Most commentators translate כְּנַעֲנִי as *merchant*, rather than the more common *Canaanite*, based on the Talmud (*Pesachim* 50a), which remarks, "Is it possible that Abraham exhorted Isaac, and Isaac Jacob [not to marry Canaanite women], yet Judah went and married one?" *Alshich* comments that the Torah uses the unusual term כְּנַעֲנִי for *merchant* because Judah's family's sojourn among the accursed Canaanites affected them adversely (*Alshich*). This would account for the sinfulness of Judah's first two children from her, as described below. Jewish tradition has always stressed the important influence of the environment on people, and Jews have always been ready to make sacrifices to raise their children among people of high moral caliber. However, *Ibn Ezra* and R' Nechemiah in the Midrash quoted above (37:35) assume that he was a Canaanite, for which Judah was punished.

3-5. Judah and the daughter of Shua had three sons in quick succession. Judah named the first Er, which, in the literal sense, means *Awaken!* The daughter of Shua named their second child Onan. The word אוֹנָן has the connotation of *complaining* and *sorrow (Ramban)*. Midrashically, the name Er alludes to premature death or childlessness, and the name Onan refers to the grief that he would cause himself and the sorrow he would cause his parents.

Rashi finds it difficult that, for no apparent reason, the Torah mentions where the third son was born. He suggests, therefore, that the place was named for the misfortune that befell her there, for after she gave birth to Shelah, she could not have more

ה וַתֹּסֶף עוֹד וַתֵּלֶד בֵּן וַתִּקְרָא אֶת־שְׁמוֹ שֵׁלָה

5 And she continued ‹ further ‹ and she bore ‹ a son; ›› and she called ‹ his name ‹ Shelah; ››

וְהָיָה בִכְזִיב בְּלִדְתָּהּ אֹתוֹ: ו וַיִּקַּח יְהוּדָה אִשָּׁה

and it was ‹ in Chezib ‹ that she bore ‹ him. ›› 6 Judah took ‹ a wife ‹

לְעֵר בְּכוֹרוֹ וּשְׁמָהּ תָּמָר: ז וַיְהִי עֵר בְּכוֹר יְהוּדָה

for Er ‹ his firstborn; ›› and her name ‹ Tamar. ›› 7 But he was ›› — Er, ‹ the firstborn ‹ of Judah — ››

רַע בְּעֵינֵי יהוה וַיְמִתֵהוּ יהוה: ח וַיֹּאמֶר יְהוּדָה

[was] bad ‹ in the eyes ‹ of HASHEM, ›› and HASHEM put him to death. ›› 8 Then Judah said ‹

לְאוֹנָן בֹּא אֶל־אֵשֶׁת אָחִיךָ וְיַבֵּם אֹתָהּ וְהָקֵם זֶרַע לְאָחִיךָ: ט וַיֵּדַע אוֹנָן

to Onan, ›› Come ‹ to ‹ the wife ‹ of your brother ‹ and enter into levirate marriage ‹ with her, ›› and establish ‹ offspring ‹ for your brother. ›› 9 But Onan knew ‹

כִּי לֹּא לוֹ יִהְיֶה הַזָּרַע וְהָיָה אִם־בָּא אֶל־אֵשֶׁת אָחִיו וְשִׁחֵת אַרְצָה

that ‹ not ‹ his ‹ would be ‹ the seed; ›› so it was, ‹ that whenever ‹ he would come ‹ to ‹ the wife ‹ of his brother, ›› he would waste [it] ‹ onto the ground ‹

לְבִלְתִּי נְתָן־זֶרַע לְאָחִיו: י וַיֵּרַע בְּעֵינֵי יהוה אֲשֶׁר עָשָׂה וַיָּמֶת גַּם־אֹתוֹ:

so as not ‹ to provide ‹ offspring ‹ for his brother. ›› 10 It was bad ‹ in the eyes ‹ of HASHEM ‹ what ‹ he did, ›› and He put to death ‹ also ‹ him. ››

ה וְאוֹסִיפַת עוֹד וִילִידַת בָּר וּקְרַת יָת שְׁמֵהּ שֵׁלָה וַהֲוָה בִכְזִיב כַּד יְלִידַת יָתֵהּ: ו וּדְבַר יְהוּדָה אִתְּתָא לְעֵר בּוּכְרֵהּ וּשְׁמַהּ תָּמָר: ז וַהֲוָה עֵר בּוּכְרָא דִיהוּדָה בִּישׁ קֳדָם יְיָ וַאֲמִיתֵהּ יְיָ: ח וַאֲמַר יְהוּדָה לְאוֹנָן עוּל לְוַת אִתַּת אָחוּךְ וְיַבֵּם יָתַהּ וַאֲקֵים בַּר זַרְעָא לְאָחוּךְ: ט וִידַע אוֹנָן אֲרֵי לָא עַל שְׁמֵהּ מִתְקְרֵי בַּר זַרְעָא וַהֲוָה כַּד עָלֵיל לְוַת אִתַּת אֲחוּהִי וּמְחַבֵּל אָרְחֵהּ עַל אַרְעָא בְּדִיל דְּלָא לְקַיָּמָא זַרְעָא לַאֲחוּהִי: י וּבְאֵישׁ קֳדָם יְיָ דִּי עֲבַד וַאֲמִית אַף יָתֵהּ:

רש"י

(ה) והיה בכזיב. שם המקום. ואומר אני על שם שפסקה מלדת נקרא כזיב, ל' היו תהיה לי כמו אכזב (ירמיה טו:יח) אשר לא יכזבו מימיו (ישעיה נח:יא), ואם לא כן מה בא להודיענו. ובב"ר (פה:ד) ראיתי ותקרא שמו שלה וגו', פסקת: (ז) רע בעיני ה'. כרעתו של אונן, משחית זרעו, שנא' באונן וימת גם אותו (פסוק י) כמיתתו של ער מיתתו של אונן ולמה היה ער משחית זרעו, כדי שלא תתעבר ויכחיש יפיה (יבמות לד:): (ח) והקם זרע. הבן יקרא על שם המת (תרגום יונתן): (ט) ושחת ארצה. דש מבפנים וזורה

children. This is alluded to by the word *Chezib*, which is from כזב, *cessation, failure,* or *falsehood (Rashi)*.

That so many of the statements of the Patriarchs and their offspring contain prophetic allusions of which the speakers were not aware indicates that they were so endowed with the prophetic spirit that they were constantly prophesying (*Sechel Tov*).

6-10. Judah's sons marry Tamar, but die for their sin. Tamar became the mother of Judah's children (see below), and the ancestress of the Davidic dynasty. According to the Midrash, she was a daughter of Noah's son Shem (*Bereishis Rabbah* 85:10). As someone who was to play such a significant role in the destiny of Israel, it is inconceivable that she was of Canaanite descent. Obviously, she, too, was the daughter of a foreigner who lived in Canaan.

The Torah states that Er and Onan died because of their wickedness, and the nature of their sin is given in verse 9. Tamar was a beautiful woman and Er and Onan did not want her beauty to be marred by pregnancy, so they wasted their seed. For this grave sin — which God considered to be even more serious because they were the grandsons of Jacob and the sons of Judah — they suffered death (*Rashi*).

8. וְיַבֵּם אֹתָהּ — *And enter into levirate marriage with her.* For details of levirate marriage, see *Deut.* 25:5 ff. Briefly, when a man dies without offspring, Torah law obliges his brother to marry the widow, and the son of this union is considered the spiritual son of the deceased. After the Torah was given, one who refuses to perform *yibum* has the option of performing the ritual of *chalitzah,* described in *Deuteronomy* (ibid.). [Today, only the ritual of *chalitzah* is performed.] *Ramban* describes the process of *yibum* [by which the soul of the dead brother gains a new life, as it were] as one of the mysteries of the Torah. Even before the Torah was given, people knew of the spiritual benefits of *yibum,* but in those early times, this obligation could be carried out by other relatives in addition to brothers, as Judah did [albeit, unwittingly] later in the narrative.

9. כִּי לֹא לוֹ יִהְיֶה הַזָּרַע — *That not his would be the seed.* Knowing the mystical significance of *yibum,* Onan knew that the children born of his union with Tamar would be a reincarnation of Er's soul, and he was too selfish to let this happen (*Ramban,* as explained by the commentaries).

11. Instead of permitting Shelah to perform *yibum* by marrying Tamar, Judah rebuffed her, saying that he wanted Shelah to

יא וַיֹּאמֶר יְהוּדָה לְתָמָר כַּלָּתוֹ שְׁבִי אַלְמָנָה בֵית־
11 Then Judah said › to › Tamar, his daughter-in-law, »» Remain › as a widow › [in] the house

אָבִיךְ עַד־יִגְדַּל שֵׁלָה בְנִי כִּי אָמַר פֶּן־יָמוּת גַּם־
of your father › until › he grow up › does Shelah › my son, »» for › he thought, »» Lest › he die »» also—›

הוּא כְּאֶחָיו וַתֵּלֶךְ תָּמָר וַתֵּשֶׁב בֵּית אָבִיהָ׃
he— »» like his brothers. »» So Tamar went › and remained › [in] the house › of her father. »»

יב וַיִּרְבּוּ הַיָּמִים וַתָּמָת בַּת־שׁוּעַ אֵשֶׁת־יְהוּדָה וַיִּנָּחֶם יְהוּדָה וַיַּעַל עַל־
12 There [passed] many › days › and the daughter of Shua died »» —the wife › of Judah; »» [when] consoled › was Judah, »» he went up › to [stand] over ›

גֹּזֲזֵי צֹאנוֹ הוּא וְחִירָה רֵעֵהוּ הָעֲדֻלָּמִי תִּמְנָתָה׃ יג וַיֻּגַּד לְתָמָר לֵאמֹר
the shearers › of his flock »» —he › and Hirah › his friend › the Adullamite— »» to Timnah. »» 13 And it was told › to Tamar, › saying, »»

הִנֵּה חָמִיךְ עֹלֶה תִמְנָתָה לָגֹז צֹאנוֹ׃ יד וַתָּסַר בִּגְדֵי אַלְמְנוּתָהּ מֵעָלֶיהָ
Indeed › your father-in-law › is going up › to Timnah › to shear › his flock. »» 14 So she removed › the garb › of her widowhood › from upon her, »»

יא וַאֲמַר יְהוּדָה לְתָמָר כַּלְּתֵהּ תִּיבִי
אַרְמְלָא בֵּית אֲבוּךְ עַד דְּיִרְבֵּי שֵׁלָה
בְרִי אֲרֵי אֲמַר דִּלְמָא יְמוּת אַף הוּא
כַּאֲחוֹהִי וַאֲזָלַת תָּמָר וִיתִיבַת בֵּית
אֲבוּהָא: יב וּסְגִיאוּ יוֹמַיָּא וּמִיתַת
בַּת שׁוּעַ אִתַּת יְהוּדָה וְאִתְנַחֵם
יְהוּדָה וּסְלִיק עַל גּוֹזְזֵי עָנֵהּ הוּא
וְחִירָה רַחֲמֵהּ עֲדֻלְּמָאָה לְתִמְנָת:
יג וְאִתְחַוָּא לְתָמָר לְמֵימָר הָא
חֲמוּךְ סָלֵק לְתִמְנָת לְמֵיגַז עָנֵהּ:
יד וְאַעְדִּיאַת לְבוּשֵׁי אַרְמְלוּתַהּ מִנַּהּ

רש"י

מבחון (יבמות סד; ב"ר פה:ה): **(יא) כי אמר וגו'.** כלומר, דוחה היה אותה בקש, שלא היה בדעתו להשיאה לו: **כי אמר פן ימות.** מוחזקת היא זו שימותו אנשיה (ב"ר שם; עי' יבמות סד:): **(יב) ויעל על גוזזי צאנו.** ויעל תמנתה לעמוד על גוזזי צאנו: **(יג) עלה תמנתה.** ובשמשון הוא אומר וירד שמשון תמנתה (שופטים יד:א). בשפוע ההר היתה

grow up first, but the verse informs us that his real reason was that he suspected Tamar of being the sort of woman whose husbands died, for whatever reason (*Rashi*). [The effect of this rebuff, however, was that Shelah could not marry anyone else, since Tamar would then demand her right to marry Shelah.]

14-19. The moral basis for the union of Tamar and Judah. The history of Man is the story of the eternal struggle of good and evil. At times when there is an enormous potential for a breakthrough of good, the forces of evil fight back furiously, just as an army with its back to the barricades will counterattack tenaciously. Tamar was a great and righteous woman, who was Divinely ordained to become the ancestress of the Davidic dynasty, and she wanted passionately to fulfill that mission. Now, at the moment when the seed of David and Messiah could come into being through the marriage of Tamar with a son of Judah, there was uncommon resistance by the Satan, representing evil, so that Er and Onan were enticed to commit sins that went beyond the normal standards of human lust.

Judah's two oldest sons were unworthy, and Judah rebuffed her from marrying Shelah, as well. In the normal course of events, therefore, she would not have been able to marry anyone from Judah's family, which would have made it impossible for her to carry out her spiritual destiny. Consequently, to bring about the union between herself and Judah, Tamar decided that she had to seek unconventional — even distasteful — means, by posing as a harlot and enticing Judah. But even that ruse would not have succeeded in the normal course of events, for the righteous Judah would never have lowered himself to immorality. As the Midrash puts it:

> *R' Yochanan said: Judah sought to pass by Tamar. The Holy One, Blessed is He, dispatched the angel of lust to trap him. The angel said to Judah, "Where are you going? From where will kings arise? From where will great men arise?" [Only then] Judah detoured to her by the road. He was coerced, against his good sense (Bereishis Rabbah* 85:8).

In the terminology of Kabbalah, the "sparks of goodness are scattered throughout Creation," and it is the task of Israel to gather them up. There was a spark in Canaan and it was lodged in Tamar. Of his own free will, Judah would never have united with her, so an angel forced him into the path of a "harlot" to begin the creation of the Davidic dynasty.

At the prospect of such an illicit union, the forces of evil did not resist, assuming that no good would come of it (*Chofetz Chaim al HaTorah*).

◆§ The halachic perspective of Judah's action.

Judah's action must be viewed in the perspective of the time in which he lived. As *Rambam* (*Hil. Ishus* 1:4) writes, harlotry was permitted in those times — just as nonkosher foods were not forbidden — before the Torah was given. Even though the Patriarchs — and presumably their families — observed the Torah before it was given, they did so *voluntarily*, so that it was conceivable that where necessary they would act according to the

וַתְּכַס בַּצָּעִיף וַתִּתְעַלָּף וַתֵּשֶׁב בְּפֶתַח עֵינַיִם אֲשֶׁר
she covered [herself] with a veil, and wrapped herself up; then she sat by the crossroads which is

עַל־דֶּרֶךְ תִּמְנָתָה כִּי רָאֲתָה כִּי־גָדַל שֵׁלָה וְהִוא
on the road toward Timnah, for she saw that Shelah had grown, and she

לֹא־נִתְּנָה לוֹ לְאִשָּׁה: טו וַיִּרְאֶהָ יְהוּדָה וַיַּחְשְׁבֶהָ
had not been given to him as a wife. 15 [When] Judah saw her, he thought her

לְזוֹנָה כִּי כִסְּתָה פָּנֶיהָ: טז וַיֵּט אֵלֶיהָ אֶל־הַדֶּרֶךְ
to be a harlot since she had covered her face. 16 So he turned aside toward her to the road

וַיֹּאמֶר הָבָה־נָּא אָבוֹא אֵלַיִךְ כִּי לֹא יָדַע כִּי כַלָּתוֹ
and said, *Get ready, please, let me come to you,* for he did not know that his daughter-in-law

הִוא וַתֹּאמֶר מַה־תִּתֶּן־לִּי כִּי תָבוֹא אֵלָי: יז וַיֹּאמֶר אָנֹכִי אֲשַׁלַּח גְּדִי־
was she. And she said, *What will you give me if you come to me?* 17 He said, *I will send [you] a kid*

עִזִּים מִן־הַצֹּאן וַתֹּאמֶר אִם־תִּתֵּן עֵרָבוֹן עַד שָׁלְחֶךָ: יח וַיֹּאמֶר מָה
of the goats from the flock. And she said, *Provided you give something as security until you send [it].* 18 And he said, *What*

הָעֵרָבוֹן אֲשֶׁר אֶתֶּן־לָּךְ וַתֹּאמֶר חֹתָמְךָ וּפְתִילֶךָ וּמַטְּךָ אֲשֶׁר בְּיָדֶךָ
is the security that I should give you? She said, *Your signet, your wrap, and your staff that is in your hand.*

וַיִּתֶּן־לָהּ וַיָּבֹא אֵלֶיהָ וַתַּהַר לוֹ: יט וַתָּקָם וַתֵּלֶךְ וַתָּסַר צְעִיפָהּ מֵעָלֶיהָ
And he gave [them] to her, and he came to her, and she conceived by him. 19 Then she arose and went, and removed her veil from upon her,

וּכְסִיאַת בְּעֵיפָא וְאִתַּקָּנַת וִיתִיבַת בְּפָרָשׁוּת עַיְנִין דִּי עַל אֹרַח תִּמְנָת אֲרֵי חֲזַת אֲרֵי רְבָא שֵׁלָה וְהִיא לָא אִתְיְהִיבַת לֵהּ לְאִנְתּוּ: טו וַחֲזָאַהּ יְהוּדָה וְחַשְׁבַהּ לְנָפְקַת בָּרָא אֲרֵי כַסִּיאַת אַפָּהָא: טז וּסְטָא לְוָתַהּ לְאָרְחָא וַאֲמַר הָבִי כְעַן אֵיעוֹל לְוָתִיךְ אֲרֵי לָא יְדַע אֲרֵי כַלְּתֵהּ הִיא וַאֲמֶרֶת מַה תִּתֵּן לִי אֲרֵי תֵיעוֹל לְוָתִי: יז וַאֲמַר אֲנָא אֲשַׁלַּח גְּדִי בַר עִזֵּי מִן עָנָא וַאֲמֶרֶת אִם תִּתֵּן מַשְׁכּוֹנָא עַד דְּתִשְׁלַח: יח וַאֲמַר מָה מַשְׁכּוֹנָא דִּי אֶתֵּן לָךְ וַאֲמֶרֶת עִזְקְתָךְ וְשׁוֹשִׁפָּךְ וְחוּטְרָךְ דִּי בִידָךְ וִיהַב לַהּ וְעַל לְוָתַהּ וְעַדִּיאַת לֵהּ: יט וְקָמַת וַאֲזָלַת וְאַעְדִּיאַת עֵיפַהּ מִנַּהּ

רש"י

יושבת, עולין לה מכאן ויורדין לה מכאן (סוטה י.): **(יד) ותתעלף.** כסתה פניה שלא יכיר בה: **ותשב בפתח עינים.** בפתיחת עינים, בפרשת דרכים שעל דרך תמנתה. ורבותינו דרשו, בפתחו של אברהם אבינו שכל עינים מצפות לראותו (שם): **כי ראתה כי גדל שלה וגו'.** לפיכך הפקירה עצמה אצל יהודה שהיתה מתאוה להעמיד ממנו בנים (הוריות י:; מגלה לתנ"י כ"י ג:יח): **(טו) ויחשבה לזונה.** לפי שיושבת בפרשת דרכים: **כי כסתה פניה.** ולא יכול לראותה ולהכירה. ומדרש רבותינו, כי כסתה פניה, כשהיתה בבית חמיה היתה צנועה לפיכך לא חשדה (סוטה י:): **(טז) ויט אליה אל הדרך.** מדרך שהיה בה נטה אל הדרך אשר היא בה. ובל' לע"ז דשטורני"ר: **הבה נא.** הכיני עצמך ודעתך לכך. כל לשון הבה ל' הזמנה הוא חוץ ממקום שיש לתרגמו בלשון נתינה, ואף אותן של הזמנה קרובים ללשון נתינה הם: **(יז) ערבון.** משכון (אונקלוס): **(יח) חתמך ופתילך.** עזקתך ושושיפך (שם). טבעת שאתה חותם בה ושמלתך שאתה מתכסה בה: **ותהר לו.** גבורים כיוצא בו לדיקים כיוצא בו (ב"ר פה:ט):

16-18. מַה־תִּתֶּן־לִי — *What will you give me?* Tamar did not want money and would have refused it if it had been offered. She wanted something that she could use later to prove that her consort was Judah, so that her pregnancy would be acknowledged as the result of a levirate union (*Sforno*). So great was the passion burning within him [as a result of the Providential intervention (*Abarbanel*)] that Judah gave her three valuable items as a pledge for a single goat (*Ibn Ezra*), and items that would so conclusively identify him.

19. וַתָּקָם — *Then she arose.* She arose spiritually, for kings and prophets would be the result of this union (*Lekach Tov*).

laws that were obligatory at the time. Consequently, if the Divine plan required Judah to cohabit with a "harlot," he would be permitted to do so. [Cf. the case of Jacob marrying two sisters which later Torah law would absolutely forbid.]

14. וְהִוא לֹא־נִתְּנָה לוֹ לְאִשָּׁה — *And she had not been given to him as a wife.* Tamar did such an undignified thing because she was determined to have children from Judah (*Rashi*). Since Judah refused Shelah to her, offspring could only come from Judah himself (*Gur Aryeh*). This was part of God's plan, for he wanted the Messianic dynasty to come from Tamar through Judah, who was more righteous and pure than his son Shelah (*Sforno*).

וַתִּלְבַּשׁ בִּגְדֵי אַלְמְנוּתָהּ׃ כ וַיִּשְׁלַח יְהוּדָה אֶת־גְּדִי

< the kid < Judah sent **20** << of her widowhood. < the garb < and she put on

הָעִזִּים בְּיַד רֵעֵהוּ הָעֲדֻלָּמִי לָקַחַת הָעֵרָבוֹן מִיַּד

< from the hand < the security items < to retrieve < the Adullamite < of his friend < in the hand < of the goats

הָאִשָּׁה וְלֹא מְצָאָהּ׃ כא וַיִּשְׁאַל אֶת־אַנְשֵׁי מְקֹמָהּ

< of her place, < the people < of < He inquired **21** << but he did not find her. << of the woman;

לֵאמֹר אַיֵּה הַקְּדֵשָׁה הִוא בָעֵינַיִם עַל־הַדָּרֶךְ

<< the road? < on < at the crossroads < the one << is the prostitute, < Where << saying,

וַיֹּאמְרוּ לֹא־הָיְתָה בָזֶה קְדֵשָׁה׃ כב וַיָּשָׁב אֶל־יְהוּדָה

< Judah < to < So he returned **22** << *a prostitute.* < *here* < *There was not* << And they said,

וּלְבֵישַׁת לְבוּשֵׁי אַרְמְלוּתַהּ׃ כ וְשַׁדַּר יְהוּדָה יָת גַּדְיָא בַּר עִזֵּי בִּידָא רַחֲמֵהּ עֲדֻלָּמָאָה לְמִסַּב מַשְׁכּוֹנָא מִידָא דְאִתְּתָא וְלָא אַשְׁכְּחַהּ׃ כא וּשְׁאִיל יָת אֱנָשֵׁי אַתְרַהּ לְמֵימַר אָן מְקַדִּשְׁתָּא הִיא בְעַיְנִין עַל אָרְחָא וַאֲמָרוּ לֵית הָכָא מְקַדִּשְׁתָּא׃ כב וְתָב לְוַת יְהוּדָה וַאֲמַר לָא אַשְׁכְּחִיתַהּ וְאַף אֱנָשֵׁי אַתְרָא אֲמָרוּ לֵית הָכָא מְקַדִּשְׁתָּא׃ כג וַאֲמַר יְהוּדָה תִּסַּב לַהּ דִּילְמָא נְהֵי לְחוּךְ הָא שַׁדָּרִית גַּדְיָא הָדֵין וְאַתְּ לָא אַשְׁכַּחְתַּהּ׃ כד וַהֲוָה כִּתְלָתוּת יַרְחַיָּא וְאִתְחַוָּא לִיהוּדָה לְמֵימַר זַנִּיאַת תָּמָר כַּלְּתָךְ וְאַף הָא מַעְדְּיָא לִזְנוּתָא וַאֲמַר יְהוּדָה אַפְּקוּהָא וְתִתּוֹקָד׃

וַיֹּאמֶר לֹא מְצָאתִיהָ וְגַם אַנְשֵׁי הַמָּקוֹם אָמְרוּ לֹא־הָיְתָה בָזֶה קְדֵשָׁה׃

<< *a prostitute.'* < *here* < *'There was not* << *said,* < *of the place* < *the men* < *and even* << *I did not find her;* << and said,

כג וַיֹּאמֶר יְהוּדָה תִּקַּח־לָהּ פֶּן נִהְיֶה לָבוּז הִנֵּה שָׁלַחְתִּי הַגְּדִי הַזֶּה וְאַתָּה

< but you < this kid, < I sent her < Indeed << a laughingstock; < we become < lest << for herself, < Let her take [them] << So Judah said, **23**

לֹא מְצָאתָהּ׃ כד וַיְהִי ׀ כְּמִשְׁלֹשׁ חֳדָשִׁים וַיֻּגַּד לִיהוּדָה לֵאמֹר זָנְתָה

< committed harlotry << saying, < to Judah < it was told << months, < after about three < And it was **24** << *find her.* < *could not*

תָּמָר כַּלָּתֶךָ וְגַם הִנֵּה הָרָה לִזְנוּנִים וַיֹּאמֶר יְהוּדָה הוֹצִיאוּהָ וְתִשָּׂרֵף׃

<< and she should be burned! < Take her out << Judah said, << *by harlotry. < she is with child < indeed < and moreover, << your daughter-in-law, < has Tamar*

רש"י

(כא) הקדשה. מקודשת ומזומנת לזנות: **(כג) תקח לה.** יהיה שלה מה שבידה: **פן נהיה לבוז.** אם תבקשנה עוד יתפרסם הדבר ויהיה גנאי כי מה עלי לעשות עוד לאמת דברי: **הנה שלחתי הגדי הזה.** ולפי שרמה יהודה את אביו בגדי עזים שהטביל כתנת יוסף בדמו, רמוהו גם אותו בגדי עזים (ב"ר פה:ט): **(כד) כמשלש חדשים.** רובו של ראשון ורובו של אחרון ואמצעי שלם (שם י). ול' כמשלש חדשים כהשתלש החדשים, כמו ומשלוח מנות (אסתר ט:כב) משלוח ידם (ישעיה יא:יד). וכן תרגם אונקלוס כתלתות ירחיא: **הרה לזנונים.** שם דבר, מעוברת, כמו אשה הרה (שמות כא:כב), וכמו ברה כחמה (שיר השירים ו:י): **ותשרף.** אמר אפרים מקשאה משום רבי מאיר, בתו של שם היתה שהוא כהן, לפיכך דנוה בשריפה (ב"ר פה:י):

20. Hirah's name is not mentioned here; he is referred to only as Judah's friend. *Bereishis Rabbasi* cites two opinions for this. According to one view, his anonymity was preserved in deference to his selflessness, for he performed this shameful mission purely out of love and friendship for Judah. According to another view, his name is omitted as a token of rebuke, because he undertook to participate in this disgraceful affair.

23. **פֶּן נִהְיֶה לָבוּז** — *Lest we become a laughingstock*, for having pledged things as valuable as a signet, wrap, and staff for such a trifle (*Ibn Ezra*).

Judah had not done anything illegal and the items in Tamar's possession were far more valuable than the kid he had promised her — so that he would have been justified in investigating further to find the harlot and retrieve his pledge. Nevertheless, Judah was ready to forfeit the pledge, for it is improper to discuss sexual matters in public, even if they do not involve forbidden conduct (*Rambam, Moreh Nevuchim*). This is in stark contrast to modern codes of propriety.

24. **וְתִשָּׂרֵף** — *And she should be burned!* As the daughter of Shem, who was a priest, Tamar was sentenced to be burned (*Rashi* citing Midrash). *Ramban* points out that a priest's unmarried daughter is *not* liable to the death penalty (*Sanhedrin* 50b), so there had to be other reasons for the death sentence. *Mizrachi* explains that there were indeed extenuating circumstances: Perhaps sexual misconduct was so rampant that extraordinary measures had been instituted to curb it, or the exalted status of

כה הִוא מוּצֵאת וְהִיא שָׁלְחָה אֶל־חָמִיהָ לֵאמֹר
25 As she was being taken out, she sent to her father-in-law, saying,
לְאִישׁ אֲשֶׁר־אֵלֶּה לּוֹ אָנֹכִי הָרָה וַתֹּאמֶר הַכֶּר־
By the man that these belong to I am with child. And she said, Identify,
נָא לְמִי הַחֹתֶמֶת וְהַפְּתִילִים וְהַמַּטֶּה הָאֵלֶּה׃
please, whose are the signet, the wrap, and the staff — these ones.
כו וַיַּכֵּר יְהוּדָה וַיֹּאמֶר צָדְקָה מִמֶּנִּי כִּי־עַל־כֵּן לֹא־נְתַתִּיהָ לְשֵׁלָה בְנִי
26 Judah recognized; and he said, She is right; it is from me, for the reason that I did not give her to Shelah my son,
וְלֹא־יָסַף עוֹד לְדַעְתָּהּ׃ כז וַיְהִי בְּעֵת לִדְתָּהּ וְהִנֵּה תְאוֹמִים בְּבִטְנָהּ׃
and he did not continue anymore to know her. 27 And it was at the time she gave birth that there were twins in her womb.
כח וַיְהִי בְלִדְתָּהּ וַיִּתֶּן־יָד וַתִּקַּח הַמְיַלֶּדֶת וַתִּקְשֹׁר עַל־יָדוֹ שָׁנִי לֵאמֹר
28 And it happened that as she gave birth, one put out a hand; the midwife took and tied on his hand a crimson [thread] saying,

כה הִיא מִתַּפְּקָא וְהִיא שְׁלַחַת לַחֲמוּהָא לְמֵימַר לִגְבַר דִּי אִלֵּין דִּילֵהּ מִנֵּהּ אֲנָא מַעְדְּיָא וַאֲמֶרֶת אִשְׁתְּמוֹדַע כְּעַן לְמָן עִזְקְתָא וְשׁוֹשִׁפָא וְחוּטְרָא הָאִלֵּין׃ כו וְאִשְׁתְּמוֹדַע יְהוּדָה וַאֲמַר זַכָּאָה מִנִּי מַעְדְּיָא אֲרֵי עַל כֵּן לָא יְהָבְתַּהּ לְשֵׁלָה בְרִי וְלָא אוֹסִיף עוֹד לְמִדְעַהּ׃ כז וַהֲוָה בְּעִדַּן דְּמֵילְדַהּ וְהָא תְיוֹמִין בִּמְעָהָא׃ כח וַהֲוָה בְּמֵילְדַהּ וִיהַב יְדָא וּנְסֵיבַת חַיְתָא וּקְטָרַת עַל יְדֵהּ זְהוֹרִיתָא לְמֵימַר

רש"י

(כה) **הוא מוצאת.** לישרף: **והיא שלחה אל חמיה.** לא רצתה להלבין פניו ולומר ממך אני מעוברת, אלא **לאיש אשר אלה לו.** אמרה, אם יודה מעצמו, יודה, ואם לאו ישרפוני, ואל אלבין פניו. מכאן אמרו נוח לו לאדם שיפיל עצמו לכבשן האש ואל ילבין פני חבירו ברבים (סוטה י:): **הכר נא.** אין נא אלא לשון בקשה, הכר נא בוראך ואל תאבד שלש נפשות (שם; ב"ר פה:יא): (כו) **צדקה.** בדבריה: **ממני.** היא מעוברת (אונקלוס; מבוא לתנ"י כ"י ג:כ). ורז"ל דרשו שיצאה בת קול ואמרה ממני ומאתי יצאו הדברים (סוטה שם). לפי שהיתה צנועה בבית חמיה גזרתי שיצאו ממנה מלכים, ומשבט יהודה גזרתי להעמיד מלכים בישראל: **כי על כן לא נתתיה.** כי בדין עשתה, על אשר לא נתתיה לשלה בני: **ולא יסף עוד.** יש אומרים לא הוסיף (ספרי בהעלתך פח) ויש אומרים לא פסק (סוטה י:), [ואחבירו גבי אלדד ומידד ולא יספו (במדבר יא:כה) ומתרגמינן ולא פסקו]: (כז) **בעת לדתה.** וברבקה הוא אומר וימלאו ימיה ללדת (לעיל כה:כד). להלן למלאים וכאן לחסרים (ב"ר פה:יג): **והנה תאומים.** מלא ולהלן (לעיל כה:כד) תומים חסר. לפי שהאחד רשע אבל אלו שניהם צדיקים (ב"ר שם): (כח) **ויתן יד.** הוציא האחד ידו לחוץ ולאחר שקשרה על ידו השני החזירה:

God repaid Judah measure for measure. With the expression הַכֶּר־נָא [*Identify, please: Whether the tunic of your son it is or not?* (37:32)], Judah had caused his father, Jacob, untold anguish. Tamar now confronted Judah with that same expression, and its impact registered solidly upon him (*Sotah* 10b).

26. צָדְקָה מִמֶּנִּי — *She is right; it is from me.* The translation follows *Rashi.* Judah's response testifies to his moral integrity. Though his public admission surely subjected him to the jibes of the populace, he did not hesitate to admit that he was the father. Nor did he pretend to pardon Tamar by showing her clemency, thereby protecting his dignity. He thought, "It is better for me to be ashamed in this transient world than to be ashamed before my righteous fathers in the World to Come ..." (*Targum Yonasan).*

Alternatively, *Rashi* cites a Midrash that a Heavenly Voice called out, *It is from Me*, that God proclaimed that He had intervened to bring the two together.

Ramban and *Rashbam* render that Judah called out, "*She is more righteous than I!*"

27-30. Tamar bears twins.

28. וַתִּקְשֹׁר — *And tied . . .*, in order to identify him as the firstborn (*Sforno*).

the families that had been shamed by Tamar — Judah's and Shem's — was sufficient to demand an unusual penalty.

Judah condemned her to this punishment because he was a great chief, and his daughter-in-law's harlotry was an affront to his status, just as a priest's daughter who commits harlotry is condemned for having "thereby profaned her father" (*Leviticus* 21:9). This judgment would not have been meted out to a commoner (*Ramban*).

25. Tamar did not shame Judah publicly by naming him as the father. She reasoned: "If he admits it voluntarily, well and good; if not, let them burn me, but let me not publicly disgrace him." Thus the Sages taught [*Sotah* 10b]: "One should let himself be thrown into a fiery furnace rather than expose his neighbor to public shame" (*Rashi*).

That Tamar sent the pledge to Judah only at the last minute is noteworthy. R' Elazar (*Midrash; Sotah* 10b) comments that, in order to prevent the Messianic dynasty from coming into the world, Satan caused her to forget where the items were. Tamar beseeched God's mercy with all her soul, and just as she was to be led to her execution, she found the pledge. Historical destinies sometimes hang by a thread and their happy outcome depends on a miracle (*R' Munk*).

זֶה יָצָא רִאשֹׁנָה׃ כט וַיְהִי | כְּמֵשִׁיב יָדוֹ וְהִנֵּה יָצָא

This one emerged first! 29 And it was, as he drew back his hand, that suddenly emerged

אָחִיו וַתֹּאמֶר מַה־פָּרַצְתָּ עָלֶיךָ פָּרֶץ וַיִּקְרָא שְׁמוֹ

his brother. And she said, "How have you breached for yourself a breach!" And he called his name

פָּרֶץ׃ ל וְאַחַר יָצָא אָחִיו אֲשֶׁר עַל־יָדוֹ הַשָּׁנִי

Perez. 30 Afterward emerged his brother who had on his hand the crimson [thread];

וַיִּקְרָא שְׁמוֹ זָרַח׃ ס חמישי [לט] א וְיוֹסֵף הוּרַד מִצְרָיְמָה וַיִּקְנֵהוּ פּוֹטִיפַר

and he called his name Zerah. 39 1 And Joseph had been brought down to Egypt. Pothiphar purchased him

סְרִיס פַּרְעֹה שַׂר הַטַּבָּחִים אִישׁ מִצְרִי מִיַּד הַיִּשְׁמְעֵאלִים אֲשֶׁר הוֹרִדֻהוּ

— an officer of Pharaoh, the Chief of the Butchers, a man of Egypt, from the hand of the Ishmaelites who had brought him down

דֵּין נְפַק בְּקַדְמֵיתָא׃ כט וַהֲוָה כַּד אֲתֵיב יְדֵהּ וְהָא נְפַק אֲחוּהִי וַאֲמֶרֶת מָא תְקוֹף סַגִּי עֲלָךְ לְמִתְקַף וּקְרָא שְׁמֵהּ פָּרֶץ׃ ל וּבָתַר כֵּן נְפַק אֲחוּהִי דִּי עַל יְדֵהּ זְהוֹרִיתָא וּקְרָא שְׁמֵהּ זָרַח׃ א וְיוֹסֵף אִתָּחַת לְמִצְרָיִם וּזְבָנֵהּ פּוֹטִיפַר רַבָּא דְפַרְעֹה רַב קָטוֹלַיָּא גְּבַר מִצְרָאָה מִידָא דַּעֲרָבָאֵי דִּי אַחְתוּהִי

רש"י

(כט) פרצת. חזקת עליך חוזק (אונקלוס): **(ל) אשר על ידו השני.** ארבע ידות כתובות כאן כנגד ארבע חרמים שמעל עכן שילא ממנו. וי"א כנגד ארבעה דברים שלקח, אדרת שנער ושני חתיכות כסף של מאתים שקלים ולשון זהב (יהושע ז:כא; ב"ר פס יד): **ויקרא שמו זרח.** על שם זריחת מראית השני: **(א) ויוסף הורד.** חוזר לענין ראשון, אלא שהפסיק בו כדי לסמוך ירידתו של יהודה למכירתו של יוסף, לומר לך שבשבילו הורידוהו מגדולתו. ועוד, כדי לסמוך מעשה אשתו של פוטיפר למעשה תמר לומר לך מה זו לשם שמים אף זו לשם שמים, שראתה באצטרולוגין שלה שעתידה להעמיד בנים ממנו, ואינה יודעת אם ממנה אם מבתה (ב"ר פה:ב):

29. That Perez pushed ahead was part of the Divine plan. Zerah desired to emerge first but God declared: "Messiah is destined to descend from Perez; is it right, then, that Zerah should emerge first? Let Zerah return to his mother's womb, and Perez shall be born first!" (*Aggadas Bereishis*).

Kabbalistically, the names Perez and Zerah have great mystical significance. *Zerah*, literally *shining* or *brightness*, alludes to the sun, which is a source of constant light. *Perez*, on the other hand, means *breach*, alluding to the moon, whose light is sometimes whole and sometimes breached, as its light wanes and waxes. It would have been logical for the brilliant, constant Zerah to be born first, but God wanted Perez to be the firstborn, to symbolize the Davidic dynasty, which is likened to the moon, because it became diminished and finally disappeared but, like the moon, it will re-emerge and grow to fullness again. Because of this similarity between the Davidic dynasty and the moon, when the Sages sent word that the New Moon had been declared (*Rosh Hashanah* 25a), they used the message "David King of Israel lives and exists" (*Ramban* citing *Sefer HaBahir).*

Judah named the child *Perez* [meaning *strength* (*Rashi*) or: *breaking forth* (*Ramban*)] because of what the midwife had said (*Radak*).

30. **זָרַח** — *Zerah* (*Brightness*). In the plain sense, the name alluded to the brightness of the crimson thread (*Rashi*).

39.

❧ Joseph in Egypt/Prelude to exile.

The Torah returns to the narrative that it had interrupted with the Judah-Tamar interlude. As noted in 38:1, Judah's degradation was inserted because his role in the sale of Joseph had caused the brothers to demote him from his leadership status. Furthermore, the close proximity of the narratives of Tamar and Potiphar's wife indicates that both women had pure motives, both of them desiring to found families in Israel. Potiphar's wife had foreseen by astrological signs that she was destined to be the ancestress of children by Joseph — but she did not know whether *she* or her daughter would have the children. [According to tradition, Joseph married her daughter. See *Rashi* to 41:45] (*Rashi*).

Joseph's descent into Egypt was the prelude to the exile foretold to Abraham at the Covenant Between the Parts [15:13]. The phrase *Joseph had been brought down to Egypt* (v. 1) has the deeper implication that Joseph *brought down* [הוריד] his father and the tribal ancestors to Egypt (*Tanchuma Yashan*). That is, God engineered Joseph's descent to Egypt and his elevation there to the position of viceroy in order to prepare an honorable way to implement His decree that Jacob and his family be exiled. [See comment after 37:28, **Why were the brothers . . .**] According to *Hadar Zekeinim,* the Divine Presence, as it were, descended with Joseph.

1-6. Joseph's success as a slave. The brothers had done their work, convinced that Joseph's dreams of kingship could never be fulfilled. But wherever he went, he ruled. As a slave of Potiphar, he was put in charge of the household; as a disgraced prisoner, he was placed in charge of the prison; as a despised Hebrew, he was rushed to interpret Pharaoh's dreams and made viceroy of all Egypt — and provider to all the surrounding countries — and his own Egyptian subjects came to him, abjectly

שָֽׁמָּה׃ ב וַיְהִ֤י יְהוָה֙ אֶת־יוֹסֵ֔ף וַיְהִ֖י אִ֣ישׁ מַצְלִ֑יחַ
who was successful; | a man | and he became | Joseph, | with | HASHEM was | 2 | there.

וַיְהִ֕י בְּבֵ֖ית אֲדֹנָ֥יו הַמִּצְרִֽי׃ ג וַיַּ֣רְא אֲדֹנָ֔יו כִּ֥י יְהוָ֖ה
HASHEM | that | His master saw | 3 | the Egyptian. | of his master | in the house | and he was

אִתּ֑וֹ וְכֹל֙ אֲשֶׁר־ה֣וּא עֹשֶׂ֔ה יְהוָ֖ה מַצְלִ֥יחַ בְּיָדֽוֹ׃
in his hand. | made succeed | HASHEM | would do | he | that | and everything | was with him,

ד וַיִּמְצָ֨א יוֹסֵ֥ף חֵ֛ן בְּעֵינָ֖יו וַיְשָׁ֣רֶת אֹת֑וֹ וַיַּפְקִדֵ֙הוּ֙
he appointed him | him; | and he served | in his eyes, | favor | Joseph found | 4

עַל־בֵּית֔וֹ וְכָל־יֶשׁ־ל֖וֹ נָתַ֥ן בְּיָדֽוֹ׃ ה וַיְהִ֡י מֵאָז֩ הִפְקִ֨יד אֹת֜וֹ בְּבֵית֗וֹ וְעַל֙
and over | in his household | him | he appointed | [that] from the time | And it was | 5 | in his hand. | he placed | to him | that belonged | and all | his household, | over

כָּל־אֲשֶׁ֣ר יֶשׁ־ל֔וֹ וַיְבָ֧רֶךְ יְהוָ֛ה אֶת־בֵּ֥ית הַמִּצְרִ֖י בִּגְלַ֣ל יוֹסֵ֑ף וַיְהִ֞י בִּרְכַּ֤ת
— the blessing | and it was | of Joseph, | on account | of the Egyptian | the house | HASHEM blessed | to him, | belonged | that | all

יְהוָה֙ בְּכָל־אֲשֶׁ֣ר יֶשׁ־ל֔וֹ בַּבַּ֖יִת וּבַשָּׂדֶֽה׃ ו וַיַּעֲזֹ֣ב כָּל־אֲשֶׁר־לוֹ֮ בְּיַ֣ד יוֹסֵף֒
of Joseph | in the hand | he had | that | all | He left | 6 | and in the field. | in the house | to him | belonged | that | in all | of HASHEM —

וְלֹא־יָדַ֤ע אִתּוֹ֙ מְא֔וּמָה כִּ֥י אִם־הַלֶּ֖חֶם אֲשֶׁר־ה֣וּא אוֹכֵ֑ל וַיְהִ֣י יוֹסֵ֔ף יְפֵה־
was handsome | Now Joseph | ate. | he | that | the bread | except for | anything, | with | given his presence — | and he did not concern himself

לְתַמָּן: ב וַהֲוָה מֵימְרָא דַייָ בְּסַעְדֵהּ דְּיוֹסֵף וַהֲוָה גְּבַר מַצְלַח וַהֲוָה בְּבֵית רִבּוֹנֵהּ מִצְרָאָה: ג וַחֲזָא רִבּוֹנֵהּ אֲרֵי מֵימְרָא דַייָ בְּסַעְדֵהּ וְכֹל דִּי הוּא עָבֵד יְיָ מַצְלַח בִּידֵהּ: ד וְאַשְׁכַּח יוֹסֵף רַחֲמִין בְּעֵינוֹהִי וְשַׁמֵּשׁ יָתֵהּ וּמַנְיֵהּ עַל בֵּיתֵהּ וְכָל דִּי אִית לֵהּ מְסַר בִּידֵהּ: ה וַהֲוָה מֵעִדַּן דְּמַנִּי יָתֵהּ בְּבֵיתֵהּ וְעַל כָּל דִּי אִית לֵהּ וּבָרִיךְ יְיָ יָת בֵּית מִצְרָאָה בְּדִיל יוֹסֵף וַהֲוָה בִּרְכְתָא דַייָ בְּכָל דִּי אִית לֵהּ בְּבֵיתָא וּבְחַקְלָא: ו וּשְׁבַק כָּל דִּי לֵהּ בִּידָא דְּיוֹסֵף וְלָא יְדַע עִמֵּהּ מִדַּעַם אֱלָהֵן לַחְמָא דִּי הוּא אָכֵל וַהֲוָה יוֹסֵף שַׁפִּיר

רש"י

(ג) **כי ה' אתו.** שם שמים שגור בפיו (תנחומא ח): (ד) **וכל יש לו.** הרי לשון קצר חסר אשר: (ו) **ולא ידע אתו מאומה.** לא היה נותן לבו לכלום: **כי אם הלחם.** היא אשתו, אלא שדבר בלשון נקייה (ב"ר פו:ו): **ויהי יוסף יפה תאר.** כיון שראה עצמו מושל התחיל אוכל ושותה ומסלסל בשערו. אמר הקב"ה אביך מתאבל ואתה מסלסל

pleading for the privilege of buying food. And finally, his entire family bowed to him. What, indeed, would become of his dreams!

2. וַיְהִי בְּבֵית אֲדֹנָיו — *And he was in the house of his master.* God intervened to have Joseph work in the house, unlike most slaves who are assigned to hard labor in the fields (*Abarbanel*). That he worked at home near Potiphar and his wife enabled Joseph's talents to be noticed and rewarded (*Ibn Caspi*).

הַמִּצְרִי — *The Egyptian.* That Potiphar was Egyptian is obvious, since he was an official in Pharaoh's court, yet the Torah mentions his nationality three times in this passage [vs. 1,2,5]; apparently this fact has special significance to the narrative. The Egyptian elite held all Canaanites in contempt and had a particular antipathy for the moral code of the Abrahamitic family. That Joseph succeeded in such an antagonistic setting, therefore, is all the more noteworthy (*R' Hirsch*). Given this fact, it is clear that he could not have been promoted unless, as this verse states, *HASHEM was with him.*

4. Perceiving that Joseph was Divinely assisted, Potiphar took a special liking to him. First he made him his personal attendant, and afterward appointed him over the household.

5. בַּבַּיִת וּבַשָּׂדֶה — *In the house and in the field.* Potiphar's affairs prospered wherever Joseph was. If Joseph was in the fields, they flourished; and if he was at home, the domestic matters did well. But the areas where he was absent did poorly, proving to Potiphar that Joseph was responsible for the blessings (*Tanchuma*).

6. כִּי אִם־הַלֶּחֶם — *Except for the bread.* This is a delicate expression; *bread* here refers to his wife (*Rashi*). The sense is that Potiphar unquestioningly entrusted to Joseph everything except for his own wife. *Tur* interprets the word literally: Potiphar trusted Joseph so completely that the only thing he concerned himself with was his personal menu, *the bread that he ate.*

תֹּאַר וִיפֵה מַרְאֶה: ששי ז וַיְהִי אַחַר הַדְּבָרִים הָאֵלֶּה

« these things, ‹ after ‹ And it was 7 « of appearance. ‹ and handsome ‹ of form

וַתִּשָּׂא אֵשֶׁת־אֲדֹנָיו אֶת־עֵינֶיהָ אֶל־יוֹסֵף וַתֹּאמֶר

« and she said, « Joseph, ‹ toward ‹ her eyes ‹ of his master ‹ did the wife ‹ lift up

שִׁכְבָה עִמִּי: ח וַיְמָאֵן ׀ וַיֹּאמֶר אֶל־אֵשֶׁת אֲדֹנָיו

« of his master, ‹ the wife ‹ to ‹ he said « But he adamantly refused; 8 « with me. ‹ Lie

הֵן אֲדֹנִי לֹא־יָדַע אִתִּי מַה־בַּבָּיִת וְכֹל אֲשֶׁר־יֶשׁ־

‹ belongs ‹ that ‹ and all « in the house, ‹ about anything « —with me present— « does not concern himself ‹ —my master « Indeed

לוֹ נָתַן בְּיָדִי: ט אֵינֶנּוּ גָדוֹל בַּבַּיִת הַזֶּה מִמֶּנִּי וְלֹא־חָשַׂךְ מִמֶּנִּי מְאוּמָה

‹ anything ‹ from me ‹ and he has not denied « than I, ‹ in this house ‹ greater ‹ There is no one 9 « in my hand. ‹ has he placed ‹ to him

כִּי אִם־אוֹתָךְ בַּאֲשֶׁר אַתְּ־אִשְׁתּוֹ וְאֵיךְ אֶעֱשֶׂה הָרָעָה הַגְּדֹלָה הַזֹּאת

‹ this great evil ‹ can I perpetrate ‹ how then « are his wife; ‹ you ‹ in that « you, ‹ except for

וְחָטָאתִי לֵאלֹהִים: י וַיְהִי כְּדַבְּרָהּ אֶל־יוֹסֵף יוֹם ׀ יוֹם וְלֹא־שָׁמַע אֵלֶיהָ

‹ to her ‹ he would not listen « [after] day, ‹ day ‹ Joseph ‹ to ‹ as she spoke « And it was, 10 « to God! ‹ and I would be sinning

לִשְׁכַּב אֶצְלָהּ לִהְיוֹת עִמָּהּ: יא וַיְהִי כְּהַיּוֹם הַזֶּה וַיָּבֹא הַבַּיְתָה לַעֲשׂוֹת

‹ to do ‹ to the house ‹ that he came ‹ [on a day] like this day ‹ And it was 11 « with her. ‹ to be « beside her, ‹ to lie

בְּרֵינָא וְיָאֵי בְחֶזְוָא: ז וַהֲוָה בָּתַר פִּתְגָּמַיָּא הָאִלֵּין וּזְקָפַת אִתַּת רִבּוֹנֵהּ יָת עֵינָהָא לְיוֹסֵף וַאֲמֶרֶת שְׁכוּב עִמִּי: ח וְסָרֵיב וַאֲמַר לְוַת אִתַּת רִבּוֹנֵהּ הָא רִבּוֹנִי לָא יָדַע עִמִּי מָא דִבְבֵיתָא וְכֹל דִּי אִית לֵהּ מְסַר בִּידִי: ט לֵית רַב בְּבֵיתָא הָדֵין מִנִּי וְלָא מְנַע מִנִּי מִדַּעַם אֱלָהֵן יָתִיךְ בְּדִיל אַתְּ אִתְּתֵהּ וְאֶכְדֵּין אֶעְבֵּד בִּישְׁתָא רַבְּתָא הָדָא וְאֵחוֹב קֳדָם יְיָ: י וַהֲוָה כַּד מַלֵּילַת עִם יוֹסֵף יוֹם יוֹם וְלָא קַבִּיל מִנַּהּ לְמִשְׁכַּב לְוָתַהּ לְמֶהֱוֵי עִמַּהּ: יא וַהֲוָה בְּיוֹמָא הָדֵין וְעַל לְבֵיתָא לְמִבְדַּק

רש"י

בשערך, אני מגרה בך את הדוב. מיד: (ז) **ותשא אשת אדוניו וגו'**, כל מקום שנא' אחר סמוך (ב"ר מד:ה; תנחומא ח; ב"ר פז:ג־ד): (ט) **וחטאתי לאלהים**. בני נח נלטוו על העריות (סנהדרין נו.): (י) **לשכב אצלה**. אפי' בלא תשמיש (ב"ר פז:ו): **להיות עמה**. לעוה"ב (שם; סוטה ג:): (יא) **ויהי כהיום הזה**. כלומר ויהי כאשר הגיע יום מיוחד, יום צחוק, יום איד שלהם שהלכו כולם לבית ע"ז, אמרה אין לי יום הגון להזקק ליוסף כהיום הזה. אמרה להם חולה אני ואיני יכולה לילך (סוטה לו:; ב"ר שם ז):

7-20. Potiphar's wife slanders Joseph. Joseph spent a year in Potiphar's service (*Seder Olam*). As verse 6 states, Joseph was exceedingly handsome, which, in the plain sense, sets the stage for the lust of Potiphar's wife (*Ramban*), but, as *Rashi* notes from the Midrash, once he became a success in his master's home, Joseph became preoccupied with his appearance and began to curl his hair. God said, "Your father is mourning and you curl your hair! I will incite the bear [Potiphar's wife] against you."

8-9. וַיְמָאֵן — *But he adamantly refused.* Joseph's refusal was constant, categorical, and definitive. He repulsed her with absolute firmness. *Haamek Davar* notes that the Torah gives no reasons for his rejection; his sense of right and wrong was so clear that he did not even consider her pleadings. To her, however, he gave an explanation, trying to convince her to stop pestering him.

It was important to him that she not be angry, because he knew full well that she could cause him great harm, so he tried to make her understand in terms that she could comprehend why he could not please her. It would have been useless to speak to an Egyptian noblewoman of Jewish religious scruples, so he explained that he must be loyal and grateful to the master who employed him, trusted him, and treated him kindly. Only then could he add, almost as an afterthought, that he *would be sinning to God*; apart from wronging your husband, I would also be sinning against God (*Mizrachi*).

10. כְּדַבְּרָהּ אֶל־יוֹסֵף — *As she spoke to Joseph.* She tried to entice him in every way possible: with words; by varying her dress; by threats of imprisonment, humiliation, and physical harm; and by offering him huge sums of money (*Yoma* 35b).

11. וַיְהִי כְּהַיּוֹם הַזֶּה — *And it was [on a day] like this day.* It was an important day — a festival when everyone went to their temple, but Potiphar's wife pleaded illness and stayed home. She reasoned, "I will never have such an opportunity to seduce Joseph כְּהַיּוֹם הַזֶּה, *like this day.*"

מְלַאכְתּ֑וֹ וְאֵ֨ין אִ֜ישׁ מֵאַנְשֵׁ֥י הַבַּ֛יִת שָׁ֖ם בַּבָּֽיִת׃
« in the house — ‹ there ‹ of the house ‹ of the staff ‹ man ‹ — and there was no « his work

12 וַתִּתְפְּשֵׂ֧הוּ בְּבִגְד֛וֹ לֵאמֹ֖ר שִׁכְבָ֣ה עִמִּ֑י וַיַּעֲזֹ֤ב
‹ Then he left « with me! ‹ Lie « saying, ‹ by his garment, ‹ that she caught hold of him 12

בִּגְדוֹ֙ בְּיָדָ֔הּ וַיָּ֖נָס וַיֵּצֵ֥א הַחֽוּצָה׃ 13 וַֽיְהִי֙ כִּרְאוֹתָ֔הּ
‹ [that] when she saw ‹ So it was 13 « to the outside. ‹ and went ‹ and he fled, « in her hand, ‹ his garment

כִּֽי־עָזַ֥ב בִּגְד֖וֹ בְּיָדָ֑הּ וַיָּ֖נָס הַחֽוּצָה׃ 14 וַתִּקְרָ֞א
‹ she called out 14 « to the outside, ‹ and fled ‹ in her hand ‹ his garment ‹ he had left ‹ that

לְאַנְשֵׁ֣י בֵיתָ֗הּ וַתֹּ֤אמֶר לָהֶם֙ לֵאמֹ֔ר רְא֗וּ הֵ֥בִיא
‹ He brought « Look! « saying, ‹ to them ‹ and said ‹ of her household ‹ to the men

לָ֛נוּ אִ֥ישׁ עִבְרִ֖י לְצַ֣חֶק בָּ֑נוּ בָּ֤א אֵלַי֙ לִשְׁכַּ֣ב עִמִּ֔י וָאֶקְרָ֖א בְּק֥וֹל גָּדֽוֹל׃
« that was loud. ‹ with a voice ‹ but I called out ‹ with me, ‹ to lie ‹ to me ‹ He came « with us! ‹ to sport ‹ a Hebrew, ‹ a man, ‹ us

15 וַיְהִ֣י כְשָׁמְע֔וֹ כִּֽי־הֲרִימֹ֥תִי קוֹלִ֖י וָאֶקְרָ֑א וַיַּעֲזֹ֤ב בִּגְדוֹ֙ אֶצְלִ֔י וַיָּ֖נָס וַיֵּצֵ֥א
‹ and went ‹ and fled, ‹ beside me, ‹ his garment ‹ he left « and called out, ‹ my voice ‹ I raised ‹ that ‹ when he heard ‹ And it was 15

הַחֽוּצָה׃ 16 וַתַּנַּ֥ח בִּגְד֖וֹ אֶצְלָ֑הּ עַד־בּ֥וֹא אֲדֹנָ֖יו אֶל־בֵּיתֽוֹ׃ 17 וַתְּדַבֵּ֣ר אֵלָ֔יו
‹ to him ‹ Then she spoke 17 « his house. ‹ to ‹ his master came ‹ until ‹ beside her ‹ his garment ‹ She laid 16 « to the outside!

כַּדְּבָרִ֥ים הָאֵ֖לֶּה לֵאמֹ֑ר בָּֽא־אֵלַ֞י הָעֶ֧בֶד הָעִבְרִ֛י אֲשֶׁר־הֵבֵ֥אתָ לָּ֖נוּ לְצַ֥חֶק
‹ to sport ‹ to us, ‹ you brought ‹ whom ‹ who is a Hebrew, ‹ did the slave ‹ to me ‹ Came « saying, « like these words,

בְּכִתְבֵי חֻשְׁבְּנֵהּ וְלֵית אֱנַשׁ מֵאֱנָשֵׁי בֵיתָא תַּמָּן בְּבֵיתָא: יב וַאֲחַדְתֵּהּ בִּלְבוּשֵׁהּ לְמֵימַר שְׁכוּב עִמִּי וְשָׁבְקֵהּ לִלְבוּשֵׁהּ בִּידַהּ וַעֲרַק וּנְפַק לְשׁוּקָא: יג וַהֲוָה כַּד חֲזַת אֲרֵי שָׁבְקֵהּ לִלְבוּשֵׁהּ בִּידַהּ וַעֲרַק לְשׁוּקָא: יד וּקְרָת לַאֲנָשֵׁי בֵיתַהּ וַאֲמֶרֶת לְהוֹן לְמֵימָר חֲזוֹ אַיְתִי לָנָא גַּבְרָא עִבְרָאָה לְחַיָּכָא בָנָא עַל לְוָתִי לְמִשְׁכַּב עִמִּי וּקְרֵית בְּקָלָא רַבָּא: טו וַהֲוָה כַּד שְׁמַע אֲרֵי אֲרֵימִית קָלִי וּקְרֵית וְשָׁבְקֵהּ לִלְבוּשֵׁהּ לְוָתִי וַעֲרַק וּנְפַק לְשׁוּקָא: טז וַאֲחִתְּתֵהּ לִלְבוּשֵׁהּ לְוָתַהּ עַד עַל רִבּוֹנֵהּ לְבֵיתֵהּ: יז וּמַלֵּילַת עִמֵּהּ כְּפִתְגָּמַיָּא הָאִלֵּין לְמֵימָר עַל לְוָתִי עַבְדָּא עִבְרָאָה דִּי אַיְתֵיתָא לָנָא לְחַיָּכָא בִי:

רש"י

לעשות מלאכתו. רב ושמואל, חד אמר מלאכתו ממש, וחד אמר לעשות צרכיו עמה, אלא שנראית לו דמות דיוקנו של אביו וכו' כדאי' במס' סוטה (שם; ב"ר שם; תנחומא ח־ט): **(יד) ראו הביא לנו.** ה"ז לשון קצרה, הביא לנו ולא פירש מי הביאו, ועל בעלה אומרת כן: **עברי.** מעבר הנהר, מבני עבר (עי' ב"ר מב:ח): **(טו) אדניו.** של יוסף: **(יז) בא**

לַעֲשׂוֹת מְלַאכְתּוֹ — *To do his work.* According to one view in the Talmud (*Sotah* 36b), Joseph's resistance had cracked, and the *work* he came to do was to yield to her advances. But then, the visage of his father appeared to him, saying that if he consorted with her, his name would not be worthy to appear with those of his brothers on the *Kohen Gadol's* Breastplate. When Joseph heard that he would be forfeiting his standing as a building block of the Jewish people, he strengthened his resolve and resisted her importunities.

12-13. וַיַּעֲזֹב בִּגְדוֹ בְּיָדָהּ — *Then he left his garment in her hand.* He could have overpowered her and retrieved his garment, but out of courtesy to his master's wife, he slipped out of it and left it in her hand (*Ramban*). This became Joseph's undoing, for she used the garment as evidence against him. When she saw that he had left his garment and fled, she was afraid that he might expose her to the household or to her husband. Anticipating this, she hurried to them first and made a scene, accusing Joseph of having removed his garment to violate her, "but when he saw that I screamed he fled in confusion" (*Ramban*).

14. הֵבִיא לָנוּ אִישׁ עִבְרִי — *He brought us a man who is a Hebrew.* She played on the prejudices of her fellow Egyptians, who abhorred the Hebrews and would not even eat with them [see 43:32]. Ordinarily, therefore, the Hebrews would never be brought into the house. Potiphar's wife charged that for her husband to have made an exception of this Hebrew slave and even to have appointed him to a position of trust was an affront to them. "No wonder the slave took advantage of it and tried to exploit his position and trifle with our sensibilities!" (*Ramban*).

בִּי: יח וַיְהִי כַּהֲרִימִי קוֹלִי וָאֶקְרָא וַיַּעֲזֹב בִּגְדוֹ אֶצְלִי

‹ beside me, ‹ his garment ‹ he left ‹ and called out, ‹ my voice ‹ *[that] when I raised* ‹ *But it was* **18** ‹‹ *with me.*

וַיָּנָס הַחוּצָה: יט וַיְהִי כִּשְׁמֹעַ אֲדֹנָיו אֶת־דִּבְרֵי

‹ the words ‹ when his master heard ‹ And it was, **19** ‹‹ *to the outside.* ‹ *and fled*

אִשְׁתּוֹ אֲשֶׁר דִּבְּרָה אֵלָיו לֵאמֹר כַּדְּבָרִים הָאֵלֶּה

‹ *Like these things* ‹‹ saying, ‹ to him, ‹ she spoke ‹ which ‹ of his wife

עָשָׂה לִי עַבְדֶּךָ וַיִּחַר אַפּוֹ: כ וַיִּקַּח אֲדֹנֵי יוֹסֵף אֹתוֹ

‹ him ‹‹ of Joseph ‹ – the master did – ‹‹ Then he took **20** ‹‹ did his anger. ‹ flare up ‹‹ *– your slave –* ‹‹ *to me* ‹ *did he do*

וַיִּתְּנֵהוּ אֶל־בֵּית הַסֹּהַר מְקוֹם אֲשֶׁר־° אֲסִירֵי

‹ the prisoners ‹ where ‹ – the place ‹‹ the prison house ‹ to ‹ and gave him over

הַמֶּלֶךְ אֲסוּרִים וַיְהִי־שָׁם בְּבֵית הַסֹּהַר: כא וַיְהִי יהוה אֶת־ [°אסורי כ׳]

‹ with ‹ But HASHEM was **21** ‹‹ in the prison house. ‹ there ‹ and he was ‹‹ were imprisoned – ‹ of the king

יוֹסֵף וַיֵּט אֵלָיו חָסֶד וַיִּתֵּן חִנּוֹ בְּעֵינֵי שַׂר בֵּית־הַסֹּהַר: כב וַיִּתֵּן שַׂר

‹ – the warden ‹‹ And he placed **22** ‹‹ of the prison house. ‹ of the warden ‹ in the eyes ‹ his favor ‹ and He put ‹‹ kindness, ‹ to him ‹ and He directed ‹‹ Joseph,

בֵּית־הַסֹּהַר בְּיַד־יוֹסֵף אֵת כָּל־הָאֲסִירִם אֲשֶׁר בְּבֵית הַסֹּהַר וְאֵת כָּל־

‹ and everything ‹‹ in the prison house, ‹ who were ‹ those imprisoned ‹ all ‹ of Joseph ‹ in the hand ‹‹ of the prison house did –

יח וַהֲוָה כַּד אֲרֵימִית קָלִי וּקְרֵית וְשַׁבְקֵהּ לִלְבוּשֵׁהּ לְוָתִי וַעֲרַק לְשׁוּקָא: יט וַהֲוָה כַּד שְׁמַע רִבּוֹנֵהּ יָת פִּתְגָּמֵי אִתְּתֵהּ דִּי מַלֵּילַת עִמֵּהּ לְמֵימַר כְּפִתְגָּמַיָּא הָאִלֵּין עֲבַד לִי עַבְדָּךְ וּתְקֵף רֻגְזֵהּ: כ וּנְסֵיב רִבּוֹנֵהּ דְּיוֹסֵף יָתֵהּ וּמַנְיֵהּ לְבֵית אֲסִירֵי אֲתַר דִּי אֲסִירֵי מַלְכָּא אֲסִירִין וַהֲוָה תַמָּן בְּבֵית אֲסִירֵי: כא וַהֲוָה מֵימְרָא דַייָ בְּסַעְדֵּהּ דְּיוֹסֵף וּנְגַד לֵהּ חִסְדָּא וִיהָבֵהּ לְרַחֲמִין בְּעֵינֵי רַב בֵּית אֲסִירֵי: כב וּמַנִּי רַב בֵּית אֲסִירֵי בִּידָא דְיוֹסֵף יָת כָּל אֲסִירַיָּא דִּי בְּבֵית אֲסִירֵי וְיָת כָּל

רש״י

אלי. לצחק בי, העבד העברי אשר הבאת לנו: (יט) ויהי כשמוע אדניו וגו׳. בשעת תשמיש אמרה לו כן. וזהו שאמרה **כדברים האלה עשה לי עבדך,** ענייני תשמיש כאלה (ב״ר פז:ט): **(כא) ויט אליו חסד.** שהיה מקובל לכל רואיו, לשון כלה נאה וחסודה שבמשנה (כתובות יז.; כרב״ת):

19. **כַּדְּבָרִים הָאֵלֶּה** — *Like these things.* To infuriate Potiphar, she described the sort of intimate conduct of which she accused Joseph (see *Rashi*).

וַיִּחַר אַפּוֹ — *Flare up did his anger.* By the standards of Egyptian society, Potiphar should have had Joseph killed. That he did not was because of his affection for Joseph; because God protected Joseph; or because — knowing Joseph's righteousness — he doubted his wife's story (*Ibn Ezra; Ramban*). According to the *Yalkut,* Potiphar's daughter Asenath swore to him that Joseph was innocent and told him what really happened. In this merit, she was eventually privileged to marry Joseph [see 41:50].

20. **וַיִּקַּח אֲדֹנֵי יוֹסֵף אֹתוֹ** — *Then he took — the master of Joseph — him.* Potiphar personally escorted Joseph to the prison, a display of his high esteem for the young Hebrew (*Abarbanel*), and an indication that he did not believe his wife's charge. He explained to Joseph that unless he punished him, people would say that his wife was routinely unfaithful and that Potiphar ignored her behavior — and he might not even be the father of their children (*Midrash, Yefeh To'ar*).

God decreed that Joseph be imprisoned for ten years: one year for each of the ten brothers whom he had slandered to Jacob [37:2]. Later, two more years were added in punishment for placing his trust in the Chief of the Cupbearers, instead of in God alone [40:14, 41:1] (*Seder Olam; Tanchuma*).

By presenting in detail the revolting injustice that resulted from a slanderer's malicious charge, the Torah portends the destiny that would befall Israel frequently in its history. As for Joseph — he accepted this misfortune as calmly and with the same unwavering faith in God as he had his ordeal at the hands of his brothers. Even during his imprisonment, his conduct inspired trust and won him honor. In prison, as in Potiphar's home, he rose to authority. Joseph's reaction is an inspiration to all future generations who would be unjustly afflicted (*R' Munk*).

21-23. Prisoner becomes master. Normally, prisoners are the dregs of society, and those accused of a crime like that attributed to Joseph are among the most degraded. But Joseph was admired by everyone, his prison warden and his fellow prisoners alike. Realizing that Joseph was innocent, that Hashem was with him, and that Hashem made him succeed in everything he undertook, the warden put Joseph in charge of the prison and never demanded an accounting of him, nor did he guard him (*Targum Yonasan*).

אֲשֶׁר עֹשִׂים שָׁם הוּא הָיָה עֹשֶׂה: כג אֵין ׀ שַׂר

‹ — the warden ‹‹ [He] did not 23 ‹‹ do. ‹ would ‹ he ‹ there, ‹ they did ‹ that

בֵּית־הַסֹּהַר רֹאֶה אֶת־כָּל־מְאוּמָה בְּיָדוֹ בַּאֲשֶׁר

‹ in that ‹ that was in his hand ‹ iota ‹ any ‹ look over ‹‹ of the prison house —

יהוה אִתּוֹ וַאֲשֶׁר־הוּא עֹשֶׂה יהוה מַצְלִיחַ: פ

‹‹ made successful. ‹ HASHEM ‹ did ‹ he ‹ and whatever ‹‹ was with him; ‹ HASHEM

[מ] שביעי א וַיְהִי אַחַר הַדְּבָרִים הָאֵלֶּה חָטְאוּ מַשְׁקֵה

‹ — the cupbearer ‹‹ that they transgressed ‹ these things ‹ after ‹ And it was 1 40

מֶלֶךְ־מִצְרַיִם וְהָאֹפֶה לַאֲדֹנֵיהֶם לְמֶלֶךְ מִצְרָיִם: ב וַיִּקְצֹף פַּרְעֹה עַל שְׁנֵי

‹ the two ‹ at ‹ Pharaoh was enraged 2 ‹‹ of Egypt. ‹ against the king ‹‹ against their master, ‹‹ and the baker — ‹ of Egypt ‹ of the king

סָרִיסָיו עַל שַׂר הַמַּשְׁקִים וְעַל שַׂר הָאוֹפִים: ג וַיִּתֵּן אֹתָם בְּמִשְׁמַר בֵּית

‹ of the house ‹ in the custody ‹ them ‹ And he put 3 ‹‹ of the Bakers. ‹ the Chief ‹ and at ‹ of the Cupbearers ‹ the Chief ‹ at ‹‹ of his officers,

שַׂר הַטַּבָּחִים אֶל־בֵּית הַסֹּהַר מְקוֹם אֲשֶׁר יוֹסֵף אָסוּר שָׁם: ד וַיִּפְקֹד

‹‹ He appointed 4 ‹‹ there. ‹ was imprisoned ‹ Joseph ‹ where ‹ the place ‹‹ the prison house, ‹ into ‹ of the Butchers, ‹ of the Chief

שַׂר הַטַּבָּחִים אֶת־יוֹסֵף אִתָּם וַיְשָׁרֶת אֹתָם וַיִּהְיוּ יָמִים בְּמִשְׁמָר:

‹‹ in custody. ‹ [for a period of] days ‹ and they were ‹‹ them ‹ and he served ‹‹ [to be] with them, ‹ Joseph ‹‹ of the Butchers — ‹ — the Chief

ה וַיַּחַלְמוּ חֲלוֹם שְׁנֵיהֶם אִישׁ חֲלֹמוֹ בְּלַיְלָה אֶחָד אִישׁ כְּפִתְרוֹן חֲלֹמוֹ

‹‹ of his dream ‹ according to the interpretation ‹ each man ‹‹ on the same night, ‹ [had] his dream ‹ each man ‹ — both of them, ‹‹ a dream ‹ They dreamt 5

דִּי עָבְדִין תַּמָּן בְּמֵימְרֵהּ הֲוָה מִתְעֲבֵד: כג לֵית רַב בֵּית אֲסִירֵי חָזֵי יָת כָּל סָרְחָן בִּידֵהּ בְּדִי מֵימְרָא דַייָ בְּסַעְדֵּהּ וְדִי הוּא עָבֵד יְיָ מַצְלַח: א וַהֲוָה בָּתַר פִּתְגָּמַיָּא הָאִלֵּין סְרָחוּ שָׁקְיָא מַלְכָּא דְמִצְרַיִם וְנַחְתּוֹמֵי לְרִבּוֹנֵיהוֹן לְמַלְכָּא דְמִצְרָיִם: ב וּרְגַז פַּרְעֹה עַל תְּרֵין רַבְרְבָנוֹהִי עַל רַב שָׁקֵי וְעַל רַב נַחְתּוֹמֵי: ג וִיהַב יָתְהוֹן בְּמַטְּרָא בֵּית רַב קָטוֹלַיָּא לְבֵית אֲסִירֵי אֲתַר דִּי יוֹסֵף אָסִיר תַּמָּן: ד וּמַנִּי רַב קָטוֹלַיָּא יָת יוֹסֵף עִמְּהוֹן וְשַׁמֵּשׁ יָתְהוֹן וַהֲווֹ יוֹמִין בְּמַטְּרָא: ה וַחֲלָמוּ חֶלְמָא תַּרְוֵיהוֹן גְּבַר חֶלְמֵהּ בְּלֵילְיָא חַד גְּבַר כְּפוּשְׁרַן חֶלְמֵהּ

רש"י

(כב) הוא היה עשה. כתרגומו, במימריה הוה מתעביד: **(כג) באשר ה' אתו.** בשביל שה' אתו (תרגום יונתן): **(א) אחר הדברים האלה.** לפי שהרגילה אותה ארורה את הצדיק בפי כלם לדבר בו בגנותו, הביא להם הקב"ה סורחנם של אלו שיפנו אליהם ולא אליו (ב"ר פח:א), ועוד שתבוא הרווחה לצדיק על ידיהם (שם ג; ברכ"ת; פס"ז): **חטאו.** זה נמצא זבוב בפיילי פוטירין שלו, וזה נמצא צרור בגלוסקין שלו (ב"ר פח:ב): **והאופה.** את פת המלך, ואין לשון אופייה אלא בפת. ובלע"ז פישטו"ר: **(ד) ויפקד שר הטבחים את יוסף.** להיות אתם: **ויהיו ימים במשמר.** שנים עשר חדש (פס"ז; עי' כתובות כז:): **(ה) ויחלמו חלום שניהם.** ויחלמו שניהם חלום זהו

40.

⇜ Joseph interprets dreams in prison.

1. חָטְאוּ מַשְׁקֵה . . . וְהָאֹפֶה — *That they transgressed — the cupbearer . . . and the baker.* In the case of the cupbearer, a fly was found in Pharaoh's goblet of wine, while in the case of the baker, a pebble was found in the king's bread (*Rashi* from Midrash).

The cupbearer's offense was less serious, since a fly could have flown into the wine at any time, and presumably was not in the goblet when the cupbearer originally prepared and served it. That is why the cupbearer was restored to his position (v. 21). The baker, however, was guilty of negligence since a pebble must have been in the dough or oven all along (*Mizrachi; Gur Aryeh*). Furthermore, the presence of a pebble was a more serious offense since it could have choked Pharaoh, whereas a dead fly, while repulsive, is harmless (*Radak*).

3. בְּמִשְׁמַר — *In the custody,* a place where they could be kept under guard (*Ibn Ezra*), pending a decision on their sentence (*Bereishis Rabbasi*). They remained in the prison for a year (*Rashi,* v. 3).

5. אִישׁ כְּפִתְרוֹן חֲלֹמוֹ — *Each man according to the interpretation*

הַמַּשְׁקֶה וְהָאֹפֶה אֲשֶׁר לְמֶלֶךְ מִצְרַיִם אֲשֶׁר
‹ who ‹‹ of Egypt, ‹ to the king ‹ who were ‹ and the baker ‹ — the cupbearer

אֲסוּרִים בְּבֵית הַסֹּהַר: ו וַיָּבֹא אֲלֵיהֶם יוֹסֵף בַּבֹּקֶר
‹‹ in the morning. ‹ did Joseph ‹ to them ‹ Come **6** ‹‹ in the prison house. ‹ imprisoned

וַיַּרְא אֹתָם וְהִנָּם זֹעֲפִים: ז וַיִּשְׁאַל אֶת־סְרִיסֵי
‹ the officers ‹ And he asked **7** ‹‹ distraught. ‹ and they were ‹ them ‹ He saw

פַרְעֹה אֲשֶׁר אִתּוֹ בְמִשְׁמַר בֵּית אֲדֹנָיו לֵאמֹר
‹‹ saying, ‹‹ of his master, ‹ of the house ‹ in the custody ‹ with him ‹ who were ‹ of Pharaoh

שָׁקְיָא וְנַחְתּוֹמֵי דִּי לְמַלְכָּא דְמִצְרַיִם דִּי אֲסִירִין בְּבֵית אֲסִירֵי: ו וַאֲתָא לְוָתְהוֹן יוֹסֵף בְּצַפְרָא וַחֲזָא יָתְהוֹן וְהָא אִנּוּן נְסִיסִין: ז וּשְׁאֵל יָת רַבְרְבֵי פַרְעֹה דִּי עִמֵּהּ בְּמַטְּרַת בֵּית רִבּוֹנֵהּ לְמֵימָר מָא דֵין אַפֵּיכוֹן בִּישִׁין יוֹמָא דֵין: ח וַאֲמָרוּ לֵהּ חֶלְמָא חֲלֵמְנָא וּפָשַׁר לֵית לֵהּ וַאֲמַר לְהוֹן יוֹסֵף הֲלָא מִן קֳדָם יְיָ פּוּשְׁרַן חֶלְמַיָּא אִשְׁתָּעוּ כְעַן לִי: ט וְאִשְׁתָּעִי רַב שָׁקֵי יָת חֶלְמֵהּ לְיוֹסֵף וַאֲמַר לֵהּ בְּחֶלְמִי וְהָא גּוּפְנָא קֳדָמָי: י וּבְגוּפְנָא תְּלָתָא שִׁבְשִׁין וְהִיא כַד אַפְרַחַת אַפֵּקַת לַבְלְבִין וַאֲנֵיצַת נֵץ בַּשִּׁילוּ אִתְכַּלְתָּהָא

מַדּוּעַ פְּנֵיכֶם רָעִים הַיּוֹם: ח וַיֹּאמְרוּ אֵלָיו חֲלוֹם חָלַמְנוּ וּפֹתֵר אֵין אֹתוֹ
‹‹ *for it.* ‹ *there is not* ‹ *but an interpreter* ‹‹ *we dreamt,* ‹ *A dream* ‹‹ to him, ‹ And they said **8** ‹‹ *today?* ‹ *downcast* ‹ *are your faces* ‹ *Why*

וַיֹּאמֶר אֲלֵהֶם יוֹסֵף הֲלוֹא לֵאלֹהִים פִּתְרֹנִים סַפְּרוּ־נָא לִי: ט וַיְסַפֵּר
‹‹ Then he recounted **9** ‹‹ *to me.* ‹ *please* ‹ *Recount [it],* ‹‹ *interpretations?!* ‹ *to God* ‹ *Are not* ‹‹ Joseph did, ‹‹ to them, ‹ So he said

שַׂר־הַמַּשְׁקִים אֶת־חֲלֹמוֹ לְיוֹסֵף וַיֹּאמֶר לוֹ בַּחֲלוֹמִי וְהִנֵּה־גֶפֶן לְפָנָי:
‹‹ *in front of me.* ‹ *a grapevine* ‹ *I beheld* ‹‹ *In my dream,* ‹‹ to him, ‹ and said ‹‹ to Joseph, ‹ his dream ‹‹ of the Cupbearers — ‹ — the Chief

י וּבַגֶּפֶן שְׁלֹשָׁה שָׂרִיגִם וְהִוא כְפֹרַחַת עָלְתָה נִצָּהּ הִבְשִׁילוּ אַשְׁכְּלֹתֶיהָ
‹ *did its clusters* ‹ *and ripen* ‹‹ *did its blossoms,* ‹ *bloom* ‹‹ *as it budded,* ‹ *and it was* ‹‹ *tendrils;* ‹ *were three* ‹ *On the grapevine* **10**

רש"י

פשוטו. ומדרשו כל אחד חלם חלום שניהם שחלם את חלומו ופתרון חבירו (ב"ר פח:ד). וזה שנאמר וירא שר האופים כי טוב פתר (ברכות נה:): **איש כפתרון חלומו.** כל אחד חלם חלום הדומה לפתרון העתיד לבא עליהם: (ו) **זועפים.** עצבים כמו סר וזעף (מלכים א כ:ד) זעף ה' אשא (מיכה ז:ט): (י) **שריגם.** זמורות ארוכות שקורין וידי"ץ:

והיא כפרחת. דומה לפורחת. והיא כפורחת, נדמה לי בחלומי כאילו היא פורחת, ואחר הפרח עלתה נצה ונעשו סמדר, אשפני"ר בלע"ז, ואחר כך הבשילו. והיא כד אפרחת אפיקת לבלבין, עד כאן תרגום של פורחת. נץ גדול מפרח, כדכתיב ובוסר גומל יהיה נצה (ישעיה יח:ה), וכתיב ויוצא פרח והדר ויצץ ציץ (במדבר יז:כג):

of his dream. The narrative and subject matter of the dream was so consistent with Joseph's later interpretations that when he explained them, the chiefs realized that he was surely right. According to the Midrash, each one dreamt what would eventually happen to his colleague (but not to himself), so that when each one heard how Joseph interpreted the other one's dream, it was clear that he was right (*Rashi*).

Ibn Ezra and *Radak* comment that each dream contained an accurate vision of the future, verifying that it was a true dream — not a fantasy.

הַמַּשְׁקֶה וְהָאֹפֶה — *The cupbearer and the baker.* No longer are they called שַׂר, *chief.* Their incarceration had broken their spirits and they felt like helpless servants, rather than officials (*Sforno*).

8. וּפֹתֵר אֵין אֹתוֹ — *But an interpreter there is not for it,* no one can explain the prophetic portents of the dream. Apparently they had sent for interpreters, or perhaps there were others with them in prison, but none could interpret it. Or the implication of their remark could be: "These dreams are so difficult that no one in the world can interpret them" (*Ramban*).

Joseph answered that just as God sends the dream, so He grants man the wisdom to interpret it; otherwise, the dream would have been in vain. Therefore *relate it to me* — perhaps God will give me the wisdom to interpret it (*Radak*). Man can interpret a dream only because he is formed in God's image. Consequently, even a despised slave in prison may be God's agent to interpret it (*Sforno*).

10. שְׁלֹשָׁה שָׂרִיגִם — *Three tendrils.* Since there are usually many more than three tendrils on a vine, Joseph perceived a special significance in this number (*Daas Sofrim*). And since the dream showed that the grapes blossomed very rapidly, he understood that the allusion was to three days rather than three months or years (*Ramban*).

עֲנָבִים: יא וְכוֹס פַּרְעֹה בְּיָדִי וָאֶקַּח אֶת־הָעֲנָבִים

« the grapes, ‹ and I took ‹ was in my hand ‹ of Pharaoh ‹ And the cup 11 « into grapes.

וָאֶשְׂחַט אֹתָם אֶל־כּוֹס פַּרְעֹה וָאֶתֵּן אֶת־הַכּוֹס

‹ the cup ‹ and I placed « of Pharaoh, ‹ the cup ‹ into ‹ them ‹ I squeezed

עַל־כַּף פַּרְעֹה: יב וַיֹּאמֶר לוֹ יוֹסֵף זֶה פִּתְרֹנוֹ

« its interpretation: ‹ This is « Joseph did, « to him, ‹ He said 12 « of Pharaoh. ‹ the palm ‹ on

שְׁלֹשֶׁת הַשָּׂרִגִים שְׁלֹשֶׁת יָמִים הֵם: יג בְּעוֹד ׀

‹ In another 13 « they are. ‹ days ‹ – three « tendrils ‹ The three

שְׁלֹשֶׁת יָמִים יִשָּׂא פַרְעֹה אֶת־רֹאשֶׁךָ וַהֲשִׁיבְךָ

‹ and he will restore you ‹ your head ‹ will Pharaoh ‹ raise up « days, ‹ three

עַל־כַּנֶּךָ וְנָתַתָּ כוֹס־פַּרְעֹה בְּיָדוֹ כַּמִּשְׁפָּט הָרִאשׁוֹן אֲשֶׁר הָיִיתָ מַשְׁקֵהוּ:

« his cupbearer. ‹ you were ‹ when ‹ originally ‹ as was the practice « in his hand, ‹ of Pharaoh ‹ the cup ‹ and you will place « your post, ‹ to

יד כִּי אִם־זְכַרְתַּנִי אִתְּךָ כַּאֲשֶׁר יִיטַב לָךְ וְעָשִׂיתָ־נָּא עִמָּדִי חָסֶד

« a kindness, ‹ to me ‹ please, ‹ and you would do, « for you, ‹ it will go well ‹ when ‹ with yourself ‹ you would think of me ‹ if ‹ For then 14

וְהִזְכַּרְתַּנִי אֶל־פַּרְעֹה וְהוֹצֵאתַנִי מִן־הַבַּיִת הַזֶּה: טו כִּי־גֻנֹּב גֻּנַּבְתִּי מֵאֶרֶץ

‹ from the land ‹ indeed I was kidnapped ‹ For 15 « this house. ‹ of ‹ you would [thereby] take me out « Pharaoh, ‹ to ‹ that you should mention me

הָעִבְרִים וְגַם־פֹּה לֹא־עָשִׂיתִי מְאוּמָה כִּי־שָׂמוּ אֹתִי בַּבּוֹר: טז וַיַּרְא

‹ See 16 « in the pit. ‹ me ‹ them to have put ‹ for ‹ anything ‹ I have not done ‹ here ‹ and even « of the Hebrews,

עִנְבִין: יא וְכַסָּא דְפַרְעֹה בִּידִי וּנְסֵיבִית יָת עִנְבַיָּא וַעֲצָרִית יָתְהוֹן עַל כַּסָּא דְפַרְעֹה וִיהָבִית יָת כַּסָּא עַל יְדָא דְפַרְעֹה: יב וַאֲמַר לֵהּ יוֹסֵף דֵּין פִּשְׁרָנֵהּ תְּלָתָא שִׁבְשִׁין תְּלָתָא יוֹמִין אִנּוּן: יג בְּסוֹף תְּלָתָא יוֹמִין יִדְכַּר פַּרְעֹה יָת רֵישָׁךְ וִיתֵיבִנָּךְ עַל שִׁמּוּשָׁךְ וְתִתֵּן כַּסָּא דְפַרְעֹה בִּידֵהּ כְּהִלְכְתָא קַדְמָאָה דִּי הֲוֵיתָא מַשְׁקֵי לֵהּ: יד אֱלָהֵן תִּדְכְּרִנַּנִי עִמָּךְ כַּד יֵיטַב לָךְ וְתַעְבֵּד כְּעַן עִמִּי טֵיבוּ וְתִדְכַּר עָלַי קֳדָם פַּרְעֹה וְתַפְּקִנַּנִי מִן בֵּית אֲסִירָא הָדֵין: טו אֲרֵי מִגְנַב גְּנֵיבְנָא מֵאַרְעָא דְעִבְרָאֵי וְאַף הָכָא לָא עֲבָדִית מִדַּעַם אֲרֵי שַׁוִּיאוּ יָתִי בְּבֵית אֲסִירֵי: טז וַחֲזָא

רש"י

(יא) ואשחט. כתרגומו ועלרית, והרבה יש בלשון משנה: **(יב) שלשת ימים הם.** סימן הם לך לשלשת ימים, ויש מדרשי אגדה הרבה (ב"ר פח:ה; חולין לב.): **(יג) ישא פרעה את ראשך.** לשון חשבון, כשיפקוד שאר עבדיו לשרת לפניו בסעודה ימנה אותך עמהם: **כנך.** בסיס שלך ומושבך: **(יד) כי אם זכרתני אתך.** אחר אם זכרתני אתך, מאחר שייטב לך כפתרוני: **ועשית נא עמדי חסד.** אין נא אלא ל' בקשה [הרי אתה עושה עמי חסד] (ברכות ט.):

13. יִשָּׂא פַרְעֹה אֶת־רֹאשֶׁךָ — *Raise up will Pharaoh your head.* The idiom *raise up your head* means *to count* [cf. *Exodus* 30:12]. The sense here is that when Pharaoh will assemble his other servants to wait upon him during the meal, *he will count you among them* (*Rashi*).

14. וְהִזְכַּרְתַּנִי אֶל־פַּרְעֹה — *That you should mention me to Pharaoh.* Your words will carry weight with the king, since you will be an important official (*Radak*). Your return to prominence in accordance with my interpretation will be so astounding that you will need merely to mention me to Pharaoh to have me freed from prison (*Rashbam*). Please tell him that I am worthy of serving kings, or ask that I be released to serve you, as I did here in prison (*Tur*).

15. כִּי־גֻנֹּב גֻּנַּבְתִּי מֵאֶרֶץ הָעִבְרִים — *For indeed I was kidnaped from the land of the Hebrews.* Joseph mentioned his background and the injustice in order to persuade the cupbearer that justice and fairness dictated that he intercede to free Joseph from prison. "Do not think you would be committing an injustice by praising me and being instrumental in securing my release from jail, for I am not a slave by birth. I am really innocent and should not have been here in the first place!" (*Rashbam; Ramban*). It is noteworthy that this was the very first time throughout all Joseph's trials that he broke his silence and protested his innocence.

Apparently, Joseph told Potiphar that he was a Hebrew [39:14]. The territory around Hebron, where the Patriarchs resided, was referred to as the land of the *Ivrim* [*Hebrews*], not because the Canaanites acknowledged it as *belonging* to a differ-

שַׂר־הָאֹפִים כִּי טוֹב פָּתָר וַיֹּאמֶר אֶל־יוֹסֵף אַף־
‹ Also ‹‹ Joseph, ‹ to ‹ so he said ‹‹ had he interpreted, ‹ favorably ‹ that ‹ of the Bakers ‹ did the Chief

אֲנִי בַּחֲלוֹמִי וְהִנֵּה שְׁלֹשָׁה סַלֵּי חֹרִי עַל־רֹאשִׁי׃
‹‹ my head. ‹ on ‹ of wicker ‹ baskets ‹ three ‹ I beheld ‹‹ In my dream, ‹‹ I!

17 וּבַסַּל הָעֶלְיוֹן מִכֹּל מַאֲכַל פַּרְעֹה מַעֲשֵׂה אֹפֶה
‹‹ of a baker— ‹ —products ‹‹ [for] Pharaoh ‹ of food ‹ [were] all kinds ‹ that was uppermost ‹ And in the basket

18 וְהָעוֹף אֹכֵל אֹתָם מִן־הַסַּל מֵעַל רֹאשִׁי׃ וַיַּעַן יוֹסֵף וַיֹּאמֶר זֶה פִּתְרֹנוֹ
‹‹ its interpretation: ‹ This is ‹‹ and said, ‹ Joseph responded 18 ‹‹ my head. ‹ above ‹ the basket ‹ from ‹ them ‹ were eating ‹ and the birds

19 שְׁלֹשֶׁת הַסַּלִּים שְׁלֹשֶׁת יָמִים הֵם׃ בְּעוֹד ׀ שְׁלֹשֶׁת יָמִים יִשָּׂא פַרְעֹה
‹ will Pharaoh ‹ lift up ‹ days, ‹ three ‹ In another 19 ‹‹ they are. ‹ days ‹ —three ‹ baskets ‹ The three

רַב נַחְתּוֹמֵי אֲרֵי יָאוּת פְּשַׁר וַאֲמַר
לְיוֹסֵף אַף אֲנָא בְּחֶלְמִי וְהָא
תְּלָתָא סַלִּין דְּחִירוּ עַל רֵישִׁי:
יז וּבְסַלָּא עִלָּאָה מִכֹּל מֵיכַל פַּרְעֹה
עוֹבַד נַחְתּוֹם וְעוֹפָא אָכֵל יָתְהוֹן
מִן סַלָּא מֵעִלָּוֵי רֵישִׁי: יח וַאֲתֵיב
יוֹסֵף וַאֲמַר דֵּין פִּשְׁרָנֵהּ תְּלָתָא
סַלִּין תְּלָתָא יוֹמִין אִנּוּן: יט בְּסוֹף
תְּלָתָא יוֹמִין יַעְדִּי פַּרְעֹה

רש"י

(טז) סלי חורי. סלים של נצרים קלופים חורין חורין, ובמקומנו יש הרבה, ודרך מוכרי פת כסנין שקורין אובלידי"ש לתתם באותם סלים:

ent nation, but because of the prominence achieved by the descendants of Abraham, who was acknowledged by the inhabitants as a *prince of God* [23:6] (*Ramban*).

Indeed, the Sages praise Joseph for proudly describing himself as a Hebrew. Because of this, he earned the privilege of being buried in *Eretz Yisrael.* Moses, however, told Jethro's daughters that he was an Egyptian (see *Exodus* 2:19), and he was denied burial in the Holy Land (*Devarim Rabbah* 2:5).

Faith and trust: the error of Joseph's request.

Because Joseph placed his trust in the Chief instead of in God Himself, his prison sentence was increased by two years (*Seder Olam; Tanchuma; Shemos Rabbah*). In a comment that seems to be contradictory, the Midrash (*Bereishis Rabbah* 89:3) describes Joseph as someone who placed his complete trust in God — and that this is *why* he was punished for asking the cupbearer to help him! But if it was wrong to ask for human intercession, how could Joseph be described as someone with trust in God?

Faith and trust cannot be defined with exactitude. There are infinite degrees of faith and trust. Someone as great as Joseph, who knew with certainty that God determines everything, should not have sought his salvation through the cupbearer or any other human agency. Just as God had caused Joseph to be imprisoned, He would cause him to be freed, if and when that was His wish. For a lesser person, it would have been *sinful* to ignore the opportunity presented by the imminent freedom of the cupbearer. An ordinary person would have been hypocritical to sit and wait for miracles; he did not have sufficient faith and trust to do so. But Joseph was praised by the Sages for his high degree of spiritual purity. He truly saw God everywhere, so he should not have relied on any human, especially his immoral, arrogant fellow prisoner.

R' Bachya comments that Joseph asked for the cupbearer's help because he realized that Providence had put the chiefs in prison with him so that they and their dreams would become the means of his freedom. He was right about God's intervention — because God customarily assists the righteous through natural means — but it was wrong for a man as great as Joseph to seek human intervention. He should have allowed God to work His way as He saw fit.

The commentators explain that there is a difference between faith [אֱמוּנָה] and trust [בִּטָּחוֹן]. "Faith" is belief that God exists. "Trust" is the conviction that God is involved in events and that their outcome accords with *His* will. In the words of the *Chazon Ish*: "Unless the future has been clarified by prophecy, the future is not definite, for who can know God's judgment or His deeds? Rather, trust involves the faith that there is no coincidence in the world and that every occurrence under the sun was by His proclamation."

16. כִּי טוֹב פָּתָר — *That favorably had he interpreted.* The implication is that the baker had not planned to tell his dream to Joseph, but when he saw that the interpretation of his colleague's dream was logical, he changed his mind. Or, it may be that he changed his mind when he heard that Joseph had interpreted the dream in a *favorable* [טוֹב] manner, and he hoped for a similarly cheerful interpretation of his own dream [especially since his dream did not seem to be as favorable as that of the cupbearer] (*Ramban*).

17. וְהָעוֹף אֹכֵל אֹתָם — *And the birds were eating them.* Not only did the birds eat Pharaoh's food, they had the impudence to eat it right off the basket on the baker's head, and he was powerless to stop them! That fearlessness on the part of the birds was a clue to the dream's meaning, for no bird would have the temerity to do that to a living person (*R' Hirsch*).

[Additionally, whereas the cupbearer was an active participant in realistic events in his dream, indicating a prophetic dream, the baker was an observer, watching an inactive image of himself in a symbolic dream.]

אֶת־רֹאשְׁךָ֙ מֵֽעָלֶ֔יךָ וְתָלָ֥ה אוֹתְךָ֖ עַל־עֵ֑ץ
« a tree; ‹ on ‹ you ‹ and he will hang ‹ from upon you ‹ your head

וְאָכַ֥ל הָע֛וֹף אֶת־בְּשָׂרְךָ֖ מֵֽעָלֶֽיךָ׃ מפטיר כ וַיְהִ֣י ׀
‹ And it was 20 « from upon you. ‹ your flesh ‹ will birds ‹ and eat

בַּיּ֣וֹם הַשְּׁלִישִׁ֗י י֚וֹם הֻלֶּ֣דֶת אֶת־פַּרְעֹ֔ה וַיַּ֥עַשׂ
‹ that he made « Pharaoh, ‹ of ‹ of the birth ‹ the day « on the third day,

מִשְׁתֶּ֖ה לְכָל־עֲבָדָ֑יו וַיִּשָּׂ֞א אֶת־רֹ֣אשׁ ׀ שַׂ֣ר הַמַּשְׁקִ֗ים וְאֶת־רֹ֛אשׁ שַׂ֥ר
‹ of the Chief ‹ and the head ‹ of the Cupbearers ‹ of the Chief ‹ the head ‹ and he counted « his servants, ‹ for all ‹ a feast

הָאֹפִ֖ים בְּת֥וֹךְ עֲבָדָֽיו׃ כא וַיָּ֛שֶׁב אֶת־שַׂ֥ר הַמַּשְׁקִ֖ים עַל־מַשְׁקֵ֑הוּ וַיִּתֵּ֥ן
‹ and he placed ‹ his cupbearing ‹ to ‹ of the Cupbearers ‹ the Chief ‹ He restored 21 « his servants. ‹ among ‹ of the Bakers

הַכּ֖וֹס עַל־כַּ֥ף פַּרְעֹֽה׃ כב וְאֵ֛ת שַׂ֥ר הָאֹפִ֖ים תָּלָ֑ה כַּאֲשֶׁ֥ר פָּתַ֛ר לָהֶ֖ם יוֹסֵֽף׃
« did Joseph. ‹ to them ‹ interpret ‹ just as « he hanged, ‹ of the Bakers ‹ But the Chief 22 « of Pharaoh. ‹ the palm ‹ on ‹ the cup

כג וְלֹֽא־זָכַ֧ר שַׂר־הַמַּשְׁקִ֛ים אֶת־יוֹסֵ֖ף וַיִּשְׁכָּחֵֽהוּ׃ פפפ קי״ב פסוקים. יב״ק סימן.
« rather, he forgot him. ‹ about Joseph, ‹ of the Cupbearers ‹ [did] the Chief « Yet remember not 23

יָת רֵישָׁךְ מִנָּךְ וְיִצְלוֹב יָתָךְ עַל צְלִיבָא וְיֵכוּל עוֹפָא יָת בִּשְׂרָךְ מִנָּךְ: כ וַהֲוָה בְּיוֹמָא תְלִיתָאָה יוֹם בֵּית וַלְדָא דְפַרְעֹה וַעֲבַד מִשְׁתְּיָא לְכָל עַבְדוֹהִי וּדְכַר יָת רֵישׁ רַב שָׁקֵי וְיָת רֵישׁ רַב נַחְתּוֹמֵי בְּגוֹ עַבְדוֹהִי: כא וַאֲתֵיב יָת רַב שָׁקֵי עַל שַׁקְיוּתֵהּ וִיהַב יָת כַּסָּא עַל יְדָא דְפַרְעֹה: כב וְיָת רַב נַחְתּוֹמֵי צְלַב כְּמָא דִי פָשַׁר לְהוֹן יוֹסֵף: כג וְלָא דְכִיר רַב שָׁקֵי יָת יוֹסֵף וְאַנְשְׁיֵהּ:

THE HAFTARAH FOR VAYEISHEV APPEARS ON PAGE 343.

When Chanukah coincides with Vayeishev, the regular Maftir is replaced with the Chanukah reading: first day Chanukah, page 355 (7:1-17); second day Chanukah page 357 (7:18-23). And the regular Haftarah is replaced with the reading for Shabbas Chanukah, page 362.

רש״י

(כ) יום הלדת את פרעה. יום לידתו וקורין לו יום גינוסיא (ב״ר פח:ו; ע״ז י.). ולשון הולדת לפי שאין הולד נולד אלא על ידי אחרים, שהחיה מילדת את האשה, ועל כן החיה נקראת מילדת. וכן ומולדותיך ביום הולדת אותך (יחזקאל טז:ד), וכן אחרי הוכבס את הנגע (ויקרא יג:נה) שכיבוסו על ידי אחרים: **וישא את ראש וגו׳.** מנאם עם שאר עבדיו, שהיה מונה המשרתים שישרתו לו בסעודתו, וזכר את אלו בתוכם, כמו שאו את ראש (במדבר א:ב) ל׳ מנין: **(כג) ולא זכר שר המשקים.** בו ביום (ב״ר פח:ז): **וישכחהו.** לאחר מכאן. מפני שתלה בו יוסף לזכרו הוזקק להיות אסור שתי שנים, שנאמר אשרי הגבר אשר שם ה׳ מבטחו ולא פנה אל רהבים (תהלים מ:ה), ולא בטח על מצרים הקרויים רהב (ב״ר פט:ג):

19. יִשָּׂא פַרְעֹה אֶת־רֹאשְׁךָ מֵעָלֶיךָ — *Lift up will Pharaoh your head from upon you.* This term יִשָּׂא רֹאשׁ, *lift up the head*, is used here in the literal sense meaning: *he will behead you.*

20. יוֹם הֻלֶּדֶת אֶת־פַּרְעֹה — *The day of the birth of Pharaoh.* According to *Rashi,* it was literally his birthday. *R' Bachya,* following *Radak,* interprets that a son was born to Pharaoh on that day. As crown prince, the baby was named Pharaoh because he would eventually ascend to the throne.

22. כַּאֲשֶׁר פָּתַר לָהֶם יוֹסֵף — *Just as interpreted to them did Joseph.* The verse implies that the fates of the chiefs were dictated by Joseph's interpretations (*Sforno*) in order to prove his veracity and pave the way for his future elevation (*Abarbanel*).

23. וְלֹא־זָכַר. . . וַיִּשְׁכָּחֵהוּ — *Yet remember not . . . about Joseph* on the day he was free; and *he forgot him* subsequently (*Rashi*).

The Midrash perceives another intent of this verse: Only the *chief* forgot Joseph, but the Holy One, Blessed is He, remembered him very well, as the events in the next *Sidrah* will graphically portray.

It is normal and proper for people to seek out avenues for their rescue, as Joseph had done. His mistake was in not recognizing that the entire episode of the chiefs' imprisonment and dreams had been brought about by God as a means of helping Joseph. He should have seen that God was in the process of saving him and so there was no need to ask for the cupbearer's help (*R' Moshe Feinstein*).

☙ **קי״ב פסוקים. יב״ק סימן.** — This Masoretic note means: There are 112 verses in *Vayeishev,* numerically corresponding to the mnemonic יַבֵּק.

The root of the word is בקק, *emptying out.* The allusion is that this *Sidrah* contains the beginning of the process which was to culminate in Israel's first exile, the process by which Jacob and his family were *emptied out* of their native land and forced to spend 210 years in Egypt (*R' David Feinstein*).

PARASHAS MIKEITZ / פרשת מקץ

[מא] א וַיְהִי מִקֵּץ שְׁנָתַיִם יָמִים וּפַרְעֹה חֹלֵם

<< was dreaming, < Pharaoh << of days: < of two years < at the end < It was 1 — 41

וְהִנֵּה עֹמֵד עַל־הַיְאֹר: ב וְהִנֵּה מִן־הַיְאֹר עֹלֹת

< were coming up < of the River < that out < when he beheld 2 << the River, < over < [that] he was standing < and he beheld

שֶׁבַע פָּרוֹת יְפוֹת מַרְאֶה וּבְרִיאֹת בָּשָׂר וַתִּרְעֶינָה

< and they were grazing < of flesh, < and robust < of appearance < beautiful < cows, < seven

בָּאָחוּ: ג וְהִנֵּה שֶׁבַע פָּרוֹת אֲחֵרוֹת עֹלוֹת אַחֲרֵיהֶן מִן־הַיְאֹר רָעוֹת

< — ugly << of the River < out < after them < coming up < other cows < seven < Then he beheld 3 << in the marshland.

מַרְאֶה וְדַקּוֹת בָּשָׂר וַתַּעֲמֹדְנָה אֵצֶל הַפָּרוֹת עַל־שְׂפַת הַיְאֹר:

<< of the River. < the bank < on < the cows < next to < and they stood << of flesh; < and gaunt < of appearance

ד וַתֹּאכַלְנָה הַפָּרוֹת רָעוֹת הַמַּרְאֶה וְדַקֹּת הַבָּשָׂר אֵת שֶׁבַע הַפָּרוֹת יְפֹת

< beautiful < cows < the seven << of flesh, < and gaunt < of appearance < ugly < did the cows, << They ate, 4

אונקלוס

א וַהֲוָה מִסוֹף תַּרְתֵּין שְׁנִין וּפַרְעֹה חָלֵם וְהָא קָאֵם עַל נַהֲרָא: ב וְהָא מִן נַהֲרָא סָלְקָן שְׁבַע תּוֹרָן שַׁפִּירָן לְמֶחֱזֵי וּפַטִּימָן בְּשַׂר וְרָעְיָן בְּאַחֲוָה: ג וְהָא שְׁבַע תּוֹרָן אָחֳרָנְיָן סָלִיקָא בַּתְרֵיהוֹן מִן נַהֲרָא בִּישָׁן לְמֶחֱזֵי וַחֲסִירַן בְּשַׂר וְקָמָן לְקִבְלֵיהוֹן דְתוֹרָן עַל כֵּיף נַהֲרָא: ד וַאֲכָלָא תוֹרָתָא בִּישָׁן לְמֶחֱזֵי וַחֲסִירַן בְּשַׂר יָת שְׁבַע תּוֹרָתָא שַׁפִּירָן

רש"י

(א) **ויהי מקץ.** כתרגומו, מסוף. וכל לשון קץ סוף הוא (עי' ערכין כח:): **על היאור.** כל שאר נהרות אינם קרוין יאורים חוץ מנילוס, מפני שכל הארץ עשויה יאורים יאורים בידי אדם ונילוס עולה בתוכם ומשקה אותם (עי' שמות ז:יט רש"י ד"ה יאריהם) לפי שאין גשמים יורדין במצרים תדיר כשאר ארצות (דברים יא:י-יא): (ב) **יפות מראה.** סימן הוא לימי השובע שהבריות נראות יפות זו לזו, שאין עין בריה צרה בחברתה (ב"ר פט:ד): **באחו.** באגם מריש"ק בלע"ז כמו ישגא אחו (איוב ח:יא): (ג) **ודקות בשר.** טינבי"ש בלע"ז ל' דק: (ד) **ותאכלנה.** סימן שתהא כל שמחת השובע נשכחת בימי הרעב (להלן פסוק ל, ורש"י שם):

PARASHAS MIKEITZ

41.

1-7. Pharaoh's dream. The time had come to free Joseph and begin the chain of events that would bring Jacob and his family to Egypt to fulfill the last part of the prophecy to Abraham that his offspring would be subjugated and persecuted (15:13-16). The events of this *Sidrah* began two years to the day after the release of the Chief of the Cupbearers — a total of twelve years since Joseph was imprisoned. At this point, Joseph was almost 30 years old, Jacob 120, and Isaac 180. Isaac died about this time.

1. עֹמֵד עַל־הַיְאֹר — *[That] he was standing over the River,* the Nile. Throughout the Torah, the Nile is referred to as **the** River, because of its overriding importance in Egyptian life (see below). According to *Rashi*, the word יְאֹר means *canal*. That name was used for the Nile because Egyptian farmers dug a network of canals from it to irrigate as much farmland as possible.

That Pharaoh dreamt of himself as standing by the River and reflecting upon it suggests that his thoughts focused on the River whose annual overflow determined the agricultural fate of Egypt for the next year (*R' Hirsch*).

The Nile, which was the source of Egypt's prosperity, was venerated as the country's god. Midrashically, therefore, Pharaoh's position "over" [עַל] the Nile suggests that he haughtily imagined himself superior to his god.

2. The symbolism of Pharaoh's dream is clear: Since famine and abundance in Egypt depend on the overflow of the Nile, Pharaoh saw the cows — which symbolize plowing [since oxen are usually harnessed for this purpose] — coming up from the River. That the fat cows, alluding to prosperity, remained near the River symbolized that the ensuing prosperity would be limited to Egypt, but the lean cows, which devoured the fat ones and alluded to years of famine, did not remain at the riverbank. This suggested that the famine would be very widespread (*Ramban*).

That the cows were *beautiful* alludes to years of plenty when people look favorably upon one another (*Rashi*). It is axiomatic that, although greed is rooted in human nature, people are less likely to resent one another when everyone is prosperous.

3. פָּרוֹת אֲחֵרוֹת — *Other cows.* These cows were symbolic of another season of plowing (*Ralbag*). The lean cows emerged from the River immediately after the seven fat cows, intimating that famine would follow immediately on the heels of the plenty (*Haamek Davar*).

4. וַתֹּאכַלְנָה — *They ate.* This symbolized that all the joy of the years of plenty would be forgotten during the famine (*Rashi*).

הַמַּרְאֶה וְהַבְּרִיאֹת וַיִּיקַץ פַּרְעֹה: ה וַיִּישָׁן וַיַּחֲלֹם
of appearance « and which were robust, « and Pharaoh awoke. 5 « He fell asleep « and he dreamt «

שֵׁנִית וְהִנֵּה | שֶׁבַע שִׁבֳּלִים עֹלוֹת בְּקָנֶה אֶחָד
a second time, « and he beheld « seven « ears of grain « were sprouting up « on a single stalk «

בְּרִיאוֹת וְטֹבוֹת: ו וְהִנֵּה שֶׁבַע שִׁבֳּלִים דַּקּוֹת
– healthy « and good. « 6 And he beheld « seven « ears of grain « – thin «

וּשְׁדוּפֹת קָדִים צֹמְחוֹת אַחֲרֵיהֶן: ז וַתִּבְלַעְנָה
and scorched « by the east wind – « were growing « after them. « 7 Then they swallowed up, «

הַשִּׁבֳּלִים הַדַּקּוֹת אֵת שֶׁבַע הַשִּׁבֳּלִים הַבְּרִיאוֹת וְהַמְּלֵאוֹת וַיִּיקַץ פַּרְעֹה
did the ears « that were thin, « the seven « ears « that were healthy « and that were full; « Pharaoh awoke «

וְהִנֵּה חֲלוֹם: ח וַיְהִי בַבֹּקֶר וַתִּפָּעֶם רוּחוֹ וַיִּשְׁלַח וַיִּקְרָא אֶת־כָּל־חַרְטֻמֵּי
and indeed! « – it had been a dream. « 8 And it was « in the morning: « Agitated « was his spirit, « so he sent « and he called « all « the necromancers «

מִצְרַיִם וְאֶת־כָּל־חֲכָמֶיהָ וַיְסַפֵּר פַּרְעֹה לָהֶם אֶת־חֲלֹמוֹ וְאֵין־פּוֹתֵר
of Egypt « and all « its wise men; « Pharaoh related « to them « his dream, « but none « could interpret «

אוֹתָם לְפַרְעֹה: ט וַיְדַבֵּר שַׂר הַמַּשְׁקִים אֶת־פַּרְעֹה לֵאמֹר אֶת־חֲטָאַי
them « for Pharaoh. « 9 Then speak up « did the Chief « of the Cupbearers « to « Pharaoh, « saying, « *My transgressions* «

לְמֶחֱזֵי וּפַטִּימָתָא וְאִתְּעַר פַּרְעֹה:
ה וּדְמוּךְ וַחֲלַם תִּנְיָנוּת וְהָא שְׁבַע
שִׁבְּלַיָּא סָלְקָן בְּקַנְיָא חַד פַּטִּימָן וְטָבָן:
ו וְהָא שְׁבַע שִׁבְּלַיָּא לָקָן וּשְׁקִיפָן קִדּוּם
צָמְחָן בַּתְרֵיהֶן: ז וּבְלָעָא שִׁבְּלַיָּא
לָקְיָתָא יָת שְׁבַע שִׁבְּלַיָּא פַּטִּימָתָא
וּמַלְיָתָא וְאִתְּעַר פַּרְעֹה וְהָא חֶלְמָא:
ח וַהֲוָה בְצַפְרָא וּמִטַּרְפָא רוּחֵהּ
וּשְׁלַח וּקְרָא יָת כָּל חָרָשֵׁי מִצְרַיִם
וְיָת כָּל חַכִּימָהָא וְאִשְׁתָּעִי פַּרְעֹה
לְהוֹן יָת חֶלְמֵהּ וְלֵית דְּפָשַׁר יָתְהוֹן
לְפַרְעֹה: ט וּמַלִּיל רַב שָׁקֵי לְפַרְעֹה
(נ״א עִם פַּרְעֹה) לְמֵימַר יָת סָרְחָנַי

רש״י

(ה) **בקנה אחד.** טודי״ל בלע״ז: **בריאות.** שיי״ם בלע״ז: (ו) **ושדופות.** השליד״ש בלע״ז. שקיפן קדום (אונקלוס) חבוטות, לשון משקוף החבוט תמיד על ידי הדלת המכה עליו: **קדים.** רוח מזרחית [דרומית] שקורין ביס״א: (ז) **הבריאות.** שיי״ם בלע״ז: **והנה חלום.** והנה נשלם חלום שלם לפניו והולרך לפותרים (עי׳ ברכ״ת): (ח) **ותפעם רוחו.** ומטרפא רוחיה (אונקלוס). מקשקשת בתוכו כפעמון. ובנבוכדנלר אומר ותתפעם רוחו (דניאל ב:א) לפי שהיו שם שתי פעימות שכחת החלום והעלמת פתרונו (ב״ר שם ה): **חרטמי.** הנחרים בטימי מתים ששואלים בעלמות (תנחומא). טימי הן עלמות בל׳ ארמי. ובמשנה, בית שהוא מלא טמיא (אהלות יז:ג) מלא עלמות: **ואין פותר אותם לפרעה.** פותרים היו אותם אבל לא לפרעה, שלא היה קולן נכנס באזניו ולא היה לו קורת רוח בפתרונם. שהיו אומרים

Ramban comments that the swallowing was what indicated to Joseph that the prosperity of the seven fat years should be stored for use in the lean years. Thus the dream itself dictated Joseph's advice that the good years provide nourishment for the bad years.

5. וַיַּחֲלֹם שֵׁנִית — *And he dreamt a second time.* The passage does not read *and he dreamt* עוֹד, *more,* but *he dreamt* שֵׁנִית, *a second time,* to intimate that it was essentially a single dream which was being repeated (*Kli Yakar*). As Joseph said in his interpretation, the repetition of the dream was to show that it would be fulfilled quickly, not that it indicated a new message (v. 32).

Grain is a symbol of harvest (*Ramban*, v. 2); that one stalk had seven ears indicated abundance (*Rashbam*).

6. דַּקּוֹת וּשְׁדוּפֹת — *Thin, and scorched.* This intimated that any attempt to harvest [symbolized, as noted, by the ears of grain] would be unsuccessful. All the new crops would be *scorched* by the east wind (*Ramban*).

7. וְהִנֵּה חֲלוֹם — *And indeed! — it had been a dream.* Pharaoh realized that it was a significant, complete dream that required interpretation (*Rashi*). The singular form indicated that he understood that the two dreams were really one (*Ramban*).

R' Hirsch comments that the expression implies that Pharaoh was surprised to realize that he had been dreaming. The visions had seemed so vivid that he thought he had seen real events.

8. וְאֵין־פּוֹתֵר אוֹתָם לְפַרְעֹה — *But none could interpret them for Pharaoh.* There *were* interpreters galore, but no one who could interpret it satisfactorily *for Pharaoh* (*Rashi*).

9-13. The Chief of the Cupbearers "remembers" Joseph. Seeing Pharaoh's anguished state, the chief realized that he would be putting himself in great danger by withholding his knowledge of someone who could interpret Pharaoh's dream

אֲנִי מַזְכִּיר הַיּוֹם׃ י פַּרְעֹה קָצַף עַל־עֲבָדָיו וַיִּתֵּן אֹתִי

< me < and he placed < his servants < at < was angry < Pharaoh **10** « today. < mention < I

בְּמִשְׁמַר בֵּית שַׂר הַטַּבָּחִים אֹתִי וְאֵת שַׂר הָאֹפִים׃

« of the Bakers. < and the Chief < — me « of the Butchers < of the Chief < of the house < in the custody

יא וַנַּחַלְמָה חֲלוֹם בְּלַיְלָה אֶחָד אֲנִי וָהוּא אִישׁ

< each man « and he; < I « on the same night, < a dream < We dreamt **11**

כְּפִתְרוֹן חֲלֹמוֹ חָלָמְנוּ׃ יב וְשָׁם אִתָּנוּ נַעַר עִבְרִי

« a Hebrew, < was a youth, < with us < And there **12** « did we dream. < of his dream < according to the interpretation

עֶבֶד לְשַׂר הַטַּבָּחִים וַנְּסַפֶּר־לוֹ וַיִּפְתָּר־לָנוּ אֶת־חֲלֹמֹתֵינוּ אִישׁ כַּחֲלֹמוֹ

< according to his dream < each man, « our dreams; < for us < and he interpreted « to him, < and we related [them] « of the Butchers; < of the Chief < a slave

פָּתָר׃ יג וַיְהִי כַּאֲשֶׁר פָּתַר־לָנוּ כֵּן הָיָה אֹתִי הֵשִׁיב עַל־כַּנִּי וְאֹתוֹ תָלָה׃

« he hanged. < and him < my post < to < he restored < me « did it happen; < so < for us < he interpreted < that just as < And it **13** « he was interpreted.

יד וַיִּשְׁלַח פַּרְעֹה וַיִּקְרָא אֶת־יוֹסֵף וַיְרִיצֻהוּ מִן־הַבּוֹר וַיְגַלַּח וַיְחַלֵּף

< and he changed < He shaved « the pit. < from < and they rushed him « Joseph, < and called [for] < So Pharaoh sent **14**

שִׂמְלֹתָיו וַיָּבֹא אֶל־פַּרְעֹה׃ שני טו וַיֹּאמֶר פַּרְעֹה אֶל־יוֹסֵף חֲלוֹם חָלַמְתִּי

« did I dream, < A dream « Joseph, < to < And Pharaoh said **15** « Pharaoh. < to < and he came « his clothes,

אֲנָא מַדְכַּר יוֹמָא דֵין׃ י פַּרְעֹה רְגִיז עַל
עַבְדוֹהִי וּמַנִּי יָתִי בְּמַטְּרַת בֵּית רַב
קָטוֹלַיָּא יָתִי וְיָת רַב נַחְתּוֹמֵי׃
יא וַחֲלַמְנָא חֶלְמָא בְּלֵילְיָא חַד אֲנָא
וָהוּא גְּבַר כְּפִשְׁרַן חֶלְמֵהּ חֲלַמְנָא׃
יב וְתַמָּן עִמָּנָא עוּלֵם עִבְרָאָה עַבְדָּא
לְרַב קָטוֹלַיָּא וְאִשְׁתָּעֵינָא לֵהּ וּפָשַׁר
לָנָא יָת חֶלְמָנָא גְּבַר כְּחֶלְמֵהּ פָּשָׁר׃
יג וַהֲוָה כְּמָא דִי פָשַׁר לָנָא כֵּן הֲוָה יָתִי
אֲתֵיב עַל שִׁמּוּשִׁי וְיָתֵהּ צְלָב׃
יד וּשְׁלַח פַּרְעֹה וּקְרָא יָת יוֹסֵף
וְאַרְהִיטוּהִי מִן בֵּית אֲסִירֵי וְסַפַּר
וְשַׁנִּי כְסוּתֵהּ וְעַל לְוַת פַּרְעֹה׃
טו וַאֲמַר פַּרְעֹה לְיוֹסֵף חֶלְמָא חֲלֵמִית

רש"י

שבע בנות אתה מוליד, שבע בנות אתה קובר (ב"ר פט:ו): **(יא) איש כפתרון חלומו.** חלום הראוי לפתרון שנפתר לנו ודומה לו (עי' ברכות נה:): **(יב) נער עברי עבד.** ארורים הרשעים שאין טובתם שלמה שמזכירו בלשון בזיון. **נער,** שוטה ואין ראוי לגדולה. **עברי,** אפילו לשוננו אינו מכיר. **עבד,** וכתוב בנימוסי מצרים שאין עבד מולך ולא לובש בגדי שרים [ס"א שיראים] (ב"ר שם ז): **איש כחלומו.** לפי החלום וקרוב לענינו (ברכות שם): **(יג) השיב על כני.** פרעה הנזכר למעלה, כמו שאמר פרעה קצף על עבדיו (לעיל י). הרי מקרא קצר לשון, ולא פירש מי השיב, לפי שאין צריך לפרש, מי השיב, מי שבידו להשיב והוא פרעה. וכן דרך כל מקראות קצרים, על מי שעליו לעשות הם סותמים את הדבר: **(יד) מן הבור.** מן בית הסוהר (אונקלוס) שהוא עשוי כעין גומא. וכן כל בור שבמקרא לשון גומא הוא, ואף אם אין בו מים קרוי בור, פוש"א בלע"ז: **ויגלח [ויחלף שמלתיו].** מפני כבוד המלכות (ב"ר שם ט):

correctly. In addition, Pharaoh seemed to be so upset that he might die — and the chief feared that if a new king took the throne, he might make wholesale changes in his retinue, thus possibly costing the cupbearer his position. Under the circumstance, the Chief of the Cupbearers decided that his own self-interest dictated that he remember Joseph and tell Pharaoh about him (*Midrash*). Obsequiously, the cupbearer began his declaration by making a point of his great devotion to the king: "Even though I will have to recall my sins to make this revelation, I will do it for the sake of your majesty — to tell you of my personal knowledge of an interpreter" (*Radak; Ibn Ezra*).

12. נַעַר עִבְרִי עֶבֶד — *A youth, a Hebrew, a slave.* Cursed are the wicked because even their favors are incomplete! The chief recalled Joseph in the most disparaging terms: נַעַר, *a youth* — ignorant and unfit for distinction; עִבְרִי, *a Hebrew* — a foreigner who does not even understand our language; עֶבֶד, *a slave* — and it is written in the laws of Egypt that a slave can neither be ruler nor wear the robes of a noble (*Rashi*).

Rashi assumes that the chief chose these words carefully in order to stigmatize Joseph because it is axiomatic that evil people act in line with their base character.

14-16. Joseph is summoned. Joseph was released from prison on Rosh Hashanah in the year 2230 from Creation (*Rosh Hashanah* 10b).

14. וַיְרִיצֻהוּ — *And they rushed him.* Every case of Divine salvation comes hastily and unexpectedly. Similarly, the coming of the Messiah will be sudden and hasty [see *Malachi* 3:1] (*Sforno*).

וּפֹתֵ֖ר אֵ֣ין אֹת֑וֹ וַאֲנִ֗י שָׁמַ֤עְתִּי עָלֶ֙יךָ֙ לֵאמֹ֔ר תִּשְׁמַ֥ע

but an interpreter — there is none for it. Now I heard about you saying that you hear [into]

חֲל֖וֹם לִפְתֹּ֥ר אֹתֽוֹ׃ טז וַיַּ֨עַן יוֹסֵ֧ף אֶת־פַּרְעֹ֛ה

a dream to interpret it. **16** *Joseph answered Pharaoh,*

לֵאמֹ֖ר בִּלְעָדָ֑י אֱלֹהִ֕ים יַעֲנֶ֖ה אֶת־שְׁל֥וֹם פַּרְעֹֽה׃

saying, That is beyond me; it is God Who will respond with the welfare of Pharaoh.

יז וַיְדַבֵּ֥ר פַּרְעֹ֖ה אֶל־יוֹסֵ֑ף בַּחֲלֹמִ֕י הִנְנִ֥י עֹמֵ֖ד עַל־

17 *Then Pharaoh spoke to Joseph, In my dream, there I was standing upon*

שְׂפַ֥ת הַיְאֹֽר׃ יח וְהִנֵּ֣ה מִן־הַיְאֹ֗ר עֹלֹת֙ שֶׁ֣בַע פָּר֔וֹת בְּרִיא֥וֹת בָּשָׂ֖ר וִיפֹ֣ת

the bank of the River. **18** *And I beheld, out of the River there came up seven cows, robust of flesh and beautiful*

תֹּ֑אַר וַתִּרְעֶ֖ינָה בָּאָֽחוּ׃ יט וְהִנֵּ֞ה שֶֽׁבַע־פָּר֤וֹת אֲחֵרוֹת֙ עֹל֣וֹת אַחֲרֵיהֶ֔ן

of form, and they were grazing in the marshland. **19** *And I beheld seven other cows came up after them*

דַּלּ֨וֹת וְרָע֥וֹת תֹּ֛אַר מְאֹ֖ד וְרַקּ֣וֹת בָּשָׂ֑ר לֹֽא־רָאִ֧יתִי כָהֵ֛נָּה בְּכָל־אֶ֥רֶץ

— scrawny and ugly of form to the extreme, and emaciated of flesh; I have not seen their like in all the land of

מִצְרַ֖יִם לָרֹֽעַ׃ כ וַתֹּאכַ֙לְנָה֙ הַפָּר֔וֹת הָֽרַקּ֖וֹת וְהָֽרָע֑וֹת אֵ֣ת שֶׁ֧בַע הַפָּר֛וֹת

Egypt for ugliness. **20** *And they ate up, did the cows that were emaciated and that were ugly, the seven cows*

וּפְשַׁר לֵית לֵהּ וַאֲנָא שְׁמַעִית עֲלָךְ לְמֵימַר דְּאַתְּ שָׁמַע חֶלְמָא לְמִפְשַׁר יָתֵהּ: טז וַאֲתֵיב יוֹסֵף יָת פַּרְעֹה לְמֵימַר בַּר מִן חָכְמְתִי אֱלָהֵן מִן קֳדָם יְיָ יִתְּתַב יָת שְׁלָמָא דְפַרְעֹה: יז וּמַלִּיל פַּרְעֹה לְיוֹסֵף (נ״א עִם יוֹסֵף) בְּחֶלְמִי הָא אֲנָא קָאֵם עַל כֵּיף נַהֲרָא: יח וְהָא מִן נַהֲרָא סָלְקָן שְׁבַע תּוֹרָן פַּטִּימָן בְּשַׂר וְשַׁפִּירָן לְמֶחֱזֵי וְרָעְיָן בְּאַחֲוָה: יט וְהָא שְׁבַע תּוֹרָן אָחֳרָנְיָן סָלְקָן בַּתְרֵיהֶן חֲסִיכָן וּבִישָׁן לְמֶחֱזֵי לַחֲדָא וַחֲסִירָן בְּשַׂר לָא חֲזֵתִי כְוָתְהֶן בְּכָל אַרְעָא דְמִצְרַיִם לְבִישׁוּ: כ וַאֲכַלָא תּוֹרָתָא חֲסִיכָתָא וּבִישָׁתָא יָת שְׁבַע תּוֹרָתָא

רש"י

(טו) תשמע חלום לפתור אתו. תאזין ותבין חלום לפתור אותו. **תשמע,** לשון הבנה והאזנה, כמו שומע יוסף (להלן מב:כג), אשר לא תשמע לשונו (דברים כח:מט), אנטנדר"א בלע"ז: **(טז) בלעדי.** אין החכמה משלי אלא **אלהים יענה,** יתן עניה בפי **לשלום פרעה:** **(יט) דלות.** כחושות. כמו מדוע אתה ככה דל (שמואל ב יג:ד) דאמנון: **ורקות בשר.** כל לשון רקות שבמקרא חסרין בשר, בלוש"ש בלע"ז:

16. **בִּלְעָדָי** — *That is beyond me.* Humbly, Joseph gave credit to the One to Whom credit was due, refusing to accept the imputation that he had any supernatural powers (*Mizrachi*). Joseph's integrity would not permit him to accept credit for himself, despite the real danger that Pharaoh might send him back to jail if there was nothing extraordinary about him.

Daniel, too, ascribed his powers solely to God (*Daniel* 2:30). Concerning such people God says (*I Samuel* 2:30), *Those that honor Me I will honor (Midrash HaGadol*).

17-24. Pharaoh recapitulates his dream. A careful comparison of the Torah's account of the dreams with Pharaoh's recapitulation of them to Joseph shows many variations, omissions, and discrepancies [see the chart in ArtScroll's *Bereishis*, vol. II, pgs. 1774-1776]. There are two primary approaches to such differences in the Torah. *Radak, Ramban,* and *Ibn Ezra* do not attach special significance to them. Midrashic literature and many of the later commentators, on the other hand, comment extensively on them, contending that since the Torah economizes on every word, one cannot easily dismiss such variations. As *Haamek Davar* observes on our passage, since it would have been sufficient for the Torah to say merely that Pharaoh repeated his dreams to Joseph, the very fact that they are repeated at length must be taken as a strong indication that every variation is significant.

It is beyond the scope of this commentary to go into all the variations, but the reader will find them discussed in ArtScroll's *Bereishis*.

According to *Tanchuma*, Pharaoh gave a changed version of the dream in order to confuse and test Joseph, but Joseph corrected him every time, until Pharaoh was amazed and exclaimed, "Were you eavesdropping on my dreams?!"

19-21. *R' Hirsch* infers from Pharaoh's elaborate description of the bad cows that they made a far stronger impression on him than did the good ones.

In repeating the dream, Pharaoh failed to mention that the emaciated cows emerged מִן־הַיְאֹר, *out of the River* (see v. 3).

הָרִאשֹׁנ֖וֹת הַבְּרִיאֹֽת׃ כא וַתָּבֹ֣אנָה אֶל־קִרְבֶּ֗נָה וְלֹ֤א
that [came] first ‹ *that were robust.* « **21** *They came* ‹ *into* ‹ *their insides,* « *but it could not* ‹

נוֹדַע֙ כִּי־בָ֣אוּ אֶל־קִרְבֶּ֔נָה וּמַרְאֵיהֶ֣ן רַ֔ע כַּאֲשֶׁ֖ר
be discerned ‹ *that* ‹ *they had come* ‹ *into* ‹ *their insides,* « *for their appearance* ‹ *[remained] as ugly* ‹ *as it was* ‹

בַּתְּחִלָּ֑ה וָאִיקָֽץ׃ כב וָאֵ֖רֶא בַּחֲלֹמִ֑י וְהִנֵּ֣ה ׀ שֶׁ֣בַע
at first. « *Then I awoke.* « **22** *I [then] saw* ‹ *in my dream:* « *I beheld* ‹ *that seven* ‹

שִׁבֳּלִ֗ים עֹלֹ֛ת בְּקָנֶ֥ה אֶחָ֖ד מְלֵאֹ֥ת וְטֹבֽוֹת׃ כג וְהִנֵּה֙
ears of grain ‹ *were sprouting up* ‹ *on a single stalk* « *—full* ‹ *and good.* « **23** *And I beheld* ‹

שֶׁ֣בַע שִׁבֳּלִ֔ים צְנֻמ֥וֹת דַּקּ֖וֹת שְׁדֻפ֣וֹת קָדִ֑ים צֹֽמְח֖וֹת אַחֲרֵיהֶֽם׃ כד וַתִּבְלַ֙עְןָ֙
seven ‹ *ears of grain,* ‹ *withered,* ‹ *thin,* ‹ *and scorched* ‹ *by the east wind* ‹ *were growing* ‹ *after them.* « **24** *Then they swallowed up,* «

הַשִׁבֳּלִ֣ים הַדַּקֹּ֔ת אֵ֖ת שֶׁ֣בַע הַשִׁבֳּלִ֣ים הַטֹּב֑וֹת וָאֹמַר֙ אֶל־הַֽחַרְטֻמִּ֔ים
did the ears ‹ *that were thin,* « *the seven* ‹ *ears* ‹ *that were good;* « *I said [this]* ‹ *to* ‹ *the necromancers,* «

וְאֵ֥ין מַגִּ֖יד לִֽי׃ כה וַיֹּ֤אמֶר יוֹסֵף֙ אֶל־פַּרְעֹ֔ה חֲל֥וֹם פַּרְעֹ֖ה אֶחָ֣ד ה֑וּא אֵ֣ת
but no one could ‹ *tell [the meaning].* ‹ *to me* « **25** *Joseph said* ‹ *to* ‹ *Pharaoh,* « *The dream* ‹ *of Pharaoh* ‹ *is [but] one;* « *that* ‹

אֲשֶׁ֧ר הָֽאֱלֹהִ֛ים עֹשֶׂ֖ה הִגִּ֥יד לְפַרְעֹֽה׃ כו שֶׁ֤בַע פָּרֹת֙ הַטֹּבֹ֔ת שֶׁ֥בַע שָׁנִ֖ים
which ‹ *God* ‹ *is doing,* ‹ *He has told* ‹ *to Pharaoh:* « **26** *The seven* ‹ *cows* ‹ *that are good* « *—seven* ‹ *years* ‹

קַדְמָיָתָא פַּטִּימָתָא: כא וְעָלָא לִמְעֵיהֶן
וְלָא אִתְיְדַע אֲרֵי עַלּוּ לִמְעֵיהֶן
וּמֶחֱזֵיהֶן בִּישׁ כַּד בְּקַדְמֵיתָא
וְאִתְעָרִית: כב וַחֲזֵית בְּחֶלְמִי וְהָא
שְׁבַע שֻׁבְּלַיָּא סָלְקָן בְּקַנְיָא חַד מָלְיָן
וְטָבָן: כג וְהָא שְׁבַע שֻׁבְּלַיָּא נָצָן לָקְיָן
שְׁקִיפָן קִדּוּם צָמְחָן בַּתְרֵיהוֹן:
כד וּבְלָעָא שֻׁבְּלַיָּא לָקְיָתָא יָת שְׁבַע
שֻׁבְּלַיָּא טָבָתָא וַאֲמָרִית לַחֲרָשַׁיָּא
וְלֵית דִּי מְחַוֵּי לִי: כה וַאֲמַר יוֹסֵף
לְפַרְעֹה חֶלְמָא (דְ)פַרְעֹה חַד הוּא יָת
דִּי יְיָ עָתִיד לְמֶעְבַּד חַוִּי לְפַרְעֹה:
כו שְׁבַע תּוֹרָתָא טָבָתָא שְׁבַע שְׁנִין

רש"י

(כג) צנמות. צונמא בלשון ארמי סלע (ב"ב יח.). הרי הן כעץ בלי לחלוח וקשות כסלע. ותרגומו נצן לקין, נצן, אין בהן אלא הקש לפי שנתרוקנו מן הזרע: **(כו) שבע שנים. ושבע שנים.** כלן אינן אלא שבע, ואשר נשנה החלום פעמים לפי שהדבר מזומן, כמו שפירש לו בסוף ועל השנות החלום וגו' (פסוק לב). בשבע שנים הטובות

Since Egypt considered the Nile a god, Pharaoh avoided the connotation that something ugly and auguring misfortune could emanate from the gods (*Kli Yakar; Akeidah*). *Kli Yakar* notes further that by saying he had never before seen such scrawny cows, Pharaoh wanted to assure Joseph that his dream was not based on daytime fantasies.

24. אֶל־הַחַרְטֻמִּים — *To the necromancers.* Pharaoh did not mention that he had summoned the *wise men* as well. He was not surprised that the wise men — who rely on logic — could not fathom the inner symbolisms of his dream. He was dismayed only that the necromancers — who could use "magic" to decipher dreams — were also unable to interpret it (*Haamek Davar*).

25-36. Joseph's interpretation. Joseph proceeded to offer a dazzling interpretation of the dream. He went so far as to tell Pharaoh that the dream itself indicated the course of action that Pharaoh should take to save his country from a disastrous famine, with the result that an unprecedented thing happened in Egypt: A foreigner, a youth, a slave — everything derogatory that the cupbearer said about Joseph — became the ruler of the land. When God wills something, nature and politics alike yield to make the impossible possible.

25. חֲלוֹם פַּרְעֹה אֶחָד הוּא — *The dream of Pharaoh is [but] one.* The dreams complement each other; they are two components of a cogent whole. The cows represent plowing, and the ears of grain represent reaping (*Abarbanel*).

אֵת אֲשֶׁר הָאֱלֹהִים עֹשֶׂה הִגִּיד לְפַרְעֹה — *That which God is doing, He has told to Pharaoh.* Since the dream concerns affairs of state — the need to prepare for the coming calamity — God revealed it to the chief of state. And since it was a Divine communication, God wished to reveal its interpretation through His own servant, rather than the wizards of Egypt (*Alshich*).

26. שֶׁבַע שָׁנִים . . . שֶׁבַע שָׁנִים — *Seven years . . . seven years.* They are not a total of fourteen; the dream was repeated to indicate the immediacy of God's plan. The matter has been set in

הֵנָּה וְשֶׁבַע הַשִּׁבֳּלִים הַטֹּבֹת שֶׁבַע שָׁנִים הֵנָּה

‹‹ they are; ‹ years ‹ — seven ‹‹ that are good ‹ ears ‹ and the seven ‹‹ they are,

חֲלוֹם אֶחָד הוּא: כז וְשֶׁבַע הַפָּרוֹת הָרַקּוֹת וְהָרָעֹת

‹ and that are ugly ‹ that are emaciated ‹ cows ‹ And the seven 27 ‹‹ it is. ‹ a single dream

הָעֹלֹת אַחֲרֵיהֶן שֶׁבַע שָׁנִים הֵנָּה וְשֶׁבַע הַשִּׁבֳּלִים

‹ ears ‹ [similarly,] the seven ‹‹ they are; ‹ years ‹ — seven ‹‹ after them ‹ that came up

הָרֵקוֹת שְׁדֻפוֹת הַקָּדִים יִהְיוּ שֶׁבַע שְׁנֵי רָעָב:

‹‹ of famine! ‹ years ‹ seven ‹ There shall be ‹‹ by the east wind. ‹ scorched ‹ that are empty,

כח הוּא הַדָּבָר אֲשֶׁר דִּבַּרְתִּי אֶל־פַּרְעֹה אֲשֶׁר

‹ What ‹‹ Pharaoh: ‹ to ‹ I have spoken ‹ that ‹ the matter ‹ This is 28

הָאֱלֹהִים עֹשֶׂה הֶרְאָה אֶת־פַּרְעֹה: כט הִנֵּה שֶׁבַע

‹ Seven ‹‹ Indeed! 29 ‹‹ Pharaoh. ‹ to ‹ He has shown ‹ is doing ‹ God

שָׁנִים בָּאוֹת שָׂבָע גָּדוֹל בְּכָל־אֶרֶץ מִצְרָיִם: ל וְקָמוּ שֶׁבַע שְׁנֵי רָעָב

‹ of famine ‹ years ‹ seven ‹ Then will arise 30 ‹‹ of Egypt. ‹ the land ‹ throughout all ‹ that is vast ‹ an abundance ‹‹ are coming — ‹ years

אַחֲרֵיהֶן וְנִשְׁכַּח כָּל־הַשָּׂבָע בְּאֶרֶץ מִצְרָיִם וְכִלָּה הָרָעָב אֶת־הָאָרֶץ:

‹‹ the land. ‹ will the famine ‹ consume ‹‹ of Egypt; ‹ in the land ‹ the abundance ‹ all ‹ and forgotten will be ‹‹ after them,

לא וְלֹא־יִוָּדַע הַשָּׂבָע בָּאָרֶץ מִפְּנֵי הָרָעָב הַהוּא אַחֲרֵי־כֵן כִּי־כָבֵד הוּא

‹ it will be ‹ severe ‹ — for ‹‹ that will be afterward ‹ of that famine ‹ in the face ‹ in the land ‹ shall be the abundance ‹ And unknown 31

מְאֹד: לב וְעַל הִשָּׁנוֹת הַחֲלוֹם אֶל־פַּרְעֹה פַּעֲמָיִם כִּי־נָכוֹן הַדָּבָר

‹ the matter ‹ ready stands ‹ it is because ‹‹ two times, ‹ Pharaoh ‹ to ‹ of the dream ‹ the repetition ‹ As for 32 ‹‹ to the extreme.

מֵעִם הָאֱלֹהִים וּמְמַהֵר הָאֱלֹהִים לַעֲשֹׂתוֹ: לג וְעַתָּה יֵרֶא פַרְעֹה אִישׁ

‹ a man ‹‹ — should Pharaoh — ‹‹ seek ‹ Now 33 ‹‹ to do it. ‹ is God ‹ and hastening ‹‹ God, ‹ from before

אִנִּין וּשְׁבַע שֻׁבְּלַיָּא טָבָתָא שְׁבַע שְׁנִין אִנִּין חֶלְמָא חַד הוּא: כז וּשְׁבַע תּוֹרָתָא חֲסִיכָתָא וּבִישָׁתָא דְּסָלְקָן בַּתְרֵיהוֹן שְׁבַע (נ״א שַׁבְעָא) שְׁנִין אִנִּין וּשְׁבַע שֻׁבְּלַיָּא לָקְיָתָא דִּשְׁקִיפָן קִדּוּם יְהֶוְיָן שְׁבַע שְׁנֵי כַפְנָא: כח הוּא פִּתְגָּמָא דִּי מַלֵּילִית יָת פַּרְעֹה דִּי יְיָ עָתִיד לְמֶעְבַּד אַחֲזֵי לְפַרְעֹה: כט הָא שְׁבַע שְׁנִין אָתְיָן שׂוֹבַע (נ״א שִׂבְעָא) רַבָּא בְּכָל אַרְעָא דְמִצְרָיִם: ל וִיקוּמוּן שְׁבַע שְׁנֵי כַפְנָא בַּתְרֵיהֶן וְיִתְנְשֵׁי כָּל שׂוֹבְעָא (נ״א שִׂבְעָא) בְּאַרְעָא דְמִצְרָיִם וִישֵׁיצֵי כַפְנָא יָת (עַמָּא דְ)אַרְעָא: לא וְלָא יִתְיְדַע שׂוֹבְעָא (נ״א שִׂבְעָא) בְּאַרְעָא מִן קֳדָם כַּפְנָא הַהוּא דִּיהֵי בָתַר כֵּן אֲרֵי תַקִּיף הוּא לַחֲדָא: לב וְעַל דְּאִתַּנִּית חֶלְמָא לְוָת פַּרְעֹה תַּרְתֵּין זִמְנִין אֲרֵי תַקִּין פִּתְגָּמָא מִן קֳדָם יְיָ וְאוֹחִי יְיָ לְמֶעְבְּדֵהּ: לג וּכְעַן יֶחֱזֵי פַרְעֹה גְּבַר

רש״י

נאמר הגיד לפרעה, לפי שהיה סמוך. ובשבע שני רעב נאמר הראה את פרעה, לפי שהיה הדבר מופלג ורחוק נופל בו ל׳ מראה: **(ל) ונשכח כל השבע.** הוא פתרון הבליעה: **(לא) ולא יודע השבע.** הוא פתרון ולא נודע כי באו אל קרבנה: **(לב) נכון.** מזומן (אונקלוס):

motion and is about to happen, as Joseph expressly told Pharaoh in verse 32 (*Rashi*).

27. שֶׁבַע שְׁנֵי רָעָב — *Seven years of famine.* Although the dream began with the good years, Joseph spoke first about the famine to attract Pharaoh's interest. In as prosperous a country as Egypt, a prediction of seven prosperous years would have elicited little interest, so Joseph concentrated on the potential disaster that Pharaoh could avoid by proper planning (*Ramban*). In dealing with people, it is essential to gain their attention; otherwise, the best arguments will go nowhere.

33-36. It would have been foolhardy for Joseph to offer unsolicited advice; he had been summoned to interpret a dream, not

נָבוֹן וְחָכָם וִישִׁיתֵהוּ עַל־אֶרֶץ מִצְרָיִם: לד יַעֲשֶׂה

< Proceed, **34** << of Egypt. < the land < over < and set him << and wise, < who is discerning

פַרְעֹה וְיַפְקֵד פְּקִדִים עַל־הָאָרֶץ וְחִמֵּשׁ אֶת־אֶרֶץ

< the land < and he shall prepare << the land, < on < appointees < and he should appoint < should Pharaoh,

מִצְרַיִם בְּשֶׁבַע שְׁנֵי הַשָּׂבָע: לה וְיִקְבְּצוּ אֶת־כָּל־

< all < And let them gather **35** << of abundance. < years < during the seven < of Egypt

אֹכֶל הַשָּׁנִים הַטֹּבֹת הַבָּאֹת הָאֵלֶּה וְיִצְבְּרוּ־בָר

< grain < let them amass << — these that are approaching; << of the good years < the food

תַּחַת יַד־פַּרְעֹה אֹכֶל בֶּעָרִים וְשָׁמָרוּ: לו וְהָיָה הָאֹכֶל

< The food will be **36** << and to safeguard it. << in the cities, < — [for] food << of Pharaoh < the hand < under

לְפִקָּדוֹן לָאָרֶץ לְשֶׁבַע שְׁנֵי הָרָעָב אֲשֶׁר תִּהְיֶיןָ בְּאֶרֶץ מִצְרָיִם וְלֹא־

< so that it will not << of Egypt, < in the land < will occur < that < of the famine < years < against the seven < for the land < a security reserve

תִכָּרֵת הָאָרֶץ בָּרָעָב: לז וַיִּיטַב הַדָּבָר בְּעֵינֵי פַרְעֹה וּבְעֵינֵי כָּל־עֲבָדָיו:

<< his servants. < of all < and in the eyes < of Pharaoh < in the eyes < did the matter < Appear good **37** << in the famine. << — the land — << perish

לח וַיֹּאמֶר פַּרְעֹה אֶל־עֲבָדָיו הֲנִמְצָא כָזֶה אִישׁ אֲשֶׁר רוּחַ אֱלֹהִים בּוֹ:

<< in him? < of God < the spirit < who has < — a man << another like him < Could we find << his servants, < to < Pharaoh said **38**

סוּכְלְתָן וְחַכִּים וִימַנִּינֵיהּ עַל אַרְעָא דְמִצְרָיִם: לד יַעְבֵּד פַּרְעֹה וִימַנֵּי מְהֵימְנִין עַל אַרְעָא וִיזָרֵז יָת אַרְעָא דְמִצְרַיִם בְּשֶׁבַע שְׁנֵי שׂוֹבְעָא (נ״א שִׂבְעָא): לה וְיִכְנְשׁוּן יָת כָּל עִיבוּר שְׁנַיָּא טַבְתָא דְּאָתְיָן הָאִלֵּין וְיִצְּרוּן (נ״א וְיִצְבְּרוּן) עִיבוּרָא תְּחוֹת יְדָא מְהֵימְנֵי דְפַרְעֹה עִיבוּר בְּקִירְוַיָּא וְיִטְּרוּן: לו וִיהֵי עִיבוּרָא גְנִיז לְאַרְעָא (נ״א לְעַמָּא דְאַרְעָא) בִּשְׁבַע שְׁנֵי כַפְנָא דִּי יֶהֶוְיָן בְּאַרְעָא דְמִצְרָיִם וְלָא יִשְׁתֵּיצֵי עַמָּא דְאַרְעָא בְּכַפְנָא: לז וּשְׁפַר פִּתְגָּמָא בְּעֵינֵי פַרְעֹה וּבְעֵינֵי כָּל עַבְדּוֹהִי: לח וַאֲמַר פַּרְעֹה לְעַבְדּוֹהִי הֲיִשְׁתְּכַח (נ״א הֲנִשְׁכַּח) כְּדֵין גְּבָר דִּי רוּחַ נְבוּאָה מִן קֳדָם יְיָ בֵּהּ:

רש״י

(לד) וחמש. כתרגומו ויזרז וכן וחמושים (שמות יג:יח): **(לה) את כל אכל.** שם דבר הוא, לפיכך טעמו באל״ף ונקוד בפתח קטן. ואוכל שהוא פועל, כגון כי כל אוכל חלב (ויקרא ז:כה), טעמו בכ׳ ונקוד קמץ קטן: **תחת יד פרעה.** ברשותו ובאוצרותיו (עי׳ מכילתא משפטים נזיקין יג; ספרי מטות קנז): **(לו) והיה האכל.** הצבור כשאר פקדון הגנוז לקיום הארץ (אונקלוס): **(לח) הנמצא כזה.** [כתרגומו] הנשכח כדין. אם נלך ונבקשנו הנמצא כמוהו (ב״ר צ:א). הנמצא לשון תמיהה, וכן כל ה״א המשמשת

become Pharaoh's minister of the economy. Yet Joseph offered his advice because it was part of the Divine message contained in the dream, as noted in the commentary to verse 4 (*Ramban).*

33. אִישׁ נָבוֹן וְחָכָם — *A man who is discerning and wise,* he must be *discerning* enough to understand how much food to store and how much to sell; and *wise* in the science of preserving the grain from spoilage. In making this recommendation, Joseph had himself in mind (*Ramban*).

34. יַעֲשֶׂה פַרְעֹה — *Proceed, should Pharaoh.* Let Pharaoh himself be active in this matter and motivate others (*Or HaChaim*).

וְחִמֵּשׁ — *And he shall prepare.* This translation follows *Rashi. Ibn Ezra* derives the word from חָמֵשׁ, *five,* according to which Joseph was recommending that Pharaoh buy a *fifth* of the land of Egypt during the seven years of abundance. Along similar lines, *Rashbam* and *Radak* observe that this was a proposal that Pharaoh double the usual one-tenth tax on grain, and have his overseers collect a *fifth* of all the produce for the royal granary during that period.

35. וְיִקְבְּצוּ — *And let them gather.* This food should be gathered as a levy from the landowners, even against their will (*Rashbam*).

The regional overseers should gather the winnowed and sifted fine grain that could be stored without rotting, and place it directly under Pharaoh's personal control in his granaries (*Rashi*). Every city should have its own royal granaries, to save transport costs and reassure the citizens that their food is not being taken for the benefit of others (*Tur; Ralbag; R' Bachya*).

37-46. Joseph's interpretation is accepted and he becomes viceroy. According to Egyptian law, a slave could not be appointed to a high position. In fact the Talmud (*Sotah* 36b) states that the royal astrologers protested, "Will you set over us a slave whose master bought him for twenty pieces of silver?"

שלישי לט וַיֹּ֤אמֶר פַּרְעֹה֙ אֶל־יוֹסֵ֔ף אַחֲרֵ֨י הוֹדִ֧יעַ אֱלֹהִ֛ים

39 Then Pharaoh said > to > Joseph, >> After > God has informed >

אוֹתְךָ֖ אֶת־כָּל־זֹ֑את אֵין־נָב֥וֹן וְחָכָ֖ם כָּמֽוֹךָ׃ מ אַתָּה֙

you > of all > this, >> there is no one > [as] discerning > and wise > as you. >> 40 You >

תִּהְיֶ֣ה עַל־בֵּיתִ֔י וְעַל־פִּ֖יךָ יִשַּׁ֣ק כָּל־עַמִּ֑י רַ֥ק הַכִּסֵּ֖א

shall be in charge > of my palace, >> and by > your command > shall be sustained > all > my people; >> only > [by] the throne >

אֶגְדַּ֥ל מִמֶּֽךָּ׃ מא וַיֹּ֥אמֶר פַּרְעֹ֖ה אֶל־יוֹסֵ֑ף רְאֵה֙ נָתַ֣תִּי

shall I be greater > than you. >> 41 Then Pharaoh said > to > Joseph, >> See! >> I have placed >

אֹֽתְךָ֔ עַ֖ל כָּל־אֶ֥רֶץ מִצְרָֽיִם׃ מב וַיָּ֨סַר פַּרְעֹ֤ה אֶת־טַבַּעְתּוֹ֙ מֵעַ֣ל יָד֔וֹ וַיִּתֵּ֥ן

you > in charge > of all > the land > of Egypt. >> 42 And Pharaoh removed > his ring > from upon > his hand > and put >

אֹתָ֖הּ עַל־יַ֣ד יוֹסֵ֑ף וַיַּלְבֵּ֤שׁ אֹתוֹ֙ בִּגְדֵי־שֵׁ֔שׁ וַיָּ֛שֶׂם רְבִ֥ד הַזָּהָ֖ב עַל־צַוָּארֽוֹ׃

it > on > the hand > of Joseph. >> He then dressed > him > in garments > of fine linen > and he placed > a chain > of gold > upon > his neck. >>

מג וַיַּרְכֵּ֣ב אֹת֗וֹ בְּמִרְכֶּ֤בֶת הַמִּשְׁנֶה֙ אֲשֶׁר־ל֔וֹ וַיִּקְרְא֥וּ לְפָנָ֖יו אַבְרֵ֑ךְ וְנָת֣וֹן

43 He had him ride > in the [royal] chariot > that was secondary > [to] the one that > was his, >> and they proclaimed > before him: >> *Avrech!* >> Thus, he put >

לט וַאֲמַר פַּרְעֹה לְיוֹסֵף בָּתַר דְּהוֹדַע יְיָ יָתָךְ יָת כָּל דָּא לֵית סָכְלְתָן וְחַכִּים כְּוָתָךְ: מ אַתְּ תְּהֵי מְמַנָּא עַל בֵּיתִי וְעַל מֵימְרָךְ יִתְּזַן כָּל עַמִּי לְחוֹד כָּרְסֵי מַלְכוּתָא הָדֵין אֵיהֵי יַקִּיר מִנָּךְ: מא וַאֲמַר פַּרְעֹה לְיוֹסֵף חֲזִי מַנֵּיתִי יָתָךְ עַל כָּל אַרְעָא דְמִצְרָיִם: מב וְאַעְדִּי פַּרְעֹה יָת עִזְקְתֵהּ מֵעַל יְדֵהּ וִיהַב יָתַהּ עַל יְדָא דְיוֹסֵף וְאַלְבֵּישׁ יָתֵהּ לְבוּשִׁין דְּבוּץ וְשַׁוִּי מָנִיכָא דְדַהֲבָא עַל צַוְּארֵהּ: מג וְאַרְכֵּיב יָתֵהּ בִּרְתִכָּא תִנְיֵתָא (נ״א תִנְיָנָא) דִּי לֵהּ וְאַכְרִיזוּ קֳדָמוֹהִי דֵּין אַבָּא לְמַלְכָּא וּמַנִּי

רש״י

ברא״ש תיבה ונקודה בחטף פתח: (לט) אין נבון וחכם כמוך. לבקש איש נבון וחכם שאמרת, לא נמצא כמוך: (מ) ישק. יתזן (אונקלוס) יתפרנס. כל צרכי עמי יהיו נעשים על ידך, כמו ובן משק ביתי (לעיל טו:ב), וכמו נשקו בר (תהלים ב:יב), גרניסו״ן בלע״ז: רק הכסא. שיהיו קורין לי מלך: כסא. לשון שם המלוכה. כמו ויגדל את כסאו מכסא אדוני המלך (מלכים א א:לז): (מא) נתתי אתך. מניתי יתך (אונקלוס). ואעפ״כ לשון נתינה הוא. כמו ולתתך עליון (דברים כו:יט), בין לגדולה בין לשפלות נופל לשון נתינה עליו, כמו נתתי אתכם נבזים ושפלים (מלאכי ב:ט): (מב) ויסר פרעה את טבעתו. נתינת טבעת המלך היא אות למי שנותנה לו להיות שני לו לגדולה: בגדי שש. דבר חשיבות הוא במצרים: רבד. ענק, ועל שהוא רצוף בטבעות קרוי רביד. וכן מרבדים רבדתי ערשי (משלי ז:טז) רצפתי ערשי מרבדים. בלשון משנה, מוקף רובדין של אבן (מדות א:ח) על הרובד שבעזרה (יומא מג:), והיא רצפה: (מג) במרכבת המשנה. השניה למרכבתו (אונקלוס) המהלכת אצל שלו: אברך. כתרגומו דין אבא למלכא. רך בלשון ארמי מלך, בהשותפין (בבא בתרא ד.) לא ריכא ולא בר ריכא. ובדברי אגדה, דרש ר׳ יהודה, אברך זה יוסף, שהוא אב בחכמה ורך בשנים. אמר לו [ר׳ יוסי] בן דורמסקית, עד מתי אתה מעוות עלינו את הכתובים, אין אברך אלא לשון ברכים, שהכל יהו נכנסין ויוצאין תחת ידו, כענין שנא׳ ונתון אותו וגו׳ (ספרי דברים סוף פסקא א):

However, realizing that only Joseph could properly implement and administer the master plan for national salvation, Pharaoh wanted to make an exception to the law. Since he knew that Joseph would not be able to function well unless he was accepted by the aristocracy, Pharaoh consulted his servants. Only after they agreed did he address Joseph directly (v. 39).

40. יִשַּׁק — *Sustained shall be.* The translation follows *Rashi* and *Onkelos. Ibn Ezra* relates the word to נְשִׁיקָה, *kiss.* He explains that Pharaoh assured Joseph that the people would love him and accept his orders with complete obedience.

42. טַבַּעְתּוֹ — *His ring,* containing the royal seal [cf. *Esther* 8:8]. By putting the ring on Joseph's hand, Pharaoh symbolized that Joseph would be the leader of the entire government and would have the authority to seal decrees, as he desired (*Ramban*).

R' Shimon ben Gamliel said: Joseph well deserved these honors because of his virtuous life. The hands, neck, and body that had refused to sin [with Potiphar's wife] were now adorned with the glorious signs of royalty (*Midrash*).

וַיַּלְבֵּשׁ אֹתוֹ בִּגְדֵי שֵׁשׁ — *He then dressed him in garments of fine linen.* Joseph's "clothes make the man." His father gave him the tunic of fine wool — a sign of leadership (see commentary 37:3); his brothers stripped him of that tunic. Then when he wore the clothes of a servant in the house of Potiphar, he was stripped of those clothes by Potiphar's wife. He reached the nadir with his prisoner's clothes during his many years in jail. When he was *rushed from the pit,* for his audience with Pharaoh, his clothes were changed to those of a freeman. Pharaoh then dressed him in the clothes befitting a ruler (*Midrash*).

43. אַבְרֵךְ — *"Avrech!"* As Joseph rode on the chariot, the servants called out before him *Avrech*, which is a composite of two words: אָב, *father* [counselor; mentor], to the *rach,* which means king in Aramaic (*Rashi; Onkelos*).

Another interpretation of the word is that it is a composite of *av* (father) in wisdom, though *rach* (tender) in years (*Midrash*).

אֹתוֹ עַל כָּל־אֶרֶץ מִצְרָיִם: מד וַיֹּאמֶר פַּרְעֹה אֶל־
< to < Pharaoh said **44** << of Egypt. < the land < all < over < him

יוֹסֵף אֲנִי פַרְעֹה וּבִלְעָדֶיךָ לֹא־יָרִים אִישׁ אֶת־יָדוֹ
< *his hand* < *a man may not lift* < *And without you* << *Pharaoh.* < *I am* << Joseph,

וְאֶת־רַגְלוֹ בְּכָל־אֶרֶץ מִצְרָיִם: מה וַיִּקְרָא פַרְעֹה
< Pharaoh called **45** << *of Egypt.* < *the land* < *in all* < *or his foot*

שֵׁם־יוֹסֵף צָפְנַת פַּעְנֵחַ וַיִּתֶּן־לוֹ אֶת־אָסְנַת בַּת־
< daughter < Asenath < him < and he gave << Zaphenath-paneah, < of Joseph < the name

פּוֹטִי פֶרַע כֹּהֵן אֹן לְאִשָּׁה וַיֵּצֵא יוֹסֵף עַל־אֶרֶץ
< the land < [with authority] over < [Thus], Joseph went out << for a wife. < of On, < Chief < of Poti-phera,

מִצְרָיִם: מו וְיוֹסֵף בֶּן־שְׁלֹשִׁים שָׁנָה בְּעָמְדוֹ לִפְנֵי פַּרְעֹה מֶלֶךְ־מִצְרָיִם
<< of Egypt; < King < Pharaoh < before < when he stood < years < thirty < was of < Now the age of Joseph **46** << of Egypt.

וַיֵּצֵא יוֹסֵף מִלִּפְנֵי פַרְעֹה וַיַּעֲבֹר בְּכָל־אֶרֶץ מִצְרָיִם: מז וַתַּעַשׂ הָאָרֶץ
< The land produced **47** << of Egypt. < the land < through all < and he passed < of Pharaoh < from the presence < Joseph left

בְּשֶׁבַע שְׁנֵי הַשָּׂבָע לִקְמָצִים: מח וַיִּקְבֹּץ אֶת־כָּל־אֹכֶל | שֶׁבַע שָׁנִים אֲשֶׁר
< that < years < of the seven < the food < all < He gathered **48** << by the handfuls. < of abundance < years < during the seven

יָתֵהּ עַל כָּל אַרְעָא דְמִצְרָיִם:
מד וַאֲמַר פַּרְעֹה לְיוֹסֵף אֲנָא פַרְעֹה
וּבַר מִמֵּימְרָךְ לָא יְרִים גְּבַר יָת יְדֵהּ
לְמֵיחַד זֵין וְיָת רַגְלֵהּ לְמִרְכַּב עַל
סוּסְיָא בְּכָל אַרְעָא דְמִצְרָיִם:
מה וּקְרָא פַרְעֹה שׁוּם יוֹסֵף גַּבְרָא
דְמִטַמְרָן גַּלְיָן לֵהּ וִיהַב לֵהּ יָת אָסְנַת
בַּת פּוֹטִי פֶרַע רַבָּא דְאוֹן לְאִתְּתָא
וּנְפַק יוֹסֵף (שַׁלִּיט) עַל אַרְעָא
דְמִצְרָיִם: מו וְיוֹסֵף בַּר תְּלָתִין שְׁנִין כַּד
קָם קֳדָם פַּרְעֹה מַלְכָּא דְמִצְרָיִם וּנְפַק
יוֹסֵף מִן קֳדָם פַּרְעֹה וַעֲבַר (שַׁלִּיט)
בְּכָל אַרְעָא דְמִצְרָיִם: מז וּכְנָשׁוּ
דָיְרֵי אַרְעָא בִּשְׁבַע שְׁנֵי שׂוֹבְעָא
(נ״א שִׂבְעָא) עִיבוּרָא לְאוֹצָרִין:
מח וּכְנַשׁ יָת כָּל עִיבוּר שְׁבַע שְׁנִין דִּי

רש"י

(מד) אני פרעה. שיש יכולת בידי לגזור גזרה על מלכותי ואני גוזר **שלא ירים איש את ידו בלעדיך,** שלא ברשותך. ד"א, אני פרעה, אני אהיה מלך, **ובלעדיך וגו',** וזהו דוגמת רק הכסא (לעיל פסוק מ) [אלא שהולך לפרשה בשעת נתינת הטבעת] (ב"ר שם ב): **את ידו ואת רגלו.** כתרגומו: **(מה) צפנת פענח.** מפרש הצפונות (שם ד; אונקלוס; תרגום יונתן). ואין לפענח דמיון במקרא: **פוטי פרע.** הוא פוטיפר, ונקרא פוטיפרע על שנסתרס מאליו לפי שחמד את יוסף למשכב זכור (סוטה יג:): **(מז) ותעש הארץ.** כתרגומו, ואין הלשון נעקר מלשון עשייה: **לקמצים.** קומץ על קומץ, יד על יד היו אוצרים:

וְנָתוֹן אֹתוֹ — *Thus, he put him.* Pharaoh did all of the above in order to demonstrate publicly that all the authority of the throne was behind his new viceroy (*HaK'sav V'HaKabbalah*).

45. צָפְנַת פַּעְנֵחַ — *Zaphenath-paneah.* Appointees to a high position were customarily assigned a name commensurate with their new eminence (*Rashbam*). *Rashi* and *Rashbam* interpret: מְפָרֵשׁ הַצְּפוּנוֹת, *he who explains what is hidden.*

Zohar comments that the name change was an instance of Divine Providence, for it helped conceal Joseph's identity from his family.

אָסְנַת בַּת־פּוֹטִי פֶרַע — *Asenath daughter of Poti-phera.* Poti-phera is identical with Potiphar [see above, 37:36], Joseph's former master. That he allowed his daughter to marry Joseph vindicated Joseph in the eyes of the Egyptians from the charge that he had assaulted Potiphar's wife (*Alshich*).

וַיֵּצֵא יוֹסֵף עַל־אֶרֶץ מִצְרָיִם — *[Thus], Joseph went out [with authority] over the land of Egypt.* Joseph emerged from his interview with Pharaoh in such a manner that it was clear to all that he was the ruler of Egypt (*Sforno*).

Although Pharaoh changed his name to Zaphenath-paneah, it was as *Joseph* that he *went out [with authority] over the land of Egypt.* Similarly, when Joseph showed his father his marriage contract (*Rashi* 48:9) he demonstrated that he had retained his original name. [Joseph thus served as a model for the Jews, who did not change their names in Egypt (*Shemos Rabbah* 1:28)] (*Chasam Sofer*).

46. וַיַּעֲבֹר בְּכָל־אֶרֶץ מִצְרָיִם — *And he passed through all the land of Egypt.* Whereas his earlier emergence (v. 46) was ceremonial, in the sense that he became known throughout the land as the new viceroy (*Ibn Ezra*), this was a "working tour." He became acquainted with the populace, learned about the country, warned the people about the impending famine, and arranged the construction of royal granaries in every city (*Akeidah*).

47-49. Joseph's plan is implemented.

47. לִקְמָצִים — *By the handfuls.* This can be understood to mean that the abundance was so great that the grain was collected

הָיוּ בְּאֶרֶץ מִצְרַיִם וַיִּתֵּן־אֹכֶל בֶּעָרִים אֹכֶל שְׂדֵה־
came to pass < in the land < of Egypt, << and he placed < food < in the cities; << the food < of the fields <

הָעִיר אֲשֶׁר סְבִיבֹתֶיהָ נָתַן בְּתוֹכָהּ: מט וַיִּצְבֹּר יוֹסֵף
of [each] city < that are < around it < he placed < within it. << 49 Joseph amassed <

בָּר כְּחוֹל הַיָּם הַרְבֵּה מְאֹד עַד כִּי־חָדַל לִסְפֹּר
grain < like the sand < of the sea < in great abundance, << until [the point] < that < he ceased < counting, <<

כִּי־אֵין מִסְפָּר: נ וּלְיוֹסֵף יֻלַּד שְׁנֵי בָנִים בְּטֶרֶם תָּבוֹא
for < there was no < number. << 50 Now to Joseph < were born < two < sons < before < there would come <

שְׁנַת הָרָעָב אֲשֶׁר יָלְדָה־לּוֹ אָסְנַת בַּת־פּוֹטִי פֶרַע כֹּהֵן אוֹן: נא וַיִּקְרָא יוֹסֵף
the year < of the famine, << whom < she bore < to him << —did Asenath < daughter < of Poti-phera, < Chief < of On. << 51 Joseph called <

אֶת־שֵׁם הַבְּכוֹר מְנַשֶּׁה כִּי־נַשַּׁנִי אֱלֹהִים אֶת־כָּל־עֲמָלִי וְאֵת כָּל־בֵּית
the name < of the firstborn < Manasseh, << for < *He made me forget* < *— God has —* << *all* < *my hardship* < *and all* < *the household* <

אָבִי: נב וְאֵת שֵׁם הַשֵּׁנִי קָרָא אֶפְרָיִם כִּי־הִפְרַנִי אֱלֹהִים בְּאֶרֶץ עָנְיִי:
of my father. << 52 And the name < of the second < he called < Ephraim, < for < *He made me fruitful* << *— God has —* << *in the land* < *of my suffering.* <<

הֲווֹ בְּאַרְעָא דְמִצְרַיִם וִיהַב עִיבוּר בְּקִרְוַיָּא עִיבוּר חֲקַל קַרְתָּא דִּי בְסַחְרָנָהָא יְהַב בְּגַוַּהּ: מט וּכְנַשׁ יוֹסֵף עִיבוּרָא כְּחָלָא דְיַמָּא סַגִּי לַחֲדָא עַד דִּי פְסַק לְמִמְנֵי אֲרֵי לֵית מִנְיָן: נ וּלְיוֹסֵף אִתְיְלִיד תַּרְתֵּין בְּנִין עַד לָא עֲלַת שַׁתָּא דְכַפְנָא דִּילִידַת לֵהּ אָסְנַת בַּת פּוֹטִי פֶרַע רַבָּא דְאוֹן: נא וּקְרָא יוֹסֵף יָת שׁוּם בּוּכְרָא מְנַשֶּׁה אֲרֵי אַנְשְׁיַנִי יְיָ יָת כָּל עַמְלִי וְיָת כָּל בֵּית אַבָּא: נב וְיָת שׁוּם תִּנְיָנָא קְרָא אֶפְרָיִם אֲרֵי אַפְּשַׁנִי יְיָ בְּאַרַע שִׁעְבּוּדִי:

רש"י

(מח) **אכל שדה העיר [אשר סביבותיה] נתן בתוכה.** שכל ארץ וארץ מעמדת פירותיה, ונותנין בתבואה מעפר המקום ומעמיד את התבואה מלירקב (ב"ר צ:ה): (מט) **עד כי חדל לספור.** עד כי חדל לו הסופר לספור, וה"ז מקרא קצר: **כי אין מספר.** לפי שאין מספר, והרי כי משמש בלשון דהא (ר"ה ג.): (נ) **בטרם תבוא שנת הרעב.** מכאן שאדם אסור לשמש מטתו בשני רעבון (תענית יא.):

"hand over fist."

R' David Feinstein comments otherwise. In order to prepare for the famine, Joseph instituted such strict controls that not even a handful of grain was overlooked. So successful was this policy that Joseph reached his predetermined goal and *there was no number* (v. 49), meaning that once that happened, it was no longer necessary to be as scrupulous in counting future acquisitions of food. As the later chapters show, Joseph's granaries were sufficient not only to feed Egypt but to enrich Pharaoh by selling food to the surrounding lands.

48-49. בָּר . . . אֹכֶל — *Food . . . grain.* According to *Ramban*, Joseph gathered *all food* of every variety to assure that there would be no waste. He apportioned rations to the people for their sustenance, and stored the rest. As for the *grain* [since grain is easier to store for long periods of time], he amassed it in storehouses *like the sand of the sea.*

50-52. Joseph's children: Manasseh and Ephraim. Verse 50 seems to stress that Asenath bore children *to him*, meaning that the sons were dedicated to the ideals of Joseph, not to those of the idolaters among whom she had been raised. As the daughter of aristocracy married to a foreign slave and former convict who owed his position to Pharaoh's whim, she might well have dominated the home atmosphere, in which case the children would have been *hers.* The Torah tells us, therefore, that she adopted Joseph's spiritual and moral outlook. To be the only Jew in Egypt, and to be married to the daughter of an idolatrous priest, yet to raise children who remain the model after whom Jewish parents bless their children — *may God make you like Ephraim and Manasseh* (48:20) — is a merit that deserves to be stressed (*R' Hirsch*).

51. כִּי־נַשַּׁנִי אֱלֹהִים . . . . — *For, "He made me forget — God has . . ."* Joseph acknowledged that God had allowed him to forget the hardships his brothers had inflicted on him in his paternal home. He was able to recognize that everything they had done was part of the Divine master plan, and consequently he bore them no ill will. For that he was grateful (*Akeidah*).

52. בְּאֶרֶץ עָנְיִי — *In the land of my suffering.* Despite all the greatness and splendor Joseph enjoyed as viceroy, he still regarded Egypt as the land of his suffering, for he was still a son of Jacob and a native of the Holy Land (*Abarbanel*).

Joseph's choice of names for his sons is the greatest proof of his loyalty to his origins and his determination not to be sucked into Egyptian culture (*R' Hirsch*).

רביעי נג וַתִּכְלֶינָה שֶׁבַע שְׁנֵי הַשָּׂבָע אֲשֶׁר הָיָה בְּאֶרֶץ

‹ in the land ‹ were ‹ that ‹ of abundance ‹ years ‹ did the seven ‹ Come to an end **53**

מִצְרָיִם: נד וַתְּחִלֶּינָה שֶׁבַע שְׁנֵי הָרָעָב לָבוֹא

« to approach, ‹ of famine ‹ years ‹ did the seven ‹ And begin **54** « of Egypt.

כַּאֲשֶׁר אָמַר יוֹסֵף וַיְהִי רָעָב בְּכָל־הָאֲרָצוֹת

« the lands, ‹ in all ‹ famine ‹ There was « Joseph had said. ‹ just as

וּבְכָל־אֶרֶץ מִצְרַיִם הָיָה לָחֶם: נה וַתִּרְעַב כָּל־אֶרֶץ

‹ the land ‹ all « It hungered, **55** « bread. ‹ there was ‹ of Egypt ‹ the land ‹ but in all

מִצְרַיִם וַיִּצְעַק הָעָם אֶל־פַּרְעֹה לַלָּחֶם וַיֹּאמֶר פַּרְעֹה לְכָל־מִצְרַיִם

« of Egypt, ‹ to all ‹ Pharaoh ‹ Said « for bread. ‹ Pharaoh ‹ to ‹ and the people cried out « of Egypt did,

לְכוּ אֶל־יוֹסֵף אֲשֶׁר־יֹאמַר לָכֶם תַּעֲשׂוּ: נו וְהָרָעָב הָיָה עַל כָּל־פְּנֵי

‹ the face ‹ all ‹ over ‹ was ‹ [When] the famine **56** « *you should do.* « *you,* ‹ *he tells* ‹ *Whatever* « *Joseph.* ‹ *to* ‹ *Go*

הָאָרֶץ וַיִּפְתַּח יוֹסֵף אֶת־כָּל־אֲשֶׁר בָּהֶם וַיִּשְׁבֹּר לְמִצְרַיִם וַיֶּחֱזַק הָרָעָב

‹ did the famine ‹ and intensified « to Egypt; ‹ and he sold provisions « had [grain] in them, ‹ that ‹ all [the storehouses] ‹ Joseph opened « of the land,

בְּאֶרֶץ מִצְרָיִם: נז וְכָל־הָאָרֶץ בָּאוּ מִצְרַיְמָה לִשְׁבֹּר אֶל־יוֹסֵף כִּי־חָזַק

‹ intensified ‹ for « Joseph, ‹ to « — to buy provisions — « to Egypt ‹ came ‹ the [surrounding] lands ‹ All **57** « of Egypt. ‹ in the land

נג וּשְׁלִימַת שְׁבַע שְׁנֵי שׂוֹבְעָא (נ״א שִׂבְעָא) דַּהֲוָה בְּאַרְעָא דְמִצְרָיִם: נד וּשְׁרִיאָה שְׁבַע שְׁנֵי כַפְנָא לְמֵיעַל כְּמָא דִי אֲמַר יוֹסֵף וַהֲוָה כַפְנָא בְּכָל אַרְעָתָא וּבְכָל אַרְעָא דְמִצְרַיִם הֲוָה לַחְמָא: נה וּכְפָנַת כָּל אַרְעָא דְמִצְרַיִם וּצְוַח עַמָּא לְפַרְעֹה לְלַחְמָא (נ״א קֳדָם פַּרְעֹה עַל לַחְמָא) וַאֲמַר פַּרְעֹה לְכָל מִצְרָאֵי אֱזִילוּ לְוַת יוֹסֵף דִּי יֵימַר לְכוֹן תַּעְבְּדוּן: נו וְכַפְנָא הֲוָה עַל כָּל אַפֵּי אַרְעָא וּפְתַח יוֹסֵף יָת כָּל (אוֹצְרַיָּא) דִּי בְהוֹן עִיבוּרָא וְזַבִּין לְמִצְרַיִם וּתְקֵיף כַּפְנָא בְּאַרְעָא דְמִצְרָיִם: נז וְכָל דָּיְרֵי אַרְעָא עַלּוּ (נ״א אֲתוֹ) לְמִצְרַיִם לְמִזְבַּן עִיבוּרָא מִן יוֹסֵף אֲרֵי תְקֵיף

רש״י

(נה) **ותרעב כל ארץ מצרים.** שהרקיבה תבואתם שאצרו חוץ משל יוסף (ב״ר מא:ה): **אשר יאמר לכם תעשו.** לפי שהיה יוסף אומר להם שימולו. וכשבאו אצל פרעה ואומרים כך הוא אומר לנו, אמר להם למה לא צברתם בר והלא הכריז לכם שבשני הרעב באים. אמרו לו אספנו הרבה והרקיבה. אמר להם אם כן כל אשר יאמר לכם תעשו, הרי גזר על התבואה והרקיבה, מה אם יגזור עלינו ונמות (שם): (נו) **על כל פני הארץ.** מי הם פני הארץ, אלו העשירים (שם): **את כל אשר בהם.** כתרגומו, די בהון עיבורא: **וישבר למצרים.** שבר לשון מכר ולשון קנין הוא. כאן משמש לשון מכר. שברו לנו מעט אוכל (להלן מג:ב) לשון קנין. ואל תאמר אינו כי אם בתבואה, שאף ביין וחלב מצינו ולכו שברו בלא כסף ובלא מחיר יין וחלב (ישעיה נה:א): (נז) **וכל הארץ באו מצרימה. אל יוסף לשבור.** ואם תדרשהו כסדרו

54. כַּאֲשֶׁר אָמַר יוֹסֵף — *Just as Joseph had said.* The Torah does not make this statement in telling of the seven prosperous years. People tend to take good times for granted. It was only when famine struck that the Egyptians acknowledged that they had a viceroy who had foretold what would happen.

55. וַתִּרְעַב כָּל־אֶרֶץ מִצְרַיִם — *It hungered, all the land of Egypt did.* During the second year of the famine *(R' Bachya)*, all the stored grain rotted, except for Joseph's *(Rashi)*. *Midrash Tanchuma* records that when that happened the people of Egypt came to Joseph demanding food, but he said that he would give them nothing unless they circumcised themselves first. They protested to Pharaoh; upon hearing that their stores of grain had rotted while Joseph's were still intact, Pharaoh told them that they must follow Joseph's orders *(Rashi* from *Tanchuma)*.

The commentators explain that Joseph was preparing for the eventual descent of his brothers to Egypt. He knew that gentiles mock Jews because they are circumcised. By making the Egyptians circumcise themselves, he made it impossible for them to ridicule the circumcised Jews (*Yafeh Toar*). According to *Shlah*, Joseph foresaw that the sexual depravity of Egypt was the reason for the punishments they would suffer in the future; indeed, the Torah warns Israel against imitating the abominations of Egypt (see *Leviticus* 18:3, *Rashi; Ramban* there). By forcing circumcision upon the Egyptians, Joseph hoped to temper their perverse lusts and thereby ease the plight of the Jews who would be exiled and oppressed there. The Egyptians abandoned the law of circumcision as soon as Joseph died.

56. עַל כָּל־פְּנֵי הָאָרֶץ — *Over all the face of the land.* The phrase פְּנֵי, *face*, refers to the prominent, well-to-do people (*Rashi*). They felt the famine first because such people are not accustomed to hunger and suffering. Poor people, unfortunately, are accustomed to hunger and take it in stride (*Yalkut Yehudah*).

57. וְכָל־הָאָרֶץ בָּאוּ — *All the [surrounding] lands came.* All the countries affected by the famine trooped to Egypt to buy food,

הָֽרָעָב בְּכָל־הָאָֽרֶץ׃ [מב] א וַיַּרְא יַעֲקֹב כִּי יֶשׁ־

< there were < that < Jacob saw 1 42 « the lands. < in all < had the famine

שֶׁבֶר בְּמִצְרָיִם וַיֹּאמֶר יַעֲקֹב לְבָנָיו לָמָּה תִּתְרָאוּ׃

« do you make yourselves conspicuous? < Why « to his sons, < so Jacob said « in Egypt; < provisions being sold

ב וַיֹּאמֶר הִנֵּה שָׁמַעְתִּי כִּי יֶשׁ־שֶׁבֶר בְּמִצְרָיִם רְדוּ־

< go down « in Egypt; < provisions being sold < there are < that < I have heard < Indeed, « And he said, 2

שָׁמָּה וְשִׁבְרוּ־לָנוּ מִשָּׁם וְנִחְיֶה וְלֹא נָמוּת׃ ג וַיֵּרְדוּ אֲחֵי־יוֹסֵף עֲשָׂרָה

« —ten [of them]— « of Joseph < did the brothers « So they went down, 3 « die. < and not < that we may live « from there, < for us < and purchase < there

לִשְׁבֹּר בָּר מִמִּצְרָיִם׃ ד וְאֶת־בִּנְיָמִין אֲחִי יוֹסֵף לֹא־שָׁלַח יַעֲקֹב אֶת־

< with < Jacob did not send < of Joseph, < the brother < But Benjamin, 4 « from Egypt. < grain < to purchase

כַּפְנָא בְּכָל אַרְעָא: א וַחֲזָא יַעֲקֹב אֲרֵי אִית עִיבוּרָא מִזְדַּבַּן בְּמִצְרַיִם וַאֲמַר יַעֲקֹב לִבְנוֹהִי לְמָא תִתְחֲזוּן: ב וַאֲמַר הָא שְׁמָעִית (אָמְרִין) אֲרֵי אִית עִיבוּרָא מִזְדַּבַּן בְּמִצְרַיִם חוּתוּ תַמָּן וּזְבוּנוּ לָנָא מִתַּמָּן וְנֵחֵי וְלָא נְמוּת: ג וּנְחָתוּ אֲחֵי יוֹסֵף עַסְרָא לְמִזְבַּן עִיבוּרָא מִמִּצְרָיִם: ד וְיָת בִּנְיָמִין אֲחוּהִי דְיוֹסֵף לָא שְׁלַח יַעֲקֹב עִם

רש"י

היה לריך לכתוב לשבור מן יוסף: (א) **וירא יעקב כי יש שבר במצרים.** ומהיכן ראה, והלא לא ראה אלא שמע, שנאמר הנה שמעתי וגו'. ומהו וירא, ראה באספקלריא של קדש שעדיין יש לו שבר במלרים ולא היתה נבואה ממש להודיעו בפי' שזה יוסף (ב"ר לא:ו): **למה תתראו.** למה תראו עלמכם בפני בני ישמעאל ובני עשו [כאילו אתם] שבעים, כי באותה שעה עדיין היה להם תבואה (תענית י:). [ול"נ פשוטו, למה תתראו, למה יהיו הכל מסתכלין בכם ומתמיהים בכם שאין אתם מבקשים לכם אוכל בטרם שיכלה מה שבידכם.] ומפי אחרים שמעתי שהוא לשון כחישה, למה תהיו כחושים ברעב. ודומה לו ומרוה גם הוא יורא (משלי יא:כה): (ב) **רדו שמה.** ולא אמר לכו, רמז למאתים ועשר שנים שנשתעבדו למלרים כמנין רד"ו (ב"ר שם ב): (ג) **וירדו אחי יוסף.** ולא כתב בני יעקב, מלמד שהיו מתחרטים במכירתו ונתנו לבם להתנהג עמו באחוה ולפדותו בכל ממון שיפסקו עליהם (ב"ר שם ו; תנחומא ח): **עשרה.** מה ת"ל, והלא כתיב ואת בנימין אחי יוסף לא שלח. אלא לענין האחוה היו חלוקין לעשרה שלא היתה אהבת כלם ושנאת כלם שוה לו. אבל לענין לשבור בר כלם לב אחד להם (ב"ר לא:ב):

with the result that Pharaoh's treasury amassed huge amounts of gold and silver. This was God's way of preparing the way for the fulfillment of the prophecy to Abraham that his offspring would leave the land of their enslavement with enormous wealth (*Zohar*).

42.

1-4. Jacob sends his sons to Egypt. It was the second year of the famine (*Seder Olam*), and although Jacob's family still had provisions (see below), Jacob was concerned and dispatched his sons to Egypt.

1. וַיַּרְא יַעֲקֹב — *Jacob saw.* But he could not actually have *seen* the events in faraway Egypt. The Sages therefore interpret the word שֶׁבֶר as if it were spelled with a *sin* — שֶׂבֶר — which means *hope.* Accordingly they comment that Jacob *saw* in a prophetic vision that there was *hope* in Egypt (*Rashi*). This is an instance of a prophet not comprehending the clear meaning of his revelation, for it is plain from the narrative that Jacob did not know the consequences of his initiative in sending his sons to Egypt. Another example is his unconscious prophecy that his family would ultimately spend 210 years in Egypt (see v. 2).

לָמָּה תִּתְרָאוּ — *Why do you make yourselves conspicuous?* Why do you show yourselves as having plenty [to eat]? Such behavior will lead to envy and ill will on the part of the families of Ishmael and Esau (*Taanis* 10b; *Rashi*). Do not travel with food in your hands lest you cause ill feelings. And do not all enter [Egypt] through one gate for fear of the evil eye [for someone might feel envy that one man should be blessed with ten such sons] (*Midrash*).

Jacob's rhetorical question has been the theme of many leaders who exhorted their fellow Jews not to flaunt their wealth and success to envious and often anti-Semitic neighbors. Whatever food Jacob's family had was honestly acquired, but even honest resources should be displayed judiciously.

2. רְדוּ — *Go down.* Jacob did not use the verb לְכוּ, *go,* but רְדוּ [*go down*], thereby alluding to the 210 years that they would be exiled in Egypt [the *gematria* (numerical value) of the word רְדוּ is 210: ר = 200; ד = 4; ו = 6] (*Rashi*). In a similar expression of unconscious prophecy, Jacob said that as a result of the foray to Egypt, *we will live*, for the Egyptian exile was an indispensable prerequisite to the spiritual life that would result from the exile and redemption.

3. אֲחֵי־יוֹסֵף עֲשָׂרָה — *The brothers of Joseph — ten [of them].* In order to prevent speculators from purchasing large amounts of grain and profiteering, as is common in times of famine and shortage, Joseph had decreed that no one could buy more food than was needed for a single household. This is why all ten brothers had to go (*Sforno*). According to the Midrash, Joseph's real reason for the decree was to assure that all of his brothers would be forced to come to him, thus fulfilling the prophecy of his dreams that they would all bow to him.

4. בִּנְיָמִין — *Benjamin.* It was destined from Above that Benjamin, who had not participated in the sale of Joseph, not accompany them so that he would be spared their tribulations before Joseph revealed his identity. Although he suffered with

אֶחָיו כִּי אָמַר פֶּן־יִקְרָאֶנּוּ אָסוֹן׃ ה וַיָּבֹאוּ בְּנֵי

his brothers, for he said, *Lest there should befall him* a disaster. 5 So came the sons

יִשְׂרָאֵל לִשְׁבֹּר בְּתוֹךְ הַבָּאִים כִּי־הָיָה הָרָעָב

of Israel to buy provisions among those arriving, for there was the famine

בְּאֶרֶץ כְּנָעַן׃ ו וְיוֹסֵף הוּא הַשַּׁלִּיט עַל־הָאָרֶץ הוּא

in the land of Canaan. 6 Now Joseph — he was the viceroy over the land, he

הַמַּשְׁבִּיר לְכָל־עַם הָאָרֶץ וַיָּבֹאוּ אֲחֵי יוֹסֵף

was the provider to all the people of the land. They came, did the brothers of Joseph,

וַיִּשְׁתַּחֲווּ־לוֹ אַפַּיִם אָרְצָה׃ ז וַיַּרְא יוֹסֵף אֶת־אֶחָיו וַיַּכִּרֵם וַיִּתְנַכֵּר

and they bowed to him with faces to the ground. 7 Joseph saw his brothers and he recognized them, but he acted like a stranger

אֲלֵיהֶם וַיְדַבֵּר אִתָּם קָשׁוֹת וַיֹּאמֶר אֲלֵהֶם מֵאַיִן בָּאתֶם וַיֹּאמְרוּ מֵאֶרֶץ

toward them and spoke with them harshly. He said to them, *From where did you come?* And they said, *From the land*

כְּנַעַן לִשְׁבָּר־אֹכֶל׃ ח וַיַּכֵּר יוֹסֵף אֶת־אֶחָיו וְהֵם לֹא הִכִּרֻהוּ׃ ט וַיִּזְכֹּר יוֹסֵף

of Canaan to buy food. 8 Joseph recognized his brothers, but they did not recognize him. 9 Joseph remembered

אֲחוֹהִי אֲרֵי אֲמַר דִּלְמָא יְעַרְעִנֵּהּ מוֹתָא׃ ה וַאֲתוֹ בְּנֵי יִשְׂרָאֵל לְמִזְבַּן עִיבוּרָא בְּגוֹ עָלַיָּא אֲרֵי הֲוָה כַפְנָא בְּאַרְעָא דִכְנָעַן׃ ו וְיוֹסֵף הוּא דְּשַׁלִּיט עַל אַרְעָא הוּא דְמַזְבֵּן עִיבוּרָא לְכָל עַמָּא דְאַרְעָא וַאֲתוֹ אֲחֵי יוֹסֵף וּסְגִידוּ לֵהּ עַל אַפֵּיהוֹן עַל אַרְעָא׃ ז וַחֲזָא יוֹסֵף יָת אֲחוֹהִי וְאִשְׁתְּמוֹדְעִנּוּן וְחַשִׁיב מָא דִימַלֵּל עִמְּהוֹן וּמַלִּיל עִמְּהוֹן קַשְׁיָן וַאֲמַר לְהוֹן מְנָן אֲתֵיתוּן וַאֲמָרוּ מֵאַרְעָא דִכְנַעַן לְמִזְבַּן עִיבוּרָא׃ ח וְאִשְׁתְּמוֹדַע יוֹסֵף יָת אֲחוֹהִי וְאִנּוּן לָא אִשְׁתְּמוֹדְעוּהִי׃ ט וּדְכִיר יוֹסֵף

רש"י

(ד) **פן יקראנו אסון.** ובבית לא יקראנו אסון, א"ר אליעזר בן יעקב מכאן שהשטן מקטרג בשעת הסכנה (ב"ר צא:ט; תנחומא ויגש א): (ה) **בתוך הבאים.** מטמינין עצמן שלא יכירום (תנחומא ו) לפי שצוה להם אביהם שלא יתראו כולם בפתח א' אלא שיכנס כל א' בפתחו כדי שלא תשלוט בהם עין הרע, שכולם נאים וכולם גבורים (תנחומא ח; ב"ר שם ו): (ו) **וישתחוו לו אפים.** נשתטחו לו על פניהם. וכן כל השתחואה פשוט ידים ורגלים הוא (מגילה כב:; שבועות טז:): (ז) **ויתנכר אליהם.** נעשה להם כנכרי בדברים לדבר קשות (תנחומא שם וב"ר שם): (ח) **ויכר יוסף וגו'.** לפי שהניחם חתומי זקן: **והם לא הכירוהו.** שיצא מאצלם בלא חתימת זקן ועכשיו מצאוהו בחתימת זקן (כתובות כז:; יבמות פח.; ב"ר צא:ז). ומ"א, ויכר יוסף את אחיו, כשנמסרו בידו הכיר שהם אחיו וריחם עליהם, והם לא

them when he joined them on their second trip, he was compensated for this by having the intense joy of meeting Joseph (*Oznaim LaTorah*).

6-13. The brothers bow to Joseph. Unknown to the brothers, Joseph had not only lived and prospered, he had set in place a plan to identify them and bring them to him when they arrived in Egypt, as he was sure they would eventually. When the lists of those entering Egypt showed that they had come, he ordered that only one storehouse be kept open, and that he would have sole authority over it. This guaranteed that he personally would meet his brothers. In addition, he instructed his trusted underlings to look for a group of men fitting their description (*Midrash*). *Ramban* offers a practical suggestion of how Joseph proceeded. He surely did not have the time to conduct every transaction; instead, he interviewed all national groups and then instructed his officials on how to deal with them. The brothers were the first to come from Canaan (*Ramban*). *Sforno* comments that it is not surprising that Joseph would be involved in every transaction, since his sales of food were the major source of governmental income.

The brothers, knowing that the original purchasers of Joseph had been bound for Egypt, wanted to find him and ransom him. They entered the country through ten different gates and spread out in the marketplaces looking for him (*Midrash*).

7. **וַיַּכִּרֵם וַיִּתְנַכֵּר אֲלֵיהֶם** — *And he recognized them, but he acted like a stranger toward them.* Joseph recognized his brothers immediately, both because he expected them and was looking for them. He, however, was beardless when they parted, so that it would have been much harder for them to recognize him, especially since he wore royal raiment and they could not have dreamt that the slave they sold would be ensconced on a throne. To assure that they would not know who he was, he took pains to behave like a stranger. *Ramban* adds that he probably lowered his hat to partially cover his face.

◆ Why Joseph concealed his identity and persecuted his brothers.

As noted before, *Ramban* explains that Joseph knew that his dreams were prophecies that had to be fulfilled, and he knew

אֶת הַחֲלֹמוֹת אֲשֶׁר חָלַם לָהֶם וַיֹּאמֶר אֲלֵהֶם
« to them, ‹ so he said « about them, ‹ he dreamed ‹ that ‹ the dreams

מְרַגְּלִים אַתֶּם לִרְאוֹת אֶת־עֶרְוַת הָאָרֶץ בָּאתֶם׃
« have you come! ‹ of the land ‹ the nakedness ‹ To see « you are! ‹ Spies

10 וַיֹּאמְרוּ אֵלָיו לֹא אֲדֹנִי וַעֲבָדֶיךָ בָּאוּ לִשְׁבָּר־
‹ to buy ‹ have come ‹ For your servants « my lord! ‹ Not so, ‹ to him, ‹ They said 10

אֹכֶל׃ 11 כֻּלָּנוּ בְּנֵי אִישׁ־אֶחָד נָחְנוּ כֵּנִים אֲנַחְנוּ לֹא־הָיוּ עֲבָדֶיךָ מְרַגְּלִים׃
« spies. ‹ have your servants been ‹ never « are we; ‹ truthful [people] « are we; ‹ of one man ‹ sons « All of us, 11 « food.

12 וַיֹּאמֶר אֲלֵהֶם לֹא כִּי־עֶרְוַת הָאָרֶץ בָּאתֶם לִרְאוֹת׃ 13 וַיֹּאמְרוּ
« And they said, 13 « to see. ‹ have you come ‹ of the land ‹ the nakedness ‹ Rather ‹ No! « to them, ‹ And he said 12

יָת חֶלְמַיָּא דִּי חֲלִים לְהוֹן וַאֲמַר לְהוֹן אַלִּילֵי אַתּוּן לְמֶחֱזֵי יָת בִּדְקָא דְאַרְעָא אֲתֵיתוּן׃ י וַאֲמָרוּ לֵהּ לָא רִבּוֹנִי וְעַבְדָךְ אֲתוֹ לְמִזְבַּן עִיבוּרָא׃ יא כֻּלָּנָא בְּנֵי גַּבְרָא חַד נָחְנָא כֵּיוָנֵי אֲנַחְנָא לָא הֲווֹ עַבְדָךְ אַלִּילֵי׃ יב וַאֲמַר לְהוֹן לָא אֱלָהֵן בִּדְקָא דְאַרְעָא אֲתֵיתוּן לְמֶחֱזֵי׃ יג וַאֲמָרוּ

רש"י

הכירוהו, כשנפל בידם לנהוג בו אחוה (ב"ר שם): (ט) **אשר חלם להם.** עליהם (תרגום יונתן) וידע שנתקיימו שהרי השתחוו לו: **ערות הארץ.** גלוי הארץ, מהיכן היא נוחה ליכבש, כמו את מקורה הערה (ויקרא כ:יח), וכמו ערום ועריה (יחזקאל טז:ז). וכן כל ערוה שבמקרא לשון גילוי. ות"א בדקא דארעא, כמו בדק הבית (מלכים ב יב:ו) רעוע הבית. אבל לא דקדק לפרשו אחר לשון המקרא: (י) **לא אדני.** לא תאמר כן, שהרי עבדיך באו לשבר אוכל: (יא) **כלנו בני איש אחד נחנו.** נצנצה בהם רוח הקדש וכללוהו עמהם שאף הוא בן אביהם (ב"ר לא:ז): **כנים.** אמתיים, כמו כן דברת (שמות י:כט) כן בנות צלפחד דוברות (במדבר כז:ז). ועברתו לא כן בדיו (ישעיה טז:ו): (יב) **כי ערות הארץ באתם לראות.** שהרי נכנסתם בעשרה שערי העיר, למה לא נכנסתם בשער אחד (תנחומא ח; ב"ר שם ו):

that he had to do all in his power to bring about that result. He also knew that the two dreams had to be fulfilled in sequence, the first and then the second. So far, *ten* brothers had bowed, but his first dream called for all eleven; therefore, he had to engineer Benjamin's appearance with the brothers, and only then could Jacob come, for the fulfillment of the second dream. Similarly, the anxiety Joseph later inflicted upon them by hiding the goblet in Benjamin's sack was for the purpose of testing their love for Benjamin before allowing him to travel with them.

Abarbanel suggests that Joseph's actions were designed to facilitate the brothers' true repentance for their sin against him. Judah's defense of Benjamin and offer of himself as a slave instead of Benjamin showed that Joseph's plan succeeded.

In another explanation of Joseph's behavior, *R' Hirsch* maintains that Joseph needed two tests before he could be reunited with his brothers: (a) Was their old rancor against him solely motivated by how they perceived the underlying motive of his dreams, or were they resentful of Rachel's special place in their father's affections? If the latter, then they could be as much of a menace to Benjamin as they had been to Joseph. And if Joseph had revealed himself now, when they were in his power, he would never know how much hatred lingered beneath the surface. Therefore, he wanted to put them into a situation where they could gain their own freedom at the expense of Benjamin's, and see how they would react. (b) If they hated Joseph when he merely *dreamed* of being a king, how much more would they hate him now that he truly had the power of life and death over them? Therefore, he wanted to show them that, after the long chain of events, he truly loved them and had only their good interests at heart. This, he was sure, would melt their long-standing resentment.

9. **מְרַגְּלִים אַתֶּם** — *Spies you are!* Joseph made this accusation to stop their attempt to learn the whereabouts of their long-lost brother, for if they were to persist in this effort, they might hear about the Hebrew slave who had become viceroy through a succession of dreams. But if they were under suspicion of spying, they would not dare circulate through the city asking questions (*Kli Yakar*).

11. **כֻּלָּנוּ בְּנֵי אִישׁ־אֶחָד נָחְנוּ** — *All of us, sons of one man are we.* The Divine Spirit was enkindled within them and they unwittingly included Joseph in their statement by saying, *"All of us* are the sons of one father" (*Midrash; Rashi*).

By mentioning that they were all sons of one man, they meant to counter the charge that they were treacherous spies. Their father Jacob, they contended, was a man of the highest repute. It would be a simple matter for Joseph to inquire about him and his family; that would be enough to dispel any notion that his sons could be spies (*Ramban*). Furthermore, no father would permit his entire family to go together on a mission as dangerous as espionage against a great power (*Daas Zekeinim*).

12-13. Joseph challenged them. "It cannot be as you say. If you are brothers traveling together, you would have entered the country together and not by ten different gates. Therefore, you must be involved in some conspiracy (*Rashi*; *Ramban*). Furthermore, how is it possible that not even one of you remained home to care for your father?" He asked this last question to determine if Benjamin was still alive, for he feared that they had done away with him, too (*Ralbag*). In reply they asserted that they came through different gates to look for their missing brother and that they had indeed left one brother at home.

שְׁנֵים עָשָׂר עֲבָדֶיךָ אַחִים | אֲנַחְנוּ בְּנֵי אִישׁ־אֶחָד

Your twelve servants » — brothers » are we, » the sons » of one man

בְּאֶרֶץ כְּנַעַן וְהִנֵּה הַקָּטֹן אֶת־אָבִינוּ הַיּוֹם וְהָאֶחָד

in the land of Canaan. » Indeed » the youngest » is with » our father » this day » and the [other] one

אֵינֶנּוּ: יד וַיֹּאמֶר אֲלֵהֶם יוֹסֵף הוּא אֲשֶׁר דִּבַּרְתִּי

is gone. 14 » But he said » to them, » Joseph did, » It is » just as » I have declared

אֲלֵכֶם לֵאמֹר מְרַגְּלִים אַתֶּם: טו בְּזֹאת תִּבָּחֵנוּ חֵי

to you, » saying: » 'Spies » you are!' 15 » By this » shall you be tested: » By the life

פַרְעֹה אִם־תֵּצְאוּ מִזֶּה כִּי אִם־בְּבוֹא אֲחִיכֶם הַקָּטֹן הֵנָּה: טז שִׁלְחוּ מִכֶּם

of Pharaoh! » If » you will leave » here » except » on condition » of the coming » of your brother » who is youngest » to here. 16 » Send » of you

אֶחָד וְיִקַּח אֶת־אֲחִיכֶם וְאַתֶּם הֵאָסְרוּ וְיִבָּחֲנוּ דִּבְרֵיכֶם הַאֱמֶת אִתְּכֶם

one, » and let him get » your brother » while you » shall remain imprisoned, » so that tested » may your words be, » whether truth » is with you;

וְאִם־לֹא חֵי פַרְעֹה כִּי מְרַגְּלִים אַתֶּם: יז וַיֶּאֱסֹף אֹתָם אֶל־מִשְׁמָר

but if » not, » by the life » of Pharaoh! » — surely » spies » you are! 17 » Then he gathered » them » into » custody

תְּרֵין עֲסַר עַבְדָיךְ אַחִין אֲנַחְנָא בְּנֵי גַבְרָא חַד בְּאַרְעָא דִכְנָעַן וְהָא זְעֵירָא עִם אֲבוּנָא יוֹמָא דֵין וְחַד לֵיתוֹהִי: יד וַאֲמַר לְהוֹן יוֹסֵף הוּא דִּי מַלֵּילִית עִמְּכוֹן לְמֵימַר אַלִּילֵי אַתּוּן: טו בְּדָא תִּתְבַּחֲרוּן חֵי פַרְעֹה אִם תִּפְקוּן מִכָּא אֱלָהֵין בְּמֵיתֵי אֲחוּכוֹן זְעֵירָא הָכָא: טז שְׁלָחוּ מִנְּכוֹן חַד וְיִדְבַּר יָת אֲחוּכוֹן וְאַתּוּן תִּתְאַסְרוּן וְיִתְבַּחֲרוּן פִּתְגָּמֵיכוֹן הַקְשׁוֹט אַתּוּן אָמְרִין וְאִם לָא חַיֵּי פַרְעֹה אֲרֵי אַלִּילֵי אַתּוּן: יז וּכְנַשׁ יָתְהוֹן לְמַטְּרָא (נ״א לְבֵית מַטְּרָא)

רש"י

(יג) **ויאמרו שנים עשר עבדיך וגו'.** ובשביל אותו א' שאיננו נתפזרנו בעיר לבקשו (שם ושם): (יד) **הוא אשר דברתי.** הדבר אשר דברתי שאתם מרגלים הוא האמת והנכון, זהו לפי פשוטו. ומדרשו, אמר להם ואילו מצאתם אותו ויפסקו עליכם ממון הרבה, תפדוהו. אמרו לו הן. אמר להם ואם יאמרו לכם שלא יחזירוהו בשום ממון מה תעשו. אמרו לכך באנו, להרוג או ליהרג. אמר להם הוא אשר דברתי אליכם, להרוג בני העיר באתם (ב"ר שם ז). מנחש אני בגביע שלי ששנים מכם החריבו כרך גדול של שכם (תנחומא שם;ב"ר שם ו): (טו) **חי פרעה.** אם יחיה פרעה. כשהיה נשבע לשקר היה נשבע בחיי פרעה (ב"ר שם ז): **אם תצאו מזה.** מן המקום הזה: (טז) **האמת אתכם.** אם אמת אתכם. לפיכך ה"א נקוד פתח שהוא כמו בלשון תימה, **ואם לא** תביאוהו **חי פרעה כי מרגלים אתם:** (יז) **משמר.** בית האסורים:

Sforno maintains that by speaking so freely about their family they hoped to prove their truthfulness, since everything they said was easily verifiable.

According to *R' Avraham ben HaRambam*, citing his grandfather, R' Maimon, their response did not counter the spying charge, but was in answer to another, unrecorded question that Joseph must have asked about their family. Such additional dialogue is alluded to by the brothers in their recapitulation of their adventures to Jacob, later in 43:7. In common Scriptural style, the Torah did not elaborate on the dialogue.

14-20. Joseph stands his ground, but offers his brothers a way out. Joseph pretended to find their protests of innocence unconvincing, and reemphasized his firm belief in their guilt. As the supreme viceroy of Egypt, he did not have to justify his accusations rationally; the brothers were in his power and it sufficed that such was his whim. However, after showing them that they were helpless, he offered them a way to prove their innocence.

15. בְּזֹאת תִּבָּחֵנוּ — *By this shall you be tested.* If your statement regarding a "youngest brother" can be verified, I will believe everything else you said as well (*B'chor Shor*). For if you are not brothers, you will never be able to find a stranger to come with you and put himself in mortal danger by posing as your brother (*Sforno*).

חֵי פַרְעֹה — *By the life of Pharaoh!* This was a formula for an oath, as if to say, "I swear by Pharaoh's life" (*Gur Aryeh*). *R' Bachya* comments that even though Joseph released nine of his brothers before Benjamin came (v. 19), he was not in violation of this oath, because he kept Simeon in the prison after he released the others.

To frighten them and make them more submissive, Joseph incarcerated them for three days, as a display of raw power.

16. שִׁלְחוּ מִכֶּם אֶחָד — *Send of you, one.* But none of the brothers volunteered to go because, seeing Joseph's unreasonable attitude, they felt that the mission would be futile, and they were fearful about Jacob's grief when he was told that nearly all of his sons were in prison (*Or HaChaim*).

18. Realizing that none of them would volunteer to fetch Benjamin, Joseph made a new proposal, which he prefaced with a soothing declaration of his concern for justice and fairness.

שְׁלֹשֶׁת יָמִים׃ יח וַיֹּאמֶר אֲלֵהֶם יוֹסֵף בַּיּוֹם הַשְּׁלִישִׁי

« on the third day, < did Joseph < to them < Say 18 « day < for a three [period].

זֹאת עֲשׂוּ וִחְיוּ אֶת־הָאֱלֹהִים אֲנִי יָרֵא׃ חמישי יט אִם־

< If 19 « fear: < do I < God « and live; < you shall do < This

כֵּנִים אַתֶּם אֲחִיכֶם אֶחָד יֵאָסֵר בְּבֵית מִשְׁמַרְכֶם

« you were in custody, < in the place < be imprisoned < let one of your brothers « you are, < truthful [people]

וְאַתֶּם לְכוּ הָבִיאוּ שֶׁבֶר רַעֲבוֹן בָּתֵּיכֶם׃

« of your households. < for the hunger < the provisions < and bring < go < while you

כ וְאֶת־אֲחִיכֶם הַקָּטֹן תָּבִיאוּ אֵלַי וְיֵאָמְנוּ דִבְרֵיכֶם וְלֹא תָמוּתוּ וַיַּעֲשׂוּ־

< And they did « and you will not die. < will be your words < thus verified « to me, < you shall bring < who is youngest < Then your brother 20

כֵן׃ כא וַיֹּאמְרוּ אִישׁ אֶל־אָחִיו אֲבָל אֲשֵׁמִים ׀ אֲנַחְנוּ עַל־אָחִינוּ אֲשֶׁר

< in that < our brother < on account of < are we < guilty < Indeed « his brother — < to < — [each] man « They [then] said 21 « so.

רָאִינוּ צָרַת נַפְשׁוֹ בְּהִתְחַנְנוֹ אֵלֵינוּ וְלֹא שָׁמָעְנוּ עַל־כֵּן בָּאָה אֵלֵינוּ

< upon us < has come < that < because of « and we did not listen; < to us < when he pleaded < of his soul < the anguish < we saw

הַצָּרָה הַזֹּאת׃ כב וַיַּעַן רְאוּבֵן אֹתָם לֵאמֹר הֲלוֹא אָמַרְתִּי אֲלֵיכֶם ׀ לֵאמֹר

« saying, < to you < Did I not speak « saying, < them < Reuben answered 22 « this anguish.

תְּלָתָא יוֹמִין: יח וַאֲמַר לְהוֹן יוֹסֵף בְּיוֹמָא תְלִיתָאָה דָּא עִיבִידוּ וְאִתְקַיָּמוּ מִן קֳדָם יְיָ אֲנָא דָחֵל: יט אִם כֵּינָנֵי אַתּוּן אֲחוּכוֹן חַד יִתְאַסַּר בְּבֵית מַטַּרְתְּכוֹן וְאַתּוּן אֱזִילוּ אוֹבִילוּ עִיבוּרָא דַּחֲסִיר בְּבָתֵּיכוֹן: כ וְיָת אֲחוּכוֹן זְעֵירָא תַּיְתוּן לְוָתִי וְיִתְהֵימְנוּן פִּתְגָמֵיכוֹן וְלָא תְמוּתוּן וַעֲבָדוּ כֵן: כא וַאֲמָרוּ גְּבַר לַאֲחוּהִי בְּקוּשְׁטָא חַיָּבִין אֲנַחְנָא עַל אָחוּנָא דִּי חֲזֵינָא עָקַת נַפְשֵׁהּ כַּד הֲוָה מִתְחַנֵּן לָנָא וְלָא קַבֵּלְנָא מִנֵּהּ עַל כֵּן אֲתָא לְוָתָנָא (נ״א אֲתַת לָנָא) עַקְתָא הָדָא: כב וַאֲתֵיב רְאוּבֵן יָתְהוֹן לְמֵימַר הֲלָא אֲמָרִית לְוָתְכוֹן לְמֵימַר

רש״י

(יט) **בבית משמרכם.** שאתם אסורים בו עכשיו: **ואתם לכו הביאו.** לבית אביכם: **שבר רעבון בתיכם.** מה שקניתם לרעבון אנשי בתיכם (תרגום יונתן): (כ) **ויאמנו דבריכם.** יתאמתו ויתקיימו, כמו אמן אמן (במדבר ה:כב), וכמו יאמן נא דבריך (מלכים א ח:כו): (כא) **אבל.** כתרגומו, בקושטא. ראיתי בב״ר (צא:ח) לישנא דרומאה [לשון בני הנגב] הוא, אבל, ברם: **באה אלינו.** טעמו בבי״ת לפי שהוא בלשון עבר, שכבר באה, ותרגומו אתת לנא:

אֶת־הָאֱלֹהִים אֲנִי יָרֵא — *God do I fear.* Accordingly, I will not keep *all* of you imprisoned while your families are starving. I will release most of you to bring provisions home while I detain only one of you as a hostage (*Ramban; Sforno*).

To the brothers, the viceroy of Egypt must have seemed like many of the rulers Jews have had to contend with throughout history, who pontificate piously about their devotion to morality and law, while their actions bespeak cruelty and hatred. No one will ever know how many Jews have bled under the lash of rulers who "feared God." Even Joseph's words implied these historic attitudes. Speaking as the viceroy and not as the righteous Joseph, he proclaimed to the brothers how ethical he was, but suggested not very subtly that they would die unless they obeyed him.

21-23. The brothers' regret. The brothers reaction at this point is illustrative of their greatness. They did not acknowledge guilt for their earlier judgment against Joseph; interpreting his actions as they did, they were convinced that they had acted properly and legally in ridding themselves of a mortal danger. To the contrary, since they felt at the time of the sale that they were obligated to remove Joseph from their midst, they felt that it would have been sinful to show compassion at a time when firmness was required. Now, however, seeing their new predicament as a punishment, they blamed themselves for their lack of compassion in how they carried out their decision. They regarded this callousness toward Joseph's entreaties — not the actual sale — as deserving punishment (*R' Aharon Kotler*).

Yafeh Toar notes that they contrasted their own behavior toward Joseph with that of the viceroy toward their hungry families. The Egyptian did not know and would never see those people in Canaan, yet he felt enough sympathy for their plight to send them food, but the brothers had been apathetic to their own flesh and blood.

אַל־תֶּחֶטְאוּ בַיֶּלֶד וְלֹא שְׁמַעְתֶּם וְגַם־דָּמוֹ הִנֵּה

‹ is now ‹ his blood ‹ Moreover, «‹ but you would not listen! «‹ against the boy,' ‹ sin ‹ 'Do not

נִדְרָשׁ: כג וְהֵם לֹא יָדְעוּ כִּי שֹׁמֵעַ יוֹסֵף כִּי הַמֵּלִיץ

‹ the interpreter ‹ for «‹ Joseph understood, ‹ that ‹ know ‹ did not ‹ They **23** «‹ being avenged.

בֵּינֹתָם: כד וַיִּסֹּב מֵעֲלֵיהֶם וַיֵּבְךְּ וַיָּשָׁב אֲלֵהֶם וַיְדַבֵּר

‹ and spoke ‹ to them ‹ then he returned «‹ and he wept; ‹ from them ‹ He turned away **24**«‹ was between them.

אֲלֵהֶם וַיִּקַּח מֵאִתָּם אֶת־שִׁמְעוֹן וַיֶּאֱסֹר אֹתוֹ

‹ him ‹ and imprisoned ‹ Simeon ‹ from them ‹ he took «‹ to them;

לְעֵינֵיהֶם: כה וַיְצַו יוֹסֵף וַיְמַלְאוּ אֶת־כְּלֵיהֶם בָּר וּלְהָשִׁיב כַּסְפֵּיהֶם אִישׁ

‹ each man ‹ their money, ‹ and to return «‹ with grain, ‹ their vessels ‹ and they filled «‹ Joseph commanded: **25** «‹ before their eyes.

אֶל־שַׂקּוֹ וְלָתֵת לָהֶם צֵדָה לַדָּרֶךְ וַיַּעַשׂ לָהֶם כֵּן: כו וַיִּשְׂאוּ אֶת־שִׁבְרָם

‹ their provisions ‹ Then they loaded **26** «‹ so. ‹ for them ‹ And he did «‹ for the journey. ‹ provisions ‹ them ‹ and to give «‹ his sack, ‹ into

עַל־חֲמֹרֵיהֶם וַיֵּלְכוּ מִשָּׁם: כז וַיִּפְתַּח הָאֶחָד אֶת־שַׂקּוֹ לָתֵת מִסְפּוֹא

‹ feed ‹ to give ‹ his sack ‹ The one [of them] opened **27** «‹ from there. ‹ and left ‹ their donkeys ‹ onto

לָא תְחוּבוּן (נ״א תֶּחֶטְאוּן) בְּעוּלֵימָא
וְלָא קַבֶּלְתּוּן וְאַף דְּמֵהּ הָא מִתְבְּעֵי:
כג וְאִנּוּן לָא יָדְעוּן אֲרֵי שְׁמִיעַ יוֹסֵף אֲרֵי
מְתֻרְגְּמָן הֲוָה בֵּינֵיהוֹן: כד וְאִסְתְּחַר
מֵעִלָּוֵיהוֹן וּבְכָא וְתָב לְוָתְהוֹן וּמַלִּיל
עִמְּהוֹן וּדְבַר מִלְוָתְהוֹן יָת שִׁמְעוֹן
וַאֲסַר יָתֵהּ לְעֵינֵיהוֹן: כה וּפַקִּיד יוֹסֵף
וּמְלוֹ יָת מָנֵיהוֹן עִיבוּרָא וּלְאָתָבָא
כַּסְפֵּיהוֹן גְּבַר לְסַקֵּהּ וּלְמִתַּן לְהוֹן זְוָדִין
לְאָרְחָא וַעֲבַד לְהוֹן כֵּן: כו וּנְטָלוּ יָת
עִיבוּרְהוֹן עַל חֲמָרֵיהוֹן וַאֲזָלוּ מִתַּמָּן:
כז וּפְתַח חַד יָת סַקֵּהּ לְמִתַּן כִּסְתָּא

רש״י

(כב) וגם דמו. אתין וגמין רבויין (ב"ר א:יד). דמו וגם דם הזקן (שם צא:ח): **(כג) והם לא ידעו כי שומע יוסף.** מבין לשונם, ובפניו היו מדברים כן (תרגום יונתן): **כי המליץ בינותם.** כי כשהיו מדברים עמו היה המליץ ביניהם היודע ל' עברי ולשון מצרי והיה מליץ דבריהם ליוסף ודברי יוסף להם, לכך היו סבורים שאין יוסף מכיר בלשון עברי (שם): **המליץ.** זה מנשה בנו (שם; ב"ר שם): **(כד) ויסב מעליהם.** נתרחק מעליהם שלא יראוהו בוכה: **ויבך.** לפי ששמע שהיו מתחרטין: **את שמעון.** הוא השליכו לבור, הוא שאמר ללוי הנה בעל החלומות הלזה בא (לעיל לז:יט; תנחומא ישן יז). ד"א, נתכוון יוסף להפרידו מלוי שמא יתיעצו שניהם להרוג אותו (תנחומא ויגש ד): **ויאסר אתו לעיניהם.** לא אסרו אלא לעיניהם וכיון שיצאו הוציאו והאכילו והשקהו (ב"ר צא:ח): **(כז) ויפתח האחד.** הוא לוי שנשאר יחיד משמעון בן זוגו (תרגום יונתן):

22. **וְגַם־דָּמוֹ** — *Moreover, his blood.* Although the brothers had not shed Joseph's blood, Reuben meant that Joseph, not accustomed to the hard life of slaves, had likely died in captivity, for which the brothers would be responsible (*Ramban*).

Following the Rabbinic rule that the word גַּם implies something *in addition* to what is mentioned explicitly, *Rashi* comments that Reuben implied that not only Joseph's blood was being avenged, but also Jacob's — because the brothers had caused him so many years of grief.

23. **כִּי הַמֵּלִיץ בֵּינֹתָם** — *For the interpreter was between them.* They had spoken to Joseph through an interpreter, so they assumed that he did not understand Hebrew. [Now the interpreter had left — for it is obvious that they would not have spoken these incriminating words had he still been present (*Radak; Mizrachi*).] According to the Midrash, the interpreter was Manasseh, Joseph's firstborn son (*Rashi*).

24. Joseph chooses his hostage. Having said that he would keep one of the brothers in Egypt as a hostage, Joseph now chose Simeon. The reason for this choice was because he was the one who had thrown Joseph into the pit and who had said derisively, "*Look! That dreamer is coming*" (37:19). Alternatively, Joseph wished to separate Simeon from Levi, lest the two of them conspire to kill him. The companionship of those two had been lethal before, since they were the ones who carried out the attack against Shechem (*Rashi*). *Ibn Ezra* suggests that, as the firstborn, Reuben would have been the logical hostage. Joseph spared Reuben in gratitude for his having been the one who tried to protect him when the brothers were planning to kill him. He took Simeon because he was the next oldest.

וַיֵּבְךְּ — *And wept.* Joseph's compassion was aroused and he wept at their distress (*Sforno*).

25-28. Joseph sends them back — with their money. On the one hand, Joseph treated them considerately, sending back food not only for the families of the nine who were going back to Canaan, but also for the family of Simeon, and even giving them extra provisions for the journey. On the other hand, he secretly had Manasseh put their money in their sacks. When they found it, they would surely suspect that it had been put there as a pretext to denounce them as thieves and sell them as slaves. Joseph did this to provide atonement — measure for measure — for those who had sold him as a slave (*Kli Yakar*).

27. **הָאֶחָד** — *The one of [them],* Levi. Now that he was separated

לַחֲמֹרוֹ בַּמָּלוֹן וַיַּרְא אֶת־כַּסְפּוֹ וְהִנֵּה־הוּא בְּפִי

‹ in the mouth ‹ it was ‹ and there « his money, ‹ he saw « at the inn, ‹ to his donkey

אַמְתַּחְתּוֹ: כח וַיֹּאמֶר אֶל־אֶחָיו הוּשַׁב כַּסְפִּי וְגַם

‹ and in addition, ‹ has my money been ‹ Returned « his brothers, ‹ to ‹ So he said 28 « of his sack.

הִנֵּה בְאַמְתַּחְתִּי וַיֵּצֵא לִבָּם וַיֶּחֶרְדוּ אִישׁ אֶל־

‹ to ‹ [each] man ‹ and they turned in trepidation, « did their hearts, ‹ Sink « in my sack! ‹ there it is

אָחִיו לֵאמֹר מַה־זֹּאת עָשָׂה אֱלֹהִים לָנוּ: כט וַיָּבֹאוּ

‹ They came 29 « to us? ‹ that God has done ‹ is this ‹ What « saying, ‹ his brother,

אֶל־יַעֲקֹב אֲבִיהֶם אַרְצָה כְּנָעַן וַיַּגִּידוּ לוֹ אֵת כָּל־

‹ of all ‹ him ‹ and they told « of Canaan, ‹ to the land ‹ their father ‹ Jacob ‹ to

הַקֹּרֹת אֹתָם לֵאמֹר: ל דִּבֶּר הָאִישׁ אֲדֹנֵי הָאָרֶץ אִתָּנוּ קָשׁוֹת וַיִּתֵּן אֹתָנוּ

‹ us ‹ and considered « harshly, ‹ to us « of the land— ‹ —the lord « The man spoke 30 « saying: ‹ to them, ‹ that had happened

כִּמְרַגְּלִים אֶת־הָאָרֶץ: לא וַנֹּאמֶר אֵלָיו כֵּנִים אֲנָחְנוּ לֹא הָיִינוּ מְרַגְּלִים:

« spies! ‹ We have never been « are we: ‹ 'Truthful [people] « to him, ‹ But we said 31 « the land. ‹ as spying out

לב שְׁנֵים־עָשָׂר אֲנַחְנוּ אַחִים בְּנֵי אָבִינוּ הָאֶחָד אֵינֶנּוּ וְהַקָּטֹן הַיּוֹם אֶת־

‹ with ‹ is now ‹ and the youngest ‹ is gone ‹ One « of our father. ‹ sons ‹ brothers, « are we, ‹ Twelve 32

אָבִינוּ בְּאֶרֶץ כְּנָעַן: לג וַיֹּאמֶר אֵלֵינוּ הָאִישׁ אֲדֹנֵי הָאָרֶץ בְּזֹאת אֵדַע

‹ I will know ‹ 'By this « of the land— ‹ the lord ‹ —the man, « to us ‹ Then he said 33 « of Canaan.' ‹ in the land ‹ our father

לַחֲמָרֵהּ בְּבֵית מְבָתָא וַחֲזָא יָת כַּסְפֵּהּ וְהָא הוּא בְּפוּם טוֹעֲנֵהּ: כח וַאֲמַר לַאֲחוֹהִי אִתּוֹתַב כַּסְפִּי וְאַף הָא בְטוֹעֲנִי וּנְפַק מַדַּע לִבְּהוֹן וּתְוָהוּ גְּבַר לַאֲחוּהִי לְמֵימַר מָה דָא עֲבַד יְיָ לָנָא: כט וַאֲתוֹ לְוַת יַעֲקֹב אֲבוּהוֹן אַרְעָא דִכְנָעַן וְחַוִּיאוּ לֵהּ יָת כָּל דְּאַרְעָן יָתְהוֹן לְמֵימָר: ל מַלִּיל גַּבְרָא רִבּוֹנָא דְאַרְעָא עִמָּנָא קַשְׁיָן וִיהַב יָתָנָא כִּמְאַלְּלֵי יָת אַרְעָא: לא וַאֲמַרְנָא לֵהּ כֵּיוָנֵי אֲנַחְנָא לָא הֲוֵינָא אַלִּילֵי: לב תְּרֵין עֲסַר אֲנַחְנָא אַחִין בְּנֵי אֲבוּנָא חַד לֵיתוֹהִי וּזְעֵירָא יוֹמָא דֵין עִם אֲבוּנָא בְּאַרְעָא דִכְנָעַן: לג וַאֲמַר לָנָא גַּבְרָא רִבּוֹנָא דְאַרְעָא בְּדָא אִדַּע

רש"י

במלון. במקום שלנו בלילה: **אמתחתו.** הוא השק: (כח) **וגם הנה באמתחתי.** גם הכסף בו עם התבואה: **מה זאת עשה אלהים לנו.** להביאנו לידי עלילה זו, שלא

from his companion Simeon, he was *the one* (*Rashi*).

According to *Abarbanel* and *Malbim,* Joseph ordered that the money of all the brothers be placed near the *bottom* of their packs, but that Levi's be near the top of his. He wanted Levi to discover the money and be distressed even during the journey, because he, Levi, was the most guilty for the sale [and this would provide him atonement, measure for measure].

28. הוּשַׁב כַּסְפִּי — *Returned has my money been.* His fright was greatest when he recognized the money as *his own* so that he was vulnerable to a personal accusation. Joseph wanted the brothers to realize how fully they were in his power and that he could do as he pleased with them (*R' Hirsch*).

מַה־זֹּאת עָשָׂה אֱלֹהִים לָנוּ — *What is this that God has done to us,* by letting us be suspected? For the money was returned only to furnish a pretext for a plot against us (*Rashi*).

According to *Sforno,* the brothers were mystified. The self-proclaimed "God-fearing" viceroy was treating them in a way that would give him an excuse to enslave them. By letting this be done to them, God seemed to be treating them measure for measure for having enslaved Joseph. But Joseph had deserved an even harsher punishment — he deserved to die! Since they had acted with mercy by reducing his sentence to enslavement, why should this be happening to them?

29-38. Their dialogue with Jacob. The Torah records how the brothers reported their experiences to Jacob, but a comparison of the following *verbatim* recapitulation with the narrative above will show that they concealed certain things, to minimize the gravity of their dilemma (*Akeidah; Ralbag*). They minimized the harshness of Joseph's ultimatums to spare Jacob unnecessary grief, and because Jacob would never allow Benjamin to return with them if he had known how relentlessly the viceroy had treated them (*Alshich, Ralbag*). For example,

כִּי כֵנִים אַתֶּם אֲחִיכֶם הָאֶחָד הַנִּיחוּ אִתִּי

<< with me; < leave < One of your brothers, << you are: < truthful [people] < that

וְאֶת־רַעֲבוֹן בָּתֵּיכֶם קְחוּ וָלֵכוּ׃ לד וְהָבִיאוּ

< And bring 34 << and go. < take < of your households < and [what is needed for] the hunger

אֶת־אֲחִיכֶם הַקָּטֹן אֵלַי וְאֵדְעָה כִּי לֹא מְרַגְּלִים

< spies < not < that < then I will know < to me; < who is youngest < your brother

אַתֶּם כִּי כֵנִים אַתֶּם אֶת־אֲחִיכֶם אֶתֵּן לָכֶם

< to you < I will give [back] < Your brother << you are. < truthful [people] < rather << are you;

וְאֶת־הָאָרֶץ תִּסְחָרוּ׃ לה וַיְהִי הֵם מְרִיקִים שַׂקֵּיהֶם וְהִנֵּה־אִישׁ צְרוֹר־

< the bundle < — for each man << they beheld! << their sacks, < were emptying < as they < Then it was, 35 << you will [be free to] circulate.' < the land < and about

כַּסְפּוֹ בְּשַׂקּוֹ וַיִּרְאוּ אֶת־צְרֹרוֹת כַּסְפֵּיהֶם הֵמָּה וַאֲבִיהֶם וַיִּירָאוּ׃

<< they were terrified. << and their father — < — they << of their money < the bundles < [When] they saw << was in his sack. < of his money

לו וַיֹּאמֶר אֲלֵהֶם יַעֲקֹב אֲבִיהֶם אֹתִי שִׁכַּלְתֶּם יוֹסֵף אֵינֶנּוּ וְשִׁמְעוֹן אֵינֶנּוּ

<< is gone, < Simeon << is gone, < Joseph << you have bereaved! < Me << their father, < did Jacob < to them < Say 36

וְאֶת־בִּנְיָמִן תִּקָּחוּ עָלַי הָיוּ כֻלָּנָה׃ לז וַיֹּאמֶר רְאוּבֵן אֶל־אָבִיו לֵאמֹר

<< saying, < his father, < to < Then Reuben said 37 << all of them! < have befallen < Upon me << you want to take away? < and [now] Benjamin

אֲרֵי כֵּיוָנֵי אַתּוּן אֲחוּכוֹן חַד שְׁבוּקוּ לְוָתִי וְיָת עִיבוּרָא דְחַסִּיר בְּבָתֵּיכוֹן סִיבוּ וְאֱזִילוּ׃ לד וְאַיְתוּ יָת אֲחוּכוֹן זְעֵירָא לְוָתִי וְאִדַּע אֲרֵי לָא אַלִילֵי אַתּוּן אֲרֵי כֵּיוָנֵי אַתּוּן יָת אֲחוּכוֹן אֶתֵּן לְכוֹן וְיָת אַרְעָא תַּעְבְּדוּן בַּהּ סְחוֹרְתָּא׃ לה וַהֲוָה אִנּוּן מְרִיקִין סַקֵּיהוֹן וְהָא גְּבַר צְרָר כַּסְפֵּהּ בְּסַקֵּהּ וַחֲזוֹ יָת צְרָרֵי כַסְפֵּיהוֹן אִנּוּן וַאֲבוּהוֹן וּדְחִילוּ׃ לו וַאֲמַר לְהוֹן יַעֲקֹב אֲבוּהוֹן יָתִי אַתְכֵּלְתּוּן יוֹסֵף לֵיתוֹהִי וְשִׁמְעוֹן לָא הֲוָה הָכָא (נ״א לֵיתוֹהִי) וְיָת בִּנְיָמִן תִּדְבְּרוּן עֲלַי הֲווֹ כֻלְּהוֹן׃ לז וַאֲמַר רְאוּבֵן לְוַת אֲבוּהִי לְמֵימַר

רש״י

הוסב אלא להתעולל עלינו: (לד) ואת הארץ תסחרו. תסובבו. וכל לשון סוחרים וסחורה על שם שמחזרים וסובבים אחר הפרקמטיא: (לה) צרור כספו. קשר כספו (תרגום יונתן): (לו) אותי שכלתם. מלמד שחשדן שמא [י]הרגוהו או [י]מכרוהו כיוסף (שם; ב״ר לא:ט): שכלתם. כל מי שבניו אבודים קרוי שכול:

they said that Joseph had judged them *as if* they were spies, not that he had made a firm accusation against them. They also omitted Joseph's strong implications that their lives were at stake, and that he had jailed them for three days.

35. וַיִּירָאוּ — *They were terrified.* They knew that money could have been left in one sack by a careless official, but the money in *all* their sacks could not possibly be an oversight. It was obvious that a plot was being implemented against them (*Alshich*).

36. אֹתִי שִׁכַּלְתֶּם — *Me you have bereaved.* This term refers to one who has lost his children. Accordingly, Jacob's remark implies that he suspected them of having slain or sold Simeon as they might have done to Joseph (*Rashi*, according to *Gur Aryeh*). [For they came back now with extra money, without their brother Simeon, just as before they came back with money, but without their brother Joseph.]

Jacob argued rather logically that since Joseph and Simeon had suffered misfortune when they had traveled in the company of their brothers, he could not be expected to submit Benjamin to the same jeopardy (*R' Hirsch*).

עָלַי — *Upon me.* Your grief, as brothers, cannot compare with mine as a father! (*Akeidah*).

Alternatively, the blame for all of their misfortune is upon me. I caused Joseph's death by sending him into danger, and I will be similarly held accountable for Simeon — and for Benjamin, as well, if I allow him to go to a place of danger (*Malbim*).

37-38. As the firstborn, Reuben felt that it was his responsibility to speak up. His frightening statement was meant figuratively, for he surely did not mean that Jacob would actually kill the two sons; rather, Reuben spoke in the sense of obligating himself under the penalty of a *curse* that he would care for Benjamin (*Ramban*). By expressing himself so emphatically, Reuben felt that he would convince Jacob of his determination to guard Benjamin zealously. Jacob did not reply directly to him; he merely said that Benjamin would not go to Egypt with them. *Rashi*, quoting the Midrash, says that Jacob said to himself, "He is a fool, this eldest son of mine. He suggests that I should kill his sons. Are not his sons also my sons?"

The reasons Jacob gave for refusing Reuben's offer were sin-

אֶת־שְׁנֵי בָנַי תָּמִית אִם־לֹא אֲבִיאֶנּוּ אֵלֶיךָ תְּנָה
Two of my sons may you put to death if I do not bring him back to you. Put
אֹתוֹ עַל־יָדִי וַאֲנִי אֲשִׁיבֶנּוּ אֵלֶיךָ: לח וַיֹּאמֶר לֹא־
him in my care and I will return him to you. 38 But he said, He shall not
יֵרֵד בְּנִי עִמָּכֶם כִּי־אָחִיו מֵת וְהוּא לְבַדּוֹ נִשְׁאָר
go down my son — with you, for his brother is dead and he alone is left.
וּקְרָאָהוּ אָסוֹן בַּדֶּרֶךְ אֲשֶׁר תֵּלְכוּ־בָהּ וְהוֹרַדְתֶּם
Should there befall him disaster on the road which you shall travel upon it, then you will have brought down
אֶת־שֵׂיבָתִי בְּיָגוֹן שְׁאוֹלָה: [מג] א וְהָרָעָב כָּבֵד בָּאָרֶץ: ב וַיְהִי כַּאֲשֶׁר
my old age in sorrow to the grave. 43 1 The famine was severe in the land. 2 And it was when
כִּלּוּ לֶאֱכֹל אֶת־הַשֶּׁבֶר אֲשֶׁר הֵבִיאוּ מִמִּצְרָיִם וַיֹּאמֶר אֲלֵיהֶם אֲבִיהֶם
they had finished eating the provisions that they had brought from Egypt, he said to them, their father did,
שֻׁבוּ שִׁבְרוּ־לָנוּ מְעַט־אֹכֶל: ג וַיֹּאמֶר אֵלָיו יְהוּדָה לֵאמֹר הָעֵד הֵעִד
Go back, buy us a little food. 3 But he said to him, Judah did, saying, Sternly warn
בָּנוּ הָאִישׁ לֵאמֹר לֹא־תִרְאוּ פָנַי בִּלְתִּי אֲחִיכֶם אִתְּכֶם: ד אִם־יֶשְׁךָ
us did the man saying, 'You shall not see my face unless your brother is with you.' 4 If you have [the will]

יָת תְּרֵין בְּנַי תְּמִית אִם לָא אַיְתִנֵּהּ לְוָתָךְ הַב יָתֵהּ עַל יְדִי וַאֲנָא אֲתֵבִנֵּהּ לָךְ: לח וַאֲמַר לָא יֵחוֹת בְּרִי עִמְּכוֹן אֲרֵי אֲחוּהִי מִית וְהוּא בִּלְחוֹדוֹהִי אִשְׁתְּאַר וִיעַרְעִנֵּהּ מוֹתָא בְּאָרְחָא דִּי תְהָכוּן בַּהּ וְתַחֲתוּן יָת שֵׂיבְתִי בְּדָווֹנָא לִשְׁאוֹל: א וְכַפְנָא תַּקִּיף בְּאַרְעָא: ב וַהֲוָה כַּד שֵׁיצִיאוּ (נ״א סַפִּיקוּ) לְמֵיכַל יָת עִיבוּרָא דְּאַיְתִיאוּ מִמִּצְרָיִם וַאֲמַר לְהוֹן אֲבוּהוֹן תּוּבוּ זְבוּנוּ לָנָא זְעֵיר עִיבוּרָא: ג וַאֲמַר לֵהּ יְהוּדָה לְמֵימָר אַסְהָדָא אַסְהֵד בָּנָא גַּבְרָא לְמֵימַר לָא תֶחֱזוּן אַפַּי אֱלָהֵן כַּד אֲחוּכוֹן עִמְּכוֹן: ד אִם אִיתָךְ

רש״י

(לח) **לא ירד בני עמכם.** לא קבל דבריו של ראובן, אמר, בכור שוטה הוא זה, הוא אומר להמית בניו, וכי בניו הם ולא בני (שם): (ב) **כאשר כלו לאכול.** יהודה אמר להם המתינו לזקן עד שתכלה פת מן הבית (תנחומא ח): **כאשר כלו.** כד שיציאו, והמתרגם כד ספיקו טועה. כאשר כלו הגמלים לשתות (לעיל כד:כב) מתורגם כד ספיקו, כשגמרו די ספוקם הוא גמר שתייתם, אבל זה, כאשר כלו לאכול, כאשר תם האוכל הוא, ומתרגמינן כד שיציאו: (ג) **העד העיד.** לשון התראה, שבשם התראה

cere, quite valid, and equally applicable to Judah's later offer [43:8]. Nevertheless, Jacob acceded to Judah's request because he had more confidence in him, and because the timing of his offer was propitious (*Ramban*).

38. **וְהוֹרַדְתֶּם אֶת־שֵׂיבָתִי בְּיָגוֹן שְׁאוֹלָה** — *Then you will have brought down my old age* (lit., white hair) *in sorrow to the grave.* I will never cease mourning. Benjamin is Rachel's only survivor; while he is with me, I find consolation for the loss of his mother and brother. If he should die, it would be as if the three of them died on the same day (see *Rashi* 44:29).

43.

1-15. Jacob sends Benjamin to Egypt.

1. **וְהָרָעָב כָּבֵד בָּאָרֶץ** — *The famine was severe in the land*, it grew more severe (*Ralbag*). In this context, the *land* refers to *Eretz Yisrael*, the land *par excellence* (*Akeidah*).

2. **כַּאֲשֶׁר כִּלּוּ לֶאֱכֹל אֶת־הַשֶּׁבֶר** — *When they had finished eating the provisions.* Presumably the issue of a return trip to Egypt arose when there was only enough food left to last until they could go there and come back (*Or HaChaim*).

Seeing how adamant Jacob had been when there was an adequate supply of food in hand, Judah had advised his brothers to wait until the household ran out of food — for then Jacob would be forced to let Benjamin go (*Rashi; Ramban* 42:37).

שֻׁבוּ — *Go back.* Although Jacob had heard them insist that they dared not go back without Benjamin, he may not have believed them. He suspected that they wanted to take Benjamin to do away with him, as they might have done to Joseph. He had implied this suspicion when he said (42:37) that they had bereaved him (*Sforno*).

3-5. Judah quoted the Egyptian viceroy in stronger terms than the brothers had used earlier (42:24). Then, they had minimized their predicament in order to spare Jacob and give him less reason to oppose Benjamin's return with them. Now that only extreme urgency would make Jacob consent, the situation demanded unabashed candor. Judah added that the brothers would refuse to go without Benjamin.

מְשַׁלֵּחַ אֶת־אָחִינוּ אִתָּנוּ נֵרְדָה וְנִשְׁבְּרָה לְךָ

‹ for you ‹ and we will buy ‹ we will go down « with us, ‹ our brother ‹ to send

אֹכֶל: ה וְאִם־אֵינְךָ מְשַׁלֵּחַ לֹא נֵרֵד כִּי־הָאִישׁ

‹ the man ‹ for « go down, ‹ we will not « send [him], ‹ you do not ‹ But if **5** *« food.*

אָמַר אֵלֵינוּ לֹא־תִרְאוּ פָנַי בִּלְתִּי אֲחִיכֶם אִתְּכֶם:

« is with you.' ‹ your brother ‹ unless ‹ my face ‹ 'You shall not see « to us, ‹ said

ו וַיֹּאמֶר יִשְׂרָאֵל לָמָה הֲרֵעֹתֶם לִי לְהַגִּיד לָאִישׁ

‹ the man ‹ by telling ‹ to me ‹ did you cause harm ‹ Why ‹ Then Israel said, **6**

מְשַׁלַּח יָת אָחוּנָא עִמָּנָא נֵיחוֹת וְנִזְבֵּן לָךְ עִיבוּרָא: ה וְאִם לֵיתָךְ מְשַׁלַּח לָא נֵיחוֹת אֲרֵי גַבְרָא אֲמַר לָנָא לָא תֶחֱזוֹן אַפַּי אֱלָהֵן כַּד אֲחוּכוֹן עִמְּכוֹן: ו וַאֲמַר יִשְׂרָאֵל לְמָא אַבְאֶשְׁתּוּן לִי לְחַוָּאָה לְגַבְרָא הַעַד כְּעַן לְכוֹן אָח: ז וַאֲמָרוּ מִשְׁאַל שָׁאֵל גַּבְרָא לָנָא וּלְיַלָּדוּתָנָא לְמֵימַר הַעַד כְּעַן אֲבוּכוֹן קַיָּם הַאִית לְכוֹן אָחָא וְחַוֵּינָא לֵהּ עַל מֵימַר פִּתְגָמַיָּא הָאִלֵּין הֲמִדַּע הֲוֵינָא יָדְעִין אֲרֵי יֵימַר אוֹחִיתוּ יָת אֲחוּכוֹן: ח וַאֲמַר יְהוּדָה לְיִשְׂרָאֵל אֲבוּהִי שְׁלַח עוּלֵימָא עִמִּי וּנְקוּם וּנְהָךְ וְנֵיחֵי וְלָא נְמוּת אַף אֲנַחְנָא אַף אַתְּ אַף טַפְלָנָא: ט אֲנָא מְעָרַבְנָא בֵּהּ מִן יְדִי תִּבְעִנֵּהּ אִם לָא אַיְתִנֵּהּ

הַעוֹד לָכֶם אָח: ז וַיֹּאמְרוּ שָׁאוֹל שָׁאַל־הָאִישׁ לָנוּ וּלְמוֹלַדְתֵּנוּ לֵאמֹר

« saying, ‹ and about our family ‹ about us ‹ did the man ‹ Persistently ask ‹ And they said, **7** *« a brother? ‹ you had ‹ that additionally*

הַעוֹד אֲבִיכֶם חַי הֲיֵשׁ לָכֶם אָח וַנַּגֶּד־לוֹ עַל־פִּי הַדְּבָרִים הָאֵלֶּה

« these words; ‹ according to ‹ him ‹ and we told « a brother?' ‹ Do you have « alive? ‹ your father ‹ 'Is yet

הֲיָדוֹעַ נֵדַע כִּי יֹאמַר הוֹרִידוּ אֶת־אֲחִיכֶם: ח וַיֹּאמֶר יְהוּדָה אֶל־יִשְׂרָאֵל

‹ Israel ‹ to ‹ Then Judah said **8** *« your brother'? ‹ 'Bring down « he would say, ‹ that ‹ could we possibly have known*

אָבִיו שִׁלְחָה הַנַּעַר אִתִּי וְנָקוּמָה וְנֵלֵכָה וְנִחְיֶה וְלֹא נָמוּת גַּם־אֲנַחְנוּ

‹ we, ‹ also « and we will not die, ‹ so we will live « and go, ‹ and let us rise up ‹ with me ‹ the lad ‹ Send « his father,

גַּם־אַתָּה גַּם־טַפֵּנוּ: ט אָנֹכִי אֶעֶרְבֶנּוּ מִיָּדִי תְּבַקְשֶׁנּוּ אִם־לֹא הֲבִיאֹתִיו

‹ I do not bring him back ‹ If « you can demand him. ‹ from my [own] hand « will [personally] guarantee him; ‹ I **9** *« our children. ‹ also ‹ you, ‹ also*

רש"י

מתרה בו בפני עדים. [וכן העידותי בכם היום (דברים ח:יט, ל:יט)] וכן העד העידותי באבותיכם (ירמיה יא:ז) רד העד בעם (שמות יט:כא): **לא תראו פני בלתי אחיכם אתכם.** לא תראוני בלא אחיכם אתכם (תרגום יונתן). ואונקלוס תרגם אלהין כד אחוכון עמכון, ויישב הדבר על אופנו ולא דקדק לתרגם אחר לשון המקרא: (ז) **לנו ולמולדתנו.** למשפחותינו. ומדרשו, אפילו עצי עריסותינו גלה לנו (ב"ר לח:י): **ונגד לו.** שיש לנו אב ואח: **על פי הדברים האלה.** ע"פ שאלותיו אשר שאל הוזקקנו להגיד: **כי יאמר.** אשר יאמר. כי משמש בלשון אם ואם משמש בלשון אשר, ה"ז שמוש אחד מארבע לשונות שמשמש כי והוא אי (ר"ה ג.), שהרי כי זה כמו אם, כמו עד אם דברתי דברי (לעיל כד:לג): (ח) **ונחיה.** נצנצה בו רוה"ק, על ידי הליכה זו תחי רוחך, שנא' ותחי רוח יעקב אביהם (להלן מה:כז): **ולא נמות.** ברעב.

6-7. וַיֹּאמֶר יִשְׂרָאֵל — *Then Israel said.* Israel is the name used to depict Jacob in his spiritual role as Patriarch of the Jewish nation. In this case, he is referred to as Israel, because he offered them a teaching for future generations: Whenever Jews are forced to appear before hostile rulers, they should not offer more information than the question requires. Since the obviously unfriendly viceroy had not asked them if they had any brothers at home, they should not have volunteered it (*Haamek Davar*). They defended themselves against Jacob's charge that they had loose tongues (*Akeidah*), saying that Joseph had questioned them exhaustively, but not in such a sinister way that they had reason to fear the consequences of a full response (*Abarbanel*).

8. וַיֹּאמֶר יְהוּדָה — *Then Judah said.* Judah argued that if Benjamin were to go, it was not definite that he would be harmed, but if Jacob's refusal made it impossible for them to purchase food, they would all surely die of hunger. It is better to set aside the doubtful in favor of the definite (*Rashi* from *Tanchuma*).

9. אָנֹכִי אֶעֶרְבֶנּוּ — *I will [personally] guarantee him.* Judah tried to remove one of Jacob's fears. If all the brothers collectively guaranteed Benjamin's safety, then no one would be responsi-

אֵלֶיךָ וְהִצַּגְתִּיו לְפָנֶיךָ וְחָטָאתִי לְךָ כָּל־הַיָּמִים׃

« time. ‹ [for] all ‹ to you ‹ then I will have sinned ‹‹ before you, ‹ and stand him ‹ to you

י כִּי לוּלֵא הִתְמַהְמָהְנוּ כִּי־עַתָּה שַׁבְנוּ זֶה פַעֲמָיִם׃

« twice. ‹ surely ‹ we could have returned ‹ [by] now ‹ then ‹‹ dallied, ‹ had we not ‹ For 10

יא וַיֹּאמֶר אֲלֵהֶם יִשְׂרָאֵל אֲבִיהֶם אִם־כֵּן ׀ אֵפוֹא

‹ here now, ‹ it must be so, ‹ If ‹‹ their father, ‹ did Israel ‹ to them ‹ Say 11

זֹאת עֲשׂוּ קְחוּ מִזִּמְרַת הָאָרֶץ בִּכְלֵיכֶם וְהוֹרִידוּ

‹ and bring it down ‹ in your vessels ‹ of the land ‹ of the choicest ‹ Take ‹‹ you shall do: ‹ this

לָאִישׁ מִנְחָה מְעַט צֳרִי וּמְעַט דְּבַשׁ נְכֹאת וָלֹט בָּטְנִים וּשְׁקֵדִים׃

« and almonds. ‹ pistachios, ‹ lotus, ‹ wax, ‹ of honey, ‹ a bit ‹ of balsam, ‹ a bit ‹‹ [as] a tribute: ‹ to the man

יב וְכֶסֶף מִשְׁנֶה קְחוּ בְיֶדְכֶם וְאֶת־הַכֶּסֶף הַמּוּשָׁב בְּפִי אַמְתְּחֹתֵיכֶם

‹ of your sacks ‹ in the mouth ‹ that was returned ‹ and the money ‹‹ in your hands, ‹ take ‹ And double the money 12

תָּשִׁיבוּ בְיֶדְכֶם אוּלַי מִשְׁגֶּה הוּא׃ יג וְאֶת־אֲחִיכֶם קָחוּ וְקוּמוּ שׁוּבוּ אֶל־

‹ to ‹ return ‹ and rise up, ‹‹ take, ‹ Your brother 13 «it was. ‹ a mistake ‹ perhaps ‹‹ in your hands; ‹ return

לָךְ וַאֲקִימִנֵּהּ קֳדָמָךְ וְאֵהֵי חָטֵי לָךְ כָּל יוֹמַיָּא׃ י אֲרֵי אִלוּלָפוֹן בְּדָא אִיתְעַכַּבְנָא אֲרֵי כְעַן תַּבְנָא דְנַן תַּרְתֵּין זִמְנִין׃ יא וַאֲמַר לְהוֹן יִשְׂרָאֵל אֲבוּהוֹן אִם כֵּן הָכָא דָא עִיבִידוּ סִיבוּ מִדִּמְשַׁבַּח אַרְעָא (נ״א בְּאַרְעָא) בְּמָנֵיכוֹן וְאוֹחִיתוּ לְגַבְרָא תִּקְרֻבְתָּא זְעֵיר קְטַף וּזְעֵיר דְּבַשׁ שְׁעַף וּלְטוֹם בָּטְנִין וְשִׁגְדִּין׃ יב וְכַסְפָּא עַל חַד תְּרֵין סִיבוּ בִּידְכוֹן וְיָת כַּסְפָּא דְּאִתּוֹתַב בְּפוּם טוֹעֲנֵיכוֹן תְּתִיבוּן בִּידְכוֹן מָאִים שָׁלוּ הוּא׃ יג וְיָת אֲחוּכוֹן דְּבָרוּ וְקוּמוּ תּוּבוּ לְוַת

רש״י

בנימין ספק יתפש ספק לא יתפש, ואנו כלנו מתים ברעב אם לא נלך. מוטב שתניח את הספק ותתפוש את הודאי (תנחומא ח): (ט) **והצגתיו לפניך.** שלא אביאנו אליך מת כי אם חי (עי' תמורה לב:): **וחטאתי לך כל הימים.** לעוה״ב (ב״ר שם): (י) **לולא התמהמהנו.** על ידך כבר היינו שבים עם שמעון ולא נצטערת כל הימים הללו: (יא) **אפוא.** כל לשון אפוא לשון יתר הוא לתקן המלה בלשון עברי. **אם כן** אזדקק לעשות שאלתנו עמכם צריך אני לחזור ולבקש איה פה תקנה ועצה להשיאכם, ואומר אני **זאת עשו: מזמרת הארץ.** מתורגם מדמשבח בארעא, שהכל מזמרים עליו כשהוא בא לעולם (ב״ר שם יא): **נכאת.** שעוה (שם): **בטנים.** לא ידעתי מה הם. ובפירוש א״ב של רבי מכיר ראיתי פיסטציא״ש, ודומה לי שהם אפרסקין: (יב) **וכסף משנה.** פי שנים כראשון (אונקלוס): **קחו בידכם.** לשבור אוכל שמא הוקר השער (ב״ר שם): **אולי משגה הוא.** שמא הממונה על הבית שכחו שוגג:

ble ultimately, because each would shift the blame to the others. Instead, Judah promised to take sole responsibility. "I will guard him from heat, cold, evil beasts, and brigands. I will offer my life for his and do anything necessary to assure his safety" (*Bechor Shor*).

In his commentary to ArtScroll *Bereishis,* R' Meir Zlotowitz suggests another reason why Judah's offer was more acceptable than Reuben's. When Jacob said, "Upon *me* has it all fallen" (42:36), he implied, as mentioned by the commentators, that only a father could realize the magnitude of the loss of two of his children. Of all the brothers, only Judah, who had lost two children (38:7,10), could appreciate his father's grief. Therefore, when he accepted responsibility for Benjamin's welfare, Jacob acquiesced.

11. וְהוֹרִידוּ לָאִישׁ מִנְחָה — *And bring it down to the man [as] a tribute.* Jacob instructed them that the gift should be sent to the viceroy before they saw him. From the way he reacted to the gift, they would then have an idea of how he would treat them (*Sforno*).

Jacob chose the gift with taste and sophistication. The ruler of a rich country would not be impressed with a large and lavish gift; he was too rich for that. Rather, Jacob selected Canaanite delicacies that were unavailable in Egypt. Some of the items listed here were identical to those brought by Ishmaelite caravans to Egypt [37:25], indicating that they were not readily available in Egypt (cf. *Sforno; Chizkuni*).

12. וְכֶסֶף מִשְׁנֶה — *And double the money*. Take twice as much money as you had on your first trip; perhaps the price of grain has risen (*Rashi*). Perhaps Jacob wanted them to buy a double ration to spare them the difficulty of an early return to Egypt for more provisions (*R' Abraham ben HaRambam*), and perhaps also to subject them to the mercurial viceroy's whims as infrequently as possible.

תָּשִׁיבוּ בְיֶדְכֶם — *Return in your hands*. Jacob meant this literally. "Do not leave the money in your sacks, nor wait until you are asked for it, but *carry it in your hands* to demonstrate immediately that you are honest men and have come to return any money not rightfully yours" (*Alshich*).

אוּלַי מִשְׁגֶּה הוּא — *Perhaps a mistake it was.* Jacob reasoned that the officials may have put the payments on top of the sacks to help them identify the owners of the sacks, and then, due to the confusion, forgotten to take the money when filling the sacks and delivering them to the customers (*Rashbam; Radak*).

הָאִישׁ: יד וְאֵל שַׁדַּי יִתֵּן לָכֶם רַחֲמִים לִפְנֵי הָאִישׁ

‹ the man ‹ before ‹ mercy ‹ you ‹ grant ‹ Shaddai ‹ And may El 14 « the man.

וְשִׁלַּח לָכֶם אֶת־אֲחִיכֶם אַחֵר וְאֶת־בִּנְיָמִין

« Benjamin. ‹ as well as « — the other one — « your brother ‹ to you ‹ that he may set free

וַאֲנִי כַּאֲשֶׁר שָׁכֹלְתִּי שָׁכָלְתִּי: טו וַיִּקְחוּ הָאֲנָשִׁים

‹ So the men took 15 « so am I bereaved. ‹ I have been bereaved, ‹ as ‹ And as for me,

אֶת־הַמִּנְחָה הַזֹּאת וּמִשְׁנֶה־כֶּסֶף לָקְחוּ בְיָדָם

‹ in their hands, ‹ they took ‹ money ‹ and double ‹ this tribute

וְאֶת־בִּנְיָמִן וַיָּקֻמוּ וַיֵּרְדוּ מִצְרַיִם וַיַּעַמְדוּ לִפְנֵי יוֹסֵף: ששי טז וַיַּרְא יוֹסֵף

‹ Joseph saw 16 « Joseph. ‹ before ‹ and they stood ‹ to Egypt ‹ and went down ‹ They rose up « Benjamin. ‹ as well as

אִתָּם אֶת־בִּנְיָמִין וַיֹּאמֶר לַאֲשֶׁר עַל־בֵּיתוֹ הָבֵא אֶת־הָאֲנָשִׁים הַבָּיְתָה

« into the house. ‹ the men ‹ Bring « of his house, ‹ in charge ‹ to the one ‹ so he said « was Benjamin; ‹ [that] with them

וּטְבֹחַ טֶבַח וְהָכֵן כִּי אִתִּי יֹאכְלוּ הָאֲנָשִׁים בַּצָּהֳרָיִם: יז וַיַּעַשׂ הָאִישׁ

‹ The man did 17 « at noon. ‹ will the men dine ‹ with me ‹ for « and prepare it, ‹ Slaughter an animal,

גַּבְרָא: יד וְאֵל שַׁדַּי יִתֵּן לְכוֹן רַחֲמִין קֳדָם גַּבְרָא וְיִפְטַר לְכוֹן יָת אֲחוּכוֹן אָחֳרָנָא וְיָת בִּנְיָמִין וַאֲנָא כְּמָא דִי אִתְכֵּלִית תְּכֵלִית: טו וּנְסִיבוּ גֻּבְרַיָּא יָת תִּקְרֻבְתָּא הָדָא וְעַל חַד תְּרֵין כַּסְפָּא נְסִיבוּ בִידֵיהוֹן וּדְבָרוּ יָת בִּנְיָמִן וְקָמוּ וּנְחָתוּ לְמִצְרַיִם וְקָמוּ קֳדָם יוֹסֵף: טז וַחֲזָא יוֹסֵף עִמְּהוֹן יָת בִּנְיָמִין וַאֲמַר לְדִי מְמַנָּא עַל בֵּיתֵהּ אָעֵיל יָת גֻּבְרַיָּא לְבֵיתָא וּנְכוֹס נִכְסְתָא וְאַתְקֵין אֲרֵי עִמִּי יֵיכְלוּן גֻּבְרַיָּא בְּשֵׁירוּתָא: יז וַעֲבַד גַּבְרָא

רש"י

(יד) **ואל שדי.** מעתה אינכם חסרים כלום אלא תפלה, הריני מתפלל עליכם (שם): **ואל שדי.** שדי בנתינת רחמיו וכדי היכולת בידו ליתן, יתן לכם רחמים, זהו פשוטו. ומדרשו, מי שאמר לעולם די יאמר די לצרותי, שלא שקטתי מנעורי, צרת לבן, צרת עשו, צרת רחל, צרת דינה, צרת יוסף, צרת שמעון, צרת בנימין (תנחומא י): **ושלח לכם.** ויפטר לכון, כתרגומו. ויפטרנו מאסוריו, ל' (שמות כא:כו) לחפשי ישלחנו. ואינו נופל בתרגום ל' וישלח, שהרי לשם הם הולכים אצלו: **את אחיכם.** זה שמעון: **אחר.** רוח הקודש נזרקה בו, לרבות יוסף (אדר"נ נו"ב פמ"ג): **ואני.** עד שובכם אהיה שכול מספק: **כאשר שכלתי.** מיוסף ומשמעון: **שכלתי.** מבנימין: (טו) **ואת בנימן.** מתרגמינן ודברו ית בנימין. לפי שאין לקיחת הכסף ולקיחת האדם שוה בלשון ארמי. בדבר הנקח ביד מתרגמינן ונסיב, ודבר הנקח בהנהגת דברים מתרגמינן ודבר: (טז) **וטבח טבח והכן.** כמו ולטבוח טבח ולהכן. ואין טבוח לשון צווי שהיה לו לומר וּטְבַח: **בצהרים.** זה מתורגם בשירותא שהוא לשון סעודה ראשונה בלשון ארמי, ובלע"ז דישני"ר. ויש הרבה

14. "Now, that you have the money, the gift, and your brother Benjamin" (*Midrash*), Jacob said, "you lack nothing but prayer. I will pray for you" (*Rashi*). As the Sages declared (*Sanhedrin* 44b), one should always pray *before* misfortune occurs (*R' Bachya).*

וְאֵל שַׁדַּי — *And may El Shaddai.* See 17:1 for a discussion of this Divine Name. It is a conjunction of שֶׁ־דַּי, *Who is sufficient* or *enough.* He is sufficient in His mercies and His hand is sufficient to give you whatever you need. "May He Who said to the world, 'Enough,' now declare that my troubles are enough. I have had no rest since my youth: trouble with Laban, trouble with Esau, the troubles of Rachel, Dinah, Joseph, Simeon — and now Benjamin" (*Rashi*).

אֲחִיכֶם אַחֵר — *Your brother the other one.* According to the Midrash, this was an instance of an unconscious prophecy. You will bring back not only Simeon, but your *other* brother — Joseph (*Rashi*).

וַאֲנִי — *And as for me.* In contrast with you, I will be in constant suspense, not knowing if I am to become even more bereaved than I already have been. As I consider myself bereft of Joseph and of Simeon, so I will now feel bereft of Benjamin *(Rashi*), a feeling I will continue to have until you return safely.

You cannot add to my bereavement. Nothing can add to the tragedy of the loss of Joseph (*Ramban*).

16-34. Joseph sees Benjamin and tests his brothers' sincerity. That Joseph was deeply moved by the sight of Benjamin is clear from the next several verses. Nevertheless, he refrained from identifying himself because he still had vital questions: Had the brothers lost their jealousy of Rachel's children? How would they react when he showed favoritism to Benjamin? What would they do when he announced his intention to detain Benjamin as a slave? Had they kidnaped Benjamin from Jacob? (*Akeidah; R' Hirsch*).

16. Joseph sent for his son Manasseh, *the one in charge of his house,* and ordered him to *have meat slaughtered, and prepare it.* According to the Sages, the expression וּטְבֹחַ טֶבַח implies that Manasseh was to expose the incision in the animal's neck to show the brothers that the meat had been slaughtered accord-

כַּאֲשֶׁר אָמַר יוֹסֵף וַיָּבֵא הָאִישׁ אֶת־הָאֲנָשִׁים
as ‹ Joseph said, ‹‹ and the man brought ‹ the men ‹
בֵּיתָה יוֹסֵף: יח וַיִּירְאוּ הָאֲנָשִׁים כִּי הוּבְאוּ בֵּית
to the house ‹ of Joseph. ‹‹ 18 But the men became frightened ‹ when ‹ they were brought ‹ to the house ‹
יוֹסֵף וַיֹּאמְרוּ עַל־דְּבַר הַכֶּסֶף הַשָּׁב בְּאַמְתְּחֹתֵינוּ
of Joseph, ‹ and they said, ‹‹ *It is because* ‹ *of the matter* ‹ *of the money* ‹ *that was returned* ‹ *in our sacks* ‹
בַּתְּחִלָּה אֲנַחְנוּ מוּבָאִים לְהִתְגֹּלֵל עָלֵינוּ
originally ‹ *that we* ‹ *are being brought,* ‹‹ *in order to fabricate a charge* ‹ *against us,* ‹
וּלְהִתְנַפֵּל עָלֵינוּ וְלָקַחַת אֹתָנוּ לַעֲבָדִים וְאֶת־חֲמֹרֵינוּ: יט וַיִּגְּשׁוּ אֶל־
and to pounce ‹ *upon us,* ‹ *and to take* ‹ *us* ‹ *for slaves* ‹ *along with* ‹ *our donkeys.* ‹‹ 19 They approached ‹ to ‹
הָאִישׁ אֲשֶׁר עַל־בֵּית יוֹסֵף וַיְדַבְּרוּ אֵלָיו פֶּתַח הַבָּיִת: כ וַיֹּאמְרוּ בִּי אֲדֹנִי
the man ‹ who was ‹ in charge ‹ of the house ‹ of Joseph ‹ and spoke ‹ to him ‹ at the entrance ‹ of the house. ‹‹ 20 And they said, ‹‹ *If you please,* ‹ *my lord:* ‹‹
יָרֹד יָרַדְנוּ בַּתְּחִלָּה לִשְׁבָּר־אֹכֶל: כא וַיְהִי כִּי־בָאנוּ אֶל־הַמָּלוֹן וַנִּפְתְּחָה
We had indeed come down ‹ *originally* ‹ *to buy* ‹ *food.* ‹‹ 21 *But it happened,* ‹ *when* ‹ *we arrived* ‹ *at* ‹ *the inn* ‹ *and opened* ‹
אֶת־אַמְתְּחֹתֵינוּ וְהִנֵּה כֶסֶף־אִישׁ בְּפִי אַמְתַּחְתּוֹ כַּסְפֵּנוּ בְּמִשְׁקָלוֹ
our sacks, ‹‹ *that we beheld* ‹ *the money* ‹ *of each one* ‹ *was in the mouth* ‹ *of his sack;* ‹‹ *it was our own money* ‹ *by its weight,* ‹‹

כְּמָא דִּי אֲמַר יוֹסֵף וְאָעֵיל גַּבְרָא יָת גֻּבְרַיָּא לְבֵית יוֹסֵף: יח וּדְחִילוּ גֻּבְרַיָּא אֲרֵי אִתַּעֲלוּ לְבֵית יוֹסֵף וַאֲמָרוּ עַל עֵסַק כַּסְפָּא דְּאִתּוֹתַב בְּטוֹעֲנָנָא בְּקַדְמֵיתָא אֲנַחְנָא מִתַּעֲלִין לְאִתְרַבְרָבָא עֲלָנָא וּלְאִסְתַּקָּפָא עֲלָנָא וּלְמִסַּב יָתָנָא לְעַבְדִין וּלְמִדְבַּר יָת חֲמָרָנָא: יט וּקְרִיבוּ לְוַת גַּבְרָא דִּי מְמַנָּא עַל בֵּית יוֹסֵף וּמַלִּילוּ עִמֵּהּ בִּתְרַע בֵּיתָא: כ וַאֲמָרוּ בְּבָעוּ רִבּוֹנִי מֵיחַת נְחֵתְנָא בְּקַדְמֵיתָא לְמִזְבַּן עִיבוּרָא: כא וַהֲוָה כַּד אֲתֵינָא לְבֵית מְבָתָא וּפְתַחְנָא יָת טוֹעֲנָנָא וְהָא כְסַף גְּבַר בְּפוּם טוֹעֲנֵהּ כַּסְפָּנָא בְּמַתְקְלֵהּ

רש"י

בגמרא, שדא לכלבא שירותיה (תענית יא:) בלע אכולא שירותא (ברכות לט:), אבל כל תרגום של צהרים טיהרא: (יח) וייראו האנשים. כתוב הוא בשני יודי"ן, ותרגומו ודחילו: כי הובאו בית יוסף. ואין דרך שאר הבאים לשבור בר ללון בבית יוסף כי אם בפונדקאות שבעיר, [על כן] וייראו, שאין זה אלא לאסרם אל משמר: אנחנו מובאים. אל תוך הבית הזה: להתגולל. להיות מתגלגלת עלינו עלילת הכסף ולהיותה נופלת עלינו. ואונקלוס שתרגם ולאסתקפא עלנא הוא ל' להתעולל, כדמתרגמינן עלילת דברים (דברים כב:יד) תסקופי מלין, ולא תרגמו אחר לשון המקרא. ולהתגולל שתרגם לאתרברבא הוא לשון גלת הזהב (קהלת יב:ו) והוצב גלתה העלתה (נחום ב:ח) שהוא לשון מלכות: (כ) בי אדוני. לשון בעיא ותחנונים הוא (אונקלוס) ובלשון ארמי בייא בייא (יומא סט:): ירד ירדנו. ירידה היא לנו, רגילים היינו לפרנס אחרים עכשיו אנו צריכים

ing to *halachah.* Although the Torah had not yet been given, Jacob's sons observed the commandments according to the tradition of their forefathers (*Chullin* 91a, *Rashi*).

18. וַיִּירְאוּ — *Became frightened.* Their fear began when they were brought to Joseph's private palace. They feared that, whereas he would be deterred from harming them publicly, he could act against them with impunity in the privacy of his home (*Akeidah*).

The *Zohar* notes how strange it is that the ten powerful brothers were afraid in the presence of a lone child. Such is the product of guilt. Because they felt guilty over their sale of Joseph [and felt that they could be subject to Divine punishment], all their courage deserted them.

וְאֶת־חֲמֹרֵינוּ — *Along with our donkeys.* The equation of their own freedom with the loss of their donkeys seems strange. *Ramban* explains that they feared the consequences of their donkeys' loss: "He will rob even our donkeys with our sacks, so that we will not be able to send grain home for our families, and they will starve to death!" (*Ramban*).

Rambam uses this as an example of the phenomenon that "people fear the loss of their property as much as their own lives — some even more — but most people hold both in the same esteem." Though this thesis may seem bizarre, the fact is that people make great sacrifices and take unusual risks for the sake of their property.

20. יָרֹד יָרַדְנוּ בַּתְּחִלָּה לִשְׁבָּר־אֹכֶל — *We had indeed come down originally to buy food.* When we came here to buy food, we had enough money to buy grain; we had no need to steal the purchase money (*Meshech Chochmah*).

21. אֶל־הַמָּלוֹן — *At the inn.* There was no way we could return

וְנָשֶׁב אֹתוֹ בְּיָדֵנוּ: כב וְכֶסֶף אַחֵר הוֹרַדְנוּ בְיָדֵנוּ

< in our hand < we have brought down < And other money 22 « in our hand. < so we have brought it back

לִשְׁבָּר־אֹכֶל לֹא יָדַעְנוּ מִי־שָׂם כַּסְפֵּנוּ

< our money < put < who < we do not know « food; < to buy

בְּאַמְתְּחֹתֵינוּ: כג וַיֹּאמֶר שָׁלוֹם לָכֶם אַל־תִּירָאוּ

« fear. < do not « with you, < Peace « He said, 23 « in our sacks.

אֱלֹהֵיכֶם וֵאלֹהֵי אֲבִיכֶם נָתַן לָכֶם מַטְמוֹן

< a hidden treasure < you < has given < of your father < and the God < Your God

בְּאַמְתְּחֹתֵיכֶם כַּסְפְּכֶם בָּא אֵלָי וַיּוֹצֵא אֲלֵהֶם

< to them < And he brought out « to me. < came < Your money « in your sacks.

וַאֲתֵיבְנָא יָתֵהּ בִּידָנָא: כב וְכַסְפָּא אָחֳרָנָא אוֹחִיתְנָא בִידָנָא לְמִזְבַּן עִיבוּרָא לָא יְדַעְנָא מָן שַׁוִּי כַּסְפָּנָא בְּטוֹעֲנָנָא: כג וַאֲמַר שְׁלָם לְכוֹן לָא תִדְחֲלוּן אֱלָהֲכוֹן וֶאֱלָהָא דַאֲבוּכוֹן יְהַב לְכוֹן סִימָא בְּטוֹעֲנֵיכוֹן כַּסְפְּכוֹן אֲתָא לְוָתִי וְאַפֵּיק לְוָתְהוֹן יָת שִׁמְעוֹן: כד וְאָעֵיל גַּבְרָא יָת גֻּבְרַיָּא לְבֵית יוֹסֵף וִיהַב מַיָּא וְאַסְחוּ רִגְלֵיהוֹן וִיהַב כִּסְתָּא לַחֲמָרֵיהוֹן: כה וְאַתְקִינוּ יָת תִּקְרֻבְתָּא עַד עַל יוֹסֵף בְּשֵׁירוּתָא אֲרֵי שְׁמָעוּ אֲרֵי תַמָּן אָכְלִין לַחְמָא: כו וְעַל יוֹסֵף לְבֵיתָא וְאַיְתִיוּ לֵהּ יָת תִּקְרֻבְתָּא דִּי בִידֵיהוֹן לְבֵיתָא וּסְגִידוּ לֵהּ עַל אַרְעָא: כז וּשְׁאֵיל לְהוֹן לִשְׁלָם וַאֲמַר הַשְׁלָם אֲבוּכוֹן סָבָא דִּי אֲמַרְתּוּן הַעַד כְּעַן קַיָּם:

אֶת־שִׁמְעוֹן: כד וַיָּבֵא הָאִישׁ אֶת־הָאֲנָשִׁים בֵּיתָה יוֹסֵף וַיִּתֶּן־מַיִם וַיִּרְחֲצוּ

< and they washed < water < He gave « of Joseph. < into the house < the men < Then the man brought 24 « Simeon.

רַגְלֵיהֶם וַיִּתֵּן מִסְפּוֹא לַחֲמֹרֵיהֶם: כה וַיָּכִינוּ אֶת־הַמִּנְחָה עַד־בּוֹא יוֹסֵף

< of Joseph < the arrival < before < the tribute < They prepared 25 « to their donkeys. < feed < and he gave « their feet,

בַּצָּהֳרָיִם כִּי שָׁמְעוּ כִּי־שָׁם יֹאכְלוּ לָחֶם: כו וַיָּבֹא יוֹסֵף הַבַּיְתָה *וַיָּבִיאּוּ

< they brought < to the house < When Joseph came 26 « bread. < they would eat < there < that < they had heard < for « at noon,

לוֹ אֶת־הַמִּנְחָה אֲשֶׁר־בְּיָדָם הַבָּיְתָה וַיִּשְׁתַּחֲווּ־לוֹ אָרְצָה: כז וַיִּשְׁאַל

< He asked 27 « to the ground. < to him < and they bowed down « into the house, « in their hands, < that was < the tribute < to him

לָהֶם לְשָׁלוֹם וַיֹּאמֶר הֲשָׁלוֹם אֲבִיכֶם הַזָּקֵן אֲשֶׁר אֲמַרְתֶּם הַעוֹדֶנּוּ חָי:

« alive? < Is he still « you spoke? < of whom < who is aged < your father « Is [he] at peace — « and he said, « of [their] peace, < them

* א' דגושה

רש"י

לך (ב"ר לב:ד): **(כג) אלהיכם.** בזכותכם, ואם אין זכותכם כדאי **אלהי אביכם,** בזכות אביכם נתן לכם מטמון (שם): **(כד) ויבא האיש.** הבאה אחר הבאה, לפי שהיו דוחפים אותו חוץ עד שדברו אליו פתח הבית (שם), ומשאמר להם שלום לכם נמשכו ובאו אחריו: **(כה) ויכינו.** הזמינו, עטרוהו בכלים נאים: **(כו) הביתה.** מפרוזדור לטרקלין:

the money then without putting our lives in jeopardy, because the viceroy had warned us not to come to Egypt again without our youngest brother (*HaK'sav V'HaKabbalah*).

23. The steward assured them that they had nothing to fear. "I did not bring you here to charge you with a crime, but as guests to dine with my master" (*Abarbanel; Malbim*). He continued, "The money you found was a Divine blessing; *your money,* however, was duly received by me — have no fears about that!" (*Radak*).

24. . . . וַיָּבֵא הָאִישׁ — *Then the man brought . . .* Although he had brought them before (v. 17), it was only after he assured them of their safety that they were willing to *enter* the house with him (*Rashi*).

25. כִּי שָׁמְעוּ — *For they had heard* from the steward and from the members of the household who were preparing the meal that they were to have a meal with Joseph. *Bread* is a general term for food (*Radak*).

26. Now, for the first time, *all* Joseph's brothers — including Benjamin — bowed down to him. This was the literal fulfillment of Joseph's first dream (37:7).

27. הַעוֹדֶנּוּ חָי — *Is he still alive?* The sequence of Joseph's questions seems strange; first he asked about Jacob's health and

כח וַיֹּאמְרוּ שָׁלוֹם לְעַבְדְּךָ לְאָבִינוּ עוֹדֶנּוּ חָי וַיִּקְּדוּ

28 They said, « At peace < is your servant < our father; « he is still < alive, « and they bowed [their head] <

וְיִּשְׁתַּחֲוּוּ [°וישתחו כ׳]: כט וַיִּשָּׂא עֵינָיו וַיַּרְא

and bowed down [to the ground]. « 29 Then he lifted up < his eyes < and saw <

אֶת־בִּנְיָמִין אָחִיו בֶּן־אִמּוֹ וַיֹּאמֶר הֲזֶה אֲחִיכֶם

Benjamin < his brother, « the son < of his mother, « and he said, « Is this < your brother <

הַקָּטֹן אֲשֶׁר אֲמַרְתֶּם אֵלָי וַיֹּאמַר אֱלֹהִים יָחְנְךָ בְּנִי: שביעי ל וַיְמַהֵר יוֹסֵף

who is 'little' < of whom < you spoke < to me? « And he said, < God < be gracious to you, < my son. « 30 Then Joseph rushed <

כִּי־נִכְמְרוּ רַחֲמָיו אֶל־אָחִיו וַיְבַקֵּשׁ לִבְכּוֹת וַיָּבֹא הַחַדְרָה וַיֵּבְךְּ שָׁמָּה:

because < enkindled < was his compassion < for < his brother < and he wanted « to weep; « so he went < into the room < and wept < there. «

לא וַיִּרְחַץ פָּנָיו וַיֵּצֵא וַיִּתְאַפַּק וַיֹּאמֶר שִׂימוּ לָחֶם: לב וַיָּשִׂימוּ לוֹ לְבַדּוֹ

31 He washed < his face < and went out; « he fortified himself < and said, « Serve < bread. « 32 They served < him < by himself <

כח וַאֲמָרוּ שְׁלָם לְעַבְדָּךְ לְאָבוּנָא עַד כְּעַן קַיָּם וּכְרָעוּ וּסְגִידוּ: כט וּזְקַף עֵינוֹהִי וַחֲזָא יָת בִּנְיָמִין אֲחוּהִי בַּר אִמֵּהּ וַאֲמַר הָדֵין אֲחוּכוֹן זְעֵירָא דִּי אֲמַרְתּוּן לִי וַאֲמַר מִן קֳדָם יְיָ יִתְרַחַם עֲלָךְ בְּרִי: ל וְאוֹחִי יוֹסֵף אֲרֵי אִתְגּוֹלְלוּ רַחֲמוֹהִי לְוַת אֲחוּהִי וּבְעָא לְמִבְכֵּי וְעַל לְאִדְרוֹן בֵּית מִשְׁכְּבָא וּבְכָא תַּמָּן: לא וְאַסְחֵי אַפּוֹהִי וּנְפַק וְאִתְחַסִּין וַאֲמַר שַׁווּ לַחְמָא: לב וְשַׁוִּיאוּ לֵהּ בִּלְחוֹדוֹהִי

רש"י

(כח) ויקדו וישתחוו. על שאלת שלום. קידה כפיפת קדקד, השתחואה משתטח לארץ (מגילה כב:): (כט) אלהים יחנך בני. בשאר שבטים שמענו חנינה, אשר חנן אלהים את עבדך (לעיל לג:ה), ובנימין עדיין לא נולד, לכך ברכו יוסף בחנינה (ב"ר לב:ה): (ל) כי נכמרו רחמיו. שאלו, יש לך אח מאם. אמר לו אח היה לי ואיני יודע היכן הוא. יש לך בנים. אמר לו יש לי עשרה. אמר לו ומה שמם. אמר לו בלע ובכר וכו'. אמר לו מה טיבן של שמות הללו. אמר לו כלם על שם אחי והצרות אשר מצאוהו. בלע שנבלע בין האומות, בכר שהיה בכור לאמו, אשבל ששבאו אל, גרא שנתגייר באכסניא, ונעמן שהיה נעים ביותר, אחי וראש אחי היה וראשי היה, מפים מפי אבי למד, וחפים שלא ראה חופתי ולא ראיתי אני חופתו, וארד שירד לבין האומות, כדאיתא במס' סוטה (לו:). מיד נכמרו רחמיו: נכמרו. נתחממו ובלשון משנה על הכומר של זיתים (בבא מציעא עד.). ובלשון ארמי משום מכמר בשרא (פסחים נח.). ובמקרא עורנו כתנור נכמרו (איכה ה:י) נתחממו ונקמטו קמטים קמטים, מפני זלעפות רעב (שם). וכן דרך כל עור כשמחממין אותו נקמט ונתכווץ: (לא) ויתאפק. נתאמץ. והוא לשון אפיקי מגנים (איוב מא:ז), חוזק, וכן ומזיח אפיקים רפה (שם יב:כא):

then whether he was still alive. *R' Hirsch* comments that this order reveals Joseph's anxiety about his father. He asked after his father's welfare as would be expected — but then he had a frightening thought: Perhaps my father has died in the interim! Quickly he adds, "He is still alive, is he not?"

Other commentators suggest that the second question does not mean: Is he still *alive?* but, is he still *vigorous*? Thus, Joseph first inquired after Jacob's general welfare, then after the state of his health.

28. וַיִּקְּדוּ וַיִּשְׁתַּחֲוּוּ — *And they bowed [their head] and bowed down [to the ground]* in gratitude for his concern about their welfare (*Rashi*), or to God for the warm reception (*Alshich*).

29. וַיַּרְא . . . אָחִיו בֶּן־אִמּוֹ — *And saw . . . his brother, the son of his mother.* He had already seen Benjamin (v. 16), but now he focused on his features and saw the resemblance to his mother, who died when he, Joseph, was but eight years old. This passage prepares us for his need to weep (*Zohar; Haamek Davar*).

הֲזֶה אֲחִיכֶם הַקָּטֹן — *Is this your brother who is 'little' . . . ?* This question about the 31-year-old Benjamin was both humorous and sarcastic. Is this the person you called too little and too fragile to bring here? (*Abarbanel*).

אֱלֹהִים יָחְנְךָ בְּנִי — *God be gracious to you, my son.* Since you are the survivor of your mother, may God grant you grace, that your brothers and others will befriend you (*Sforno*).

All the other brothers had been blessed with grace [see 33:5] before Benjamin was born. Now Joseph gave that blessing to Benjamin (*Rashi*).

30-31. His first conversation with Benjamin was an intensely emotional experience for Joseph. Benjamin told him that he had ten children, each of whom he had named to commemorate the tragedy of his lost brother. When Joseph heard the extent of Benjamin's devotion to his memory, his feelings became *enkindled (Midrash)*. And when Joseph realized that he still could not reveal his true identity to Benjamin and that he would inflict further suffering on him in the matter of the goblet [Ch. 44], he became very emotional and had to leave the room to cry (*Haamek Davar*). When he regained control of his emotions, Joseph washed his face and ordered that the meal be served.

32. Joseph did not eat with the brothers. *They served him by himself* in deference to his royal rank (*B'chor Shor; Radak*), and because Egyptians and Hebrews did not dine together, as noted further in this verse. *R' Hirsch* notes that this shows that Joseph

וְלָהֶם לְבַדָּם וְלַמִּצְרִים הָאֹכְלִים אִתּוֹ לְבַדָּם כִּי
‹ for «by themselves, ‹ with him ‹ who ate ‹ and the Egyptians ‹ by themselves ‹ and them

לֹא יוּכְלוּן הַמִּצְרִים לֶאֱכֹל אֶת־הָעִבְרִים לֶחֶם
« bread, ‹ the Hebrews ‹ with ‹ to eat « the Egyptians could not bear

כִּי־תוֹעֵבָה הִוא לְמִצְרָיִם: לג וַיֵּשְׁבוּ לְפָנָיו הַבְּכֹר
‹ the firstborn « before him, ‹ They were seated 33 « to Egypt. ‹ it is ‹ loathsome ‹ for

כִּבְכֹרָתוֹ וְהַצָּעִיר כִּצְעִרָתוֹ וַיִּתְמְהוּ הָאֲנָשִׁים אִישׁ אֶל־רֵעֵהוּ: לד וַיִּשָּׂא
‹ He served 34 « his fellow. ‹ to ‹ [each] man « were the men, ‹ and astonished « according to his youth, ‹ and the youngest ‹ according to his seniority

מַשְׂאֹת מֵאֵת פָּנָיו אֲלֵהֶם וַתֵּרֶב מַשְׂאַת בִּנְיָמִן מִמַּשְׂאֹת כֻּלָּם חָמֵשׁ
‹ five ‹ of all of them ‹ over the portions ‹ of Benjamin ‹ the portion ‹ and increased was « to them, « his face — ‹ — that had been before « portions

יָדוֹת וַיִּשְׁתּוּ וַיִּשְׁכְּרוּ עִמּוֹ: [מד] א וַיְצַו אֶת־אֲשֶׁר עַל־בֵּיתוֹ לֵאמֹר
« saying, ‹ of his house, ‹ in charge ‹ who is ‹ the one ‹ Then he instructed 1 44 « with him. ‹ and became intoxicated ‹ They drank « times.

וּלְהוֹן בִּלְחוֹדֵיהוֹן וּלְמִצְרָאֵי דְּאָכְלִין
עִמֵּהּ בִּלְחוֹדֵיהוֹן אֲרֵי לָא יָכְלִין
מִצְרָאֵי לְמֵיכַל עִם עִבְרָאֵי לַחְמָא אֲרֵי
בְעִירָא (נ״א מְרַחֲקָא) דְמִצְרָאֵי דָחֲלִין
לֵהּ עִבְרָאֵי אָכְלִין: לג וְאַסְחָרוּ קֳדָמוֹהִי
רַבָּא כְּרַבְיוּתֵהּ וּזְעֵירָא כִּזְעֵרוּתֵהּ
וּתְמָהוּ גֻבְרַיָּא גְּבַר לְחַבְרֵהּ: לד וּנְטַל
חֳלָקִין מִלְוָת אַפּוֹהִי לְוָתְהוֹן וּסְגִיאַת
חֲלָקָא דְבִנְיָמִן מֵחֲלָקֵי דְכָלְּהוֹן
חַמְשָׁא חֳלָקִין וּשְׁתִיאוּ וּרְוִיאוּ עִמֵּהּ:
א וּפַקִּיד יָת דִּי מְמַנָּא עַל בֵּיתֵהּ לְמֵימַר

רש״י

(לב) **כי תועבה היא.** דבר שנאוי הוא למצרים לאכול את העברים, ואונקלוס נתן טעם לדבר: (לג) **הבכר כבכרתו.** מכה בגביע וקורא ראובן שמעון לוי יהודה יששכר וזבולון בני אם אחת, הסבו כסדר הזה שהוא סדר תולדתכם, וכן כלם. כיון שהגיע לבנימין אמר זה אין לו אם ואני אין לי אם, ישב אצלי (ב״ר צב:ה): (לד) **משאות.** מנות (תנחומא ויגש ד): **חמש ידות.** חלקו עם אחיו ומשאת יוסף ואסנת ומנשה ואפרים (שם): **וישכרו עמו.** ומיום שמכרוהו לא שתו יין ולא הוא שתה יין

did not disown his Jewish origin and that notwithstanding his supreme position of authority, the Egyptians would not eat with Joseph the Jew! The verse singles out *Hebrews* as the object of Egyptian loathing, which, as *R' Hirsch* notes, is a remarkable testimony to the prominence of Jacob's family, which consisted of less than seventy people at the time. The fame of Abraham's descendants had spread as far as Egypt, and that hotbed of moral perversion loathed the family that represented standards of chastity and morality that stood in marked opposition to the Egyptian way of life.

Most commentators, however, agree that the Egyptians despised *all* foreigners who ate foods that the Egyptians abhorred, and our verse specifies Hebrews only because that happened to be the nationality of the brothers. *Onkelos* specifies that the problem was that the brothers ate meat, while the Egyptians worshiped animals.

33. הַבְּכֹר כִּבְכֹרָתוֹ וְהַצָּעִיר כִּצְעִרָתוֹ — *The firstborn according to his seniority and the youngest according to his youth.* According to *Tanchuma,* Joseph assigned the seating at the banquet by tapping his goblet and calling out, "Reuben, Simeon, Levi, and so on, sons of one mother, be seated in that order." He did the same with the sons of Bilhah and Zilpah, but when he came to Benjamin, he said, "He has no mother and I have no mother — let him sit nearest to me" (*Rashi*). For someone who did not know the family, this was a remarkable feat, because the ten oldest brothers were born within seven years of one another, and their appearances could not have indicated their seniority.

This use of the "magic" goblet was to set the stage for the later arrest of Benjamin for having "stolen" it.

34. The meal was a battle of wits. Joseph lavished affection on Benjamin as the beginning of his test to see if the brothers would be jealous of him. As will be seen below, Joseph's spotlight would glare much more strongly on Benjamin, so that if the brothers still harbored ill feelings toward the sons of Jacob's favored wife, it would explode in hostility.

וַיִּשְׁכְּרוּ — *They . . . became intoxicated. Tur* suggests that this was part of Joseph's plan — to get them drunk so that they would not realize what was being put in their sacks. Further, he sent them off early in the morning (43:3) so that they would not have time to inspect their laden donkeys.

44.

⇨ The final test. Benjamin is accused of thievery.

The brothers' attitude toward the privileged treatment afforded Benjamin convinced Joseph that they were no longer spiteful, but not all his doubts had been resolved. Would they be ready to fight and sacrifice for the sake of a child of Rachel? To test them, he arranged for Benjamin to be arrested for theft and sentenced to a lifetime of slavery. Possibly, too, there was enmity between them because Benjamin may have known or suspected what they had done to Joseph (*Ramban*). Thus, Joseph was about to create a situation that was parallel to his own. He

מַלֵּ֤א אֶת־אַמְתְּחֹ֨ת הָאֲנָשִׁ֜ים אֹ֗כֶל כַּאֲשֶׁ֛ר יוּכְל֖וּן

< they are able < as much as < with food < of the men < the sacks < Fill

שְׂאֵ֑ת וְשִׂ֥ים כֶּֽסֶף־אִ֖ישׁ בְּפִ֥י אַמְתַּחְתּֽוֹ׃ ב וְאֶת־

< And 2 << of his sack. < in the mouth < of [each] man < the money < and put << to carry,

גְּבִיעִ֞י גְּבִ֣יעַ הַכֶּ֗סֶף תָּשִׂים֙ בְּפִ֣י אַמְתַּ֣חַת הַקָּטֹ֔ן

<< of the youngest one, < of the sack < in the mouth < place << of silver— < —the goblet << my goblet

וְאֵ֖ת כֶּ֣סֶף שִׁבְר֑וֹ וַיַּ֕עַשׂ כִּדְבַ֥ר יוֹסֵ֖ף אֲשֶׁ֥ר דִּבֵּֽר׃

<< he had spoken. < that < of Joseph < according to the word < And he did << of his purchase. < the money < along with

ג הַבֹּ֖קֶר א֑וֹר וְהָאֲנָשִׁ֣ים שֻׁלְּח֔וּ הֵ֖מָּה וַחֲמֹרֵיהֶֽם׃ ד הֵ֠ם יָֽצְא֣וּ אֶת־הָעִיר֮

<< the city, < had left < They 4 << and their donkeys. < they << were sent off, < and the men < was light < The morning 3

לֹ֣א הִרְחִ֒יקוּ֒ וְיוֹסֵ֣ף אָמַר֮ לַאֲשֶׁ֣ר עַל־בֵּיתוֹ֒ ק֥וּם רְדֹ֖ף אַחֲרֵ֣י הָאֲנָשִׁ֑ים

<< the men; < after < chase < Rise up, << of his house, < in charge < to the one < said < when Joseph << they had not gone far,

וְהִשַּׂגְתָּם֙ וְאָמַרְתָּ֣ אֲלֵהֶ֔ם לָ֛מָּה שִׁלַּמְתֶּ֥ם רָעָ֖ה תַּ֥חַת טוֹבָֽה׃ ה הֲל֣וֹא זֶ֗ה

< this the one < Is not 5 << good? < in place of < evil < have you repaid < 'Why << to them, < you are to say < [when] you overtake them,

אֲשֶׁ֨ר יִשְׁתֶּ֤ה אֲדֹנִי֙ בּ֔וֹ וְה֕וּא נַחֵ֥שׁ יְנַחֵ֖שׁ בּ֑וֹ הֲרֵעֹתֶ֖ם אֲשֶׁ֥ר עֲשִׂיתֶֽם׃

<< you have done!' < in what < You have done evil << with it? < regularly divines < and he << from it, < my master drinks < that

מְלֵי יָת טוֹעֲנֵי גֻבְרַיָּא עִיבוּרָא כְּמָה דִי יָכְלִין לְמִיטְעַן וְשַׁוִּי כְּסַף גְּבַר בְּפוּם טוֹעֲנֵהּ: ב וְיָת כַּלִידִי כַּלִידָא דְכַסְפָּא תְּשַׁוֵּי בְּפוּם טוֹעֲנָא דִזְעֵירָא וְיָת כַּסְפָּא זְבִינוֹהִי וַעֲבַד כְּפִתְגָמָא דְיוֹסֵף דִּי מַלִּיל: ג צַפְרָא נְהַר וְגֻבְרַיָּא אִתְפַּטָּרוּ אִנּוּן וַחֲמָרֵיהוֹן: ד אִנּוּן נְפָקוּ מִן קַרְתָּא לָא אַרְחִיקוּ וְיוֹסֵף אֲמַר לְדִי מְמַנָּא עַל בֵּיתֵהּ קוּם רְדַף בָּתַר גֻּבְרַיָּא וְתַדְבְּקִנּוּן וְתֵימַר לְהוֹן לְמָא אַשְׁלֶמְתּוּן בִּישָׁא חֲלָף טַבְתָּא: ה הֲלָא דֵין דְּשָׁתֵי רִבּוֹנִי בֵּהּ וְהוּא בָּדָקָא מְבָדֵק בֵּהּ אַבְאֶשְׁתּוּן דִּי עֲבַדְתּוּן:

רש"י

ואותו היום שתו (שם שבת קלט.): (ב) גביע. כוס ארוך וקורין לו מדריג"ש:

had been carted off to slavery because of his brothers; would they now permit Benjamin to become a slave?

1. אֹכֶל כַּאֲשֶׁר יוּכְלוּן שְׂאֵת — *With food as much as they are able to carry,* more than their money's worth. This placing of each man's money in his sack was to be done with the brothers' knowledge, ostensibly in reparation for Joseph's earlier harsh treatment. The official who filled the grain sacks would close and seal them; therefore the brothers did not open their sacks and discover the silver goblet that had been slipped into Benjamin's sack (*Ramban*).

Thus, his graciousness at the meal and his generosity in sending so much food would accentuate the brothers' baseness in repaying his kindness by "stealing his goblet" (*Alshich*).

Abarbanel claims that the brothers were not aware that the money was placed in their sacks. Joseph had it put there as a crucial part of his "test of the goblet." For even if the brothers had no enmity or jealousy toward Benjamin, they might have been justified in believing that he actually had stolen the goblet and deserved his punishment. They could point to his mother Rachel who stole the *teraphim* from Laban and incurred Jacob's unwitting curse that led to her death (31:19,32 and *Rashi* there). The money in their sacks proved beyond any doubt that items were put in each sack without the owner's knowledge. Thus if they chose to leave Benjamin as a slave to Joseph, it would only be due to their ill will toward him.

4. קוּם רְדֹף אַחֲרֵי הָאֲנָשִׁים — *Rise up, chase after the men*, while the fear of the city is still upon them (*Tanchuma*), as long as they were still under the jurisdiction of the city. Otherwise, they might have attacked the official sent after them and simply fled.

5. הֲלוֹא זֶה אֲשֶׁר יִשְׁתֶּה אֲדֹנִי בּוֹ — *Is not this the one that my master drinks from it.* By stressing the importance of the goblet, the official made the point that their offense was unpardonable. Someone who would dare steal the royal cup from which a monarch drinks demonstrates disdain for the ruler — any bribe or ransom is inadequate to pardon him (*Ramban*).

הֲרֵעֹתֶם אֲשֶׁר עֲשִׂיתֶם — *You have done evil in what you have done.* By taking the cup, you have destroyed the reputation for honesty that you gained by returning the money (*Or HaChaim*).

ו וַיַּשִּׂגֵם וַיְדַבֵּר אֲלֵהֶם אֶת־הַדְּבָרִים הָאֵלֶּה׃

« those words. ‹ to them ‹ and spoke ‹ He overtook **6** them

ז וַיֹּאמְרוּ אֵלָיו לָמָּה יְדַבֵּר אֲדֹנִי כַּדְּבָרִים הָאֵלֶּה

« *these?* ‹ *such words as* ‹ *does my lord say* ‹ *Why* « to him, ‹ And they said 7

חָלִילָה לַעֲבָדֶיךָ מֵעֲשׂוֹת כַּדָּבָר הַזֶּה׃ ח הֵן כֶּסֶף

‹ *the money* « *Indeed!* **8** « *this!* ‹ *such a thing as* ‹ *to do* ‹ *for your servants* ‹ *It would be sacrilegious*

אֲשֶׁר מָצָאנוּ בְּפִי אַמְתְּחֹתֵינוּ הֱשִׁיבֹנוּ אֵלֶיךָ

‹ *to you* ‹ *we brought back* ‹ *of our sacks* ‹ *in the mouth* ‹ *we found* ‹ *that*

מֵאֶרֶץ כְּנַעַן וְאֵיךְ נִגְנֹב מִבֵּית אֲדֹנֶיךָ כֶּסֶף אוֹ זָהָב׃

« *gold?* ‹ *or* ‹ *[any] silver* ‹ *of your master* ‹ *from the house* ‹ *could we have stolen* ‹ *How then* « *of Canaan.* ‹ *from the land*

ו וְאַדְבֵּיקִנּוּן וּמַלִּיל עִמְּהוֹן יָת פִּתְגָּמַיָּא הָאִלֵּין: ז וַאֲמָרוּ לֵהּ לְמָא יְמַלֵּל רִבּוֹנִי כְּפִתְגָּמַיָּא הָאִלֵּין חַס לְעַבְדָּךְ מִלְּמֶעְבַּד כְּפִתְגָּמָא הָדֵין: ח הָא כַּסְפָּא דִּי אַשְׁכַּחְנָא בְּפוּם טוֹעֲנָנָא אֲתֵיבְנוּהִי לָךְ מֵאַרְעָא דִכְנָעַן וְאֶכְדֵּין נִגְנוּב מִבֵּית רִבּוֹנָךְ כַּסְפָּא אוֹ דַהֲבָא (נ״א מָנִין דִּכְסַף אוֹ מָנִין דִּדְהָב): ט דִּי יִשְׁתְּכַח עִמֵּהּ מֵעַבְדָּךְ וִימוּת (נ״א יִתְקְטֵל) וְאַף אֲנַחְנָא נְהֵי לְרִבּוֹנִי לְעַבְדִין: י וַאֲמַר אַף כְּעַן כְּפִתְגָּמֵיכוֹן כֵּן הוּא דִּי יִשְׁתְּכַח עִמֵּהּ יְהֵי לִי עַבְדָּא וְאַתּוּן תְּהוֹן זַכָּאִין: יא וְאוֹחִיאוּ וְאוֹחִיתוּ גְּבַר יָת טוֹעֲנֵהּ לְאַרְעָא וּפְתָחוּ גְּבַר טוֹעֲנֵהּ: יב וּבְלַשׁ בְּרַבָּא שָׁרִי וּבִזְעֵירָא שֵׁיצִי וְאִשְׁתְּכַח כַּלִּידָא

ט אֲשֶׁר יִמָּצֵא אִתּוֹ מֵעֲבָדֶיךָ וָמֵת וְגַם־אֲנַחְנוּ נִהְיֶה לַאדֹנִי לַעֲבָדִים׃

« *slaves.* ‹ *to my lord* ‹ *will be* ‹ *we* ‹ *and also* « *shall die,* ‹ *of your servants* ‹ *with him* ‹ *it is found* ‹ *Whomever* **9**

י וַיֹּאמֶר גַּם־עַתָּה כְדִבְרֵיכֶם כֶּן־הוּא אֲשֶׁר יִמָּצֵא אִתּוֹ יִהְיֶה־לִּי עָבֶד

« *a slave,* ‹ *to me* ‹ *shall be* ‹ *with him* ‹ *it is found* ‹ *[Nevertheless,] whomever* « *it should be.* ‹ *so* « *according to what you say,* ‹ *now* ‹ *Also* « He said, **10**

וְאַתֶּם תִּהְיוּ נְקִיִּם׃ יא וַיְמַהֲרוּ וַיּוֹרִדוּ אִישׁ אֶת־אַמְתַּחְתּוֹ אָרְצָה וַיִּפְתְּחוּ

« and they opened « to the ground, ‹ his sack ‹ and [each] man lowered ‹ They hurried **11** « *exoner-ated.* ‹ *shall be* ‹ *and [the rest of] you*

אִישׁ אַמְתַּחְתּוֹ׃ יב וַיְחַפֵּשׂ בַּגָּדוֹל הֵחֵל וּבַקָּטֹן כִּלָּה וַיִּמָּצֵא הַגָּבִיעַ

‹ was the goblet ‹ and found « he ended; ‹ and with the youngest ‹ he began ‹ with the oldest « He searched; **12** « his sack. « — [each] man —

רש״י

(ז) **חלילה לעבדיך.** חולין הוא לנו, לשון גנאי. ותרגום, חס לעבדיך, חס מאת הקב״ה יהי עלינו מעשות זאת. והרבה יש בתלמוד חס ושלום: (ח) **הן כסף אשר מצאנו.** זה אחד מעשרה קל וחומר האמורים בתורה, וכלן מנויין בבראשית רבה (לב:ז): (י) **גם עתה כדבריכם.** אף זו מן הדין אמת כדבריכם כן הוא שכלכם חייבים בדבר, עשרה שנמצאת גניבה ביד אחד מהם כלם נתפסים. אבל אני אעשה לכם לפנים משורת הדין, אשר ימצא אתו יהיה לי עבד (שם ח): (יב) **בגדול החל.** שלא ירגישו

7-9. At first the brothers responded with shock and indignation; then they used a logical argument to try and prove that the charge was ridiculous. Their argument, known in Talmudic parlance as *kal vachomer [a fortiori]*, was a deduction from minor to major: If they had come all the way back from Canaan to return money that they had not even taken, how could they now be accused of having stolen? *Ramban* comments that their response revealed that they were totally ignorant of the import of the charge. They spoke of being innocent of taking *silver or gold*, implying that they did not even realize that the subject of the charge was a goblet.

The brothers did not stop at vehemently denying the charge. So certain were they that none of them was guilty, they volunteered to accept an unusually harsh punishment if any stolen item was found among them.

10. The steward's counteroffer implied that only the thief would be detained, but the others would not even have to come back to the city; they would be free to go on their way and return home. This was part of the test, to see whether they would willingly leave Benjamin behind (*Haamek Davar*).

11. . . . וַיְמַהֲרוּ — *They hurried . . .* So eager were the brothers to prove their innocence that they did not wait for him to open their sacks; each one opened his own and offered to be searched first (*Bereishis Rabbasi*).

12. בַּגָּדוֹל הֵחֵל וּבַקָּטֹן כִּלָּה — *With the oldest he began and with the youngest he ended.* In the plain meaning, Manasseh searched them all in order, so that it would not be obvious that

בְּאַמְתַּחַת בִּנְיָמִן׃ יג וַיִּקְרְעוּ שִׂמְלֹתָם וַיַּעֲמֹס אִישׁ
in the sack of Benjamin. 13 They rent their garments. They reloaded — [each] man

עַל־חֲמֹרוֹ וַיָּשֻׁבוּ הָעִירָה׃ מפטיר יד וַיָּבֹא יְהוּדָה
on his donkey — and they returned to the city. 14 Judah arrived

וְאֶחָיו בֵּיתָה יוֹסֵף וְהוּא עוֹדֶנּוּ שָׁם וַיִּפְּלוּ לְפָנָיו
with his brothers to the house of Joseph and he was still there. They fell before him

אָרְצָה׃ טו וַיֹּאמֶר לָהֶם יוֹסֵף מָה־הַמַּעֲשֶׂה הַזֶּה
to the ground. 15 Say to them did Joseph, What is this deed

אֲשֶׁר עֲשִׂיתֶם הֲלוֹא יְדַעְתֶּם כִּי־נַחֵשׁ יְנַחֵשׁ אִישׁ אֲשֶׁר כָּמֹנִי׃
that you have done? Do you not know that divination will be practiced [by] a man who is like me!

טז וַיֹּאמֶר יְהוּדָה מַה־נֹּאמַר לַאדֹנִי מַה־נְּדַבֵּר וּמַה־נִּצְטַדָּק הָאֱלֹהִים
16 Judah said, What can we say to my lord? What can we speak? And how can we justify ourselves? God

מָצָא אֶת־עֲוֹן עֲבָדֶיךָ הִנֶּנּוּ עֲבָדִים לַאדֹנִי גַּם־אֲנַחְנוּ גַּם אֲשֶׁר־נִמְצָא
has found the sin of your servants. Here we are as slaves to my lord — also we and also the one that was found [to have]

בְּטוֹעֲנָא דְבִנְיָמִן׃ יג וּבְזָעוּ לְבוּשֵׁיהוֹן וּרְמוֹ גְּבַר עַל חֲמָרֵהּ וְתָבוּ לְקַרְתָּא׃ יד וַאֲתָא יְהוּדָה וַאֲחוֹהִי לְבֵית יוֹסֵף וְהוּא עַד דְּהוּא (נ״א כְּעַן) תַּמָּן וּנְפָלוּ קֳדָמוֹהִי עַל אַרְעָא׃ טו וַאֲמַר לְהוֹן יוֹסֵף מָה עוֹבָדָא הָדֵין דִּי עֲבַדְתּוּן הֲלָא יְדַעְתּוּן אֲרֵי בָדָקָא מְבָדֵק גַּבְרָא דִּי כְוָתִי׃ טז וַאֲמַר יְהוּדָה מַה נֵּימַר לְרִבּוֹנִי מַה נְּמַלֵּל וּמַה נִּזְכֵּי מִן קֳדָם יְיָ אִשְׁתְּכַח יָת חוֹבָא דְעַבְדָיךְ הָא אֲנַחְנָא עַבְדִין לְרִבּוֹנִי אַף אֲנַחְנָא אַף דְּאִשְׁתְּכַח

רש״י

שהיה יודע היכן הוא (שם): (יג) **ויעמס איש על חמורו.** בעלי זרוע היו ולא הוצרכו לסייע זה את זה לטעון (תנחומא ו; ב״ר צב:ח): **וישובו העירה.** מטרפולין היתה והוא אומר העירה, העיר כל שהוא. אלא שלא היתה חשובה בעיניהם אלא כעיר בינונית של עשרה בני אדם לענין המלחמה (ב״ר שם): (יד) **עודנו שם.** שהיה ממתין להם: (טו) **הלא ידעתם כי נחש ינחש וגו׳.** הלא ידעתם כי איש חשוב כמוני יודע לנחש ולדעת מדעת ומסברא ובינה כי אתם גנבתם הגביע (עי׳ אונקלוס): (טז) **האלהים מצא.** יודעים אנו שלא סרחנו, אבל מאת המקום נהיתה להביא לנו זאת. מצא בעל חוב מקום לגבות שטר חובו (ב״ר שם ט): **ומה נצטדק.** לשון צדק, וכן כל תיבה שתחלת יסודה צד״י והיא באה לדבר בלשון מתפעל או נתפעל נותן טי״ת במקום תי״ו, ואינו נותנה לפני אות ראשונה של יסוד התיבה אלא באמצע אותיות העיקר, כגון נצטדק מגזרת צדק. ויצטבע

he knew the whereabouts of the goblet (*Rashi*). *Maharil Diskin* cites a strange Midrash that he searched only the sacks of Simeon and Benjamin. He explains that the brothers had attempted to prove their honesty by referring to their return of the money that had been planted in their sacks. To this the Egyptian official retorted that they were right — but that their logic did not apply to Simeon and Benjamin. Since Simeon had been imprisoned in Egypt and Benjamin had been at home in Canaan, neither of them had returned money to Egypt. If so, only their sacks needed to be searched, beginning with the older one [בַּגָּדוֹל] and concluding with the younger one [בַּקָּטֹן].

13. **וַיִּקְרְעוּ שִׂמְלֹתָם** — *They rent their garments.* In addition to the obvious reason for their distress — that they faced possible imprisonment and slavery, and, at the very least, Benjamin would lose his freedom — they were grief-stricken over the effect this development could have on Jacob. If, indeed, Benjamin were to become a slave of the Egyptian viceroy, the shock might kill Jacob (*Ralbag*). The Midrash notes that the brothers were being punished measure for measure. By sending Joseph's bloodstained tunic home to Jacob, they caused him to rend his garment in grief. Now they rent their own garments.

14. **בֵּיתָה יוֹסֵף** — *To the house of Joseph.* Manasseh directed them to Joseph's house to spare them the shame of appearing before other Egyptians (*Midrash HaGadol*).

וַיִּפְּלוּ לְפָנָיו אָרְצָה — *They fell before him to the ground,* in obeisance. According to *Tanchuma,* it was now that Joseph's dream of the eleven bowing stars [37:9] was fulfilled.

15. With affected indignation, Joseph reproached them for what they had done, but he avoided Manasseh's criticism of their ingratitude, for it would have been beneath the dignity of the supreme ruler of a great land to imply that he needed their thanks. Instead, he deplored their foolishness. Did they think that a great practitioner of the art of divination would not know that they were the culprits? Did they think that by depriving him of his goblet they would make him helpless?

16. Judah, the leader of the brothers, spoke on behalf of all. He attempted no excuse, for the facts seemed to allow none (*Abarbanel*). Though they insisted they were innocent, how could they refute the apparently conclusive evidence? (*Sforno*).

Judah's remarks referred not only to his helplessness in replying to Joseph's rebuke, but alluded also to Jacob: *What can we speak* to my own father to whom I assured Benjamin's safety? *And how can we justify ourselves* before the Divine Presence? (*Tanchuma Yashan*).

הַגָּבִיעַ בְּיָדוֹ׃ יז וַיֹּאמֶר חָלִילָה לִּי מֵעֲשׂוֹת זֹאת

« *this.* ‹ *to do* ‹ *for me* ‹ *It would be sacrilegious* « *But he said,* 17 « *in his hand.* ‹ *the goblet*

הָאִישׁ אֲשֶׁר נִמְצָא הַגָּבִיעַ בְּיָדוֹ הוּא יִהְיֶה־לִּי

‹ *to me* ‹ *shall be* ‹ *[only] he* « *in his hand,* ‹ *the goblet* ‹ *was found [to have]* ‹ *who* ‹ *The man*

עָבֶד וְאַתֶּם עֲלוּ לְשָׁלוֹם אֶל־אֲבִיכֶם׃ ססס

« *your father.* ‹ *to* ‹ *in peace* ‹ *— go up* « *and [as for] you* « *a slave,*

כַּלִּידָא בִּידֵהּ׃ יז וַאֲמַר חַס לִי מִלְּמֶעְבַּד דָּא גַּבְרָא דִּי אִשְׁתְּכַח כַּלִּידָא בִּידֵהּ הוּא יְהֵי לִי עַבְדָּא וְאַתּוּן סָקוּ לִשְׁלָם לְוַת אֲבוּכוֹן׃

קמ"ו פסוקים. יחזקיה"ו סימן. אמצי"ה סימן. יהי"ה ל"י עב"ד סימן. ותיבות אלפים כ"ה.

THE HAFTARAH FOR MIKEITZ APPEARS ON PAGE 344.

When Chanukah coincides with Mikeitz, the regular Maftir is replaced with the Chanukah reading: third day Chanukah, page 357 (7:24-29); fourth day Chanukah, page 358 (7:30-35); sixth day Chanukah — Mikeitz is divided into six *aliyos*, the Rosh Chodesh reading (page 352, 28:9-15) is the seventh aliyah, and the Chanukah reading (page 358, 7:42-47) is read as the Maftir; seventh day Chanukah, page 358 (7:48-53). On all of these days, the Haftarah reading is replaced with the reading of Shabbas Chanukah, page 362. When the last day of Chanukah coincides with this Shabbos, the Chanukah readings are: Maftir, page 359 (7:54-8:4); Haftarah, page 364.

רש"י

(דניאל ד:ל) מגזרת צבע. ויצטירו (יהושע ט:ד) מגזרת ציר אמונים (משלי יג:יז). הצטיידנו (יהושע ט:יב) מגזרת צדה לדרך. ותיבה שתחלתה סמ"ך או שי"ן כשהיא מתפעלת התי"ו מפרדת את אותיות העיקר, כגון ויסתבל החגב (קהלת יב:ה) מגזרת סבל. מסתכל הוית בקרניא (דניאל ז:ח) מגזרת סכל. וישתמר חקות עמרי (מיכה ו:טז) מגזרת שמר. וסר מרע משתולל (ישעיה נט:טו) מגזרת מוליך יועצים שולל (איוב יב:יז). מסתולל בעמי (שמות ט:יז) מגזרת דרך לא סלולה (ירמיה יח:טו):

"We know we committed no wrong in this matter. Rather the matter emanates from God, Who caused all of this to befall us because He wishes to punish us for an earlier sin. It is as if the previous misdeed had lain in abeyance, but now it is *uncovered — found,* as it were — to be dealt with. 'The Creditor has found an opportunity to collect His debt' " (*Rashi* from *Midrash*).

17. Joseph pressed his advantage. To make them realize more keenly their precarious position, he declared that he would retain only Benjamin.

חָלִילָה לִּי מֵעֲשׂוֹת זֹאת — *It would be sacrilegious for me to do this.* In response to Judah's contrite statement that God was punishing the brothers for an old sin, Joseph replied that he would never punish people for a sin that they had not committed against him. The only guilty party, from his point of view, was Benjamin, and only he would be punished. The others would go free (*Sforno*).

To Judah, however, Joseph's answer made it apparent that this was not a Divine punishment for their former sins or else *all* of them would have been enslaved. It was either the viceroy's capriciousness, or the result of some sin of Benjamin. Therefore, from this point on, Judah began exercising his responsibility to do whatever he could for Benjamin (*Haamek Davar*).

Meshech Chochmah observes that Joseph's ruling implied that he knew Benjamin to be innocent — otherwise he would never have allowed a thief to be a servant in his household. If so, the charge was fabricated, nothing but an excuse to deprive an innocent man of his freedom. This gave Judah the courage to speak up against Joseph.

☙ **קמ"ו פסוקים. יחזקיה"ו סימן. אמצי"ה סימן. יהי"ה ל"י עב"ד סימן. ותיבות אלפים כ"ה** — This Masoretic note means: There are 146 verses in the *Sidrah,* numerically corresponding to the mnemonics יְחִזְקִיָּה"וּ [*Yechizkiyahu*], אֲמַצְיָ"ה [*Amatziah*], יִהְיֶ"ה לִ"י עֶבֶ"ד [*he shall be My slave*]. And the *Sidrah* contains 2,025 words.

The names *Yechizkiyahu* and *Amatziah* are the same as the mnemonics used for the *Sidrah Bereishis,* implying that the two portions have common themes. *Bereishis,* the portion of Creation, proclaims God's all-powerful majesty; as Creator of the universe, only He sustains it and determines its course, whatever pretensions man may have to the contrary. In *Sidrah Mikeitz,* we find Pharaoh considering himself a god and Egypt worshiping the Nile as its deity. Through the devices of abundance and famine, God displayed beyond doubt that only *His* is the power. Pharaoh and his people were forced to acknowledge that they were subservient to Joseph whose distinction was that whatever his position — slave or viceroy — he remained but a servant of God: *He shall be My slave* (*R' David Feinstein*).

Only in this *Sidrah* is a mnemonic provided for the number of words, in this case 2025. This alludes to Chanukah, which usually falls in the week of *Sidrah Mikeitz.* On Chanukah, we light a new נֵר, *lamp,* for each of the eight nights. The numerical value of נֵר is 250; accordingly, the eight lights of Chanukah give a total of 2000. Chanukah begins on the *twenty-fifth* of Kislev. Thus, 2025 is an allusion to the lights and the date of Chanukah (*Torah Temimah*).

The theme of Chanukah is especially appropriate to *Mikeitz.* We commemorate even the first day's burning, even though the oil in the jug was enough to burn for a day without miraculous intervention. By doing so, we testify to our belief that even the seemingly "natural" process of burning oil is in essence a miracle, because it is a manifestation of God's will.

PARASHAS VAYIGASH / פרשת ויגש

יח וַיִּגַּ֨שׁ אֵלָ֜יו יְהוּדָ֗ה וַיֹּאמֶר֮ בִּ֣י אֲדֹנִי֒ יְדַבֶּר־נָ֨א

< please, < speak, << my lord, < If you please, << and he said, < did Judah < him < Then approach 18

עַבְדְּךָ֤ דָבָר֙ בְּאָזְנֵ֣י אֲדֹנִ֔י וְאַל־יִ֥חַר אַפְּךָ֖ בְּעַבְדֶּ֑ךָ

<< at your servant < your anger < flare up < and let not << of my lord, < in the ears < a word < may your servant

כִּ֥י כָמ֖וֹךָ כְּפַרְעֹֽה׃ יט אֲדֹנִ֣י שָׁאַ֔ל אֶת־עֲבָדָ֖יו לֵאמֹ֑ר הֲיֵשׁ־לָכֶ֥ם אָ֖ב אוֹ־

< or < a father < you < 'Have << saying, < his servants < has asked < My lord 19 << like Pharaoh. << like you, < — for

אָֽח׃ כ וַנֹּ֙אמֶר֙ אֶל־אֲדֹנִ֔י יֶשׁ־לָ֙נוּ֙ אָ֣ב זָקֵ֔ן וְיֶ֥לֶד זְקֻנִ֖ים קָטָ֑ן וְאָחִ֣יו מֵ֗ת

<< has died, < and his brother << who is young; < of [his] old age < and a child < who is old < a father < 'We have << my lord, < to < And we said 20 << a brother?'

אונקלוס

יח וּקְרֵב לְוָתֵהּ יְהוּדָה וַאֲמַר בְּבָעוּ רִבּוֹנִי יְמַלֵּל כְּעַן עַבְדָּךְ פִּתְגָמָא קֳדָם רִבּוֹנִי וְלָא יִתְקֵף רוּגְזָךְ בְּעַבְדָּךְ אֲרֵי כְּפַרְעֹה כֵּן אַתְּ: יט רִבּוֹנִי שְׁאֵיל יָת עַבְדוֹהִי לְמֵימָר הַאִית לְכוֹן אַבָּא אוֹ אָחָא: כ וַאֲמַרְנָא לְרִבּוֹנִי אִית לָנָא אַבָּא סָבָא וּבַר סִיבְתִּין זְעֵיר וַאֲחוּהִי מִית

רש"י

(יח) ויגש אליו. דבר באזני אדני. יכנסו דברי באזניך (ב"ר נג:ו): **ואל יחר אפך.** מכאן אתה למד שדבר אליו קשות: **כי כמוך כפרעה.** חשוב אתה בעיני כמלך, זהו פשוטו. ומדרשו סופך ללקות עליו בצרעת כמו שלקה פרעה על ידי זקנתו שרה על לילה אחת שעכבה (שם). ד"א, מה פרעה גוזר ואינו מקיים מבטיח ואינו עושה אף אתה כן, וכי זו היא שימת עין שאמרת לשום עינך עליו. ד"א, כי כמוך כפרעה, אם תקניטני אהרוג אותך ואת אדונך (שם): **(יט) אדני שאל את עבדיו.** מתחלה בעלילה באת עלינו, למה היה לך לשאול כל אלה, בתך היינו מבקשים או אחותנו אתה מבקש, ואע"פ כן ונאמר אל אדוני, לא כחדנו ממך דבר (שם ח): **(כ) ואחיו מת.** מפני

PARASHAS VAYIGASH

18-34. At the conclusion of the previous *Sidrah,* Benjamin was an apprehended thief who had been caught red-handed with the viceroy's goblet. He and his brothers stood abjectly at the mercy of the hostile, indignant all-powerful Egyptian, who ruled that Benjamin would have to remain in Egypt as a slave while his brothers could return to their father. *All* the brothers were dumbfounded, but only Judah stepped forward, risking his life to intercede. His speech was simple yet eloquent; controlled yet emotional; respectful yet firm. Judah petitioned without debasing himself. He could not protest the fairness of the verdict, because the goblet *was* found in Benjamin's sack. Instead, Judah offered *himself* as a slave — not realizing that he was speaking to the very person whom he had once sold into slavery. The Midrash teaches that the brothers shrank away as Joseph and Judah confronted one another. They sensed that this was a confrontation not merely between two strong men, but between two opposing philosophies. Ultimately, both antagonists triumphed, for Joseph and Judah, and the ideas they represented, remained integral parts of the Jewish people [see Overview to *Vayigash,* ArtScroll *Bereishis*].

The Torah states that Judah *approached* Joseph (v. 18), which means, according to *Zohar* and the Midrash, that Judah penetrated Joseph's innermost depths. Buried in Joseph's heart was a plan to conceal his identity until the appropriate moment when he would tell them that he was their brother — but Judah tied together narrative, appeal, and argument until he drew the secret from Joseph. Then the news burst forth that not only was he still alive but he was their *brother*, with all the love and devotion the word implies.

18. **בְּאָזְנֵי אֲדֹנִי** — *In the ears of my lord.* May my words penetrate into your ears, may my request convince you (*Rashi*).

When Judah spoke about a *word* that he wanted Joseph to accept, he alluded to the plea he was about to make (v. 33), that Joseph free Benjamin and allow Judah to take his place as a slave (*Ramban*).

וְאַל־יִחַר אַפְּךָ בְּעַבְדֶּךָ — *And let not flare up your anger at your servant.* The implication was that Judah was ready to speak in a blunt manner that could well arouse Joseph's ire (*Rashi*), so he wanted Joseph not to be caught by surprise and react angrily.

Sforno is more specific. Judah meant to say, "Do not be angry when I imply that you *forced* us into this predicament."

כִּי כָמוֹךָ כְּפַרְעֹה — *For like you, like Pharaoh.* I consider you as important as the king. The Midrash interprets the inner connotation of the phrase to imply: You will be smitten with leprosy for detaining Benjamin, just as an earlier Pharaoh was smitten for detaining his great-grandmother, Sarah, for only one night [above, 12:17]. Another Midrashic interpretation is, "You are like Pharaoh in that neither of you keeps promises. You said you wanted to 'set eyes on him' — is this what you call 'setting eyes on someone'?" *(Rashi)*.

Ramban disagrees with the last interpretation, for in the plain sense of the narrative, Joseph could not be blamed for treating the "thief" harshly. When Benjamin had first come, Joseph had treated him with unusual warmth and courtesy; now it was Benjamin, not Joseph, who was at fault. Therefore, Judah's argument should be understood as an appeal for compassion on the part of Joseph, a self-proclaimed God-fearing man [42:18]. Accordingly, at great personal risk, Judah presented an emotional argument that was impelled by his pledge to, and love of, his father. He concluded by saying, "If only one of us must remain as a slave let it be me, so that our aged and anxious father may again see his beloved youngest son. Because I guaranteed Ben-

וַיִּוָּתֵר הוּא לְבַדּוֹ לְאִמּוֹ וְאָבִיו אֲהֵבוֹ: כא וַתֹּאמֶר
‹ *Then you said* **21** « *loves him.'* ‹ *and his father* « *from his mother,* ‹ *alone* ‹ *is he* ‹ *and left*

אֶל־עֲבָדֶיךָ הוֹרִדֻהוּ אֵלָי וְאָשִׂימָה עֵינִי עָלָיו:
« *on him.'* ‹ *my eye* ‹ *and I will set* ‹ *to me,* ‹ *'Bring him down* ‹ *your servants,* ‹ *to*

כב וַנֹּאמֶר אֶל־אֲדֹנִי לֹא־יוּכַל הַנַּעַר לַעֲזֹב
‹ *to leave* ‹ *is the youth* ‹ *'Unable* « *my lord,* ‹ *to* ‹ *We said* **22**

אֶת־אָבִיו וְעָזַב אֶת־אָבִיו וָמֵת: כג וַתֹּאמֶר אֶל־
‹ *to* ‹ *But you said* **23** « *he will die.'* ‹ *his father* ‹ *for should he leave* « *his father,*

עֲבָדֶיךָ אִם־לֹא יֵרֵד אֲחִיכֶם הַקָּטֹן אִתְּכֶם
« *with you,* « *who is youngest —* ‹ *— your brother* « *he does not come down* ‹ *'If* « *your servants,*

לֹא תֹסִפוּן לִרְאוֹת פָּנָי: כד וַיְהִי כִּי עָלִינוּ אֶל־עַבְדְּךָ אָבִי וַנַּגֶּד־לוֹ
‹ *him* ‹ *we told* « *my father,* ‹ *your servant* ‹ *to* ‹ *we went up* ‹ *when* ‹ *And it was,* **24** « *my face!'* ‹ *see* ‹ *you will not again*

אֵת דִּבְרֵי אֲדֹנִי: כה וַיֹּאמֶר אָבִינוּ שֻׁבוּ שִׁבְרוּ־לָנוּ מְעַט־אֹכֶל: כו וַנֹּאמֶר
« *We said,* **26** « *food.'* ‹ *a little* ‹ *us* ‹ *buy* ‹ *'Go back,* « *Our father said,* **25** « *of my lord.* ‹ *the words*

לֹא נוּכַל לָרֶדֶת אִם־יֵשׁ אָחִינוּ הַקָּטֹן אִתָּנוּ וְיָרַדְנוּ כִּי־לֹא נוּכַל לִרְאוֹת
‹ *see* ‹ *we cannot* ‹ *for* « *then we will go down,* ‹ *with us,* ‹ *who is youngest* ‹ *our brother* ‹ *there is* ‹ *[only] if* « *go down;* ‹ *'We cannot*

פְּנֵי הָאִישׁ וְאָחִינוּ הַקָּטֹן אֵינֶנּוּ אִתָּנוּ: כז וַיֹּאמֶר עַבְדְּךָ אָבִי אֵלֵינוּ אַתֶּם
‹ *'You* « *to us,* « *my father —* ‹ *— your servant* « *Then he said* **27** « *with us.'* ‹ *is not* ‹ *who is youngest* ‹ *if our brother* ‹ *of the man* ‹ *the face*

יְדַעְתֶּם כִּי שְׁנַיִם יָלְדָה־לִּי אִשְׁתִּי: כח וַיֵּצֵא הָאֶחָד מֵאִתִּי וָאֹמַר אַךְ
‹ *Alas,* « *and I presumed:* ‹ *from me* ‹ *The one has gone away* **28** « *— my wife.* ‹ *to me* ‹ *she bore* ‹ *two [sons]* ‹ *that* ‹ *know*

וְאִשְׁתָּאַר הוּא בִּלְחוֹדוֹהִי לְאִמֵּהּ
וַאֲבוּהִי רָחֵים לֵהּ: כא וַאֲמַרְתָּ לְעַבְדָּיךְ
אַחֲתוּהִי לְוָתִי וְאֱשַׁוִּי עֵינִי עֲלוֹהִי:
כב וַאֲמַרְנָא לְרִבּוֹנִי לָא יִכּוֹל עוּלֵימָא
לְמִשְׁבַּק יָת אֲבוּהִי וְאִם יִשְׁבּוֹק יָת
אֲבוּהִי וּמִית: כג וַאֲמַרְתְּ לְעַבְדָּיךְ אִם
לָא יֵחוֹת אֲחוּכוֹן זְעֵירָא עִמְּכוֹן לָא
תוֹסְפוּן לְמֶחֱזֵי אַפָּי: כד וַהֲוָה כַּד
סְלֵיקְנָא לְעַבְדָּךְ אַבָּא וְחַוֵּינָא לֵהּ יָת
פִּתְגָּמֵי רִבּוֹנִי: כה וַאֲמַר אֲבוּנָא תּוּבוּ
זְבוּנוּ לָנָא זְעֵיר עִיבוּרָא: כו וַאֲמַרְנָא לָא
נִכּוּל לְמֵיחַת אִם אִית אֲחוּנָא זְעֵירָא
עִמָּנָא וְנֵחוֹת אֲרֵי לָא נִכּוּל לְמֶחֱזֵי
אַפֵּי גַבְרָא וַאֲחוּנָא זְעֵירָא לֵיתוֹהִי
עִמָּנָא: כז וַאֲמַר עַבְדָּךְ אַבָּא לָנָא אַתּוּן
יְדַעְתּוּן אֲרֵי תְרֵין יְלִידַת לִי אִתְּתִי:
כח וּנְפַק חַד מִלְּוָתִי וַאֲמָרִית בְּרַם

רש"י

היראה היה מוציא דבר שקר מפיו. אמר אם אומר לו שהוא קיים יאמר הביאהו אצלי (שם): **לבדו לאמו.** מאותה האם אין לו עוד אח (תרגום יונתן): **(כב) ועזב את אביו ומת.** אם יעזוב את אביו דואגים אנו שמא ימות בדרך, שהרי אמו בדרך מתה:

jamin's safety, I cannot return home without him, *lest I see the tragedy that will befall my father."*

19. Implicit in Judah's extended recapitulation of the events is a suspicion that the affair of the goblet was a sinister conspiracy against Benjamin and the brothers.

22-23. וְעָזַב אֶת־אָבִיו וָמֵת — *For should he leave his father [then] he will die.* Jacob reasoned, "It may have been decreed that the sons of Rachel should perish on the road. I sent Joseph on a journey and he did not return; the same might happen to Benjamin if I send him, for their mother, too, died on the road" (*Midrash HaChafetz*). But, Judah contended to Joseph, you ignored our fears. Instead, you capriciously demanded that we bring him to you (*Alshich*).

24. עַבְדְּךָ אָבִי — *Your servant my father.* The Sages (*Sotah* 13b) criticize Joseph for remaining silent when his father was described in this degrading manner. He lost ten years of his life in punishment for doing so. For Judah, this was not a sin because he thought he was addressing the royalty of Egypt, and such obeisance is the required etiquette in such circumstances. Joseph, however, would not have revealed his identity by saying that a resident of Canaan was not his servant.

27-28. This passage was not recorded in the original account of Jacob's response (43:6-7). This is in keeping with the rule that the Torah is brief in one place and expansive in another,

טָרֹף טֹרָף וְלֹא רְאִיתִיו עַד־הֵנָּה: כט וּלְקַחְתֶּם

he has been torn to pieces, ‹ and I have not seen him ‹ until ‹ now! « 29 So should you take ‹

גַּם־אֶת־זֶה מֵעִם פָּנַי וְקָרָהוּ אָסוֹן וְהוֹרַדְתֶּם

also ‹ this one ‹ from ‹ before me ‹ and there should befall him ‹ a disaster, « then you will [thereby] have brought down ‹

אֶת־שֵׂיבָתִי בְּרָעָה שְׁאֹלָה: ל וְעַתָּה כְּבֹאִי אֶל־

my old age ‹ in tragedy ‹ to the grave.' « 30 And now, « if I come ‹ to ‹

עַבְדְּךָ אָבִי וְהַנַּעַר אֵינֶנּוּ אִתָּנוּ וְנַפְשׁוֹ קְשׁוּרָה

your servant ‹ my father ‹ and the youth ‹ is not ‹ with us « —since his soul ‹ is so bound up ‹

בְנַפְשׁוֹ: שני לא וְהָיָה כִּרְאוֹתוֹ כִּי־אֵין הַנַּעַר וָמֵת

with his soul— « 31 it will happen ‹ that when he sees ‹ that ‹ not [with us] ‹ is the youth ‹ he will die, «

וְהוֹרִידוּ עֲבָדֶיךָ אֶת־שֵׂיבַת עַבְדְּךָ אָבִינוּ בְּיָגוֹן שְׁאֹלָה: לב כִּי עַבְדְּךָ

and your servants will have brought down ‹ the old age ‹ of your servant ‹ our father ‹ in sorrow ‹ to the grave. « 32 For ‹ your servant ‹

עָרַב אֶת־הַנַּעַר מֵעִם אָבִי לֵאמֹר אִם־לֹא אֲבִיאֶנּוּ אֵלֶיךָ וְחָטָאתִי

guaranteed ‹ the youth ‹ unto ‹ my father ‹ saying, « 'If ‹ I do not bring him back ‹ to you ‹ then I will have sinned ‹

לְאָבִי כָּל־הַיָּמִים: לג וְעַתָּה יֵשֶׁב־נָא עַבְדְּךָ תַּחַת הַנַּעַר עֶבֶד לַאדֹנִי

to my father ‹ [for] all ‹ the days.' « 33 And now, ‹ let [me] remain, ‹ please, ‹ [me] your servant ‹ in place of ‹ the youth ‹ [as] a servant ‹ to my lord, «

וְהַנַּעַר יַעַל עִם־אֶחָיו: לד כִּי־אֵיךְ אֶעֱלֶה אֶל־אָבִי וְהַנַּעַר אֵינֶנּוּ

and the youth ‹ will go up ‹ with ‹ his brothers. « 34 For ‹ how ‹ can I go up ‹ to ‹ my father ‹ if the youth ‹ is not ‹

מִקְטַל קְטִיל וְלָא חֲזִתֵּהּ עַד כְּעָן: כט וְתִדְבְּרוּן אַף יָת דֵּין מִן קֳדָמַי וִיעַרְעִנֵּהּ מוֹתָא וְתַחֲתוּן יָת שֵׂבְתִי בְּבִישְׁתָא לִשְׁאוֹל: ל וּכְעַן כְּמֵיתִי לְוַת עַבְדָּךְ אַבָּא וְעוּלֵימָא לֵיתוֹהִי עִמָּנָא וְנַפְשֵׁהּ חֲבִיבָא לֵהּ כְּנַפְשֵׁהּ: לא וִיהֵי כַּד חָזֵי אֲרֵי לֵית עוּלֵימָא וִימוּת וְיַחֲתוּן עַבְדָיךְ יָת שֵׂיבַת עַבְדָּךְ אֲבוּנָא בְּדַאֲבוֹנָא (נ״א בְּדָווֹנָא) לִשְׁאוֹל: לב אֲרֵי עַבְדָּךְ מְעָרַב בְּעוּלֵימָא מִן אַבָּא לְמֵימַר אִם לָא אַיְתִנֵּהּ לְוָתָךְ וָאֱהֵי חָטֵי לְאַבָּא כָּל יוֹמַיָּא: לג וּכְעַן יִתֵּב כְּעַן עַבְדָּךְ תְּחוֹת עוּלֵימָא עַבְדָּא לְרִבּוֹנִי וְעוּלֵימָא יִסַּק עִם אֲחוֹהִי: לד אֲרֵי אֶכְדֵּין אֶסַּק לְוַת אַבָּא וְעוּלֵימָא לֵיתוֹהִי

רש"י

(כט) וקרהו אסון. שהשטן מקטרג בשעת הסכנה (ב"ר צא:ט): **והורדתם את שיבתי וגו'.** עכשיו כשהוא אצלי אני מתנחם בו על אמו ועל אחיו ואם ימות זה דומה עלי ששלשתן מתו ביום אחד (שם ח): **(לא) והיה כראותו כי אין הנער ומת.** אביו מצרתו (ברב"ת): **(לב) כי עבדך ערב את הנער [וגו'].** וא"ת למה אני נכנס לתגר יותר משאר אחי. הם כולם מבחוץ, ואני נתקשרתי בקשר חזק להיות מנודה בב' עולמות (ב"ר צג:ח; תנחומא ישן ד): **(לג) ישב נא עבדך וגו'.** לכל

reserving details for wherever they would be more pertinent.

30-31. **וְעַתָּה** — *And now.* Especially now that our father had warned us that any mishap affecting Benjamin would not be attributable to simple happenstance, but that he would blame us for having brought misfortune upon him (*Sforno*) . . . and he will die immediately. If we could have a chance to tell him that Benjamin had stolen your goblet, our law-abiding, righteous father would accept the justice of your decree, but when he sees that Benjamin is not with us, he will die before we have a chance to tell him (*Dubno Maggid*).

The question arises: Why didn't Judah mention the grief that Benjamin's ten children would experience at *their* father's absence? R' Menachem Mendel of Kotzk used this as an example of the truism that parents have more compassion for their children than children have for their parents.

32. Judah proceeds to explain why he was the only one of all the brothers pleading Benjamin's cause.

33. **יֵשֶׁב־נָא עַבְדְּךָ תַּחַת הַנַּעַר** — *Let [me] remain, please,]me] your servant in place of the youth*. One who buys a slave and discovers that he is a thief sends him back, yet you would force a thief to be your servant! You must have some sinister design. If you want him as a personal attendant, I am more skilled than he; if you need him as a fighter, I can fight better than he. Therefore, please let me remain as a slave in place of the youth (*Tanchuma Yashan*).

אִתִּי פֶּן אֶרְאֶה בָרָע אֲשֶׁר יִמְצָא אֶת־אָבִי׃

with me, ‹ lest ‹ I see ‹ the tragedy ‹ that ‹ will befall ‹ my father!

45 [מה] 1 א וְלֹא־יָכֹל יוֹסֵף לְהִתְאַפֵּק לְכֹל הַנִּצָּבִים

[Now] unable ‹ was Joseph ‹ to restrain himself ‹ [in the presence] of all ‹ who stood

עָלָיו וַיִּקְרָא הוֹצִיאוּ כָל־אִישׁ מֵעָלָי וְלֹא־עָמַד

before him, ‹ so he called out, ‹ Clear out ‹ every ‹ man ‹ from before me! ‹ Thus there stood no

אִישׁ אִתּוֹ בְּהִתְוַדַּע יוֹסֵף אֶל־אֶחָיו׃ ב וַיִּתֵּן אֶת־קֹלוֹ בִּבְכִי וַיִּשְׁמְעוּ

man ‹ with him ‹ when Joseph made himself known ‹ to ‹ his brothers. 2 He gave out ‹ his voice ‹ in weeping. ‹ And they heard,

מִצְרַיִם וַיִּשְׁמַע בֵּית פַּרְעֹה׃ ג וַיֹּאמֶר יוֹסֵף אֶל־אֶחָיו אֲנִי יוֹסֵף הַעוֹד

did Egypt, ‹ and hear ‹ did the household ‹ of Pharaoh. 3 And Joseph said ‹ to ‹ his brothers, ‹ I am ‹ Joseph. ‹ Is yet

אָבִי חָי וְלֹא־יָכְלוּ אֶחָיו לַעֲנוֹת אֹתוֹ כִּי נִבְהֲלוּ מִפָּנָיו׃ ד וַיֹּאמֶר יוֹסֵף

my father ‹ alive? ‹ But unable were ‹ his brothers ‹ to answer ‹ him ‹ because ‹ they were dismayed ‹ before him. 4 Then Joseph said

עִמִּי דִלְמָא אֶחֱזֵי בְּבִישׁוּ דְּיִשְׁכַּח יָת אַבָּא: א וְלָא יְכִיל יוֹסֵף לְאִתְחַסָּנָא לְכֹל דְּקָיְמִין עִלָּווֹהִי וּקְרָא אַפִּיקוּ כָל גְּבַר מִלְּוָתִי וְלָא קָם אֱנַשׁ עִמֵּהּ כַּד אִתְיְדַע יוֹסֵף לְוַת אֲחוֹהִי: ב וִיהַב יָת קָלֵהּ בִּבְכִיתָא וּשְׁמָעוּ מִצְרַיִם וּשְׁמַע אֱנַשׁ בֵּית פַּרְעֹה: ג וַאֲמַר יוֹסֵף לַאֲחוֹהִי אֲנָא יוֹסֵף הַעַד כְּעַן אַבָּא קַיָּם וְלָא יְכִילוּ אֲחוֹהִי לַאֲתָבָא יָתֵהּ פִּתְגָּם אֲרֵי אִתְבְּהִילוּ מִן קֳדָמוֹהִי: ד וַאֲמַר יוֹסֵף

רש"י

דבר אני מעולה ממנו לגבורה ולמלחמה ולשמש (ב"ר שם ו): **(א) ולא יכול יוסף להתאפק לכל הנצבים.** לא היה יכול לסבול שיהיו מצרים נצבים עליו ושומעין שאחיו מתביישין בהודעו להם (תנחומא ה): **(ב) וישמע בית פרעה.** ביתו של פרעה, כלומר עבדיו ובני ביתו (אונקלוס). ואין זה לשון בית ממש אלא כמו בית ישראל (תהלים קטו:יב) בית יהודה (מלכים א יב:כא). מיסניד"א בלע"ז: **(ג) נבהלו מפניו.** מפני הבושה (תנחומא שם):

45.

1-15. Joseph identifies himself and conciliates his brothers. With Judah's selfless offer of himself as a substitute for Benjamin, Joseph finally had irrefutable proof of his brothers' new attitude, as exemplified by their filial devotion to Jacob, their love for Benjamin, and their sincere contrition for their crime against Joseph himself. It was to ascertain this that he had subjected them to all these tribulations to begin with. Moreover, his brothers had already had their share of the expiatory humiliation they deserved. Joseph felt, therefore, that the time of reconciliation had at last arrived (*Akeidah; Abarbanel; R' Hirsch*).

1. וְלֹא־יָכֹל יוֹסֵף לְהִתְאַפֵּק — *[Now] unable was Joseph to restrain himself.* The verse associates the presence of Joseph's attendants with his inability to restrain himself. Among the explanations are:

— He was ready to reveal himself, but he could not bear to let his brothers be embarrassed in the presence of so many bystanders (*Rashi*).

— He was concerned with his own image, not that of his brothers. It would have been unseemly for him to break into tears in the presence of so many outsiders (*Rashbam*).

— Joseph's multitude of attendants were moved by Judah's plea and they joined in pleading for Benjamin's freedom. Joseph could not resist their combined pleas (*Ramban*).

2. Joseph's uncontrollable weeping was heard by the courtiers whom he had expelled from his presence. Word quickly spread to Pharaoh's court, and the entire power structure of the country was concerned.

It is indicative of Joseph's rank and the high esteem in which he was held that his weeping caused such universal concern (*R' Hirsch*).

3. אֲנִי יוֹסֵף הַעוֹד אָבִי חָי — *I am Joseph! Is yet my father alive?* Joseph's primary concern was his father. Emotionally, he wondered how Jacob could have survived the years of sorrow (*Sforno*). Alternatively, Joseph was asking whether his father was still *vigorous (Tur)*. Or, he was wondering whether all their talk about an aging father was true, or whether they were merely trying to win Joseph's sympathy so that they could escape from the country without further torment (*Ralbag*).

This could also be taken as an implied rebuke of his brothers. After listening to Judah's impassioned protestations that Jacob could not survive the loss of Benjamin, Joseph wondered why Judah was not similarly concerned when he tore Joseph away from Jacob.

When Joseph said "I am Joseph," God's master plan became clear to the brothers. They had no more questions. Everything that had happened for the last twenty-two years fell into perspective. So, too, will it be in the time to come when God will reveal Himself and announce, "I am HASHEM!" The veil will be lifted from our eyes and we will comprehend everything that transpired throughout history (*Chofetz Chaim*).

4-5. Seeing that his brothers shrank from him in shame, he

אֶל־אֶחָיו גְּשׁוּ־נָא אֵלַי וַיִּגָּשׁוּ וַיֹּאמֶר אֲנִי יוֹסֵף
‹ Joseph ‹ I am « And he said, « and they came close. « to me, ‹ please, ‹ Come close, « his brothers, ‹ to

אֲחִיכֶם אֲשֶׁר־מְכַרְתֶּם אֹתִי מִצְרָיְמָה: ה וְעַתָּה ׀
‹ And now, 5 « into Egypt. ‹ me ‹ you sold ‹ that « your brother

אַל־תֵּעָצְבוּ וְאַל־יִחַר בְּעֵינֵיכֶם כִּי־מְכַרְתֶּם אֹתִי
‹ me ‹ you sold ‹ because ‹ in your own eyes ‹ be angry ‹ and do not ‹ be upset, ‹ do not

הֵנָּה כִּי לְמִחְיָה שְׁלָחַנִי אֱלֹהִים לִפְנֵיכֶם: ו כִּי־
‹ For 6 « ahead of you. ‹ that God sent me ‹ it was to be a source of sustenance ‹ for « to this place,

זֶה שְׁנָתַיִם הָרָעָב בְּקֶרֶב הָאָרֶץ וְעוֹד חָמֵשׁ שָׁנִים
‹ years ‹ five ‹ and there are yet « of the land, ‹ in the midst ‹ of the famine ‹ two years ‹ this has been

אֲשֶׁר אֵין־חָרִישׁ וְקָצִיר: ז וַיִּשְׁלָחֵנִי אֱלֹהִים לִפְנֵיכֶם לָשׂוּם לָכֶם שְׁאֵרִית
‹ a remnant ‹ for you ‹ to establish ‹ ahead of you ‹ Thus God has sent me 7 « and harvest. ‹ plowing ‹ there shall be no ‹ in which

בָּאָרֶץ וּלְהַחֲיוֹת לָכֶם לִפְלֵיטָה גְּדֹלָה: שלישי ח וְעַתָּה לֹא־אַתֶּם שְׁלַחְתֶּם
‹ who sent ‹ you ‹ It was not « And now: 8 « that is great. ‹ for a deliverance ‹ for you ‹ and to provide sustenance ‹ in the land

אֹתִי הֵנָּה כִּי הָאֱלֹהִים וַיְשִׂימֵנִי לְאָב לְפַרְעֹה וּלְאָדוֹן לְכָל־בֵּיתוֹ וּמֹשֵׁל
‹ and ruler « household, ‹ to his entire ‹ and as a master « to Pharaoh, ‹ as a father ‹ He has made me « God; ‹ but « to this place, ‹ me

בְּכָל־אֶרֶץ מִצְרָיִם: ט מַהֲרוּ וַעֲלוּ אֶל־אָבִי וַאֲמַרְתֶּם אֵלָיו כֹּה אָמַר בִּנְךָ
‹ your son ‹ said ‹ 'So « to him, ‹ and you should say ‹ my father ‹ to ‹ —go up ‹ Hurry 9 « of Egypt. ‹ land ‹ throughout the entire

יוֹסֵף שָׂמַנִי אֱלֹהִים לְאָדוֹן לְכָל־מִצְרָיִם רְדָה אֵלַי אַל־תַּעֲמֹד: י וְיָשַׁבְתָּ
‹ You will reside 10 « delay. ‹ do not « to me; ‹ Come down « Egypt. ‹ of all ‹ master ‹ "God has made me « Joseph:

לַאֲחוֹהִי קְרִיבוּ כְעַן לְוָתִי וּקְרִיבוּ וַאֲמַר אֲנָא יוֹסֵף אֲחוּכוֹן דִּי זַבֵּנְתּוּן יָתִי לְמִצְרָיִם: ה וּכְעַן לָא תִתְנַסְסוּן וְלָא יִתְקֵף בְּעֵינֵיכוֹן אֲרֵי זַבֵּנְתּוּן יָתִי הָכָא אֲרֵי לְקַיָּמָא שַׁלְחַנִי יְיָ קֳדָמֵיכוֹן: ו אֲרֵי דֵין תַּרְתֵּין שְׁנִין כַּפְנָא בְּגוֹ אַרְעָא וְעוֹד חָמֵשׁ שְׁנִין דִּי לֵית זְרוֹעָא וַחֲצָדָא: ז וְשַׁלְחַנִי יְיָ קֳדָמֵיכוֹן לְשַׁוָּאָה לְכוֹן שְׁאָרָא בְּאַרְעָא וּלְקַיָּמָא לְכוֹן לְשֵׁיזָבָא רַבְּתָא: ח וּכְעַן לָא אַתּוּן שְׁלַחְתּוּן יָתִי הָכָא אֱלָהֵן מִן קֳדָם יְיָ וְשַׁוְּיַנִי לְאַבָּא לְפַרְעֹה וּלְרִבּוֹן לְכָל אֱנָשׁ בֵּיתֵהּ וְשַׁלִּיט בְּכָל אַרְעָא דְמִצְרָיִם: ט אוֹחוּ וּסְקוּ לְוַת אַבָּא וְתֵימְרוּן לֵהּ כִּדְנַן אֲמַר בְּרָךְ יוֹסֵף שַׁוְּיַנִי יְיָ לְרִבּוֹן לְכָל מִצְרָיִם חוּת לְוָתִי לָא תִתְעַכַּב: י וְתֵתֵיב

רש"י

(ד) **גשו נא אלי.** ראה אותם נסוגים לאחור אמר עכשיו אחי נכלמים קרא להם בלשון רכה ותחנונים והראה להם שהוא מהול (שם; ב"ר שם ח): (ה) **למחיה.** להיות לכם למחיה (תרגום יונתן): (ו) **כי זה שנתים הרעב.** עברו משני הרעב: (ח) **לאב.** לחבר ולפטרון (ב"ר צג:י): (ט) **ועלו אל אבי.** ארץ ישראל גבוהה מכל

called them lovingly, and comforted them by saying that their selling him was part of God's plan. "God, not you, sent me here. You need not be dismayed, because His purpose was to implant me here to preserve life; you were but His instrument. All of us were destined to descend to Egypt in fulfillment of God's decree that Abraham's descendants would be aliens in a foreign land (15:13). Normally we would have gone to Egypt in iron fetters [in the manner of all enslaved exiles], but He chose to spare Father and you from the harshness of a *forced descent* into hostile conditions. He sent me here to prepare the way and provide for you in honor" (gathered from *Tanchuma; Lekach Tov*).

10. Joseph had good reason to choose Goshen as the future home of his family, the place where they lived throughout their stay in Egypt: He wanted to keep them segregated from the mainstream of Egypt's idolatrous, immoral life, and to allow them to freely pursue their shepherding, an activity that was hateful to the Egyptians. Goshen was a fertile region in northeast Egypt, east of the Nile delta, which contained the country's

בְּאֶרֶץ־גֹּשֶׁן וְהָיִיתָ קָרוֹב אֵלַי אַתָּה וּבָנֶיךָ וּבְנֵי
in the land of Goshen · and you will be · near · to me · — you, · your children, · the children

בָנֶיךָ וְצֹאנְךָ וּבְקָרְךָ וְכָל־אֲשֶׁר־לָךְ: יא וְכִלְכַּלְתִּי
of your children, · your flocks · and your cattle, · and all · that is · yours. · 11 And I will provide

אֹתְךָ שָׁם כִּי־עוֹד חָמֵשׁ שָׁנִים רָעָב פֶּן־תִּוָּרֵשׁ
for you · there · — for · there are yet · five · [more] years · of famine · — lest · you become destitute,

אַתָּה וּבֵיתְךָ וְכָל־אֲשֶׁר־לָךְ: יב וְהִנֵּה עֵינֵיכֶם רֹאוֹת
you, · your household, · and all · that is · yours.'" · 12 Indeed! · Your eyes · see

וְעֵינֵי אָחִי בִנְיָמִין כִּי־פִי הַמְדַבֵּר אֲלֵיכֶם: יג וְהִגַּדְתֶּם לְאָבִי אֶת־כָּל־
as do the eyes · of my brother · Benjamin · that · it is my mouth · that is speaking · to you. · 13 You shall tell · my father · of all

כְּבוֹדִי בְּמִצְרַיִם וְאֵת כָּל־אֲשֶׁר רְאִיתֶם וּמִהַרְתֶּם וְהוֹרַדְתֶּם אֶת־אָבִי
my glory · in Egypt · and all · that · you have seen; · but you must hurry, · and bring down · my father

הֵנָּה: יד וַיִּפֹּל עַל־צַוְּארֵי בִנְיָמִן־אָחִיו וַיֵּבְךְּ וּבִנְיָמִן בָּכָה עַל־צַוָּארָיו:
to this place. · 14 Then he fell · upon · the neck · of Benjamin · his brother · and wept; · and Benjamin · wept · upon · his neck.

טו וַיְנַשֵּׁק לְכָל־אֶחָיו וַיֵּבְךְּ עֲלֵהֶם וְאַחֲרֵי כֵן דִּבְּרוּ אֶחָיו אִתּוֹ: טז וְהַקֹּל
15 He then kissed · all · his brothers · and wept · upon them; · and after · that · his brothers talked · with him. · 16 The report

בְּאַרְעָא דְגֹשֶׁן וּתְהֵי קָרִיב לִי אַתְּ
וּבְנָיךְ וּבְנֵי בְנָיךְ וְעָנָךְ וְתוֹרָךְ וְכָל
דִּי לָךְ: יא וְאֵזוּן יָתָךְ תַּמָּן אֲרֵי
עוֹד חֲמֵשׁ שְׁנִין כַּפְנָא דִּלְמָא
תִתְמַסְכַּן אַתְּ וֶאֱנַשׁ בֵּיתָךְ וְכָל דִּי
לָךְ: יב וְהָא עֵינֵיכוֹן חָזְן וְעֵינֵי אָחִי
בִנְיָמִין אֲרֵי בְּלִישָׁנְכוֹן אֲנָא מְמַלֵּל
עִמְּכוֹן: יג וּתְחַוּוּן לְאַבָּא יָת כָּל
יְקָרִי בְּמִצְרַיִם וְיָת כָּל דִּי חֲזֵיתוּן
וְתוֹחוּן וְתַחֲתוּן יָת אַבָּא הָכָא:
יד וּנְפַל עַל צַוְּארֵי בִנְיָמִן אֲחוּהִי
וּבְכָא וּבִנְיָמִן בְּכָא עַל צַוְּארֵהּ:
טו וְנַשִּׁיק לְכָל אֲחוּהִי וּבְכָא עֲלֵיהוֹן
וּבָתַר כֵּן מַלִּילוּ אֲחוּהִי עִמֵּהּ: טז וְקָלָא

רש"י

האראות (זבחים נד:): (יא) **פן תורש.** דלמא תתמסכן (אונקלוס). לשון מוריש ומעשיר (שמואל א ב:ז): (יב) **והנה עיניכם רואות.** בכבודי (ברב"ת) ושאני אחיכם שאני מהול ככם, ועוד **כי פי המדבר אליכם** בלשון הקדש (ב"ר שם; תנחומא ה): **ועיני אחי בנימין.** השוה את כולם יחד, לומר שכשם שאין לי שנאה על בנימין אחי, שהרי לא היה במכירתי, כך אין בלבי שנאה עליכם (מגילה טז:):

(יד) **ויפל על צוארי בנימין אחיו ויבך.** על שני מקדשות שעתידין להיות בחלקו של בנימין וסופן להחרב (שם): **ובנימין בכה על צואריו.** על משכן שילה שעתיד להיות בחלקו של יוסף וסופו להחרב (שם): (טו) [**וינשק.** הוסיף בנשיקה, מנשק והולך, דיבייש"ר בלע"ז:] **ואחרי כן.** מאחר שראוהו בוכה ולבו שלם עמהם: **דברו אחיו אתו.** שמתחלה היו בושים ממנו (תנחומא שם):

most fertile soil and is described as *the best of the land* (47:6). Its major city was Rameses.

12. The brothers had been standing dumbfounded before him all this time. Joseph was apprehensive that they still might be doubtful about his true identity, so he wanted to reassure them again that he was really Joseph. He did so by referring to his *mouth that is speaking to you.* Most commentators say that Joseph pointed out that he was speaking Hebrew, a language that was unknown in Egypt. *Ramban* differs, for the ruling and commercial classes surely knew Hebrew, the language of a neighboring country. Rather, Joseph meant to say that he spoke as the viceroy who had the power to carry out his lavish promises of the previous verses. *Sforno* comments that he quoted their discussion at the time of his sale, something that was done in Hebrew and that the slave merchants could not have understood.

14. When Joseph revealed himself to his brothers, he had cried tears of joy; now he wept in sadness and foreboding, for he foresaw that the exile into which he was now summoning his family would not be their last. He knew that many trials and hardships lay in store for the nation, and he felt the mixture of joy and sadness that has been typical of the Jewish people ever since (*R' Munk*).

The Midrash comments that Joseph and Benjamin wept over the destruction of the sanctuaries that would be built in their respective territories: the two Temples that would stand in Benjamin's portion of Jerusalem, and the Tabernacle of Shiloh, in the portion of Joseph's son Ephraim. According to the *Zohar,* he

נִשְׁמַע בֵּית פַּרְעֹה לֵאמֹר בָּאוּ אֲחֵי יוֹסֵף וַיִּיטַב

‹ And it was good « of Joseph! ‹ — the brothers « They have come « saying, ‹ of Pharaoh ‹ in the palace ‹ was heard

בְּעֵינֵי פַּרְעֹה וּבְעֵינֵי עֲבָדָיו: יז וַיֹּאמֶר פַּרְעֹה

‹ Pharaoh said 17 « of his servants. ‹ and in the eyes ‹ of Pharaoh ‹ in the eyes

אֶל־יוֹסֵף אֱמֹר אֶל־אַחֶיךָ זֹאת עֲשׂוּ טַעֲנוּ

‹ Load up « you shall do: ‹ 'This « your brothers, ‹ to ‹ Say « Joseph, ‹ to

אֶת־בְּעִירְכֶם וּלְכוּ־בֹאוּ אַרְצָה כְּנָעַן: יח וּקְחוּ

‹ Bring 18 « of Canaan. ‹ to the land ‹ [so that] you come ‹ and go ‹ your animals

אֶת־אֲבִיכֶם וְאֶת־בָּתֵּיכֶם וּבֹאוּ אֵלָי וְאֶתְּנָה לָכֶם

‹ you ‹ I will give « to me. ‹ and come ‹ and your households ‹ your father

אֶת־טוּב אֶרֶץ מִצְרַיִם וְאִכְלוּ אֶת־חֵלֶב הָאָרֶץ:

« of the land.' ‹ the fat ‹ and you will eat ‹ of Egypt ‹ of the land ‹ the best

רביעי יט וְאַתָּה צֻוֵּיתָה זֹאת עֲשׂוּ קְחוּ־לָכֶם מֵאֶרֶץ מִצְרַיִם עֲגָלוֹת לְטַפְּכֶם

‹ for your small children ‹ wagons ‹ of Egypt ‹ from the land ‹ for yourselves ‹ Take « you shall do: ‹ 'This « are commanded [to say], ‹ And you 19

וְלִנְשֵׁיכֶם וּנְשָׂאתֶם אֶת־אֲבִיכֶם וּבָאתֶם: כ וְעֵינְכֶם אַל־תָּחֹס עַל־

‹ on ‹ take pity ‹ should not ‹ And your eye 20 « and come. ‹ your father ‹ and you should carry « and for your wives;

כְּלֵיכֶם כִּי־טוּב כָּל־אֶרֶץ מִצְרַיִם לָכֶם הוּא: כא וַיַּעֲשׂוּ־כֵן בְּנֵי יִשְׂרָאֵל

« of Israel, ‹ — the sons « so ‹ They did 21 « it is.' ‹ — yours « of Egypt ‹ the land ‹ of all ‹ the best ‹ for « your belongings,

וַיִּתֵּן לָהֶם יוֹסֵף עֲגָלוֹת עַל־פִּי פַרְעֹה וַיִּתֵּן לָהֶם צֵדָה לַדָּרֶךְ: כב לְכֻלָּם

‹ To all of them 22 « for the journey. ‹ provisions ‹ them ‹ and he gave « of Pharaoh, ‹ the word ‹ by ‹ wagons ‹ Joseph « to them, ‹ and he did, gave

אִשְׁתְּמַע לְבֵית פַּרְעֹה לְמֵימַר אֲתוֹ אֲחֵי יוֹסֵף וּשְׁפַר בְּעֵינֵי פַרְעֹה וּבְעֵינֵי עַבְדוֹהִי: יז וַאֲמַר פַּרְעֹה לְיוֹסֵף אֱמַר לַאֲחָךְ דָּא עִיבִידוּ טְעוּנוּ יָת בְּעִירְכוֹן וְאֱזִילוּ אוֹבִילוּ לְאַרְעָא דִכְנָעַן: יח וּדְבָרוּ יָת אֲבוּכוֹן וְיָת אֱנַשׁ בָּתֵּיכוֹן וְעוּלוּ לְוָתִי וְאֶתֵּן לְכוֹן יָת טוּב אַרְעָא דְמִצְרָיִם וְתֵיכְלוּן יָת טוּבָא דְאַרְעָא: יט וְאַתְּ מְפַקַּד דָּא עִיבִידוּ סִיבוּ לְכוֹן מֵאַרְעָא דְמִצְרַיִם עֶגְלָן לְטַפְלְכוֹן וְלִנְשֵׁיכוֹן וְתִטְלוּן יָת אֲבוּכוֹן וְתֵיתוּן: כ וְעֵינְכוֹן לָא תְחוּס עַל מָנֵיכוֹן אֲרֵי טַב כָּל אַרְעָא דְמִצְרַיִם דִּלְכוֹן הוּא: כא וַעֲבָדוּ כֵן בְּנֵי יִשְׂרָאֵל וִיהַב לְהוֹן יוֹסֵף עֶגְלָן עַל מֵימַר פַּרְעֹה וִיהַב לְהוֹן זְוָדִין לְאָרְחָא: כב לְכָלְּהוֹן

רש"י

(טז) והקל נשמע בית פרעה. כמו בבית פרעה, וזהו לשון בית ממש: **(יז) טענו את בעירכם.** תבואה: **(יח) את טוב ארץ מצרים.** ארץ גושן (להלן מז:ו). ניבא, ואינו יודע מה ניבא סופה לעשותה כמצולה שאין בה דגים (ברכות ט:): **חלב הארץ.** כל חלב לשון מיטב הוא (אונקלוס): **(יט) ואתה צויתה.** מפי לומר להם: **זאת עשו.** כך

wept over his brothers, as well, because he foresaw that the Ten Tribes would be exiled and scattered among the nations.

16-21. Pharaoh joins in the welcome.

16. וַיִּיטַב בְּעֵינֵי פַּרְעֹה — *And it was good in the eyes of Pharaoh.* Pharaoh was happy that Egypt would no longer bear the stigma of being ruled by an ex-slave and ex-convict of unknown origins. Now it was known that Joseph was a member of a prominent and respected family (*Ramban*). Furthermore, now that Joseph's family would be coming to Egypt, he would surely stop thinking of himself as an alien and be even more devoted to the best interests of the land (*Sforno*).

19-20. Joseph's integrity and honesty were so unimpeachable that Pharaoh knew he would never abuse his high office for personal advantage [especially in this case, since the export of wagons from Egypt was prohibited (*Abarbanel*)]; thus, Joseph might not send his father anything. Therefore Pharaoh specifically *commanded* him to send a large complement of wagons, which would contain a generous supply of provisions and enough cargo space to bring back all their necessary belongings (*Ramban*). He added the admonition that they not be concerned with items that they would be forced to leave behind, for the abundance of Egypt would be at their disposal.

R' Yosef Dov Soloveitchik conjectures that the reason Pharaoh

נָתַן לְאִישׁ חֲלִפוֹת שְׂמָלֹת וּלְבִנְיָמִן נָתַן שְׁלֹשׁ

< three < he gave < but to Benjamin << of clothing; < changes < to [each] man < he gave

מֵאוֹת כֶּסֶף וְחָמֵשׁ חֲלִפֹת שְׂמָלֹת: כג וּלְאָבִיו שָׁלַח

< he sent < And to his father **23** << of clothing. < changes < and five < pieces of silver < hundred

כְּזֹאת עֲשָׂרָה חֲמֹרִים נֹשְׂאִים מִטּוּב מִצְרָיִם

< of Egypt < from the best < laden < he-donkeys < ten << as follows:

וְעֶשֶׂר אֲתֹנֹת נֹשְׂאֹת בָּר וָלֶחֶם וּמָזוֹן לְאָבִיו לַדָּרֶךְ: כד וַיְשַׁלַּח אֶת־אֶחָיו

< his brothers, < And he sent off **24** << for the journey. < for his father < and food < bread, < with grain, < laden < she-donkeys < and ten

וַיֵּלֵכוּ וַיֹּאמֶר אֲלֵהֶם אַל־תִּרְגְּזוּ בַּדָּרֶךְ: כה וַיַּעֲלוּ מִמִּצְרָיִם וַיָּבֹאוּ אֶרֶץ

< to the land < and came < from Egypt < They went up **25** << *on the way.* < *become agitated* < *Do not* < to them, < He said << and they went.

כְּנַעַן אֶל־יַעֲקֹב אֲבִיהֶם: כו וַיַּגִּדוּ לוֹ לֵאמֹר עוֹד יוֹסֵף חַי וְכִי־הוּא מֹשֵׁל

< ruler < he is < and that < *lives,* < *Joseph* < *Yet* << saying, < him, < And they told **26** << their father. < Jacob < to < of Canaan

יְהַב לִגְבַר אִצְטְלַוָן דִּלְבוּשִׁין וּלְבִנְיָמִן יְהַב תְּלָת מְאָה סִלְעִין דִּכְסַף וַחֲמֵשׁ אִצְטְלַוָן דִּלְבוּשִׁין: כג וְלַאֲבוּהִי שְׁלַח כְּדָא עַסְרָא חֲמָרִין טְעִינִין מִטּוּבָא דְמִצְרָיִם וַעֲסַר אַתְנָן טְעִינָן עִיבוּר וּלְחֵם וּזְוָדִין לַאֲבוּהִי לְאָרְחָא: כד וְשַׁלַּח יָת אֲחוּהִי וַאֲזָלוּ וַאֲמַר לְהוֹן לָא תִתְנַצּוּן בְּאָרְחָא: כה וּסְלִיקוּ מִמִּצְרָיִם וַאֲתוֹ לְאַרְעָא דִכְנַעַן לְוַת יַעֲקֹב אֲבוּהוֹן: כו וְחַוִּיאוּ לֵהּ לְמֵימַר עוֹד כְּעַן יוֹסֵף קַיָּם וַאֲרֵי הוּא שַׁלִּיט

רש"י

אמור להם שברשותי הוא (תרגום יונתן): **(כג) שלח כזאת.** כחשבון הזה ומהו החשבון עשרה חמורים וגו': **מטוב מצרים.** מצינו בגמרא ששלח לו יין ישן שדעת זקנים נוחה הימנו (מגילה טז:). ומ"א, גריסין של פול (ב"ר צד:ב): **בר ולחם.** כתרגומו: **ומזון.** ליפתן (שם): **(כד) אל תרגזו בדרך.** אל תתעסקו בדבר הלכה שלא תרגז עליכם הדרך. ד"א, אל תפסיעו פסיעה גסה, והכנסו בחמה לעיר (תענית י:; ב"ר צד:ב). ולפי פשוטו של מקרא יש לומר לפי שהיו נכלמים היה דואג שמא יריבו בדרך על דבר מכירתו להתוכח זה עם זה ולומר על ידך נמכר אתה ספרת לשון הרע עליו וגרמת לנו לשנאתו (אונקלוס; תרגום יונתן): **(כו) וכי הוא מושל.** ואשר הוא מושל:

was so anxious for Joseph's family to come and was so generous in receiving them was because of his great respect for Joseph's political and economic acumen. Pharaoh assumed that there must be others in the family who were brilliant and could be impressed into Egyptian national service.

22-24. Joseph dispenses gifts and sends his brothers off.

22. לְכֻלָּם נָתַן . . . וּלְבִנְיָמִן נָתַן — *To all of them he gave . . . but to Benjamin he gave.* To each of the ten brothers he gave two sets of clothing (*Ibn Ezra*), so that they would be dressed in an elegance befitting their position as brothers of the viceroy (*R' Avraham ben HaRambam*), and to replace the garments they had torn in grief [44:13] (*R' Tam*). But to Benjamin, he gave more lavishly. Such largess to his only full brother was understandable and probably would not have aroused jealousy on the part of the others. The Talmud (*Megillah* 16b), however, questions how Joseph, the victim of jealousy, could have done such a thing. It explains that Joseph's gifts were meant to allude to the future success of Benjamin's descendant Mordechai, who would emerge from King Ahasuerus's presence attired in five royal garments (see *Esther* 8:15). This episode, therefore, is yet another instance of the events in the lives of the Patriarchal family alluding to future Jewish history.

24. אַל־תִּרְגְּזוּ בַּדָּרֶךְ — *Do not become agitated on the way. Rashi* offers three interpretations of our passage: (a) Do not become involved in halachic discussion lest the road become "angry" at you, a figurative expression, meaning: lest you become so engrossed that you lose your way; (b) do not be impatient on the journey, lest you travel too quickly or travel into the night before stopping to rest; (c) according to the plain sense of the passage, however, Joseph feared that the brothers would quarrel with each other and engage in mutual recrimination over who was responsible for selling him. He cautioned them, therefore, not to quarrel on the way.

25-28. Jacob receives the news. One can barely imagine the tremendous emotional impact upon Jacob of the news that Joseph was still alive and that, despite his long isolation from his family and the harmful influence of Egyptian society, Joseph was still a loyal son of Jacob. Fearing that a sudden announcement might shock and harm Jacob, the brothers sent one of his granddaughters, Serach daughter of Asher, to prepare him for it. She played her harp and sang gently that Joseph was still alive and that he was the ruler of Egypt. Slowly, Jacob's long sadness evaporated and he blessed her for having lifted his spirits. As a result, she was still alive centuries later, and eventually entered the Garden of Eden alive (*Pirkei d'R' Eliezer*). While she was still with Jacob, the brothers entered and proclaimed the astounding news. Although Serach had prepared the way, at

בְּכָל־אֶרֶץ מִצְרָיִם וַיָּפָג לִבּוֹ כִּי לֹא־הֶאֱמִין לָהֶם׃
« them. ‹ he did not believe ‹ for « did his heart, ‹ but turn away « of Egypt; ‹ the land ‹ over all

כז וַיְדַבְּרוּ אֵלָיו אֵת כָּל־דִּבְרֵי יוֹסֵף אֲשֶׁר דִּבֶּר
‹ he had spoken ‹ that ‹ of Joseph ‹ the words ‹ all ‹ to him ‹ When they told 27

אֲלֵהֶם וַיַּרְא אֶת־הָעֲגָלוֹת אֲשֶׁר־שָׁלַח יוֹסֵף
‹ Joseph had sent ‹ that ‹ the wagons ‹ and he saw ‹ to them,

לָשֵׂאת אֹתוֹ וַתְּחִי רוּחַ יַעֲקֹב אֲבִיהֶם׃ חמישי כח וַיֹּאמֶר יִשְׂרָאֵל רַב
« How great! ‹ And Israel said, 28 « their father. ‹ of Jacob ‹ the spirit ‹ then revived was « him, ‹ to carry

עוֹד־יוֹסֵף בְּנִי חָי אֵלְכָה וְאֶרְאֶנּוּ בְּטֶרֶם אָמוּת׃ [מו] א וַיִּסַּע יִשְׂרָאֵל
‹ So Israel journeyed 1 46 « I die. ‹ before ‹ and see him ‹ I shall go « lives! ‹ my son ‹ Joseph ‹ Yet

וְכָל־אֲשֶׁר־לוֹ וַיָּבֹא בְּאֵרָה שָּׁבַע וַיִּזְבַּח זְבָחִים לֵאלֹהֵי אָבִיו יִצְחָק׃
« Isaac. ‹ of his father ‹ to the God ‹ sacrifices ‹ He slaughtered « to Beer-sheba. ‹ and he came ‹ was his ‹ that ‹ with all

בְּכָל אַרְעָא דְמִצְרָיִם וַהֲווֹ מִלַּיָּא פָּיְגָן עַל לִבֵּהּ אֲרֵי לָא הֵימִין לְהוֹן: כז וּמַלִּילוּ עִמֵּהּ יָת כָּל פִּתְגָּמֵי יוֹסֵף דִּי מַלִּיל עִמְּהוֹן וַחֲזָא יָת עֲגָלָתָא דִּשְׁלַח יוֹסֵף לְמִטַּל יָתֵהּ וּשְׁרַת רוּחַ נְבוּאָה עַל יַעֲקֹב אֲבוּהוֹן: כח וַאֲמַר יִשְׂרָאֵל סַגִּי לִי חֶדְוָא עַד כְּעַן יוֹסֵף בְּרִי קַיָּם אֵזִיל וְאֶחֱזְנֵהּ עַד לָא אֵמוּת: א וּנְטַל יִשְׂרָאֵל וְכָל דִּי לֵהּ וַאֲתָא לִבְאֵר שָׁבַע וּדְבַח דִּבְחִין לֵאלָהָא דַאֲבוּהִי יִצְחָק:

רש"י

ויפג לבו. נחלף לבו והלך מלהאמין, לא היה לבו פונה אל הדברים, ל' מפיגין טעמן בלשון משנה (ביצה יד.), וכמו מאין הפוגות (איכה ג:מט) וריחו לא נמר (ירמיה מח:יא) מתרגמינן וריחיה לא פג: **(כז) את כל דברי יוסף.** סימן מסר להם במה היה עוסק כשפירש ממנו, בפרשת עגלה ערופה (ב"ר לד:ג; לה:ג; תנחומא יא). וזהו שנאמר **וירא את העגלות אשר שלח יוסף,** ולא נאמר אשר שלח פרעה: **ותחי רוח יעקב.** שרתה עליו שכינה שפירשה ממנו (אונקלוס; תנחומא וישב ג): **(כח) רב [עוד].** רב לי [עוד] שמחה וחדוה הואיל **ועוד יוסף בני חי: (א) בארה שבע.** כמו לבאר שבע. ה"א בסוף תיבה במקום למ"ד בתחלתה (יבמות יג:): **לאלהי אביו יצחק.** חייב אדם בכבוד אביו יותר מבכבוד זקנו (ב"ר לד:ה) לפיכך תלה ביצחק ולא באברהם:

first Jacob found it intellectually impossible to believe them. Finally, they offered incontrovertible proof. They repeated to Jacob the last Torah lesson he had studied with Joseph. That was something they could have known only if Joseph himself had told them.

26. **כִּי לֹא־הֶאֱמִין לָהֶם** — *For he did not believe them.* This is the fate of a liar: He is disbelieved even when he tells the truth! Jacob had believed them when they came and showed him Joseph's bloodstained tunic, indicating that a wild beast had devoured him; but now, even though they were telling the truth, he did not believe them (*Avos d'Rabbi Nassan*).

27. To prove to Jacob that Joseph had sent these messages, Joseph directed his brothers to say that the last topic he and Jacob had studied together was that of *eglah arufah* [the calf whose neck was broken in expiation of an unsolved murder (see *Deut.* 21:1-9)]. The word עֲגָלוֹת, *wagons,* can also be translated *calves,* thus alluding to that topic. Therefore it is written [further in this verse], *And he saw the agalos* [wagons] *that "Joseph" had sent;* it does not say . . . that *Pharaoh* had sent (*Rashi*).

וַתְּחִי — *Revived.* During the years of Joseph's absence Jacob was in grief and the Divine spirit had left him, for it rests only amid joy. Now that Jacob was happy again, he *was revived* spiritually (*Rashi*; *Rambam*). Therefore, in the next verse he is called *Israel*, the name that stands for his spiritual nobility.

28. The news that brought rejoicing to Jacob was not merely that Joseph was physically alive, or even that he had risen to greatness in the land of his captivity, for Jacob defined life in spiritual terms. What resuscitated Jacob's — *Israel's* — spirit was the assurance that the viceroy of Egypt was the same Joseph who had left Canaan twenty-two years before and that he even remembered the Torah he had studied with his father. But Jacob was not yet satisfied, for only he could recognize the full extent of Joseph's spiritual stature. Great though his sons were, only he was the ultimate judge of the soul, and for that reason, he announced, *"I shall go and see him before I die."* He wanted to see for himself if Joseph was truly still the same, and, Jacob's words implied, if it was indeed the same Joseph, he was ready to die, for his mission of raising a perfect family would have been fulfilled.

46.

1-27. Jacob undertakes the journey to Joseph. On his way to Egypt, Jacob stopped to express his gratitude to God. Then he accepted the Divine command that he go to Egypt, despite his frightening premonition that he was embarking on an exile that would cause his family incalculable harm.

1. **זְבָחִים לֵאלֹהֵי אָבִיו יִצְחָק** — *Sacrifices to the God of his father Isaac. Rashi* comments that Jacob associated his offerings only with Isaac, not Abraham, because a son owes more honor to his father than to his grandfather.

Ramban and *R' Bachya*, however, offer a deeper reason. In His

ב וַיֹּאמֶר אֱלֹהִים ׀ לְיִשְׂרָאֵל בְּמַרְאֹת הַלַּיְלָה
‹ of the night ‹ in visions ‹ to Israel ‹ God said 2

וַיֹּאמֶר יַעֲקֹב ׀ יַעֲקֹב וַיֹּאמֶר הִנֵּנִי: ג וַיֹּאמֶר אָנֹכִי
‹ *I am* «And He said, 3 « *Here I am.* ‹ And he said, « *Jacob.* ‹ *Jacob,* « and He said,

הָאֵל אֱלֹהֵי אָבִיךָ אַל־תִּירָא מֵרְדָה מִצְרַיְמָה כִּי־
‹ *for* « *to Egypt,* ‹ *of descending* ‹ *fear* ‹ *Do not* « *of your father.* ‹ *— God* « *the God*

לְגוֹי גָּדוֹל אֲשִׂימְךָ שָׁם: ד אָנֹכִי אֵרֵד עִמְּךָ מִצְרַיְמָה
« *to Egypt,* ‹ *with you* ‹ *shall descend* ‹ *I* 4 « *there.* ‹ *I shall establish you* ‹ *that is great* ‹ *as a nation*

וְאָנֹכִי אַעַלְךָ גַם־עָלֹה וְיוֹסֵף יָשִׁית יָדוֹ עַל־עֵינֶיךָ: ה וַיָּקָם יַעֲקֹב
‹ So Jacob rose up 5 « *your eyes.* ‹ *on* ‹ *his hand* ‹ *shall place* ‹ *and Joseph* « *shall surely bring you up also;* ‹ *and I*

מִבְּאֵר שָׁבַע וַיִּשְׂאוּ בְנֵי־יִשְׂרָאֵל אֶת־יַעֲקֹב אֲבִיהֶם וְאֶת־טַפָּם
‹ [as well as] their young children « their father, ‹ Jacob « of Israel did — ‹ — the sons « and they carried « from Beer-sheba;

וְאֶת־נְשֵׁיהֶם בָּעֲגָלוֹת אֲשֶׁר־שָׁלַח פַּרְעֹה לָשֵׂאת אֹתוֹ: ו וַיִּקְחוּ
‹ They took 6 « him. ‹ to carry ‹ Pharaoh had sent ‹ which ‹ in the wagons ‹ and their wives,

אֶת־מִקְנֵיהֶם וְאֶת־רְכוּשָׁם אֲשֶׁר רָכְשׁוּ בְּאֶרֶץ כְּנַעַן וַיָּבֹאוּ מִצְרָיְמָה
« to Egypt ‹ and they came ‹ of Canaan ‹ in the land ‹ they had amassed ‹ that ‹ and their possessions ‹ their livestock

ב וַאֲמַר יְיָ לְיִשְׂרָאֵל בְּחֶזְוֵי דְלֵילְיָא וַאֲמַר יַעֲקֹב יַעֲקֹב וַאֲמַר הָא אֲנָא: ג וַאֲמַר אֲנָא אֵל אֱלָהָא דַאֲבוּךְ לָא תִדְחַל מִלְּמֵיחַת לְמִצְרַיִם אֲרֵי לְעַם סַגִּי אֲשַׁוִּנָּךְ תַּמָּן: ד אֲנָא אֵחוֹת עִמָּךְ לְמִצְרַיִם וַאֲנָא אַסֶּקִנָּךְ אַף אַסָּקָא וְיוֹסֵף יְשַׁוֵּי יְדוֹהִי עַל עֵינָךְ: ה וְקָם יַעֲקֹב מִבְּאֵרָא דְשָׁבַע וּנְטָלוּ בְּנֵי יִשְׂרָאֵל יָת יַעֲקֹב אֲבוּהוֹן וְיָת טַפְלְהוֹן וְיָת נְשֵׁיהוֹן בַּעֲגָלָתָא דִּי שְׁלַח פַּרְעֹה לְמִטַּל יָתֵהּ: ו וּנְסִיבוּ יָת גֵּיתֵיהוֹן וְיָת קִנְיָנְהוֹן דִּי קְנוֹ בְּאַרְעָא דִכְנַעַן וַאֲתוֹ לְמִצְרָיִם

רש"י

(ב) **יעקב יעקב.** לשון חבה (תורת כהנים ויקרא א:יב): (ג) **אל תירא מרדה מצרימה.** לפי שהיה מצר על שנזקק לצאת לחוצה לארץ (פדר"א פל"ט): (ד) **ואנכי אעלך.** הבטיחו להיות נקבר בארץ (ירושלמי סוטה א:י; קה"ר ז:ג): (ו) **אשר רכשו בארץ כנען.** אבל מה שרכש בפדן ארם נתן הכל לעשו בשביל חלקו במערת המכפלה, אמר, נכסי חוצה לארץ אינן כדאי לי. וזהו אשר כריתי לי (להלן נ:ה), העמיד לו צבורין של זהב ושל כסף כמין כרי ואמר לו טול את אלו (תנחומא ישן וישלח יא):

relationship to Isaac, God is called פַּחַד יִצְחָק, *the Fear of Isaac* (31:42), a name that denotes awe and justice, for this was the attribute that characterized Isaac's service of God. Now that Jacob recognized that a harsh exile lay ahead, a manifestation of extreme judgment, he invoked Isaac in his prayer for a softening of the ordeal. He stressed this request further by the sort of offerings he brought. The term *zevachim* usually refers to peace-offerings, which symbolize the harmony between God and Israel.

R' Shlomo Ashtruc (*Midrashei HaTorah*) writes that without doubt Jacob was aware of the prophecy that Abraham's descendants would be aliens and slaves in a strange land, and he was fearful that the literal exile and servitude would begin with him. He prayed to *the God of his father Isaac,* because, even though the four hundred years of alien status commenced with his birth, Isaac had been spared the travails of physical exile and slavery. Now Jacob prayed and offered these sacrifices, imploring God to grant him the same dispensation.

2. בְּמַרְאֹת הַלַּיְלָה — *In visions of the night.* This is the only place where a vision is described in this manner, which implies impending darkness. At this moment, Jacob was poised to leave *Eretz Yisrael* for a long, long Egyptian exile, and he was right to be afraid of what would happen to his family there. The night of exile, when hope is enveloped in darkness, was about to begin, so God came *in visions of the night* to symbolize to him that though Jews would be exiled from their land, they would never be exiled from their God; He would always be with them. Therefore, Jacob, the Patriarch of exile, originated *Maariv,* the evening prayer, to show his children that the exile/night might be the epilogue to one day, but it is prologue to another, even better one (*Meshech Chochmah*).

3-4. אַל־תִּירָא — *Do not fear.* When asked why he was afraid to go to Egypt, Jacob said, "I am afraid that my family will succumb there, that the *Shechinah* will no longer dwell among us, that I will not be buried with my ancestors, and that I will not see the redemption of my children." God reassured him on all counts (*Zohar*). In addition, God promised him that Joseph would *place his hand on your eyes*, an idiomatic expression referring to closing the eyes of one who dies (*Ibn Ezra*). Thus, God

יַעֲקֹב וְכָל־זַרְעוֹ אִתּוֹ: ז בָּנָיו וּבְנֵי בָנָיו אִתּוֹ בְּנֹתָיו

‹ his daughters ‹‹ with him, ‹ of his sons ‹ and the sons ‹ His sons 7 ‹‹ with him. ‹ his offspring ‹ and all ‹ — Jacob

וּבְנוֹת בָּנָיו וְכָל־זַרְעוֹ הֵבִיא אִתּוֹ מִצְרָיְמָה: ס

‹‹ to Egypt. ‹ with him ‹ he brought ‹ his offspring ‹ and all ‹ of his sons ‹ and the daughters

ח וְאֵלֶּה שְׁמוֹת בְּנֵי־יִשְׂרָאֵל הַבָּאִים מִצְרַיְמָה

‹‹ to Egypt ‹ who were coming ‹ of Israel ‹ of the children ‹ the names ‹ Now these are 8

יַעֲקֹב וּבָנָיו בְּכֹר יַעֲקֹב רְאוּבֵן: ט וּבְנֵי רְאוּבֵן חֲנוֹךְ

‹ Hanoch, ‹‹ of Reuben: ‹ The sons 9 ‹‹ Reuben. ‹‹ of Jacob, ‹ the firstborn ‹‹ and his children: ‹ — Jacob

וּפַלּוּא וְחֶצְרֹן וְכַרְמִי: י וּבְנֵי שִׁמְעוֹן יְמוּאֵל וְיָמִין וְאֹהַד וְיָכִין וְצֹחַר

‹ Zohar, ‹ Jachin, ‹ Ohad, ‹ Jamin, ‹ Jemuel, ‹‹ of Simeon: ‹ The sons 10 ‹‹ and Carmi. ‹ Hezron, ‹ Pallu,

וְשָׁאוּל בֶּן־הַכְּנַעֲנִית: יא וּבְנֵי לֵוִי גֵּרְשׁוֹן קְהָת וּמְרָרִי: יב וּבְנֵי יְהוּדָה עֵר

‹ Er, ‹‹ of Judah: ‹ The sons 12 ‹‹ and Merari. ‹ Kohath, ‹ Gershon, ‹‹ of Levi: ‹ The sons 11 ‹‹ of the Canaanite woman. ‹ son ‹ and Shaul,

וְאוֹנָן וְשֵׁלָה וָפֶרֶץ וָזָרַח וַיָּמָת עֵר וְאוֹנָן בְּאֶרֶץ כְּנַעַן וַיִּהְיוּ בְנֵי־פֶרֶץ

‹‹ of Perez — ‹ — the sons ‹‹ and they were ‹‹ of Canaan, ‹ in the land ‹ as well as Onan ‹ — Er ‹‹ but he died ‹‹ and Zerah; ‹ Perez, ‹ Shelah, ‹ Onan,

חֶצְרֹן וְחָמוּל: יג וּבְנֵי יִשָּׂשכָר תּוֹלָע וּפֻוָּה וְיוֹב וְשִׁמְרֹן: יד וּבְנֵי זְבֻלוּן

‹‹ of Zebulun: ‹ The sons 14 ‹‹ and Shimron. ‹ Iov, ‹ Puvah, ‹ Tola, ‹‹ of Issachar: ‹ The sons 13 ‹‹ and Hamul. ‹ Hezron

סֶרֶד וְאֵלוֹן וְיַחְלְאֵל: טו אֵלֶּה | בְּנֵי לֵאָה אֲשֶׁר יָלְדָה לְיַעֲקֹב בְּפַדַּן אֲרָם

‹‹ in Paddan-aram, ‹ to Jacob ‹ she bore ‹ that ‹ of Leah ‹ the sons ‹ These are 15 ‹‹ and Jahleel. ‹ Elon, ‹ Sered,

יַעֲקֹב וְכָל בְּנוֹהִי עִמֵּהּ: ז בְּנוֹהִי וּבְנֵי בְנוֹהִי עִמֵּהּ בְּנָתֵהּ וּבְנַת בְּנוֹהִי וְכָל זַרְעֵהּ אַיְתִי עִמֵּהּ לְמִצְרָיִם: ח וְאִלֵּין שְׁמָהַת בְּנֵי יִשְׂרָאֵל דְּעַלּוּ לְמִצְרַיִם יַעֲקֹב וּבְנוֹהִי בּוּכְרָא דְיַעֲקֹב רְאוּבֵן: ט וּבְנֵי רְאוּבֵן חֲנוֹךְ וּפַלּוּא וְחֶצְרֹן וְכַרְמִי: י וּבְנֵי שִׁמְעוֹן יְמוּאֵל וְיָמִין וְאֹהַד וְיָכִין וְצֹחַר וְשָׁאוּל בַּר כְּנַעֲנֵיתָא: יא וּבְנֵי לֵוִי גֵּרְשׁוֹן קְהָת וּמְרָרִי: יב וּבְנֵי יְהוּדָה עֵר וְאוֹנָן וְשֵׁלָה וָפֶרֶץ וָזָרַח וּמִית עֵר וְאוֹנָן בְּאַרְעָא דִכְנַעַן וַהֲווֹ בְנֵי פֶרֶץ חֶצְרוֹן וְחָמוּל: יג וּבְנֵי יִשָּׂשכָר תּוֹלָע וּפֻוָּה וְיוֹב וְשִׁמְרוֹן: יד וּבְנֵי זְבֻלוּן סֶרֶד וְאֵלוֹן וְיַחְלְאֵל: טו אִלֵּין בְּנֵי לֵאָה דִּי יְלִידַת לְיַעֲקֹב בְּפַדַּן אֲרָם

רש"י

(ז) ובנות בניו. סרח בת אשר ויוכבד בת לוי: **(ח) הבאים מצרימה.** על שם השעה קורא להם הכתוב באים. ואין לתמוה על אשר לא כתב אשר באו: **(י) בן הכנענית.** בן דינה שנבעלה לכנעני. כשהרגו את שכם לא היתה דינה רוצה לצאת עד שנשבע לה שמעון שישאנה (ב"ר פ:יא): **(טו) אלה בני לאה**

assured Jacob that Joseph would outlive him, relieving him of the fear he had had that Joseph would die in Jacob's lifetime (*Or HaChaim*).

7. The Torah goes on to specify those who were included in the general designation of Jacob's offspring, grouping them according to their respective mothers.

10. וְשָׁאוּל בֶּן־הַכְּנַעֲנִית — *And Shaul, son of the Canaanite woman.* In the most literal sense, this verse is tacit proof that, of all the brothers, only Simeon married a woman of Canaanite descent. The Torah therefore singles him out for taking a Canaanite wife. [The Canaanites were an accursed nation, and one must recall Abraham's intense efforts to assure that Isaac would not marry a Canaanite woman (see 24:3), and Isaac's similar charge to Jacob (28:1)] (*Ibn Ezra*).

According to the predominant Rabbinic view, however, this term refers to Dinah, who is called a Canaanite woman because she had been ravished by the Canaanite Shechem. When her brothers killed Shechem, Dinah refused to accompany them until Simeon agreed to marry her (*Rashi; Midrash*), and before the Torah was given, it was permitted to marry a sister (*Matnos Kehunah*). Generally speaking, the families of the Patriarchs observed the Torah before it was given, but under exceptional circumstances — such as the need to show compassion to Dinah — they permitted themselves to observe the prevailing Halachah.

15. The "hidden miracle" of Jochebed's birth. The verse gives the total of Leah's offspring as thirty-three; however, the foregoing account lists only thirty-*two* names. The thirty-third

וְאֵת דִּינָה בִתּוֹ כָּל־נֶפֶשׁ בָּנָיו וּבְנוֹתָיו שְׁלֹשִׁים
< [were] thirty << and his daughters — < — his sons < the souls < All << his daughter. < Dinah < and in addition

וְשָׁלֹשׁ׃ טז וּבְנֵי גָד צִפְיוֹן וְחַגִּי שׁוּנִי וְאֶצְבֹּן עֵרִי
< Eri, < Ezbon, < Shuni, < Haggi, < Ziphion, << of Gad: < The sons **16** << and three.

וַאֲרוֹדִי וְאַרְאֵלִי׃ יז וּבְנֵי אָשֵׁר יִמְנָה וְיִשְׁוָה וְיִשְׁוִי
< Ishvi, < Ishvah, < Imnah, << of Asher: < The sons **17** << and Areli. < Arodi,

וּבְרִיעָה וְשֶׂרַח אֲחֹתָם וּבְנֵי בְרִיעָה חֶבֶר
< Heber << of Beriah, < and the sons << their sister; < and Serah < Beriah,

וּמַלְכִּיאֵל׃ יח אֵלֶּה בְּנֵי זִלְפָּה אֲשֶׁר־נָתַן לָבָן לְלֵאָה בִתּוֹ וַתֵּלֶד אֶת־אֵלֶּה
< these < She bore << his daughter. < to Leah < Laban had given < whom < of Zilpah < the sons < These are **18** << and Malchiel.

לְיַעֲקֹב שֵׁשׁ עֶשְׂרֵה נָפֶשׁ׃ יט בְּנֵי רָחֵל אֵשֶׁת יַעֲקֹב יוֹסֵף וּבִנְיָמִן׃ כ וַיִּוָּלֵד
< There were born **20** << and Benjamin. < Joseph << of Jacob: < the wife << Rachel, < The sons of **19** << souls. < — sixteen << to Jacob

לְיוֹסֵף בְּאֶרֶץ מִצְרַיִם אֲשֶׁר יָלְדָה־לּוֹ אָסְנַת בַּת־פּוֹטִי פֶרַע כֹּהֵן אֹן
<< of On — < Chief < of Poti-phera < daughter < — Asenath << to him < she bore < that << of Egypt, < in the land < to Joseph

אֶת־מְנַשֶּׁה וְאֶת־אֶפְרָיִם׃ כא וּבְנֵי בִנְיָמִן בֶּלַע וָבֶכֶר וְאַשְׁבֵּל גֵּרָא וְנַעֲמָן
< Naaman, < Gera, < Ashbel, < Becher, < Bela, << of Benjamin: < The sons **21** << and Ephraim. < Manasseh

וְיָת דִּינָה בְּרַתֵּהּ כָּל נֶפֶשׁ בְּנוֹהִי וּבְנָתֵהּ תְּלָתִין וּתְלָת: טז וּבְנֵי גָד צִפְיוֹן וְחַגִּי שׁוּנִי וְאֶצְבּוֹן עֵרִי וַאֲרוֹדִי וְאַרְאֵלִי: יז וּבְנֵי אָשֵׁר יִמְנָה וְיִשְׁוָה וְיִשְׁוִי וּבְרִיעָה וְשֶׂרַח אֲחַתְהוֹן וּבְנֵי בְרִיעָה חֶבֶר וּמַלְכִּיאֵל: יח אִלֵּין בְּנֵי זִלְפָּה דִּי יְהַב לָבָן לְלֵאָה בְּרַתֵּהּ וִילִידַת יָת אִלֵּין לְיַעֲקֹב שִׁית עֶשְׂרֵי נַפְשָׁא: יט בְּנֵי רָחֵל אִתַּת יַעֲקֹב יוֹסֵף וּבִנְיָמִן: כ וְאִתְיְלִיד לְיוֹסֵף בְּאַרְעָא דְמִצְרַיִם דִּי יְלִידַת לֵהּ אָסְנַת בַּת פּוֹטִי פֶּרַע רַבָּא דְאוֹן יָת מְנַשֶּׁה וְיָת אֶפְרָיִם: כא וּבְנֵי בִנְיָמִן בֶּלַע וָבֶכֶר וְאַשְׁבֵּל גֵּרָא וְנַעֲמָן

רש"י

ואת דינה בתו. הזכרים תלה בלאה והנקבות תלה ביעקב, ללמדך, אשה מזרעת תחלה יולדת זכר, איש מזריע תחלה יולדת נקבה (נדה לא.): **שלשים ושלש.** ובפרטן אי אתה מוצא אלא ל"ב. אלא זו יוכבד שנולדה בין החומות בכניסתן לעיר שנא' אשר ילדה אותה ללוי במצרים (במדבר כו:נט) לידתה במצרים ואין הורתה במצרים (ב"ב קכג.): **(יט) בני רחל אשת יעקב.** ובכלן לא נאמר בהן אשת, אלא שהיתה עיקרו של בית (ב"ר עג:ב; תנחומא ישן ויגש טו):

child was Jochebed, the future mother of Moses, who was born as they entered the gateway between the walls, on the way into the city. Although *Numbers* 26:59 states that she was born in Egypt, she had been conceived in Canaan (*Rashi*).

Ibn Ezra is troubled by this interpretation, however, for if Jochebed was born at this point, she would have been 130 years old when she gave birth to Moses — as was indeed the case according to Rabbinic tradition (see *Rashi* to *Exodus* 2:1). If so, why did the Torah publicize the miracle that Sarah gave birth at the age of 90 while ignoring the greater miracle of Jochebed's fertility at the age of 130? Consequently, *Ibn Ezra* comments that the "thirty-third" person alluded to in this verse is Jacob himself, who was included in the count of his family. That he was included with Leah's offspring, rather than with any of the other wives, may be because her branch of the family was by far the largest.

Ramban disagrees sharply. First, he contends, even if Jochebed had not been born "between the walls," *Ibn Ezra* could not deny that the birth of Moses involved a great miracle. Levi was 43 at the time of the descent to Egypt and Moses was born 130 years later, 80 years before the Exodus; neither of these facts is in question. Thus, even if Jochebed had been born to Levi much afterward, say 57 years later, Levi would have been 100. Jochebed would then have been 73 when she gave birth to Moses — surely two miraculous events!

Why, then, did the Torah not mention the miracle of Jochebed? In a fundamental treatise, *Ramban* differentiates between hidden and open miracles. It must be understood that in the final analysis *everything* is a miracle, because nature does not function independently of God. The reward of the righteous and the punishment of the wicked are hardly "natural" occurrences, because the deeds of people cannot be shown in a laboratory to change the course of the heavens or the agricultural cycle. What we call nature is nothing more than what we are *accustomed* to see, and we do not consider it to be a manifestation of God's controlling hand because, generally, He prefers to govern the world in ways that appear to be normal. Thus the prosperity of the Patriarchs or even the extended fertility of people such as Jochebed, who *remained* youthful and vigorous at an advanced age, do not *clearly* show Divine intervention; they are

אֵחִי וָרֹאשׁ מֻפִּים וְחֻפִּים וָאָרְדְּ: כב אֵלֶּה בְּנֵי רָחֵל
Ehi, Rosh, Muppim, Huppim, and Ard. 22 These are the sons of Rachel

אֲשֶׁר יֻלַּד לְיַעֲקֹב כָּל־נֶפֶשׁ אַרְבָּעָה עָשָׂר: כג וּבְנֵי־
who were born to Jacob — all the souls, fourteen. 23 The sons

דָן חֻשִׁים: כד וּבְנֵי נַפְתָּלִי יַחְצְאֵל וְגוּנִי וְיֵצֶר
of Dan: Hushim. 24 The sons of Naphtali: Jahzeel, Guni, Jezer,

וְשִׁלֵּם: כה אֵלֶּה בְּנֵי בִלְהָה אֲשֶׁר־נָתַן לָבָן לְרָחֵל
and Shillem. 25 These are the sons of Bilhah whom Laban had given to Rachel

בִּתּוֹ וַתֵּלֶד אֶת־אֵלֶּה לְיַעֲקֹב כָּל־נֶפֶשׁ שִׁבְעָה:
his daughter. She bore these to Jacob — all the souls, seven.

כו כָּל־הַנֶּפֶשׁ הַבָּאָה לְיַעֲקֹב מִצְרַיְמָה יֹצְאֵי יְרֵכוֹ מִלְּבַד נְשֵׁי בְנֵי־יַעֲקֹב
26 All the souls coming that were belonging to Jacob — to Egypt, that issued from his loins, aside from the wives of the sons of Jacob

כָּל־נֶפֶשׁ שִׁשִּׁים וָשֵׁשׁ: כז וּבְנֵי יוֹסֵף אֲשֶׁר־יֻלַּד־לוֹ בְמִצְרַיִם נֶפֶשׁ שְׁנָיִם
— all the souls, sixty-six. 27 And the sons of Joseph who were born to him in Egypt two souls.

כָּל־הַנֶּפֶשׁ לְבֵית־יַעֲקֹב הַבָּאָה מִצְרַיְמָה שִׁבְעִים: ס ששי כח וְאֶת־יְהוּדָה
All the souls belonging to the household of Jacob who came to Egypt — seventy. 28 And Judah

שָׁלַח לְפָנָיו אֶל יוֹסֵף לְהוֹרֹת לְפָנָיו גֹּשְׁנָה וַיָּבֹאוּ אַרְצָה גֹּשֶׁן:
he sent ahead of him to Joseph, to oversee before him in Goshen; and they arrived in the land of Goshen.

אֵחִי וָרֹאשׁ מֻפִּים וְחֻפִּים וָאָרְדְּ: כב אִלֵּין בְּנֵי רָחֵל דִּי אִתְיְלִידוּ לְיַעֲקֹב כָּל נַפְשָׁתָא אַרְבְּעָה עֲשָׂר: כג וּבְנֵי דָן חֻשִׁים: כד וּבְנֵי נַפְתָּלִי יַחְצְאֵל וְגוּנִי וְיֵצֶר וְשִׁלֵּם: כה אִלֵּין בְּנֵי בִלְהָה דִּי יְהַב לָבָן לְרָחֵל בְּרַתֵּהּ וִילִידַת יָת אִלֵּין לְיַעֲקֹב כָּל נַפְשָׁתָא שִׁבְעָא: כו כָּל נַפְשָׁא (נ״א נַפְשָׁתָא) דְּעָלָא לְיַעֲקֹב לְמִצְרַיִם נָפְקֵי יַרְכֵּהּ בַּר מִנְּשֵׁי בְנֵי יַעֲקֹב כָּל נַפְשָׁתָא שִׁתִּין וְשִׁית: כז וּבְנֵי יוֹסֵף דִּי אִתְיְלִידוּ לֵהּ בְּמִצְרַיִם נַפְשָׁתָא תַּרְתֵּין כָּל נַפְשָׁתָא לְבֵית יַעֲקֹב דְּעַלָּא לְמִצְרַיִם שִׁבְעִין: כח וְיָת יְהוּדָה שְׁלַח קֳדָמוֹהִי לְוַת יוֹסֵף לְפַנָּאָה קֳדָמוֹהִי לְגֹשֶׁן וַאֲתוֹ לְאַרְעָא דְגֹשֶׁן:

רש״י

(כו) כל הנפש הבאה ליעקב. שיצאו מארץ כנען לבא למצרים. ואין הבאה זו לשון עבר אלא לשון הווה, כמו בערב היא באה (אסתר ב:יד), וכמו והנה רחל בתו באה עם הצאן (לעיל כט:ו), לפיכך טעמו למטה באל״ף, לפי שכשיצאו לבוא מארץ כנען לא היו אלא ששים ושש. והשני, כל הנפש לבית יעקב הבאה מצרימה שבעים, הוא לשון עבר, לפיכך טעמו למעלה בבי״ת. לפי שמשבאו שם היו שבעים, שמצאו שם יוסף ושני בניו ונתוספה להם יוכבד בין החומות. ולדברי האומר תאומות נולדו עם השבטים (ב״ר פב:ח; עי׳ לעיל לה:יז) צריכים אנו לומר שמתו לפני ירידתן למצרים, שהרי לא נמנו כאן. [מצאתי בויקרא רבה (ד:ו) עשו שש נפשות היו לו והכתוב קורא אותן נפשות ביתו (לעיל לו:ו) לשון רבים, לפי שהיו עובדין לאלהות הרבה. יעקב שבעים היו לו והכתוב קורא אותן נפש, לפי שהיו עובדים לאל אחד]: **(כח) להורות לפניו.** כתרגומו. לפנות לו מקום ולהורות היאך יתיישב בה: **לפניו.** קודם שיגיע לשם. ומ״א, להורות לפניו, לתקן לו בית תלמוד שמשם תצא הוראה (תנחומא יא; ב״ר

“hidden” miracles, and the Torah does not stress them. The miracles that are highlighted in the Torah are those that are foretold by a prophet or that *clearly* contravene the natural order, such as the prophecy of the angels that Sarah would give birth and the Splitting of the Sea. Why God chose to highlight some events and not others is a product of the Divine wisdom.

26-27. The grand total of seventy descendants. The total consisted of the following: All the persons who set out on the journey from Canaan to Egypt numbered sixty-six — Leah’s thirty-two listed descendants, Zilpah’s sixteen, Rachel’s eleven, and Bilhah’s seven — Joseph and his two sons were in Egypt, and Yocheved was born en route, for a total of seventy.

There are other views of who was the seventieth: Jacob himself is counted among the group as implied by the expression *Jacob and his children* [v. 8] (*Ibn Ezra* v. 15).

The *Shechinah* [Divine Presence] was the seventieth, for God joined their group, as it were, in fulfillment of His promise to Jacob [in v. 4]: *I shall descend with you.*

In the simple sense, no one is “missing,” since the Torah commonly rounds off a number when just one unit is lacking (*Rosh*).

28. Judah’s mission. Jacob sent Judah ahead of the family to oversee the proper arrangements for their arrival and settlement

כט וְטַכֵּיס יוֹסֵף רְתִכּוֹהִי וּסְלֵיק
לְקַדָּמוּת יִשְׂרָאֵל אֲבוּהִי לְגֹשֶׁן
וְאִתְגְּלִי לֵהּ וּנְפַל עַל צַוְּרֵהּ וּבְכָא עַל
צַוְּרֵהּ עוֹד: ל וַאֲמַר יִשְׂרָאֵל לְיוֹסֵף אִלּוּ
אֲנָא מָיִת זִמְנָא הָדָא מְנַחַם אֲנָא בָּתַר

כט וַיֶּאְסֹר יוֹסֵף מֶרְכַּבְתּוֹ וַיַּעַל לִקְרַאת־יִשְׂרָאֵל
29 Joseph harnessed ‹ his chariot ‹ and went up ‹ toward ‹ Israel ‹
אָבִיו גֹּשְׁנָה וַיֵּרָא אֵלָיו וַיִּפֹּל עַל־צַוָּארָיו וַיֵּבְךְּ
his father ‹ to Goshen. ‹‹ He appeared ‹ before him, ‹ and he fell ‹ upon ‹ his neck, ‹ and he wept ‹
עַל־צַוָּארָיו עוֹד: ל וַיֹּאמֶר יִשְׂרָאֵל אֶל־יוֹסֵף אָמוּתָה הַפָּעַם אַחֲרֵי
upon ‹ his neck ‹ yet more. ‹‹ 30 Then Israel said ‹ to ‹ Joseph, ‹‹ *I can die* ‹ *at this time,* ‹‹ *after* ‹

רש"י

לה:ג): **(כט) ויאסר יוסף מרכבתו.** הוא עצמו אסר את הסוסים למרכבה להזדרז לכבוד אביו (מכילתא בשלח פ"א; ב"ר נה:ח): **וירא אליו.** יוסף נראה אל אביו: **ויבך על צואריו עוד.** לשון הרבות בכיה, וכן כי לא על איש ישים עוד (איוב לד:כג) ל' רבוי הוא, אינו שם עליו עלילות נוספות על חטאיו, אף כאן הרבה והוסיף בבכי יותר על הרגיל. אבל יעקב לא נפל על צוארי יוסף ולא נשקו, ואמרו רבותינו שהיה קורא את שמע (מס' דא"ז (היגער) א:י): **(ל) אמותה הפעם.** פשוטו כתרגומו. ומדרשו סבור הייתי למות שתי מיתות, בעוה"ז ולעולם הבא, שנסתלקה ממני שכינה והייתי אומר שיתבעני הקב"ה מיתתך. עכשיו שעודך חי לא אמות אלא פעם אחת

in Goshen. Of all his sons, he chose Judah who was the proven leader of the family and who had demonstrated his prowess in the confrontation with the "viceroy" who had threatened Benjamin's freedom. *Rashi* cites the Midrashic interpretation of Judah's mission. The Midrash interprets לְהוֹרֹת as *to teach*, which implies that Jacob dispatched Judah to Goshen to establish a house of study. This set a precedent for all Jewish history. Historically, the first priority of Jewish communities has always been Torah education, for the soul of the nation is the Torah; without it we are not a nation.

29. וַיִּפֹּל . . . וַיֵּבְךְּ — *[He] fell . . . and he wept.* Joseph wept greatly and continuously. Jacob, however, did not fall upon Joseph's neck, nor did he kiss him, for, as the Sages say, Jacob was reciting the *Shema* at that moment (*Rashi*). *Gur Aryeh* explains why Jacob chose just this moment to recite the *Shema.* Supremely righteous people utilize every opportunity and resource to serve God, so that when Jacob felt a surge of joy and love at the sight of his beloved son after a long and painful separation, he submerged his personal feelings and offered all his love to God. The recitation of the *Shema* represents acceptance of God's sovereignty; that is what Jacob did at this moment of supreme emotion.

Rambam implies a more specific reason for Jacob to recite the *Shema* at the moment he saw Joseph. In describing the intensity of the love one should have for God, *Rambam* states*: It is like the love of a certain woman where he has a consuming focus on her constantly, whether he is sitting or standing, eating or drinking — greater than that should be his love for God ... as we are commanded "with all your heart and with all your soul" [phrase from Shema]...* (*Laws of Teshuvah* 10:3). What is the prime example of *the love of a certain woman* if not that of Jacob and Rachel? As noted in the commentary to 42:38 and 43:14, Jacob's mourning for Joseph included mourning for the loss of Rachel — mourning that caused the Divine spirit to leave him for 22 years (commen-

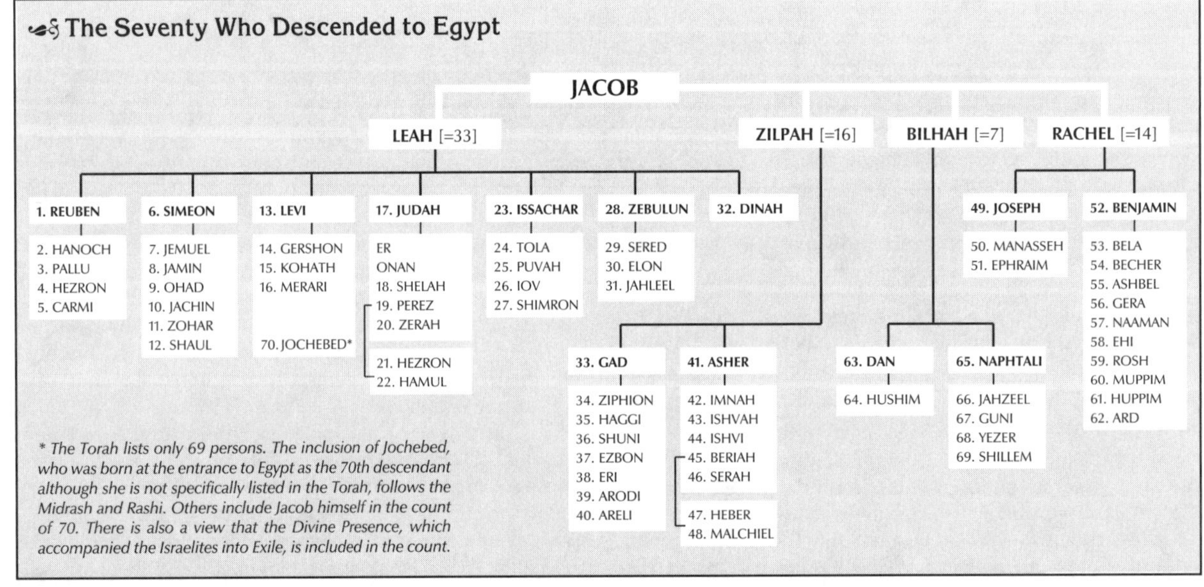

** The Torah lists only 69 persons. The inclusion of Jochebed, who was born at the entrance to Egypt as the 70th descendant although she is not specifically listed in the Torah, follows the Midrash and Rashi. Others include Jacob himself in the count of 70. There is also a view that the Divine Presence, which accompanied the Israelites into Exile, is included in the count.*

רְאוֹתִי אֶת־פָּנֶיךָ כִּי עוֹדְךָ חָי: לא וַיֹּאמֶר יוֹסֵף אֶל־
< to < And Joseph said 31 « alive. < you are still < in that « your face, < my having seen

אֶחָיו וְאֶל־בֵּית אָבִיו אֶעֱלֶה וְאַגִּידָה לְפַרְעֹה
« to Pharaoh, < and I will report < I will go up « of his father, < the household < and to < his brothers

וְאֹמְרָה אֵלָיו אַחַי וּבֵית־אָבִי אֲשֶׁר בְּאֶרֶץ־כְּנַעַן
< of Canaan < in the land < who were < of my father < and the household < 'My brothers « to him, < and I will say

בָּאוּ אֵלָי: לב וְהָאֲנָשִׁים רֹעֵי צֹאן כִּי־אַנְשֵׁי מִקְנֶה
< herdsmen < for « of flocks, < are herders < And the men 32 « to me. < have come

הָיוּ וְצֹאנָם וּבְקָרָם וְכָל־אֲשֶׁר לָהֶם הֵבִיאוּ: לג וְהָיָה כִּי־יִקְרָא לָכֶם
< you < summon < when < And it shall be, 33 « they have brought.' < is theirs < that < and everything < and their cattle, < their sheep, « have they [ever] been;

פַּרְעֹה וְאָמַר מַה־מַּעֲשֵׂיכֶם: לד וַאֲמַרְתֶּם אַנְשֵׁי מִקְנֶה הָיוּ עֲבָדֶיךָ
< have your servants been < 'Herdsmen « Then you are to say, 34 « is your occupation?' < 'What < and he will say, < will Pharaoh,

מִנְּעוּרֵינוּ וְעַד־עַתָּה גַּם־אֲנַחְנוּ גַּם־אֲבֹתֵינוּ בַּעֲבוּר תֵּשְׁבוּ בְּאֶרֶץ גֹּשֶׁן
« of Goshen, < in the land < you may settle < so that « our forefathers,' < also < we, < also « now, < until < from our youth

כִּי־תוֹעֲבַת מִצְרַיִם כָּל־רֹעֵה צֹאן: [מז] א וַיָּבֹא יוֹסֵף וַיַּגֵּד לְפַרְעֹה
< to Pharaoh, < and reported < Then Joseph came 1 47 « of flocks. < herder < is every < of Egypt < the abomination < for

דַּחֲזֵיתִינוּן לְאַפָּיךְ אֲרֵי עַד כְּעַן אַתְּ קַיָּם: לא וַאֲמַר יוֹסֵף לַאֲחוֹהִי וּלְבֵית אֲבוּהִי אֶסַּק וְאֶחַוֵּי לְפַרְעֹה וְאֵימַר לֵהּ אַחַי וּבֵית אַבָּא דִּי בְאַרְעָא דִכְנַעַן אֲתוֹ לְוָתִי: לב וְגֻבְרַיָּא רָעֵי עָנָא אֲרֵי גֻבְרֵי מָרֵי גֵיתֵי הֲווֹ וְעָנְהוֹן וְתוֹרְהוֹן וְכָל דִּי לְהוֹן אַיְתִיאוּ: לג וִיהֵי אֲרֵי יִקְרֵי לְכוֹן פַּרְעֹה וְיֵימַר מָה עוֹבָדֵיכוֹן: לד וְתֵימְרוּן גֻּבְרֵי מָרֵי גֵיתֵי הֲווֹ עַבְדָּיךְ מֵעוּלֵמָנָא וְעַד כְּעַן אַף אֲנַחְנָא אַף אֲבָהָתָנָא בְּדִיל דִּי תֵיתְבוּן בְּאַרְעָא דְגֹשֶׁן אֲרֵי בְעִירָא דְמִצְרָאֵי דָחֲלִין לֵהּ (נ״א אֲרֵי מְרַחֲקִין מִצְרָאֵי) כָּל רָעֵי עָנָא: א וַאֲתָא יוֹסֵף וְחַוִּי לְפַרְעֹה

רש"י

(תנחומא ט): (לא) ואמרה אליו אחי וגו'. ועוד אומר לו והאנשים רועי צאן וגו': (לד) בעבור תשבו בארץ גשן. והיא צריכה לכם שהיא ארץ מרעה. וכשתאמרו לו שאין אתם בקיאין במלאכה אחרת ירחיקכם מעליו ויושיבכם שם: כי תועבת מצרים כל רעה צאן. לפי שהם להם אלהות:

tary to 45:27)! In recognition of that loss, at the moment when he felt that rekindled love in its highest degree, he recited the *Shema* because *greater than that should be his love for God.*

However, *Ramban* maintains that, in the literal sense, the subject of the verb *wept* is not Joseph but Jacob, who is the antecedent of the preceding pronoun אֵלָיו, *to him.* Accordingly he interprets: *And he* [Jacob] *fell on* [Joseph's] *neck and he* [Jacob] *wept . . . Ramban* sums up his interpretation: "It is well known whose tears are more present, the aged parent who finds his long-lost son alive after having despaired and mourned for him, or the young son who rules."

30. אָמוּתָה הַפָּעַם — *I can die at this time.* See commentary to 45:28.

31-34. Joseph ensures his family's settlement in Goshen. Joseph wanted to guarantee that his family would live in Goshen, where they would be apart from the corrupting influence of Egyptian society. *Chiddushei HaRim* remarks that Joseph was establishing a pattern for his successors to follow in every generation: Do not seek the grace of gentile rulers; neither emulate their ways nor mingle with them socially. Knowing that Pharaoh would wish to recruit officials and courtiers from the brilliant and talented family that had produced his viceroy, Joseph counseled his brothers on how to respond to the king: They should be truthful, but in a way that would deter him from associating with them. Knowing that the animal-worshiping Egyptians detested shepherds, Joseph had them introduce themselves as herdsmen. Thus, Pharaoh would shun them and let them settle in the relative isolation of Goshen.

R' Hirsch finds in the phenomenon of their respective occupations a basic difference between Jewish and Egyptian society. Because a shepherd is involved with dependent living creatures, he develops the traits of kindness and generosity. Because his possessions are unstable he learns not to place too much value on wealth. And his work allows him the time to think of Godli-

וַיֹּאמֶר אָבִי וְאַחַי וְצֹאנָם וּבְקָרָם וְכָל־אֲשֶׁר לָהֶם
and he said, My father and my brothers, their sheep, their cattle, and everything that is theirs,

בָּאוּ מֵאֶרֶץ כְּנָעַן וְהִנָּם בְּאֶרֶץ גֹּשֶׁן: ב וּמִקְצֵה
have arrived from the land of Canaan, and they are [now] in the land of Goshen. 2 From the least

אֶחָיו לָקַח חֲמִשָּׁה אֲנָשִׁים וַיַּצִּגֵם לִפְנֵי פַרְעֹה:
of his brothers he took five men and presented them before Pharaoh.

ג וַיֹּאמֶר פַּרְעֹה אֶל־אֶחָיו מַה־מַּעֲשֵׂיכֶם וַיֹּאמְרוּ
3 Pharaoh said to his brothers, What is your occupation? They said

אֶל־פַּרְעֹה רֹעֵה צֹאן עֲבָדֶיךָ גַּם־אֲנַחְנוּ גַּם־אֲבוֹתֵינוּ: ד וַיֹּאמְרוּ אֶל־
to Pharaoh, Herders of flocks are your servants — also we, also our forefathers. 4 And they said to

פַּרְעֹה לָגוּר בָּאָרֶץ בָּאנוּ כִּי־אֵין מִרְעֶה לַצֹּאן אֲשֶׁר לַעֲבָדֶיךָ כִּי־
Pharaoh, To sojourn in the land have we come, since there is no pasture for the flocks that belong to your servants, for

כָבֵד הָרָעָב בְּאֶרֶץ כְּנָעַן וְעַתָּה יֵשְׁבוּ־נָא עֲבָדֶיךָ בְּאֶרֶץ גֹּשֶׁן:
severe is the famine in the land of Canaan; now, let dwell, please, your servants in the land of Goshen.

ה וַיֹּאמֶר פַּרְעֹה אֶל־יוֹסֵף לֵאמֹר אָבִיךָ וְאַחֶיךָ בָּאוּ אֵלֶיךָ: ו אֶרֶץ
5 And Pharaoh said to Joseph saying, Your father and your brothers have come to you. 6 The land

וַאֲמַר אַבָּא וְאַחַי וְעָנְהוֹן וְתוֹרְהוֹן
וְכָל דִּי לְהוֹן אֲתוֹ מֵאַרְעָא דִכְנָעַן
וְהָא אִנּוּן בְּאַרְעָא דְגֹשֶׁן: ב וּמִקְצַת
מִן אֲחוֹהִי דְּבַר חַמְשָׁא גֻבְרִין
וַאֲקֵימִנּוּן קֳדָם פַּרְעֹה: ג וַאֲמַר פַּרְעֹה
לַאֲחוֹהִי מָה עוּבָדֵיכוֹן וַאֲמָרוּ
לְפַרְעֹה רָעֵי עָנָא עַבְדָּךְ אַף
אֲנַחְנָא אַף אֲבָהָתָנָא: ד וַאֲמָרוּ לְוַת
פַּרְעֹה לְאִתּוֹתָבָא בְּאַרְעָא אֲתֵינָא
אֲרֵי לֵית רַעֲיָא לְעָנָא דִּי לְעַבְדָּךְ
אֲרֵי תַקִּיף כַּפְנָא בְּאַרְעָא דִכְנָעַן
וּכְעַן יִתְבוּן כְּעַן עַבְדָּךְ בְּאַרְעָא
דְגֹשֶׁן: ה וַאֲמַר פַּרְעֹה לְיוֹסֵף לְמֵימַר
אֲבוּךְ וַאֲחָךְ אֲתוֹ לְוָתָךְ: ו אַרְעָא

רש"י

(ב) **ומקצה אחיו.** מן הפחותים שבהם לגבורה שאין נראים גבורים, שאם יראה אותם גבורים יעשה אותם אנשי מלחמתו. ואלה הם, ראובן שמעון לוי יששכר ובנימין, אותן שלא כפל משה שמותם כשברכן. אבל שמות הגבורים כפל. וזאת ליהודה שמע ה' קול יהודה (דברים לג:ז). ולגד אמר ברוך מרחיב גד (שם כ). ולנפתלי אמר נפתלי (שם כג). ולדן אמר דן (שם כב). וכן לזבולון. וכן לאשר. זהו לשון בראשית רבה (צה:ד) שהיא אגדת ארץ ישראל. אבל בגמרא בבלית שלנו מצינו שאותן שכפל משה שמותן הם החלשים ואותן הביא לפני פרעה, ויהודה שהוכפל שמו לא הוכפל משום חלשות אלא טעם יש בדבר, כדאיתא בבבא קמא (לב.). ובברייתא דספרי

ness and goodness. Given the nature of Egyptian culture, it is quite understandable that the nation hated shepherds. Egypt's agricultural economy encouraged slavery and disregard of human dignity, and the resultant perversions and excesses of the country have been well documented.

47.

1-6. Joseph carried out the strategy he had outlined to his brothers above. In his own conversation with Pharaoh, he noted that his family had settled in Goshen, as if to implant the idea in the king's mind that he should officially designate that area as their home. And he orchestrated their formal audience with Pharaoh in such a way that he would judge them to be unsuitable for royal service.

2. וּמִקְצֵה אֶחָיו — *From the least of his brothers.* Afraid that if Pharaoh were to be introduced to robust, powerful men, he would enlist them in his military, Joseph chose the five brothers who were least impressive physically *(Rashi)*.

וַיַּצִּגֵם — *And presented them.* Joseph wanted Pharaoh to see for himself, from their words and general demeanor, that they were suitable only for shepherding (*Sforno*).

4. לָגוּר בָּאָרֶץ בָּאנוּ — *To sojourn in the land have we come.* Familiar from the Passover *Haggadah,* this statement represents the nation's resolve that its true home is *Eretz Yisrael*. The family had come to Egypt only temporarily, until the time when God would permit them to return where they belonged.

Or HaChaim comments that their intent in saying this was to present themselves as people who were humbly seeking Pharaoh's good will, not as a privileged family that was entitled to special treatment because they were the viceroy's brothers.

5-6. Pharaoh responded as graciously as Joseph had hoped, giving Joseph full authority to provide his family with the best that Egypt had to offer.

מִצְרַיִם לְפָנֶיךָ הוּא בְּמֵיטַב הָאָרֶץ הוֹשֵׁב
‹ settle ‹ of the land ‹ In the best part ‹‹ it is. ‹ – before you ‹‹ of Egypt

אֶת־אָבִיךָ וְאֶת־אַחֶיךָ יֵשְׁבוּ בְּאֶרֶץ גֹּשֶׁן וְאִם־
‹ and if ‹‹ of Goshen, ‹ in the land ‹ let them settle ‹‹ and your brothers; ‹ your father

יָדַעְתָּ וְיֶשׁ־בָּם אַנְשֵׁי־חַיִל וְשַׂמְתָּם שָׂרֵי מִקְנֶה עַל־
‹ over ‹ of livestock ‹ as chiefs ‹ appoint them ‹‹ who are capable, ‹ men ‹ among them ‹ that there are ‹ you know

אֲשֶׁר־לִי׃ ז וַיָּבֵא יוֹסֵף אֶת־יַעֲקֹב אָבִיו וַיַּעֲמִדֵהוּ
‹ and stood him ‹ his father, ‹ Jacob, ‹ Then Joseph brought 7 ‹‹ belongs to me. ‹ that which

לִפְנֵי פַרְעֹה וַיְבָרֶךְ יַעֲקֹב אֶת־פַּרְעֹה׃ ח וַיֹּאמֶר פַּרְעֹה אֶל־יַעֲקֹב כַּמָּה
‹ How many ‹‹ Jacob, ‹ to ‹ Pharaoh said 8 ‹‹ Pharaoh. ‹ and Jacob blessed ‹‹ Pharaoh, ‹ before

יְמֵי שְׁנֵי חַיֶּיךָ׃ ט וַיֹּאמֶר יַעֲקֹב אֶל־פַּרְעֹה יְמֵי שְׁנֵי מְגוּרַי שְׁלֹשִׁים וּמְאַת
‹ and one hundred ‹ have been thirty ‹ of my sojourns ‹ of the years ‹ The days ‹‹ Pharaoh, ‹ to ‹ Jacob said 9 ‹‹ of your life? ‹ of the years ‹ are the days

שָׁנָה מְעַט וְרָעִים הָיוּ יְמֵי שְׁנֵי חַיַּי וְלֹא הִשִּׂיגוּ אֶת־יְמֵי שְׁנֵי חַיֵּי
‹ of the lives ‹ of the years ‹ the days ‹ and they have not reached ‹‹ of my life, ‹ of the years ‹ the days ‹ have been ‹ and bad ‹ few ‹‹ years;

אֲבֹתַי בִּימֵי מְגוּרֵיהֶם׃ י וַיְבָרֶךְ יַעֲקֹב אֶת־פַּרְעֹה וַיֵּצֵא מִלִּפְנֵי פַרְעֹה׃
‹‹ Pharaoh. ‹ from before ‹ and he went out ‹‹ Pharaoh, ‹ Then Jacob blessed 10 ‹‹ of their sojourns. ‹ in the days ‹ of my forefathers

דְמִצְרַיִם קֳדָמָךְ הִיא בִּדְשַׁפִּיר בְּאַרְעָא אוֹתֵיב יָת אֲבוּךְ וְיָת אֲחָיךְ יֵתְבוּן בְּאַרְעָא דְגֹשֶׁן וְאִם יְדַעְתְּ וְאִית בְּהוֹן גֻּבְרִין דְּחֵילָא וּתְמַנִּנּוּן רַבָּנֵי גֵיתֵי עַל דִּי לִי׃ ז וְאָעֵיל יוֹסֵף יָת יַעֲקֹב אֲבוּהִי וַאֲקִימִנֵּהּ קֳדָם פַּרְעֹה וּבָרִיךְ יַעֲקֹב יָת פַּרְעֹה׃ ח וַאֲמַר פַּרְעֹה לְיַעֲקֹב כַּמָּה יוֹמֵי שְׁנֵי חַיָּיךְ׃ ט וַאֲמַר יַעֲקֹב לְפַרְעֹה יוֹמֵי שְׁנֵי תוֹתָבוּתַי מְאָה וּתְלָתִין שְׁנִין זְעֵירִין וּבִישִׁין הֲווֹ יוֹמֵי שְׁנֵי חַיַּי וְלָא אַדְבִּיקוּ יָת יוֹמֵי שְׁנֵי חַיֵּי אֲבָהָתַי בְּיוֹמֵי תוֹתָבוּתְהוֹן׃ י וּבָרִיךְ יַעֲקֹב יָת פַּרְעֹה וּנְפַק מִן קֳדָם פַּרְעֹה׃

רש"י

בזאת הברכה (שנד) שניתו כמו בגמרא שלנו: (ו) **אנשי חיל.** בקיאין באומנותן לרעות צאן: **על אשר לי.** על צאן שלי (אונקלוס): (ז) **ויברך יעקב.** הוא שאילת שלום, כדרך כל הנראים לפני המלכים לפרקים, שלוד"ר בלע"ז: (ט) **שני מגורי.** ימי גרותי. כל ימי הייתי גר בארץ (תרגום יונתן): **ולא השיגו.** בטובה: (י) **ויברך יעקב.** כדרך כל הנפטרים מלפני שרים מברכים אותם ונוטלים רשות. ומה ברכה ברכו, שיעלה נילוס לרגליו, לפי שאין ארץ מצרים שותה מי גשמים אלא נילוס עולה

7-10. Jacob and Pharaoh meet. Joseph presented his great father to the king of Egypt. The nature of this meeting was far different, of course, from the earlier one with the brothers. Although Jacob showed every deference due to Pharaoh, this was an instance of two monarchs greeting one another, a monarch of the spirit and a monarch of a world power. As will be noted below, *R' Hirsch* derives from the nuances of the dialogue that as Pharaoh spoke to the elderly man in front of him he realized that this was no ordinary commoner or supplicant, and, indeed, Jacob was accorded great honor throughout the remaining seventeen years of his life.

8-9. The commentators note the apparent incongruity of a king inquiring about the age of a visitor. In the plain sense, Pharaoh was struck by the appearance of the man, who seemed to be older than anyone he had ever seen before; hence his question. In reply, Jacob said that he had not yet lived nearly as long as Abraham or Isaac, but he had aged due to a life filled with travail (*Rashbam; Ramban).* He said, the days that I have lived as a גֵּר, *stranger* or *alien,* have totaled 130 years, for I have been a stranger in other people's lands all my life (*Rashi*).

R' Hirsch notes also that both Pharaoh and Jacob spoke of *days* and *years*, as if they represented separate concepts. He explains that Pharaoh, the king of a great country, must be regarded as a wise and perceptive man, who had a good reason for asking such a personal question and for differentiating between days and years. Pharaoh understood very well that though a person may live a very long life, he has probably made full and productive use of only few of his days, since most people fall far short of their potential. Seeing before him a man of incomparable stature, he asked Jacob, *How many are the "days" of the years of your life,* tell me how many truly meaningful days have you had in your long life. In response, Jacob assessed the qualitative content of his life modestly. "My life is not comparable to the lives of my fathers. They lived *more,* in the sense that every day of their existence was *living,* and they were able to carry out their missions under cheerful conditions."

10. וַיְבָרֶךְ יַעֲקֹב אֶת־פַּרְעֹה — *Then Jacob blessed Pharaoh.* As a result of Jacob's blessing, the famine ended after only two years,

שביעי יא וַיּוֹשֵׁב יוֹסֵף אֶת־אָבִיו וְאֶת־אֶחָיו וַיִּתֵּן לָהֶם

‹ them ‹ and he gave ‹ and his brothers ‹ his father ‹ So Joseph settled **11**

אֲחֻזָּה בְּאֶרֶץ מִצְרַיִם בְּמֵיטַב הָאָרֶץ בְּאֶרֶץ

‹ in the land ‹ of the land, ‹ in the best part « of Egypt, ‹ in the land ‹ a possession

רַעְמְסֵס כַּאֲשֶׁר צִוָּה פַרְעֹה׃ יב וַיְכַלְכֵּל יוֹסֵף

‹ Joseph sustained **12** « Pharaoh had commanded. ‹ as « of Rameses,

אֶת־אָבִיו וְאֶת־אֶחָיו וְאֵת כָּל־בֵּית אָבִיו לֶחֶם

‹ [with] bread ‹ of his father ‹ of the household ‹ and all ‹ and his brothers ‹ his father

לְפִי הַטָּף׃ יג וְלֶחֶם אֵין בְּכָל־הָאָרֶץ כִּי־כָבֵד הָרָעָב

‹ was the famine ‹ severe ‹ for « the land, ‹ in all ‹ — there was none « Now bread **13** « according to the children.

מְאֹד וַתֵּלַהּ אֶרֶץ מִצְרַיִם וְאֶרֶץ כְּנַעַן מִפְּנֵי הָרָעָב׃ יד וַיְלַקֵּט יוֹסֵף

‹ Joseph gathered **14** « the famine. ‹ because of ‹ of Canaan ‹ and the land ‹ of Egypt ‹ the land ‹ was weary « to an extreme;

אֶת־כָּל־הַכֶּסֶף הַנִּמְצָא בְאֶרֶץ־מִצְרַיִם וּבְאֶרֶץ כְּנַעַן בַּשֶּׁבֶר אֲשֶׁר־הֵם

‹ they ‹ that ‹ through the provisions ‹ of Canaan ‹ and in the land ‹ of Egypt ‹ in the land ‹ that was to be found ‹ the money ‹ all

שֹׁבְרִים וַיָּבֵא יוֹסֵף אֶת־הַכֶּסֶף בֵּיתָה פַרְעֹה׃ טו וַיִּתֹּם הַכֶּסֶף מֵאֶרֶץ

‹ from the land ‹ was the money ‹ And [when] depleted **15** « of Pharaoh. ‹ into the palace ‹ the money ‹ and Joseph brought « were purchasing,

מִצְרַיִם וּמֵאֶרֶץ כְּנַעַן וַיָּבֹאוּ כָל־מִצְרַיִם אֶל־יוֹסֵף לֵאמֹר הָבָה־לָּנוּ

‹ *us* ‹ *Give* « saying, ‹ Joseph, ‹ to ‹ of Egypt ‹ all ‹ then came « of Canaan, ‹ and from the land ‹ of Egypt

יא וְאוֹתֵיב יוֹסֵף יָת אֲבוּהִי וְיָת אֲחוּהִי
וִיהַב לְהוֹן אַחֲסָנָא בְּאַרְעָא דְמִצְרַיִם
בִּדְשַׁפִּיר בְּאַרְעָא בְּאַרְעָא דְרַעְמְסֵס
כְּמָא דִי פַּקִּיד פַּרְעֹה: יב וְזָן יוֹסֵף יָת
אֲבוּהִי וְיָת אֲחוּהִי וְיָת כָּל בֵּית אֲבוּהִי
לַחְמָא לְפוּם טַפְלָא: יג וְלַחְמָא לֵית
בְּכָל אַרְעָא אֲרֵי תַקִּיף כַּפְנָא לַחֲדָא
וְאִשְׁתַּלְהֵי עַמָּא דְאַרְעָא דְמִצְרַיִם
וְעַמָּא דְאַרְעָא דִכְנַעַן מִן קֳדָם כַּפְנָא:
יד וְלַקִּיט יוֹסֵף יָת כָּל כַּסְפָּא
דְּאִשְׁתְּכַח בְּאַרְעָא דְמִצְרַיִם
וּבְאַרְעָא דִכְנַעַן בְּעִיבוּרָא דִּי אִנּוּן
זָבְנִין וְאַיְתִי יוֹסֵף יָת כַּסְפָּא לְבֵית
פַּרְעֹה: טו וּשְׁלִים כַּסְפָּא מֵאַרְעָא
דְמִצְרַיִם וּמֵאַרְעָא דִכְנַעַן וַאֲתוֹ כָל
מִצְרַיִם לְוַת יוֹסֵף לְמֵימַר הַב לָנָא

רש"י

ומשקה, ומברכתו של יעקב ואילך היה פרעה בא אל נילוס והוא עולה לקראתו ומשקה את הארץ. (תנחומא נשא כו; תנחומא ישן נשא כו): **(יא) רעמסס.** מארץ גושן היא: **(יב) לפי הטף.** לפי הצריך לכל בני ביתם (תרגום יונתן): **(יג) ולחם אין בכל הארץ.** חוזר לענין הראשון לתחלת שני הרעב: **ותלה.** כמו ותלאה. לשון עיפות, כתרגומו, ודומה לו כמתלהלה היורה זקים (משלי כו:יח): **(יד) בשבר אשר הם שברים.** נותנין לו את הכסף:

instead of the seven years foretold by Joseph (*Midrash*).

12. לֶחֶם לְפִי הַטָּף — *[With] bread according to the children.* Joseph provided them with enough food to satisfy the needs of every member of the household (*Rashi*), even the children who need a bit more because they are prone to scatter and waste (*Mizrachi*).

13-27. Joseph's agrarian policy enriches Pharaoh. The narrative reverts to the beginning of the famine and describes how Joseph used his immense economic power to accumulate nearly all the wealth and all the land of Egypt for Pharaoh. Since only Joseph had preserved food in sufficient quantity to feed the masses — and he had Pharaoh's full backing — the population had no choice but to accede to his every demand. *R' Munk* cites historical descriptions of similar famines in Egypt during which people practiced cannibalism and the route from Syria to Egypt resembled a vast field strewn with corpses.

14. בַּשֶּׁבֶר אֲשֶׁר־הֵם שֹׁבְרִים — *Through the provisions that they were purchasing.* Actually the farmers themselves had contributed this grain to the royal granaries. Why, then, were they now forced to pay for their own grain? Either Joseph had bought the grain from them when the prices were depressed during the seven years of abundance, or Pharaoh had forced them to give it up during those years and now claimed that he was entitled to charge for it since it had been preserved only due to Joseph's foresight (*Ramban* to 41:18).

Not all the money of the Egyptian citizens was used up at the same time. Obviously the poor used up their savings before the rich. This verse speaks of the time when even the money of the rich was depleted (*Tur*). In order to emphasize Joseph's loyalty and honesty, the Torah makes a point of saying that he brought all the money to Pharaoh (*Ramban*).

לֶחֶם וְלָמָּה נָמוּת נֶגְדֶּךָ כִּי אָפֵס כָּסֶף׃ טז וַיֹּאמֶר

< And say 16 << money! < there is no [more] < — for << in front of you? < should we die < why < bread;

יוֹסֵף הָבוּ מִקְנֵיכֶם וְאֶתְּנָה לָכֶם בְּמִקְנֵיכֶם אִם־

< if < in return for your livestock, < for you < and I will provide < your livestock < Give over << did Joseph,

אָפֵס כָּסֶף׃ יז וַיָּבִיאוּ אֶת־מִקְנֵיהֶם אֶל־יוֹסֵף וַיִּתֵּן

< and he gave << Joseph, < to < their livestock < So they brought 17 << money. < there is no [more]

לָהֶם יוֹסֵף לֶחֶם בַּסּוּסִים וּבְמִקְנֵה הַצֹּאן וּבְמִקְנֵה

< for the livestock < of flocks, < for the livestock < in exchange for the horses, < bread < Joseph did, << them,

הַבָּקָר וּבַחֲמֹרִים וַיְנַהֲלֵם בַּלֶּחֶם בְּכָל־מִקְנֵהֶם

< their livestock < in exchange for all < with bread < thus he provided them << and for the donkeys; < of cattle,

בַּשָּׁנָה הַהִוא׃ יח וַתִּתֹּם הַשָּׁנָה הַהִוא וַיָּבֹאוּ אֵלָיו בַּשָּׁנָה הַשֵּׁנִית וַיֹּאמְרוּ

< and they said < in the second year < to him < they came < that year, < And [when] concluded was 18 << during that year.

לוֹ לֹא־נְכַחֵד מֵאֲדֹנִי כִּי אִם־תַּם הַכֶּסֶף וּמִקְנֵה הַבְּהֵמָה אֶל־אֲדֹנִי לֹא

< nothing << my lord, < to [give to] < of the animals < and the herds < the money < depleted is < if < that < from my lord < We will not withhold << to him,

נִשְׁאַר לִפְנֵי אֲדֹנִי בִּלְתִּי אִם־גְּוִיָּתֵנוּ וְאַדְמָתֵנוּ׃ יט לָמָּה נָמוּת לְעֵינֶיךָ

<< before your eyes, < should we die < Why 19 << and our land. < our bodies < perhaps < except < my lord < before < is left

גַּם־אֲנַחְנוּ גַּם־אַדְמָתֵנוּ קְנֵה־אֹתָנוּ וְאֶת־אַדְמָתֵנוּ בַּלָּחֶם וְנִהְיֶה אֲנַחְנוּ

< — we << and we will become << for bread; < and our land < us < Buy << our land? < also < we < also

וְאַדְמָתֵנוּ עֲבָדִים לְפַרְעֹה וְתֶן־זֶרַע וְנִחְיֶה וְלֹא נָמוּת וְהָאֲדָמָה לֹא תֵשָׁם׃

<< become desolate. < will not < and the land << die, < and not < so that we may live < seed < and provide << to Pharaoh; < serfs << with our land —

לַחְמָא וּלְמָא נְמוּת לְקִבְלָךְ אֲרֵי שְׁלִים כַּסְפָּא: טז וַאֲמַר יוֹסֵף הָבוּ גֵּיתֵיכוֹן וְאֶתֵּן לְכוֹן בְּגֵיתֵיכוֹן אִם שְׁלִים כַּסְפָּא: יז וְאַיְתִיוּ יָת גֵּיתֵיהוֹן לְוַת יוֹסֵף וִיהַב לְהוֹן יוֹסֵף לַחְמָא בְּסוּסָוָתָא וּבְגֵיתֵי עָנָא וּבְגֵיתֵי תוֹרִין וּבַחֲמָרִין וְזָנְנוּן בְּלַחְמָא בְּכָל גֵּיתֵיהוֹן בְּשַׁתָּא הַהִיא: יח וּשְׁלִימַת שַׁתָּא הַהִיא וַאֲתוֹ לְוָתֵהּ בְּשַׁתָּא תִנְיֵתָא וַאֲמָרוּ לֵהּ לָא נְכַסֵּי מִן רִבּוֹנִי אֱלָהֵן שְׁלִים כַּסְפָּא וְגֵיתֵי בְעִירָא לְוַת רִבּוֹנִי לָא אִשְׁתְּאַר קֳדָם רִבּוֹנִי אֱלָהֵן גְּוִיָּתָנָא וְאַרְעֲנָא: יט לְמָא נְמוּת לְעֵינָךְ אַף אֲנַחְנָא אַף אַרְעֲנָא קְנֵי יָתָנָא וְיָת אַרְעֲנָא בְּלַחְמָא וּנְהֵי אֲנַחְנָא וְאַרְעֲנָא עַבְדִּין לְפַרְעֹה וְהַב בַּר זַרְעָא וְנֵיחֵי וְלָא נְמוּת וְאַרְעָא לָא תְבוּר:

רש"י

(טו) אפס. כתרגומו, שליס: **(יז) וינהלם.** כמו וינהגם. ודומה לו אין מנהל לה (ישעיה נא:יח) על מי מנוחות ינהלני (תהלים כג:ב): **(יח) בשנה השנית.** שנית לשני הרעב: **כי אם תם הכסף וגו׳.** כי אשר תם הכסף והמקנה ובא הכל אל יד אדוני: **בלתי אם גויתנו.** כמו אם לא גויתנו: **(יט) ותן זרע.** לזרוע האדמה. ואע"פ שאמר יוסף ועוד חמש שנים אשר אין חריש וקציר מכיון שבא יעקב למצרים באה ברכה לרגליו והתחילו לזרוע. וכלה הרעב וכן שנינו בתוספתא דסוטה (י:ג): **לא תשם.** לא תהא

16. Joseph's master plan was to impoverish the Egyptians and make them totally dependent upon the king. In response to their pleas for food, he said, "To *give* you bread is not within my authority. However, if indeed your money is used up, then bring me your cattle and I will give you food in exchange. If you still have livestock, you have no right to ask for charity."

18. בַּשָּׁנָה הַשֵּׁנִית — *In the second year,* the second year of the famine. Although Joseph had said to his brothers (45:6): *And there are yet five years in which there shall be no plowing and harvest,* as soon as Jacob arrived a blessing came with him. The Egyptians began to sow and the famine came to an end [see v.10 above] *(Tosefta Sotah* 10:9).

19. גַּם־אַדְמָתֵנוּ — *Also our land.* The Egyptians spoke of the death of the land because, as many commentators note, when

כ וַיִּקֶן יוֹסֵף אֶת־כָּל־אַדְמַת מִצְרַיִם לְפַרְעֹה כִּי־
‹ since ‹‹ for Pharaoh, ‹ of Egypt ‹ the land ‹ all ‹ Thus Joseph acquired **20**
מָכְרוּ מִצְרַיִם אִישׁ שָׂדֵהוּ כִּי־חָזַק עֲלֵהֶם הָרָעָב
‹‹ had the famine; ‹ them ‹ overwhelmed ‹ because ‹‹ his field — ‹ [each] man ‹‹ Egypt sold
וַתְּהִי הָאָרֶץ לְפַרְעֹה׃ כא וְאֶת־הָעָם הֶעֱבִיר אֹתוֹ
‹ it ‹ he transferred ‹‹ the nation, ‹ As for **21** ‹‹ Pharaoh's. ‹ and the land became
לֶעָרִים מִקְצֵה גְבוּל־מִצְרַיִם וְעַד־קָצֵהוּ׃ כב רַק
‹ Only **22** ‹‹ the [other] end. ‹ unto ‹ of Egypt ‹ of the borders ‹ from [one] end ‹‹ by cities,
אַדְמַת הַכֹּהֲנִים לֹא קָנָה כִּי חֹק לַכֹּהֲנִים מֵאֵת פַּרְעֹה וְאָכְלוּ אֶת־חֻקָּם
‹ their stipend ‹ and they ate ‹‹ Pharaoh, ‹ from ‹ for the priests ‹ there was a stipend ‹ since ‹‹ he did not acquire, ‹ of the priests ‹ the land
אֲשֶׁר נָתַן לָהֶם פַּרְעֹה עַל־כֵּן לֹא מָכְרוּ אֶת־אַדְמָתָם׃ כג וַיֹּאמֶר יוֹסֵף
‹ Joseph said **23** ‹‹ their land. ‹ they did not sell ‹ therefore ‹‹ Pharaoh had; ‹‹ them, ‹ he gave ‹ that

כ וּזְבַן יוֹסֵף יָת כָּל אַרְעָא דְמִצְרַיִם
לְפַרְעֹה אֲרֵי זַבִּינוּ מִצְרַיִם גְּבַר
חַקְלֵהּ אֲרֵי תְקֵיף עֲלֵיהוֹן כַּפְנָא
וַהֲוַת אַרְעָא לְפַרְעֹה׃ כא וְיָת עַמָּא
אַעְבַּר יָתֵהּ מִקְרֵי לִקְרֵי מִסְיָפֵי תְחוּם
מִצְרַיִם וְעַד סוֹפֵהּ׃ כב לְחוֹד אַרְעָא
דְכֻמָרַיָּא לָא קְנָא אֲרֵי חֲלָקָא
לְכֻמָרַיָּא מִלְוַת פַּרְעֹה וְאָכְלִין יָת
חֲלָקְהוֹן דִּי יְהַב לְהוֹן פַּרְעֹה עַל כֵּן
לָא זַבִּינוּ יָת אַרְעֲהוֹן׃ כג וַאֲמַר יוֹסֵף

רש"י

שממה, לא תבור (אונקלוס) לשון שדה בור (פאה ב:א) שאינו חרוש: **(כ) ותהי הארץ לפרעה.** קנויה לו: **(כא) ואת העם העביר.** יוסף מעיר לעיר (אונקלוס) לזכרון שאין להם עוד חלק בארץ והושיב של עיר זו בחברתה. ולא הוצרך הכתוב לכתוב זאת אלא להודיעך שבחו של יוסף שנתכוין להסיר חרפה מעל אחיו שלא יהיו קורין אותם גולים (חולין ס:): **מקצה גבול מצרים וגו'.** כן עשה לכל הערים אשר במלכות מצרים מקצה גבולה ועד קצה גבולה: **(כב) הכהנים.** הכומרים (אונקלוס). כל לשון כהן משרת לאלהות הוא חוץ מאותן שהם לשון גדולה, כמו כהן מדין (שמות ב:טז) כהן און (לעיל מא:מה): **חק לכהנים.** חק כך וכך לחם ליום (ביצה טז.):

the land is allowed to lay waste, without being plowed and planted, it is tantamount to its death. The same is true of people who squander their potential. As the Sages put it with regard to sinners, the wicked are called dead even in their lifetimes. Life is synonymous with productivity.

20. In practice, Joseph took possession of the land, but not of the people. According to *Haamek Davar,* Joseph did not make them slaves for the welfare of the state: He wanted them to remain self-supporting and not become wards of the government.

21. וְאֶת־הָעָם הֶעֱבִיר אֹתוֹ לֶעָרִים — *As for the nation, he transferred it by cities.* That is, Joseph transferred the population from one city to the other to establish the monarchy's undisputed ownership of the land, and to demonstrate that individuals no longer had claim to their former property. He was concerned that if he let them remain in their old homes, each would cling tenaciously to his former property as if it were still his, and Joseph wanted it absolutely clear that anyone's association with a certain piece of state property was exclusively at the king's pleasure (*Rashi; Radak; Chizkuni; Meshech Chochmah*).

However, the verse implies that Joseph executed this policy wisely. Had he split up groups of people, he would have broken down the social and community structure with harmful effects to the nation. Instead, he moved entire communities *en masse* so that old friends and neighbors would remain together.

22. רַק אַדְמַת הַכֹּהֲנִים לֹא קָנָה — *Only the land of the priests he did not buy.* The verse explains that the priests had no need to sell their land for food because they received a stipend from Pharaoh, despite the famine. Verse 26 reiterates that only the priestly lands did not become Pharaoh's. The Torah's stress on the royal provision for the priests is seen by the commentators as a lesson for future generations of Israel: Jews should never be reluctant to give their tithes and contributions to the Kohanim, Levites, and the poor. God says, "See how Pharaoh did not take the land of his idol-worshiping priests and he freed them from paying a fifth of their produce to the crown. But to you, My children, I have given *Eretz Yisrael* as an outright gift — surely you, who are children of the Living God, should graciously contribute a fifth" (*Moshav Zekeinim).*

Joseph prophetically established a precedent that would later benefit Israel while it was in Egypt. By giving a privileged status to the clergy, Joseph made it possible for the tribe of Levi — the Jewish "clerics" — to be exempt from the servitude to which the Egyptians later subjected the other tribes, so that there would be a strong nucleus of people who kept alive the teachings of the Patriarchs (*R' Yaakov Kamenetzky*).

23-24. Joseph told the people the conditions under which they would be permitted to work the newly acquired royal lands and thereby earn their livelihood. Although he had refused their offer to become slaves (see v. 20), he required them to work the land as sharecroppers. He said, "Under our arrangement it would have been proper for the king, who now owns the land, to take *four*-fifths of the harvest and leave only the remaining fifth for you, but I will be generous: *You* will take the portion due to the owner of the land — four-fifths — and Pharaoh will receive

אֶל־הָעָם הֵן קָנִיתִי אֶתְכֶם הַיּוֹם וְאֶת־אַדְמַתְכֶם
< your land < with < this day < you < — I have acquired << Indeed << the people, < to
לְפַרְעֹה הֵא־לָכֶם זֶרַע וּזְרַעְתֶּם אֶת־הָאֲדָמָה׃
<< the land. < — you shall sow << seed < to you < here is << for Pharaoh;
כד וְהָיָה בַּתְּבוּאֹת וּנְתַתֶּם חֲמִישִׁית לְפַרְעֹה
<< to Pharaoh; < a fifth < you will give < when the crops come in < And it will be 24
וְאַרְבַּע הַיָּדֹת יִהְיֶה לָכֶם לְזֶרַע הַשָּׂדֶה וּלְאָכְלְכֶם
<< and for your food, << for the field, < — for seed << for you < shall be < parts < the [other] four
וְלַאֲשֶׁר בְּבָתֵּיכֶם וְלֶאֱכֹל לְטַפְּכֶם׃ מפטיר כה וַיֹּאמְרוּ הֶחֱיִתָנוּ נִמְצָא־חֵן
< favor < may we find << You have given us life; << And they said, 25 « to your young ones. < and [to give] to eat << in your household, < and for those
בְּעֵינֵי אֲדֹנִי וְהָיִינוּ עֲבָדִים לְפַרְעֹה׃ כו וַיָּשֶׂם אֹתָהּ יוֹסֵף לְחֹק עַד־
< until < as a statute < Joseph did, << it, < So he imposed 26 « to Pharaoh. < serfs < and we will be < of my lord, < in the eyes,
הַיּוֹם הַזֶּה עַל־אַדְמַת מִצְרַיִם לְפַרְעֹה לַחֹמֶשׁ רַק אַדְמַת הַכֹּהֲנִים
< of the priests < the land < only << for the fifth; < It was to Pharaoh << of Egypt: < the land < upon < this day
לְבַדָּם לֹא הָיְתָה לְפַרְעֹה׃ כז וַיֵּשֶׁב יִשְׂרָאֵל בְּאֶרֶץ מִצְרַיִם בְּאֶרֶץ גֹּשֶׁן
<< of Goshen; < in the land < of Egypt < in the land < And Israel settled 27 « Pharaoh's. < become < did not < alone
וַיֵּאָחֲזוּ בָהּ וַיִּפְרוּ וַיִּרְבּוּ מְאֹד׃ בס"ת אין כאן פיסקא אלא אות אחת. ק"ו פסוקים. יהללא"ל סימן.
« greatly. < and multiplied < and they were fruitful < in it < they acquired [property]

לְעַמָּא הָא קָנִיתִי (נ"א זְבַנִית) יָתְכוֹן יוֹמָא דֵין וְיָת אַרְעֲכוֹן לְפַרְעֹה הֵא לְכוֹן בַּר זַרְעָא וְתִזְרְעוּן יָת אַרְעָא׃ כד וִיהֵי בְּאָעוֹלֵי עֲלַלְתָּא וְתִתְּנוּן חַד מִן חַמְשָׁא לְפַרְעֹה וְאַרְבַּע חֻלָקִין יְהֵא לְכוֹן לְבַר זְרַע חַקְלָא וּלְמֵיכַלְכוֹן וְלֶאֱנַשׁ בָּתֵּיכוֹן וּלְמֵיכַל לְטַפְלְכוֹן׃ כה וַאֲמָרוּ קַיֵּמְתָּנָא נַשְׁכַּח רַחֲמִין בְּעֵינֵי רִבּוֹנִי וּנְהֵי עַבְדִין לְפַרְעֹה׃ כו וְשַׁוִּי יָתַהּ יוֹסֵף לִגְזֵרָא עַד יוֹמָא הָדֵין עַל אַרְעָא דְמִצְרַיִם דִּיהוֹן יָהֲבִין חַד מִן חַמְשָׁא לְפַרְעֹה לְחוֹד אַרְעָא דְכֻמְרַיָּא בִּלְחוֹדֵיהוֹן לָא הֲוַת לְפַרְעֹה׃ כז וִיתֵיב יִשְׂרָאֵל בְּאַרְעָא דְמִצְרַיִם בְּאַרְעָא דְגֹשֶׁן וְאִתְחֲסִינוּ בַהּ וּנְפִישׁוּ וּסְגִיאוּ לַחֲדָא׃

THE HAFTARAH FOR VAYIGASH APPEARS ON PAGE 346.

רש"י

(כג) **הא.** כמו הנה [כמו וגם אני הא דרכך בראש נתתי (יחזקאל טז:מג)]: (כד) **לזרע השדה.** שבכל שנה: **ולאשר בבתיכם.** ולאכול העבדים והשפחות אשר בבתיכם: **טפכם.** בנים קטנים: (כה) **נמצא חן.** לעשות לנו זאת כמו שאמרת: **והיינו עבדים לפרעה.** להעלות לו המס הזה בכל שנה: (כו) **לחק.** שלא יעבור: (כז) **וישב ישראל בארץ מצרים.** והיכן, **בארץ גשן,** שהיא מארץ מצרים: [**ויאחזו בה.** לשון אחיזה [ס"א אחוזה] (תרגום יונתן)]:

only the portion due to the tenant — one-fifth. The only restriction will be that you must remain to work the fields and cannot leave them" (*Ramban*).

27. וַיֵּאָחֲזוּ בָהּ — *They acquired [property] in it.* Not content with the land that Joseph had given them, they bought more and more land (*Ibn Ezra*), an indication that they were no longer regarding themselves as aliens who were sojourning in Egypt, but as permanent residents (*Kli Yakar*).

The Midrash renders *they were grasped* by the land of Egypt — implying that they could not leave — to make sure that they would remain there as long as was necessary to fulfill the prophecy made to Abraham about persecution and enslavement.

This has the further implication that Israel slowly became grasped by Egyptian culture, in the sense that they had begun the slide into assimilation.

בס"ת אין כאן פיסקא. ק"ו פסוקים. יהללא"ל סימן. — This Masoretic note means: In the Torah Scroll there is no break at this point (see notes, 'The "closed" section,' page 268); there are 106 verses in *Vayigash*, numerically corresponding to the mnemonic יְהַלֵּל אֵ־ל, *he shall praise God.*

This refers to the praises due God for having spared Joseph and reuniting Jacob's family. It further alludes to the praise due to God for orchestrating the events that led to the Egyptian bondage. For just as the Jew is obligated to praise God for the goodness He bestows, so must we praise Him for that which appears evil (*R' David Feinstein*).

PARASHAS VAYECHI / פרשת ויחי

אונקלוס

כח וַחֲיָא יַעֲקֹב בְּאַרְעָא דְמִצְרַיִם
שְׁבַע עַשְׂרֵי שְׁנִין וַהֲווֹ יוֹמֵי יַעֲקֹב
שְׁנֵי חַיּוֹהִי מְאָה וְאַרְבְּעִין וּשְׁבַע
שְׁנִין: כט וּקְרִיבוּ יוֹמֵי יִשְׂרָאֵל
לִמְמָת וּקְרָא לִבְרֵהּ לְיוֹסֵף וַאֲמַר

כח וַיְחִי יַעֲקֹב בְּאֶרֶץ מִצְרַיִם שְׁבַע עֶשְׂרֵה שָׁנָה

28 Jacob lived ‹ in the land ‹ of Egypt ‹ seventeen ‹ years; ‹‹

וַיְהִי יְמֵי־יַעֲקֹב שְׁנֵי חַיָּיו שֶׁבַע שָׁנִים וְאַרְבָּעִים

and they were ‹‹ the days ‹– of Jacob, ‹ the years ‹ of his life – ‹‹ seven ‹ years ‹ and forty ‹

וּמְאַת שָׁנָה: כט וַיִּקְרְבוּ יְמֵי־יִשְׂרָאֵל לָמוּת וַיִּקְרָא ׀ לִבְנוֹ לְיוֹסֵף וַיֹּאמֶר

and one hundred ‹ years. ‹‹ 29 Draw near ‹ did the days ‹ for Israel ‹ to die, ‹‹ so he called ‹ for his son, ‹ for Joseph, ‹ and he said ‹

רש"י

(כח) ויחי יעקב. למה פרשה זו סתומה, לפי שכיון שנפטר יעקב אבינו נסתמו עיניהם ולבם של ישראל מצרת השעבוד, שהתחילו לשעבדם. ד"א, שבקש לגלות את הקץ לבניו ונסתם ממנו. בב"ר (צו:א): **(כט) ויקרבו ימי ישראל למות.** כל מי שנאמר בו קריבה למות לא הגיע לימי אבותיו (שם ד) [יצחק חי ק"פ ויעקב קמ"ז. בדוד נאמר קריבה אביו חי ת' [ס"א פ'] שנים והוא חי ע']: **ויקרא לבנו ליוסף.** למי שהיה יכולת בידו לעשות (שם ה):

PARASHAS VAYECHI

☙ The "closed" section.

In the entire Torah Scroll, *Vayechi* is unique in that there is no extra space between it and the preceding *parashah*, in contrast to the general rule that a *Sidrah* begins on a new line or that it is separated from the previous one by at least a nine-letter space. *Rashi,* therefore, describes *Vayechi* as סְתוּמָה, *closed*, a condition that is meant to teach something about the mood of Jacob's children when he died. At that moment, the hearts of the Children of Israel were "closed" in expectation of the suffering and despair of the impending bondage. Immediately after his death, the *spiritual* exile began, even though the physical and emotional travails of *enslavement* did not commence until the death of all his sons (*Tur*). Another reason: Jacob wanted to tell his children the time of the "End," i.e., the Messianic age when Israel's exiles would finally end, but he was prevented from doing so because his prophetic vision was *closed*, i.e., it was concealed from him (*Rashi*).

The Sages in *Toras Kohanim* teach that the spaces in the Torah indicate that God paused in order to allow Moses — and later students, as well — to reflect upon the preceding verses. Consequently, the "closure" of *Vayechi* implies that in the aftermath of Jacob's death his offspring did not have the capacity to perceive the significance or draw the proper conclusions from the event (*R' Gedaliah Schorr).*

28-31. Jacob's request of Joseph. Feeling that his death was drawing near, Jacob sent for Joseph — the only one of his sons who held power — and asked Joseph to swear that he would bring him to *Eretz Yisrael* for burial in the Cave of Machpelah, in Hebron. He had several reasons for insisting on this: (a) He knew that the soil of Egypt would one day be plagued with כִּנִּים, *lice* [*Exodus* 8:12], which would have swarmed beneath his body if he had been buried in Egypt; (b) those who are buried outside of *Eretz Yisrael* will not come to life at the Resurrection until they roll through the earth to *Eretz Yisrael;* (c) Jacob did not want the Egyptians to make his tomb a shrine of idol worship (*Rashi*).

In addition, he wanted to establish for his offspring the principle that only *Eretz Yisrael* was their heritage, no matter how successful or comfortable they might be in some other land. This was especially important then, for he saw that his family had begun to feel at home in Egypt, that they were *being grasped* by it [see commentary to v. 27 above]. Soon they might substitute the Nile for the Jordan [as *Meshech Chochmah* wrote of the assimilated Jews of the ninth century: "they substituted Berlin for Jerusalem"], so that it was necessary for him to demonstrate in an impressive manner that Egypt was not their homeland (*R' Munk*).

28. וַיְחִי יַעֲקֹב בְּאֶרֶץ מִצְרַיִם — *Jacob lived in the land of Egypt.* The Torah informs us that although Jacob's original intention had been to sojourn in Egypt only until the end of the famine, God commanded him to remain there for the rest of his life (*Abarbanel*).

That the Torah uses the term *lived* [וַיְחִי], rather than *sojourned* [וַיָּגָר], indicates that the Torah speaks of the *quality* of Jacob's life in Egypt. In the plain sense, the implication is that after a lifetime of difficulty — Esau's hatred, Laban's conniving, and Joseph's disappearance — Jacob was finally able to enjoy the tranquility and harmony he had longed for. As the saying goes, "If one's end is good, all is good" (*Akeidah*).

In line with the theme that the deeds of the Patriarchs formed a pattern for the future of their descendants, it may be said that the closing years of Jacob — the symbol of Torah and truth — were a living lesson that Jews can survive and even thrive in exile if they maintain their allegiance to the ideals Jacob represented.

שֶׁבַע שָׁנִים . . . — *Seven years . . .* Normally the Torah gives the greater numbers first [see 23:1 and 25:7]. Here, the Torah reverses the order so that the number forty-seven will be in proximity to *the years of his life.* This suggests that the best years of his life totaled forty-seven, for those were the years that he was in the company of Rachel and/or Joseph, plus the first six years of his life, which were carefree (*Or HaChaim*).

לוֹ אִם־נָא מָצָאתִי חֵן בְּעֵינֶיךָ שִׂים־נָא יָדְךָ תַּחַת
to him, If, please, I have found favor in your eyes, place, now, your hand under

יְרֵכִי וְעָשִׂיתָ עִמָּדִי חֶסֶד וֶאֱמֶת אַל־נָא תִקְבְּרֵנִי
my thigh and do with me kindness and truth — do not, please, bury me

בְּמִצְרָיִם: ל וְשָׁכַבְתִּי עִם־אֲבֹתַי וּנְשָׂאתַנִי מִמִּצְרַיִם
in Egypt. 30 For I will lie down with my fathers and you shall transport me out of Egypt

וּקְבַרְתַּנִי בִּקְבֻרָתָם וַיֹּאמַר אָנֹכִי אֶעֱשֶׂה כִדְבָרֶךָ:
and bury me in their tomb. He said, I myself will do as you have said.

לא וַיֹּאמֶר הִשָּׁבְעָה לִי וַיִּשָּׁבַע לוֹ וַיִּשְׁתַּחוּ יִשְׂרָאֵל עַל־רֹאשׁ הַמִּטָּה:
31 He said, Swear to me, and he swore to him; then Israel bowed down upon the head of the bed.

[מח] א וַיְהִי אַחֲרֵי הַדְּבָרִים הָאֵלֶּה וַיֹּאמֶר לְיוֹסֵף הִנֵּה אָבִיךָ חֹלֶה
48 1 And it came to pass after these things that someone said to Joseph, Indeed, your father is ill.

וַיִּקַּח אֶת־שְׁנֵי בָנָיו עִמּוֹ אֶת־מְנַשֶּׁה וְאֶת־אֶפְרָיִם: ב וַיַּגֵּד לְיַעֲקֹב וַיֹּאמֶר
So he took his two sons with him, Manasseh and Ephraim. 2 Someone told Jacob and said,

לֵהּ אִם כְּעַן אַשְׁכַּחִית רַחֲמִין בְּעֵינָיךְ שַׁוִּי כְעַן יְדָךְ תְּחוֹת יַרְכִּי וְתַעְבֵּד עִמִּי טִיבוּ וּקְשׁוֹט לָא כְעַן תִּקְבְּרִנַּנִי בְּמִצְרָיִם: ל וְאֶשְׁכּוּב עִם אֲבָהָתַי וְתִטְלִנַּנִי מִמִּצְרַיִם וְתִקְבְּרִנַּנִי בִּקְבֻרְתְּהוֹן וַאֲמַר אֲנָא אֶעְבֵּד כְּפִתְגָּמָךְ: לא וַאֲמַר קַיֵּם לִי וְקַיֵּים לֵהּ וּסְגִיד יִשְׂרָאֵל עַל רֵישׁ עַרְסָא: א וַהֲוָה בָּתַר פִּתְגָּמַיָּא הָאִלֵּין וַאֲמַר לְיוֹסֵף הָא אֲבוּךְ שְׁכִיב מְרָע וּדְבַר יָת תְּרֵין בְּנוֹהִי עִמֵּהּ יָת מְנַשֶּׁה וְיָת אֶפְרָיִם: ב וְחַוִּי לְיַעֲקֹב וַאֲמַר

רש"י

שים נא ידך. והשבע (תנחומא ישן חיי שרה ו; פדר"א פל"ט): **חסד ואמת.** חסד שעושין עם המתים הוא חסד של אמת שאינו מצפה לתשלום גמול (ב"ר שם): **אל נא תקברני במצרים.** סופה להיות עפרה כנים [ומרחשין תחת גופי]. ושאין מתי חוצה לארץ חיים אלא בצער גלגול מחילות. ושלא יעשוני מצרים עבודת כוכבים (שם): **(ל) ושכבתי עם אבותי.** וי"ו זו מחובר למעלה לתחלת המקרא, שים נא ידך תחת ירכי והשבע לי ואני סופי לשכב עם אבותי ואתה תשאני ממצרים. ואין לומר ושכבתי עם אבותי השכיבני עם אבותי במערה, שהרי כתיב אחריו ונשאתני ממצרים וקברתני בקבורתם. ועוד מצינו בכל מקום ל' שכיבה עם אבותיו היא הגויעה ולא הקבורה, כמו וישכב דוד עם אבותיו, ואחר כך, ויקבר בעיר דוד (מלכים א ב:י): **(לא) וישתחו ישראל.** תעלא בעידניה סגיד ליה (מגילה טז:): **על ראש המטה.** הפך עצמו לצד השכינה (תנחומא ג), [מכאן אמרו שהשכינה למעלה מראשותיו של חולה (שבת יב:). ד"א, על ראש המטה, על שהיתה מטתו שלימה ולא היה בה רשע (ספרי ואתחנן לא), שהרי יוסף מלך היה ועוד שנשבה לבין הגוים, והרי הוא עומד בצדקו (שם האזינו שלד): **(א) ויאמר ליוסף.** אחד מן המגידים (עי' פס"ר פי"ב, מט:) והרי זה מקרא קצר. ויש אומרים, אפרים היה רגיל לפני יעקב בתלמוד, וכשחלה יעקב בארץ גושן הלך אפרים אצל אביו למצרים להגיד לו (תנחומא ו): **ויקח את שני בניו עמו.** כדי שיברכם יעקב לפני מותו (שם ה): **(ב) ויגד.** המגיד ליעקב ולא פירש מי, והרבה מקראות קצרי לשון:

29. . . . שִׂים־נָא יָדְךָ — *Place, now, your hand* . . . This was the means of taking an oath; see 24:2-3. As indicated by verse 31, Jacob insisted upon an oath, and would not accept an informal promise. This did not imply a lack of trust in Joseph. Rather, Jacob made a realistic assessment of the political problem that would arise when Joseph sought permission for the burial outside of Egypt. Pharaoh would take it as an insult to the land that had given generous hospitality to Jacob and his family, and he would understand the request as a demonstration that Israel's allegiance did not belong to Egypt. Only if Joseph were to take a solemn oath would Pharaoh deem it improper to stand in the way. Indeed, when Pharaoh gave permission to Joseph, he emphasized that he was doing so because Joseph had sworn to do so [see 50:6] (*Ramban, Sforno*).

חֶסֶד וֶאֱמֶת — *Kindness and truth.* The kindness shown to the dead is the true *kindness of truth* — sincerely altruistic kindness — in that the beneficiary will never be able to return the favor (*Rashi*).

31. וַיִּשְׁתַּחוּ יִשְׂרָאֵל — *Then Israel bowed down* [to Joseph]. As the proverb says, תַּעֲלָא בְּעִדָּנֵיהּ סְגִיד לֵיהּ, "*When the fox has his hour, bow down to him*" (*Rashi*). Normally it would have been improper for a father to bow to his son, but in this case, Joseph was the reigning viceroy, so that Jacob was bowing to royalty. He felt he had to show his gratitude, because, as noted above, he was fully aware that Joseph would incur Pharaoh's displeasure by acceding to this request.

48.

1-7. Jacob's illness and Joseph's birthright. After Joseph returned from Goshen, Jacob became ill. When Joseph was informed, he brought his two sons so that Jacob would bless them

הִנֵּה בִּנְךָ יוֹסֵף בָּא אֵלֶיךָ וַיִּתְחַזֵּק יִשְׂרָאֵל וַיֵּשֶׁב

‹ and he sat up ‹ did Israel ‹ So exert himself « to you. ‹ has come ‹ Joseph ‹ — your son « Indeed!

עַל־הַמִּטָּה׃ ג וַיֹּאמֶר יַעֲקֹב אֶל־יוֹסֵף אֵל שַׁדַּי

‹ Shaddai ‹ El « Joseph, ‹ to ‹ Jacob said **3** *« the bed. ‹ on*

נִרְאָה־אֵלַי בְּלוּז בְּאֶרֶץ כְּנָעַן וַיְבָרֶךְ אֹתִי׃

« me. ‹ and He blessed ‹ of Canaan ‹ in the land ‹ in Luz ‹ to me ‹ had appeared

ד וַיֹּאמֶר אֵלַי הִנְנִי מַפְרְךָ וְהִרְבִּיתִךָ וּנְתַתִּיךָ לִקְהַל עַמִּים וְנָתַתִּי

‹ and I will give « of nations, ‹ into a congregation ‹ I will make you « and I will make you numerous; ‹ will make you fruitful ‹ 'Indeed, I ‹ to me, ‹ He said **4**

אֶת־הָאָרֶץ הַזֹּאת לְזַרְעֲךָ אַחֲרֶיךָ אֲחֻזַּת עוֹלָם׃ ה וְעַתָּה שְׁנֵי־בָנֶיךָ

‹ your two sons « And now, **5** *« that is eternal.' ‹ as a possession ‹ after you ‹ to your offspring ‹ this land*

הַנּוֹלָדִים לְךָ בְּאֶרֶץ מִצְרַיִם עַד־בֹּאִי אֵלֶיךָ מִצְרַיְמָה לִי־הֵם אֶפְרַיִם

‹ Ephraim « shall they be; ‹ mine « to Egypt, ‹ to you ‹ my coming ‹ before ‹ of Egypt ‹ in the land ‹ to you ‹ who were born

הָא בְּרָךְ יוֹסֵף אֲתָא לְוָתָךְ וְאִתַּקַּף יִשְׂרָאֵל וִיתֵיב עַל עַרְסָא׃ ג וַאֲמַר יַעֲקֹב לְיוֹסֵף אֵל שַׁדַּי אִתְגְּלִי לִי בְּלוּז בְּאַרְעָא דִכְנָעַן וּבָרִיךְ יָתִי׃ ד וַאֲמַר לִי הָא אֲנָא מַפֵּישׁ לָךְ וְאַסְגִּנָּךְ וְאֶתְּנִנָּךְ לִכְנִשַׁת שִׁבְטִין וְאֶתֵּן יָת אַרְעָא הָדָא לִבְנָיךְ בַּתְרָךְ אַחֲסָנַת עָלַם׃ ה וּכְעַן תְּרֵין בְּנָיךְ דְּאִתְיְלִידוּ לָךְ בְּאַרְעָא דְמִצְרַיִם עַד מֵיתִי לְוָתָךְ לְמִצְרַיִם דִּילִי אִנּוּן אֶפְרַיִם

רש"י

ויתחזק ישראל. אמר, אע"פ שהוא בני מלך הוא, אחלק לו כבוד, מכאן שחולקין כבוד למלכות. וכן משה חלק כבוד למלכות, וירדו כל עבדיך אלה אלי (שמות יא:ח), וכן אליהו וישנס מתניו וגו' (מ"א יח:מו; מכילתא בא פי"ג; תנחומא בא ז; זבחים קב.): (ד) **ונתתיך לקהל עמים.** בשרני שעתידים לצאת ממני עוד קהל ועמים. ואע"פ שאמר לי גוי וקהל גוים (לעיל לה:יא). גוי אמר לי על בנימין. קהל גוים הרי שנים לבד מבנימין ושוב לא נולד לי בן. למדני שעתיד אחד משבטי להחלק ועתה אותה מתנה אני נותן לך (ב"ר פב:ד; פס"ר פ"ג): (ה) **הנולדים לך וגו' עד בואי אליך.** לפני בואי אליך כלומר שנולדו משפרשת ממני עד שבאתי אצלך: **לי הם.** בחשבון שאר בני הם

(*Ramban* 47:29). The blessing included a major change in the composition of the Jewish people, in that Jacob elevated Manasseh and Ephraim to the status of his own sons — in effect adopting them as his own — thereby transferring to Joseph a double portion of the inheritance. Thus Jacob removed the first-born status from Reuben and gave it to Joseph.

4. **קְהַל עַמִּים** — *A congregation of nations.* Jacob explained why he had made the decision to add Manasseh and Ephraim to the list of tribes. When he had returned to *Eretz Yisrael* from his twenty years with Laban, he already had eleven sons. At that time God blessed him, saying that *a nation and a congregation of nations* (35:11) would descend from him, meaning that he would have more children, since each tribe is considered a nation in its own right. The promise of a *nation* was fulfilled with the birth of Benjamin. The further blessing of a *congregation of nations*, in the plural, intimated that two more sons *besides* Benjamin would descend from him. Since no more sons were born to him after Benjamin, Jacob assumed that one of his existing sons would branch out into two tribes — and he was now about to confer that blessing upon Joseph (*Rashi* from *Pesikta*).

◆§ The extent of the territory that would go to each of the tribes.

The Sages (*Bava Basra* 121b) disagree on whether or not the new status of Ephraim and Manasseh had any bearing on how much land they would receive in *Eretz Yisrael.* Those two views are expressed by *Rashi* and *Ramban* in their respective commentaries. All agree that as a result of Jacob's gift, each of the two would have the title of a separate tribe, have its own banner/flag in the Wilderness, and cast separate lots to determine the location of their respective portions of the Land, i.e., who would live in the plains or mountains, north or south and so on. They differ, however, as follows:

According to *Rashi*, although *Eretz Israel* would be divided into twelve portions, these territories would not be of equal size. Rather, the size of a tribe's portion depended on its population, with each eligible Jew receiving an equal portion of the Land, so that, for example, a tribe of 80,000 would receive twice as much land as a tribe of 40,000. Thus, Joseph's offspring would receive the same amount of land whether they were one tribe or two, and in terms of their portions of the Land, lots were drawn only to determine *where* they would be.

According to *Ramban,* all twelve tribes received equal portions, which were then subdivided among its members. Consequently, large and small tribes had equal shares, but the individual member of a large tribe would receive less land than his cousin of a small tribe. Thus, the combined tribes of Joseph received a double portion of land, since Manasseh and Ephraim each received portions the same size as those of the other tribes.

The above is but a brief summary of the two views, which are based on Scriptural exegesis, and which involve much complex discussion.

וּמְנַשֶּׁה כִּרְאוּבֵן וְשִׁמְעוֹן יִהְיוּ־לִי׃ 6 וּמוֹלַדְתְּךָ
< But your progeny 6 << mine. < shall be < and Simeon, < like Reuben < and Manasseh,

אֲשֶׁר־הוֹלַדְתָּ אַחֲרֵיהֶם לְךָ יִהְיוּ עַל שֵׁם אֲחֵיהֶם
< of their brothers < the name < by << shall they be; < —yours << after them < you beget < whom

יִקָּרְאוּ בְּנַחֲלָתָם׃ 7 וַאֲנִי | בְּבֹאִי מִפַּדָּן מֵתָה עָלַי
<< on me, < she died << from Paddan, < —when I came << But as for me 7 << with regard to their inheritance. < they will be called

רָחֵל בְּאֶרֶץ כְּנַעַן בַּדֶּרֶךְ בְּעוֹד כִּבְרַת־אֶרֶץ לָבֹא אֶפְרָתָה וָאֶקְבְּרֶהָ
< and I buried her << to Ephrath; < to come < of land < a stretch < while there was yet << on the road, < of Canaan < in the land < Rachel did,

שָּׁם בְּדֶרֶךְ אֶפְרָת הִוא בֵּית לָחֶם׃ 8 וַיַּרְא יִשְׂרָאֵל אֶת־בְּנֵי יוֹסֵף וַיֹּאמֶר
< and he said, << of Joseph < the sons < Then Israel saw 8 << Bethlehem. < which is < to Ephrath, < on the road < there

מִי־אֵלֶּה׃ 9 וַיֹּאמֶר יוֹסֵף אֶל־אָבִיו בָּנַי הֵם אֲשֶׁר־נָתַן־לִי אֱלֹהִים בָּזֶה
<< here. < [by] God < to me < [were] given < who < they are < My sons << his father, < to < Joseph < Said 9 << are these? < Who

וּמְנַשֶּׁה כִּרְאוּבֵן וְשִׁמְעוֹן יְהוֹן קֳדָמָי: ו וּבְנִין דִּי תוֹלִיד בַּתְרֵיהוֹן דִּילָךְ יְהוֹן עַל שׁוּם אֲחוּהוֹן יִתְקְרוֹן בְּאַחֲסַנְתְּהוֹן: ז וַאֲנָא בְּמֵיתִי מִפַּדָּן מֵיתַת עֲלַי רָחֵל בְּאַרְעָא דִכְנַעַן בְּאָרְחָא בְּעוֹד כְּרוּבָא דְאַרְעָא (נ״א כְּרוּב אַרְעָא) לְמֵיעַל לְאֶפְרָת וּקְבַרְתַּהּ תַּמָּן בְּאֹרַח אֶפְרָת הִיא בֵּית לָחֶם: ח וַחֲזָא יִשְׂרָאֵל יָת בְּנֵי יוֹסֵף וַאֲמַר מַן אִלֵּין: ט וַאֲמַר יוֹסֵף לַאֲבוּהִי בְּנַי אִנּוּן דִּי יְהַב לִי יְיָ הָכָא

רש״י

ליטול חלק בארץ איש כנגדו: (ו) **ומולדתך וגו׳.** אם תוליד עוד (אונקלוס) לא יהיו במנין בני אלא בתוך שבטי אפרים ומנשה יהיו נכללים ולא יהא להם שם בשבטים לענין הנחלה. ואע״פ שנחלקה הארץ למנין גלגולתם, כדכתיב לרב תרבו נחלתו (במדבר כו:נד) וכל איש ואיש נטל בשוה חוץ מן הבכורים (ספרי פנחס קלה), מכל מקום לא נקראו שבטים אלא אלו [להטיל גורל הארץ למנין שמות השבטים ונשיא לכל שבט ושבט ודגלים לזה ולזה] (עי׳ הוריות ו:): (ז) **ואני בבואי מפדן וגו׳.** ואע״פ שאני מטריח עליך להוליכני להקבר בארץ כנען ולא כך עשיתי לאמך שהרי מתה סמוך לבית לחם: **כברת ארץ.** מדת ארץ והם אלפים אמה כמדת תחום שבת כדברי ר׳ משה הדרשן. ולא תאמר שעכבו עלי גשמים מלהוליכה ולקברה בחברון, עת הגריד היה שהארץ חלולה ומנוקבת ככברה: **ואקברה שם.** לא הולכתיה אפילו לבית לחם להכניסה לארץ וידעתי שיש בלבך עלי. אבל דע לך שעל פי הדיבור קברתיה שם, שתהא לעזרה לבניה כשיגלה אותם נבוזראדן והיו עוברים דרך שם, יצאת רחל על קברה ובוכה ומבקשת עליהם רחמים. שנאמר קול ברמה נשמע וגו׳ (ירמיה לא:יד), והקב״ה משיבה, יש שכר לפעולתך נאם ה׳ וגו׳ ושבו בנים לגבולם (שם לא:טו־טז; ב״ר פב:י; פסיקתא רבתי פ״ג). ואונקלוס תרגם כרוב ארעא כדי שיעור חרישת יום [ס״א ארץ] ואומר אני שהיה להם קצב שהיו קורין אותו כדי מחרישה א׳, קרואיד״א בלע״ז. כדאמרי׳ כרוב ותני (בבא מציעא קז.). כמה דמסיק תעלא מבי כרבא (יומא מג:): (ח) **וירא ישראל את בני יוסף.** בקש לברכם ונסתלקה שכינה ממנו, לפי שעתיד ירבעם ואחאב לצאת מאפרים ויהוא ובניו ממנשה (תנחומא ו): **ויאמר מי אלה.** מהיכן יצאו אלו (עי׳ תרגום יונתן) שאינן ראוין לברכה: (ט) **בזה.** הראה לו שטר אירוסין ושטר כתובה (מסכת כלה ג:טו).

7. וַאֲנִי בְּבֹאִי מִפַּדָּן — *But as for me — when I came from Paddan. Rashi* connects this statement with Jacob's earlier request that Joseph inter him in Canaan. In fairness, how could Jacob ask to be buried in the Cave of Machpelah when he did not do the same for Rachel, who died on the way home from Paddan, only a short distance from Hebron? Apparently Jacob sensed that Joseph might have harbored resentment about this, and he took this opportunity to explain his action: Even though she died but a short distance from Bethlehem, God commanded Jacob to bury her by the roadside so that she could help the Jewish people when Nebuzaradan, the chief general of King Nebuchadnezzar of Babylon (see *II Kings* 25:8 ff), would lead Israel into captivity after the destruction of the First Temple. When the Jews were passing along the road to Bethlehem, tormented, hungry, and exhausted, Rachel's soul came to her grave, and wept, beseeching God's mercy upon them [see *Jeremiah* 31:14 ff]. God heard her plea. As the prophet relates, *A voice is heard on high, the sound of lamentation . . . Rachel weeping for her children . . . [God replied to her] Withhold your voice from weeping and your eyes from tears, for your work will be rewarded, says* HASHEM *. . . and your children will return to their border* (*Rashi*).

To this very day, the tomb of "Mother Rachel" is a place of prayer where Jews come to pray and ease their grieving hearts in times of personal and national need.

8-21. The blessing of Manasseh and Ephraim. Jacob now prepared to give his special blessing to Joseph's sons. As stated in verse 15, this was a blessing for Joseph as well, because the greatest mark of his success in maintaining his spiritual integrity in Egypt was that his sons, born on foreign soil, were worthy of this lofty status. Jacob's blessing also included an aspect that surprised Joseph; Jacob gave priority to the younger son Ephraim, for, as he explained to Joseph, both sons would be great, but Ephraim would be the greater of the two.

8-9. מִי־אֵלֶּה — *Who are these?* Following the Midrash, *Rashi* explains that Jacob wished to bless the children, but the Divine Spirit departed from him because Jacob *saw* [prophetically] that wicked kings would descend from them — Jeroboam and Ahab from Ephraim; Jehu and his sons from Manasseh. Shocked, he said to Joseph, "*Who are these?*" meaning: Where did these sons, who are apparently unworthy of a blessing, come from? Joseph assured him that the children were begotten from a marriage of holiness, and worthy of being blessed notwith-

וַיֹּאמַ֕ר קָחֶם־נָ֥א אֵלַ֖י וַאֲבָרְכֵֽם׃ שני י וְעֵינֵ֤י יִשְׂרָאֵל֙

‹ of Israel ‹ Now the eyes **10** « *and I will bless them.* ‹ *to me* ‹ *please,* ‹ *Bring them,* ‹ He said,

כָּבְד֣וּ מִזֹּ֔קֶן לֹ֥א יוּכַ֖ל לִרְא֑וֹת וַיַּגֵּ֤שׁ אֹתָם֙ אֵלָ֔יו

‹ to him ‹ so he brought them near « to see; ‹ he was not able « from old age, ‹ were heavy

וַיִּשַּׁ֥ק לָהֶ֖ם וַיְחַבֵּ֥ק לָהֶֽם׃ יא וַיֹּ֤אמֶר יִשְׂרָאֵל֙ אֶל־

‹ to ‹ Israel ‹ Said **11** « them. ‹ and he hugged ‹ them ‹ and he kissed

יוֹסֵ֔ף רְאֹ֥ה פָנֶ֖יךָ לֹ֣א פִלָּ֑לְתִּי וְהִנֵּ֨ה הֶרְאָ֥ה אֹתִ֛י

« *me,* ‹ *He has shown* ‹ *and indeed* « *I did not [even] think,* ‹ *your face* ‹ *[That I would] see* « Joseph,

אֱלֹהִ֖ים גַּ֥ם אֶת־זַרְעֶֽךָ׃ יב וַיּוֹצֵ֥א יוֹסֵ֛ף אֹתָ֖ם מֵעִ֣ם בִּרְכָּ֑יו וַיִּשְׁתַּ֥חוּ לְאַפָּ֖יו

‹ with his face ‹ and he bowed down ‹ his knees ‹ from between ‹ Then Joseph brought them out **12** « *your offspring!* ‹ *also* ‹ *God has,*

אָֽרְצָה׃ יג וַיִּקַּ֣ח יוֹסֵף֮ אֶת־שְׁנֵיהֶם֒ אֶת־אֶפְרַ֤יִם בִּֽימִינוֹ֙ מִשְּׂמֹ֣אל יִשְׂרָאֵ֔ל

« of Israel, ‹ to the left ‹ with his right [hand], ‹ — Ephraim « the two of them ‹ Joseph took **13** « toward the ground.

וְאֶת־מְנַשֶּׁ֥ה בִשְׂמֹאל֖וֹ מִימִ֣ין יִשְׂרָאֵ֑ל וַיַּגֵּ֖שׁ אֵלָֽיו׃ יד וַיִּשְׁלַח֩ יִשְׂרָאֵ֨ל

‹ But Israel extended **14** « to him. ‹ and he brought [them] near « of Israel — ‹ to the right ‹ with his left [hand], ‹ and Manasseh

אֶת־יְמִינ֜וֹ וַיָּ֨שֶׁת עַל־רֹ֤אשׁ אֶפְרַ֙יִם֙ וְה֣וּא הַצָּעִ֔יר וְאֶת־שְׂמֹאל֖וֹ עַל־

‹ on ‹ and his left [hand] « was the younger ‹ though he « of Ephraim ‹ the head ‹ on ‹ and placed [it] ‹ his right [hand]

רֹ֣אשׁ מְנַשֶּׁ֑ה שִׂכֵּל֙ אֶת־יָדָ֔יו כִּ֥י מְנַשֶּׁ֖ה הַבְּכֽוֹר׃ טו וַיְבָ֥רֶךְ אֶת־יוֹסֵ֖ף

‹ Joseph ‹ He blessed **15** « was the firstborn. ‹ Manasseh ‹ for ‹ his hands, ‹ He wisely directed « of Manasseh. ‹ the head

וַאֲמַר קָרֵבְנוּן כְּעַן לְוָתִי וַאֲבָרֵכִנּוּן: י וְעֵינֵי יִשְׂרָאֵל יְקָרָן מִסֵּיבוּ לָא יָכוֹל לְמֶחֱזֵי וְקָרִיב יָתְהוֹן לְוָתֵהּ וְנַשִּׁיק לְהוֹן וְגַפִּיף לְהוֹן: יא וַאֲמַר יִשְׂרָאֵל לְיוֹסֵף לְמֶחֱזֵי אַפָּיךְ לָא סְבָרִית וְהָא אַחֲזִי יָתִי יְיָ אַף יָת בְּנָיךְ: יב וְאַפֵּיק יוֹסֵף יָתְהוֹן מִן קֳדָמוֹהִי וּסְגֵיד עַל אַפּוֹהִי עַל אַרְעָא: יג וּדְבַר יוֹסֵף יָת תַּרְוֵיהוֹן יָת אֶפְרַיִם בִּימִינֵהּ מִשְּׂמָאלָא דְיִשְׂרָאֵל וְיָת מְנַשֶּׁה בִּשְׂמָאלֵהּ מִימִינָא דְיִשְׂרָאֵל וְקָרִיב לְוָתֵהּ: יד וְאוֹשִׁיט יִשְׂרָאֵל יָת יְמִינֵהּ וְשַׁוִּי עַל רֵישָׁא דְאֶפְרַיִם וְהוּא זְעֵירָא וְיָת שְׂמָאלֵהּ עַל רֵישָׁא דִמְנַשֶּׁה אַחְכְּמִנּוּן לִידוֹהִי אֲרֵי מְנַשֶּׁה בּוּכְרָא: טו וּבָרִיךְ יָת יוֹסֵף

רש"י

ובקש יוסף רחמים על הדבר ונחה עליו רוח הקודש (תנחומא שם): **ויאמר קחם נא אלי ואברכם.** זה שאמר הכתוב ואנכי תרגלתי לאפרים קחם על זרועותיו (הושע יא:ג), תרגלתי רוחי ביעקב בשביל אפרים עד שלקחן על זרועותיו (תנחומא שם): **(יא) לא פללתי.** לא מלאני לבי לחשוב [ס"א לחקור] מחשבה שאראה פניך עוד: **פללתי.** לשון מחשבה, כמו הביאי עצה עשי פלילה (ישעיה טז:ג): **(יב) ויוצא יוסף אתם.** לאחר שנשקם הוציאם יוסף מעם ברכיו כדי ליטבם זה לימין וזה לשמאל לסמוך ידיו עליהם ולברכם: **וישתחו לאפיו.** כשחזר לאחוריו מלפני אביו: **(יג) את אפרים בימינו משמאל ישראל.** הבא לקראת חברו ימינו כנגד שמאל חברו. וכיון שיהא הבכור מיומן לברכה: **(יד) שכל את ידיו.** כתרגומו, אחכמינון, בהשכל וחכמה השכיל את ידיו לכך, ומדעת, כי יודע היה כי מנשה הבכור ואעפ"כ לא שת ימינו עליו:

standing the fact that they — not unlike Jacob's other sons — would be the ancestors of certain wicked descendants.

Or HaChaim suggests that since the Divine Presence rests where there is joy, Jacob's question was motivated by a desire to enhance the quality of his subsequent blessing by discussing his grandsons in a positive and loving way. This would account for the affectionate words and deeds of verses 9 and 10.

13. Traditionally, one blesses another by laying one's hand on the person's head. The right hand has spiritual primacy and is the preferred one for the performance of *mitzvos.* Consequently, if both sons were to be blessed simultaneously, Jacob's right hand would be on the head of Manasseh, the firstborn, and his left on Ephraim's. Therefore, Joseph positioned Ephraim on his own right side, facing Jacob's left. However, as *R' David Feinstein* observes, by placing Ephraim at his own right hand, Joseph unwittingly affirmed Ephraim's supremacy.

14. שִׂכֵּל אֶת־יָדָיו — *He wisely directed his hands.* Jacob crossed his hands, extending his right hand diagonally toward Ephraim, who was on his left side (*Akeidah*).

כִּי מְנַשֶּׁה הַבְּכוֹר — *For Manasseh was the firstborn.* That Jacob

וַיֹּאמַ֑ר הָֽאֱלֹהִ֡ים אֲשֶׁר֩ הִתְהַלְּכ֨וּ אֲבֹתַ֤י לְפָנָיו֙

<< and he said, < The God < that < walk < did my forefathers < before Him <<

אַבְרָהָ֣ם וְיִצְחָ֔ק הָֽאֱלֹהִים֙ הָרֹעֶ֣ה אֹתִ֔י מֵעוֹדִ֖י עַד־

< —Abraham < and Isaac— << the God < Who shepherds < me < from my inception < until

הַיּ֥וֹם הַזֶּֽה׃ 16 הַמַּלְאָךְ֩ הַגֹּאֵ֨ל אֹתִ֜י מִכָּל־רָ֗ע יְבָרֵךְ֮

this day: << 16 The angel < who redeems < me < from all < evil, << may he bless <

אֶת־הַנְּעָרִים֒ וְיִקָּרֵ֤א בָהֶם֙ שְׁמִ֔י וְשֵׁ֥ם אֲבֹתַ֖י

the lads; << and there shall be declared < upon them < my name < and the names < of my forefathers, <

אַבְרָהָ֣ם וְיִצְחָ֑ק וְיִדְגּ֥וּ לָרֹ֖ב בְּקֶ֥רֶב הָאָֽרֶץ׃ שלישי 17 וַיַּ֣רְא יוֹסֵ֗ף כִּֽי־יָשִׁ֨ית

< Abraham < and Isaac; << and may they proliferate like fish < to abundance < within < the land. << 17 Joseph saw < that < he was about to place <<

אָבִ֧יו יַד־יְמִינ֛וֹ עַל־רֹ֥אשׁ אֶפְרַ֖יִם וַיֵּ֣רַע בְּעֵינָ֑יו וַיִּתְמֹ֣ךְ יַד־אָבִ֗יו לְהָסִ֥יר

his father was, < his right hand < on < the head < of Ephraim < and it was wrong < in his eyes; << so he supported < the hand < of his father < to remove <

אֹתָ֛הּ מֵעַ֥ל רֹאשׁ־אֶפְרַ֖יִם עַל־רֹ֥אשׁ מְנַשֶּֽׁה׃ 18 וַיֹּ֧אמֶר יוֹסֵ֛ף אֶל־אָבִ֖יו

it < from upon < the head < of Ephraim < [to put it] on < the head < of Manasseh. << 18 And said < Joseph < to < his father, <<

לֹא־כֵ֣ן אָבִ֑י כִּי־זֶ֣ה הַבְּכֹ֔ר שִׂ֥ים יְמִינְךָ֖ עַל־רֹאשֽׁוֹ׃ 19 וַיְמָאֵ֤ן אָבִיו֙ וַיֹּ֔אמֶר

Not < so, < Father, << for < this is < the firstborn; << place < your right [hand] < on < his head. << 19 But his father refused, < saying, <<

וַאֲמַר יְיָ דִּי פְלָחוּ אֲבָהָתַי קֳדָמוֹהִי אַבְרָהָם וְיִצְחָק יְיָ דְּזַן יָתִי מִדְּאִיתִי עַד יוֹמָא הָדֵין: טז מַלְאָכָא דִּי פְרַק יָתִי מִכָּל בִּישָׁא יְבָרֵךְ יָת עוּלֵמַיָּא וְיִתְקְרֵי בְהוֹן שְׁמִי וְשׁוּם אֲבָהָתַי אַבְרָהָם וְיִצְחָק וּכְנוּנֵי יַמָּא יִסְגּוֹן בְּגוֹ בְּנֵי אֱנָשָׁא עַל אַרְעָא: יז וַחֲזָא יוֹסֵף אֲרֵי שַׁוִּי אֲבוּהִי יַד יְמִינֵהּ עַל רֵישָׁא דְאֶפְרַיִם וּבְאֵישׁ בְּעֵינוֹהִי וּסְעָדָא יְדָא דַאֲבוּהִי לְאַעֲדָאָה יָתַהּ מֵעַל רֵישָׁא דְאֶפְרַיִם לְאַנָּחוּתַהּ עַל רֵישָׁא דִמְנַשֶּׁה: יח וַאֲמַר יוֹסֵף לַאֲבוּהִי לָא כֵן אַבָּא אֲרֵי דֵין בּוּכְרָא שַׁוִּי יְמִינָךְ עַל רֵישֵׁהּ: יט וְסָרֵיב אֲבוּהִי וַאֲמַר

רש"י

(טז) המלאך הגואל אותי. מלאך הרגיל להשתלח אלי בצרתי, כענין שנא' ויאמר אלי מלאך האלהים בחלום יעקב וגו' אנכי האל בית אל (לעיל לא:יא־יג): **יברך את הנערים.** מנשה ואפרים: **וידגו.** כדגים הללו שפרים ורבים ואין עין הרע שולטת בהם (ב"ר לז:ג; ברכות כ.): **(יז) ויתמך יד אביו.** הרימה מעל ראש בנו ותמכה בידו:

had to cross his hands instead of extending them straight ahead was *because* Manasseh was the firstborn, but Jacob did not wish to bless him with the right hand (*Rashi*).

16. **הַמַּלְאָךְ** — *The angel.* This is the essence of the prayer that began with the previous verse: May You, O God, assign Your "emissary" — the angel whom You always dispatched to redeem me from all evil — to bless the lads, etc. Jacob's prayer was certainly not addressed to the angel himself, for angels have no power to act except as agents of the Holy One, to Whom Jacob referred in the previous verse. This translation, which combines both verses, follows *R' Avraham ben Ha-Rambam* and avoids many difficulties encountered by other translations that imply that the angel had independent power.

The present tense, *Who shepherds . . . who redeems*, is indicative of Jacob's faith. To him, Divine Providence is present eternally, always near to man, always merciful. God's love is inexhaustible and knows neither past nor future — only the present (*R' Munk*).

וְיִקָּרֵא בָהֶם שְׁמִי וְשֵׁם אֲבֹתַי — *And declared upon them may my name be, and the names of my forefathers.* May they deserve to have their names coupled with those of the Patriarchs (*Rashi*). Jacob mentioned himself first as if to imply, "May they act so righteously that not only I, but even my more illustrious forebears would be proud of them" (*R' David Feinstein*).

It is common that when someone acts commendably, people associate him with his righteous ancestors, but if one behaves wickedly, people say that he is the offspring of his evil forebears. Thus, Jacob's blessing was that in the future, people would always identify the tribes of Manasseh and Ephraim as the descendants of the Patriarchs (*Sforno*). Similarly, Jacob prayed that he not be identified as the ancestor of Korach and his fellow rebels (see commentary to 49:6).

וְיִדְגּוּ לָרֹב — *And like fish may they proliferate to abundance.* May they be like fish, which are fruitful and multiply and which are not affected by the evil eye [since they live calmly, unseen by man (*Berachos* 20a)] (*Rashi*). The Talmud (ibid.) explains that

יָדַעְתִּי בְנִי יָדַעְתִּי גַּם־הוּא יִהְיֶה־לְּעָם וְגַם־הוּא

‹ he ‹ and also ‹ a people, ‹ will become ‹ he ‹ also ‹‹ I know; ‹ my son, ‹ I know,

יִגְדָּל וְאוּלָם אָחִיו הַקָּטֹן יִגְדַּל מִמֶּנּוּ וְזַרְעוֹ יִהְיֶה

‹ will be ‹ and [the fame of] his offspring ‹ than he, ‹ shall become greater ‹ who is younger ‹ his brother ‹ yet ‹‹ will become great;

מְלֹא־הַגּוֹיִם׃ כ וַיְבָרְכֵם בַּיּוֹם הַהוּא° לֵאמוֹר בְּךָ

‹ By you ‹‹ saying, ‹ that day, ‹ So he blessed them **20** *‹‹ the nations. ‹ such as fills*

יְבָרֵךְ יִשְׂרָאֵל לֵאמֹר יְשִׂמְךָ אֱלֹהִים כְּאֶפְרַיִם וְכִמְנַשֶּׁה וַיָּשֶׂם

‹ —and he put ‹‹ and like Manasseh' ‹ like Ephraim ‹ 'May God make you ‹‹ saying, ‹ shall Israel invoke blessing

אֶת־אֶפְרַיִם לִפְנֵי מְנַשֶּׁה׃ כא וַיֹּאמֶר יִשְׂרָאֵל אֶל־יוֹסֵף הִנֵּה אָנֹכִי מֵת

‹‹ about to die; ‹ I am ‹ Indeed ‹‹ Joseph, ‹ to ‹ Then Israel said **21** *‹‹ Manasseh. ‹ before ‹ Ephraim*

וְהָיָה אֱלֹהִים עִמָּכֶם וְהֵשִׁיב אֶתְכֶם אֶל־אֶרֶץ אֲבֹתֵיכֶם׃ כב וַאֲנִי נָתַתִּי

‹ I have given ‹ And as for me, **22** *‹‹ of your fathers. ‹ the land ‹ to ‹ and will bring you back ‹ with you ‹ God will be*

° מלא ו'

יָדַעְנָא בְּרִי יָדַעְנָא אַף הוּא יְהֵי לְעַמָּא וְאַף הוּא יִסְגֵּי וּבְרַם אֲחוּהִי זְעֵירָא יִסְגֵּי מִנֵּהּ וּבְנוֹהִי יְהוֹן שַׁלִּיטִין בְּעַמְמַיָּא׃ כ וּבָרֵיכִנּוּן בְּיוֹמָא הַהוּא לְמֵימַר בָּךְ יְבָרֵךְ יִשְׂרָאֵל לְמֵימַר יְשַׁוִּינָךְ יְיָ כְּאֶפְרַיִם וְכִמְנַשֶּׁה וְשַׁוִּי יָת אֶפְרַיִם קֳדָם מְנַשֶּׁה׃ כא וַאֲמַר יִשְׂרָאֵל לְיוֹסֵף הָא אֲנָא מָאִית וִיהֵי מֵימְרָא דַייָ בְּסַעְדְּכוֹן וְיָתֵיב יָתְכוֹן לְאַרְעָא דַּאֲבָהַתְכוֹן׃ כב וַאֲנָא יְהָבִית

רש"י

(יט) **ידעתי בני ידעתי.** שהוא הבכור: **גם הוא יהיה לעם. ויגדל,** שעתיד גדעון לצאת ממנו שהקב"ה עושה נס על ידו (תנחומא ו): **ואולם אחיו הקטן יגדל ממנו.** שעתיד יהושע לצאת ממנו שינחיל את הארץ וילמד תורה לישראל (שם): **וזרעו יהיה מלא הגוים.** כל העולם יתמלא בצאת שמעו ושמו כשיעמיד חמה בגבעון וירח בעמק אילון (ב"ר שם ד; ע"ז כה.): (כ) **בך יברך ישראל.** הבא לברך את בניו יברכם בברכתם ויאמר איש לבנו ישימך אלהים כאפרים וכמנשה: **וישם את אפרים.** בברכתו לפני מנשה, להקדימו בדגלים ובחנוכת הנשיאים (ב"ר צז:ה): (כב) **ואני נתתי לך.** לפי שאתה טורח להתעסק בקבורתי וגם אני נתתי לך נחלה שתקבר בה, ואיזו, זו שכם, שנא'

Joseph earned this blessing of immunity against the evil eye because he averted his own eyes from the advances of Potiphar's wife.

19. **יָדַעְתִּי בְנִי יָדַעְתִּי** – *I know, my son, I know* that he is the firstborn (*Rashi*). According to the Midrash, Jacob repeated the expression to imply that he knew many things of which Joseph was unaware, and if he chose to give the primary blessing to Ephraim, it was for good and sufficient reason.

Haamek Davar explains that Ephraim's preeminence was not the *result* of Jacob's blessing. Rather, it was *because* Ephraim was destined for more greatness that he required a more intensive blessing, for prominent people need a blessing to carry out their mission successfully. Not Jacob's blessing, but Ephraim's upbringing was the source of his future greatness, for Ephraim spent his life studying Torah with Jacob (see *Rashi* to 48:1), while Manasseh was Joseph's assistant in governing the country. Thus, Ephraim's accomplishments in Torah study earned him the primary blessing. This contrasts with the experience of the tribes of Issachar and Zebulun. Although Issachar was the tribe that excelled in Torah scholarship while Zebulun was a merchant tribe, Jacob gave precedence to Zebulun (49:13), because Issachar's spiritual growth was made possible only because Zebulun shared his wealth with the scholars of Issachar.

20. **וַיְבָרְכֵם בַּיּוֹם הַהוּא** — *So he blessed them that day.* It may be inferred by extension that the term *that day* refers to the day, whenever it is, that Jewish parents would wish to bless their children. Whenever such days arrive, they will use the text of Jacob's blessing. *Targum Yonasan* explains that the term alludes to the day when a newborn child is circumcised, and Sephardic communities pronounce Jacob's blessing on such occasions. It is customary in many families that parents bless their sons on the Sabbath eve with the formula: *May God make you like Ephraim and Manasseh.* [They bless their daughters by saying, "*May God make you like Sarah, Rebecca, Rachel, and Leah.*"]

בְּךָ יְבָרֵךְ יִשְׂרָאֵל — *By you shall Israel invoke blessing.* Jacob assured Joseph that for all time Jewish parents would remember that he was the father of sons who were elevated to the status of full-fledged tribal fathers. Longing that their own children would rise to such heights, parents would bless them accordingly. Another reason for the choice of Ephraim and Manasseh as the models for all future generations is that they demonstrated the strength to maintain their Jewishness in the face of the hostility and temptation of Egyptian culture and society. Jewish parents, especially in exile, have ample cause to hope that their children show comparable commitment to their heritage.

21. Having blessed Joseph's sons, Jacob turned to Joseph and awarded him an additional portion of *Eretz Yisrael,* that would become the possession of his offspring (*Ramban).* This special gift to Joseph was in gratitude for his readiness to bring Jacob's remains to *Eretz Yisrael* for burial (*Maharshal*).

It is illustrative and inspiring that Jacob prefaced his gift with the declaration that he was about to die. At the very moment

לְךָ שְׁכֶם אַחַד עַל־אַחֶיךָ אֲשֶׁר לָקַחְתִּי מִיַּד

< you < [Shechem as] one portion < more than << your brothers, < which < I took < from the hand

הָאֱמֹרִי בְּחַרְבִּי וּבְקַשְׁתִּי׃ פ רביעי [מט] א וַיִּקְרָא

< of the Amorite < with my sword < and with my bow. >> 49 1 Then he called >>

יַעֲקֹב אֶל־בָּנָיו וַיֹּאמֶר הֵאָסְפוּ וְאַגִּידָה לָכֶם אֵת אֲשֶׁר־יִקְרָא אֶתְכֶם

< Jacob did, < to < his sons << and he said, < Assemble yourselves < and I will tell < you < that < which < will happen < to you

לָךְ חוּלַק חַד יַתִּיר עַל אַחָיךְ דִּי נְסֵיבִית מִידָא דֶאֱמוֹרָאָה בִּצְלוֹתִי וּבְבָעוּתִי: א וּקְרָא יַעֲקֹב לִבְנוֹהִי וַאֲמַר אִתְכַּנָּשׁוּ וַאֲחַוֵּי לְכוֹן יָת דִּי יְעָרַע יָתְכוֹן

רש"י

ואת עצמות יוסף אשר העלו וגו' ממצרים קברו בשכם (יהושע כד:לב): **שכם אחד על אחיך.** שכם ממש. היא תהיה לך חלק אחד יתירה על אחיך (ב"ר שם ו): **בחרבי ובקשתי.** כשהרגו שמעון ולוי את אנשי שכם נתכנסו כל סביבותיהם להזדווג להם. וחגר יעקב כלי מלחמה כנגדן (שם פ:י). ד"א, שכם אחד היא הבכורה, שיטלו בניו שני חלקים (שם לז:ו). ושכם ל' חלק הוא, כתרגומו, והרבה יש לו דומים במקרא, כי תשיתמו שכם (תהלים כא:יג) תשית שונאי לפני לחלקים. אחלקה שכם (שם ס:ח) דרך ירצחו שכמה (הושע ו:ט) איש חלקו. לעבדו שכם אחד (צפניה ג:ט): **אשר לקחתי מיד האמורי.** מיד עשו שעשה מעשה אמורי (ב"ר לז:ו). ד"א, שהיה צד אביו באמרי פיו (עי' רש"י לעיל כה:כח): **בחרבי ובקשתי.** היא חכמתי ותפלתי (עי' ב"ב קכג.; תנחומא בשלח ט): (א) **ואגידה לכם.** בקש לגלות את הקץ ונסתלקה ממנו שכינה

when he was ready to leave this world, he presented a gift to Joseph — a gift that his descendants would not have until the nation entered the Land, more than two hundred years later. This legacy of hope and confidence in better times to come remained the soul of Jewish history.

22. **שְׁכֶם אַחַד עַל־אַחֶיךָ** — *[Shechem as] one portion more than your brothers. Rashi* offers two interpretations of the word *Shechem*: It means literally the city of Shechem, which Jacob ceded to Joseph, beyond the territory that would fall to his offspring when the Land was divided among the tribes. Alternatively, it means *portion*, referring to the gift of the birthright, which entitled Joseph's children to receive two portions of *Eretz Yisrael.*

According to the first interpretation, Shechem became his at the time when Simeon and Levi slew the inhabitants of the city and all the surrounding nations gathered together against them. Jacob took up arms to do battle with them and triumphed in a hidden miracle (*Rashi*).

According to the second interpretation, the birthright became his because he wrested it from Esau, who is here called *the Amorite.* If so, *my sword and my bow* are figurative names for the spiritual weapons that gave Jacob the birthright and its blessings. Accordingly, the *sword* represents "sharp" wisdom, and the *bow* represents prayer, which propels the supplicant's plea to God *(Rashi)*. In another view, the prayer of the righteous is like a *sword* because it "pierces" barriers, and it is like a *bow* because, just as an arrow's swiftness, power, and distance depend on the pressure exerted on the bow, so too the efficacy of a prayer depends on the degree of the supplicant's intense concentration and sincerity (*Gur Aryeh*).

The use of these similes reveals another aspect of the righteous. To them, strength depends not on armaments and sheer physical force, but on their spiritual strength. As the Psalmist said, *Some with chariots and some with horses; but we, in the Name of HASHEM, our God — call out. They dropped to their knees and fell, but we arose and were invigorated (Psalms* 20:8-9).

49.

◆ Jacob blesses his children.

Blessings occupy a prominent place in the Torah and particularly in the Book of *Genesis.* From the time Abraham was given the power to bless whomever he wanted (*Rashi* to 12:2), the concept of blessing played an increasingly important role. That the righteous can confer a blessing is a God-given privilege, for He provides the metaphysical force that makes the blessing efficacious . . . At this moment in Egypt, Jacob's progeny were embarking on the historic task of creating an independent nation. Before he died, the Patriarch wished to confer the Divine blessing for their success in this critical undertaking (*R' Munk*).

Jacob was about to bless the tribes individually, each in line with its own character and ability, so that they would be directed toward the paths for which God had suited them, for his blessings would make clear that each of the tribes had its own unique mission. Only Jacob could perceive this. In a sense he was like Adam at the beginning of time, giving names to all living creatures. As the one closest to God and with an all-encompassing vision, Adam understood what each animal's role was in the scheme of the cosmos, and he named it accordingly. Jacob, too, as the zenith of the Patriarchal era, had this ability, and he assigned his sons to their respective missions accordingly.

Far from breeding disunity, however, their separate missions were to bring them together, because they were like the spokes of a wheel; though the spokes point in different directions, they are all part of the same wheel and essential to its function. So, too, the tribes of Israel. Their roles would be different — royalty, priesthood, scholarship, commerce, and so on — but all would contribute their talents and accomplishments to the national mission of serving God and glorifying His Name.

1. **הֵאָסְפוּ** — *Assemble yourselves.* In addition to the literal call that his children come to him to receive his blessings, Jacob intimated to his family that only if they avoided dissension — if they *assembled* and *gathered* together at all times — would they merit the final Redemption. This message was especially important then, for Jacob's "family" was becoming a "nation" composed of separate tribes, and the potential for divergence was very great. Indeed, after the death of King Solomon, the nation split into two kingdoms, with disastrous results.

אֵת אֲשֶׁר־יִקְרָא אֶתְכֶם — *That which will happen to you.* Literally,

בְּאַחֲרִית הַיָּמִים: ב הִקָּבְצוּ וְשִׁמְעוּ בְּנֵי יַעֲקֹב

‹ of Jacob, ‹ O sons ‹ and listen, ‹ Gather yourselves **2** *« of Days. ‹ in the End*

וְשִׁמְעוּ אֶל־יִשְׂרָאֵל אֲבִיכֶם: ג רְאוּבֵן בְּכֹרִי אַתָּה

« are you, ‹ my firstborn ‹ Reuben, **3** *« your father. ‹ Israel ‹ to ‹ and listen*

כֹּחִי וְרֵאשִׁית אוֹנִי יֶתֶר שְׂאֵת וְיֶתֶר עָז: ד פַּחַז

‹ Impetuous **4** *« in power. ‹ and exceeding ‹ in rank ‹ exceeding « of my vigor, ‹ and the first ‹ my strength*

כַּמַּיִם אַל־תּוֹתַר כִּי עָלִיתָ מִשְׁכְּבֵי אָבִיךָ אָז חִלַּלְתָּ יְצוּעִי עָלָה: פ

« would ascend. ‹ [Him Who above] my couch ‹ you desecrated ‹ then « of your father; ‹ the bed ‹ you mounted ‹ because « — you cannot exceed, « like water

בְּסוֹף יוֹמַיָּא: ב אִתְכַּנָּשׁוּ וּשְׁמָעוּ בְּנֵי
יַעֲקֹב וְקַבִּילוּ אוּלְפַן מִן יִשְׂרָאֵל
אֲבוּכוֹן: ג רְאוּבֵן בּוּכְרִי אַתְּ חֵילִי
וְרֵישׁ תָּקְפִּי לָךְ הֲוָה חָזֵי לְמִסַּב
תְּלָתָא חוּלָקִין בְּכֵירוּתָא כְּהֻנְּתָא
וּמַלְכוּתָא: ד עַל דַּאֲזַלְתָּא לָקֳבֵל
אַפָּיךְ הָא כְּמַיָּא בְּרַם לָא
אַהֲנֵיתָא חוּלָק יַתִּיר לָא תִסַּב אֲרֵי
סְלֶקְתָּא בֵּית מִשְׁכְּבֵי אֲבוּךְ בְּכֵן
אַחֲלֶתָּא לְשִׁוּוּיֵי בְּרִי סְלֶקְתָּא:

רש"י

והתחיל אומר דברים אחרים (פסחים נו.; ב"ר לח:ב): (ג) **וראשית אוני.** היא טפה ראשונה שלו, שלא ראה קרי מימיו (ב"ר שם ד; יבמות עו.): **אוני.** כוחי. כמו מצאתי און לי (הושע יב:ט) מרוב אונים (ישעיה מ:כו) ולאין אונים (שם כט): **יתר שאת.** ראוי היית להיות יתר על אחיך בכהונה, לשון נשיאות כפים (ב"ר לט:ו): **ויתר עז.** במלכות (שם), כמו ויתן עז למלכו (שמואל א ב:י). ומי גרם לך להפסיד כל אלה: (ד) **פחז במים.** הפחז והבהלה אשר מהרת להראות כעסך כמים הללו הממהרים למרוצתם, לכך: **אל תותר.** אל תרבה ליטול כל היתרונות הללו שהיו ראויות לך (תנחומא ט). ומהו הפחז אשר פחזת: **כי עלית משכבי אביך אז חללת.** אותו שם שעלה על יצועי, והיא השכינה שהיה דרכו להיות עולה על יצועי (שבת נה:): **פחז.** שם דבר הוא, לפיכך טעמו למעלה וכלו נקוד פתח, ואילו היה לשון עבר היה נקוד חציו קמץ וחציו פתח וטעמו למטה: **יצועי.** ל' משכב. ע"ש שמציעים אותו על ידי לבדין וסדינין. והרבה דומים לו, אם זכרתיך על יצועי (תהלים סג:ז) אם אעלה על ערש יצועי (שם קלב:ג):

what will call to you. By using the root קרא, *call,* instead of קרה, *happen*, Jacob taught that whatever event may happen, it must be understood as a *call* from God, for nothing is haphazard; everything has a purpose. It is for us to "hear" and seek to understand the call (*R' Hirsch*). The commentators generally concur that *the End of Days* refers to the Messianic era.

Following the Midrash, *Rashi* comments that Jacob wished to tell his children when Messiah would come [presumably to comfort them and their descendants during times of exile] — but the Divine Presence deserted him. Jacob did not know why. He thought that perhaps one of them was unworthy, a new Ishmael or Esau! He asked if this could be so — to which they responded with the first verse of the *Shema: "Hear, O Israel* [our father]. . . just as there is only One in your heart, so there is only One in our heart." Upon hearing that the reason for his lapse of prophecy was not due to any shortcomings within his family, Jacob exclaimed in gratitude, בָּרוּךְ שֵׁם כְּבוֹד מַלְכוּתוֹ לְעוֹלָם וָעֶד, *Blessed be the name of His glorious kingdom for ever and ever.*

Then he realized that God did not want the time of the End to be known. Israel would find its comfort not in deadlines but in faith and performance of God's commandments.

3-4. Reuben. Jacob rebuked his older sons. He had waited until now before doing so because, he explained, "Reuben, my son, I did not rebuke you all these years so that you should not leave me and stay with my brother Esau" (*Sifre Devarim).* This implies a general rule for those who wish to admonish others in a constructive way. They must weigh their words carefully, lest their sincere comments do more harm than good.

3. בְּכֹרִי אַתָּה — *My firstborn are you.* Jacob begins by recounting that, as the firstborn, Reuben *should* have been entitled to priesthood [שְׂאֵת, *rank*] and kingship [עָז, *power*], but instead these privileges went to Levi and Judah, respectively. Reuben forfeited them, because . . .

4. פַּחַז כַּמַּיִם — *Impetuous like water.* Jacob told Reuben, "You lost your right to national leadership because of the *impetuosity* with which you rushed to vent your anger" [in the incident with Bilhah when you *mounted the bed of your father*; see 35:22]. It was hasty recklessness *like that of fast-flowing waters*, which rush ahead and cause damage without a thought to the consequences; therefore אַל־תּוֹתַר, *you cannot exceed,* "you do not deserve to serve in the superior positions that were designated for you" (*Rashi*). Following the Midrash, *Targum Yonasan* renders interpretively: "But because you sinned, my son, the birthright is given to Joseph, the kingship to Judah, and the priesthood to Levi."

Ramban comments that Reuben was punished measure for measure. He wanted to prevent Jacob from having children by Bilhah, who would share in the family heritage. His punishment was that he lost the firstborn's share of the heritage.

The tragedy of Reuben is informative. He did not mean to sin; to the contrary, he thought he was acting virtuously in defending his mother's honor. Moreover, Reuben repented sincerely, and was held up as a model of sincere repentance, but this did not save his status as the firstborn. A leader cannot be impetuous. He must think through his decisions and reckon their consequences. The Midrash adds that Jacob *comforted* Reuben, saying that he was still a respected member of Israel and that Moses would bless him along with the other tribes (*Deuteronomy* 33:6).

5-7. Simeon and Levi. Having explained why Reuben forfeited the prerogatives of the birthright, Jacob then explained why Simeon and Levi, the next oldest, were also unworthy to succeed him as rulers: The Levites had the status of servants of God, but they did not have authority over the nation; to the contrary, for their livelihood they depended on the tithes of their brethren. They had attacked the males of Shechem, and men of the sword are unworthy of being "the king who by *justice* estab-

ה שִׁמְעוֹן וְלֵוִי אַחִים כְּלֵי חָמָס מְכֵרֹתֵיהֶם׃
5 Simeon < and Levi < are brothers, < tools < stolen [from Esau] < are their weaponry. »

ו בְּסֹדָם אַל־תָּבֹא נַפְשִׁי בִּקְהָלָם אַל־תֵּחַד
6 Into their conspiracy, < let not < my soul enter! « Into their congregation < do not < join, <

כְּבֹדִי כִּי בְאַפָּם הָרְגוּ אִישׁ וּבִרְצֹנָם עִקְּרוּ־שׁוֹר׃ ז אָרוּר אַפָּם כִּי עָז
O my honor! « For < in their rage < they murdered < a man < and in their desire < they crippled < an ox. » 7 Accursed < is their rage < for < it is intense, <

וְעֶבְרָתָם כִּי קָשָׁתָה אֲחַלְּקֵם בְּיַעֲקֹב וַאֲפִיצֵם בְּיִשְׂרָאֵל׃ פ ח *יְהוּדָה
and their wrath < for < it is harsh; « I will separate them < within Jacob, « and I will disperse them < in Israel. » 8 Judah »

*בראש עמוד בי״ה שמ״ו סימן

ה שִׁמְעוֹן וְלֵוִי אַחִין גַּבְרִין גִּבָּרִין בְּאַרַע תּוֹתָבוּתְהוֹן עֲבָדוּ גְבוּרָא: ו בְּרָזְהוֹן לָא הֲוַת נַפְשִׁי בְּאִתְכַּנְשֵׁהוֹן לְמִהַךְ לָא נְחָתִית מִן יְקָרִי אֲרֵי בְרָגְזְהוֹן קְטָלוּ קְטוֹל וּבִרְעוּתְהוֹן תַּרָעוּ שׁוּר סַנְאָה: ז לִיט רָגְזְהוֹן אֲרֵי תַקִּיף וְחִמַתְהוֹן אֲרֵי קַשְׁיָא אֲפַלְּגִנּוּן בְּיַעֲקֹב וְאֲבַדְּרִנּוּן בְּיִשְׂרָאֵל: ח יְהוּדָה

רש״י

(ה) **שמעון ולוי אחים.** בעלה אחת על שכם ועל יוסף, ויאמרו איש אל אחיו וגו' ועתה לכו ונהרגהו (לעיל לז:יט־כ). מי הם, אם תאמר ראובן או יהודה, הרי לא הסכימו בהריגתו. אם תאמר בני השפחות, הרי לא היתה שנאתן שלמה, שנאמר והוא נער את בני בלהה ואת בני זלפה וגו' (שם פסוק ב). יששכר וזבולון לא היו מדברים בפני אחיהם הגדולים מהם. על כרחך שמעון ולוי הם שקראם אביהם אחים: **בלי חמס.** אומנות זו של רציחה חמס הוא בידכם, מברכת עשו היא זו, אומנות שלו היא ואתם חמסתם אותה הימנו (תנחומא ט; ב״ר צט:ו): **מכר תיהם.** לשון כלי זיין הסייף בל' יוני מכי״ר (תנחומא שם). דבר אחר, מכרתיהם, בארץ מגורתם נהגו עצמן בכלי חמס, כמו מכורותיך ומולדותיך (יחזקאל טז:ג), וזה תרגום של אונקלוס: (ו) **בסדם אל תבא נפשי.** זה מעשה זמרי. כשנתקבצו שבטו של שמעון להביא את המדינית לפני משה ואמרו לו זו אסורה או מותרת, אם תאמר אסורה, בת יתרו מי התירה לך (סנהדרין פב.) אל יזכר שמי בדבר, שנאמר זמרי בן סלוא נשיא בית אב לשמעוני (במדבר כה:יד) ולא כתב בן יעקב (ב״ר צט:ו): **בקהלם.** כשיקהיל קרח שהוא משבטו של לוי את כל העדה על משה ועל אהרן: **אל תחד כבודי.** שם אל יתיחד עמהם שמי, שנאמר קרח בן יצהר בן קהת בן לוי (במדבר טז:א) ולא נאמר בן יעקב. אבל בדברי הימים (א ו:כב־כג) כשנתיחסו בני קרח על הדוכן נאמר בן קרח בן יצהר בן קהת בן לוי בן ישראל (ב״ר נח:ה): **אל תחד כבודי.** כבוד לשון זכר הוא, ועל כרחך אתה צריך לפרש כמדבר אל הכבוד ואומר אתה כבודי אל תתיחד עמהם, כמו לא תחד אתם בקבורה (ישעיה יד:כ): **כי באפם הרגו איש.** אלו חמור ואנשי שכם, ואינן חשובין כולם אלא כאיש אחד. וכן הוא אומר בגדעון והכית את מדין כאיש אחד (שופטים ו:טז), וכן במצרים סוס ורוכבו רמה בים (שמות טו:א). זהו מדרשו (ב״ר צט:ו). ופשוטו אנשים הרבה קורא איש כל אחד לעצמו, באפס הרגו כל איש שכעסו עליו, וכן וילמד לטרף טרף אדם אכל (יחזקאל יט:ג): **וברצונם עקרו שור.** רצו לעקור את יוסף שנקרא שור, שנאמר בכור שורו הדר לו (דברים לג:יז; עי' תרגום ירושלמי). עקרו אשיירטי״ר בלע״ז, לשון את סוסיהם תעקר (יהושע יא:ו): (ז) **ארור אפם כי עז.** אפילו בשעת תוכחה לא קלל אלא את אפם, וזהו שאמר בלעם מה אקוב לא קבה אל (במדבר כג:ח; ב״ר שם): **אחלקם ביעקב.** אפרידם זה מזה שלא יהא לוי במנין השבטים, והרי הם חלוקים (ב״ר נח:ה). ד״א, אין לך עניים וסופרים ומלמדי תינוקות אלא משמעון, כדי שיהיו נפוצים, ושבטו של לוי עשאו מחזר על הגרנות

lishes the land" [*Proverbs* 29:4] (*Sforno; Abarbanel).* Jacob spoke to all the other sons individually, but he grouped Simeon and Levi together, describing them as *brothers,* because, as he explained in poetic terms, they joined together in conspiracy and violence. They perpetrated the violence against Shechem and they instigated the sale of Joseph.

5. כְּלֵי חָמָס מְכֵרֹתֵיהֶם — *Tools stolen [from Esau] are their weaponry.* Simeon and Levi's preoccupation with the *weaponry* of violence is a trait they have stolen from Esau. He, not Jacob, was the brother who lived by the sword (*Rashi*). Jacob's *sword* is prayer, as above, 48:22.

6. בְּסֹדָם אַל־תָּבֹא נַפְשִׁי — *Into their conspiracy, let not my soul enter!* The commentators differ on which conspiracy Jacob had in mind, a past or a future one. According to *Ramban,* Jacob disavowed any part in their conspiracy to attack Shechem when its men were ill after their circumcision. According to *Rashi*, Jacob made a prophetic reference to two future rebellions in the Wilderness, after the Exodus. Elements of the tribe of Simeon followed one of their leaders, Zimri, in leading people into sin (*Numbers* 25:14). Korach, a Levite, also led a rebellion (ibid. 16:1). Jacob now prayed that his name not be mentioned in connection with either *conspiracy.*

וּבִרְצֹנָם עִקְּרוּ־שׁוֹר — *And in their desire they crippled an ox.* Simeon and Levi sought to disable Joseph, who is figuratively likened to an *ox;* see *Deuteronomy* 33:17 (*Rashi*). *Ramban* interprets *ox* literally, as a reference to the livestock of Shechem. Not only did they kill the men of Shechem, they destroyed its cattle.

7. אָרוּר אַפָּם — *Accursed is their rage.* Even when Jacob was chastising his sons, he did not curse *them,* but their *rage* (*Rashi*).

Haamek Davar explains the difference between אַף, *rage,* and עֶבְרָה, *wrath,* in the context of this verse. *Rage* was the fury that caused them to lash out when they lost their tempers, but even when the initial rage was spent, they remained *wrathful* enough to continue their destructiveness, as in the case of the livestock of Shechem.

8-12. Judah. When Judah heard Jacob's rebuke of his three older brothers, he drew back, afraid that Jacob might chastise him over the affair of Tamar. So Jacob called him soothingly, "Judah — *you* [this word is emphatic] are not like them. *You,* your brothers shall acknowledge!" (*Midrash; Rashi*). Judah would be the source of Jewish leadership and royalty, of the Davidic dynasty and Messiah.

So admired will you be by all your brothers that Jews will not say, I am a Reubenite or a Simeonite, but I am a Yehudi [Judahite; Jew] (*Midrash*). Thus we find that Mordechai, in the Book of *Esther,* was known as a *Yehudi*, even though he was from the

אַתָּה יוֹדוּךָ אַחֶיךָ יָדְךָ בְּעֹרֶף אֹיְבֶיךָ יִשְׁתַּחֲווּ

‹ bow down ‹‹ of your enemies; ‹ [will be] at the nape ‹ your hand ‹‹ shall your brothers; ‹ acknowledge ‹‹ — you — you

לְךָ בְּנֵי אָבִיךָ׃ ט גּוּר אַרְיֵה יְהוּדָה מִטֶּרֶף בְּנִי

‹‹ my son, ‹‹ from the prey, ‹‹ is Judah; ‹ of a lion ‹ A cub **9** ‹‹ of your father. ‹ will the sons ‹ to you

עָלִיתָ כָּרַע רָבַץ כְּאַרְיֵה וּכְלָבִיא מִי יְקִימֶנּוּ׃

‹‹ provoke him? ‹ who would ‹ and like an awesome lion, ‹ like a lion, ‹ he lied down ‹ He crouched, ‹‹ you have risen.

אַתְּ אוֹדֵיתָא וְלָא בְהֵיתְתָא בָּךְ יוֹדוּן אֲחָיךְ יְדָךְ תִּתְקֵף עַל בַּעֲלֵי דְבָבָךְ יִתְבַּדְּרוּן סַנְאָךְ יְהוֹן מְחַזְּרִין קְדָל קֳדָמָךְ וִיהוֹן מְקַדְּמִין לְמִשְׁאַל בִּשְׁלָמָךְ בְּנֵי אֲבוּךְ׃ ט שִׁלְטוֹן יְהֵי בְשֵׁרוּיָא וּבְסוֹפָא יִתְרַבָּא מַלְכָּא מִדְּבֵית יְהוּדָה אֲרֵי מִדִּין קַטְלָא בְּרִי נַפְשָׁךְ סְלֶקְתָּא יְנוּחַ יִשְׁרֵי בִתְקוֹף כְּאַרְיָא וּכְלֵיתָא וְלֵית מַלְכוּ דִּתְזַעְזְעִינֵהּ׃ י לָא יַעֲדֵי עָבֵד שָׁלְטָן מִדְּבֵית יְהוּדָה וְסָפְרָא מִבְּנֵי בְנוֹהִי עַד עָלְמָא עַד דְּיֵיתֵי מְשִׁיחָא

י לֹא־יָסוּר שֵׁבֶט מִיהוּדָה וּמְחֹקֵק מִבֵּין רַגְלָיו עַד כִּי־יָבֹא שִׁילֹה

‹‹ Shiloh, ‹ arrives ‹ when ‹ until ‹ his descendants, ‹ from among ‹ [nor] a legislator ‹ from Judah ‹ shall the scepter ‹ pass ‹ Not **10**

רש"י

לתרומות ולמעשרות, נתן לו תפולתו דרך כבוד (שם לט:ו): **(ח) יהודה אתה יודוך אחיך.** לפי שהוכיח את הראשונים בקנטורים התחיל יהודה לסוג לאחוריו [שלא יוכיחנו על מעשה תמר], וקראו יעקב בדברי רצוי, יהודה לא אתה כמותם (ב"ר לח:ה, לט:ח): **ידך בערף איביך.** בימי דוד, ואויבי תתה לי ערף (שמואל ב כב:מא; ב"ר לט:ח): **בני אביך.** על שם שהיו מנשים הרבה לא אמר בני אמך כדרך שאמר יצחק (לעיל כז:כט; ב"ר שם): **(ט) גור אריה.** על דוד נתנבא. בתחלה גור, בהיות שאול מלך עלינו אתה היית המוציא והמביא את ישראל (שמואל ב ה:ב). ולבסוף אריה כשהמליכוהו עליהם. וזהו שתרגם אונקלוס שלטון יהא בשרויא, בתחלתו: **מטרף.** ממה שחשדתיך בטרוף טורף יוסף חיה רעה אכלתהו (לעיל לז:לג) וזהו יהודה שנמשל לאריה (ב"ר צה:ב; תנחומא ויגש ט): **בני עלית.** סלקת את עצמך ואמרת מה בצע וגו' (לעיל לז:כו), וכן בהריגת תמר שהודה צדקה ממני (לעיל לח:כו; תנחומא י; ב"ר לח:ז, לט:ח). לפיכך: **כרע רבץ וגו'.** בימי שלמה איש תחת גפנו וגו' (מלכים א ה:ה): **(י) לא יסור שבט מיהודה.** מדוד ואילך, אלו ראשי גליות שבבבל שרודים את העם בשבט, שממונים [היו] ע"פ המלכות (סנהדרין ה.): **ומחקק מבין רגליו.** תלמידים, אלו נשיאי א"י (שם): **עד כי יבא שילה.** מלך המשיח שהמלוכה שלו (ב"ר צט:ח), וכן ת"א. ומדרש אגדה, שילו, שי לו, שנאמר יובילו שי למורא (תהלים עו:יב; ילק"ש קס):

tribe of Benjamin. *Chiddushei HaRim* comments that the reason for this honor was Leah's motive in giving Judah his name. She gave it to express her gratitude to God for having given her more than her share [see 29:35]. It is characteristic of a Jew that he thanks God for everything, never feeling that he is entitled to Divine benevolence.

9. גּוּר אַרְיֵה — *A cub of a lion.* In the future, Judah would be like a *lion*, the king of beasts, but when Jacob blessed him he was still a *cub*, for his greatest moments, when he would reign over the nation, were still in the future (*Sforno*). You combine the courage of youth with the prudence of age (*R' Hirsch*).

מִטֶּרֶף בְּנִי עָלִיתָ — *From the prey, my son, you have risen.* Jacob had suspected Judah of responsibility for Joseph's murder, a deed he described with the word טֶרֶף, literally *tearing apart* [see 37:33]. Thus, *Rashi* perceives our passage to say: *You, my son, had risen above the act of tearing your prey,* of which I had suspected you; to the contrary, you were instrumental in sparing him (*Rashi*). Jacob had suspected Judah more than the others because he, as the one destined for kingship, would be the one who felt most threatened by Joseph's dreams (*Gur Aryeh*).

Tur comments that Jacob referred prophetically to Judah's greatest descendant, David, who first displayed his strength and courage as a lad, when he killed a lion and a bear (*I Samuel* 17:34 ff.).

10. לֹא־יָסוּר שֵׁבֶט מִיהוּדָה — *Not pass shall the scepter from Judah.* The privilege of providing Israel's sovereign ruler — symbolized by the royal scepter — shall not pass from the House of Judah (*Onkelos*). This blessing did not take effect immediately, however, for the first Jewish king was Saul, a Benjaminite. However, Jacob's blessing applied uninterruptedly from the time that the monarchy went to David, and it continued even after the demise of the royalty, for after the destruction of the Second Temple, the Exilarchs, or heads of the Babylonian exile, were appointed from the tribe of Judah (*Rashi*). As to present times and before the time of David, when kings did not come from Judah, *Gur Aryeh* explains as follows: Jacob's blessings applied only when there would be a legally constituted king. The times of Saul and the Judges were temporary aberrations. Similarly, the current exile, too, will be followed by a return of the Davidic dynasty, proving that Jacob's blessing remains in force.

וּמְחֹקֵק — *[Nor] a legislator,* an allusion to Hillel's descendants, the *Nesiim*, or Princes in *Eretz Yisrael,* whose greatness in Torah was enhanced by their descent from the royal line of Judah (*Sanhedrin* 5a).

עַד כִּי־יָבֹא שִׁילֹה — *Until when arrives Shiloh. Onkelos,* followed by *Rashi*, renders: until the Messiah comes, to whom the kingdom belongs. The Midrash explains that the word Shiloh is a composite of the words שַׁי לוֹ, *a gift to him*, a reference to the King Messiah, to whom all nations will bring gifts. This verse is a primary Torah source for the belief that the Messiah will come, and the rabbis always referred to it in the Middle Ages, when they were forced to debate with clerics of other religions.

The word *until* does not mean that Judah's ascendancy will end with the coming of Messiah. To the contrary, the sense of the verse is that once Messiah begins to reign, Judah's blessing of kingship will become fully realized and go to an even higher plateau (*Shlah*). At that time, all the nations will assemble to acknowledge his greatness and pay homage to him.

וְל֖וֹ יִקְּהַ֥ת עַמִּֽים׃ יא אֹסְרִ֤י לַגֶּ֙פֶן֙ עִירֹ֔ה וְלַשֹּׂרֵקָ֖ה

and to him < shall assemble < [the] nations. « 11 He will tie < to the vine < his donkey; « to the vine branch <

בְּנִ֣י אֲתֹנ֑וֹ כִּבֵּ֤ס בַּיַּ֙יִן֙ לְבֻשׁ֔וֹ וּבְדַם־עֲנָבִ֖ים סוּתֹֽה׃

the foal < of his donkey; « he will wash < in wine < his garment, « and in the blood < of grapes < his clothing. «

יב חַכְלִילִ֥י עֵינַ֖יִם מִיָּ֑יִן וּלְבֶן־שִׁנַּ֖יִם מֵחָלָֽב׃ פ

12 Reddened < are [his] eyes < from wine, « and whitened < are [his] teeth < from milk. «

יג זְבוּלֻ֕ן לְח֥וֹף יַמִּ֖ים יִשְׁכֹּ֑ן וְהוּא֙ לְח֣וֹף אֳנִיֹּ֔ת וְיַרְכָת֖וֹ עַל־צִידֹֽן׃ פ

13 Zebulun < by the shore < of the seas < shall settle. « And he [shall be] < by the shore, < [the harbor] of the ships; « and his border < will [reach] unto < Zidon. «

דְּדִילֵהּ הִיא מַלְכוּתָא וְלֵהּ יִשְׁתַּמְעוּן עַמְמַיָּא: יא יַסְחַר יִשְׂרָאֵל לְקַרְתֵּהּ עַמָּא יִבְנוּן הֵיכְלֵהּ יְהוֹן צַדִּיקַיָּא סְחוֹר סְחוֹר לֵהּ וְעָבְדֵי אוֹרַיְתָא בְּאוּלְפַן עִמֵּהּ יְהֵי אַרְגְּוָן טַב לְבוּשׁוֹהִי כְּסוּתֵהּ מֵילָא מֵילָא צְבַע זְהוֹרִי וְצִבְעוֹנִין: יב יִסַּמְקוּן טוּרוֹהִי בְּכַרְמוֹהִי יְטוּפוּן נַעֲווֹהִי בַּחֲמָר יְחַוְּרָן בִּקְעָתֵיהּ בְּעִיבוּר וּבְעֶדְרֵי עָנָא: יג זְבוּלֻן עַל סְפַר יַמְמַיָּא יִשְׁרֵי וְהוּא יְכַבֵּשׁ מְחוֹזִין בִּסְפִינַן וְטוּב יַמָּא יֵיכוּל וּתְחוּמֵהּ יְהֵי מָטֵי עַל צִידוֹן:

רש"י

ולו יקהת עמים. אסיפת העמים. שהיו"ד עיקר היא ביסוד, כמו יפעתך (יחזקאל כח:יז), ופעמים שנופלת ממנו. וכמה אותיות משמשות בל' זה והם נקראים עיקר נופל, כגון נו"ן של נוגף ושל נושך, ואל"ף שבאחותי באזניכם (איוב יג:יז) ושבאבחת חרב (יחזקאל כא:כ), ואסוך שמן (מלכים ב ד:ב). אף זה, יקהת עמים, אסיפת עמים, שנא' אליו גוים ידרושו (ישעיה יא:י; ב"ר שם). ודומה לו עין תלעג לאב ותבוז ליקהת אם (משלי ל:יז), לקבוץ קמטים שבפניה מפני זקנתה. ובתלמוד, דיתבי ומקהו אקהתא בשוקי דנהרדעא [ס"א דפומבדיתא] במסכת יבמות (קי:). ויכול היה לומר קהיית עמים: **(יא) אסרי לגפן עירה.** נתנבא על ארץ יהודה שתהא מושכת יין כמעין. איש יהודה יאסור לגפן עיר אחד ויטעננו מגפן אחת, ומשורק אחד בן אתון אחד (ב"ר צח:ט): **שרקה.** זמורה ארוכה, קוריי"דא בלע"ז: **כבס ביין.** כל זה לשון רבוי יין (ב"ר צט:ח; תנחומא י): **סותה.** לשון מין בגד הוא (אונקלוס) ואין לו דמיון במקרא: **אסרי.** כמו אוסר. דוגמתו מקימי מעפר דל (תהלים קיג:ז) היושבי בשמים (שם קכג:א), וכן בני אתונו כענין זה. ואונקלוס תרגם במלך המשיח, **גפן** הם ישראל, **עירה** זו ירושלים, **שורקה** אלו ישראל, ואנכי נטעתיך שורק (ירמיה ב:כא), **בני אתנו** יבנון היכליה, ל' שער האיתון בס' יחזקאל (מ:טו). ועוד תרגמו בפנים אחרים, **גפן** אלו צדיקים, **בני אתנו** עבדי אורייתא באולפן, על שם רוכבי אתונות צחורות (שופטים ה:י), **כבס ביין** יהא ארגוון טב לבושוהי, שלבושו דומה ליין. וצבעונין הוא לשון **סותה**, שהאשה לובשתן ומסיתה בהן את הזכר ליתן עיניו בה. ואף רבותינו פירשו בגמרא לשון הסתת שכרות, במסכת כתובות (קיא:), ועל היין שמא תאמר אינו מרוה, ת"ל סותה: **(יב) חכלילי.** לשון אודם, כתרגומו. וכן למי חכלילות עינים (משלי כג:כט) שכן דרך שותי יין עיניהם מאדימין: **מחלב.** מרוב חלב, שיהא בארצו מרעה טוב לעדרי צאן. וכן פירוש המקרא, אדום עינים יהא מרוב יין, ולבן שנים יהא מרוב חלב. ולפי תרגומו, עינים ל' הרים, שמשם צופים למרחוק. ועוד תרגמו בפנים אחרים, לשון מעיינות וקילוח היקבים, נעווהי, יקבים שלו, ולשון ארמי הוא במס' עבודה זרה (עד:) נעוה ארעתו. יחוורן בקעתיה, תרגם שנים לשון שני הסלעים (עי' שמואל א יד:ד): **(יג) זבלון לחוף ימים.** על חוף ימים תהיה ארצו. חוף כתרגומו ספר, מרק"א בלע"ז. **והוא** יהיה מצוי תדיר אל **חוף אניות** במקום הנמל שאניות מביאות שם פרקמטיא, שהיה זבולון עוסק בפרקמטיא וממציא מזון לשבט יששכר והם עוסקים בתורה. הוא שאמר משה שמח זבולון בצאתך ויששכר באהליך (דברים לג:יח), זבולון יוצא בפרקמטיא ויששכר עוסק בתורה באהלים (תנחומא יא; ב"ר צט:ט): **וירכתו על צידן.** סוף גבולו יהיה סמוך לצידון. ירכתו, סופו, כמו ולירכתי המשכן (שמות כו:כב):

Alternatively, until the tabernacle in Shiloh is destroyed, the kingship of David will not begin — since David's dynasty is inextricably linked to the Temple in Jerusalem (*Midrash Aggadah*).

Others suggest that Jacob is referring to the establishment of the competing kingship of Jeroboam son of Nebat over the Ten Tribes that took place under the direction of the prophet Ahijah the Shilonite [*I Kings* 11:29] in Shechem, near Shiloh [12:1,20] (*Rashbam, Chizkuni*).

11-12. Though Jacob could not reveal the "End" to his sons, he did provide them with tiny glimpses of the Messianic era (*Abarbanel*). Judah's district will be productive and flow with wine like a fountain. So lush will his vineyards be that a farmer will tie his donkey to a single vine, for it will produce as many grapes as a donkey can carry (*Rashi, Rashbam*). The passage continues hyperbolically with more illustrations of the productivity of Judah's land.

Messiah is associated with a donkey rather than a horse ready for battle, because he is depicted not as a warrior but as a man of peace who represents prosperity; thus the simile of the vineyard. His wars will be won by God, not through force of arms (*Sforno*).

13. Zebulun precedes Issachar. Having given a glimpse of the Messianic era and of Judah as a fitting leader of the future House of Israel, the Patriarch turns to his other children. He bestows his blessings upon each according to his particular role in the harmony of the twelve tribes (*Abarbanel*). Although Issachar was older, Jacob gave precedence to Zebulun because [as *Rashi* notes] Issachar's Torah-learning was made possible by Zebulun, who engaged in commerce and supported Issachar (*Tanchuma;* cf. *Ibn Ezra*). *Sforno* elaborates that one cannot engage in Torah study without material necessities, as the Sages said, "If there is no flour there is no Torah" (*Avos* 3:17). This is why the Torah commands the nation to provide gifts for the Kohanim and Levites, who devote themselves to the study and teaching of Torah.

The verse describes the tribe of Zebulun as seafaring merchants. Its territory would be in the Galil, between the Sea of Kinereth and the Mediterranean, and its border would extend to Zidon, a famed center of commerce at the northwest boundary of *Eretz Yisrael*.

14-15. Issachar. Although the simile of *a donkey of [strong] bones* and the references to *land* seem to allude to agricultural pursuits — a view indeed expressed by one Sage in the Midrash and followed by several commentators — *Rashi* favors the tradi-

יד יִשָּׂשכָר חֲמֹר גָּרֶם רֹבֵץ בֵּין הַמִּשְׁפְּתָיִם: טו וַיַּרְא

< He saw **15** *<< the boundaries. < between < he rests << of [strong] bones; < is a donkey < Issachar* **14**

מְנֻחָה כִּי טוֹב וְאֶת־הָאָרֶץ כִּי נָעֵמָה וַיֵּט שִׁכְמוֹ

< his shoulder < yet he bent << it is pleasant, < that < and the land << it is good, < that < tranquility

לִסְבֹּל וַיְהִי לְמַס־עֹבֵד: ס טז דָּן יָדִין עַמּוֹ כְּאַחַד

< equal to the unique one << [for] his people, < will exact just vengeance < Dan **16** *<< of service. < [to pay] the levy < and he became [the one] < to bear*

שִׁבְטֵי יִשְׂרָאֵל: יז יְהִי־דָן נָחָשׁ עֲלֵי־דֶרֶךְ שְׁפִיפֹן

< a viper << the highway, < along < a serpent < Dan will be **17** *<< of Israel. < of the tribes*

עֲלֵי־אֹרַח הַנֹּשֵׁךְ עִקְּבֵי־סוּס וַיִּפֹּל רֹכְבוֹ אָחוֹר:

<< backward. < shall its rider < so that fall << of a horse, < the heels < one that bites << the path, < along

יד יִשָּׂשכָר עַתִּיר בְּנִכְסִין וְאַחֲסַנְתֵּהּ בֵּין תְּחוּמַיָּא: טו וַחֲזָא חוּלָקָא אֲרֵי טַב וְיָת אַרְעָא אֲרֵי מְעַבְּדָא פֵּירִין וִיכַבֵּשׁ מָחוֹזֵי עַמְמַיָּא וִישֵׁיצֵי יָת דַּיָּרֵיהוֹן וּדְאִשְׁתַּאֲרוּן בְּהוֹן יְהוֹן לֵהּ פַּלְחִין וּמַסְּקֵי מַסִּין: טז מִדְּבֵית דָּן יִתְבְּחַר וִיקוּם גַּבְרָא בְּיוֹמוֹהִי יִתְפְּרֵק עַמֵּהּ וּבִשְׁנוֹהִי יְנוּחוּן כַּחֲדָא שִׁבְטַיָּא דְיִשְׂרָאֵל: יז יְהֵי גַבְרָא דְיִתְבְּחַר וִיקוּם מִדְּבֵית דָּן אֵימְתֵהּ תִּתְרְמֵי עַל עַמְמַיָּא וּמְחָתֵהּ תִּתְקֵף בִּפְלִשְׁתָּאֵי כְּחִיוֵי חוּרְמָן יִשְׁרֵי עַל אָרְחָא וּכְפִתְנָא יִכְמוֹן עַל שְׁבִילָא יְקַטֵּל גִּבָּרֵי מַשְׁרִית פְּלִשְׁתָּאֵי פָּרָשִׁין עִם רַגְלָאִין יְעַקֵּר סוּסָוָן וּרְתִכִּין וִימַגַּר רוֹכְבֵיהוֹן לַאֲחוֹרָא:

רש"י

(יד) **ישׂשכר חמור גרם.** חמור בעל עצמות, סובל עול תורה כחמור חזק שמטעינין אותו משא כבד (ב"ר שם י): **רבץ בין המשפתים.** כחמור המהלך ביום ובלילה ואין לו לינה בבית. וכשהוא רוצה לנוח רובץ בין התחומין (אונקלוס) בתחומי העיירות שמוליך שם פרקמטיא: (טו) **וירא מנוחה כי טוב.** ראה לחלקו ארץ מבורכת וטובה להוציא פירות (שם): **ויט שכמו לסבל.** עול תורה: **ויהי.** לכל אחיו ישראל: **למס עבד.** לפסוק להם הוראות של תורה וסדרי עבורין, שנא' ומבני יששכר יודעי בינה לעתים לדעת מה יעשה ישראל ראשיהם מאתים (דברי הימים א יב:לג). מאתים ראשי סנהדראות העמיד, וכל אחיהם על פיהם (שם; ב"ר עב:ה, צח:יב, צט:י; תנחומא יא; שהש"ר ו:ד): **ויט שכמו.** השפיל שכמו. כמו ויט שמים (שמואל ב כב:י) הטו אזנכם (תהלים עח:א). ואונקלוס תרגם בפנים אחרים, ויט שכמו לסבול מלחמות ולכבוש מחוזות, שהם יושבים על הספר, ויהיה האויב כבוש תחתיו למס עובד: (טז) **דן ידין עמו.** ינקום נקמת עמו מפלשתים, כמו כי ידין ה' עמו (דברים לב:לו): **כאחד שבטי ישראל.** כל ישראל יהיו כאחד עמו ואת כלם ידין, ועל שמשון נבא נבואה זו. ועוד יש לפרש, כאחד שבטי ישראל, כמיוחד שבשבטים, הוא דוד שבא מיהודה (ב"ר צט:יא; תנחומא יב): (יז) **שפיפן.** הוא נחש ואומר אני שקרוי כן על שם שהוא נושף, כמו ואתה תשופנו עקב (לעיל ג:טו): **הנושך עקבי סוס.** כך דרכו של נחש, ודמהו לנחש הנושך עקבי סוס, **ויפל רכבו אחור,** שלא נגע בו. ודוגמתו מצינו בשמשון וילפת וגו' את שני עמודי התוך וגו' (שופטים טז:כט) ושעל הגג מתו. ואונקלוס תרגם כחיוי חורמן, שם מין נחש שאין רפואה לנשיכתו והוא לפעוני, וקרוי חורמן על שם שעושה הכל חרם, וכפיתנא, כמו פתן, יכמון, יארוב:

tional Rabbinic interpretation that this reflects Issachar's *spiritual* role as bearer of the yoke of Torah and cultivator of the spiritual treasures of the people.

14. רֹבֵץ בֵּין הַמִּשְׁפְּתָיִם — *He rests between the boundaries.* The Torah Sages toil day and night in their studies without *formal* rest, but they are spiritually tranquil (*Shaarei Aharon*).

15. This verse, too, can be taken literally as a reference to agricultural prosperity, or as a symbolic allusion to the tranquility and pleasantness of the hard but rewarding task of Torah study.

וַיְהִי לְמַס־עֹבֵד — *And he became [the one] [to pay] the levy of service. Rashi*, following the Midrash, comments that Issachar's dedication to the Torah made him a servant of the people, rendering decisions and teaching the complex regulations concerning the fixing of leap years. Two hundred heads of Sanhedrins came from this tribe, and their halachic pronouncements were accepted as authoritative [see *I Chronicles* 12:33].

16-18. Dan. Having concluded his blessings of Leah's six sons, Jacob went on to the older son of Bilhah, Rachel's maidservant. He left the sons of Rachel for last.

Jacob alluded prophetically to Dan's descendant Samson, who single-handedly fought and defeated the Philistines — *equal to the unique one of the tribes of Israel,* meaning that Samson would be like David, a member of Judah, the most distinguished of the tribes. An alternate translation — still referring to Samson — in his time, he brought unity [כְּאַחַד] to the people (*Rashi*).

17. נָחָשׁ עֲלֵי־דֶרֶךְ — *A serpent along the highway. Rashi* and *Ramban* apply the words to Samson, whose single-handed battle tactics corresponded closely to Jacob's description. Like a serpent leaving its lair to attack travelers and then slithering back to its hiding place, Samson waged a personal, guerrilla-like war against the Philistines, catching them by surprise and going into hiding before they could counterattack.

R' Hirsch notes that Jacob said, "*Dan will be a serpent,*" not that Dan, i.e., Samson, *is* a serpent — as he said that Judah is a lion and Issachar a powerful donkey — because the treacherous nature of the serpent is distasteful and un-Jewish. The implication is that Samson had no choice but to adopt such tactics in battle, but his nature remained pure.

וַיִּפֹּל רֹכְבוֹ — *So that fall shall its rider.* The allusion is to Samson's final victory, when — blind and in chains — he pulled down the pillars of the Philistine idol's temple and caused it to collapse, killing himself and three thousand Philistines. Like a snake biting a horse and indirectly killing its rider, Samson struck indi-

יח לִישׁוּעָתְךָ קִוִּיתִי יְהוָה׃ ס חמישי יט גָּד גְּדוּד יְגוּדֶנּוּ

18 For Your salvation › do I long, » O HASHEM! » 19 Gad – » a troop › will troop forth ›

וְהוּא יָגֻד עָקֵב׃ ס כ מֵאָשֵׁר שְׁמֵנָה לַחְמוֹ וְהוּא

and it › will troop back › on [its own] footsteps. » 20 From Asher » will be rich – › his bread, » and he ›

יִתֵּן מַעֲדַנֵּי־מֶלֶךְ׃ ס כא נַפְתָּלִי אַיָּלָה שְׁלֻחָה הַנֹּתֵן אִמְרֵי־שָׁפֶר׃ ס

will provide › delicacies › for the king. » 21 Naphtali › is a deer › sent forth › who delivers › sayings › that are beautiful. »

יח לְפוּרְקָנָךְ סַבָּרִית יְיָ: יט דְּבֵית גָּד מַשִּׁרְיַת מְזַיְּנִין כַּד יַעַבְרוּן יָת יַרְדְּנָא קֳדָם אֲחֵיהוֹן לִקְרָבָא וּבְנִכְסִין סַגִּיאִין יְתוּבוּן לְאַרְעֲהוֹן: כ דְּאָשֵׁר טָבָא אַרְעֵהּ וְהוּא מְרַבֵּי (נ״א וְהִיא מְרַבְּיָא) תַּפְנוּקֵי מַלְכִין: כא נַפְתָּלִי בְּאַרַע טָבָא יִתְרְמֵי עַדְבֵהּ וְאַחְסַנְתֵּהּ תְּהֵי מַעְבְּדָא פֵּירִין יְהוֹן מוֹדַן וּמְבָרְכִין עֲלֵיהוֹן:

רש״י

(יח) לישועתך קויתי ה׳. נתנבא שינקרו פלשתים את עיניו וסופו לומר זכרני נא וחזקני נא אך הפעם (שם טז:כח): **(יט) גד גדוד יגודנו.** כלם לשון גדוד הם וכך חברו מנחם. ואם תאמר אין גדוד בלא שני דלתי״ן. יש לומר, גדוד שם דבר צריך שני דלתי״ן, שכן דרך תיבה בת שתי אותיות לכפול בסופה ואין יסודה אלא שתי אותיות. וכן אמר כצפור לנוד (משלי כו:ב) מגזרת ושבעתי נדודים (איוב ז:ד), שם נפל שדוד (שופטים ה:כז) מגזרת ישוד צהרים (תהלים צא:ו), אף יגוד יגודנו וגדוד מגזרה אחת הם. וכשהוא מדבר בלשון יפעל אינו כפול, כמו יגוד, ינוד, ירום, ישוד, ישוב. וכשהוא מתפעל או מפעיל אחרים הוא כפול, כמו יתגודד, יתרומם, יתבולל, יתעודד. ובלשון מפעיל, יתום ואלמנה יעודד (שם קמו:ט) לשובב יעקב אליו (ישעיה מט:ה) משובב נתיבות (שם נח:יב). אף יגודנו האמור כאן אין ל׳ שיפעילוהו אחרים אלא כמו יגוד הימנו, כמו בני יצאוני (ירמיה י:כ) יצאו ממני, גד גדוד יגודנו, גדודים יגודו הימנו שיעברו הירדן עם אחיהם למלחמה כל חלוץ עד שנכבשה הארץ: **והוא יגד עקב.** כל גדודיו ישובו על עקבם לנחלתם שלקחו בעבר הירדן ולא יפקד מהם איש (תרגום ירושלמי): **עקב.** בדרכם ובמסילותם שהלכו ישובו, כמו ועקבותיך לא נודעו (תהלים עז:כ), וכן בעקבי הצאן (שיר השירים א:ח). בלשון לע״ז טרצי״ש: **(כ) מאשר שמנה לחמו.** מאכל הבא מחלקו של אשר יהא שמן, שיהיו זיתים מרובים בחלקו והוא מושך שמן כמעין. וכן ברכו משה, וטובל בשמן רגלו (דברים לג:כד), כמו ששנינו במנחות (פה:) פעם אחת הוצרכו אנשי לודקיא לשמן וכו׳: **(כא) אילה שלחה.** זו בקעת גינוסר שהיא קלה לבשל פירותיה כאילה זו שהיא קלה לרוץ (ב״ר צט:יב). אילה שלוחה, אילה משולחת לרוץ: **הנתן אמרי שפר.** כתרגומו. ד״א, על מלחמת סיסרא נתנבא, ולקחת עמך עשרת אלפים איש מבני נפתלי וגו׳ (שופטים ד:ו) והלכו שם בזריזות. וכן נאמר שם ל׳ שלוח, בעמק שלח ברגליו (שם ה:טו): **הנתן אמרי שפר.** על ידם שרו דבורה וברק שירה (ב״ר צח:יז). ורבותינו דרשוהו על יום קבורת יעקב כשערער עשו על המערה במסכת סוטה (יג.). ותרגומו יתרמי עדביה, יפול חבלו,

rectly at his tormentors [*Judges* 16:29] (*Rashi; Ramban*).

18. לִישׁוּעָתְךָ קִוִּיתִי ה׳ — *For Your salvation do I long, O HASHEM!* Jacob prophesied that Samson would utter a heartfelt plea to God, begging for the strength to tear down the Philistine temple, a prayer that was answered (*R' Bachya*) to such an extent that the Philistines were afraid to harass Israel for twenty years.

R' Moshe Feinstein sees this prayer of Samson as the paradigm of his greatness. R' Yochanan expounded homiletically that Samson would lead Israel all alone, just as God is the lone Sovereign of the world (*Sotah* 10a). The impact of this teaching is that Samson's sometimes incomprehensible behavior must be understood as emanating from the loftiest ideals and purest motives, just as we know that God is just, even when we fail to understand His ways. This is exemplified by Samson's prayerful declaration that his salvation and hope were all from God, not from any prowess of his own. Even his phenomenal physical strength was not his own; it was a gift from God for the service of Israel.

19. Gad. Jacob went from Bilhah's older son to Zilpah's. Although the Gadites' territory was on the east of the Jordan, they nobly crossed the Jordan to assist their brothers in conquering the Land. They fought the Canaanites valiantly and did not return home until the Land was won. Jacob prophesied that after the conquest, Gad will return safely *on [its own] footsteps* — by the same roads and paths upon which it had initially traveled — and not one of the troops will be missing (*Rashi*).

20. Asher. Asher's land will be so rich in olive groves that it will flow with oil like a fountain (*Rashi*); *and he will provide delicacies for the king,* his rich produce will be worthy of royal tables and will be sought by kings (*Radak*).

Asher was the second son of Zilpah. Jacob blessed Zilpah's younger son before Bilhah's in order to suggest that Gad would be free to devote himself to the defense of the nation because Asher would make available his rich produce whenever the Gadites were in need (*Daas Zekeinim*).

21. Naphtali. Having blessed Zilpah's sons, Jacob blessed Bilhah's younger son, and thus concluded the sons of the maidservants.

אַיָּלָה שְׁלֻחָה — *A deer sent forth.* The simile carries a connotation of swiftness, for which *Rashi* offers three Midrashic interpretations: (a) Naphtali's *territory,* its crops, will ripen swiftly, like a deer sent forth to run free. (b) In the war against Sisera [during the time of Deborah the prophetess (*Judges* 4 ff.)], the valiant warriors of Naphtali were nimble as deer, and played a leading role in the battle. (c) On the day Jacob was buried, the swift Naphtali ran with proof that Jacob, not Esau, was entitled to be buried in the Cave of Machpelah. As related in *Sotah* 13a, when Jacob's sons came to bury him, Esau tried to stop them, claiming that as the firstborn he had a prior claim to the last remaining grave site in the cave. He demanded, "Produce your deed to the cave!" Thereupon the fleet Naphtali ran like a deer to Egypt and brought the deed.

אִמְרֵי־שָׁפֶר — *Sayings that are beautiful.* Based on the above three interpretations, the verse concludes by referring to: (a) Naphtali's beautiful praises to God in gratitude for the abundant crops; (b) Deborah's song of praise to God for the victory in which Naphtali's troops were instrumental; (c) the deed to the cave, which contained the *beautiful* confirmation of Jacob's ownership.

כב בֵּן פֹּרָת יוֹסֵף בֵּן פֹּרָת עֲלֵי־עָיִן בָּנוֹת צָעֲדָה

22 A son / of grace / is Joseph, / a son / of grace / to / the eye; / [each of] the daughters / climbed [heights]

עֲלֵי־שׁוּר: כג וַיְמָרְרֻהוּ וָרֹבּוּ וַיִּשְׂטְמֻהוּ בַּעֲלֵי

in order to / gaze. **23** They embittered him / and they antagonized; / hate him / did the masters

חִצִּים: כד וַתֵּשֶׁב בְּאֵיתָן קַשְׁתּוֹ וַיָּפֹזּוּ זְרֹעֵי יָדָיו

of arrows. **24** But emplaced / with firmness / was his bow / and gilded were / the arms / of his hands,

מִידֵי אֲבִיר יַעֲקֹב מִשָּׁם רֹעֶה אֶבֶן יִשְׂרָאֵל:

from the hands / of the Mighty Power / of Jacob / — from there / he shepherded / the stone / of Israel.

כב בְּרִי דִּיסְגֵּי יוֹסֵף בְּרִי דְּיִתְבָּרַךְ כְּגֻפַן דִּנְצִיב עַל עֵינָא דְּמַיָּא תְּרֵין שִׁבְטִין יִפְּקוּן מִבְּנוֹהִי יְקַבְּלוּן חוּלָקָא וְאַחֲסַנְתָּא: כג וְאִתְמָרָרוּ יָתֵהּ וְנַקְמוּהִי וְאָעִיקוּ לֵהּ גֻּבְרִין גִּבָּרִין בַּעֲלֵי (נ״א מָרֵי) פַּלְגּוּתָא: כד וְתָבַת בְּהוֹן נְבִיאוּתֵהּ עַל דְּקַיֵּם אוֹרָיְתָא בְּסִתְרָא וְשַׁוִּי בְּתוּקְפָּא רוּחֲצָנֵהּ בְּכֵן יִתְרְמָא דְהַב עַל דְּרָעוֹהִי אַחֲסִין מַלְכוּתָא וּתְקֵיף דָּא הֲוָת לֵהּ מִן קֳדָם אֵל תַּקִּיפָא דְּיַעֲקֹב דִּי בְמֵימְרֵהּ זָן אֲבָהָן וּבְנִין זַרְעָא דְיִשְׂרָאֵל:

רש״י

והוא יודה על חלקו אמרים נאים ושבח: (כב) **בן פרת.** בן חן. והוא ל׳ ארמי, אפריון [ס״א אפריין] נמטייה לרבי שמעון, בסוף בבא מציעא (קיט.): **בן פרת עלי עין.** חנו נטוי על העין הרואה אותו: **בנות צעדה עלי שור.** בנות מצרים היו צועדות על החומה להסתכל ביפיו (עי׳ ב״ר שם יח), בנות הרבה צעדה כל אחת ואחת במקום שתוכל לראותו משם. ד״א, עלי שור, על ראייתו, כמו אשורנו ולא קרוב (במדבר כד:יז). ומדרש אגדה יש רבים וזה נוטה ליישוב המקרא: **פרת.** ת״ו שבו הוא תקון הלשון, כמו על דברת בני האדם (קהלת ג:יח): **שור.** כמו לשור. ד״א, עלי שור, בשביל לשור. ותרגום של אונקלוס בנות צעדה עלי שור, תרין שבטין יפקון מבנוהי וכו׳. וכתב בנות על שם בנות מנשה בנות צלפחד שנטלו חלק בשני עברי הירדן (תנחומא פנחס ט). ברי דיסגי יוסף פורת ל׳ פריה ורביה. ויש מ״א בו המתישבים על הלשון, בשעה שבא עשו לקראת יעקב בכלן קדמו האמהות ללכת לפני בניהם להשתחוות, וברחל כתיב נגש יוסף ורחל וישתחוו (לעיל לג:ז). אמר יוסף, הרשע הזה עינו רמה שמא יתן עיניו באמי, יצא לפניה ושרבב קומתו לכסותה. והוא שברכו אביו, **בן פרת,** הגדלת עצמך **יוסף עלי עין** של עשו, לפיכך זכית לגדולה, **בנות צעדה עלי שור** להסתכל בך בצאתך על מצרים (ב״ר שם, עח:י). ועוד דרשוהו לענין שלא ישלוט בזרעו עין הרע, ואף כשברך מנשה ואפרים ברכם כדגים שאין עין הרע שולטת בהם (ברכות כ.): (כג) **וימררהו ורבו.** וימררוהו אחיו ומררוהו פוטיפר ואשתו לאסרו, לשון וימררו את חייהם (שמות א:יד; ב״ר לח:יט): **ורבו.** נעשו לו אחיו אנשי ריב. ואין הלשון הזה לשון פָּעֲלוּ שא״כ היה לו לינקד וְרָבוּ, כמו המה מי מריבה אשר רבו וגו׳ (במדבר כ:יג), ואף אם לשון רביית חצים הוא כן היה לו להנקד. ואינו אלא לשון פוּעֲלוּ, כמו שֹׁמּוּ שמים (ירמיה ב:יב) שהוא לשון הוּשַּׁמּוּ, וכן רוֹמּוּ מעט (איוב כד:כד) שהוא לשון הוּרְמוּ. אלא שלשון הורמו והושמו ע״י אחרים, ול׳ שמו רמו רבו מאליהם הוא, מסוממים את עצמם, נתרוממו מעצמם, נעשו אנשי ריב. וכן דמו יושבי אי (ישעיה כג:ב) כמו נָדַמּוּ. וכן תרגם אונקלוס ונקמוהי: **בעלי חצים.** שלשונם כחץ (ב״ר שם). ותרגומו מרי פלגותא, לשון ותהי המחלה (במדבר לא:לו) אותן שהיו ראוים לחלוק עמו נחלה: (כד) **ותשב באיתן קשתו.** נתישבה בחוזק. קשתו, חזקו: **ויפזו זרעי ידיו.** זו היא נתינת טבעת על ידו, לשון זהב מופז (מלכים א י:יח). זאת היתה לו **מידי** הקב״ה שהוא **אביר יעקב. ומשם** עלה להיות **רועה אבן ישראל** עקרן של ישראל, לשון האבן הראשה (זכריה ד:ז) לשון מלכות. ואונקלוס אף הוא כך תרגמו. ותשב, ותבת בהון נביאותיה, החלומות אשר חלם להם. על דקיים אורייתא בסתרא תוספת הוא ולא מל׳ עברי שבמקרא. ושוי בתוקפא רוחצניה תרגום של באיתן קשתו. וכך לשון התרגום על העברי ותשב נביאותו בשביל שאיתנו של הקב״ה היתה לו לקשת ולמבטח. בכן יתרמא דהב על דרעוהי, לכך ויפזו זרועי ידיו, לשון פז. אבן ישראל לשון נוטריקון אב ובן אבהן ובנין יעקב ובניו:

22-26. Joseph. Jacob now turned to the sons of Rachel, who were born last and who were his comfort after the loss of his beloved wife. He began with ecstatic praise of Joseph, whose talent and purity survived hatred and temptation.

22. **בֵּן פֹּרָת יוֹסֵף** — *A son of grace is Joseph.* So handsome was Joseph that Egyptian girls climbed atop walls to catch a glimpse of his beauty when he passed by (*Rashi*).

Others interpret the verse as comparing Joseph to a prolific vine or tree growing luxuriantly by a spring, whose boughs or vines surge upward over the surrounding walls. This alludes to Joseph's offspring or to Joseph himself, who was revealed after a disappearance of twenty-two years, when his family thought he was dead or hopelessly swallowed up by some unknown society.

23-24. According to *Rashi* (as understood by the commentaries), these two verses are linked: Joseph rose to prominence despite the hatred he suffered. His brothers and Potiphar and his wife all *embittered him and became antagonists.* People with arrow-like tongues — a Scriptural allusion to purveyors of malicious slander and gossip — dealt bitterly with Joseph, but, by the grace of God, he rose to prominence despite them . . . (*Rashi*).

Abarbanel sees in this verse the reason why Judah, not Joseph, became the leader of the nation: Noble though he was, Joseph provoked jealousy in people, while Judah enjoyed undisputed popularity. *R' Munk* observes, on the other hand, that in Jewish literature and tradition, only Joseph is called הַצַּדִּיק, *the Righteous One* (*Yoma* 35b), because of his grandeur of soul and high moral caliber. Therefore, even though Jacob had assigned royalty to Judah, he praised Joseph as the *crown among his brothers.*

24. **וַתֵּשֶׁב בְּאֵיתָן קַשְׁתּוֹ** — *But emplaced with firmness was his bow. Bow* alludes to *his power*, notwithstanding the attacks and hatred of his foes, Joseph's power as regent of Egypt was firmly established, when Pharaoh "gilded his arms," by placing the royal signet ring on his hand (*Rashi*). All this happened to Joseph thanks to God — *the Mighty Power of Jacob* — Whose help overcame all the obstacles to Joseph's rise (*Rashi*).

מִשָּׁם רֹעֶה אֶבֶן יִשְׂרָאֵל — *From there, he shepherded the stone of Israel. From there* — his God-given position as viceroy, or from his position as the victim of slander — Joseph became *the shepherd* who provided sustenance for Jacob, *the stone of Israel.* The word *stone* denotes kingship, the primary personage of the

כה מֵאֵל אָבִיךָ וְיַעְזְרֶךָּ וְאֵת שַׁדַּי וִיבָרְכֶךָּ בִּרְכֹת

< [with] blessings < — and He will bless you << Shaddai < and with << and He will help you, < of your father < [That was] from the God 25

שָׁמַיִם מֵעָל בִּרְכֹת תְּהוֹם רֹבֶצֶת תָּחַת בִּרְכֹת

< blessings << below, < crouching < of the deep < [and] blessings < from above, < of heaven

שָׁדַיִם וָרָחַם: כו בִּרְכֹת אָבִיךָ גָּבְרוּ עַל־בִּרְכֹת

< the blessings < beyond < have surpassed < of your father < The blessings 26 << and the womb. < of the bosom

הוֹרַי עַד־תַּאֲוַת גִּבְעֹת עוֹלָם תִּהְיֶיןָ לְרֹאשׁ יוֹסֵף וּלְקָדְקֹד נְזִיר אֶחָיו:

<< [from] his brothers. < of the one separated < and upon the head < of Joseph < upon the head < Let them be << eternal. < of the hills < the [endless] bounds < unto < of my parents

פ ששי כז בִּנְיָמִין זְאֵב יִטְרָף בַּבֹּקֶר יֹאכַל עַד וְלָעֶרֶב יְחַלֵּק שָׁלָל:

<< spoils. < he will distribute < and in the evening < prey < he will devour < in the morning << that tears [its prey]; < is a wolf < Benjamin 27

כה מֵימַר אֱלָהָא דַאֲבוּךְ יְהֵי בְסַעֲדָךְ וְיָת
שַׁדַּי וִיבָרְכִנָּךְ בִּרְכָן דְּנָחֲתָן מִטַּלָּא
דִשְׁמַיָּא מִלְּעֵלָּא בִּרְכָן דְּנָגְדָן מִמַּעֲמַקֵּי
אַרְעָא מִלְּרַע בִּרְכְתָא דַאֲבוּךְ וּדְאִמָּךְ:
כו בִּרְכָתָא דַאֲבוּךְ יִתּוֹסְפָן עַל בִּרְכָתָא
דְלִי בָּרִיכוּ אֲבָהָתִי דְּחַמִּידוּ לְהוֹן רַבְרְבַיָּא
דְּמִן עָלְמָא יְהֶוְיָן כָּל אִלֵּין לְרֵישָׁא דְיוֹסֵף
וּלְגַבְרָא פְּרִישָׁא דַאֲחוֹהִי: כז בִּנְיָמִין
בְּאַרְעֵהּ תִּשְׁרֵי שְׁכִנְתָּא וּבְאַחְסַנְתֵּהּ
יִתְבְּנֵי מַקְדְּשָׁא בְּצַפְרָא וּבְפַנְיָא יְהוֹן
מְקָרְבִין כָּהֲנַיָּא קֻרְבָּנָא וּלְעִדָּן רַמְשָׁא יְהוֹן
מְפַלְּגִין מוֹתַר חוּלָקְהוֹן מִשְּׁאַר קֻדְשַׁיָּא:

רש"י

(כה) מאל אביך. היתה לך זאת, והוא **יעזרך: ואת שדי.** ועם הקב"ה היה לבך כשלא שמעת לדברי אדונתך והוא **יברכך** (ב"ר פז:ז): **ברכת שדים ורחם.** ברכתא דאבא ודאמא [כתרגום אונקלוס]. כלומר יתברכו המולידים והיולדות, שיהיו הזכרים מזריעין טיפה הראויה להריון והנקבות לא ישכלו את רחם שלהן להפיל עובריהן: **שדים.** ירה יירה (שמות יט:יג) מתרגמינן אישתדאה ישתדי, אף שדים כאן על שם שהזרע יורה כחץ: **(כו) ברכת אביך גברו וגו'.** הברכות שברכני הקב"ה גברו והלכו על הברכות שבירך את הורי (ברב"ת): **עד תאות גבעת עולם.** לפי שהברכות שלי גברו עד סוף גבולי גבעות עולם, שנתן לי ברכה פרוצה בלי מצרים מגעת עד ד' קצות העולם, שנאמר ופרצת ימה וקדמה וגו' (לעיל כח:יד) מה שלא אמר לאברהם אבינו וליצחק. לאברהם א"ל שא נא עיניך וראה צפונה וגו' כי את כל הארץ אשר אתה רואה לך אתננה (שם יג:יד-טו) ולא הראהו אלא ארץ ישראל בלבד. ליצחק אמר לו כי לך ולזרעך אתן את כל הארצות האל והקימותי את השבועה וגו' (שם כו:ג). זהו שאמר ישעיה (נח:יד) והאכלתיך נחלת יעקב אביך ולא אמר נחלת אברהם (שבת קיח.): **תאות.** אשמול"ץ, כך חברו מנחם בן סרוק: **הורי.** לשון הריון שהורוני במעי אמי. כמו הורה גבר (איוב ג:ג): **עד תאות.** עד קצות. כמו והתאויתם לכם לגבול קדמה (במדבר לד:י) תתאו לבא חמת (שם ח): **תהיין.** כלם **לראש יוסף: נזיר אחיו.** פרישא דאחוהי (אונקלוס) שנבדל מאחיו. כמו וינזרו מקדשי בני ישראל (ויקרא כב:ב) נזורו אחור (ישעיה א:ד). ור"ד, **ותשב באיתן קשתו,** על כבישת יצרו באשת אדוניו, וקוראו קשת ע"ש שהזרע יורה כחץ. **ויפזו זרועי ידיו,** כמו ויפוצו, שיצא הזרע מבין אצבעות ידיו. **מידי אביר יעקב,** שנראתה לו דמות דיוקנו של אביו וכו', כדאיתא בסוטה (לו:). ואונקלוס תרגם תאות עולם לשון תאוה וחמדה, וגבעות עולם ל' מצוקי ארץ (שמואל א ב:ח), [והם הברכות] שחמדתן אמו והזקיקתו לקבלם: **(כז) בנימין זאב יטרף.** זאב הוא אשר יטרף. נבא על שיהיו עתידין להיות חטפנין, וחטפתם לכם איש אשתו (שופטים כא:כא) בפלגש בגבעה. ונבא על שאול שיהיה נוצח באויביו סביב שנא' ושאול לכד המלוכה וגו' וילחם וגו' במואב ובאדום וגו' ובכל אשר יפנה ירשיע (שמואל א יד:מז; תנחומא יד): **בבקר יאכל עד.** לשון בזה ושלל המתורגם עדאה (אונקלוס במדבר לא:יא). ועוד יש לו דומה בלשון עברית אז חולק עד שלל (ישעיה לג:כג). ועל שאול הוא אומר שעמד בתחלת בוקרן [ס"א פריחתן] וזריחתן של ישראל: **ולערב יחלק שלל.** אף משתשקע שמשן של ישראל על ידי נבוכדנצר שיגלם לבבל: **יחלק שלל.** מרדכי ואסתר שהם מבנימין יחלקו את שלל המן, שנאמר הנה בית המן נתתי לאסתר (אסתר ח:ז; אסת"ר

nation, as it is used in *Zechariah* 4:7. Alternatively, אֶבֶן can be seen as a contraction of the words אָב וּבֵן, *father and son,* thus alluding to Joseph's support of the entire family (*Rashi*). The above contraction also alludes to the family, for it is the building block — the *stone* — with which the nation is built.

25. **וְאֵת שַׁדַּי** — *And with Shaddai.* When Joseph was tempted by Potiphar's wife, his heart remained *with* God and he overcame his desire *(Rashi).* The Name *Shaddai*, often translated as All-Sufficient, refers to God as the One Who sets the proper limits of all things, good or bad. In the context of this verse, when Joseph needed God's help to maintain his spiritual integrity — and in the future when Israel cries out to Him as Joseph did in his time of spiritual anguish — God will provide sufficient blessing for the people to prevail.

בִּרְכֹת . . . — *Blessings* . . . God will bring blessings of irrigation from subterranean springs, so that Joseph's land would be fertile even in times of scarce rainfall. The *womb* will be blessed so that women will carry to term and give birth to healthy babies, and the *bosom* will provide enough milk to nourish them (see *Targum Yonasan*).

26. Jacob ends his blessing of Joseph with the hope that he would be the beneficiary of the very same boundless blessings that Jacob had received from his own forefathers.

27. Benjamin. Benjamin's descendants — likened to a wolf — were mighty, fearless warriors, as depicted in the affair of the Concubine at Gibeah [*Judges* Chs. 19-20] (*Radak*), as was King Saul, a Benjaminite, who, in his short reign, defeated Moab, Edom, and Philistia. The *morning* refers to Saul who rose as Israel's champion during the early years of Israel's history, when the nation began to flourish and shine. In the national *evening* of decline, when the people were exiled to Babylonia and Persia, Benjamin's offspring will triumph over Israel's enemies and divide the spoils of victory. This is an allusion to Mordechai and Esther, of the tribe of Benjamin, who defeated Haman and were awarded his estate [see *Esther* 8:7] (*Rashi* from *Tanchuma*).

כח כָּל־אֵלֶּה שִׁבְטֵי יִשְׂרָאֵל שְׁנֵים עָשָׂר וְזֹאת
< and this << — twelve — << of Israel < are the tribes < these < All 28

אֲשֶׁר־דִּבֶּר לָהֶם אֲבִיהֶם וַיְבָרֶךְ אוֹתָם אִישׁ אֲשֶׁר
< what was < [each] man << them; < and he blessed << — their father — << to them < he spoke < is what

כְּבִרְכָתוֹ בֵּרַךְ אֹתָם: כט וַיְצַו אוֹתָם וַיֹּאמֶר אֲלֵהֶם
<< to them, < and he said << them; < Then he instructed 29 << them. < he blessed < his [appropriate] blessing

אֲנִי נֶאֱסָף אֶל־עַמִּי קִבְרוּ אֹתִי אֶל־אֲבֹתָי אֶל־
< in < my fathers < with < me < bury << my people; < to < shall be gathered < I

הַמְּעָרָה אֲשֶׁר בִּשְׂדֵה עֶפְרוֹן הַחִתִּי: ל בַּמְּעָרָה אֲשֶׁר בִּשְׂדֵה הַמַּכְפֵּלָה
< of Machpelah, < in the field < that is < In the cave 30 << the Hittite. < of Ephron < in the field < that is < the cave

אֲשֶׁר־עַל־פְּנֵי מַמְרֵא בְּאֶרֶץ כְּנָעַן אֲשֶׁר קָנָה אַבְרָהָם אֶת־הַשָּׂדֶה מֵאֵת
< from < the field < with < Abraham bought < which << of Canaan, < in the land < Mamre, < faces < which

עֶפְרֹן הַחִתִּי לַאֲחֻזַּת־קָבֶר: לא שָׁמָּה קָבְרוּ אֶת־אַבְרָהָם וְאֵת שָׂרָה אִשְׁתּוֹ
<< his wife; < and Sarah < Abraham < they buried < There 31 << for a burial site. < as [land] legally possessed < the Hittite < Ephron

שָׁמָּה קָבְרוּ אֶת־יִצְחָק וְאֵת רִבְקָה אִשְׁתּוֹ וְשָׁמָּה קָבַרְתִּי אֶת־לֵאָה:
<< Leah. < I buried < and there << his wife; < and Rebecca < Isaac < they buried < there

כח כָּל אִלֵּין שִׁבְטַיָּא דְיִשְׂרָאֵל תְּרֵין עֲסַר וְדָא דִּי מַלִּיל לְהוֹן אֲבוּהוֹן וּבָרִיךְ יָתְהוֹן גְּבַר דִּי כְבִרְכְתֵהּ בָּרִיךְ יָתְהוֹן: כט וּפַקֵּד יָתְהוֹן וַאֲמַר לְהוֹן אֲנָא מִתְכְּנֵשׁ לְעַמִּי קְבָרוּ יָתִי לְוַת אֲבָהָתַי בִּמְעַרְתָּא דִּי בַּחֲקַל עֶפְרוֹן חִתָּאָה: ל בִּמְעַרְתָּא דִּי בַּחֲקַל כָּפֶלְתָּא דִּי עַל אַפֵּי מַמְרֵא בְּאַרְעָא דִכְנָעַן דִּי זְבַן אַבְרָהָם יָת חַקְלָא מִן עֶפְרֹן חִתָּאָה לְאַחֲסָנַת קְבוּרָא: לא תַּמָּן קְבָרוּ יָת אַבְרָהָם וְיָת שָׂרָה אִתְּתֵהּ תַּמָּן קְבָרוּ יָת יִצְחָק וְיָת רִבְקָה אִתְּתֵהּ וְתַמָּן קְבָרִית יָת לֵאָה:

רש"י

י:ג). ואונקלוס תרגם על שלא הכהנים בקדשי המקדש: **(כח) וזאת אשר דבר להם אביהם ויברך אותם.** והלא יש מהם שלא ברכם אלא קנטרן. אלא כך פירושו. וזאת אשר דבר להם אביהם, מה שנאמר בענין. יכול שלא ברך לראובן שמעון ולוי, ת"ל ויברך אותם, כלם במשמע (פסיקתא רבתי ז (כח.); במ"ר יג:ח): **איש אשר כברכתו.** ברכה העתידה לבא על כל אחד ואחד: **ברך אתם.** לא היה לו לומר אלא איש אשר כברכתו ברך אותו, מה ת"ל ברך אותם. לפי שנתן ליהודה גבורת ארי ולבנימין חטיפתו של זאב ולנפתלי קלותה של אילה, יכול שלא כללן כלם בכל הברכות, ת"ל ברך אותם (תנחומא טז): **(כט) נאסף אל עמי.** על שם שמכניסין הנפשות אל מקום גניזתן (עי' שבת קנב:). שיש אסיפה בלשון עברי שהיא ל' הכנסה, כגון ואין איש מאסף אותם הביתה (שופטים יט:טו) ואספתו אל תוך ביתך (דברים כב:ב) באספכם את תבואת הארץ (ויקרא כג:לט) הכנסתם לבית מפני הגשמים, באספך את מעשיך (שמות כג:טז), וכל אסיפה האמורה במיתה אף היא לשון הכנסה: **אל אבתי.** עם אבותי:

28. שְׁנֵים עָשָׂר — *Twelve.* The Torah reiterates the point made in 35:22, that there were twelve tribes — even though the tribe of Joseph had been divided into two tribes. The connotation is not that the twelve full-fledged tribes are only those mentioned in Jacob's blessings, in which Manasseh and Ephraim are not counted separately. Rather, there were always twelve tribes; if Levi was reckoned as one of them, Manasseh and Ephraim were combined and listed as the tribe of Joseph. If Levi was omitted, Manasseh and Ephraim were reckoned as two tribes. Accordingly, on the breastplate of the Kohen Gadol and in the blessings that would be pronounced at Mount Gerizim and Mount Ebal when the nation entered the Land (see *Deuteronomy* 18:1 ff.), the offspring of Joseph would be counted as one tribe. However, in the division of the Land and in the twelve tribal encampments in the Wilderness, Manasseh and Ephraim were counted as separate tribes. In both of those cases, Levi was omitted, because as the special servants of God the Levites encamped around the Tabernacle and received no territory in *Eretz Yisrael* (except for forty-eight towns as living quarters).

29-32. Jacob's final request. Although Joseph had already sworn to bury Jacob in the Cave of Machpelah, Jacob now imposed this duty upon the rest of his sons as well, because he feared that Pharaoh might forbid Joseph to leave the country, but would be amenable to allowing the others to go. Regarding Joseph, Jacob's apprehension was justified, because Joseph felt that he needed Pharaoh's courtiers to intercede for him, and Pharaoh agreed to let him go only, or primarily, because Joseph had taken an oath to do so [see 50:4-6]. Furthermore, Jacob emphasized the importance of burial in the cave by stating that the Patriarchs and Matriarchs had been buried there (*Ramban*).

30. According to the commentaries, Jacob described the cave in great detail because he was afraid that during their seventeen years of absence from *Eretz Yisrael*, his sons might have forgotten where it was, or he feared that the area had been seized by one of the local people. Also, he reiterated that Abraham had *bought* the site, not merely occupied it on his own.

לב מִקְנֵה הַשָּׂדֶה וְהַמְּעָרָה אֲשֶׁר־בּוֹ מֵאֵת בְּנֵי־

‹the Sons ‹was from ‹within it ‹which is ‹ and the cave ‹ of the field ‹ Purchase 32

חֵת: לג וַיְכַל יַעֲקֹב לְצַוֹּת אֶת־בָּנָיו וַיֶּאֱסֹף רַגְלָיו

‹ his feet ‹ and he gathered ‹ his sons, ‹ instructing ‹ Then Jacob finished 33 «of Heth.

אֶל־הַמִּטָּה וַיִּגְוַע וַיֵּאָסֶף אֶל־עַמָּיו: [נ] א וַיִּפֹּל

« Then he fell, 1 50 « his people. ‹ to ‹ and was gathered ‹ he expired « the bed; ‹ into

יוֹסֵף עַל־פְּנֵי אָבִיו וַיֵּבְךְּ עָלָיו וַיִּשַּׁק־לוֹ: ב וַיְצַו יוֹסֵף אֶת־עֲבָדָיו

‹ his servants, ‹ Joseph ordered 2 « him. ‹ and he kissed ‹ over him ‹ he wept « of his father; ‹ the face ‹ upon ‹ Joseph did,

אֶת־הָרֹפְאִים לַחֲנֹט אֶת־אָבִיו וַיַּחַנְטוּ הָרֹפְאִים אֶת־יִשְׂרָאֵל: ג וַיִּמְלְאוּ־

‹ There were completed 3 « Israel. ‹ so the physicians embalmed « his father; ‹ to embalm ‹ the physicians,

לוֹ אַרְבָּעִים יוֹם כִּי כֵּן יִמְלְאוּ יְמֵי הַחֲנֻטִים וַיִּבְכּוּ אֹתוֹ מִצְרַיִם שִׁבְעִים

‹ for seventy ‹ Egypt did, « for him, ‹ and they cried « of embalming; ‹ the days ‹ are completed ‹ thus ‹ for « days, ‹ forty ‹ for him

לב וְזַבִּינֵי חַקְלָא וּמְעַרְתָּא דִּי בֵהּ מִן בְּנֵי חִתָּאָה: לג וְשֵׁיצִי יַעֲקֹב לְפַקָּדָא יָת בְּנוֹהִי וּכְנַשׁ רַגְלוֹהִי לְעַרְסָא וְאִתְנְגִיד וְאִתְכְּנֵישׁ לְעַמֵּהּ: א וּנְפַל יוֹסֵף עַל אַפֵּי אֲבוּהִי וּבְכָא עֲלוֹהִי וּנְשַׁק לֵהּ: ב וּפַקֵּיד יוֹסֵף יָת עַבְדוֹהִי יָת אַסְוָתָא לְמֶחְנַט יָת אֲבוּהִי וַחֲנַטוּ אַסְוָתָא יָת יִשְׂרָאֵל: ג וּשְׁלִימוּ לֵהּ אַרְבְּעִין יוֹמִין אֲרֵי כֵּן שַׁלְמִין יוֹמֵי חֲנִטַיָּא וּבְכוֹ יָתֵהּ מִצְרָאֵי שַׁבְעִין

רש"י

(לג) ויאסף רגליו. הכניס רגליו: ויגוע ויאסף. ומיתה לא נאמרה בו, ואמרו רז"ל יעקב אבינו לא מת (תענית ה:): (ב) לחנט את אביו. ענין מרקחת בשמים הוא (תרגום יונתן): (ג) וימלאו לו. השלימו לו ימי חניטתו עד שמלאו לו ארבעים יום: ויבכו אותו מצרים שבעים יום. ארבעים לחניטה ושלשים לבכיה, לפי שבאה להם

33. וַיְכַל יַעֲקֹב — *Then Jacob finished.* Jacob lived until he had finished whatever he had to do in this world. His final task was to charge his sons, and until he did so, his soul did not leave him.

◆§ "Our father Jacob did not die" (*Taanis* 5b).

R' Yochanan maintains that Jacob did not die, even though the Torah relates below that he was mourned, embalmed, and buried. He cites the verse, *"Do not fear, O Jacob, My servant," said HASHEM, "and do not be dismayed, O Israel; for I will save you from afar and your descendants from captivity"* (*Jeremiah* 30:10). Thus, the prophet equates Jacob with his descendants; this implies that just as his descendants live on, so does he. *Tosafos* there notes also that the Torah does not say explicitly that he died, as it does of the passing of Abraham and Isaac. Most commentators understand this statement to imply that Jacob lives on spiritually because his offspring maintain his heritage.

Resisei Laylah comments that Jacob had so perfected his body that it was no contradiction to his soul. Death is a wrenching, painful concept only because — and to the extent that — it involves the soul's removal from a material existence that it has come to crave. The more materially lustful a person is, the less he can bear to part from this life to the holier one awaiting him. Conversely, the more spiritual his earthly life has become, the less he is encumbered by his body's animal demands and instincts. Jacob had so perfected himself that leaving this life meant no more to him than removing a coat means to us. His soul simply discarded its earthly raiment — his body — and continued essentially unchanged. In the deepest sense, therefore, death did not exist for him — so he did not die in the conventional sense.

50.

1-3. Jacob is mourned by all Egypt.

1. וַיִּפֹּל יוֹסֵף עַל־פְּנֵי אָבִיו — *Then he fell, Joseph did, upon the face of his father.* Although the other brothers were surely as aggrieved as Joseph, only he is mentioned because his presence in Jacob's final moments was a fulfillment of God's promise [46:4] that *Joseph shall place his hand on your eyes* (*Sechel Tov*). It may also be that Joseph was nearest to Jacob at the time, listening to the final whispered instructions and Divine secrets that were not known to his brothers (*Haamek Davar*).

2. לַחֲנֹט אֶת־אָבִיו — *To embalm his father.* Embalming was an Egyptian custom based on the teachings of the nation's idolatrous beliefs. Under Torah law, however, it is strictly forbidden. The Torah requires that the body be permitted to decompose naturally, as quickly as possible and without impediment. The soul rises to God, but its physical habitat, which had been taken from the earth, returns to its source, as God told Adam, *For dust you are, and to dust shall you return* (3:19).

That Joseph had Jacob's body embalmed was surely not for compliance with the pagan rite of Egypt. Rather, he wished to show respect to his father by preventing decay in view of the very long delay before burial, since the Egyptians observed a long period of mourning (v. 3) and then there was a long journey to Canaan, in a warm climate.

Or HaChaim, however, comments that since the body of a

יוֹם: ד וַיַּעַבְרוּ יְמֵי בְכִיתוֹ וַיְדַבֵּר יוֹסֵף אֶל־בֵּית

‹ the household ‹ to ‹ Joseph spoke ‹‹ of weeping for him — ‹ — the days ‹‹ [When] they passed **4** ‹‹ days.

פַּרְעֹה לֵאמֹר אִם־נָא מָצָאתִי חֵן בְּעֵינֵיכֶם

‹‹ in your eyes, ‹ favor ‹ I have found ‹ please, ‹ If, ‹‹ saying, ‹ of Pharaoh,

דַּבְּרוּ־נָא בְּאָזְנֵי פַרְעֹה לֵאמֹר: ה אָבִי הִשְׁבִּיעַנִי

‹ had made me swear, ‹ My father **5** *‹‹ saying: ‹ of Pharaoh, ‹ in the ears ‹ now ‹ speak*

לֵאמֹר הִנֵּה אָנֹכִי מֵת בְּקִבְרִי אֲשֶׁר כָּרִיתִי לִי

‹ for myself ‹ I have dug ‹ which ‹ in my grave, ‹‹ about to die; ‹ I am ‹ 'Indeed, ‹ saying,

בְּאֶרֶץ כְּנַעַן שָׁמָּה תִּקְבְּרֵנִי וְעַתָּה אֶעֱלֶה־נָּא וְאֶקְבְּרָה אֶת־אָבִי

‹ my father; ‹ and I will bury ‹ please, ‹ I will go up, ‹ Now, ‹‹ you are to bury me.' ‹ — there ‹‹ of Canaan ‹ in the land

וְאָשׁוּבָה: ו וַיֹּאמֶר פַּרְעֹה עֲלֵה וּקְבֹר אֶת־אָבִיךָ כַּאֲשֶׁר הִשְׁבִּיעֶךָ:

‹‹ he made you swear. ‹ as ‹ your father ‹ and bury ‹ Go up ‹‹ And Pharaoh said, **6** *‹‹ then I will return.*

ז וַיַּעַל יוֹסֵף לִקְבֹּר אֶת־אָבִיו וַיַּעֲלוּ אִתּוֹ כָּל־עַבְדֵי פַרְעֹה זִקְנֵי בֵיתוֹ

‹‹ of his household, ‹ the elders ‹‹ of Pharaoh, ‹ the servants ‹ — all ‹‹ with him ‹ and they went up ‹ his father, ‹ to bury ‹ So Joseph went up 7

וְכֹל זִקְנֵי אֶרֶץ־מִצְרָיִם: ח וְכֹל בֵּית יוֹסֵף וְאֶחָיו וּבֵית אָבִיו רַק טַפָּם

‹ their young children, ‹ only ‹‹ of his father; ‹ and the household ‹ and his brothers, ‹‹ of Joseph ‹ of the household ‹ and all **8** ‹‹ of Egypt, ‹ of the land ‹ the elders ‹ and all

יוֹמִין: ד וַעֲבָרוּ יוֹמֵי בְכִיתֵהּ וּמַלִּיל יוֹסֵף עִם בֵּית פַּרְעֹה לְמֵימָר אִם כְּעַן אַשְׁכָּחִית רַחֲמִין בְּעֵינֵיכוֹן מַלִּילוּ כְעַן קֳדָם פַּרְעֹה לְמֵימָר: ה אַבָּא קַיִּים עָלַי לְמֵימַר הָא אֲנָא מָיֵית בְּקִבְרִי דִּי אַתְקֵינִית לִי בְּאַרְעָא דִכְנַעַן תַּמָּן תִּקְבְּרִנַּנִי וּכְעַן אֶסַּק כְּעַן וְאֶקְבַּר יָת אַבָּא וְאֵיתוּב: ו וַאֲמַר פַּרְעֹה סַק וּקְבוֹר יָת אֲבוּךְ כְּמָא דִי קַיִּים עֲלָךְ: ז וּסְלֵיק יוֹסֵף לְמִקְבַּר יָת אֲבוּהִי וּסְלִיקוּ עִמֵּהּ כָּל עַבְדֵי פַרְעֹה סָבֵי בֵיתֵהּ וְכֹל סָבֵי אַרְעָא דְמִצְרָיִם: ח וְכֹל בֵּית יוֹסֵף וַאֲחוֹהִי וּבֵית אֲבוּהִי לְחוֹד טַפְלְהוֹן

רש"י

ברכה לרגלו, שכלה הרעב והיו מי נילוס מתברכין (עי' רש"י לעיל מז:י, יט) (ה) **אשר כריתי לי.** כפשוטו כמו כי יכרה איש (שמות כא:לג; תרגום יונתן). ומדרשו עוד מתישב על הלשון, כמו אשר קניתי. אמר ר' עקיבא כשהלכתי לכרכי הים היו קורין למכירה כירה (ר"ה השנה כו.). ועוד מדרשו ל' כרי, דגור, שנטל יעקב כל כסף וזהב שהביא מבית לבן ועשה אותו כרי ואמר לעשו טול זה בשביל חלקך במערה (שמות רבה לא:יז): (ו) **כאשר השביעך.** ואם לא בשביל השבועה לא הייתי מניחך. אבל ירא לומר עבור על השבועה, שלא יאמר א"כ אעבור על שבועה שנשבעתי לך שלא אגלה על לשון הקודש שאני מכיר עודף על שבעים לשון ואתה אינך מכיר בו, כדאיתא במסכת סוטה (לו:):

completely righteous person never putrefies, Joseph was afraid that the Egyptians, upon noting this phenomenon, would venerate Jacob's body as a god and turn it into an idol. In order to spare his father that awful indignity, Joseph had the body embalmed, so that the Egyptians would attribute its preservation to their own skill.

4-6. Permission for burial. As the ruler of the land, Joseph could not leave the country for an extended period without his absence affecting the administration of government. Furthermore, if it became apparent that Jacob and his family still considered Canaan to be their true home, Pharaoh might well suspect that Joseph would remain there and not return to Egypt. [To allay this suspicion, Joseph promised Pharaoh that he would return without delay (v. 5).] It was necessary, therefore, for Joseph to secure Pharaoh's permission to leave (*Ramban*).

As indicated by verse 4, Joseph did not go directly to Pharaoh; instead, he had members of the royal household make the initial approach. The Midrash comments that Joseph expected opposition from Pharaoh's courtiers, so he acted according to the proverb, "Win the accuser to your cause if you want him not to act against you." First he spoke to the queen's lady-in-waiting, who influenced her mistress, who intervened with Pharaoh.

6. כַּאֲשֶׁר הִשְׁבִּיעֶךָ — *As he made you swear.* Pharaoh's implication was clear: Had Joseph not sworn to do so, he would not have been permitted to go (*Rashi*).

7-13. The burial procession.

7. וַיַּעַל יוֹסֵף — *So Joseph went up.* Although all the brothers went, Joseph is singled out because he personally attended to his father's burial even though he was the greatest man of the time. In reward for this — measure for measure — Moses, the greatest of all, personally attended to Joseph's remains when Israel left Egypt (*Sotah* 9b).

Joseph was accompanied by the leading citizens of Egypt,

וְצֹאנָם וּבְקָרָם עָזְבוּ בְּאֶרֶץ גֹּשֶׁן: ט וַיַּעַל עִמּוֹ גַּם־
‹ also ‹ And with him went up 9 « of Goshen. ‹ in the land ‹ did they leave ‹ and their cattle ‹ their flocks,

רֶכֶב גַּם־פָּרָשִׁים וַיְהִי הַמַּחֲנֶה כָּבֵד מְאֹד: י וַיָּבֹאוּ
‹ They came 10 « to the extreme. ‹ imposing ‹ and the assemblage was « horsemen; ‹ and also ‹ chariots

עַד־גֹּרֶן הָאָטָד אֲשֶׁר בְּעֵבֶר הַיַּרְדֵּן וַיִּסְפְּדוּ־שָׁם
‹ there ‹ and they eulogized « of the Jordan, ‹ on the other side ‹ which is ‹ Goren HaAtad, ‹ to

מִסְפֵּד גָּדוֹל וְכָבֵד מְאֹד וַיַּעַשׂ לְאָבִיו אֵבֶל שִׁבְעַת
‹ of seven ‹ a mourning period ‹ for his father ‹ and he observed « to the extreme; ‹ and imposing ‹ great ‹ a eulogy,

יָמִים: יא וַיַּרְא יוֹשֵׁב הָאָרֶץ הַכְּנַעֲנִי אֶת־הָאֵבֶל בְּגֹרֶן הָאָטָד וַיֹּאמְרוּ
« they said, ‹ in Goren HaAtad, ‹ the mourning « the Canaanites, ‹ of the land, ‹ did the inhabitants « When they saw, 11 « days.

אֵבֶל־כָּבֵד זֶה לְמִצְרָיִם עַל־כֵּן קָרָא שְׁמָהּ אָבֵל מִצְרַיִם אֲשֶׁר בְּעֵבֶר
‹ on the other side ‹ which is « Avel Mizraim, ‹ its name ‹ he called ‹ Therefore, « *for Egypt.* ‹ *is this* ‹ *that is imposing* ‹ *A mourning*

הַיַּרְדֵּן: יב וַיַּעֲשׂוּ בָנָיו לוֹ כֵּן כַּאֲשֶׁר צִוָּם: יג וַיִּשְׂאוּ אֹתוֹ בָנָיו אַרְצָה
‹ to the land ‹ did his sons, « him, ‹ They carried 13 « he had instructed them. ‹ as ‹ exactly ‹ for him ‹ His sons did 12 « of the Jordan.

וְעָנְהוֹן וְתוֹרֵיהוֹן שְׁבָקוּ בְּאַרְעָא דְגֹשֶׁן: ט וּסְלִיקוּ עִמֵּהּ אַף רְתִכִּין אַף פָּרָשִׁין וַהֲוָה מַשְׁרִיתָא סַגִּי לַחֲדָא: י וַאֲתוֹ עַד בֵּית אִדְרֵי דְאָטָד דִּי בְּעִבְרָא דְיַרְדְּנָא וּסְפָדוּ תַּמָּן מִסְפֵּד רַב וְתַקִּיף לַחֲדָא וַעֲבַד לַאֲבוּהִי אֶבְלָא שִׁבְעַת יוֹמִין: יא וַחֲזָא יָתֵב אַרְעָא כְּנַעֲנָאָה יָת אֶבְלָא בְּבֵית אִדְרֵי דְאָטָד וַאֲמָרוּ אָבֵל תַּקִּיף דֵּין לְמִצְרָיִם עַל כֵּן קְרָא שְׁמַהּ אָבֵל מִצְרַיִם דִּי בְּעִבְרָא דְיַרְדְּנָא: יב וַעֲבָדוּ בְנוֹהִי לֵהּ כֵּן כְּמָא דִי פַקֵּדנוּן: יג וּנְטָלוּ יָתֵהּ בְּנוֹהִי לְאַרְעָא

רש"י

(י) **גרן האטד.** מוקף אטדין היה. ורבותינו דרשו על שם המאורע, שבאו כל מלכי כנען ונשיאי ישמעאל למלחמה, וכיון שראו כתרו של יוסף תלוי בארונו של יעקב עמדו כלן ותלו בו כתריהם והקיפוהו כתרים כגרן המוקף סייג של קוצים (סוטה יג.): (יב) **כאשר צום.** מהו אשר צום: (יג) **וישאו אתו בניו.** ולא בני בניו. שכך צום, אל ישאו

who came both in his honor and as a token of respect for Jacob, who was universally admired as a wise and great man, and as the one whose presence in Egypt had caused the famine to end (*Sforno*).

8. רַק טַפָּם . . . עָזְבוּ — *Only their young children . . . did they leave.* According to many commentators, the first subtle aspects of the Egyptian bondage began as soon as Jacob died. The brothers had wanted to take everyone along, but Pharaoh would not permit it, as if to show them that they were not free agents. This is why Joseph had to reassure his brothers (v. 24) that God would remember them and bring them out of Egypt (*Malbim*).

[This may have served as a precedent, for when Moses asked Pharaoh to permit the Jews to leave for three days to worship God, Pharaoh insisted that the children remain.]

10. גֹּרֶן הָאָטָד — *Goren HaAtad.* Literally, *the field,* or *threshing floor, of thorns*, implying that the field was surrounded by thorns. The Sages (*Sotah* 13a), however, give another derivation of the name. The kings of Canaan and the princes of Ishmael massed to prevent the burial, but when they saw Joseph's crown hanging on Jacob's coffin, they relented and hung their own crowns on the coffin in tribute to the Patriarch. With a total of thirty-six crowns hanging from it, the coffin resembled a field surrounded by thorns, and the area was named for that event (*Rashi*).

מִסְפֵּד גָּדוֹל וְכָבֵד מְאֹד — *A eulogy that was great and imposing.* Never before had there been such an imposing eulogy (*Sechel Tov*). It was *great* because there were many hours of eulogies, and it was *imposing* because the eulogies penetrated the inner recesses of the heart (*Haamek Davar*).

אֵבֶל שִׁבְעַת יָמִים — *A mourning period of seven days,* the seven-day mourning period [*shivah*] that begins immediately after burial (*Ibn Ezra*).

11. אֵבֶל־כָּבֵד זֶה לְמִצְרָיִם — *"A mourning that is imposing is this for Egypt."* This was an instance of people prophesying without realizing the import of their words. It was indeed a cause of mourning for Egypt that Jacob was no longer with them, for his presence in their land had brought prosperity and blessing. Had they continued to revere his memory by honoring his offspring, they would have continued to benefit, but instead, they began to despise the Jewish people and eventually enslaved them. As a result, Egypt was to be punished with plagues that destroyed it as a great nation — truly a cause of mourning (*Or HaTorah*).

13. וַיִּשְׂאוּ אֹתוֹ בָּנָיו — *They carried him, did his sons.* After the

כְּנַעַן וַיִּקְבְּרוּ אֹתוֹ בִּמְעָרַת שְׂדֵה הַמַּכְפֵּלָה אֲשֶׁר

< that < of Machpelah, < of the field < in the cave < him < and they buried < of Canaan

קָנָה אַבְרָהָם אֶת־הַשָּׂדֶה לַאֲחֻזַּת־קֶבֶר מֵאֵת עֶפְרֹן

< Ephron < from < for a burial site < as [land] legally possessed < the field < Abraham had bought

הַחִתִּי עַל־פְּנֵי מַמְרֵא: יד וַיָּשָׁב יוֹסֵף מִצְרַיְמָה הוּא

< —he, << to Egypt < Joseph returned **14** << Mamre. < facing << the Hittite,

וְאֶחָיו וְכָל־הָעֹלִים אִתּוֹ לִקְבֹּר אֶת־אָבִיו אַחֲרֵי קָבְרוֹ אֶת־אָבִיו:

<< his father. < he buried < after << his father — < to bury < with him < who had gone up < and all < and his brothers,

טו וַיִּרְאוּ אֲחֵי־יוֹסֵף כִּי־מֵת אֲבִיהֶם וַיֹּאמְרוּ לוּ יִשְׂטְמֵנוּ יוֹסֵף

< *Joseph will harbor hatred against us* < *Perhaps* << and they said, << their father had died, < that << of Joseph, < did the brothers << They saw, **15**

וְהָשֵׁב יָשִׁיב לָנוּ אֵת כָּל־הָרָעָה אֲשֶׁר גָּמַלְנוּ אֹתוֹ: טז וַיְצַוּוּ אֶל־יוֹסֵף

< Joseph < to [tell] < So they instructed **16** << *him.* < *we dealt* < *that* < *the evil* < *all* < *us* < *and then he will surely repay*

דִכְנַעַן וּקְבָרוּ יָתֵהּ בִּמְעָרַת חֲקַל כָּפֶלְתָּא דִּי זְבַן אַבְרָהָם יָת חַקְלָא לְאַחֲסָנַת קְבוּרָא מִן עֶפְרוֹן חִתָּאָה עַל אַפֵּי מַמְרֵא: יד וְתַב יוֹסֵף לְמִצְרַיִם הוּא וַאֲחוֹהִי וְכָל דִּסְלִיקוּ עִמֵּהּ לְמִקְבַּר יָת אֲבוּהִי בָּתַר דִּקְבַר יָת אֲבוּהִי: טו וַחֲזוֹ אֲחֵי יוֹסֵף אֲרֵי מִית אֲבוּהוֹן וַאֲמָרוּ דִּלְמָא יִטַּר לָנָא דְבָבוּ יוֹסֵף וַאֲתָבָא יָתֵיב לָנָא יָת כָּל בִּישְׁתָא דִּי גְמַלְנָא יָתֵהּ: טז וּפַקִּידוּ לְוַת יוֹסֵף

רש"י

מטתי לא איש מצרי ולא אחד מבניכם שהם מבנות כנען אלא אתם. וקבע להם מקום ג' למזרח וכן לארבע רוחות. וכסדרן למסע ומחנה של דגלים נקבעו כאן. לוי לא ישא, שהוא עתיד לשאת את הארון, ויוסף לא ישא, שהוא מלך, מנשה ואפרים יהיו תחתיהם, וזהו איש על דגלו באותות (במדבר ב:ב) באות שמסר להם אביהם לישא מטתו (תנחומא במדבר יב; ב"ר ק:ב): **(יד) הוא ואחיו וכל העולים אתו.** בחזרתן כאן הקדים אחיו למצרים העולים אתו, ובהליכתן הקדים מצרים לאחיו, שנאמר ויעלו אתו כל עבדי פרעה וגו' ואחר כך וכל בית יוסף ואחיו. אלא לפי שראו כבוד שעשו מלכי כנען, שתלו כתריהם בארונו של יעקב, נהגו בהם כבוד (סוטה שם): **(טו) ויראו אחי יוסף כי מת אביהם.** מהו ויראו, הכירו במיתתו אצל יוסף, שהיו רגילים לסעוד על שולחנו של יוסף והיה מקרבן בשביל כבוד אביו, ומשמת יעקב לא קרבן (תנחומא ישן שמות ב; ב"ר ק:ח): **לו ישטמנו.** שמא ישטמנו. לו מתחלק לענינים הרבה יש לו משמש בלשון בקשה ולשון הלואי, כגון לו יהיה כדברך (לעיל ל:לד) לו שמעני (שם כג:יג) ולו הואלנו (יהושע ז:ז) לו מתנו (במדבר יד:ב). ויש לו משמש בלשון אם ואולי, כגון לו חכמו (דברים לב:כט) לו הקשבת למצותי (ישעיה מח:יח) ולו אנכי שוקל על כפי (שמואל ב יח:יב). ויש לו משמש בלשון שמא, לו ישטמנו ואין לו עוד דומה במקרא, והוא לשון אולי כמו אולי לא תלך האשה אחרי (לעיל כד:לט) ל' שמא הוא. ויש אולי ל' בקשה, כגון אולי יראה ה' בעיני (שמואל ב טז:יב) אולי ה' אותי (יהושע יד:יב), הרי הוא כמו לו יהי כדברך (לעיל ל:לד). ויש אולי לשון אם, אולי יש חמשים צדיקים (לעיל יח:כד):

eulogies were over, his sons carried the coffin on their shoulders to the Cave of Machpelah (*Abarbanel*).

Jacob had assigned his sons to their respective positions around his bier, exactly as they would later encamp in the Wilderness around the Tabernacle (see *Numbers* Ch. 2). As in that instance, Levi did not participate. Nor did Joseph, for Ephraim and Menasseh took his place at the bier. Jacob said that Levi should not be a bearer because his offspring were destined to carry the Ark, and it was not proper for him to carry human remains. Nor should Joseph carry the bier, for it would be disrespectful for a ruler to do so (*Rashi*).

The Talmud relates that Esau contested Jacob's right to be interred in the cave, whereupon the fleet-footed Naphtali dashed all the way back to Egypt to bring the deed (as noted above, 49:21). When Chushim, the deaf son of Dan, realized what was happening, he became infuriated and shouted, "Shall my grandfather lie there in disgrace until Naphtali returns from Egypt!" Thereupon, Chushim took a club and struck Esau so hard that he killed him (*Sotah* 13a). According to *Pirkei d'Rabbi Eliezer* 36, the force of the blow decapitated Esau, and his head rolled into the cave, at Jacob's feet.

Since Esau studied Torah under Abraham and Isaac, he deserved some reward. But his study was only a mental exercise that never entered his bloodstream or his organs. He never took the Torah to heart, or used it to guide his actions. Thus, only his head could enter the cave for burial, but not his limbs and other organs *(R' Aharon Kotler)*.

15-21. Joseph reassures his brothers. Joseph's brothers *saw that their father was dead*, in the sense that it seemed to them that with Jacob's death, Joseph's attitude toward them had changed. While he used to invite the family to dine with him very often during Jacob's lifetime and received them all very warmly, he now stopped doing so. To them this meant that once Joseph no longer had to show deference to Jacob, he was revealing his lingering animosity toward them, and they feared that he would avenge himself against them for having sold him. They were wrong, however. His real reason for stopping the invitations was that Jacob used to insist that Joseph sit at the head of the table. Now, however, Joseph felt uncomfortable about taking precedence over Reuben and Judah. On the other hand,

לֵאמֹר אָבִיךָ צִוָּה לִפְנֵי מוֹתוֹ לֵאמֹר: יז כֹּה־
‹ 'Thus 17 « saying: ‹ his death, ‹ before ‹ instructed ‹ Your father « saying,

תֹאמְרוּ לְיוֹסֵף אָנָּא שָׂא נָא פֶּשַׁע אַחֶיךָ וְחַטָּאתָם
‹ and their sin ‹ of your brothers ‹ the flagrant offense ‹ please, ‹ forgive, ‹ "O please, « to Joseph: ‹ shall you say

כִּי־רָעָה גְמָלוּךָ וְעַתָּה שָׂא נָא לְפֶשַׁע עַבְדֵי אֱלֹהֵי
‹ of the God ‹ of the servants ‹ the flagrant offense ‹ please, ‹ forgive, ‹ so now, « they have dealt ‹ evil ‹ for you" ';

אָבִיךָ וַיֵּבְךְּ יוֹסֵף בְּדַבְּרָם אֵלָיו: יח וַיֵּלְכוּ גַּם־אֶחָיו
« — his brothers also — « They went 18 « to him. ‹ when they spoke ‹ And Joseph wept « of your father.

וַיִּפְּלוּ לְפָנָיו וַיֹּאמְרוּ הִנֶּנּוּ לְךָ לַעֲבָדִים: יט וַיֹּאמֶר אֲלֵהֶם יוֹסֵף אַל־
‹ Do not « did Joseph, ‹ to them ‹ But say 19 « as slaves. ‹ [ready to be] to you ‹ Here we are « and they said, ‹ before him ‹ and fell down

תִּירָאוּ כִּי הֲתַחַת אֱלֹהִים אָנִי: כ וְאַתֶּם חֲשַׁבְתֶּם עָלַי רָעָה אֱלֹהִים
‹ God « harm, ‹ me ‹ intended ‹ Although you 20 « am I? ‹ of God ‹ is it that in the place ‹ for « fear,

חֲשָׁבָהּ לְטֹבָה לְמַעַן עֲשֹׂה כַּיּוֹם הַזֶּה לְהַחֲיֹת עַם־רָב: שביעי כא וְעַתָּה
‹ So now, 21 « that is numerous. ‹ a people ‹ keeping alive « — it is as [clear as] this day — ‹ to accomplish ‹ in order « for good: ‹ intended it

לְמֵימָר אָבוּךְ פַּקֵּד קֳדָם מוֹתֵהּ לְמֵימָר: יז כְּדֵין תֵּימְרוּן לְיוֹסֵף בְּבָעוּ שְׁבוֹק כְּעַן חוֹבָא אַחָיךְ וְחֶטָאֲהוֹן אֲרֵי בִישָׁא גְמָלוּךְ וּכְעַן שְׁבוֹק כְּעַן לְחוֹבָא עַבְדֵי אֱלָהָא דְאָבוּךְ וּבְכָא יוֹסֵף בְּמַלָּלוּתְהוֹן עִמֵּהּ: יח וַאֲזָלוּ אַף אֲחוֹהִי וּנְפָלוּ קֳדָמוֹהִי וַאֲמָרוּ הָא אֲנַחְנָא לָךְ לְעַבְדִין: יט וַאֲמַר לְהוֹן יוֹסֵף לָא תִדַּחֲלוּן אֲרֵי דַחֲלָא דַייָ אֲנָא: כ וְאַתּוּן חֲשַׁבְתּוּן עֲלַי בִּישָׁא מִן קֳדָם יְיָ אִתְחַשְׁבָא לְטָבָא בְּדִיל לְמֶעְבַּד כְּיוֹמָא הָדֵין לְקַיָּמָא עַם סַגִּי: כא וּכְעַן

רש"י

(טז) **ויצוו אל יוסף.** כמו ויצום אל בני ישראל (שמות ו:יג) צוה למשה ולאהרן להיות שלוחים אל בני ישראל. אף זה ויצוו אל שלוחם להיות שליח אל יוסף לומר לו כן. ואת מי צוו, את בני בלהה שהיו רגילין אצלו (עי' תנחומא ישן שמות ב), שנאמר והוא נער את בני בלהה (לעיל לז:ב): **אביך צוה.** שינו בדבר מפני השלום, כי לא צוה יעקב כן שלא נחשד יוסף בעיניו (יבמות סה:; תנחומא תולדות א; ב"ר ק:ח): (יז) **שא נא לפשע עבדי אלהי אביך.** אם אביך מת אלהיו קיים (תנחומא ישן שמות ב) והם עבדיו: (יח) **וילכו גם אחיו.** מוסף על השליחות: (יט) **כי התחת אלהים אני.** שמא במקומו אני, בתמיה, אם הייתי רוצה להרע לכם כלום אני יכול, והלא אתם כולכם חשבתם עלי רעה והקב"ה חשבה לטובה, והיאך אני לבדי יכול להרע לכם (ב"ר שם ט):

it would be a violation of protocol for the viceroy to relinquish his position — so he stopped issuing the invitation (*Tanchuma*). Alternatively, Joseph knew that, with Jacob gone, there was a serious danger that Egyptian persecution could begin at any time, and that it could be provoked if the Egyptians suspected that the Jews were seeking power and influence. To prevent the Egyptians from harboring such suspicions, Joseph stopped inviting them to his palace (*Gur Aryeh*).

R' Hirsch notes that without parents as a focal point of the family, it is unfortunately natural for siblings to meet less often and even to drift apart. That happened after Jacob died, but the brothers interpreted it as portending something sinister.

16. וַיְצַוּוּ אֶל־יוֹסֵף — *So they instructed [to tell] to Joseph*. Fearful of Joseph's reaction, they dispatched the sons of Bilhah — with whom he had always been very friendly — to tell him that Jacob had given instructions regarding such a situation before he died. This was not true, for Jacob knew that Joseph would not seek vengeance, but, as the Sages state (*Yevamos* 65b), one may alter the truth for the sake of peace. After the emissaries delivered their message, the rest of the brothers came to him (v. 18) and pleaded for mercy (*Rashi*).

17. וְחַטָּאתָם . . . פֶּשַׁע — *The flagrant offense . . . and their sin.* The first term implies an intentional, very serious transgression, while the second one implies an unintentional sin. What the brothers did was both. It was intentional. On the other hand, they believed that they were justified because they sincerely felt endangered by what they perceived to be Joseph's "attitude" and ambitions (*Akeidah*).

19-20. Joseph reassured his brothers, saying that he could not harm them even if he wanted to. If God would not permit them — a large group of righteous people — to harm him, how could he as an individual succeed in harming them? (*Rashi*). Am I a judge with the power to take God's place in analyzing whether His decree was proper and punish those who carried it out? You were nothing more than His agents! You erred in thinking that I was your enemy, but God used your actions to bring about the ultimate good (*Sforno*).

אַל־תִּירָאוּ אָנֹכִי אֲכַלְכֵּל אֶתְכֶם וְאֶת־טַפְּכֶם
<< and your young ones. < you < will sustain < — I << fear < do not

וַיְנַחֵם אוֹתָם וַיְדַבֵּר עַל־לִבָּם: כב וַיֵּשֶׁב יוֹסֵף
< Joseph dwelt 22 << their heart. < to < and spoke < them < Thus he comforted

בְּמִצְרַיִם הוּא וּבֵית אָבִיו וַיְחִי יוֹסֵף מֵאָה וָעֶשֶׂר
< and ten < one hundred < and Joseph lived << of his father — < and the household < — he << in Egypt

שָׁנִים: מפטיר כג וַיַּרְא יוֹסֵף לְאֶפְרַיִם בְּנֵי שִׁלֵּשִׁים גַּם
< also << of the third [generation]; < children < through Ephraim < Joseph saw 23 << years.

לָא תִדַּחֲלוּן אֲנָא אֵזוּן יָתְכוֹן וְיָת
טַפְלְכוֹן וְנַחֵם יָתְהוֹן וּמַלֵּל תַּנְחוּמִין
עַל לִבְּהוֹן: כב וִיתֵיב יוֹסֵף בְּמִצְרַיִם
הוּא וּבֵית אֲבוּהִי וַחֲיָא יוֹסֵף מְאָה
וַעֲסַר שְׁנִין: כג וַחֲזָא יוֹסֵף לְאֶפְרַיִם
בְּנִין תְּלִיתָאִין אַף בְּנֵי מָכִיר בַּר
מְנַשֶּׁה אִתְיְלִידוּ וְרַבִּי יוֹסֵף: כד וַאֲמַר
יוֹסֵף לַאֲחוֹהִי אֲנָא מָאִית וַייָ מִדְכַּר
דְּכִיר יָתְכוֹן וְיַסִּיק יָתְכוֹן מִן אַרְעָא
הָדָא לְאַרְעָא דִּי קַיִּים לְאַבְרָהָם
לְיִצְחָק וּלְיַעֲקֹב: כה וְאוֹמֵי יוֹסֵף

בְּנֵי מָכִיר בֶּן־מְנַשֶּׁה יֻלְּדוּ עַל־בִּרְכֵּי יוֹסֵף: כד וַיֹּאמֶר יוֹסֵף אֶל־אֶחָיו
<< his brothers, < to < Joseph said 24 << of Joseph. < the knees < on < were born < of Manasseh < son < of Machir < the sons

אָנֹכִי מֵת וֵאלֹהִים פָּקֹד יִפְקֹד אֶתְכֶם וְהֶעֱלָה אֶתְכֶם מִן־הָאָרֶץ הַזֹּאת
< of this land < out < and bring you up < you < will surely remember < but God << about to die, < I am

אֶל־הָאָרֶץ אֲשֶׁר נִשְׁבַּע לְאַבְרָהָם לְיִצְחָק וּלְיַעֲקֹב: כה וַיַּשְׁבַּע יוֹסֵף
<< Then Joseph made them swear 25 << and to Jacob. < to Isaac, < to Abraham, < He swore < that < the land < to

רש"י

(כא) וידבר על לבם. דברים המתקבלים על הלב. עד שלא ירדתם לכאן היו מרננים עלי שאני עבד ועל ידיכם נודע שאני בן חורין, ואני הורג אתכם, מה הבריות אומרות, כת של בחורים ראה ונשתבח בהם ואמר אחי הם ולבסוף הרג אותם, יש לך אח שהורג את אחיו (תנחומא ישן שם; ב"ר שם). ד"א, עשרה נרות לא יכלו לכבות נר אחד כו' (מגילה טז:): **(כג) על ברכי יוסף.** כתרגומו, גדלן בין ברכיו:

23. בְּנֵי שִׁלֵּשִׁים — *Children of the third generation.* Although Joseph was the first of the brothers to die, he lived to see Ephraim's children, grandchildren, and great-grandchildren.

The point has been made that Machir's sons were contemporaries of Moses (*Numbers* 26:29), and they were among the fourth generation that God had promised to liberate from Egypt (15:16). When they were children, they had seen Joseph, the greatest of his generation, and they would live to enter *Eretz Yisrael*.

24. Signs of the redemption. Joseph told his brothers a secret sign of the redemption that Jacob had confided to him in the last moments of his life. Some day — Jacob was prevented from saying when — a redeemer would come to the enslaved Jews in Egypt. He would tell them that God had declared פָּקֹד פָּקַדְתִּי, *I have indeed remembered you (Exodus* 3:16), just as Joseph now promised his brothers, וֵאלֹהִים פָּקֹד יִפְקֹד אֶתְכֶם, *But God will surely remember you (Mizrachi).* The implication of the term is that after a long period of time during which it seemed as if God had "forgotten" His people, He would manifest His Presence, as if He had "remembered" them once more. This "password" was transmitted to the leaders of the people, and when Moses came and proclaimed those words, they knew that he was truly speaking in God's Name. On the surface, one might wonder why some charlatan could not have come and used the same pre-ordained words, but it is the very nature of prophecy that it is above logic. The fact is that no one but Moses ever used this term, and when he came and uttered the words, the nation knew and believed.

וְהֶעֱלָה אֶתְכֶם — *And bring you up.* Joseph meant this quite literally; not only the generations of the future but the remains of all his brothers — *you* — would be brought from Egypt to the Land (*Sechel Tov*).

25. Joseph knew that his brothers and children would not have the power to bury him in *Eretz Yisrael* — Pharaoh and his people would not have permitted it — but he exacted this pledge that when the time came for the nation to leave the land of their servitude, they should take his remains with them. *Meshech Chochmah* suggests that he did not impose this pledge on his own children because he knew that a large part of the Manasseh half of his tribe would settle on the eastern side of the Jordan, not in *Eretz Yisrael* proper, and that is not where he wanted to be buried.

Ultimately, Joseph was buried in Shechem, either because Jacob gave him that city as a personal gift (see 48:22), or because his brother tribes wanted to make amends for their mistreatment of him in that very place, for it was in Shechem that they sold him (*Sotah* 13b).

אֶת־בְּנֵי יִשְׂרָאֵל לֵאמֹר פָּקֹד יִפְקֹד אֱלֹהִים
‹ — the children ‹ of Israel — « saying, « God will surely remember ‹
אֶתְכֶם וְהַעֲלִתֶם אֶת־עַצְמֹתַי מִזֶּה: כו וַיָּמָת יוֹסֵף
you, « then you must bring up ‹ my bones ‹ from this [place]. « 26 Joseph died ‹

בֶּן־מֵאָה וָעֶשֶׂר שָׁנִים וַיַּחַנְטוּ אֹתוֹ וַיִּישֶׂם בָּאָרוֹן בְּמִצְרָיִם:
at the age of ‹ one hundred ‹ and ten ‹ years; « they embalmed ‹ him ‹ and he was placed ‹ in a coffin ‹ in Egypt. «

יָת בְּנֵי יִשְׂרָאֵל לְמֵימַר מִדְכַּר דְּכִיר יְיָ יָתְכוֹן וְתַסְּקוּן יָת גַּרְמַי מִכָּא: כו וּמִית יוֹסֵף בַּר מְאָה וַעֲסַר שְׁנִין וַחֲנַטוּ יָתֵהּ וְשָׂמוּהִי בְּאָרוֹנָא בְּמִצְרָיִם:

It is customary for the congregation followed by the reader to proclaim:

חֲזַק! חֲזַק! וְנִתְחַזֵּק!

Be strong! ‹ Be strong! ‹ And may we be strengthened! «

פ״ה פסוקים. פ״ה אל פ״ה סימן. סכום פסוקי דספר בראשית אלף וחמש מאות ושלשים וארבעה. א״ך לד׳ סימן.

THE HAFTARAH FOR VAYECHI APPEARS ON PAGE 348.

פ״ה פסוקים. פ״ה אל פ״ה סימן — This Masoretic note means: There are 85 verses in the *Sidrah,* corresponding to the mnemonic פֶּ״ה אֶל פֶּ״ה [literally, *mouth to mouth* (the word פֶּה equals 85)].

This alludes to the theme of our *Sidrah,* in which Jacob spoke to his children, relating to them the blessings that would form the core of their mission for all time. In the mnemonic of our *Sidrah, R' David Feinstein,* who interprets these Masoretic notes, finds support for his contention that they are meant not only as convenient memory devices but to encapsulate the message of the *Sidrah.* If nothing were intended except a reminder that there are 85 verses, it would have been sufficient to use only the word פֶּה, *mouth,* or פֹּה, *here* — but this would tell us nothing about the *sidrah* itself, therefore it was expanded to פֶּה אֶל פֶּה, *mouth to mouth.*

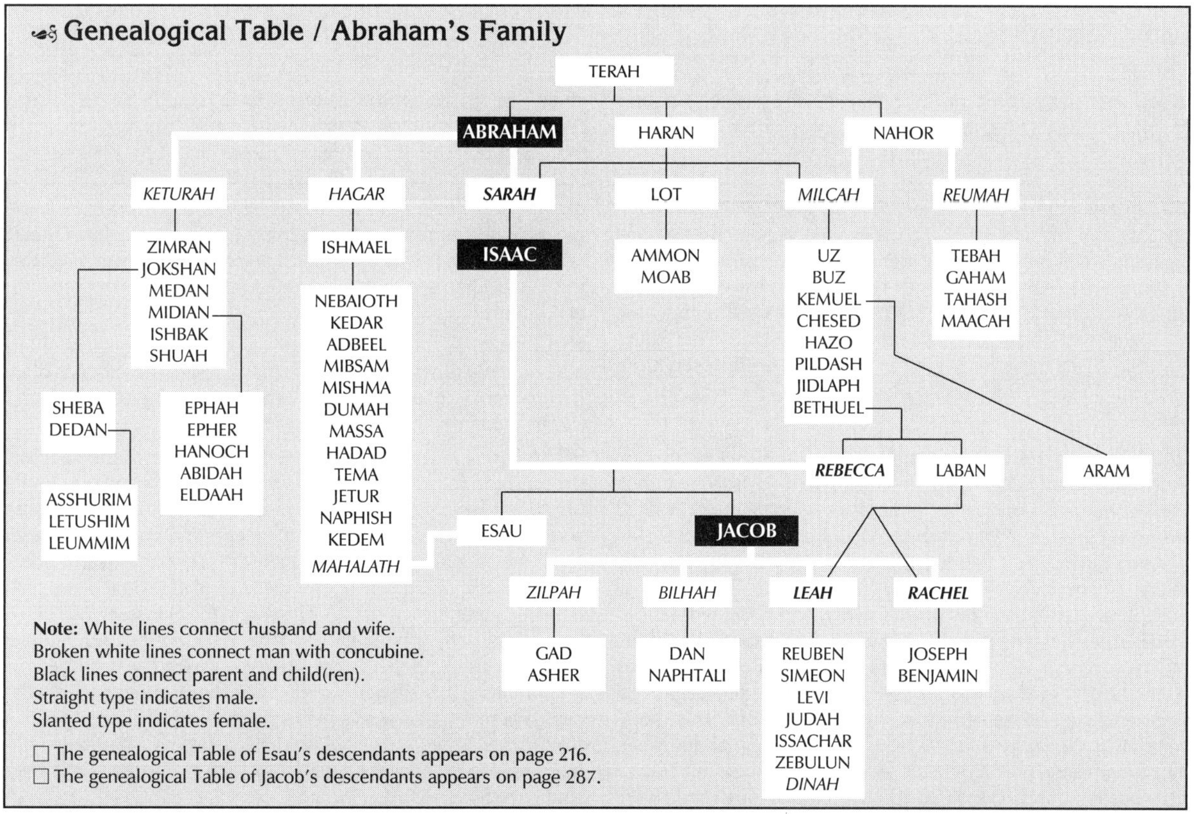

Genealogical Table / Abraham's Family

- TERAH
  - **ABRAHAM**
    - *KETURAH*: ZIMRAN, JOKSHAN, MEDAN, MIDIAN, ISHBAK, SHUAH
      - JOKSHAN: SHEBA, DEDAN
        - DEDAN: ASSHURIM, LETUSHIM, LEUMMIM
      - MIDIAN: EPHAH, EPHER, HANOCH, ABIDAH, ELDAAH
    - *HAGAR*: ISHMAEL
      - ISHMAEL: NEBAIOTH, KEDAR, ADBEEL, MIBSAM, MISHMA, DUMAH, MASSA, HADAD, TEMA, JETUR, NAPHISH, KEDEM, *MAHALATH*
    - ***SARAH***: **ISAAC**
      - **ISAAC** – ***REBECCA***: ESAU, **JACOB**
        - ESAU – *MAHALATH*
        - **JACOB**
          - *ZILPAH*: GAD, ASHER
          - *BILHAH*: DAN, NAPHTALI
          - ***LEAH***: REUBEN, SIMEON, LEVI, JUDAH, ISSACHAR, ZEBULUN, *DINAH*
          - ***RACHEL***: JOSEPH, BENJAMIN
  - HARAN: ***SARAH***, LOT, *MILCAH*
    - LOT: AMMON, MOAB
  - NAHOR
    - *MILCAH*: UZ, BUZ, KEMUEL, CHESED, HAZO, PILDASH, JIDLAPH, BETHUEL
      - KEMUEL: ARAM
      - BETHUEL: ***REBECCA***, LABAN
        - LABAN: ***LEAH***, ***RACHEL***
    - *REUMAH*: TEBAH, GAHAM, TAHASH, MAACAH

Note: White lines connect husband and wife.
Broken white lines connect man with concubine.
Black lines connect parent and child(ren).
Straight type indicates male.
Slanted type indicates female.

☐ The genealogical Table of Esau's descendants appears on page 216.
☐ The genealogical Table of Jacob's descendants appears on page 287.

הפטרות
The Haftaros

BLESSINGS OF THE HAFTARAH / ברכות ההפטרה

AFTER THE TORAH SCROLL HAS BEEN WOUND, TIED AND COVERED, THE *OLEH* FOR *MAFTIR* RECITES THE *HAFTARAH* BLESSING:

בָּרוּךְ אַתָּה יהוה אֱלֹהֵינוּ מֶלֶךְ
‹ King ‹ our God, ‹ HASHEM, ‹ are You, ‹ Blessed
הָעוֹלָם, אֲשֶׁר בָּחַר בִּנְבִיאִים טוֹבִים,
‹ good prophets ‹ has chosen ‹ Who « of the universe,
וְרָצָה בְדִבְרֵיהֶם הַנֶּאֱמָרִים בֶּאֱמֶת,
« with truth. ‹ that were uttered ‹ with their words ‹ and was pleased

בָּרוּךְ אַתָּה יהוה, הַבּוֹחֵר בַּתּוֹרָה
‹ the Torah ‹ Who chooses ‹ HASHEM, ‹ are You, ‹ Blessed
וּבְמֹשֶׁה עַבְדּוֹ, וּבְיִשְׂרָאֵל עַמּוֹ,
‹ His people, ‹ and Israel, ‹ His servant, ‹ and Moses,
וּבִנְבִיאֵי הָאֱמֶת וָצֶדֶק: (CONG. – אָמֵן.)
« (Amen.) « and righteousness. ‹ of truth ‹ and the prophets

AFTER THE *HAFTARAH* IS READ, THE *OLEH* RECITES THE FOLLOWING BLESSINGS:

בָּרוּךְ אַתָּה יהוה אֱלֹהֵינוּ מֶלֶךְ
‹ King ‹ our God, ‹ HASHEM, ‹ are You, ‹ Blessed
הָעוֹלָם, צוּר כָּל הָעוֹלָמִים, צַדִּיק
‹ Righteous ‹ the worlds, ‹ of all ‹ Rock « of the universe,
בְּכָל הַדּוֹרוֹת, הָאֵל הַנֶּאֱמָן הָאוֹמֵר
‹ Who says « Who is trustworthy, ‹ the God « generations, ‹ in all
וְעוֹשֶׂה, הַמְּדַבֵּר וּמְקַיֵּם, שֶׁכָּל דְּבָרָיו
‹ of His words ‹ Who all « and fulfills, ‹ Who speaks « and does,
אֱמֶת וָצֶדֶק. נֶאֱמָן אַתָּה הוּא יהוה
‹ HASHEM, ‹ are You ‹ Trustworthy « and righteous. ‹ are true
אֱלֹהֵינוּ, וְנֶאֱמָנִים דְּבָרֶיךָ, וְדָבָר אֶחָד
‹ [even] one word « are Your words; ‹ and trustworthy ‹ our God,
מִדְּבָרֶיךָ אָחוֹר לֹא יָשׁוּב רֵיקָם,
« unfulfilled, ‹ reverts ‹ never ‹ back « of Your words
כִּי אֵל מֶלֶךְ נֶאֱמָן (וְרַחֲמָן) אָתָּה.
« are You. ‹ (and compassionate) ‹ trustworthy ‹ King, ‹ a God, ‹ for
בָּרוּךְ אַתָּה יהוה, הָאֵל הַנֶּאֱמָן בְּכָל
‹ in all ‹ Who is trustworthy ‹ the God « HASHEM, ‹ are You, ‹ Blessed
דְּבָרָיו. (CONG. – אָמֵן)
« (Amen.) « His words.

רַחֵם עַל צִיּוֹן כִּי הִיא בֵּית חַיֵּינוּ,
« [that is the focus] of our life; ‹ is the place ‹ it ‹ for ‹ Zion, ‹ on ‹ Have mercy
וְלַעֲלוּבַת נֶפֶשׁ תּוֹשִׁיעַ בִּמְהֵרָה
‹ speedily, ‹ bring salvation ‹ to her very soul, ‹ and to [Israel,] who is humiliated
בְיָמֵינוּ. בָּרוּךְ אַתָּה יהוה, מְשַׂמֵּחַ
‹ Who gladdens « HASHEM, ‹ are You, ‹ Blessed « in our days.
צִיּוֹן בְּבָנֶיהָ. (CONG. – אָמֵן)
« (Amen.) « through her children. ‹ Zion

שַׂמְּחֵנוּ יהוה אֱלֹהֵינוּ בְּאֵלִיָּהוּ
‹ with Elijah ‹ our God, ‹ HASHEM, ‹ Gladden us,
הַנָּבִיא עַבְדֶּךָ, וּבְמַלְכוּת בֵּית דָּוִד
‹ of David, ‹ of the House ‹ and with the kingdom « Your servant, ‹ the prophet,
מְשִׁיחֶךָ, בִּמְהֵרָה יָבֹא וְיָגֵל לִבֵּנוּ, עַל
‹ On « and then our hearts will rejoice. ‹ may he come, ‹ speedily « Your anointed one;
כִּסְאוֹ לֹא יֵשֶׁב זָר וְלֹא יִנְחֲלוּ עוֹד
‹ any longer ‹ and let not inherit « any stranger, ‹ sit ‹ may there never ‹ his throne
אֲחֵרִים אֶת כְּבוֹדוֹ, כִּי בְשֵׁם קָדְשְׁךָ
‹ of your Holiness ‹ by the Name ‹ for « his honor, ‹ others

נִשְׁבַּעְתָּ לוֹ, שֶׁלֹּא יִכְבֶּה נֵרוֹ לְעוֹלָם

‹ forever ‹ would ‹ extinguished ‹ that not ‹‹ to him ‹ You swore his lamp be

וָעֶד. בָּרוּךְ אַתָּה יהוה, מָגֵן דָּוִד.

« of David. ‹ Shield ‹‹ HASHEM, ‹ are You, ‹ Blessed « and ever.

(אָמֵן – CONG.)

« (Amen.)

ON A REGULAR SABBATH:

עַל הַתּוֹרָה, וְעַל הָעֲבוֹדָה,

‹ the prayer service, ‹ for ‹ the Torah reading, ‹ For

וְעַל הַנְּבִיאִים, וְעַל יוֹם הַשַּׁבָּת הַזֶּה,

‹ this Sabbath Day ‹ and for ‹ the reading from the Prophets ‹ for

שֶׁנָּתַתָּ לָּנוּ יהוה אֱלֹהֵינוּ, לִקְדֻשָּׁה

‹ for holiness ‹‹ our God, ‹ HASHEM, ‹ to us, ‹ that You have given

וְלִמְנוּחָה, לְכָבוֹד וּלְתִפְאָרֶת. עַל

‹ – for ‹‹ and splendor ‹ for glory ‹ and rest,

הַכֹּל, יהוה אֱלֹהֵינוּ, אֲנַחְנוּ מוֹדִים

‹ thank ‹ we ‹‹ our God, ‹ HASHEM, ‹‹ everything,

לָךְ, וּמְבָרְכִים אוֹתָךְ, יִתְבָּרַךְ שִׁמְךָ

‹ May Your Name be blessed « You. ‹ and bless ‹ You

בְּפִי כָּל חַי תָּמִיד לְעוֹלָם וָעֶד. בָּרוּךְ

‹ Blessed ‹‹ and ever. ‹ for ever ‹ always, ‹‹ the living, ‹ of all ‹ by the mouth

אַתָּה יהוה, מְקַדֵּשׁ הַשַּׁבָּת. (אָמֵן – CONG.)

«(Amen.) « the Sabbath. ‹ Who sanctifies ‹‹ HASHEM, ‹ are You,

There are various customs regarding the *Haftaros*. We have noted the prevalent customs of the *Ashkenazic* and *Sephardic* communities. *Chabad Chassidim* follow the *Ashkenazic* custom unless otherwise noted.

HAFTARAS BEREISHIS / הפטרת בראשית

Isaiah 42:5-43:10 / ישעיה מב:ה–מג:י

מב ה כֹּה־אָמַר הָאֵל ׀ יְהוָה בּוֹרֵא

‹ He [Who] creates ‹‹ HASHEM, ‹ the God, ‹ said ‹ So 5 [42]

הַשָּׁמַיִם וְנוֹטֵיהֶם רֹקַע הָאָרֶץ

‹ the earth ‹ He [Who] spreads out ‹‹ and [Who] stretches them forth; ‹ the heavens

וְצֶאֱצָאֶיהָ נֹתֵן נְשָׁמָה לָעָם עָלֶיהָ וְרוּחַ

‹ and a spirit ‹‹ [that are] upon it, ‹ to the people ‹ a soul ‹ He [Who] gives ‹‹ and its produce;

לַהֹלְכִים בָּהּ: ו אֲנִי יְהוָה קְרָאתִיךָ

‹ *I have called you* ‹‹ *HASHEM:* ‹ *I am* 6 ‹‹ on it: ‹ to those [creatures] that go about

בְצֶדֶק וְאַחְזֵק בְּיָדֶךָ וְאֶצָּרְךָ וְאֶתֶּנְךָ

‹ *and I will set you* ‹‹ *and I will protect you;* ‹‹ *by your hand;* ‹ *and I will hold [you]* ‹‹ *in righteousness*

לִבְרִית עָם לְאוֹר גּוֹיִם: ז לִפְקֹחַ עֵינַיִם

‹ *eyes* ‹ *to open* 7 ‹‹ *[for] the nations;* ‹ *as a light* ‹‹ *[for] the people,* ‹ *as a covenant*

עִוְרוֹת לְהוֹצִיא מִמַּסְגֵּר אַסִּיר מִבֵּית

‹ *from a house* ‹‹ *a prisoner;* ‹ *from jail* ‹ *to take out* ‹‹ *that are blind;*

כֶּלֶא יֹשְׁבֵי חֹשֶׁךְ: ח אֲנִי יְהוָה הוּא שְׁמִי

‹‹ *My Name;* ‹ *that is* ‹ *HASHEM,* ‹ *I am* 8 ‹‹ *in darkness.* ‹ *those dwelling* ‹ *of detention,*

וּכְבוֹדִי לְאַחֵר לֹא־אֶתֵּן וּתְהִלָּתִי

‹ *[nor] My praise* ‹‹ *I shall not give,* ‹ *to another* ‹ *and My glory*

לַפְּסִילִים: ט הָרִאשֹׁנוֹת הִנֵּה־בָאוּ

‹‹ *they have come about;* ‹ *— behold! —* ‹ *The first [prophecies]* 9 ‹‹ *to the graven idols.*

וַחֲדָשׁוֹת אֲנִי מַגִּיד בְּטֶרֶם תִּצְמַחְנָה

‹ *they will sprout* ‹ *Before* ‹‹ *relate [now].* ‹ *[that] I* ‹ *and [it is] new ones*

אַשְׁמִיעַ אֶתְכֶם: י שִׁירוּ לַיהוָה שִׁיר

‹ a song, ‹ to HASHEM ‹ Sing 10 ‹‹ *you [of them].* ‹ *I shall inform*

חָדָשׁ תְּהִלָּתוֹ מִקְצֵה הָאָרֶץ יוֹרְדֵי הַיָּם

‹ [to] the sea ‹ [you] who go down ‹‹ of the earth; ‹ from the end ‹ [sing] His praise ‹‹ a new one;

וּמְלֹאוֹ אִיִּים וְיֹשְׁבֵיהֶם: יא יִשְׂאוּ מִדְבָּר

‹ the desert ‹ Let them raise [their] voices: 11 ‹‹ and their inhabitants. ‹ [settled] islands ‹‹ and [you creatures] that fill it;

וַעֲרָיו חֲצֵרִים תֵּשֵׁב קֵדָר יָרֹנּוּ יֹשְׁבֵי

‹ those who dwell ‹‹ Let them sing out, ‹‹ Kedar. ‹ where dwells ‹ the open places ‹ and its cities;

סֶלַע מֵרֹאשׁ הָרִים יִצְוָחוּ: יב יָשִׂימוּ

‹ Let them render 12 ‹‹ let them shout. ‹ of mountains ‹ from the summit ‹‹ on bedrock;

לַיהוָה כָּבוֹד וּתְהִלָּתוֹ בָּאִיִּים יַגִּידוּ:

‹‹ they shall declare ‹ in the islands ‹ and His praise ‹‹ glory; ‹ to HASHEM

יג יְהוָה כַּגִּבּוֹר יֵצֵא כְּאִישׁ מִלְחָמוֹת

‹ of wars ‹ like a man ‹‹ He shall go forth, ‹ like a warrior ‹ HASHEM, 13

יָעִיר קִנְאָה יָרִיעַ אַף־יַצְרִיחַ עַל־אֹיְבָיו

‹ His enemies, ‹ over ‹‹ even roar; ‹ He shall shout [triumphantly], ‹‹ [His] vengeance; ‹ He shall arouse

יִתְגַּבָּר: יד הֶחֱשֵׁיתִי מֵעוֹלָם אַחֲרִישׁ

‹‹ *I have been quiet;* ‹‹ *from times of old;* ‹ *I have been silent* 14 ‹‹ He shall prevail.

אֶתְאַפָּק כַּיּוֹלֵדָה אֶפְעֶה אֶשֹּׁם וְאֶשְׁאַף

‹ *and I will swallow [them] up,* ‹ *I will lay waste [to My enemies],* ‹‹ *I will cry out;* ‹ *— [But, now,] like a woman in childbirth* ‹‹ *I have restrained Myself.*

◆ Haftaras Bereishis

The *Sidrah* began with the story of Creation and the august role of man in bringing God's goal to fruition; of his downfall and God's mercy in allowing him a new life in which he could redeem himself. The *Haftarah's* theme is similar.

Creation is not a phenomenon that took place in primeval times and then was left to proceed of its own inertia. The first verse of the *Haftarah* speaks of Creation in the present tense, because God must renew it constantly; otherwise the universe would cease to exist. So He does. His purpose is for Israel to guide mankind to His service: *to bring the people to the covenant, to be a light to the nations;* to help them remove the impediments that prevent their eyes and ears from seeing and hearing the truth.

But Israel falters. It sins, and God allows it to be plundered as a result of its failure. The downfall is not permanent; although God may look from afar, He remains vigilant and seeks the opportunity to restore Israel to its eminence. No one seems to care, to see, but God always keeps His original purpose in mind, and only Israel is equal to it. Can the nations or their gods match Israel's loyalty, despite its frequent lapses? Is there any other nation that can bear witness to God's greatness, His mercy, and the fulfillment of His prophecies?

Ultimately, Israel can, and because it does it will be redeemed and be the instrument for the triumph of the spirit.

יַחַד׃ טו אַחֲרִיב הָרִים וּגְבָעוֹת וְכָל

together. 15 I will destroy [their] mountains and [their] hills; and all

עֶשְׂבָּם אוֹבִישׁ וְשַׂמְתִּי נְהָרוֹת לָאִיִּים

their herbage I will cause to wither; I will make [their] rivers into islands,

וַאֲגַמִּים אוֹבִישׁ׃ טז וְהוֹלַכְתִּי עִוְרִים

and [their] marshes I will dry up. 16 I will walk the blind

בְּדֶרֶךְ לֹא יָדָעוּ בִּנְתִיבוֹת לֹא־יָדְעוּ

on a way they did not know; on paths they did not know

אַדְרִיכֵם אָשִׂים מַחְשָׁךְ לִפְנֵיהֶם לָאוֹר

I will lead them. I will make the darkness before them into light,

וּמַעֲקַשִּׁים לְמִישׁוֹר אֵלֶּה הַדְּבָרִים

and the crooked places straight. — These things

עֲשִׂיתִם וְלֹא עֲזַבְתִּים׃ יז נָסֹגוּ אָחוֹר

I will do and I will not neglect them. 17 They will be turned back;

יֵבֹשׁוּ בֹשֶׁת הַבֹּטְחִים בַּפָּסֶל הָאֹמְרִים

they will be humiliated with shame, those who trust in the graven idol; those who say

לְמַסֵּכָה אַתֶּם אֱלֹהֵינוּ׃ יח הַחֵרְשִׁים

to a molten idol, 'You are our gods.' 18 O deaf ones,

שְׁמָעוּ וְהַעִוְרִים הַבִּיטוּ לִרְאוֹת׃ יט מִי

listen; and blind ones, gaze to see! 19 Who is

עִוֵּר כִּי אִם־עַבְדִּי וְחֵרֵשׁ כְּמַלְאָכִי

blind, but My servant, and [who is] deaf like My agent

אֶשְׁלָח מִי עִוֵּר כִּמְשֻׁלָּם וְעִוֵּר כְּעֶבֶד

whom I would send? Who is blind like the perfect one; and [who is] blind like the servant

יהוה׃ כ רָאוֹת [ראית כ׳] רַבּוֹת וְלֹא תִשְׁמֹר

of Hashem? 20 — Seeing much, yet you do not heed!

פָּקוֹחַ אָזְנַיִם וְלֹא יִשְׁמָע׃ כא יהוה חָפֵץ

Opening ears, yet he would not hear! 21 Hashem desires

לְמַעַן צִדְקוֹ יַגְדִּיל תּוֹרָה וְיַאְדִּיר׃

for the sake of His righteousness that He magnify the Torah and that He glorify [it].

Sephardim, the community of Frankfurt am Main, and *Chabad Chassidim* conclude the *Haftarah* here. Others continue.

כב וְהוּא עַם־בָּזוּז וְשָׁסוּי הָפֵחַ בַּחוּרִים

22 But it is a people, looted and oppressed, trapped in holes,

כֻּלָּם וּבְבָתֵּי כְלָאִים הָחְבָּאוּ הָיוּ לָבַז

all of them; and in houses of detention they are hidden. They have become as booty,

וְאֵין מַצִּיל מְשִׁסָּה וְאֵין־אֹמֵר הָשַׁב׃

but there is no rescuer; [they are] oppressed, but there is no one who says, Give back!

כג מִי בָכֶם יַאֲזִין זֹאת יַקְשִׁב וְיִשְׁמַע

23 Who among you will give ear to this? [Who] will hearken and hear

לְאָחוֹר׃ כד מִי־נָתַן לִמְשִׁסָּה [למשוסה כ׳]

[what will be] at the end? 24 Who gave over to the oppressor,

יַעֲקֹב וְיִשְׂרָאֵל לְבֹזְזִים הֲלוֹא יהוה זוּ

Jacob, and Israel to looters? Was it not Hashem? This [it is],

חָטָאנוּ לוֹ וְלֹא־אָבוּ בִדְרָכָיו הָלוֹךְ

[for] we have sinned against Him. They have not been willing in His ways to walk;

וְלֹא שָׁמְעוּ בְּתוֹרָתוֹ׃ כה וַיִּשְׁפֹּךְ עָלָיו

and they have not hearkened to His Torah. 25 So He poured upon him

חֵמָה אַפּוֹ וֶעֱזוּז מִלְחָמָה וַתְּלַהֲטֵהוּ

fury, His wrath, and the power of war, and He set him on fire

מִסָּבִיב וְלֹא יָדָע וַתִּבְעַר־בּוֹ וְלֹא־יָשִׂים

all around, yet he did not know; it burned within him, yet he did not set [it]

עַל־לֵב׃ מג א וְעַתָּה כֹּה־אָמַר יהוה

upon [his] heart. [43] 1 And now, so said Hashem,

בֹּרַאֲךָ יַעֲקֹב וְיֹצֶרְךָ יִשְׂרָאֵל אַל־תִּירָא

He Who created you, O Jacob; He Who fashioned you, O Israel: Do not fear,

כִּי גְאַלְתִּיךָ קָרָאתִי בְשִׁמְךָ לִי־אָתָּה׃

for I have redeemed you; I have called [you] by your name; Mine are you.

ב כִּי־תַעֲבֹר בַּמַּיִם אִתְּךָ אָנִי וּבַנְּהָרוֹת

2 When you pass through water, with you am I; and [when you pass] through rivers,

לֹא יִשְׁטְפוּךְ כִּי־תֵלֵךְ בְּמוֹ־אֵשׁ
they will not flood you. When you walk through fire,

לֹא תִכָּוֶה וְלֶהָבָה לֹא תִבְעַר־בָּךְ: ג כִּי
you will not be burned; and a flame will not burn you. 3 For

אֲנִי יְהוָה אֱלֹהֶיךָ קְדוֹשׁ יִשְׂרָאֵל
I am HASHEM, your God, the Holy One of Israel,

מוֹשִׁיעֶךָ נָתַתִּי כָפְרְךָ מִצְרַיִם כּוּשׁ
your Savior; I gave as your ransom Egypt; [and] Kush

וּסְבָא תַּחְתֶּיךָ: ד מֵאֲשֶׁר יָקַרְתָּ בְעֵינַי
and Seba, instead of you. 4 Because you were precious in My eyes,

נִכְבַּדְתָּ וַאֲנִי אֲהַבְתִּיךָ וְאֶתֵּן אָדָם
you were honored, and as for Me, I loved you; so I gave a person

תַּחְתֶּיךָ וּלְאֻמִּים תַּחַת נַפְשֶׁךָ:
instead of you and regimes instead of your soul.

ה אַל־תִּירָא כִּי אִתְּךָ אָנִי מִמִּזְרָח
5 Do not fear, for with you am I; from the east

אָבִיא זַרְעֶךָ וּמִמַּעֲרָב אֲקַבְּצֶךָּ: ו אֹמַר
I will bring your offspring, and from the west I will gather you. 6 I shall say

לַצָּפוֹן תֵּנִי וּלְתֵימָן אַל־תִּכְלָאִי הָבִיאִי
to the north, 'Give [back],' and to the south, 'Do not withhold'; bring

בָנַי מֵרָחוֹק וּבְנוֹתַי מִקְצֵה הָאָרֶץ: ז כֹּל
My sons from afar and My daughters from the end of the earth; 7 everyone

הַנִּקְרָא בִשְׁמִי וְלִכְבוֹדִי בְּרָאתִיו
who is called by My Name, and for My glory I have created him,

יְצַרְתִּיו אַף־עֲשִׂיתִיו: ח הוֹצִיא עַם־עִוֵּר
I have fashioned him, indeed, I have perfected him; 8 taking out the nation that is blind,

וְעֵינַיִם יֵשׁ וְחֵרְשִׁים וְאָזְנַיִם לָמוֹ: ט כָּל
though eyes are there; and [they are] deaf though [there are] ears, for them. 9 [Were] all

הַגּוֹיִם נִקְבְּצוּ יַחְדָּו וְיֵאָסְפוּ לְאֻמִּים מִי
the nations gathered together, and assembled were the countries, who

בָהֶם יַגִּיד זֹאת וְרִאשֹׁנוֹת יַשְׁמִיעֻנוּ
among them would declare this? [Would] the early [prophecies] declare for us?

יִתְּנוּ עֵדֵיהֶם וְיִצְדָּקוּ וְיִשְׁמְעוּ וְיֹאמְרוּ
Let them set forth their witnesses and they will be vindicated; else let them hear and they will say,

אֱמֶת: י אַתֶּם עֵדַי נְאֻם־יְהוָה וְעַבְדִּי
It is true. 10 You are My witnesses — the word of HASHEM — and My servant,

אֲשֶׁר בָּחָרְתִּי לְמַעַן תֵּדְעוּ וְתַאֲמִינוּ לִי
whom I have chosen, so that you will know and you will believe in Me,

וְתָבִינוּ כִּי־אֲנִי הוּא לְפָנַי לֹא־נוֹצַר אֵל
and you will understand that I am He; before Me nothing was created by a god,

וְאַחֲרַי לֹא יִהְיֶה:
and after Me it shall not be!

HAFTARAS NOACH / הפטרת נח

Isaiah 54:1-55:5 / ישעיה נד:א־נה:ה

נד א רָנִּי עֲקָרָה לֹא יָלָדָה פִּצְחִי רִנָּה
[54] 1 Sing out, O barren one, who has not given birth, break out into glad song

וְצַהֲלִי לֹא־חָלָה כִּי־רַבִּים בְּנֵי־
and be jubilant, O one who had no labor pains, for more numerous are the children

שׁוֹמֵמָה מִבְּנֵי בְעוּלָה אָמַר יְהוָה:
of the desolate [Jerusalem] than the children of the inhabited [city], said HASHEM.

ב הַרְחִיבִי ׀ מְקוֹם אָהֳלֵךְ וִירִיעוֹת
2 Broaden the place of your tent, and the curtains

מִשְׁכְּנוֹתַיִךְ יַטּוּ אַל־תַּחְשֹׂכִי הַאֲרִיכִי
of your dwellings stretch out, do not skimp; lengthen

מֵיתָרַיִךְ וִיתֵדֹתַיִךְ חַזֵּקִי: ג כִּי־יָמִין
your cords, and your tent pegs strengthen. 3 For southward

Haftaras Noach

Man has infinite capacity to save the world and to destroy it. And he has an equal capacity to perceive the truth and to see right through it and miss it entirely.

The generation of the Flood continued man's slide into immorality until God's mercy had reached its limit. It is instructive that the last straw was thievery; as the Sages teach: Even if there is a bushel of sins, it is thievery that leads the condemnations. So man had taken the universe and pushed it over the brink of destruction, but there was one man, Noah, who saved the race and

וּשְׂמֹאול תִּפְרֹצִי וְזַרְעֵךְ גּוֹיִם יִירָשׁ
and northward you shall spread out mightily, your offspring will inherit the nations,

וְעָרִים נְשַׁמּוֹת יוֹשִׁיבוּ: ד אַל־תִּירְאִי
and cities that are desolate they will settle. 4 Do not fear,

כִּי־לֹא תֵבוֹשִׁי וְאַל־תִּכָּלְמִי כִּי־
for you will not be shamed, do not feel humiliated for

לֹא תַחְפִּירִי כִּי בֹשֶׁת עֲלוּמַיִךְ תִּשְׁכָּחִי
you will not be mortified; for the shame of your youth you will forget,

וְחֶרְפַּת אַלְמְנוּתַיִךְ לֹא תִזְכְּרִי־עוֹד:
and the mortification of your widowhood you will not remember any more.

ה כִּי בֹעֲלַיִךְ עֹשַׂיִךְ יהוה צְבָאוֹת שְׁמוֹ
5 For your Master is your Maker — HASHEM, Master of Legions is His Name;

וְגֹאֲלֵךְ קְדוֹשׁ יִשְׂרָאֵל אֱלֹהֵי כָל־הָאָרֶץ
your Redeemer is the Holy One of Israel — God of all the world

יִקָּרֵא: ו כִּי־כְאִשָּׁה עֲזוּבָה וַעֲצוּבַת רוּחַ
shall He be called. 6 For like a wife who had been forsaken and of melancholy spirit

קְרָאָךְ יהוה וְאֵשֶׁת נְעוּרִים כִּי תִמָּאֵס
will HASHEM have called you, and like a wife of one's youth when she had become despised

אָמַר אֱלֹהָיִךְ: ז בְּרֶגַע קָטֹן עֲזַבְתִּיךְ
— said your God. 7 For [but] a moment that is brief have I forsaken you,

וּבְרַחֲמִים גְּדֹלִים אֲקַבְּצֵךְ: ח בְּשֶׁצֶף
and with mercy that is abundant I shall gather you in. 8 With a slight

קֶצֶף הִסְתַּרְתִּי פָנַי רֶגַע מִמֵּךְ וּבְחֶסֶד
wrath have I concealed My countenance for a moment from you, but with kindness

עוֹלָם רִחַמְתִּיךְ אָמַר גֹּאֲלֵךְ יהוה:
that is eternal I shall show you mercy, said your Redeemer, HASHEM.

ט כִּי־מֵי נֹחַ זֹאת לִי אֲשֶׁר נִשְׁבַּעְתִּי
9 For [like] the waters of Noah shall this be to Me: As I have sworn

מֵעֲבֹר מֵי־נֹחַ עוֹד עַל־הָאָרֶץ כֵּן
never to [let] pass the waters of Noah again over the earth, so

נִשְׁבַּעְתִּי מִקְּצֹף עָלַיִךְ וּמִגְּעָר־בָּךְ:
have I sworn not to be wrathful with you or rebuke you.

י כִּי הֶהָרִים יָמוּשׁוּ וְהַגְּבָעוֹת תְּמוּטֶינָה
10 For the mountains may move and the hills may falter,

וְחַסְדִּי מֵאִתֵּךְ לֹא־יָמוּשׁ וּבְרִית
but My kindness from you shall not move away and My covenant

שְׁלוֹמִי לֹא תָמוּט אָמַר מְרַחֲמֵךְ
of peace shall not falter, says the One Who shows you mercy,

יהוה:
HASHEM.

Sephardim and *Chabad Chassidim* conclude the *Haftarah* here. *Ashkenazim* continue:

יא עֲנִיָּה סֹעֲרָה לֹא נֻחָמָה הִנֵּה אָנֹכִי
11 O afflicted, storm-tossed, unconsoled one, behold! I

מַרְבִּיץ בַּפּוּךְ אֲבָנַיִךְ וִיסַדְתִּיךְ
shall lay upon pearls your [floor] stones, and make your foundation

בַּסַּפִּירִים: יב וְשַׂמְתִּי כַּדְכֹד שִׁמְשֹׁתַיִךְ
of sapphires. 12 I shall make of rubies your sun windows,

וּשְׁעָרַיִךְ לְאַבְנֵי אֶקְדָּח וְכָל־גְּבוּלֵךְ
and your gates of stones of garnet, and your entire boundary

לְאַבְנֵי־חֵפֶץ: יג וְכָל־בָּנַיִךְ לִמּוּדֵי יהוה
of stones that are precious. 13 All your children will be students of HASHEM,

וְרַב שְׁלוֹם בָּנָיִךְ: יד בִּצְדָקָה תִּכּוֹנָנִי
and abundant will be the peace of your children. 14 Through righteousness establish yourself,

רַחֲקִי מֵעֹשֶׁק כִּי־לֹא תִירָאִי וּמִמְּחִתָּה
distance yourself from oppression, for you need not fear it, and from panic

---

the world. Thanks to his righteousness, humanity survived — proof that no one should ever consider himself too insignificant to make a difference.

One would expect the survivors of the Flood and their immediate descendants to have learned that immortality is not assured. When the generation that built the Tower of Babel thought that it could do battle with God, it did not need fallible history books to tell it about the Flood. Noah and his children were still alive, eyewitnesses who had lived through man's foolishness and its consequences. But, overcome with delusions of their own power and rationalizing that the Flood had been a natural, coincidental disaster, they built the Tower anyway.

History repeats itself for those who refuse to learn from it.

כִּי לֹא־תִקְרַב אֵלָיִךְ: טו הֵן גּוֹר יָגוּר
‹ one certainly need fear ‹ Indeed, 15 « you. ‹ come near ‹ it will not ‹ for

אֶפֶס מֵאוֹתִי מִי־גָר אִתָּךְ עָלַיִךְ יִפּוֹל:
« will fall. ‹ because of you « against you, ‹ gathers to provoke a war ‹ whoever « from Me; ‹ if he has nothing

טז הִנֵּה [הן כ׳] אָנֹכִי בָּרָאתִי חָרָשׁ נֹפֵחַ
‹ who blows ‹ the smith ‹ have created ‹ I ‹ Indeed! 16

בְּאֵשׁ פֶּחָם וּמוֹצִיא כְלִי לְמַעֲשֵׂהוּ
« for his labor, ‹ a tool ‹ and withdraws ‹ from charcoal ‹ on a flame

וְאָנֹכִי בָּרָאתִי מַשְׁחִית לְחַבֵּל: יז כָּל־
‹ Any 17 « to ruin. ‹ the destroyer ‹ have created ‹ and I

כְּלִי יוּצַר עָלַיִךְ לֹא יִצְלָח וְכָל־לָשׁוֹן
‹ tongue ‹ and any « succeed, ‹ shall not ‹ against you ‹ sharpened ‹ weapon

תָּקוּם־אִתָּךְ לַמִּשְׁפָּט תַּרְשִׁיעִי זֹאת
‹ this « you shall condemn; ‹ in judgment, ‹ against you ‹ that shall rise

נַחֲלַת עַבְדֵי יהוה וְצִדְקָתָם מֵאִתִּי
« is from Me, ‹ and their righteousness « of HASHEM, ‹ of the servants ‹ is the heritage

נְאֻם־יהוה: נה א הוֹי כָּל־צָמֵא לְכוּ
‹ go ‹ who is thirsty, ‹ everyone ‹ Ho, 1 [55] « of HASHEM. ‹ the words

לַמַּיִם וַאֲשֶׁר אֵין־לוֹ כָּסֶף לְכוּ שִׁבְרוּ
‹ buy, ‹ go, « money; ‹ who has no ‹ [even] one « to the water,

וֶאֱכֹלוּ וּלְכוּ שִׁבְרוּ בְּלוֹא־כֶסֶף וּבְלוֹא
‹ and without ‹ money ‹ without ‹ and buy, ‹ go, « and eat,

מְחִיר יַיִן וְחָלָב: ב לָמָּה תִשְׁקְלוּ־כֶסֶף
‹ money ‹ do you weigh out ‹ Why 2 « and milk. ‹ wine ‹ barter,

בְּלוֹא־לֶחֶם וִיגִיעֲכֶם בְּלוֹא לְשָׂבְעָה
« satisfy? ‹ for that which does not ‹ and [the fruit of] your toil, « bread, ‹ for that which is not

שִׁמְעוּ שָׁמוֹעַ אֵלַי וְאִכְלוּ־טוֹב וְתִתְעַנַּג
‹ and let delight « what is good, ‹ and eat ‹ to Me ‹ Listen well

בַּדֶּשֶׁן נַפְשְׁכֶם: ג הַטּוּ אָזְנְכֶם וּלְכוּ אֵלַי
« to Me, ‹ and come ‹ your ear ‹ Incline 3 « your soul. ‹ in abundance

שִׁמְעוּ וּתְחִי נַפְשְׁכֶם וְאֶכְרְתָה לָכֶם
‹ with you ‹ I shall seal « your soul; ‹ and rejuvenated will be ‹ listen

בְּרִית עוֹלָם חַסְדֵי דָוִד הַנֶּאֱמָנִים:
‹ that are enduring. ‹ [promised to] David ‹ the kindnesses « that is eternal, ‹ a covenant

ד הֵן עֵד לְאוּמִּים נְתַתִּיו נָגִיד וּמְצַוֵּה
‹ and a commander ‹ a prince « I have appointed him, ‹ to the regimes ‹ as a witness ‹ Indeed 4

לְאֻמִּים: ה הֵן גּוֹי לֹא־תֵדַע תִּקְרָא וְגוֹי
‹ and a nation « will you call, ‹ that you did not know ‹ a nation ‹ Indeed! 5 « to the regimes.

לֹא־יְדָעוּךָ אֵלֶיךָ יָרוּצוּ לְמַעַן יהוה
‹ of HASHEM, ‹ for the sake « will run, ‹ toward you ‹ know you, ‹ that did not

אֱלֹהֶיךָ וְלִקְדוֹשׁ יִשְׂרָאֵל כִּי פֵאֲרָךְ:
« He has glorified you! ‹ for ‹ of Israel, ‹ and [for the sake of] the Holy One « your God,

HAFTARAS LECH LECHA / הפטרת לך לך

Isaiah 40:27-41:16 / ישעיה מ:כז־מא:טז

מ כז לָמָּה תֹאמַר יַעֲקֹב וּתְדַבֵּר יִשְׂרָאֵל
« O Israel: ‹ and [why should] you declare, ‹ O Jacob, ‹ you say, ‹ Why should 27 [40]

נִסְתְּרָה דַרְכִּי מֵיהוה וּמֵאֱלֹהַי מִשְׁפָּטִי
‹ *my cause* ‹ *and from my God* « *from HASHEM;* ‹ *is my way* ‹ *Hidden*

יַעֲבוֹר: כח הֲלוֹא יָדַעְתְּ אִם־לֹא שָׁמַעְתְּ
‹ you have not heard [from others], ‹ [even] if ‹ [that] you have known, ‹ Is it not [true] 28 « *has been passed over?*

אֱלֹהֵי עוֹלָם ׀ יהוה בּוֹרֵא קְצוֹת הָאָרֶץ
« of the earth; ‹ of the ends ‹ [that] He is Creator « is HASHEM; ‹ of eternity ‹ [that] God

Haftaras Lech Lecha

God gave Abraham the mission of bringing His will to fruition and His message to the nations. The *Haftarah* encourages Israel to maintain its optimistic spirit even in the face of its own failure and exile, and stubborn resistance on the part of the nations.

"God gives strength to the weary. . ." Isaiah proclaims; those who trust Him will find new strength and ultimately prevail. Rather than focus on the shortcomings of people — Jews and gentiles —

לֹא יִיעַף וְלֹא יִיגָע אֵין חֵקֶר לִתְבוּנָתוֹ:

« to His understanding? ‹ [that] there is no limit « and He does not tire; ‹ [that] He does not weary,

כט נֹתֵן לַיָּעֵף כֹּחַ וּלְאֵין אוֹנִים עָצְמָה

‹ [their] might ‹ power, ‹ and to those without « strength; ‹ to the weary ‹ He gives 29

יַרְבֶּה: ל וְיִעֲפוּ נְעָרִים וְיִגָעוּ וּבַחוּרִים

‹ and young men « and they may tire; ‹ — the youths — ‹ They may weary 30 « He will increase.

כָּשׁוֹל יִכָּשֵׁלוּ: לא וְקוֹיֵ יהוה יַחֲלִיפוּ כֹחַ

« [their] strength, ‹ will renew ‹ [to] HASHEM, ‹ But those who hope 31 « they will falter. ‹ faltering,

יַעֲלוּ אֵבֶר כַּנְּשָׁרִים יָרוּצוּ וְלֹא יִיגָעוּ

« but they will not tire; « they will run ‹ like the eagles; ‹ a wing ‹ they will grow

יֵלְכוּ וְלֹא יִיעָפוּ: מא א הַחֲרִישׁוּ אֵלַי

‹ to [hear] me, ‹ Be silent 1 [41] « but they will not grow weary. ‹ they will walk,

אִיִּים וּלְאֻמִּים יַחֲלִיפוּ כֹחַ יִגְּשׁוּ אָז

‹ then ‹ let them approach, « [their] strength; ‹ that would renew ‹ and countries ‹ O [inhabitants of] islands,

יַדְבֵּרוּ יַחְדָּו לַמִּשְׁפָּט נִקְרָבָה: ב מִי

‹ Who 2 « let us approach. ‹ toward judgment, ‹ — together, « let them speak;

הֵעִיר מִמִּזְרָח צֶדֶק יִקְרָאֵהוּ לְרַגְלוֹ יִתֵּן

‹ [Who] would place « at his [every] footstep. ‹ would [Abraham] proclaim ‹ Righteousness « from the east? ‹ aroused [Abraham]

לְפָנָיו גּוֹיִם וּמְלָכִים יַרְדְּ יִתֵּן כֶּעָפָר

‹ like dust, ‹ [Who] would make « [that] he would dominate? ‹ And [Who would set] kings, « nations? ‹ before him

חַרְבּוֹ כְּקַשׁ נִדָּף קַשְׁתּוֹ: ג יִרְדְּפֵם יַעֲבוֹר

‹ he would pass through ‹ [so that] he would pursue them, 3 « [the victims of] his bow, ‹ — wind-driven — ‹ and like straw « [the victims of] his sword;

שָׁלוֹם אֹרַח בְּרַגְלָיו לֹא יָבוֹא: ד מִי־

‹ Who 4 « have never come? ‹ where his feet ‹ [on] a path ‹ [in] peace,

פָּעַל וְעָשָׂה קֹרֵא הַדֹּרוֹת מֵרֹאשׁ אֲנִי

‹ — [It is] I, « from the beginning. ‹ the generations ‹ [It is] He Who called « and [Who] has accomplished [it]? ‹ has wrought

יהוה רִאשׁוֹן וְאֶת־אַחֲרֹנִים אֲנִי־הוּא:

« He. ‹ I am ‹ the last [generations], ‹ and with « [with] the first [generation], ‹ HASHEM,

ה רָאוּ אִיִּים וְיִירָאוּ קְצוֹת הָאָרֶץ יֶחֱרָדוּ

« will shudder, ‹ of the earth ‹ [those at] the ends « and they will fear; ‹ — the [inhabitants of the] islands — ‹ They will have seen 5

קָרְבוּ וַיֶּאֱתָיוּן: ו אִישׁ אֶת־רֵעֵהוּ יַעְזֹרוּ

« they would help [build idols], ‹ to his fellow ‹ — [Each] man 6 « and they will have come [to involve their idols]. ‹ they will have approached

וּלְאָחִיו יֹאמַר חֲזָק: ז וַיְחַזֵּק חָרָשׁ

« — [he,] the crafter [of idols] — « He would encourage 7 « *Be strong.* ‹ he would say, ‹ and to his brother

אֶת־צֹרֵף מַחֲלִיק פַּטִּישׁ אֶת־הוֹלֶם

‹ the one who strikes ‹ with a hammer [would encourage] ‹ the one who smooths « the goldsmith;

פָּעַם אֹמֵר לַדֶּבֶק טוֹב הוּא וַיְחַזְּקֵהוּ

‹ But he would strengthen it « *it is!* ‹ *[How good* ‹ of the soldering, ‹ he would say « the anvil;

בְּמַסְמְרִים לֹא יִמּוֹט: ח וְאַתָּה יִשְׂרָאֵל

‹ O Israel, ‹ And [as for] you, 8 « that it not slip. ‹ with nails

עַבְדִּי יַעֲקֹב אֲשֶׁר בְּחַרְתִּיךָ זֶרַע

‹ O offspring « I have chosen; ‹ whom ‹ O Jacob, « My servant;

אַבְרָהָם אֹהֲבִי: ט אֲשֶׁר הֶחֱזַקְתִּיךָ

‹ I have supported ‹ [you] whom 9 « who loved Me; ‹ of Abraham,

מִקְצוֹת הָאָרֶץ וּמֵאֲצִילֶיהָ קְרָאתִיךָ

« I have called you, ‹ and from among its nobles « of the earth; ‹ from the ends

וָאֹמַר לְךָ עַבְדִּי־אַתָּה בְּחַרְתִּיךָ

‹ I have chosen you « *are you!* ‹ *My servant* ‹ to you, ‹ and I said

וְלֹא מְאַסְתִּיךָ: י אַל־תִּירָא כִּי עִמְּךָ

‹ with you ‹ for ‹ fear, ‹ Do not 10 « and I have not despised you.

אֲנִי אַל־תִּשְׁתָּע כִּי־אֲנִי אֱלֹהֶיךָ

« your God; ‹ I am ‹ for ‹ go astray ‹ do not « am I;

we should look to the obvious manifestations of God's sovereignty and recognize that, despite what transitory events may sometimes indicate, the only intelligent course is to serve God.

But what do unthinking people do in the face of these manifestations? They persist in their idol worship, exhort their comrades to be firm in their misdirection. Israel will triumph in the end.

אִמַּצְתִּיךָ אַף־עֲזַרְתִּיךָ אַף־תְּמַכְתִּיךָ
‹ I have supported you ‹ moreover, « I have helped you, ‹ moreover, « I have strengthened you,

בִּימִין צִדְקִי: יא הֵן יֵבֹשׁוּ וְיִכָּלְמוּ כֹּל
‹ all ‹ and they shall be humiliated, ‹ They shall be shamed ‹ Behold! 11 « of My righteousness. ‹ with the right hand

הַנֶּחֱרִים בָּךְ יִהְיוּ כְאַיִן וְיֹאבְדוּ אַנְשֵׁי
‹ —the men « and they shall perish ‹ like nothingness ‹ they shall be « against you; ‹ who are seething

רִיבֶךָ: יב תְּבַקְשֵׁם וְלֹא תִמְצָאֵם אַנְשֵׁי
‹ —the men « but you shall not find them ‹ You shall seek them 12 « who contend against you.

מַצֻּתֶךָ יִהְיוּ כְאַיִן וּכְאֶפֶס אַנְשֵׁי
‹ —the men « and naught ‹ like nothingness ‹ they shall be « who fight against you;

מִלְחַמְתֶּךָ: יג כִּי אֲנִי יהוה אֱלֹהֶיךָ
‹ your God, ‹ HASHEM, ‹ I am ‹ For 13 « who do battle against you.

מַחֲזִיק יְמִינֶךָ הָאֹמֵר לְךָ אַל־תִּירָא אֲנִי
‹ *[for] I,* ‹ *fear,* ‹ *Do not* « to you: ‹ He Who says « your right hand; ‹ supporting

עֲזַרְתִּיךָ: יד אַל־תִּירְאִי תּוֹלַעַת יַעֲקֹב
« Jacob, ‹ O [weak as a] worm ‹ fear, ‹ Do not 14 « *have helped you.*

מְתֵי יִשְׂרָאֵל אֲנִי עֲזַרְתִּיךָ נְאֻם־יהוה
« of HASHEM — ‹ —the word « have helped you ‹ I « of Israel; ‹ O people

וְגֹאֲלֵךְ קְדוֹשׁ יִשְׂרָאֵל: טו הִנֵּה שַׂמְתִּיךְ
‹ I have set you « Behold! 15 « of Israel. ‹ the Holy One ‹ and [I am] your Redeemer,

לְמוֹרַג חָרוּץ חָדָשׁ בַּעַל פִּיפִיּוֹת תָּדוּשׁ
‹ you shall thresh « many-bladed; ‹ new, ‹ sharp, ‹ as a threshing board,

הָרִים וְתָדֹק וּגְבָעוֹת כַּמֹּץ תָּשִׂים:
« you shall make them. ‹ —like chaff « and [as for the] hills « and grind [them]; ‹ mountains

טז תִּזְרֵם וְרוּחַ תִּשָּׂאֵם וּסְעָרָה תָּפִיץ
‹ will scatter ‹ and the storm « will carry them off, ‹ and the wind ‹ You shall winnow them, 16

אֹתָם וְאַתָּה תָּגִיל בַּיהוה בִּקְדוֹשׁ
‹ in the Holy One ‹ in HASHEM, ‹ will rejoice ‹ but you « them;

יִשְׂרָאֵל תִּתְהַלָּל:
« you will glory! ‹ of Israel

HAFTARAS VAYEIRA / הפטרת וירא

II Kings 4:1-37 / מלכים ב ד:א-לז

ד א וְאִשָּׁה אַחַת מִנְּשֵׁי בְנֵי־הַנְּבִיאִים
‹ of the prophets ‹ of the disciples ‹ of the wives ‹ A [certain] woman 1 [4]

צָעֲקָה אֶל־אֱלִישָׁע לֵאמֹר עַבְדְּךָ
‹ *Your servant,* ‹ saying, ‹ Elisha, ‹ to ‹ cried out

אִישִׁי מֵת וְאַתָּה יָדַעְתָּ כִּי עַבְדְּךָ הָיָה
‹ *was* ‹ *your servant* ‹ *that* ‹ *know* ‹ *and you* « *has died;* ‹ *my husband,*

יָרֵא אֶת־יהוה וְהַנֹּשֶׁה בָּא לָקַחַת
‹ *to take* ‹ *has come* ‹ *But the creditor* « HASHEM. ‹ *one who fears*

אֶת־שְׁנֵי יְלָדַי לוֹ לַעֲבָדִים: ב וַיֹּאמֶר
‹ Say 2 « *as slaves.* ‹ *for himself* ‹ *my two sons*

אֵלֶיהָ אֱלִישָׁע מָה אֶעֱשֶׂה־לָּךְ הַגִּידִי לִי
‹ *me,* ‹ *Tell* « *for you?* ‹ *shall I do* ‹ *What* « did Elisha, ‹ to her

מַה־יֶּשׁ־לָךְ [לכי כ׳] בַּבָּיִת וַתֹּאמֶר אֵין
‹ *There is not* « She said, « *in the house?* ‹ *for you* ‹ *is there* ‹ *what*

לְשִׁפְחָתְךָ כֹל בַּבַּיִת כִּי אִם־אָסוּךְ
‹ *a cruse* ‹ *except for* ‹ *in the house,* ‹ *anything* ‹ *for your maidservant*

שָׁמֶן: ג וַיֹּאמֶר לְכִי שַׁאֲלִי־לָךְ כֵּלִים מִן־
‹ *from* ‹ *vessels* ‹ *for yourself* ‹ *borrow* ‹ *Go* He said, 3 « *of oil.*

הַחוּץ מֵאֵת כָּל־שְׁכֵנָיִךְ [שכניכי כ׳] כֵּלִים
‹ *vessels* ‹ *your neighbors,* ‹ *all* ‹ *from* ‹ *the outside,*

Haftaras Vayeira

Elisha, like Abraham, embodied the nobility of Judaism for his generation, and, as it does to Abraham, Scripture expresses Elisha's greatness by setting forth his compassion for others. The *Haftarah* cites two such episodes: The first involves a destitute widow who has no one to help her, and the second involves a wealthy, influential woman who needs no favors from anyone.

It may be that the case of the widow was chosen because her plight seemed to be like that of a visitor to Sodom, so unconcerned did her neighbors seem to be. According to the Sages, she was the widow of the prophet Obadiah, who risked his life and spent his fortune to support and shelter hundreds of prophets from the sword of Ahab and Jezebel. Yet when his widow was confronted with a creditor who was about to seize her children as slaves in

רֵקִים אַל־תַּמְעִיטִי: ד וּבָאת וְסָגַרְתְּ
‹ *and shut* ‹ *[Then] go in* **4** « *be sparing.* ‹ *do not* ‹ *that are empty;*

הַדֶּלֶת בַּעֲדֵךְ וּבְעַד־בָּנַיִךְ וְיָצַקְתְּ עַל
‹ *over* ‹ *and you shall pour [from the cruse]* « *your sons;* ‹ *and upon* ‹ *upon yourself* ‹ *the door*

כָּל־הַכֵּלִים הָאֵלֶּה וְהַמָּלֵא תַּסִּיעִי:
« *you shall remove.* ‹ *and each full one* ‹ *these vessels,* ‹ *all*

ה וַתֵּלֶךְ מֵאִתּוֹ וַתִּסְגֹּר הַדֶּלֶת בַּעֲדָהּ
‹ upon herself ‹ the door ‹ and she shut ‹ from him ‹ She went **5**

וּבְעַד בָּנֶיהָ הֵם מַגִּשִׁים אֵלֶיהָ וְהִיא
‹ and she ‹ to her, ‹ were bringing [vessels] ‹ They « her sons: ‹ and upon

מוֹצָקֶת [מיצקת כ׳]: ו וַיְהִי | כִּמְלֹאת הַכֵּלִים
‹ were the vessels ‹ when nearly filled ‹ Then it was **6** « was pouring.

וַתֹּאמֶר אֶל־בְּנָהּ הַגִּישָׁה אֵלַי עוֹד כֶּלִי
« *vessel.* ‹ *another* ‹ *to me* ‹ *Bring* ‹ her son, ‹ to ‹ she said

וַיֹּאמֶר אֵלֶיהָ אֵין עוֹד כֶּלִי וַיַּעֲמֹד
‹ And stopped « *vessel.* ‹ *another* ‹ *There is not* ‹ to her, ‹ And he said

הַשָּׁמֶן: ז וַתָּבֹא וַתַּגֵּד לְאִישׁ הָאֱלֹהִים
« of God. ‹ the man ‹ and she told ‹ She came **7** « did the oil.

וַיֹּאמֶר לְכִי מִכְרִי אֶת־הַשֶּׁמֶן וְשַׁלְּמִי
‹ *and pay* ‹ *the oil* ‹ *sell* ‹ *Go* ‹ And he said,

אֶת־נִשְׁיֵךְ [נשיכי כ׳] וְאַתְּ וּבָנַיִךְ [בניכי כ׳]
‹ *and your sons* ‹ *and you* ‹ *your creditors;*

תִּחְיִי בַּנּוֹתָר: ח וַיְהִי הַיּוֹם וַיַּעֲבֹר
‹ And travel « one day: ‹ It happened **8** « *on the remainder.* ‹ *will live*

אֱלִישָׁע אֶל־שׁוּנֵם וְשָׁם אִשָּׁה גְדוֹלָה
« who was prominent; ‹ a woman, ‹ And there [dwelt] « Shunem. ‹ to ‹ did Elisha

וַתַּחֲזֶק־בּוֹ לֶאֱכָל־לָחֶם וַיְהִי מִדֵּי עָבְרוֹ
‹ of his traveling through, ‹ each time ‹ And [so] it was « bread. ‹ to eat ‹ him ‹ and she pressed

יָסֻר שָׁמָּה לֶאֱכָל־לָחֶם: ט וַתֹּאמֶר אֶל־
‹ to ‹ She said **9** « bread. ‹ to eat ‹ there ‹ he would turn

אִישָׁהּ הִנֵּה־נָא יָדַעְתִּי כִּי אִישׁ אֱלֹהִים
‹ *of God,* ‹ *[he is] a man* ‹ *that* ‹ *— I know* « *now!* ‹ *Behold* ‹ her husband,

קָדוֹשׁ הוּא עֹבֵר עָלֵינוּ תָּמִיד: י נַעֲשֶׂה־
‹ *Let us make* **10** « *regularly.* ‹ *to us* ‹ *he travels* « *is he;* ‹ *holy*

נָּא עֲלִיַּת־קִיר קְטַנָּה וְנָשִׂים לוֹ שָׁם
‹ *there* ‹ *for him* ‹ *and let us place* ‹ *that is small,* ‹ *[enclosed by] a wall,* ‹ *an upstairs area,* ‹ *now*

מִטָּה וְשֻׁלְחָן וְכִסֵּא וּמְנוֹרָה וְהָיָה בְּבֹאוֹ
‹ *when he comes* ‹ *And it will be* « *and a candelabrum.* ‹ *and a chair,* ‹ *and a table,* ‹ *a bed,*

אֵלֵינוּ יָסוּר שָׁמָּה: יא וַיְהִי הַיּוֹם וַיָּבֹא
‹ He came ‹ one day: ‹ It happened **11** « *[into] there.* ‹ *he can turn* ‹ *to us,*

שָׁמָּה וַיָּסַר אֶל־הָעֲלִיָּה וַיִּשְׁכַּב־שָׁמָּה:
« there. ‹ and he lay down ‹ the upstairs area ‹ to ‹ and he turned « there;

יב וַיֹּאמֶר אֶל־גֵּיחֲזִי נַעֲרוֹ קְרָא
‹ *Call* « his attendant, ‹ Gehazi ‹ to ‹ He said **12**

לַשּׁוּנַמִּית הַזֹּאת וַיִּקְרָא־לָהּ וַתַּעֲמֹד
‹ and she stood ‹ her, ‹ He called « *this Shunammite woman.*

לְפָנָיו: יג וַיֹּאמֶר לוֹ אֱמָר־נָא אֵלֶיהָ הִנֵּה
« *Indeed!* ‹ *to her,* ‹ *now* ‹ *Say* ‹ to [Gehazi], ‹ [Elisha] said **13** « before him.

חֲרַדְתְּ | אֵלֵינוּ אֶת־כָּל־הַחֲרָדָה הַזֹּאת
« *of this concern.* ‹ *all* ‹ *about us* ‹ *— You have concerned yourself*

מֶה לַעֲשׂוֹת לָךְ הֲיֵשׁ לְדַבֶּר־לָךְ אֶל־
‹ *to* ‹ *on your behalf* ‹ *to be spoken* ‹ *Is there [something]* « *for you?* ‹ *to do* ‹ *What is there*

---

payment for her debts, she had nowhere to turn, but to Elisha. Where was Abraham's legacy of mercy? But in the kingdom of the Ten Tribes, where that legacy had apparently been squandered, Elisha was still there to listen, empathize, and help.

The second episode involves the Shunammite woman who had everything — but no children. Elisha shows his gratitude for her hospitality by blessing her with a son, as God blessed Sarah with a son.

When the child died suddenly, Elisha revived him by placing himself upon the lifeless little body, and injecting his own soul, as it were, into the child. This has become an eternal lesson for those who wish to teach and inspire Jewish children — to breathe life into them. A teacher must give himself over to his charges if he hopes to succeed.

הַמֶּ֫לֶךְ א֖וֹ אֶל־שַׂ֣ר הַצָּבָ֑א וַתֹּ֕אמֶר
« She said, « of the army? ‹ the commander ‹ to ‹ or ‹ the king

בְּת֥וֹךְ עַמִּ֖י אָנֹכִ֥י יֹשָֽׁבֶת׃ יד וַיֹּ֕אמֶר וּמֶ֖ה
‹ What is there ‹ So he said [to Gehazi], 14 « dwell. ‹ do I « my people ‹ Among

לַעֲשׂ֣וֹת לָ֑הּ וַיֹּ֣אמֶר גֵּיחֲזִ֔י אֲבָ֛ל בֵּ֥ן אֵֽין־
‹ there is not ‹ a child ‹ In truth, ‹ Gehazi said, « for her? ‹ [for us] to do

לָ֖הּ וְאִישָׁ֥הּ זָקֵֽן׃ טו וַיֹּ֖אמֶר קְרָא־לָ֑הּ
« her. ‹ Call ‹ [Elisha] said, 15 « is old. ‹ and her husband « unto her,

וַיִּ֨קְרָא־לָ֔הּ וַֽתַּעֲמֹ֖ד בַּפָּֽתַח׃ טז וַיֹּ֗אמֶר
‹ [Elisha] said, 16 « in the doorway. ‹ and she stood ‹ her, ‹ [Gehazi] called

לַמּוֹעֵ֤ד הַזֶּה֙ כָּעֵ֣ת חַיָּ֔ה אַ֖תְּ [אתי כ׳]
‹ you [will be] ‹ next year, ‹ At this season

חֹבֶ֣קֶת בֵּ֑ן וַתֹּ֗אמֶר אַל־אֲדֹנִי֙ אִ֣ישׁ
‹ O man ‹ my master, ‹ Do not, ‹ She said, « a son. ‹ embracing

הָאֱלֹהִ֔ים אַל־תְּכַזֵּ֖ב בְּשִׁפְחָתֶֽךָ׃ יז וַתַּ֥הַר
‹ Conceive 17 « about your maidservant! ‹ speak falsely ‹ do not ‹ of God,

הָאִשָּׁ֖ה וַתֵּ֣לֶד בֵּ֑ן לַמּוֹעֵ֤ד הַזֶּה֙ כָּעֵ֣ת חַיָּ֔ה
‹ the next year, ‹ at that season ‹ a son ‹ and she bore ‹ did the woman,

אֲשֶׁר־דִּבֶּ֥ר אֵלֶ֖יהָ אֱלִישָֽׁע׃ יח וַיִּגְדַּ֖ל
‹ And grow up 18 « — Elisha. ‹ to her ‹ he had spoken ‹ as

הַיָּ֑לֶד וַיְהִ֣י הַיּ֔וֹם וַיֵּצֵ֥א אֶל־אָבִ֖יו אֶל־
‹ to ‹ his father ‹ to ‹ [that] he went out ‹ one day, ‹ and it happened « did the boy;

הַקֹּצְרִֽים׃ יט וַיֹּ֥אמֶר אֶל־אָבִ֖יו רֹאשִׁ֣י ׀
‹ My head! ‹ his father, ‹ to ‹ He said 19 « the reapers.

רֹאשִׁ֑י וַיֹּ֙אמֶר֙ אֶל־הַנַּ֔עַר שָׂאֵ֖הוּ אֶל־
‹ to ‹ Carry him ‹ the servant, ‹ to ‹ [His father] said « My head!

אִמּֽוֹ׃ כ וַיִּשָּׂאֵ֔הוּ וַיְבִיאֵ֖הוּ אֶל־אִמּ֑וֹ וַיֵּ֧שֶׁב
‹ He sat « his mother. ‹ to ‹ and he brought him ‹ He carried him 20 « his mother.

עַל־בִּרְכֶּ֛יהָ עַד־הַצָּהֳרַ֖יִם וַיָּמֹֽת׃
« then he died. ‹ noontime; ‹ until ‹ her lap ‹ on

כא וַתַּ֗עַל וַתַּשְׁכִּבֵ֖הוּ עַל־מִטַּ֣ת אִ֣ישׁ
‹ of the man ‹ the bed ‹ upon ‹ and she laid him ‹ She went up 21

הָאֱלֹהִ֑ים וַתִּסְגֹּ֥ר בַּעֲד֖וֹ וַתֵּצֵֽא׃
« and she left. ‹ upon him ‹ she shut [the door] ‹ of God;

כב וַתִּקְרָא֙ אֶל־אִישָׁ֔הּ וַתֹּ֗אמֶר שִׁלְחָ֨ה
‹ Send ‹ and she said, ‹ her husband ‹ to ‹ Then she called 22

נָ֥א לִ֛י אֶחָ֥ד מִן־הַנְּעָרִ֖ים וְאַחַ֣ת
‹ and one ‹ the servants ‹ of ‹ one ‹ to me ‹ now

הָאֲתֹנ֑וֹת וְאָר֛וּצָה עַד־אִ֥ישׁ הָאֱלֹהִ֖ים
‹ of God ‹ the man ‹ to ‹ so that I may run « of the donkeys

וְאָשֽׁוּבָה׃ כג וַיֹּ֡אמֶר מַדּ֜וּעַ אַ֣תְּ הֹלֶ֣כֶת
‹ going ‹ are you ‹ Why ‹ He said, 23 « and I will return.

[אתי הלכתי כ׳] אֵלָיו֙ הַיּ֔וֹם לֹא־חֹ֖דֶשׁ וְלֹ֣א
‹ and it is not ‹ a [New] Moon ‹ It is not « today? ‹ to him

שַׁבָּ֑ת וַתֹּ֖אמֶר שָׁלֽוֹם׃
« It is well. ‹ She said, « a Sabbath!

Sephardim, the community of Frankfurt am Main, and *Chabad Chassidim* conclude the *Haftarah* here. Others continue.

כד וַֽתַּחֲבֹשׁ֙ הָאָת֔וֹן וַתֹּ֥אמֶר אֶֽל־נַעֲרָ֖הּ
‹ her servant, ‹ to ‹ and she said ‹ the donkey ‹ She saddled 24

נְהַ֣ג וָלֵ֑ךְ אַל־תַּעֲצָר־לִ֣י לִרְכֹּ֔ב
‹ to ride, ‹ for me ‹ stop ‹ Do not « and go. ‹ Lead

כִּ֖י אִם־אָמַ֥רְתִּי לָֽךְ׃ כה וַתֵּ֨לֶךְ וַתָּב֧וֹא
‹ and she came « She went; 25 « you. ‹ I tell ‹ if ‹ except

אֶל־אִ֥ישׁ הָאֱלֹהִ֖ים אֶל־הַ֣ר הַכַּרְמֶ֑ל
« Carmel. ‹ Mount ‹ at ‹ of God ‹ the man ‹ to

וַיְהִי֩ כִּרְא֨וֹת אִישׁ־הָאֱלֹהִ֤ים אוֹתָהּ֙
‹ her ‹ of God ‹ did the man ‹ when see ‹ And it was

מִנֶּ֔גֶד וַיֹּ֙אמֶר֙ אֶל־גֵּיחֲזִ֣י נַעֲר֔וֹ הִנֵּ֖ה
« Behold! ‹ his attendant, ‹ Gehazi, ‹ to ‹ he said ‹ from afar,

הַשּׁוּנַמִּ֥ית הַלָּֽז׃ כו עַתָּה֙ רֽוּץ־נָ֣א
‹ please, ‹ run, « Now, 26 « That Shunammite woman.

לִקְרָאתָ֔הּ וֶאֱמָר־לָ֔הּ הֲשָׁל֥וֹם לָ֖ךְ
« with you? ‹ 'Is it well ‹ to her, ‹ and say ‹ toward her,

הֲשָׁלוֹם לְאִישֵׁךְ הֲשָׁלוֹם לַיָּלֶד וַתֹּאמֶר
‹ And she said, « with the boy?' ‹ Is it well « with your husband? ‹ Is it well

שָׁלוֹם: כז וַתָּבֹא אֶל־אִישׁ הָאֱלֹהִים אֶל
‹ at ‹ of God ‹ the man ‹ to ‹ She came 27 « It is well.

הָהָר וַתַּחֲזֵק בְּרַגְלָיו וַיִּגַּשׁ גֵּיחֲזִי
‹ did Gehazi ‹ Approach « of his feet. ‹ and she took hold ‹ the mountain

לְהָדְפָהּ וַיֹּאמֶר אִישׁ הָאֱלֹהִים הַרְפֵּה־
‹ Leave ‹ of God, ‹ the man ‹ but said ‹ to push her off,

לָהּ כִּי־נַפְשָׁהּ מָרָה־לָהּ וַיהוה הֶעְלִים
‹ has hidden [it] ‹ but HASHEM « within her, ‹ is bitter, ‹ her soul ‹ for ‹ her

מִמֶּנִּי וְלֹא הִגִּיד לִי: כח וַתֹּאמֶר
‹ She said, 28 « me. ‹ told ‹ and has not ‹ from me

הֲשָׁאַלְתִּי בֵן מֵאֵת אֲדֹנִי הֲלֹא אָמַרְתִּי
‹ that I said, ‹ Is it not « my master? ‹ of ‹ a son ‹ Did I request

לֹא תַשְׁלֶה אֹתִי: כט וַיֹּאמֶר לְגֵיחֲזִי
‹ to Gehazi, ‹ He said 29 « me!'? ‹ mislead ‹ 'Do not

חֲגֹר מָתְנֶיךָ וְקַח מִשְׁעַנְתִּי בְיָדְךָ
‹ in your hand ‹ my staff ‹ and take ‹ your waist, ‹ Gird

וָלֵךְ כִּי־תִמְצָא־אִישׁ לֹא תְבָרְכֶנּוּ וְכִי־
‹ and if « greet him; ‹ do not ‹ a man, ‹ you will meet ‹ If « and go.

יְבָרֶכְךָ אִישׁ לֹא תַעֲנֶנּוּ וְשַׂמְתָּ
‹ And you shall place « respond to him. ‹ do not ‹ a man will greet you,

מִשְׁעַנְתִּי עַל־פְּנֵי הַנָּעַר: ל וַתֹּאמֶר אֵם
‹ did the mother ‹ And say 30 « of the lad. ‹ the face ‹ upon ‹ my staff

הַנַּעַר חַי־יהוה וְחֵי־נַפְשְׁךָ אִם־אֶעֶזְבֶךָּ
« [that] I will leave you! ‹ it shall not happen ‹ of your soul, ‹ and [by] the life ‹ [I swear,] as HASHEM lives ‹ of the lad,

וַיָּקָם וַיֵּלֶךְ אַחֲרֶיהָ: לא וְגֵחֲזִי עָבַר
‹ had traveled on ‹ Gehazi 31 « after her. ‹ and he went ‹ So he stood up

לִפְנֵיהֶם וַיָּשֶׂם אֶת־הַמִּשְׁעֶנֶת עַל־פְּנֵי
‹ the face ‹ on ‹ the staff ‹ he placed ‹ before them;

הַנַּעַר וְאֵין קוֹל וְאֵין קָשֶׁב וַיָּשָׁב
‹ [Gehazi] returned « audible. ‹ and there was nothing ‹ a sound ‹ but there was not ‹ of the lad,

לִקְרָאתוֹ וַיַּגֶּד־לוֹ לֵאמֹר לֹא הֵקִיץ
‹ awakened ‹ Not ‹ saying, ‹ to him, ‹ and reported ‹ toward [Elisha]

הַנָּעַר: לב וַיָּבֹא אֱלִישָׁע הַבַּיְתָה וְהִנֵּה
‹ and behold! ‹ into the house ‹ Elisha came 32 « has the lad.

הַנַּעַר מֵת מֻשְׁכָּב עַל־מִטָּתוֹ: לג וַיָּבֹא
‹ He entered 33 « his bed. ‹ upon ‹ laid out ‹ is dead, ‹ the lad

וַיִּסְגֹּר הַדֶּלֶת בְּעַד שְׁנֵיהֶם וַיִּתְפַּלֵּל אֶל־
‹ to ‹ and he prayed ‹ the two of them, ‹ upon ‹ the door ‹ and he shut

יהוה: לד וַיַּעַל וַיִּשְׁכַּב עַל־הַיֶּלֶד וַיָּשֶׂם
‹ he placed ‹ the boy; ‹ upon ‹ and he lay ‹ Then he went up 34 « HASHEM.

פִּיו עַל־פִּיו וְעֵינָיו עַל־עֵינָיו וְכַפָּיו עַל־
‹ upon ‹ and his palms ‹ his eyes, ‹ upon ‹ and his eyes ‹ his mouth, ‹ upon ‹ his mouth

כַּפָּיו [כפו כ׳] וַיִּגְהַר עָלָיו וַיָּחָם בְּשַׂר
‹ did the flesh ‹ and become warm ‹ over him; ‹ and he stretched ‹ his palms,

הַיָּלֶד: לה וַיָּשָׁב וַיֵּלֶךְ בַּבַּיִת אַחַת הֵנָּה
‹ this way ‹ once ‹ inside the house, ‹ and he walked ‹ He withdrew 35 « of the boy.

וְאַחַת הֵנָּה וַיַּעַל וַיִּגְהַר עָלָיו וַיְזוֹרֵר
‹ and sneeze ‹ over him; ‹ and stretched ‹ then he went up « that way; ‹ and once

הַנַּעַר עַד־שֶׁבַע פְּעָמִים וַיִּפְקַח הַנַּעַר
‹ then the lad opened « times; ‹ seven ‹ until [he had sneezed] ‹ did the lad

אֶת־עֵינָיו: לו וַיִּקְרָא אֶל־גֵּיחֲזִי וַיֹּאמֶר
‹ and he said, ‹ Gehazi ‹ to ‹ [Elisha] called 36 « his eyes.

קְרָא אֶל־הַשֻּׁנַמִּית הַזֹּאת וַיִּקְרָאֶהָ
« He called her; « this Shunammite woman. ‹ to ‹ Call

וַתָּבֹא אֵלָיו וַיֹּאמֶר שְׂאִי בְנֵךְ: לז וַתָּבֹא
‹ She came 37 « your son! ‹ Pick up ‹ and he said, ‹ to him; ‹ she came

וַתִּפֹּל עַל־רַגְלָיו וַתִּשְׁתַּחוּ אָרְצָה
« to the ground; ‹ and bowed down ‹ his feet ‹ at ‹ and she fell

וַתִּשָּׂא אֶת־בְּנָהּ וַתֵּצֵא:
« and she left. ‹ her son ‹ she picked up

HAFTARAS CHAYEI SARAH / הפטרת חיי שרה

I Kings 1:1-31 / מלכים א א:א-לא

א אוְהַמֶּלֶךְ דָּוִד זָקֵן בָּא בַּיָּמִים וַיְכַסֻּהוּ

[1] 1 And King David was old, advanced in years; they covered him

בַּבְּגָדִים וְלֹא יִחַם לוֹ׃ ב וַיֹּאמְרוּ לוֹ

with garments, but he could not warm himself. 2 Say to him

עֲבָדָיו יְבַקְשׁוּ לַאדֹנִי הַמֶּלֶךְ נַעֲרָה

did his servants, *Let there be sought for my lord, the king, a girl,*

בְתוּלָה וְעָמְדָה לִפְנֵי הַמֶּלֶךְ וּתְהִי־לוֹ

a virgin, and she will stand before the king, and she will be for him

סֹכֶנֶת וְשָׁכְבָה בְחֵיקֶךָ וְחַם לַאדֹנִי

[as] a warmer; she will lie in your bosom, and it will be warm, for my lord

הַמֶּלֶךְ׃ ג וַיְבַקְשׁוּ נַעֲרָה יָפָה בְּכֹל גְּבוּל

the king. 3 They sought a beautiful girl throughout the boundary

יִשְׂרָאֵל וַיִּמְצְאוּ אֶת־אֲבִישַׁג הַשּׁוּנַמִּית

of Israel, and they found Abishag the Shunammite,

וַיָּבִאוּ אֹתָהּ לַמֶּלֶךְ׃ ד וְהַנַּעֲרָה יָפָה עַד־

and they brought her to the king. 4 The girl was beautiful to

מְאֹד וַתְּהִי לַמֶּלֶךְ סֹכֶנֶת וַתְּשָׁרְתֵהוּ

the extreme; and she was to the king [as] a warmer; and she served him;

וְהַמֶּלֶךְ לֹא יְדָעָהּ׃ ה וַאֲדֹנִיָּה בֶן־חַגִּית

but the king was not intimate with her. 5 Adonijah son of Haggith

מִתְנַשֵּׂא לֵאמֹר אֲנִי אֶמְלֹךְ וַיַּעַשׂ לוֹ

exalted himself, saying, *I shall reign!* He provided for himself

רֶכֶב וּפָרָשִׁים וַחֲמִשִּׁים אִישׁ רָצִים

a chariot and riders, with fifty men running

לְפָנָיו׃ ו וְלֹא־עֲצָבוֹ אָבִיו מִיָּמָיו לֵאמֹר

before him. 6 Not distress him did his father [ever] in his lifetime by saying,

מַדּוּעַ כָּכָה עָשִׂיתָ וְגַם־הוּא טוֹב־תֹּאַר

Why in this way have you acted? Moreover, he was handsome

מְאֹד וְאֹתוֹ יָלְדָה אַחֲרֵי אַבְשָׁלוֹם׃

very much so; and him [his mother] bore after Absalom.

ז וַיִּהְיוּ דְבָרָיו עִם יוֹאָב בֶּן־צְרוּיָה וְעִם

7 His conspiracies were with Joab son of Zeruiah and with

אֶבְיָתָר הַכֹּהֵן וַיַּעְזְרוּ אַחֲרֵי אֲדֹנִיָּה׃

Abiathar the Kohen; and they lent support, following Adonijah.

ח וְצָדוֹק הַכֹּהֵן וּבְנָיָהוּ בֶן־יְהוֹיָדָע וְנָתָן

8 But Zadok the Kohen, and Benaiahu son of Jehoiada, and Nathan

הַנָּבִיא וְשִׁמְעִי וְרֵעִי וְהַגִּבּוֹרִים אֲשֶׁר

the prophet, and Shimi, and Rei, and the mighty men who

לְדָוִד לֹא הָיוּ עִם־אֲדֹנִיָּהוּ׃ ט וַיִּזְבַּח

[had been] David's were not with Adonijah. 9 And slaughter

אֲדֹנִיָּהוּ צֹאן וּבָקָר וּמְרִיא עִם אֶבֶן

did Adonijah sheep, and cattle, and fatted bull at the stone

הַזֹּחֶלֶת אֲשֶׁר־אֵצֶל עֵין רֹגֵל וַיִּקְרָא

of Zoheleth that was near En-rogel, and he called

Haftaras Chayei Sarah

Like that of the *Sidrah*, the theme of the *Haftarah* deals with succession. Abraham needed to find a mother for the Jewish people, and David had to select the new head of the dynasty that would lead Israel and the world to God's appointed destiny. But there the similarity ends.

Isaac and Eliezer were devoted to the desires of Abraham, because they knew that he, in turn, represented only the will of God. As the Sages teach, when one nullifies his will before God's, God will nullify the will of others before his will (*Avos* 2:4). Abraham's will was paramount, because those nearest him knew that he spoke for God.

But as a nation grows and prospers, there are new challenges. When there is wealth, power, and influence, there are people who crave position. The great King David, as he lay old, weak, and unaware, became the victim of a cabal. Prince Adonijah, the senior son, handsome and well connected, tried to seize the throne. Pushed aside would be Solomon, the wise and devoted son whom David had designated. Can one imagine how the history of Israel would have been harmed if the king had been the imperious prince to whom monarchy meant lavish feasting amid fawning courtiers, instead of the wisest of men, whose legacy was the Temple, and the Books of *Proverbs, Song of Songs,* and *Ecclesiastes?*

אֶת־כָּל־אֶחָיו֙ בְּנֵ֣י הַמֶּ֔לֶךְ וּלְכָל־אַנְשֵׁ֥י
‹ the men for all ‹ and « of the king; ‹ the sons ‹ of his brothers, ‹ for all

יְהוּדָ֖ה עַבְדֵ֥י הַמֶּֽלֶךְ׃ י וְאֶת־נָתָ֨ן הַנָּבִ֜יא
‹ the prophet, ‹ But Nathan 10 « of the king. ‹ servants ‹ of Judah,

וּבְנָיָ֗הוּ וְאֶת־הַגִּבּוֹרִ֛ים וְאֶת־שְׁלֹמֹ֥ה
‹ and Solomon ‹ and the mighty men, ‹ and Benaiahu,

אָחִ֖יו לֹ֥א קָרָֽא׃ יא וַיֹּ֣אמֶר נָתָ֗ן אֶל־
‹ to ‹ Nathan said 11 « he did not call. ‹ his brother

בַּת־שֶׁ֤בַע אֵם־שְׁלֹמֹה֙ לֵאמֹ֔ר הֲל֣וֹא
‹ *Have not* « saying, ‹ of Solomon, ‹ mother ‹ Bathsheba,

שָׁמַ֔עַתְּ כִּ֥י מָלַ֖ךְ אֲדֹנִיָּ֣הוּ בֶן־חַגִּ֑ית
« *of Haggith?* ‹ *son* ‹ *has Adonijah* ‹ *reigned* ‹ *that* ‹ *you heard*

וַאֲדֹנֵ֥ינוּ דָוִ֖ד לֹ֥א יָדָֽע׃ יב וְעַתָּ֛ה לְכִ֥י
‹ *go,* ‹ *So now* **12** « *does not know.* ‹ *David* ‹ *—Yet our lord*

אִיעָצֵ֥ךְ נָ֖א עֵצָ֑ה וּמַלְּטִי֙ אֶת־נַפְשֵׁ֔ךְ
‹ *your life* ‹ *and you will be saving* « *[this] advice;* ‹ *now,* ‹ *I will counsel you*

וְאֶת־נֶ֖פֶשׁ בְּנֵ֥ךְ שְׁלֹמֹֽה׃ יג לְ֠כִי וּבֹ֣אִי ׀
‹ *and come* ‹ *Go,* **13** « *Solomon.* ‹ *of your son* ‹ *and the life*

אֶל־הַמֶּ֣לֶךְ דָּוִ֗ד וְאָמַ֤רְתְּ אֵלָיו֙ הֲלֹֽא־
‹ *'Is it not true,* « *to him,* ‹ *and you shall say* ‹ *David* ‹ *King* ‹ *to*

אַתָּ֞ה אֲדֹנִ֣י הַמֶּ֗לֶךְ נִשְׁבַּ֤עְתָּ לַאֲמָֽתְךָ֙
‹ *to your maidservant* ‹ *have sworn* ‹ *the king,* ‹ *my lord,* ‹ *[that] you,*

לֵאמֹ֔ר כִּֽי־שְׁלֹמֹ֤ה בְנֵךְ֙ יִמְלֹ֣ךְ אַחֲרַ֔י
‹ *after me,* ‹ *will reign* ‹ *your son* ‹ *"Solomon* ‹ *that* ‹ *saying,*

וְה֖וּא יֵשֵׁ֣ב עַל־כִּסְאִ֑י וּמַדּ֖וּעַ מָלַ֥ךְ
‹ *has reigned* ‹ *So why* « *my throne?"* ‹ *on* ‹ *who will sit* ‹ *and it is he*

אֲדֹנִיָֽהוּ׃ יד הִנֵּ֗ה עוֹדָ֛ךְ מְדַבֶּ֥רֶת שָׁ֖ם עִם־
‹ *with* ‹ *there* ‹ *speaking* ‹ *you will still be* ‹ *Indeed!* **14** « *Adonijah?'*

הַמֶּ֑לֶךְ וַאֲנִי֙ אָב֣וֹא אַחֲרַ֔יִךְ וּמִלֵּאתִ֖י
‹ *and I will complement* ‹ *after you* ‹ *will come in* ‹ *and I* « *the king,*

אֶת־דְּבָרָֽיִךְ׃ טו וַתָּבֹ֨א בַת־שֶׁ֤בַע אֶל־
‹ to ‹ did Bathsheba ‹ So come **15** « *your words.*

הַמֶּ֙לֶךְ֙ הַחַ֔דְרָה וְהַמֶּ֖לֶךְ זָקֵ֣ן מְאֹ֑ד
« to the extreme; « was old, ‹ Now, the king « into the chamber. ‹ the king

וַאֲבִישַׁג֙ הַשּׁ֣וּנַמִּ֔ית מְשָׁרַ֖ת אֶת־הַמֶּֽלֶךְ׃
« the king. ‹ attending ‹ the Shunammite ‹ with Abishag

טז וַתִּקֹּ֤ד בַּת־שֶׁ֙בַע֙ וַתִּשְׁתַּ֖חוּ לַמֶּ֑לֶךְ
« to the king. ‹ and she prostrated herself ‹ did Bathsheba ‹ And bow **16**

וַיֹּ֥אמֶר הַמֶּ֖לֶךְ מַה־לָּֽךְ׃ יז וַתֹּ֣אמֶר ל֗וֹ
‹ to him, ‹ She said **17** « *for you?* ‹ *What [can I do]* ‹ And the king said,

אֲדֹנִי֙ אַתָּ֞ה נִשְׁבַּ֜עְתָּ בַּיהוָ֤ה אֱלֹהֶ֙יךָ֙
‹ *your God,* ‹ *by* HASHEM, ‹ *have sworn* ‹ *you* ‹ *My lord,*

לַאֲמָתֶ֔ךָ כִּֽי־שְׁלֹמֹ֥ה בְנֵ֖ךְ יִמְלֹ֣ךְ אַחֲרָ֑י
‹ *after me;* ‹ *will reign* ‹ *your son,* ‹ *'Solomon,* ‹ *that* ‹ *to your maidservant,*

וְה֖וּא יֵשֵׁ֥ב עַל־כִּסְאִֽי׃ יח וְעַתָּ֕ה הִנֵּ֥ה
« *indeed!* ‹ *But now,* **18** « *my throne.'* ‹ *on* ‹ *will sit* ‹ *and he*

אֲדֹנִיָּ֖ה מָלָ֑ךְ וְעַתָּ֛ה אֲדֹנִ֥י הַמֶּ֖לֶךְ
‹ *the king,* ‹ *my lord,* ‹ *Yet now* « *has reigned.* ‹ *Adonijah*

לֹ֥א יָדָֽעְתָּ׃ יט וַ֠יִּזְבַּח שׁ֥וֹר וּֽמְרִיא־וְצֹאן֙
‹ *and sheep,* ‹ *and fatted bull,* ‹ *ox,* ‹ *He has slaughtered* **19** « *you have not known!*

לָרֹ֔ב וַיִּקְרָא֙ לְכָל־בְּנֵ֣י הַמֶּ֔לֶךְ וּלְאֶבְיָתָר֙
‹ *and for Abiathar* ‹ *of the king,* ‹ *the sons* ‹ *for all* ‹ *and he has called* « *in abundance;*

הַכֹּהֵ֔ן וּלְיֹאָ֖ב שַׂ֣ר הַצָּבָ֑א וְלִשְׁלֹמֹ֥ה
‹ *But for Solomon* « *of the army.* ‹ *the commander* ‹ *and for Joab* ‹ *the Kohen,*

עַבְדְּךָ֖ לֹ֥א קָרָֽא׃ כ וְאַתָּה֙ אֲדֹנִ֣י הַמֶּ֔לֶךְ
‹ *the king,* ‹ *my lord,* ‹ *And you,* **20** « *called.* ‹ *he has not* ‹ *your servant*

עֵינֵ֥י כָל־יִשְׂרָאֵ֖ל עָלֶ֑יךָ לְהַגִּ֣יד לָהֶ֔ם מִ֗י
‹ *who* ‹ *them* ‹ *to tell* ‹ *are upon you,* ‹ *Israel* ‹ *of all* ‹ *the eyes*

יֵשֵׁ֛ב עַל־כִּסֵּ֥א אֲדֹנִֽי־הַמֶּ֖לֶךְ אַחֲרָֽיו׃
« *after him.* ‹ *the king,* ‹ *of my lord,* ‹ *the throne* ‹ *on* ‹ *will sit*

But the Guardian of Israel neither slumbers nor sleeps. Nathan and Bathsheba bring the planned travesty to David's sickbed, and the elderly king arouses his greatness once more. He promises them that his pledge remains in effect and that Solomon *will* reign. It is indicative of the inherent goodness of the nation that it was not necessary for the *Haftarah* to include the outcome. Adonijah and his cabal were an aberration that represented only their own small group. Solomon became king.

כא וְהָיָה כִּשְׁכַּב אֲדֹנִי־הַמֶּלֶךְ עִם־אֲבֹתָיו
‹ his ‹ with ‹ the king, ‹ does ‹ that when ‹ It will be 21
ancestors, my lord, sleep

וְהָיִיתִי אֲנִי וּבְנִי שְׁלֹמֹה חַטָּאִים:
« [considered ‹ Solomon, ‹ and my ‹ I ‹ that I will be,
as] criminals. son

כב וְהִנֵּה עוֹדֶנָּה מְדַבֶּרֶת עִם־הַמֶּלֶךְ וְנָתָן
‹ when ‹ the king ‹ with ‹ speaking ‹ She was « And 22
Nathan still behold!

הַנָּבִיא בָּא: כג וַיַּגִּידוּ לַמֶּלֶךְ לֵאמֹר הִנֵּה
« Behold! ‹ saying, ‹ the king, ‹ [The serv- 23 « arrived. ‹ the
ants] told prophet

נָתָן הַנָּבִיא וַיָּבֹא לִפְנֵי הַמֶּלֶךְ וַיִּשְׁתַּחוּ
‹ and prostrated ‹ the king ‹ before ‹ He « the ‹ Nathan
himself came prophet!

לַמֶּלֶךְ עַל־אַפָּיו אָרְצָה: כד וַיֹּאמֶר נָתָן
« Nathan said, 24 « to the ‹ his face, ‹ upon ‹ to the king
ground.

אֲדֹנִי הַמֶּלֶךְ אַתָּה אָמַרְתָּ אֲדֹנִיָּהוּ
‹ 'Adonijah ‹ said, ‹ have you ‹ the king, ‹ My lord,

יִמְלֹךְ אַחֲרָי וְהוּא יֵשֵׁב עַל־כִּסְאִי: כה כִּי ׀
‹ For 25 « my ‹ on ‹ will sit ‹ and he ‹ after me ‹ will reign
throne?'

יָרַד הַיּוֹם וַיִּזְבַּח שׁוֹר וּמְרִיא־וְצֹאן
‹ and ‹ and fatted ‹ ox, ‹ and he has ‹ today ‹ he has
sheep, bull, slaughtered gone down

לָרֹב וַיִּקְרָא לְכָל־בְּנֵי הַמֶּלֶךְ וּלְשָׂרֵי
‹ and for the ‹ of the ‹ the ‹ for all ‹ and he « in abun-
commanders king, sons has called dance;

הַצָּבָא וּלְאֶבְיָתָר הַכֹּהֵן וְהִנָּם אֹכְלִים
‹ are ‹ and they ‹ the ‹ and for Abiathar ‹ of the army,
eating indeed Kohen,

וְשֹׁתִים לְפָנָיו וַיֹּאמְרוּ יְחִי הַמֶּלֶךְ
‹ the King ‹ '[Long] ‹ and they « before ‹ and they
live have said, him; are drinking

אֲדֹנִיָּהוּ: כו וְלִי אֲנִי־עַבְדֶּךָ וּלְצָדֹק הַכֹּהֵן
‹ the ‹ and for ‹ your ‹ I who ‹ But 26 « Adonijah!'
Kohen, Zadok servant, am for me,

וְלִבְנָיָהוּ בֶן־יְהוֹיָדָע וְלִשְׁלֹמֹה עַבְדְּךָ
‹ your ‹ and for ‹ of Jehoiada, ‹ son ‹ and for
servant, Solomon Benaiahu

לֹא קָרָא: כז אִם מֵאֵת אֲדֹנִי הַמֶּלֶךְ נִהְיָה
‹ has come ‹ the ‹ my lord, ‹ that ‹ Is it 27 « he did
about king, from possible not call.

הַדָּבָר הַזֶּה וְלֹא הוֹדַעְתָּ אֶת־עַבְדְּךָ
‹ your servant ‹ informed ‹ but you ‹ this matter,
have not

[עבדיך כ׳] מִי יֵשֵׁב עַל־כִּסֵּא אֲדֹנִי־הַמֶּלֶךְ
‹ the king, ‹ of my ‹ the ‹ on ‹ will sit ‹ who
lord, throne

אַחֲרָיו: כח וַיַּעַן הַמֶּלֶךְ דָּוִד וַיֹּאמֶר
‹ and he ‹ David ‹ did King ‹ And 28 « after him?
said, answer

קִרְאוּ־לִי לְבַת־שָׁבַע וַתָּבֹא לִפְנֵי
‹ before ‹ She came « for Bathsheba. ‹ for me ‹ Call

הַמֶּלֶךְ וַתַּעֲמֹד לִפְנֵי הַמֶּלֶךְ: כט וַיִּשָּׁבַע
‹ And swear 29 « the king. ‹ before ‹ and she stood ‹ the king

הַמֶּלֶךְ וַיֹּאמַר חַי־יהוה אֲשֶׁר־פָּדָה
‹ redeemed ‹ [He] ‹ As HASHEM lives, « and he said, ‹ did the king
Who has

אֶת־נַפְשִׁי מִכָּל־צָרָה: ל כִּי כַּאֲשֶׁר
‹ as ‹ That 30 « trouble: ‹ from every ‹ my soul

נִשְׁבַּעְתִּי לָךְ בַּיהוה אֱלֹהֵי יִשְׂרָאֵל
‹ of Israel, ‹ God ‹ by HASHEM, ‹ to you ‹ I have sworn

לֵאמֹר כִּי־שְׁלֹמֹה בְנֵךְ יִמְלֹךְ אַחֲרַי
‹ after me, ‹ will reign ‹ your son ‹ 'Solomon ‹ that ‹ saying,

וְהוּא יֵשֵׁב עַל־כִּסְאִי תַּחְתָּי כִּי כֵּן
‹ thus ‹ that ‹ in my ‹ my ‹ on ‹ will sit ‹ and he
place,' throne

אֶעֱשֶׂה הַיּוֹם הַזֶּה: לא וַתִּקֹּד בַּת־שֶׁבַע
« did Bathsheba, ‹ And bow 31 « this very day. ‹ shall I do

אַפַּיִם אֶרֶץ וַתִּשְׁתַּחוּ לַמֶּלֶךְ וַתֹּאמֶר
« and she « to the ‹ and she ‹ [to] the ‹ face
said, king; prostrated herself ground,

יְחִי אֲדֹנִי הַמֶּלֶךְ דָּוִד לְעֹלָם:
« forever! ‹ David, ‹ King ‹ my lord, ‹ [Long]
live,

HAFTARAS TOLDOS / הפטרת תולדות

Malachi 1:1-2:7 / מלאכי א:א־ב:ז

א א מַשָּׂא דְבַר־יהוה אֶל־יִשְׂרָאֵל בְּיַד
[1] 1 The communication of the word of HASHEM to Israel, by the hand

מַלְאָכִי: ב אָהַבְתִּי אֶתְכֶם אָמַר יהוה
of Malachi: 2 'I have loved you,' said HASHEM;

וַאֲמַרְתֶּם בַּמָּה אֲהַבְתָּנוּ הֲלוֹא־
and you said, 'In what way have You loved us?' 'Is it not [true that]

אָח עֵשָׂו לְיַעֲקֹב נְאֻם־יהוה וָאֹהַב
a brother was Esau to Jacob?' — the word of HASHEM: 'Yet I loved

אֶת־יַעֲקֹב: ג וְאֶת־עֵשָׂו שָׂנֵאתִי וָאָשִׂים
Jacob, 3 but Esau I hated; and I made

אֶת־הָרָיו שְׁמָמָה וְאֶת־נַחֲלָתוֹ
his mountains a desolation, and his heritage

לְתַנּוֹת מִדְבָּר: ד כִּי־תֹאמַר אֱדוֹם
for the serpents of the desert.' 4 Perhaps Edom will say

רֻשַּׁשְׁנוּ וְנָשׁוּב וְנִבְנֶה חֳרָבוֹת כֹּה
'We have become destitute, but we shall return and we shall rebuild the ruins.' So

אָמַר יהוה צְבָאוֹת הֵמָּה יִבְנוּ וַאֲנִי
said HASHEM, Master of Legions, 'They shall build; but I

אֶהֱרוֹס וְקָרְאוּ לָהֶם גְּבוּל רִשְׁעָה
will tear down!' [People] will call them, 'The boundary of wickedness,'

וְהָעָם אֲשֶׁר־זָעַם יהוה עַד־עוֹלָם:
and 'the people against whom HASHEM is angry to eternity.'

ה וְעֵינֵיכֶם תִּרְאֶינָה וְאַתֶּם תֹּאמְרוּ יִגְדַּל
5 Your eyes shall see and you shall say, 'May exalted be

יהוה מֵעַל לִגְבוּל יִשְׂרָאֵל: ו בֵּן יְכַבֵּד
HASHEM beyond the boundary of Israel.' 6 'A son will honor

אָב וְעֶבֶד אֲדֹנָיו וְאִם־אָב אָנִי אַיֵּה
[his] father and a slave his master; if a Father am I, where is

כְבוֹדִי וְאִם־אֲדוֹנִים אָנִי אַיֵּה מוֹרָאִי
My honor? And if a Master am I, where is My reverence?'

אָמַר ׀ יהוה צְבָאוֹת לָכֶם הַכֹּהֲנִים בּוֹזֵי
says HASHEM, Master of Legions, to you, the Kohanim who scorn

שְׁמִי וַאֲמַרְתֶּם בַּמֶּה בָזִינוּ אֶת־שְׁמֶךָ:
My Name: But you would say, 'In what way have we scorned Your Name?'

ז מַגִּישִׁים עַל־מִזְבְּחִי לֶחֶם מְגֹאָל
7 — bringing upon My Altar, bread that is defiled.

וַאֲמַרְתֶּם בַּמֶּה גֵאַלְנוּךָ בֶּאֱמָרְכֶם
And you would say, 'In what way have we defiled [Your bread]?' — by your saying,

שֻׁלְחַן יהוה נִבְזֶה הוּא: ח וְכִי־תַגִּשׁוּן
'The table of HASHEM, repulsive it is.' 8 And when you bring

עִוֵּר לִזְבֹּחַ אֵין רָע וְכִי תַגִּישׁוּ פִּסֵּחַ
a blind [animal] to slaughter, is it not evil? And when you bring a lame [animal]

וְחֹלֶה אֵין רָע הַקְרִיבֵהוּ נָא לְפֶחָתֶךָ
or a sick [animal], is it not evil? Offer it, please, if you to your governor.

הֲיִרְצְךָ אוֹ הֲיִשָּׂא פָנֶיךָ אָמַר יהוה
Will he be pleased with you? Or would he show favor toward you? — said HASHEM,

צְבָאוֹת: ט וְעַתָּה חַלּוּ־נָא פְנֵי־אֵל
Master of Legions. 9 And now, pray, if you please, before God,

וִיחָנֵנוּ מִיֶּדְכֶם הָיְתָה זֹּאת הֲיִשָּׂא מִכֶּם
that He be gracious to us. [For] from your hand has come about this [curse]. Will He show some among you

---

Haftaras Toldos

The *Sidrah* depicts perhaps the major turning point in the spiritual history of the world — the choice of Jacob over Esau to receive the Torah and bear the Patriarchal legacy. But the choice was not automatic. Esau was the firstborn and, however one understands Isaac's motives, he wished to confer the blessings upon Esau. Only God's will, as set in motion by Rebecca, secured the blessings for Jacob.

The *Haftarah* says at the outset that God's choice of Jacob was a sign of God's love for Jacob and His hatred for Esau. Because of this hatred, the prophet states that Edom, the nation that stems from Esau, will not prosper eternally; that it is doomed to destruc-

פָּנִים אָמַר יהוה צְבָאוֹת: י מִי גַם־בָּכֶם

‹—from among you— ‹[who] also ‹Who is there 10 « Master of Legions. ‹ HASHEM, ‹ says « a [favorable] countenance?

וְיִסְגֹּר דְּלָתַיִם וְלֹא־תָאִירוּ מִזְבְּחִי חִנָּם

« in vain! ‹ My Altar ‹ so that you could not kindle ‹ the doors ‹ would shut

אֵין־לִי חֵפֶץ בָּכֶם אָמַר יהוה צְבָאוֹת

‹ Master of Legions, ‹ HASHEM, ‹ said « for you, ‹ desire within Me ‹ There is not

וּמִנְחָה לֹא־אֶרְצֶה מִיֶּדְכֶם: יא כִּי

‹ For 11 « from your hand. ‹ I will not accept ‹ and an offering

מִמִּזְרַח־שֶׁמֶשׁ וְעַד־מְבוֹאוֹ גָּדוֹל שְׁמִי

‹ is My Name ‹ great « its setting, ‹ until ‹ of the sun ‹ from the rising

בַּגּוֹיִם וּבְכָל־מָקוֹם מֻקְטָר מֻגָּשׁ לִשְׁמִי

‹ for My Name's sake, ‹ it is offered ‹ incense is burned, ‹ place ‹ and in every « among the nations;

וּמִנְחָה טְהוֹרָה כִּי־גָדוֹל שְׁמִי בַּגּוֹיִם

« among the nations, ‹ is My Name ‹ great ‹ for « that is pure; ‹ an offering

אָמַר יהוה צְבָאוֹת: יב וְאַתֶּם מְחַלְּלִים

‹ desecrate ‹ But you 12 « Master of Legions. ‹ HASHEM, ‹ said

אוֹתוֹ בֶּאֱמָרְכֶם שֻׁלְחַן אֲדֹנָי מְגֹאָל הוּא

‹ it is'; ‹ defiled ‹ of the Lord, ‹ 'The table ‹ by your saying, ‹ it

וְנִיבוֹ נִבְזֶה אָכְלוֹ: יג וַאֲמַרְתֶּם הִנֵּה

‹ 'Here is ‹ And you would say, 13 « is His food.' ‹ 'Repulsive ‹ and his expression is,

מַתְּלָאָה וְהִפַּחְתֶּם אוֹתוֹ אָמַר יהוה

‹ HASHEM, ‹ said « 'You have made [Me] him disconsolate,' « a sickly [animal].'

צְבָאוֹת וַהֲבֵאתֶם גָּזוּל וְאֶת־הַפִּסֵּחַ

‹ and the lame, ‹ the stolen, ‹ And you would bring « Master of Legions.

וְאֶת־הַחוֹלֶה וַהֲבֵאתֶם אֶת־הַמִּנְחָה

« as an offering. ‹ and you would bring [it] ‹ and the sick,

הַאֶרְצֶה אוֹתָהּ מִיֶּדְכֶם אָמַר יהוה:

« HASHEM. ‹ said « from your hand? ‹ it ‹ Shall I accept

יד וְאָרוּר נוֹכֵל וְיֵשׁ בְּעֶדְרוֹ זָכָר וְנֹדֵר

‹ [yet] he pledges ‹ a [superior] ram, ‹ in his flock ‹ There is « the fraud: ‹ Accursed 14 is

וְזֹבֵחַ מָשְׁחָת לַאדֹנָי כִּי מֶלֶךְ גָּדוֹל אָנִי

« am I, ‹ great, ‹ a King, ‹ For ‹ to the Lord. ‹ a blemished one, ‹ and he slaughters

אָמַר יהוה צְבָאוֹת וּשְׁמִי נוֹרָא בַגּוֹיִם:

« among the nations. ‹ awesome ‹ and My Name is « Master of Legions, ‹ HASHEM, ‹ said

ב א וְעַתָּה אֲלֵיכֶם הַמִּצְוָה הַזֹּאת

‹ is this commandment, ‹ upon you ‹ And now, 1 [2]

הַכֹּהֲנִים: ב אִם־לֹא תִשְׁמְעוּ וְאִם־

‹ and if ‹ you will not listen ‹ If 2 « O Kohanim.

לֹא תָשִׂימוּ עַל־לֵב לָתֵת כָּבוֹד לִשְׁמִי

« to My Name, ‹ honor ‹ to render ‹ heart ‹ to ‹ you will not take

אָמַר יהוה צְבָאוֹת וְשִׁלַּחְתִּי בָכֶם

‹ among you ‹ I shall send « Master of Legions, ‹ HASHEM, ‹ said

אֶת־הַמְּאֵרָה וְאָרוֹתִי אֶת־בִּרְכוֹתֵיכֶם

« your blessings; ‹ and I shall curse ‹ the curse,

וְגַם אָרוֹתִיהָ כִּי אֵינְכֶם שָׂמִים עַל־לֵב:

« heart. ‹ to ‹ take ‹ you do not ‹ because ‹ I have cursed it, ‹ indeed,

ג הִנְנִי גֹעֵר לָכֶם אֶת־הַזֶּרַע וְזֵרִיתִי פֶרֶשׁ

‹ dung ‹ and I scatter ‹ the seed; «—because of you— « rebuke ‹ Behold! 3 I

עַל־פְּנֵיכֶם פֶּרֶשׁ חַגֵּיכֶם וְנָשָׂא אֶתְכֶם

‹ you ‹ [your sin] will carry « of your festival offerings; ‹ the dung « your faces, ‹ upon

אֵלָיו: ד וִידַעְתֶּם כִּי שִׁלַּחְתִּי אֲלֵיכֶם

‹ to you ‹ I have sent ‹ that ‹ And you shall know 4 « to itself.

---

tion, as indeed the evil that is incarnated in Edom will ultimately be destroyed. It will take time. The Roman Empire that brought about the current exile and most of the powers that have persecuted Israel during its long, long duration are regarded by the Rabbinic tradition as descendants — spiritual, if not direct — of Edom. Like most prophecies, we do not know when this one will be fulfilled; we know only that it will.

But this is not enough. Israel cannot achieve its destiny merely because of Esau's downfall. A chosen people must deserve its chosenness. Thus the prophet chastises Israel severely for the hypocrisy of those who think that they, encouraged and abetted by their self-serving priests, can turn their service of God into an insincere practice. How dare they offer their old, crippled, and ill animals as offerings to God, while retaining the best for themselves? Would they dare do the same for their human rulers?

In closing, the prophet exhorts the Kohanim to live up to their calling as teachers and models. Only then can they pull the people

אֶת הַמִּצְוָה הַזֹּאת לִהְיוֹת בְּרִיתִי
‹ My covenant ‹ so that it be ‹ this commandment,

אֶת־לֵוִי אָמַר יהוה צְבָאוֹת: ה בְּרִיתִי ׀
‹ My covenant 5 « Master of Legions. ‹ HASHEM, ‹ said « Levi, ‹ with

הָיְתָה אִתּוֹ הַחַיִּים וְהַשָּׁלוֹם וָאֶתְּנֵם־לוֹ
‹ to him ‹ I gave them « and peace; ‹ life « with him, ‹ was

מוֹרָא וַיִּירָאֵנִי וּמִפְּנֵי שְׁמִי נִחַת הוּא:
« was he. ‹ awestruck ‹ My Name, ‹ and before « and he revered Me; ‹ [for the sake of his] reverence,

ו תּוֹרַת אֱמֶת הָיְתָה בְּפִיהוּ וְעַוְלָה
‹ and injustice ‹ in his mouth, ‹ was ‹ of truth ‹ The teaching 6

לֹא־נִמְצָא בִשְׂפָתָיו בְּשָׁלוֹם וּבְמִישׁוֹר
‹ and in fairness ‹ in peace « on his lips; ‹ was not found

הָלַךְ אִתִּי וְרַבִּים הֵשִׁיב מֵעָוֹן:
« from iniquity. ‹ did he turn away ‹ and many « with Me, ‹ he walked

ז כִּי־שִׂפְתֵי כֹהֵן יִשְׁמְרוּ־דַעַת וְתוֹרָה
‹ and teaching « knowledge, ‹ should safeguard ‹ of a Kohen ‹ the lips ‹ For 7

יְבַקְשׁוּ מִפִּיהוּ כִּי מַלְאַךְ יהוה־צְבָאוֹת
‹ Master of Legions, ‹ of HASHEM, ‹ an agent ‹ for « from his mouth, ‹ they should seek

הוּא:
« is he.

HAFTARAS VAYEITZEI / הפטרת ויצא

Hosea 11:7-14:10 / הושע יא:ז־יד:י

Sephardim and *Chabad Chassidim* begin the *Haftarah* here. *Ashkenazim* begin below.

יא ז וְעַמִּי תְלוּאִים לִמְשׁוּבָתִי וְאֶל־עַל
‹ the Supreme One ‹ [though] unto « concerning returning to Me; ‹ wavers ‹ My people 7 [11]

יִקְרָאֻהוּ יַחַד לֹא יְרוֹמֵם: ח אֵיךְ אֶתֶּנְךָ
‹ shall I give you up [to destruction], ‹ How 8 « exalt [Him]. ‹ it will not ‹ [nevertheless] as one, ‹ [the prophets] summon it,

אֶפְרַיִם אֲמַגֶּנְךָ יִשְׂרָאֵל אֵיךְ אֶתֶּנְךָ
‹ shall I give you up ‹ How « O Israel? ‹ [How] shall I hand you over, « O Ephraim?

כְאַדְמָה אֲשִׂימְךָ כִּצְבֹאיִם נֶהְפַּךְ עָלַי
‹ upon Me ‹ Turned about « like Zeboim? ‹ [How] shall I set you « like Admah?

לִבִּי יַחַד נִכְמְרוּ נִחוּמָי: ט לֹא אֶעֱשֶׂה
‹ I will not carry out 9 « My regrets. ‹ were kindled ‹ together « is My heart;

חֲרוֹן אַפִּי לֹא אָשׁוּב לְשַׁחֵת אֶפְרָיִם
« Ephraim; ‹ to destroy ‹ I will not return « of My wrath; ‹ the heat

כִּי אֵל אָנֹכִי וְלֹא־אִישׁ בְּקִרְבְּךָ קָדוֹשׁ
‹ [am I] the Holy One, ‹ in your midst « a man; ‹ and not ‹ am I, ‹ God ‹ for

וְלֹא אָבוֹא בְּעִיר: י אַחֲרֵי יהוה יֵלְכוּ
« they will go. ‹ HASHEM ‹ Following 10 « into [another] city. ‹ and I will not come

כְּאַרְיֵה יִשְׁאָג כִּי־הוּא יִשְׁאַג וְיֶחֶרְדוּ
‹ and they shall hasten ‹ shall roar ‹ He ‹ for « He shall roar; ‹ Like a lion

בָנִים מִיָּם: יא יֶחֶרְדוּ כְצִפּוֹר מִמִּצְרַיִם
‹ out of Egypt; ‹ like a bird ‹ They will hasten 11 « from the west. ‹ — [His] children

וּכְיוֹנָה מֵאֶרֶץ אַשּׁוּר וְהוֹשַׁבְתִּים עַל
‹ in ‹ and I will settle them « of Assyria; ‹ out of the land ‹ and like a dove

---

up with them. The same remonstrance applies to all leaders — they have the duty to teach and lead by example.

Haftaras Vayeitzei

Hosea was one of the greatest prophets. A contemporary of Isaiah, he too cried out vainly against the rapidly deteriorating Kingdom of Samaria, the Ten Tribes of Israel. Hosea contrasts God's mercies of the past with Israel's failure to recognize that everything they have is due to God's kindness. Despite Israel's shortcomings, God says poignantly that He will never desert Ephraim, the wayward leader of the Ten Tribes. Like a spurned but still merciful Father, God confesses that He will not make a permanent end of Ephraim, because He has pledged that Israel will remain His people and because Israel is innately good and will eventually heed God's call to repent and resume its mission. When God will *roar like a lion* that the End has come, even Ephraim's children will rush to declare their renewed allegiance to Him.

The prophet declares that Judah, too, will falter, and will be punished. It will be a sad outcome for the people who descended from a Patriarch who defeated Esau's angel, but God's justice must be served. Thus Judah will join Ephraim in an exile that will recall the origins of the nation in Egypt.

The prophet continues his rebuke of the Ten Tribes, which had come to think that it was invincible. It had forgotten that Jacob had once been a humble shepherd in order to earn the right to his

בָּתֵּיהֶם נְאֻם־יהוה: יב א סְבָבֻנִי בְכַחַשׁ
‹ with falsehood ‹ He has surrounded Me 1 [12] « of HASHEM. ‹ – the word « their homes

אֶפְרַיִם וּבְמִרְמָה בֵּית יִשְׂרָאֵל וִיהוּדָה
‹ But Judah « of Israel. ‹ the House ‹ and with deceit, « – Ephraim [has];

עֹד רָד עִם־אֵל וְעִם־קְדוֹשִׁים נֶאֱמָן:
« he is faithful. ‹ the Holy One, ‹ and with ‹ God; ‹ with ‹ has ruled ‹ still

ב אֶפְרַיִם רֹעֶה רוּחַ וְרֹדֵף קָדִים כָּל־
‹ all « the east wind; ‹ and chases « [on] wind, ‹ grazes ‹ Ephraim 2

הַיּוֹם כָּזָב וָשֹׁד יַרְבֶּה וּבְרִית עִם־אַשּׁוּר
‹ Assyria ‹ with ‹ and a covenant « he would increase; ‹ and violence ‹ falseness ‹ the day,

יִכְרֹתוּ וְשֶׁמֶן לְמִצְרַיִם יוּבָל: ג וְרִיב
‹ But there is contention 3 « is brought. ‹ to Egypt ‹ and oil « they would seal;

לַיהוה עִם־יְהוּדָה וְלִפְקֹד עַל־יַעֲקֹב
‹ Jacob ‹ upon ‹ to visit « Judah; ‹ against ‹ unto HASHEM

כִּדְרָכָיו כְּמַעֲלָלָיו יָשִׁיב לוֹ: ד בַּבֶּטֶן
‹ In the womb, 4 « him. ‹ He will repay ‹ according to his deeds, « according to his ways;

עָקַב אֶת־אָחִיו וּבְאוֹנוֹ שָׂרָה אֶת־
‹ with ‹ he struggled ‹ and with his power, « of his brother; ‹ he held the heel

אֱלֹהִים: ה וַיָּשַׂר אֶל־מַלְאָךְ וַיֻּכָל בָּכָה
‹ [the angel] wept ‹ and he triumphed; ‹ an angel ‹ with ‹ He struggled 5 « [an angel of] God.

וַיִּתְחַנֶּן־לוֹ בֵּית־אֵל יִמְצָאֶנּוּ וְשָׁם
‹ *and there* ‹ *He will find us,* ‹ *[In] Beth-el* « him: ‹ and it entreated

יְדַבֵּר עִמָּנוּ: ו וַיהוה אֱלֹהֵי הַצְּבָאוֹת
« of Legions, ‹ the God ‹ And HASHEM is 6 « *with us.* ‹ *He will speak*

יהוה זִכְרוֹ: ז וְאַתָּה בֵּאלֹהֶיךָ תָשׁוּב
« you shall return; ‹ by [the promise of] your God ‹ And as for you 7 « is His remembrance. ‹ HASHEM

חֶסֶד וּמִשְׁפָּט שְׁמֹר וְקַוֵּה אֶל־אֱלֹהֶיךָ
‹ your God ‹ place your hope in « you shall observe; ‹ and justice ‹ kindness

תָּמִיד: ח כְּנַעַן בְּיָדוֹ מֹאזְנֵי מִרְמָה
« of deceit; ‹ are scales ‹ in whose hand ‹ [Yet you are like] a trader 8 « constantly.

לַעֲשֹׁק אָהֵב: ט וַיֹּאמֶר אֶפְרַיִם אַךְ
‹ *Surely* ‹ Ephraim said, 9 « [is his] love. ‹ to defraud

עָשַׁרְתִּי מָצָאתִי אוֹן לִי כָּל־יְגִיעַי
‹ *my toil* ‹ *[In] all* « *for myself.* ‹ *power* ‹ *I have found* ‹ *I have grown wealthy,*

לֹא יִמְצְאוּ־לִי עָוֺן אֲשֶׁר־חֵטְא: י וְאָנֹכִי
‹ But I am 10 « *[my] sin.* ‹ *that is* ‹ *iniquity* ‹ *in me* ‹ *they will not find*

יהוה אֱלֹהֶיךָ מֵאֶרֶץ מִצְרָיִם עֹד
‹ once again « of Egypt; ‹ [Who took you] from the land ‹ your God, ‹ HASHEM,

אוֹשִׁיבְךָ בָאֳהָלִים כִּימֵי מוֹעֵד:
« of yore. ‹ as in days ‹ in tents ‹ I shall settle you

יא וְדִבַּרְתִּי עַל־הַנְּבִיאִים וְאָנֹכִי חָזוֹן
‹ – prophecy ‹ and I ‹ the prophets, ‹ to ‹ I have spoken 11

הִרְבֵּיתִי וּבְיַד הַנְּבִיאִים אֲדַמֶּה: יב אִם־
‹ If 12 « I have conveyed allegory. ‹ of the prophets ‹ and by the hand « have I increased;

גִּלְעָד אָוֶן אַךְ־שָׁוְא הָיוּ בַּגִּלְגָּל שְׁוָרִים
‹ oxen ‹ in Gilgal « were they; ‹ false ‹ [it is] because ‹ [suffered] destruction, ‹ Gilead

זִבֵּחוּ גַּם מִזְבְּחוֹתָם כְּגַלִּים עַל תַּלְמֵי
‹ the furrows ‹ on ‹ [were] like heaps [of stone] ‹ their altars ‹ even ‹ they slaughtered;

שָׂדָי:
« of the fields.

Most *Sephardim* conclude the *Haftarah* here; some continue until 13:6. *Ashkenazim* begin the *Haftarah* here.

יג וַיִּבְרַח יַעֲקֹב שְׂדֵה אֲרָם וַיַּעֲבֹד
‹ and labor « of Aram; ‹ to the field ‹ did Jacob ‹ Flee 13

יִשְׂרָאֵל בְּאִשָּׁה וּבְאִשָּׁה שָׁמָר:
« he guarded [the sheep]. ‹ and for a wife ‹ for a wife, ‹ did Israel

---

bride, and that Ephraim had achieved eminence only because it *spoke harshly* against Solomon's successor, Rehoboam, who abused his holy calling. Thus Ephraim should have known that success is a gift of God, and not acquired by strength or guile.

But Ephraim sinned through arrogance and idolatry, and therefore was condemned to defeat, exile, and death. God does not forget sins; He stores them, to punish the perpetrators when they are no longer entitled to Divine forbearance. Israel's sins are serious because the nation forgot that God made them a nation.

Nevertheless, God does not abandon Israel. The prophet's ghastly warning concludes with a loving call to repentance. The same passage begins the *Haftarah* of *Shabbos Shuvah*, the Sabbath of Repentance. True, Israel has sinned grievously, but its essence remains good; it has *stumbled* into sin. The potential for repentance remains, and God is ready to forgive.

יד וּבְנָבִיא הֶעֱלָה יְהוָה אֶת־יִשְׂרָאֵל

14 Through a prophet did HASHEM bring up Israel

מִמִּצְרָיִם וּבְנָבִיא נִשְׁמָר׃

from Egypt, and through a prophet it was guarded.

Chabad Chassidim conclude the *Haftarah* here.

טו הִכְעִיס אֶפְרַיִם תַּמְרוּרִים וְדָמָיו

15 Ephraim provoked [upon himself] bitterness; his bloodshed

עָלָיו יִטּוֹשׁ וְחֶרְפָּתוֹ יָשִׁיב לוֹ אֲדֹנָיו׃

upon him will be cast; and his disgrace He will return to him — his Lord.

יג א כְּדַבֵּר אֶפְרַיִם רְתֵת נָשָׂא הוּא

[13] 1 When Ephraim speak [with] trembling, exalted was he

בְּיִשְׂרָאֵל וַיֶּאְשַׁם בַּבַּעַל וַיָּמֹת׃ ב וְעַתָּה ׀

in Israel; but he became guilty of Baal-worship and he died. 2 Yet now

יוֹסִפוּ לַחֲטֹא וַיַּעֲשׂוּ לָהֶם מַסֵּכָה

they continue to sin, and they made for themselves a molten idol

מִכַּסְפָּם כִּתְבוּנָם עֲצַבִּים מַעֲשֵׂה

from their silver, according to their design, idols, the work

חָרָשִׁים כֻּלֹּה לָהֶם הֵם אֹמְרִים זֹבְחֵי

of artisans, all of it. Of them they say, *Those who sacrifice*

אָדָם עֲגָלִים יִשָּׁקוּן׃ ג לָכֵן יִהְיוּ כַּעֲנַן

man: The calves they shall kiss. 3 Therefore, they shall be like the cloud

בֹּקֶר וְכַטַּל מַשְׁכִּים הֹלֵךְ כְּמֹץ יְסֹעֵר

of the morning; and like the dew, early passing on; like chaff wind-driven

מִגֹּרֶן וּכְעָשָׁן מֵאֲרֻבָּה׃ ד וְאָנֹכִי יְהוָה

from the threshing floor, and like smoke from a chimney. 4 Yet I am HASHEM,

אֱלֹהֶיךָ מֵאֶרֶץ מִצְרָיִם וֵאלֹהִים זוּלָתִי

your God, [Who took you] from the land of Egypt; and gods other than Me

לֹא תֵדָע וּמוֹשִׁיעַ אַיִן בִּלְתִּי׃ ה אֲנִי

you shall not know; for a Savior does not exist except for Me. 5 [And] I,

יְדַעְתִּיךָ בַּמִּדְבָּר בְּאֶרֶץ תַּלְאֻבוֹת׃

knew you in the wilderness, in a land of droughts.

Sephardim conclude the *Haftarah* here. *Ashkenazim* continue.

ו כְּמַרְעִיתָם וַיִּשְׂבָּעוּ שָׂבְעוּ וַיָּרָם לִבָּם

6 When at their pasturing, they became satiated; they became [so] satiated [that] haughty was their heart,

עַל־כֵּן שְׁכֵחוּנִי׃ ז וָאֱהִי לָהֶם כְּמוֹ־שָׁחַל

because of this they forgot Me. 7 So I have been toward them like a lion;

כְּנָמֵר עַל־דֶּרֶךְ אָשׁוּר׃ ח אֶפְגְּשֵׁם כְּדֹב

like a leopard on the road, I will look [to ambush]. 8 I will encounter them as a bear

שַׁכּוּל וְאֶקְרַע סְגוֹר לִבָּם וְאֹכְלֵם שָׁם

bereft and I will tear open their closed heart; I will devour them there

כְּלָבִיא חַיַּת הַשָּׂדֶה תְּבַקְּעֵם׃ ט שִׁחֶתְךָ

like a lioness; a beast of the field will split them apart. 9 You have destroyed yourself,

יִשְׂרָאֵל כִּי־בִי בְעֶזְרֶךָ׃ י אֱהִי מַלְכְּךָ

O Israel, for [you have rebelled] against Me, against your Helper. 10 I shall be! [But,] your king,

אֵפוֹא וְיוֹשִׁיעֲךָ בְּכָל־עָרֶיךָ וְשֹׁפְטֶיךָ

where is he, that he may save you in all your cities? And [where are] your judges

אֲשֶׁר אָמַרְתָּ תְּנָה־לִּי מֶלֶךְ וְשָׂרִים׃

of whom you have said, *Give me a king and princes?*

יא אֶתֶּן־לְךָ מֶלֶךְ בְּאַפִּי וְאֶקַּח בְּעֶבְרָתִי׃

11 I would give to you a king in My anger, and would take [him away] in My wrath.

יב צָרוּר עֲוֹן אֶפְרָיִם צְפוּנָה חַטָּאתוֹ׃

12 Bound up is the iniquity of Ephraim; hidden away is his sin.

יג חֶבְלֵי יוֹלֵדָה יָבֹאוּ לוֹ הוּא־בֵן לֹא

13 The pangs of a laboring woman shall come upon him; he is a son [who is] not

חָכָם כִּי־עֵת לֹא־יַעֲמֹד בְּמִשְׁבַּר בָּנִים׃

wise, for [when] the time [comes], he will not endure on the birthstool of children.

יד מִיַּד שְׁאוֹל אֶפְדֵּם מִמָּוֶת אֶגְאָלֵם אֱהִי

14 From the clutch of the grave I would ransom them; from death I would redeem them. [But now:] I will be

דְּבָרֶיךָ מָוֶת אֱהִי קָטָבְךָ שְׁאוֹל נֹחַם
‹ Reconsideration ‹ *[to] the grave.* ‹ your destroyer ‹ I will be « *Death!* ‹ [the speaker] to you of:

יִסָּתֵר מֵעֵינָי: טו כִּי הוּא בֵּין אַחִים
‹ the marsh plants, ‹ among ‹ he [Ephraim], ‹ For 15 « from My eyes. ‹ will be hidden

יַפְרִיא יָבוֹא קָדִים רוּחַ יהוה מִמִּדְבָּר
‹ from the desert ‹ of HASHEM, ‹ the wind ‹ the east wind [Assyria], ‹ [but] there shall come « would flourish;

עֹלֶה וְיֵבוֹשׁ מְקוֹרוֹ וְיֶחֱרַב מַעְיָנוֹ הוּא
‹ He [Assyria], « his well-spring, ‹ and it will parch ‹ his fountain, ‹ it will dry up « it will ascend;

יִשְׁסֶה אוֹצַר כָּל־כְּלִי חֶמְדָּה:
« that is desirable. ‹ vessel ‹ of every ‹ the treasure-trove ‹ will plunder

יד א תֶּאְשַׁם שֹׁמְרוֹן כִּי מָרְתָה בֵּאלֹהֶיהָ
« against her God. ‹ she has rebelled ‹ because ‹ Samaria shall be desolate 1 [14]

בַּחֶרֶב יִפֹּלוּ עֹלְלֵיהֶם יְרֻטָּשׁוּ וְהָרִיּוֹתָיו
‹ and its pregnant women « will be dashed; ‹ their infants « [its inhabitants] will fall; ‹ By the sword

יְבֻקָּעוּ: ב שׁוּבָה יִשְׂרָאֵל עַד יהוה
‹ HASHEM, ‹ unto ‹ O Israel, ‹ Return, 2 « will be torn asunder.

אֱלֹהֶיךָ כִּי כָשַׁלְתָּ בַּעֲוֺנֶךָ: ג קְחוּ עִמָּכֶם
‹ with you ‹ Take 3 « in your iniquity. ‹ you have stumbled ‹ for « your God,

דְּבָרִים וְשׁוּבוּ אֶל־יהוה אִמְרוּ אֵלָיו
‹ to Him, ‹ Say « HASHEM. ‹ to ‹ and return ‹ words

כָּל־תִּשָּׂא עָוֺן וְקַח־טוֹב וּנְשַׁלְּמָה פָרִים
‹ *bull-offerings* ‹ *and let us replace* « *goodness;* ‹ *and accept* ‹ *iniquity* ‹ *Forgive every*

שְׂפָתֵינוּ: ד אַשּׁוּר | לֹא יוֹשִׁיעֵנוּ עַל־סוּס
‹ *[the Egyptian] horse* ‹ *upon* « *cannot help us;* ‹ *Assyria* 4 « *[with the words of] our lips.*

לֹא נִרְכָּב וְלֹא־נֹאמַר עוֹד אֱלֹהֵינוּ
‹ *'[You are] our god,'* ‹ *again,* ‹ *and we will not say* ‹ *we will not ride*

לְמַעֲשֵׂה יָדֵינוּ אֲשֶׁר־בְּךָ יְרֻחַם יָתוֹם:
« *for an orphan.* ‹ *will there be compassion* ‹ *in You* ‹ *For [only]* « *of our hands.* ‹ *to the work*

ה אֶרְפָּא מְשׁוּבָתָם אֹהֲבֵם נְדָבָה כִּי שָׁב
‹ withdrawn is ‹ for ‹ freely, ‹ I shall love them « their waywardness; ‹ I shall heal 5

אַפִּי מִמֶּנּוּ: ו אֶהְיֶה כַטַּל לְיִשְׂרָאֵל יִפְרַח
‹ it will blossom « to Israel; ‹ like dew ‹ I shall be 6 « from them. ‹ My wrath.

כַּשּׁוֹשַׁנָּה וְיַךְ שָׁרָשָׁיו כַּלְּבָנוֹן: ז יֵלְכוּ
‹ Go forth 7 « like the [cedars of] Lebanon. ‹ its roots ‹ and it will strike ‹ like the rose;

יֹנְקוֹתָיו וִיהִי כַזַּיִת הוֹדוֹ וְרֵיחַ לוֹ
‹ unto it ‹ with a fragrance ‹ [in] its glory; ‹ like an olive tree ‹ and it will be ‹ will its shoots

כַּלְּבָנוֹן: ח יָשֻׁבוּ יֹשְׁבֵי בְצִלּוֹ יְחַיּוּ דָגָן
‹ [like] grain ‹ they shall revive « in its shade; ‹ those who sit ‹ They shall return, 8 « like that of the [cedars of] Lebanon.

וְיִפְרְחוּ כַגָּפֶן זִכְרוֹ כְּיֵין לְבָנוֹן: ט אֶפְרַיִם
« Ephraim [will say], 9 « of Lebanon. ‹ like the wine ‹ Its fame [will be] « like the grapevine. ‹ and they shall blossom

מַה־לִּי עוֹד לָעֲצַבִּים אֲנִי עָנִיתִי
‹ I have responded ‹ And as for Me, « *with idols?* ‹ *anymore* ‹ *have I* ‹ *What [to do]*

וַאֲשׁוּרֶנּוּ אֲנִי כִּבְרוֹשׁ רַעֲנָן מִמֶּנִּי פֶּרְיְךָ
‹ your fruit ‹ from Me « ever-fresh; ‹ like a cypress, ‹ I am « and I will gaze upon him.

נִמְצָא: י מִי חָכָם וְיָבֵן אֵלֶּה נָבוֹן וְיֵדָעֵם
« to know them? ‹ [Who is] discerning, « these? ‹ to understand ‹ wise, ‹ Who is 10 « will be found.

כִּי־יְשָׁרִים דַּרְכֵי יהוה וְצַדִּקִים יֵלְכוּ בָם
‹ in them, ‹ will walk ‹ Righteous people « of HASHEM: ‹ are the ways ‹ just ‹ For

וּפֹשְׁעִים יִכָּשְׁלוּ בָם:
« on them. ‹ will stumble ‹ but sinners

Some congregations have the custom to add the following verses from *Joel* (2:26-27).

כו וַאֲכַלְתֶּם אָכוֹל וְשָׂבוֹעַ וְהִלַּלְתֶּם
‹ and you shall praise « and being satiated — ‹ eating — « And you shall eat 26

אֶת־שֵׁם יהוה אֱלֹהֵיכֶם אֲשֶׁר־עָשָׂה
‹ had done ‹ Who ‹ Your God ‹ of HASHEM ‹ the Name

עִמָּכֶם לְהַפְלִיא וְלֹא־יֵבֹשׁוּ עַמִּי
‹ [shall] My people be ‹ and not put to shame « wondrously; ‹ with you

לְעוֹלָם: כז וִידַעְתֶּם כִּי בְקֶרֶב יִשְׂרָאֵל
‹ of Israel ‹ in the midst ‹ that ‹ Then you shall know 27 « ever.

אָנִי וַאֲנִי יהוה אֱלֹהֵיכֶם וְאֵין עוֹד | וְלֹא־יֵבֹשׁוּ עַמִּי לְעוֹלָם׃

« other. ‹ and there is no ‹ Your God ‹ HASHEM ‹ and I am « am I, | « ever. ‹ [shall] My people be ‹ And not put to shame

HAFTARAS VAYISHLACH / הפטרת וישלח

Obadiah 1:1-21 / עובדיה א:א־כא

א א חֲזוֹן עֹבַדְיָה כֹּה־אָמַר אֲדֹנָי יֱהֹוִה
‹ HASHEM/ELOHIM ‹ the Lord ‹ said ‹ — So « of Obadiah: ‹ The vision 1 [1]

לֶאֱדוֹם שְׁמוּעָה שָׁמַעְנוּ מֵאֵת יהוה
« HASHEM, ‹ from ‹ have we heard ‹ tidings « against Edom;

וְצִיר בַּגּוֹיִם שֻׁלָּח קוּמוּ וְנָקוּמָה עָלֶיהָ
‹ against her, ‹ Let us rise ‹ Arise! « has been sent [saying,] ‹ among the nations ‹ and an envoy

לַמִּלְחָמָה׃ ב הִנֵּה קָטֹן נְתַתִּיךָ בַּגּוֹיִם
« among the nations; ‹ have I made you ‹ small ‹ Indeed! 2 « to [do] battle!

בָּזוּי אַתָּה מְאֹד׃ ג זְדוֹן לִבְּךָ הִשִּׁיאֶךָ
« has misled you. ‹ of your heart ‹ The wickedness 3 « exceedingly. ‹ are you, ‹ despised

שֹׁכְנִי בְחַגְוֵי־סֶלַע מְרוֹם שִׁבְתּוֹ אֹמֵר
‹ who says ‹ is his abode, ‹ lofty ‹ of a rock, ‹ in clefts ‹ [You] who dwells

בְּלִבּוֹ מִי יוֹרִדֵנִי אָרֶץ׃ ד אִם־תַּגְבִּיהַּ
‹ you raise yourself ‹ If 4 « *to earth?* ‹ *can bring me down* ‹ *Who* « in his heart,

כַּנֶּשֶׁר וְאִם־בֵּין כּוֹכָבִים שִׂים קִנֶּךָ
‹ your nest, ‹ you place ‹ the stars ‹ among ‹ and if ‹ like the eagle,

מִשָּׁם אוֹרִידְךָ נְאֻם־יהוה׃ ה אִם־גַּנָּבִים
‹ thieves ‹ If 5 « of HASHEM. ‹ — the word « I will bring you down! ‹ from there

בָּאוּ־לְךָ אִם־שׁוֹדְדֵי לַיְלָה אֵיךְ
‹ how « of the night; ‹ robbers ‹ if « upon you, ‹ had come

נִדְמֵיתָה הֲלוֹא יִגְנְבוּ דַּיָּם אִם־בֹּצְרִים
‹ grape harvesters ‹ If « their fill? ‹ they would steal ‹ Is it not [true that] « cut off you had been!

בָּאוּ לָךְ הֲלוֹא יַשְׁאִירוּ עֹלֵלוֹת׃ ו אֵיךְ
‹ How 6 « the [grape] gleanings? ‹ they would leave ‹ is it not [true that] ‹ upon you, ‹ had come

נֶחְפְּשׂוּ עֵשָׂו נִבְעוּ מַצְפֻּנָיו׃ ז עַד־הַגְּבוּל
‹ the border ‹ Just until 7 « his hidden [treasures]! ‹ [How] revealed « Esau! ‹ searched was

שִׁלְּחוּךָ כֹּל אַנְשֵׁי בְרִיתֶךָ הִשִּׁיאוּךָ
‹ [But] they misled you, « of your covenant. ‹ the men ‹ all ‹ they escorted you,

יָכְלוּ לְךָ אַנְשֵׁי שְׁלֹמֶךָ לַחְמְךָ יָשִׂימוּ
‹ emplaced ‹ [Those who ate] your bread « who seemed at peace with you. ‹ the men ‹ against you, ‹ [for] they prevailed

מָזוֹר תַּחְתֶּיךָ אֵין תְּבוּנָה בּוֹ׃ ח הֲלוֹא
‹ Shall it not be 8 « within him [Esau]. ‹ understanding ‹ There is no « in your place. ‹ sickness

בַּיּוֹם הַהוּא נְאֻם־יהוה וְהַאֲבַדְתִּי
‹ [that] I will eradicate « of HASHEM — ‹ — the word « on that day

חֲכָמִים מֵאֱדוֹם וּתְבוּנָה מֵהַר עֵשָׂו׃
« Esau? ‹ from Mount ‹ and [men of] understanding ‹ from Edom, ‹ wise men

ט וְחַתּוּ גִבּוֹרֶיךָ תֵּימָן לְמַעַן יִכָּרֶת־אִישׁ
‹ [every] man ‹ cut down will be ‹ so that « O Teman, ‹ your mighty ones, ‹ Smashed shall be 9

מֵהַר עֵשָׂו מִקָּטֶל׃ י מֵחֲמַס אָחִיךָ יַעֲקֹב
‹ Jacob, ‹ [against] your brother ‹ For [your] violence 10 « by slaughter. ‹ Esau, ‹ from Mount

תְּכַסְּךָ בוּשָׁה וְנִכְרַתָּ לְעוֹלָם׃ יא בְּיוֹם
‹ On the day 11 « forever. ‹ and you will be cut off « by disgrace; ‹ you will be covered

◆§ Haftaras Vayishlach

The Book of *Obadiah* is read in its entirety as the *Haftarah* of the *Sidrah* that deals with the climactic encounter between Jacob and Esau. Its subject is God's wrath against Edom, the descendants of Esau. Of all the prophets, this vision was left for Obadiah for two reasons: (a) He was a descendant of an Edomite proselyte (*Yalkut*, *Job* 897; *Zohar*); and, (b) Obadiah was the antithesis of Esau. Esau lived among two righteous people, Isaac and Rebecca, yet he did not learn from them. Obadiah, on the other hand, was a courtier of two of the wickedest people in the annals of our people, King Ahab and Queen Jezebel, yet he remained righteous. Moreover, at a time when the king and queen murdered nearly all of the prophets of God, Obadiah risked his life to shelter and feed a hundred surviving prophets.

The *Haftarah* follows Edom through various periods of its history, culminating in its eventual defeat and final downfall in Messianic times. Edom began as a small and insignificant kingdom to the south of *Eretz Yisrael*, that, like a jackal, despoiled Israel in the wake of the triumphs of others. It enjoyed the travails and suffering of its "cousin," instead of feeling compassion. Then, in a vision

עֲמָדְךָ מִנֶּגֶד בְּיוֹם שְׁבוֹת זָרִים חֵילוֹ
of your standing afar, on the day of the plundering by strangers of his wealth,

וְנָכְרִים בָּאוּ שְׁעָרָיו [שערו כ׳] וְעַל־
and [when] foreigners entered his gates, and upon

יְרוּשָׁלַםִ יַדּוּ גוֹרָל גַּם־אַתָּה כְּאַחַד
Jerusalem they cast a lottery — even you were like one

מֵהֶם: יב וְאַל־תֵּרֶא בְיוֹם־אָחִיךָ בְּיוֹם
of them. 12 Do not gaze on the day of your brother, on the day

נָכְרוֹ וְאַל־תִּשְׂמַח לִבְנֵי־יְהוּדָה בְּיוֹם
of his estrangement; and do not rejoice over the children of Judah, on the day

אָבְדָם וְאַל־תַּגְדֵּל פִּיךָ בְּיוֹם צָרָה:
of their destruction; and do not open wide your mouth, on the day of [their] distress!

יג אַל־תָּבוֹא בְשַׁעַר־עַמִּי בְּיוֹם אֵידָם
13 Do not enter through the gate of My people, on the day of their calamity;

אַל־תֵּרֶא גַם־אַתָּה בְּרָעָתוֹ בְּיוֹם אֵידוֹ
do not gaze, even you, upon his misfortune, on the day of his calamity;

וְאַל־תִּשְׁלַחְנָה בְחֵילוֹ בְּיוֹם אֵידוֹ:
and do not send forth [your hands] against his wealth, on the day of his calamity.

יד וְאַל־תַּעֲמֹד עַל־הַפֶּרֶק לְהַכְרִית
14 And do not stand at the crossroads to cut down

אֶת פְּלִיטָיו וְאַל־תַּסְגֵּר שְׂרִידָיו בְּיוֹם
his refugees; and do not imprison his survivors on the day

צָרָה: טו כִּי־קָרוֹב יוֹם־יהוה עַל־כָּל־
of [his] distress. 15 For near is the day of HASHEM upon all

הַגּוֹיִם כַּאֲשֶׁר עָשִׂיתָ יֵעָשֶׂה לָּךְ גְּמֻלְךָ
the nations; just as you did, so shall be done to you; your recompense

יָשׁוּב בְּרֹאשֶׁךָ: טז כִּי כַּאֲשֶׁר שְׁתִיתֶם
shall return upon your head. 16 For just as you drank

עַל־הַר קָדְשִׁי יִשְׁתּוּ כָל־הַגּוֹיִם תָּמִיד
on the mountain of My holiness, [so] shall drink all the nations always;

וְשָׁתוּ וְלָעוּ וְהָיוּ כְּלוֹא הָיוּ: יז וּבְהַר
they shall drink, and they shall swallow, and they shall be, as if never had they been. 17 But on Mount

צִיּוֹן תִּהְיֶה פְלֵיטָה וְהָיָה קֹדֶשׁ וְיָרְשׁוּ
Zion there shall be refuge, and it shall be holy; and they will repossess,

בֵּית יַעֲקֹב אֵת מוֹרָשֵׁיהֶם: יח וְהָיָה בֵית־
the House of Jacob [will] [the property of] their dispossessors. 18 And it will be, the House

יַעֲקֹב אֵשׁ וּבֵית יוֹסֵף לֶהָבָה וּבֵית עֵשָׂו
of Jacob [will be], a fire, and the House of Joseph [will be] a flame; and the House of Esau

לְקַשׁ וְדָלְקוּ בָהֶם וַאֲכָלוּם וְלֹא־יִהְיֶה
[will be] straw; they will burn in them and they will consume them; and there will not be

שָׂרִיד לְבֵית עֵשָׂו כִּי יהוה דִּבֵּר:
any survivor of the House of Esau — for HASHEM has spoken!

יט וְיָרְשׁוּ הַנֶּגֶב אֶת־הַר עֵשָׂו וְהַשְּׁפֵלָה
19 They [the House of Jacob] shall inherit the south — the mountain of Esau; and the lowland

אֶת־פְּלִשְׁתִּים וְיָרְשׁוּ אֶת־שְׂדֵה אֶפְרַיִם
— Philistia; and they shall inherit the field of Ephraim

וְאֵת שְׂדֵה שֹׁמְרוֹן וּבִנְיָמִן אֶת־הַגִּלְעָד:
and the field of Samaria; and Benjamin [shall inherit] the Gilead.

כ וְגָלֻת הַחֵל־הַזֶּה לִבְנֵי יִשְׂרָאֵל אֲשֶׁר־
20 And the exile of this host, of the Children of Israel that are

כְּנַעֲנִים עַד־צָרְפַת וְגָלֻת יְרוּשָׁלַםִ אֲשֶׁר
[with] the Canaanites as far as Zarephath, and the exile of Jerusalem that is

בִּסְפָרַד יִרְשׁוּ אֵת עָרֵי הַנֶּגֶב: כא וְעָלוּ
in Sepharad — they will inherit the cities of the south. 21 And there will come up

מוֹשִׁעִים בְּהַר צִיּוֹן לִשְׁפֹּט אֶת־הַר
saviors on Mount Zion to judge Mount

עֵשָׂו וְהָיְתָה לַיהוה הַמְּלוּכָה:
Esau; and there will be unto HASHEM the kingdom.

---

of the future, Obadiah turns to the Roman Empire and its barbaric treatment of the Jews under its control. True to Isaac's blessing, Rome lived by the sword, and its sword drank thirstily of Jewish blood.

HAFTARAS VAYEISHEV / הפטרת וישב

Amos 2:6-3:8 / עמוס ב:ו־ג:ח

ב ו כֹּה אָמַר יְהוָה עַל־שְׁלֹשָׁה פִּשְׁעֵי
‹ transgressions ‹ three ‹ For « HASHEM: ‹ said ‹ So 6 [2]
יִשְׂרָאֵל וְעַל־אַרְבָּעָה לֹא אֲשִׁיבֶנּוּ עַל
‹ For « I will not pardon them: ‹ four ‹ but for « of Israel, [I have pardoned them]
מִכְרָם בַּכֶּסֶף צַדִּיק וְאֶבְיוֹן בַּעֲבוּר
‹ for ‹ and a destitute man « a righteous man, ‹ for silver ‹ their selling
נַעֲלָיִם: ז הַשֹּׁאֲפִים עַל־עֲפַר־אֶרֶץ
‹ of the earth ‹ the dust ‹ for ‹ They yearn 7 « a pair of shoes.
בְּרֹאשׁ דַּלִּים וְדֶרֶךְ עֲנָוִים יַטּוּ וְאִישׁ
‹ A man « they pervert! ‹ of the humble, ‹ the path [of justice] « of the poor; ‹ [to be] upon the head
וְאָבִיו יֵלְכוּ אֶל־הַנַּעֲרָה לְמַעַן חַלֵּל
‹ to desecrate ‹ in order « the [same] maiden, ‹ to ‹ would go [together] ‹ and his father
אֶת־שֵׁם קָדְשִׁי: ח וְעַל־בְּגָדִים חֲבֻלִים
‹ held as security ‹ garments ‹ Upon 8 « of My Holiness. ‹ the Name
יַטּוּ אֵצֶל כָּל־מִזְבֵּחַ וְיֵין עֲנוּשִׁים יִשְׁתּוּ
‹ they drink ‹ bought with [unjust] fines ‹ and wine « [idolatrous] ‹ every altar; ‹ beside ‹ they recline,
בֵּית אֱלֹהֵיהֶם: ט וְאָנֹכִי הִשְׁמַדְתִּי
‹ destroyed ‹ Yet, I 9 « of their gods. ‹ [in] the temple
אֶת־הָאֱמֹרִי מִפְּנֵיהֶם אֲשֶׁר כְּגֹבַהּ אֲרָזִים
‹ of cedars ‹ like the height ‹ [the Amorite] who « from before them; ‹ the Amorite
גָּבְהוֹ וְחָסֹן הוּא כָּאַלּוֹנִים וָאַשְׁמִיד
‹ yet I destroyed « as the oaks; ‹ was he ‹ and mighty « was his height;
פִּרְיוֹ מִמַּעַל וְשָׁרָשָׁיו מִתָּחַת: י וְאָנֹכִי
‹ And I 10 « from below. ‹ and his roots ‹ from above ‹ his fruit
הֶעֱלֵיתִי אֶתְכֶם מֵאֶרֶץ מִצְרָיִם וָאוֹלֵךְ
‹ and I led « of Egypt, ‹ out of the land ‹ brought you up

אֶתְכֶם בַּמִּדְבָּר אַרְבָּעִים שָׁנָה לָרֶשֶׁת
‹ to take possession of ‹ years ‹ [for] forty ‹ in the wilderness ‹ you
אֶת־אֶרֶץ הָאֱמֹרִי: יא וָאָקִים מִבְּנֵיכֶם
‹ some of your children ‹ And I established 11 « of the Amorite. ‹ the land
לִנְבִיאִים וּמִבַּחוּרֵיכֶם לִנְזִרִים הַאַף
‹ Can it even be [said,] « as nazirites. ‹ and some of your youths « as prophets,
אֵין־זֹאת בְּנֵי יִשְׂרָאֵל נְאֻם־יְהוָה:
« of HASHEM. ‹ — the word « *of Israel?* ‹ *O Children* ‹ *so,* ‹ *It is not*
יב וַתַּשְׁקוּ אֶת־הַנְּזִרִים יָיִן וְעַל־
‹ and upon « [with] wine; ‹ the nazirites ‹ But you plied 12
הַנְּבִיאִים צִוִּיתֶם לֵאמֹר לֹא תִּנָּבְאוּ:
‹ *prophesy!* ‹ *Do not* « saying, ‹ you commanded, ‹ the prophets
יג הִנֵּה אָנֹכִי מֵעִיק תַּחְתֵּיכֶם כַּאֲשֶׁר
‹ as ‹ in your place, ‹ press [you] down ‹ I ‹ Indeed, 13
תָּעִיק הָעֲגָלָה הַמְלֵאָה לָהּ עָמִיר:
« [with] sheaves. ‹ it is ‹ when filled ‹ is the wagon ‹ pressed down
יד וְאָבַד מָנוֹס מִקָּל וְחָזָק לֹא־יְאַמֵּץ
‹ fortify ‹ will not ‹ and the strong one « for the fleet; ‹ flight ‹ Lost will be 14
כֹּחוֹ וְגִבּוֹר לֹא־יְמַלֵּט נַפְשׁוֹ: טו וְתֹפֵשׂ
‹ and he who grasps 15 « his soul; ‹ save ‹ will not ‹ and the mighty one « his strength;
הַקֶּשֶׁת לֹא יַעֲמֹד וְקַל בְּרַגְלָיו לֹא יְמַלֵּט
« save [himself]; ‹ will not ‹ of foot ‹ and he who is fleet « stand fast; ‹ will not ‹ the bow
וְרֹכֵב הַסּוּס לֹא יְמַלֵּט נַפְשׁוֹ: טז וְאַמִּיץ
‹ and the boldest 16 « his soul; ‹ save ‹ will not ‹ of the horse ‹ and the rider
לִבּוֹ בַּגִּבּוֹרִים עָרוֹם יָנוּס בַּיּוֹם־הַהוּא
« on that day ‹ will he ‹ naked « among the ‹ in his

Finally, however, Edom will be repaid in kind. *On Mount Zion there shall be a remnant:* Despite all its suffering and persecutions, Israel and its land will survive and haughty Edom will be cast down. Israel will return to its land and its Temple Mount. It will judge Edom for its horrors and all the world will know that the *kingdom will be HASHEM's.*

Haftaras Vayeishev

The prophet Amos began his prophecies with explanations of the reasons for the downfall of the kingdoms surrounding *Eretz Yisrael*. In each case, there are three sins that God was willing to overlook, at least for a time, but then there was a fourth, which went beyond His willingness to delay the full extent of judgment.

נְאֻם־יְהוָה: ג א שִׁמְעוּ אֶת־הַדָּבָר הַזֶּה
‹ this matter ‹ Hear 1 [3] « of HASHEM. ‹ – the word

אֲשֶׁר דִּבֶּר יְהוָה עֲלֵיכֶם בְּנֵי יִשְׂרָאֵל
« of Israel, ‹ O Children ‹ against you, « HASHEM [has] « He has spoken, ‹ that

עַל כָּל־הַמִּשְׁפָּחָה אֲשֶׁר הֶעֱלֵיתִי
‹ I have brought out ‹ that ‹ family ‹ the entire ‹ against

מֵאֶרֶץ מִצְרַיִם לֵאמֹר: ב רַק אֶתְכֶם
‹ you ‹ Only 2 « saying: ‹ of Egypt, ‹ of the land

יָדַעְתִּי מִכֹּל מִשְׁפְּחוֹת הָאֲדָמָה עַל־כֵּן
‹ this ‹ because of « of the earth; ‹ the families ‹ of all ‹ have I known

אֶפְקֹד עֲלֵיכֶם אֵת כָּל־עֲוֺנֹתֵיכֶם:
« your iniquities. ‹ all ‹ upon you ‹ I will visit

ג הֲיֵלְכוּ שְׁנַיִם יַחְדָּו בִּלְתִּי אִם־נוֹעָדוּ:
« they have so arranged? ‹ when ‹ if not ‹ together, ‹ two ‹ Can people travel, 3

ד הֲיִשְׁאַג אַרְיֵה בַּיַּעַר וְטֶרֶף אֵין לוֹ הֲיִתֵּן
« Give forth « his? ‹ was not ‹ if prey « in the forest – ‹ – a lion « Would he roar 4

כְּפִיר קוֹלוֹ מִמְּעֹנָתוֹ בִּלְתִּי אִם־לָכָד:
« he has caught [prey]? ‹ when ‹ if not ‹ from his den, ‹ his voice « would a young lion –

ה הֲתִפֹּל צִפּוֹר עַל־פַּח הָאָרֶץ וּמוֹקֵשׁ
‹ if a snare ‹ on the earth, ‹ a trap ‹ into ‹ a bird ‹ Would there fall 5

אֵין לָהּ הֲיַעֲלֶה־פַּח מִן־הָאֲדָמָה וְלָכוֹד
‹ if a capture, ‹ the ground, ‹ from ‹ a trap ‹ Would there rise ‹ hers? ‹ was not

לֹא יִלְכּוֹד: ו אִם־יִתָּקַע שׁוֹפָר בְּעִיר
‹ in a city, ‹ a shofar ‹ there would blow ‹ If 6 « captured? ‹ it has not

וְעָם לֹא יֶחֱרָדוּ אִם־תִּהְיֶה רָעָה בְּעִיר
‹ in a city ‹ misfortune ‹ there would be ‹ If « tremble? ‹ not ‹ [would] the people

וַיהוָה לֹא עָשָׂה: ז כִּי לֹא יַעֲשֶׂה אֲדֹנָי
‹ – [He,] the Lord « He will not do ‹ For 7 « have caused [it]? ‹ not ‹ [could] HASHEM

יֱהוִֹה דָּבָר כִּי אִם־גָּלָה סוֹדוֹ אֶל־עֲבָדָיו
‹ His servants ‹ to ‹ his secret ‹ He has revealed ‹ if ‹ except ‹ a thing, « HASHEM/ELOHIM –

הַנְּבִיאִים: ח אַרְיֵה שָׁאָג מִי לֹא יִירָא
« fear? ‹ would not ‹ who « has roared; ‹ A lion 8 « the prophets.

אֲדֹנָי יֱהוִֹה דִּבֶּר מִי לֹא יִנָּבֵא:
« prophesy? ‹ would not ‹ who « has spoken; ‹ HASHEM/ELOHIM ‹ The Lord

HAFTARAS MIKEITZ / הפטרת מקץ

I Kings 3:15-4:1 / מלכים א ג:טו-ד:א

ג טו וַיִּקַץ שְׁלֹמֹה וְהִנֵּה חֲלוֹם וַיָּבוֹא
‹ Then he came « [it was] a dream. ‹ and Indeed! ‹ Solomon awoke 15 [3]

יְרוּשָׁלַם וַיַּעֲמֹד | לִפְנֵי | אֲרוֹן בְּרִית־
‹ of the Covenant ‹ the Ark ‹ before ‹ and he stood ‹ to Jerusalem

אֲדֹנָי וַיַּעַל עֹלוֹת וַיַּעַשׂ שְׁלָמִים וַיַּעַשׂ
‹ and he made « peace-offerings; ‹ and he made ‹ burnt-offerings ‹ and he brought up [onto the Altar] « of the Lord;

מִשְׁתֶּה לְכָל־עֲבָדָיו: טז אָז תָּבֹאנָה
‹ came ‹ Then, 16 « his servants. ‹ for all ‹ a banquet

שְׁתַּיִם נָשִׁים זֹנוֹת אֶל־הַמֶּלֶךְ
‹ the king ‹ to ‹ innkeepers ‹ women, ‹ two

וַתַּעֲמֹדְנָה לְפָנָיו: יז וַתֹּאמֶר הָאִשָּׁה
‹ The woman said, 17 « before him. ‹ and they stood

הָאַחַת בִּי אֲדֹנִי אֲנִי וְהָאִשָּׁה הַזֹּאת
‹ *and this woman* ‹ *I* ‹ *my lord,* ‹ *Please,* « the [first] one,

Finally, the prophet comes to Israel, and again, he proclaims that God would forbear despite the three cardinal sins of idolatry, adultery, and murder (*Radak*), but there was a fourth sin that burst His endurance, as it were. The fourth was the persecution of the poor, and the greed that caused the rich and powerful to take advantage of the helpless and to pervert justice in order to get their way. This characteristic was more than God would bear, and it led to the downfall of the nation. They would sell the legal rights of poor people for a few pieces of silver — as Joseph's brothers did when they disposed of the problem he posed for them by selling him into slavery — and they would grind the poor into the ground, figuratively, and cover their heads with dust.

Lest these leaders continue to delude themselves that they are too powerful to be brought to justice, the prophet warns them that the Amorite inhabitants of Canaan were even more powerful, but God had swept them away when He wished to give the land to Israel. In "gratitude," Israel had prevented prophets from teaching God's word and nazirites from maintaining their holy standard of

יֹשְׁבֹת בְּבַיִת אֶחָד וָאֵלֵד עִמָּהּ בַּבָּיִת׃

« in the ‹ [while] ‹ and I « in one house, ‹ dwell
house. with her gave birth

יח וַיְהִי בַּיּוֹם הַשְּׁלִישִׁי לְלִדְתִּי וַתֵּלֶד גַּם

‹ too, ‹ that she ‹ after my ‹ on the third day, ‹ And 18
gave birth, giving birth, it was

הָאִשָּׁה הַזֹּאת וַאֲנַחְנוּ יַחְדָּו אֵין־זָר

‹ out- ‹ there « together, ‹ Now we « this woman.
sider was no were

אִתָּנוּ בַּבַּיִת זוּלָתִי שְׁתַּיִם־אֲנַחְנוּ בַּבָּיִת׃

« [were] in ‹ of us ‹ the two ‹ only « in the ‹ with us
the house. house;

יט וַיָּמָת בֶּן־הָאִשָּׁה הַזֹּאת לָיְלָה אֲשֶׁר

‹ because ‹ [during « of this woman — ‹ — the « And he 19
the] night, son died,

שָׁכְבָה עָלָיו׃ כ וַתָּקָם בְּתוֹךְ הַלַּיְלָה

‹ the night, ‹ during ‹ She arose 20 « upon him. ‹ she lay

וַתִּקַּח אֶת־בְּנִי מֵאֶצְלִי וַאֲמָתְךָ יְשֵׁנָה

‹ slept, ‹ while your ‹ from next ‹ my son ‹ and she
maidservant to me, took

וַתַּשְׁכִּיבֵהוּ בְּחֵיקָהּ וְאֶת־בְּנָהּ הַמֵּת

‹ the dead one, ‹ and her son, « in her bosom; ‹ and she lay him

הִשְׁכִּיבָה בְחֵיקִי׃ כא וָאָקֻם בַּבֹּקֶר

‹ in the ‹ When 21 « in my bosom. ‹ she lay
morning I arose

לְהֵינִיק אֶת־בְּנִי וְהִנֵּה־מֵת וָאֶתְבּוֹנֵן

‹ Then I « He was ‹ and there « my son, ‹ to nurse
studied dead! it was!

אֵלָיו בַּבֹּקֶר וְהִנֵּה לֹא־הָיָה בְנִי אֲשֶׁר

‹ whom ‹ my son ‹ he was not ‹ and ‹ in the ‹ him
indeed! morning,

יָלָדְתִּי׃ כב וַתֹּאמֶר הָאִשָּׁה הָאַחֶרֶת לֹא

‹ It is « — the other woman « Then 22 « I had
not [said] — she said, borne.

כִי בְּנִי הַחַי וּבְנֵךְ הַמֵּת וְזֹאת אֹמֶרֶת

‹ says, ‹ But this « is the ‹ and your ‹ is the ‹ My ‹ so!
one dead one. son live one, son

לֹא כִי בְּנֵךְ הַמֵּת וּבְנִי הֶחָי וַתְּדַבֵּרְנָה

‹ [Thus] they « is the ‹ and my ‹ is the ‹ Your « so! ‹ It is
spoke live one! son dead one, son not

לִפְנֵי הַמֶּלֶךְ׃ כג וַיֹּאמֶר הַמֶּלֶךְ זֹאת

‹ This one ‹ The king said, 23 « the king. ‹ before

אֹמֶרֶת זֶה־בְּנִי הַחַי וּבְנֵךְ הַמֵּת וְזֹאת

‹ And « is the ‹ and your ‹ the living ‹ my ‹ 'This « says,
this one dead one.' son one, son, is

אֹמֶרֶת לֹא כִי בְּנֵךְ הַמֵּת וּבְנִי הֶחָי׃

« is the ‹ and my ‹ is the ‹ Your « so! ‹ 'It is « says,
living one.' son dead one, son not

כד וַיֹּאמֶר הַמֶּלֶךְ קְחוּ לִי־חָרֶב וַיָּבִאוּ

‹ And they « a sword! ‹ me ‹ Fetch « So the king said, 24
brought

הַחֶרֶב לִפְנֵי הַמֶּלֶךְ׃ כה וַיֹּאמֶר הַמֶּלֶךְ

« And the king said, 25 « the king. ‹ before ‹ the sword

גִּזְרוּ אֶת־הַיֶּלֶד הַחַי לִשְׁנָיִם וּתְנוּ

‹ and give ‹ in two, ‹ the living one, ‹ the boy, ‹ Cut

אֶת־הַחֲצִי לְאַחַת וְאֶת־הַחֲצִי לְאֶחָת׃

« to one ‹ and the [other] half ‹ to one ‹ the [one] half
[woman]. [woman]

כו וַתֹּאמֶר הָאִשָּׁה אֲשֶׁר־בְּנָהּ הַחַי אֶל־

‹ to ‹ was [in truth] ‹ son ‹ whose ‹ The woman said, 26
the living one,

---

service — as if God's will could be ignored if it were not proclaimed openly. But the fleet-footed often cannot escape and the mighty cannot always prevail — should it not be clear that the power is God's alone?

The prophet closes with ringing rhetoric destined to wake up the people to the obvious. They use their logic to determine the significance of daily events. They *knew* that a *lion's roar* means that prey is at hand, that a trap lifted from the sand means that a snared bird or animal is tugging vainly to free itself — should they not perceive that God is roaring for their repentance through His mastery of events?

⁂ Haftaras Mikeitz

Like the *Sidrah*, the *Haftarah* deals with royal dreams and their aftermath. In the *Sidrah*, Pharaoh had a portentous dream and Joseph applied his God-given wisdom to its interpretation, with the result that he became acknowledged as the most qualified person to rule Egypt.

The *Haftarah* begins by saying that Solomon awoke from a dream. It was a dream that set the tone of his reign and had implications for the future of the Jewish people. In his prophetic dream, the twelve-year-old, newly crowned Solomon had been asked by God what blessing he desired for his new position. Solomon had requested wisdom so that he could judge his people well. Pleased that Solomon had altruistically asked for wisdom, and not selfishly requested longevity, wealth or power, God promised him not only unprecedented wisdom, such as had never been before and would never be again, but also the wealth and honor that he did not ask for.

Shortly after the dream came proof of its fulfillment, in the form of a seemingly insoluble dilemma. Solomon's verdict gained the admiration and respect of the nation, and displayed a degree of wisdom that became the hallmark of his reign and an augury of the three inspiring and enlightening books he would contribute to Scripture: *Proverbs, Song of Songs,* and *Ecclesiastes*.

הַמֶּלֶךְ כִּֽי־נִכְמְרוּ רַחֲמֶיהָ עַל־בְּנָהּ

« her son, ‹ for ‹ her feelings of compassion ‹ aroused were ‹ for « the king,

וַתֹּאמֶר ׀ בִּי אֲדֹנִי תְּנוּ־לָהּ אֶת־הַיָּלוּד

‹ the newborn, ‹ to her ‹ give ‹ my lord, ‹ Please, « and she said,

הַחַי וְהָמֵת אַל־תְּמִיתֻהוּ וְזֹאת

‹ And this [other] one « put him to death! ‹ Do not « But put [him] to death!? « the living one.

אֹמֶרֶת גַּם־לִי גַם־לָךְ לֹא יִהְיֶה גְּזֹרוּ׃

« Cut! « he shall not be! ‹ to you ‹ Also ‹ to me, ‹ Also « said,

כז וַיַּעַן הַמֶּלֶךְ וַיֹּאמֶר תְּנוּ־לָהּ אֶת־הַיָּלוּד

‹ the newborn, ‹ to her ‹ Give « and he said, ‹ The king spoke up 27

הַחַי וְהָמֵת לֹא תְמִיתֻהוּ הִיא אִמּוֹ׃

« his mother. ‹ [For] she is « put him to death: ‹ do not ‹ But to death, « the living one.

כח וַיִּשְׁמְעוּ כָל־יִשְׂרָאֵל אֶת־הַמִּשְׁפָּט

‹ the judgment « of Israel [did], ‹ all « They heard, 28

אֲשֶׁר שָׁפַט הַמֶּלֶךְ וַיִּרְאוּ מִפְּנֵי הַמֶּלֶךְ

« the king, ‹ before ‹ and they were awe-struck ‹ the king decided ‹ that

כִּי רָאוּ כִּֽי־חָכְמַת אֱלֹהִים בְּקִרְבּוֹ

‹ is within him, ‹ of God ‹ the wisdom ‹ that ‹ they saw ‹ for

לַעֲשׂוֹת מִשְׁפָּט׃ ד א וַיְהִי הַמֶּלֶךְ שְׁלֹמֹה

‹ And King Solomon was 1 [4] « justice. ‹ to do

מֶלֶךְ עַל־כָּל־יִשְׂרָאֵל׃

« Israel. ‹ all ‹ over ‹ king

HAFTARAS VAYIGASH / הפטרת ויגש

Ezekiel 37:15-28 / יחזקאל לז:טו-כח

לז טו וַיְהִי דְבַר־יְהֹוָה אֵלַי לֵאמֹר׃

« saying: ‹ unto me, ‹ of HASHEM ‹ the word ‹ And there was 15 [37]

טז וְאַתָּה בֶן־אָדָם קַח־לְךָ עֵץ אֶחָד

‹ one stick, ‹ unto yourself ‹ take ‹ of Man, ‹ Son ‹ O you, 16

וּכְתֹב עָלָיו לִיהוּדָה וְלִבְנֵי יִשְׂרָאֵל

« of Israel, ‹ and for the Children ‹ For Judah ‹ upon it, ‹ and write

חֲבֵרָיו [חברו כ׳] וּלְקַח עֵץ אֶחָד וּכְתוֹב עָלָיו

‹ upon it, ‹ and write ‹ one [other] stick, ‹ Then take « his comrades.

לְיוֹסֵף עֵץ אֶפְרַיִם וְכָל־בֵּית יִשְׂרָאֵל

‹ of Israel, ‹ the House ‹ and all ‹ of Ephraim, ‹ the stick ‹ For Joseph,

חֲבֵרָיו [חברו כ׳]: יז וְקָרַב אֹתָם אֶחָד אֶל־

‹ to ‹ one ‹ them, ‹ And juxtapose 17 « his comrades.

אֶחָד לְךָ לְעֵץ אֶחָד וְהָיוּ לַאֲחָדִים

‹ one ‹ and they shall be « they were as one stick; ‹ [so that] to you ‹ one,

בְּיָדֶךָ׃ יח וְכַאֲשֶׁר יֹאמְרוּ אֵלֶיךָ בְּנֵי עַמְּךָ

« of your people, ‹ will the children « unto you, ‹ they will say ‹ And when 18 « in your hand.

לֵאמֹר הֲלוֹא־תַגִּיד לָנוּ מָה־אֵלֶּה לָּךְ׃

« to you? ‹ these are ‹ what ‹ us ‹ Will you not tell « saying,

יט דַּבֵּר אֲלֵהֶם כֹּה־אָמַר אֲדֹנָי יֱהֹוִה הִנֵּה

« Behold! « HASHEM/ELOHIM: ‹ the Lord ‹ said ‹ Thus « to them, ‹ Speak 19

אֲנִי לֹקֵחַ אֶת־עֵץ יוֹסֵף אֲשֶׁר בְּיַד

‹ in the hand ‹ which is ‹ of Joseph, ‹ the stick ‹ am taking ‹ — I

אֶפְרַיִם וְשִׁבְטֵי יִשְׂרָאֵל חֲבֵרָיו [חברו כ׳]

‹ his comrades, ‹ of Israel ‹ and the tribes « of Ephraim,

וְנָתַתִּי אוֹתָם עָלָיו אֶת־עֵץ יְהוּדָה

« of Judah; ‹ the stick ‹ with ‹ alongside him, ‹ them ‹ and I shall place

וַעֲשִׂיתִם לְעֵץ אֶחָד וְהָיוּ אֶחָד בְּיָדִי׃

« in My hand. ‹ one ‹ for they shall become « into one stick; ‹ and I will make them

Haftaras Vayigash

A *Sidrah* that tells of the reunification of Jacob's sons is followed by a *Haftarah* that prophesies the eventual unification of the twelve tribes of Israel. The prophet Ezekiel, like Jeremiah, was one of the main prophets of the Destruction, and he actually joined his exiled brethren in Babylonia. The destruction of the Temple took place 140 years after the exile of the ten tribes, so that the prophecy of this *Haftarah* was a source of great comfort to the tribes of Judah and Benjamin, for if even their long-lost comrades of the Northern Kingdom were assured that they would again become part of the nation, surely the two southern tribes could be certain that God was not forsaking them.

According to *Maharal (Gur Aryeh, Genesis* 45:14), the tears that accompanied the embrace of Joseph and Benjamin when Joseph revealed himself in Egypt were tears of joy, because the long-separated brothers foresaw the prophecy of Ezekiel. Joseph was the

כ וְהָיוּ הָעֵצִים אֲשֶׁר תִּכְתֹּב עֲלֵיהֶם
‹ upon them, ‹ you will write ‹ that ‹ those sticks ‹ And they shall be, 20

בְּיָדְךָ לְעֵינֵיהֶם: כא וְדַבֵּר אֲלֵיהֶם כֹּה־
‹ Thus « to them, ‹ Then speak 21 « before their eyes. ‹ in your hand,

אָמַר אֲדֹנָי יֱהֹוִה הִנֵּה אֲנִי לֹקֵחַ אֶת־בְּנֵי
‹ the Children ‹ am taking ‹ I « Behold! « HASHEM/ELOHIM: ‹ the Lord ‹ said

יִשְׂרָאֵל מִבֵּין הַגּוֹיִם אֲשֶׁר הָלְכוּ־שָׁם
« there, ‹ they went ‹ that ‹ the nations ‹ from among ‹ of Israel

וְקִבַּצְתִּי אֹתָם מִסָּבִיב וְהֵבֵאתִי אוֹתָם
‹ them ‹ and I shall bring « from all around; ‹ them ‹ and I shall gather

אֶל־אַדְמָתָם: כב וְעָשִׂיתִי אֹתָם לְגוֹי אֶחָד
‹ into one nation, ‹ them ‹ I shall make 22 « their land. ‹ to

בָּאָרֶץ בְּהָרֵי יִשְׂרָאֵל וּמֶלֶךְ אֶחָד יִהְיֶה
‹ shall there be ‹ and one king, « of Israel, ‹ upon the hills ‹ in the land

לְכֻלָּם לְמֶלֶךְ וְלֹא יִהְיוּ־עוֹד [יהיה־עוד כ׳]
‹ any longer ‹ and they shall not be « as a king; ‹ for them all

לִשְׁנֵי גוֹיִם וְלֹא יֵחָצוּ עוֹד לִשְׁתֵּי
‹ into two ‹ any longer, ‹ and they shall not [be] divided « nations; ‹ as two

מַמְלָכוֹת עוֹד: כג וְלֹא יִטַּמְּאוּ עוֹד
‹ any longer ‹ And they will not be contaminated 23 « any longer. ‹ kingdoms

בְּגִלּוּלֵיהֶם וּבְשִׁקּוּצֵיהֶם וּבְכֹל פִּשְׁעֵיהֶם
« their sins; ‹ and with all ‹ and with their abominations, ‹ with their idols,

וְהוֹשַׁעְתִּי אֹתָם מִכֹּל מוֹשְׁבֹתֵיהֶם
‹ their habitations ‹ from all ‹ them ‹ and I shall save

אֲשֶׁר חָטְאוּ בָהֶם וְטִהַרְתִּי אוֹתָם וְהָיוּ
‹ and they shall be ‹ them, ‹ then I shall purify ‹ within them; ‹ they have sinned, ‹ that

לִי לְעָם וַאֲנִי אֶהְיֶה לָהֶם לֵאלֹהִים:
« for a God. ‹ unto them ‹ will be ‹ and I, ‹ for a people; ‹ unto Me

כד וְעַבְדִּי דָוִד מֶלֶךְ עֲלֵיהֶם וְרוֹעֶה אֶחָד
‹ and one shepherd, « over them; ‹ [will be] king ‹ David ‹ And My servant 24

יִהְיֶה לְכֻלָּם וּבְמִשְׁפָּטַי יֵלֵכוּ וְחֻקֹּתַי
‹ and My decrees ‹ they will go; ‹ In [the way of] My ordinances « for all of them. ‹ will there be

יִשְׁמְרוּ וְעָשׂוּ אוֹתָם: כה וְיָשְׁבוּ עַל־
‹ upon ‹ They will dwell 25 « them. ‹ and they will perform ‹ they will observe

הָאָרֶץ אֲשֶׁר נָתַתִּי לְעַבְדִּי לְיַעֲקֹב אֲשֶׁר
‹ that ‹ to Jacob, ‹ to My servant ‹ I gave ‹ that ‹ the land

יָשְׁבוּ־בָהּ אֲבוֹתֵיכֶם וְיָשְׁבוּ עָלֶיהָ
« upon it, ‹ and they shall dwell « did your forefathers, « within it, ‹ they dwelt

הֵמָּה וּבְנֵיהֶם וּבְנֵי בְנֵיהֶם עַד־עוֹלָם
« forever; ‹ of their children, ‹ and the children ‹ and their children, ‹ — they,

וְדָוִד עַבְדִּי נָשִׂיא לָהֶם לְעוֹלָם:
« forever. ‹ for them, ‹ [will be] a leader ‹ My servant, ‹ and David,

כו וְכָרַתִּי לָהֶם בְּרִית שָׁלוֹם בְּרִית עוֹלָם
‹ eternal ‹ a covenant ‹ of peace, ‹ a covenant ‹ with them, ‹ I shall seal 26

יִהְיֶה אוֹתָם וּנְתַתִּים וְהִרְבֵּיתִי אוֹתָם
‹ them, ‹ and I shall increase ‹ and I shall emplace them « with them; ‹ shall it be

וְנָתַתִּי אֶת־מִקְדָּשִׁי בְּתוֹכָם לְעוֹלָם:
« forever. ‹ among them ‹ My Sanctuary ‹ and I shall place

כז וְהָיָה מִשְׁכָּנִי עֲלֵיהֶם וְהָיִיתִי
‹ and I shall be « upon them; ‹ And My Tabernacle shall be, 27

לָהֶם לֵאלֹהִים וְהֵמָּה יִהְיוּ־לִי לְעָם:
« for a people. ‹ unto Me ‹ shall be ‹ and they « for a God; ‹ unto them

כח וְיָדְעוּ הַגּוֹיִם כִּי אֲנִי יְהֹוָה מְקַדֵּשׁ
‹ Who sanctifies ‹ HASHEM, ‹ I am ‹ that ‹ [Then] the nations shall know, 28

אֶת־יִשְׂרָאֵל בִּהְיוֹת מִקְדָּשִׁי בְּתוֹכָם
‹ among them ‹ My Sanctuary ‹ when there will be ‹ Israel,

לְעוֹלָם:
« forever.

father of Ephraim, leader of the Ten Tribes, and Benjamin's descendants remained loyal to the Davidic dynasty of Judah; thus their reunion in Egypt was a precursor of that foretold by Ezekiel.

The *Haftarah* goes on to make clear what sort of unified nation the twelve tribes of the future would be. The prophecy speaks not of a mere political union, free from the wars and rivalry that marred the era of the First Temple. Rather, it speaks of an era under a king from the House of David, who will be a servant of God

HAFTARAS VAYECHI / הפטרת ויחי

I Kings 2:1-12 / מלכים א ב:א-יב

ב א וַיִּקְרְבוּ יְמֵי־דָוִד לָמוּת וַיְצַו
‹ so he commanded ‹‹ [for him] to die, ‹ of David ‹ did the days ‹ Draw near, **1** **[2]**
אֶת־שְׁלֹמֹה בְנוֹ לֵאמֹר: ב אָנֹכִי הֹלֵךְ
‹ am going ‹ I **2** ‹‹ saying: ‹ his son, ‹ Solomon,
בְּדֶרֶךְ כׇּל־הָאָרֶץ וְחָזַקְתָּ וְהָיִיתָ לְאִישׁ:
‹‹ a man. ‹ and you shall be ‹ you shall be strong, ‹‹ the earth; ‹ of all ‹ in the way
ג וְשָׁמַרְתָּ אֶת־מִשְׁמֶרֶת ׀ יהוה אֱלֹהֶיךָ
‹ your God, ‹ of HASHEM, ‹ the charge ‹ You shall safeguard **3**
לָלֶכֶת בִּדְרָכָיו לִשְׁמֹר חֻקֹּתָיו מִצְוֺתָיו
‹ His commandments, ‹ His decrees, ‹ to observe ‹‹ in His ways; ‹ to walk
וּמִשְׁפָּטָיו וְעֵדְוֺתָיו כַּכָּתוּב בְּתוֹרַת
‹ in the Torah ‹ as it is written ‹ and His testimonies, ‹ and His ordinances,
מֹשֶׁה לְמַעַן תַּשְׂכִּיל אֵת כׇּל־אֲשֶׁר
‹ that ‹ all ‹ in ‹ you will act wisely ‹ so that ‹‹ of Moses;
תַּעֲשֶׂה וְאֵת כׇּל־אֲשֶׁר תִּפְנֶה שָׁם:
‹‹ there. ‹ you turn ‹ that ‹ everything ‹ and in ‹ you do
ד לְמַעַן יָקִים יהוה אֶת־דְּבָרוֹ אֲשֶׁר
‹ that ‹ His word ‹ HASHEM will uphold, ‹ So that **4**
דִּבֶּר עָלַי לֵאמֹר אִם־יִשְׁמְרוּ בָנֶיךָ
‹ your children will observe, ‹ 'If ‹‹ saying, ‹ regarding me, ‹ He spoke
אֶת־דַּרְכָּם לָלֶכֶת לְפָנַי בֶּאֱמֶת בְּכׇל־
‹ with all ‹ in truth, ‹ before Me ‹ to walk ‹ their way,
לְבָבָם וּבְכׇל־נַפְשָׁם לֵאמֹר לֹא־יִכָּרֵת
‹ 'There will not be cut off ‹‹ [and] saying, ‹‹ their soul,' ‹ and with all ‹ their heart
לְךָ אִישׁ מֵעַל כִּסֵּא יִשְׂרָאֵל: ה וְגַם
‹ Moreover, **5** ‹‹ of Israel. ‹ the throne ‹ from upon ‹ a man ‹ from your [descendants]
אַתָּה יָדַעְתָּ אֵת אֲשֶׁר־עָשָׂה לִי יוֹאָב בֶּן־
‹ son ‹‹ Joab did, ‹‹ to me, ‹ he did ‹ what ‹ have known ‹ you

צְרוּיָה אֲשֶׁר עָשָׂה לִשְׁנֵי־שָׂרֵי צִבְאוֹת
‹ of the armies ‹ leaders ‹ to two ‹ he did ‹ [by] what ‹ of Zeruiah,
יִשְׂרָאֵל לְאַבְנֵר בֶּן־נֵר וְלַעֲמָשָׂא בֶן־
‹ son ‹ and to Amasa ‹ of Ner ‹ son ‹ to Abner ‹‹ of Israel,
יֶתֶר וַיַּהַרְגֵם וַיָּשֶׂם דְּמֵי־מִלְחָמָה
‹ of war ‹ the blood ‹ and he shed ‹ [when] he murdered them, ‹ of Jether,
בְּשָׁלֹם וַיִּתֵּן דְּמֵי מִלְחָמָה בַּחֲגֹרָתוֹ
‹ on his belt ‹ of war ‹ the blood ‹ and he [thus] placed ‹ in [time of] peace;
אֲשֶׁר בְּמׇתְנָיו וּבְנַעֲלוֹ אֲשֶׁר בְּרַגְלָיו:
‹‹ on his feet. ‹ that was ‹ and on his shoe ‹ on his waist, ‹ that was
ו וְעָשִׂיתָ כְּחׇכְמָתֶךָ וְלֹא־תוֹרֵד שֵׂיבָתוֹ
‹ of his old age ‹ allow the descent ‹ and do not ‹ according to your wisdom, ‹ You shall do **6**
בְּשָׁלֹם שְׁאֹל: ז וְלִבְנֵי בַרְזִלַּי הַגִּלְעָדִי
‹ the Gileadite ‹ of Barzilai ‹ Toward the children **7** ‹‹ [to the] grave. ‹ in peace
תַּעֲשֶׂה־חֶסֶד וְהָיוּ בְּאֹכְלֵי שֻׁלְחָנֶךָ כִּי־
‹ for ‹‹ at your table; ‹ among those who eat ‹ and they shall be ‹‹ [with] kindness; ‹ you should act
כֵן קָרְבוּ אֵלַי בְּבׇרְחִי מִפְּנֵי אַבְשָׁלוֹם
‹ Absalom ‹ from ‹ in my fleeing ‹ unto me, ‹ did they draw near ‹ so
אָחִיךָ: ח וְהִנֵּה עִמְּךָ שִׁמְעִי בֶן־גֵּרָא
‹ of Gera, ‹ son ‹ Shim'i ‹ —With you ‹‹ And there is **8** ‹‹ your brother.
בֶן־הַיְמִינִי מִבַּחֻרִים וְהוּא קִלְלַנִי
‹ cursed me ‹ he ‹‹ from Bahurim; ‹ the Benjamite
קְלָלָה נִמְרֶצֶת בְּיוֹם לֶכְתִּי מַחֲנָיִם
‹‹ [to] Mahanaim; ‹ I went ‹ on the day ‹ with a powerful curse,
וְהוּא־יָרַד לִקְרָאתִי הַיַּרְדֵּן וָאֶשָּׁבַע לוֹ
‹ to him ‹ and I swore ‹ at the Jordan, ‹ to greet me ‹ came down ‹ but he
בַיהוה לֵאמֹר אִם־אֲמִיתְךָ בֶּחָרֶב:
‹‹ by the sword!' ‹ that I will not put you to death ‹‹ saying, ‹ by HASHEM,

---

and who will unify the people in allegiance to the Torah. Idolatry will be gone and the Temple will stand; the standard of life will be obedience to the laws of the Torah and the result will be that the entire world will know that HASHEM is God.

⇜ Haftaras Vayechi

Like the *Sidrah*, the *Haftarah* describes the last will and testament of one of the greatest figures in history. In the *Sidrah*, Jacob gives his final commands and blessings, first to Joseph and then

ט וְעַתָּה אַל־תְּנַקֵּהוּ כִּי אִישׁ חָכָם אָתָּה
‹ are you, ‹ [who is] wise ‹ a man ‹ for ‹‹ hold him guiltless, ‹ do not ‹ But now, 9

וְיָדַעְתָּ אֵת אֲשֶׁר תַּעֲשֶׂה־לּוֹ וְהוֹרַדְתָּ
‹ You shall bring down ‹ to him: ‹ you are to do ‹ what ‹ and you will know

אֶת־שֵׂיבָתוֹ בְּדָם שְׁאוֹל: י וַיִּשְׁכַּב דָּוִד
‹ Then David lay, 10 ‹‹ to the grave. ‹ in blood ‹ his old age

עִם־אֲבֹתָיו וַיִּקָּבֵר בְּעִיר דָּוִד: יא וְהַיָּמִים
‹ The days 11 ‹‹ of David. ‹ in the City ‹ and he was buried ‹‹ his forefathers; ‹ with

אֲשֶׁר מָלַךְ דָּוִד עַל־יִשְׂרָאֵל אַרְבָּעִים
‹ [were] forty ‹ Israel ‹ over ‹ David reigned ‹ that

שָׁנָה בְּחֶבְרוֹן מָלַךְ שֶׁבַע שָׁנִים
‹ years ‹ seven ‹ he reigned ‹ in Hebron ‹‹ years;

וּבִירוּשָׁלַיִם מָלַךְ שְׁלֹשִׁים וְשָׁלֹשׁ שָׁנִים:
‹‹ years. ‹ and three ‹ thirty ‹ he reigned ‹ and in Jerusalem

יב וּשְׁלֹמֹה יָשַׁב עַל־כִּסֵּא דָּוִד אָבִיו
‹ his father, ‹ of David, ‹ the throne ‹ on ‹ sat ‹ And Solomon 12

וַתִּכֹּן מַלְכֻתוֹ מְאֹד:
‹‹ very [firmly]. ‹ was his kingship ‹ and established

HAFTARAS SHABBAS EREV ROSH CHODESH / הפטרת שבת ערב ראש חודש

שמואל א כ:יח־מב / *I Samuel 20:18-42*

כ יח וַיֹּאמֶר־לוֹ יְהוֹנָתָן מָחָר חֹדֶשׁ
‹ is the [New] Moon, ‹ Tomorrow ‹‹ did Jonathan, ‹‹ to him ‹ He said 18 [20]

וְנִפְקַדְתָּ כִּי יִפָּקֵד מוֹשָׁבֶךָ: יט וְשִׁלַּשְׁתָּ
‹ You shall wait three [days], 19 *‹‹ your seat. ‹ empty will be ‹ because ‹ and you will be missed*

תֵּרֵד מְאֹד וּבָאתָ אֶל־הַמָּקוֹם אֲשֶׁר
‹ where ‹ the place ‹ to ‹ and you shall come ‹ very [deep] ‹ you shall descend

נִסְתַּרְתָּ שָּׁם בְּיוֹם הַמַּעֲשֶׂה וְיָשַׁבְתָּ
‹ and you shall camp ‹‹ of the deed; ‹ on the day ‹ there ‹ you hid yourself

אֵצֶל הָאֶבֶן הָאָזֶל: כ וַאֲנִי שְׁלֹשֶׁת
‹ three ‹ And I, 20 *‹‹ of the wayfarer. ‹ the stone ‹ near*

הַחִצִּים צִדָּה אוֹרֶה לְשַׁלַּח־לִי
‹ for myself ‹ [as if] shooting ‹ I will shoot, ‹ in that direction ‹ arrows

to all the brothers, assigning each of them his specific role in Jewish history. David issues his commands to only one son, his anointed successor Solomon.

David's exhortations that Solomon follow the commandments of the Torah and that only thereby can he assure success for himself and his progeny are to be expected. So is his urging that Solomon show kindness to the family of Barzilai, who stood by David during the hardest period of his life. Obedience to the Torah is the *raison d'etre* of the Jewish people; without it the nation can look forward only to enmity, defeat, and exile. Acknowledging gratitude, too, is a basic Jewish value. But the rest of his will is surprising. David commanded Solomon to exact the death penalty against Joab and Shim'i. Was vengeance a prerequisite of Jewish leadership?

It may be that David's last words were concerned with communicating to Solomon the attitudes he must have regarding such character traits as treachery, loyalty, and duplicity. As the commanding general of David's army, Joab was one of the most important people in the kingdom and in David's own accession to the throne. But in a cowardly and treacherous way, he had murdered Abner and Amasa after gaining their confidence. David had admitted that his position was not strong enough to permit him to punish Joab, but he urged Solomon not to permit the attitude to fester that the mighty have a different law than the weak, and to dispel the notion that David may have conspired with Joab to do away with the competing generals. Barzilai's loyalty, in contrast, must be rewarded in a public way, so that the people would draw the proper lessons for their own behavior.

◆§ Shabbas Erev Rosh Chodesh

The Sages teach that any love which is pure and not founded on selfishness will last forever. "And [which love] did not depend on a specific cause? — The love of David and Jonathan" (*Avos* 5:19). Our *Haftarah* is the story that best demonstrates the nature of this quintessential friendship.

No two people were more natural rivals than David and Jonathan. Jonathan was the crown prince, the natural successor to his father Saul as king of Israel. And he was a man of great stature, beloved by the people, and righteous as well — he would have been a source of pride to the nation. David was the rival, the interloper who had been anointed by Samuel to take away the throne that should have been Jonathan's. And King Saul was incensed, overcome by a hatred that had brought him to attempt to do away with David. Yet David and Jonathan were dear friends. In the story of the *Haftarah,* Jonathan ignores his selfish interests — even his father's fury — and devises a plan to warn David of danger and, as the narrative shows, to save his life.

In a sense, the *Haftarah* was chosen for the day before Rosh Chodesh because of the mere coincidence that the conversation that begins it took place the day before Rosh Chodesh. It may be, however, that there is a deeper reason.

The New Moon alludes to the history of Israel and the Davidic dynasty. The moon grows to fullness over a period of fifteen days and then declines for the next fifteen until it disappears. So, too, there were fifteen generations from Abraham to Solomon, while the Jewish people grew spiritually and physically. Then began the decline, until, fifteen generations later, the monarchy came to an

לַמַּטָּרָה: כא וְהִנֵּה אֶשְׁלַח אֶת־הַנַּעַר
« the servant, ‹ I will send « And, then, 21 « at a target.
לֵךְ מְצָא אֶת־הַחִצִּים אִם־אָמֹר אֹמַר
‹ I will have said ‹ If « the arrows.' ‹ Find ‹ [saying,] 'Go!
לַנַּעַר הִנֵּה הַחִצִּים | מִמְּךָ וָהֵנָּה
« and here,' ‹ between you ‹ The arrows are « 'Behold! ‹ to the servant,
קָחֶנּוּ וָבֹאָה כִּי־שָׁלוֹם לְךָ וְאֵין
‹ and there is no ‹ with you, ‹ it is well ‹ for « and come, ‹ take him
דָּבָר חַי־יהוה: כב וְאִם־כֹּה אֹמַר לָעֶלֶם
« to the youth, ‹ I will say ‹ thus ‹ But if 22 « [I swear,] as HASHEM lives. « concern,
הִנֵּה הַחִצִּים מִמְּךָ וָהָלְאָה לֵךְ כִּי
‹ for ‹ go [away], ‹ and beyond!' ‹ between you ‹ The arrows are « 'Behold!
שִׁלַּחֲךָ יהוה: כג וְהַדָּבָר אֲשֶׁר דִּבַּרְנוּ אֲנִי
‹ I ‹ we have spoken, ‹ of which ‹ And [concerning] the matter 23 « HASHEM has sent you away.
וָאָתָּה הִנֵּה יהוה בֵּינִי וּבֵינְךָ עַד־
‹ for ‹ and between you ‹ between me ‹ HASHEM [shall witness] « Behold! ‹ and you:
עוֹלָם: כד וַיִּסָּתֵר דָּוִד בַּשָּׂדֶה וַיְהִי הַחֹדֶשׁ
‹ the [New] Moon ‹ It was « in the field. ‹ So David concealed himself 24 « eternity.
וַיֵּשֶׁב הַמֶּלֶךְ אֶל־ [על־ כ׳] הַלֶּחֶם לֶאֱכוֹל:
« to eat. ‹ the meal ‹ at ‹ and the king sat
כה וַיֵּשֶׁב הַמֶּלֶךְ עַל־מוֹשָׁבוֹ כְּפַעַם |
‹ as time ‹ his seat ‹ upon ‹ The king sat 25
בְּפַעַם אֶל־מוֹשַׁב הַקִּיר וַיָּקָם יְהוֹנָתָן
« And Jonathan stood up; « [by] the wall. ‹ the seat ‹ and time [again],
וַיֵּשֶׁב אַבְנֵר מִצַּד שָׁאוּל וַיִּפָּקֵד מְקוֹם
‹ the place ‹ but empty was ‹ of Saul, ‹ at the side ‹ [so that] Abner sat
דָּוִד: כו וְלֹא־דִבֶּר שָׁאוּל מְאוּמָה
‹ anything ‹ Saul did not speak 26 « of David.

בַּיּוֹם הַהוּא כִּי אָמַר מִקְרֶה הוּא בִּלְתִּי
‹ not « it is; ‹ A coincidence « he said [to himself], ‹ for « on that day,
טָהוֹר הוּא כִּי־לֹא טָהוֹר: כז וַיְהִי
‹ And it was 27 « clean. ‹ [he is] not ‹ it is that « is he, ‹ clean
מִמָּחֳרַת הַחֹדֶשׁ הַשֵּׁנִי וַיִּפָּקֵד מְקוֹם דָּוִד
« of David. ‹ the place ‹ and [still] empty was ‹ the second [day], ‹ the [New] Moon, ‹ on the day after
וַיֹּאמֶר שָׁאוּל אֶל־יְהוֹנָתָן בְּנוֹ מַדּוּעַ
‹ Why ‹ his son, ‹ Jonathan, ‹ to ‹ Saul said
לֹא־בָא בֶן־יִשַׁי גַּם־תְּמוֹל גַּם־הַיּוֹם
‹ today ‹ nor ‹ yesterday ‹ neither « of Jesse, ‹ [that] son ‹ did he not come,
אֶל־הַלָּחֶם: כח וַיַּעַן יְהוֹנָתָן אֶת־שָׁאוּל
« Saul, ‹ Jonathan answered 28 « the meal? ‹ to
נִשְׁאֹל נִשְׁאַל דָּוִד מֵעִמָּדִי עַד־
‹ [to go] to ‹ from me ‹ did David request ‹ A quest
בֵּית לָחֶם: כט וַיֹּאמֶר שַׁלְּחֵנִי נָא כִּי זֶבַח
‹ an offering ‹ for ‹ please, ‹ 'Send me, « He said, 29 « Bethlehem.
מִשְׁפָּחָה לָנוּ בָּעִיר וְהוּא צִוָּה־לִי אָחִי
« my brother did. ‹ me, ‹ has commanded ‹ and he « in the city; ‹ we have ‹ [by] the family
וְעַתָּה אִם־מָצָאתִי חֵן בְּעֵינֶיךָ אִמָּלְטָה
‹ let me get away, ‹ in your eyes, ‹ favor ‹ I have found ‹ if ‹ So now,
נָּא וְאֶרְאֶה אֶת־אֶחָי עַל־כֵּן לֹא־בָא
‹ he did not come ‹ of this ‹ Because « my brothers.' ‹ that I may see ‹ please,
אֶל־שֻׁלְחַן הַמֶּלֶךְ: ל וַיִּחַר־אַף שָׁאוּל
‹ of Saul ‹ the anger ‹ Then flared 30 « of the king. ‹ the table ‹ to
בִּיהוֹנָתָן וַיֹּאמֶר לוֹ בֶּן־נַעֲוַת הַמַּרְדּוּת
‹ rebellious woman: ‹ of a perverse ‹ Son « to him, ‹ and he said ‹ at Jonathan,
הֲלוֹא יָדַעְתִּי כִּי־בֹחֵר אַתָּה לְבֶן־יִשַׁי
‹ of Jesse, ‹ the son ‹ do you ‹ choose ‹ that ‹ [what] I have known, ‹ Is it not [true]

end, with the destruction of the Temple and the Babylonian Exile. But the heavens do not remain dark; the moon reappears. So, too, there will be a time of redemption, and the Davidic family will reign again. This is why the monthly *Kiddush Levanah/* Sanctification of the Moon includes the verse *David, King of Israel, is alive and enduring.*

It is prophetic that Jonathan's plan to save David begins with the words *"Tomorrow is the New Moon."* Indeed, there is a New Moon for David. And his New Moon is the rebirth of the nation, as well.

לְבָשְׁתְּךָ וּלְבֹשֶׁת עֶרְוַת אִמֶּךָ: לא כִּי כָל־
‹ all ‹ For 31 « of your mother! ‹ of the nakedness ‹ and to the shame ‹ to your own shame

הַיָּמִים אֲשֶׁר בֶּן־יִשַׁי חַי עַל־הָאֲדָמָה
‹ the earth, ‹ on ‹ lives ‹ of Jesse ‹ the son ‹ that ‹ the days

לֹא תִכּוֹן אַתָּה וּמַלְכוּתֶךָ וְעַתָּה
« And now, « and your kingdom! ‹ you ‹ be established, ‹ there shall not

שְׁלַח וְקַח אֹתוֹ אֵלַי כִּי בֶן־מָוֶת
‹ death ‹ deserving of ‹ for « to me, ‹ him ‹ and bring ‹ send [for him]

הוּא: לב וַיַּעַן יְהוֹנָתָן אֶת־שָׁאוּל אָבִיו
‹ his father ‹ to Saul, ‹ And Jonathan replied 32 « is he.

וַיֹּאמֶר אֵלָיו לָמָּה יוּמַת מֶה עָשָׂה:
« has he done? ‹ What « should he die? ‹ Why « to him, ‹ and he said

לג וַיָּטֶל שָׁאוּל אֶת־הַחֲנִית עָלָיו לְהַכֹּתוֹ
« to strike him; ‹ at him ‹ the spear ‹ Then Saul hurled 33

וַיֵּדַע יְהוֹנָתָן כִּי־כָלָה הִיא מֵעִם אָבִיו
‹ his father ‹ from ‹ was it ‹ final ‹ that ‹ and Jonathan realized

לְהָמִית אֶת־דָּוִד: לד וַיָּקָם יְהוֹנָתָן מֵעִם
‹ from ‹ Jonathan arose 34 « David. ‹ to put to death

הַשֻּׁלְחָן בָּחֳרִי־אָף וְלֹא־אָכַל בְּיוֹם
‹ on the day ‹ he did not eat « of anger; ‹ in a flare ‹ the table

הַחֹדֶשׁ הַשֵּׁנִי לֶחֶם כִּי נֶעְצַב אֶל־
‹ over ‹ he was saddened ‹ for « [any] food, « — the second — « of the month

דָּוִד כִּי הִכְלִמוֹ אָבִיו: לה וַיְהִי בַבֹּקֶר
« in the morning: ‹ And it was 35 « his father had humiliated him. ‹ because ‹ David,

וַיֵּצֵא יְהוֹנָתָן הַשָּׂדֶה לְמוֹעֵד דָּוִד וְנַעַר
‹ and a servant, ‹ [with] David, ‹ for [his] appointment ‹ to the field ‹ Jonathan went out

קָטֹן עִמּוֹ: לו וַיֹּאמֶר לְנַעֲרוֹ רֻץ מְצָא־
‹ Find, ‹ Run! « to his servant, ‹ He said 36 « was with him. ‹ a young one,

נָא אֶת־הַחִצִּים אֲשֶׁר אָנֹכִי מוֹרֶה
« shoot. ‹ I ‹ that ‹ the arrows ‹ please,

הַנַּעַר רָץ וְהוּא־יָרָה הַחֵצִי לְהַעֲבִרוֹ:
« to go beyond him. ‹ the arrow ‹ shot ‹ and he ‹ ran, ‹ The servant

לז וַיָּבֹא הַנַּעַר עַד־מְקוֹם הַחֵצִי אֲשֶׁר
‹ that ‹ of the arrow ‹ the place ‹ to ‹ The servant came 37

יָרָה יְהוֹנָתָן וַיִּקְרָא יְהוֹנָתָן אַחֲרֵי הַנַּעַר
‹ the servant, ‹ after ‹ and Jonathan called out ‹ Jonathan had shot;

וַיֹּאמֶר הֲלוֹא הַחֵצִי מִמְּךָ וָהָלְאָה:
« and beyond? ‹ between you ‹ the arrow ‹ Is not « and he said,

לח וַיִּקְרָא יְהוֹנָתָן אַחֲרֵי הַנַּעַר מְהֵרָה
‹ Quickly, « the servant, ‹ after ‹ And Jonathan called out 38

חוּשָׁה אַל־תַּעֲמֹד וַיְלַקֵּט נַעַר יְהוֹנָתָן
« of Jonathan did, ‹ the servant ‹ He gathered, « stand still! ‹ do not ‹ hurry,

אֶת־הַחִצִּים [החצי כ׳] וַיָּבֹא אֶל־אֲדֹנָיו:
« his master. ‹ to ‹ and he came ‹ the arrows

לט וְהַנַּעַר לֹא־יָדַע מְאוּמָה אַךְ יְהוֹנָתָן
‹ Jonathan ‹ only « anything; ‹ know ‹ did not ‹ Now the servant 39

וְדָוִד יָדְעוּ אֶת־הַדָּבָר: מ וַיִּתֵּן יְהוֹנָתָן
‹ Jonathan gave 40 « of the matter. ‹ knew ‹ and David

אֶת־כֵּלָיו אֶל־הַנַּעַר אֲשֶׁר־לוֹ וַיֹּאמֶר
‹ and he said ‹ his ‹ who was ‹ the servant ‹ to ‹ his gear

לוֹ לֵךְ הָבֵיא הָעִיר: מא הַנַּעַר בָּא וְדָוִד
‹ and David ‹ went ‹ The servant 41 « [to] the city. ‹ Bring [this] ‹ Go! « to him,

קָם מֵאֵצֶל הַנֶּגֶב וַיִּפֹּל לְאַפָּיו אַרְצָה
‹ to the ground ‹ on his face ‹ and he fell ‹ the south [of the stone], ‹ from near ‹ stood up

וַיִּשְׁתַּחוּ שָׁלֹשׁ פְּעָמִים וַיִּשְּׁקוּ | אִישׁ
‹ [each] man ‹ They kissed, « times. ‹ three ‹ and prostrated himself

אֶת־רֵעֵהוּ וַיִּבְכּוּ אִישׁ אֶת־רֵעֵהוּ עַד
‹ until ‹ his companion, ‹ with ‹ [each] man ‹ and they wept, ‹ his companion;

דָּוִד הִגְדִּיל: מב וַיֹּאמֶר יְהוֹנָתָן לְדָוִד לֵךְ
‹ Go « to David, ‹ Jonathan said 42 « [wept] greatly. ‹ David

לְשָׁלוֹם אֲשֶׁר נִשְׁבַּעְנוּ שְׁנֵינוּ אֲנַחְנוּ
‹ we, ‹ the two of us, ‹ we have sworn, ‹ What « unto peace.

בְּשֵׁם יהוה לֵאמֹר יהוה יִהְיֶה | בֵּינִי
‹ between me ‹ shall be [the witness] ‹ 'HASHEM « saying, ‹ of HASHEM, ‹ in the Name

וּבֵינֶךָ וּבֵין זַרְעִי וּבֵין זַרְעֲךָ עַד־עוֹלָם:
« eternity. ‹ [shall be] for ‹ your offspring, ‹ and between ‹ my offspring ‹ and between ‹ and between you,

MAFTIR OF SHABBAS ROSH CHODESH / מפטיר לשבת ראש חודש

Numbers 28:9-15 / במדבר כח:ט-טו

ט וּבְיוֹם הַשַּׁבָּת שְׁנֵי־כְבָשִׂים בְּנֵי־שָׁנָה

‹ first year, ‹ in their ‹ [male] lambs ‹ two « And on the day of the Sabbath [the *mussaf*-offering is]: 9

תְּמִימִם וּשְׁנֵי עֶשְׂרֹנִים סֹלֶת מִנְחָה

« for a meal-offering, ‹ of fine flour ‹ tenths [of an *ephah*] ‹ two « unblemished,

בְּלוּלָה בַשֶּׁמֶן וְנִסְכּוֹ: י עֹלַת שַׁבַּת

‹ of each Sabbath ‹ The burnt-offering 10 « and its [wine-]libation. « with ‹ mixed [olive] oil,

בְּשַׁבַּתּוֹ עַל־עֹלַת הַתָּמִיד וְנִסְכָּהּ:

« and its [wine-]libation. ‹ the continual burnt-offering ‹ in addition to « on its own Sabbath,

יא וּבְרָאשֵׁי חָדְשֵׁיכֶם תַּקְרִיבוּ עֹלָה

‹ a burnt-offering ‹ you shall bring ‹ of your months ‹ On the first [day] 11

לַיהוָה פָּרִים בְּנֵי־בָקָר שְׁנַיִם וְאַיִל אֶחָד

« one ram, « two; « of the herd, ‹ young ones ‹ bulls, « to HASHEM:

כְּבָשִׂים בְּנֵי־שָׁנָה שִׁבְעָה תְּמִימִם:

« unblemished. « — seven, « first year ‹ in their ‹ [male] lambs

יב וּשְׁלֹשָׁה עֶשְׂרֹנִים סֹלֶת מִנְחָה

‹ for a meal-offering ‹ of fine flour ‹ tenths [of an *ephah*] ‹ And three 12

בְּלוּלָה בַשֶּׁמֶן לַפָּר הָאֶחָד וּשְׁנֵי

‹ and two « for each bull; ‹ with [olive] oil, ‹ mixed

עֶשְׂרֹנִים סֹלֶת מִנְחָה בְּלוּלָה בַשֶּׁמֶן

‹ with [olive] oil, ‹ mixed ‹ for a meal-offering ‹ of fine flour ‹ tenths [of an *ephah*]

לָאַיִל הָאֶחָד: יג וְעִשָּׂרֹן עִשָּׂרוֹן סֹלֶת

‹ of fine flour ‹ And a tenth-*ephah* each 13 « for the single ram.

מִנְחָה בְּלוּלָה בַשֶּׁמֶן לַכֶּבֶשׂ הָאֶחָד

« for each lamb ‹ with [olive] oil, ‹ mixed ‹ for a meal-offering,

עֹלָה רֵיחַ נִיחֹחַ אִשֶּׁה לַיהוָה:

« to HASHEM. ‹ a fire-offering ‹ that is satisfying, ‹ an aroma ‹ — a burnt-offering,

יד וְנִסְכֵּיהֶם חֲצִי הַהִין יִהְיֶה לַפָּר

‹ for a bull, ‹ shall be ‹ of a *hin* ‹ a half « And their [wine-]libations: 14

וּשְׁלִישִׁת הַהִין לָאַיִל וּרְבִיעִת הַהִין

‹ of a *hin* ‹ and a quarter « for the ram, ‹ of a *hin* ‹ and a third

לַכֶּבֶשׂ יָיִן זֹאת עֹלַת חֹדֶשׁ בְּחָדְשׁוֹ

‹ upon its renewal ‹ of the month ‹ the burnt-offering ‹ This is « — of wine. « for a lamb

לְחָדְשֵׁי הַשָּׁנָה: טו וּשְׂעִיר עִזִּים אֶחָד

‹ one, ‹ of the goats, ‹ And a male 15 « of the year. ‹ for the months

לְחַטָּאת לַיהוָה עַל־עֹלַת הַתָּמִיד

‹ the continual burnt-offering ‹ in addition to « to HASHEM, ‹ for a sin-offering

יֵעָשֶׂה וְנִסְכּוֹ:

« and its [wine-]libation. « shall it be made,

HAFTARAS SHABBAS ROSH CHODESH / הפטרת שבת ראש חודש

Isaiah 66:1-24 / ישעיה סו:א-כד

סו א כֹּה אָמַר יהוה הַשָּׁמַיִם כִּסְאִי

‹ *My throne* ‹ *The heaven is* « HASHEM: ‹ *said* ‹ *So* 1 [66]

תִּבְנוּ־לִי וְאֵי־זֶה מָקוֹם מְנוּחָתִי:

« *of My resting?* ‹ *place* ‹ *that* ‹ *And where is* « *for Me?* ‹ *you would build*

וְהָאָרֶץ הֲדֹם רַגְלָי אֵי־זֶה בַיִת אֲשֶׁר

‹ *that* ‹ *House* ‹ *that* ‹ *Where is* « *for My feet.* ‹ *the stool* ‹ *and the earth is*

ב וְאֶת כָּל־אֵלֶּה יָדִי עָשָׂתָה וַיִּהְיוּ כָל־

‹ *all* ‹ *and there came into being* « *has made,* ‹ *My hand* ‹ *these* ‹ *And all* 2

Shabbas Rosh Chodesh

This chapter is the last one in the stirring Book of *Isaiah.* It was chosen as the *Haftarah* of the Sabbath Rosh Chodesh because its penultimate verse (which is repeated after the chapter is concluded) speaks of the homage that will be paid to God on every Sabbath and Rosh Chodesh.

The chapter gives hope and comfort to the Jewish people, as Isaiah foresees the ultimate downfall of the nations that will do battle against one another and against Israel in the climactic War of Gog and Magog, the war that will precede the final redemption. Isaiah speaks of the defeat of the nations and the universal recognition of the greatness of God and His people. But there are stern

אֵלֶּה נְאֻם־יהוה וְאֶל־זֶה אַבִּיט אֶל־עָנִי

the poor | to | I look: | this | — But to | of HASHEM. | the word | these —

וּנְכֵה־רוּחַ וְחָרֵד עַל־דְּבָרִי: ג שׁוֹחֵט

One who slaughters 3 | My Word. | regarding | who is zealous | of spirit | and broken

הַשּׁוֹר מַכֵּה־אִישׁ זוֹבֵחַ הַשֶּׂה עֹרֵף כֶּלֶב

a dog; | [is like] one who beheads | the sheep [offering] | one who sacrifices | a person; | [is like] one who smites | the ox [offering]

מַעֲלֵה מִנְחָה דַּם־חֲזִיר מַזְכִּיר לְבֹנָה

frankincense | one who censes | of a swine; | [is like] the blood | a meal-offering | he who brings up

מְבָרֵךְ אָוֶן גַּם־הֵמָּה בָּחֲרוּ בְּדַרְכֵיהֶם

their ways, | have chosen | they | also | of extortion; | [is like] one who brings a gift

וּבְשִׁקּוּצֵיהֶם נַפְשָׁם חָפֵצָה: ד גַּם־אֲנִי

I, | Also 4 | have desired. | their souls | and their abominations

אֶבְחַר בְּתַעֲלֻלֵיהֶם וּמְגוּרֹתָם אָבִיא

I will bring | so their fears | in [the manner of] their deeds, | will choose [to act]

לָהֶם יַעַן קָרָאתִי וְאֵין עוֹנֶה דִּבַּרְתִּי

I spoke, | response; | but there was no | I called, | because | upon them;

וְלֹא שָׁמֵעוּ וַיַּעֲשׂוּ הָרַע בְּעֵינַי וּבַאֲשֶׁר

and what | in My eyes, | what is evil | and they did | but they did not hear;

לֹא־חָפַצְתִּי בָּחָרוּ: ה שִׁמְעוּ דְּבַר־יהוה

of HASHEM, | to the Word | Listen 5 | they chose. | I did not desire

הַחֲרֵדִים אֶל־דְּבָרוֹ אָמְרוּ אֲחֵיכֶם

did your brethren | They said, | His Word. | at | O [you] who tremble

שֹׂנְאֵיכֶם מְנַדֵּיכֶם לְמַעַן שְׁמִי יִכְבַּד

[that] glorified will be | my name | 'It is for the sake of | who distance you [from them], | who hate you,

יהוה וְנִרְאֶה בְשִׂמְחַתְכֶם וְהֵם יֵבֹשׁוּ:

will be shamed. | and they | your gladness | — But we shall see | HASHEM.'

ו קוֹל שָׁאוֹן מֵעִיר קוֹל מֵהֵיכָל קוֹל

the sound | from the Sanctuary, | a sound | [comes] from the city, | of tumult | A sound 6

יהוה מְשַׁלֵּם גְּמוּל לְאֹיְבָיו: ז בְּטֶרֶם

Before 7 | to His enemies. | retribution | paying | of HASHEM

תָּחִיל יָלָדָה בְּטֶרֶם יָבוֹא חֵבֶל לָהּ

to her, | pain will come | Before | she will have given birth! | she will labor,

וְהִמְלִיטָה זָכָר: ח מִי־שָׁמַע כָּזֹאת מִי

Who | anything like this? | has heard | Who 8 | a son! | she will have delivered

רָאָה כָּאֵלֶּה הֲיוּחַל אֶרֶץ בְּיוֹם אֶחָד

in one day? | a land | Will there be born | anything like these? | has seen

אִם־יִוָּלֵד גּוֹי פַּעַם אֶחָת כִּי־חָלָה גַּם

even | she went through labor, | that | at once, | a nation | there be born | Will

יָלְדָה צִיּוֹן אֶת־בָּנֶיהָ: ט הַאֲנִי אַשְׁבִּיר

bring [a woman] to the birthstool | 'Would I 9 | to her children? | did Zion, | gave birth,

וְלֹא אוֹלִיד יֹאמַר יהוה אִם־אֲנִי

I, | Would | HASHEM would say. | allow [her] to give birth?' | and not

הַמּוֹלִיד וְעָצַרְתִּי אָמַר אֱלֹהָיִךְ: י שִׂמְחוּ

Be glad 10 | your God. | — said | hold [it] back? | the One Who causes birth,

אֶת־יְרוּשָׁלַיִם וְגִילוּ בָהּ כָּל־אֹהֲבֶיהָ

who love her; | all | in her, | and exult | Jerusalem | with

---

lessons for Israel, as well.

The chapter begins by declaring that all the world is but God's throne and His footstool. Can anyone think that the Jewish people can build a Temple that will encompass His Glory? Surely the purpose of the Temple is not to honor God — Who is above any honor we can render Him — but to serve as our vehicle to elevate ourselves. People who seek to appease God with insincere, meaningless service are considered like those who kill and maim people, and who offer unclean animals and contaminated blood upon His Altar. And they do so consciously, having *chosen* this form of blasphemous service. God will respond in kind, punishing those who ill serve Him. But that will not be the end. Those who are loyal to God will be acknowledged and rewarded in a miraculous manner. The rebirth of Israel will be as astounding as that of a nation being born in a single day, without even labor pains. If God decides to give new life to His people, can it be otherwise?

Thus, all who have been loyal to Jerusalem and mourned her will rejoice with her. Blessings will flow to them in torrents, but their enemies will suffer ignominious defeat, as God pours out His wrath upon them. The survivors will bring word of His greatness to the furthest corners of the world, and in the process they will bring back the straggling Jews who seemed to have been irretrievably lost in the long, hard exile.

Then all will come to the rebuilt Temple — the eternal Temple — to prostrate themselves in devout and loyal service to God. History will have reached its goal and those who were loyal to God will be vindicated.

שִׂישׂוּ אִתָּהּ מָשׂוֹשׂ כָּל־הַמִּתְאַבְּלִים
‹ who mourned ‹ all ‹ [in] joyousness, ‹ with her ‹ rejoice

עָלֶיהָ: יא לְמַעַן תִּינְקוּ וּשְׂבַעְתֶּם מִשֹּׁד
‹ from the breast ‹ and you may be sated ‹ you may nurse ‹ so that **11** « for her;

תַּנְחֻמֶיהָ לְמַעַן תָּמֹצּוּ וְהִתְעַנַּגְתֶּם מִזִּיז
‹ from the glow ‹ and you may delight ‹ you may suck ‹ so that « of her consolations;

כְּבוֹדָהּ: יב כִּי־כֹה ׀ אָמַר יהוה הִנְנִי
‹ Behold! I shall « HASHEM: ‹ said ‹ so ‹ For **12** « of her glory.

נֹטֶה־אֵלֶיהָ כְּנָהָר שָׁלוֹם וּכְנַחַל שׁוֹטֵף
‹ surging ‹ and a [veritable] stream, « [of] peace; ‹ a [veritable] river ‹ to her ‹ extend

כְּבוֹד גּוֹיִם וִינַקְתֶּם עַל־צַד תִּנָּשֵׂאוּ
« you will be carried, ‹ [her] side ‹ at « and you shall nurse; ‹ of nations ‹ [with] the honor

וְעַל־בִּרְכַּיִם תְּשָׁעֳשָׁעוּ: יג כְּאִישׁ אֲשֶׁר
‹ whom ‹ Like a man **13** « you will be dandled. ‹ [her] knees ‹ and on

אִמּוֹ תְּנַחֲמֶנּוּ כֵּן אָנֹכִי אֲנַחֶמְכֶם
‹ console you, ‹ [will] I ‹ so ‹ would console him, ‹ his mother

וּבִירוּשָׁלַםִ תְּנֻחָמוּ: יד וּרְאִיתֶם וְשָׂשׂ
‹ and rejoice ‹ You shall see **14** « you will be consoled. ‹ and in Jerusalem

לִבְּכֶם וְעַצְמוֹתֵיכֶם כַּדֶּשֶׁא תִפְרַחְנָה
« will flourish. ‹ like grass ‹ and your bones; ‹ will your heart

וְנוֹדְעָה יַד־יהוה אֶת־עֲבָדָיו וְזָעַם אֶת־
‹ with ‹ and He will be angry ‹ His servants; ‹ to ‹ And the hand of HASHEM will be known,

אֹיְבָיו: טו כִּי־הִנֵּה יהוה בָּאֵשׁ יָבוֹא
« will arrive, ‹ in fire ‹ HASHEM, « behold! ‹ For **15** « His enemies.

וְכַסּוּפָה מַרְכְּבֹתָיו לְהָשִׁיב בְּחֵמָה אַפּוֹ
‹ of His anger, ‹ with the wrath ‹ to repay « His chariots; ‹ and like the whirlwind,

וְגַעֲרָתוֹ בְּלַהֲבֵי־אֵשׁ: טז כִּי בָאֵשׁ יהוה
‹ HASHEM ‹ with fire ‹ For **16** « of fire. ‹ through flames ‹ and His rebuke

נִשְׁפָּט וּבְחַרְבּוֹ אֶת־כָּל־בָּשָׂר וְרַבּוּ
‹ many will be « flesh; ‹ all ‹ against ‹ and with His sword « will judge,

חַלְלֵי יהוה: יז הַמִּתְקַדְּשִׁים וְהַמִּטַּהֲרִים
‹ and those who purify themselves ‹ Those who prepare themselves **17** « by HASHEM. ‹ those slain

אֶל־הַגַּנּוֹת אַחַר אַחַת [אחד כ׳] בַּתָּוֶךְ
« in the middle [of the garden]; ‹ each one [is another] ‹ behind ‹ the [idols'] gardens; ‹ to [enter]

אֹכְלֵי בְּשַׂר הַחֲזִיר וְהַשֶּׁקֶץ וְהָעַכְבָּר
‹ and the mouse, ‹ and the abominable creature, ‹ of the swine, ‹ of the flesh ‹ eaters

יַחְדָּו יָסֻפוּ נְאֻם־יהוה: יח וְאָנֹכִי
‹ I [know] **18** « of HASHEM. ‹ — the word « they will be consumed ‹ together

מַעֲשֵׂיהֶם וּמַחְשְׁבֹתֵיהֶם בָּאָה לְקַבֵּץ
‹ to gather ‹ [the time] has come « and their thoughts; ‹ their deeds

אֶת־כָּל־הַגּוֹיִם וְהַלְּשֹׁנוֹת וּבָאוּ וְרָאוּ
‹ and they shall see ‹ and they shall come « and [all] the tongues; ‹ the nations ‹ all

אֶת־כְּבוֹדִי: יט וְשַׂמְתִּי בָהֶם אוֹת
‹ a sign, ‹ upon them ‹ I will place **19** « My glory.

וְשִׁלַּחְתִּי מֵהֶם ׀ פְּלֵיטִים אֶל־הַגּוֹיִם
« nations: ‹ to ‹ as survivors, ‹ some of them, ‹ and I will send

תַּרְשִׁישׁ פּוּל וְלוּד מֹשְׁכֵי קֶשֶׁת תֻּבַל
‹ [to] Tubal ‹ the bow, ‹ those who draw « and Lud — ‹ Pul ‹ Tarshish,

וְיָוָן הָאִיִּים הָרְחֹקִים אֲשֶׁר לֹא־שָׁמְעוּ
‹ heard ‹ have not ‹ who ‹ that are far away, ‹ [and to] the islands ‹ and [to] Javan

אֶת־שִׁמְעִי וְלֹא־רָאוּ אֶת־כְּבוֹדִי וְהִגִּידוּ
‹ and they will relate « My glory; ‹ seen ‹ and have not ‹ of My fame

אֶת־כְּבוֹדִי בַּגּוֹיִם: כ וְהֵבִיאוּ אֶת־כָּל־
‹ all ‹ They will bring **20** « among the nations. ‹ My glory

אֲחֵיכֶם מִכָּל־הַגּוֹיִם ׀ מִנְחָה ׀ לַיהוה
« to HASHEM, ‹ as an offering ‹ the nations ‹ from all ‹ your brethren

בַּסּוּסִים וּבָרֶכֶב וּבַצַּבִּים וּבַפְּרָדִים
‹ and by mules, ‹ and by covered wagons, ‹ and by chariot, ‹ by horses,

וּבַכִּרְכָּרוֹת עַל הַר קָדְשִׁי יְרוּשָׁלִָם
« Jerusalem ‹ of My holiness, ‹ the mount ‹ onto ‹ and by camels

אָמַר יהוה כַּאֲשֶׁר יָבִיאוּ בְנֵי יִשְׂרָאֵל
« of Israel, ‹ do the Children « they bring, ‹ just as « HASHEM — ‹ — said

אֶת־הַמִּנְחָה בִּכְלִי טָהוֹר בֵּית יהוה:
« of HASHEM. ‹ [to] the House ‹ a pure one, ‹ in a vessel, ‹ the offering

כא וְגַם־מֵהֶם אֶקַּח לַכֹּהֲנִים לַלְוִיִּם אָמַר

‹ — said « and [as] Levites ‹ [as] Kohanim ‹ I will take ‹ from [among] them ‹ Then even 21

יְהוָֹה: כב כִּי כַאֲשֶׁר הַשָּׁמַיִם הַחֲדָשִׁים

‹ that are new, ‹ the heavens, ‹ just as ‹ For 22 « HASHEM.

וְהָאָרֶץ הַחֲדָשָׁה אֲשֶׁר אֲנִי עֹשֶׂה

‹ am making ‹ I ‹ that ‹ that is new, ‹ and the earth,

עֹמְדִים לְפָנַי נְאֻם־יְהוָֹה כֵּן יַעֲמֹד

‹ will endure ‹ so « — the word of HASHEM — « before Me ‹ endure

זַרְעֲכֶם וְשִׁמְכֶם: כג וְהָיָה מִדֵּי־חֹדֶשׁ

‹ month ‹ each ‹ And it shall be, 23 « and your name. ‹ your offspring

בְּחָדְשׁוֹ וּמִדֵּי שַׁבָּת בְּשַׁבַּתּוֹ יָבוֹא כָל־

‹ all ‹ there shall come ‹ in its week, ‹ week ‹ and each ‹ in its month

בָּשָׂר לְהִשְׁתַּחֲוֹת לְפָנַי אָמַר יְהוָֹה:

« HASHEM. ‹ — said « before Me ‹ to prostrate [themselves] ‹ flesh

כד וְיָצְאוּ וְרָאוּ בְּפִגְרֵי הָאֲנָשִׁים הַפֹּשְׁעִים

‹ who rebel ‹ of the people ‹ the corpses ‹ and they shall see ‹ They shall go out 24

בִּי כִּי תוֹלַעְתָּם לֹא תָמוּת וְאִשָּׁם לֹא

‹ will not ‹ and their fire ‹ die, ‹ will not ‹ their worm ‹ for ‹ against Me,

תִכְבֶּה וְהָיוּ דֵרָאוֹן לְכָל־בָּשָׂר: וְהָיָה

‹ And it shall be, « flesh. ‹ for all ‹ a disgrace ‹ and they shall be ‹ go out,

מִדֵּי־חֹדֶשׁ בְּחָדְשׁוֹ וּמִדֵּי שַׁבָּת בְּשַׁבַּתּוֹ

‹ in its week, ‹ week ‹ and each ‹ in its month ‹ month ‹ each

יָבוֹא כָל־בָּשָׂר לְהִשְׁתַּחֲוֹת לְפָנַי אָמַר

‹ — said « before Me ‹ to prostrate [themselves] ‹ flesh ‹ all ‹ there shall come

יְהוָֹה:

« HASHEM.

When the second day Rosh Chodesh falls on Sunday, some congregations add the first and last verses of the *Haftarah* for *Shabbos* Erev Rosh Chodesh:

וַיֹּאמֶר־לוֹ יְהוֹנָתָן מָחָר חֹדֶשׁ וְנִפְקַדְתָּ

‹ and you will be missed ‹ is the [New] Moon, ‹ To-morrow « did Jonathan, « to him ‹ He said

כִּי יִפָּקֵד מוֹשָׁבֶךָ: וַיֹּאמֶר יְהוֹנָתָן לְדָוִד

« to David, ‹ Jonathan said « your seat. ‹ empty will be ‹ because

לֵךְ לְשָׁלוֹם אֲשֶׁר נִשְׁבַּעְנוּ שְׁנֵינוּ אֲנַחְנוּ

‹ we, ‹ the two of us, ‹ we have sworn, ‹ What « unto peace. ‹ Go

בְּשֵׁם יְהוָֹה לֵאמֹר יְהוָֹה יִהְיֶה | בֵּינִי

‹ between me ‹ shall be [the witness] ‹ 'HASHEM « saying, ‹ of HASHEM, ‹ in the Name

וּבֵינֶךָ וּבֵין זַרְעִי וּבֵין זַרְעֲךָ עַד־עוֹלָם:

« eternity. ‹ [shall be] for ‹ your offspring, ‹ and between ‹ my offspring ‹ and between ‹ and between you,

MAFTIR OF SHABBAS CHANUKAH / מפטיר לשבת חנוכה

FIRST DAY CHANUKAH / א׳ חנוכה

Numbers (6:22) 7:1-17 / במדבר (ו:כב) ז:א-יז

(כב וַיְדַבֵּר יְהוָֹה אֶל־מֹשֶׁה לֵּאמֹר: כג דַּבֵּר

‹ Speak 23 « saying, ‹ Moses ‹ to ‹ HASHEM spoke 22

אֶל־אַהֲרֹן וְאֶל־בָּנָיו לֵאמֹר כֹּה

‹ 'So « saying: ‹ his sons ‹ and to ‹ Aaron ‹ to

תְבָרְכוּ אֶת־בְּנֵי יִשְׂרָאֵל אָמוֹר לָהֶם:

« to them: ‹ saying « of Israel, ‹ the Children ‹ shall you bless

כד יְבָרֶכְךָ יְהוָֹה וְיִשְׁמְרֶךָ: כה יָאֵר יְהוָֹה |

‹ May HASHEM illuminate 25 « and safe-guard you. « "May HASHEM bless you 24

פָּנָיו אֵלֶיךָ וִיחֻנֶּךָּ: כו יִשָּׂא יְהוָֹה | פָּנָיו

‹ His countenance ‹ May HASHEM turn 26 « and be gracious to you. ‹ for you ‹ His countenance

אֵלֶיךָ וְיָשֵׂם לְךָ שָׁלוֹם: כז וְשָׂמוּ

‹ Let them place 27 « peace." ' ‹ for you ‹ and establish ‹ to you

אֶת־שְׁמִי עַל־בְּנֵי יִשְׂרָאֵל וַאֲנִי

‹ and I « of Israel, ‹ the Children ‹ upon ‹ My Name

אֲבָרְכֵם:) [ז] א וַיְהִי בְּיוֹם כַּלּוֹת מֹשֶׁה

‹ that Moses finished ‹ on the day ‹ It was 1 [7] « shall bless them.

לְהָקִים אֶת־הַמִּשְׁכָּן וַיִּמְשַׁח

‹ that he anointed ‹ the Tabernacle ‹ erecting

אֹתוֹ וַיְקַדֵּשׁ אֹתוֹ וְאֶת־כָּל־כֵּלָיו

« its utensils, ‹ and all ‹ it ‹ and he sanctified ‹ it,

וְאֶת־הַמִּזְבֵּחַ וְאֶת־כָּל־כֵּלָיו וַיִּמְשָׁחֵם
‹ and he anointed them « its utensils, ‹ and all ‹ and the Altar

וַיְקַדֵּשׁ אֹתָם: ב וַיַּקְרִיבוּ נְשִׂיאֵי יִשְׂרָאֵל
« of Israel, ‹ — the princes « And they brought forward offerings 2 « them. ‹ and he sanctified

רָאשֵׁי בֵּית אֲבֹתָם הֵם נְשִׂיאֵי הַמַּטֹּת
« of the tribes, ‹ the princes ‹ they were « of their fathers; ‹ of the House ‹ the heads

הֵם הָעֹמְדִים עַל־הַפְּקֻדִים: ג וַיָּבִיאוּ
‹ They brought 3 « the countings. ‹ at ‹ those who stand ‹ they were

אֶת־קָרְבָּנָם לִפְנֵי יהוה שֵׁשׁ־עֶגְלֹת צָב
‹ that were covered ‹ wagons ‹ six « HASHEM: ‹ before ‹ their offering

וּשְׁנֵי עָשָׂר בָּקָר עֲגָלָה עַל־שְׁנֵי
‹ [each] two ‹ to ‹ — a wagon « oxen ‹ and twelve

הַנְּשִׂאִים וְשׁוֹר לְאֶחָד וַיַּקְרִיבוּ אוֹתָם
‹ them ‹ and they brought « to [each] one ‹ and an ox ‹ princes

לִפְנֵי הַמִּשְׁכָּן: ד וַיֹּאמֶר יהוה אֶל־
‹ to ‹ HASHEM said 4 « the Tabernacle. ‹ before

מֹשֶׁה לֵּאמֹר: ה קַח מֵאִתָּם וְהָיוּ
‹ *and they shall be* « *from them,* ‹ *Take* 5 « saying, ‹ Moses

לַעֲבֹד אֶת־עֲבֹדַת אֹהֶל מוֹעֵד וְנָתַתָּה
‹ *you shall give* « *of Meeting;* ‹ *of the Tent* ‹ *the work* ‹ *to perform*

אוֹתָם אֶל־הַלְוִיִּם אִישׁ כְּפִי עֲבֹדָתוֹ:
« *his work.* ‹ *according to* ‹ *[each] man* « *the Levites,* ‹ *to* ‹ *them*

ו וַיִּקַּח מֹשֶׁה אֶת־הָעֲגָלֹת וְאֶת־הַבָּקָר
« and the oxen ‹ the wagons ‹ So Moses took 6

וַיִּתֵּן אוֹתָם אֶל־הַלְוִיִּם: ז אֵת ׀ שְׁתֵּי
‹ Two 7 « the Levites. ‹ to ‹ them ‹ and gave

הָעֲגָלוֹת וְאֵת אַרְבַּעַת הַבָּקָר נָתַן לִבְנֵי
‹ to the sons ‹ he gave ‹ of the oxen ‹ and four ‹ of the wagons

גֵּרְשׁוֹן כְּפִי עֲבֹדָתָם: ח וְאֵת ׀ אַרְבַּע
‹ And four 8 « their work. ‹ in accordance with « of Gershon,

הָעֲגָלֹת וְאֵת שְׁמֹנַת הַבָּקָר נָתַן לִבְנֵי
‹ to the sons ‹ he gave ‹ of the oxen ‹ and eight ‹ of the wagons

מְרָרִי כְּפִי עֲבֹדָתָם בְּיַד אִיתָמָר
‹ of Ithamar, ‹ under the supervision ‹ their work, ‹ in accordance with « of Merari,

בֶּן־אַהֲרֹן הַכֹּהֵן: ט וְלִבְנֵי קְהָת
‹ of Kohath ‹ And to the sons 9 « the Kohen. ‹ Aaron ‹ son of

לֹא נָתָן כִּי־עֲבֹדַת הַקֹּדֶשׁ עֲלֵהֶם
« was upon them, ‹ of the sacred [vessels] ‹ the service ‹ since « he did not give;

בַּכָּתֵף יִשָּׂאוּ: י וַיַּקְרִיבוּ הַנְּשִׂאִים
‹ Then, the princes brought forward [offerings] 10 « they were to carry. ‹ on the shoulder

אֵת חֲנֻכַּת הַמִּזְבֵּחַ בְּיוֹם הִמָּשַׁח אֹתוֹ
« of it, ‹ of the anointing ‹ on the day ‹ of the Altar ‹ the dedication ‹ to serve for

וַיַּקְרִיבוּ הַנְּשִׂיאִם אֶת־קָרְבָּנָם לִפְנֵי
‹ before ‹ their offering ‹ and the princes brought

הַמִּזְבֵּחַ: יא וַיֹּאמֶר יהוה אֶל־מֹשֶׁה
« Moses, ‹ to ‹ HASHEM said 11 « the Altar.

נָשִׂיא אֶחָד לַיּוֹם נָשִׂיא אֶחָד לַיּוֹם
‹ *to [each] day,* ‹ *one prince* ‹ *to [each] day,* ‹ *One prince*

יַקְרִיבוּ אֶת־קָרְבָּנָם לַחֲנֻכַּת הַמִּזְבֵּחַ:
« *of the Altar.* ‹ *for the dedication* ‹ *their offering* ‹ *shall they bring*

יב וַיְהִי הַמַּקְרִיב בַּיּוֹם הָרִאשׁוֹן
‹ on the first day ‹ [that] the one who brought ‹ And it was 12

אֶת־קָרְבָּנוֹ נַחְשׁוֹן בֶּן־עַמִּינָדָב לְמַטֵּה
‹ of the tribe ‹ Amminadab, ‹ son of ‹ [was] Nahshon ‹ his offering

יְהוּדָה: יג וְקָרְבָּנוֹ קַעֲרַת־כֶּסֶף אַחַת
« — one, ‹ of silver ‹ a bowl ‹ His offering was: 13 « of Judah.

שְׁלֹשִׁים וּמֵאָה מִשְׁקָלָהּ מִזְרָק אֶחָד
‹ and one basin « was its weight; ‹ and one hundred [*shekels*] ‹ thirty

כֶּסֶף שִׁבְעִים שֶׁקֶל בְּשֶׁקֶל הַקֹּדֶשׁ
« of the sanctuary; ‹ in the *shekel* ‹ *shekels* ‹ of seventy « of silver,

שְׁנֵיהֶם ׀ מְלֵאִים סֹלֶת בְּלוּלָה בַשֶּׁמֶן
‹ with [olive] oil ‹ mixed ‹ with fine flour ‹ filled ‹ both of them

לְמִנְחָה: יד כַּף אַחַת עֲשָׂרָה זָהָב מְלֵאָה
‹ filled ‹ of gold ‹ of ten [*shekels*] ‹ one ladle 14 « for a meal-offering;

קְטֹֽרֶת: טו פַּר אֶחָד בֶּן־בָּקָר אַיִל אֶחָד
« one ram; « of the cattle; ‹ a calf ‹ one bull, **15** « with incense;

כֶּֽבֶשׂ־אֶחָד בֶּן־שְׁנָתוֹ לְעֹלָה: טז שְׂעִיר־
‹ a male **16** « —for a burnt-offering; « first year ‹ in its ‹ one [male] lamb

עִזִּים אֶחָד לְחַטָּאת: יז וּלְזֶבַח הַשְּׁלָמִים
« of the peace-offering: ‹ and for the sacrifice **17** « for a sin-offering; ‹ —one, ‹ of the goats

בָּקָר שְׁנַיִם אֵילִם חֲמִשָּׁה עַתּוּדִים
‹ he-goats « —five, ‹ rams « —two, ‹ cattle

חֲמִשָּׁה כְּבָשִׂים בְּנֵי־שָׁנָה חֲמִשָּׁה זֶה
‹ This is « —five. ‹ first year ‹ in their ‹ sheep « —five,

קָרְבַּן נַחְשׁוֹן בֶּן־עַמִּינָדָב:
« Amminadab. ‹ son of ‹ of Nachshon ‹ the offering

SECOND DAY CHANUKAH / ב׳ חנוכה

Numbers 7:18-23 / במדבר ז:יח־כג

יח בַּיּוֹם הַשֵּׁנִי הִקְרִיב נְתַנְאֵל בֶּן־צוּעָר
‹ Zuar, ‹ son of ‹ Nethanel ‹ offered ‹ On the second day, **18**

נְשִׂיא יִשָּׂשכָר: יט הִקְרִב אֶת־קָרְבָּנוֹ
‹ his offering: ‹ He brought **19** « of Issachar. ‹ the Prince

קַֽעֲרַת־כֶּסֶף אַחַת שְׁלֹשִׁים וּמֵאָה
‹ and one hundred [*shekels*] ‹ thirty « —one, ‹ of silver ‹ a bowl

מִשְׁקָלָהּ מִזְרָק אֶחָד כֶּסֶף שִׁבְעִים שֶׁקֶל
‹ *shekels* ‹ of seventy « of silver, ‹ and one basin « was its weight;

בְּשֶׁקֶל הַקֹּדֶשׁ שְׁנֵיהֶם ׀ מְלֵאִים סֹלֶת
‹ with fine flour ‹ filled ‹ both of them « of the sanctuary; ‹ in the *shekel*

בְּלוּלָה בַשֶּׁמֶן לְמִנְחָה: כ כַּף אַחַת
‹ one ladle **20** « for a meal-offering; ‹ with [olive] oil ‹ mixed

עֲשָׂרָה זָהָב מְלֵאָה קְטֹרֶת: כא פַּר אֶחָד
‹ one bull, **21** « with incense; ‹ filled ‹ of gold ‹ of ten [*shekels*]

בֶּן־בָּקָר אַיִל אֶחָד כֶּֽבֶשׂ־אֶחָד בֶּן־
‹ in its ‹ one [male] sheep « one ram; « of the cattle; ‹ a calf

שְׁנָתוֹ לְעֹלָה: כב שְׂעִיר־עִזִּים אֶחָד
‹ —one, ‹ of the goats ‹ a male **22** « —for a burnt-offering; « first year

לְחַטָּאת: כג וּלְזֶבַח הַשְּׁלָמִים בָּקָר שְׁנַיִם
« —two, ‹ cattle « of the peace-offering: ‹ and for the sacrifice **23** « for a sin-offering;

אֵילִם חֲמִשָּׁה עַתֻּדִים חֲמִשָּׁה כְּבָשִׂים
‹ sheep « —five, ‹ he-goats « —five, ‹ rams

בְּנֵי־שָׁנָה חֲמִשָּׁה זֶה קָרְבַּן נְתַנְאֵל
‹ of Nethanel ‹ the offering ‹ This is « —five. ‹ first year ‹ in their

בֶּן־צוּעָר:
« Zuar. ‹ son of

THIRD DAY CHANUKAH / ג׳ חנוכה

Numbers 7:24-29 / במדבר ז:כד־כט

כד בַּיּוֹם הַשְּׁלִישִׁי נָשִׂיא לִבְנֵי זְבוּלֻן
« of Zebulun, ‹ of the children ‹ the Prince ‹ On the third day, **24**

אֱלִיאָב בֶּן־חֵלֹן: כה קָרְבָּנוֹ קַֽעֲרַת־
‹ a bowl ‹ His offering was **25** « Helon. ‹ son of ‹ Eliab

כֶּסֶף אַחַת שְׁלֹשִׁים וּמֵאָה מִשְׁקָלָהּ
« was its weight; ‹ and one hundred [*shekels*] ‹ thirty « —one, ‹ of silver

מִזְרָק אֶחָד כֶּסֶף שִׁבְעִים שֶׁקֶל בְּשֶׁקֶל
‹ in the *shekel* ‹ *shekels* ‹ of seventy « of silver, ‹ and one basin

הַקֹּדֶשׁ שְׁנֵיהֶם ׀ מְלֵאִים סֹלֶת בְּלוּלָה
‹ mixed ‹ with fine flour ‹ filled ‹ both of them « of the sanctuary;

בַשֶּׁמֶן לְמִנְחָה: כו כַּף אַחַת עֲשָׂרָה זָהָב
‹ of gold ‹ of ten [*shekels*] ‹ one ladle **26** « for a meal-offering; ‹ with [olive] oil

מְלֵאָה קְטֹרֶת: כז פַּר אֶחָד בֶּן־בָּקָר
« of the cattle; ‹ a calf ‹ one bull, **27** « with incense; ‹ filled

אַיִל אֶחָד כֶּֽבֶשׂ־אֶחָד בֶּן־שְׁנָתוֹ לְעֹלָה:
« —for a burnt-offering; « first year ‹ in its ‹ one [male] sheep « one ram;

כח שְׂעִיר־עִזִּים אֶחָד לְחַטָּאת:
« for a sin-offering; ‹ —one, ‹ of the goats ‹ a male **28**

כט וּלְזֶבַח הַשְּׁלָמִים בָּקָר שְׁנַיִם אֵילִם
‹ rams « —two, ‹ cattle « of the peace-offering: ‹ and for the sacrifice **29**

חֲמִשָּׁה עַתֻּדִים חֲמִשָּׁה כְּבָשִׂים בְּנֵי־
‹ in their ‹ sheep « —five, ‹ he-goats « —five,

שָׁנָה חֲמִשָּׁה זֶה קׇרְבַּן אֱלִיאָב בֶּן־חֵלֹן׃
« Helon. ‹ son of ‹ of Eliab ‹ the offering ‹ This is « — five. ‹ first year

FOURTH DAY CHANUKAH / ד׳ חנוכה

Numbers 7:30-35 / במדבר ז:ל-לה

ל בַּיּוֹם הָרְבִיעִי נָשִׂיא לִבְנֵי רְאוּבֵן
« of Reuben, ‹ of the children ‹ the Prince ‹ On the fourth day, **30**

אֱלִיצוּר בֶּן־שְׁדֵיאוּר׃ לא קׇרְבָּנוֹ קַעֲרַת־
‹ a bowl ‹ His offering was: **31** « Shedeur. ‹ son of ‹ Elizur

כֶּסֶף אַחַת שְׁלֹשִׁים וּמֵאָה מִשְׁקָלָהּ
« was its weight; ‹ and one hundred [*shekels*] ‹ thirty « — one, ‹ of silver

מִזְרָק אֶחָד כֶּסֶף שִׁבְעִים שֶׁקֶל בְּשֶׁקֶל
‹ in the *shekel* ‹ *shekels* ‹ of seventy « of silver, ‹ and one basin

הַקֹּדֶשׁ שְׁנֵיהֶם ׀ מְלֵאִים סֹלֶת בְּלוּלָה
‹ mixed ‹ with fine flour ‹ filled ‹ both of them « of the sanctuary;

בַשֶּׁמֶן לְמִנְחָה׃ לב כַּף אַחַת עֲשָׂרָה זָהָב
‹ of gold ‹ of ten [*shekels*] ‹ one ladle **32** « for a meal-offering; ‹ with [olive] oil

מְלֵאָה קְטֹרֶת׃ לג פַּר אֶחָד בֶּן־בָּקָר
« of the cattle; ‹ a calf ‹ one bull, **33** « with incense; ‹ filled

אַיִל אֶחָד כֶּבֶשׂ־אֶחָד בֶּן־שְׁנָתוֹ לְעֹלָה׃
« — for a burnt-offering; « first year ‹ in its ‹ one [male] sheep « one ram;

לד שְׂעִיר־עִזִּים אֶחָד לְחַטָּאת׃ לה וּלְזֶבַח
‹ and for the sacrifice **35** « for a sin-offering; ‹ — one, ‹ of the goats ‹ a male **34**

הַשְּׁלָמִים בָּקָר שְׁנַיִם אֵילִם חֲמִשָּׁה
« — five, ‹ rams « — two, ‹ cattle « of a peace-offering:

עַתֻּדִים חֲמִשָּׁה כְּבָשִׂים בְּנֵי־שָׁנָה
‹ first year ‹ in their ‹ sheep « — five, ‹ he-goats

חֲמִשָּׁה זֶה קׇרְבַּן אֱלִיצוּר בֶּן־שְׁדֵיאוּר׃
« Shedeur. ‹ son of ‹ of Elizur ‹ the offering ‹ This is « — five.

SIXTH DAY CHANUKAH / ו׳ חנוכה

Numbers 7:42-47 / במדבר ז:מב-מז

מב בַּיּוֹם הַשִּׁשִּׁי נָשִׂיא לִבְנֵי גָד אֶלְיָסָף
‹ Eliasaph « of Gad, ‹ of the children ‹ the Prince ‹ On the sixth day, **42**

בֶּן־דְּעוּאֵל׃ מג קׇרְבָּנוֹ קַעֲרַת־כֶּסֶף אַחַת
« — one, ‹ of silver ‹ a bowl ‹ His offering was: **43** « Deuel. ‹ son of

שְׁלֹשִׁים וּמֵאָה מִשְׁקָלָהּ מִזְרָק אֶחָד
‹ and one basin « was its weight; ‹ and one hundred [*shekels*] ‹ thirty

כֶּסֶף שִׁבְעִים שֶׁקֶל בְּשֶׁקֶל הַקֹּדֶשׁ
« of the sanctuary; ‹ in the *shekel* ‹ *shekels* ‹ of seventy « of silver,

שְׁנֵיהֶם ׀ מְלֵאִים סֹלֶת בְּלוּלָה בַשֶּׁמֶן
‹ with [olive] oil ‹ mixed ‹ with fine flour ‹ filled ‹ both of them

לְמִנְחָה׃ מד כַּף אַחַת עֲשָׂרָה זָהָב מְלֵאָה
‹ filled ‹ of gold ‹ of ten [*shekels*] ‹ one ladle **44** « for a meal-offering;

קְטֹרֶת׃ מה פַּר אֶחָד בֶּן־בָּקָר אַיִל אֶחָד
« one ram; « of the cattle; ‹ a calf ‹ one bull, **45** « with incense;

כֶּבֶשׂ־אֶחָד בֶּן־שְׁנָתוֹ לְעֹלָה׃ מו שְׂעִיר־
‹ a male **46** « — for a burnt-offering; « first year ‹ in its ‹ one [male] sheep

עִזִּים אֶחָד לְחַטָּאת׃ מז וּלְזֶבַח
‹ and for the sacrifice **47** « for a sin-offering; ‹ — one, ‹ of the goats

הַשְּׁלָמִים בָּקָר שְׁנַיִם אֵילִם חֲמִשָּׁה
« — five, ‹ rams « — two, ‹ cattle « of the peace-offering:

עַתֻּדִים חֲמִשָּׁה כְּבָשִׂים בְּנֵי־שָׁנָה
‹ first year ‹ in their ‹ sheep « — five, ‹ he-goats

חֲמִשָּׁה זֶה קׇרְבַּן אֶלְיָסָף בֶּן־דְּעוּאֵל׃
« Deuel. ‹ son of ‹ of Eliasaph ‹ the offering ‹ This is « — five.

SEVENTH DAY CHANUKAH / ז׳ חנוכה

Numbers 7:48-53 / במדבר ז:מח-נג

מח בַּיּוֹם הַשְּׁבִיעִי נָשִׂיא לִבְנֵי אֶפְרָיִם
« of Ephraim, ‹ of the children ‹ the Prince ‹ On the seventh day, **48**

אֱלִישָׁמָע בֶּן־עַמִּיהוּד׃ מט קׇרְבָּנוֹ
‹ His offering was: **49** « Ammihud. ‹ son of ‹ Elishama

קַעֲרַת־כֶּסֶף אַחַת שְׁלֹשִׁים וּמֵאָה
‹ and one hundred [*shekels*] ‹ thirty « — one, ‹ of silver ‹ a bowl

מִשְׁקָלָהּ מִזְרָק אֶחָד כֶּסֶף שִׁבְעִים שֶׁקֶל
‹ *shekels* ‹ of seventy « of silver, ‹ and one basin « was its weight;

בְּשֶׁקֶל הַקֹּדֶשׁ שְׁנֵיהֶם ׀ מְלֵאִים סֹלֶת
‹ with fine flour ‹ filled ‹ both of them ‹‹ of the sanctuary; ‹ in the *shekel*

בְּלוּלָה בַשֶּׁמֶן לְמִנְחָה: נ כַּף אַחַת
‹ one ladle **50** ‹‹ for a meal-offering; ‹ with [olive] oil ‹ mixed

עֲשָׂרָה זָהָב מְלֵאָה קְטֹרֶת: נא פַּר אֶחָד
‹ one bull, **51** ‹‹ with incense; ‹ filled ‹ of gold ‹ of ten [*shekels*]

בֶּן־בָּקָר אַיִל אֶחָד כֶּבֶשׂ־אֶחָד בֶּן
‹ in its ‹ one [male] sheep ‹‹ one ram; ‹‹ of the cattle; ‹ a calf

שְׁנָתוֹ לְעֹלָה: נב שְׂעִיר־עִזִּים אֶחָד
‹ —one, ‹ of the goats ‹ a male **52** ‹‹ —for a burnt-offering; ‹‹ first year

לְחַטָּאת: נג וּלְזֶבַח הַשְּׁלָמִים בָּקָר שְׁנַיִם
‹‹ —two, ‹ cattle ‹ of the peace-offering: ‹ and for the sacrifice **53** ‹‹ for a sin-offering;

אֵילִם חֲמִשָּׁה עַתֻּדִים חֲמִשָּׁה כְּבָשִׂים
‹ sheep ‹‹ —five, ‹ he-goats ‹‹ —five, ‹ rams

בְּנֵי־שָׁנָה חֲמִשָּׁה זֶה קָרְבַּן אֱלִישָׁמָע
‹ of Elishama ‹ the offering ‹ This is ‹‹ —five. ‹ first year ‹ in their

בֶּן־עַמִּיהוּד:
‹‹ Ammihud. ‹ son of

EIGHTH DAY CHANUKAH / ח׳ חנוכה

Numbers 7:54-8:4 / במדבר ז:נד-ח:ד

נד בַּיּוֹם הַשְּׁמִינִי נָשִׂיא לִבְנֵי מְנַשֶּׁה
‹‹ of Manasseh, ‹ of the children ‹ the Prince ‹ On the eighth day, **54**

גַּמְלִיאֵל בֶּן־פְּדָהצוּר: נה קָרְבָּנוֹ קַעֲרַת־
‹ a bowl ‹ His offering was: **55** ‹‹ Pedahzur. ‹ son of ‹ Gamaliel

כֶּסֶף אַחַת שְׁלֹשִׁים וּמֵאָה מִשְׁקָלָהּ
‹‹ was its weight; ‹ and one hundred [*shekels*] ‹ thirty ‹‹ —one, ‹ of silver

מִזְרָק אֶחָד כֶּסֶף שִׁבְעִים שֶׁקֶל בְּשֶׁקֶל
‹ in the *shekel* ‹ *shekels* ‹ of seventy ‹‹ of silver, ‹ and one basin

הַקֹּדֶשׁ שְׁנֵיהֶם ׀ מְלֵאִים סֹלֶת בְּלוּלָה
‹ mixed ‹ with fine flour ‹ filled ‹ both of them ‹‹ of the sanctuary;

בַּשֶּׁמֶן לְמִנְחָה: נו כַּף אַחַת עֲשָׂרָה זָהָב
‹ of gold ‹ of ten [*shekels*] ‹ one ladle **56** ‹‹ for a meal-offering; ‹ with [olive] oil

מְלֵאָה קְטֹרֶת: נז פַּר אֶחָד בֶּן־בָּקָר
‹‹ of the cattle; ‹ a calf ‹ one bull, **57** ‹‹ with incense; ‹ filled

אַיִל אֶחָד כֶּבֶשׂ־אֶחָד בֶּן־שְׁנָתוֹ לְעֹלָה:
‹‹ —for a burnt-offering; ‹ first year ‹ in its ‹ one [male] sheep ‹‹ one ram;

נח שְׂעִיר־עִזִּים אֶחָד לְחַטָּאת: נט וּלְזֶבַח
‹ and for the sacrifice **59** ‹‹ for a sin-offering; ‹ —one, ‹ of the goats ‹ a male **58**

הַשְּׁלָמִים בָּקָר שְׁנַיִם אֵילִם חֲמִשָּׁה
‹‹ —five, ‹ rams ‹‹ —two, ‹ cattle ‹ of the peace-offering:

עַתֻּדִים חֲמִשָּׁה כְּבָשִׂים בְּנֵי־שָׁנָה
‹ first year ‹ in their ‹ sheep ‹‹ —five, ‹ he-goats

חֲמִשָּׁה זֶה קָרְבַּן גַּמְלִיאֵל בֶּן־פְּדָהצוּר:
‹‹ Pedahzur. ‹ son of ‹ of Gamaliel ‹ the offering ‹ This is ‹‹ —five.

ס בַּיּוֹם הַתְּשִׁיעִי נָשִׂיא לִבְנֵי בִנְיָמִן
‹‹ of Benjamin, ‹ of the children ‹ the Prince ‹ On the ninth day, **60**

אֲבִידָן בֶּן־גִּדְעֹנִי: סא קָרְבָּנוֹ קַעֲרַת־
‹ a bowl ‹ His offering was: **61** ‹‹ Gideoni. ‹ son of ‹ Abidan

כֶּסֶף אַחַת שְׁלֹשִׁים וּמֵאָה מִשְׁקָלָהּ
‹‹ was its weight; ‹ and one hundred [*shekels*] ‹ thirty ‹‹ —one, ‹ of silver

מִזְרָק אֶחָד כֶּסֶף שִׁבְעִים שֶׁקֶל בְּשֶׁקֶל
‹ in the *shekel* ‹ *shekels* ‹ of seventy ‹‹ of silver, ‹ and one basin

הַקֹּדֶשׁ שְׁנֵיהֶם ׀ מְלֵאִים סֹלֶת בְּלוּלָה
‹ mixed ‹ with fine flour ‹ filled ‹ both of them ‹‹ of the sanctuary;

בַשֶּׁמֶן לְמִנְחָה: סב כַּף אַחַת עֲשָׂרָה זָהָב
‹ of gold ‹ of ten [*shekels*] ‹ one ladle **62** ‹‹ for a meal-offering; ‹ with [olive] oil

מְלֵאָה קְטֹרֶת: סג פַּר אֶחָד בֶּן־בָּקָר
‹‹ of the cattle; ‹ a calf ‹ one bull, **63** ‹‹ with incense; ‹ filled

אַיִל אֶחָד כֶּבֶשׂ־אֶחָד בֶּן־שְׁנָתוֹ
‹‹ first year ‹ in its ‹ one [male] sheep ‹‹ one ram;

לְעֹלָה: סד שְׂעִיר־עִזִּים אֶחָד לְחַטָּאת:
‹‹ for a sin-offering; ‹ —one, ‹ of the goats ‹ a male **64** ‹‹ —for a burnt-offering;

סה וּלְזֶבַח הַשְּׁלָמִים בָּקָר שְׁנַיִם אֵילִם
‹ rams ‹‹ —two, ‹ cattle ‹ of the peace-offering: ‹ and for the sacrifice **65**

חֲמִשָּׁה֙ עַתֻּדִ֣ים חֲמִשָּׁ֔ה כְּבָשִׂ֥ים בְּנֵֽי
‹ in their ‹ sheep ‹‹ —five, ‹ he-goats ‹‹ —five,

שָׁנָ֖ה חֲמִשָּׁ֑ה זֶ֛ה קָרְבַּ֥ן אֲבִידָ֖ן בֶּן־גִּדְעֹנִֽי׃
‹‹ Gideoni. ‹ son of ‹ of Abidan ‹ the offering ‹ This is ‹‹ —five. ‹ first year

סו בַּיּוֹם֙ הָֽעֲשִׂירִ֔י נָשִׂ֖יא לִבְנֵ֣י דָ֑ן
‹‹ of Dan, ‹ of the children ‹ the Prince ‹ On the tenth day, 66

אֲחִיעֶ֖זֶר בֶּן־עַמִּֽישַׁדָּֽי׃ סז קָרְבָּנ֞וֹ קַֽעֲרַת־
‹ a bowl ‹ His offering was: 67 ‹‹ Ammishaddai. ‹ son of ‹ Ahiezer

כֶּ֣סֶף אַחַ֗ת שְׁלֹשִׁ֣ים וּמֵאָה֮ מִשְׁקָלָהּ֒
‹‹ was its weight; ‹ and one hundred [*shekels*] ‹ thirty ‹‹ —one, ‹ of silver

מִזְרָ֤ק אֶחָד֙ כֶּ֔סֶף שִׁבְעִ֥ים שֶׁ֖קֶל בְּשֶׁ֣קֶל
‹ in the *shekel* ‹ *shekels* ‹ of seventy ‹‹ of silver, ‹ and one basin

הַקֹּ֑דֶשׁ שְׁנֵיהֶ֣ם ׀ מְלֵאִ֗ים סֹ֛לֶת בְּלוּלָ֥ה
‹ mixed ‹ with fine flour ‹ filled ‹ both of them ‹‹ of the sanctuary;

בַשֶּׁ֖מֶן לְמִנְחָֽה׃ סח כַּ֥ף אַחַ֛ת עֲשָׂרָ֥ה זָהָ֖ב
‹ of gold ‹ of ten [*shekels*] ‹ one ladle 68 ‹‹ for a meal-offering; ‹ with [olive] oil

מְלֵאָ֥ה קְטֹֽרֶת׃ סט פַּ֣ר אֶחָ֞ד בֶּן־בָּקָ֗ר
‹‹ of the cattle; ‹ a calf ‹ one bull, 69 ‹‹ with incense; ‹ filled

אַ֧יִל אֶחָ֛ד כֶּֽבֶשׂ־אֶחָ֥ד בֶּן־שְׁנָת֖וֹ לְעֹלָֽה׃
‹‹ —for a burnt-offering; ‹‹ first year ‹ in its ‹ one [male] sheep ‹‹ one ram;

ע שְׂעִיר־עִזִּ֥ים אֶחָ֖ד לְחַטָּֽאת׃ עא וּלְזֶ֣בַח
‹ and for the sacrifice 71 ‹‹ for a sin-offering; ‹ —one, ‹ of the goats ‹ a male 70

הַשְּׁלָמִים֮ בָּקָ֣ר שְׁנַ֒יִם֒ אֵילִ֤ם חֲמִשָּׁה֙
‹‹ —five, ‹ rams ‹‹ —two, ‹ cattle ‹ of a peace-offering:

עַתֻּדִ֣ים חֲמִשָּׁ֔ה כְּבָשִׂ֥ים בְּנֵי־שָׁנָ֖ה
‹ first year ‹ in their ‹ sheep ‹‹ —five, ‹ he-goats

חֲמִשָּׁ֑ה זֶ֛ה קָרְבַּ֥ן אֲחִיעֶ֖זֶר בֶּן־עַמִּֽישַׁדָּֽי׃
‹‹ Ammishaddai. ‹ son of ‹ of Ahiezer ‹ the offering ‹ This is ‹‹ —five.

עב בְּיוֹם֙ עַשְׁתֵּ֣י עָשָׂ֣ר י֔וֹם נָשִׂ֖יא לִבְנֵ֣י
‹ of the children ‹ the Prince ‹ day, ‹ the eleventh ‹ On the day, 72

אָשֵׁ֑ר פַּגְעִיאֵ֖ל בֶּן־עָכְרָֽן׃ עג קָרְבָּנ֞וֹ
‹ His offering was: 73 ‹‹ Ochran. ‹ son of ‹ Pagiel ‹‹ of Asher,

קַֽעֲרַת־כֶּ֣סֶף אַחַ֗ת שְׁלֹשִׁ֣ים וּמֵאָה֮
‹ and one hundred [*shekels*] ‹ thirty ‹‹ —one, ‹ of silver ‹ a bowl

מִשְׁקָלָהּ֒ מִזְרָ֤ק אֶחָד֙ כֶּ֔סֶף שִׁבְעִ֥ים שֶׁ֖קֶל
‹ *shekels* ‹ of seventy ‹‹ of silver, ‹ and one basin ‹‹ was its weight;

בְּשֶׁ֣קֶל הַקֹּ֑דֶשׁ שְׁנֵיהֶ֣ם ׀ מְלֵאִ֗ים סֹ֛לֶת
‹ with fine flour ‹ filled ‹ both of them ‹‹ of the sanctuary; ‹ in the *shekel*

בְּלוּלָ֥ה בַשֶּׁ֖מֶן לְמִנְחָֽה׃ עד כַּ֥ף אַחַ֛ת
‹ one ladle 74 ‹‹ for a meal-offering; ‹ with [olive] oil ‹ mixed

עֲשָׂרָ֥ה זָהָ֖ב מְלֵאָ֥ה קְטֹֽרֶת׃ עה פַּ֣ר אֶחָ֞ד
‹ one bull, 75 ‹‹ with incense; ‹ filled ‹ of gold ‹ of ten [*shekels*]

בֶּן־בָּקָ֗ר אַ֧יִל אֶחָ֛ד כֶּֽבֶשׂ־אֶחָ֥ד בֶּן־
‹ in its ‹ one [male] sheep ‹‹ one ram; ‹‹ of the cattle; ‹ a calf

שְׁנָת֖וֹ לְעֹלָֽה׃ עו שְׂעִיר־עִזִּ֥ים אֶחָ֖ד
‹ —one, ‹ of the goats ‹ a male 76 ‹‹ —for a burnt-offering; ‹‹ first year

לְחַטָּֽאת׃ עז וּלְזֶ֣בַח הַשְּׁלָמִים֮ בָּקָ֣ר שְׁנַ֒יִם֒
‹‹ —two, ‹ cattle ‹ of the peace-offering: ‹ and for the sacrifice 77 ‹‹ for a sin-offering;

אֵילִ֤ם חֲמִשָּׁה֙ עַתֻּדִ֣ים חֲמִשָּׁ֔ה כְּבָשִׂ֥ים
‹ sheep ‹‹ —five, ‹ he-goats ‹‹ —five, ‹ rams

בְּנֵי־שָׁנָ֖ה חֲמִשָּׁ֑ה זֶ֛ה קָרְבַּ֥ן פַּגְעִיאֵ֖ל
‹ of Pagiel ‹ the offering ‹ This is ‹‹ —five. ‹ first year ‹ in their

בֶּן־עָכְרָֽן׃ עח בְּיוֹם֙ שְׁנֵ֣ים עָשָׂ֣ר י֔וֹם נָשִׂ֖יא
‹ the Prince ‹ day, ‹ the twelfth ‹ On the day, 78 ‹‹ Ochran. ‹ son of

לִבְנֵ֣י נַפְתָּלִ֑י אֲחִירַ֖ע בֶּן־עֵינָֽן׃ עט קָרְבָּנ֞וֹ
‹ His offering was: 79 ‹‹ Enan. ‹ son of ‹ Ahira ‹‹ of Naphtali, ‹ of the children

קַֽעֲרַת־כֶּ֣סֶף אַחַ֗ת שְׁלֹשִׁ֣ים וּמֵאָה֮
‹ and one hundred [*shekels*] ‹ thirty ‹‹ —one, ‹ of silver ‹ a bowl

מִשְׁקָלָהּ֒ מִזְרָ֤ק אֶחָד֙ כֶּ֔סֶף שִׁבְעִ֥ים שֶׁ֖קֶל
‹ *shekels* ‹ of seventy ‹‹ of silver, ‹ and one basin ‹‹ was its weight;

בְּשֶׁקֶל הַקֹּדֶשׁ שְׁנֵיהֶם ׀ מְלֵאִים סֹלֶת
‹ with fine flour ‹ filled ‹ both of them « of the sanctuary; ‹ in the *shekel*

בְּלוּלָה בַשֶּׁמֶן לְמִנְחָה׃ פ כַּף אַחַת
‹ one ladle 80 « for a meal-offering; ‹ with [olive] oil ‹ mixed

עֲשָׂרָה זָהָב מְלֵאָה קְטֹרֶת׃ פא פַּר אֶחָד
‹ one bull, 81 « with incense; ‹ filled ‹ of gold ‹ of ten [*shekels*]

בֶּן־בָּקָר אַיִל אֶחָד כֶּבֶשׂ־אֶחָד בֶּן־
‹ in its ‹ one [male] sheep « one ram; « of the cattle; ‹ a calf

שְׁנָתוֹ לְעֹלָה׃ פב שְׂעִיר־עִזִּים אֶחָד
‹ —one, ‹ of the goats ‹ a male 82 «—for a burnt-offering; « first year

לְחַטָּאת׃ פג וּלְזֶבַח הַשְּׁלָמִים בָּקָר
‹ cattle ‹ of the peace-offering: ‹ and for the sacrifice 83 « for a sin-offering;

שְׁנַיִם אֵילִם חֲמִשָּׁה עַתֻּדִים חֲמִשָּׁה
« —five, ‹ he-goats « —five, ‹ rams « —two,

כְּבָשִׂים בְּנֵי־שָׁנָה חֲמִשָּׁה זֶה קָרְבַּן
‹ the offering ‹ This is « —five. ‹ first year ‹ in their ‹ sheep

אֲחִירַע בֶּן־עֵינָן׃ פד זֹאת ׀ חֲנֻכַּת
‹ the dedication ‹ This was 84 « Enan. ‹ son of ‹ of Ahira

הַמִּזְבֵּחַ בְּיוֹם הִמָּשַׁח אֹתוֹ מֵאֵת נְשִׂיאֵי
‹ the princes ‹ from « of it, ‹ of the anointing ‹ on the day ‹ of the Altar,

יִשְׂרָאֵל קַעֲרֹת כֶּסֶף שְׁתֵּים עֶשְׂרֵה
« —twelve, ‹ of silver ‹ bowls « of Israel:

מִזְרְקֵי־כֶסֶף שְׁנֵים עָשָׂר כַּפּוֹת זָהָב
‹ of gold ‹ ladles « —twelve, ‹ of silver ‹ basins

שְׁתֵּים עֶשְׂרֵה׃ פה שְׁלֹשִׁים וּמֵאָה
‹ and one hundred, ‹ thirty 85 « —twelve;

הַקְּעָרָה הָאַחַת כֶּסֶף וְשִׁבְעִים
‹ and seventy « [in] silver [*shekels*] ‹ each bowl,

הַמִּזְרָק הָאֶחָד כֹּל כֶּסֶף הַכֵּלִים אַלְפַּיִם
‹ was two thousand, ‹ of the vessels ‹ the silver ‹ all « each basin;

וְאַרְבַּע־מֵאוֹת בְּשֶׁקֶל הַקֹּדֶשׁ׃ פו כַּפּוֹת
‹ Ladles 86 « of the sanctuary. ‹ in the *shekel* ‹ hundred ‹ four

זָהָב שְׁתֵּים־עֶשְׂרֵה מְלֵאֹת קְטֹרֶת
« with incense, ‹ filled ‹ twelve ‹ of gold

עֲשָׂרָה עֲשָׂרָה הַכַּף בְּשֶׁקֶל הַקֹּדֶשׁ
« of the sanctuary; ‹ in the *shekel* ‹ was the ladle ‹ ten each

כָּל־זְהַב הַכַּפּוֹת עֶשְׂרִים וּמֵאָה׃
« and one hundred [*shekels*]. ‹ was twenty ‹ of the ladles ‹ the gold ‹ all

פז כָּל הַבָּקָר לָעֹלָה שְׁנֵים עָשָׂר פָּרִים
« bulls, ‹ twelve « for the burnt-offering: ‹ the livestock ‹ All 87

אֵילִם שְׁנֵים־עָשָׂר כְּבָשִׂים בְּנֵי־שָׁנָה
‹ first year ‹ in their ‹ lambs « twelve, ‹ rams

שְׁנֵים עָשָׂר וּמִנְחָתָם וּשְׂעִירֵי עִזִּים
‹ of the goats ‹ and males « and their meal-offerings; ‹ —twelve,

שְׁנֵים עָשָׂר לְחַטָּאת׃ פח וְכֹל בְּקַר ׀ זֶבַח
‹ for the sacrifice ‹ the livestock ‹ All 88 « for a sin-offering. ‹ —twelve

הַשְּׁלָמִים עֶשְׂרִים וְאַרְבָּעָה פָּרִים
« bulls, ‹ and four ‹ twenty « of the peace-offering:

אֵילִם שִׁשִּׁים עַתֻּדִים שִׁשִּׁים כְּבָשִׂים
‹ sheep « —sixty, ‹ he-goats « —sixty, ‹ rams

בְּנֵי־שָׁנָה שִׁשִּׁים זֹאת חֲנֻכַּת הַמִּזְבֵּחַ
‹ of the Altar ‹ the dedication ‹ This was « —sixty. ‹ first year ‹ in their

אַחֲרֵי הִמָּשַׁח אֹתוֹ׃ פט וּבְבֹא מֹשֶׁה
‹ When Moses entered 89 « of it. ‹ the anointing ‹ after

אֶל־אֹהֶל מוֹעֵד לְדַבֵּר אִתּוֹ וַיִּשְׁמַע
‹ he heard « with Him, ‹ to speak ‹ of Meeting ‹ the Tent ‹ into

אֶת־הַקּוֹל מִדַּבֵּר אֵלָיו מֵעַל הַכַּפֹּרֶת
‹ the Cover ‹ from atop ‹ to him ‹ speaking ‹ the Voice

אֲשֶׁר עַל־אֲרֹן הָעֵדֻת מִבֵּין שְׁנֵי
‹ the two ‹ from between « of the Testimony, ‹ the Ark ‹ upon ‹ that was

הַכְּרֻבִים וַיְדַבֵּר אֵלָיו׃ [ח] א וַיְדַבֵּר יהוה
‹ HASHEM spoke 1 [8] « to him. ‹ and He spoke « Cherubim,

אֶל־מֹשֶׁה לֵּאמֹר׃ ב דַּבֵּר אֶל־אַהֲרֹן
‹ *Aaron* ‹ *to* ‹ *Speak* 2 « saying, ‹ Moses ‹ to

וְאָמַרְתָּ אֵלָיו בְּהַעֲלֹתְךָ אֶת־הַנֵּרֹת
« *the lamps,* ‹ *When you kindle* « *to him:* ‹ *and say*

אֶל־מוּל֙ פְּנֵ֣י הַמְּנוֹרָ֔ה יָאִ֖ירוּ שִׁבְעַ֥ת
‹ toward ‹ the face ‹ of the Menorah ‹ shall they cast light « the seven —›

הַנֵּרֽוֹת׃ ג וַיַּ֤עַשׂ כֵּן֙ אַהֲרֹ֔ן אֶל־מוּל֙
lamps. » 3 So, did › Aaron [do]; » toward ›

פְּנֵ֣י הַמְּנוֹרָ֔ה הֶעֱלָ֖ה נֵרֹתֶ֑יהָ כַּאֲשֶׁ֛ר
the face › of the Menorah › he kindled › its lamps, » as ›

צִוָּ֥ה יהוה אֶת־מֹשֶֽׁה׃ ד וְזֶ֨ה מַעֲשֵׂ֤ה
HASHEM had commanded › Moses. » 4 This › is the crafting ›

הַמְּנֹרָה֙ מִקְשָׁ֣ה זָהָ֔ב עַד־יְרֵכָ֥הּ עַד־
of the Menorah, › hammered-out › gold, » to › its base, › to ›

פִּרְחָ֖הּ מִקְשָׁ֣ה הִ֑וא כַּמַּרְאֶ֗ה אֲשֶׁ֨ר
its flower, › hammered out › it is; » according to the vision › that ›

הֶרְאָ֤ה יהוה֙ אֶת־מֹשֶׁ֔ה כֵּ֖ן עָשָׂ֥ה
HASHEM showed › Moses, › so › did he make ›

אֶת־הַמְּנֹרָֽה׃
the Menorah. »

HAFTARAS SHABBAS CHANUKAH (I) / הפטרת שבת שבת חנוכה (א)

Zechariah 2:14-4:7 / זכריה ב:יד-ד:ז

ב יד רָנִּ֥י וְשִׂמְחִ֖י בַּת־צִיּ֑וֹן כִּ֧י הִנְנִי־בָ֛א
14 [2] Sing › and be glad, › O daughter of Zion, » for › behold! › I come ›

וְשָׁכַנְתִּ֥י בְתוֹכֵ֖ךְ נְאֻם־יהוה׃ טו וְנִלְווּ֩ גוֹיִ֨ם
and I will dwell › in your midst » — the word › of HASHEM. » 15 And attach themselves › will nations ›

רַבִּ֤ים אֶל־יהוה֙ בַּיּ֣וֹם הַה֔וּא וְהָ֥יוּ לִ֖י
that are many, › to › HASHEM › on that day, › and they shall be › unto Me ›

לְעָ֑ם וְשָׁכַנְתִּ֣י בְתוֹכֵ֔ךְ וְיָדַ֕עַתְּ כִּֽי־יהוה
for a people; » but I will dwell › in your midst. » Then you will know › that › HASHEM, ›

צְבָא֖וֹת שְׁלָחַ֥נִי אֵלָֽיִךְ׃ טז וְנָחַ֨ל יהוה
Master of Legions, › has sent me › to you. » 16 HASHEM shall inherit ›

אֶת־יְהוּדָה֙ חֶלְק֔וֹ עַ֖ל אַדְמַ֣ת הַקֹּ֑דֶשׁ
Judah › [as] His portion › upon › the land › of holiness, »

וּבָחַ֥ר ע֖וֹד בִּירוּשָׁלָֽ͏ִם׃ יז הַ֥ס כָּל־בָּשָׂ֖ר
and He shall choose › again › Jerusalem. » 17 Be silent, › all › flesh, ›

מִפְּנֵ֣י יהוה כִּ֥י נֵע֖וֹר מִמְּע֥וֹן קָדְשֽׁוֹ׃
before › HASHEM, » for › He is awakened › from the habitation › of His holiness! »

ג א וַיַּרְאֵ֗נִי אֶת־יְהוֹשֻׁ֙עַ֙ הַכֹּהֵ֣ן הַגָּד֔וֹל
1 [3] Then He showed me › Joshua › the Kohen Gadol ›

עֹמֵ֕ד לִפְנֵ֖י מַלְאַ֣ךְ יהוה וְהַשָּׂטָ֛ן עֹמֵ֥ד
standing › before › an angel › of HASHEM; » with the Satan › standing ›

עַל־יְמִינ֖וֹ לְשִׂטְנֽוֹ׃ ב וַיֹּ֨אמֶר יהוה אֶל־
at › his right › to accuse him. » 2 And [the angel of] HASHEM said, › to ›

הַשָּׂטָ֗ן יִגְעַ֨ר יהוה בְּךָ֙ הַשָּׂטָ֔ן וְיִגְעַ֤ר
the Satan, » HASHEM shall rebuke › you, › O Satan; » and He shall [again] rebuke, ›

יהוה֙ בְּךָ֔ הַבֹּחֵ֖ר בִּירוּשָׁלָ֑͏ִם הֲל֛וֹא זֶ֥ה
HASHEM, › shall › against you, » [for] He chooses › Jerusalem » Is not › this one [Joshua] ›

א֖וּד מֻצָּ֥ל מֵאֵֽשׁ׃ ג וִיהוֹשֻׁ֕עַ הָיָ֥ה לָבֻ֖שׁ
a brand › rescued › from the fire? » 3 But Joshua › was › dressed ›

בְּגָדִ֣ים צוֹאִ֑ים וְעֹמֵ֖ד לִפְנֵ֥י הַמַּלְאָֽךְ׃
[in] garments › [that were] soiled, » and was standing › before › the angel. »

ד וַיַּ֣עַן וַיֹּ֗אמֶר אֶל־הָעֹמְדִ֤ים לְפָנָיו֙
4 [The angel] spoke up › and he said › to › those standing › before him, ›

Shabbas Chanukah (I)

The *Haftarah* of Chanukah is read even if Rosh Chodesh falls on the same Sabbath.

On the Sabbath of Chanukah, the *Haftarah* speaks of an earlier Chanukah, when the Menorah of the Second Temple was inaugurated. The Kohen Gadol was Joshua; the leader of the nation was Zerubbabel, scion of the Davidic dynasty; and the prophet who conveyed this vision was Zechariah. The prophet begins by looking ahead to the times when all the world will acknowledge Israel's primacy as God's chosen people under the leadership of the tribe of Judah, the tribe of David.

Then the prophet turns to Joshua, who was victim of the same sin that plagued much of the nation in the wake of the Babylonian Exile: His sons had married gentile women and Joshua had failed to chastise them. In his vision, Zechariah sees the Satan condemning Joshua for this lapse, which was symbolized by the soiled garments he was wearing. But God defends Joshua on the grounds that he is a *firebrand rescued from the flames;* he was immersed in

לֵאמֹר הָסִירוּ הַבְּגָדִים הַצֹּאִים מֵעָלָיו

« from upon him. ‹ that are soiled, ‹ the garments, ‹ Remove « saying,

וַיֹּאמֶר אֵלָיו רְאֵה הֶעֱבַרְתִּי מֵעָלֶיךָ

‹ from upon you ‹ I have removed ‹ See, « to him [Joshua], ‹ Then [the angel] said

עֲוֺנֶךָ וְהַלְבֵּשׁ אֹתְךָ מַחֲלָצוֹת: ה וָאֹמַר

« Then I said, 5 « in fresh garments. ‹ you ‹ dressing « your iniquity,

יָשִׂימוּ צָנִיף טָהוֹר עַל־רֹאשׁוֹ וַיָּשִׂימוּ

‹ And they placed « his head. ‹ on ‹ a pure one, ‹ a turban, ‹ Let them place

הַצָּנִיף הַטָּהוֹר עַל־רֹאשׁוֹ וַיַּלְבִּשֻׁהוּ

‹ and they dressed him ‹ his head, ‹ on ‹ that was pure, ‹ the turban,

בְּגָדִים וּמַלְאַךְ יהוה עֹמֵד: ו וַיָּעַד מַלְאַךְ

‹ did the angel ‹ Then he warned, 6 « standing [there]. ‹ of HASHEM ‹ with the angel ‹ in [fresh] garments;

יהוה בִּיהוֹשֻׁעַ לֵאמֹר: ז כֹּה־אָמַר

‹ said ‹ So 7 « saying, ‹ to Joshua, « of HASHEM,

יהוה צְבָאוֹת אִם־בִּדְרָכַי תֵּלֵךְ

‹ you will walk, ‹ in My ways ‹ 'If « Master of Legions: ‹ HASHEM,

וְאִם אֶת־מִשְׁמַרְתִּי תִשְׁמֹר וְגַם־

‹ and also, ‹ you will observe, ‹ My charge ‹ and if

אַתָּה תָּדִין אֶת־בֵּיתִי וְגַם תִּשְׁמֹר

‹ you will guard ‹ and also, ‹ My Temple, ‹ will administer ‹ you

אֶת־חֲצֵרָי וְנָתַתִּי לְךָ מַהְלְכִים בֵּין

‹ between ‹ the ability to work ‹ you ‹ then I shall give « My courtyards,

הָעֹמְדִים הָאֵלֶּה: ח שְׁמַע־נָא יְהוֹשֻׁעַ |

‹ O Joshua ‹ now, ‹ Listen, 8 « – these [angels]. « the standing [beings]

הַכֹּהֵן הַגָּדוֹל אַתָּה וְרֵעֶיךָ הַיֹּשְׁבִים

‹ that sit ‹ and your companions ‹ you « the Kohen Gadol –

לְפָנֶיךָ כִּי־אַנְשֵׁי מוֹפֵת הֵמָּה כִּי־הִנְנִי

‹ behold! – I am ‹ for « are they – ‹ [worthy] of a miracle ‹ men ‹ for « before you,

מֵבִיא אֶת־עַבְדִּי צֶמַח: ט כִּי | הִנֵּה הָאֶבֶן

‹ the stone « behold! – ‹ For, 9 « Zemach [the flourishing one]. ‹ My servant, ‹ bringing

אֲשֶׁר נָתַתִּי לִפְנֵי יְהוֹשֻׁעַ עַל־אֶבֶן אַחַת

‹ one stone ‹ toward ‹ Joshua, ‹ before ‹ I have placed ‹ that

שִׁבְעָה עֵינָיִם הִנְנִי מְפַתֵּחַ פִּתֻּחָהּ

« its inscription ‹ engraving ‹ behold! – I am « eyes; ‹ seven

נְאֻם יהוה צְבָאוֹת וּמַשְׁתִּי אֶת־עֲוֺן

‹ the iniquity ‹ and I will remove « Master of Legions – ‹ of HASHEM, ‹ – the word

הָאָרֶץ־הַהִיא בְּיוֹם אֶחָד: י בַּיּוֹם הַהוּא

« On that day, 10 « in one day. ‹ of that land,

נְאֻם יהוה צְבָאוֹת תִּקְרְאוּ אִישׁ לְרֵעֵהוּ

‹ his neighbor, ‹ [each] man ‹ you will invite, « Master of Legions – ‹ of HASHEM, ‹ – the word

אֶל־תַּחַת גֶּפֶן וְאֶל־תַּחַת תְּאֵנָה:

« a fig tree. ‹ under ‹ and to [join him] ‹ a vine ‹ under ‹ to [join him]

ד א וַיָּשָׁב הַמַּלְאָךְ הַדֹּבֵר בִּי וַיְעִירֵנִי

‹ and he wakened me, « with me, ‹ that was speaking ‹ did the angel « Then he returned, 1 [4]

כְּאִישׁ אֲשֶׁר־יֵעוֹר מִשְּׁנָתוֹ: ב וַיֹּאמֶר

‹ He said 2 « from his sleep. ‹ is awakened ‹ who ‹ as a man

אֵלַי מָה אַתָּה רֹאֶה וָאֹמַר [ויאמר כ׳]

« I said, « see? ‹ do you ‹ What « to me,

רָאִיתִי | וְהִנֵּה מְנוֹרַת זָהָב כֻּלָּהּ וְגֻלָּהּ

‹ and its bowl ‹ in its entirety, ‹ of gold; ‹ a Menorah ‹ and there is ‹ I see,

עַל־רֹאשָׁהּ וְשִׁבְעָה נֵרֹתֶיהָ עָלֶיהָ

« upon it, ‹ are its lamps ‹ and seven ‹ its top, ‹ is on

שִׁבְעָה וְשִׁבְעָה מוּצָקוֹת לַנֵּרוֹת אֲשֶׁר

‹ that are ‹ to [each of] the lamps ‹ are its pipes ‹ [and] seven each

---

the flames of the exile's physical and spiritual destruction, and as such cannot be condemned for the past. The angel garbs him in the pure vestments and turban of the high priesthood — but warns him that henceforth he must obey the commandments. Only then can he be assured that his heirs will succeed him as Kohen Gadol. And only then can he be assured constant progress among the angels, who are *immobile*, in the sense that they can do only what God commands them, but can not choose and grow, as man can. Joshua's comrades — Chananiah, Mishael, and Azariah — will join him in welcoming Zerubbabel, *the flourishing one,* and in seeing the cornerstone of the Temple, which, figuratively, has all eyes upon it and is adorned with beautiful carvings.

Finally, Zechariah is shown a Menorah, complete with a bowl containing oil, tubes bringing oil to its seven lamps, and even two olive trees to provide a continuous supply of fuel. This symbolizes that all man's needs are provided by God — man, however, must have the eyes to see it. Impassable mountains become hospitable plains if God so wills.

A fitting message for Chanukah, not only because of the Menorah, but because Chanukah, too, shows that a small band of righteous warriors, putting their faith in God, overcame one of the world's superpowers and brought purity back to the Temple.

עַל־רֹאשָׁהּ: ג וּשְׁנַיִם זֵיתִים עָלֶיהָ אֶחָד
‹ one « are near it; ‹ olive trees ‹ And two 3 « its top. ‹ on

מִימִין הַגֻּלָּה וְאֶחָד עַל־שְׂמֹאלָהּ:
« its left. ‹ to ‹ and one ‹ of the bowl ‹ to the right

ד וָאַעַן וָאֹמַר אֶל־הַמַּלְאָךְ הַדֹּבֵר בִּי
‹ to me, ‹ that was speaking ‹ the angel ‹ to ‹ and I said ‹ And I spoke up 4

לֵאמֹר מָה אֵלֶּה אֲדֹנִי: ה וַיַּעַן הַמַּלְאָךְ
‹ did the angel ‹ Spoke up 5 « my lord? ‹ these, ‹ What are « saying,

הַדֹּבֵר בִּי וַיֹּאמֶר אֵלַי הֲלוֹא יָדַעְתָּ מָה
‹ what ‹ Do you not know « to me, ‹ and he said ‹ to me, ‹ that was speaking

הֵמָּה אֵלֶּה וָאֹמַר לֹא אֲדֹנִי: ו וַיַּעַן
‹ He spoke up 6 « my lord. ‹ No, « And I said, « these are?

וַיֹּאמֶר אֵלַי לֵאמֹר זֶה דְּבַר־יהוה
‹ of HASHEM ‹ the word ‹ This is « saying, ‹ to me, ‹ and he said

אֶל־זְרֻבָּבֶל לֵאמֹר לֹא בְחַיִל וְלֹא
‹ and not ‹ through army, ‹ 'Not « saying, ‹ Zerubbabel, ‹ to

בְכֹחַ כִּי אִם־בְּרוּחִי אָמַר יהוה צְבָאוֹת:
« Master of Legions. ‹ HASHEM, ‹ — said « through My spirit' ‹ only ‹ but ‹ through might,

ז מִי־אַתָּה הַר־הַגָּדוֹל לִפְנֵי זְרֻבָּבֶל
‹ Zerubbabel ‹ Before « that is great? ‹ O mountain ‹ are you, ‹ Who 7

לְמִישֹׁר וְהוֹצִיא אֶת־הָאֶבֶן הָרֹאשָׁה
‹ of the chief [builder] ‹ the [plumb] stone ‹ He shall bring out « [you shall turn] into a plain!

תְּשֻׁאוֹת חֵן ׀ חֵן לָהּ:
« for it! ‹ 'Grace!' ‹ 'Grace!' ‹ to shouts of,

When *Shabbos*, Rosh Chodesh, and Chanukah coincide, some congregations add the first and last verses of the *Haftaros* for *Shabbos* Rosh Chodesh and for *Shabbos* Erev Rosh Chodesh.

כֹּה אָמַר יהוה הַשָּׁמַיִם כִּסְאִי
‹ My throne ‹ The heaven is « HASHEM: ‹ said ‹ So

וְהָאָרֶץ הֲדֹם רַגְלָי אֵי־זֶה בַיִת אֲשֶׁר
‹ that ‹ House ‹ that is ‹ Where « for My feet. ‹ the stool ‹ and the earth is

תִּבְנוּ־לִי וְאֵי־זֶה מָקוֹם מְנוּחָתִי:
« of My resting? ‹ place ‹ that ‹ And where is « for Me? ‹ you would build

וְהָיָה מִדֵּי־חֹדֶשׁ בְּחָדְשׁוֹ וּמִדֵּי שַׁבָּת
‹ week ‹ and each ‹ in its month ‹ month ‹ each ‹ And it shall be,

בְּשַׁבַּתּוֹ יָבוֹא כָל־בָּשָׂר לְהִשְׁתַּחֲוֹת
‹ to prostrate [themselves] ‹ flesh ‹ all ‹ there shall come ‹ in its week,

לְפָנַי אָמַר יהוה:
« HASHEM. ‹ — said « before Me

וַיֹּאמֶר־לוֹ יְהוֹנָתָן מָחָר חֹדֶשׁ וְנִפְקַדְתָּ
‹ and you will be missed ‹ is the [New] Moon, ‹ To-morrow « did Jonathan, « to him ‹ He said

כִּי יִפָּקֵד מוֹשָׁבֶךָ: וַיֹּאמֶר יְהוֹנָתָן לְדָוִד
« to David, ‹ Jonathan said « your seat. ‹ empty will be ‹ because

לֵךְ לְשָׁלוֹם אֲשֶׁר נִשְׁבַּעְנוּ שְׁנֵינוּ אֲנַחְנוּ
‹ we, ‹ the two of us, ‹ we have sworn, ‹ What « unto peace. ‹ Go

בְּשֵׁם יהוה לֵאמֹר יהוה יִהְיֶה ׀ בֵּינִי
‹ between me ‹ shall be [the witness] ‹ 'HASHEM « saying, ‹ of HASHEM, ‹ in the Name

וּבֵינְךָ וּבֵין זַרְעִי וּבֵין זַרְעֲךָ עַד־עוֹלָם:
« eternity. ‹ [shall be] for offspring, ‹ your offspring, ‹ and between ‹ my offspring ‹ and between ‹ and between you,

HAFTARAS SHABBAS CHANUKAH (II) / הפטרת שבת שבת חנוכה (ב)

I Kings 7:40-50 / מלכים א ז:מ-נ

ז מ וַיַּעַשׂ חִירוֹם אֶת־הַכִּיֹּרוֹת וְאֶת־
‹ and ‹ the lavers, ‹ Hiram made 40 [7]

הַיָּעִים וְאֶת־הַמִּזְרָקוֹת וַיְכַל חִירָם
‹ and Hiram finished « the basins; ‹ and ‹ the shovels,

לַעֲשׂוֹת אֶת־כָּל־הַמְּלָאכָה אֲשֶׁר עָשָׂה
‹ he did ‹ that ‹ the work ‹ all ‹ doing

לַמֶּלֶךְ שְׁלֹמֹה בֵּית יהוה: מא עַמֻּדִים
‹ Pillars — 41 « of HASHEM: ‹ [for] the House ‹ Solomon ‹ for King

Shabbas Chanukah (II)

This *Haftarah* is the same as that of *Vayakhel*, which discusses the construction of the Tabernacle; thus it is appropriate for Chanukah, as well, when the Temple was rededicated. Much of the *Haftarah* describes the Temple vessels that were made by King Hiram of Tyre, a friend and collaborator of King Solomon. The Second Temple as a whole is often ascribed to King Cyrus, for he merited the privilege of giving permission for its construction, and even of contributing significant resources toward the work. In contrast, the desecration of the Temple prior to the mir

שְׁנַיִם וְגֻלֹּת הַכֹּתָרֹת אֲשֶׁר־עַל־רֹאשׁ
‹ the top ‹ on ‹ that were ‹ of the capitals ‹ and the bowls ‹ two;

הָעַמֻּדִים שְׁתָּיִם וְהַשְּׂבָכוֹת שְׁתַּיִם
‹ — two, ‹ and the nettings ‹ — two; ‹ of the pillars

לְכַסּוֹת אֶת־שְׁתֵּי גֻּלּוֹת הַכֹּתָרֹת
‹ of the capitals ‹ bowls ‹ the two ‹ to cover

אֲשֶׁר עַל־רֹאשׁ הָעַמּוּדִים׃ מב וְאֶת־
‹ and 42 ‹‹ of the pillars; ‹ the top ‹ on ‹ that were

הָרִמֹּנִים אַרְבַּע מֵאוֹת לִשְׁתֵּי הַשְּׂבָכוֹת
‹‹ nettings; ‹ for the two ‹ hundred, ‹ — four ‹ the pomegranates

שְׁנֵי־טוּרִים רִמֹּנִים לַשְּׂבָכָה הָאֶחָת
‹ for each netting, ‹ of pomegranates ‹ rows ‹ two

לְכַסּוֹת אֶת־שְׁתֵּי גֻּלֹּת הַכֹּתָרֹת
‹ of the capitals ‹ bowls ‹ the two ‹ to cover

אֲשֶׁר עַל־פְּנֵי הָעַמּוּדִים׃ מג וְאֶת־
‹ and 43 ‹‹ of the pillars; ‹ the [upper] face ‹ on ‹ that were

הַמְּכֹנוֹת עֶשֶׂר וְאֶת־הַכִּיֹּרֹת עֲשָׂרָה
‹ — ten, ‹ the lavers ‹ and ‹ — ten; ‹ the bases

עַל־הַמְּכֹנוֹת׃ מד וְאֶת־הַיָּם הָאֶחָד וְאֶת־
‹ and ‹ the one sea; ‹ and 44 ‹‹ the bases; ‹ upon

הַבָּקָר שְׁנֵים־עָשָׂר תַּחַת הַיָּם׃ מה וְאֶת־
‹ and 45 ‹‹ the sea; ‹ under ‹ — twelve, ‹ the oxen

הַסִּירוֹת וְאֶת־הַיָּעִים וְאֶת־הַמִּזְרָקוֹת
‹ the basins; ‹ and ‹ the shovels, ‹ and ‹ the pots,

וְאֵת כָּל־הַכֵּלִים הָאֵלֶּה [האהל כ׳]
‹ these vessels ‹ all ‹ and

אֲשֶׁר עָשָׂה חִירָם לַמֶּלֶךְ שְׁלֹמֹה בֵּית
‹ [for] the House ‹ Solomon ‹ for King ‹ Hiram made ‹ that

יְהֹוָה נְחֹשֶׁת מְמֹרָט׃ מו בְּכִכַּר הַיַּרְדֵּן
‹ of the Jordan ‹ In the plain 46 ‹‹ burnished. ‹ were of copper, ‹ of HASHEM,

יְצָקָם הַמֶּלֶךְ בְּמַעֲבֵה הָאֲדָמָה בֵּין סֻכּוֹת
‹ Succoth ‹ between ‹ of the ground, ‹ in the thick [clay] ‹ the king cast them

וּבֵין צָרְתָן׃ מז וַיַּנַּח שְׁלֹמֹה אֶת־כָּל־
‹ all ‹ Solomon left 47 ‹‹ Zarethan. ‹ and between

הַכֵּלִים מֵרֹב מְאֹד מְאֹד לֹא נֶחְקָר
‹ calculated ‹ not ‹‹ very [great]; ‹ very, ‹ [was] abundance ‹ because [their] ‹‹ the vessels [unweighed]

מִשְׁקַל הַנְּחֹשֶׁת׃ מח וַיַּעַשׂ שְׁלֹמֹה
‹ Solomon made 48 ‹‹ of the copper. ‹ [was] the weight

אֵת כָּל־הַכֵּלִים אֲשֶׁר בֵּית יְהֹוָה
‹‹ of HASHEM: ‹ in the House ‹ that were ‹ the vessels ‹ all

אֵת מִזְבַּח הַזָּהָב וְאֶת־הַשֻּׁלְחָן אֲשֶׁר
‹ which ‹ the Table, ‹ and ‹ of gold; ‹ the Altar

עָלָיו לֶחֶם הַפָּנִים זָהָב׃ מט וְאֶת־הַמְּנֹרוֹת
‹ the candelabra, ‹ and 49 ‹‹ — of gold; ‹ was the showbread ‹ upon it

חָמֵשׁ מִיָּמִין וְחָמֵשׁ מִשְּׂמֹאל לִפְנֵי
‹ before ‹ to the left, ‹ and five ‹ to the right ‹ five

הַדְּבִיר זָהָב סָגוּר וְהַפֶּרַח וְהַנֵּרֹת
‹ and the lamps, ‹ and the blossom, ‹‹ refined; ‹ — of gold, ‹ the Devir

וְהַמֶּלְקָחַיִם זָהָב׃ נ וְהַסִּפּוֹת וְהַמְזַמְּרוֹת
‹ and the musical instruments, ‹ and the jugs, 50 ‹‹ — of gold; ‹ and the tongs

וְהַמִּזְרָקוֹת וְהַכַּפּוֹת וְהַמַּחְתּוֹת זָהָב
‹ — of gold, ‹ and the pans ‹ and the spoons, ‹ and the basins,

סָגוּר וְהַפֹּתוֹת לְדַלְתוֹת הַבַּיִת הַפְּנִימִי
‹ of the inner House [the Sanctuary], ‹ for the doors ‹ and the hinges ‹‹ refined;

לְקֹדֶשׁ הַקֳּדָשִׁים לְדַלְתֵי הַבַּיִת לְהֵיכָל
‹ into the Temple [the Sanctuary] ‹ of the House [the Hall], ‹ [and] for the doors ‹‹ of Holies, ‹ entering the Holy

זָהָב׃
‹‹ — of gold.

---

acle of Chanukah was ordered by King Antiochus. This shows the contrast between the ideal state and the perverted one that has caused so much grief since the dawn of Jewish history. Israel was charged with the task of being a magnet to the nations, drawing them toward a recognition of God's majesty and service. Hiram and Cyrus saw and responded. Antiochus did not. When Israel is worthy, it is instrumental in leading society toward this state. Indeed, in the aftermath of Chanukah, when the family of Hasmoneans inspired the Jewish people to risk their lives to renew the glory and purity of the Temple, the result was that the Jewish commonwealth expanded, in size, wealth, and spiritual influence.

⸎ Bibliography of Sources Cited in the Commentary

Abarbanel — (1437-1508) Philosopher, statesman, leader of Spanish Jewry at the time of the Expulsion in 1492. Wrote massive commentary on nearly the entire *Tanach.*

Aderes Eliyahu — Commentary on the Pentateuch by the Vilna Gaon, R' Eliyahu ben Shlomo Zalman (1720-1797).

Aggadas Bereishis — A midrash on Genesis, apparently compiled from earlier sources around the tenth century.

Ahavas Yehonasan — Commentary on the weekly *Haftaros* by R' Yehonasan Eybeschutz (1690?-1764), of Prague, Metz, and Altona, one of the leading rabbis of the eighteenth century.

Akeidas Yitzchak — Profound philosophical-homiletical commentary on the Pentateuch by R' Yitzchak Arama (1420-1494), one of the leading rabbis of fifteenth-century Spain.

R' Akiva — (died circa 138) One of leading Tannaim; martyred by the Romans.

Alshich — Extremely popular commentary on the *Tanach* by R' Moshe Alsheich (1508-1593?), *dayan* and preacher in Safed during its golden age.

Alter of Slabodka — R' Nassan Tzvi Finkel (1849-1927), spiritual head of the Slabodka Yeshiva; one of the giants of the Lithuanian Mussar movement. His discourses are collected in *Or Hatzafun.*

Arachin — Talmudic tractate in *Seder Kodashim.*

Aruch HaShalem — Expanded version of the *Aruch* of R. Nasan ben Yechiel of Rome (c.1045-1103), the famous medieval dictionary/compendium of Talmudic literature, by the nineteenth-century scholar A. Kohut.

Astruc, R' Shlomo — Author of *Midreshei Torah,* a commentary on the Pentateuch, cited by Abarbanel and Sforno. He is believed to have been martyred in the Spanish massacres of 1391.

Avnei Nezer — Title of the responsa collection of R' Avraham Borenstein of Sochachov (1839-1910), a foremost Chassidic Rebbe and Torah scholar of the nineteenth century; frequently cited in *Shem MiShmuel,* the discourses of his son (see below).

Avodah Zarah — Talmudic tractate in *Seder Nezikin.*

Avos — Mishnah tractate in *Seder Nezikin,* which is unique in that it is devoted exclusively to the ethical teachings of the Sages.

Avos D'Rabbi Nassan — One of the fourteen so-called "Minor Tractates." A collection of *Baraisos* which forms a commentary to the Mishnah tractate *Avos.*

R' Avraham Ben HaRambam — (1186-1237) Successor to his illustrious father as Naggid, or official leader, and Chief Rabbi of Egyptian Jewry. Wrote commentary on the Pentateuch in Arabic of which only the sections on Genesis and Exodus have survived.

Baal Halachos Gedolos — One of the earliest codes of Jewish law, composed by R' Shimon Kayyara, who is believed to have lived in Babylonia in the ninth century and to have studied under the *Geonim* of Sura.

Baal HaTurim — Commentary on the Pentateuch by R' Yaakov the son of the Rosh (c.1275-c.1340). The commentary is composed of two parts: a) a brief one based on gematria and Masoretic interpretations (known as *Baal HaTurim*); b) an extensive exegetical commentary, known as *Peirush HaTur HaAruch.*

Bais HaLevi — Commentary on the Pentateuch by R' Yosef Dov Halevi Soloveitchik (1820-1892), Rosh Yeshiva in Volozhin and afterward Rabbi of Slutzk and Brisk. Considered one of the most brilliant Talmudists of the nineteenth century.

Bais Yosef — Commentary by R' Yosef Caro (1488-1575) on the law code *Arba'ah Turim.* He was also the author of the *Shulchan Aruch* and *Kessef Mishneh*, a classic commentary on *Rambam's* code.

Bamidbar Rabbah — The section of *Midrash Rabbah* on the Book of Numbers.

Baraisa D'Meleches HaMishkan — Tannaitic work on the building of the Tabernacle in the desert described in the Book of Exodus.

Bava Basra — Talmudic tractate in *Seder Nezikin.*

Bava Kamma — Talmudic tractate in *Seder Nezikin.*

Bava Metzia — Talmudic tractate in *Seder Nezikin.*

B'chor Shor — Commentary on the Pentateuch by the Tosafist R' Yosef B'chor Shor (1140-1190), disciple of Rabbeinu Tam, see above.

Be'er BaSadeh — A supercommentary on Rashi's Pentateuch commentary and the supercommentary of Mizrachi, by R' Meir Binyamin Menachem Danon, Chief Rabbi of Sarejevo, Bosnia in the early nineteenth century.

Be'er HaGolah — a work composed by the Maharal of Prague (1526-1609) to explain certain *aggados*, which superficially seem to contradict science.

Be'er Mayim Chaim — Supercommentary on Rashi's commentary on the Pentateuch by R' Chaim ben Betzalel (1515-1588), Chief Rabbi of Worms, older brother of Maharal.

Be'er Mayim Chaim — Commentary on the Torah by the Chassidic master R' Chaim of Czernowitz (1760-1818).

Be'er Moshe — Chassidic commentary on the Pentateuch by R' Moshe Yechiel HaLevi Epstein of Ozharov (1890-1971).

Be'er Yitzchok — Supercommentary on Rashi's commentary on the Pentateuch by R' Yitzchak Yaakov Horowitz of Yaroslav (died 1864).

Beitzah — Talmudic tractate in *Seder Moed.*

Berachos — Talmudic tractate in *Seder Zeraim.*

Bereishis Rabbah — The section of *Midrash Rabbah* on the Book of Genesis.

Bereishis Rabbasi — A midrash on Genesis either composed by, or based on the teachings of, R' Moshe HaDarshan (circa 1050).

Bertinoro, R' Ovadiah of — (c.1440-1516) Leading rabbi in Italy and Jerusalem; author of the most popular commentary on the Mishnah, commonly referred to as "the Rav" or "the Bartinura"; author of *Amar Nekeh*, a supercommentary on Rashi's Pentateuch commentary.

R' Bunam of P'schis'cha — (1765-1827) Leading Chassidic Rebbe in Poland in the early-nineteenth century. Some of his teachings are collected in *Chedvas Simchah, Kol Simchah,* and *Ramasayim Tzofim.*

R' Chananel — (died c.1055) Rosh Yeshiva and Rabbi of the Jewish community of Kairouan, North Africa; author of famous Talmud commentary and commentary on the Pentateuch which is quoted by Ramban, R' Bachya, and others.

Chasam Sofer — Title of the many works of R' Moshe Sofer (1762-1839), Rabbi of Pressburg and acknowledged leader of Hungarian Jewry who led the battle against Reform.

Chazon Ish — Title of the works of R' Avraham Yeshaya Karelitz (1878-1953), Lithuanian scholar who spent his last twenty years in Bnei Brak. He held no official position, but was acknowledged as a foremost leader of Jewry. His works cover all aspects of Talmud and Halachah.

Chiddushei HaRim — Title of the works of R' Yitzchak Meir of Ger or Gur (1799-1866), founder of Ger Chassidism and one of the outstanding Talmudic scholars of the nineteenth century.

Chizkuni — Commentary on the Pentateuch by R' Chizkiyah Chizkuni, who lived in the thirteenth century, probably in France.

Chofetz Chaim — Title of one of the works of R' Yisrael Meir HaKohen of Radin (1838-1933), author of basic works in *halachah, hashkafah,* and *mussar,* famous for his saintly qualities, acknowledged as a foremost leader of Jewry.

Chullin — Talmudic tractate in *Seder Kodashim.*

Daas Sofrim — Contemporary commentary on the entire *Tanach* (excluding the Five *Megillos*) by the noted Israeli Bible scholar and lecturer, Rabbi Chaim D. Rabinowitz (born 1911).

Daas Tevunos — Work of religious philosophy in the form of a dialogue between the soul and the intellect, by R' Moshe Chaim Luzzato (1707-1746), Kabbalist, poet, and author of, among other works, the basic Mussar text, *Mesillas Yesharim.*

Daas Zekeinim — Collection of comments on the Pentateuch by the Tosafists of the twelfth and thirteenth centuries.

Degel Machaneh Ephraim — Chassidic commentary on the Pentateuch by R' Moshe Chaim Ephraim of Sudylkov (1748-1800), grandson of the Baal Shem Tov.

Derech Eretz Rabbah — One of the fourteen so-called "Minor Tractates." A collection of *Baraisos* dealing with marital laws, proper conduct, and ethical principles.

Derech Hashem — See *Daas Tevunos.*

Divrei David — Supercommentary on Rashi's commentary on the Pentateuch by R' David ben Samuel HaLevi (1586-1667), known as the *Taz* after his classic commentary on the *Shulchan Aruch, Turei Zahav.*

Drashos HaRan — A collection of discourses by R' Nissim of Gerona, Spain (c.1290-c.1375). A classic exposition of the fundamentals of Judaism.

Dubno Maggid — R' Yaakov Krantz (1741-1804), the most famous of the Eastern European *maggidim,* or preachers. Best known for his parables, his discourses were collected and published in *Ohel Yaakov* and other works.

R' Elazar ben Azaria — First-generation Tanna; Nasi of the Sanhedrin (c.90).

Eruvin — Talmudic tractate in *Seder Moed.*

Feinstein, R' David — Rosh Yeshiva of Mesivtha Tifereth Jerusalem; one of contemporary Jewry's foremost halachic decisors. Some of his comments on the Torah are collected in *Kol Dodi.*

Feinstein, R' Moshe — (1895-1986) Rosh Yeshiva of Mesivtha Tifereth Jerusalem in New York City; the leading halachic decisor of his time, and a foremost leader of Jewry; author of *Igros Moshe* (responsa) and *Dibros Moshe* (studies in Talmud). Some of his comments on the Pentateuch have been collected and published as *Darash Moshe*.

Goldwurm, R' Hersh — (1937-1993) Brilliant Torah scholar and contributing editor to this volume. See appreciation in acknowledgments.

Gur Aryeh — Supercommentary on Rashi's Pentateuch commentary by the Maharal of Prague (1526-1609).

Haamek Davar — Commentary on the Pentateuch by R' Naftali Zvi Yehudah Berlin (1817-1893), Rosh Yeshiva of the famous yeshiva of Volozhin in Russia; popularly known as the Netziv.

Hadar Zekeinim — A work on the Pentateuch containing commentaries by the eleventh- and twelfth-century Tosafists and the Rosh, R' Asher ben Yechiel (c.1250-1327).

HaK'sav V'HaKabbalah — Comprehensive commentary on the Pentateuch by R' Yaakov Tzvi Mecklenburg (1785-1865), Chief Rabbi of Koenigsberg in Germany. It demonstrates how the *Kabbalah,* the Oral Tradition, derives from the *K'sav,* the written text of the Pentateuch.

HaRechasim LeBik'ah — Eighteenth-century commentary on the Pentateuch by R' Yehudah Leib Shapira ("Loeb Frankfurter"), great-uncle of Samson Raphael Hirsch.

Heidenheim, R' Wolf — (1757-1832) Philologist; Bible scholar; liturgical scholar; famous for his accurate editions of the Chumash, Siddur and Machzorim; author of *Havanas Hamikra,* a supercommentary on Rashi.

Hirsch, R' Samson Raphael — (1808-1888) Rabbi in Frankfurt-am-Main; great leader of modern German-Jewish Orthodoxy and battler against Reform; author of many works, including a six-volume commentary on the Pentateuch.

Hoffmann, R' David Zvi — (1843-1921) Leading German decisor; headed Orthodox Rabbinical Seminary of Berlin (1899-1921); refuted revisionist Bible Criticism. Author of numerous works, including commentaries (in German) on much of the Pentateuch.

Horayos — Talmudic tractate in *Seder Nezikin.*

Ibn Caspi, R' Yosef — (1280-1340) Controversial philosopher; Bible commentator; grammarian. Among his many works is *Mishneh Kessef,* a commentary on the Pentateuch.

Ibn Ezra, R' Avraham — (1089-c.1164) Bible commentator; *paytan.* Composed classic commentary on entire *Tanach,* famous for its grammatical and linguistic analysis.

Iggeres Teiman — Rambam's famous letter to the Jews of Yemen urging them to remain steadfast in their faith in the face of false messianism and Moslem religious persecution. An exposition of many fundamental aspects of *hashkafah*.

Igros Moshe — See R' Moshe Feinstein.

Imrei Emes — Chassidic discourses on the Pentateuch by R' Avraham Mordechai Alter, the third Gerrer Rebbe (1865-1948), and foremost leader of Polish Jewry.

Imrei Shefer — Commentary on the Pentateuch by R' Shlomo Kluger (1785-1869), Rabbi of Brody in Galicia, one of the leading Torah scholars of the nineteenth century.

Kafich, R' Yosef — (born 1917) Noted Israeli Yemenite scholar and translator; translated and annotated many of the Arabic works of the Rishonim into Hebrew, including a new edition of the Rambam's (see below) *Commentary to the Mishnah* with an extensive commentary.

Kaftor VaFerach — Famous work on the history, geography, and Halachos of Eretz Yisrael, by R' Eshtori HaFarchi (c.1282-c.1357), a disciple of the *Rosh* (see above).

Kamenetsky, R' Yaakov — (1891-1986) Rav of Tzitevian, Lithuania and of Toronto, and Rosh Yeshiva of Mesivta Torah Vodaath; a foremost thinker and leader of Jewry. His comments and discourses on the Pentateuch have been published as *Emes L'Yaakov (Iyunim BeMikra).*

Kavanos HaTorah — Introductory essay to the Pentateuch by R' Ovadiah Sforno (see above), discussing such matters as the purpose of the narratives in the Torah, certain commandments, and the Tabernacle.

Kedushas Levi — Chassidic discourses of R' Levi Yitzchak of Berditchev (1740-1809) on the Torah, Festivals, Talmud, Midrash, and *Pirkei Avos.*

Kereisos — Talmudic tractate in *Seder Kodashim.*

Kesubos — Talmudic tractate in *Seder Nashim.*

K'sav Sofer — Title of the responsa collection and of the Pentateuch commentary of R' Avraham Shmuel Binyomin Sofer of Pressburg (1815-1879), son and successor of the Chasam Sofer (see above), and the leader of non-Chassidic Hungarian Jewry in the middle decades of the nineteenth century.

Kitzur Mizrachi — Abridged version of the supercommentary *Mizrachi* (see below), by R' Yitzchak HaKohen of Ostrava, Moravia.

Kli Yakar — Popular commentary on the Pentateuch by R' Shlomo Ephraim Lunshitz (c.1550-1619), Rosh Yeshiva in Lemberg and Rabbi of Prague, one of the leading Polish rabbis of the early-seventeenth century.

Kluger, R' Shlomo — (1785-1869) Rabbi of Brody in Galicia, author of numerous works, one of the leading Torah scholars of the nineteenth century.

Kol Bo — Anonymous Halachic compendium (late- 13th — early-14th cent.).

Kopitchinitz, R' Avraham Yehoshua Heschel of — (1888-1967) Prominent Chasidic Rebbe, Galicia, Vienna, New York.

Korban Aharon — Basic commentary on the *Sifra* by R' Aharon ben Avraham ibn Chaim (1545-1632) of Morocco.

Kotler, R' Aharon — (1892-1962) Rosh Yeshiva of Kletzk, Poland, and founder of Beth Medrash Govoha in Lakewood; a foremost leader and propounder of the primacy of Torah.

Kotzk, R' Menachem Mendel of — (1787-1859) One of the leading Chassidic Rebbes in the mid-nineteenth century; his pithy comments are published in *Emes V'Emunah,* in *Ohel Torah,* and in the numerous works of his disciples.

Kuzari — Basic work of Jewish religious philosophy in the form of a dialogue; by R' Yehudah Halevi (c.1080-c.1145), the most famous of the medieval Jewish liturgical poets in Spain.

Lekach Tov — Contemporary anthology of Mussar and Hashkafah writings arranged according to the Pentateuchal weekly readings, by R' Yaakov Yisrael Beifus.

Levin, R' Aryeh — (1885-1969) Acclaimed by religious and non-religious Jews in Israel as "The Tzaddik of Jerusalem"; famous as the voluntary chaplain to the Leper Hospital and to Jewish political prisoners in British Mandatory jails.

Magen Avraham — Basic commentary on *Shulchan Aruch Orach Chaim,* by R' Avraham Gombiner (1634-1682) of Kalisch, Poland.

Maharal — Acronym for *R' Yehudah Loewe* ben Bezalel (1526-1609), one of the seminal figures in Jewish thought in the last five centuries. Chief Rabbi in Moravia, Posen, and Prague. Author of numerous works in all fields of Torah.

Maharam — Acronym for *Moreinu HaRav Meir* ben Gedaliah of Lublin, Poland (1558-1616), Rabbi and rosh yeshiva in a number of leading communities in Poland; author of a commentary on the Talmud; responsa; and *Torah Or,* sermons based on the Torah.

Maharil Diskin — Acronym of *Moreinu HaRav Yehoshua Leib* Diskin (1818-1898), one of the leading Torah scholars of the nineteenth century, Rabbi in several Lithuanian communities, especially Brisk; subsequently settled in Jerusalem. Among his works is a commentary on the Pentateuch.

Maharit — Acronym for *Moreinu HaRav Yosef Trani* (1568-1639), Rosh Yeshiva and Chief Rabbi of Constantinople; the leading Sephardic Halachist of the early-seventeenth century. His responsa collection, *She'elos U'Teshuvos Maharit*, is considered a classic.

Maharsha — Acronym for *Moreinu HaRav Shlomo Eidel's* of Ostroh, Poland (1555-1632), Rosh Yeshiva and Rabbi in a number of the leading communities of Poland. Author of monumental commentaries on the Halachic and Aggadic sections of the Babylonian Talmud.

Maharshal — Acronym for *Moreinu HaRav Shlomo Luria* (1510-1573), one of the leading Rabbis of Poland in the sixteenth century; author of numerous works on Talmud and Halachah, as well as a supercommentary on Rashi's Pentateuch commentary.

Maharzu — Acronym for *Moreinu HaRav Zeev Wolf* Einhorn of Vilna (died 1862), author of a comprehensive commentary on the *Midrash Rabbah.*

Makkos — Talmudic tractate in *Seder Nezikin.*

Malbim —Acronym for *Meir Leibush ben Yechiel Michel* (1809-1879), Rabbi in Germany, Romania, and Russia, leading Torah scholar and one of the preeminent Bible commentators of modern times. Demonstrated how the Oral tradition is implicit in the Biblical text.

Maskil L'David — Supercommentary on Rashi's Pentateuch commentary by R' David Pardo (1710-1792), Rabbi in Sarajevo and Jerusalem, author of many important works; one of the leading Sephardic Torah scholars of the eighteenth century.

R' Masya Ben Charash — (c.90) One of the Tannaim of the first generation; headed a yeshiva in Rome.

Matanos Kehunah — Commentary on the *Midrash Rabbah* by R' Yissachar Ber HaKohen (c.1520-1590), a student of the Rama.

Me'am Loez — Monumental Ladino commentary on the entire *Tanach* begun by R' Yaakov Culi of Constantinople (1689-1732), a disciple of the Mishneh LeMelech. The most popular Torah work ever published in Ladino, it has won great popularity in its Hebrew and English translations as well.

Mechilta — Tannaitic Halachic midrash to the Book of Exodus.

Megillah — Talmudic tractate in *Seder Moed.*

R' Menachem Mendel of Kotzk — See above, Kotzk.

Menachos — Talmudic tractate in *Seder Kodashim.*

Meshech Chochmah — Commentary on the Pentateuch by R' Meir Simcha HaKohen of Dvinsk (1843-1926), a foremost Torah scholar of his time and author of the classic *Or Sameach* on the Rambam's *Mishneh Torah.*

Michtav MeEliyahu — Collected writings and discourses of R' Eliyahu Eliezer Dessler (1891-1954) of London and Bnei Brak, one of the outstanding personalities and thinkers of the Mussar movement.

Midrash — Genre of Rabbinical literature, selections from the Halachic and/or Aggadic teachings of the Tannaim and Amoraim arranged according to the verses of the Torah.

Midrash Aggadah — Midrashic collection based on the works of R' Moshe HaDarshan, see below.

Midrashei HaTorah — Commentary on the Pentateuch composed by R' Shlomo Astruc, cited by Abarbanel and Sforno. He is believed to have been martyred in the Spanish massacres of 1391.

Midrash HaCheifetz — Midrashic anthology of the Pentateuch and the *Haftaros,* by R' Zechariah ben Shlomo HaRofei (early-15th century).

Midrash HaGadol — Monumental compilation of Halachic and Aggadic material gleaned from Talmudic sources and arranged according to the verses of the Torah, by R' Dovid al-Adeni of Aden in South Arabia (late-13th century). This midrash, discovered in this century, contains much otherwise unknown material.

Midrash HaNe'elam — Kabbalistic midrash, part of the *Zohar.*

Midrash Lekach Tov — Midrashic work on the Pentateuch and the Five *Megillos* compiled by R' Toviah (ben Eliezer) HaGadol (1036-1108) of Greece and Bulgaria. This work is also known as *Pesikta Zutrasa.*

Midrash Or Ha'Afelah — Midrashic collection by R' Naftali ben Yeshaya of Yemen.

Midrash Tadshei — A midrash attributed to R' Pinchas ben Yair (c.130).

Midrash Tanchuma — See below, *Tanchuma.*

Midrash Tehillim — Ancient midrash on the Psalms, also known as *Midrash Shochar Tov.*

Minchah Belulah — Commentary on the Pentateuch by R' Avraham Rapa of Porto and Venice, Italy (died 1593).

Minchas Yehudah — Commentary on the Pentateuch by R' Yehudah ben Eliezer (early-fourteenth century). The author cites many interpretations of the Tosafists.

Mishnah Rosh Hashanah — Tractate in *Seder Moed.*

Mizrachi — Basic supercommentary on Rashi's Pentateuch commentary by R' Eliyahu Mizrachi (1450-1525) of Constantinople, Chief Rabbi of the Turkish Empire.

Moed Kattan — Talmudic tractate in *Seder Moed.*

Moshav Zekeinim — Collection of comments on the Pentateuch by the Tosafists of the twelfth and thirteenth centuries.

R' Moshe HaDarshan — Eleventh-century compiler of midrashic anthology known as *Yesod R' Moshe HaDarshan,* cited by Rashi and other Rishonim.

R' Elie Munk — (1900-1980) Rabbi in Paris, prolific author of many works, including the popular *World of Prayer,* and a commentary on the Pentateuch in French, translated into English as *The Call of the Torah.*

Nachalas Yaakov — Commentary on the Pentateuch by R' Yaakov Loerberbaum (d. 1832), Rabbi of Lissa in Prussian Poland. Famous Torah scholar and author of *Nesivos HaMishpat* and *Chavos Daas* on *Shulchan Aruch.*

Nachalas Yitzchok — Supercommentary on Rashi.

Nefesh HaChaim — Basic work of religious philosophy by R' Chaim of Volozhin (1749-1821), primary disciple of the Vilna Gaon; founder of the famous yeshiva of Volozhin.

Nefesh HaGer — Commentary on *Targum Onkelos* by R' Mordechai Levenstein. Does not include the Book of Deuteronomy.

Ne'os HaDesheh — Collection of comments on the Pentateuch of R' Avraham of Sochachov, see above, *Avnei Nezer.*

Netziv — See above, *Haamek Davar.*

Noam Elimelech — Collection of Chassidic discourses on the Pentateuch by R' Elimelech of Lizhensk (1717-1787).

Onkelos — See below, *Targum Onkelos.*

Or HaChaim — Commentary on the Pentateuch by the famous Kabbalist and Talmudic scholar R' Chaim ben Attar (1696-1743), Rabbi and Rosh Yeshiva in Livorno, Italy, and subsequently in Jerusalem.

Oznaim L'Torah — Commentary on the Pentateuch by R' Zalman Sorotzkin (1881-1966), one of the leading Rabbis in Lithuania (popularly known as "the Lutzker Rav") and subsequently in Israel. Has been published in English as *Insights in the Torah.*

Pachad Yitzchak — The collected discourses of R' Yitzchak Hutner (1907-1980), Rosh Yeshiva of Mesivta R' Chaim Berlin in New York, and a foremost thinker and leader of Jewry. His works are based in great measure on those of the Maharal.

Panim Yafos — Commentary on the Pentateuch by R' Pinchas Horowitz (1730-1805), one of the leading Torah scholars of the eighteenth century, Rabbi in Frankfurt-am-Main, author of the classic works *Haflaah* and *Hamakneh* on the Talmud.

Pesachim — Talmudic tractate in *Seder Moed.*

Pesikta D'Rav Kahana — Ancient midrashic collection on certain portions of the Pentateuch as well as on the *Haftaros* of the festivals and special Sabbaths, by R' Kahana, probably the Amora R' Kahana, the disciple of Rav (second century).

Pesikta Rabbasi — Midrashic collection of homilies compiled in the Geonic era on parts of the weekly Torah reading, certain *Haftaros,* and certain special Sabbaths.

Pesikta Zutrasa — Midrashic work on the Pentateuch and the Five *Megillos* compiled by R' Toviah (ben Eliezer) HaGadol (1036-1108) of Greece and Bulgaria. This work is also known as *Midrash Lekach Tov.*

Pirkei D'Rabbi Eliezer — Midrash composed by the school of the Tanna R' Eliezer ben Hyrcanus (c. 100). An important commentary on this midrash was composed by R' David Luria (1798-1855), one of the leading Torah scholars in Russia in the early nineteenth century.

Pis'chei Teshuvah — Digest of responsa arranged according to the order of the *Shulchan Aruch* (excluding *Orach Chaim*), forming a kind of commentary to that law-code, by R' Avraham Tzvi Hirsch Eisenstadt (1813-1868), Rabbi of Utian, Lithuania.

Pri Megadim — Monumental supercommentary on the *Shulchan Aruch* commentaries *Magen Avraham, Turei Zahav,* and *Sifsei Cohen,* by R' Yoseph Teomim (1727-1792), *dayan* in Lemberg and Rabbi in Frankurt an der Oder.

Rabbeinu Bachya — (1263-1340) Student of the *Rashba*, author of a commentary on the Pentateuch containing four modes of interpretation: plain meaning of the text, and midrashic, philosophical, and kabbalistic exegeses.

Rabbeinu Tam — (1100-1171) Grandson of Rashi, and one of the foremost Tosafists.

Radak — Acronym for *R' Dovid Kimchi* (1160-1235) of Provence, leading Bible commentator and grammarian. Of his famous commentary on *Tanach,* only the sections to Genesis, the Prophets, Psalms, Proverbs, and Chronicles have survived.

Radvaz — Acronym for *R' Dovid ibn Zimra* (c.1480-1573), Chief Rabbi of Egypt, one of the leading rabbis of the sixteenth century; his responsa collection is considered a classic.

Ralbag — Acronym for *R' Levi ben Gershom* [Gersonides] (1288-1344) of Provence. According to some, he was a grandson of Ramban. Composed rationalistic commentary on the Scriptures which explains the text, and then sums up the philosophical ideas and moral lessons contained in each section.

Rambam — Acronym for *R' Moshe ben Maimon* ["Maimonides"] (1135-1204), one of the leading Torah scholars of the Middle Ages. His three major works are: *Commentary to the Mishnah* in Arabic; *Mishneh Torah,* a comprehensive code of Jewish law; and *Moreh Nevuchim* ("Guide for the Perplexed"), a major work of Jewish philosophy.

Ramban — Acronym for *R' Moshe ben Nachman* ["Nachmanides"] (1194-1270) of Gerona, Spain, one of the leading Torah scholars of the Middle Ages; successfuly defended Judaism at the dramatic debate in Barcelona in 1263; author of numerous basic works in all aspects of Torah, including a classic commentary on the Pentateuch.

Ran — Acronym for *R' Nissim* of Gerona, Spain (c.1290-c.1375), famous for his Talmudic commentary, see above, *Drashos HaRan.*

Rashash — Acronym for *R' Shmuel Strashun* of Vilna (1794-1872). His annotations and glosses on nearly every tractate of the Mishnah, Talmud, and *Midrash Rabbah* are printed in the Romm (Vilna) editions of the Talmud and the *Midrash Rabbah.*

Rashba — Acronym for *R' Shlomo Ibn Aderes* (1235-1310), the leading rabbi in Spain in the late-thirteenth century. Famous for his many classic works in all branches of Torah learning, including thousands of responsa dealing with all aspects of Bible, Aggadah, Talmud, and Halachah.

Rashbam — Acronym for *R' Shlomo ben Meir* (c.1085-1174), grandson of Rashi and brother of Rabbeinu Tam, leading Tosafist and Talmud commentator, author of a literalist commentary on the Pentateuch.

Rashi — Acronym for *R' Shlomo Yitzchaki* (1040-1105), considered *the* commentator par excellence. Rashi's commentary on the Pentateuch as well as his commentary on the Talmud are considered absolutely basic to the understanding of the text to this very day.

Ravad — Acronym for *R' Avraham ben David* of Posquieres, Provence (c.1120-c.1197), one of the leading Torah scholars of the twelfth century, famous for his critical notes on the *Mishneh-Torah* of the Rambam, as well as many other works on Talmud and Halachah.

R' Menachem Recanati — (late-13th — early-14th cent.) Italian Kabbalist who composed a mystical commentary on the Pentateuch.

Resisei Laylah — Collection of essays by R' Tzaddok HaCohen (1823-1900), see below.

Ritva — Acronym for *R' Yom Tov Ben Avraham* al-Asevilli (1248-1330), Rabbi in Saragossa, Spain, one of the leading Rabbis in Spain in his day; famous for his classic novellae on the Talmud.

Rokeach — Guide to ethics and halachah, by R' Elazar Rokeach of Worms (c.1160-c.1238), a leading scholar and mystic of the medieval *Chachmei Ashkenaz* (German Pietists); author of many works, including a commentary on the Pentateuch.

Rosh — Acronym for *R' Asher ben Yechiel* (c.1250-1327), disciple of Maharam Rottenberg. He fled to Spain from Germany and became Rabbi of Toledo and one of the leading authorities of his era; author of a classic halachic commentary on the Talmud, as well as other works, including a commentary on the Pentateuch, see above, *Hadar Zekeinim.*

Rosh Hashanah — Talmudic tractate in *Seder Moed.*

R' Saadiah Gaon — (882-942) Head of the famous yeshiva of Pumbedisa, zealous opponent of Karaism; author of many works in all areas of Torah learning, including the philosophical work, *Emunos v'Deos,* as well as an Arabic translation of the Pentateuch.

Sanhedrin — Talmudic tractate in *Seder Nezikin.*

Schorr, R' Gedaliah — (1910-1979) Rosh Yeshiva of Mesivta Torah Vodaath in Brooklyn, New York; described as first American-trained *gadol*. Three volumes of his discourses on Genesis, Exodus, and the festivals have been published under the title *Or Gedalyahu.*

Sechel Tov — Compilation of midrashim, arranged on each verse of the Pentateuch and the Five *Megillos,* interspersed with halachic notes and original comments, by R' Menachem ben Shlomo of Italy (12th century).

Seder Olam — Ancient chronological work quoted by the Gemara, attributed to the Tanna R' Yosei ben Chalafta.

Sefer Chassidim — Classic miscellaneous work of Mussar, Halachah, customs, Bible commentary, and Kabbalah, by R' Yehudah HaChassid of Germany (c.1150-1217).

Sefer Habahir — Ancient Kabbalistic work attributed to the Tanna R' Nechunya ben HaKana.

Sefer HaChinuch — The classic work on the 613 commandments, their rationale and their regulations, by an anonymous author in thirteenth-century Spain.

Sefer HaMitzvos — Listing and explanation of the 613 commandments, with a seminal preface explaining the principles of how to classify which Biblical precepts are to be included in the list, by Rambam, see above.

Sefer HaPardes — Halachic compendium, from the school of Rashi (see above); includes certain of his legal decisions.

Sefer HaParshiyos — Anthology of Rabbinic literature arranged according to the weekly Torah readings, by the noted Israeli educator R' Eliyahu Kitov (1912-1976).

Sefer HaZikaron — Supercommentary on Rashi's Pentateuch commentary by R' Avrahaham Bakrat, who lived at the time of the Expulsion from Spain of 1492.

Sfas Emes — Discourses on the Pentateuch and other subjects, by R' Yehudah Leib Alter (1847-1905), the second Gerrer Rebbe and leader of Polish Jewry.

Sforno — Classic commentary on the Pentateuch by R' Ovadiah Sforno of Rome and Bolgna, Italy (1470-1550).

Shaarei Aharon — A contemporary encyclopedic commentary on the Pentateuch by R' Aharon Yeshaya Rotter of Bnei Brak.

Shabbos — Talmudic tractate in *Seder Moed.*

Shem MiShmuel — Chassidic discourses on the Pentateuch and other subjects, by R' Shmuel of Sochachov (1856-1920), son of R' Avraham of Sochachov, see above.

Shemos Rabbah — The section of *Midrash Rabbah* on the Book of Exodus.

Sheurin Shel Torah — Commentary on halachic measurements by Rabbi Yaakov Yisrael Kanievsky, a major contemporary scholar and Torah leader, popularly known as "The Steipler" (d. 1985 in Bnei Brak).

Shevuos — Talmudic tractate in *Seder Nezikin.*

Shibbolei HaLekket — Halachic compendium, by R' Tzidkiyah HaRofei of Rome (c.1230-c.1300).

Sh'lah — Acronym for *Shnei Luchos Habris* ("The two Tablets of the Covenant"), by R' Yeshayah Hurwitz (1560-1630), Rabbi in Poland, Frankfurt, Prague, and Jerusalem, one of the leading Torah scholars of the early-seventeenth century. It includes fundamental tenets of Judaism, basic instruction in Kabbalah, and a commentary on the Pentateuch.

Shorashim — Alphabetical encyclopedia of the roots of all words found in the Bible. A seminal work by the famous grammarian R' Yonah Ibn Janach (c.990-c.1055) of Cordoba and Saragossa. Written in Arabic, it became available in Hebrew only in the last century.

Sidduro Shel Shabbos — Chassidic work on the sanctity of the Sabbath, by R' Chaim Tyrer of Czernowitz (1760-1818), author of *Be'er Mayim Chaim,* see above.

Sifra — Tannaitic halachic midrash to the Book of Leviticus; also known as *Toras Kohanim.*

Sifre — Tannaitic halachic midrash to the Books of Numbers and Deuteronomy.

Sifsei Chachamim — Popular supercommentary on Rashi's Pentateuch comentary, by R' Shabsai Bass (1641-1718), well-known publisher.

Sifsei Kohen — Mystical commentary on the Pentateuch by R' Mordechai HaKohen of Safed (16th century).

R' Simcha Zissel Ziv of Kelm — "The Alter of Kelm" (1824-1898). One of the foremost disciples of R' Yisrael Salanter; founder and head of the famous Mussar yeshiva, the Talmud Torah of Kelm, Lithuania. His discourses were published as *Daas Chochmah U'Mussar* (2 volumes).

Soloveitchik, R' Chaim — (1853-1918) "Reb Chaim Brisker"; Rosh Yeshiva in Volozhin and subsequently Rabbi of Brisk. Equally renowned for his genius in Torah learning and his saintly qualities, he was one of the most seminal Torah scholars of his day.

Soloveitchik, R' Yitzchak Zev — (1886-1959). Successor of his father as Rabbi of Brisk, he was also a teacher of the foremost Lithuanian Torah scholars, a practice he continued when he settled in Jerusalem in 1940; major leader of world Jewry.

Soloveitchik, R' Yosef Dov — (1903-1993), Rosh Yeshivah of Yeshivas R' Yitzchak Elchanan, and rabbi of the Boston Orthodox community. A scion of the Brisk Torah dynasty, he was an original Talmudic scholar, thinker and leader.

R' Zalman Sorotzkin — See above, *Oznaim L'Torah.*

Sotah — Talmudic tractate in *Seder Nashim.*

Taanis — Talmudic tractate in *Seder Moed.*

Talmud Yerushalmi — The Talmud composed by the Amoraim of *Eretz Yisrael* in the second-fourth centuries. Although traditionally called the Talmud of Jerusalem, it was composed in the Galilee, since the Romans did not permit the Jews to reside in Jerusalem in that era.

Tanchuma — Aggadic midrash on the Pentateuch, attributed to the school of the Amora R' Tanchuma bar Abba of Eretz Yisrael (late-fourth century). There are two published versions of this Midrash: a) *Tanchuma Yashan,* the only one extant until the late nineteenth century; b) *Tanchuma Buber,* manuscript discovered by the scholar S. Buber in 1885.

Targum or ***Targum Onkelos*** — Authoritative Aramaic translation of the Pentateuch by the proselyte Onkelos (c. 90). This work, which earned the approbation of his teachers, the Tannaim R' Eliezer and R' Yehoshua, is an interpretive translation.

Targum Yonasan — Aramaic paraphrase of the Pentateuch, attributed by some to Yonasan ben Uziel, the disciple of Hillel. Others maintain that the initials ת״י signify *Targum Yerushalmi,* meaning that it was composed in Eretz Yisrael, and ascribe a later date to its composition.

Taz — Acronym for *Turei Zahav* ("Rows of Gold"), a basic commentary on the *Shulchan Aruch* by R' Dovid ben Shmuel HaLevi (1586-1667), one of the foremost Rabbinical authorities in seventeenth-century Poland.

Tevuos Ha'aretz — Geographical work describing the history and borders of Eretz Yisrael, its topography, Biblical and Talmudic locations, flora and fauna, and other matters, by R' Yehosef Schwartz (1804-1865) of Jerusalem.

Tiferes Yisrael — Comprehensive commentary on the Mishnah, by R' Yisrael Lipschutz (1782-1860), Rabbi in a number of Jewish communities in Germany.

Torah Sheleimah — Monumental multi-volume encyclopedia of all Talmudic and Midrashic sources on the Pentateuch, with explanations, scholarly notes and essays by R' Menachem Kasher (1895-1983), noted Israeli Torah scholar. He published thirty-eight volumes, up to *Parashas Beha'aloscha* before his death. *Torah Sheleimah* is currently being completed by his disciples.

Toras Kohanim — See *Sifra.*

Tosafos — The Talmudic glosses of the French and German rabbis of the twelfth and thirteen centuries on the Babylonian Talmud printed in all editions of that work alongside the text of the Gemara.

Tosefta — Tannaitic collection of *Baraisos,* traditionally attributed to R' Chiya and his circle (*Iggeres R' Shrira Gaon*); a kind of parallel work to the Mishnah.

Tur — Code of Jewish law composed by R' Yaakov, the son of the Rosh (c.1275-c.1340). The *Arba Turim* (which is its full title) is composed of four parts: *Tur Orach Chaim, Tur Yoreh Deah, Tur Even HaEzer,* and *Tur Choshen Mishpat.*

R' Tzaddok HaCohen — (1823-1900) Chassidic sage and thinker; prolific author in many aspects of Torah; one of the leading Torah scholars of the nineteenth century. Largest of his many works is *Pri Tzadik*, a collection of his discourses on the Pentateuch.

Tzror HaMor — Homiletic commentary on the Pentateuch by R' Avraham Saba (c.1440-c.1508). Fear of the Inquisition forced him to bury the book in Portugal; he subsequently rewrote it from memory when he escaped to Morocco.

Vayikra Rabbah — The section of *Midrash Rabbah* on the Book of Leviticus.

Vilna Gaon — R' Eliyahu ben Shlomo Zalman (1720-1797), also known as R' Eliyahu HaChassid (R' Eliyahu the Saintly). Considered the greatest Torah scholar in many centuries; acknowledged leader of non-Chassidic Jewry of Eastern Europe; see above, *Aderes Eliyahu.*

Volozhin, R' Chaim of — (1749-1821) Leading disciple of the Vilna Gaon and founder of the famous yeshiva of Volozhin. Acknowledged leader of non-Chassidic Jewry of Russia and Lithuania, see above, *Nefesh HaChaim.*

Wolbe, R' Shlomo — Leading contemporary Israeli Mussar personality, author of *Alei Shur* (2 volumes) and other *hashkafah* works.

R' Yaakov of Orleans — (d. 1189); disciple of Rabbeinu Tam (see above); martyred in London, author of a commentary on the Pentateuch (ms.) which is cited in other collections.

Yafeh To'ar — Classic massive commentary on the *Midrash Rabbah,* by R' Shmuel Yafeh Ashkenazi (1525-1595) of Constantinople. The sections on *Bamidbar Rabbah* and *Devarim Rabbah* remain unpublished.

Yalkut — See below, *Yalkut Shimoni.*

Yalkut Shimoni — The best-known and most comprehensive Midrashic anthology, covering the entire *Tanach;* attributed to R' Shimon HaDarshan of Frankfurt (13th century).

R' Yehudah HaLevi — See above, *Kuzari.*

Yerushalmi — See *Talmud Yerushalmi.*

Yerushalmi Shekalim — Talmudic tractate found only in the *Talmud Yerushalmi.*

Yevamos — Talmudic tractate in *Seder Nashim.*

R' Yisrael of Rizhin — (1797-1851) One of the foremost Chassidic Rebbes in Poland; his comments are found in *Irin Kadishin, Knesses Yisrael, Beis Yisrael,* and *Niflaos Yisrael*, among others.

R' Yochanan Ben Zakkai — Leading sage at the time of the destruction of the Second Temple (c.70); youngest of the disciples of Hillel.

Yohel Ohr — Supercommentary on Ibn Ezra's Pentateuch commentary, by Yehudah Leib Krinsky of Minsk, published in 1907.

Yoma — Talmudic tractate in *Seder Moed.*

Zevachim — Talmudic tractate in *Seder Kodashim.*

Zohar — The basic work of Kabbalah, compiled by R' Shimon ben Yochai and his disciples in the form of a commentary on the Pentateuch and the *Megillos.* Hidden for centuries, it was first published in the late-thirteenth century by R' Moshe de Leon (c.1250-1305), in Spain.

Zohar Chadash — Kabbalistic Midrash, part of the *Zohar.*

◂§ Scriptural Index for the Book of Bereishis/Genesis

Abel,
murder of, 4:8
offering, 4:3*ff.*
Abimelech,
abduction of Sarah, *Ch.* 20
alliance with Abraham, 21:22*ff.*
appeases Abraham, 20:14*ff.*
meets Isaac, 26:1*ff.*
reaffirms treaty with Isaac, 26:26*ff.*
Abraham,
Abimelech appeases, 20:14*ff.*
Akeidah (Binding of Isaac), *Ch.* 22
alliance with Abimelech, 21:22*ff.*
angels appear to, *Ch.* 18
birth, 11:26
birth of Isaac, 21:2*ff.*
birth of Ishmael, *Ch.* 16
blessed by Malchizedek, 14:18
builds altar, 12:7
buys Cave of Machpelah, 23:9*ff.*
childlessness, *Ch.* 15-16
circumcises Isaac, 21:4
circumcision, 17:3-23*ff.*
commandment to move to Canaan, 12:1*ff.*
Covenant Between the Parts, 15:7*ff.*
death, 25:7*ff.*
departure from Ur Kasdim, 11:31
eulogizes Sarah, 23:2
expells Ishmael, 21:9*ff.*
finding a wife for Isaac, *Ch.* 24
God's reassurance to, 15:1*ff.*
intercedes for Sodom, 18:23*ff.*
marries Keturah, 25:1
marries Sarah, 11:29
name changed, 17:5
prayer, 19:27, 20:17
promise of Isaac's birth, 17:19
quarrel with Lot, 13:5*ff.*
saving Lot, 14:13*ff.*
sojourns to Egypt, 13:1
trial: ten tests of faith, 12:1, *comm.*
war of the kings, 14:1*ff.*
Abram, *see* Abraham
Adam,
curse, 3:17*ff.*, 4:25, 5:1*ff.*
see man
Adullamite, 38:1
Ai, 12:8, 13:3
altar,
Abraham builds, 12:7, 4:2*ff.*, 4:25
Jacob, 33:20, 35:14
Noah, 8:20
Ammon, conception, 19:38
Amorah [Gemorrah]; *see* Sodom
Amorites, 10:16, 14:7, 15:21,
Amraphel, 14:1*ff.*
angels,
appear to Abraham, *Ch.* 18
visiting Lot, 19:1*ff.*
Aram Naharaim, 24:10
Ararat, 8:4
Arioch, 14:1*ff.*
Ark, Noah's, command to build, 6:14*ff.*
– entering, 7:1*ff.*
– leaving, 8:18
Asenath, wife of Joseph, 41:45
Asher,
birth, 30:13
blessed by Jacob, 49:20
Ashur, 10:11

Babel, 10:10
tower, 11:4*ff.*
Beer-sheba, 21:14, 21:31, 22:19, 26:23, 26:33, 28:10, 46:1
Benjamin,
birth, 35:18
blessed by Jacob, 49:27
meets Joseph, 43:16
sent to Egypt, 43:13*ff.*
Bera, 14:2*ff.*
Bethel, 12:8, 13:3, 28:19, 35:6, 35:15
Jacob journeys to, 35:1
Bethlehem; *see* Ephrath,
Bethuel,
birth, 22:22
offers Rebecca for Isaac, 24:50
Bilhah, 29:29, 30:3*ff.*
birds,
creation of, 1:20*ff.*
dove, 8:8*ff.*
raven, 8:7
Birsha, 14:2*ff.*
birthright, sale of, 25:33

Cain, 4:1*ff.*, 4:25
killed by Lamech, 4:23
murder of Abel, 4:8
offering, 4:3*ff.*
punishment, 4:11*ff.*
Canaan,
curse of, 9:25*ff.*
descendants, 10:15*ff.*
sees father's nakedness 9:22
Canaan, land, 11:31, 13:12
cattle, creation, 1:24*ff.*
Cave of Machpelah, 23:9, 25:9, 49:30
Chanoch, 4:17*ff.*, 5:18*ff.*
Charan, 11:31, 12:4*ff.*
Chedorlaomer, 14:1*ff.*
childlessness,
Rachel 30:1*ff.*
Sarah, 16:1*ff.*
circumcision, 17:3*ff.*,
Abraham, 17:23*ff.*
Isaac, 21:4
Ishmael, 17:25
Covenant Between the Parts, 15:7*ff.*
covenant
Abraham, 15:7*ff.*
Noah, 9:9
Creation, 1:1*ff.*
birds, 1:20*ff.*
cattle, 1:24*ff.*
fifth day, 1:23
first day, 1:5
fourth day, 1:19
man, 1:26*ff.*, 2:7, 5:1*ff.*
naming of animals, 2:19*ff.*
second day, 1:8
seventh day, 2:2*ff.*
sixth day, 1:31
third day, 1:13
trees and plants, 1:11, 1:29
woman, 2:21*ff.*, 5:1*ff.*
curse, Adam, 3:17*ff.*
Canaan, 9:25*ff.*
Eve, 3:16
serpent, 3:14*ff.*

Dan,
birth of, 30:6
blessed by Jacob, 49:16*ff.*
Deborah, Rebecca's nurse, 35:8
Dinah,
abduction, 34:2*ff.*
birth, 30:21
dispersion, *see* Babel, tower of
Dothan, 37:17
dove, 8:8*ff.*,
dream
Jacob, 28:12*ff.*
Joseph, 37:5*ff.*
Pharaoh, 41:1*ff.*
Pharaoh's chamberlain's, 40:8*ff.*
drunkenness, Noah, 9:21
dudaim, 30:14*ff.*

Eber, 10:24*ff.*, 11:15*ff.*
Eden, Garden of, 2:8*ff.*
expulsion, 3:23*ff.*
rivers, 2:10*ff.*
Tree of Knowledge, 2:9, 2:17
Tree of Life, 2:9, 2:17, 3:24

Edom, 32:4, 36:1
Egypt,
  Abraham sojourns to, 12:10
  Jacob journeys to, 46:1*ff.*
  Jacob sends sons to, 42:1
  Joseph brought to, 37:28
  mourns Jacob, 50:3
Eliezer, 15:2
  finds wife for Isaac, *Ch.* 24
El Shaddai, 35:11,
embalming
  Jacob, 50:2
  Joseph, 50:26
End of Days, *Ch.* 49,
Enoch, 4:17*ff.*, 5:16*ff.*
Enosh, 4:26, 5:6*ff.*
Ephraim,
  birth, 41:52
  blessing, 48:5, 48:20
Ephrath, 48:7
  Rachel's death, 35:16*ff.*
Ephron, 23:8*ff.*
Er, birth, 38:3
  death, 38:7
  marries Tamar, 38:6
Esau,
  birth, 25:25
  descendants, *Ch.* 36
  encounter with Jacob, *Ch.* 33
  hatred of Jacob, 27:41
  marriage, 26:34, 28:9
  sale of birthright, 25:29*ff.*
  tribute from Jacob, 32:14*ff.*
Esek, well, 26:20
esrog; *see* citron
Eve, 3:20
  curse, 3:16
  see also Woman
expulsion, 3:22*ff.*

famine, 12:10*ff.*, 41:54, 43:1, 47:13
Flood,
  beginning, 7:6
  completion, 8:1*ff.*
  date, 7:11

Gad,
  birth, 30:11
  blessed by Jacob, 49:19
Garden of Eden; *see* Eden, Garden of
Gerar, 20:1,26:6
Gomorrah; *see* Sodom
Goshen, 45:10
  Israel settles, 47:27
  Jacob arrives, 46:29

Hagar,
  birth of Ishmael, *Ch.* 16
  conflict with Sarah, 16:5
  exiled, 16:6*ff.*
  expelled, 21:9*ff.*
Ham, 5:32, 6:10, 7:13, 9:18,
  descendants, 10:1, 10:6*ff.*
  sin, 9:22
Haran, birth, 11:26
  death, 11:28
Hebron, 13:18 23:2, 35:27

Isaac,
  Akeidah (Binding of Isaac), *Ch.* 22
  birth, 21:2*ff.*
  birth of Jacob and Esau, 25:26
  blesses Jacob, 27:28*ff.*, 28:1*ff.*
  buries Abraham, 25:9
  death, 35:28
  famine, 26:1*ff.*
  God's promise to, 26:2*ff.*, 26:24
  marries Rebecca, 24:67
  prayer, 24:63, 25:21
  promise of his birth, 17:19
  reaffirms treaty with Abimelech, 26:26*ff.*
  sends Jacob away, 28:5
Ishmael,
  birth, *Ch.* 16
  blessing, 17:20*ff.*
  buries Abraham, 25:9
  circumcision, 17:25
  death, 25:17
  descendants, 25:12*ff.*
  Egypt, 46:8*ff.*
  expelled, 21:9*ff.*
Issachar, birth, 30:14*ff.*
  blessed by Jacob, 49:14*ff.*

Jacob, Abrahamitic blessing, 28:1*ff.*
  acquisition of birthright, 25:29*ff.*
  arrives in Shechem, 33:18
  birth, 25:26
  blesses children, *Ch.* 49
  buried in Cave of Machpelah, 50:13
  confrontation with Laban, 31:25*ff.*
  covenant with Laban, 31:44*ff.*
  death, 49:33
  decides to flee Laban, 31:1*ff.*
  descendants 35:23ff.
  departs from Beer-sheba, 28:10
  dream, 28:12*ff.*
  embalmed, 50:2
  encounter with Esau, *Ch.* 33
  final request, 49:29*ff.*
  flees Laban, 31:17*ff.*
  gives Joseph Shechem, 48:22
  God's blessing, 35:9*ff.*
  hired by Laban, 29:15*ff.*
  Isaac's blessing, 27:28*ff.*
  journeys to Bethel, 35:1
  journeys to Egypt, 46:1*ff.*
  marries Leah, 29:23
  marries Rachel, 29:28
  meets Joseph, 46:29
  meets Laban, 29:13
  meets Pharaoh, 47:7
  meets Rachel, 29:9*ff.*
  mourned by Egypt, 50:3
  mourns Joseph's death, 37:34
  name changed to Israel, 32:29, 35:10
  prayer, 32:10
  prohibition of eating sciatic nerve, 32:33
  promise from God, 46:2*ff.*
  promise to Joseph, 48:3*ff.*
  request to Joseph, 47:29*ff.*
  sends Benjamin to Egypt, 43:13*ff.*
  sends sons to Egypt, 42:1
  sent away by Isaac, 28:5
  told that Joseph is alive, 45:25
  tribute to Esau, 32:14*ff.*
  wrestles with Angel, 32:25*ff.*

Laban, 24:29
  confrontation with Jacob, 31:25*ff.*
  covenant with Jacob, 31:44*ff.*
  meets Jacob, 29:13
  offers Rebecca, 24:50
Lamech, 4:18, 4:23*ff.*, 6:28*ff.*
Leah, 29:16
  burial, 49:31
  conceives, 29:32*ff.*, 30:19*ff.*
  marries Jacob, 29:23
Levi, birth, 29:34
  blessed by Jacob, 49:5*ff.*
  massacre of Shechem, 34:25*ff.*
Lot, birth, 11:27
  capture, 14:12
  leaving Egypt, 13:1
  quarreling with Abraham, 13:5*ff.*
  saved by Abraham, 14:13*ff.*
  saved with family, *Ch.* 19
  sin with daughters, 19:32*ff.*
  traveling with Abraham, 12:4*ff.*
  wife turned to salt, 19:26

Machpelah, Cave, 23:9, 25:9, 49:30
Mahanaim, 32:3
Malchizedek, blessing Abraham, 14:18
Manasseh,
  birth, 41:51
  Jacob's blessing, 48:5, 48:20
man, creation, 1:26*ff.*, 2:7, 5:1
  see Adam
meat, permission to eat, 9:3,
Menashe, *see* Manasseh
Methusael, 4:18, 6:21*ff.*
Midian, 25:4
Midianites, 37:28,36

Milcah, 11:29, 22:20
Moab, conception, 19:37
mourning,
  Jacob, 50:10
  Sarah, 23:2

Nahor, 22:20
  birth, 11:24, 11:26*ff.*
  marriage, 11:29
Naphtali,
  birth, 30:8
  blessed by Jacob, 49:21
Nephilim, 6:4
Nimrod, birth, 10:8*ff.*
Nineveh, 10:11*ff.*
Noah, 5:29*ff.*, 6:8*ff.*
  altar, 8:20
  ark, 6:14*ff.*, 7:1*ff.*
  birth, 5:29
  blessing, 9:1*ff.*
  covenant, 9:12*ff.*
  death, 9:29
  descendants, 10:1
  drunkenness, 9:21
  leaving the ark, 8:18
  Noahide laws, 9:4*ff.*
  see also Flood
Noahide laws, 9:4*ff.*
Nod, 4:16

oaths, Isaac and Philistines, 26:31
olive leaf, 8:11
Onan, birth, 38:4
  death, 38:10

Peleg, 10:25, 11:16*ff.*
Peniel, 32:31
Perez, birth, 38:29
Pharaoh,
  afflicted with plagues, 12:17
  dealings with Abraham, 15*ff.*
  dream, 41:1*ff.*
  dream interpreted by Joseph, 41:25*ff.*
  enriched by Joseph, 47:20*ff.*
  Joseph viceroy of Egypt, 41:40
  meets Jacob, 47:7
Philistines, 21:34,
Plain of Moreh, 12:6
Plains of Mamre; *see* Hebron,
plants, creation, 1:11, 1:29
Potiphar,
  purchases Joseph, 37:36, 39:1
Potiohar's wife,
  slanders Joseph, 39:7*ff.*
prayer,
  Abraham, 19:27 [*Shacharis*],20:17
  Isaac, 24:63 [*Minchah*], 25:21
  Jacob, 28:11 [*Maariv*], 32:10

Rachel,
  barreness, 29:31, 30:1
  death, 35:18
  gives birth, 30:22*ff.*
  marries Jacob, 29:28
  meets Jacob, 29:9*ff.*
  steals *teraphim*, 31:19
rainbow, 9:13*ff.*
rain; *see* flood
Rameses, city, 47:11,
raven, 8:7
Rebecca,
  beautiful, 26:7
  birth, 22:23
  birth of Jacob and Esau, 25:25*ff.*
  marries Isaac, 24:67
  meets Eliezer, 24:15
Rehoboth, well, 26:22
Reuben,
  birth, 29:32
  blessed by Jacob, 49:3*ff.*
  dudaim, 30:14*ff.*
  forfeits seniority, 35:22, 49:6
  incident with Bilhah, 35:22
  saves Joseph, 37:21*ff.*

Sabbath, 2:2*ff.*
Sacrifice,
  Cain and Abel, 4:3*ff.*
  Noah, 8:20
  see also offering
salt, pillar, 19:26
Salt Sea, Valley of Siddim, 14:3
Sarah,
  abducted by Abimelech, *Ch.* 20
  abducted by Pharaoh, 12:15*ff.*
  appearance of angels, 18:9*ff.*
  birth of Isaac, 21:2*ff.*
  childlessness, 11:30, 17:19, 18:10
  death, 23:1*ff.*
  departure, 11:31
  laughs, 18:12
  marriage, 11:29
  name changed, 17:15
  sends away Hagar, 16:6*ff.*
  sojourns to Egypt, 12:11
Sarai; *see* Sarah
sciatic nerve, 32:33
sea giants, 1:21
seasons, 8:22
Seir, 32:4, 33:16
serpent, 3:1*ff.*, 3:13*ff.*
Seth, 4:25*ff.*, 5:3*ff.*, 9:18
Shechem, 12:6, 37:12*ff.*
  abduction of Dinah, 34:2*ff.*
  given to Joseph, 48:22
  Jacob arrives in, 33:18
  massacre, 34:25*ff.*
  son of Hamor, 34:2
Shekel, 23:15, 24:22
Shelah son of Judah, birth, 38:5
Shem, 5:32, 6:10, 7:13, 9:23
  blessing, 9:26
  descendants, 10:1, 10:21*ff.*, 11:10*ff.*
Shemeber, 14:2*ff.*
Shibah, well, 26:33
Shinab, 14:2*ff.*
Shinar, 10:10, 11:2
Shua, Judah marries daughter, 38:2
Simeon,
  birth, 29:33
  blessed by Jacob, 49:5*ff.*
  imprisoned, 42:24
  massacre of Shechem, 34:25*ff.*
Sitnah, well, 26:20
Sodom, 13:10, 13:12*ff.*
  destruction, 19:24*ff.*
  promise of destruction, 18:20*ff.*
stars, creation, 1:16
Succoth, 33:17
sword, Eden, 3:24

Tamar,
  and Judah, 38:15*ff.*
  marries Er, 38:6
Ten Trials of Abraham's faith,
    12:1, *comm.*
Terah,
  birth, 11:24
  death, 11:32
  departure, 11:31
  genealogy, 11:27
teraphim, Rachel steals, 31:19
Tidal, 14:1*ff.*
Timnah, 38:13*ff.*
Tree of Knowledge, 2:9, 2:17
Tree of Life, 2:9, 2:17, 3:24

Ur Kasdim, 11:28, 11:31, 15:7

Valley of Siddim, 14:3
  see also Salt Sea
vineyard, wine, 9:20

war of the Kings, *Ch.* 14
well,
  Esek, 26:20
  Rehoboth, 26:22
  Shibah, 26:33
  Sitnah, 26:21
Wine, vineyard, 9:20
woman, creation, 1:27, 2:21*ff.*, 5:2*ff.*

Zaphenath-paneah, *see* Joseph
Zebulun, birth, 30:20
  blessed by Jacob, 49:13
Zerah, birth, 38:30
Zilpah, 29:24 30:10*ff*
Zoar, 19:22*ff.*, 19:30

CHUMASH
INTERLINEAR
MW01620576